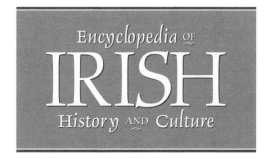

Encyclopedia OF

IRISH

History AND Culture

Ireland

- –·–·– International boundary
- ▬▬▬ Provincial boundary
- –·–·– County boundary
- ☐ County borough
- ● County town

Donegal
Lifford

Londonderry
Londonderry

Antrim
Ballymena

Tyrone
Omagh

Belfast

Down
Downpatrick

U L S T E R

Leitrim
Sligo

Enniskillen
Fermanagh

Armagh
Armagh

Monaghan
Monaghan

Sligo

Carrick on Shannon

Cavan
Cavan

Dundalk

Louth

Mayo
Castlebar

C O N N A C H T

Roscommon

Longford
Longford

Navan
Meath

Roscommon

Galway
Galway

Westmeath
Mullingar

Dublin

Kildare
Naas

Dublin

Offaly
(King's County)
Tullamore

L E I N S T E R

Clare
Ennis

Nenagh

Tipperary
(North Riding)

Port Laoise

Laois
(Queen's County)

Wicklow
Wicklow

Limerick
Limerick

Tipperary
(South Riding)

Kilkenny
Kilkenny

Carlow
Carlow

Wexford

M U N S T E R

Clonmel

Waterford

Wexford
Wexford

Tralee

Kerry

Cork

Dungarvan

Waterford

Cork

N

0   20   40 mi.
0   20   40 km

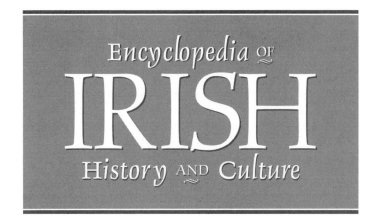

Encyclopedia of IRISH History and Culture

James S. Donnelly, Jr.
EDITOR IN CHIEF

Karl S. Bottigheimer, Mary E. Daly, James E. Doan, and David W. Miller
ASSOCIATE EDITORS

Volume

2

P–Z
PRIMARY DOCUMENTS
INDEX

MACMILLAN REFERENCE USA
An imprint of Thomson Gale, a part of The Thomson Corporation

THOMSON
★
GALE

Detroit • New York • San Francisco • San Diego • New Haven, Conn. • Waterville, Maine • London • Munich

Encyclopedia of Irish History and Culture
James S. Donnelly, Jr., Editor in Chief

LIBRARY OF CONGRESS CATALOGING-IN-PUBLICATION DATA

Encyclopedia of Irish history and culture / James S. Donnelly Jr., editor in chief.
  p. cm.
  Includes bibliographical references and index.
  ISBN 0-02-865902-3 (set hardcover : alk. paper) — ISBN 0-02-865699-7 (volume 1) — ISBN 0-02-865903-1 (volume 2) — ISBN 0-02-865989-9 (e-book)
  1. Ireland—History—Encyclopedias.
  2. Ireland—Civilization—Encyclopedias. I. Donnelly, James S.

DA912.E53 2004
941.5'003—dc22   2004005353

This title is also available as an e-book.
ISBN 0-02-865989-9
Contact your Gale sales representative for ordering information

Printed in the United States of America
10 9 8 7 6 5 4 3 2 1

Contents

Volume 1

LIST OF MAPS
ix

PREFACE
xi

LIST OF ARTICLES
xiii

LIST OF CONTRIBUTORS
xix

CHRONOLOGY
xxvii

Encyclopedia of Irish History and Culture

A–O
1

Volume 2

P–Z
517

LIST OF PRIMARY DOCUMENTS
773

PRIMARY DOCUMENTS
777

INDEX
1027

Paisley, Ian

Ian Paisley (1926–), fundamentalist and unionist political leader, was born in Armagh city on 6 April. His father, a Baptist minister, formed a breakaway congregation in 1933. After training at evangelical colleges in Wales and Belfast, Ian Paisley became minister of an east Belfast fundamentalist congregation in 1946. In 1951 he founded the Free Presbyterian Church of Ulster, attracting defectors from mainstream Protestant churches. Its non-Presbyterian features include Paisley's status as "moderator for life." (Paisley's ordination is unrecognized by mainstream Presbyterians.) During the 1950s Paisley was active in working-class unionist politics. An outspoken opponent of religious ecumenism and Northern Ireland's prime minister, Terence O'Neill, Paisley was briefly imprisoned for public-order offenses in 1966. Paisley reacted to the civil-rights movement with provocative counter-demonstrations that further destabilized Northern Ireland.

In 1970 Paisley won the Stormont by-election that was prompted by O'Neill's resignation, then took the North Antrim seat at the 1970 Westminster general election. In 1971 he founded the Democratic Unionist Party (DUP). Throughout the 1970s the DUP grew by denouncing compromise, deploying menacing street protests against any hint of compromise, and outmaneuvering less adroit rival hardliners. (Paisley is frequently accused of inciting loyalists and sanctimoniously dissociating himself when they get caught.) Some officials hoped that Paisley might deliver compromise where moderates had failed, but he remained a reactive and opportunistic figure unwilling to risk his popularity. In 1979 Paisley topped the Northern Ireland poll in the European Parliament elections, his personal popularity far outstripping that of his party. By the 1981 local elections, the DUP had drawn level with the Ulster Unionist Party in votes received and had acquired several talented young activists associated with Paisley's deputy and quasi-rival Peter Robinson. (Paisley's immediate family are prominent in both his party and church.) Paisley dominated the unionist front against the 1985 Anglo-Irish Agreement; the perceived impotence of his street politics convinced some unionists that they needed to influence future developments by participating in negotiations. Paisley walked out of the talks leading to the 1998 Belfast Agreement, marking the final breakdown of the unionist front. Despite his defeat in the 1998 referendum and health problems, Paisley retained the support of half the unionist community; the DUP benefited by denouncing the Belfast Agreement while taking advantage of devolution. (Paisley characteristically refused ministerial office.) Paisley is seen by international audiences as embodying unionism; his booming Ballymena voice (cultivated as a contrast to the strangulated tones of upper-class unionism) was frequently caricatured. His good-humored image conceals a reactive, irresponsible, and ultimately destructive career.

SEE ALSO Loyalist Paramilitaries after 1965; Presbyterianism; Ulster Politics under Direct Rule

Bibliography

Bruce, Steve. *God Save Ulster! The Religion and Politics of Paisleyism.* 1986.

Cooke, Denis. *Persecuting Zeal: A Portrait of Ian Paisley.* 1996.

Moloney, Ed, and Andy Pollak. *Paisley.* 1986.

Smyth, Clifford. *Ian Paisley: Voice of Protestant Ulster.* 1987.

Patrick Maume

Parker, Dame Dehra

A prominent Unionist politician and the first and only woman to hold ministerial office in the Parliament of Northern Ireland, Dame Dehra Parker (1882–1963) was named after the place of her birth, Dehra Doon in India. In 1901 she married Lieutenant Colonel Robert Spencer Chichester from Castledawson in County Londonderry. Parker's early career showed both a public spirit and a commitment to the Unionist cause. She organized Ulster Volunteer Force nursing units during the third Home Rule crisis of 1911 to 1914 and was awarded an Order of the British Empire for her war work in 1918. She was a vice-chairman of the Ulster Women's Unionist Council from 1911 to 1930 and also served as a justice of the peace, a rural district councillor in Magherafelt, Co. Londonderry, and as a member of Magherafelt board of guardians, serving as chair of this body from 1924 to 1927. In 1921 she was elected as an Unionist MP for Londonderry in the newly established Parliament of Northern Ireland, one of only two women to be elected. Her maiden speech was received with cheers from the Northern Ireland Commons on 1 December 1921, and she quickly became recognized as a staunch defender of the Unionist government, particularly its premier, Sir James Craig. Her standing was such that in 1924 she was selected as the first woman in Britain to present the annual address on behalf of the Commons following the king's speech at the opening of the parliamentary session.

Widowed in 1921, she married Rear Admiral Henry Parker in 1928 and stepped down from her parliamentary seat in favor of her son-in-law, James Chichester-Clark, in the following year. She returned to politics after Chichester-Clark's death in 1933 and remained an MP for South Londonderry until she retired from politics in 1960. A stalwart Unionist, Parker was appointed Northern Ireland parliamentary secretary for education in 1937, retaining this post until 1944. In 1949 she was appointed Northern Ireland minister of health and local government, becoming the first woman in Northern Ireland to hold a cabinet position. She held this post until 1957. She was also grandmother to two prime ministers of Northern Ireland: James Chichester-Clark and Terence O'Neill.

A voluble orator with a wry wit, Parker was the most prominent and long-serving woman in the Parliament of Northern Ireland. Made a Dame of the British Empire (DBE) in 1949, she retired from politics after a thirty-five-year career in June 1960 because of ill health. She died in November 1963 and was aptly re-membered by one former colleague, J. A. Oliver, as "capricious, an adroit politician and a most formidable operator" (Oliver 1974, p. 81).

SEE ALSO Ulster Unionist Party in Office; Women's Parliamentary Representation since 1922

Bibliography

Hansard, Northern Ireland House of Commons Debates. 1921–1960.

Oliver, J. A. Working at Stormont. 1974.

Urquhart, Diane. Women in Ulster Politics, 1890–1940: A History Not Yet Told. 2000.

Diane Urquhart

Parnell, Charles Stewart

Irish Parliamentary Party leader Charles Stewart Parnell (1846–1891) was born on 27 June 1846 at his family's estate at Avondale, Co. Wicklow. Parnell went to school in England and attended Cambridge University but did not graduate. He was elected Home Rule MP for Meath in 1875 and made a name for himself by obstructing the business of Parliament. After Isaac Butt's death in 1879, Parnell became the de facto leader of the Irish Parliamentary Party (IPP), but he came to lead the wider nationalist movement only when agricultural depression revived the land question in the late 1870s. When Michael Davitt organized the Irish Land League in 1879, Parnell, himself a Protestant landowner, realized the league's political potential and became its president. Widespread agrarian violence characterized the ensuing Land War of 1879 to 1881, and Ireland seemed on the verge of revolution. Capitalizing on British fears, Parnell wrested the Land Act of 1881 from the British government. This legislation finally granted Irish tenants the "three Fs"—fair rent, fixity of tenure, and free sale.

Fearing continued agrarian instability, in 1882 Parnell shifted his focus to winning Home Rule in the British Parliament. Parnell gave the IPP a national organization by creating the Irish National League and established greater discipline and loyalty to himself within the IPP. These steps paid off when the IPP won a record eighty-six seats in the 1885 election. This electoral mandate gave Parnell the leverage necessary to

Charles Stewart Parnell (1846–1891) pursued a political career that belied his background as a Wicklow landlord and an English-educated Protestant. He became president of the Land League at its foundation (October 1879) and chairman of the Irish Parliamentary Party (May 1880). He fought for agrarian reform until 1882, when he switched the emphasis of the Irish national movement to Home Rule. His political alliance with the Liberal leader William Gladstone failed to bring Home Rule in 1886, and his love affair with Katharine O'Shea eventually destroyed Parnell's career. Photograph c. 1885 by William Lawrence. © HULTON ARCHIVE/GETTY IMAGES. REPRODUCED BY PERMISSION.

convince the British Liberal Party to support Home Rule. Although the 1886 Home Rule bill failed to pass, Parnell had placed Irish self-government on the Liberal agenda.

Parnell rapidly fell from the heights that he had reached in 1886. The new Conservative government's fierce opposition to Home Rule left Parnell with less political flexibility. Parnell also faced a public outcry in 1887 when *The Times* incorrectly linked him to the infamous Phoenix Park murders. But it was Parnell's personal life that ultimately ended his career. In December 1890 British Liberals and Irish Catholics turned on Parnell after news surfaced of his long-standing love affair with Katharine O'Shea, the wife of a Home Rule MP. Most members of the IPP repudiated Parnell's leadership, and although he fought to maintain his position, his political career was over. Physically exhausted, Par-

nell died on 6 October 1891. Parnell was an exceptional figure: a Protestant landlord who advocated land reform for Irish Catholic tenants and a distant and rather difficult man who during the 1880s was the charismatic uncrowned king of Ireland.

SEE ALSO Butt, Isaac; Davitt, Michael; Home Rule Movement and the Irish Parliamentary Party: 1870 to 1891; Home Rule Movement and the Irish Parliamentary Party: 1891 to 1918; Ladies' Land League; Land Acts of 1870 and 1881; Land War of 1879 to 1882; Newspapers; Plan of Campaign; Protestant Ascendancy: Decline, 1800 to 1930; **Primary Documents:** Establishment of the National Land League of Mayo (16 August 1879); Call at Ennis for Agrarian Militancy (19 September 1880); Land Law (Ireland) Act (22 August 1881); On Home Rule and the Land Question at Cork (21 January 1885); On Home Rule at Wicklow (5 October 1885); The Irish Parliamentary Party Pledge (30 June 1892)

Bibliography

Bew, Paul. *C. S. Parnell.* 1980.

Kee, Paul. *The Laurel and the Ivy.* 1993.

Lyons, F. S. L. *Charles Stewart Parnell.* 1977.

Patrick F. Tally

Peace Movement in Northern Ireland

Even during the early 1970s, the darkest days of the "Troubles," there were people committed to the pursuit of peace. Spontaneous outbursts of protest frequently followed in the wake of local hijackings or murders, but organizations also emerged, usually headed by women, to bring the call for peace to the forefront of public attention; for example, Women Together was formed in 1970 and the Women Caring Trust two years later. Individuals as well as groups regularly led peace rallies, marches, and prayer meetings, particularly at times of paramilitary truce, and local peace committees were set up in many areas. Most peace activists declared themselves, like Women Together, to be "not political, just sick of violence" (*Women Together*). This was not an easy stance to maintain in a country dominated by politically inspired disturbances, and peace activists frequently met hostility from paramilitaries and their supporters.

The names most usually associated with the Northern Ireland peace movement are Betty Williams and Máiréad Corrigan, whose campaign followed a particularly tragic incident. On 10 August 1976 Corrigan's sister Anne Maguire was walking with her four children when the getaway car of a wounded gunman crashed into them, killing three of the children and leaving their mother seriously injured. Corrigan and Williams's call for an end to such senseless deaths and their subsequent campaign for peace drew wide public support. Tens of thousands gathered to sign petitions and join a group that became known as the Peace People, led by the two women with the assistance of reporter Ciaran McKeown. As many as 20,000 people attended rallies in Belfast during that first month, and 25,000 turned up in Derry in September. Marches held every weekend in the different cities of Northern Ireland, England, and the Republic during the following months continued to attract large crowds and massive media attention, as the frustration and despair of years was transformed into a wave of hope and optimism.

The high point of the movement came with the award of the Nobel Peace Prize to Corrigan and Williams in 1977, but the leaders of the movement, constantly in the public spotlight and seemingly out of touch with the wider membership, were increasingly divided over organization and direction, and Williams left in 1979. Moreover, lacking an agreed political agenda, they were prone to attack from both sides of the religious and political divide, and by 1980 growing popular disillusionment had led to a rapid decline in membership. The movement had blossomed during a period of political stalemate, and although it offered a ray of hope in a seemingly irresolvable situation, it lacked a policy of sufficient strength to sustain its growth. While individuals and organizations continued to work for peace in their localities, fundamental political issues had to be addressed before large-scale progress would be possible.

SEE ALSO Women's Movement in Northern Ireland

Bibliography

Deutsch, Richard. *Mairead Corrigan and Betty Williams.* 1977.

Wilson, Rhoda, ed. *Along the Road to Peace: Fifteen Years with the Peace People.* 1991.

Women Together 1, no. 1 (December 1971).

Myrtle Hill

Pearse, Patrick

Educator, poet, journalist, and leader of the Easter Rising, Patrick Pearse (1879–1916) was born in Dublin on 10 November. Although he received a bachelor of law degree from the Royal University of Ireland, Pearse managed his late father's church-statuary business while pursuing his love of native culture.

A member of the Gaelic League since 1897, he edited its weekly newspaper *An Claidheamh Soluis* from 1903 until 1909. Contrary to his later disingenuous claims, Pearse did not use his post to undermine the nonpolitical stance of the organization. His most important writings from this period focused on education. Pearse was not an original thinker, but he energetically pursued concepts that interested him, and in 1908 he established his own school, Saint Enda's, based on the bilingual schools in Belgium. Innovative in an Irish context, the venture was financially draining and increased Pearse's growing personal desperation after 1910.

A proponent of Home Rule until 1912, he came to believe that constitutional agitation was ineffectual, and his growing affinity for Robert Emmet, Theobald Wolfe Tone, and John Mitchel led him to gravitate toward militant expressions of nationalism. Critically, his writings from this period reflect that he—like others in contemporary Europe—became fixated on the idea that a blood sacrifice was needed to "cleanse" and reinvigorate the national spirit.

By December 1913, his public speeches had convinced skeptical Irish Republican Brotherhood (IRB) leaders that he had developed into an "advanced" nationalist, and one month after Pearse helped to found the Irish Volunteers, Bulmer Hobson swore him into the IRB. When the Volunteers split over whether to fight alongside Britain in the Great War, Pearse was a central figure in surreptitiously securing control of the smaller, breakaway faction for the IRB. He was also part of a secret military council within the IRB that planned to use the Volunteers in an armed revolt at Easter 1916.

Alongside labor activist James Connolly, Pearse commanded forces in Dublin during the six days of fighting, proclaiming that they fought on behalf of an existing Irish republic. In contrast to his more disappointed comrades, Pearse believed that the failed Rising fulfilled his vision of blood sacrifice and positioned himself centrally as a Christ figure. Although the public was initially hostile toward the insurgents, the court-martials and executions of their leaders, including Pearse on 3 May 1916, did gradually turn public sentiment against the existing regime.

Subsequent idealizations emphasized Pearse's piety and his romantic commitment to Gaelic culture and militant republicanism, but his true legacy is both more pragmatic and more ambiguous: He was a gifted teacher whose last days facilitated the foundation of an independent Irish state and perpetuated the use of the gun in politics.

SEE ALSO Gaelic Revivalism: The Gaelic League; Hyde, Douglas; Home Rule Movement and the Irish Parliamentary Party: 1891 to 1918; Sinn Féin Movement and Party to 1922; Struggle for Independence from 1916 to 1921; **Primary Documents:** O'Donovan Rossa Graveside Panegyric (1 August 1915); The Proclamation of the Irish Republic (24 April 1916)

Bibliography

Dudley Edwards, Ruth. *Patrick Pearse: The Triumph of Failure.* 1977.

Moran, Sean Farrell. *Patrick Pearse and the Politics of Redemption: The Mind of the Easter Rising, 1916.* 1994.

Ó Buachalla, Séamus, ed. *A Significant Educationalist: The Educational Writings of P. H. Pearse.* 1980.

Pearse, Mary Brigid, ed. *The Home Life of Padraig Pearse.* 1934, 1979.

Timothy G. McMahon

Penal Laws

The penal laws may be described as the corpus of legislation that created and maintained the confessionalism of the early modern Irish state. As such, they include legislation against Protestant dissent as well as anti-Catholic legislation. They also include all the legislation of the sixteenth and seventeenth centuries that formed the Anglican establishment and undermined Catholic economic and political power by land confiscation. However, late-eighteenth-century Catholic activists were anxious to assure Protestants that they sought to overthrow neither the religious establishment nor the existing distribution of property. They thus complained only of such anti-Catholic measures as were enacted in the period after the extension to Ireland of the successful Dutch invasion of Britain in 1688. This gave a more limited and still generally accepted meaning to the term *penal laws.*

The elements of the penal code have parallels in the contemporary bodies of law enacted against religious dissenters elsewhere in Europe. However, the rise of democratic and nationalist sentiment in the nineteenth century rendered the Irish legislation, in retrospect, particularly objectionable. Democratic thought held the nation to be constituted by its population, and because the penal laws had affected the greater part of that population, they came to be regarded as among the most notable of the Irish nation's historical grievances. Sectarian social and political divisions also ensured that the "penal era" did not lose its importance in popular historiography. Historians of the late twentieth century, in contrast, have worked hard to place the condition of eighteenth-century Catholics in a more favorable light.

Insecurity was the dominant feature of the new British regime established in the wake of the Dutch invasion. Many Anglicans feared that with the establishment of Presbyterianism in Scotland, the terrible events of mid-century were beginning to repeat themselves. Irish Presbyterians consequently found themselves excluded from much of public life and subject to irksome legal restrictions, though their situation was improved in the reign of George I. As always, however, fear of popery was much greater and was intensified by the real threat of a restoration by force of the deposed James II or, from 1701, his son—known to his foreign allies and domestic supporters as James III. For some seventy years after the usurpation of 1688, the Glorious Revolution, as its partisans named the event, was by no means irreversible. The anti-Catholic legislation of the late Stuart and early Hanoverian period may be attributed simply to the fear that this engendered. Legislation enacted in 1695 answered the immediate need to disarm potential insurgents. The assault on Catholic landownership, most notably in the Popery Act of 1704, was intended to ensure, in a society in which the right to power was often held to depend on property, that no Catholic party would ever again exist. Legislation directly aimed at the Catholic Church, such as the Bishops' Banishment Act of 1697, is similarly explained by the desire to defend an insecure regime. The perception of Catholicism as primarily a political conspiracy was deeply embedded in the British Protestant mind. Equally, however, the measures that were not ostensibly concerned with the church itself might be justly seen as having a primarily religious motivation. In an age in which religion was by no means a matter for the individual, particularly in the lower ranks of society, it was assumed that the now exclusively Protestant character of the elite would determine the religion of those outside it. This view received support from the proponents of the early Enlightenment who held naive beliefs about what might be expected of education.

In reality, there was little religious change in the population at large. The established church was incapable of a sustained campaign of proselytism, while the Catholic clergy restored a restricted but effective pastoral presence in the country within decades. The poverty of the lowest ranks of society gave them immunity against the penal code's threats and bribes, and their linguistic and cultural separation from the Protestant elites served as further protection, if one was needed. However, among those who, their Catholicism aside, had claims or aspirations to be included in the elite, a degree of religious change was affected. The stick of the imposition of a humiliating status, involving exclusion from public office or the more desirable professions, and the carrot of economic advantage were recognized by the Catholic community as sufficiently persuasive to prevent great opprobrium falling on those who chose conversion. For those who remained Catholic, there were difficulties, but by no means were all paths to increased prosperity and influence in society barred. A Catholic economic environment, with varying degrees of self-sufficiency, was constructed and extended to the European mainland. Trade was attractive because land, in the early eighteenth century, was not a particularly good investment, quite apart from the restrictions on Catholic ownership of it. Still, short leases of up to thirty-one years were perfectly legal and often economically advantageous. Moreover, restrictions on more permanent forms of possession could be circumvented.

With the British victory in the Seven Years' War the threat to the ruling dynasty was gone. The alienation of the Catholic population in the British Isles was not merely needless, but politically and militarily foolish. Thus, toward the end of the 1770s, the dismantling of the penal code began. Yet in breaking Catholic power in Ireland, it had served the later Stuarts and the Hanoverians well. Unlike Scotland, Ireland never at any time after 1691 became the base for assaults on the regime established by William III. The penal code's importance lies also in its enduring effects on Irish society. The importance of religious affiliation in the distribution of privilege in the Irish ancien régime did much to produce a very extended elite, eventually held by many to encompass the whole Protestant community—the "plebeian oligarchy," which Edmund Burke attacked. Its enduring strength as an oligarchy, together with its fears of Catholicism and the secularizing British state, played a major role in forming the sectarian politics of the nineteenth century and beyond.

SEE ALSO Catholic Committee from 1756 to 1809; Eighteenth-Century Politics: 1690 to 1714—Revolution Settlement; Eighteenth-Century Politics: 1714 to 1778—Interest Politics; Eighteenth-Century Politics: 1778 to 1795—Parliamentary and Popular Politics; Eighteenth-Century Politics: 1795 to 1800—Repression, Rebellion, and Union; Government from 1690 to 1800; O'Conor, Charles, of Balenagare; Politics: 1690 to 1800—A Protestant Kingdom; Protestant Ascendancy: 1690 to 1800; Religion: Since 1690; Roman Catholic Church: 1690 to 1829; **Primary Documents:** An Act to Prevent the Further Growth of Popery (1704)

Bibliography

Burns, Robert E. "The Irish Penal Code and Some of Its Historians." *Review of Politics* 21 (1959): 276–299.

Burns, Robert E. "The Irish Popery Laws: A Study of Eighteenth-Century Legislation and Behavior." *Review of Politics* 24 (1962): 485–508.

Cullen, Louis M., and Paul Butel, eds. *Négoce et Industrie en France et en Irlande aux XVIIIe et XIXe Siècles (Trade and Industry in France and Ireland between the Eighteenth and Nineteenth Centuries).* 1980.

Leighton, Cadoc D. A. *Catholicism in a Protestant Kingdom: A Study of the Irish Ancien Régime.* 1994.

Power, Thomas, and Kevin Whelan, eds. *Endurance and Emergence: Catholics in Eighteenth-Century Ireland.* 1990.

Wall, Maureen. *Catholic Ireland in the Eighteenth Century: Collected Essays of Maureen Wall.* 1989.

C. D. A. Leighton

Petty, Sir William

Sir William Petty (1623–1687), scientist and statistician, first came to public notice in Ireland in the 1650s. He was set on the path of scientific inquiry after having been taught mathematics by Jesuits in Normandy. Back in England, he was influenced by a group of reformers around Samuel Hartlib, a Protestant refugee from central Europe eager for social and educational changes. In 1651 the new regime first made Petty professor of anatomy at the University of Oxford and then in 1652, physician to the army in Ireland. He soon took over the survey of lands confiscated by the English state between 1649 and 1653. The result, the Down Survey, although not without flaws, provided the basis for the Cromwellian land settlement. Besides benefiting many military and Protestant civilians, the land redistribution also enriched Petty: He received £9,000 and substantial estates with annual rentals approaching £6,000 by the 1680s.

The Dublin administration, appreciative of his skills, made him clerk to the council and after 1655 secretary to the effective ruler of the island, Henry Cromwell, the younger son of Oliver Cromwell. Petty shared Cromwell's wish to move toward civilian instead of military government; this provoked radicals and soldiers to attack him in the Westminster Parliament of 1659, of which he was a member. He readily submitted to the restored Charles II, hopeful of high employment, but what he received—a knighthood in 1661, a place on the Irish privy council and its council of trade, and the judgeship of the Irish admiralty court in 1676—hardly matched his high estimate of his own abilities. He directed his energies into science and technology. A founder-member of the Royal Society of London, he was intermittently active in its affairs. He also pioneered, with John Graunt, the analysis of mortality rates in London and Dublin, and extrapolated both trends and population totals. His interest in quantification (although his figures were not always accurate) led to more sustained treatments of the natural and human geography of Ireland. On his own estates, especially in remote Kerry, he sought to demonstrate the merits of a methodical approach in exploiting iron ore, water power, timber, and the sea. The results failed to live up to his extravagant hopes.

Embittered by what he saw as his own neglect, Petty could be intemperate. In private he delighted friends with his irreverence. He wrote, sometimes obsessively and repetitively, about the politics, economy, and society of Ireland and England. Much was utopian or merely outrageous: He happily contemplated the enforced exchange of peoples from the two kingdoms. He was excessively optimistic that his unsentimental ideas about Ireland would recommend him to the Catholic James II, but a deluge of proposals failed to return Petty to the influence that he had briefly enjoyed between 1655 and 1659. He left behind a body of writings, many focused on Ireland, that showed him to be an unusually disciplined analyst. He also prepared the first county maps of Ireland, published in 1685 as *Hiberniae Delineatio*. The scope of Petty's interests and the scale of his achievements were fully apparent after his death: His *Political Arithmetic* was published in 1690, his *Political Anatomy* in 1691. The publication of all of his significant works has still to be completed. His writings, if sometimes repetitive and impractical, provide abundant details of the physical and human geography of seventeenth-century Ireland and England. They also show Petty's formidable intellectual prowess, especially as the originator of the statistical method known as political arithmetic.

Sir William Petty (1623–1687) was an English-born polymath who went to Ireland in 1652 as Physician General to the Commonwealth Army there. He stayed to carry out the pathbreaking "Down Survey" of Irish land (1654–1659), was enriched with confiscated estates in Kerry by Cromwell, and knighted (1662) by Charles II. He later divided his time between England and Ireland and was a founding member of both the Royal Society in London and the Dublin Philosophical Society, two important early academies of natural and social science. BY COURTESY OF THE NATIONAL PORTRAIT GALLERY, LONDON. REPRODUCED BY PERMISSION.

SEE ALSO Agriculture: 1500 to 1690; Boyle, Robert; Cromwellian Conquest; Dublin Philosophical Society; Restoration Ireland

Bibliography

Barnard, T. C. "Sir William Petty, Irish Landowner." In *History and Imagination: Essays in Honor of H. R. Trevor-Roper*, edited by Hugh Lloyd-Jones, Valerie Pearl, and Blair Worden. 1981.

Fitzmaurice, Lord E. *The Life of Sir William Petty, 1623–1687.* 1895.

Harris, Frances. "Ireland as a Laboratory: The Archive of Sir William Petty." In *Archives of the Scientific Revolution: The Formation and Exchange of Ideas in Seventeenth-Century Europe*, edited by Michael Hunter. 1998.

Hull, Charles Henry, ed. *The Economic Writings of Sir William Petty.* 2 vols. 1899.

Larcom, Sir Thomas, ed. *The History of the Survey of Ireland, Commonly Called the Down Survey, by Dr. William Petty*, A.D. 1655–6. 1851.

Petty-Fitzmaurice, H. W. E., marquess of Lansdowne, ed. *The Petty Papers*. 2 vols. 1927.

Petty-Fitzmaurice, H. W. E., marquess of Lansdowne, ed. *The Petty-Southwell Correspondence, 1676–1687*. 1928.

Petty Papers. ADD MSS 72850–72908. British Library.

Toby Barnard

~

Plan of Campaign

The Plan of Campaign was the second of three phases of land agitation that occurred in Ireland between 1879 and 1903. Like the Land League before it, the Plan of Campaign was a reaction to falling agricultural production and prices that made it difficult for many tenant farmers to pay their customary rents. An increase in the late summer and early autumn of 1886 in the number of legal and forcible dispossessions of defaulting tenants, more commonly known as evictions, and the seeming indifference of the newly elected Conservative government to the tenants' economic plight, sparked the agitation, which in essence was a refusal to pay the contracted rents on selected estates.

The Plan of Campaign manifesto was published in the nationalist newspaper *United Ireland* on 23 October 1886. According to the manifesto, tenants on individual properties were to decide the percentage rent reduction they required. If the landlords refused their demands, the tenants were to entrust their rents, less the desired reduction, to individuals known only to themselves. This money, which was known as "the estate fund" or "the campaign fund," was to pay general expenses and to support evicted tenants. Campaigners were strongly urged not to pay legal costs, to publicize and resist evictions, and to boycott those responsible for them.

The Plan of Campaign affected a mere one percent of Irish estates during its five-year existence. It was implemented on at least 203 properties—75 in Munster, 71 in Connacht, 33 in Leinster, and 24 in Ulster. Although the heaviest concentration was in the poorer western half of the country, the Plan of Campaign was not simply the reaction of an impoverished peasantry to adverse economic circumstances. The evidence suggests that virtually all of the crucial Plan of Campaign struggles were fought on estates that had notoriously insecure financial bases. If tenant farmers, by withholding rents, could bring landlords to the verge of bankruptcy and force them to sell at sacrificial prices, the occupying tenants might be the beneficiaries.

The leadership of the movement was drawn from the more radical, agrarian wing of the Irish Parliamentary Party that regarded landlords as parasites and landlordism as alien. Additionally, and perhaps more significantly, the landlords were seen, and largely saw themselves, as part of the English garrison in Ireland, and as such, they were a considerable barrier to the establishment of a Home Rule parliament in Dublin. The leading proponents of land agitation in the 1880s made no secret of the fact that Home Rule was their ultimate aim, and thus the Plan of Campaign had a political dimension from the beginning.

The agitation was exclusively Catholic. With some exceptions, the Catholic hierarchy and clergy shared the nationalist community's attitude toward the landlords and the Plan of Campaign. They took their lead from the two most influential churchmen of the day, Dr. William Walsh, archbishop of Dublin, and his archiepiscopal colleague in Cashel, Dr. Thomas Croke, both of whom, after initial misgivings, defended the morality of the agitation. Their position was challenged by the more conservative members of the Catholic hierarchy, notably the redoubtable bishop of Limerick, Dr. Edward Thomas O'Dwyer. He and a handful of like-minded colleagues regarded the refusal to pay rent as illegal and morally wrong—a violation of the sacrosanctity of contract as enshrined in the Land Act of 1881. Their objections were strengthened in late December 1886 when the Irish executive proclaimed the agitation "an unlawful and criminal conspiracy," and made absolute in April 1888 when a papal rescript condemned the Plan of Campaign on the grounds that it was unlawful to break contracts freely entered into by landlords and tenants, that the land courts were available to those who believed that their rents were unfair, and that funds collected under the Plan had been extorted from tenants. The pope decreed that boycotting was contrary to charity and justice, depicting it as a tactic designed to intimidate individuals who were willing to pay their rents or who were exercising their legal rights in taking farms from which other tenants had been evicted.

The general response to the papal decree was great indignation. John Dillon, William O'Brien, and other Catholic leaders acknowledged Rome's religious and spiritual jurisdiction but rejected the pope's condemnation of boycotting and the Plan of Campaign as unwarranted meddling in Irish political affairs. In their reaction to the rescript and in the ensuing debate on the question of church-state relations, Irish Catholics demonstrated impressive political maturity and firmly indicated that, in an independent Ireland, Home Rule would not necessarily mean Rome Rule.

In the late 1880s tenants on some 200 Irish estates adopted the "Plan of Campaign" and deprived their landlords of the usual rents by concerted action. In striking back, some landlords, including Captain Hector Vandeleur of Kilrush House, Co. Clare, made use of a battering ram to oust resisting tenants, as depicted in this 1888 photograph. © SEAN SEXTON COLLECTION/CORBIS. REPRODUCED BY PERMISSION.

An ironic exception to the broad nationalist consensus on the Plan of Campaign was Charles Stewart Parnell, the charismatic leader and embodiment of Irish nationalism. His attitude was one of undisguised antipathy, and he disavowed the agitation publicly on several occasions, notably in a press release in December 1886 and more comprehensively in a major address to the Liberal Party hierarchy at the Eighty Club in London on 8 May 1888. Parnell was opposed to the agitation on political and tactical grounds rather than on moral ones; he was concerned that certain aspects of the Plan would have an adverse affect on English public opinion and on the political situation generally. Agrarian agitation endangered the alliance that Parnell had forged between Irish nationalists and English Liberals, and thus it threatened the prospect of Home Rule for Ireland, Parnell's overriding political ambition.

The Plan of Campaign came through the twin traumas of the papal rescript and Parnell's Eighty Club address more or less unscathed. However, the leaders of the agitation could not escape the crippling shortage of funds and the financial demands of an ever-increasing number of evicted tenants, and their difficulties became more acute as the government and the landlords sharpened and coordinated their responses. But the blow that precipitated the collapse of the agitation was the London divorce-court verdict against Mrs. Katharine O'Shea and Parnell on 17 November 1890. The subsequent rending of nationalist Ireland into pro- and anti-Parnellite camps was reflected in the ranks of the campaigners. Several of the Plan's leading advocates sided with Parnell, but the majority lined up against him. The tribulations in the nationalist camp demoralized the tenants, and by mid-1891 many had settled with their landlords, accepting terms that many observers regarded as ruinous. A small number of disputes dragged on for several years, but to all intents and purposes the agitation was moribund by the time of Parnell's death in October 1891.

Despite its precipitous and less than glorious termination, the Plan of Campaign was successful on most of the estates on which it was implemented and secured sizeable rent reductions for many tenants. In addition, the agitation had a considerable, if incalculable, indirect

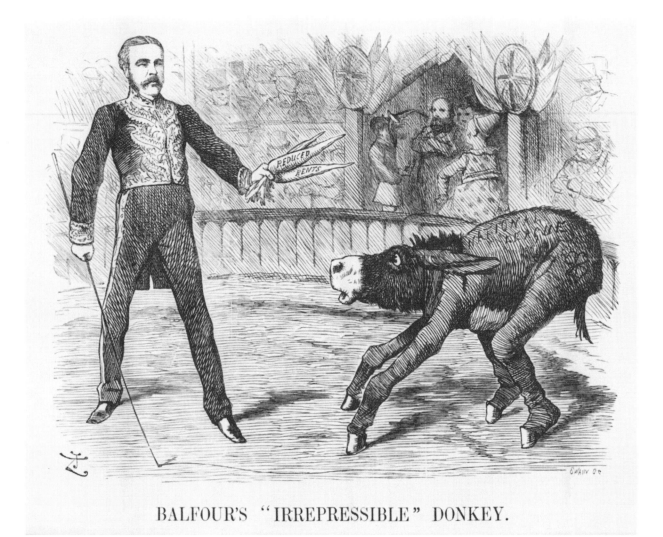

BALFOUR'S "IRREPRESSIBLE" DONKEY.

Coercion and conciliation were standard elements in the Tory government's response to the land war in the late 1880s. Agrarian activists were jailed while the land courts forced landlords to lower the rents of leaseholders. In this Punch *cartoon of 1888 the Irish chief secretary A. J. Balfour holds out the carrot of reduced rents to the "irrepressible donkey" of the Irish National League.* FROM PUNCH, 14 JANUARY 1888.

influence on rent movements—many landlords conceded to their tenants' demands when threatened with the Plan or after seeing it take root in their area. The agitation exposed the fallacy of dual ownership in the soil by landlord and tenant, and it signalled that peasant proprietorship was the only long-term solution to the Irish land question. In the wake of the Plan of Campaign the political and social isolation of the mainly Protestant landed class was almost complete.

SEE ALSO Congested Districts Board; Home Rule Movement and the Irish Parliamentary Party: 1870 to 1891; Land Questions; Land War of 1879 to 1882; Parnell, Charles Stewart; Protestant Ascendancy: Decline, 1800 to 1930; United Irish League Campaigns

Bibliography

Donnelly, James S., Jr. *The Land and People of Nineteenth-Century Cork: The Rural Economy and the Land Question.* 1975.

Geary, Laurence M. *The Plan of Campaign, 1886–1891.* 1986.

Larkin, Emmet. *The Roman Catholic Church and the Plan of Campaign, 1886–1888.* 1978.

Lyons, F. S. L. "John Dillon and the Plan of Campaign, 1886–1890." *Irish Historical Studies* 14 (September 1965): 313–47.

Lyons, F. S. L. *John Dillon: A Biography.* 1968.

Shannon, Catherine B. *Arthur J. Balfour and Ireland, 1874–1922.* 1988.

Warwick-Haller, Sally. *William O'Brien and the Irish Land War.* 1990.

Laurence M. Geary

Plunkett, Oliver

(Saint) Oliver Plunkett (1625–1681), the martyred Roman Catholic archbishop of Armagh, was born in Loughcrew, Co. Meath, on 1 November. After an early education in Ireland, Plunkett traveled to study in the Irish College in Rome in 1647. He was ordained on 1 January 1654, and in 1657 was appointed professor of theology at Propaganda College. He was later transferred to the chair of controversies, the branch of theology dealing with items at issue between the Christian denominations.

Plunkett was elevated to the archiepiscopal see of Armagh in 1669 and consecrated in Ghent. After arriving in Ireland in March 1670, he quickly set about visiting and reorganizing his archdiocese and reforming abuses. He worked to improve the education and lifestyles of his parochial clergy, discouraging such vices as drinking and womanizing, removing factious clerics from their posts, and ordaining more suitable candidates. His ongoing attempts to regulate the size, training, activities, and rivalries of the religious orders in his province, as well as his opposition to Jansenism (a Catholic ideological movement frequently denounced as heretical), led him into conflict with the Franciscans in particular. In his dealings with the laity his major concerns were with confirmation, regularizing marriages not contracted in full conformity with Canon Law, and restraining "tories" (bandit members of the dispossessed gentry). He was particularly concerned with education and sponsored Jesuit-run schools that were later forcibly closed by the Protestant authorities. In 1672 he wrote *Jus Primatiale*, a defense of the primacy within Ireland of the see of Armagh, in response to the rival claims of Peter Talbot, archbishop of Dublin. A practical and effective administrator, he held several synods and dispatched numerous letters to his superiors on the continent detailing his achievements and recommendations for the Irish church. The poverty of his see led him to complain of financial hardship, and outbreaks of persecution beginning in late 1673 occasionally forced him into hiding.

During the fallout from the Popish Plot (a fictitious conspiracy to assassinate Charles II and replace him with his Catholic brother) Plunkett was arrested, imprisoned successively in Dublin and London, accused of treason, and tried and convicted on 8 June 1681 on the perjured evidence of several Irish witnesses, including priests and friars from his own province. He was executed at Tyburn on 1 July. His body was buried in Saint Giles's churchyard, London, but it was subsequently

Oliver Plunkett (1625–1681), Catholic archbishop of Armagh from 1669, had the misfortune to be caught up in the so-called Popish Plot in 1679. Tried in London on dubious charges, he was convicted and executed there in 1681. He was canonized by the Roman Catholic Church in 1975. NATIONAL GALLERY OF IRELAND, CAT. NO. 11 073. REPRODUCED BY PERMISSION.

translated to Lamspringe, Germany, and thence to Downside Abbey, England. His head is preserved in Saint Peter's Church, Drogheda, Co. Louth. Plunkett was declared venerable on 9 December 1886, beatified on 23 May 1920, and canonized on 12 October 1975. His feast day is 11 July.

SEE ALSO Council of Trent and the Catholic Mission; English Political and Religious Policies, Responses to (1534–1690); Restoration Ireland

Bibliography

Hanly, John, ed. *The Letters of Saint Oliver Plunkett.* 1979.

Moran, Patrick Francis. *Memoir of the Ven. Oliver Plunket.* 1861. Reprint, 1895.

Ó Fiaich, Tomás. *Oliver Plunkett: Ireland's New Saint.* 1975.

Clodagh Tait

Plunkett, Sir Horace Curzon

Sir Horace Curzon Plunkett (1854–1932) was born in Gloucestershire, England on 24 October 1854, the son of the sixteenth Baron Dunsany and his wife, the Honorable Anne Constance Dutton. He was educated at Eton and Oxford and devoted his life principally to agricultural reform in Ireland.

As agent for his father at Dunsany Castle, Co. Meath, Plunkett took the initiative in 1878 of establishing a Dunsany Co-operative Society, the germ of the idea that was to dominate his life. Influenced by the British cooperative movement, ranching experience in the U.S. west, and the agricultural modernization of Denmark, he developed a concept of cooperation appropriate to the needs of the Irish small farmer. He saw in cooperation a means of establishing improved agricultural production, processing and distribution, a new sense of community, and an alternative social and moral order able to fill the gap that had been opened by the demise of the landlord system. However, a lack of political acumen compromised his achievements, and he attracted enmity within both major communities in Ireland: By antagonizing unionist voters, he lost the parliamentary seat on which his long-term vice-presidency of the Irish Department of Agriculture and Technical Instruction depended; by attacking nationalist parliamentarians and the Catholic clergy, he alienated those who most directly represented the class on whom the success of his reforms depended. In addition, his ideas threatened the shopkeeper and money-lending class, which provided much of the rural leadership of the nationalist movement. Perversely, he took pride in this multipartisan opposition, comparing his popularity to that of "a dog on a tennis court."

The escalating crisis in Ireland after 1916 brought much more into the open the covert nationalism that Plunkett had long disguised. He sought, particularly through his chairing of the Irish Convention (1917–1918), to avert the partition of Ireland, and in 1919 he founded the Irish Dominion League in a further futile effort to that end. His achievements and contributions, however, were notable. The Irish Agriculture and Technical Instruction Department was created in 1899 as a result of his efforts. He was a member of the Congested Districts Board between 1891 and 1918, and in 1922 he became a senator of the Irish Free State. An adviser on agriculture to United States governments, he had an especially close relationship with President Theodore Roosevelt. Most notably of all, the Irish Agricultural Organisation Society, which he founded in 1894, not only devised practical improvements to Irish farming but also enriched a relatively impoverished rural environment by increasing opportunities for social intercourse and a shared sense of community.

SEE ALSO Agriculture: 1845 to 1921; Congested Districts Board; Home Rule Movement and the Irish Parliamentary Party: 1891 to 1918; Land Questions; Protestant Ascendancy: Decline, 1800 to 1930; Rural Life: 1850 to 1921; Struggle for Independence from 1916 to 1921; Unionism from 1885 to 1922

Bibliography

Digby, Margaret. *Horace Plunkett: An Anglo–American Irishman.* 1949.

Ehrlich, Cyril. "Horace Plunkett and Agricultural Reform." In *Irish Population, Economy, and Society*, edited by J. M. Goldstrom and L. A. Clarkson. 1981.

West, Trevor. *Horace Plunkett: Co-operation and Politics, An Irish Biography.* 1986.

Philip Bull

Poetry, Modern

In modern Irish poetry certain important themes recur and are explored, defined, and refined throughout the twentieth century. Irish poets have continued to focus on their relation to place, politics, history, the private world, and those points where the public and the private collide. The early agenda was set by William Butler Yeats, whose figure and achievement continue to cast a large shadow. The principal themes in Yeats's work are Irish mythology; the revolutionary and post-revolutionary periods in Ireland, with their attendant heroes and villains; and love, mortality, and the poet's search for immortality through mysticism and art. Although he produced compelling work throughout his career, his greatest achievements are found in the second half, in such landmark poems as "Easter 1916," his poem about the Easter Rising; "The Wild Swans at Coole," a vision of rural paradise; and "Sailing to Byzantium," a profound meditation on aging and the quest for immortality. Yeats was awarded the Nobel Prize for literature in 1923.

The middle period of twentieth-century Irish poetry is dominated by Austin Clarke, Louis MacNeice, and

Patrick Kavanagh. Clarke is best known for his long poems *Mnemosyne Lay in Dust* and *Tiresias*, and for the short, often pointed, lyrics which comprise the major part of his *Selected Poems*. In the early part of his career much of the material of his poetry was derived from Irish mythology and concerned with faith and loss of faith. His best work explores, with a satiric eye, the political, cultural, and sexual inadequacies of Irish life between the 1950s and 1970s. Louis MacNeice was born in Belfast, educated in England, and spent much of his adult life in London as a contemporary of W. H. Auden, Stephen Spender, and the British poets of the 1930s. He has written many memorable Irish poems, the most famous being "Carrickfergus," an autobiographical account of his Ulster upbringing. Patrick Kavanagh, born and raised on a farm in County Monaghan, is the most important poet of this period, whose work has had an enormous influence on many poets who were to follow, Seamus Heaney and Eavan Boland in particular. In his long poems *The Great Hunger* and *Lough Derg*, Kavanagh shows that the romantic version of rural life presented by Yeats does not match reality. The rural world, in Kavanagh's view, is dominated by social, intellectual, sexual, and economic hungers. Toward the end of his life, after successful cancer surgery, Kavanagh produced his great lyric poems: "Canal Bank Walk," "Lines Written on a Seat on the Grand Canal, Dublin . . . ," and "The Hospital." Other notable poets of the period include the trio of modernists Denis Devlin, Thomas MacGreevy, and Brian Coffey; and Máirtín Ó Direáin and Seán Ó Ríordáin, the most prominent Irish-language poets.

In the 1950s a new generation finally brought Irish poetry out from under the shadow of Yeats and provided it with a new agenda: exploring and defining the new, more prosperous, and more outgoing Ireland that replaced the isolated post-independence nation. In *The Rough Field* John Montague provides the first extended poetic meditation on the role of history and place in the developing "Troubles" in Northern Ireland and in *The Dead Kingdom* he explores the lives of those Irish who were lost in America as part of the Irish Diaspora. Thomas Kinsella, a more hermetic poet than Montague, has explored the loss of language and of one's place in the world in work that takes daring risks with poetic form, becoming more avant-garde as his career has progressed. James Liddy is the most exuberant poet of this generation. His work is influenced primarily by the American Beat poets; it is through his work that the Beat influence is introduced into Irish poetry. Kinsella's and Liddy's best works are gathered in their respective volumes of *Collected Poems*. Richard Murphy is a poet associated primarily with the west of Ireland, County Galway in particular, and is known for his exploration of the natural world and of the lives of men who make

their living as fishermen. With the publication of Murphy's *High Island*, an Irish literature of the environment begins to emerge. Another notable poet of this generation is Pearse Hutchinson, whose poetry, written in both English and Irish, is concerned with the vanishing language and vanishing culture of rural, Gaelic Ireland. Also associated with the writers of this generation is Anthony Cronin, whose *New and Selected Poems* is a significant volume that explores the Irish social and political conscience.

POETRY FROM NORTHERN IRELAND

The 1960s saw the resumption of the "Troubles" in Northern Ireland and the emergence of an important group of poets who have dominated Irish poetry since their first work began to appear. The best known of these poets is Seamus Heaney, who was awarded the Nobel Prize for literature in 1995. Heaney, who was born in Mossbawn, about thirty miles northwest of Belfast, has produced a remarkable body of varied work. The political turmoil of Northern Ireland has an important place in his poetry, but it does not overwhelm it. Heaney also examines the natural world and its points of intersection with the world of men and women. He is a poet of bogs, hills, and fields, and of the people who interact with this world and violate it with violence. In *Opened Ground: Selected Poems, 1966–1996*, one is struck both by the remarkable quality of Heaney's lyric poems, in which he extols the quiet virtues of ordinary people. In contrast, Derek Mahon's complex work, influenced by Samuel Beckett and the French existentialist writers, takes note of the loss of order in the contemporary world. It is elegant and highly structured. His best-known poem is "A Disused Shed in Co. Wexford," which is found in his *Collected Poems*. Michael Longley's poetry is classical in tone and influence. In looking at Belfast, he gazes through the prism of classical literature and philosophy to help define the city, its people, and their predicaments. Longley's *Poems, 1963–1983* also reveals a deep attachment to the natural world of the west of Ireland. In *Poems, 1956–1986*, James Simmons mixes the lyric and the comic as he seeks to describe the tangled personal and public realities of Northern Ireland.

In the 1980s a second wave of poets from the North emerged; the most prominent figures in this group are Paul Muldoon, Ciaran Carson, Medbh McGuckian, Tom Paulin, and Frank Ormsby. Muldoon's work is set both in Ireland, where he grew up and was raised, and in the United States, where he now lives, and it ranges widely in themes, forms, and attitudes. Muldoon provides his readers with an ironic and postmodern view of the Irish experience in such collections as *Meeting the British* and

Madoc. Ciaran Carson's best-known book is *Belfast Confetti*, a volume of narrative verse that reveals the vital essences present in contemporary Belfast. Medbh McGuckian's work is sometimes considered inscrutable by readers. In her luminous poetry, she reveals the interiors of experience. It is as if everything is reversed: instead of describing the world as we see it, McGuckian presents a deep-rooted vision of how the exterior world is recreated by the female psyche and body. Frank Ormsby's most prominent work is found in *A Northern Spring. Fivemiletown* is Tom Paulin's best-known work.

WOMEN POETS AND THE CONTEMPORARY SCENE

Until recently, many women poets have felt excluded and marginalized in the Irish literary world, but a brilliant generation of women poets appeared in the 1980s. To date, the most important figure, as writer and influence, is Eavan Boland. Raised in Dublin, London, and New York, Boland articulated the struggles she faced as a young woman, mother, and poet in her prose memoir *Object Lessons: The Life of the Woman and the Poet in Her Time.* She has also published many volumes of poetry, including *The Journey, A Woman in a Time of Violence,* and *The Lost Land.* Throughout the 1980s, she conducted workshops for women in rural Ireland that encouraged them to write and publish. Nuala Ní Dhomhnaill has published a number of important volumes, the best known being *Pharaoh's Daughter* and *The Astrakhan Cloak,* in which Irish mythology is wedded to an original feminist outlook to produce a new Irish poetic vision. Ní Dhomhnaill writes in Irish, and her success has encouraged other Irish-language poets (including her male contemporaries Michael Davitt and Cathal Ó Searcaigh, both of whom have published distinguished work). Mary O'Malley, in such volumes as *The Knife in the Wave* and *Asylum Road,* has also introduced mythology into her work. In addition, her explorations of the west of Ireland are the first sustained feminist interpretation of the western landscape. Paula Meehan has written many fine love poems and poems of family, and poems in which ordinary Dubliners are given voice; her book *The Man Who Was Marked by Winter* has had wide influence in Ireland. Other women who have produced important poetry in recent years include Mary O'Donnell, Rita Ann Higgins, Sara Berkeley, and Moya Cannon. The poetic vision of these women has been influenced by poets from the United States, particularly Adrienne Rich. With the exception of Medbh McGuckian, all of these women are from the Republic, from where most of the most significant new writers have come.

The following distinguished collections by men were published in the 1990s: Theo Dorgan's *Rosa Mundi,* Tony Curtis's *Three Songs of Home,* Greg Delanty's *The Hell Box,* Philip Casey's *The Year of the Knife,* Sean Lysaght's *The Clare Island Survey,* Gerard Donovan's *The Lighthouse,* Dennis O'Driscoll's *Weather Permitting,* Michael Coady's *All Souls,* and Pat Boran's *The Shape of Water.* These works are often united by a common desire to escape what we understand to be the traditional themes of Irish poetry—they are more likely to be concerned with social issues than with historical though, overall, the world they depict is more private than public. It is poetry inspired by Kavanagh that also shows the influences of European and American poets. Contemporary Irish poets, male and female, have produced work that is both exciting and unpredictable, that steps out from under the great canopies of the past.

SEE ALSO Arts: Modern Irish and Anglo-Irish Literature and the Arts since 1800; Drama, Modern; Fiction, Modern; Heaney, Seamus; Literature: Twentieth-Century Women Writers; Yeats, W. B.; **Primary Documents:** "Easter 1916" (1916); "Burial of an Irish President (Dr. Douglas Hyde)" (c. 1949); "An Irishman in Coventry" (1960); "Punishment" (1975)

Bibliography

Bolger, Dermot, ed. *The Bright Wave: An Tonn Ghael.* 1986.

Brown, Terence. *Ireland: A Social and Cultural History, 1922–79.* 1981.

Deane, Seamus. *Celtic Revivals.* 1985.

Deane, Seamus. *A Short History of Irish Literature.* 1986.

Fallon, Peter, and Derek Mahon. *The Penguin Book of Contemporary Irish Poetry.* 1990.

Heaney, Seamus. *Opened Ground: Selected Poems, 1966–1996.* 1998.

Kiberd, Declan. *Inventing Ireland: The Literature of the Modern Nation.* 1995.

Kinsella, Thomas. *The New Oxford Book of Irish Verse.* 1986.

Yeats, William Butler. *The Yeats Reader,* edited by Richard J. Finneran. 1997.

Eamonn Wall

Elected members of Fianna Fáil walking to Dáil Éireann in 1927. Their decision to take their seats in Dáil Éireann in August 1927 consolidated parliamentary democracy in the Irish Free State. © RTÉ STILLS LIBRARY, REF. NO. 504/100. REPRODUCED BY PERMISSION.

Political Parties in Independent Ireland

The party system of independent Ireland is atypical of Europe. Instead of the configuration of liberal, Christian democratic and socialist parties that characterizes other predominantly Catholic societies, there is one set of parties that originated in the nationalist Sinn Féin (We ourselves) movement and another that grew out of sectional interests or alternative perspectives. The electoral support bases and ideological standpoints of all of these parties are unusual.

SINN FÉIN AND ITS SUCCESSORS

Although the party that became known as Sinn Féin was founded by nationalist journalist Arthur Griffith (1871–1922) and others in 1905, it was not until the British general election of 14 December 1918 that it moved to the center of the Irish political stage. By that time, what had been a marginal political force had become a broad national movement, a change marked by the accession of Eamon de Valera (1882–1975) as party leader in October 1917.

Having won 73 of Ireland's 105 parliament seats (including 69 of the 74 seats that were located in what is now the Republic of Ireland) in 1918, the success of Sinn Féin's campaign to force the British to the negotiating table left the party poised to become the dominant political force in the new Ireland. But disagreement over the terms of the Anglo-Irish Treaty of 6 December 1921 provoked a split in Sinn Féin. With de Valera's resignation as president of the revolutionary regime on 9 January 1922, he and other opponents of the treaty parted with their colleagues, arguing that the treaty, in addition to excluding Northern Ireland from the new state, failed to assert full Irish independence. The antitreaty group, which retained the name Sinn Féin, was roundly defeated in a general election on 16 June 1922, and its IRA supporters were crushed in the Civil War of 1922 to 1923.

Rejecting the legitimacy of the new state and its institutions, Sinn Féin remained in the political wilderness in the early 1920s. At the party's convention in March 1926, however, when de Valera's advocacy of a more pragmatic approach was rejected, he and his supporters withdrew from the party. On 16 May 1926 they founded a new party, Fianna Fáil (Soldiers of Destiny). In spite of its uncompromising stand for Irish unity and independence, Fianna Fáil entered the Dáil on 11 August 1927 and went on to register a series of landmark political victories. In the general election of February 1932 it became Ireland's largest party and formed a government that lasted for sixteen years. Notwithstanding a significant drop in support in the 1990s, Fianna Fáil's average support in general elections during the period 1932 to 2002 was 45.3 percent.

The victorious protreaty section of Sinn Féin reorganized itself as Cumann na nGaedheal (Party of the Irish) on 8 April 1923. Although it formed the government until 1932, it never won an overall majority, and a further decline began after its loss of power. On 8 September 1933 it merged with two smaller groups to form Fine Gael (Family or Tribe of the Gaels), which headed Ireland's first coalition government (beginning 18 February 1948) and subsequently participated in five other coalitions. Between 1932 and 2002 average support for this political stance has been 30.1 percent.

The Sinn Féin rump that remained after de Valera's withdrawal in 1926 shifted to the left following the collapse of an IRA campaign in Northern Ireland between 1956 and 1962, and limped on until the outbreak of the Northern Ireland troubles. It split again on 11 January 1970. The "official" group that retained control of the party led it further to the left, later abandoned the name Sinn Féin (becoming the Workers' Party), and eventually faded away. Most of its parliamentarians ultimately joined the Labour Party. The "provisional" group that seceded set down deep roots in Northern Ireland and is now known simply as Sinn Féin in both parts of Ireland.

OTHER PARTIES

Two distinctive sets of sectional interests have also been significant since 1922. First, a small Labour Party appeared in 1922 as an offshoot of the trade-union movement, and has been continuously represented since then; its average support between 1932 and 2002 has been 11 percent. Second, a Farmers' Party—originating from the Farmers' Union, an organization of larger farmers—existed between 1922 and 1932; average support during its lifetime was 7.7 percent. A more extensive agrarian party, Clann na Talmhan (Party of the Land), was founded on 29 June 1939 and

later participated in two coalition governments. Its support tended to come from smaller farmers, especially in the western counties, but this gradually tapered off; the party's average support from 1943 to 1961 was 5.5 percent.

Few other parties disturbed the pattern of relatively stable party support. The radical left has been very weak, and only one communist-linked deputy has ever been elected (James Larkin, in September 1927). Some minor nationalist parties existed in the 1920s, but on 6 July 1946 a more vigorous radical party appeared—Clann na Poblachta (Party of the Republic), which took support from Fianna Fáil and allowed the formation of the first coalition government on 18 February 1948. Clann na Poblachta proved to be ephemeral; it disappeared in the 1960s; its average support between 1948 and 1961 was 6.5 percent. Since then, the most significant new arrival has been the Progressive Democrats, founded on 21 December 1985, whose origins lay in divisions within Fianna Fáil over the leadership of Charles Haughey but which also attracted support from other parties. The party's share of the vote has slipped since its first electoral outing in 1987, but it averaged 6.1 percent over the four elections between 1987 and 2002. It has participated in coalition governments with Fianna Fáil from 1989 to 1992 and since 1997.

PARTIES AND VOTERS

The three main parties had long been considered atypical of Europe because they reflected underlying social divisions only weakly. Fianna Fáil has traditionally been a catchall party, with more pronounced support in the small-farming areas of the western counties in its early years. Fine Gael has had a slightly more middle-class support base and has traditionally been strongly represented among large farmers. The Labour Party's areas of greatest strength are in the south and east of the country, with farm laborers as one of its more distinctive traditional components and some urban working-class support in more recent years.

Parallel to the weak link between the parties and social structure, there is a near-absence of ideological distinctiveness. In its early days Fianna Fáil was more socially radical, and Fine Gael more conservative, but since the late twentieth century the two parties have contested the middle ground. The Labour Party originally represented itself as a relatively cautious wing of the trade-union movement, but it swung sharply to the left in the late 1960s, then returned decisively to the center in the 1980s.

By the end of the twentieth century the similarity of Irish political parties mirrored developments in other

European countries. The bitter differences that led to the formation of the party system in the 1920s were substantially purged when in 1948 Fine Gael appeared to appropriate Fianna Fáil's cause and broke the remaining tenuous link with the United Kingdom by ending Ireland's membership of the Commonwealth. Since then, although the imprint of Fianna Fáil's more nationalist history is still plain, competition between parties has been based on pragmatic rather than ideological arguments.

SEE ALSO Anglo-Irish Treaty of 1921; Civil War; Clarke, Kathleen; Cosgrave, W. T.; de Valera, Eamon; Irish Republican Army (IRA); Lemass, Seán; Mother and Child Crisis; Politics: Impact of the Northern Ireland Crisis on Southern Politics; Politics: Independent Ireland since 1922; Proportional Representation; Trade Unions; Women's Parliamentary Representation since 1922; **Primary Documents:** Provisional Government Proclamation at the Beginning of the Civil War (29 June 1922); Republican Cease-Fire Order (28 April 1923); "Aims of Fianna Fáil in Office" (17 March 1932); From the 1937 Constitution; Letter to John A. Costello, the Taoiseach (5 April 1951)

Bibliography

Busteed, M. A. *Voting Behaviour in the Republic of Ireland: A Geographical Perspective.* 1990.

Coakley, John, and Michael Gallagher, eds. *Politics in the Republic of Ireland.* 3d edition, 1999.

Gallagher, Michael. *Political Parties in the Republic of Ireland.* 1985.

Mair, Peter. *The Changing Irish Party System.* 1987.

Marsh, Michael, and Paul Mitchell. *How Ireland voted 1997.* 1999.

Sinnott, Richard. *Irish Voters Decide: Voting Behaviour in Elections and Referendums since 1918.* 1995.

John Coakley

Politics

1500 TO 1690	**STEVEN G. ELLIS**
1690 TO 1800—A PROTESTANT KINGDOM	**DAVID W. MILLER**
1800 TO 1921— CHALLENGES TO THE UNION	**D. GEORGE BOYCE**
INDEPENDENT IRELAND SINCE 1922	**DIARMAID FERRITER**
NATIONALIST POLITICS IN NORTHERN IRELAND	**ÉAMON PHOENIX**
IMPACT OF THE NORTHERN IRELAND CRISIS ON SOUTHERN POLITICS	**JOHN COAKLEY**

1500 TO 1690

In large measure political divisions in late medieval Ireland still reflected the pattern of earlier English colonization. This in turn had been shaped by geographical divisions between arable lowlands and predominantly pastoral regions of mountain, wood, and bog. Medieval English settlement had been concentrated in the eastern and southern lowlands, which remained the heartland of the English lordship into early Tudor times. By then, however, little remained of the less heavily colonized regions of English Connacht and Ulster. English rule in these parts had mostly been swept away by the Gaelic revival (c. 1300–1460), leaving small coastal strips around Galway and extending north from Carlingford to Carrickfergus; and even the English heartland had been somewhat reduced by Gaelic military pressure on the frontier borders. Thus, by 1500, Ireland as seen by English officials was divided politically and culturally into three main regions. First, there was the "English Pale," first so described in 1494. In the narrow sense, this meant the fortified area of English law, language, and culture around Dublin—the "four obedient shires" of the eastern coastal plain inhabited by "the king's loyal English lieges," although even here Gaelic customs retained a hold. The Pale also referred more loosely to the wider English lordship, particularly the royal port-towns and cities, and other densely settled areas like south Wexford and the Barrow-Nore-Suir river basin, which were readily accounted part of the Tudor state. Second, there was the area of the "king's English rebel," that is, various lordships of mixed English and Gaelic law and custom ruled by families of English descent, which were effectively independent or only intermittently answerable to royal government. Finally, there were those regions inhabited by "the king's Irish enemies," the Gaelic clans and chiefs who ruled over sixty independent lordships and a host of dependent chieftaincies by Gaelic law and custom.

Politically, therefore, Ireland around 1500 was a highly fragmented land, in which the effective unit of authority was the lordship. English kings usually governed their Irish territories—like other Tudor borderlands—by appointing as their deputy the most powerful magnate among the local English, in this case, the earl of Kildare. By this means the Crown could harness to defend the English both the earl's personal *manraed* ("counsel of men," including his tenants, members of his household, and other supporters) on the Pale's southern borders and also his extensive political connections elsewhere, so as to supplement the meager resources traditionally available to the Dublin administration. With royal support successive Kildare earls had gradually built up an effective system of peels (tower-houses), dikes, and fortified bridges to defend the Pale. They had also reduced and recolonized key outposts long reoccupied by the Irish in exposed marchlands. Thus English rule was consolidated during the Kildare ascendancy, and the English lordship was again made financially and militarily self-sufficient.

To the Tudors, however, there were also disadvantages in this system of devolved administration through a powerful regional magnate (known as aristocratic Home Rule to an earlier generation of nationalist historians). As long as Henry Tudor concentrated on reestablishing royal authority in lowland England, and Kildare refrained from backing Yorkist pretenders, the arrangement worked well; and initially too, Henry VIII was far more interested in reviving the Hundred Years' War against France than in fostering good rule in remote borderlands. By 1520, however, when the earl of Surrey led a reconnaissance in force to establish "by which means and ways your grace might reduce this land to obedience and good order," Tudor expectations of their ruling magnates had advanced beyond the mere preservation of a precarious peace in the Pale. Moreover, English merchants and gentry of the *maghery* (Pale heartland) increasingly demanded "good English order and rule" instead of march law (a local hybrid of English and Gaelic law specific to the borderland) and feudal excesses that left the king's subjects "in no better case than the wild Irish." The Kildares therefore became a victim of their own success. An effective system of defenses fostered the growth in the Pale *maghery* of an ordered society akin to that in lowland England, and with like expectations of "good rule." Yet, so long as Ireland remained overall a turbulent society—with a military frontier between two nations, cultures, and political systems—defensive needs necessarily remained paramount.

THE ORIGINS OF THE TUDOR CONQUEST

The Kildare rebellion of 1534 to 1535 was in effect precipitated by growing tensions between traditional magnate power and the heightened expectations of Tudor monarchy and Pale society. Hitherto, the Tudors had generally declined the option of an English-born outsider as governor, with the consequent expense of supplying a military retinue to enforce royal authority. Yet the crushing of the rebellion also destroyed the earl's political connection by which the English in Ireland had been defended, thus bringing the Tudor monarchy for the first time into direct contact with the turbulent border chieftaincies hitherto controlled by Kildare. This left the Crown with little option but to retain as a standing garrison the nucleus of the English relief army sent to crush the rebellion, together with its administrative backbone, the financial officials, and army captains headed by the successive military commanders (Sir William Skeffington, deputy, 1534–1535, and Lord Leonard Grey, deputy, 1536–1540).

Government through an English-born outsider transformed the Crown's immediate problem from supervising a wayward deputy to finding additional revenues to meet the extra expenses of what some historians have termed *direct rule*. The so-called Irish Reformation Parliament (1536–1537) not only applied to Ireland Henry VIII's religious initiatives and arrangements for the royal succession but also attempted to put the Irish revenues on a more secure footing. Acts for the attainder of Kildare and his supporters, the dissolution of the monasteries, and the confiscation of the lands of English absentees all swelled the supply of Crown lands, nominally tripling the annual Irish revenues. In practice, however, much of this land was marchland that the new regime, lacking Kildare's cross-border connections, was unable properly to defend. Lord Leonard Grey worked wonders with the small army at his disposal, but the events surrounding the Geraldine League underlined the fact that both financially and militarily his administration was seriously undersupplied.

The long rule of Sir Anthony Saint Leger as governor (1540–1548, 1550–1551, 1553–1556) provided more continuity in the Dublin administration and a more consistent attempt to adapt for Ireland the characteristic Tudor reform policies—reducing outlying parts to good rule. The ground was prepared by the so-called surrender and regrant initiative. A statute of 1541 in the Irish Parliament confirmed Henry VIII as king of Ireland—so that what had been a mere land or lordship annexed to the Crown was now erected into a separate kingdom. By these means a mechanism was belatedly established for turning Irish enemies into English subjects and incorporating Gaelic lordships into the Tudor state. Gaelic chiefs would hold their lands from the Crown, with leading clansmen transformed into tenants by a process of subinfeudation; Gaelic lordships would become English shires; and English law and administrative structures would replace Gaelic law and customs. In short, the extension of English government throughout Ireland would eliminate the traditional constitutional divisions between the Irish and the English.

Administratively, this initiative closely resembled the so-called Welsh act of union (1536–1543), whereby Welsh marcher lordships had been shired (made into counties or shires) and the "mere Welsh" granted English law. Yet Wales had been conquered by 1283, was part of the same land mass, and its peoples regarded the Tudors as Welsh. Ireland, by contrast, was not only a separate island four times as large, but more than half of it was inhabited by hostile clans—part of a wider Gaelic world extending into Scotland—that had no natural ties with the Tudors. The decision to turn Ireland into a second Tudor kingdom (albeit still a dependency, not a sovereign kingdom) perhaps reflected some appreciation of these essential differences that Ireland could not simply be submerged into a greater England. Yet the Tudor aim was nothing less than to erect on the flimsy foundations of medieval English settlement—a mere patchwork of lordships and port-towns scattered through Leinster and Munster—a centralized early modern kingdom comprehending the whole island, which was also thoroughly English in law, government, culture and, eventually too, in religion. This was probably the most ambitious project that the Tudors ever attempted. Yet for much of the century Ireland ranked a bad fourth, after English domestic concerns, continental developments, and relations with Scotland, in the priorities of Tudor government, and so also in the resources which successive monarchs were prepared to commit to this enterprise.

The inevitable result of scanty resources matched to great ambition was very slow progress. Paradoxically, this worked initially in the government's favor. With only five hundred men available and the old king already grumbling about an annual deficit of IR£5,000, Saint Leger had little option in his dealings with Gaelic chiefs but to prefer inexpensive compromise and conciliation over coercion. Henry VIII's death (in January 1547) saw surrender and regrant completed only in regard to three of the more powerful chieftaincies: O'Brien and O'Neill were created earls of Thomond and Tyrone respectively, and MacGiolla Phádraig was ennobled as Lord Fitzpatrick of Upper Ossory. In addition, two lords of English descent were reconciled to the Crown: James FitzGerald, earl of Desmond, and Ulick Bourke, who was created earl of Clanrickard. Yet transforming Gaelic chiefs into feudal magnates like Kildare did little to foster the kind of ordered society that Tudor officials increasingly saw as the only authentic expression of English civility. The deployment of Gaelic kerne (unarmored, variously armed foot soldiers) in France and Scotland in 1544 to 1545 temporarily eased the problem of underemployed professional soldiers in these lordships, but the replacement of Gaelic succession and inheritance customs by English tenures and primogeniture, as envisaged by surrender and regrant, proved very divisive in the erstwhile ruling clan. Thus Ireland still looked very disturbed and disorderly to English observers, despite the optimism engendered by these new initiatives. And not until 1557 was any Gaelic lordship actually shired, and then only in very different circumstances.

The English saw the Irish as living in idleness and brutality in mountains, woods, and bogs, in insubstantial dwellings, and practicing other, apparently bizarre customs, and officials automatically relegated them to the lower rungs of the great chain of being. Surrender and regrant accordingly presented a great opportunity to adopt a better way of life. Yet, instead of eager acceptance of this generous offer, English officials detected reluctance on the part of Gaelic nobles to embrace the benefits of English civility. The slow progress of Tudor reform was soon blamed on the malice of chiefs and clansmen who seemingly wished to preserve their privileges and tyranny over the poor earthtillers who were without rights in the lands they worked. Thus, once Henry VIII's death had eased the purse strings, the regency council of the young Edward VI developed more coercive strategies to force the pace, and was prepared to pay for results. The army was quadrupled in size, military control south of a line running from Carlingford to the Shannon was quickly established, and, following disturbances by the O'Mores and O'Connors in the Gaelic midlands, Leix and Offaly were declared forfeit to the Crown. Having established Forts Governor and Protector to control these lordships, the government then took steps to plant them with colonies of Englishmen—Pale gentry or New English servitors—in a bid to screen the Pale.

Yet increased coercion proved both expensive and counterproductive. By 1552 the annual deficit had soared to IR£52,000, which the government could not afford. The army's lack of discipline and the increased cost of purveyance to support it alienated the local English, as did other sporadic attempts to shift the financial burden onto them: the disastrous Tudor experiment of debasing the coinage, which ruined trade; and various attempts into the 1580s to commute purveyance (called *cess* in Ireland), which was opposed as a system of military taxation without parliamentary consent.

An English depiction (c. 1581) of Irish life by John Derricke. It shows Irish kerne—or brigands—bands of lightly armed, loosely organized toughs who preyed on civilians and contributed (particularly from an English point of view) to the instability of the countryside. FROM JOHN DERRICKE'S *THE IMAGE OF IRELANDE* (1581).

The Irish too were unsettled by the activities of an enlarged army, seeing its exploits, particularly the Leix-Offaly plantation, not as a development of Tudor reform but as a reversion to the more traditional English ambition of military conquest. Moreover, although Leix and Offaly were shired as queen's and king's counties in 1557, the struggling English settlement of soldier-colonists proved both a financial drain and a military liability. The expropriated Gaelic clans never accepted this purported oasis of English civility planted in their midst, and these new shires, lying beyond the standing defenses of the Pale, also proved difficult to defend.

By the time the young Queen Elizabeth tried to rein in costs—following a second bout of military adventures in Ulster by Saint Leger's successor, the enthusiastic but inexperienced earl of Sussex—an army of fifteen hundred was about the minimum force that could be contemplated to maintain order. And in the longer period of peace down to the outbreak of the Spanish war (1585–1604), the Irish service was almost the only outlet for younger sons of English aristocrats bent on soldiering to make their fortunes.

Contrary to the contention that English captains were swayed by ethnological and anthropological distinctions between Irish and English, research from the 1990s suggests that they thought conventionally in terms of good subjects and rebels, and generally felt themselves bound by the normal rules of war as practiced elsewhere. Yet the increasing resort to martial law did nothing to promote respect among the *Gaedhil* (Gaelic Irish) for English law and government; and neither ministers in London nor in Dublin could effectively check the abrasive conduct of local captains and officials more concerned to establish themselves as landed gentry than to advance Tudor reform. Growing political and military pressure exerted by the Dublin administration mainly prompted disaffected Gaelic chiefs and feudal magnates to band together to resist Tudor centralization. Late Tudor politics was punctuated by major rebellions as native opposition became more generalized and ideological. And by 1579 originally distinct movements of political and religious opposition were coalescing. Widespread withdrawal from Church of Ireland services fostered a settled recusancy among Gaelic and Old English peoples alike.

In appealing to Gaelic chiefs for support James Fitzmaurice combined the appeal of faith with fatherland. Likewise, Hugh O'Neill, earl of Tyrone, who mounted the most serious challenge to Tudor rule during the Nine Years War (1594–1603), courted Old English support from 1596 onwards by attributing to Ireland and the Irish a common faith and a common fatherland. Within thirty years this new nationalist ideology was to erode earlier differences of race and culture, but in the 1590s Gaelic particularism and the traditional politics of ethnicity proved insuperable obstacles in Tyrone's efforts to build a national movement against the Tudor conquest. Despite English fears of an Old English rising in support of their fellow Catholics, or the Spanish landing at Kinsale, Lord Deputy Mountjoy's commanders at the decisive battle of Kinsale (1601) included the Gaelic earl of Thomond and the Old English earl of Clanrickard.

A BRITISH KINGDOM

Tyrone's surrender to Mountjoy at Mellifont in March 1603 brought the Tudor conquest to completion at the same time as the accession of James VI of Scotland to the English Crown created a new multiple monarchy extending throughout the British Isles. These twin developments transformed the character of Irish politics. In the first place, Ireland was now governed as a centralized early modern kingdom. Within three years the normal officials of English shire government were operating in the erstwhile Gaelic lordships, and English laws and customs had ousted Gaelic ones. Similar moves against Gaelic law and custom in Scotland removed the political underpinning of the Gaelic system there too, thus facilitating the partition of medieval Gaeldom between two composite kingdoms. Behind these changes lay a subtle redirection of Crown policy. King James sought the gradual assimilation of his patrimony into a British polity following best practice in politics, government, and religion. Rather than imposing "civility" like the Tudors by a rigid enforcement of English norms and values, his aim of erecting a "perfect union" on the union of the crowns envisaged detailed differences between his three kingdoms. He was also more familiar with, and indulgent of, Gaelic traditions. Gaelic bards were indeed conscious of the Stewart dynasty's Gaelic lineage, extolling James in traditional praise poetry as "our true king."

In consequence, early Stuart Ireland witnessed the rapid advance of what might be described as national politics in the modern sense, focused on king and country, faith and fatherland. The Crown and institutions of English government were soon accepted in Gaelic Ireland, so much so that during the War of the Three Kingdoms (1638–1652) support for a restoration of the old Gaelic system was negligible. A striking indication of this change was the creation of a new political vocabulary in Gaelic, attuned to the changed circumstances, with terms like *dúthaigh* and *athartha* now denoting *native land* and *fatherland*. The poets quietly decided that the *Gaill* (foreigners) were Irish Catholics like the *Gaedhil*. Accordingly, the common denomination

Éireannaigh (the people of Ireland) now applied to these Catholic descendants of medieval *Gaedhil* and *Gaill*, whether of English or Gaelic speech and culture. The real foreigners, for whom the term *Gaill* was now reserved, were the New English, followers of Luther and Calvin and other Protestant heretics. Also excluded were the *Gaedhil* of Scotland: though no less Gaelic in language, law, and customs, these *Gaedhil* were neither Catholic (in many cases) nor living in Ireland. Yet surviving Gaelic landowners increasingly adopted English law and language to protect their estates in the new Ireland. The descent of the Gaelic learned classes into poverty mirrored the language's declining status. By 1700 a series of predominantly spoken dialects had ousted the standard literary language, common classical Gaelic.

These changes engendered real bitterness among the Gaelic literati: In satires such as *Parliament Chloinne Tomáis* (The parliament of Thomas's clan) they denounced the accompanying social revolution that transformed oppressed Gaelic laborers into smallholding tenants of New English landlords. By contrast with the autocratic Gaelic system, the model of English local government envisaged comparatively humble freeholders and copyholders (yeomen, husbandmen, and even artisans) serving as parish constables, churchwardens, and members of grand and petty juries. Similarly, English tenures held out the prospect of protection at common law for erstwhile Gaelic laborers. In practice, however, the parallel intrusion through plantation projects of numerous British settlers frustrated English efforts to build an ordered society and an English pattern of politics. In the aftermath of the Desmond rebellion (1579–1583) earlier experiments with small-scale plantation projects gave place to more sweeping measures. The expropriation of native landowners was still more thorough in the Ulster plantation of 1610, covering six escheated counties in the northwest, even though many native smallholders remained on the land. Thus the apparent success of anglicization masked growing tensions within the political system, focusing on land and religion.

Throughout James I's reign the basis of support for Crown policy remained disturbingly narrow, with central government dominated by an unrepresentative clique of New English adventurers, backed by a small standing army, fixed initially at eleven hundred men. Under the English model, local government was traditionally run by the major landowners acting as justices of the peace and sheriffs; but outside the major plantation districts, these remained predominantly Catholic, whether Gaelic or Old English. The government's difficulty was highlighted by the events of the 1613 to 1615 Parliament (repeated in the 1634–1635 Parliament), when most shires and traditional boroughs elected Catholic members (temporal peers in the Lords were also predominantly Catholic) and the government was forced to create new boroughs to engineer a compliant and Protestant Commons majority. Further plantations (as proposed, most sweepingly, for Connacht in 1635) gradually produced more Protestant landowners, but also deepened the divisions between Catholic tenants, threatened or dispossessed landowners, and Protestant newcomers, thus highlighting the regime's predominantly colonial character.

With Charles I's firm backing, the able but unscrupulous Viscount Wentworth (deputy, 1633–1640) was able to recover some freedom of maneuver for the Crown by balancing natives against planters, but when the king's policies of centralist "personal rule" collapsed in his other two kingdoms and Wentworth was recalled, the weakly directed Dublin administration proved quite unable to contain the ensuing Ulster rising (1641). Catholics exploited the political paralysis in England to launch a preemptive strike in a bid to disarm the Protestant communities of Ulster and the Pale. The revolt quickly got out of hand, precipitating the worst civilian massacres ever seen in the British Isles: perhaps three thousand Protestants were slaughtered, and many more fled to England. The ensuing civil war (1641–1649) was nakedly sectarian: English and Scots armies were sent over to prop up the Protestant and settler interest still holding out in small pockets; the "Confederate Catholics of Ireland" (from July 1642) established control elsewhere. Yet the Confederates were riven by internal dissentions, chiefly between the Old English anxious for a speedy settlement with the king to safeguard their estates and the already dispossessed *Gaedhil* who were more eager to prosecute the war. These divisions in turn prevented the Confederates from supporting the king effectively against the English parliamentarians and Scots, with the result that, following Charles's defeat and execution (1649), Oliver Cromwell was able to redeploy the New Model Army to accomplish the military subjugation of Ireland and the restoration of English authority (1649–1651).

IRELAND UNDER CROMWELL

With the important exception of the land settlement, the establishment of Ireland's first republic (1653–1660) had little long-term impact on the political system. Over one-third of the land was confiscated and redistributed to English soldiers or investors, but even with a large army of occupation, the republic's efforts to transplant the Catholics to Connacht proved beyond its administrative capacity. In 1653 Ireland and Scotland were accorded representation in the 460-member English parliament, but the 30 Irish members who sat in the three succeeding parliaments were chiefly army officers. The republic's speedy collapse following Cromwell's death (1658) not only discredited what little antimonarchical sentiment had existed in Ireland but also occasional proposals in the settler community for a parliamentary union.

THE RESTORATION

With the monarchy's restoration (1660) came also a return of the old constitutional relationship with England, the Church of Ireland, and the early Stuart system of politics and government. What was not restored, however, was the land confiscated from Irish Catholics. While his throne remained insecure, Charles II dared not alienate the Irish Cromwellians (who had supported the Restoration). Thus, despite the king's sympathy for the dispossessed, and despite the selective restoration of lands to a few leading royalists like the duke of Ormond, the most that could be achieved was a piecemeal modification of the Cromwellian settlement. In 1641 Catholics had still held 59 percent of the land; by 1688, the Catholic proportion had fallen to 22 percent. Moreover, when Parliament first met in 1661, very few restorations had occurred, and so the Cromwellian interest dominated an exclusively Protestant Commons. Restoration Ireland had the form of a parliamentary constitution, but it was essentially a colony governed through deputy and council.

Under the circumstances, political stability depended on the English connection. As before, many of the dispossessed soon departed to Catholic Europe or took to banditry. Protestants feared another Catholic insurrection, as in 1641. The hysteria surrounding the Popish Plot (1678–1681) prompted the execution of the Catholic archbishop of Armagh for treason, and new orders for the expulsion of Catholic clergy and the surrender of arms by Catholics. With the accession in 1685 of a Catholic king, James II, however, the Restoration settlement soon unraveled. Initially, James denied any intention to alter the land settlement and moved cautiously to admit Catholics to office and replace Protestant army officers, but Catholic expectations of great changes arose. Many Protestant merchants sold up and moved to England. The pace of change quickened considerably in 1687 after a Catholic deputy, Richard Talbot, earl of Tyrconnell, was appointed. In preparation for Parliament, Tyrconnell selected Catholic sheriffs, remodeled the corporations, and greatly increased the size of the now Catholic army.

THE GLORIOUS REVOLUTION AND THE SUBJUGATION OF IRELAND

By the time Parliament met in the summer of 1689, however, James had been deposed in England in favor of William of Orange. Tyronnell still held Ireland (excepting Londonderry and Enniskillen) for James who had since arrived in person. The overwhelmingly Catholic Parliament asserted Ireland's legislative independence, removed civil disabilities imposed on religious grounds, overturned the land settlement, and attainted over 2,400 Protestants, including almost all the landowners. Yet this program could only be implemented by military victory since a Williamite army had meanwhile landed near Belfast and recovered Ulster for William. The Jacobite forces were strengthened by 7,000 French troops in March 1690, but William's arrival tipped the balance. William's victory at the Boyne did not end the campaign, but with James's immediate departure for France the issue was no longer in doubt. The Boyne restored Protestant political control, and Catholic influence was soon reduced still further by renewed expropriation of Catholic landlords. It also marked the climax of a political conflict that had grown steadily more explicit and intense since the mid-Tudor period.

SEE ALSO Colonial Theory from 1500 to 1690; Land Settlements from 1500 to 1690; Legal Change in the Sixteenth and Seventeenth Centuries; Monarchy; Surrender and Regrant; **Primary Documents:** From *Solon His Follie* (1594); On Catholic Ireland in the Early Seventeenth Century; From *A Direction for the Plantation of Ulster* (1610); Ferocity of the Irish Wars (1580s–1590s)

Bibliography

Beckett, James C. *The Making of Modern Ireland, 1603–1923.* 1966.

Canny, Nicholas. *Making Ireland British, 1580–1650.* 2001.

Ellis, Steven G. *Ireland in the Age of the Tudors.* 1998.

Moody, T. W., F. X. Martin, and F. J. Byrne, eds. *A New History of Ireland.* Vol. 3, *Early Modern Ireland, 1534–1691.* 1976.

Steven G. Ellis

1690 TO 1800—A PROTESTANT KINGDOM

Politics is contention for power, and we may call that subset of the population within which a country's poli-

tics takes place the "polity." Ireland's political history over this period of eleven decades begins with the expulsion from the polity of one of the major groups of contenders in the politics of the previous era—propertied (or previously propertied) Catholics. It ends with the collapse of that polity in the face of demands not only by the heirs of those contenders but also by various other groups for admission to the polity, and with a decision by the government to replace the old polity with an entirely new one.

A polity is always more than just the government but less than the whole population. The government is one contender for power; other contenders in an early modern European polity typically include elite coalitions organized around some interest—economic, religious, dynastic, ideological, and so on—and the object of their contention is usually some degree of influence in or upon the government. Normally, however, all members of the polity regard themselves as entitled to protection by the combined resources of the whole polity, including those of the government, whenever threatened by those outside its geographic or social boundaries. There are, however, abnormal times when members of the polity seek alliances with entities outside the polity—for example, domestic nonelite groups or foreign powers. We call such times "revolutionary."

The process by which a government gained a monopoly of one particular component of power—physical coercion—has a special name in the historiography of early modern Europe: "the rise of the state." In the modern world we measure the legitimacy of a state by the extent to which its population recognizes the right of its government to such a monopoly. Two successive polities embracing Ireland—the "Kingdom of Ireland" in its Protestant-dominated phase (1691–1800) and the "United Kingdom of Great Britain and Ireland" (1801–1922)—spectacularly failed to attain legitimacy by this standard. Just what sort of a state was the eighteenth-century Irish polity, and why did it fail?

THE COMPOSITION OF THE IRISH POLITY

The Irish polity in this period consisted of the Protestant landed class (who, together with their clergy, came to be known as the "Ascendancy") and a government headquartered in Dublin Castle. The fact that the Irish polity excluded the great majority of the population—the "lower orders"—was quite normal in ancien régime Europe. It had, however, two quite peculiar features. First, it excluded a large and important elite: those members of the nobility and gentry who were Roman Catholics. Second, its government was extraterritorial—that is, government officials owed their appoint-

The Irish House of Commons *(1780) by Francis Wheatley. The member standing to the right of the table is Henry Grattan. The theatrical character of the chamber is emphasized by the gallery of fashionably dressed spectators.* LEEDS MUSEUMS AND GALLERIES (LOTHERTON HALL) U.K./BRIDGEMAN ART LIBRARY. REPRODUCED BY PERMISSION.

ments to the workings of the polity of another country, Great Britain (or England prior to 1707).

The ideal of a nonmartial politics was symbolized in Ireland by the existence of a parliament modelled on its English counterpart. During the late Middle Ages the geographic range within which the government might dare to hope that local elites could be trusted to engage in politics with voices rather than with swords was reflected in the territory that had been "shired"—that is, carved up into counties entitled to send representatives to the House of Commons. It was not until the 1690s, however, that the government was forced by financial needs to summon Parliament with sufficient frequency to make it the primary venue of contention within the polity.

The first object of contention was the composition of the polity itself. At the end of the seventeenth century, of course, it went without saying that membership

in the polity would be limited to the landed. Confiscations had reduced the Catholic land ownership to 22 percent of the land in Ireland by 1688. In 1691 William consented to terms of Jacobite surrender at Limerick whose leniency toward Catholic landowners enraged Protestants. Catholics having been barred from sitting in the Irish parliament in 1691, Protestants used their control of that institution to put pressure on the king to restrict implementation of provisions favorable to continued Catholic landowning. By 1703 the Catholic share of Irish land had been reduced to 14 percent. Furthermore, the Irish parliament insisted upon enactment of a series of anti-Catholic penal laws toward which the government was lukewarm. While this legislation seemed to envisage the complete elimination of the Roman Catholic Church from Irish soil, restrictions on the exercise of the Catholic religion came to be rarely implemented. Patterns of enforcement suggest that the Ascendancy's real objective was to reduce the property of wealthy Catholic laymen even further and to prevent them from ever acquiring more land.

Thus by about 1710 the composition of the polity seemed decided: It would consist of the Protestant Ascendancy and the government and no one else. So long as that remained true, no monarch would be able to play off the Catholics against the Protestants in the manner of several earlier Stuart kings. For the foreseeable future the principal object of contention within the polity would be the power relationships between the Ascendancy and the government. The principal mechanism regulating those relationships was Poynings' Law, which had been enacted in 1494 to prevent Ireland from being used as a launching pad for pretenders to the English crown. In the eighteenth century its practical effect was to give the king's ministers in London the power to amend or veto legislation proposed by the Irish parliament. In the Declaratory Act of 1720 the British parliament further asserted its right to pass legislation binding on Ireland. Members of the Ascendancy generally acquiesced in these arrangements, though a Patriot Party opposed to the subordinate status of the Irish parliament emerged in mid-century. Most of the time the government was able to manage the Irish parliament through the same arts of influence and patronage that were perfected in the British parliament in this period.

How well did this curious polity work? Certainly, it did succeed for eight decades in averting violent contention for power among its own members: Differences among gentlemen might lead to duels, but not to civil wars. Of course, the Catholic side in the violent contentions of the previous century had been decisively weakened by the penal laws as well as by the departure of many of their gentry to the continent. However, even when a reversal of their fortunes seemed possible during the invasions of Scotland in 1715 and 1745 by the Stuart pretenders (nominally recognized as the legitimate royal line by the Catholic Church), Catholic gentry in Ireland lay very low indeed.

But how well did the polity succeed in gaining the acquiescence of those who were outside it not because of their religion (or at least not solely because of it) but because of their social class? Outbreaks of violence involving either Catholic peasants in southern districts or their Protestant counterparts in parts of Ulster became especially frequent from around 1760. These disturbances, however, were focused on local grievances and did not threaten the authority of the polity itself. Indeed, there is evidence that rioters had a "moral economy" perspective on their plight—a deferential expectation that the gentry could and should be expected to redress their grievances on principles of social justice.

To the extent that there was a cultural "glue" that legitimated the eighteenth-century polity it was not nationalism (however fervently patriot orators might espouse the cause of the "Irish nation") but a political culture based on patron-client relationships. To sustain cordial relations with their local tenants and other dependents, members of the polity practiced various sorts of reciprocity, ranging from rent abatements to generous provision of popular festivities. In addition, reliable Protestant retainers participated in a special ritual of clientage in times of alarm, foreign or domestic: Their patron might assemble them as an ad hoc military force upon which the government might (or might not) confer the official status of a militia.

During the late 1770s some unofficial local militias, which had been mobilized in recent years to deal with agrarian disturbances, were suddenly supplemented by the formation of numerous other "volunteer" units throughout the country in response to rumors of a possible invasion by the French allies of the U.S. rebels. Though the original purpose of these forces was security and the maintenance of public order, the Volunteers quickly became a political movement allied with the Patriot Party. Volunteer agitation contributed both to the British government's decision in 1779 to yield to the Irish parliament's demand for an end to restrictions on Irish trade with Britain and the colonies and to its 1782 concession of a drastic amendment of Poynings' Law. Although it is easy to overstate the importance of this move to "legislative independence," it was clearly a major victory for the patrons of the rank-and-file Volunteers in the former's contention with the government.

A THEATER STATE?

The anthropologist Clifford Geertz has proposed the term *theater state* to describe polities remote from the modern western state conceived as an entity that commands virtually unanimous consent for a government having a monopoly of coercive force within the national territory (Geertz 1980). It would be hard to find a better example of political theater than the parade of the Dublin Volunteers outside the Parliament House on 4 November 1779, with a cannon bearing a sign which read "Free Trade or this!" The gun was a prop that no one actually expected would be fired in anger. In this exercise—as in all their countless parades, reviews, drills, and mock battles—Volunteers were acting out their understanding of their place in the polity. For the officers, these military performances symbolized the honor-laden right and duty of the Protestant male elite to defend the polity, and the reciprocal duty of the government to grant their political demands.

Ireland's lack of a resident monarch did leave it relatively impoverished in some particular types of ritual performance that have interested students of various other early modern European countries. Moreover, the fact that the religion of the polity was rejected by the overwhelming majority of the population made it difficult for the established church to play the role of sacralizing the polity as effectively as did her counterparts in other theater states in early modern Europe. Nevertheless, the Irish polity managed to affirm itself in various ceremonial ways, ranging from processions by high officials to the exemplary spectacles of capital and corporal punishment. The flamboyant oratorical performances of leading politicians gave the Irish parliament a theatrical character confirmed by the audience of fashionable ladies in the gallery in Francis Wheatley's famous painting of the *The Irish House of Commons* (1780). However, it was the martial spectacles of the Volunteers that in most parts of Ireland most faithfully reflected the patron-client relationship that underpinned the political system. Nevertheless, by taking their act onto the stage of national politics, Volunteer leaders unwittingly placed the boundaries of the polity in question.

While Volunteer performances symbolized essential features of the political system, Volunteer activities in defense of public order, as well as political advocacy by Volunteer gatherings, exposed some of the anomalies and ambiguities of that system. An important ambiguity in the boundaries of the polity was the status of the wealthy Presbyterian elite of Belfast. Although they had not suffered from such severe legal disabilities as had elite Catholics, in practice they were excluded from the governance of their own town by an Anglican landlord who owned the land on which it was situated. The Volunteers in Belfast and its immediate hinterland (as well as those in and around Derry) had been an exception to the general rule that Volunteering embodied and celebrated the patron-client culture. Since Presbyterians had long been welcomed into militia arrays at times of crisis, their enthusiastic volunteering was a way of demonstrating the claim of their lay and clerical leaders to full membership in the polity. A few respectable Catholics, eager to demonstrate their loyalty by taking a stand against French invasion and internal commotion, were welcomed into certain Volunteer units; and after the attainment of legislative independence in 1782 some Volunteer meetings began to pass resolutions in favor of restoring civil and political rights to Catholics.

Did willingness to defend the polity call for admission to its membership? The question was perhaps less urgent with respect to elite Catholics and Presbyterians than to rank-and-file Protestant Volunteers, who might already have had the right to vote but lacked political influence because the system of representation ensured that a majority of seats in the House of Commons were controlled by a small number of wealthy Protestant landowners. Volunteer meetings began to pass resolutions in favor of parliamentary reforms that would mainly have benefited neither the Ascendancy nor their disenfranchised Catholic gentry rivals, but rather their clients—nonelite Protestants. Accordingly, in 1784 Ascendancy leaders took steps to put a stop to political advocacy by the Volunteers.

Even this suppression of Volunteer meetings, however, did not resolve all problems over the social boundaries of the polity. During the mid-1780s in the County Armagh linen country, young Protestant males, most of whom were probably too poor to have been considered fit material for the Volunteers, began attacking Catholic homes. Angered by reports of Catholics being admitted to Volunteer units, they implicitly claimed membership in the polity by asserting that they were enforcing the penal laws against possession of arms by Catholics. Catholic "Defenders" responded to the sectarian aggression of these "Peep o' Day Boys," and in counties south and west of Armagh growing sectarian threats prompted the spread of a network of Defender cells on the model of agrarian secret societies.

Other types of politically charged ritual existed alongside the "patriotic" performance of the Volunteers. The Whiteboys and other agrarian combinations practiced "communitarian" rituals whose purposes were to enforce communal solidarity upon fellow peasants in a given locality and to remind the elite of their duties of reciprocity toward their dependents. So long as the moral economy was intact, communitarian ritual tacitly supported the patron-client political culture. Two other species of ritual, however, challenged that culture. Freemasonry, whose lodges were multiplying in the last third of the century, practiced "enlightenment" rituals that anticipated the replacement of birth by merit and tradition by reason in political culture; its adherents envisaged something like modern civil society as an alternative to the patron-client culture. A fourth variety of political ritual was associated with the rapidly growing conservative Presbyterian sects in rural Ulster that harked back to the theocratic political order advocated by the Scottish Covenanters. In revisions and renewals of seventeenth-century covenants and in open-air festal communions, "theocratic" ritual celebrated an alternative system of governance by neither the well-born nor the enlightened, but by the godly. They shared with Freemasonry a suspicion of the existing political order, but while the former looked to the past for an alternative, the latter looked forward.

Thus by the late 1780s the theatrical character of the Irish state was abundantly manifest. It was members of the polity who, by sponsoring patriotic ritual on a grand scale, had initiated an era of performance politics on the national level. Those excluded from the polity, however, had rich repertoires of ritual to contribute to the spectacle that was the theater state.

WHY THE IRISH POLITY FAILED

The French Revolution, which began in 1789, would profoundly change the situation. Northern Presbyterians, who had sympathized with the American rebels (many of them their own kinsmen) a decade earlier, tended to welcome the news from France. By 1791 the local Volunteer units were being revived, and celebrations of anniversaries of the fall of the Bastille were initiated. In that same year a group of Belfast radicals organized the Society of United Irishmen, in conscious imitation of the Masonic lodges, to advocate reform of the system of representation and equality of rights for members of all religious persuasions.

The government was increasingly alarmed at the course of the revolution and in 1793 joined other European powers in a war against France. In this situation the government was especially concerned both with placating Catholics in Ireland, whose leaders were vigorously lobbying for concessions, and with maximizing the Irish contribution to defense. Under government pressure, in 1793 the Irish parliament granted Catholics the right to vote and established a new militia that would conscript by lot from all religions. These measures stopped short of full admission of Catholics to the polity: Catholics were still prohibited from sitting in Parliament. However, the grant of both the franchise and the right to bear arms certainly blurred the sharp line that had hitherto excluded them. Perhaps surprisingly, there was widespread violent resistance by Catholic peasants, often within the organizational framework of the Defenders, to conscription for the militia. It has been powerfully argued (Bartlett 1983) that these disturbances marked a decisive end to the moral economy that had tempered earlier peasant disturbances but that had been under stress in recent decades as landlords increasingly privileged market forces over paternalistic considerations.

The end of the moral economy facilitated a profound reconfiguration of ritual systems. Communitarian ritual in its current manifestation—Defenderism—no longer supported the patron-client culture. Older histories represent the politically sophisticated United Irishmen as manipulating the backwoods Defenders, but recent students have seen the latter as much more politicized and proactive. In any event, the enlightenment repertoire of United Irish ritual and the communitarian repertoire of Defender performance tended to merge during the mid-1790s. Efforts in Belfast to revive the Volunteers for a radical agenda, plus the manifest lack of enthusiasm on the part of Catholics for the role of defending the polity in the new militia, prompted some Ascendancy leaders to sponsor new institutions as bearers of the patriotic ritual tradition. Reaffirmation of the patron-client culture and defense of the polity were entrusted to the Loyal Orange Order (established in 1795) and a yeomanry force of cavalry (set up in 1796) completely separate from the new militia. These developments reflected Ascendancy recognition that their reliable clientage now extended no further than the nonradical subset of nonelite Protestants—essentially Anglican tenants.

In the mounting excitement from 1795 to 1798 the principal form of political ritual was oath-taking. Solemn oaths of secrecy and obedience were central to both the United Irish and the Defender projects, and the government's principal legal weapon against them was a provision of the Insurrection Act of 1796 making the administration of such oaths a capital felony. Conversely, magistrates often offered suspects the opportunity to clear their names by taking the official oath of allegiance, which radicals might scruple to take on the grounds that it constituted acceptance of recent repressive legislation. As performance politics, swearing had an improvisational character. Local United Irish societies might devise variations upon the oath prescribed by their national convention, and local magistrates might recast official oaths either to create snares for tender consciences or to remove them, as suited the occasion. This orgy of reliance upon and fascination with oaths was symptomatic of the rupture of whatever social bonds had earlier existed; the prospect of divine retribution had to be invoked where human trust was lacking.

These changes in the structure and content of ritual performance were portents of the end of the Irish theater state. Whatever social cohesion had been generated by the patron-client political culture (beyond cohesion among Anglicans) had now been shattered. Performance politics had called into question all the social assumptions upon which rested such authority as the polity enjoyed, and it was reduced to its final resource: naked coercion. In the spring following the December 1796 attempt of the French fleet to land an expeditionary force in Bantry Bay (thwarted only by weather), government and Ascendancy forces carried out a systematic campaign to disarm the countryside of Ulster, which was perceived to be the most disaffected province. Routinely employing public torture, this campaign was typical of the terroristic methods to which weak regimes resort when they know they have lost all popular claim to authority.

Despite disappointment of their hopes for another French expedition and penetration of their organization by government spies, United Irish leaders initiated a rebellion in May 1798. Hostilities were concentrated mainly in three theaters. In the southeast, especially County Wexford, rebels enjoyed the able leadership of a number of liberal Protestant and Catholic gentry, who were, however, unable to prevent some sectarian atrocities against Protestant loyalists. It was in this region that the rebels made their most impressive stand against the Crown forces. In the northeast, rebels had a few minor victories before being soundly defeated. Their cause no doubt suffered from the effects of the terror campaign of the previous years, from hardheaded calculation on the part of the Belfast elite that the cause was now hopeless, and from the reports of atrocities from Wexford. On the other hand, rebel numbers were probably augmented somewhat by the tendency of some rural Presbyterians to rely more on millenarian hopes than on hardheaded calculation. Finally, after both the southeastern and northeastern rebellions had been suppressed, the French landed forces near Killala, County Mayo. Together with forces raised locally, the French conducted a two-week campaign before the Crown forces engaged and defeated them at Ballinamuck in early September.

Although policymakers in London no doubt breathed a sigh of relief at the defeat of the rebels, they gave scant credit to the Ascendancy. The Irish polity had manifestly failed, and the government decided that it should be replaced by a different polity. In particular, it proposed an Act of Union providing for a single parliament for the entire British Isles in which Irish Protestant landlords—or Irishmen of any description—would never constitute a majority. The idea was attractive to prominent Catholics, who were quietly promised that once the union was implemented, Catholic Emancipation (i.e., legislation to allow Catholics to sit in the new parliament) would be introduced. Many members of the Ascendancy, however, were bitterly hostile to the union, and they mobilized their sole remaining reliable clients, the Orangemen, in opposition to it—a special irony from the perspective of later generations, when the Orange Order was the union's staunchest defender.

Two separate parliamentary sessions—1799 and 1800—were required to secure passage of the act by the Irish parliament. The government succeeded only through a massive distribution of patronage to Protestant politicians. On 1 January 1801 a new polity—the United Kingdom of Great Britain and Ireland—came into existence. One immediate result was a measure of parliamentary reform comparable to that sought by the United Irishmen, for many of the least democratic boroughs represented in the Irish House of Commons were not given seats in the united parliament. The other principal demand of the United Irishmen did not fare so well; early in 1801 George III, who had not been apprised of the plan to introduce Catholic Emancipation, angrily refused to assent to such legislation. Prime Minister Pitt resigned, and the issue remained unresolved for nearly three decades, a delay that contributed significantly to the eventual failure of the new polity.

SEE ALSO Act of Union; Eighteenth-Century Politics: 1690 to 1714—Revolution Settlement; Eighteenth-Century Politics: 1714 to 1778—Interest Politics; Eighteenth-Century Politics: 1778 to 1795—Parliamentary and Popular Politics; Eighteenth-Century Politics: 1795 to 1800—Repression, Rebellion, and Union; Government from 1690 to 1800; Penal Laws; Protestant Ascendancy: 1690 to 1800; **Primary Documents:** An Act to Prevent the Further Growth of Popery (1704); The Declaratory Act (1720); The Catholic Relief Act (1778); The Catholic Relief Act (1782); Yelverton's Act (1782); The Renunciation Act (1783); The Catholic Relief Act (1793)

Bibliography

Bartlett, Thomas. "An End to Moral Economy: The Irish Militia Disturbances of 1793." *Past and Present* 99 (1983): 41–64.

Bartlett, Thomas. *The Fall and Rise of the Irish Nation: The Catholic Question, 1690–1830.* 1992.

Connolly, S. J. *Religion, Law, and Power: The Making of Protestant Ireland, 1660–1760.* 1992.

Cullen, Louis. "The 1798 Rebellion in Wexford: United Irishman Organisation, Membership, Leadership." In *Wexford: History and Society*, edited by Kevin Whelan. 1987.

Curtin, Nancy J. *The United Irishmen: Popular Politics in Ulster and Dublin, 1791–1798.* 1994.

Dickson, David. *New Foundations: Ireland, 1660–1800.* 1987.

Dickson, David, Dáire Keogh, and Kevin Whelan, eds. *The United Irishmen: Republicanism, Radicalism, and Rebellion.* 1993.

Donnelly, James S., Jr. "The Rightboy Movement, 1785–8." *Studia Hibernica* 17–18 (1977–1978): 120–202.

Donnelly, James S., Jr. "The Whiteboy Movement, 1761–5." *Irish Historical Studies* 21 (1978): 20–54.

Donnelly, James S., Jr. "Hearts of Oak, Hearts of Steel." *Studia Hibernica* 21 (1981): 7–73.

Donnelly, James S., Jr. "Irish Agrarian Rebellion: The Whiteboys of 1769–76." *Proceedings of the Royal Irish Academy* section C, 83, no. 12 (1983): 293–331.

Elliott, Marianne. *Wolfe Tone, Prophet of Irish Independence.* 1989.

Geertz, Clifford. *Negara: The Theatre State in Nineteenth-Century Bali.* 1980.

McDowell, R. B. *Ireland in the Age of Imperialism and Revolution, 1760–1801.* 1979.

Miller, David W. "The Armagh Troubles, 1784–95." In *Irish Peasants: Violence and Political Unrest, 1780–1914,* edited by Samuel Clark and James S. Donnelly, Jr. 1983.

Miller, David W. "Non-Professional Soldiery, c. 1600–1800." In *A Military History of Ireland,* edited by Thomas Bartlett and Keith Jeffery. 1996.

Miller, David W. "The Origins of the Orange Order in County Armagh." In *Armagh: History and Society,* edited by A. J. Hughes and William Nolan. 2001.

Stewart, A. T. Q. *A Deeper Silence: The Hidden Origins of the United Irish Movement.* 1993.

Smyth, Jim. *The Men of No Property: Irish Radicals and Popular Politics in the Late Eighteenth Century.* 1992.

Smyth, Jim, ed. *Revolution, Counter-Revolution, and Union: Ireland in the 1790s.* 2000.

Wall, Maureen. *Catholic Ireland in the Eighteenth Century.* Edited by Gerard O'Brien. 1989.

Whelan, Kevin. *The Tree of Liberty: Radicalism, Catholicism, and the Construction of Irish Identity, 1760–1830.* 1996.

David W. Miller

1800 TO 1921—CHALLENGES TO THE UNION

The Act of Union of 1800 was not a wholly new beginning for Ireland. The political manifestations of the late eighteenth century—Protestant nationalism, Catholic political advances, Presbyterian radicalism, Irish republicanism, and the sharpening of sectarian tension—all were carried forward into the new United Kingdom. Protestant enthusiasm, initially limited, soon blossomed as the union was seen as a bulwark against Catholic power. Catholic belief that the union would provide justice was weakened by the British failure to carry Catholic Emancipation in 1800. The British government hoped that the new system would provide stable political arrangements and bring prosperity to Ireland. But Ireland in the 1820s and 1830s saw a renewal of agrarian violence and a revival of the agitation for Catholic Emancipation that boded ill for the British connection.

DANIEL O'CONNELL'S OLD IRELAND

The Catholic Emancipation campaign shaped challenges to the union for decades to come. Its leader, Daniel O'Connell, denounced what most European states would have regarded as a reasonable settlement of the issue, the right of the British government to exercise a veto on episcopal appointments. He gathered the sup-

port of the Catholic Church for his stand and used its considerable influence in his victory in the County Clare by-election in 1828 against a liberal Protestant, William Vesey Fitzgerald. Yet O'Connell was also a political pragmatist who saw the advantage of working with British political parties if they could deliver reforms to assuage Catholic grievances regarding the payment of tithes to the Church of Ireland; municipal corporations in need of restructuring; and unjust Protestant and Orange influence at Dublin Castle. This might make Irishmen (by which he meant Catholics) "West Britons" again; but it would definitely shift some power in Ireland from Protestants to Catholics. O'Connell's tactics did not divert him from the greater goal of repeal of the union, which he believed was compatible with loyalty to the Crown, but which would hasten the process by which Protestants would (to use his own word) "melt" into the nation.

This prospect occasioned another challenge to the union, though one mounted to reserve a safe place for Ireland's Protestant minority (as it was fast becoming in political terms). The Young Ireland movement was deeply influenced by European (especially German) Romanticism, with its emphasis on language and culture as defining the nation. Thomas Davis, its most influential figure, hoped to stop English domination of Ireland, but he also believed that the Irish Protestants (of whom he was one) could provide cultural leadership and stave off a Catholic ascendancy. He and his colleagues clashed with O'Connell's "Old Ireland" and came off worse. Most Protestants feared that repeal of the union would mean their destruction anyway. But this struggle set the scene for future conflicts between Protestants and Catholics, with the British government, of whatever political complexion, calculating how each conflict could best be managed in the interest of the British state.

EFFECTS OF THE GREAT FAMINE

O'Connell's cause was soon lost in the Great Famine that struck Ireland between 1845 and 1851, which had a lasting impact on the character and aims of Irish nationalism. It closed the chapter that had begun as far back as the 1760s, when the Catholic middle class started to challenge its total exclusion from political power. It revealed the need for a political party and movement to be founded on a more secure electoral base. It also inspired a hopeless (but by later generations, revered) rebellion by the Young Irelanders in 1848. And it provoked some nationalists to criticize the British for their alleged callous indifference to the suffering of the people: Despite the reality of a limited but by no means unimportant official response to the famine, the British belief that it was the visitation of God that would shove

Ireland into modernization was a brutal response to a human tragedy. There is no reason to assume that Ireland was destined for a revival of nationalism after the famine; on the contrary, the 1850s saw a Conservative revival (among Protestant landlords), and the attempt by the Tenant League, which had been founded in 1850, to unite Catholic and Protestant farmers in a common cause.

But the famine had two significant influences on the recovery of Irish nationalism. The Fenian Brotherhood, which aimed at establishing an Irish republic by force of arms, was founded in 1858. Its failure to organize and to maintain secrecy, and the opposition of the Catholic hierarchy, all contributed to its failure. The suppression of sporadic violence in Great Britain and a failed uprising in Ireland in 1867 suggested that there was little future in this kind of attack upon the union. But Fenianism provided an inspiration for later would-be revolutionaries, and it produced a group of activists whose dedication surpassed their numbers. A silent revolution was of more immediate importance. The Great Famine resulted in major changes in the pattern of landholding in Ireland, with the consolidation of land in fewer hands and the rise of an important tenant-farming class—or rather classes, for the tenant farmers were not a uniform entity. There were large farmers in some areas, small farmers in others. But social change gave rural Ireland a chance to assert itself, and nationalist leaders had to take account of their fears and hopes. Rural Ireland was soon to demonstrate its power in the 1870s, as the Irish land question became at times *the* Irish Question, and it was always on the political agenda until the beginning of the twentieth century.

This was shown by the placing of land ownership on the agenda by even such a moderate challenger to the union as Isaac Butt, founder of the Home Government Association in 1870. Butt was a Protestant Conservative who had bitterly opposed Daniel O'Connell in the 1840s, but who had become disillusioned with the British government's response to the Great Famine. He was also looking for a new direction to his political career, but he had defended Fenian prisoners in the 1860s and there is no reason to doubt his sincere desire to reform the government of Ireland. He did not seek an independent Ireland, and his federal scheme for the United Kingdom envisaged an Irish parliament based on the existing restricted franchise, with an upper house to represent Irish property. His leadership has been contrasted unfavorably with that of his famous successor, Charles Stewart Parnell, but Butt was leading a party in the British parliament eulogized by Walter Bagehot, with its loose and shifting party ties. He did overestimate the power of rational argument in that parliament, but he

was aware of the kind of issue that might help to broaden the popular base of his party. The land question was one such issue, and Butt referred to it frequently. Tenant right was now moving into the political debate, and William Ewart Gladstone's Land Act of 1870 showed a recognition that some reform of the relations between landlord and tenant was necessary.

THE LAND LEAGUE, PARNELL, AND HOME RULE

The land question burst dramatically upon the British and Irish political scene in the late 1870s and retained its centrality for decades. In 1878 agrarian life in Ireland was threatened with recession, and even, some thought, with a recurrence of famine. The worldwide agrarian depression that began in 1878 had a particular impact upon the west of Ireland, and it was here that local agitators and organizers went to work to create one of the most remarkable resistance movements not only in Irish but in European history. The Land League, founded in 1879, was a genuine locally inspired movement, well organized, popular, and able to impose its will on large parts of the countryside. It called for lower rents and other concessions while the crisis lasted, but the agitation tapped into one of the core beliefs that motivated challenges to the union—that of dispossession. It was easy to turn a demand for reform into an attack upon the alien landlord class. This was not merely the result of the admittedly skillful Land League propaganda; it derived its strength from the genuine belief that the older, Catholic landlords had the real title to the land. But the Land League had no intention of seeking out and transferring the land to these lost leaders. The cry, "the land for the people," meant the tenant farmers. The result was a struggle between the Land League and the British government that was taken advantage of by the rising star of the Home Rule Party, the Protestant landlord Charles Stewart Parnell.

Parnell took the risky step of allying himself with the Land League and its aims. Although he was a landlord, he was prepared to defy the unionist politics of the vast majority of his class. Yet he was anxious to include them in a self-governing Ireland, which could be done all the better by removing the land problem that stood between them and their tenants like a sword. Parnell was prepared to place himself in direct confrontation not only with the British government, but with most of his own party members, who feared where his extremism was leading him—and them. Parnell was prepared to take that risk, and he had already caught the eye of Fenians through his obstructive behavior in the British House of Commons and his willingness to give public approval to the Fenian martyrs who had been hanged for the murder of a policeman in Manchester. In 1879 he gained the support of Fenian leaders in the New Departure, which he may not have formally accepted but which united Fenianism and the constitutional movement behind a "national parliament," peasant proprietorship, and Home Rule MPs forming an absolutely independent party. His support of the Land League brought the agrarian agitation under his leadership as well. Yet there was a real risk that the Land League agitation would spin out of control, and especially that it would alienate the important bulwark that Daniel O'Connell had fashioned, the support of the Catholic hierarchy.

Parnell was skillful enough to keep this potentially fragile alliance together, at least for a time. He used the land agitation to help his bid for the leadership of the Home Rule Party, which he gained in May 1880. He then used the party to subsume the Land League into the broader nationalist movement, and thus reinforced, he presented the British government with a dilemma: It could use coercive legislation to keep Parnell in check, but British liberal sentiment was unlikely to regard coercion as a long-term solution to the Irish problem. Gladstone, for his part, saw no reason to let anarchy prevail, but he came to believe that there must be an alternative to coercion, and he hoped that that would be to support the Conservative Party (which had dallied with the idea of a reconciliation with nationalist Ireland) in bringing in a Home Rule measure for Ireland. His hand was forced through the premature disclosure of his intentions, and in 1886 Gladstone introduced his Irish Home Rule bill in the House of Commons.

In 1869, when he disestablished the Church of Ireland, Gladstone had claimed that he based his policy on the government of Ireland by Irish ideas. He did not easily arrive at his Home Rule policy, however, and he hoped that it would end the challenge to the union by giving Ireland a settled constitution in which the Irish Protestant gentry would play their rightful part. Parnell responded by talking about a union of hearts—a final settlement of the Irish Question. It is hard to establish how likely this outcome might have been. Irish Catholics who would have received the benefits of Gladstone's Home Rule bill might not have been prepared to draw a line under a modest measure of self-government. But there was in any event the resistance of Irish Protestants to be taken into account. Gladstone had a great affection for the Irish gentry, who might be won back to public life under Home Rule, but he rejected any claims by Ulster unionists that they should be given special treatment under his Home Rule scheme, claiming that they were no more different from the Irish nation than Scottish Highlanders were from the rest of the Scottish nation. The problem was compounded by the democratization of Irish politics in the 1880s, which gave public voice and electoral power to the deeply divided people of Ulster. Sectarian divisions were becoming more deeply rooted in the north, not only in politics but in many walks of life, including the great industrial factories and shipbuilding works of Belfast. The urban working classes were most divided of all. Thus the challenge to the union represented by Parnell and his party was met by a formidable counterchallenge. The inevitable clash was postponed by Parnell's fall from grace in 1889 to 1891 because of his association with Mrs. Katharine O'Shea, his mistress and the wife of a member of his own party. Gladstone's second Home Rule bill of 1893 was defeated in the House of Lords, and the danger subsided. But Home Rule was still part of the political agenda of British Liberals, however much of an encumbrance it might be. And even while Home Rulers themselves split and split again, nationalist Ireland was tightening its grip on local government (reformed on a wholly elected basis in 1898), and on the land, through a series of land acts in the 1880s and 1890s. Nationalists found it hard to sustain the former enthusiasm for Home Rule. But they did not use the lacuna after 1893 to ponder what the Irish nation was; instead, they contented themselves with regarding unionist opposition as a kind of false consciousness, or as the artificial product of British Conservative resistance to Irish self-government.

THE GAELIC REVIVAL AND SINN FÉIN

Challenges to the union were not confined to the political sphere. In 1884 the Gaelic Athletic Association was founded to recover and popularize Ireland's national games and pastimes, thus encouraging the youth of Ireland to eschew foreign games likes soccer, rugby, and above all, cricket. Its exclusion of policemen and soldiers from its ranks and its ban on members watching foreign games provided a remarkable form of social control in rural areas, where native sports were most popular. In 1893 the Gaelic League was established to revive the Irish language and to save Ireland from anglicization and the swamping of its culture by cheap and nasty English newspapers, magazines and books, with their emphasis on sex, crime, and sensationalism. In a strict sense—but in that sense only—these were nonpolitical organizations, but they provided a clarion call for a new kind of nationalism that would not go begging to the "Saxon" Parliament, and would not equate the nation with a mere parliament, but that would regenerate Ireland from within and prevent its degeneration from without. The new nationalism of the 1890s and early 1900s sought to persuade the younger generation that

Old Ireland had failed it and would fail it again unless the Irish people took their destiny into their own hands. The political aspect of this mood was the Sinn Féin movement, which aimed at saving Ireland by its own exertions. The Sinn Féin leader Arthur Griffith exhorted the Irish to look to themselves for salvation, and he appealed to Protestants to follow the example of their illustrious forebears Jonathan Swift, Theobald Wolfe Tone, and Robert Emmet, and join hands with their Catholic fellow-countrymen in the national cause. This movement, these ideas, amounted to very little at the time, but they signified new points of resistance to what were now regarded as the all-too-enveloping grasp of the union and the destruction of all that made Ireland a nation.

But for the moment the Home Rule Party, reunited under John Redmond's leadership in 1900, could claim that it had won many battles, and would one day win the last battle—for self-government for Ireland. It could even be said that Home Rulers were no longer challenging the union but seeking to give it a new lease on life. The Liberal alliance might yet deliver Home Rule, so Redmond strove to convince the British public that he could be a loyal imperial statesman in the mode of the Canadian, Australian, and New Zealander prime ministers. The nationalist political elite was ready to complete a century of concessions to Ireland by taking control of an Irish executive and parliament, and by 1911 that promised land seemed well within its grasp. The Home Rule Party supported H. H. Asquith's government in its attack upon the Conservative-dominated House of Lords, thus demonstrating that it was no longer challenging the union, but using its power in the British Parliament to exploit the union in order to get Home Rule.

THE ULSTER VOLUNTEER FORCE AND THE IRISH VOLUNTEERS

But for Irish unionists the challenge was still real. They declared that the Home Rulers, whatever the professed moderation of their aims, were separatists at heart, and that they would use their powers to establish a priest-ridden, England- (and Protestant-) hating ascendancy. The 1911 Parliament Act, by destroying the Lords' veto, would open the way to this dire consequence. Now came a different kind of challenge to the union, one which the British government was awkwardly positioned to oppose. The Ulster unionists formed the Ulster Volunteer Force (UVF) to deny Home Rule to Ireland (they claimed that they were doing so to defend the union and their loyalty to the Crown). They did not deny the legitimacy of the United Kingdom, but they refused to accept the authority of the Liberal government. Nationalists held that the United Kingdom itself was, as

far as Ireland was concerned, not a legitimate entity; it had, after all, been carried by bribery and corruption in 1799 and 1800. Now they argued, as Parnell had argued from 1886 to 1889, that a "union of hearts" would found the government of Ireland on a true constitutional base.

The result was a paradox: The union now faced two challenges from two groups, both of whom claimed that they were acting in its defense, for the UVF was followed in 1913 by the Irish Volunteers, founded by nationalists to defend the Home Rule settlement. It was a measure of the mistrust of the British government by both sides in Ireland that matters had come to this head. The danger of civil war was revealed when a gun-running enterprise by the UVF in April 1914 was emulated by the Irish Volunteers in July, only this time nationalist blood was spilt in a clash with British troops.

The outbreak of the Great War in August 1914 seemed to offer a way out of the crisis, for both Ulster and Irish Volunteers, after some initial hesitation, were placed at the disposal of the British army. The minority that split from the Irish Volunteers seemed isolated, but it was this minority, together with James Connolly's Citizen Army, that formed the nucleus of the Easter Rising of April 1916. The three leading figures in the Rising—Tom Clarke, James Connolly, and Patrick Pearse—all had different motives for seeking to break the union. Clarke was from Fenian stock, dedicated to securing the Irish republic; Connolly wanted to use republicanism to create a socialist state in Ireland; Pearse wanted an Ireland not merely free but Gaelic as well. This curious amalgam of eighteenth-century French Enlightenment, twentieth-century revolutionary socialism, and nineteenth-century romantic nationalism proved to be a more dynamic force than might have been supposed. It set the scene for Irish republicanism after the Rising, and although it failed to ignite the country in 1916, its brave sacrifice, followed by the British government's failure to intervene to stop the military executions of the leaders of the Rising, gave republicanism a promising start. The clumsy attempt to impose conscription on Ireland in 1918 gave the reconstituted Sinn Féin party the chance to exploit the predicament and win a victory in the general election of December 1918.

THE IRA, THE "TROUBLES," AND THE END OF UNION

The last phase of the union was marked by serious violence and disorder. The Irish Volunteers, now calling themselves the Irish Republican Army (IRA), were under no political control, and they gave their allegiance to a state that was not yet established, and almost certainly could not be established—a united Irish republic. Their character was no doubt influenced by the numbers of young men (many, ex-soldiers) with little to do but fall into troublesome ways, but the vast majority thought that they were fighting to free Ireland after centuries of repression—nationalist rhetoric had done its job only too well. The British response was two-fold: to pass a Government of Ireland Act establishing two new states, Northern Ireland and Southern Ireland, each with a Home Rule Parliament; and to wage war against the IRA. But the war was self-defeating: Nothing could be more condemnatory of the union than the British expedient of raising a force of ex-soldiers and letting them use whatever means might be thought necessary to defeat the guerrilla and terrorist campaign. Equally, it would be hard to find a more futile role for republicans than seeking to coerce Ulster unionists into a united Ireland. The result was the "Troubles," a euphemistic, but in its own way accurate, term to describe this mixture of state violence and civil war.

The British government eventually acknowledged that it had to negotiate with Sinn Féin, and between October and December 1921 Lloyd George and his team engaged in hard bargaining with Arthur Griffith, Michael Collins, and other Sinn Féin representatives. But by now the debate on the union had moved to a wider plane, for statesmen from the British empire, such as General Smuts of South Africa, urged the British to follow the instinct and the constitutional practice that had led to the dominions of the empire becoming equal partners with the mother country. This imperialization of the union question led the British to offer, under threat, dominion status to Ireland. On 6 December the Irish plenipotentiaries accepted what they had known all along—that the British offer could not be rejected without renewal of war, and that it was final; yet not so final, for dominion status on the Canadian model gave Ireland the "freedom to achieve freedom." It was on this still evolving stage that the last great Irish nationalist challenge to the union ended.

The end of the union can be seen in two ways: as the result of contingency, of the British lack of "feel" for Ireland, exemplified in the events of 1914 to 1921; or in a more deterministic way, as the outcome of an Irish nationalist quest for freedom that would change, but never go away. The truth lies somewhere in between. The most useful test is to consider the way in which Irish Catholics switched their political allegiance from Liberalism (which, after Gladstone's disestablishment of the Church of Ireland in 1869, seemed likely to hold both Catholic and Presbyterian loyalties) to the Home Rule movement, which Catholics believed would best serve their interests, and which Presbyterians firmly

held would not serve theirs. A self-conscious political community, told from O'Connell's time that it was the rightful master of Ireland and the majority that must and would have its way, was likely to challenge a constitution that excluded it or otherwise used it badly. The form of challenge varied, and no one could have foreseen the 1921 end of the affair. Paradoxically, it was Protestant attempts to divert or control the march of the Catholic nation that helped to create cultural nationalism, and indeed before that, Irish republicanism, the two greatest, and in the end triumphant, challenges to the union.

SEE ALSO Anglo-Irish Treaty of 1921; Catholic Emancipation Campaign; Electoral Politics from 1800 to 1921; Fenian Movement and the Irish Republican Brotherhood; Gaelic Revivalism: The Gaelic Athletic Association; Gaelic Revivalism: The Gaelic League; Home Rule Movement and the Irish Parliamentary Party: 1870 to 1891; Home Rule Movement and the Irish Parliamentary Party: 1891 to 1918; Independent Irish Party; Irish Republican Army (IRA); O'Connell, Daniel; Parnell, Charles Stewart; Protestant Ascendancy: Decline, 1800 to 1930; Repeal Movement; Sinn Féin Movement and Party to 1922; Struggle for Independence from 1916 to 1921; Unionism from 1885 to 1922; Veto Controversy; Young Ireland and the Irish Confederation; **Primary Documents:** Speech from the Dock (19 September 1803); Origin of the "Catholic Rent" (18 February 1824); The Catholic Relief Act (1829); Letter Advocating Federalism as an Alternative to Repeal (November 1844); Two Fenian Oaths (1858, 1859); "God Save Ireland" (1867); Resolutions Adopted at the Home Rule Conference (18–21 November 1873); On Home Rule and the Land Question at Cork (21 January 1885); On Home Rule at Wicklow (5 October 1885); On the Home Rule Bill of 1886 (8 April 1886); Address at the First Annual Convention of the National Council of Sinn Féin (28 November 1905); Resolutions Adopted at the Public Meeting Following the First Annual Convention of the National Council of Sinn Féin (28 November 1905); Declaration against Home Rule (10 October 1911); "Solemn League and Covenant" Signed at the "Ulster Day" Ceremony in Belfast (28 September 1912); Address on the Ulster Question in the House of Commons (11 February 1914); O'Donovan Rossa Graveside Panegyric (1 August 1915); "What Is Our Programme?" (22 January 1916); The Proclamation of the Irish Republic (24 April 1916); Declaration of Irish Independence (21 January 1919); The "Democratic Programme" of the Dáil Éireann (21 January 1919); Government of Ireland Act (23 December 1920); "Time Will Tell" (19 December 1921); Speech in Favor of the Anglo-Irish Treaty of December 1921 (7 January 1922); Proclamation Issued by IRA Leaders at the Beginning of the Civil War (29 June 1922)

Bibliography

Augustejn, J. *From Public Defiance to Guerrilla Warfare.* 1996.

Bew, Paul. *C. S. Parnell.* 1980.

Bew, Paul. *Conflict and Conciliation in Ireland, 1890–1910.* 1987.

Boyce, D. George. *Nationalism in Ireland.* 1995.

Buckland, P. *Ulster Unionism and the Origins of Northern Ireland, 1886–1922.* 1973.

Comerford, Vincent. *The Fenians in Context: Irish Politics and Society, 1848–1882.* 1985.

Coogan, Tim Pat. *Michael Collins: A Biography.* 1990.

Curtis, L. P., Jr. *Conflict and Conciliation in Ireland.* 1963.

Edwards, Owen Dudley, and Fergus Pyle, eds. *1916: The Easter Rising.* 1968.

Fitzpatrick, David. *Politics and Irish Life, 1913–21: Provincial Experience of War and Revolution.* 1977.

Garvin, Tom. *Nationalist Revolutionaries in Ireland, 1858–1928.* 1987.

Hart, Peter. *The IRA and Its Enemies: Violence and Community in Cork, 1916–23.* 1990.

Hennessey, Thomas. *Dividing Ireland: World War I and Partition.* 1998.

Hutchinson, J. *The Dynamics of Cultural Nationalism: The Gaelic Revival and the Creation of the Irish Nation State.* 1987.

Kerr, Donal. *"A Nation of Beggars"? Priests, People, and Politics in Famine Ireland, 1846–52.* 1994.

MacDonagh, O. *The Hereditary Bondsman: Daniel O'Connell, 1775–1829.* 1988.

MacDonagh, O. *The Emancipist: Daniel O'Connell, 1830–1847.* 1989.

MacIntyre, A. *The Liberator: Daniel O'Connell and the Irish Party, 1830–47.* 1965.

Mansergh, N. *The Irish Question, 1840–1921.* 1975.

Mitchell, Arthur. *Revolutionary Government in Ireland: Dáil Éireann, 1919–22.* 1995.

Ó Broin, Leon. *Fenian Fever: An Anglo-American Dilemma.* 1971.

O'Day, Alan. *Parnell and the First Home Rule Episode.* 1986.

O'Callaghan, Margaret. *British High Politics and a Nationalist Ireland.* 1994.

O'Halpin, Eunan. *The Decline of the Union: British Government in Ireland, 1892–1920.* 1991.

Sheehy, J. *The Rediscovery of Ireland's Past.* 1980.

Townshend, Charles. *Political Violence in Ireland: Government and Resistance since 1848.* 1983.

Ward, Alan. *The Easter Rising and Revolutionary Irish Nationalism.* 1980.

Vaughan, W. E., ed. *Ireland under the Union: I, 1801–70; II, 1870–1921, New History of Ireland.* Vol. 5. 1989, 1996.

D. George Boyce

INDEPENDENT IRELAND SINCE 1922

The cease-fire of July 1921 between the Irish Republican Army (IRA) and the British government and the subsequent negotiation and signing of the Anglo-Irish Treaty on 6 December by delegates from the British and Irish governments brought an end to the Irish war of independence begun in 1919. The bitter and divisive debates that followed the signing of the treaty commenced on 14 December 1921 and ended in January 1922 when the Dáil Éireann ratified the treaty by 64 votes to 57, after which the country slid into a civil war that began formally in June 1922 and ended in a cease-fire in May 1923, with the antitreaty republicans decisively beaten by the new Free State army. The years between 1918 and 1923 were thus five of the most extraordinary in the development of modern Ireland. That Ireland had been partitioned by the implementation of the Government of Ireland Act of 1920 was a point scarcely alluded to during the treaty debates. Rather, what hopelessly divided Irish republicans was the constitutional status of the new southern Free State and in particular the oath of allegiance to the British Crown that had formed part of the treaty agreement.

ANGLO-IRISH TREATY

Modern scholarship has done much to challenge some of the myths associated with these years, in particular the idea that the only issues retarding the development of a modern, prosperous, and egalitarian independent Ireland were the contradictions, inconsistencies, and undemocratic approach of British government policy on Ireland. Although it is difficult to refute the charge of British misgovernment, it is also the case that early-twentieth-century Irish republicanism had its own fair share of contradictions and inconsistencies, perhaps the inevitable product of war and revolution.

It is perhaps unsurprising that many historians have been more sympathetic to the protreaty side, depicting them as defenders of democracy against a school of idealistic republicans who summoned up the memory of blood shed by different generations of Irish patriots in order to gain support for their antitreaty position. Many such republicans disregarded the Irish electorate's firm backing of the protreaty Sinn Féin, winning 58 seats in the general election of June 1922. The Labour Party, Ireland's oldest political party, and Independent and Farmer candidates received 17 and 10 seats respectively, leaving the antitreaty party with just 36 seats.

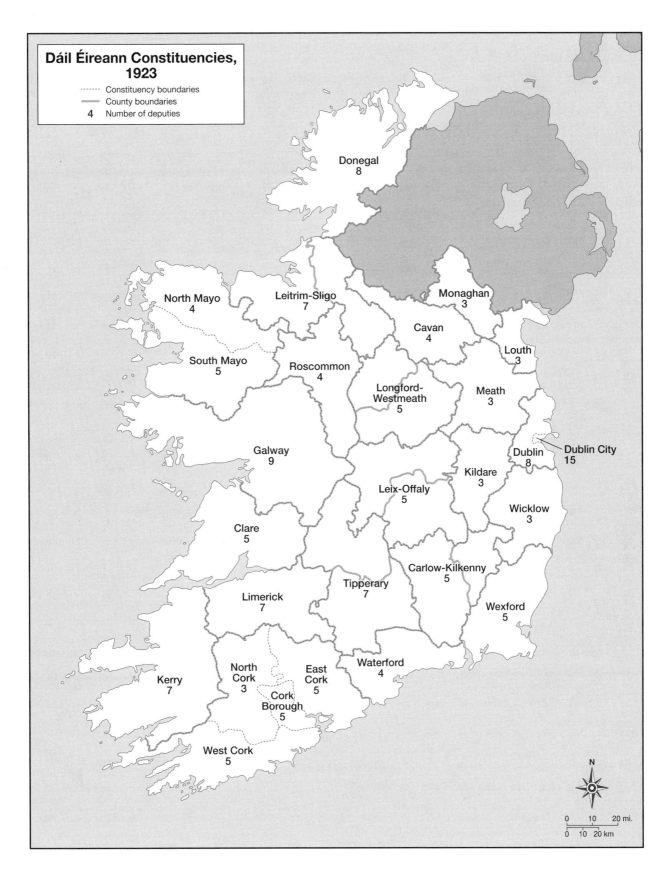

Dáil Éireann Constituencies, 1923

-------- Constituency boundaries
———— County boundaries
  4   Number of deputies

Donegal
8

North Mayo
4

Leitrim-Sligo
7

Monaghan
3

Cavan
4

Louth
3

South Mayo
5

Roscommon
4

Longford-
Westmeath
5

Meath
3

Galway
9

Dublin
8

Dublin City
15

Kildare
3

Leix-Offaly
5

Wicklow
3

Clare
5

Carlow-Kilkenny
5

Tipperary
7

Wexford
5

Limerick
7

Waterford
4

Kerry
7

North
Cork
3

East
Cork
5

Cork
Borough
5

West Cork
5

N

0   10   20 mi.

0 10 20 km

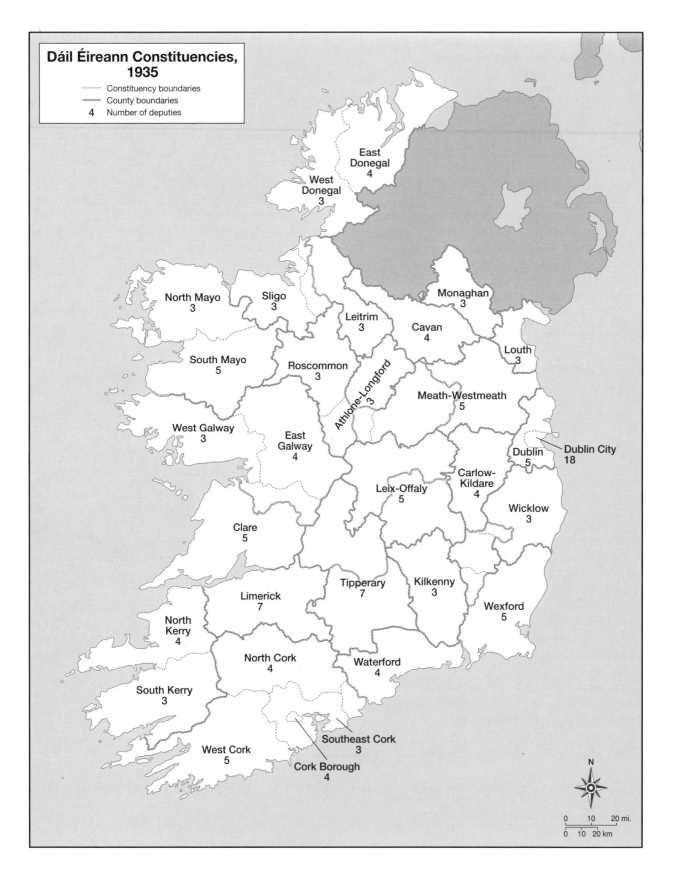

Dáil Éireann Constituencies, 1935

- .... Constituency boundaries
- ———— County boundaries
- 4   Number of deputies

East Donegal 4

West Donegal 3

Monaghan 3

North Mayo 3

Sligo 3

Leitrim 3

Cavan 4

Louth 3

South Mayo 5

Roscommon 3

Athlone-Longford 3

Meath-Westmeath 5

West Galway 3

East Galway 4

Dublin 5

Dublin City 18

Leix-Offaly 5

Carlow-Kildare 4

Wicklow 3

Clare 5

Tipperary 7

Kilkenny 3

Limerick 7

Wexford 5

North Kerry 4

North Cork 4

Waterford 4

South Kerry 3

Southeast Cork 3

Cork Borough 4

West Cork 5

N

0   10   20 mi.

0   10 20 km

CIVIL WAR

The Irish Civil War was a conflict that the republicans had neither the resources, nor the soldiers, nor the popular support to win. For the first three decades of independence these differences over the treaty shaped party politics, by becoming the prism through which elections were fought and political opponents abused. In the 1920s the dominant protreaty establishment was represented by a new party, Cumann na nGaedheal, which needed to secure popular legitimacy as it attempted to rescue an economy on the verge of bankruptcy. The party's political balance sheet contained a fair share of successes and failures, but perhaps the ultimate testament of its achievement was the relative marginalization of extreme republicanism, the assertion of the primacy of the Irish parliament and the Free State army, and the creation of an unarmed Irish police force, the Garda Síochana.

After the killing of Michael Collins and the death of Arthur Griffith during the Civil War (the two leaders between them embodied the generational compromise within Irish nationalism), governments in the 1920s were led by William T. Cosgrave, a politician who under enormous pressures presided over administrations that had to deal with the continual problem of security and defense, a bloated army, and the blurring of the lines between military and civilian power as violence had not ceased with the end of the Civil War, but continued into the 1920s. Fiscal policies in the main were conservative, with those who argued for protection sidelined by the advocates of free trade and policies attractive to those with a stake in dairy farming. This situation led to the belief that the governments of the 1920s favored the more prosperous sections of the Irish agricultural economy. Whereas the Labour Party gained seats in the Irish parliament in the general election of 1922, it was unable to build on it. The left in Ireland remained weak and frequently divided, and it was 1992 before the Labour Party won more than 30 seats in a Dáil Éireann of 166 members.

FIANNA FÁIL PARTY

Eamon de Valera's antitreaty Fianna Fáil Party, which was formed in 1926 and entered Dáil Éireann in 1927, came to power after the vitriolic and tense general election of 1932. Its success was built on demeaning Cumann na nGaedheal Party for failing to use the treaty to further Irish independence, on promises to accommodate the needs of small farmers and the working classes, and on a commitment to end the partition of Ireland, which had been further cemented by the leaked report of the Boundary Commission of 1925. This body, established by Article 12 of the treaty, and expected by republicans to recommend a revision of the border favoring the Free State, made it clear that there would be little alteration of the border. The report was subsequently abandoned, with both the British and Irish governments agreeing to leave the border untouched. Opponents of Fianna Fáil attempted to depict them as communist sympathizers.

Although many republican prisoners were released, de Valera, eager in the 1930s to place distance between himself and the IRA, was quick to use the same emergency legislation that had been used in the 1920s. By the time of Irish neutrality during World War II he was prepared to see IRA men die on hunger strikes rather than tolerate threats to the security of the state. This strategy confirmed democracy's hold in Ireland; further proof was the effective resistance offered to the Blueshirts, a proto-fascist group of disgruntled Cumann na nGaedheal supporters, who were the main victims of de Valera's "economic war" with Britain over the refusal to continue paying land annuities to the British government.

The Eucharistic Congress in Dublin in 1932 seemed to confirm that whatever divided Irish people politically, they were firmly united when it came to their Catholic faith, with a million devotees in attendance. The dominant themes proclaimed on this occasion were the unswerving devotion and institutional loyalty of Irish Catholics amid centuries of suffering and their eventual triumph. Fianna Fáil also built on the legislation that had emerged in the 1920s to safeguard Irish Catholic morality through censorship, discouraging the importation of foreign literature and culture as well as banning the importation and sale of contraceptives. The church, through its largest lay organization, the Pioneer Total Abstinence Association, succeeded in getting many Irish Catholics to abstain from alcohol, but alcoholism remained a huge problem throughout the century.

Fianna Fáil's economic policies did not succeed in achieving self-sufficiency in the agricultural and industrial sectors owing to Ireland's reliance on imports for industrial raw materials and dependence on Britain to take its agricultural produce. The economic war was eventually settled in 1938 with the Anglo-Irish Trade Agreement, which safeguarded and regularized the export trade between the two countries. Aside from de Valera's other initiatives in Anglo-Irish relations and his dismantling of the treaty—most notably the abolition of the oath of allegiance and the External Relations Act of 1936, which removed the role of the Crown from Irish affairs—he was also capable of pursuing independent lines in foreign policy. The government supported sanctions against Italy in 1935 following the invasion of Abyssinia, and urged nonintervention in the Spanish Civil War, indicating that de Valera was not going to allow foreign policy to be dictated by the Catholic bishops.

The Irish constitution of 1937 was another significant legacy of de Valera's tenure in government. Although de Valera consulted widely in preparing the constitution, it was too liberal for some of the more extremist clerics in Ireland, who wanted Catholicism to be recognized as "the one true church," rather than having the "special position" afforded it by de Valera. The constitution attempted to combine the essence of a liberal secular democracy with an emphasis on family values and a sense of community. It created a largely ceremonial office of president and a new senate, and contained controversial articles stipulating the importance of a woman's place in the home. In Articles 2 and 3, the constitution maintained that the de jure government of Ireland was a 32-county one, not just the 26 counties of the Free State, while conceding that the de facto government extended only to 26 counties. These latter articles, which infuriated Ulster unionists, were not deleted until the electorate voted overwhelmingly in 1998 in favor of the Good Friday Agreement (which also created a power-sharing executive and assembly and cross-border bodies). The Irish constitution was a document that endured partly because it contained scope for review through referendum and a commitment to human rights, though its repeated use of the word *sovereignty* would lead to much future debate.

In terms of a wider foreign policy the governments of the 1920s and 1930s used the League of Nations (which the Free State had joined in 1923) to define its international standing; the Free State was a member of the League Council from 1930 to 1933. Ireland's concerns were largely centered on league policy, commonwealth policy, as well as Anglo-Irish affairs, indicating that Ireland's foreign policy during this period did not only concern Anglo-Irish relations. De Valera's support of the League was a sign that Ireland would use it as a forum for international groupings of small and weaker states. Foreign policy was more eurocentric in the 1930s, though the failure of economic sanctions against Italy after the invasion of Abyssinia illustrated its limitations, and neutrality became more significant than the belief in the primacy of collective security under the League's covenant.

De Valera showed himself more adept than any other party leader of his era in knowing when to draw a line between church and state. Although he cultivated close relations with the most powerful man in independent Ireland's Catholic Church, John Charles McQuaid,

archbishop of Dublin from 1940 to 1972, he also viewed with distaste the idea that Ireland needed to "reconstruct" itself as a Catholic power, given that by 1946, 94 percent of the population was Catholic. Though the Irish state became extremely confessional, it was not a clerical state or theocracy.

Members of the Fianna Fáil Party, in tandem with many Catholic social theorists, indulged in much rhetoric concerning the idea of a rural and self-sufficient utopia, but despite some success in creating indigenous employment, the notion was dramatically falsified by the continued depopulation of rural Ireland through emigration. Fianna Fáil also maintained the relentless crusade to centralize state power, begun by Cumann na nGaedheal, and it continued to strip away the powers of local government.

Although de Valera's steadfast course of neutrality for Ireland during World War II earned him huge respect at home, as did his verbal battles with British Prime Minister Winston Churchill (one indication of his considerable media skills), his concept of neutrality was conveniently ambiguous enough to allow a great deal of cooperation with Britain. At times Irish neutrality greatly annoyed the U.S. government, particularly after de Valera offered his sympathies to the German ambassador in Dublin following the death of Hitler—a move that he was almost forced to make in view of his principles. Nor did Ireland show itself to be generous on the issue of taking in Jewish refugees; the friendship between de Valera and the Jewish community was overshadowed by the paranoia and parsimony of the Department of Justice. But the end of de Valera's first phase of power was ultimately decided by economic issues and by the continuing poverty of much of the country, and it was significant that the new party that challenged Fianna Fáil's record in 1948 and won ten seats, Clann na Poblachta, tended to mirror Fianna Fail's election promises from the early 1930s. Its success enabled the formation of the first interparty government.

That government lasted until 1951 and helped to reaffirm support for Fine Gael (the new name for Cumann na nGaedheal after 1934) and the Labour Party as well as the continuing relevance to the Irish political scene of Independent and Farmers' Party candidates. A government once seen as a shaky hybrid administration whose importance lay only in its breaking Fianna Fáil's dominance is now recognized by historians as having been significant for developing important fiscal policy. The coalition, under the leadership of John A. Costello of Fine Gael, comprised five different parties, not to mention independents, but it was ultimately undermined by the absence of collective responsibility.

THE IRISH REPUBLIC

While the circumstances surrounding the declaration of the Irish republic in 1949 remain unclear, particularly the issue as to whether or not it had been agreed by the Irish cabinet, it was a move which Fianna Fáil representatives did not oppose, despite suggestions that the reason they had not done it when in office was that they feared that it would prevent the ending of partition.

The absence of collective cabinet harmony was also a factor in the defeat of Health Minister Noël Browne's Mother and Child scheme, an effort to introduce free medical health care. The scheme was defeated by the determination of the Irish Medical Association to safeguard their members' private income and their ability to gain Catholic Church's support. What has often been presented as a church-state clash was in fact a much more stratified conflict that had strong class undertones, and there was concerted opposition in Ireland to the concept of the welfare state from many quarters. In any case, disagreements over the price of milk brought this government down—an indication that Irish elections were no longer being fought on issues of sovereignty or Anglo-Irish relations.

Economic depression, emigration, and unemployment dominated the records of the other governments of the 1950s. The Fianna Fáil government returned to power in 1951 and again in 1957, and the coalition government was again in power from 1954 to 1957. Some cultural historians have rightly criticized the view of Ireland in the 1950s as a cultural wasteland and have pointed to the achievements in the arts, creative writing, and the critical questioning of Irish nationalism. This is a significant revision in that it suggests that the prosperity of the 1960s was propelled by not only questioning and frustration but also by an enlightenment that belongs to the 1950s and not just the 1960s.

Still, the 1950s was the decade in which emigration devastated the national psyche and the rural hinterland and made a mockery of much of the rhetoric concerning the ideal rural life and the merits of self-sufficiency. In the postwar period down to 1981 over 500,000 people emigrated from the Irish Republic. In 1958 alone almost 60,000 left the country. During the 1950s the power of the Catholic Church peaked in terms of the influence of individual bishops, and the force of collective institutional adherence—though it was also the case that an unquestioning acceptance of clerical domination was under some strain—as the unifying thread that it had provided after the political divisions of the earlier part of the twentieth century became less relevant. Ireland was also increasingly exposed to outside influence, and the adoption of the Programmes for Economic Expansion (1958–1963) finally ended any lingering attachment to the virtues of economic and cultural isolationism.

The prosperity that accrued in the 1960s, marked by the decline in unemployment and the development of a robust export trade, indicated the merits of a more open economy. With de Valera's retirement in 1959, his successor as taoiseach, Seán Lemass, began to implement change that was long overdue, and Ireland successfully caught up with many of the economies of western Europe that had boomed under postwar reconstruction plans. The introduction of free secondary education in 1966 demonstrated a commitment to change Ireland's exceptionally narrow and class-based educational system that had been dominated by an unsuccessful mission to restore the Irish language.

Prosperity in turn exposed many of the class divisions and gaps in income that continued to operate in Irish life. Particularly disturbing was the practice of church and state in showing scant regard for Ireland's most vulnerable populations, particularly in its sometimes savage treatment of children in institutions such as the industrial schools, in which over 150,000 children were housed from their foundation in 1868 to their closure in the early 1970s. Memoirs of Irish childhood became something of a publishing phenomenon in the 1990s and exposed the poverty, hardship, and ill-treatment that many endured, though these accounts were balanced by other memoirs of childhood marked by relative security and comfort.

Lemass, by meeting the Northern Irish prime minister Terence O'Neill in January 1965, also began to recognize the reality of the Northern Irish State. One of the reasons that Ireland had refused to join NATO in 1949 was because of fears that it would prevent the eventual reunification of Ireland, but Ireland became a full participant in the United Nations in 1955. Ireland's participation in the UN was inspired by national interests but it also influenced foreign policy, developing from an initial pro-Western, pro-Christian, anticommunist stance to a more independent line in the context of reducing internal tensions, opposing apartheid, and mediating international disputes. There was an eventual return to a pro-Western bias in an effort to harmonize relations between Ireland and the United States and European Economic Community (EEC) members, mostly for economic reasons. Nonetheless, given its small size, Ireland's proposals could be successful only if they managed to secure the support of the great powers. Largely as a result of the initiative of Frank Aiken, minister for external affairs, Ireland was an important contributor to what became the nuclear nonproliferation treaty in 1968. This was the same period that saw the emergence of Ireland's contribution to peacekeeping, and there was a recognition that Ireland's economic and political future also rested in the emerging power of the EEC, particularly after Britain's decision to apply for membership in 1961.

Domestically, the 1960s also witnessed the emergence of a small group of politicians who began to abuse politics to create personal wealth, though most of their endeavors and unhealthy links with prominent business people were exposed only at the very end of the twentieth century by various tribunals of inquiry, which focused on corruption and the links between politicians, businessmen, and land speculators.

Whereas the Civil War divisions in Irish politics and Irish life were becoming less relevant by the 1960s, and Ireland was approaching both Northern Ireland and the rest of the world with greater maturity, many Irish were still ready to indulge in unbridled triumphalism about the bloody birth of the state, as witnessed by the fiftieth-anniversary commemorations of the 1916 Rising. These were sentiments that the outbreak of the modern "Troubles" in Northern Ireland tempered, as did the crisis in the Fianna Fáil Party and questions about the essential security of the state as revealed in the arms trial of 1970, when senior Fianna Fáil ministers were accused (and acquitted) of assisting in the importation of arms to aid northern republicans. The impact of the northern crisis was also reflected in draconian emergency legislation passed by the Dáil Éireann during the 1970s, increased monitoring of paramilitaries, and accusations of the operation of a "heavy gang" in the police force that ignored the due process of law. The increased level of violence impinged more directly on the south, particularly in May 1974 when loyalist bombs caused carnage on the streets of Dublin and Monaghan, killing thirty-one people and helping to swing public opinion against violence. Despite limited electoral success in the south at the time of the IRA hunger strikes in the Maze prison, extreme republicans did not fare well in southern elections, and there were increasing divisions between Fianna Fáil and Fine Gael on the issue, particularly after Garret FitzGerald took over leadership of Fine Gael in 1977 and advocated a more conciliatory approach to northern unionists.

The beginnings of the peace process can be traced to the after-effects of the Hunger Strikes of 1981 and the winning of seats by Sinn Féin in the south that deprived Fianna Fáil of a majority in the same year. Whereas Fianna Fáil under Charles Haughey attempted to adopt a more pro-republican stance in relation to the north, the report of the New Ireland Forum in 1984, established under pressure from John Hume and the Social Democratic and Labour Party (SDLP), sought to give credence to the legitimacy of unionist identity and acknowledged the necessity of a new agreed constitution in the event of Irish unity. Unionists emphatically rejected the report, as they did the Anglo-Irish Agreement of 1985 that sought to give the Republic a say in the affairs of Northern Ireland through an intergovernmental conference. But many of the most important government moves in relation to the North, particularly in terms of engaging with republicans in an attempt to end the IRA campaign, were done in secret. Albert Reynolds, who succeeded Haughey as leader of Fianna Fáil in 1992, sought to pursue the issue more energetically and was less concerned with the ideology of Irish unity than with the pressing need for an IRA cease-fire and a guarantee that both the Irish and British governments would respond positively. The reality was that most of the Republic's electorate by the end of the twentieth century had little practical interest in a united Ireland. By the time of the Good Friday Agreement in 1998, they were ready to vote overwhelmingly to delete Articles 2 and 3 of the Irish constitution.

AN AGE OF COALITIONS

Although comparatively little has been written by historians on Ireland in the post-1970 period, partly because under Ireland's National Archives Act of 1986 state files can be released only under a thirty-year rule, certain themes are discernible. Fine Gael and Labour managed to oust Fianna Fáil from power in 1973, and despite Fianna Fáil winning a huge majority under the populist Jack Lynch in 1977 coalitions were to be the hallmark of the last twenty-five years of the twentieth century and included those of Fine Gael and Labour (1982–1987) and Fianna Fáil and Labour (1992–1995). A small new party, the Progressive Democrats, composed of Fianna Fáil dissidents who were unhappy with the leadership of Haughey and were committed to liberal economic and social policies, was established in 1985. The party was able to take advantage of Fianna Fáil's failure to form a single-party government and to present itself as an important and modernizing coalition partner. Fine Gael's move to the left and support for greater social liberalization under Garret FitzGerald from 1977 onwards expanded its appeal to the urban middle classes, while by the early 1990s, the Labour Party under the leadership of Dick Spring moved toward the center, presenting itself as a modernizing party of government rather than a force of social opposition. These general moves toward the center ground in Irish politics prevented Fianna Fáil from achieving an overall majority in successive elections, though it continued to command the allegiance of at least 40 percent of the electorate. The absence of serious ideological divisions in Irish politics also facilitated the formation of the first Fianna Fáil/Labour coalition in 1992 and allowed a broad consensus on economic policy to emerge.

JOINING THE EUROPEAN ECONOMIC COMMUNITY/EUROPEAN UNION

The economic fortunes of the country had continued to fluctuate after Ireland joined the EEC in 1972 with a vote of 83 percent in favor, and it was significant that debates about politics were not to figure largely in discussions about the European Union (EU) in Ireland. Most Irish people continued to believe that the most important aspect of the EEC/EU was not political but economic, particularly access to assistance for farmers and to the social and regional funds, which at least partly justified the image of Ireland in Europe as the country with the begging bowl. Issues of sovereignty were not widely debated until the very end of the century, though governments were forced to develop policies on international issues that they had not done prior to joining the EEC. Membership had serious and positive consequences for the status of women in Irish society in the area of equal rights, with the adoption of an equal-pay directive adopted in 1975 and the passage of the Employment Equality Act of 1977.

The decade of the 1980s was disastrous for the economy, with huge unemployment (close to 300,000 by the early 1990s) and mass emigration, as Ireland felt the effects of the global oil crisis and the failure of traditional industry to retain competitiveness. The national debt rose inexorably as governments in the pursuit of electoral victory resorted to borrowing for current expenditure and to disastrous give-away economic manifestoes that paid scant regard to long-term planning. The huge increase in the size of the public sector and spiraling wage inflation also contributed to the problem, as did the increase in the number of young job seekers who were entering a shrinking labor market. There were three general elections between 1981 and 1982 that were fought primarily on the basis of the economic crisis and the need to keep government spending and borrowing under control.

LIBERALIZATION OF IRISH SOCIETY

By the late 1980s, however, very little divided the main political parties when it came to economic and social policy, and the election of Mary Robinson as president in 1990 was regarded as a huge breakthrough for the left in Ireland and part of a wider liberalization in Irish society. The visit of the pope in 1979 had on the surface illustrated the continued appeal of the Catholic Church in Ireland, but it masked a steep fall in religious vocations and a decline in Marian devotion; the church's

ability to dictate the moral and sexual lives of the population was slowly dissipating. While the church helped to secure an ultimately disastrous prolife amendment to the constitution in 1983 and successfully resisted the introduction of divorce in 1986, by the end of the twentieth century contraceptives, divorce, and homosexuality had been decriminalized, thus fulfilling what was termed the "liberal agenda," though both legislators and voters failed to solve the abortion issue, seeking instead to export this problem rather than solve it in a domestic context.

The end of the twentieth century was also marked by accusations of clerical child abuse, regular sex scandals in the church, and the exposing of political corruption, particularly in relation to one of the most divisive but talented of twentieth-century leaders, Fianna Fáil's Charles Haughey, who amassed a fortune through his links with business leaders. The twentieth century ended with Ireland enjoying the phenomenal success of what was dubbed its "Celtic Tiger" economy. In stark contrast to its general record since independence, Ireland became one of the fastest-growing economies in the world. Yet the extent to which it succeeded in combating poverty and the class inequities in Irish society is seriously open to the question, as tax cuts favored the already wealthy, and despite a fall in unemployment from 16 to 4 percent and rises in real wages after 1993, Ireland's healthcare, childcare, housing, and transport problems were not solved.

From 1987 until the end of the century economic growth (GNP) averaged over 5 percent annually, while in some years growth was over 10 percent. In a dozen years the growth in employment amounted to almost 60 percent. The boom was a result of a switch to a directed approach to economic policy on the part of government, extremely low corporation taxes, and a series of social-partnership agreements between governments and trade unions. By 1997 nearly half of all manufacturing jobs were in foreign-owned companies, illustrating the importance of an export-oriented approach (helped by EU funding), investments by multinational corporations, and the revolution in communications and the information technology sector. Monopolies faced competition through commercialization rather than privatization. The impact of EU competition and state aids was also important, as were decisions to invest in education and to encourage foreign investment and a healthy demographic structure, though there was little radicalism in undertaking redistributive taxation or in tackling long-term unemployment.

While the conflict in the north had a notable impact on the writing of Irish history in the form of a growing revisionism that critically questioned the merits of the violent tradition of Irish republicanism, or else chose to ignore it, this thinking had rectified itself by the end of the twentieth century. Scholars showed themselves capable of depicting both the noble and uglier sides of the Irish struggle for independence, as well as the neglected aspects of social history, and the experiences of women and minorities. They sought to cultivate a more detached perspective on Ireland's full range of snobberies, hypocrisies, and class divisions as well as the nobility and dignity of aspiration that had colored both politics and society in the twentieth century.

SEE ALSO Boundary Commission; Civil War; Clarke, Kathleen; Constitution; Cosgrave, W. T.; Declaration of a Republic and the 1949 Ireland Act; de Valera, Eamon; Eucharistic Congress; European Union; Gaelic Catholic State, Making of; Jewish Community; Kennedy, John F., Visit of; Lemass, Seán; McQuaid, John Charles; Mother and Child Crisis; Neutrality; Political Parties in Independent Ireland; Politics: Impact of the Northern Ireland Crisis on Southern Politics; Presidency; Proportional Representation; Robinson, Mary; United Nations; **Primary Documents:** Speech in Favor of the Anglo-Irish Treaty of December 1921 (7 January 1922); Provisional Government Proclamation at the Beginning of the Civil War (29 June 1922); Speech at the Opening of the Free State Parliament (11 September 1922); Constitution of the Irish Free State (5 December 1922); Republican Cease-Fire Order (28 April 1923); Speech on Ireland's Admission to the League of Nations (10 September 1923); "Aims of Fianna Fáil in Office" (17 March 1932); "Failure of the League of Nations" (18 June 1936); "German Attack on Neutral States" (12 May 1940); From the 1937 Constitution; On the Republic of Ireland Bill (24 November 1948); Letter to John A. Costello, the Taoiseach (5 April 1951); Speech to Ministers of the Governments of the Member States of the European Economic Community (18 January 1962)

Bibliography

Brown, Terence. *Ireland: A Social and Cultural History, 1922–1985.* 1981.

Coakley, John, and Michael Gallagher. *Politics in the Republic of Ireland.* 1999.

Cooney, John. *John Charles McQuaid: Ruler of Catholic Ireland.* 1999.

Cronin, Mike. *The Blueshirts and Irish Politics.* 1997.

Delaney, Enda. *Demography, State, and Society: Irish Migration to Britain, 1921–1971.* 2000.

Dunphy, Richard. *The Making of Fianna Fáil Power in Ireland, 1923–1948.* 1995.

Fallon, Brian. *An Age of Innocence: Irish Culture, 1930–1960.* 1998.

Ferriter, Diarmaid. *A Nation of Extremes: The Pioneers in Twentieth-Century Ireland.* 1999.

Ferriter, Diarmaid. *Lovers of Liberty? Local Government in Twentieth-Century Ireland.* 2001.

Fanning, Ronan. *Independent Ireland.* 1983.

Hart, Peter. *The IRA and Its Enemies: Violence and Community in Cork, 1916–1923.* 1998.

Hopkinson, Michael. *Green against Green: The Irish Civil War.* 1988.

Horgan, John. *Noël Browne: Passionate Outsider.* 1999.

Kennedy, Michael. *Ireland at the League of Nations, 1919–1946.* 1995.

Keogh, Dermot. *Twentieth-Century Ireland: Nation and State.* 1994.

Keogh, Dermot. *Jews in Twentieth-Century Ireland.* 1998.

Lee, Joe. *Ireland, 1912–1985: Politics and Society.* 1989.

Lee, Joe, ed. *Ireland, 1945–1970.* 1979.

McCourt, Frank. *Angela's Ashes: A Memoir of a Childhood.* 1996.

McCullagh, David. *Makeshift Majority: Ireland's First Inter-Party Government, 1948–1951.* 1998.

Murphy, John A., and John P. O'Carroll. *De Valera and His Times.* 1986.

Ó Gráda, Cormac. *A Rocky Road: The Irish Economy since the 1920s.* 1997.

Raftery, Mary, and Eoin O'Sullivan. *Suffer the Little Children: The Inside Story of Ireland's Industrial Schools.* 1999.

Regan, John. *The Irish Counter-Revolution, 1921–1936.* 2000.

Skelly, Joseph. *Irish Diplomacy at the United Nations, 1945–1965.* 1997.

Sweeney, Paul. *The Celtic Tiger: Ireland's Economic Miracle Explained.* 1998.

Whyte, John. *Church and State in Modern Ireland, 1923–1979.* 1984.

Diarmaid Ferriter

NATIONALIST POLITICS IN NORTHERN IRELAND

From 1900 until the 1916 Easter Rising, Ulster Catholics, in common with their coreligionists in the rest of Ireland, gave their allegiance to the Irish Parliamentary Party (IPP) and its goal of a united, self-governing Ireland. In the north the party was controlled by the West Belfast MP Joseph Devlin (1872–1934). A captivating orator and superb organizer, Devlin's iron grip on Ulster Catholics was closely associated with his revival in 1904 of the Ancient Order of Hibernians (AOH), a sectarian fraternal society formed to counteract Orangeism.

Northern nationalist hopes of inclusion in a Home Rule Ireland were dashed by unionist resistance after

1912 and by the IPP's acceptance of British prime minister Lloyd George's scheme for the exclusion of the six Ulster counties of Antrim, Armagh, Derry, Down, Fermanagh, and Tyrone in June 1916. This split northern nationalism along east–west lines and paved the way for the rise of Sinn Féin in the nationalist-majority counties of Tyrone and Fermanagh and in Derry city. Only in Devlin's power base of east Ulster did the IPP retain a substantial following.

PARTITION

Northern nationalists saw partition, rather than "Home Rule versus Republic," as the critical issue between 1918 and 1921, and fears of unionist domination resulted in a Sinn Féin–IPP pact in Ulster in the 1918 election. Despite the Sinn Féin landslide, Devlin's invincibility in the northern constituency of the Belfast Falls enabled him to defeat the Sinn Féin leader Eamon de Valera. Rejecting the First Dáil, the native parliament established by the victorious Sinn Féin MPs in January 1919, Devlin attended the British parliament in London, opposing partition and demanding minority safeguards in the new Northern Irish (N.I.) state created in 1921. Catholic hostility to partition was intensified by vicious sectarian violence in northeast Ulster between 1920 and 1922 and by the aggressively sectarian Ulster Special Constabulary (1920), though the IRA enjoyed only limited support in the north.

Because of an electoral pact Devlin's party and Sinn Féin each won six seats in the first N.I. elections of May 1921 on a platform of abstaining from attending the new Northern Ireland parliament. Northern nationalists looked to Sinn Féin to undo partition, but the 1921 treaty (which ended the Anglo-Irish War) contained only an ambiguous Boundary Commission to redraw the 1920 border. This merely deepened internal nationalist divisions, with the border section—mainly supporters of Sinn Féin—campaigning for the transfer of large areas to the Irish Free State and the East Ulster nationalists who feared fearing permanent minority status. During 1922 the nationalist position was further eroded by the treaty split between a protreaty majority led by Michael Collins and a Republican faction identified with de Valera, and Michael Collins's confusing blend of "nonrecognition" diplomacy and IRA violence toward Northern Ireland. His two pacts with Craig dissolved in violence, but the abortive March Agreement was the only serious attempt between 1922 and 1968 to involve the minority in the workings of the state.

The Irish Civil War (1922–1923), Collins's death, and Craig's use of internment shattered nationalist mo-

rale, while the Cosgrave government abandoned Collins's aggressive policy in favor of accelerating the Boundary Commission. Meanwhile, the minority's boycott of the N.I. parliament during 1922 to 1925 ensured that the basic framework of the state was laid without any constructive nationalist input. The abolition of proportional representation (PR) for local elections in 1922, which had the effect of consolidating unionist domination, together with the 1923 Education Act (which penalized voluntary/Catholic schools), underlined the indifference of the unionist administration to minority interests. Under pressure from the Catholic hierarchy Devlin took his seat in April 1925.

The Boundary Commission's collapse in November 1925, leaving the border unaltered, dealt a major blow to the border nationalists, and, by 1928 their MPs, led by the Sinn Féin leader Cahir Healy of County Fermanagh, had joined Devlin in a new united party, the National League, dedicated to Irish unity by constitutional means. Devlin now led a party of ten in the regional parliament, but his appeals for redress were repeatedly rejected by the unionist majority, and his hopes of a new political alignment along class lines were destroyed by the total abolition of PR in 1929. Devlin's death in 1934 marked the effective end of the National League, as abstentionism again set in and nationalists enlisted de Valera's aid, most dramatically to prevent the extension of conscription with the advent of World War II to Northern Ireland in 1939.

Despite its overriding responsibility for Northern Ireland, the British government rebuffed nationalist appeals to intervene, and by the 1930s the minority had formed a "state within a state," equipped with its own social and political infrastructure. During World War II only the two Belfast nationalist MPs attended Stormont (the seat of the N.I. parliament near Belfast) which regarded the minority as "a fifth column," in Northern Ireland Prime Minister Lord Brookeborough's phrase.

In 1945 the return of a British Labour government signaled a major upsurge of antipartitionist activity as the nationalists launched a new mass movement, the Anti-Partition League (APL), adopting a policy of active opposition at Stormont and Westminster, and coordinating a worldwide campaign against partition. However, its single focus on the constitutional issue, rather than on well-founded grievances, alienated the British Labour government of Clement Atlee, while the Irish government rejected its demand for representation in the Dáil. The subsequent Ireland Act (1949), reinforcing partition, undermined the APL, which rapidly declined, challenged as it was by a revived IRA.

THE OPPOSITION

The postwar years saw "change without change" in Northern Ireland despite the introduction of the British welfare state after 1945. By the 1950s the Nationalist Party had lost its former Belfast base to the socialist-inclined Republican Labour Party under Harry Diamond and Gerry Fitt, who seemed more attuned to the needs of urban Catholics. The Nationalist Party remained a loose, rural "association of local notables," lacking even a formal party organization.

Mounting nationalist frustration was reflected in 1955 when Sinn Féin—the political wing of the IRA—secured 152,000 votes, though the IRA's subsequent border campaign (1956–1962) lacked sizable Catholic support. By the early 1960s, nationalist politics were being transformed by the more liberal policies of the new unionist prime minister, Terence O'Neill (1963–1969), the conciliatory policy toward the Northern Ireland of Seán Lemass (taoiseach, 1959–1966) and the demand for equality from the growing Catholic middle classes, products of the 1947 N.I. Education Act, some of whom formed the progressive National Democratic Party in 1965.

Following the groundbreaking O'Neill-Lemass meeting of January 1965 (the first north–south summit since 1925) the nationalists under Edward McAteer assumed "official opposition" status for the first time. However, O'Neill's failure to introduce much-needed reform angered nationalists, whereas the old Nationalist Party's "rigid immobility" was being assailed by the rising young Derry schoolteacher, John Hume, the Campaign for Social Justice (CSJ), a middle-class pressure group, and radical MPs such as Gerry Fitt. A Republican Labour MP at Westminster from 1966, Fitt effectively raised civil-rights demands with the new Labour government of Harold Wilson.

The Nationalist Party's belated efforts to modernize its image were soon overtaken in 1967 to 1968 by the mobilization of Catholic protest in the Northern Ireland Civil Rights Association (NICRA) with its inclusive slogan, "British rights for British subjects." Worldwide reaction to the batoning of a civil-rights march in Derry on 5 October 1968 ended Westminster's indifference to N.I. affairs. As the unionist government hurriedly introduced reforms, it seemed that NICRA had achieved more in forty days of agitation than the nationalists had in forty years of constitutionalism. The N.I. general election of February 1969 saw the nationalists' eclipsed by civil-rights candidates, who included Hume, and which reflected Catholic support for the new style of politics.

The scene was set for the formation of left-of-center Social Democratic and Labour Party (SDLP) under Fitt's leadership in August 1970. The new party was wedded to political participation and constructive reform, and as such it helped to negotiate the Sunningdale Agreement (1973) and participated in the short-lived power-sharing executive of 1974. For the next twenty-five years the SDLP would be the voice of moderate nationalist opinion in Northern Ireland.

SEE ALSO Irish Republican Army (IRA); Northern Ireland: Policy of the Dublin Government from 1922 to 1969; Ulster Unionist Party in Office; **Primary Documents:** On Community Relations in Northern Ireland (28 April 1967); Irish Republican Army (IRA) Cease-Fire Statement (31 August 1994); Text of the IRA Cease-Fire Statement (19 July 1997)

Bibliography

Farrell, Michael. *Northern Ireland: The Orange State.* 1976.

Lynn, B. *Holding the Ground: The Nationalist Party in Northern Ireland, 1945–1972.* 1997.

McCluskey, Conn. *Up Off Their Knees: A Commentary on the Civil Rights Movement in Northern Ireland.* 1989.

Phoenix, Éamon. *Northern Nationalism.* 1994.

Purdie, Bob. *Politics in the Streets: The Origins of the Civil Rights Movement in Northern Ireland.* 1990.

Éamon Phoenix

IMPACT OF THE NORTHERN IRELAND CRISIS ON SOUTHERN POLITICS

When the Northern Ireland "Troubles" began in 1968, the political system of the Republic was unprepared for the consequent challenges to its own system. The call for an end to partition and for the establishment of a united Irish state had been a mainstream nationalist demand since 1922 and had in effect been written into the Republic's constitution in 1937. They were the defining principles of the state's official stance, but political elites and parties had given little thought to mechanisms for actually implementing this policy. Northern Ireland intruded little in political debate in the Republic and had virtually no impact on the electoral performance of the parties. In the decades that followed, though, life in the Republic changed in all three of these respects—constitutional, party political, and electoral.

CONSTITUTIONAL REALITIES

The wording of Article 2 of the 1937 constitution, which declared that "the national territory consists of the whole island of Ireland, its islands and the territorial seas," combined with Article 3, which confined the jurisdiction of the state's political institutions to the area of the former Irish Free State "pending the reintegration of the national territory," was generally interpreted by constitutional lawyers up to 1990 as a statement of political aspiration. It reflected a widespread domestic view that the Republic had a vested interest in Northern Ireland, an interest that had found expression in periodic demands from Dublin that the British government take steps to bring about Irish unity.

The outbreak of civil unrest in Northern Ireland in the late 1960s resulted initially in a hardening of this position, with the southern Irish government insisting that the roots of the problem lay in the partition of the island and that unity was the obvious solution. In the early 1970s, as the IRA's military campaign for Irish unity intensified, successive administrations distanced themselves from this position to avoid any allegation that they endorsed the IRA's methods. The Sunningdale Agreement (between the Irish and British governments and the moderate Northern Ireland parties) on 9 December 1973 was the first clear indication of this shift. The Irish government "fully accepted and solemnly declared that there could be no change in the status of Northern Ireland until a majority of the people of Northern Ireland desired a change in that status." Subsequent Irish administrations have adhered to this position, with varying degrees of emphasis, while continuing to express a desire for unity in the long term.

On 1 March 1990 the Irish Supreme Court ruled in favor of a more assertive interpretation of the constitution that construed Articles 2 and 3 as amounting to a claim of legal right. Consequently, the explicit recognition of Northern Ireland as a part of the United Kingdom that was written into the Good Friday Agreement of 10 April 1998 made necessary a change in the Irish constitution's articles. This change had considerable value as a symbolic gesture to northern unionists, and it was made part of the peace agreement. In a referendum on 22 May 1998 Irish voters approved the change by a majority of 94 percent; the amendment took effect on 2 December 1999. The "national territory" is no longer defined in the constitution, which now incorporates a guarantee to unionists that "a united Ireland shall be brought about only by peaceful means with the consent of a majority of the people, democratically expressed, in both jurisdictions in the island."

The Good Friday Agreement also brought about further institutional changes, including the creation of a British-Irish Council linking the British and Irish governments; the Scottish, Welsh, and Northern Irish ad-

The killing of thirteen civilians in Derry by British forces on "Bloody Sunday" (30 January 1972) led to mass protests in Dublin, which culminated in the burning of the British Embassy on 2 February 1972. PHOTOGRAPH COURTESY OF THE *IRISH TIMES.*

ministrations; and the governments of Man, Jersey, and Guernsey. More significantly, it set up a small network of North-South bodies designed to encourage cooperation in specific areas (such as economics, certain marine matters, and language), under the political control of a North/South Ministerial Council made up of representatives of the Irish government and the Northern Ireland executive.

PARTY POLICIES

These constitutional and institutional changes reflected shifts in the positions of the Republic's main parties. The two largest parties had long advocated Irish unity as a major goal but had differed in emphasis. From its formation in 1926 the first aim of Fianna Fáil, as specified in its constitution, was "to secure the unity and independence of Ireland as a republic," and this objective had featured from time to time in party rhetoric. A notable shift in direction took place under the leadership of Jack Lynch (1966–1979), who stressed that unity must be brought about only with the consent of Northern Ireland. Later leaders adhered to this policy, notwithstanding the more nationalist tone of Lynch's successor Charles Haughey (1979–1992).

Fine Gael had traditionally supported Irish unity too (the official English version of its name was "the United Ireland party"), but less insistently than Fianna Fáil. Under the leadership of Liam Cosgrave (1965–1977), the party began to deemphasize its nationalist past and stress that unity could come about only by agreement between the two parts of Ireland. The party has since adhered to this position, though other leaders have pushed it in rather different directions: Garret FitzGerald (1977–1987) committed the party to a vision of new constitutional structures for the island of Ireland, and John Bruton (1990–2001), according to his critics, displayed more sensitivity to the unionist case than to the nationalist.

Other parties have undergone similar transitions. The Labour Party had been formally committed to the establishment of an all-Ireland republic, but in the course of the 1970s it increasingly accepted the long-term reality of partition. The official Sinn Féin party (as opposed to provisional Sinn Féin, which broke away from the official party in 1970 and is now known as Sinn Féin *simpliciter*) changed even more radically than Labour, eventually renaming itself the Workers' Party and altogether rejecting the mainstream nationalist position (but eventually becoming entirely politically marginalized). The very birth of the Progressive Democrats in 1985 suggested strains over policy in relation to Northern Ireland—the new party was founded partly to oppose the more aggressively nationalist Fianna Fáil.

These changes indicated (and, to some extent, also influenced) a profound shift in public attitudes. As the economic and political costs of absorbing Northern Ireland have become obvious, popular enthusiasm in the Republic has waned. The cooling of public opinion has been reinforced by revulsion at the IRA's campaign of violence and by the increasing differentiation of northern from southern Irish society, itself a long-term consequence of partition.

ELECTORAL COMPETITION

There is little evidence that the Northern Ireland issue was significant in electoral politics in the south after the 1920s, except possibly in 1948, when a radical nationalist party, Clann na Poblachta ("Party of the Republic"), made a dramatic but ephemeral dent in the support base of Fianna Fáil. The evidence of more recent elections, opinion polls, and party electoral strategies suggests that the Northern Ireland issue attracts little interest. Indeed, in the November 1982 election Charles Haughey, sensing widespread popular suspicion of any interference with the status quo, used Garret FitzGerald's advocacy of an all-Ireland security force as a weapon against Fine Gael.

Attempts by newer parties to mobilize support for North-South unification have not been notably successful. None of the small radical nationalist parties has won a sizeable bloc of electoral support. Although Sinn Féin won a large share of the nationalist vote in Northern Ireland in the 1980s and 1990s (about 50% by the beginning of the twenty-first century), it has had little impact in the Republic (less than 3% in 1997). Although opinion polls registered an increase in Sinn Féin's popularity in the Republic after the Good Friday Agreement of 1998, it is likely that this owes more to the party's increasing moderation on the issue of partition and its involvement in domestic social issues than to nationalist enthusiasm; by 2002 it built its share of the vote up to 6.5 percent.

SEE ALSO Political Parties in Independent Ireland; Politics: Independent Ireland since 1922; **Primary Documents:** From the 1937 Constitution; Statement by the Taoiseach (13 August 1969); "Towards Changes in the Republic" (1973); Anglo-Irish Agreement (15 November 1985)

Bibliography

Arthur, Paul. *Special Relationships: Britain, Ireland, and the Northern Ireland Problem.* 2000.

Bowman, John. *De Valera and the Ulster Question, 1917–1973.* 1982.

Cox, Michael, Adrian Guelke, and Fiona Stephen, eds. *A Farewell to Arms? From "Long war" to Long Peace in Northern Ireland.* 2000.

Kennedy, Michael J. *Division and Consensus: The Politics of Cross-Border Relations in Ireland.* 2000.

O'Halloran, Clare. *Partition and the Limits of Irish Nationalism: An Ideology under Stress.* 1987.

O'Leary, Brendan, and John McGarry. *The Politics of Antagonism: Understanding Northern Ireland.* 2d edition, 1996.

Ruane, Joseph, and Jennifer Todd. *The Dynamics of Conflict in Northern Ireland: Power, Conflict, and Emancipation.* 1996.

John Coakley

Landlords took advantage of the "Gregory clause" in the Poor Law Amendment Act of 1847 to evict bankrupt tenants en masse. Such tenants were disqualified from official relief unless they surrendered their holdings (above a quarter-acre) to their landlords. This 1848 sketch depicts a grieving father standing at the entrance to his roadside hut while a daughter points toward their former dwelling. FROM ILLUSTRATED LONDON NEWS, 16 DECEMBER 1848.

~

Poor Law Amendment Act of 1847 and the Gregory Clause

The Poor Law Amendment Act of 1847 marked a major shift in British government policy with respect to famine distress in Ireland. Under the new act Irish property owners and tenants would henceforth bear the full burden of fiscal responsibility for relief, which was to be administered solely by the Irish poor-law system.

The main provisions of the act accommodated these changes by allowing the poor-law authorities, for the first time, to extend relief to destitute persons without necessarily obliging them to become inmates of a workhouse. In the case of relief applicants adjudged ablebodied, this outdoor relief was to be made available only under the most stringent conditions, mainly where insufficient accommodation existed within the workhouses. One important qualification of the right to relief, however, was outlined in the Gregory clause of the act, which required that relief applicants surrender all but a quarter acre of their land. Because workhouse accommodation was not remotely sufficient for the huge numbers entitled to relief, and because poor-law administrators refused to sanction outdoor relief on the scale necessary, the act was calamitous for the poor. The workhouse system was engulfed in a tide of destitution, and hunger, disease, and death increased sharply in the hinterland.

In addition to this, the Poor Law Amendment Act itself created new levels of destitution, because fear of incurring a huge new tax liability to fund the amended poor law propelled landlords into a massive campaign of evictions. As things were, the property tax that paid for the poor law, the poor-law rate, was levied on each rented holding, and already fell heavily on the landlord; for the smallest holdings his liability was total. Now faced with a hugely increased tax burden at a time when famine distress was severely affecting rents, many landlords chose to eliminate the rate-bearing holdings altogether by evicting their occupiers and destroying their dwellings. The Gregory clause greatly facilitated these famine clearances; it forced tenants to part with almost all their land in order to obtain relief, but in practice, landlords often refused to accept surrenders unless the entire holding was yielded, together with the dwelling. Commonly, tenants starved to death rather than surrender their land, because entitlement to relief was no guarantee of its availability. Even more frequently, tenants who surrendered all but the required quarter acre had their dwellings razed in their absence, often while they were at the workhouse applying for relief.

Not surprisingly, the evictions that it facilitated and the abuses to which it led lent the Gregory clause a notoriety unique in the history of British legislation for Ireland.

SEE ALSO Agriculture: 1845 to 1921; Famine Clearances; Great Famine; Indian Corn or Maize; Land Questions; Potato and Potato Blight (*Phytophthora infestans*); Subdivision and Subletting of Holdings

Bibliography

Donnelly, James S., Jr. "Mass Eviction and the Great Famine." In *The Great Irish Famine*, edited by Cathal Portéir. 1995.

Donnelly, James S., Jr. *The Great Irish Potato Famine.* 2001.

Kinealy, Christine. *This Great Calamity: The Irish Famine, 1845–1852.* 1994.

Ó Gráda, Cormac. *Black '47 and Beyond: The Great Irish Famine in History, Economy, and Memory.* 1999.

O'Neill, Timothy P. "Famine Evictions." In *Famine, Land and Culture in Ireland*, edited by Carla King. 2000.

Ciarán Ó Murchadha

~

Population, Economy, and Society from 1750 to 1950

In the century before the Great Famine of the 1840s Ireland had one of the fastest-growing populations in Europe. In the century after, Ireland was the only European country to decrease in population in every decade. Therein lies the drama of Irish population change. Explaining these great swings in Irish population is no easy task. Interactions between the Irish and international economies are relevant, as are changes within Irish society itself. In the 1740s Ireland was a thinly populated island, in the process of recovering from the devastating famine of 1740 through 1741. The dominant economic sector was agriculture. Ireland's mild, damp climate naturally predisposed its inhabitants toward livestock farming rather than tillage. The former tended to use more land and less labor per unit of output as compared with the production of cereal or root crops, and hence was more consistent with a low population density.

The people numbered perhaps 2 million, or a little more. Then, in one of the most remarkable transforma-

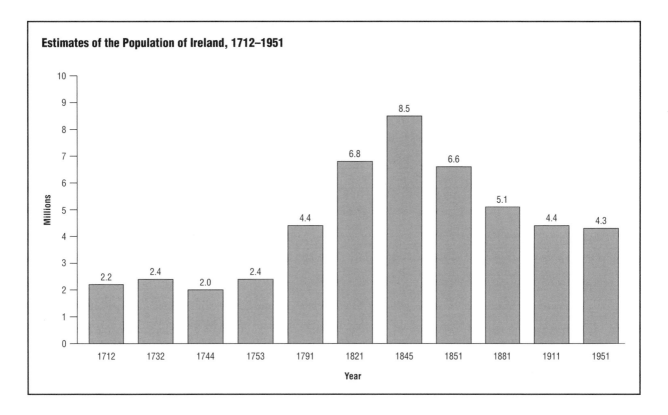

Estimates of the Population of Ireland, 1712–1951

tions in European population history, the inhabitants of the island quadrupled from 2 million to 8.5 million in the space of a century (1745–1845). Concerns with overpopulation rather than the longer-standing observations of underpopulation began to creep into the consciousness and vocabulary of contemporaries. How this explosive multiplication of people came about, and its ultimate consequences, goes to the heart of modern Irish social history.

FERTILITY AND MORTALITY FLUCTUATIONS

The surge in population must have been due either to a rise in fertility (more births) or a fall in mortality (increased life expectancy), or a combination of the two. The only other possibility—a rise in numbers due to an influx of people—can be excluded as there was a net outflow from Ireland during the eighteenth century, particularly from Ulster to North America. Most writers would agree that population change was composed of both changes in fertility and mortality, though there is no settled view on the relative importance of the two. An argument by analogy—drawing on the contemporaneous experience in England where the causal mechanisms of population increase are better understood—would place the main emphasis on rising fertility rather than mortality decline. A fertility-based explanation for Irish population growth is also compatible with some indirect indicators: changes in the market economy and

increasing dependence on potato cultivation in Ireland during the second half of the eighteenth century.

The norm governing household formation in Ireland, as in western Europe more generally, was that before entering marriage the couple should possess the means of an independent livelihood for themselves and any children they might have. For the mass of the people this meant a cottage and access to land (at the very least a potato plot). For others, a livelihood might be derived from trade, crafts or commerce, or some mixture of these and agriculture. By all accounts the condition of the Irish economy during the second half of the eighteenth century favored marriage and the multiplication of households.

THE INFLUENCE OF THE ECONOMY AND EXPANDING EXPORT MARKETS Many population changes were market driven, reflecting the deepening commercialization of Irish society in the eighteenth century. Between the 1740s and the end of the French Wars in 1815 the Irish economy experienced a long wave of expansion. This was powered initially by demand for Irish foodstuffs—beef, butter, and pork—in the British colonies of North America and in Britain itself. As Britain was at war during much of this period, wartime conditions gave rise to additional demands for Irish produce. The result was a secular rise in prices, employment, and Irish national income, though the fruits of this expansion were unevenly divided as between different social groups. From the later eighteenth century, demand also shifted in favor of Irish tillage products, cereals in particular, in response to the food needs of a rapidly growing British population, and, to a lesser extent, those of a growing nonfarming population in Ireland. Labor-intensive tillage production amplified the demand for labor, creating additional incomes and thereby enhancing the prospects of marriage and household formation.

The agricultural sector was not the only one stimulated by buoyant external and internal demand. Incomes and employment in industry—as yet largely organized on a handicraft basis—also experienced growth. The eighteenth-century linen industry was a spectacular example of export-led growth, with flax cultivation, spinning, weaving, and bleaching generating extensive demand for labor in the cottages and small farms of the northern counties. The traditional woolen industry, located in many of the towns of the south of Ireland and geared predominantly to the domestic market, underwent fluctuating fortunes but was also a source of significant employment. Other industries included food processing, brewing, and distilling. These benefited from expanding markets at home and abroad. Overall, therefore, growing opportunities to make a livelihood facilitated marriage, possibly (though there is little direct evidence on this) at earlier ages than had been customary prior to 1750.

CULTIVATION OF THE POTATO A further factor, less directly connected to market processes, was the diffusion of the potato, which changed radically the domestic economy and ecology of the countryside. From being a supplement to the people's diet, potatoes had become by the end of the century the dominant element in the food of the rural poor (the small farmers, cottiers, and laborers). The likelihood is that it increased fertility within marriage and, by virtue of improving the food supply, also reduced mortality.

But the cheap, nutritious potato was not only the manna of the Irish masses, it was also a new technology. Its cultivation needed less land relative to the acreages required by other food sources. This made the subdivision of holdings more practicable, a movement also facilitated by the swing toward labor-intensive tillage from the 1760s onwards. Thus new household formation and the subdivision of holdings went hand in hand, each cause and effect of the other. The potato also aided the creation of new landholdings because of its effectiveness in reclaiming marginal or wasteland. Potato cultivation in effect increased the supply of land and lowered the threshold of viability for landholdings. It added to the land area in a further sense, by abolishing fallow periods through its incorporation into new crop rotations. A huge increase after 1750 in the ecological niches for making a living was now available to individuals and families. In an odd way, the potato both caused and accommodated population growth.

It would be wrong, however, to give the impression that the whole of the Irish countryside was now being parceled up into dwarf-sized holdings as a result of interactions between the subdivision of holdings, potato cultivation, land reclamation and population growth. This was true of parts of south Ulster, where the symbiosis of linen manufacture and farming resulted in a patchwork of very small farms. It was also true of the poorer lands of the west of Ireland, where communal farming added a further twist to the landholding system. But on the more fertile lowlands where commercial farming, particularly livestock production, was well established, medium-sized and large farms survived intact from generation to generation. On the edges of these lowland areas, and up in the hills, an increasingly potato-dependent cottier and laboring class reproduced energetically. Thus in the Golden Vale region of south Tipperary, for instance, there coexisted substantial farms and, on their fringes, dense settlements of the rural poor who supplied the labor needs of a commercializing agriculture.

It seems, therefore, that there were at least three demographic regimes in the later eighteenth century. In the northern counties of Ireland the opportunities afforded by the rapidly expanding linen industry and the partial adoption of a potato diet relaxed the constraints on land division and family formation. It is no coincidence that the most rapid growth of population in the period between 1753 and 1791—the formative phase of the population explosion—was to be found in Ulster, the rate of increase being in the region of 2 percent per annum. This was well above the national average, estimated at somewhere between 1.4 and 1.9 percent. Along the Atlantic seaboard population increase was also rapid, whereas in the more urbanized and commercialized east of Ireland population gain was relatively moderate. The differences were not purely regional, however: the rural poor seem to have engaged in less restrained reproduction by comparison with the commercial farming class, where dowry payments and carefully calculated marriage alliances were more in evidence.

EFFECT ON SOCIETY

Rapid population increase gave rise to social tensions, often centering on access to land—the renting of potato plots in particular—but extending also to the pay and condition of laborers, tithe payments, and disputes between neighbors and kinfolk. A more crowded countryside intensified competition for material and symbolic resources, resulting in collective as well as personal conflicts. The first major outbreak of agrarian violence, for instance, that of the Whiteboys in south Tipperary in 1761, involved confrontations between landowners and land-poor cottiers and laborers. The immediate provocation was the enclosure of common land, a traditional resource of the poor and all the more valuable under conditions of population increase. In the northern counties religious affiliation and its associated trappings were much more likely to be the bone of contention. But competition for land and other resources, itself linked to population growth, was never far beneath the surface. The Ulster county of Armagh had the highest density of rural population of any of the Irish counties in 1841. Armagh was also notorious for intense and sustained sectarian violence. The two were connected.

SLOW DOWN IN POPULATION BEFORE THE FAMINE

Population levels continued to rise in the decades before the Great Famine, but there is clear evidence that the demographic escalator was slowing down. By the 1830s the rate of population increase had dipped below 1 percent per annum, and was now in line with the mainstream European experience. Emigration was the major source of this adjustment. Between 1815 and 1845 1.5 million people sought their fortunes in Britain or North America. Rapid population growth had been accompanied by the immiseration of the poorer strata of Irish society, now almost wholly dependent on a potato diet. Decline in the handicraft textile industries stripped away other sources of income, as handicraft production came under intense competition from factory-produced goods. To take the primary example, while huge, power-driven spinning mills emerged in Belfast and along the Lagan Valley from the close of the 1820s, cottage-based hand spinning ceased in tens of thousands of cabins in the Ulster countryside.

Ireland in 1841, on the eve of the Great Famine, was a country of contrasts. Much economic and technological progress had been made in the preceding decades. Modern banking institutions had emerged, communications by land and waterway were much improved, the country was on the eve of the railway age, modern industrialization had taken hold in east Ulster, literacy levels were rising, a poor-law system ensured against the more cruel vagaries of life, and a centralized police force had come into being. Landlords, commercial farmers, the new industrialists, and the professional classes were growing in economic strength. But signs of progress should not be allowed to obscure the more perva-

sive reality of uneven social development and mass poverty. Perhaps as many as four million individuals lived impoverished lives, close to the edge of subsistence, using primitive spade cultivation and dependent for survival on a slender lifeline: the potato.

In the eyes of many contemporary commentators this immense population of potato eaters had arisen because the Irish poor had entered recklessly into early and fertile marriage: seizing the pleasure of the moment out of despair for the future. The census of 1841 offers a more sober assessment. Age at marriage averaged twenty-eight years for men and twenty-five to twenty-six years for women, much the same as elsewhere in western Europe. There is no sign here of early and profligate marriage. Still, it is earlier periods that matter most, and evidence is limited. There is a strong presumption that marriage ages had been lower in the late eighteenth century and had then risen in the decades before the famine. Moreover, marriage was available to virtually all in Irish society: Among the older age groups in 1841 only 10 percent of men and 12 percent of women were still unmarried and there is no reason to believe marriage had been any less universal in earlier decades. It is noticeable, though, that in some of the southeastern counties the proportions of single individuals were considerably higher on the eve of the debacle, prefiguring a drift toward permanent celibacy that was to be such a feature of postfamine society. (Permanent celibacy is conventionally and somewhat arbitrarily defined as the proportion of single individuals in the age group forty-five to fifty-four years, which is the measure used here.) Further reinforcing the image of a society with formidable reproductive powers, calculations made in the 1990s confirm the opinions of contemporaries that Irish couples were remarkably fertile. Conversely, births outside marriage were low by the standards of other societies, a position that was to be maintained in the century after the famine. The oft-proclaimed chastity of the Irish, and the sometimes brutal treatment of single mothers which was its accompaniment, probably owed more to the fragility of the peasant household economy and a dearth of opportunities for making an independent living than to deep moral or religious values.

PHYTOPHTHORA INFESTANS Malthusian tendencies, or an increasing tension between population increase and living standards, were evident in prefamine society. A narrowing diet and rising emigration suggest as much. Yet, paradoxically, the Great Famine was not itself a case of a Malthusian crisis. Population had not outrun the capacity of the Irish economy to sustain these numbers. It partook more of the character of an

IRELAND.

There were serious potato shortages in some years before the Great Famine. A large deficiency caused great suffering because about half of the population depended heavily on the potato for food. The shortages of 1839–1841 led to food riots, including the attack on a potato store in Galway town portrayed in this engraving of June 1842. FROM ILLUSTRATED LONDON NEWS, 25 JUNE 1842.

ecological disaster. The then mysterious potato blight, caused by *Phytophthora infestans*, struck suddenly and without warning in the summer of 1845. There was a partial failure of the potato crop, but revealingly, Irish society was capable of absorbing this severe challenge without any noticeable loss of life. The return of the blight in more virulent form in the following season opened the floodgates to mass destitution, malnutrition, famine, and famine-related diseases. In "Black '47," although blight was absent, the potato crop was severely deficient. Blight returned in 1848 and again in some areas in 1849. Cruelly, Irish society had been visited, not by one famine, but by repeated famines within the space of five years. This was unprecedented in modern European experience, as was the severity of the food loss. By the end of the famine, which in some districts occurred

as late as 1850, sections of Irish society lay devastated. In excess of one million women, men, and children had died of starvation or starvation-related diseases, the great bulk of these belonging to the poorer strata of society. Another one million had fled the country. This great stream of economic refugees flowed to Britain and, in even greater numbers, to the United States.

THE RESPONSIBILITY OF THE BRITISH The source of the massive failure of the food supply lay in the world of botany and plant disease. But responsibility for the mass mortality is altogether more controversial. After all, these deaths took place in the environs of the world's most industrially advanced society, and Ireland, under the Act of Union of 1800, was an integral part of that nation state. The charge, therefore, is not that the Brit-

Many poor Irish smallholders, such as those depicted in this illustration of 1881, had long traveled to England for harvest work. The wages earned there permitted them to eke out a bare subsistence on marginal land in Ireland. Mayo and Donegal provided the great bulk of migrant workers. Their numbers declined substantially after the 1860s. FROM ILLUSTRATED LONDON NEWS, 28 MAY 1881.

ish sent the blight but that they failed to offer humanitarian aid on a scale sufficient to contain the crisis.

The problem is that once the famine-related diseases of typhus, typhoid, and dysentery had secured a grip, massive mortality was inevitable. Still, there is no doubt that more could have been done. The public-works programs were seriously misguided for undernourished and famished laborers. More constructive initiatives, such as the provision of soup kitchens, which at their peak in the summer of 1847 fed some three million souls, were withdrawn when they could have helped to prolong life. It is clear, therefore, that the Parliament at Westminster could have acted more humanely in relation to the tragedy (though the allegation that the state was engaged in some form of genocide has a reality only in the fevered imagination of political ideologues). It is also the case that many in the propertied strata of Irish society—the landlords, strong farmers, merchants, and ecclesiastics—could have done more to help their starving compatriots of the lower orders. Then, as now, human sympathies trickled only slowly across boundaries of family, social class, ethnicity, religion, and region.

Unlike earlier famines (where population bounced back soon afterwards), the Great Famine inaugurated a century of population decline. From a population of 6.6 million in 1851, in the immediate aftermath of the famine, the numbers had fallen to 4.4 million by 1911, and were marginally lower at 4.3 million in 1951. The last is about half the prefamine level. Some of the more melodramatic writers in the 1950s went so far as to warn against "race suicide" on the part of the Irish. Taking the longer view, however, we can see that major population decline belonged to the nineteenth century. The large loss of population, when millions were uprooted from their tiny holdings, was concentrated in the two decades after 1845, as if a long-evolving imbalance between population and resources was being corrected with indecent haste. The wave of population decline gradually subsided thereafter, and had largely leveled off by 1911. (The politically and economically troubled decade of the 1880s interrupted but did not reverse the decelerating pace of population loss.)

Falling population was wholly due to emigration. Birth rates still comfortably exceeded death rates. In 1880, for instance, the number of births per thousand of the population was twenty-five, while the corresponding death rate was twenty, yielding a natural increase of five per thousand, or a net addition of 25,180 in that year. In a typical year, therefore, emigration topped off the natural increase and more. The source of most of this emigration was rural Ireland, reflecting the large gap between the earnings of servants, agricultural laborers, and small farmers at home and the alternatives available to able-bodied men and women in Britain and more especially in North America. The famine exodus smoothed the pathways of subsequent Irish emigration, particularly from western Ireland where barriers of culture and poverty had previously inhibited migration to America. The prospect of life outside Ireland became increasingly part of the psyche of the Irish family. Thus between 1841 and 1921 more than six million Irish settled abroad, mainly in the United States but also in Britain, Canada, Australasia, and elsewhere around the globe. No other country experienced such a massive exodus of its people. Remarkably also, women were equally represented with men, which is quite at variance with the male-dominated emigration streams from other European societies. Some writers have interpreted this rough equality of movement as indicative of the lowly status of women in Irish society; an alternative reading might be to suggest the relatively fewer restrictions on Irish women.

MALTHUS AND POPULATION CHANGE The volume of emigration might well have been greater still. But in a posthumous and no doubt unconscious tribute to the father of modern population studies, the Irish settled enthusiastically on some of the preventive checks favored by the Reverend Thomas Malthus. Age at marriage edged upwards in the decades after the Great Famine, as parents and children calculated more carefully the costs and benefits of the marriage bed. The more widespread adoption of dowries and the diffusion of the match, or arranged marriage, were indicative of growing social controls over erotic energies. By 1911 the average age at marriage for women was twenty-nine (as compared with twenty-five to twenty-six on the eve of the Great Famine), and this mature age was still the norm as late as the mid-twentieth century, when the Irish Republic topped the late-marrying league for European women. The lengthening of the male age at marriage was even more marked, though from the viewpoint of reproduction is less significant.

THE INCREASE IN CELIBACY It was not, however, delayed marriage so much as a wholesale retreat from marriage that marked Ireland off from the other countries of Europe. By 1911 a quarter of Irish women were destined never to marry; the proportion of permanently celibate men was higher still at 27 percent. Or to take an extreme example, in the fertile farming county of Meath permanent celibacy among men was at the extraordinary level of 41 percent. This remarkable pattern of behavior placed Ireland at the extreme of the European marriage system. These outcomes were little changed by 1951 when rates of permanent celibacy in Ireland were double, or more, those to be found in countries such as England, France, Italy, or the United States. Some wondered—neglecting the deeper economic and social forces at play—if there might not be a peculiar Irish aversion to marriage, rooted perhaps in Gaelic asceticism or puritanical forms of Catholicism.

A TRANSFORMED DEMOGRAPHY

In the century after the Great Famine, Irish society was transformed demographically. That is, in all but one respect: fertility. The ready availability of emigration for economically surplus sons and daughters absolved Irish parents of the need either to curtail family size or to accept steep reductions in living standards. It is true that some middle-class families, particularly Protestant families, practiced family limitation from around 1900, but Irish society as a whole was a slow and unenthusiastic participant in the European fertility transition.

These new demographic patterns were heavily conditioned by changes in Irish economy and society. These in turn reflected powerful impulses generated by labor, capital, commodity, and information flows in the international economy, during what some see as the first phase of globalization (1840s–1914). The Irish rural economy needed less labor as relative prices, dictated by international food markets, moved in favor of livestock production. Falling transport costs for passengers helped to integrate British, Irish, and North American labor markets, easing the flow of workers out of the Irish economy. The feedback of information on wages and living conditions abroad fueled expectations regarding acceptable living standards at home. While incomes, on average, rose sharply in the second half of the nineteenth century, faster than in industrializing Britain in the same period, material expectations may have risen faster still. Early and fruitful marriage threatened these gains, particularly on the family-run farms. Not infrequently, notions of postponed marriage drifted on into the lonely reality of permanent celibacy. Little wonder that the poet Patrick Kavanagh, describing social life in Ireland between the two world wars, was moved to speak of another Great Hunger, that of sexual frustration. In the 1930s the countryside of his native county of Monaghan teemed with bachelors and spinsters, with little promise of marriage, its intimacies, or its responsibilities.

The pace of demographic change did vary regionally. Most exceptional were the remote western districts of Ireland, where prefamine patterns of early and frequent marriage survived the onslaught of modernization until at least the 1880s. Even in the decades after 1880 western Ireland merged only slowly with the national mainstream. An economically peripheral status, limited social stratification, and a degree of cultural autonomy (based on Gaelic speaking) help to explain the resilience of traditional practices.

The north east of Ireland constituted a very different kind of region. Ulster was the most ethnically diverse of the Irish provinces, with a large Protestant population. Unusually in the Irish context it experienced the twin processes of industrialization and urbanization, which might also suggest the basis for a different demography. The early phase of the industrial revolution (1780s–1830) had touched the Lagan Valley, but the effects were largely confined to the new, factory-based cotton industry. In the second half of the nineteenth century industrialization proceeded on a much wider front. Heavy industry in the form of shipbuilding and engineering, in addition to the traditional but now technologically transformed linen textiles, flourished. Was there, as a result, a distinctive Ulster demography? Differences between north and south were evident by the eve of the World War I, but only in some areas of behavior. Thus in Belfast, permanent celibacy among women was almost as high as in the rest of Ireland generally in the census year of 1911. In the case of men, however, there was a marked contrast. The incidence of permanent celibacy or non-marriage was very low: at 13 percent it was only half the national level. The crowded workplaces of the female-dominated linen industry and its feisty "millies" improved the chaps' chances of a match, or so it would seem. In the northern metropolis age at marriage was also lower than elsewhere. For women it was some two years below the national average; for men the difference, at almost four years, was even more pronounced. Differences in fertility, as already noted, were beginning to open up, as between north and south, and within Ulster as between Catholic and Protestant couples. The industrialization of the north, and the livelihoods it created, also succeeded in reducing the rate of emigration from the northern counties. This was especially true of Ulster Protestants, who by the turn of the twentieth century had consolidated their position economically, demographically, and politically in the northeast of the island. Protestant demographic strength underpinned the political resolve of Ulster unionists to resist Home Rule for Ireland, or the breakup of the United Kingdom as they viewed it.

PATTERNS IN THE TWENTIETH CENTURY

The course of Irish population change following World War I and the partition of the island in 1921 consisted to a large extent of the working out of trends, which had been apparent since the 1850s. Despite the political convulsions, the century after the famine can, with some change of detail, be viewed as a unified period in demographic terms. Indeed, at mid-twentieth century, Northern Ireland and the Irish Republic looked rather old-fashioned by comparison with other western societies. While the number of children born to the typical Irish family had undergone some decline since 1900, the fall was minor compared with that experienced by neighboring societies. Similarly, while the incidence of marriage had risen from its nadir during the Great Depression of 1929 through 1932, the Irish Republic and Northern Ireland still featured at the bottom of the European marriage stakes. Birth and death rates were, admittedly, closer to the European norm, though the former were the product of two abnormal forces: a low marriage rate but a high incidence of fertility within marriage. Emigration, that great constant in modern Irish population history, remained high in both jurisdictions. The situation was to get worse before it got better. During the 1950s the Irish Republic witnessed the greatest mass exodus since the 1880s, with an average of 40,000 people taking the emigrant boat each year. The term the *vanishing Irish* came into vogue, as some sympathetic outsiders worried that the Irish—by which they meant the Catholic Irish—were set to disappear from the face of the earth. But such is the mystery and the magic of population growth dynamics that this dark episode can be seen in hindsight as the hour before dawn: the threshold of a new era in Irish population history.

SEE ALSO Agriculture: 1690 to 1845; Agriculture: 1845 to 1921; American Wakes; Family: Marriage Patterns and Family Life from 1690 to 1921; Great Famine; Indian Corn or Maize; Migration: Emigration from the Seventeenth Century to 1845; Migration: Emigration from 1850 to 1960; Migration: Seasonal Migration; Population Explosion; Potato and Potato Blight (*Phytophthora infestans*); Rural Life: 1690 to 1845; Rural Life: 1850 to 1921; Subdivision and Subletting of Holdings; Town Life from 1690 to the Early Twentieth Century; **Primary Documents:** On Irish Rural Society and Poverty (1780); On Irish Society before the Famine (1841–1843); On Rural Society on the Eve of the Great Famine (1844–1845); From *Narrative of a Recent Journey* (1847)

Bibliography

Connell, Kenneth H. *The Population of Ireland, 1750–1845.* 1950.

Fitzpatrick, David. *Irish Emigration, 1801–1921.* 1990.

Guinnane, Timothy W. *The Vanishing Irish: Households, Migration, and the Rural Economy in Ireland, 1850–1914.* 1997

Ó Grada, Cormac. *Ireland: A New Economic History, 1780–1939.* 1994.

Kennedy, Liam, et al. *Mapping the Great Irish Famine: A Survey of the Famine Decades.* 1999.

Kennedy, Robert E. *The Irish: Emigration, Marriage and Fertility.* 1973.

Vaughan, William E., and A. J. Fitzpatrick. *Irish Historical Statistics: Population, 1821–1971.* 1978.

Liam Kennedy

≈

Population Explosion

In the seventeenth century, Ireland was one of the more thinly populated regions of western Europe. Population growth was typically slow and subject to reversals owing to war, harvest failure, famine, and disease. Modest population growth was apparent during the first four decades of the eighteenth century but there was a savage setback between 1740 and 1741 as a result of crop failure, bitterly cold weather, hunger, and famine diseases. By the end of that catastrophe the number of people on the island approximated only two million, much the same level as a half century earlier. But that picture of slow change in the numbers of families, households, and individuals inhabiting the island was to change dramatically and unexpectedly.

In the century between the 1740s and the 1840s Ireland experienced an explosive growth of population. In fact, the expansion was the fastest in Europe, with the possible exception of Finland (another thinly populated country with large reserves of wasteland). In 1750, in round figures, there were two million inhabitants. By 1800 this total had swollen to five million. The mighty wave of population increase continued into the nineteenth century, reaching its highest level in 1845. By then the island was peopled by 8.5 million beings, a remarkable figure never achieved before or since.

An alternative way of expressing this headlong surge of population is to capture it in terms of proportional change on an annual basis. Before looking at the Irish figures, it is worth bearing in mind that a sustained population increase of more than 1 percent per annum is rapid by the standards of preindustrial societies. The most authoritative estimates for Ireland suggest an annual growth rate of 1.5 percent or more for the period 1753 to 1791, and 1.4 percent (possibly 1.6%) for the years from 1791 to 1821. In the poorest, most westerly province of Connacht reproduction was at its most exuberant, with the population increasing by close on 2 percent each year, on average, up to 1821.

So, why this astonishing turnaround in demographic fortunes? It certainly had nothing to do with an influx of people, as in the case of other immigration-prone societies. There was a small but significant outflow of people from Ireland, and Ulster in particular, during the eighteenth century. Between 1815 and 1845 perhaps a further 1.5 million Irish emigrated to Britain or North America. In view of this movement of population, the problem to be explained is all the greater.

INCREASED FERTILITY AS A CAUSE

Logically, there are only two remaining possible sources of population increase: a rise in births or a fall in mortality over time. The two are not of course mutually exclusive. Historians have tended to place the primary emphasis on increased births (or fertility). Change might have come about because of a variety of shifts in the economic and ecological systems of Irish society. First, there was the increasing use of the miracle food—the potato. The famous spud was not only nutritious: In the production of a given level of calories it was at least twice as economical in its use of land as other food sources such as oats or wheat (not to mention dairy or beef farming, which used land extravagantly). In effect, under a regime of potato cultivation much higher population densities became possible. Subdivision of holdings among two or more children also became feasible without threatening, at least for a generation or two, the viability of the farm holding. In addition, potatoes proved to be well adapted to the poorer soils, allowing reclamation of bog lands and mountainsides. This in turn allowed population to spill out onto the wastelands in a process of internal colonization of the countryside.

It is possible, as the pioneering work of Kenneth H. Connell suggested, that potato cultivation lowered the age at which men and, more importantly, women married in the second half of the eighteenth century. The argument is that the potato crop lowered the barriers to marriage by assuring young couples of at least a mini-

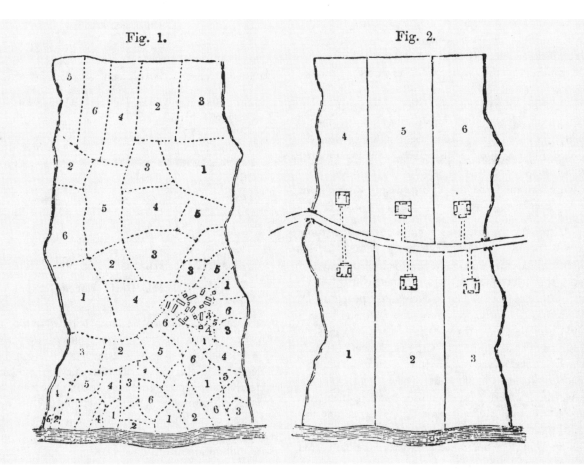

Agricultural reformers wanted to make Irish farming more efficient by eliminating such traditional practices as rundale. This illustration shows diagrams of land held in rundale (scattered pieces) by six tenants, and of the same land held in compact farms by the same tenants. Rundale was declining in some places before 1845, but the Great Famine accelerated the process enormously. FROM MR. AND MRS. SAMUEL CARTER HALL, IRELAND: ITS SCENERY, CHARACTER, ETC. (1841–1843).

mum subsistence, even when access to a patch of land was all that was available. In a noncontraceptive society early female marriage would have led inevitably to larger families. There is a small number of local studies that indicate that this is indeed what happened in the later eighteenth century but there is no comprehensive evidence as yet on age at marriage and how this may have changed over time. In addition to possible changes in the age at marriage, it is also possible that the proportions of the population that married increased over time as potato cultivation relaxed the restraints on the formation of households. Even more speculatively, a baby food of mashed potatoes and milk may have allowed children to be weaned at an earlier age. The effect on mothers would have been to shorten the sterile period after birth and thus boost fertility.

The potato also acted on mortality by helping prolong the lives of children and adults. It reduced mortality not only by virtue of its high nutritional content but also because it added a cheap and apparently reliable food to the people's diet. In time, of course, with a descent into monoculture, dependence on the potato would prove a source of vulnerability. But for at least the two generations after 1750, when it was used in conjunction with oatmeal, milk, or other foodstuffs, it must have added to the reliability of the food supply. Further influences favoring a decline in mortality in the century before the Great Famine of the 1840s may have included medical advances in the fight against infectious diseases, with smallpox perhaps as the only significant candidate for consideration. It is also possible that the virulence of infectious diseases naturally waned over time; if so, the reasons belong to the natural rather than to the social world.

SOCIOECONOMIC CONTEXT

But the social world was fundamental. The prerequisite to an ever-increasing population was an expanding economic base, as the early classical economists Adam

Smith and the Reverend Thomas Malthus reminded their readers. The Irish economy experienced a long wave of expansion between the 1740s and 1815. Potato cultivation played its variety of roles. A rising demand for Irish agricultural produce on the British and overseas markets, in particular for labor-intensive products such as oats, wheat, butter, and pork, created livings for more and more people. Handicraft industry also expanded, most notably in Ulster, where the linen industry achieved spectacular gains. Manufacturing and subsistence farming coexisted side by side, multiplying the possibilities of making a living.

Ulster also illustrates the point that there was more to Irish population history than the potato. In this northerly province the potato never achieved the dominance that it attained in the south and west of the island. Oatmeal was used extensively in the people's diet, yet during the early decades of population growth it was Ulster that experienced the most rapid increase in numbers of any of the four provinces. Similarly, it may be noted that population growth was common to other European societies at the time, where cereals were the stable food. Clearly, then, pan-European rather than purely Irish forces were at play. Still, in explaining Ireland's place at the top of the European growth league, it is tempting to conclude that it was the potato that made the difference.

A Downward Trend

Irish population lurched forward in the century before the Great Famine, in a manner that had no precedent in Irish history. But it is also clear that at least three decades before that awful event, the rate of population growth was slackening and adjusting downward. The tragedy is that potato failure and famine struck at an inflated population before it had time to complete the adjustment to a new equilibrium between population and food resources.

SEE ALSO Agriculture: 1690 to 1845; Family: Marriage Patterns and Family Life from 1690 to 1921; Great Famine; Land Questions; Migration: Emigration from the Seventeenth Century to 1845; Population, Economy, and Society from 1750 to 1950; Potato and Potato Blight (*Phytophthora infestans*); Rural Life: 1690 to 1845; Subdivision and Subletting of Holdings; Town Life from 1690 to the Early Twentieth Century

Bibliography

Connell, Kenneth H. *The Population of Ireland, 1750–1845.* 1950.

Daultrey, Stuart, David Dickson, and Cormac Ó Grada. "Eighteenth-Century Irish Population: New Perspectives from Old Sources." *Journal of Economic History* 41, no. 3 (1981): 601–628.

Liam Kennedy

~

Potato and Potato Blight (*Phytophthora infestans*)

The potato (*Solanum tuberosum*) originated in the South American Andes and from there it was brought to Europe by Spanish traders about the year 1570. Sir Walter Raleigh has been credited with introducing the potato to Ireland, but it appears more likely that it was imported from Spain sometime between 1586 and 1600. The potato proved highly adaptable to the Irish soil and Ireland's cool, damp climate. In its first hundred years or so of cultivation, until about 1700, the potato was used as a supplementary food and as a bulwark against famine during years of poor corn yields. During the next fifty years, it became the staple food of the poorer classes during the winter months from October to March. The years between 1750 and 1810 saw dramatic growth in potato tillage and consumption, as the potato supported a rapidly growing population that increasingly depended on its sustenance for the greater part of the year. By 1845 some three million people had come to rely primarily on the potato as their staple food.

From about 1810 to 1845 a growing gap between food supply and demand led to increasing distress among the poorer classes, with ever more marginal land being pressed into service, little or no use of manures, and the increasing cultivation of the bulky but inferior quality "lumper" potato variety. The "lumper" had become the dominant variety in much of the country by 1845, and it was to prove highly susceptible to potato blight.

Potato blight is caused by the fungus phytophthora infestans, which attacks and rots the leaves and tubers of affected plants. Mild, humid, and wet weather conditions, common in Ireland, are particularly favorable to the spread of the disease. The blight that was to devastate Ireland was first seen in the United States in 1843 and in Belgium in June 1845. From there it spread rap-

Enough potatoes were grown in Ireland on the eve of the famine to supply about 60 percent of national food needs. The deadly fungus Phytophthora infestans *reduced potato production after 1845 to only a fraction of its former level. This 1849 sketch shows people scratching desperately for potatoes in a stubble field in hopes of staying alive.* FROM ILLUSTRATED LONDON NEWS, 22 DECEMBER 1849.

idly across northwestern Europe, appearing in Ireland in August 1845. Its late arrival in Ireland reduced the impact on the 1845 harvest, but the yield was still about one-third below that required to feed the population. The following two years produced only about one-tenth of the prefamine harvest. With the ending of the blight after 1849 the potato supply slowly recovered, but it never again achieved its prefamine dominance in the Irish diet.

The decimation of the staple food source of at least three million people had inevitable and appalling consequences. About one million people died in the Great Famine; two million more left the country forever in the years between 1845 and 1855, many emigrating to the

United States, Canada, and Australia, and others to Britain.

SEE ALSO Agriculture: 1690 to 1845; Agriculture: 1845 to 1921; Family: Marriage Patterns and Family Life from 1690 to 1921; Famine Clearances; Great Famine; Indian Corn or Maize; Migration: Emigration from the Seventeenth Century to 1845; Migration: Emigration from 1850 to 1960; Poor Law Amendment Act of 1847 and the Gregory Clause; Population, Economy, and Society from 1750 to 1950; Population Explosion; Rural Life: 1690 to 1845; Rural Life: 1850 to 1921; Subdivision and Subletting of Holdings; Town Life from 1690 to the Early Twentieth Century; **Primary Documents:** On Irish Rural Society and Poverty (1780); On Rural Society on the Eve of the Great Famine (1844–1845)

Bibliography

Burke, Austin. *"The visitation of God"? The Potato and the Great Irish Famine*. 1993.

Clarkson, Leslie A., and E. Margaret Crawford, eds. *Feast and Famine: A History of Food and Nutrition in Ireland, 1500–1920*. 2001.

Matthew Lynch

Prehistoric and Celtic Ireland

In about 7000 B.C.E. small Stone Age Mesolithic communities in Ireland hunted wild pig, deer, and wood grouse in the forests with composite harpoons and spears (armed with tiny flints similar to those found in Britain and northern Europe) and fished the rivers near their settlements for the abundant salmon and eel in season. Three millennia later, the descendants of these first colonists were joined by much larger Neolithic communities of farmers who cleared the forests with polished stone axeheads. They set up farmsteads on the newly established grasslands to rear imported cattle and sheep, making field systems enclosed by double-faced stone walls, many of which were preserved under later blanket peat in the west of Ireland. They grew imported wheat and oats, which they ground into meal in saddle-querns and cooked in pottery vessels to make porridge.

MEGALITHIC TOMBS

COURT TOMBS The tombs of the Neolithic period are spaced apart over the cleared landscape. Built of very large stones and thus termed "megalithic," they required communal effort and were places for communal burial. Called "court tombs" after the distinctive open enclosed-courts in front of the burial chambers, they were built with orthostats and aligned east and west. Court and burial-chambers were integrated within a long trapezoid cairn between 15 and 55 meters long. More than 400 of these court tombs now exist on the coastal plains and on the uplands north of a line drawn from Clifden in Galway to Dundalk in Louth.

PASSAGE TOMBS More than forty excavated tombs have yielded both cremated and inhumed burials of people of all ages and both sexes. There is no distinction in type between the material deposited with these burials and that found in the habitations: shouldered pottery vessels and characteristic flint lozenge arrowheads and tools. Bones of cattle, sheep, and red deer found with the burials document funeral feasts.

Under the court tomb at Ballyglass, near the shore of Bunatrahir Bay in north Mayo, the foundations of a rectangular timber building 13 meters by 6 meters were discovered. The entrance was through a porch in the northwest façade into a partitioned hallway, above which were the sleeping-quarters. Within was a large open area 6 meters by 5.5 meters, with a fireplace close to the wall at its southeast end and with a high A-roof above. The pottery and stone implements found were of the same types as those from court tombs. Similar houses were excavated at Ballynagilly in Tyrone and Tankardstown in Limerick. These rectangular dwellings, the largest of the whole Irish prehistoric period, appear to have housed substantial social units like extended families, possibly headed by matriarchs.

More than 300 "passage tombs" are grouped in large cemeteries on hilltops, mainly in the north and east of the country. The chambers are simple or complex in shape, enclosed within round cairns girdled by megalithic kerbs. The finest architectural achievements of their builders are found in such monuments as Newgrange in the Boyne Valley, erected about 3000 B.C.E.; other major cemeteries are known on the Loughcrew Hills in north Meath and at Carrowkeel and Knocknarea-Carrowmore in Sligo. The lopsided cruciform chamber of Newgrange, over 6 meters wide, is approached by a passage 19 meters long; both are lined with tall orthostats. A great hexagonal corbelled vault built of large ice-boulders rises 6 meters above the floor of the chamber. This is covered by a pear-shaped mound of layered earth and stones 85 meters in diameter and averaging 12 meters in height, standing on a low knoll and containing a quarter of a million tons of material.

In Ireland, as on the Atlantic façade of Europe from Iberia north, these tombs are distinguished by a set of art motifs engraved on the orthostats, lintels, and roof-slabs of the tomb and on the kerbstones set around the mound in an early public display of art. The simplest canon merely represents these devices on the stones; another, more ambitious, combines elements to enhance the architectural effect, as on the lintel stones at Newgrange and Fourknocks; a later canon blends complex designs with the undulations of the stone to achieve a sophisticated plastic effect, as on orthostats and kerbstones at Newgrange and Knowth nearby. Many of these complex designs on tombs in Ireland and Anglesey and around the Gulf of Morbihan in Brittany are abstractions of the human face or figure; some are frankly female, representing a goddess of death and regeneration stationed at the threshold of the otherworld.

A rectangular fanlight or roof-box with a decorated upper lintel specially constructed over the doorway of Newgrange directs the rising sun at midwinter into the chamber, dramatically embodying the principle of regeneration in marking the death of the old year and the coming of the new.

The people buried in these tombs were generally cremated—as many as 200 persons of all ages and both sexes have been found in a single tomb at Tara—and the remains were interred with their ornaments, pendants, and beads carved of semiprecious stones and strung in necklaces. Their pottery, known as Carrowkeel ware, was a hemispherical bowl, ornamented all over the surface with chevrons and nested arcs. The most significant feature of their burial ritual in Ireland is the complete absence of stone tools and weapons from their burial chambers, contrasting with the burial deposits of all other megalithic tombs in west and north Europe. This suggests that these mundane items were prohibited from the sacred burial places, being allowed only in the habitations. The size and number of these tombs in the Boyne Valley suggests a workforce of several hundred people living in agglomerated settlements. They betray their ancestry in Atlantic Europe, particularly in Brittany, in their unique fondness for shellfish—periwinkle, mussel, oyster, and pecten—which constitute the remains of funeral meals found at sites far inland.

LATER NEOLITHIC COMMUNITIES, HILLTOP DEFENDED SETTLEMENTS, AND CONTACTS WITH CENTRAL EUROPE AND THE CAUCASUS

A later Neolithic tradition, dramatically different in its origin in the Caucasus via central Europe and Scandinavia, was a new burial rite—the individual burial of a man deposited in the central closed cist (a small stone box roofed with a flat slab roof, designed to take a single crouched burial) of an earthen mound up to thirty-six meters in diameter. The departure from communal burial indicates a radical change in society: Now each sept had a single male leader or ruler at its head. The burial was normally accompanied by a highly decorated pottery vessel that could have belonged to one of four newly introduced classes.

The followers of this new group occupied the coastal islands of the Clyde area of Scotland and the river valleys of the lands on both sides of the Irish Sea and were strongly represented in south Leinster. Their arrival in Ireland can be dated to early in the third millennium B.C.E.; their cultural contacts with central Europe were thriving as late as 1800 B.C.E., when bone-barbell pins of Únĕtice type were imported directly from central Europe to Dublin, Kilkenny, and Limerick. These people introduced the horse into Ireland, ultimately from the Caucasus. Their portal tombs—200 single-chambered megalithic tombs in long cairns derived from court tombs—follow similar patterns on both sides of the Irish Sea.

The new arrivals lived in defended settlements built on moderately high hills in the northeast, such as Lyles Hill north of Belfast, where a broad palisaded earthen bank enclosed a pear-shaped area of six hectares, within which stood a cairn probably containing a classic individual burial. The naturally defended promontory of Knockadoon extending into Lough Gur in Limerick was also chosen for settlement, along with artificial lake-dwellings in Tyrone, Derry, and Meath. The salmon fisheries of the River Bann and the coastal sites in the sandhills in Derry, Antrim, and Down, and on the offshore islands of Rathlin, Bute, Man, Lambay, and Dalkey, also attracted them. This new group's Scandinavian, central European, and Caucasian background, their introduction of the horse, and the timing of their arrival in Ireland (from the third millennium into the second), all suggest a close relationship with speakers of a proto-Indo-European language spreading from their homeland in the Caucasus via Scandinavia to the far west.

THE BRONZE AGE

With the Early Bronze Age came the art of transforming new materials in a radically innovative way into personal ornaments, weapons, and tools. Copper mined in Leinster as well as in Waterford, Cork, and Kerry, was smelted and cast in open molds into knives, daggers, and flat axeheads from about 2000 B.C.E.; copper was later alloyed with tin to make a harder metal, bronze. Gold was hammered into flat sheets to make earrings, lunulae (neck ornaments shaped like the crescent moon), and breast ornaments. Settlements were established near the sources of these metals; as a result, west Munster became prominent for the first time.

Beaker metalworkers, named for their distinctive bell-shaped redware vessels, settled on the European continent at three great nodes rich in metal ores: near Lisbon, in central Europe along the Danube north of the Alps, and in Ireland and Britain. Their dead were buried alone in cists or pits with a single beaker, a conical V-perforated button, and a wrist-bracer, which was a flat plate of stone perforated at the ends to protect an archer's wrist from the bowstring. With these classic accoutrements of the archer-warrior went flint barbed-and-tanged arrowheads. These people wore gold basket-shaped earrings and pairs of sun-discs, along with tanged knife-daggers cast in open stone molds. Only a few classic beakers have been found in Ireland, the finest of them at Moytirra near Sligo town.

Whereas in Britain and on the Continent single males were buried in cists, in Bronze Age Ireland and Brittany the dead were buried in late megalithic tombs, allées couvertes (gallery graves) and "wedge tombs." Irish wedge tombs number more than 500 and are found mainly in the west, with a great concentration in the metal-rich areas of Cork and Kerry. One hundred have been found on the limestone uplands of the Burren in County Clare, where winter grazing is widely available. Wedge tombs were economically designed, with long burial galleries opening to the west, low orthostats that converge and slope downward toward the east end, and roofs with flat lintels.

Archeologists have discovered more than 1,300 single burials deposited in pit graves and cists, mainly in Leinster and in east and central Ulster—the obverse of the wedge tomb distribution. The pottery normally found at these sites are food vessels and urns—provincial and hybrid derivatives of beakers, with contributions from some Late Neolithic types. Sometimes the cists have been found grouped together in cemetery cairns and in flat cemeteries.

About forty round cairns housing several cists have been discovered. They probably developed from using Neolithic passage tombs to take secondary cist burials, as at the "Mound of the Hostages" at Tara. Here, secondary burials with food-vessel and urn pottery extended from the end of the Neolithic period to about 1500 B.C.E., when the remains of a prince aged fourteen wearing a necklace of bronze tubular beads were inserted into the mound. A royal scepter of five cylinders of animal bone with toothed edges was found with a cremated burial in the multiple-cist cairn of Knockast in County Westmeath.

Cinerary urns (large, coarse vessels designed to contain and protect the cremated remains of a single individual, frequently inverted over them) became the standard funerary pottery of the early Irish Bronze Age, displacing to an extent the earlier food vessel. Predominantly associated with such urns from about 1500 B.C.E. are bronze razors with ovoid blades sharpened to a keen edge, apparently designed for the removal of facial or cranial hair. Of forty-four Irish razors discovered, thirty-one were found with burials, apparently of males—possibly barber-surgeons or medicine men.

Between about 1250 and 1000 B.C.E., while dramatic changes in the eastern Mediterranean marked the disintegration of civilizations and empires, the scene was set for the magnificence of the Final Bronze Bishopsland phase in Ireland. Among the treasures from this phase are palstaves—implements developed from the flat axehead, with flanges at the edges terminating in a stopridge halfway between butt and blade. Finely made new tools of bronze for metalworking and woodworking—the hammer, anvil, vice, punch, graver, and chisel—also made their debut; they are the first such tools to be found in Ireland. More than twenty hoards of this period, found mainly in the north and east, consist of new types of gold ornaments including delicate finger-rings and feminine gold earrings, which were molded or twisted, copying east Mediterranean techniques. Heavy gold torcs were also developed in Ireland from bronze prototypes of Baltic origin. The dramatic increase in the availability of gold bullion suggests the discovery of a mother lode, possibly in Wicklow.

Excavations at Haughey's Fort, located on a hilltop three kilometers west of Emain Macha in Armagh and covering an area of about twenty acres, yielded evidence of a bank faced by a palisade inside the innermost ditch, dating from about 1100 B.C.E. Storage pits on the site yielded carbonized barley. Animal remains indicate that cattle, pigs, and a small number of sheep or goats had been eaten there, as well as leftovers of an apple. The great size of two circular post-built houses, each over twenty-five meters in diameter, suggests that this was the seat of a potentate.

THE FINAL BRONZE AGE

After 1000 B.C.E. the metal industries of Ireland burgeoned, flourishing under the influence of the late European Urnfield phase (from 900 B.C.E.), so called after the great bronze hoard of Dowris found near Birr in County Offaly. The large number of individual tool and weapon types and the quantities of metal found in the posses-

sion of individual craftsmen attest to a society that controlled mining and distribution, satisfied a demanding market, and supported the rise of important smiths, merchants, and potentates. A hundred hoards provide convincing evidence of great personal riches. The Great Clare Gold Find of 1854 consisted of at least 150 ornaments weighing 5.5 kilograms—the largest find of prehistoric gold objects in northern or western Europe. Claymolds, which were used exclusively by 1000 B.C.E., made possible the manufacture of new socketed axeheads, socketed knives, and chisels in great numbers.

A brilliant new school of artists who worked in gold devised a far more extensive range of personal ornaments than had been available before—gorgets, dress-fasteners, cuff links and pins, bracelets, and a variety of new hair ornaments, some of which seem to have been invented to satisfy a discriminating home market. The delicacy of the gold ornaments contrasts with the rude weaponry, spears, and slashing swords of the military heroes. Braying martial horns were part of the new military panoply, and horse-trappings and rattle-pendants denote a society given to parades. Large sheet-metal cauldrons and cast flesh-forks attest to princely hospitality. A northern province yielding cauldrons, buckets, horns, and gold sleeve-fasteners contrasts with a southwestern province (extending up to Banagher on the Shannon) in which horns decorated with conical pseudo-rivets, gold lock-rings, gorgets, and repoussé bowls are distinctive types. Ireland's contacts with the Urnfield area of Central Europe were at this time through northern and southern Britain, and also via the Atlantic with the Mediterranean.

Great stone fortresses like those on the Aran Islands, some surrounded by defensive zones of multiple walls or *chevaux-de-frise* (protective areas made of stone spikes set at an angle in the ground), appeared seemingly overnight in the southwest and west of Ireland at this time, probably from Galicia in northwest Spain. Promontory forts on the coast provided well-garrisoned lookout posts. Suddenly, society assumed a new military character; the times were troubled. Lake-dwellings became common, some of them with bronze workshops. Bronze crotals, metal objects resembling bull's testicles, may be evidence of a bull fertility cult at this time. A tall, wooden god preserved in the bog at Ralaghan in County Cavan foreshadowed the iconic gods and the La Tène aniconic (nonrepresentational) fertility stones that appeared at the end of this last millennium B.C.E. Important dwellings and temples emerged on sites such as Emain Macha—structures that in the early centuries C.E. were recognized as sacred royal centers.

HALLSTATT AND LA TÈNE TRADITIONS

In Ireland and Britain there are few Iron Age artifacts of the Hallstatt tradition (750 to 450 B.C.E.), when immensely rich leaders lived in princely strongholds such as the defended hilltop of the Heuneberg overlooking the Danube in southern Germany. During the fifth century B.C.E. the late Iron Age La Tène culture developed out of the Hallstatt tradition in the Champagne area of France and the middle Rhine valley and Bohemia. The princely dead were buried with splendid weapons and ornaments on two-wheeled chariots under huge mounds. The people of this culture congregated in impressive hillforts and in enormous proto-urban oppida (towns) such as the Heuneburg in southern Germany and Alesia in eastern France. Their new art style was disseminated widely from Asia Minor to Britain and Ireland. In this style, Greek palmettes and tendrils were subtly distorted into elegant and sophisticated abstract shapes presented on curved surfaces with a charming ambiguity.

In about 300 B.C.E. this heroic tradition arrived in Ireland and established itself in a northern province over the broad territory of Ulster, Connacht, and north Leinster. Ironworking was then fully established in Ireland, though gold and bronze were still used in making luxury objects. Examples of the distinctive La Tène neck-torc and brazen horn representing the "Dying Gaul" have been found in Broighter in Derry and Ardbrin in Down. Warriors were equipped with leaf-shaped spearheads, at that point made of iron and mounted on wooden shafts up to 2.4 meters long, and with swords, scabbards, and shields. Only a very small number of cauldrons and bronze bowls have been recovered, along with a single stave-built 1.4-liter tankard from Carrickfergus. Bronze fibulae (safety pin ornaments with tightly coiled springs, decorated with relief ornament to the bow) along with beads of colored glass appeared as new kinds of personal ornament.

The great royal sites of the period are located in the northern La Tène province: Tara and Tailtiu in Meath, Emain Macha near Armagh, Uisneach in Westmeath, and Cruachain west of the Shannon in Roscommon. The history of Tara and Cruachain begins with the burial monuments and the found objects dating from the Neolithic and Early Bronze Age; in the late prehistoric period ring-barrows appeared in great numbers and in a range of shapes and sizes. An excellent example of a ring-barrow is found at the royal site at Tara, where a large oval enclosure, 210 by 175 meters across, was formed from a double row of stout posts on the northern slope of the ridge, surrounding the "Rath of the Synods" and the "Mound of the Hostages." Ring-barrows are also found at Tailtiu, on the hilltop of Emain Macha, within the hilltop enclosure at Clogher in Tyrone, and

at Uisneach. Thus these royal sites were in part conceived of as cemeteries, sanctified by the bones of ancestors. The other characteristic monument is a great mound, the forradh, as at Tara, on which the king sat to exercise his judicial functions at the periodic assembly, or oenach. Massive composite monuments—Ráith Airthir at Donaghpatrick in the Tailtiu complex, the Mote of Downpatrick, and the monument at Granard in Longford—all relate to this forradh.

It appears that while the Iron Age La Tène tradition developed in the north, the Final Bronze Age tradition lived on in Munster and south Leinster. The greatest impact of the Irish La Tène tradition may have been on the landscape around royal sites and in massive defensive earthworks of the last two centuries B.C.E., such as the Dorsey in County Armagh and the Black Pig's Dyke running from south Armagh through Monaghan as far as north Leitrim. Despite its relative paucity, La Tène art continued in Ireland and Britain after the Romans, finding ultimate expression in the hands of early Christian artists.

LA TÈNE GODS AND RELIGION

Practices related to Celtic rituals have survived through the Christian period and up to the present day. Midsummer and midwinter rituals began in time immemorial. The quarter-days—the first days of February, May, August, and November (respectively, Imbolc, Bealtaine, Lughnasa, and Samhain)—each had their own rituals. High hilltops were visited at Lughnasa, a practice surviving to the present in the pilgrimage to the summit of Croagh Patrick in Mayo. The element dair, meaning oak, which appears in many place-names (as in Brigit's Cill Dara, the modern Kildare) may commemorate druidic sanctuaries sited at oak groves.

Representations in stone of godlike figures are known: The three-faced Corleck granite head from Cavan may have been part of a composite icon; the horned Tanderagee idol, from the cathedral site at Armagh, has mask-like features, a great open mouth, thick-lipped and screaming, and stylized arms. At that site there are also representations of a sun god, a bearded head, and a family of three benign bears, the largest with a wolf-head between its fore and hind legs. On Boa Island in Fermanagh a pair of belted warrior-gods, described by Françoise Henry as "terrifying in their inhumanity," stand back-to-back, staring severely out from the otherworld with large almond eyes.

Three aniconic carvings decorated with the characteristic abstract swirling curves, spirals, and trumpets of the Irish La Tène style celebrate male potency at Killycluggin in the territory of the legendary Crom Cruach at Mágh Sleacht in north Cavan, at Castlestrange in Roscommon, and at Turoe in Galway. Plain phallic pillars are more numerous: They are found on the Hill of Tara and beside Dún Dealgan as well as at Kilkieran in Kilkenny, Killadeas in Fermanagh, and Clear Island in Cork, where they were later purposely incorporated in early Christian sites.

ROMAN IRON AGE AND CHRISTIANITY

Roman material borne by visitors from Wales and Scotland appeared in Ireland from the first century C.E. onwards, and have been found between the Liffey and the Boyne as well as along the northeastern and northern coasts. A hoard of 500 valuable silver coins of the first and second centuries from Feigh Mountain in Antrim was found in a leather bag concealed under a flagstone. No Roman roads, towns, temples, or military camps were built in Ireland. After a marked hiatus in the third century, Roman material again found its way into the country. Evidence of visitors to Newgrange in this later period has been documented by coins of Theodosius, Constantine I, and Valentinian I, dating from about the year 400, together with a number of disc-brooches and the inscribed terminal of a Bishopsland bar-torc. Roman silver found at Balline in Limerick and Ballinrees in Derry was brought back to Ireland by Irish pirates from the crumbling periphery of the Roman empire in the fourth and fifth centuries. Numerous shards of Samian ware document visits by native Irish to the Roman world.

Christianity, already tolerated in Roman Britain and Gaul from the time of Constantine after 312 C.E., was present in Ireland by about 400. Ogham writing based on the Roman alphabet also appeared about this time. With Christianity came the Bible and a certain degree of literacy. It was about this time that the young (Saint) Patrick, son of a Roman decurion, was seized by Irish pirates in Britain and enslaved by Milchú, who put him to herding sheep on Slemish Mountain in Antrim. It was this Patrick, author of our earliest texts, who returned in the second half of the fifth century with a mission to organize and extend the already growing Irish church.

SEE ALSO Bronze Age Culture; Celtic Migrations; Cruachain; Cú Chulainn; Dún Ailinne; Emain Macha (Navan Fort); Myth and Saga; Stone Age Settlement; *Táin Bó Cúailnge*; Tara

Bibliography

Bateson, J. D. "Roman Material in Ireland: A Reconsideration." *Proceedings of the Royal Irish Academy* 73 (1973): 21–97.

de Valera, Ruaidhrí, and S. Ó Nualláin. *Megalithic Survey of Ireland: I, Co. Clare*. 1961.

de Valera, Ruaidhrí, and Seán Ó Nualláin. *Megalithic Survey of Ireland: II, Co. Mayo*. 1964.

Eogan, George. *Hoards of the Irish Later Bronze Age*. 1983.

Eogan, George. *The Accomplished Art: Gold and Gold Working in Britain and Ireland during the Bronze Age*. 1994.

Harbison, Peter. "The Axes of the Early Bronze Age in Ireland." *Prähistorische Bronzefunde* 9, no. 1 (1969).

Herity, Michael. *Irish Passage Graves*. 1974.

Herity, Michael. "Irish Decorated Neolithic Pottery." *Proceedings of the Royal Irish Academy* 82C (1982): 247–404.

Herity, Michael. "The Finds from Irish Court Tombs." *Proceedings of the Royal Irish Academy* 87C (1987): 103–281.

Herity, Michael. "Motes and Mounds at Celtic Royal Sites in Ireland." *Journal of the Royal Society of Antiquaries of Ireland* 123 (1993): 127–51.

Kavanagh, Rhoda M. "The Encrusted Urn in Ireland." *Proceedings of the Royal Irish Academy* 73C (1973): 507–617.

Kavanagh, Rhoda M. "Collared and Cordoned Cinerary Urns in Ireland." *Proceedings of the Royal Irish Academy* 76C (1976): 293–403.

Ó Ríordáin, Breandán, and John Waddell. *The Funerary Bowls and Vases of the Irish Bronze Age*. 1993.

Raftery, Barry. *Pagan Celtic Ireland: The Enigma of the Irish Iron Age*. 1984.

Waddell, John. *The Prehistoric Archaeology of Ireland*. 1998.

Michael Herity

~

Presbyterianism

Irish Presbyterianism is largely the result of a movement of population from Scotland to Ireland in the seventeenth century. The defeat of the Ulster Gaelic chieftains after a long struggle against English rule and the inexorable process of anglicization in Ireland had left the northern Irish province devastated and depopulated, ripe for colonization. James VI of Scotland had succeeded Elizabeth I on the English throne. This enabled Scots to settle in Ulster, and some Presbyterian ministers followed them, taking parishes in the state Church of Ireland, which was extending its structures into Ulster. James VI had restored episcopacy in Scotland, some of the Church of Ireland bishops in Ulster were Scots, and in a fluid ecclesiastical situation it was not too difficult for Scottish Presbyterian ministers to become parish ministers in the Irish church. Inevitably, this was a temporary situation, and when the Church of Ireland, under government pressure, began to enforce Anglican discipline, the Presbyterian ministers were expelled from their parishes. This followed a remarkable revival of religion among the settlers, anticipating similar revivals in colonial America a century later.

LAYING THE FOUNDATIONS OF AN IRISH PRESBYTERIAN CHURCH

There might never have been a Presbyterian Church in Ireland had not the Catholic Irish risen in rebellion in 1641. It was the chaplains of the Scots army that arrived in Ulster in 1642 to save the colony who formed the first presbytery on Irish soil and began the formal history of Irish Presbyterianism. During the Cromwellian interregnum Presbyterian congregations multiplied, and five presbyteries, or meetings of what had become the Ulster presbytery, emerged. Also during this period a number of congregations were formed in Dublin and in the south and west of Ireland, some of them originally Independent or Baptist, which later became Presbyterian. Their background was often English, rather than Scottish, Presbyterian. The restoration of monarchy and the established Episcopal Church of Ireland in 1660 brought eviction from their parishes and outlawry for some seventy Presbyterian ministers, but the colonial government in Ireland could not afford to alienate what was the majority Protestant denomination in Ulster, and Presbyterianism was allowed a precarious and restricted existence as Dissent with a small state subvention, the *regium donum* (royal bounty), for their ministers. They in turn supported William III against James II in the crisis for the British colony in 1689 to 1690 and were rewarded with an increased royal bounty and some small improvement in their position as Dissenters. Their five presbyteries formed a Synod of Ulster and its records are available from 1691.

THE EIGHTEENTH CENTURY

In the eighteenth century Presbyterians experienced continuing disabilities as Dissenters, and many of them suffered economic hardship as tenant farmers, with rising rents and tithes to pay to the established Church of Ireland. Large numbers emigrated to colonial America, where they were known as the Scotch-Irish, and some of them played significant parts in the colonists' fight for independence from Britain. Inspired by events in America, some Ulster Presbyterians became leaders in the United Irish movement for reform in Ireland and independence from Britain, culminating in the disastrous rebellion of 1798. Also in the eighteenth century Irish

Presbyterians were divided by tensions between conservative Calvinists, known as Old Lights, and theological liberals, or New Lights, often centering on the issue of subscription to the Westminster Confession of Faith by ordinands (ministers on ordination), the Synod having followed the Church of Scotland in adopting the Confession as its official statement of faith. The advance of the New Lights was resisted by conservative church members, who welcomed more conservative Scottish Presbyterian dissenters, Seceders, and Covenanters, who formed congregations and presbyteries in Ulster.

THE NINETEENTH CENTURY

The Old Light versus New Light controversy entered a new phase in the nineteenth century when evangelicalism breathed new life into the Old Light party, and some of the New Light, nonsubscribing ministers declared themselves Arians, querying the divinity of Christ. After a bitter conflict in the Synod in the 1820s the small minority of Arians and nonsubscribers withdrew to form a separate synod, which later united with other nonsubscribing Presbyterians as the Non-Subscribing Irish Presbyterian Church. The Old Light victory in the Synod of Ulster led in 1840 to a union with the Secession Synod in the General Assembly of the Presbyterian Church in Ireland. The new united church displayed great creative energy in outreach at home and abroad, forming new congregations, evangelizing in the south and west of Ireland, initiating a foreign mission, and founding two theological colleges and new institutions of social service such as the Kinghan Mission to the Deaf and Dumb. Evangelicalism, which had contributed so much to these developments, reached a climax of influence in the Ulster revival of 1859, recalling the revival of the early seventeenth century. In politics Irish Presbyterians maintained their essential liberalism, supporting education and land reforms and advancing democracy and social justice. Yet they were also unwavering in their commitment to the parliamentary union with Britain that had followed the 1798 rebellion, opposing the nationalist campaign for Irish Home Rule.

THE TWENTIETH CENTURY

That opposition to Home Rule led to the partition of Ireland in 1921, with Presbyterians as the majority Protestant population in Northern Ireland. The estimated 650,000 Irish Presbyterians in 1840 have now been reduced by at least half, and numbers in what is now the Republic of Ireland have fallen from 50,000 to 15,000 since partition, though that decline seems recently to have been reversed. Most Presbyterians in the Republic of Ireland regard themselves as Irish, not British, while most Presbyterians in Northern Ireland see no contradiction between their Irishness and Britishness, of which they are equally proud. Within the existing political context the Presbyterian Church, which remains undivided in Ireland, endeavors to promote peace, justice, and reconciliation between the two communities in both parts of the island. Relations between different churches in Ireland are better today than in previous centuries, although the theologically conservative Irish Presbyterians remain wary of relationships that they believe would compromise their distinctive Reformed witness.

SEE ALSO Abernethy, John; Cooke, Henry; Education: Primary Public Education—National Schools from 1831; Education: University Education; Evangelicalism and Revivals; Overseas Missions; Paisley, Ian; Religion: Since 1690; Second Reformation from 1822 to 1869; Temperance Movements

Bibliography

Beckett, James C. *Protestant Dissent in Ireland, 1687–1780.* 1948.

Brooke, Peter. *Ulster Presbyterianism.* 1987.

Dunlop, John. *A Precarious Belonging: Presbyterians and the Conflict in Ireland.* 1995.

Holmes, R. Finlay. *Our Irish Presbyterian Heritage.* 1992.

Holmes, R. Finlay. *The Presbyterian Church in Ireland: A Popular History.* 2000.

Kilroy, Phil. *Protestant Dissent and Controversy in Ireland, 1660–1714.* 1994.

McBride, I. R. *Scripture Politics: Ulster Presbyterians and Irish Radicalism in the Late Eighteenth Century.* 1998.

Miller, David. "Presbyterianism and 'Modernization' in Ulster." *Past and Present* 80 (1978): 66–90.

Westerkamp, Marilyn. *The Triumph of the Laity: Scots-Irish Piety and the Great Awakening, 1620–1760.* 1988.

Finlay Holmes

Presidency

Articles 12 to 14 of Eamon de Valera's constitution of 1937 detail the powers of the office of president and stipulate that the president be directly elected for a seven-year term in a national vote, or, if the political parties so choose, nomination procedures can be used to agree on a candidate and avoid a vote. Although the articles allow for outgoing presidents to nominate themselves for a second term, other potential candidates need to be proposed either by twenty members of the Oireachtas (TDs or senators), or the councils of four counties or county boroughs. Given that these local authorities are composed on party lines, this route was rarely feasible and was not used until 1997.

On five occasions—1938, 1952, 1974, 1976, and 1983—only one candidate was nominated, while there have been six contested elections in 1945, 1959, 1966, 1973, 1990, and 1997. Although the constitution prevents the president from participating in party politics or the day-to-day running of the government, there are six discretionary powers for use in specific circumstances; three give the president an adjudicatory role in disputes between Dáil and Senate (which have never arisen), and a fourth gives the president power to convene a meeting of either or both of the houses of the Oireachtas.

The president can also refer a bill passed by the Oireachtas to the Supreme Court to judge its constitutionality, before which the president must consult but is not bound by the Council of State, an advisory body containing past and present senior politicians and seven people appointed by the president. In 1976 President Cearbhall Ó Dálaigh referred the Emergency Powers Bill on this basis and resigned after vicious criticism by the minister for defense.

The sixth power relates to the dissolution of the Dáil, and does not require consultation, although Article 13.2.2 states most ambiguously that the president "may in his absolute discretion refuse to dissolve Dáil Éireann on the advice of a Taoiseach who has ceased to retain the support of a majority in Dáil Éireann." No president has ever exercised this power, though pressure in 1981 was brought to bear on Patrick Hillery to do so.

The office of president has been likened to that of a relatively powerless constitutional monarch and in the earlier years was frequently used as a retirement post for distinguished male senior politicians, most notably de Valera, who was aged 76 when elected president. In 1990 Mary Robinson, aged 46, and a candidate nominated by the Labour Party, shattered this convention following an electrifying campaign, making Ireland only the second country in Europe after Iceland to have a woman as elected head of state. Hoping to expand the role of the office, she certainly gave it an increased profile and championed the plight of minorities and the status of women in Irish society, though ultimately she had to accept the limitations of the office and abstain from interfering in matters that were the prerogative of the government.

SEE ALSO Constitution; de Valera, Eamon; Politics: Independent Ireland since 1922; Robinson, Mary

Bibliography

Gallagher, Michael, and John Coakley, eds. *Politics in the Republic of Ireland.* 1992.

Finlay, Fergus. *Mary Robinson: A President with a Purpose.* 1991.

Diarmaid Ferriter

Proportional Representation

Proportional representation (PR) is an electoral mechanism designed to ensure that the distribution of votes between various interests in an election to a collective body is reflected proportionally in the distribution of seats on that body. In its typical form, in continental Europe "list" systems, it ensures that the share of votes cast for party lists in elections is fairly accurately translated into share of seats.

Under the less common "single transferable vote" (STV) system of PR, voters rank candidates (in practice, party is the most important consideration, but other criteria such as region or gender may also count). These preference votes are then converted into seats on the basis of an electoral quota; "surplus" votes of candidates reaching this quota are redistributed according to lower preferences, and less popular candidates are progressively eliminated and their lower preferences are redistributed until all vacancies have been filled.

The STV form of PR has been the "normal" one in English-speaking countries. First implemented in Tasmania in 1896, it was introduced for local elections in Ireland in 1919 and for elections to the parliaments of Northern Ireland and Southern Ireland in 1920. Election of the Dáil by PR has been a constitutional requirement since 1922 (the 1937 constitution specifies that the STV system be used). Notwithstanding efforts to replace it with the U.K.- and U.S.-style plurality system in 1959 and 1968, this system has survived in the Republic of Ireland. It is also used in elections to the senate, in local elections, and in Irish elections to the European parliament.

In Northern Ireland, PR was abolished for local elections in 1922 and for domestic parliamentary elections in 1929. The reinstituted plurality system helped to preserve unionist hegemony, and when Northern Ireland's institutions were reformed following the outbreak of civil unrest, PR was brought back in 1973 for elections to local authorities and to the Northern Ireland assembly and its successors (apart from the Forum elected in 1996, when a modified "list" system was used).

The primary reason for the introduction of PR in Ireland was to ensure minority representation. One alleged side effect of the STV form is that it promotes intraparty divisions and, by placing a premium on electoral competition *within* rather than *between* parties, encourages clientelist politics, with candidates offering to do favors for constituents rather than engaging with issues of national policy; evidence on this issue is inconclusive. A second criticism of PR is that it inhibits strong government by promoting a multiparty system; but its defenders argue that non-PR systems violate basic principles of electoral justice. Since the political stakes are high, this debate is likely to continue.

SEE ALSO Northern Ireland: History since 1920; Political Parties in Independent Ireland; Politics: Independent Ireland since 1922

Bibliography

Bogdanor, Vernon. *What Is Proportional Representation?* 1984.

Sinnott, Richard. "The Electoral System." In *Politics in the Republic of Ireland*, edited by John Coakley and Michael Gallagher. 1999.

John Coakley

Protestant Ascendancy

1690 TO 1800	JAMES KELLY
DECLINE, 1800 TO 1930	JACQUELINE HILL

1690 TO 1800

The anglophone landed elite, whose command of the political, economic, and social structures of Ireland was

---

at its most complete in the period between the defeat in 1690 to 1691 of the Jacobite armies and the enactment of an Anglo-Irish union in 1800, is familiarly known as the Protestant Ascendancy. Significantly, this term was neither coined nor popularized until the late eighteenth century, when conservative elements within the elite, perceiving that it was at risk, rallied to defend the "Protestant constitution" in the face of external threat. As it was famously defined by Dublin Corporation in 1792, Protestant Ascendancy encompassed "a Protestant king of Ireland—a Protestant parliament—a Protestant hierarchy—Protestant electors and government—the bench of justice—the army and the revenue—through all their branches and details Protestant." Though ostensibly just a list of those elements of church and state that Protestant ideologues were determined to preserve unaltered, it reflected the actuality of the command that Protestants enjoyed of the levers of power from the mid-seventeenth century.

The emerging Protestant elite was well placed to consolidate its dominant position in the kingdom of Ireland when, following the restoration of the monarchy in 1660, Charles II confirmed them in possession of three-quarters of the land and acknowledged the Church of Ireland as the established church. Yet the fact that they chose to describe themselves variously as the "Protestant interest" or "the English interest" provides a reliable pointer to their imperfectly developed sense of identity. They were, for a ruling elite, also surprisingly lacking in confidence, arising out of the conviction, annually reinforced by ceremonies recalling the "massacres" perpetrated during the early phases of the 1641 Rebellion, that the Catholic population was committed to their extirpation. Their unease was heightened during the late 1680s when, in the course of James II's unsuccessful attempt to use Ireland as a base from which to regain the throne, it seemed not just that the Catholic Church would be elevated to a position above that of the Church of Ireland but that Irish Protestants would be obliged to forfeit the lands that they currently occupied. As a result, they determined, having overcome this challenge, to take the measures necessary to protect themselves in the future. To this end they oversaw the introduction of a body of anti-Catholic legislation commonly known as the penal laws. Parallel with this, the command that the Protestant elite already possessed over the wealth of the country was increased as a result of the Williamite land settlement, which ensured the transfer of a further 14 percent of the land from Catholic to Protestant ownership.

In an environment where Irish Protestants were genuinely fearful of the Jacobitism and Catholicism of the population at large, the maintenance of a secure connection with England was of obvious importance. At the same time, Irish Protestants remained convinced that as the "English in Ireland" they were entitled to the same rights and privileges as Englishmen. To this end they repeatedly asserted the right of the Irish parliament to possess greater powers than the government in London was willing to concede. Despite this refusal to admit the Irish Protestants' constitutional claims, the centrality of the ascendancy to the effective rule of Ireland was confirmed by the English government's growing reliance on certain Irish Protestant leaders ("undertakers") to manage the Irish parliament.

The confidence that Irish Protestants vested in their legislature was augmented from the 1720s by the reinforcement of the culture of improvement already established among the elite. This was given institutional expression by the foundation of the Dublin Society in 1731. The mid-eighteenth century witnessed a striking acceleration in the range and variety of schemes and initiatives that were pursued both to increase the generation of wealth and to model the Irish landscape to reflect a familiar anglicized ideal. The construction of villages and towns, the development of the main cities, and the laying out of elegant demesnes created an appropriate milieu for the scores of Palladian and neoclassical houses that came to occupy the remodeled urban and rural landscape. As all this activity suggests, the Anglo-Irish elite were the arbiters of taste as well as the patrons of the architects, artists, book binders, silversmiths, mapmakers, tailors, and others whose handiwork has proved so influential in shaping the prevailing positive impression of the Georgian era. In practice, most of what was achieved was provincial in scale as well as standard, but this must not obscure the fact that the Anglo-Irish elite constituted Ireland's equivalent of an ancien régime aristocracy. The enthusiasm that they showed for dueling, that emblem of aristocratic exceptionalism throughout Europe, is merely the most obvious manifestation, but it is also exemplified in the general embrace of the ideals of civic virtue and, in the political sphere, of patriotism.

The Patriots' belief in the virtue of self-government climaxed during the late 1770s and early 1780s, when the Irish parliament secured the right to free trade within the empire (1780) and the right to make law untrammeled by restriction (1782). The late-eighteenth-century Irish parliament was legislatively active, but the atavistic incapacity of a majority of the Irish Protestant elite to perceive how they could possibly broaden the parameters of their constitution to admit Catholics caused many of their number to seek security in the rhetoric of Protestant Ascendancy from the mid-1780s. The popularity of this ideology, misleadingly attributed

Castletown House, Co. Kildare, the most splendid of the great houses of the Protestant Ascendancy. Built (1722–1732) for William Connolly, Speaker of the House of Commons, it was designed by Alessandro Galilei and Sir Edward Pearce. © DEPARTMENT OF ENVIRONMENT, HERITAGE & LOCAL GOVERNMENT PHOTO UNIT. REPRODUCED BY PERMISSION.

to mercantile and urban interests by William J. McCormack, extended across the Protestant elite. It was tangibly increased in the 1790s by the admission of Catholics to the franchise as well as by the emergence of republican separatism with the United Irishmen. Faced with the implications of redefining their constitution and identity to accommodate Catholics and with the threat of separation from Great Britain, many Irish Protestants found the rhetoric of continued Protestant Ascendancy more compelling. They found it more acceptable indeed to accede to the abolition of the Irish parliament, even though this body had been critical to their capacity to express their vision for Ireland when their influence was at its greatest during the mid-eighteenth century. The enactment of an Anglo-Irish union whereby, from 1 January 1801, Ireland sent one hundred MPs to the newly formed imperial parliament at Westminster paradoxically represented a milestone in the decline of the Protestant Ascendancy as a historical phenomenon.

SEE ALSO Church of Ireland: Since 1690; Eighteenth-Century Politics: 1690 to 1714—Revolution Settlement; Eighteenth-Century Politics: 1714 to 1778—Interest Politics; Eighteenth-Century Politics: 1778 to 1795—Parliamentary and Popular Politics; Eighteenth-Century Politics: 1795 to 1800—Repression, Rebellion, and Union; Penal Laws; Politics: 1690 to 1800—A Protestant Kingdom; Protestant Ascendancy: Decline, 1800 to 1930; Religion: Since 1690

Bibliography

Connolly, Sean. *Religion, Law, and Power: The Making of Protestant Ireland, 1660–1760.* 1992.

Cullen, Louis M. *The Emergence of Modern Ireland, 1600–1900.* 1981.

Kelly, James. "Eighteenth-Century Ascendancy: A Commentary." *Eighteenth-Century Ireland* 5 (1990): 173–187.

Lady Gilbert. Vol. 8 of *Calendar of Ancient Records of Dublin.* 1906.

McCormack, William J. *Ascendancy and Tradition in Anglo-Irish Literature from 1789 to 1939.* 1985.

MacDonagh, Oliver. *States of Mind: A Study in Anglo-Irish Conflict, 1780–1980.* 1983.

McGrath, Charles I. *The Making of the Eighteenth-Century Irish Constitution: Government, Parliament and the Revenue, 1692–1714.* 2000.

McNally, Patrick. *Parties, Patriots, and Undertakers: Parliamentary Politics in Early Hanoverian Ireland.* 1997.

James Kelly

DECLINE, 1800 TO 1930

During the course of the nineteenth century the term *ascendancy*—whether *Protestant* or *Anglo-Irish*—gradually shed its earlier connotations of a political condition reflecting Protestant hegemony and came to be applied almost exclusively to the Protestant landed class, ignoring those in other walks of life. The landed class (comprising up to ten thousand families in the mid-nineteenth century) was itself far from homogeneous; the estates of most landlords could be measured in hundreds rather than thousands of acres, but a few hundred landlords owned over ten thousand acres each. Recent scholarship has tended to qualify the stereotypical nationalist depiction of the rack-renting landlord, and casts doubt on the view that Catholic landlords, whose numbers were increasing in the postfamine era, were in general more sympathetic toward their tenants.

The Act of Union of 1800 weakened the Ascendancy by removing a parliament that they had been able to monopolize, and which had served to enhance their Irish credentials. A further blow came with the granting of Catholic Emancipation in 1829, which allowed Catholics to sit in Parliament, but until the 1880s the very limited franchise meant that the bulk of Irish seats were still filled by propertied Protestants. Of greater immediate consequence for the Protestant community was the passing of the Irish Municipal Corporations Act of 1840, which abolished the bulk of the urban corporations—town governments created by the Crown. Despite being legally open to Catholics since 1793, their composition had remained almost exclusively Protestant. A uniform £10 household vote was introduced for the remainder. The act facilitated the transfer of control of the surviving corporations (except in Ulster) from Protestants to Catholics. Together with the legacy of the 1798 rebellion and a postwar agricultural slump, it prompted emigration among middle-class and poorer Protestants. It has been estimated that up to half a million Protestants left Ireland during the first half of the nineteenth century. In Ulster, Protestant numbers were sufficiently high to enable such losses to be absorbed without much effect on the social structure. Elsewhere, the middle-class hemorrhage left the landed class dangerously exposed. Overall, the Protestant proportion of the population dropped from well over one-quarter in the eighteenth century to little over one-fifth by 1861, and in the three southern provinces the proportion was only about 10 percent (Vaughan and Fitzpatrick 1978).

In 1869 the disestablishment of the Church of Ireland removed a serious grievance of Catholics and (some) Presbyterians, but after the initial shock, it had an invigorating effect. Church members took advantage of the financial arrangements for compensation to secure the church's future, and it was to remain an important and influential institution, particularly for southern Protestants, four-fifths of whom were members. At this time Protestant landlords still enjoyed dominance in rural local government through the grand-jury system and boards of poor-law guardians. However, the advent of competitive examinations for the civil service in the 1850s, together with the establishment of the Queen's Colleges, gradually improved the prospects of Catholics for state employment.

The cause of land reform first made significant headway in the aftermath of the Great Famine, which had highlighted the lack of security of tenure for tenants. A limited land act was passed in 1870. Subsequently, a run of poor harvests created serious hardship for small tenant farmers in the west of Ireland and led to the formation in 1879 of the Irish National Land League, which pledged to resist rack rents and landlordism, an institution portrayed as anti-Irish. The ensuing land-reform agitation, which continued intermittently until the 1920s, witnessed rent strikes and other tactics designed to weaken landlord control, and prompted a series of measures from government (in 1881, 1885, 1891, 1903, and 1909) that facilitated the purchase by tenants of their holdings, a process that was still not fully complete by 1921. The Local Government Act of 1898, substituting elected county councils for Protestant-controlled grand juries and extending the vote in local government elections, further marginalized the Ascendancy.

The land issue helped to drive the Ascendancy toward the Conservative Party, and this was reinforced when the advent of an effective Irish Nationalist Party at Westminster in the 1880s prompted successive Liberal governments to back Home Rule. Protestants in the three southern provinces were the first to mobilize in defense of the Union, but the extension of the vote in 1884 to all male householders enabled Nationalists, with the backing of many of the Catholic clergy, to win 85 percent of the Irish seats in Parliament. Only in Ulster could Unionists win significant electoral support. Their sup-

Douglas Hyde (1860–1949), son of a Protestant clergyman, collector and translator of folklore and poetry in the Irish language, one of the founders of the Gaelic League, and president of Ireland from 1937 to 1945. Shown here with his daughter Mrs. Sealy and children. © HULTON-DEUTSCH COLLECTION/CORBIS. REPRODUCED BY PERMISSION.

port for the Union, predicated on the assumption that "Home Rule was Rome Rule," was reinforced by economic considerations, especially trade with Britain and the empire; the industrialization of linen manufacture and the rise of the shipyards had contributed to the spectacular growth of Belfast's population from about 25,000 in 1800 to 350,000 in 1901, of whom three-quarters were Protestants (Vaughn and Fitzpatrick 1978). With a Home Rule measure due to come into effect after World War I, the decision of Ulster Unionists to accept partition for six of the nine counties in the historic province (embodied in the Government of Ireland Act of 1920 and the Anglo-Irish Treaty of 1921) had the effect of leaving Protestants in the twenty-six counties resentful and largely leaderless.

Although the territorial and political powers of the Ascendancy had been greatly reduced even before the

revolutionary period (1919–1923), Protestants were not exempt from the troubles of those years. Many suffered intimidation and even murder; their houses often were raided for arms, and some were burned. Some Protestant businesses were boycotted. The Gaelic and Catholic ethos of the Irish Free State was uncongenial to most Protestants, and all this tended to deter them from participating fully in public life, though the Senate afforded some opportunities for Protestant representation in the *Oireachtas* (legislature). The transition to independence in the south led to a marked exodus of Protestant residents (not only British army personnel), some of whom moved to Northern Ireland, increasing the concentration of Protestants there. The Protestant population of the Free State dropped from 10 percent in 1911 to 7 percent in 1926, with the greatest losses occurring in areas where their numbers had been fewest (Vaughn and Fitzpatrick 1978). However, their small numbers, generally comfortable circumstances, and the partial earlier transfer of land ownership to tenants helped somewhat to protect southern Protestants in the new state, and for some time to come they were regarded by the Catholic majority with a mixture of deference, resentment, and envy.

SEE ALSO Agriculture: 1690 to 1845; Agriculture: 1845 to 1921; Anglo-Irish Treaty of 1921; Catholic Emancipation Campaign; Church of Ireland: Since 1690; Electoral Politics from 1800 to 1921; Famine Clearances; Great Famine; Great War; Home Rule Movement and the Irish Parliamentary Party: 1870 to 1891; Home Rule Movement and the Irish Parliamentary Party: 1891 to 1918; Hyde, Douglas; Irish Tithe Act of 1838; Land Acts of 1870 and 1881; Land Purchase Acts of 1903 and 1909; Land Questions; Land War of 1879 to 1882; Local Government since 1800; Parnell, Charles Stewart; Plan of Campaign; Plunkett, Sir Horace Curzon; Politics: 1800 to 1921—Challenges to the Union; Protestant Ascendancy: 1690 to 1800; Protestant Community in Southern Ireland since 1922; Struggle for Independence from 1916 to 1921; Tenant Right, or Ulster Custom; Tithe War (1830–1838); Unionism from 1885 to 1922; United Irish League Campaigns; **Primary Documents:** Irish Act of Union (1 August 1800)

Bibliography

Bowen, Kurt. *Protestants in a Catholic State: Ireland's Privileged Minority.* 1983.

Dooley, Terence. *The Plight of Monaghan Protestants, 1912–1926.* 2000.

Hurley, Michael, ed. *Irish Anglicanism, 1869–1969.* 1970.

McDowell, R. B. *Crisis and Decline: The Fate of the Southern Unionists.* 1997.

Miller, Kerby A. "No Middle Ground: The Erosion of the Protestant Middle Class in Southern Ireland during the Pre-Famine Era." *Huntingdon Library Quarterly* 49 (1986): 295–306.

Moffitt, Miriam. *The Church of Ireland Community of Killala and Achonry, 1870–1940.* 1999.

Vaughan, W. E. *Landlords and Tenants in Mid-Victorian Ireland.* 1994.

Vaughan, W. E., and A. J. Fitzpatrick, eds. *Irish Historical Statistics.* 1978

Jacqueline Hill

Protestant Community in Southern Ireland since 1922

The Irish Free State was born in a period of great political and community turbulence, but when it had been legally constituted in 1922, Archbishop Gregg of Dublin urged his church to obey the laws of the new state and to work for its peace and prosperity. Some Protestants with a conspicuous unionist record, or closely identified with the British armed services and other agencies of the Crown, suffered violence to their persons and property, and many felt themselves to be in a vulnerable position as members of the former landed ascendancy class. While physical violence against Protestants was not endemic, many felt pain in adjusting to the new regime in which their cultural heritage was to be relegated to second place in favor of a Gaelic Ireland, and society regulated according to Vatican precepts. Many of those who could do so emigrated to Britain or migrated to Northern Ireland, thus accelerating the decline in the Protestant population that had affected in particular the western and southern counties long before partition. The withdrawal from Ireland of military personnel, many of whom had been Protestant, together with casualties in World War I, contributed to the demographic decline. The "mixed marriage" regulations of the Roman Catholic Church, whereby the partners promised that all children of the marriage would be brought up in the Catholic tradition, also had an impact. Eventually Protestants constituted less than 5 percent of the population. Consequently the Protestant community endeavored to provide separate educational and recreational opportunities for its youth that would minimize social contact with Catholics; this policy, when seen in the context of a popular view that Protestants belonged to an ascendancy class, caused them sometimes to be regarded as aloof and disdainful of the Catholic community, which indeed some of them were.

Southern Irish Protestants, while law-abiding citizens of the new state, found much that was alien to them in the early decades of independence. The unique status given to Irish in the educational system was uncongenial to many—if not most—Protestants, who felt little sympathy with the compulsion used to restore the language. Social legislation, particularly in the areas of divorce, family planning, and censorship of publications, reflected Vatican teaching, and claims by unionist leaders in Northern Ireland that they had a Protestant parliament for a Protestant people were matched by public statements by some southern politicians equating Irish Catholics with the Irish people.

However, Protestants did not readily surrender their claim to Irish identity, conscious that the leaders of Irish political and cultural nationalism included Protestant names such as Theobold Wolfe Tone, Thomas Russell, Robert Emmet, the Sheares brothers, Napper Tandy, Lord Edward Fitzgerald, Charles Stewart Parnell, Lady Gregory, J. M. Synge, Sean O'Casey, and W.B. Yeats. The view that to be truly Irish one also must be Catholic was impossible to sustain in the case of President Douglas Hyde, son of a Church of Ireland rector and a cofounder of the Gaelic League, which was dedicated to the revival of the Irish language. Protestants could therefore have confidence in their Irish credentials. This sense of confidence was enhanced by a secure position in Irish intellectual, professional, and commercial life, and by an awareness that despite evidence that there was a confessional character to much public policy, particularly in the first half of the twentieth century, their contribution to Irish life was valued.

The late twentieth century saw radical changes in both Protestant attitudes and attitudes toward Protestants. They welcomed liberalizing changes in public policy, largely supported by public opinion. Protestants claimed to have played some part in achieving these changes, not least through the opening up of political and social discourse by such erstwhile Protestant and unionist fastnesses as Trinity College, Dublin, and the *Irish Times*. An increasingly independent broadcasting environment played its part: television audiences were thrilled by public discussion of issues, moral and theological, previously regarded as the exclusive preserve of the ecclesiastical authorities, while both television and radio conveyed the excitement of Vatican II to the people of the Republic (as the Free State had become in 1949) at a time of greatly improved economic development and enhanced educational opportunity. Vatican II, which created unease in some conservative circles north and south, was a major catalyst in the emergence of a society in which Protestants have felt increasingly comfortable.

SEE ALSO Church of Ireland: Since 1690; Ecumenism and Interchurch Relations; Eucharistic Congress; Gaelic Catholic State, Making of; Jewish Community; Protestant Ascendancy: Decline, 1800 to 1930; Politics: Independent Ireland since 1922; Religion: Since 1690

Bibliography

Akenson, Donald H. *A Mirror to Kathleen's Face: Education in Independent Ireland, 1922–1060*. 1975.

Bowen, Kurt. *Protestants in a Catholic State: Ireland's Privileged Minority*. 1983.

Lee, J. J. *Ireland, 1912–1985: Politics and Society*. 1989. Reprint, 2001.

Lyons, F. S. L. "The Minority Problem in the 26 Countries." In *The Years of the Great Test, 1926–36*, edited by Francis MacManus. 1967.

Lyons, F. S. L. *Culture and Anarchy in Ireland, 1890–1939*. 1979.

McDowell, R. B. *Crisis and Decline: The Fate of the Southern Unionists*. 1997.

Milne, Kenneth. "Brave New World." In *To-morrow's Church*, edited by Stephen R. White. 1999.

Milne, Kenneth. "The Protestant Churches in Independent Ireland." In *Religion and Politics in Ireland at the Turn of the Millennium*, edited by J. P. Mackey and Enda McDonagh. 2003.

Kenneth Milne

Protestant Immigrants

Among the groups of continental Protestants who migrated to Ireland in the seventeenth and eighteenth centuries, the Huguenots from France were the single largest group. This article focuses on their settlement and also discusses another major immigrant group, the Palatines from Germany.

In 1685 Louis XIV of France issued the Edict of Fontainebleau, thereby finally ending a nearly hundred-year period of religious coexistence between Protestants and Catholics in his realm. The edict had been preceded by harsh government measures to force the Huguenots into conformity with the Catholic Church, among them the so-called *dragonnades*. As a consequence, there was a mass exodus of Huguenots, who settled in Europe from east to west—in Protestant territories of the Holy Roman Empire, such as Brandenburg, as well as in Switzerland, the Netherlands, Britain, and Ireland. Although the number of immigrants to each of these countries can only be estimated, about 7,000 to 10,000 Huguenots settled in Ireland, compared with between 14,000 and 20,000 in Brandenburg-Prussia and about 50,000 to 80,000 in England.

The Huguenot immigration to Ireland occurred in three distinct phases. During the first phase, between 1662 and 1680, the viceroy of Ireland, James Butler, first duke of Ormonde, was the driving force behind the establishment of a Huguenot community. Ormonde hoped for economic stimuli and a bolstering of Protestantism by encouraging Huguenots to settle in Ireland. An "Act for encouraging Protestant strangers and others to inhabit and plant in the kingdom of Ireland" was passed by the Irish parliament in 1662, thus providing a legal basis for immigration. During this first phase only about 180 Huguenots came to Ireland. This community was overwhelmingly mercantile and settled exclusively in Dublin. It dwindled to sixty persons just before the second phase of settlement began in 1680.

The second phase of Huguenot settlement in Ireland, between 1681 and 1691, coincided with the dragonnades and the Edict of Fontainebleau. By 1687 about 400 to 650 Huguenots lived in Dublin. Only the third phase of immigration, after 1692, resulted in the settlement of a substantial Huguenot population in Ireland. In 1692, the Irish parliament passed an "Act for encouragement of Protestant strangers to settle in this kingdom of Ireland." The refugees settled mainly in the harbor towns of Ireland—in Cork, Waterford, Wexford, Dundalk, Belfast, and of course Dublin.

Two settlement projects, one successful and one unsuccessful, stand out in this otherwise scattered migration. Both projects were initiated by the leading Huguenot refugee in Ireland, Henry Massue, marquis de Ruvigny, baron of Portarlington (from 1691), and earl of Galway (from 1697). The successful one was the settlement of Huguenot veterans from William III's armies in the town of Portarlington from 1692 onwards. The unsuccessful one intended to transport thousands of Huguenots stranded in Switzerland to Ireland. Entitled "le projet d'Irlande," it was initiated by Ruvigny in 1693, but English and Swiss funds for the project were withdrawn and it came to nothing.

Compared to steps taken in other European countries, notably German territories such as Brandenburg-Prussia where the Huguenots were given extensive special rights, the Irish acts of parliament did not make provision for separating the "Protestant strangers" from the rest of Irish society. The Huguenot refugees in Ireland were not granted their own jurisdiction, but had to avail themselves of the Irish courts of law. Although they were granted some economic privileges, these were far less extensive than those in states such as Brandenburg. All in all, the Irish immigration laws guided Huguenot refugees toward integration into Irish society, not separation from it. Apart from Portarlington, where French traditions survived into the nineteenth century, Huguenots quickly integrated into Irish Protestant society.

In terms of religion the position of the Huguenots in Irish society was deeply influenced by the complex religious makeup of their host country, where the Anglican established church, the Church of Ireland, was in a minority position and was confronted with a Catholic majority on the one hand and a substantial Nonconformist presence, mostly Presbyterians in Ulster, on the other. The first act of 1662 required Huguenots to swear the oath of supremacy, thereby accepting the king as head of the Church of Ireland. Viceroy Ormonde was determined to integrate the refugees into the state church. After the example of the conformist "French Church of the Savoy," which had been founded in London some years earlier, he established a conformist Huguenot church in Dublin in 1666. This was called "French Patrick" because it held its services in the Ladychapel of Saint Patrick's Cathedral. Its pastors were paid by the state church. In return for using a French translation of the *Book of Common Prayer* and accepting the authority of the bishops of the Church of Ireland, "French Patrick" was allowed to hold its services in French and to establish a Presbyterian church order. However, this compromise was not acceptable to many Huguenots, who started to drift away from "French Patrick" to form Nonconformist conventicles elsewhere.

The act of 1692 completely changed the religious conditions for refugees by granting them "the free exercise of their religion in their own several rites used in their own countries, any law or statute to the contrary notwithstanding" ("An act for encouragement of Protestant strangers to settle in this kingdom of Ireland" [1692]). This led to the establishment of conformist as well as Nonconformist Huguenot churches in Ireland. Despite the granting of religious freedom, the Nonconformist groups came repeatedly under pressure from the established church, notably in Portarlington.

It is generally difficult to gauge the contribution that refugees make to the cultural and economic development of their adopted country. However, with regard to the Huguenots, there are some areas where their role was palpable, although recent historiography is less certain about it. The large Huguenot contribution of soldiers and officers in William III's armies, including at the Battle of the Boyne, is part of the story. Economically, Huguenot influence was also significant: Besides Huguenot merchants operating successfully in Irish cities, Huguenots rapidly assumed importance in the Irish linen and banking industries. Louis Crommelin successfully established the linen industry in the north of Ireland, and David Digues La Touche began a highly successful banking business in Dublin. The La Touche family also established the silk- and poplin-weaving industries in Dublin. Moreover, Huguenots were active as silversmiths and goldsmiths as well as in the learned professions. They also contributed to the cultural development of Ireland. One of the more enduring traditions of Portarlington was the creation of boarding schools, which had a very high reputation in the late eighteenth and early nineteenth centuries. In addition, the promotion of gardening is attributed to Huguenot influence.

In contrast to the Huguenots, whose settlement in Ireland can be called a success and who were quickly integrated into Irish Protestant society, the intended settlement of another major group of foreign Protestant immigrants, the Palatines, caused many problems. In 1708 and 1709 about 11,000 to 13,500 people left the Palatinate and other regions in southwestern Germany as a consequence of the invasions of Louis XIV's armies. They made their way to England via the Netherlands with the intention of moving on to the North American colonies of the British Crown. While a substantial number of these so-called Palatines made it to North America, others remained in England and about 3,000 persons were sent to Ireland. Although there had also been Catholics among the original refugees (southwestern Germany was a confessionally mixed area), they had been sent back to Germany by the British government, and only Protestants were allowed to acquire lands under the British Crown.

When the suggestion was first made to settle Palatines in Ireland, the Irish parliament was enthusiastic about the idea, arguing that "they will prove an occasion of strength to the Protestant interest of this nation, especially considering the disproportion between the Protestants and the Papists in this kingdom" (Hick 1989, p. 120). With substantial financial support from the government and private donors in Ireland, 821 families were sent to Dublin in September and October 1709.

It quickly turned out that most of them could not be settled in Ireland successfully. The exact reasons for this are difficult to ascertain, but it seems that the Palatines might have been led to expect very favorable conditions in Ireland (e.g., rent-free lands). In any case, they were so discontented that about 60 percent of them returned to England, and from there, many made their way back to Germany. By November 1711 only 312 Palatine families (1,218 persons) remained in Ireland; the number further decreased to 185 families by 1720. While some stayed in Dublin and others were scattered about the country, most—115 families—were settled on the lands of Sir Thomas Southwell in County Limerick. In spite of continuing financial difficulties and conflicts, they became permanently settled there, growing hemp and flax and conforming to the established church. However, the language barrier between the Palatines and their English and Irish neighbors in Ireland was not overcome for a long time. The Palatines continued to intermarry and formed a distinct community,

retaining their language and cultural traditions at least until the beginning of the nineteenth century.

SEE ALSO Economy and Society from 1500 to 1690; Urban Life, Crafts, and Industry from 1500 to 1690

Bibliography

Caldicott, C. E. J., Hugh Gough, and Jean-Paul Pittion, eds. *The Huguenots and Ireland: Anatomy of an Emigration.* 1987.

Gwynn, Robin D. *Huguenot Heritage: The History and Contribution of the Huguenots in Britain.* 1985.

Hick, Vivien. "The Palatine Settlement in Ireland: The Early Years." *Eighteenth-Century Ireland* 4 (1989): 113–131.

Knox, S. J. *Ireland's Debt to the Huguenots.* 1959.

Lee, Grace Lawless. *The Huguenot Settlements in Ireland.* 1936.

Saint Leger, Alice. *Silver, Sail, and Silk: Huguenots in Cork, 1685–1850.* 1991.

Vigne, Randolph, and Charles Littleton, eds. *From Strangers to Citizens: The Integration of Immigrant Communities in Britain, Ireland, and Colonial America, 1550–1750.* 2001.

Ute Lotz-Heumann

Protestant Reformation in the Early Sixteenth Century

The failure of the Protestant Reformation in Ireland was not inevitable. There was a considerable degree of (at least nominal) conformity to the initial stages of the Tudors' reformation, especially among the Old English. It was not until Elizabeth I's reign that a passive antipathy to religious change was galvanized into a general adherence to the Counter-Reformation.

EVE OF REFORMATION

The fortunes of the Irish Church revived from the mid-fifteenth century, particularly in the English lordship. There was considerable investment in parish churches, and many chantries were founded. Contemporary wills reflect a strong piety. In the case of Armagh diocese it has been shown that the church provided pastoral care through a dense network of churches and chapels staffed with resident priests. Diocesan synods (meetings of clergy) were used to raise standards. Episcopal visitations were conducted regularly and the church courts processed suits to some effect. In the most anglicized parts of Ireland the diocesan church was in relatively good order, and the laity engaged in forms of piety that would have been familiar to Christians elsewhere in Europe.

The foundation of no fewer than ninety new friaries after 1400 is further evidence of the religious revival. Many of the new communities were "observant," committed to a stricter observance of ascetic rules, and observantism won over most of the existing communities in Ireland. In the diocesan church across much of the country the greatest problem was not the prevalence of clerical concubinage or the tendency of clergymen's sons to seek preferment in the church, but rather the poverty of the institution. The practice of subsistence agriculture among the Irish, and the frequency of petty wars and general lawlessness, depressed clerical incomes. Consequently, church buildings were often in a poor state. Few Irish clergymen could afford a university education, which could only be obtained abroad. Yet there were generally resident clergy in place to meet the pastoral needs of the laity, except in districts wasted by war.

THE ADVENT OF REFORMATION

Henry VIII sent a new lord deputy, Sir William Skeffington, to Ireland in June 1534 with instructions to terminate the pope's jurisdiction. That contributed to the outbreak of rebellion. The rebel leader, Lord Thomas Fitzgerald, eldest son of the ninth earl of Kildare, was not motivated primarily by religious concerns, but he exploited popular opposition to Henry VIII's assault on the church to maximize his support within Ireland and to attract help from the pope and the Holy Roman Emperor. Clergy throughout Ireland roused support for his avowed crusade and its initial success owed something to the popular distaste for religious change. The rebellion failed for want of support from Catholic Europe, yet it demonstrated the widespread hostility toward Henry VIII's innovations. In the immediate aftermath of the suppression of the rebellion there was a large garrison of English troops quartered in Ireland, a guarantee that the English Crown's wishes could not be ignored.

The Irish Reformation Parliament was convened on 1 May 1536, and within a month the lords and Commons had endorsed bills altering the church. The justification offered for the king's supremacy over the Irish Church (replacing that of the pope) was political rather than religious. There was significant lay opposition to the bill for the suppression of monasteries, but the parliamentarians bowed to Henry VIII's determination to dissolve these religious communities.

There was little Protestant preaching in Ireland, apart from the efforts of George Browne, archbishop of Dublin (1536–1554). Browne found that his words fell on deaf ears. He could not persuade his senior clergy to endorse the Henrician reformation, and, indeed, they worked against it behind the scenes. He also encountered considerable hostility from "observant" friars. Nonetheless, Browne conducted a visitation and subsequently issued a set of injunctions early in 1538 that promoted the royal supremacy; otherwise he was fairly conservative. Vicegerent Thomas Cromwell's second set of injunctions were published in October 1538, not only in Dublin but also in much of southeastern Ireland. His injunction against notable images or relics was widely implemented in the Pale, but often evaded elsewhere.

Archbishop Browne's efforts to promote religious change were hampered by Lord Deputy Grey, who treated the unpopular archbishop with open contempt. Grey calculated that the political costs of rigorously enforcing the king's reformation in Ireland were impracticably high. His successor, Anthony Saint Leger, lord deputy from July 1540, took advantage of the temporary retreat from Protestant doctrine in the English parliament's Six Articles of 1539 to promote a royal supremacy in Ireland shorn of doctrinal or liturgical innovation. It was a strategy that worked well and won wide acceptance for a schismatic but still very conservative religious settlement.

IMPACT OF THE REFORMATION

All of the Reformation statutes sanctioned by the Irish parliament were enforced with varying degrees of success. Over much of Ireland the English Crown displaced the papacy in terms of taxation and faculties and as the final court of appeal in ecclesiastical causes. The religious houses were dissolved with the cooperation of local juries. This was the most dramatic feature of the Henrician reformation. In terms of pastoral care the suppression of the mendicant orders impoverished the spiritual lives of the people in a direct fashion. Yet the loss was not complete. Some mendicant communities continued to maintain their ministry in the Pale, while others took refuge beyond the Pale, to return in Mary Tudor's reign.

Henry VIII did nothing to reform the diocesan church. The poverty of the benefices and the dismal stipends available to unbeneficed curates made it extremely difficult to promote graduate priests who might have favored the Reformation. The failure to establish a university in Ireland (until 1592), or a training college for the ministers of the Henrician church added to the staffing problems of the reformed church. Throughout the early Tudor reformation most of the Irish clergy were trained in the late medieval manner, inclining them toward the practice of traditional religion.

The Edwardian reformation got off to a very slow start in Ireland while Saint Leger remained as lord deputy. However, after the deputy's recall in May 1548, Archbishop Browne promoted a "book of Reformation" in the ecclesiastical province of Dublin and introduced the first *Book of Common Prayer* in the following year. Bishop Edward Staples distinguished himself by preaching Protestantism in the diocese of Meath—much to the chagrin of his congregations. The fiery Protestant Bishop John Bale was very active in Kilkenny. The Protestant *Book of Common Prayer* was widely used in churches in Old English areas of Ireland. However, with the connivance of Saint Leger (he returned as deputy in August 1550) Primate George Dowdall of Armagh resisted the Edwardian reformation until the summer of 1551, when Saint Leger's final recall left him exposed to the likelihood of arrest and imprisonment. Dowdall fled and took refuge in the monastery at Centre in the Netherlands. His Protestant successor never reached Armagh, and the diocese may have escaped the imposition of the Edwardian reformation altogether before King Edward VI died in July 1553.

Henry VIII largely succeeded in displacing the papacy's jurisdiction over the church in the Pale and beyond. The first Jesuits in Ireland in 1542 formed a very bleak impression of the prospects for the Catholic Church there. With hindsight it is clear that they were unduly pessimistic: the church in Ireland proved to be open to reinvigoration by the Counter-Reformation. Nonetheless, as long as the senior clergy and secular elites were prepared to acquiesce in the Tudors' royal supremacy over the church, and generally conform to the Edwardian *Book of Common Prayer*, there was a distinct possibility that a Protestant Reformation might eventually succeed, at least in the most English part of Ireland.

SEE ALSO Church of Ireland: Elizabethan Era; Edwardian Reform; Marian Restoration; Monarchy; Religion: 1500 to 1690

Bibliography

Bottigheimer, Karl S., and Lotz-Heumann, Ute. "The Irish Reformation in European Perspective." *Archive for Reformation History* 89 (1998): 268–309.

Bradshaw, Brendan. *The Dissolution of the Religious Orders in Ireland under Henry VIII.* 1974.

Ford, Alan, James McGuire, and Kenneth Milne, eds. *As By Law Established: The Church of Ireland since the Reformation.* 1995.

Jefferies, Henry A. *Priests and Prelates of Armagh in the Age of Reformations.* 1997.

Jefferies, Henry A. "The Early Tudor Reformations in the Irish Pale." *Journal of Ecclesiastical History* 52 (2001): 34–62.

Lennon, Colm. *The Lords of Dublin in the Age of Reformation.* 1989.

Lyons, Mary Ann. *Church and Society in County Kildare, c. 1470–1547.* 2000.

Henry A. Jefferies

Puritan Sectaries

Protestantism in Ireland was precariously established among a minority of its inhabitants in the sixteenth and seventeenth centuries. For the most part it remained the confession of the immigrants from England, Wales, and Scotland, but just as they brought their Protestantism with them, so too they arrived with a variety of forms of worship. In particular, those from Scotland often came with the Presbyterian preferences that marked the national church in Scotland after the Reformation. The resultant diversity in doctrine and ritual among Irish Protestants offended Charles I and his archbishop of Canterbury, William Laud. Their agents in Ireland—Lord Deputy Wentworth and John Bramhall, bishop of Derry—attempted to achieve religious uniformity among the Protestants of Ireland. This drive was resisted by Scots Presbyterians in Ulster, who were prosecuted for their nonconformity. Soon, the uprising of 1641 brought Scottish armies into Ulster. The commanders protected Presbyterianism on the Scottish model, so that it survived and then thrived. By 1659 five presbyteries in Antrim, Down, the Route, Laggan, and Tyrone oversaw the separate churches. By 1689, seventy-two separate sessions or congregations attracted perhaps 18,000 worshipers.

Scottish Presbyterianism was merely one component in an increasingly fragmented Protestant community. Separatism had not been a problem elsewhere in Ireland before 1641. However, the presence in the island throughout the 1640s of forces dispatched from England and Wales rapidly introduced a multiplicity of religious practices. In 1647 the Directory of Worship, a religious formulary imposed by the English parliament, replaced the ceremonies and government by bishops enshrined in the now banned *Book of Common Prayer*. In Ireland spontaneous enthusiasm for these changes was limited because Protestants were primarily worried about containing and defeating the insurgent Catholics. However, the arrival in 1649 of a large army from England brought sectaries as its chaplains and provided them with auditors. As English authority was reintroduced across the island, Protestantism was again actively promoted. Ministers, mainly English but also some Welsh and Scots, were invited to officiate in Ireland. In England the collapse of episcopacy and the proscription of the old Anglican liturgy had produced a confused situation in which Presbyterians, religious Independents (the future Congregationalists), and General and Particular Baptists all flourished. Adherents of each of these sects came to Ireland. Some were formally invited and were given state stipends. The best paid were installed in Dublin, where the most Protestants were concentrated. The favored served as chaplains to the parliamentary commissioners who governed the country, or (after 1653) to the lord deputy and councillors in Dublin. Notable among them was Samuel Winter, minister of the Independent congregation that assembled in the former Christ Church cathedral, and head of Dublin University as provost of Trinity College from 1652 to 1660.

As in England, so too in Ireland, different practices continued, although there were attempts to silence those who professed unorthodox beliefs. Some groups resented the freedom and favor allowed to their rivals and schemed to curtail them. In addition, divergences in confessional affiliation frequently coincided with and sometimes aggravated political differences. The religious Independents and Baptists, for example, were associated with the permissive attitudes of the lord deputy, Charles Fleetwood. Some Presbyterians looked to Fleetwood's rival Henry Cromwell as their particular patron. The Presbyterians, moreover, split between those who favored the Scottish and English schemes of church government. By the 1650s the Scottish Presbyterians in Ireland had reproduced the divisions between Resolutioners and Remonstrants in Scotland. The situation was further complicated when new groups of English origin, such as the Ranters, Fifth Monarchists, and Quakers, appeared in Ireland. Of these, the Quakers made the most headway and became a permanent presence. Like other sectaries, they owed their initial successes to support within the occupying army. But more than most of their rivals, the Quakers prospered by widening their appeal to embrace civilians in towns and countryside.

The longer history of the Quakers as a distinct confession in Protestant Ireland illustrates the problem bequeathed by the interregnum. Efforts to check the most disruptive and unorthodox preachers had had only limited success. After 1660, in Ireland as in England, the restoration of the Stuart monarchy was quickly followed by the restoration of the established episcopal church. By 1666 attendance at and conformity with the services of the Church of Ireland were required, and nonconformists (i.e., sectarians) were punished. At moments of panic, known leaders might be rounded up and imprisoned. In addition, those who broke the law by refusing to pay tithes toward the maintenance of the clergy of the established church (notably the Quakers) had goods seized and were sometimes imprisoned.

The need for Protestant solidarity in the face of the danger from the large Catholic majority persuaded some former sectaries to conform to the state church. Among them were two ministers, Henry Jones and Edward Worth, who had accepted salaries from the Cromwellians and then bishoprics from Charles II. In a similar spirit, some bishops, conscious of the need to include as many Protestants as possible, did not enquire too closely into the practices of erstwhile dissenters. Yet, despite these accommodations and concessions, sectarian congregations survived after 1660. The most tenacious were in Ulster, Dublin, and the larger towns.

In Ulster the Scottish Presbyterians built on the foundations established in the 1640s and 1650s. They were assisted by the continuing emigration from Scotland to the north of Ireland, especially in the 1690s. Also, a degree of indulgence was accorded to the group, which technically was outside the law. From 1672 onwards, the Irish state was authorized to supplement the stipends of docile Presbyterian pastors through a grant known as the king's gift (*regium donum*). Strictly defined, the Scottish Presbyterians in Ulster were not sectaries. They believed as firmly as the adherents of the Church of Ireland in a state church—technically, they were an offshoot of the Presbyterian kirk of Scotland, the legally established church of that kingdom, and organized as such through the Synod of Ulster. The Presbyterians in Ireland were subjected to further serious legal inhibitions when in 1704 a Test Act was passed. This confined many important public offices and the full exercise of citizenship to the communicant members of the Church of Ireland. Thereafter, the Presbyterians were treated more like the Irish Catholics than like their conformist Protestant neighbors.

Other Dissenters also felt the effects of the Test Act. Through strategies such as occasional conformity—taking holy communion according to the Church of Ireland's rites at least once a year—and through the forbearance of the authorities in not insisting on certificates of such conformity, it was possible for some Protestant Dissenters to evade the ban. Nevertheless, since 1660 they had faced potential and sometimes actual discrimination. This grievance drew them into political activism, but hopes of the repeal of penalties were disappointed. A Toleration Act was delayed until 1719 and did not remove the disabilities in the Test Act.

The inability of the Dissenters in Ireland to obtain the favors granted to their compatriots in Scotland and England after 1690 suggested a lack of political influence. Few within the Irish landed elite still adhered to the sectaries by 1700. Their strength came from the renewed influx of Scottish Presbyterians into Ulster and the continuing attractions of English Presbyterianism, religious Independency, and Quakerism for the merchants, craft-workers, and artisans of the towns. Some groups from the 1650s, such as the Baptists, Independents, and English Presbyterians, dwindled into near invisibility. Their fate contrasted with that of the Scottish Presbyterians and Quakers, and—from the 1740s—the newly arrived Methodists. These contrasts owed much to whether or not the sects developed institutions through which they could train and pay ministers and discipline and relieve their adherents. In turn, success in these spheres reflected not only the numbers, commitment, and prosperity of the congregations in Ireland, but also their links with associates in Britain, Holland, and North America.

SEE ALSO Butler, James, Twelfth Earl and First Duke of Ormond; Calvinist Influences in Early Modern Ireland; Church of Ireland: Elizabethan Era; Cromwellian Conquest; Restoration Ireland; Solemn League and Covenant

Bibliography

Barnard, T. C. *Cromwellian Ireland: English Government and Reform in Ireland, 1649–1660.* 1975. Reprint, 2000.

Gillespie, Raymond. "The Presbyterian Revolution in Ulster, 1600–1690." In *The Churches, Ireland and the Irish*, edited by W. J. Shiels and D. Wood. 1989.

Greaves, Richard L. *God's Other Children: Protestant Nonconformists and the Emergence of Denominational Churches in Ireland, 1660–1700.* 1997.

Kilroy, Philomena. *Protestant Dissent and Controversy in Ireland, 1660–1714.* 1994.

Seymour, St. John D. *The Puritans in Ireland, 1647–1661.* 1921. Reprint, 1961.

Toby Barnard

R

Raiftearaí (Raftery), Antaine

A native of Mayo, the Irish-language poet Antaine Raiftearaí (anglicized Anthony Raftery, 1779–1835) spent most of his life in east Galway and his home county. Contemporary manuscript copies of his work and later oral tradition suggest that he was well remembered throughout Connacht. He came posthumously to national prominence in the early 1900s as one of the few nineteenth-century Gaelic composers whose output attracted scholarly notice. His first modern editor, Douglas Hyde (1903), heard Raiftearaí's verse recited in County Roscommon during his youth in the 1870s. Hyde assembled written and spoken versions of his poems, rendered them into English, and did much to shape interpretation of their author's career. Subsequent anthologization for school curricula of items like his lament for a boating tragedy in Annaghdown on the southeastern shores of Lough Corrib in 1828, when twenty-eight people were drowned, led to ongoing awareness of Raiftearaí throughout the twentieth century. In 1987 Ciarán Ó Coiglígh provided the authoritative up-to-date edition of his poems, complete with critical apparatus and extensive annotation, but without English translations. Some fifty more of Raiftearaí's compositions survive, amounting to about 4,000 lines of verse. Because only one-fifth of them can be dated, editors have grouped the works thematically. The poems and extant folk memories are an impressive record of their creator's culture and community. They furnish the relatively sparse surviving details of his own life.

Raiftearaí apparently lost his sight when he was five years old. He made his living as a wandering musician and poet, traveling extensively throughout a cluster of adjacent Connacht baronies, walking mainly, as references to the appalling state of his footwear indicate. Claims of his having been in various Munster venues are probably literary inventions. His disability would appear to have prevented him from visiting locations like the pilgrimage mountain, Croagh Patrick, where he had been advised to go to atone for his sins. He was often attracted to his destinations by accounts of the hospitality that he might receive there. Minor local gentry like the Taaffes of Killeden, Co. Mayo, or the Lynches of Lavally, Co. Galway, welcomed him. Praise of their towns, villages and homes, and of the individuals themselves, is a major strand of his work. He mentions the Catholic clergy, but there is less evidence that they supported him. Raiftearaí seems to have received much assistance from successful or prosperous tradesmen whom he extolled. Some of them, such as the Galway carpenter Seán Mac Conraoi, were literate, and they may have begun writing down his output. Certain of his numerous verse portraits of women might also have been commissions. His vagrant lifestyle and evident fondness for taverns and good company may have overtaken him eventually; he already described himself as aged in a composition from 1832. A serious cholera outbreak, which lasted in the west until 1835, was possibly responsible for his demise, although the precise reasons for his death are unknown.

Raiftearaí's poetry is a rich source of information concerning those with whom he came into contact. It outlines the lives of his landowning benefactors, their estates, demesnes, livestock and fauna, houses, furnishings, tableware and other accoutrements, and their feasting and alternative pastimes. Proximity to coastal and lakeland settings is reflected in his patrons' varied marine and freshwater food supplies. The manufacturing processes and output of his tradesmen supporters—tailors, weavers, smiths, and joiners, among others—

are also set out in detail. The inventory of what his carpenter friend Mac Conraoi could produce by way of farm implements, house fittings, and boating equipment amounts to over fifty items. Intellectual as well as material subjects figure in his work. Raftery shows residual familiarity with and sympathy for the revolutionary republican ideology of 1798. By the 1820s he supported Catholic Emancipation, as seen in his endorsement of the "Catholic rent" and his satisfaction at O'Connell's County Clare by-election victory in 1828. He approved of the antitithe protests in the early 1830s, having earlier been an opponent of Protestant proselytizing societies. Because of their focus on public events, these writings can be dated more accurately than his others.

Whether personal or political, a standard Raiftearaí poem has an easily recognizable configuration. Most of his works are six to eight stanzas, eight lines each, in *ochtfhoclach* meter, based on the stress patterns of contemporary speech. Because detailed description is such a pronounced feature of his style, incremental listing (of the contents of a patron's home, or details of a tradesman's craft, for example) is a dominant characteristic. This may have served as a mnemonic device for its unsighted author, and suggests an interaction with oral compositional techniques. In this connection his strategies deserve to be compared with those of another blind nineteenth-century composer, the Listowel-based D. C. Hennessy (de Brún 2001). Raiftearaí's efforts to secure credit as the originator of a work can be seen in first- or third-person references to his own surname at the beginning or end of many poems, in a pattern similar to a painter's signature. This device and the recitation of his poems to evocative song (*amhrán*) airs and melodies might have ensured accurate ascription of certain compositions to him in oral memory. His more extensive works deal with religious topics like the imminence of death, or retell the history of Ireland. The historical poems are informed by items from traditional handwritten sources, thus hinting at the presence of manuscript materials in Connacht. They also attest to the methods of assimilation and subsequent recreation of these sources.

Raiftearaí often depicts himself as a skilled composer of verse in Irish and an authoritative spokesperson for his audience (Denvir 2000). He implicitly contrasts his attainments with the artistic shortcomings (not to mention venality) of other Galway-based poets such as the Calnans, whom he criticizes in poems of considerable length and satirical invective. All of these indicators suggest that he was an active participant in a cultural community of considerable vitality, diversity, and self-awareness. Much of its vigor may have derived from the obviously enduring strength of the Irish language in the poet's day. Borrowed or adapted English terms do figure in the details of what his tradesmen patrons could produce, but even here an indigenous technical vocabulary remains prominent. Raiftearaí's own ability to generate acceptable new word formations (for instance, noun compounds) is noteworthy. This linguistic creativity mirrors his own lively intelligence, alertness, and conviviality as well as the enduring resourcefulness of his tradition. Such an image contrasts with the impression which the poem *Mise Raiftearaí* (doubtfully attributed to him) conveys, that of a forlorn and desolate individual. Those characteristics more accurately describe the Ireland which witnessed the collapse of Gaelic civilization in 1845, ten years after his death, rather than the dynamism of the composer's actual life and times.

SEE ALSO Gaelic Revivalism: The Gaelic League; Hyde, Douglas; Language and Literacy: Decline of Irish Language; Literacy and Popular Culture

Bibliography

de Brún, Pádraig, ed. *The Lays of North Kerry & Other Poems and Sketches [by] D. C. Hennessy.* 2001.

Denvir, Gearóid. "Filíocht Antaine Raiftearaí." In *Saoi na hÉigse: Aistí in Ómós do Sheán Ó Tuama*, edited by in Pádraigín Riggs, Breandán Ó Conchúir, and Seán Ó Coileáin. 2000.

Hyde, Douglas. *Poems Ascribed to Raftery.* 1903.

Ó Coigligh, Ciarán. *Raiftearaí: Amhráin agus Dánta.* 1987.

Neil Buttimer

Raths

With an estimated 45,000 examples, raths (also known as ringforts) represent the most common form of ancient monument in Ireland. Dating to the early Christian period, they are circular earthworks defined by a deep ditch and internal bank, enclosing an area of twenty to forty meters in diameter. Within their interiors the remains of houses and other structures have been discovered. Raths with two or more sets of banks and ditches are also known, and these are considered the probable homes of the upper echelons of society. Raths are often associated with souterrains, artificial caves used for refuge and storage purposes, whereas cashels, the stone equivalents of raths, were constructed in hilly upland areas.

The origins of the rath remain uncertain; only a small number of sites have been investigated by archaeological excavation. Scientific dating suggests that the majority date to between 600 C.E. and 900 C.E., and that they fell out of use by medieval times. Finbar McCormick has proposed that during the early Christian period Ireland underwent an agricultural revolution generated by the advent of dairying. This was a time when wealth was measured in cattle, and the endemic form of warfare was raiding. Raths may therefore have developed as a means of protecting the farming family and their valuable livestock. Their defensive capacity, however, has been questioned by Jim Mallory and Tom McNeill, but their argument has been countered by Matthew Stout, who considers raths to have been adequate for the everyday security needs of the inhabitants.

A body of folklore grew up around these monuments and they were regarded as the homes of the *sídhe* (fairies), earning them the title "fairy forts." Until recent decades superstitious fear of retribution from the fairy-folk dissuaded country people from damaging the monuments and, as a consequence, protected many from destruction.

SEE ALSO Clachans; Landscape and Settlement; Rural Settlement and Field Systems

Bibliography

McCormick, Finbar. "Cows, Ringforts, and the Origins of Early Christian Ireland." *Emania* 13 (1995): 33–37.

Mallory, James P., and Thomas E. McNeill. *The Archaeology of Ulster.* 1991.

Stout, Matthew. *The Irish Ringfort.* 1997.

Eileen M. Murphy

Rebellion of 1641

Both the Old English and the Irish harbored grievances relating to land and religion that reached back to the English conquest of Ireland during the sixteenth century and the associated policy of plantation. Plantation had injected English and Scottish settlers into various parts of Ireland, but particularly Ulster, to the disadvantage of the former inhabitants. However, a rebellion was not inevitable, and it took most contemporary observers by surprise. In 1628, with the granting of the Graces, it appeared that the king was prepared to address the issues of security of land tenure, and even though the confirmation of these concessions into law was long delayed, in August 1641 bills giving them effect had been forwarded to Ireland. Even on the matter of religion, Catholicism enjoyed a degree of informal toleration. What transformed the situation was the successful Scottish challenge to the Crown from 1637 to 1641. As many Irish leaders remarked, they learned how to use force from the Scots. Moreover, the Scottish crisis diminished the Crown's authority in both Ireland and England, and in the latter the consequence was the rise in influence of extreme Protestants whose rhetoric aroused fears in Ireland of the intention to extirpate all Catholics.

The plotting of preemptive action by the Irish was complex and is much debated by historians, but it is generally agreed that by October 1641 Sir Phelim O'Neill and other Irish gentry in Ulster had agreed to seize many English-controlled centers in that province. Simultaneously, colonels, who had recently arrived in Dublin to recruit soldiers for Spanish service, were to surprise Dublin Castle with the aid of some other Irish gentry from Ulster. Sir Phelim struck on 22 October, and by the next day such towns as Dungannon, Charlemont, Portadown, and Newry had fallen to the insurgents. Meanwhile, the MacMahons in Monaghan, the Maguires in Fermanagh, and the O'Reillys in Cavan seized centers of power in their counties. Thus, by early November the Irish controlled most of five northern counties. Had Dublin also been taken, English authority in Ireland might have been overwhelmed quickly, but this venture was betrayed to the government at the last moment.

Before he knew that Dublin had not been taken, Sir Phelim indicated that he intended to negotiate with the king from a position of strength, on the Scottish model, while leaving settlers in possession of their estates. But news of the failure in Dublin necessitated a forceful effort to gain as much additional territory as possible. O'Neill, who at first managed to create division between Scottish and English settlers, advanced as far north as Strabane and to Lurgan in the east by December, but as news that Dublin had not fallen reached the north, settler resistance prevented further Irish expansion in Ulster at this stage. To the south, the MacMahons had penetrated Louth by 1 November, and by 21 November they, with the assistance of the O'Reillys, had begun to

Woodcut of atrocities associated with Irish rising of 1641, massacre of Protestants. BY PERMISSION OF THE BRITISH LIBRARY, E. 1175(3).

invest Drogheda. An English relief force was intercepted at Julianstown and routed on 29 November.

Julianstown persuaded the Old English lords of the Pale to join with the northern insurgents at a meeting held on Crofty Hill on 7 December. They had become deeply suspicious that the Dublin government intended to use the crushing of the rebellion as an excuse both to extend plantation at the expense of the Catholic community as a whole and to end the tacit toleration of their religion. Important as these fears were, their action must also have been influenced by the popular support of the rebellion beyond Ulster before they met with the Irish leaders at Crofty. Leitrim, in Connacht, and Longford, in Leinster, had risen almost simultaneously with Ulster, and popular support, as demonstrated by attacks on settlers, was manifest in Louth, Meath, and Westmeath as early as October. By the end of November Catholic elements had begun to move against Protestants and the government's authority in virtually every county in Leinster save County Dublin. In Connacht the situation was more complex. The earl of Clanricarde, though Catholic, remained loyal and delayed rebellion in Galway, but in counties Sligo, Mayo, and Roscommon there was support for the rising before the meeting at Crofty. Only in Munster was there delay in providing support on the popular level, and, significantly, when

the rebellion did break out in the province, it was usually the Catholic proprietors who led it. By May 1642 the Catholic community was sufficiently united that, in conjunction with the church, it was able to create the Confederation of Kilkenny, and in July it received reinforcement in the north with the arrival of Owen Roe O'Neill, the leader of the Irish exiles on the continent and a man of proven military ability.

Reference to the popular dimension of the rebellion raises one of the most contentious issues associated with it, namely, the treatment of Protestant settlers. Economic conditions had already deteriorated when the Scottish crisis interrupted trade, and almost as soon as the rebellion began, the Irish population below the level of the gentry began to rob their Protestant neighbors, to whom they were often in debt. Thus, although Sir Phelim and many other Irish leaders had not intended spoliation, they had in effect unleashed a peasant rising over which they had little control. After about two weeks, there were instances of settlers being killed, particularly when they attempted to resist robbery. There were also reports by settlers of torture being applied to those who would not reveal where they had hidden their wealth. Large numbers of settlers fled after they were attacked, with those in the north often crossing to Scotland, and those leaving the southern counties of Ulster finding refuge in Dublin and then sometimes crossing to England. Some, however, never reached sanctuary because they had been stripped naked and died of exposure in the cold weather. Others died while in captivity at the hands of their captors, although many remained captive for months or even years without being harmed. It is impossible to calculate the number who died during the first months of the rebellion. The number was not insignificant, but some additional points relating to these noncombatant casualties require emphasis. First, Irish leaders generally opposed atrocities, though local commanders sometimes initiated them. Owen Roe O'Neill put an end to them on his arrival. Second, there were relatively few cases of mass murder. Such incidents did occur, usually after an Irish defeat, when some thirty to one hundred colonists were killed at one time. The most notable instances were those at Augher, Portadown, Belturbet, and Monaghan in Ulster, and at Sligo and Shrule in Connacht. Third, some Protestants reported that priests and sometimes laypeople intervened on their behalf, though there were other reports in which priests were described as justifying atrocity or as denouncing Protestant accoutrements, such as Bibles, in a manner that encouraged hostility toward their owners. Fourth, contemporary accounts of the rebellion by Englishmen, such as Sir John Temple's, published in 1646, vastly exaggerated the number of British murdered and claimed that the killings were premeditated. The purpose of these accounts was to encourage a reconquest of Ireland by the English. Fifth, the intensity of the Irish reaction at the popular level toward the settlers (which in some instances extended even to the slaughter of English-type cattle) reflected a level of hostility toward the settlements that is hard to detect in sources predating the rebellion, and that substantially exceeded the animosities harbored towards the British within the Catholic elite. Finally, settler treatment of the Irish in quelling the rebellion equaled the ferocity that had been displayed against them.

SEE ALSO Bedell, William; Confederation of Kilkenny; English Political and Religious Policies, Responses to (1534–1690); Graces, The; Old English; O'Neill, Owen Roe; Rinuccini, Giovanni Battista; Solemn League and Covenant; Wentworth, Thomas, First Earl of Strafford; **Primary Documents:** Confederation of Kilkenny (1642); Speech to the Speaker of the House of Commons (1642); From *A True and Credible Relation* (1642); From *A Remonstrance . . . Being the Examinations of Many Who Were Eye-Witnesses of the Same, and Justified upon Oath by Many Thousands* (1643); On the Capture of Drogheda (17 September 1649); From *The Interest of England in the Irish Transplantation Stated* (1655)

Bibliography

Bradshaw, Brendan. "The Invention of the Irish: Was the Ulster Rising Really a Bolt from the Blue?" *Times Literary Supplement* 4 (October 1994): 8–10.

Canny, Nicholas. *Making Ireland British, 1580–1650.* 2001.

Clarke, Aidan. *The Old English in Ireland, 1625–42.* 1966.

Clarke, Aidan. "The Genesis of the Ulster Rising of 1641." In *Plantation to Partition*, edited by Peter Roebuck. 1981.

Gillespie, Raymond. "The End of an Era: Ulster and the Outbreak of the 1641 Rising." In *Natives and Newcomers: The Making of Irish Colonial Society, 1534–1641*, edited by Ciaran Brady and Raymond Gillespie. 1986.

MacCuarta, Brian, ed. *Ulster 1641: Aspects of the Rising.* 1993.

Perceval-Maxwell, Michael. *The Outbreak of the Irish Rebellion of 1641.* 1994.

Michael Perceval-Maxwell

Redmond, John

Born in County Wexford, John Redmond (1856–1918) was the leader of Irish constitutional nationalism in the first decades of the twentieth century. An effective parliamentarian throughout his career, Redmond was a loyal follower of Charles Stewart Parnell, becoming one of his chief supporters in Parnell's final years. Because he was never tightly associated with Parnell's divisive legacy, Redmond was able to take on the mantle of leadership of the minority Parnellite faction.

Redmond's political career can be divided into two periods. In the first phase, which lasted from 1900 to 1914, Redmond achieved a number of important successes for Irish nationalists. The first of these occurred in 1900, when Redmond's gentlemanly diplomacy reunited the Irish Parliamentary Party, which had been shattered and ineffectual for the previous decade. Taking advantage of the favorable political conditions provided by the election of 1910 and the Parliament Act of 1911, Redmond was able to force a Liberal Party dependent on nationalist votes to pass the Third Home Rule Bill into law in 1914. Redmond seemingly had won Home Rule for Ireland.

The outbreak of the war in August 1914 put Redmond in a very difficult spot, for the implementation of

John Redmond (1856–1918) led the minority Parnellite wing of the Home Rule party for a decade after the famous split in December 1890. He was generally accepted as leader after the party was reunited in 1900. He was still at the helm when the third Home Rule bill was nominally placed on the statute book in 1914, but already by then the Ulster question made Irish national unity seem unlikely. COURTESY OF THE GRADUATE LIBRARY, UNIVERSITY OF MICHIGAN.

Home Rule was delayed until after the war ended. The logic of Redmond's position meant that he had to support the British war effort, a difficult balancing act for an Irish nationalist. As the war dragged on, the radicalization of Irish politics increasingly left Redmond behind, particularly after British blundering transformed the leaders of the Easter Rising of 1916 into heroes and martyrs. But Redmond was not simply a victim of circumstance. His public calls of support for the British war effort provided ammunition for his separatist opponents, and his attitude toward partition proved to be an even more serious problem. Desperate to achieve some form of tangible victory, Redmond reluctantly agreed in 1916 to accept Ulster's temporary exclusion from a Home Rule Ireland in exchange for immediate implementation of his cherished legislation. When the deal fell through, Redmond was tarred by his seeming willingness to accept partition. Election results in 1917 and 1918 made clear how far his party had fallen: In 1918 the once proud political machine won only six seats to Sinn Féin's seventy-three. His hopes crushed, Redmond died in March 1918. The war had transformed Irish attitudes, making Redmond's goal of Home Rule increasingly irrelevant as Irish nationalist men and women pressed for something closer to independence.

SEE ALSO Carson, Sir Edward; Electoral Politics from 1800 to 1921; Great War; Home Rule Movement and the Irish Parliamentary Party: 1891 to 1918; Parnell, Charles Stewart; Sinn Féin Movement and Party to 1922; Struggle for Independence from 1916 to 1921; Unionism from 1885 to 1922; United Irish League Campaigns

Bibliography

Bew, Paul. *The Life and Times of John Redmond*. 1996.

Fitzpatrick, David. *The Two Irelands, 1912–39*. 1998.

Laffan, Michael. *The Partition of Ireland, 1911–1925*. 1987.

O'Day, Alan. *Irish Home Rule, 1867–1921*. 1998.

Sean Farrell

Reformation

See Protestant Reformation in the Early Sixteenth Century; Second Reformation from 1822 to 1869.

Religion

THE COMING OF CHRISTIANITY	DÁIBHÍ Ó CRÓINÍN
1500 TO 1690	UTE LOTZ-HEUMANN
SINCE 1690	DAVID W. MILLER
TRADITIONAL POPULAR RELIGION	DIARMUID Ó GIOLLÁIN

THE COMING OF CHRISTIANITY

The year 431 marks the date of the official introduction of Christianity to Ireland. That was the year (according to Prosper of Aquitaine, *Chronicle*) in which Pope Celestine I dispatched the newly ordained Palladius as "first bishop to the Irish believing in Christ" (*primus episcopus ad Scottos in Christum credentes*). Nothing else is known about Palladius or his mission from official Roman sources, but Prosper appears to allude to both in his *Contra Collatorem* (written in the later 430s in defense of Celestine against his detractors) when he refers to the pope's having made Britain ("the Roman island") Catholic, whereas he made Ireland ("the barbarous island") Christian. This was in reference to an earlier episode, in 429, when Celestine dispatched Germanus, bishop of Auxerre, to Britain in order to overthrow those in that island who had espoused the views of the heresiarch Pelagius. That mission (again according to Prosper) had been undertaken at the instigation of the same Palladius, who was at that time still a deacon.

It is generally assumed that the mission to Ireland in 431 followed on from the one to Britain in 429, though there is no definite proof. Nor was anything more known about Palladius himself until a 2000 discovery that casts new light on his youthful years, especially those apparently spent in Rome about 417, following which he made a "conversion" to radical Christianity. There is a general consensus that Palladius did reach Ireland, presumably with a party of helpers (Augustine of Canterbury journeyed to England in 596 or 597 with an entourage of forty), and established his mission probably in the area around the present-day County Meath. The place names Dunshaughlin and Killashee are understood to derive from the Irish *dún* ("fort") and *cell* (Latin *cella*) and Secundinus and Auxilius, respectively (in their Irish forms Sechnall and Ausille), denoting early foundations by the continental missionaries. No church dedicated to Palladius, however, has survived.

At just this point, however, Palladius disappears entirely from view, his role and that of his followers completely submerged by the legend surrounding Saint Patrick. Native tradition associates the beginnings of Irish Christianity with Patrick, not Palladius, who was written out of history in the seventh century. Patrick, a Briton by birth and upbringing, was captured when aged sixteen by Irish pirates in a raid on his family's estate (*uillula*), "along with many thousands of others" (as he says himself), and brought to Ireland as a slave. His account of that episode, and of the events that unfolded because of it, has survived in his famous *Confession*, which is a unique testimony to the experiences of a Roman citizen snatched from his home by alien marauders and who lived to tell the tale. The *Confession* and the only other writing of Patrick's to survive, his letter addressed to the soldiers of Coroticus, offer unique insights into the everyday experiences of a man in the front-line of missionary activity beyond the frontiers of the Roman Empire.

Unfortunately, the dates of Patrick's mission in Ireland are not known. In fact, no dates exist at all for the saint, for the simple reason that he offers none, and no other reliable contemporary source exists that might fill that gap. Irish historians in the seventh century and after maintained that Patrick came in 432 to replace Palladius, who was assumed to have either failed or been killed, or else to have abandoned the missionary effort. Neither scenario seems likely, however, as Prosper appears to indicate that the continental mission was successful, at least in its initial stages. But no document from the Palladian mission survived, whereas Patrick's two writings became the foundation for a body of legends, which turned the Briton into an all-powerful, conquering Christian hero. In the process, however, the true character of the man was sacrificed for the purpose of creating a mythological figure whose heroic deeds formed the basis for the claims made by his followers in the centuries after him. Next to nothing is known about the progress of Christianity in Ireland in the fifth century, and Patrick emerges into the light of history only in 632, in the famous Paschal letter of Cummian, who refers to the saint (*sanctus Patricius*) as *papa noster* (our father)—the earliest indication that Patrick enjoyed a special status in the Irish Church.

Historians have been troubled, however, that nowhere in Patrick's writings is there a reference to Palladius or anyone else involved in missionary activity in Ireland, but Patrick constantly reiterates the claim that he has gone where no man has gone before. It is not at all impossible, therefore, that Patrick came to Ireland before Palladius, rather than after him, perhaps in the late fourth century or in the generation before Palladius was dispatched by Pope Celestine to those "Irish believing in Christ." That would perhaps offer the most satisfactory explanation for Patrick's otherwise inexplicable silence about the work of others before him on the Christian mission in Ireland, for modern readers of his words are unanimous that his writings reveal an individual of genuine spiritual greatness, one unlikely to be mean-spirited about others. An earlier missionary period for Patrick would also account for the presence in Ireland of Christians before 431, those "Irish believing in Christ" to whom Palladius was sent as first bishop. Certain expressions in Patrick's writings would seem to add weight to this surmise because he appears to be writing at a time when the Roman presence is still all-pervasive in his native Britain. On the other hand, the more traditional dating of his career (arrival in 432; death in 461 or 493), runs up against the difficulty that the Roman legions had long since departed what in the 440s was becoming the "Saxon shore" as Britain was prey to Anglo-Saxon invaders. Since Patrick makes no mention of these cataclysmic events, it seems reasonable to infer that his silence on the subject is due to the fact that he had left his native home long before the Anglo-Saxon occupation of Britain, which did not become complete until the sixth century.

Palladius's mission made nothing like the same impression on the Irish historical mind as Patrick's did, and yet there are occasional traces of a transitional period during which Christianity was still finding its feet, not yet securely established as the national religion. In fact, that was probably not to be the case until the late sixth or early seventh century. The earlier phase of missionary activity is represented, for example, by a remarkable survival: a list of the days of the week in a mixture of Irish and Latin, a witness to the first faltering attempts by Irish Christians to adapt to the new concepts introduced by the Roman religion. This phase of conversion is evident also in the way that Irish converts simply recycle the terminology of the older native beliefs in their earliest Christian vocabulary. Thus the Irish terms for *God, belief, faith, grace*, and so on, are all words used to express similar concepts in the pre-Christian religion. In time, of course, the newer religion was to replace the earlier one entirely, but not before the latter had left an indelible mark on the Irish Christian mind. How much of the new Irish Christian religion was due to the activities of Palladius and his continental comrades, and how much to Patrick and the efforts of later British clergy, is difficult to judge. The neighboring church (and doubtless also the Irish settlements in the neighboring island from the fourth century on) had a profound impact on the Irish Church in the sixth century, not only in terms of its structures and organization but also on the Irish language and the ways in which that language was first given expression. That the older formal Roman scripts of late antiquity (*capitalis* and *uncial*) never took hold in Ireland strongly suggests that the books brought to Ireland by the continental missionaries failed to find any imitators. The form of writing favored by Irish scribes and stonemasons from about the seventh century on, and even their orthography and pronunciation, both of their own language and of Latin, seem to indicate that the British influence in the longer term was the stronger of the two.

SEE ALSO Early Medieval Ireland and Christianity; Hagiography; Latin and Old Irish Literacy; Saint Patrick, Problem of; **Primary Documents:** *Confessio* (Declaration) (c. 450); From Muirchú's *Life of St. Patrick* (c. 680)

Bibliography

Binchy, Daniel A. "Patrick and His Biographers, Ancient and Modern." *Studia Hibernica* 2 (1962): 7–173.

Ó Cróinín, Dáibhí. *Early Medieval Ireland*. 1995.

Ó Cróinín, Dáibhí. "Who Was Palladius, 'First Bishop of the Irish'?" *Peritia* 14 (2000 [2001]): 205–237.

Thompson, Edward A. *Who Was Saint Patrick?* 1985.

Dáibhí Ó Cróinín

1500 TO 1690

In 1500 there was only one religion in Ireland—medieval Catholicism. By 1690 this situation had changed completely: There were the three major churches, the Roman Catholic Church, the Church of Ireland, and the Presbyterian Church, as well as numerous sects like the Baptists and Quakers. The religious makeup of Ireland had been substantially changed through the long-term effects of the Protestant Reformation of the sixteenth century, although in terms of winning the majority of the population of Ireland to Protestantism, the Reformation had undoubtedly failed and Catholicism had succeeded.

The chronology of the failure of the Protestant Reformation in Ireland has been much debated in Irish historiography and the discussion has certainly not led to a *consensus* about the exact chronology of the failure of Protestantism and the success of Catholicism among the Irish. Whereas an older, Catholic nationalist historiography saw Ireland as naturally and unchangeably Catholic, scholars since World War II have come to ask why and how the Protestant Reformation failed in Ireland. The suggestions regarding the time frame of this development have varied considerably: from a suggestion that the failure of the Reformation was already determined in the reign of the Protestant Edward VI (1547–1553) (as proposed by Brendan Bradshaw), to the thesis that neither the failure of Protestantism nor the success of Catholicism was decided during the early modern period (1500–1800), but that the die was cast in the nineteenth century (Nicholas Canny). However, these periodizations have not been widely accepted, and in the 1990s a consensus evolved which sees the 1580s and 1590s as a watershed in the religious development of Ireland. The following, therefore, is an interpretive summary of the religious and ecclesiastical development of Ireland between 1500 and 1690 based on this rough consensus chronology.

ETHNIC, CULTURAL, AND POLITICAL DIVISIONS

The religious evolution of Ireland between 1500 and 1690 was deeply influenced by the long-standing ethnic and cultural divisions of the island and by its troubled political development. In consequence of the Anglo-Norman conquest between 1169 and 1170, late medieval Ireland was ethnically and culturally divided between the indigenous Gaelic-Irish population on the one hand and the medieval Anglo-Norman colonizers, the so-called Anglo-Irish, on the other hand. The Anglo-Irish consisted of essentially two groups: the aristocracy, many of whom frequently intermarried with the Gaelic-Irish nobility and who were thus gradually integrated into the social and political structure of Gaelic Ireland; and the gentry and burghers in the English Pale and the Anglo-Irish towns. The Pale, the region around Dublin, and the towns, most of which were situated in the east and southeast of Ireland, were the only areas effectively under English government control in the fifteenth and for most of the sixteenth centuries. The Anglo-Irish gentry and burghers retained a firm separate identity, seeing themselves as upholders of English culture in Ireland.

IRELAND UNDER ENGLAND'S RULE

In the early sixteenth century, Ireland came under "direct rule" from England, that is, government by Anglo-Irish noblemen was replaced by government by English-born lord deputies and other English officials. In 1541 the Irish parliament declared Henry VIII "King of Ireland," thereby superseding the title "lord" granted by Pope Adrian IV in 1155. Subsequent efforts at building a state and commonwealth in Ireland after the model of the English kingdom foundered. English policy toward Ireland was not systematic and consistent, but vacillating. Although the aim of creating a unified "Irish kingdom" remained unchanged, policies varied considerably—from peaceful integration of Gaelic and Anglo-Irish lords to military campaigns to suppress them. When in the sixteenth century Gaelic and Anglo-Irish lords rebelled against English efforts at state formation, the English administration responded by deploying a standing army and by opting for the policy of "plantation," settling "New English" planters on the confiscated lands of defeated lords. This policy was pursued into the seventeenth century, with the plantation of Ulster from 1607 as the largest colonization project to date. In the early seventeenth century Ireland seemed at last to be peaceful, but this changed when the so-called Irish rebellion broke out in 1641. Ireland was then drawn into the British Civil War and was conquered by Cromwell between 1649 and 1650. In the following years Ireland participated in the vicissitudes of the British state. In 1660 Charles II was restored as monarch, and in 1685 he was succeeded by his Catholic brother James II. It was Ireland to which James came when fleeing William

of Orange's invasion of England (the so-called Glorious Revolution). Here were fought the battles in which James was defeated, namely, the Battle of the Boyne.

POLITICAL AND LEGAL REFORMATION (1534–1558)

In constant interaction with these political and cultural developments, the religious makeup of Ireland was changing dramatically. The first phase of change from 1534 to 1558 brought political and legal Reformation through Henry VIII's break with Rome, which was legalized by the Irish parliament in 1536 and the act of 1541 declaring him king of Ireland in 1541. This period was not characterized by religious changes at the popular level. Henry VIII's Reformation was political, dynastic, and legal, and the two subsequent reigns in Ireland, that of Edward VI (1549–1553) and Mary Tudor (1553–1558), were too short to allow religious identities in Ireland to become fixed. There were signs of resistance to a Protestant Reformation in the reign of Edward, and, according to the Protestant Bishop John Bale, people in Kilkenny rejoiced over the return of Catholicism in Mary's reign, but as the research of the 1990s on England has shown, they also welcomed the return of the Mass in England.

POLITICAL TENSIONS AND RELIGIOUS UNCERTAINTY (1558–1580)

Largely owing to dynastic coincidences, the religious future of Ireland remained undetermined when Elizabeth I acceded to the throne in 1558, and in this respect Ireland was not so different from England and Wales. It was, however, different with regard to its political situation. Ireland was clearly not under the control of the English monarchs, but was politically fragmented between the Gaelic Irish, the Anglo-Irish lordships and the "English districts," that is, the Pale and the Anglo-Irish towns. This political complexity was crucial for Ireland's religious development in the later sixteenth century.

The following phase between 1558 and about 1580 was characterized by increasing political tensions in an atmosphere of religious uncertainty. After the accession of Elizabeth I in 1558 it soon became clear that she would separate her dominions from the Catholic Church. This became law in Ireland when in 1560 the Irish parliament adopted the English Act of Supremacy, declaring the Church of Ireland independent of Rome and Elizabeth "supreme governor" of this state church. The English *Book of Common Prayer* was introduced to Ireland through an Act of Conformity. At least theoretically, the Church of Ireland took control of the medieval church, its fabric, and its personnel. This political and legal Reformation was followed up by an attempted religious Reformation. It was hoped that the Church of Ireland would gradually be transformed into a true Protestant church and that the people of Ireland would be educated in the new faith. However, Protestant reform strategies of all kinds, whether persuasive or coercive, lacked the means to be fully implemented. The principle of "one monarch, one faith," which was successfully applied in many, if not all, European countries, did not succeed in Ireland; or rather the "mechanisms" necessary to achieve this were never really set in motion.

This situation had two important consequences: First, the all-embracing, but not all-controlling Church of Ireland produced a vacuum, which was filled by traditional Roman Catholic religion. This vacuum was most obvious in areas that were not politically controlled by the Dublin government. But even where the queen's writ more or less ran, a similar situation prevailed: There was no active resistance to Protestantism, some conformity, little enthusiasm, and a lot of "clinging to the old ways." Catholic survivalism—also called crypto-Catholicism or church papistry—thrived in a church that, while having to rely on the existing personnel, did not have the means to ensure that personnel's conformity with the new ecclesiastical laws. From the point of view of the government and the Church of Ireland, this period was one of "missed opportunities," which afforded "a crucial breathing space" to Catholicism in Ireland (Ford 1997, p. 222).

However, this phase saw important developments in the political sphere. The Desmond rebellions of 1569 and 1579 brought together two forms of noble resistance that would prove explosive in the future: Resistance to expansionary English rule on the one hand and militant Counter-Reformation with backing from the papacy and continental Catholic powers like Spain on the other. The aim and justification of this kind of opposition was a combination of political resistance with the idea of religious war against Protestantism.

The second decisive political development was the Anglo-Irish resistance to the so-called cess, a particularly galling and burdensome tax. Owing to the financial strain on them caused by the English military presence, the loyal Anglo-Irish burghers and gentry, who had originally been in favor of increased English involvement in Ireland, developed a political grievance and began to resist English power in Ireland. Although the religious climate was still preconfessional (i.e., not yet marked by sectarian antagonism), political opposition to the cess became intense.

TRANSITION TO A RELIGIOUSLY DIVIDED SOCIETY (1580–1603)

The subsequent phase of religious development in Ireland from about 1580 to 1603 was marked by a gradual transition to a religiously divided society. This phase began with the Baltinglass and Nugent rebellions of 1580 and 1581, two highly symbolic events whose psychological consequences exceeded their real political significance. The government was shocked that the kind of fusion between political resistance and Catholicism, which they had previously associated only with the "unruly" lordships not under government control, now suddenly occurred so close to Dublin. Its reaction was swift and harsh, but in its turn shocked and antagonized the loyal Anglo-Irish community of the Pale. Moreover, the executions following the rebellion produced the first Catholic martyrs in Ireland, as some of the convicted declared on the scaffold that they died for their religion, not for the political crime of treason.

A fusion of religion and politics had begun: Political opposition, which focused on the traditional rights and privileges of the Anglo-Irish community, coalesced with religious opposition, understood as the defense of liberty of conscience. Catholicism, the "old religion," was seen as an integral part of the traditions, rights, and privileges to be guarded from an encroaching government. As a consequence, important decisions for the future were taken: Sons of Anglo-Irish families were increasingly sent to Catholic universities on the continent and a decisive "generation shift" occurred. The children came back imbued with Tridentine Catholicism and often as missionaries for the Roman Catholic Church in Ireland.

In terms of aims and justification, the Nine Years War (1593–1603) was a climax of the fusion between political and military resistance and the idea of a "religious war" against Protestantism. This was powerfully propagated by the Gaelic lord Hugh O'Neill, but not persuasively for the Anglo-Irish burghers and gentry who sided with the government and preferred constitutional opposition in parliament to open rebellion.

During this phase both the Catholic Church in Ireland and the Protestant Church of Ireland took their first steps toward church formation, that is, toward building fully developed confessional churches—processes that would come to fruition in the early seventeenth century. The religious vacuum left by the state church was increasingly filled by seminary priests and missionaries returning from the Continent, who brought with them a well-defined confessional alternative in the form of Catholicism as articulated by the Council of Trent (1545–1563). In contrast to the Catholicism that was customary among the Anglo-Irish and Gaelic Irish up to this point, Tridentine Catholicism precluded conformity or any other compromises with the state church. Toward the end of the sixteenth century the most important order of reformed Catholicism, the Jesuits, successfully and permanently established themselves in Ireland.

Meanwhile, the Church of Ireland's status as an all-embracing state church was literally crumbling. Older conformist clergy died out or clergy even left their Church of Ireland benefices to live and work as Catholic priests. Recusancy (that is, the refusal to attend the services of the state church) increased drastically. The Church of Ireland had difficulty recruiting clergy in Ireland and increasingly resorted to "importing" Protestant clergymen from England and Scotland. As a consequence, the Church of Ireland became a colonial church, embracing only the "New English" community in Ireland. This was the phase in Irish religious history, which, through gradual church formation on both sides, eliminated a conservative "middle way" within the state church. While the religious divide hardened, clergy and people were forced to decide "which side they were on."

OPPOSITION OF OLD ENGLISH TO THE STATE CHURCH (1603–1632)

The next phase of Irish religious development from 1603 until 1632 was one in which the religious divide between Protestantism and Catholicism grew even sharper, although the period was on the whole peaceful because the London government often exercised a moderating influence from fear of rebellion. The year 1603 saw the end of the Nine Years War and the period that followed was—from the point of view of the government—characterized by a sense of new possibilities. In the early years of the reign of James I the Irish government believed that, as a consequence of the complete military conquest of Ireland, political and religious control could now be established effectively and completely.

But particularly with regard to the Church of Ireland's claim to a religious monopoly in Ireland, this reform program did not succeed. After the demise of the great Gaelic and Anglo-Irish lords in the Nine Year's War, the religious conflicts focused on the Anglo-Irish gentry and burghers, who from the late sixteenth century onwards called themselves the "Old English" in order to stress their difference from the more recent Protestant settlers, the "New English." They were still a very powerful group in Irish society, controlling the towns and much of the land and wielding great political influence, not least in the Irish Parliament. Their reli-

gious allegiance was the issue at stake, for, as a political elite, their religious conformity was essential to establish the Church of Ireland in the whole island. Protestant efforts to force this group into conformity with the state church achieved effects that were the opposite of their intentions: It provoked fundamental opposition of the Old English to church and state.

Again, the political and the religious aspects of this confrontation coalesced, particularly in the towns. Whereas the Protestant effort "from above" to enforce conformity was combined with an attack on urban political and economic privileges, Catholic resistance "from below" also meant defending urban liberties against state encroachment. For example, the recusancy revolt of 1603 in the Munster towns was sparked by a combination of political, economic, and religious grievances. This also suggests that strong Catholic identities had been formed during the preceding period.

In 1626 English foreign-policy considerations brought about a new development in Irish history. In return for their financial support of the army, Charles I offered the Old English "graces," concessions which would have made life easier for the Catholics in Ireland by, for example, abolishing recusancy fines and enabling the Old English to inherit property and practice law despite their religion. The graces could have prepared the way for an official toleration of Catholicism and a biconfessional settlement in the Irish kingdom. However, the failure of the graces was inherent in that they did not grow out of, and thus did not find sufficient support in, Irish society as a whole. They had been suggested by the monarch as a response to foreign policy and without consultation from the "New English" elite; therefore, "New English" opposition against them was massive, and the Crown eventually retracted.

This period of religious development also saw an unprecedented level of rival church formation in Ireland. The Church of Ireland had become a Protestant minority church, with its personnel recruited in England and Scotland. In 1615 the convocation (the assembly of the Church of Ireland clergy) agreed upon the markedly Calvinist 104 Articles. Thus the Church of Ireland was put on a consciously broad, but nevertheless clearly defined, Protestant footing. For the time being, Scottish Presbyterians and their ministers, who had settled in Ulster in the course of the plantation there, were kept within the hierarchical structure of the Church of Ireland.

After establishing a Tridentine mission at the end of the sixteenth century, Catholic Church formation accelerated in the early seventeenth century. Major synods were held in 1614 and 1618 to ensure acceptance of the decrees of the Council of Trent and to regulate Catholic

Church formation in Ireland along Tridentine lines. And by establishing a resident hierarchy, Catholicism developed from a mission into a visible "underground" but institutionalized church.

POLITICAL AND RELIGIOUS UPHEAVAL (1632–1660)

The last phase of religious development in Ireland, between 1632 and 1660, was mainly determined by influences and developments from outside Ireland, namely, by the British and European contexts of Irish political and religious history. From 1633 to 1641, the new lord deputy, Thomas Wentworth, attempted to transform the Church of Ireland into an all-embracing state church. Wentworth believed that Catholic strength and the economic weakness of the Church of Ireland had produced a situation where conformity with the state church could not be successfully enforced. Moreover, he realized that the Church of Ireland could not be effectively controlled by the state because of the strong New English lay influence over it. Therefore, Wentworth intended to transform the Church of Ireland into an institution that could be controlled by the state and become a formidable opponent to Catholicism. This program was to advance in two steps.

The first step required condoning Catholicism for the time being and meanwhile transforming the Church of Ireland. The state church was to be put on a sound financial footing and at the same time New English lay influence was to be reduced. The Church of Ireland's theological and doctrinal basis was to be tightened, and at the same time it was to be given greater capacity to control its own personnel. Despite vigorous resistance, Wentworth succeeded in forcing convocation in 1634 to replace the 104 Irish by the 39 English Articles, thereby removing the broad Calvinist consensus on which the Irish state church had been based since 1615. As a consequence, Puritan and Presbyterian-minded clergy were forced out of the parishes of the Church of Ireland.

The second step of Wentworth's program targeted Catholicism. First, he wanted to render the Old English elite politically and economically powerless, a means to which were additional "plantations." Second, with the help of a "streamlined" Church of Ireland, Wentworth intended eventually to suppress Catholicism in Ireland. But his attempt at this transformation ended when he was impeached in England and into the power vacuum he left behind came the rising of 1641.

The period after 1641 was marked by political and religious upheaval of the most extreme kind. In political terms, the rising of 1641 led to the Irish Confederate War (also called the Irish Civil War) between 1641 and 1653. After the outbreak of the rising, which was initiated by the Ulster Irish, the Old English of the Pale for the first time joined a Catholic war in Ireland and consequently made possible the so-called Confederation of Kilkenny, which met in 1642. In the territory that was controlled by the confederation, Catholicism experienced a new phase of church formation. During his presence as papal nuncio to the confederation, Archbishop Rinuccini of Fermo in Italy was an agent of Tridentine Catholicism in Ireland. The aims of Rinuccini's mission were derived from his continental background. On the one hand, he advocated a militant Counter-Reformation, aiming at the establishment of Catholicism as the state religion in Ireland. This, however, caused the latent differences of opinion within the Confederation of Kilkenny to intensify. Whereas the Old English sought an accommodation with the Protestant king, the Gaelic Irish refused to accept such a solution and were strongly backed by the nuncio. On the other hand, Rinuccini also brought his strict Tridentine convictions to bear on his Irish mission. Consequently, he criticized the Catholic Church in Ireland for adapting to its underground status and compromising Tridentine principles.

The political and social upheaval of this period also resulted in massive religious changes on the Protestant side of the religious divide. The Scottish Presbyterians in Ulster, who had previously been part of the Church of Ireland, set up a separate Presbyterian Church structure. And in the south of Ireland, soldiers and new settlers, especially after the Cromwellian invasion of 1649, brought with them the religious pluralism that had developed in England during the Civil Wars. Thus the Quakers, Baptists, and Independents came to Ireland, adding to its religious diversity.

THE PROTESTANT-CATHOLIC DIVIDE AFTER 1660

With the Restoration of the monarchy in 1660, another phase of religious history in Ireland began because the ecclesiastical settlement resulted in the reestablishment of the Church of Ireland as an episcopal state church. Other Protestant groups, notably the Scottish Presbyterians, were henceforth regarded as "Dissenters" because they did not accept the newly restored state church. The Presbyterians, however, made up a substantial number of the Protestants in Ireland, and the government did not want to alienate them. In fact, from 1672 they were granted a fixed sum of money by the Crown for the maintenance of their ministers, the so-called *regium donum*. The Church of Ireland thus became even more of a minority church in Ireland.

Although some land was returned to Catholics after the Restoration, the Old English elite had lost their political and economic power as a result of the Cromwellian land settlement. And the Catholic Church after 1660 became again a "visible underground church," whose situation was in many ways precarious. For example, during the so-called Remonstrance controversy of the 1660s it was again debated whether Irish Catholics could declare their loyalty to the Protestant King Charles II. Moreover, anti-Catholic measures were, just as in the early seventeenth century, periodically adapted by the government, especially during the Popish Plot scare of 1678 to 1681.

The tide turned again for a short time when the Catholic James II acceded to the throne in 1685. The new king made it clear that he intended to promote the Catholic Church in Ireland, and the Church of Ireland was clearly in danger of losing its status and privileges as state church. However, the victory of William of Orange in 1690 meant that the Church of Ireland continued to be the Irish state church until its disestablishment in 1869. The Catholic Church remained an illegal underground church. Although the rule of Mary Tudor, the Confederation of Kilkenny, and the reign of James II were the only short periods in early modern Irish history in which Catholicism was practiced publicly and openly, Catholicism remained the religion of the vast majority of the population of Ireland.

SEE ALSO Burial Customs and Popular Religion from 1500 to 1690; Church of Ireland: Elizabethan Era; Edwardian Reform; Marian Restoration; Protestant Reformation in the Early Sixteenth Century; **Primary Documents:** On Catholic Ireland in the Early Seventeenth Century; Confederation of Kilkenny (1642)

Bibliography:

Bottigheimer, Karl S. "The Failure of the Reformation in Ireland. *Une Question Bien Posée.*" *Journal of Ecclesiastical History* 36 (1985): 196–207.

Bottigheimer, Karl S., and Ute Lotz-Heumann. "The Irish Reformation in European Perspective." *Archiv für Reformationsgeschichte* 89 (1998): 268–309.

Bradshaw, Brendan. "The Reformation in the Cities. Cork, Limerick, and Galway, 1534–1603." In *Settlement and Society in Medieval Ireland: Studies Presented to F. X. Martin, O.S.A.*, edited by J. Bradley. 1988.

Canny, Nicholas P. "Why the Reformation Failed in Ireland. *Une Question Mal Posée.*" *Journal of Ecclesiastical History* 30 (1979): 423–450.

Connolly, S. J. *Religion, Law, and Power: The Making of Protestant Ireland, 1660–1760.* 1992.

Ford, Alan. *The Protestant Reformation in Ireland, 1590–1641.* 1997.

Gillespie, Raymond. *Devoted People: Belief and Religion in Early Modern Ireland.* 1997.

Lennon, Colm. *The Lords of Dublin in the Age of Reformation.* 1989.

Lennon, Colm. *Sixteenth-Century Ireland: The Incomplete Conquest.* 1994.

Lotz-Heumann, Ute. *Die doppelte Konfessionalisierung in Irland. Konflikt und Koexistenz im 16. und in der ersten Hälfte des 17. Jahrhunderts* [The dual confessionalization process in Ireland: Conflict and coexistence in the sixteenth and the first half of the seventeenth century]. 2000.

Meigs, Samantha A. *The Reformations in Ireland: Tradition and Confessionalism, 1400–1690.* 1997.

Ó hAnnracháin, Tadhg. *Catholic Reformation in Ireland: The Mission of Rinuccini, 1645–1649.* 2001.

Ute Lotz-Heumann

SINCE 1690

The Irish Republic has been widely regarded, until recently, as a Catholic confessional state founded on a nationalism mainly confined to its Catholic community; Northern Ireland remains bitterly divided into two ethnic communities defined largely by religious affiliation. Many observers therefore regard group identity in ethnic communities as the key to understanding the role of religion in modern Ireland.

RELIGION AND COMMUNITY

Those who link religion to community formation in Ireland usually have in mind a special type of community called the "nation." The nation, a modern construct that became politically important in Ireland and elsewhere in the nineteenth century, is an "imagined" community. It posits that each individual enjoys relationships with millions of fellow-countryfolk whom he or she has never met, comparable to relationships experienced in a traditional local community in which all relationships are personal and face-to-face. Most of the population of late seventeenth-century Ireland identified primarily with the latter sort of community—for example, a village or kin group—and not with the modern imagined community of the nation.

There was, however, another type of community present in early modern Ireland that was different from both the traditional local community and the modern imagined community. Every landed gentleman in seventeenth-century Ireland belonged to one of the two elite confessional communities—Catholic or Protestant—contending for power at the national level. When the Protestant landed elite decisively won this contest at the end of that century, they set about excluding not only Catholics but also Protestant Dissenters from power. There were relatively few Dissenters who owned enough land to be serious contenders for power in any event, but during the course of the eighteenth century they too developed an elite which formed a third confessional community.

There was therefore a well-understood tripartite division of Irish society into three religious systems known to contemporaries as Protestant, Catholic, and Dissenting. This use of the term *Protestant* can confuse modern readers because what it really connoted was the Anglican Church of Ireland, the established church until 1869. The term *Dissenter* also obscures the true situation. A scattering of English Protestant Dissenting groups—Quakers, Independents, Baptists, and so on—had survived from Cromwellian times, but the Presbyterians were by far the most numerous Dissenters by the mid-eighteenth century, when approximately two-thirds of the population were Catholic, and the remaining one-third were divided appoximately equally between Anglicanism and Presbyterianism. Apart from a few exceptions—notably some Old English elite families that had remained Catholic—the tripartite system delineated three ethnic groups: native Irish Catholics, New English members of the Protestant Established Church, and Ulster-Scot Presbyterians.

The Williamite victory of 1691 confirmed the huge transfers of land from Catholic to Protestant ownership that had occurred during the preceding century, ensuring that there would be an Anglican presence in virtually every part of the Irish countryside, though in many localities it consisted of little more than the families of the landlord (or his agent) and the Church of Ireland minister. In most areas the great majority of the rural population was Catholic, but in Ulster there was a substantial Protestant population engaged in agricultural and protoindustrial pursuits. Anglicans were most numerous in a swath of rural territory across south Ulster, and Presbyterians dominated the countryside in the north and east of the province.

Though a primary objective of the Anglican elite was to deprive Catholics of landownership and thus exclude them from access to political power, some Catholics managed to maintain gentry status and even to exercise modest political influence in eighteenth-century Ireland. Moreover, a number of Catholics in the towns became quite prosperous merchants, sometimes taking advantage of relationships with kinsmen who had migrated to continental Europe following the Williamite victory. In Belfast and Derry the Presbyterians made up somewhat for their almost total lack of landed property by similar mercantile success.

So each of the three religious systems—Anglican, Catholic, and Presbyterian—was led by a confessional community of clergy and elite laity. In the Anglican case this community came to be called the "Ascendancy," and it used its victory in the contests of the previous century to make its central religious ritual—taking communion "according to the usage of the Church of Ireland"—a test for full membership in the civil polity. In 1760 the Catholic elite community founded an organization known as the Catholic Committee to agitate for their own admission to that polity. The Presbyterian elite developed a principled aversion (not necessarily shared by country Presbyterians) to confessional politics, so when they set up an analogous organization in Belfast in 1791, they called it the "Society of United Irishmen" rather than the "Presbyterian Committee."

During the 1790s the revolution in France generated high hopes among the proponents of change in Ireland and alarm among the defenders of the status quo. Radicals from both the Catholic and Presbyterian elites were pitted against the government and the Anglican Ascendancy. The confrontation culminated in an insurrection in 1798 for which the elite radicals mobilized both Catholic and Presbyterian foot soldiers. The rebels were soundly defeated, and in the aftermath of the rebellion the government sought to craft policies that would win the adherence of the Catholic and Presbyterian confessional communities to a new civil polity—the United Kingdom of Great Britain and Ireland—in which the Irish Ascendancy would be a permanent minority.

The government's policy was frustrated in one important particular by the king, George III, who refused to consent to the prompt admission of Catholics into the new united Parliament. The resulting delay of Catholic Emancipation for nearly three decades contributed to a crucial change in the structure of community in Ireland. During the 1820s Daniel O'Connell developed a daring political strategy by replacing the old elite Catholic Committee with a new Catholic Association with dues of one penny a month, collected at the gates of Catholic chapels throughout the country. This strategy transformed the elite Catholic confessional community into an "imagined" nationwide community, an empty vessel into which modern nationalism flowed as soon as the (essentially elite) issue of admission to Parliament was resolved in 1829. From 1832, when O'Connell proposed the repeal of the Act of Union, the attainment of some sort of national autonomy would be the consensus goal of a Catholic community that now transcended class lines.

In a sense the Ascendancy was also well on the way to reinventing itself as a confessional community transcending class lines. The Loyal Orange Order, which emerged in 1795 out of a squalid sectarian conflict in County Armagh, had promptly been taken over by landlords throughout the country as a means of mobilizing their reliable Protestant tenants in opposition to radicalism. Although the Order opposed the Act of Union in 1800, the admission of Catholics to Parliament in 1829 made it plain that any repeal of the Union would result in a Catholic-dominated parliament in Dublin and ensured that the expanded Anglican confessional community would oppose Repeal as strongly as its Catholic counterpart demanded it.

The position of the Presbyterian community around 1840 is less clear. Most Presbyterians certainly opposed Repeal, but respectable Presbyterians continued to view the Orange Order with contempt. As late as the 1870s there were a few constituencies in which Presbyterian and Catholic voters cooperated to elect reformist candidates. The espousal of Home Rule for Ireland by the Liberal Party in 1886 made a Catholic-dominated government in Dublin a realistic eventuality and terminated the last vestiges of Presbyterian political independence. The tripartite array of confessional communities had been transformed into a bipolar arrangement in which virtually all Catholics were nationalists and virtually all Protestants were unionists.

RELIGION AND SOCIETY

While the process of ethnic-community formation certainly helps us to understand how the political alignments of religious groups emerged, it is not as helpful in explaining the character and depth of religious devotion. We must look not only at the differences between the ethnoreligious groups but also at the divisions within them. The most important of these divisions is social class, which, insofar as the clergy are seldom drawn from the poorest classes, is closely related to (but not identical with) the division between clergy and laity.

In a rural society religion is a commodity which, like whiskey, can easily be manufactured by the consumers; the licensed purveyor, when he cannot rely upon the government to stamp out illicit competition, must persuade consumers to buy his product and perhaps to modify it to accommodate their tastes. In early modern Catholic Europe the official product was Tridentine Catholicism as promulgated by the Council of Trent (1545–1563). A uniform hierarchical structure based on the territorial parish was imposed upon Catholic Europe, making the parish church the exclusive venue for the central acts of religion, especially for regular mass attendance and Easter communion.

Late medieval Ireland, where feuding might militate against the peaceable gathering of a parish population

for mass and where church resources were often controlled by kinship groups, presented especially egregious examples of the noncanonical practices that Trent was trying to supplant (Bossy 1971). Outside the towns the official rituals of confession and communion may well have been less central to religious life than the seasonal or occasional pilgrimage to sites associated with local religious figures. In such observances the clergy were dispensable. Indeed, if later folk tradition can be trusted, a clergyman in good standing may have been regarded as a less reliable conduit to the supernatural than one who had distanced himself from the church by misconduct (Taylor 1995). Religion in early modern Ireland, as Raymond Gillespie (Donnelly and Miller 1998, pp. 30–49) has suggested, was the product of dialogue between the systems on offer from the religious professionals and the religious needs and practices of ordinary folk.

By 1690 the heroic efforts of missionaries and of clergy trained in continental seminaries had effected some progress toward the establishment of a parish system that could function at least at a minimal level when not prevented from doing so by persecution or warfare. It appears unlikely, however, that many individual Catholics in the countryside had yet adjusted their behavior very far toward compliance with the Tridentine norms by this time. From then until the third quarter of the twentieth century, when social scientists found that almost 100 percent of Catholics who were canonically obligated to attend mass were doing so each week, we have nationwide data on mass attendance for only one year: In 1834 the government collected data on religious practice which enables us to estimate that about 40 percent of the Catholic population (or, arguably, a somewhat higher percentage of Catholic adults) attended mass on a typical Sunday. Attendance varied from more than 80 percent in parts of the southeast to less than 30 percent in some areas of the northwest (Brown and Miller 2000, pp. 158–179).

Between 1690 and about 1775 Irish Catholicism did make some progress toward compliance with Tridentine norms, but during the population explosion from that period until the 1840s canonical practice seems to have declined to the levels reflected in the 1834 census (Corish 1985, p. 167). During this decline the church was obliged to compromise the Tridentine ideal of a parish chapel-based set of rituals by admitting the household-based piety reflected in the practice of "stations"—confession and communion held on a rotating basis at the homes of various Catholic farmers throughout the parish. Certainly there were local efforts in the late eighteenth and early nineteenth centuries to implement Tridentine reforms, but it was the Great Famine of the late 1840s which, by dramatically reducing the ratio of layfolk to priests, made possible a "devotional revolution" throughout the country. From about 1850, disciplinary reforms introduced by Paul Cardinal Cullen, the conduct of parish missions by members of religious orders, and the introduction of a variety of continental devotional practices led to a sustained rise in compliance with canonical norms (Larkin 1984).

The linkage of long-term change in canonical practice with demographic change raises further questions. It is fairly clear that members of the huge rural underclass of the landless and near-landless were disproportionately represented among the lax mass attenders before the famine. The elimination of much of this underclass by the famine and its aftermath may account for a significant share of any rise in formal religious practice (Hynes 1978). So should we see those who failed to attend mass prior to the famine as deterred more by their poverty or by their class? Were remote residences, bad roads, and lack of energy owing to austere diet their principal obstacles to attending mass? Or did ragged clothes and the stench and vermin of a destitute rural existence render them out of place in the chapels erected by their better-off neighbors? These questions remain unanswered, but recent studies of postfamine Catholicism make plain its predominantly middle-class character (Rafferty 1999; Murphy 1997) and suggest that the interaction between class formation and religious behaviors is a promising area for further investigation. Certainly, there continued to be tension between official and popular Catholicism, but the postfamine Church found it much easier to coopt popular devotional movements—notably the flowering of Marian devotions between about 1860 and 1960 (Brown and Miller 2000, pp. 252–283).

Indeed, changes in class structure affected the relationship between popular and official religion in all three systems—Catholic, Anglican, and Presbyterian. Although ordinary Protestants had shown interest during the seventeenth century in some of the same sorts of "magical" folk practices that Tridentine reformers tried to eliminate or coopt in Catholic peasant life, in eighteenth-century Protestantism we should look in a different domain for the popular side of the ongoing dialogue between ordinary folk and religious professionals. Both English and Scottish settler communities manifested vocabularies and ritual repertoires for challenging local elite dominance in their respective ethnic religions, thereby defending the communal rather than class character of their religious systems.

The prime challengers of elite hegemony within Anglicanism were the Methodist preachers who offered a generous religion of the heart as an alternative to the cold and self-interested outlook of many established clergy. Although a separate Methodist denomination was erected in 1816, a more significant development for the Church of Ireland was the adoption of evangelical attitudes promoted by Methodism on the part of numerous landlords and ministers in the aftermath of the 1798 rebellion. This development together with the elite patronage of the Orange Order—an organization that enabled working-class Anglicans to proclaim loudly their Protestantism without the inconvenience of regular church attendance—helped Anglicanism to retain its communal character. The Church of Ireland managed to remain a church for rich and poor, devout and indifferent, for perhaps two centuries of dizzying changes in class structure.

Methodism made few inroads in Ulster-Scot settlements because Presbyterians had their own ritual repertoire for challenging their elite. Presbyterian polity provided a more or less democratic process for selection of a local minister, which offered ample opportunities for literate but unreflective folk to tax the candidate and their betters more generally with defection from the seventeenth-century standards of orthodoxy. Moreover, from the 1740s the Secession Synods, imported from Scotland, facilitated such challenges to the dominance of the well-heeled and the well-read. In open-air communions, drawing both the godly and the worldly from a wide area, Seceders celebrated a vision of Presbyterian solidarity reminiscent of the covenanting days of the seventeenth century and unconstrained by the tidy respectability of the mainstream meeting houses.

So Presbyterianism, despite its institutionally divisive tendencies (indeed, because of them) was socially comprehensive within the Ulster-Scot settlements of the eighteenth century. The mechanisms that enabled Presbyterianism to function as a communal religion, however, were dismantled between 1829 and 1840. By requiring unqualified subscription to the Westminster Confession from all its ministers and then by merging with the Seceding Synod, the General Synod removed the question of doctrinal orthodoxy from the arena of congregational politics. It thereby facilitated the conversion of a religious system in which the unwashed and the unlettered had once had their say into a system that primarily addressed the needs of the respectable. This was happening just as Belfast, the recipient of considerable migration from Presbyterian country districts, became aware that, like many British cities, it faced a serious problem of unchurched workers. Furthermore, deindustrialization of the countryside would create an underclass of unemployed linen weavers comparable to the Catholic underclass whose miseries became so evident during the Great Famine.

Presbyterian leaders groped for a strategy to cope with this reality, and in 1859 some thought that Providence had provided a solution in the form of a huge revival that dominated the life of Ulster for some months. Suddenly, young working-class converts, female and male, were perceived as more in touch with the supernatural than were the ministers. Clergy moved decisively to gain control of the movement and give it a satisfactory spin. Although very few Presbyterians spoke ill of the revival in public, over the succeeding generation those who preferred the emotional style of religiosity that it represented tended to drift into Methodism and a number of smaller evangelical sects that arose in the north. The transformation of Ulster Presbyterianism from a communal religion to a class religion was virtually complete by the end of the century—a development that confirmed the transformation of the tripartite system of religious communities into the bipolar system with which we are so familiar in contemporary Northern Ireland.

CHURCH AND STATE

The extraordinarily high levels of religious observance that prevailed among Catholics in the southern Irish state (compared with other European countries) until the 1980s, and the sectarian character of the Northern Ireland state from 1921 to 1972, have led observers to use the term *confessional state* in discussions of twentieth-century Ireland. Recently, historians have been using the same term to characterize eighteenth-century political structures throughout the British Isles. Like England and Scotland, eighteenth-century Ireland was a confessional state; to avoid confusion, we should perhaps refer to it more specifically as an "Erastian" state. In other words, the Church of Ireland, like its counterparts the Church of England and the (Presbyterian) Church of Scotland, was expected to act as the religion department of the state. The prime function of a state church, in the eyes of the government and the governing classes, was to sacralize the civil polity and instill in the lower orders obedience to the Lord's commandments, especially the one that forbade coveting the goods of one's neighbor. In principle an Erastian state church was supposed to minister to the whole population, not just to the devout.

Since more than 80 percent of the population were either Catholics or Presbyterians, the Church of Ireland was in no position to fulfill this function. In one respect the government acknowledged this fact by paying modest stipends (the *regium donum*) to Presbyterian clergy, who took this gesture as a recognition, albeit an imperfect one, of their status as ministers of an established church, to the great annoyance of Anglican ecclesiastics.

One reason for a controversy among Presbyterians in the 1720s over subscription to the Westminster Confession of Faith was a desire on the part of the "subscribers" to demonstrate their institution's fitness to play the role of an established church.

In the early eighteenth century, of course, there could be no thought of an Erastian role for the Catholic clergy, whose bishops were appointed on nomination of the Jacobite Pretender until the death of "James III" in 1766. Indeed, certain penal laws, if enforced, would have eliminated the Catholic clergy in one generation and left their Anglican counterparts as the sole Christian ministers in most parts of Ireland. Moreover, early in the century some Anglican churchmen tried to launch a program to convert the Catholics through the medium of the Irish language. In general, however, the Ascendancy had little zeal for enforcing the laws against the Catholic clergy and ritual system (as opposed to those designed to limit the property and power of Catholic gentry) and little interest in providing the resources to convert the Catholics.

Predictably, the Church of Ireland was a dismal failure in the role of sacralizing the polity assigned to it by Erastianism. Among the lower orders only the Anglican minority could be relied upon to oppose rebellion in the 1790s. Government policy reflected an understanding of this dysfunctionality and showed a determination to enlist the other churches in the duty on which the state church had defaulted. Both the establishment of a state-funded Catholic theological seminary at Maynooth in 1795 and an increase and restructuring of the *regium donum* to Presbyterian clergy after the 1798 rebellion were prompted by that determination. The threat of disorder from the Presbyterians faded in succeeding decades, but the same cannot be said of the Catholics. Throughout the nineteenth century the government regularly sought to encourage the appointment of "loyal" bishops by the Holy See and to persuade bishops to constrain the behavior of priests suspected of "agitation."

In the eighteenth century none of the three religious systems had tried very hard to make converts from the other two. This pattern was changing dramatically by the 1820s, when Anglicans, inspired by evangelicalism and probably prompted also by liberal criticism of their church for its failure to serve more than a minority, launched a movement to convert Catholics known as the Second Reformation. At the same time, Anglican-dominated, government-subsidized societies were actively establishing schools for poor children. Some Catholic clergy, generally lacking the resources to provide schools for their parishioners' children, were initially willing to sanction such schools, but the Catholic hierarchy was increasingly wary of them.

A Liberal government responded in 1831 to the resulting tensions by establishing the National Education Board (composed of prominent members of all three religious communities) to make grants to local interdenominational committees of clergy and laity who would undertake to establish mixed schools under the inspection of the board's staff. Catholic clergy generally welcomed the plan, and Anglican clergy largely refused to participate in what they saw, rightly, as a major attack on their Erastian entitlements. At the time of the initiative the General Synod of Ulster was under the demagogic influence of the Reverend Henry Cooke, who cherished a vision of a reconfigured Irish Protestant establishment that would somehow embrace Presbyterians as well as Anglicans. Cooke was counting on Sir Robert Peel and the Tory Party to implement this vision. In the early 1840s, however, the Tory government adopted policies toward the established Church of Scotland (as well as the Irish Presbyterian Church) that were interpreted as deliberately anti-Presbyterian. Peel was blamed for the dramatic 1843 schism in the Church of Scotland known as the Great Disruption. Cooke's vision was discredited and his grip on Irish Presbyterianism was broken. Meanwhile, however, Cooke had kept the General Synod from sanctioning the national schools until 1840, when they extracted from the board concessions that seriously compromised its original goal of nonsectarian education. These concessions made it difficult for the board and the government to resist further demands over succeeding decades—notably from the Catholic Church—to compromise the original nonsectarian ideal. By the end of the century the system basically consisted of a separate clerically controlled, government-funded, de facto denominational school wherever there were enough children of a given denomination to warrant it.

In 1869 a Liberal government enacted legislation disestablishing the Church of Ireland and replacing the regium donum and the annual grant to Maynooth with lump-sum payments to the Presbyterian and Catholic churches respectively. This action formally ended the Erastian system, but the continued heavy involvement of the churches in state-financed education means that we should think of the resulting arrangement less as a secular state than as a multiconfessional polity. By imposing order and discipline upon a previously fractious hierarchy, Paul Cullen was rendering the Catholic Church an increasingly capable contender for influence within the civil polity.

In the years following Cullen's death in 1878, that polity came to include not only a government at Westminster but a government-in-waiting for a new civil polity to be based in Dublin—the Home Rule Party. In 1884 the hierarchy struck a deal with Charles Stewart Parnell in which the bishops agreed to support the party and the party promised to defer to the bishops in the vital matter of education. This arrangement set the conventions followed by Parnell's generation of nationalist leaders, and these conventions were instilled in key leaders of the next political generation who supplanted the Home Rule Party in 1916 to 1921.

Both of the new polities created from 1920 to 1922—the Irish Free State and Northern Ireland—are sometimes described as "confessional" states. Whatever this label may have meant in twentieth-century Ireland, it definitely did not connote the Erastianism of the eighteenth-century confessional state. It might make more sense to refer to Northern Ireland as a confessional "society"—the dysfunctional product of the bipolar division of Irish society in the nineteenth century in which religion, far from sacralizing the civil polity, became the principal obstacle to the emergence of such a polity capable of enjoying support in both confessional communities.

Those who describe the post-1921 southern Irish state as "confessional" do not have in mind a church which, like the Church of Ireland two centuries earlier, exists to buttress the authority of the state. Rather, they tend to envisage the Roman Catholic Church as dictating policy to the state. A better-supported formulation is that until the 1980s southern Ireland was certainly not a theocracy, but the church did have more influence on policy than an ordinary interest group, particularly in those domains such as education, which the church claimed as within her sphere (Whyte 1971). In recent years that influence, and the devotional commitment that underlay it, have diminished significantly, and the Catholic Church has begun to share the concern of other Irish churches for recovering their traditional constituencies.

SEE ALSO Ancient Order of Hibernians; Catholic Committee from 1756 to 1809; Church of Ireland: Since 1690; Ecumenism and Interchurch Relations; Education: Primary Private Education—"Hedge Schools" and Other Schools; Education: Primary Public Education—National Schools from 1831; Education: Secondary Education, Female; Education: Secondary Education, Male; Education: University Education; Gaelic Catholic State, Making of; Marianism; Maynooth; Methodism; Mother and Child Crisis; Overseas Missions; Penal Laws; Presbyterianism; Protestant Ascendancy: 1690 to 1800; Protestant Ascendancy:

Decline, 1800 to 1930; Protestant Community in Southern Ireland since 1922; Religious Orders: Men; Religious Orders: Women; Roman Catholic Church: 1690 to 1829; Roman Catholic Church: 1829 to 1891; Roman Catholic Church: Since 1891; Secularization; Sodalities and Confraternities; Temperance Movements; **Primary Documents:** An Act to Prevent the Further Growth of Popery (1704); The Catholic Relief Act (1778); The Catholic Relief Act (1782); The Catholic Relief Act (1793); On Presbyterian Communities in Ulster (1810, 1812); From the 1937 Constitution; Letter to John A. Costello, the Taoiseach (5 April 1951)

Bibliography

Acheson, Alan. *A History of the Church of Ireland.* 1997.

Bossy, John. "The Counter-Reformation and the People of Catholic Ireland, 1596–1641." *Historical Studies VIII* (1971): 155–69.

Brown, Stewart J., and David W. Miller, eds. *Piety and Power in Ireland, 1760–1960: Essays in Honour of Emmet Larkin.* 2000.

Carroll, Michael P. *Irish Pilgrimage: Holy Wells and Popular Catholic Devotion.* 1999.

Corish, Patrick. *The Irish Catholic Experience: A Historical Survey.* 1985.

Donnelly, James S., Jr., and K. A. Miller, eds. *Irish Popular Culture, 1650–1850.* 1998.

Hempton, David, and Myrtle Hill. *Evangelical Protestantism in Ulster Society, 1740–1890.* 1992.

Holmes, Finlay. *The Presbyterian Church in Ireland: A Popular History.* 2000.

Hynes, Eugene. "The Great Hunger and Irish Catholicism." *Societas* 8 (1978): 137–156.

Kerr, Donal A. *Peel, Priests, and Politics: Sir Robert Peel's Administration and the Roman Catholic Church in Ireland, 1841–1846.* 1992.

Larkin, Emmet. *The Roman Catholic Church and the Creation of the Modern Irish State, 1878–1886.* 1975.

Larkin, Emmet. *The Historical Dimensions of Irish Catholicism.* 1984.

Leighton, C. D. A. *Catholicism in a Protestant Kingdom: A Study of the Irish Ancien Regime.* 1994.

McBride, Ian. *Scripture Politics: Ulster Presbyterians and Irish Radicalism in the Late Eighteenth Century.* 1998.

Magray, Mary Peckham. *The Transforming Power of the Nuns: Women, Religion, and Cultural Change in Ireland, 1750–1900.* 1998.

Miller, David W. *Church, State, and Nation in Ireland, 1898–1921.* 1973.

Miller, David W. "Irish Presbyterians and the Great Famine." In *Luxury and Austerity*, edited by Jacqueline Hill and Colm Lennon. 1999.

Murphy, James H. *Catholic Fiction and Social Reality in Ireland, 1873–1922.* 1997.

Rafferty, Oliver P. *The Church, the State, and the Fenian Threat, 1861–75.* 1999.

Taylor, Lawrence J. *Occasions of Faith: An Anthropology of Irish Catholics.* 1995.

Whyte, J. H. *Church and State in Modern Ireland, 1923–1970.* 1971.

David W. Miller

TRADITIONAL POPULAR RELIGION

The popular historically is defined not by any inherent quality but by its subordinate (or subaltern) position in a wider social system. It must be understood in its social and political context, and changing configurations of power hence may entail the changing of the content of the popular. Traditional popular religion seeks to distinguish those aspects of popular religion that have long been established in agrarian society and are associated with a particular way of life, especially that of peasants, from more recent and nonrural forms, particularly those characteristic of industrial society. The latter, of course, may be traditional too, but are seen as being a product of modern society (usually defined in opposition to "traditional society"), whereas the former are seemingly premodern in origin or at least are conventionally so constructed. The traditional–modern polarity can obscure the reality of hybrid cultural forms in the present as well as in the past.

Sources for traditional popular religion include the huge archives assembled by the Irish Folklore Commission (1935–1970), largely representing the remembered traditional culture of the postfamine period; the writings of eighteenth- and nineteenth-century antiquarians and nineteenth- and twentieth-century folklorists (the term *folklore* was coined in 1846); travel writings of the eighteenth and nineteenth centuries; eighteenth- and nineteenth-century statistical inquiries (note the etymological relationship between state, statist, and statistic); and the "literature of confutation" (to use Alberto Mario Cirese's words) of church documents. None of these sources engaged with traditional popular religion in its own right as a legitimate religious phenomenon. Mostly, they were the work of men and had a distinct patriarchal bias. A social and often sectarian condescension influences many of the eighteenth- and nineteenth-century sources. Enlightenment discourses of progress and improvement influenced the observations of statisticians and sometimes of churchmen. Romanticism was a strong influence on folklorists and often on travel writers. Folklorists were frequently informed by a nation-building discourse that sought to rescue the elements of traditional popular culture, which could be adjusted to that project, or, in the case

Pilgrims to a holy well near Galway. From Harper's Weekly, *14 October 1871.* COURTESY OF THE WISCONSIN HISTORICAL SOCIETY. REPRODUCED BY PERMISSION.

of those who were also creative writers, such as W. B. Yeats, by a notion of folklore as a source of artistic inspiration that transcended a prosaic modern world. Travel writers were usually in search of local color, provided by cultural difference in its more spectacular forms.

Traditional popular religion is a shifting object of study over time. It includes cultural elements of pre-Christian, often Celtic, and Christian origin, which were articulated in a worldview framed ultimately by Christian notions. The evidence for it in the eighteenth and nineteenth centuries came from within a state that had an official religion (the Church of Ireland until 1869) and its projects of modernization, and from within a society that had its social stratifications and a majority religion that differed from that of the state and hence shared in the wider derogatory connotations of the popular. Within this context pressures on popular religion grew in the course of the late eighteenth and nineteenth centuries from the state, from state religion, and from

Roman Catholic elites influenced by Tridentine reform (which aimed to strengthen church discipline and attack "superstition") as well as by their own projects of modernization (of which nationalism was one). In 1852 Sir William Wilde in *Irish Popular Superstitions* could quote a Catholic acquaintance of his as having complained that "the tone of society in Ireland is becoming more and more 'Protestant' every year; the literature is a Protestant one, and even the priests are becoming more Protestant in their conversation and manners" (p. 17n). Here, then, Protestant values become synonymous with modernity in Ireland, as anglicization was to be for a later generation.

Localism is a defining characteristic of traditional popular religion, in contradistinction to the centralizing and hierarchizing organization of institutional religion and particularly of the Roman Catholic Church. This is attested to by scores of thousands of sacred sites from ring forts ("fairy forts") to holy wells and by supernatural beings with specific local associations, from named fairy leaders to local patron saints. Mircea Eliade in *Patterns in Comparative Religion* pointed out how in traditional societies the supreme divinities "are constantly pushed to the periphery of religious life where they are almost ignored; other sacred forces, nearer to man, more accessible to his daily experience, more useful to him, fill the leading role" (1958, p. 43). The numerous recorded traditions of the intervention of fairies in people's lives, such as bringing bad luck, blighting crops, and abducting humans and animals and their propitiation with gifts or their containment with charms, exemplify that. The modernization of religion meant the "disenchantment" of the landscape and the limiting of the sacred to relatively few sites, more subject to institutional control.

Traditional popular religion shared common religious concepts with institutional religion, but unlike the latter, it did not coexist to the same extent with the abstract rationalism of modern society. It has been argued that traditional societies have no real historical consciousness. Their history, preserved and transmitted through myths and rituals, is the work of supernatural beings and mythical heroes, whose actions are the model for all significant human actions. Thus the present moment constantly intersects with the time of origins. Mythical time recurs, is cyclical, and can be exemplified by the festival, which interrupts the passage of profane time, allowing the supernatural and the mortal to intersect. This can also be exemplified by St. Brigid's presence on the eve of her festival (St. Brigid's Day, Lá 'le Bríde), blessing a ribbon (*brat Bríde*) left on the windowsill and endowing it with healing powers, or by the dangers of May Day (Bealtaine) or Hallowe'en (Samhain), when supernatural beings were about and interacted with mortals.

Holy-well pilgrimages and wake customs were a constant source of fascination to travelers and were widely condemned by churchmen. This interest was largely due to the apparent unseemly and scandalous mixing of boisterous entertainment with the sober piety of a religious occasion. Scholarly writing on festival has emphasized the importance of its role as a form of release in hierarchical societies, allowing the temporary suspension of norms and distinctions and a concomitant sense of communion and comradeship, *communitas* in Victor Turner's terminology, thus helping to renew social order. Mikhail Bakhtin has argued that the boisterous festivities were a coequal part of such rituals, without which they could not reveal their true meaning. "The material bodily principle," as he called it, with its emphasis on feasting, drinking, and sexual license, emphasized a biological humanity, which is immortal and thus pointed to the relativity of authority.

A "pattern" (from "patron [saint]") was a type of pilgrimage normally held on a saint's day and involved visiting a sacred site, which usually included ecclesiastical ruins, a holy well, and other features such as a cairn (mound of stones). The pattern entailed arduous devotions at the sacred site, fasting, numerous circumambulations of well, ruin, and cairns, and prayer. These were followed by eating, drinking, and storytelling, and the playing of music, dancing, and fighting, which sometimes led to fatalities. Thomas Crofton Croker (1824), visiting the pattern at Gougane Barra, County Cork, in 1813, sympathized with the simple devotion of the common people, but observed that "drunken men and the most depraved women mingled with those whose ideas of piety brought them to this spot; and a confused uproar of prayers and oaths, of sanctity and blasphemy sounded in the same instant on the ear." This sums up the commonest objections to the pattern and helps to explain why a "civilizing offensive'" of clerical and civil power helped finally to abolish it altogether or largely to reduce it to its devotions by the second half of the nineteenth century.

The wake was a key funerary custom lasting at least a night and involving the laying out of the body, usually in the family home of the deceased, so that respect could be paid by family, friends, and neighbors, and the deceased could be "keened" (ritually lamented). Alcohol, whiskey or *poitín*, and tobacco were provided to visitors, and after the saying of prayers amusements began and usually included storytelling, singing, dancing, the playing of music, card playing, contests of strength and agility, and merriment varying from practical jokes and mock sacraments to catch games and games of forfeit and the hide-and-seek kind. The Catholic Church vigorously opposed the ritual public mourning and the license, particularly of a sexual nature, of the wake. As with the pattern, the wake can also be seen as renewing social order, not at a fixed temporal and calendrical point but after the crisis and disruption caused by death. Gearóid Ó Crualaoich argues that the "merry wake" "became a focus in eighteenth- and nineteenth-century Irish popular culture for the carnivalesque element of social life," increasingly subject to new forms of civil and ecclesiastical control (1998, p. 193). The merry wake rarely survived into the twentieth century and is illustrative of a continuous process, ultimately coercive, in the modern period of shifting the population away from traditional popular religion and toward more orthodox religious forms.

SEE ALSO Burial Customs and Popular Religion from 1500 to 1690; Devotional Revolution; Religion: Since

1690; Roman Catholic Church: 1690 to 1829; Roman Catholic Church: 1829 to 1891

Bibliography

Bourke, Angela. *The Burning of Bridget Cleary: A True Story.* 1999.

Carroll, Michael P. *Irish Pilgrimage: Holy Wells and Popular Catholic Devotion.* 1999.

Connolly, S. J. *Priests and People in Pre-Famine Ireland, 1780–1845.* 1982. New edition, 2001.

Croker, T. Crofton. *Researches in the South of Ireland.* 1824.

Danaher, Kevin. *The Year in Ireland.* 1972.

Eliade, Mircea. *Patterns in Comparative Religion.* 1958.

Ó Crualaoich, Gearóid. "The 'Merry Wake.'" In *Irish Popular Culture, 1650–1850,* edited by James S. Donnelly, Jr., and Kerby A. Miller. 1998.

Ó Giolláin, Diarmuid. "The Pattern." In *Irish Popular Culture: 1650–1850,* edited by James S. Donnelly, Jr., and Kerby A. Miller. 1998.

Ó Súilleabháin, Seán. *Irish Wake Amusements.* 1967.

Ó Súilleabháin, Seán. *Irish Folk Custom and Belief.* 1967.

Taylor, Lawrence J. *Occasions of Faith: An Anthropology of Irish Catholics.* 1995.

Wilde, Sir William. *Irish Popular Superstitions.* 1852.

Diarmuid Ó Giolláin

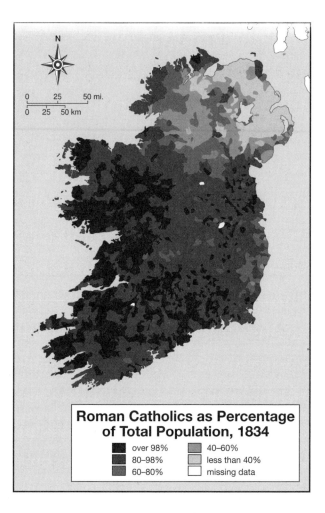

Roman Catholics as Percentage of Total Population, 1834

- over 98%
- 80–98%
- 60–80%
- 40–60%
- less than 40%
- missing data

~

Religious Geography

The general pattern of geographic distribution of the major religious denominations in modern Ireland was established by events of the sixteenth to eighteenth centuries. Native Irish "occupiers" of the land generally were Roman Catholic, but many of them were displaced from certain areas by Protestant settlers from England and Scotland. Meanwhile, the "ownership" of the land in most areas was transferred from Gaelic and Old English elites, who were still largely Catholic in the seventeenth century, to a New English elite composed of members of the Protestant Established Church. These transfers—together with some conversions of Catholic landlords in the eighteenth century—ensured that there was at least a small Protestant minority composed of landlord families and their retainers in nearly every part of Ireland in the nineteenth century.

The earliest census that provides reliable and consistent parish-level data on adherence to each of the major religious denominations throughout Ireland was con-

ducted in 1834. The first map here is based on these data and offers a snapshot of Irish religious geography about halfway through the period since the general pattern was established. The proportion of Protestants in the population, which may have been higher in the eighteenth century, was declining in many areas by the mid-nineteenth century, and that decline was accelerated in southern Ireland after independence in 1922. At present Protestants constitute less than 5 percent of the population of the Irish Republic.

The religious geography of Ulster reflects not only the displacement of Catholics by Protestant settlers but also the division among those Protestants between immigrants from England, who generally adhered to the Church of Ireland, and those from Scotland, who mostly retained the Presbyterianism of their mother country. At least as late as the 1790s that division within Protestantism was very important politically. Anglicanism dominated a zone based in the Erne valley in the southwest of the province and another zone in the lowlands around the southern shore of Lough Neagh. Usually, lowland territory is agriculturally more desirable;

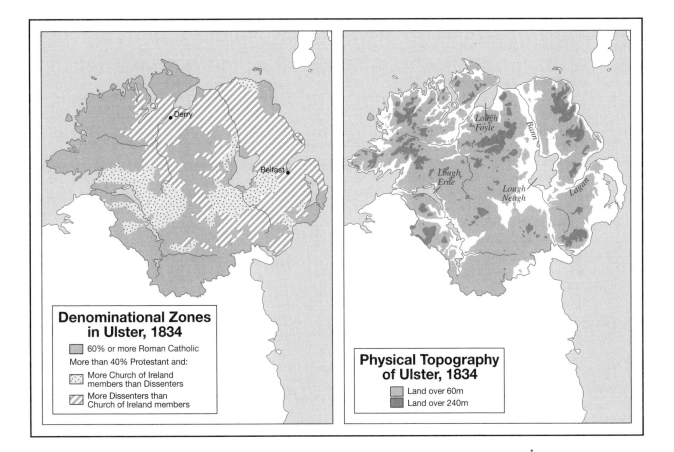

**Denominational Zones
in Ulster, 1834**

- 60% or more Roman Catholic

More than 40% Protestant and:

- More Church of Ireland members than Dissenters
- More Dissenters than Church of Ireland members

**Physical Topography
of Ulster, 1834**

- Land over 60m
- Land over 240m

significantly, Catholics and Presbyterians had to settle for the less desirable uplands adjacent to these zones. Presbyterians did, however, dominate the mouth of the River Lagan as well as the Lower Bann valley (known locally as "the Route") and the Foyle valley (known, confusingly, as "the Laggan"). As a result, the two leading towns that developed in post-plantation Ulster, Belfast and Derry, were Presbyterian strongholds in the eighteenth century.

The industrialization of Belfast in the nineteenth century led to heavy migration from the countryside, including both Anglican and Catholic workers. As Presbyterians lost their majority position in the city, and as the political tensions between Anglicans and Presbyterians lost their salience, Belfast developed more or less clearly demarcated Protestant and Catholic working-class neighborhoods. A similar process happened in Derry, which is now a predominantly Catholic city. Such segregation became even more thorough during the "Troubles" that began in the late 1960s. Although the refusal of many persons to state their religion in recent censuses makes precision impossible, it appears that the present population of Northern Ireland is about 42 percent Catholic (compared with about 35 percent in the 1960s).

SEE ALSO Landscape and Settlement

Bibliography

Compton, Paul A. *Northern Ireland: A Census Atlas.* 1978.

Vaughan, W. E., and A. J. Fitzpatrick, eds. *Irish Historical Statistics: Population, 1821–1971.* 1978.

David W. Miller

Religious Orders

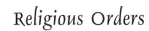

| MEN | TONY FLANNERY |
| WOMEN | MARY PECKHAM MAGRAY |

MEN

Though the nineteenth century opened with some of the penal laws still on the statute books, and though Catholic Emancipation did not become law until 1829, in fact the "emancipation" of Catholics in Ireland had been substantially achieved by the turn of the century. Traditional religious orders, such as the Jesuits, re-emerged after the persecution, and by the middle of the century they were joined by many new orders, both native and from continental Europe.

Possibly the most significant of such new orders was that founded by Edmund Ignatius Rice in 1802, when he set up a school to educate the sons of poor families. This was the beginning of the Irish Christian Brothers, a congregation which came to have immense influence in Ireland for nearly two hundred years. With other groups, such as the Presentation and Franciscan Brothers, they gradually provided both primary and secondary schools for the sons of the poor. Similar development occurred among women's orders to provide for the needs of girls.

Around the middle of the century a number of male religious orders came to Ireland from the Continent. The Passionists (1848) and the Redemptorists (1853) brought with them many of the devotional practices of Italy. Along with the Oblates of Mary Immaculate (1851) and a group of native priests who eventually came under the umbrella of the Vincentians, they began an intense period of missions around the country. These missions were enormously popular and led to an upsurge in religious practice and devotional exercises. Confraternities and sodalities were set up in parish churches. The Redemptorist Archconfraternity of the Holy Family, a confraternity for men in Limerick city, was the largest of its type in the world for many years. The Passionists had a similar one for boys at Mount Argus in Dublin that at its peak had a membership of close to 2,500. Devotion to the Miraculous Medal and the Sacred Heart of Jesus spread widely. These movements in popular piety changed the face of Irish Catholicism and led to a significant increase in the power and influence of the church. In fact, by the 1880s Catholic life and practice was dominated by its clergy to a greater degree than ever before, and this continued for almost one hundred years.

By the latter part of the nineteenth century Ireland had become a fertile ground for vocations, and other religious orders from the Continent, especially France, began to arrive. The Holy Ghost Fathers (1859) and the Society of African Missions (1877) were two of the most important. Their coming coincided with a period of great nationalist fervor, leading up to the establishment of the Irish Free State in 1922. The clergy had been closely associated with the nationalist movement, and they benefited from this development. They had considerable status in the emerging society, religious orders thrived, and a period of enormous missionary expansion began. In the minds of many Irish people the mission of the "Island of Saints and Scholars," which had restored the faith to Europe in the eighth century, was being reenacted with great pride. Maynooth, the national seminary, was overflowing with candidates for the priesthood, and out of this abundance two new missionary institutes were founded, the Columbans in 1916 and the Kiltegan Fathers in 1932. A society that had become very religious and church-centered sent thousands of Irish missionaries to Africa, the Far East, and South and North America. To be a priest, and especially a missionary, was presented as a life of great service and idealism, superior to married life. In a poor Ireland with little opportunity for its young, becoming a priest or female religious was for many the best way of obtaining an education and having a chance to travel, living an interesting life, and stepping up the social ladder.

This period of growth for religious orders lasted until the 1960s, when a sudden change occurred. Vocations quickly dried up, and within a few years only a handful were joining. The Catholic Church was changing as Ireland became prosperous and economic opportunities abounded. The traditional power of the church began to be resented, and church attendance eventually fell sharply. People became more materially minded, the notion of service was no longer so attractive to the young, and scandals, particularly involving child abuse, further eroded the church's influence. By the end of the twentieth century nearly all male religious orders in Ireland were in serious decline, with some already dying out.

SEE ALSO Devotional Revolution; Education: Secondary Education, Male; Overseas Missions; Religion: Since 1690; Rice, Edmund; Roman Catholic Church: 1690 to 1829; Roman Catholic Church: 1829 to 1891; Roman Catholic Church: Since 1891; Sodalities and Confraternities; Temperance Movements; **Primary Documents:** An Act to Prevent the Further Growth of Popery (1704)

Bibliography

Corish, Patrick. *The Irish Catholic Experience.* 1985.

Keenan, Desmond. *The Catholic Church in Nineteenth-Century Ireland.* 1983.

Sharp, John. *Reapers of the Harvest.* 1989.

Whyte, J. H. *Church and State in Modern Ireland, 1923–1979.* New edition, 1980.

Tony Flannery

WOMEN

In 1771 the wealthy Catholic woman Nano Nagle paid for a foundation of the French Ursuline order in her native city of Cork, the first new convent in Ireland since the early seventeenth century. It proved to be a very significant event. Over the next century and a half, Irish women of means and ability created an immense network of institutions that became indispensable to the functioning of the Irish church and Irish society. In the process they were instrumental in constructing the devout, modern Irish-Catholic culture.

The significance of their lives and work has been much debated. They have been described variously as powerless subordinates who carried out the wishes of their male superiors, and also as resourceful women who took advantage of an opportunity (given to few women at the time) to create, finance, and run institutions, thereby effecting real social and religious change. Contemporary women have held them responsible for disseminating and inculcating a powerful gender ideology that continues to limit women's cultural authority and personal autonomy. In fact, all these assessments are valid. However, to focus exclusively on their subordinate position within the church or their maintenance of the traditional gender hierarchy is to overlook their influence on the world in which they lived. The women's orders helped to transform church and society in the nineteenth and twentieth centuries. As a consequence, it is impossible to discuss religious and cultural change in Ireland without discussing women religious.

NINETEENTH-CENTURY GROWTH

In 1750 there were just twelve houses of religious women in Ireland, which belonged to four old, established orders that had managed to survive despite two centuries of legal proscription and harassment. By the late eighteenth century, however, great change was under way, precipitated by canonical modifications in the organization of women's communities. In 1749, Pope Benedict XIV issued a precedent-setting ruling that conceded (after centuries of pressure) the right of religious women to form a new style of uncloistered, socially engaged women's community, ending the era of enforced enclosure in place since 1299. Although freedom of movement was still restricted, the new congregations did afford women the right to undertake a range of religious and charitable activities within the community.

Wealthy Irish women (like many other women of their class in Europe at this time who sought a life dedicated to philanthropic work) were quick to take advantage of this development. In just a few decades they revi-

talized the religious life for women. Old religious orders like the Dominicans (who became prominent educators of the daughters of wealthier Catholics) and the Poor Clares (who took up the institutional care of orphans) were revived, and dynamic new Irish congregations (whose ministry was primarily to the poor) were formed. The most important of these were Nano Nagle's Sisters of the Presentation, founded in 1775; the Sisters of Charity, begun in 1815 by Mary Aikenhead; the Loreto Sisters (an Irish foundation of Mary Ward's Institute of the Blessed Virgin Mary), founded in 1820 by Frances Ball; the Sisters of Mercy, created by Catherine McAuley in 1831; Margaret Aylward's Sisters of the Holy Faith, founded in 1867; and the Medical Missionaries of Mary, founded by Marie Martin in 1936. In addition, many European congregations made foundations in Ireland, including the Sisters of the Sacred Heart, the Daughters of Charity of Saint Vincent de Paul, the Good Shepherd Sisters, and the Saint Louis Sisters. Following the establishment of the first houses, branch foundations were made, gradually expanding the convent network throughout Ireland between 1775 and 1850. By 1900 there were 368 convents in the country, belonging to thirty-five different orders. Numbers of vowed women continued increasing until the middle of the twentieth century, and at their peak they comprised almost 75 percent of the total Irish Catholic workforce of priests, monks, and nuns.

INSTITUTIONAL DEVELOPMENT

From large and imposing buildings (often the most prominent local landmarks) in Ireland's cities and towns, the women's orders developed and managed large and complex enterprises. During the first half of the nineteenth century out-of-doors relief to the sick and poor was a principal occupation of the Irish orders. They were later quick to utilize state subsidies to develop institutional care. Orphanages, industrial-training schools, reformatories, hospitals, hospices, and asylums (for the blind, the aged, the homeless, the mentally impaired, and those marginalized in other ways) all appeared in increasing numbers after 1850.

During the last half of the nineteenth century some orders took up nursing, managing their own private hospitals and health-care facilities as well as providing nurses at state institutions. They did not undertake professional medical or nurses' training, however, until well into the twentieth century after the canonical prohibition on the study of medicine (1917–1936) was rescinded. Their relatively recent access to professional training notwithstanding, by the twentieth century women religious managed to own, operate, and staff Ireland's major hospitals.

Perhaps their most significant work was in education. Beginning early in the nineteenth century, women's orders accepted state funding to establish a network of national primary schools and, later, secondary schools. After 1922, with the full financial and ideological support of the new southern Irish state, women religious came to control Catholic female education in the country.

Finally, the expansion of Irish orders outside of the country that had begun in the nineteenth century (principally in North America and Australia) continued in the twentieth. Irish women religious played a prominent role in the missionary movement, starting new orders and opening new convents in Africa and Asia.

TWENTIETH-CENTURY DECLINE

The decade of the 1950s proved to be the high-water mark of devotional Catholicism in Ireland. Thereafter, the conventual movement suffered a precipitous decline. Though religious life had long been a fulfilling and highly sought-after avocation for women—a chance for many to hold positions of responsibility and authority not available to them in secular society—by the 1960s it no longer offered the opportunity it once had. A century after women began to demand access to education, employment, and political and civil rights, Irish women's lives were irrevocably changed. And in the increasingly secularized world within which those lives were lived, the conservative brand of Catholicism that the women's orders helped to create now came under scrutiny. Women's educational and professional credentials were no longer a luxury but, in some cases, a necessity, and in this regard women religious fell far short. Long eschewing the need for advanced education and training, relying instead on their moral and spiritual authority, women religious now seemed to be ill-educated, poorly compensated, and seriously outdated vestiges of a society that no longer existed. Burdened by archaic restrictions on their personal freedom on the one hand, and by a serious (and highly critical) reinterpretation of the benefit and impact of their work by young Irish women on the other, the Irish women's orders began to contract in the 1960s. By the 1980s they were forced to begin closing convents around the country in response to the sharp decline in their numbers. The Irish witnessed again what had not been seen in a hundred and fifty years—towns without convents.

SEE ALSO Devotional Revolution; Education: Women's Education; Nagle, Honora (Nano); Overseas Missions; Religion: Since 1690; Roman Catholic Church: 1690 to 1829; Roman Catholic Church: 1829 to 1891; Roman Catholic Church: Since 1891; Secularization; Sodalities and Confraternities; **Primary Documents:** An Act to Prevent the Further Growth of Popery (1704)

Bibliography

Clear, Caitriona. *Nuns in Nineteenth-Century Ireland.* 1987.

MacCurtain, Margaret. "Godly Burden: The Catholic Sisterhoods in Twentieth-Century Ireland." In *Gender and Sexuality in Modern Ireland*, edited by Anthony Bradley and Maryann Gialanella Valiulis. 1997.

Magray, Mary Peckham. *The Transforming Power of the Nuns: Women, Religion, and Cultural Change in Ireland, 1750–1900.* 1998.

Mary Peckham Magray

Religious Society of Friends (Quakers)

Established in Ireland by 1654, the Religious Society of Friends (Quakers) is remembered for its unprecedented relief during the Great Famine of 1845 to 1851. Never numbering more than about 3,000, Irish Quakers had an impact on social policies and the relief of distress far greater than their proportion in the population. English in origin, some were farmers, others artisans and merchants. Upon moving into manufacturing, the professions, commerce, and shipping, they won respect for their rectitude in business. After the Restoration of 1660, Irish Quakers were considered a threat to the supremacy of the established Church of Ireland, and they endured a century of persecution, distraint of their goods, and imprisonment. In response they developed systems to care for oppressed members, which they soon extended outside of the sect. About 1680, Quaker Anthony Sharp of Dublin prepared a plan to care for the indigent and beggars. During the Williamite war pacifist Quakers cared impartially for the wounded and distressed, inspiring the memorable cry "Spare the Quakers, they do good to all and harm to none." In the 1798 rebellion Quaker women organized soup kitchens, the distinctive manifestation of Quaker practicality. In the famine of 1821 to 1822, Quakers worked on relief committees. By documenting and publicizing distress during the Great Famine in the late 1840s, Quakers defined the limits of philanthropy and state responsibility, challenging official policies with irrefutable statistics and contravening government relief procedures. They brought an awareness of the true condition of Ireland to North America. Through their Central Relief Committee they coordinated the outpouring of famine relief materials and money (amounting to about 6 million dollars in modern funds) directed to their care. Quakers tackled the Irish Fisheries Board over inappropriate legislation for fishing seasons, made interest-free loans to bring waste land into production, revitalized the fishing industry, led the establishment of linen manufacture in parts of the west and south, undertook the provision of employment for women as well as men, and carried out two massive distributions of green-crop seeds to provide immediate food and an alternative to potatoes. A model farm was set up to train Irish farmers in the management of new crops. Quaker relief policies were institutionalized in the sect and have become the methodology in Third World relief and development today.

In the postfamine years the Quakers, led most visibly by Jonathan Pim (MP, Dublin city, 1865–1874), pressed land-reform campaigns through legislation from the Encumbered Estates Act of 1849 to the great 1881 Land Act. The Friends mounted relief campaigns during the acute distress of 1860 to 1863 and 1880 to 1881, and yet again during the war of 1919 to 1921. In the 1980s Quakers led a campaign to find homes for itinerants and to get their children into school. The relief work that is remembered in the phrase, "They fed us in the famine," is only one aspect of major services to Ireland in 350 years of Irish Quakerism.

SEE ALSO Great Famine

Bibliography

Central Relief Committee of the Society of Friends. *Transactions of the [CRC] . . . during the Famine in Ireland in 1846 and 1847.* 1852.

Hatton, Helen E. *The Largest Amount of Good: Quaker Relief in Ireland, 1654–1921.* 1993.

O'Neill, Thomas P. "The Organisation and Distribution of Relief." In *The Great Famine: Studies in Irish History, 1845–52,* edited by R. D. Edwards and T. D. Williams. 1956.

Pim, Jonathan. *The Condition and Prospects of Ireland.* 1848.

Richardson, J. M. *Six Generations [of Quakers] in Ireland, 1655–1890.* 1893.

Helen E. Hatton

~

Repeal Movement

Many Irish people, including Daniel O'Connell, opposed the Act of Union (1800) from its inception, but it was not until the late 1830s that nationalists began an organized campaign to bring about its repeal and to develop a form of self-government for Ireland. O'Connell launched the Precursor Society of Ireland in 1838 as a preliminary to forming the Loyal National Repeal Association in July 1840. By 1843 this organization, whose general structure resembled that of the Catholic Association of the 1820s, had drawn thousands into its ranks and had become the vehicle for mass agitation on an unprecedented scale.

The repeal movement differed from the campaign for Catholic emancipation in a number of ways. First, the Repeal Association brought political organization to a new level of sophistication. It boasted a permanent staff of nearly sixty people who formed departments and committees that specialized in particular issues and activities; it featured a three-tiered membership, each with its own identification card and annual dues; it operated at the parish level through "repeal wardens" who were in regular contact with the central organization and who supervised repeal reading rooms and collected the "repeal rent." The latter, a national fundraising scheme, was crucial to the functioning of the organization; in 1843 and 1844 alone it brought in £92,590 (this compared with around £55,000 collected for the "Catholic rent" between 1826 and 1829). Second, O'Connellites were more skilled in politics by the 1840s than they had been in the 1820s. The campaigns for Catholic emancipation, tithe reform, tenant right, and other issues had turned countless numbers of them into experienced activists and politicians. As well, the Municipal Corporations Act of 1840 created Catholic-nationalist majorities on the town councils and corporations of more than a half-dozen large municipalities. Third, it was easier to mobilize the Catholic population in the 1840s than it had been two decades earlier. Thanks to a slow but steady growth in literacy and an expanded nationalist press—by 1843 the Young Ireland weekly, the *Nation*, enjoyed the largest circulation of any newspaper in the country—repeal supporters were better informed about national issues and could be reached more easily. Father Theobald Mathew's temperance crusade in the early 1840s had produced a more sober population and, through its mass assemblies, showed the enthusiasm that immense public gatherings could generate. Finally, a substantial majority of the Catholic hierarchy endorsed the repeal movement, as did most ordinary parish priests, many of whom be-

Depicted here is the "monster meeting" staged in August 1843 at Tara, site of the ancient Irish high kings near Dublin. It was the largest of about forty vast gatherings organized in that year. Supporters of repeal of the Union with Britain exaggerated the size of the crowds, but they were still among the biggest political assemblies ever seen in Ireland. FROM ILLUSTRATED LONDON NEWS, 26 AUGUST 1843.

came the key organizers in their parishes. "Do nothing without the clergy," was the advice that O'Connell gave to his colleagues in the field.

MONSTER MEETINGS

When a Tory government took office in 1841, the prospects of gaining repeal solely through Parliament appeared to fade. O'Connell believed that some sort of extraparliamentary pressure was needed and, with the conclusion of his term as lord mayor of Dublin in late 1842, he and his aides focused their attentions on obtaining repeal. The plan they developed involved the staging of a series of large open-air meetings in the three southern provinces (O'Connellite support was weakest in Ulster) that would attract as many people as possible. As O'Connell put it, the purpose of these "monster meetings" was not to convince Irish nationalists of the need for repeal, "but to convince our enemies—to con-

vince the British statesmen. . . . I want to make all Europe and America know it—I want to make England feel her weakness if she refuses to give the justice we require—the restoration of our domestic parliament."

During a six-month period in 1843—the "Repeal Year"—O'Connell and his followers organized more than thirty repeal gatherings. Some of the sites that they chose, such as the Hill of Tara (the seat of the ancient high kings of Ireland), Clontarf (where Brian Boru defeated a Danish army in 1014), and the Rath of Mullaghmast (where English soldiers slaughtered Irish leaders in 1577), were intended to evoke a sense of continuity with Ireland's past. Other meetings took place in the larger cities and provincial towns in order to blanket Leinster, Munster, and Connacht and thereby enable everyone in these areas to attend at least one of them. The number of people who *did* attend has always been a subject of debate. Nationalists naturally gave inflated estimates, invariably reporting crowds in the hundreds of thousands and, in the case of the Tara meeting, claiming that more than a million people attended. The government and the Tory press, by contrast, downplayed the size of the meetings. Precise figures are impossible to come by, but it is certain that the assemblies were huge by any standard. Even reducing nationalist figures by as much as 75 percent would mean that about one and a half million people—or approximately one-quarter of the total population of the three southern provinces—attended monster meetings in 1843. This in itself constituted an unparalleled achievement in political mobilization in Europe and North America. The meetings were spectacular events that commenced with massive processions that numbered in the thousands and that featured bands, elaborate banners, floats, and street theater. By including townsfolk and people from the surrounding countryside, the parades symbolized the way that the repeal movement had united the urban middle classes and small farmers. This was also apparent when the same crowds later gathered in a large open area to hear O'Connell and other dignitaries speak on the subject of repeal. There were additional speeches at an evening banquet, this time to a smaller, more select group of the local elite in a hotel or special pavilion.

THE END OF REPEAL

Despite their color and excitement, the monster meetings failed in their objective. British opinion remained steadfastly opposed to granting self-government for Ireland in any form because it seemed to threaten the very existence of the United Kingdom and the empire. The government banned the monster meeting scheduled for Clontarf on 8 October 1843 and charged O'Connell and eight of his associates with conspiring to alter the government and constitution by unlawful means. After a lengthy trial they were found guilty, fined, and sent to Richmond prison for nine months to a year. An appeal to the House of Lords gained their early release in September 1844, after which O'Connell renewed the repeal campaign. He appeared at a few more monster meetings in the summer of 1845, but at age seventy his physical strength and mental powers were obviously waning. Leadership of the Repeal Association fell increasingly to his son John, whose tactlessness and arrogance alienated many nationalists.

Most important, rifts opened up in the repeal movement between the Young Irelanders and O'Connellites who proudly styled themselves as "Old Ireland." Their differences were generational and ideological, but they were fought out over specific issues such as the Queen's Colleges Bill of 1845. This measure, which established three colleges in Ireland, also placed restrictions on theological education and thereby appealed to Thomas Davis and other Young Irelanders who believed that it would promote an all-inclusive nationality. By contrast, O'Connell and his supporters condemned the "godless colleges." The split grew wider after Davis died in September 1845; it became irreparable a year later when the O'Connellites introduced resolutions calling upon all repealers to renounce the use of physical force as a means of obtaining Irish self-government. John Mitchel, William Smith O'Brien, and other Young Irelanders soon left the Repeal Association, and in January 1847 they formed a rival organization, the Irish Confederation. These events, coupled with the death of O'Connell in May, the devastation of the Great Famine, and the abortive Young Ireland rising of July 1848, effectively ended the repeal movement. Nevertheless, it established a potent legacy that found expression in the Home Rule movement of the late nineteenth century.

SEE ALSO Davis, Thomas; Electoral Politics from 1800 to 1921; Mitchel, John; Newspapers; O'Connell, Daniel; Politics: 1800 to 1921—Challenges to the Union; **Primary Documents:** On Repeal of the Act of Union at the "Monster Meeting" at Mullingar (14 May 1843)

Bibliography

Cronin, Maura. "'Of One Mind'? O'Connellite Crowds in the 1830s and 1840s." In *Crowds in Ireland, c. 1720–1920*, edited by Peter Jupp and Eoin Magennis. 2000.

MacDonagh, Oliver. *O'Connell: The Life of Daniel O'Connell, 1775–1847*. 1991.

Nowlan, K. B. *The Politics of Repeal: A Study in the Relations between Great Britain and Ireland, 1841–50*. 1965.

Owens, Gary. "Nationalism Without Words: Spectacle and Ritual in the Repeal 'Monster Meetings' of 1843–45." In *Irish Popular Culture, 1650–1850*, edited by James S. Donnelly, Jr., and Kerby Miller. 1998.

Gary Owens

Republic of Ireland, Declaration of

See Declaration of a Republic and the 1949 Ireland Act.

~

Restoration Ireland

The Cromwellian conquest of Ireland (1649–1653) had resulted in massive transfers of land, but not commensurate immigration, and in the months preceding the restoration of Charles II in May 1660, the established settlers, who had been the principal beneficiaries of the recent confiscation of Catholic estates, asserted themselves to seize the political initiative. Their desire for the return of monarchy was sincere, but it was qualified by their determination to preserve the land settlement and to defend it by excluding Catholics from political power. Catholics in Ireland sought the overthrow of the settlement and the benefits of the Ormond peace of 1649, which had granted to individual Catholics the free exercise of their religion and made them eligible for appointment to public office. Although Charles was conscious of an obligation to Catholics who had been loyal to his father, he was mindful that his political circumstances did not allow him to favor Catholics over Protestants. The Act of Settlement (1662) incorporated a compromise that aimed to restore their estates to those Catholics who established their innocence of involvement in the rebellion of 1641 before a court of claims and to compensate (or "reprise") their Protestant successors with grants of reserve lands that had not been distributed in the 1650s. The impracticality of this scheme was revealed when the success rate of the first batch of Catholic claimants proved so unexpectedly high as to exceed the reserve lands available. The court was abruptly adjourned, leaving thousands of claims unheard. An alternative approach was adopted in an Act of Explanation (1665), which required grantees to each relinquish one-third of their land to provide sufficient land reserves to make room for the reinstatement not only of those dispossessed Catholics who had received decrees of innocence from the court of claims,but also for new land grants for a number of prominent Catholics nominated by the king. This act made no provision for further hearings of claims of innocence—when a new court of claims opened to administer the act in 1666, its operating principle was that those who had not already been declared innocent were irredeemably guilty. The result was the permanent disinheritance of those Catholics who had not already benefited. When the court concluded its business in 1669, the proportion of land owned by Catholics, which had fallen from 60 percent in 1640 to about 10 percent in 1660, stood at 22 percent (Simms 1956, p. 195).

Charles's own priority in 1660 was the restoration of the Church of Ireland, and this was accomplished expeditiously through a complete set of appointments to vacant bishoprics and the passage of a new Act of Uniformity (1666). Those who hoped for a policy of accommodation with the Presbyterian community were disappointed. A three-tier system emerged in which only members of the Protestant Established Church, who constituted perhaps 40 percent of the Protestant community, enjoyed full privileges. Presbyterians, who accounted for about one-third of Irish Protestants and whose numbers increased steadily with continued migration from Scotland to Ulster, were subject to religious and civil disabilities, as were other Protestant dissenters. In practice, they were allowed to worship freely, but their marriages and the legitimacy of their children were not recognized and their conscientious refusal to take an oath acknowledging the king as the supreme governor of the church excluded them from appointment to public office. Catholics, who amounted to some three-quarters of the population, were tolerated at the Crown's discretion. Though there were instances of Catholic persecution, and a sustained period of repression during the "Popish Plot" crisis in England (1678–1681), in general Charles's tolerant inclinations and his devious foreign policy combined to favor freedom of worship, and the reconstruction of both the regular and secular components of the Catholic Church proceeded without official opposition.

At the insistence of Protestants in Ireland, who recognized that the preservation of the land settlement depended upon the retention of political power, Catholics ceased to be admitted to membership in the Irish parliament. The right to vote was not withheld, but Catholic voting strength was greatly reduced by the loss of property and by a related shift of control in the towns, which had become Protestant enclaves. The complementary mainstay of the settlement was the control of military force. The standing army, at between 5,000 and 7,000 men, was twice as large as the prewar army and was deployed widely in small garrisons as an internal security force. At first undenominationally Protestant, and a source of official anxiety because many of the soldiers had served in Cromwellian armies, the introduction of obligatory attendance at divine service converted it gradually into a predominantly Anglican force. It was supplemented by local militia forces that were organized on a county basis and attracted a degree of participation that indicated both the priority that Protestant proprietors attached to defense and their unwillingness to leave the entire responsibility for it in the hands of the central authority.

The restoration arrangements rested upon force, and the main routine business of government was to find the money to pay for the security that the system required. After initial problems of adjustment this did not prove difficult. The prewar regime, which had relied on archaic feudal taxes for its ordinary revenue, had been dominated by financial problems. The restored government drew its revenue principally from a hearth tax, customs duties, and the introduction of internal excise duties. These were largely consumer taxes, and the effect was to redistribute the costs of government from the property-holding classes to the community at large. The policy was both politically shrewd and fiscally successful. The period proved to be one of fairly constant economic expansion, revenue was buoyant, the expense of the military was easily borne, and the government was absolved from the need to summon Parliament again after its dissolution in 1666. Economic growth suffered an apparent and deeply resented setback in 1667 when the export of Irish cattle, sheep, and pork to England and Scotland was prohibited, but in reality the diversification of Irish pastoral exports was already under way and proved more profitable than the traditional supply of store cattle to the English market. Wool exports to England increased, exports to the French market expanded, and the provision trade with the transatlantic colonies was developed. The profits of expanding trade were closely associated with landownership, either directly through large-scale production for export markets or indirectly through increased rents, which meant that the Protestant community enjoyed a disproportionate benefit, all the more so because international trade was largely in Protestant hands. Nonetheless, vigorous population growth suggests that there was some trickle-down effect. Prosperity underpinned government by providing the revenue that supported the army that upheld the established order.

An important element of the new order was novel. Faced with the imperialist claims of the English Parliament in the 1640s, both Protestants and Catholics had protested that Ireland was a separate kingdom under the same crown and was not subject to the authority of the English legislature. They had not changed their minds by 1660, but Protestants were reluctant to offend Parliament and embarrass Charles by pressing the point. They raised no objection to English acts regulating Irish trade and disposing of Irish land, and their silence condoned a significant change in the legal relationship of the two kingdoms.

Outwardly, Restoration Ireland witnessed a remarkable recovery from the disruptions brought about by war and political uncertainty. By Charles's death in 1685, the government was solvent and stable, the established church was firmly in place, the land settlement and its associated social order had been maintained, trade was flourishing, and the population was growing. All of this was secured by a Protestant monopoly of administrative and political power, the protection of a large military force, and the support of the English government. The structure, however, was under a variety of strains. The most obtrusive was the discontent of those who had been deprived of land, office, and influence, most particularly the members of the Old English community. The defenses against disaffection were elaborate, but they depended ultimately on what had come to be recognized as the vital stress point—the reliability of English support. Since the early 1670s, when the conversion to Catholicism of James, Charles's brother and heir, had become public knowledge, the prospect of his succession had been a destabilizing influence in Ireland. From their different perspectives, all parties feared or hoped that the accession of a Catholic monarch would make the Protestant monopoly of power unsustainable and open the way to a sympathetic reconsideration of the inequities of the land settlement of the 1660s. As a result, the second half of Charles's reign was not the period of consolidation that it seemed to be on the surface, but a period of marking time until his death inexorably reopened the fundamental issues of land and religion that divided the communities of Ireland.

SEE ALSO Agriculture: 1500 to 1690; Boyle, Robert; Butler, James, Twelfth Earl and First Duke of Ormond; Petty, Sir William; Plunkett, Oliver; Puritan Sectaries; Smith, Erasmus

Bibliography

Arnold, Lawrence J. "The Irish Court of Claims of 1663." *Irish Historical Studies* 24 (November 1985): 417–430.

Arnold, Lawrence J. *The Restoration Land Settlement in County Dublin, 1660–1688.* 1993.

Barnard, Toby C. "New Opportunities for British Settlement: Ireland, 1650–1700." In *The Origins of Empire*, edited by Nicholas Canny. 1998.

Clarke, Aidan. *Prelude to Restoration in Ireland: The End of the Commonwealth, 1659–1660.* 1999.

Connolly, Sean. *Religion, Law and Power: The Making of Protestant Ireland, 1660–1760.* 1992.

Gillespie, Raymond. *The Transformation of the Irish Economy, 1550–1700.* 1991.

Moody, T. W., F. X. Martin, and F. J. Byrne, eds. *Early Modern Ireland, 1534–1691.* Vol. 3 of *A New History of Ireland.* 1976. Reprint, 1991.

Simms, J. G. *The Williamite Confiscation in Ireland, 1690–1703.* 1956.

Aidan Clarke

Rice, Edmund

Edmund Rice (1762–1844), educator, founder of Presentation Brothers and Irish Christian Brothers, was born at Callan, Co. Kilkenny, and educated at a local "hedge school" before being apprenticed to his uncle, a merchant in Waterford, in 1779. Rice amassed a fortune in the provisioning trade at Waterford, where he joined the campaign of the Catholic Committee for emancipation. In 1785 he married Mary Elliott; their only child, Mary, was mentally handicapped, and Rice suffered additional heartbreak in 1789 with the death of his wife.

This tragedy radically changed Rice's priorities and from that point he became increasingly involved in pious and charitable pursuits. Initially he devoted his attention to the plight of prisoners and orphans, assisting in the foundation of the Trinitarian Orphan Society (1793) and the Society for the Relief of Distressed Roomkeepers (1794). His greatest contribution, however, was to Catholic education. Prompted by a pastoral address of Bishop Thomas Hussey, in 1802 Rice established a religious community of laymen dedicated to teaching poor boys, modeled upon the Nano Nagle's Presentation Sisters. The schools followed a plan devised by Rice. The curriculum was a pragmatic combination of best practice of the time, but from the outset the Brothers were determined to preserve the exclusively Catholic character of their schools. In time this led to acrimonious relations with the National Board and the eventual withdrawal of Rice's schools from the system. By the time of Rice's death in 1844 the Brothers had forty-three schools, including six in England. Besides founding the schools, Rice played a key role in the revival of the institutional church following the dislocation of the penal era. A collaborator of Daniel O'Connell, Theobald Mathew, and Charles Bianconi, Edmund Rice was a key figure in the modernization of Irish society; he was beatified by Pope John Paul II in 1996.

SEE ALSO Education: Primary Private Education—"Hedge Schools" and Other Schools; Education: Primary Public Education—National Schools from 1831; Education: Secondary Education, Male; Religious Orders: Men; Roman Catholic Church: 1690 to 1829; Roman Catholic Church: 1829 to 1891

Bibliography

Keogh, Dáire. *Edmund Rice, 1762–1844.* 1996.

Dáire Keogh

Richard II in Ireland

Richard II, the only king of England to visit Ireland between 1210 and 1689, did so in order to retain his lordship there in the face of two threats: a mounting Gaelic recovery, particularly in Leinster under Art MacMurrough, and a dangerous depopulation of the English colony, caused partly by plague and by the flight of colonists before the Irish advance. Richard used the opportunity of peace with France and Scotland in 1394 to lead an expedition in person, as had long been called for by the Anglo-Irish. Having proclaimed that all men of Irish birth should return there, he assembled a fleet of perhaps 500 ships and set sail from Haverfordwest in late September. When joined by Anglo-Irish troops upon his arrival, he had an army of 8,000 to 10,000 men, the largest that had ever been sent to Ireland.

Richard landed at Waterford on 2 October, but he waited until the end of the month before marching against MacMurrough, having first established a ring of garrisons around his territory. MacMurrough was attacked by force and eventually compelled to submit, as did his vassal kings, O'Byrne, O'Toole, and O'Nolan. In the following months, amid heavy fighting in some areas, negotiations ensued with the other Irish kings, most of whom, seeing the ease of Richard's success in Leinster, decided to submit on terms. Some did so voluntarily, hoping that by becoming his subjects he would shield them from colonial aggression, and Richard too seems to have arrived at a greater understanding of Irish grievances, and was intent on a more conciliatory approach.

The problem was that Richard's policy involved strengthening the colony by resettlement of land held by absentee lords, whose interests were in direct conflict with the Irish. The earldom of Ulster, for instance, was now the possession of Richard's heir, Roger Mortimer, and when Richard left Ireland after having appointed him as lieutenant, a clash with O'Neill was inevitable, since the latter had overrun much of the territory of the earldom. The settlement that Richard had imposed was therefore fragile and superficial, and it had collapsed by

Richard II's fleet sails from Ireland (c. 1399). From Jean Creton's verse chronicle of the campaign, Histoire du Roy d'Angleterre Richard II *. . . (c. 1400–1425).* © THE BRITISH LIBRARY/TOPHAM-HIP/THE IMAGE WORKS. REPRODUCED BY PERMISSION.

the time Mortimer was killed in 1398. When Richard made a second expedition to Ireland in 1399, it was with vengeance in mind, however his weaker force met with hardened Irish resistance, and was probably doomed even before news arrived from England of the coup by his cousin, the future Henry IV, which ended both his reign and his life.

SEE ALSO English Government in Medieval Ireland; Gaelic Recovery; Gaelic Society in the Late Middle Ages; Norman Invasion and Gaelic Resurgence; **Primary Documents:** King Richard II in Ireland (1395)

Bibliography

Curtis, Edmund. *Richard II in Ireland, 1394–1395, and Submissions of the Irish Chiefs.* 1927.

Johnston, Dorothy. "Richard II and the Submissions of Gaelic Ireland." *Irish Historical Studies* 22 (1980): 1–20.

Johnston, Dorothy. "The Interim Years: Richard II and Ireland, 1395–1399." In *England and Ireland in the Later Middle Ages*, edited by James Francis Lydon. 1981.

Lydon, James Francis. "Richard II's Expedition to Ireland." *Journal of the Royal Society of Antiquaries of Ireland* 93 (1963): 135–149.

Seán Duffy

Rinuccini, Giovanni Battista

Archbishop of Fermo and papal nuncio to the Confederate Catholics of Ireland, Giovanni Battista Rinuccini (1592–1653) was born in Rome on 15 September 1592 (new style). After a glittering scholastic career he received a doctorate of *Utrumque Ius* from the University of Pisa and was employed as a referendary in the Roman Curia before being promoted to the archbishopric of Fermo in Italy on 17 November (ns) 1625. In March 1645, with considerable fanfare he was appointed nuncio to the Confederate Catholics of Ireland and began his journey to the island. After a stay of several months in Paris in an unsuccessful attempt to thaw diplomatic relations between France and the Holy See, he eventually landed in Kenmare Bay, Co. Kerry, in October and entered the de facto Confederate capital in Kilkenny on 12 November (old style).

For most of his first year in Ireland, Rinuccini attempted to prevent the conclusion of the first Ormond Peace between the Confederate Catholics and Charles I's lord lieutenant, the marquis of Ormond, because it failed to guarantee rights to property and jurisdiction to the Catholic clergy. Military successes in June and July of that year, partially owing to the 50,000 scudi that the pope had provided for the Irish mission, confirmed his belief that a more militant policy would enjoy both practical success and divine favor. When the peace was finally published in Confederate quarters in early August 1646, Rinuccini led the Irish clergy in the synod of Waterford, which repudiated the peace and overthrew the government that the treaty had established. The nuncio became president of a new Confederate Supreme Council, which launched an unsuccessful assault on Ormond in Dublin. From this point on, his influence began to wane. He resigned his presidency in early 1647, confident that his supporters still dominated Confederate government, but a succession of military disasters, partially attributable to the alienation of the Confederate faction that had supported the peace, severely eroded his influence. He was tempted to leave Ireland in March 1648 but elected to remain and resist the Inchiquin truce, which he considered a device to prepare the way for the reintroduction of the Ormond Peace. His excommunication of the supporters of the truce in May 1648 triggered a Confederate civil war that his partisans eventually lost. This paved the way to the negotiation of the second Ormond Peace of January 1649. Bitterly disappointed and resentful, the nuncio left Ireland in the following month.

During his career in Ireland Rinuccini was animated by a distrust of the Confederate peace party, which he believed ready to abandon the interests of the clergy for private gain, and by a belief that genuine commitment to war in the Catholic interest offered real possibilities of success, not least because it would attract large-scale papal assistance. In the event he was able neither to unify the Confederates around a militant strategy nor to attract substantial investment from the pope. Instead, he served merely to delay the completion of peace between the Royalist and Confederate parties and to ensure that the forces that opposed invasion from England in 1649 not only lacked possession of Dublin but were weaker and less united than they would have been without his mission.

SEE ALSO Confederation of Kilkenny; Darcy, Patrick; English Political and Religious Policies, Responses to (1534–1690); O'Mahony, Conor, S. J.; Rebellion of 1641

Bibliography

Aiazzi, Giuseppe. *Nunziatura in Irlanda di Monsignor Gio. Baptista Rinuccini arcivescovo di Fermo negli anni 1645 à 1649* [The nunciature in Ireland of Monsignor G. B. Rinuccini, archbishop of Fermo, in the years 1645–1649]. 1844.

Corish, Patrick. "The Crisis in Ireland in 1648: The Nuncio and the Supreme Council: Conclusions." *Irish Theological Quarterly* 22 (1955): 231–257.

Kavanagh, Stanislaus, ed. *Commentarius Rinuccianus, de sedis apostolicae legatione ad foederatos Hiberniae Catholicos per annos 1645–1649* [The Rinuccini memoirs concerning the mission from the Apostolic See to the Confederate Catholics of Ireland during the years 1645–1649], 6 vols. 1932–1949.

Ó hAnnracháin, Tadhg. *Catholic Reformation in Ireland: The Mission of Rinuccini, 1645–1649.* 2002.

Tadhg Ó hAnnracháin

Robinson, Mary

First female president of Ireland, long-time human-rights campaigner, and United Nations (UN) Commissioner for Human Rights, Mary Robinson (née Bourke) was born in Ballina, Co. Mayo, in 1944. Mary attended a private primary school, and her secondary education was gained at the Sacred Heart Convent at Mount Anville in Dublin. She also attended a finishing school in Paris. At Trinity College, Dublin, she studied law and won a postgraduate fellowship to Harvard in 1967. After practicing for a year as a barrister, she was appointed Reid Professor of Law at Trinity College in 1969. In the same year she was elected a senator on the Trinity College panel, and in the following year introduced a bill to repeal the laws banning the importation and sale of contraceptives. This was to be the first of three unsuccessful private member's bills that she introduced on this subject. In 1975 she acted for Mairin de Burca and Mary Anderson when they successfully took the state to the Supreme Court for its exclusion of women from jury duty. She campaigned on a broad spectrum of human-rights and feminist issues—against internment in Northern Ireland, against the Emergency Powers Act in the Republic, and for greater support for unmarried mothers who wanted to keep their children. In 1979 she took a successful case against the Irish government to the European Court of Human Rights in Strasbourg for its failure to provide free legal aid in a family-law matter. She also worked to abolish the status of illegitimacy and campaigned against the 1983 antiabortion amendment to the constitution. In 1986 she defended freedom of information about abortion. She was involved in the campaign to preserve Viking Dublin, served on the Dublin Vocational Education Committee, and participated in the Divorce Action Group, founded in 1980.

In 1976 she joined the Labour Party and stood unsuccessfully for election to the Dáil in 1977 and 1981, but she regained her senate seat on both occasions. In 1985 she resigned from the Labour Party in protest over its support for the Hillsborough Anglo-Irish Agreement, yet in 1990 the party adopted her as its candidate for the presidency. In November 1990 she was elected the first female president of Ireland. She made the first working visit of an Irish president to Belfast in 1992 and traveled to other trouble spots all over the globe. In 1997 she announced that she would not be seeking a second term as president, and was appointed UN Commissioner for Human Rights, a position that she held until 2002.

She married Nicholas Robinson in 1970, and they have three children—Tessa (born in 1972), William (1974), and Aubrey (1981).

SEE ALSO Equal Economic Rights for Women in Independent Ireland; Politics: Independent Ireland since 1922; Presidency; Women's Parliamentary Representation since 1922; **Primary Documents:** On the Family Planning Bill (20 February 1974)

Bibliography

Bourke, Helen, and Olivia O'Leary. *Mary Robinson: The Authorised Biography.* 1998.

Horgan, John. *Mary Robinson.* 1997.

Caitriona Clear

Roman Catholic Church

1690 TO 1829	**C. D. A. LEIGHTON**
1829 TO 1891	**OLIVER P. RAFFERTY**

SINCE 1891	DAVID W. MILLER AND JAMES S. DONNELLY, JR.

1690 TO 1829

From the sixteenth century until 1800, Ireland was singular among European states in that the greater part of the population adhered to a religion that was regarded with intense hostility by the ruling elite and the organs of government. The position of the Catholic Church, embraced by this majority, was rendered even more difficult in the wake of the defeat in 1691 of the cause of the dethroned Catholic monarch James II. The Irish parliament's relevant legislation of this period was, ostensibly, largely directed toward securing the Protestant character of the establishment, by destroying the economic, political, and military capacity of the surviving Catholic part of the elite. However, legislation was also directed against the Catholic Church itself. Further, the assumptions of the age about the ability of the elite to determine the religion of the inferior ranks of society allow it to be said that the penal code, as it came to be known, sought the destruction of the Catholic religion.

The anti-Catholic legislation proved impossible to enforce in its entirety, and disruption of fundamental Catholic practice was restricted to the decades around the turn of the century. As the eighteenth century wore on, conversions from Catholicism were numerous; but the weakness of the established religion and the poverty and distinct culture of most Catholics served as barriers to any major change in affiliation. In the long term, this experience assisted Catholicism in adapting to the changing circumstances of the late eighteenth and the nineteenth centuries. Catholic Ireland was largely immune to the contagion of the Enlightenment—always an elite affair—but was enthusiastic in embracing its notions of religious toleration, propagated by Charles O'Conor of Belanagare and later publicists in the Catholic cause. The way was paved for the turbulent religious pluralism of the nineteenth century. The hostility of an essentially Protestant ancien régime, which survived well into the nineteenth century, had the singular effect of ensuring that Catholicism was the firm ally of the liberalism of the period.

The government of the Irish church was singularly constituted. Though Ireland fell under the jurisdiction of the Roman congregation (Propaganda) responsible for non-Catholic countries, it continued to possess a national hierarchy. It was the exiled Stuart sovereign who nominated its members until 1766. Thereafter, Irish bishops were, in effect, very often able to nominate their

THE STATION.

UR readers are to suppose the Reverend Philemy M'Guirk, parish priest of Tir-neer, to be standing upon the altar of the chapel, facing the congregation, after having gone through the canon of the Mass; and having nothing more of the service to perform, than the usual prayers with which he closes the ceremony.

"Take notice, that the Stations for the following week will be held as follows :——

VOL. I.   I,

A "station" mass celebrated in a private home remote from the nearest Catholic chapel. In the late eighteenth and early nineteenth centuries this was a common arrangement to deal with shortages of clergy and inaccessible church accommodation. Illustration from William Carleton (1794–1869), Traits and Stories of the Irish Peasantry *(1830).* COURTESY OF THE GRADUATE LIBRARY, UNIVERSITY OF MICHIGAN.

own successors. From about 1780 the question of the nomination of bishops was central to a conflict, which lasted some fifty years, about who was to exercise the greatest influence over the church as it emerged from its repressed condition. From 1808 attempts by politicians to gain influence for the state were firmly resisted by the bishops; but their clerical and lay subjects also entered the fray. Substantially, victory went to the bishops, and the nineteenth-century Irish church was free of both excessive political influence and internal factionalism.

The Banishment Act of 1697 did come close to obliterating its targets, the episcopal bench and the regular clergy. However, both bodies recovered quickly. By the middle of the century friars had become numerous enough to be seen as undermining the diocesan and parochial structures of the church, and Roman decrees of 1743 and 1751 restricted their activities and reduced their numbers. The episode is indicative of the reasonably healthy condition and satisfactory circumstances of the clerical body as a whole by this time. Certainly, clerical numbers did not constitute a serious problem; but despite the establishment of seminaries within Ireland, notably at Maynooth, toward the end of the century, they did not manage to match the population growth in the famous gap between the famines (1740s to 1840s). The penal legislation did not advert to religious women; but life was in fact difficult for them, and for most of the eighteenth century there were not more than about a dozen convents in the country. They generally presented themselves as girls' boarding schools. New, indigenous foundations, beginning with Nano Nagle's Presentation Sisters, marked the beginnings of spectacular growth thereafter.

The history of Irish Catholic practice in the period conforms to a general European picture: There was a diffusion of Tridentine patterns of religious behavior, which were particularly slow to reach poorer rural regions. As elsewhere, this regional variation was magnified by linguistic difference. The oral and scribal culture of Gaelic Ireland certainly produced a distinctive religious life, albeit that this too was nourished by the religion of the Counter-Reformation. However, the chief local variations were simply the consequences of relative prosperity and poverty. In some places the parish gathered in a chapel rather than around a Mass rock and possessed a well-educated priest, a fixed residence for him, and a parish school. Here the Tridentine vision of the parish as the focus of the sacramentally based Catholic life of a well-instructed laity was clearly much easier to realize. The provision of this plant and personnel seems to have been normal by the middle of the eighteenth century in the more prosperous agricultural regions of Leinster and Munster, as well as in the towns.

Here Catholic life, though conducted with the minimum of ostentation, differed very little from the norms aspired to anywhere else in the western church.

The emergence of O'Connellite politics has been taken as the chief sign that the era of Catholic self-effacement was at an end. However, other signs, such as the provision of capacious new Dublin churches, might have been observed (and certainly were by an anxious Protestant community) well before the O'Connellite agitation of the 1820s. Such change had much to do with the general Catholic revival in postrevolutionary Europe and the increasing frequency with which the population was taken into account in political calculations in the era. However, it was also a reflection of very considerable growth and advance in many areas of the life of the Irish church, notably in education at all levels and in religious life among women. And these were but the consolidation and expansion of Irish Catholicism's remarkable achievement in the face of its penal-era adversity.

SEE ALSO Catholic Committee from 1756 to 1809; Doyle, James Warren; MacHale, John; Maynooth; Murray, Daniel; Nagle, Honora (Nano); Penal Laws; Religion: Since 1690; Religion: Traditional Popular Religion; Religious Orders: Men; Religious Orders: Women; Rice, Edmund; Troy, John; **Primary Documents:** An Act to Prevent the Further Growth of Popery (1704); The Catholic Relief Act (1778); The Catholic Relief Act (1782); The Catholic Relief Act (1793); Origin of the "Catholic Rent" (18 February 1824); The Catholic Relief Act (1829)

Bibliography

Brady, John, and Patrick J. Corish. *The Church under the Penal Code.* Vol. 4, fasc. 2, of *A History of Irish Catholicism.* 1971.

Connolly, Sean. *Priests and People in Pre-Famine Ireland, 1780–1845.* 1982.

Corish, Patrick J. *The Irish Catholic Experience: A Historical Survey.* 1985.

Leighton, Cadoc D. A. *Catholicism in a Protestant Kingdom: A Study of the Irish Ancien Régime.* 1994.

C. D. A. Leighton

1829 TO 1891

The period from Catholic Emancipation in 1829 to the fall of Charles Stewart Parnell in 1890 to 1891 saw profound transformation in the Catholic Church in Ireland.

At an institutional level the church moved from a relatively weak position to one where organized Catholicism came to dominate the social and to some extent the political lives of most Irish Roman Catholics. In the process ecclesiastical leadership passed from the hands of accommodating and politically retiring individuals such as Daniel Murray, archbishop of Dublin (1823–1852), and James Doyle, bishop of Kildare and Leighlin (1817–1834), to more robust defenders of the church's prerogatives like Cardinal Paul Cullen (1849–1878) and Archbishop John MacHale (1825–1881).

Cullen and MacHale were unlikely bedfellows, and they frequently clashed on matters of policy. MacHale tended to represent a romantic Gallican and advanced nationalist strain within the church, compared with Cullen's brash ultramontane tendencies. For Cullen, political aspirations were to be placed at the service of the church, and Catholicism itself was the only permissible ideology.

The political coming of age represented by Emancipation coincided with growing social expectations on the part of Irish Catholics, and in 1869 the first Catholic lord chancellor, Thomas O'Hagan, was appointed. This fed Cullen's hopes that at last Catholicism would begin to play a role commensurate with its strength in Irish society.

Political advancement went hand in hand with specific religious developments in the church. Although it is clear that Catholic mores had begun to change early in the nineteenth century, the "devotional revolution" which is particularly associated with Cullen's ministry developed in earnest from 1850 to 1875. In time the church building replaced the home as the center of Irish religious life, and ultimately, Tridentine Counter-Reformation Catholicism triumphed over traditional popular religion. Many of the features of modern Irish Catholicism, such as sodalities and confraternities, have their beginnings in this period. Other, more traditional aspects of Irish Catholic devotional life were greatly strengthened, such as Marianism, which was helped in part by the reputed apparition of the Blessed Virgin Mary at Knock, Co. Mayo, in the summer of 1879.

Like many other changes in Irish society, the transformation of Irish Catholicism into a recognizable product of ultramontane exuberance was facilitated by the Great Famine. The ratio of priests to laypeople dramatically improved, and an emphasis on improving the church's infrastructure meant that more people had access to churches than at any other time in Irish history. The education and training of the clergy received a new impetus with the increase of the state grant to Maynooth College in 1845. The average product of the college was not necessarily an academic high-flyer, but he

was nonetheless solidly grounded in Catholic culture and rites. The Maynooth-trained clergy also assisted in the political gains of Catholicism, and Daniel O'Connell's skillful manipulation of the clergy as political agitators helped to ensure the political successes he achieved. The priests also worked to keep the more militant aspects of growing Irish nationalism at bay. Ironically, it was precisely what he regarded as the overpoliticized and anti-Roman elements in the Maynooth education that led Cullen to set up his own seminary in Dublin in 1859.

If the clergy by mid-century were better educated, so too, relatively speaking, were the laity. The national school system set up in 1831 was a major factor. The system was not always to the liking of the Catholic authorities, but policy disagreements among the bishops concerning the system meant that the schools were not as vigorously opposed as they might have been. Even opponents such as MacHale were eventually forced to accept the system as the only means of securing primary education in poor dioceses. The system ultimately replaced the "hedge schools" and on the whole provided a higher standard of education. The popularity of both the hedge schools and the national system is testimony to the high value that Irish peasant society placed on education.

State provision always exceeded the church's ability to meet popular educational demands, despite the activities of religious orders such as the Irish Christian Brothers, founded by Edmund Ignatius Rice in 1802, or the Presentation Sisters, founded by Nano Nagle in 1775. The education of the Catholic middle classes was relatively well provided for by such groups as the Jesuits and, from 1860, by the Holy Ghost Fathers. Individual dioceses also began to build and run secondary schools, and these often were recruiting grounds for the major seminaries such as Maynooth. The education of middle-class girls was facilitated by the expansion of communities of female religious such as the Sisters of Mercy and the Sacred Heart order.

The attempt by the church to immerse itself in university education was not especially successful. Despite the involvement of John Henry Newman and subsequently the Society of Jesus, the hoped-for Catholic University paid for by the public purse never emerged in nineteenth-century Ireland. The Irish Universities Act of 1908 gave the Catholic Church considerable scope to influence the shape of third-level education, at least in what became the Irish Free State. This new authority was, from an ecclesiastical perspective, an enormous improvement over the Queen's Colleges established by an act of Parliament in 1845.

The leading figure in shaping educational policy at its various levels was William Walsh, archbishop of Dublin (1885–1921). Walsh's ascendancy marked the increasing rapprochement between official Catholicism and militant Irish nationalism, which reached its apogee, especially in Ulster, in the activities of the explicitly Catholic-directed Ancient Order of Hiberians. Walsh's tenure as archbishop also saw the foundation of the most successful and enduring of the temperance movements, the Pioneers of the Sacred Heart, which doubtless built on the mid-nineteenth-century work of the "apostle of temperance," Father Theobald Mathew.

The consolidation of Catholicism in Ireland was complemented by its expansion overseas. At any given time, up to a third of the soldiers in the British army were Irish Catholics. Meeting their spiritual needs in the far-flung corners of the British empire produced as a by-product the strengthening of Catholicism wherever the Union Jack was raised. Such considerations also involved official Vatican pronouncements on Irish political affairs, including the condemnation of Fenianism in 1870 by Pope Pius IX, which was welcomed by Irish bishops, and the condemnation of the Plan of Campaign and of boycotting by Pope Leo XIII in 1888, which was a grave embarrassment to Irish ecclesiastics.

Perhaps the most remarkable aspect of Irish Catholicism in the whole period was its gradual shift toward conformity. Between the late 1820s and the early 1890s the church was characterized by two decisive features: strict obedience to Roman authority and an inclination to identity itself with aggressively nationalist politics. As the downfall of Parnell illustrated, at some level, nationalism had to be firmly under the control of ecclesiastical hierarchy.

SEE ALSO Ancient Order of Hibernians; Cullen, Paul; Devotional Revolution; Doyle, James Warren; Education: Primary Private Education—"Hedge Schools" and Other Schools; Education: Primary Public Education—National Schools from 1831; Education: Secondary Education, Female; Education: Secondary Education, Male; Education: University Education; MacHale, John; Marianism; Maynooth; Murray, Daniel; Overseas Missions; Religion: Since 1690; Religion: Traditional Popular Religion; Religious Orders: Men; Religious Orders: Women; Rice, Edmund; Sodalities and Confraternities; Temperance Movements; Walsh, William Joseph; **Primary Documents:** The Catholic Relief Act (1829); On Irish Catholicism (1839)

Bibliography

Bew, Paul. "A Vision to the Dispossessed? Popular Piety and Revolutionary Politics in the Irish Land War, 1879–82." In *Religion and Rebellion. Historical Studies, XX,* edited by Judith Devlin and Ronan Fanning. 1997.

Callanan, Frank. *The Parnell Split, 1890–91.* 1992.

Corish, Patrick J. *The Irish Catholic Experience.* 1985.

Corish, Patrick J. *Maynooth College, 1795–1995.* 1995.

Elliott, Marianne. *The Catholics of Ulster: A History.* 2000.

Larkin, Emmet. *The Roman Catholic Church and the Plan of Campaign, 1886–1888.* 1978.

Macaulay, Ambrose. *The Holy See, British Policy, and the Plan of Campaign in Ireland, 1885–93.* 2002.

Magray, Mary P. *The Transforming Power of the Nuns: Women, Religion, and Cultural Change in Ireland, 1750–1900.* 1998.

Morrissey, Thomas J. *William J. Walsh: Archbishop of Dublin, 1841–1921.* 2000.

Rafferty, Oliver P. *Catholicism in Ulster, 1603–1983.* 1994.

Rafferty, Oliver P. *The Church, the State, and the Fenian Threat, 1861–1875.* 1999.

Oliver P. Rafferty

SINCE 1891

By the 1890s Irish Catholics displayed extraordinary levels of religious practice thanks to the devotional revolution of the mid-century. Ecclesiastics were well aware, however, that intense devotion to Catholicism existed in uneasy alliance with another popular passion—nationalism. Though most clergy, including nearly all the bishops, shared the popular aspiration for Home Rule, over the preceding two generations the church had acquired important interests under British rule, foremost among which was a network of clerically managed but state-funded primary schools that had become denominationally segregated despite the government's original intent that they be nonsectarian. The Catholic hierarchy's problem was how to protect its interests within the existing political system while retaining the confidence and fidelity of a laity committed to the abolition of that system and its replacement with one in which Ireland would be self-governed.

LATE NINETEENTH AND EARLY TWENTIETH CENTURIES

During the career of Charles Stewart Parnell as leader of the Irish Nationalist Party in Parliament, the Catholic hierarchy had addressed the difficulty of protecting its interests in an 1884 arrangement to support the party's effort to gain Home Rule for the Irish nation on condition that the latter defer to the bishops' judgment in matters relating to the church's educational interests.

This arrangement was able to survive the crisis in 1890 and 1891 over Parnell's divorce because, contrary to an important strain of popular memory, it was not the bishops but the party itself (prompted by the English Liberal Party leader, W. E. Gladstone) that deposed Parnell from the leadership. Two legacies from the period of Parnell's dominance of Irish politics, however, made the 1884 arrangement problematic for the church over the next three decades.

The first of these legacies was that all parliamentary constituencies with Catholic majorities had become permanent "safe" seats for nationalists. As a result, a cohort of politicians only a few years younger than Parnell continued to dominate nationalist politics from the latter's death in 1891 until the party's humiliating defeat in the 1918 general election by a new generation of politicians. Therefore, to the extent that the bishops adhered to the 1884 arrangement, they risked alienating younger Catholic nationalists frustrated by the party's failure to deliver Home Rule. The second legacy was Gladstone's commitment of the Liberal Party to Home Rule, which meant that the Nationalist Party had no practical alternative to some sort of alliance with the Liberals. The latter's increasingly secularist outlook toward education made some bishops deeply suspicious of Nationalist Party leaders.

During the decade-long split in the party following Parnell's fall, some ecclesiastics were enthusiastic supporters of Timothy Healy, one of the anti-Parnellite leaders whose policies seemed to promise greater clerical influence in party affairs. The 1900 reunion of the party under the leadership of the Parnellite John Redmond, with the support of Healy's anti-Parnellite rival John Dillon, isolated Healy politically. Cardinal Logue of Armagh had never really abandoned his Healyite sympathies, but Archbishop Walsh of Dublin, the subtlest intellect in the hierarchy, did correspond candidly with Redmond in the years immediately following the reunion. Around 1905, however, Walsh became alienated from the party under Redmond's leadership. Communication between the hierarchy and the party leaders generally devolved upon one of Logue's suffragans, Patrick O'Donnell, bishop of Raphoe, who had become rather deeply involved in party affairs.

Although the 1884 arrangement remained the basis for the relationship between the bishops and the party, unease over the Liberal alliance, as well as some popular disillusion with the party, meant that the hierarchy increasingly tended to conduct that relationship at arm's length. Of course, the outcome of the two 1910 general elections, which seemed to give the party leverage to force enactment of Home Rule, restored some of its popularity. Popular disenchantment with the party returned, however, after Ulster Unionist threats to secede from any Home Rule government in Dublin resulted, at the outbreak of World War I, in the mere pro forma enactment of Home Rule coupled with an act suspending it for the duration of the war.

EASTER RISING THROUGH WORLD WAR II

The distancing of the bishops from the party during the preceding decade or more worked very much to their advantage during the revolutionary developments of 1914 to 1923. Nineteenth-century experience might have led one to expect the hierarchy to rally around the party's constitutional nationalism in opposition to "physical force" nationalism in the wake of the 1916 Easter Rising. Certainly a number of bishops condemned the violence immediately after the event, but the hierarchy avoided any ringing endorsement of the party. Meanwhile British execution of most of the rebel leaders left a sort of tabula rasa upon which an alternative to the party would be constructed under the label Sinn Féin ("we ourselves"). The young Sinn Féiners were unsullied by the old party's associations with the Liberals, and the fact that many of them were associated with movements celebrating rural Gaelic society resonated with the bishops' anxiety over the dangers of modern urban popular culture.

In the spring of 1918, by promoting a nationwide anticonscription movement in which the party and Sinn Féin were nominally coequal partners, the hierarchy sent a message that the latter was a legitimate claimant to the former's role as representative of the nation. During the hostilities of 1919 to 1921, bishops deplored the violence of both the Irish Republican Army (IRA) and crown forces without calling into question the legitimacy of Dáil Éireann, the alternative legislature constituted by the Sinn Féiners elected to Parliament in late 1918. The hierarchy rejoiced at the 1921 treaty settlement and came down very hard on the side of the new Free State government by excommunicating the antitreaty side in the Civil War of 1922 to 1923.

Given this ecclesiastical support at such a critical moment, it is not surprising that the new state quickly enacted into civil law Catholic moral teachings in such matters as divorce and contraception. More significant is the fact that antitreaty politicians, after they reentered the Dáil in 1927 as the Fianna Fáil Party led by Eamon de Valera, proved themselves equally committed to the confessional character of the state despite their harsh treatment by the church during the Civil War. When de Valera as head of government set about redrafting the constitution in 1937, he relied heavily on the advice of Father John Charles McQuaid, who became archbishop of Dublin in 1940. The new constitution was influenced by contemporary Catholic social teaching and recognized "the special position of the Holy Catholic Apostolic and Roman Church as the guardian of the Faith professed by the great majority of the citizens."

THE 1950S

By the 1950s the Irish Catholic Church had settled into certain grooves and seemed likely to preserve this combination of features far into the future. It was thoroughly hierarchical in its governance, with its bishops and priests expecting the laity to accept a distinctly subordinate role. It occupied a position of enormous power and influence primarily because, with vocations at floodtide, priests, brothers, and nuns in great profusion staffed schools, hospitals, and other public services. Most politicians—and Catholics generally—readily acknowledged its authority over public and private morality. The celebrated "Mother and Child" crisis of 1951 was remarkable not because the church succeeded in blocking implementation of a system to provide prenatal and pediatric care and instruction but because the minister of health insisted on making a public issue of his disagreement with the hierarchy.

Taking a deeply pessimistic view of the secular world, church leaders saw moral danger lurking almost everywhere, and nowhere more menacingly than in the sexual realm. Other Christians in Ireland (not to mention Jews), outside the "one true church," were regarded as fit only for conversion; otherwise their very salvation was in doubt. To the discomfort of Irish Protestants, the cult of the Virgin Mary had long occupied a central position in the devotional life of most Irish Catholics. Rituals and ceremonies focused on Our Lady of Fatima, Our Lady of Lourdes, and the rosary were especially widespread and exuberant in the 1950s, when devotees were stimulated by the Marian Year (1954), the centenary of the Lourdes apparitions (1958), and the rosary "crusades" of the Irish Dominicans and Father Patrick Peyton. There was no scriptural tradition either in popular piety or in scholarship, and Irish Catholics were encouraged to observe with great strictness the iron laws of a punitive God and "his" church if they wished to escape everlasting damnation.

IRISH CATHOLICISM SINCE VATICAN II

All of these characteristic features of Irish Catholicism were challenged forcefully by the very different winds that blew from Rome during and after the Second Vatican Council (1962–1965). In its sweeping reform program Vatican II called for giving the laity a much-

expanded role in the governance of the church. It expressed considerable optimism about the nature of the modern world. It strongly encouraged dialogue with other Christians and indeed with representatives of other major religious traditions. It discouraged popular religious beliefs associated with miraculous cults, and it sought to put the life of Christ and the boundless love of God at the core of personal religious experience, thus relegating the Virgin Mary to a subordinate position. And the Scriptures were to become the touchstone of both theological inquiry and popular piety.

Over the next quarter-century Irish Catholicism was substantially reshaped by the reforms associated with Vatican II. In some important areas, admittedly, change came very slowly and in small doses. The hierarchy was unwilling to share much power with either priests or the laity, and the roles of both in church governance expanded more in form than in practice. On the other hand, clergy and laity alike readily accepted numerous liturgical changes—Mass in the vernaculars (English and Irish), hymn singing, lay Scripture readers, lay ministers of the Eucharist, and Communion in the hand. Marian devotions and Marian organizations such as Our Lady's Sodality and the Legion of Mary soon dwindled into insignificance. Relations between the churches vastly improved. Laying aside its earlier conversionist mentality, the institutional Catholic Church entered into respectful theological discussions with representatives of other Christian traditions in Ireland and began to view certain kinds of interfaith religious services as not only acceptable but even highly desirable.

But Vatican II did not only reshape the Catholic Church in Ireland; it also weakened it and helped to precipitate its decline. The development that has proved most debilitating has been the dramatic fall in vocations to the priesthood and the religious life. Of course, the causes of this development include the materialist values arising from economic prosperity and the spread of modern sexuality since the 1960s, but the emphasis placed by Vatican II on human freedom, the development of the whole human person, and the dignity and beauty of married love worked strongly in the same direction. The requirement of celibacy now seemed to entail too great a sacrifice. Whatever arguments there might be about the relative weight of the different factors involved, the results have long been all too plain. By 1998 there were only 44 ordinations to the priesthood in Ireland, as compared with the peak of 412 in 1965. The total number of priests, brothers, and nuns in Ireland plummeted from almost 34,000 in 1967 to fewer than 20,000 in 1998 (a fall of 41 percent), with the heaviest declines coming among the orders of religious brothers.

If the recent past and the present have been bleak, the future is even darker. In 1966, at the crest of the floodtide of vocations, some 1,400 people in Ireland were registered as beginning formal preparation for the priesthood or the religious life, but by 1998 the corresponding number had fallen to 92. The dramatic decline in vocations has hardly been limited to Ireland, but its consequences there have been more far-reaching than almost anywhere else owing to the historic role of Irish Catholicism. Because of this radical contraction in its personnel, the institutional Irish Church has been unable to staff schools, hospitals, and other public services to anything like the same degree as in the period up to the mid-1960s, and in the process much of its old power and influence has been lost.

Other factors have undoubtedly contributed to this loss of power and influence. One is that the Catholic laity of Ireland have been made more independent of clerical authority by their rising levels of education. Between 1970 and 1998 the number of students enrolled in third-level education in the Irish Republic increased from about 25,000 to over 112,000. The statistics for secondary-school education tell an equally dramatic story. The moral authority of the church has also been badly damaged by poor leadership. In Ireland as elsewhere, the Catholic laity generally repudiated the teaching of *Humanae Vitae*, the notorious papal encyclical of 1968 banning all forms of "artificial" birth control. On this issue the Catholic bishops of Ireland took a hard line in accord with Roman orthodoxy and prohibited priests from engaging in public dissent. The obvious fact that many priests did dissent and yet pretended to accept the ban fostered an image of clerical hypocrisy among the laity and cost the institutional church dearly in credibility with most Irish Catholics.

Crippling the moral authority of the church even more seriously has been the avalanche of clerical scandals since the early 1990s, beginning with the case of Bishop Eamonn Casey of Galway (who resigned in 1992 when it was discovered that he had fathered a son years earlier), and extending to the case of Bishop Brendan Comiskey of Ferns (who resigned in 2002 after his role in failing to stop the activities of a pedophile priest—the suicide Father Sean Fortune—came under intense public scrutiny). Among these scandals none caused more public outrage than the disclosure of the widespread physical and sexual abuse of children and adolescents in residential institutions conducted by male and female religious orders. This particular scandal, magnified in its public impact by a powerful television documentary in spring 1999, led to the appointment of a government commission of investigation and eventually to a huge financial settlement in 2002 by the religious orders to compensate victims of abuse. The clerical sex-abuse scandal in Ireland, as in the United States, eventually focused on the failure of church leaders to remove priests from active ministry or contact with children after the receipt of credible evidence of serious wrongdoing. Cardinal Desmond Connell, the archbishop of Dublin, came under pressure to resign for this reason. The Irish Catholic hierarchy promised a thorough diocese-by-diocese investigation of clerical sex abuse, to be followed by a public report.

As if the seemingly endless drumbeat of scandals were not depressing enough, church leaders have also had to confront much evidence that a basic feature of Irish Catholic life—regular Sunday Mass attendance—has become imperiled. Surveys indicate that during the 1990s Mass attendance rates declined significantly—from 85 percent in 1990 to 65 percent in 1997. Although even the lower rate is quite impressive by European standards, what is especially worrisome is that when these figures are broken down by age and location, it emerges that a majority of young people in urban areas "have turned their backs on a part of Irish life which was almost universal a generation ago." It should not be assumed, however, that there is a causal connection between the scandals and the drop in Sunday Mass attendance. Persuasive evidence exists that Irish Catholics have not substantially changed their religious beliefs or practices in reaction against the scandals. Nevertheless, the aura of serious moral misconduct attaching to numerous servants of the church since the early 1990s can only worsen the problems of the dearth of vocations and the poverty of moral credibility. It will be years before the Irish Catholic Church could recover even a semblance of its former authority in the moral sphere, and its old political power is gone for good.

SEE ALSO Ancient Order of Hibernians; Ecumenism and Interchurch Relations; Education: Primary Public Education—National Schools from 1831; Education: Secondary Education, Female; Education: Secondary Education, Male; Education: University Education; Gaelic Catholic State, Making of; McQuaid, John Charles; Marianism; Maynooth; Mother and Child Crisis; Overseas Missions; Religion: Since 1690; Religious Orders: Men; Religious Orders: Women; Secularization; Social Change since 1922; Sodalities and Confraternities; Temperance Movements; Walsh, William Joseph; **Primary Documents:** From the 1937 Constitution; Letter to John A. Costello, the Taoiseach (5 April 1951)

Bibliography

Bradshaw, Brendan, and Dáire Keogh, eds. *Christianity in Ireland: Revisiting the Story.* 2002.

Cooney, John. *John Charles McQuaid: Ruler of Catholic Ireland.* 1999.

Donnelly, James S., Jr. "The Peak of Marianism in Ireland, 1930–60." In *Piety and Power in Ireland, 1760–1960: Essays in Honour of Emmet Larkin,* edited by Stewart J. Brown and David W. Miller. 2000.

Falconer, Alan, Enda McDonagh, and Seán Mac Réamoinn, eds. *Freedom to Hope? The Catholic Church in Ireland Twenty Years after Vatican II.* 1985.

Hug, Chrystel. *The Politics of Sexual Morality in Ireland.* 1999.

Miller, David W. *Church, State, and Nation in Ireland, 1898–1921.* 1973.

Raftery, Mary, and Eoin O'Sullivan. *Suffer the Little Children: The Inside Story of Ireland's Industrial Schools.* 1999.

Whyte, John H. *Church and State in Modern Ireland, 1923–1979.* 2d edition, 1980.

James S. Donnelly, Jr., and David W. Miller

~

Royal Ulster Constabulary (including Specials)

The police force of Northern Ireland, the Royal Ulster Constabulary (RUC), came into existence on 1 June 1922 upon the disbandment of the Royal Irish Constabulary (RIC). It was preceded by local paramilitary defense forces that were officially recognized in June 1920 as the Ulster Special Constabulary (USC) and divided into "A" (full-time), "B" (part-time), and "C" (reserve) sections. The USC was seen as violent, ill-disciplined, and sectarian. After the demise of the Boundary Commission in 1925, the "A" Specials were disbanded and the "C" force lapsed. The "B" Specials survived as a police auxiliary force, whose main advantages were its low cost and local knowledge. Its unofficial activities included bitterly resented harassment of local Catholics.

Nationalist attempts to secure proportionate Catholic membership of the RUC in the early 1920s failed. Protestant predominance increased as older Catholic members recruited from the RIC retired; the RUC had 23 percent Catholic membership in 1922, 10 percent in 1970. From the 1920s to the 1960s the RUC was a small provincial police force. Its politicization and lack of professionalism were exposed by its violent response to civil-rights demonstrations in 1968 and 1969; its inability to contain rioting in August 1969 led to direct British intervention. The 1969 Hunt Commission recommended that the RUC should be restructured, modernized, and disarmed, with the "B" Specials replaced by the Ulster Defence Regiment (UDR). The UDR inherited the "B" Specials' reputation as a semiprofessionalized Protestant defense force; some UDR members were implicated in loyalist paramilitarism. (The UDR merged with the Royal Irish Regiment in 1992.)

The Troubles precluded disarmament; "Ulsterization" of security policy beginning in the mid-1970s placed the RUC on the frontline. It was professionalized and trebled in size, and it suffered an increasing proportion of security-force casualties. (303 RUC officers were killed; many were severely injured or traumatized.) The RUC remained predominantly Protestant (republican paramilitaries targeted Catholic members). Controversy surrounded its interrogation techniques and the role of double agents who were sometimes accused of becoming agent provocateurs or licensed murderers within paramilitary organizations. However, the RUC arrested and secured the convictions of numerous loyalists as well as republicans.

The Patten Commission, established under the 1998 Belfast Agreement, recommended a reformed police force whose name and emblems would be neutral between communities On 4 November 2001 the RUC became the Police Service of Northern Ireland. Republicans complained that the old culture of the RUC persisted; unionists protested that the changes retrospectively dishonored the RUC, and that the loss of experienced officers compromised policing. The history of the RUC illustrates the difficulties of policing a deeply divided society.

SEE ALSO Special Powers Act; **Primary Documents:** The Belfast/Good Friday Agreement (10 April 1998)

Bibliography

Farrell, Michael. *Arming the Protestant: The Formation of the Ulster Special Constabulary and the Royal Ulster Constabulary, 1920–27.* 1983.

Follis, Bryan. *A State under Siege: The Establishment of Northern Ireland, 1920–25.* 1985.

Ryder, Chris. *The RUC, 1922–1997: A Force under Fire.* 1989. Rev. edition, 1997.

Patrick Maume

Rural Industry

Until the introduction of cotton in the late eighteenth century, wool and linen were the raw materials from which cloth was woven in Ireland. For more than a century, skilled craftsmen were concentrated in Dublin and the country towns under the patronage of local landowners, but in the countryside many people prepared the raw materials, spun yarn, wove coarse cloths, and sold them in local fairs to supplement their family incomes. The woollen industry in its long history in the south of the country from Kilkenny to Waterford and Bandon had developed cloths to suit local markets, but the success of the linen industry in Ulster was due to increasing demand from England and its colonies.

The ready supply of flax, a traditional crop in Ireland, was exploited by immigrants from Britain during the plantation of Ulster in the seventeenth century. Several landlords encouraged their tenants to spin and weave linen in their cottages and assisted in marketing the products. Some merchants carried their linen to market in Dublin, and its improving quality attracted attention even in London. The King's and Queen's Corporation for the Linen Manufacture in England, incorporated in 1690, promoted a subsidiary company in Ireland in 1692. An employee, George Stead of Lisburn, informed the Board of Trade and Plantations in 1697 that there were then from 500 to 1,000 looms working commercially in the counties of Down, Antrim, Armagh, Tyrone, and Londonderry. To promote the industry in Ireland, the London government encouraged a Huguenot, Louis Crommelin, to establish a colony in Lisburn in 1698 and made him Overseer of the Royal Linen Manufacture. Because his project had limited success, however, the Dublin parliament in 1711 set up the Board of Trustees of the Linen and Hempen Manufactures to regulate and supervise the development of the industry. Especially in its early years it played an important role by developing contacts in London and by employing craftsmen to copy not only patterns and qualities of European cloths then fashionable in London, but also techniques for bleaching and finishing the linen webs. In 1728 the trustees established a White Linen Hall in Dublin to accommodate the commerce in linens with visiting English merchants.

By 1730 Ulster linen was competing successfully with continental linens on the London market. In that decade it strengthened its grip further by reducing the cost of bleaching when its bleachers adapted for linen the processes used in the tuck mills for finishing woollen cloths. Water power was harnessed to drive the wash-

The weaving of linen on the type of handloom typically found in the weaver's own cottage. Detail from an engraving by William Hincks, c. 1783. PHOTOGRAPH COURTESY OF DAVID W. MILLER.

mills, rubbing-boards, and beetling engines in their bleachmills. The temperate climate of eastern Ulster provided lakes and rivers in the hills with a regular supply of water during the summer bleaching season as well as power to drive scutch mills every autumn for separating the fiber from the woody sheath of the flax plant. The bleachers were entrepreneurs, quick to adopt chemicals for bleaching by importing sulphuric acid (oil of vitriol) and barilla ash. Fierce competition led them to slash the bleaching time, increase the throughput of webs, and cut their overheads to reduce the cost of bleaching, and smaller concerns were forced out of business.

With growing confidence the bleachers began to take over the direction of the industry. In Ulster the marketing of domestically manufactured linens had grafted itself onto the traditional pattern of markets and fairs. A 1719 act had stipulated that all linen cloth and yarn had to be sold publicly in open markets or at lawful fairs, and had appointed lappers to inspect the finished linen cloths and stamp them as a guarantee of their quality. For several decades, however, the enforcement of these laws was opposed by the weavers, who viewed it as a plot to enslave them, until in 1764 Parliament passed a fresh act for the regulation of the trade. The Linen Board appointed sealmasters to inspect and

Women spinning, boiling, and reeling linen yarn in the home, County Down. Engraving by William Hincks, c. 1783. PHOTOGRAPH COURTESY OF DAVID W. MILLER.

stamp the brown (unbleached) linens brought in by the weavers before the commencement of each market. Although these brown sealmasters were selected from among the weavers themselves, individuals were liable to summary dismissal for failing to enforce the act. The bleachers appreciated this measure of quality control because it enabled them to send their linendrapers on circuit through the weekly markets in the provincial towns to purchase the variety of linen webs required for the English and American markets. In 1782 they asserted themselves by rejecting new regulations introduced by the board. This independence they consolidated by opening two new white-linen halls, in Belfast and Newry.

Great quantities of both linen and wool were spun by country people to supplement the incomes of their families. On the periphery of the Ulster linen-weaving counties were regions where women spun linen yarn. Men known as "grey yarn jobbers" carried some of it to the weaving districts in east Ulster, but much was ex-

ported either from the east coast through Dublin and Drogheda or from the north coast through Londonderry, which itself sent more than 10,000 hundredweights per annum in the 1760s to Lancashire. This same decade saw exports of woollen yarn for the English market from Cork and west Leinster peak at 150,000 stones per annum. Afterward, exports of worsted yarn from Ireland declined rapidly as its price rose. Nevertheless, during the 1760s as many as 60,000 women may have been employed by the southern clothiers in spinning wool for the market.

Both the linen and woollen industries were affected after 1770 by the rapid growth of the cotton industry, which was more profitable than either of them. Since the newer industry relied on imports of cotton wool into Dublin, Cork, and Belfast, cotton-spinning mills were built there and the yarn put out to weavers. Key individuals in the Cork wool-spinning trade moved into the cotton industry, which itself failed to grow after the 1820s. By contrast, the survival of the Ulster linen industry was due to the skill of rural weavers in weaving fine-quality linens, notably damasks and cambrics, and to the business skills of the bleachers, who continued to dominate the industry.

SEE ALSO Brewing and Distilling; Factory-Based Textile Manufacture; Industrialization; Markets and Fairs in the Eighteenth and Nineteenth Centuries; Transport—Road, Canal, Rail; Women and Children in the Industrial Workforce

Bibliography

Clarkson, Leslie A. "The Carrick-on-Suir Woollen Industry in the Eighteenth Century." *Irish Economic and Social History* 16 (1989): 23–41.

Crawford, William H. "The Evolution of the Linen Trade before Industrialisation." *Irish Economic and Social History* 15 (1988): 32–53.

Crawford, William H. *The Handloom Weavers and the Ulster Linen Industry.* 1994.

Dickson, David J. "Aspects of the Rise and Decline of the Irish Cotton Industry." In *Comparative aspects of Scottish and Irish Economic and Social History, 1600–1900,* edited by Louis M. Cullen and T. Christopher Smout. 1977.

William H. Crawford

Rural Life

| 1690 TO 1845 | W. A. MAGUIRE |
| 1850 TO 1921 | DAVID FITZPATRICK |

1690 TO 1845

Throughout the period 1690 to 1845 Ireland was predominantly rural. Though towns expanded or developed to meet the needs of what was a rapidly growing population and greater trade, since at least the mid-eighteenth century the great majority of Irish people continued to live and work in the countryside rather than in urban areas. In 1725 only about one-eighth of Ireland's total population of two million or so lived in the eight largest towns. Apart from Dublin and Cork most of these urban centers were small places. The smallest, Lisburn in County Antrim, had fewer than eight hundred houses (Cullen 1972). At that time much of Ireland's industrial activity was, in any case, rurally located, being concerned with processing agricultural products.

The problems created by prolonged population growth fell much more heavily on certain areas of the country than on others, and more on some classes of the rural population than on others. The traditional view of eighteenth-century Ireland is of a chronically depressed society, but as L. M. Cullen has shown, the wealth of the country as a whole—to judge by the value of its trade—increased considerably while other parts of Europe were as unfortunate, or more so, in the bad years that threatened all agricultural societies. "Bad harvests," he writes, "feature disproportionately in contemporary literature. Better harvests in the intervening years were often taken for granted"; and the particularly bad 1720s were "a period of prolonged agricultural depression everywhere . . . . Ireland's circumstances were not exceptional" (Cullen, Davis Lecture 1968, p. 11). When famines occurred—as in the periods 1728 to 1729 and 1740 to 1741—they did so when food was in short supply everywhere in Europe. The famine of 1740 to 1741, largely forgotten but proportionately as severe in its effects as the Great Famine of the late ·1840s, caused the deaths of somewhere between 310,000 and 480,000 people (Dickson 1997). Even the lower death toll estimate is higher than that of the Great Famine, and the deaths occurred in a much shorter time.

Rural society was complex, with many gradations at every level. At the very bottom of the heap were laborers with no access to land. Some of them were employed as live-in servants on a pittance wage but at least with the security of bed and board. Others, called cottiers, were employed by the farmers when needed, paying the rent of their small potato gardens in labor rather than in cash. Worst off of all were those forced to rent each season, for cash, plots of potato ground called "conacre." Such laborers got whatever work and wages they could find by migrating seasonally to different parts of the country. By 1830 only one-third of the laboring poor could find steady employment (Cullen 1968).

Above the laborers were tenant farmers of various degrees. Most were smallholders living at subsistence level. On the eve of the Great Famine, the Devon commission report (1845) revealed, nearly one-quarter of all holdings consisted of a mere five acres or fewer. Another quarter were between five and ten acres; a similar proportion were ten to twenty. Farms of fifty acres or more, most of which were in the province of Leinster, accounted for less than 10 percent of the total of all holdings (Donnelly 2001).

Above the farmer class were gentry. Sir Jonah Barrington, who came from the top layer, famously identified three categories of gentry, in ascending order of gentility: "half-mounted gentlemen," "gentlemen every

Cottiers and laborers occupied the meanest houses in Ireland. In most of the west before the Great Famine, half or more of all houses were cramped one-room cabins, like that of the Kerry cottier shown here in 1846. In the clearances of the famine years these huts were generally unroofed or demolished altogether. FROM ILLUSTRATED LONDON NEWS, 10 JANUARY 1846.

inch of them," and "gentlemen to the backbone" (Staples 1968, p. 31). From such people came most of the "middlemen"—holders of long leaseholds who typically lived on the profits from subletting their estates. Their numbers were declining well before the Great Famine, however.

The top of the pyramid of rural society was occupied by a small number of aristocrats and wealthy commoners, owners of freehold estates, who were leaders in county affairs and dispensers of patronage. Contrary to the popular view at the time and later, most of the major absentees were careful to maintain and cultivate their Irish "interests" and to keep an eye on their resident agents. The vast amount of estate correspondence generated by such men as the eighth earl of Abercorn shows that absenteeism did not necessarily mean neglect or oppression.

From the end of the seventeenth century through to the middle of the nineteenth century and even later,

most Irish people lived in a countryside that has been aptly described as "a multitude of rural islands, each dominated by its Big House" (MacDonagh, p. xxx). A Big House was not necessarily a grand one, but some were, for the eighteenth century was the golden age of country houses in the classical style, from Castletown in County Kildare (begun in 1722) to Castle Coole in Fermanagh (started in 1793). Most so-called Big Houses were more modest in size and architectural ambition, however, with the gentry who owned them often acting as their own architects.

By contrast, housing conditions for the rural poor deteriorated as population continued to increase (though at a slower rate after 1815), as domestic industry declined, and as poverty in consequence became more widespread. The 1841 census figures show that on the eve of the Great Famine 40 percent of houses in Ireland (in some areas up to 75 percent) were one-room mud cabins without windows. The next class of dwelling, of two to four rooms with windows, accounted for another 37 percent. The furniture in these hovels was sparse, if any. One parish in County Donegal had only 10 beds, 93 chairs, and 243 stools among its 9,000 inhabitants (Cullen 1968).

More ominous still than the increasing impoverishment of the rural population was its growing dependence on a more or less exclusive diet of potatoes. But the assumption that this dependence was a fact even before 1800 is wrong. For most of the eighteenth century the potato, though widely cultivated everywhere, was not the only food: Even the poor ate oat bread in the months between potato crops (Cullen 1972). The reliance of the poorest classes on the potato increased as the population went on rising, however, to the point where a male laborer on average consumed twelve to fourteen pounds of potatoes a day and little else (Donnelly 2001). Fortunately, such a diet, if supplemented by milk, was remarkably nutritious. Recent research (based on military and convict records) shows that during the period 1770 to 1845 potato-eating Irishmen were on average taller than Englishmen, and concludes that they may have been healthier and better fed (Mokyr and Ó Gráda 1989, 1990; Ó Gráda 1991). This confirms the impressions reported by many visitors to Ireland at the time. But over-dependence by so many people on a single source of food, however good, would eventually prove fatal.

Lastly, two cultural changes affecting rural society are worth noting. The first was the growing presence and prestige of the Catholic Church, evident in the doubling of the number of parish priests between 1800 and 1845 (Cullen 1968) and in the part played by many clergy in O'Connell's campaign for emancipation. The second change was a marked decline in the use of the Irish language, from about 50 percent of the population in 1800 to about half that figure in 1851. By then, only 5 percent spoke no English (Cullen 1968).

SEE ALSO Agriculture: 1690 to 1845; Family: Marriage Patterns and Family Life from 1690 to 1921; Great Famine; Land Questions; Migration: Emigration from the Seventeenth Century to 1845; Migration: Seasonal Migration; Population, Economy, and Society from 1750 to 1950; Population Explosion; Potato and Potato Blight (*Phytophthora infestans*); Subdivision and Subletting of Holdings; **Primary Documents:** On Irish Rural Society and Poverty (1780); On Rural Society on the Eve of the Great Famine (1844–1845); From *Narrative of a Recent Journey* (1847)

Bibliography

Crawford, W. H. *The Management of a Major Ulster Estate in the Late Eighteenth Century: The Eighth Earl of Abercorn and his Irish Agents.* 2001.

Cullen, L. M. "The Irish Economy in the Eighteenth Century." In *The Formation of the Irish Economy*, edited by L. M. Cullen. 1968.

Cullen, L. M. *Life in Ireland.* 1968.

Cullen, L. M. *An Economic History of Ireland since 1660.* 1972.

Cullen, L. M. *The Emergence of Modern Ireland.* 1998.

Dickson, David. *Arctic Ireland.* 1997.

Donnelly, James S., Jr. *The Great Irish Potato Famine.* 2001.

MacDonagh, Oliver. *The Nineteenth-Century Novel and Social History.* 1970.

Mokyr, Joel, and Cormac Ó Gráda. "The Height of Irishmen and Englishmen in the 1770's: Some Evidence from the East India Company Army Records." *Eighteenth-Century Ireland/Iris an dá chultúr* 4 (1989): 83–92.

Mokyr, Joel, and Cormac Ó Gráda. "The Heights of the Irish and the British during the Napoleonic Wars: Evidence from the East India Company Army." In *UCD Centre for Economic Research Working Paper.* 1990.

Ó Gráda, Cormac. "The Heights of Clonmel Prisoners, 1845–49: Some Dietary Implications." *Irish Economic and Social History* 18 (1991): 24–33.

Ó Gráda, Cormac. *Ireland: A New Economic History, 1780–1939.* 1999.

Staples, Hugh B., ed. *The Ireland of Sir Jonah Barrington.* 1968.

W. A. Maguire

1850 TO 1921

Between 1851 and 1911 the urban proportion of Ireland's ever-declining population doubled. Even so, on the eve of World War I, only one-third of the people lived in towns with more than two thousand inhabitants. Despite rapid urbanization in the Belfast region, Ulster was still predominantly rural, though less so than Munster or especially Connacht. Even in Leinster the urban population was only 47 percent in 1911. Farming still accounted for the majority of occupied men, though the proportion had fallen from two-thirds in 1951 to 55 percent in 1911. Though not immune to the urban drift transforming Britain, western Europe, the United States, and Australasia, the Irish economy had retained its rural character to a remarkable degree. This anomaly was a by-product of massive emigration, which had enabled up to half of each generation to urbanize itself overseas rather than at home.

The character of rural life in postfamine Ireland was likewise shaped by emigration, which enabled the remaining labor force to exploit the land more efficiently. As the population shrank, the mean size of farms gradually grew, despite the persistent problem of "conges-

The Land Act of 1870 aimed to increase tenants' security by encouraging the granting of leases. Landlords issued thousands of new leases after 1870, but under many of them tenants were denied legal rights. The backlash came during the land war, as when in 1881 the Duke of Leinster's leases were contemptuously burned at a Land League meeting in Kildare town. FROM ILLUSTRATED LONDON NEWS, 8 JANUARY 1881.

tion" in Connacht and along the western seaboard. The continuous shift from tillage to pasturage raised profits and output per capita, but reduced the demand for labor. This factor, along with significant if unspectacular technological breakthroughs (such as the displacement of sickles by scythes), fundamentally altered the rural class structure. Paid laborers, already depleted by the Great Famine, lost out to farmers and their unpaid family assistants as agriculture became less labor-intensive. By 1912, 70 percent of the agricultural workforce was made up of family members, while less than two-thirds of paid workers were permanently employed. Though real earnings rose for those laborers who remained, the laboring class disintegrated. Even female service declined, except for the widespread practice of young girls spending a year or so on a neighboring farm before emigration or marriage. The concentration of farming into small family-based units, with low labor costs, was most marked in Connacht and least prevalent in Leinster. Yet throughout Ireland the pattern of prewar agriculture bore little resemblance to

rural Britain, where farming was increasingly conducted by large landowners with substantial workforces.

Rural class structure lost much of its top as well as its bottom layer during the later nineteenth century. Tenant agitation, legislation, and economic setbacks accomplished what the Great Famine had failed to achieve, the emasculation of the landlord class. Though retaining their home farms and leaseholds, most landlords had begun to sell tenanted farms to the occupiers before 1914. Fairly generous state compensation ensured that such landlords were not pauperized, and many gentry continued to live beyond their means through reliance on bonuses and easy credit, facilitating their subsequent ruin in the aftermath of World War I and civil conflict.

For the mass of small farmers and their families, the half century after the famine was a period of cultural retrieval, whereby they salvaged much of the supposedly archaic style of life which the famine (according to the providential interpretation) should have destroyed. In much of rural Ireland the potato, far from being discredited, remained the major staple of diet, along with buttermilk and "kitchen" in the form of salted herring. Meat was seldom eaten except at festivals, even in rural Ulster where oats still reigned supreme. The enduring preference for potatoes reflected justified faith in their nutritional value as well as taste, and prevailed despite the fact that unblighted potatoes were now much more expensive to grow or buy. By the late nineteenth century imported foods and home-produced meats were more widely disseminated, yet the rural diet remained astonishingly simple and healthy.

This helps to account for the exceptionally low level of rural mortality, by comparison with urban Britain and America as well as urban Ireland. Statistics based on the frequency of deaths registered after 1864, though somewhat unreliable, suggest a gradual but steady decline up to the World War I. This decline, marked among infants, reflected the reduced incidence of many infectious diseases despite the alarming spread of tuberculosis. There was little variation in welfare between men and women, mortality being lowest paradoxically in the poorest counties of Connacht. Income is indeed inadequate as an index of human well-being.

Residential conditions gradually improved, as slate and stone or brick displaced thatch and mud. The greatest advance in housing benefited the few remaining regular laborers, many of whom were able from the 1880s onwards to rent excellent cottages subsidized by the state and local authorities. Farmers, whose houses were often older, less comfortable, and less up-to-date, resented both the extra rate-burden and the novel prestige secured by the humble laborer. Even so, in most of rural Ireland farmers lived in adequate if simple dwellings with two or three rooms, a chimney, and an expanding stock of furniture and delft. The pig-infested hovels celebrated in *Punch* had virtually disappeared. Whereas a growing proportion of city-dwellers lived in cramped and unsanitary tenements, the quality of rural vernacular housing was improving.

Intrinsic to human happiness and therefore to welfare is the support available from family and neighbors. By the mid-twentieth century, rural Ireland seemed to many of its surviving inhabitants, isolated by widespread "celibacy" (nonmarriage) and inexorable emigration, a lonely and abandoned terrain. Before 1914, however, Irish families continued to reproduce themselves quite efficiently, with remarkably high levels of fertility within marriage, and moderate though increasing celibacy. Illegitimate births remained unusual and the negotiated property "match" was still the normal form of marriage, though "shotgun" alliances were tolerated on the principle that it was better to marry than to burn. In 1911, when median completed family size in Britain and Australia was down to about two children, seven offspring remained typical in rural Ireland. These large families, made practicable by the prospect of emigration, provided a reserve of unpaid labor and, more importantly, of personal sustenance. Women, though ever more excluded from the paid labor force, derived enhanced influence and often satisfaction from their control of the expanding household economy. Mutual support among relatives and neighbors compensated for low income and deprivation of career options for those staying at home.

Between 1914 and 1920 rural Ireland experienced unexampled prosperity as a consequence of the European war. Irish farmers, hitherto struggling to compete with European and North American food imports in the British market, relished their comparative advantage as long-distance merchant shipping was curtailed. During the boom, which ended only in late 1920, farmers gained more than their laborers. Yet increased demand for tillage, along with state controls over food prices and farm wages, generated a minor revival of paid agricultural labor. The decline of the gentry, accelerated by wartime enlistment and losses, was crowned by land seizures, arson, and sometimes murderous attacks by acquisitive neighbors.

Since the late nineteenth century, state intervention had benefited rural welfare through housing subsidies, the work of the Congested Districts Board, and technical innovations fostered by the Department of Agriculture. Desperate to augment human capital and consolidate the home front, wartime governments proved even more energetic in fostering welfare. In a successful effort to reduce infant mortality, midwifery was professionalized, advice centers opened, and free milk supplied to schools. As the world economy slid towards recession, and as Ireland slipped into revolution, the impulse for reform faltered. Yet rural Ireland was a far richer, healthier, and more comfortable environment in 1921 than seventy years earlier. Remarkably, modernization had been achieved without sacrificing the simple yet satisfying ways of living that the survivors of famine had conspired so ingeniously to perpetuate.

SEE ALSO Agriculture: 1845 to 1921; American Wakes; Congested Districts Board; Family: Marriage Patterns and Family Life from 1690 to 1921; Great Famine; Indian Corn or Maize; Migration: Emigration from 1850 to 1960; Migration: Seasonal Migration; Plunkett, Sir Horace Curzon; Population, Economy, and Society from 1750 to 1950; Potato and Potato Blight (*Phytophthora infestans*); **Primary Documents:** From *Narrative of a Recent Journey* (1847)

Bibliography

Bourke, Joanna. *Husbandry to Housewifery: Women, Economic Change, and Housework in Ireland, 1890–1914*. 1993.

Guinnane, Timothy W. *The Vanishing Irish: Households, Migration, and the Rural Economy in Ireland, 1850–1914*. 1997.

Kennedy, Líam, et al. *Mapping the Great Irish Famine*. 1999.

Kennedy, Robert E., Jr. *The Irish: Emigration, Marriage, and Fertility*. 1973.

Ó Gráda, Cormac. *Ireland before and after the Famine*. 1988.

Ó Gráda, Cormac. *Ireland: A New Economic History, 1780–1939*. 1994.

David Fitzpatrick

~

Rural Settlement and Field Systems

Rural settlement and field systems refer to the arrangements of farmsteads and their associated landholdings. Although the geographical and economic contexts of rural landscapes in Ireland have been substantially modified in the decades since World War II, earlier cultural and historical processes have been fundamental in shaping the template of rural settlement.

Rural settlement in Ireland at present is predominantly one of dispersal of houses across the face of the countryside. There are also limited examples of a variety of nucleated settlements in parts of the country. In restricted coastal districts of the west of Ireland and in isolated parts of mountainous regions elsewhere (in Tyrone, Louth, and Wicklow), there are remnants of house clusters of late origin; some localities in south Leinster have farm clusters of a different origin. Throughout rural Ireland there are also chapel villages, which are informal nucleations of school, shop, public house, and post office around Catholic churches. Finally, there are small, more formally planned villages that are often legacies of a local landed estate.

This legacy of rural settlement has been modified in the twentieth century by the Irish planning system, which has an important function in conserving or expanding the inherited settlement pattern. In many ways the dispersed pattern of settlement has resulted in local demand for further building in the countryside, and many pressured countrysides, especially around towns and cities, are characterized by ribbon development along the road network.

Through all these changes, however, the texture and scale of the rural settlement pattern reflect its evolution over time. Although the single isolated farm was a characteristic form of settlement in early historic Ireland, where the rath or ringfort predominated, modern settlement patterns largely originated in the eighteenth and nineteenth centuries, when distances were short and communities were largely self-sufficient. Houses were sited in the midst of their farmland. Settlement growth was usually organic, reflecting the processes of farm fragmentation. The operation of the estate system locally may have been important in influencing the nature of settlement dispersal. The clustering of laborers' houses on some estates frequently accompanied dispersed large farmsteads, and although huge sections of the landless population emigrated in the nineteenth century, county-council cottage schemes in the east mirror these settlements in the early twenty-first century. In large parts of the west and many more marginal areas, where the controlling hand of the estates was largely absent (like the landlord himself), local clustered settlements grew up haphazardly in response to adverse environmental conditions. Many of these clusters (or *clachans*) grew out of one or two original houses, with land being fragmented and subdivided among offspring, until clusters of thirty or forty cabins resulted, with a few surnames predominating. Most of these experienced attrition in the postfamine years, and only in places like Achill (in Mayo) or Gweedore (in Donegal), can residual features of this historical pattern be seen. In some regions of Norman colonization, especially in south Leinster and east Munster, older farm villages developed from manorial times, many of which were abandoned in the later medieval period or were dispersed during eighteenth-century improvements.

Rural settlement was closely connected with various methods of managing the farm holdings that were associated with the settlement. The basic ingredient of patchwork and hedged fields in the modern Irish countryside is largely a product of local tenant initiative as well as of landlord commitment to the modernization of agriculture from the eighteenth century. Enclosure of the land with farmhouses located centrally in their fields became the hallmark of improvement. Field size, ranging from miniscule plots of stone wall–enclosed gardens in Connemara to extensive enclosures of twenty or thirty acres with drainage ditches in parts of Leinster, reflects the historical impact of the local agricultural economy and estate management, as well as the consequences of local demographic expansion or contraction. Commercial tillage, dairying, and cattle grazing all required varying arrangements of fields and farmhouses. Areas of rapid population expansion in the prefamine period also resulted in fragmentation of farms and fields, and periods of continuous emigration subsequently resulted in consolidation or abandonment of settlement landscapes.

This essentially modern individualized field system succeeded earlier systems that accompanied premodern settlement structures. As in much of Europe, open-field systems were most prevalent before the eighteenth century, when the land lay largely unenclosed, with each farmer's portion held in scattered intermingled plots, usually separated by low baulks. In the richer eastern portions of the island, where the manorial system flourished, the open fields resembled those of Europe, with the strips of land belonging to the village farmers lying in two or more extensive "fields," each cultivated with the same crop on an agreed cycle. Subsequently, piecemeal enclosure of these open fields occurred, so that in some parts of the Pale the long, narrow medieval strips were fossilized as modern hedged enclosures. In general however, from the eighteenth century wholesale land reform saw the obliteration of the open fields and their nucleated villages.

The other form of open field in Ireland was associated with the nineteenth-century farm clusters on more marginal landscapes—clusters that developed as late responses to population growth in these poorer places. These small peasant communities worked their surrounding open fields on a simple "infield" and "outfield" system, called the rundale system. The most productive land close to the village was the infield, in which scattered small plots of the farmers were worked communally. The outfield farther out was cultivated occasionally but more frequently as population expanded. Plots consisted of ridges termed *lazy beds* (because of the simple way in which they were made) separated by small boundary markers. Both areas were symbiotically linked with extensive commonage, frequently sur-rounding moorland or mountain, which was often used for summer pasturing of animals in a transhumance system known in parts of the country as *booleying* (from *bó* for cow). A farm cluster at Rathlackan in County Mayo in the early twentieth century had fifty-six families whose land was scattered in 1,500 small fragments. These rundale field systems were generally remodeled in the postfamine decades either by landlords who wished to reform their estates on more efficient lines or by the state's Congested Districts Board. In all cases the small, scattered plots of land were consolidated into modern fields enclosed by a hedge or stone wall to make up contiguous fields, which were then allocated to individual farmers relocated in houses strung out along new roads. This process frequently accompanied the granting of outright ownership of the farms to the farmers under the Land Acts and represented a revolution in the Irish rural landscape.

SEE ALSO Bogs and Drainage; Clachans; Estates and Demesnes; Landscape and Settlement; Raths

Bibliography

Aalen, Frederick H. A., and Kevin Whelan. "Fields." In *Atlas of the Irish Rural Landscape*, edited by Frederick H. A. Aalen, Kevin Whelan, and Mathew Stout. 1997.

Duffy, Patrick J. "Trends in Nineteenth- and Twentieth-Century Settlement." In *A History of Settlement in Ireland*, edited by Terry Barry. 2000.

Evans, Estyn. *Irish Folk Ways*. 1957.

Whelan, Kevin. "Towns and Villages." In *Atlas of the Irish Rural Landscape*, edited by Frederick H. A. Aalen, Kevin Whelan, and Mathew Stout. 1997.

Patrick J. Duffy

S

Saint Patrick, Problem of

Two documents written by this fifth-century British-born missionary to Ireland survive. One is a letter to the British chieftain named Coroticus concerning a raid by his henchmen who had seized some Irish Christians. The other, known as the *Confessio*, is a self-defense of Patrick's own missionary career, apparently submitted to an ecclesiastical body of some kind conducting a disciplinary review or formal inquiry. Most of what is known about the man comes from these two pieces. The evolving legend of the saint is reflected in a series of medieval lives and stories about him, the earliest of those extant dating to the late seventh century.

Patrick is presumed to have lived and worked in Ireland from the middle to the latter part of the fifth century, though some scholars have argued for both earlier and later dates. The continental chronicle of Prosper of Aquitaine in the year 431 reports that Pope Celestine had ordained Palladius as the first bishop to the Irish. According to the Irish hagiographical tradition, Palladius failed in his mission and was succeeded by Patrick, but we have no independent contemporary confirmation of the claim.

In the *Confessio*, Patrick provides a brief sketch of his own life in the course of describing his personal spiritual evolution. He was born to a prosperous Romano-British Christian family of some local prominence. When he was sixteen, Patrick was seized by raiders and sold as a slave in Ireland, where he experienced an intense spiritual conversion. He was able to escape and return to his family, but some time later (how much later Patrick does not say) he returned to Ireland in obedience to a divine summons received in a dream vividly described in the *Confessio*.

It is not known what official ecclesiastical backing Patrick had for his mission to Ireland. He refers to his ordination as a bishop but does not say where or by whom he was made one, nor does he name associates in his mission. The persons to whom the *Confessio* is addressed are never named. What does emerge very clearly from the *Confessio* is Patrick's own conviction that the authority for his ministry in Ireland was divine in origin and therefore not subject to question because of his own personal failings. The letter to Coroticus adds little information about Patrick himself, but it attests to the hardships of his mission and the perilous environment for his converts. In both documents Patrick shows a particular concern for the women among them, respecting their courage and the strength of their faith, and fearing for them.

The two earliest surviving lives of the saint were composed in Ireland in the late seventh century, nearly two hundred years after Patrick's time. Most scholars consider the career of the saint presented in these early lives as an amalgam drawn from the careers of Patrick, the shadowy Palladius mentioned by Prosper, and perhaps other members of their missions. Both accounts are also highly colored by the political environment of their authors' own time, in which the ecclesiastical community at Armagh was vigorously asserting itself as the seat of the saint's cult and therefore as leader of the Christian church in Ireland. This claim was more explicitly and stridently asserted in the anonymous work called the *Tripartite Life*, which was probably composed in the tenth century at Armagh and certainly reflects the views of the community's members. This life seeks to establish Patrick as the apostle to all of Ireland and, by doing so, make Armagh the administrative head of all of its ecclesiastical institutions, despite Ireland's political fragmentation. All these early lives were composed in Ireland for an Irish audience and depict the saint as a

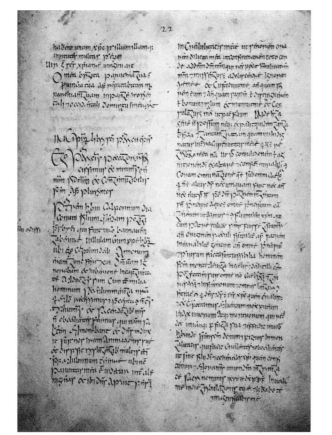

The beginning of St. Patrick's Confessio *from the* Book of Armagh, *created by the scribe Ferdomnach for the Abbot Torbach (early ninth century).* THE BOARD OF TRINITY COLLEGE DUBLIN. REPRODUCED BY PERMISSION.

powerful miracle worker whose deeds serve political ends as often as spiritual ones. In these lives Patrick blesses kings and dynasties, or curses their opponents, as often as he cures the sick and helps the poor.

The medieval lives of Patrick from the English and continental tradition are in marked contrast to the earlier Irish ones. They use the Irish tradition but are more in conformity with continental hagiography: The topographical and political details are reduced, and the intimidating ferocity of the Irish saint is tempered with a more decorous Christian humility. This trend was greatly advanced in the late twelfth century, after the Norman conquest of Ireland, when the professional hagiographer Jocelyn of Furness was commissioned by John de Courcy in 1185 to write a life of Patrick. It was this life that was widely circulated and eventually selected by the Catholic religious order known as the Bollandists for their great collection of saints' lives, the *Acta Sanctorum*. Another highly influential text of the late twelfth century was the *Tractatus de Purgatorio Sancti Patricii* (Tract on Saint Patrick's purgatory) written by

a Cistercian monk at Saltrey. Although this tract was a literary vision of hell, not a life of the saint, its popularity helped to spread the reputation of the saint and his cult outside of Ireland.

SEE ALSO Hagiography; Hiberno-Latin Culture; Latin and Old Irish Literacy; Religion: The Coming of Christianity; **Primary Documents:** *Confessio* (Declaration) (c. 450); From Muirchú's *Life of St. Patrick* (c. 680)

Bibliography

Hanson, Richard Patrick Crosland. *The Life and Writings of the Historical Saint Patrick*. 1983.

Ó Cróinín, Dábhí. *Early Medieval Ireland, 400–1200*. 1995.

Picard, Jean-Michael, trans. *Saint Patrick's Purgatory: A Twelfth-Century Tale of a Journey to the Other World*. Introduction by Yolande de Pontfarcy. 1985.

Dorothy Africa

Sarsfield, Patrick

Patrick Sarsfield (1655?–1693) was born, probably in 1655, into a prominent old English Catholic family, whose estates in counties Dublin and Kildare had been confiscated in the Cromwellian settlement (though partly restored in Charles II's reign). Nothing is known of his early life. A second son, in 1675 he went soldiering. Debarred by his Roman Catholicism from being an officer in England, he served with the duke of Monmouth's regiment of foot in France until the recall of British regiments. The London to which he came in 1678 was about to be engulfed in the anti-Catholic hysteria of the "popish plot," and he found himself unemployable as an army officer. His time in London gave him a reputation for duelling and womanizing, but after a visit to Ireland in 1681 he returned to London with the prospect of income from the Sarsfield estate at Lucan, Co. Kildare, which he eventually inherited in 1683.

With the accession of the Catholic James II in 1685, it was again possible for Sarsfield to serve in the army, and opportunity was provided by Monmouth's rebellion against James in the English west country. At the battle of Sedgefield, Sarsfield suffered severe wounds and gained a reputation for loyalty and daring which James II rewarded with promotion and trust. In 1688 he was given command of Irish troops in England. Shortly after the king fled London in December 1688, Sarsfield joined him in France. Back in Ireland in 1689, he was promoted to brigadier and given command of a cavalry regiment. In August he failed to prevent the rout of Jacobites at Enniskillen, though he did take Sligo in October and helped to hold much of Connacht for James II. Some time during the winter of 1689 to 1690 he found time to marry Lord Clanricarde's fifteen-year-old daughter, Honora Burke. Promoted to major-general, he did not see much action at the battle of the Boyne and subsequently escorted the defeated James II to Dublin. His posthumous reputation is built on his successful surprise attack at Ballyneety on a Williamite siege train en route to Limerick (August 1690). This success prevented the Williamites' first siege of Limerick from turning into a full-scale attack. It also provided an important boost for Jacobite morale, thereby strengthening the hand of the antipeace party among the Jacobites, of whom Sarsfield was the most prominent. Created earl of Lucan early in 1691, he commanded the reserve forces at the battle of Aughrim (July 1691), after which he withdrew to Limerick. Not long after Tyrconnell's sudden death in August, Sarsfield too concluded that it was necessary to sue for peace. He was both a negotiator and a signatory of the Articles of Limerick (3 October 1691). The military articles were a considerable achievement, allowing him to take to France as many of his troops as were prepared to travel. Appointed a marshal in the French army, he fought creditably at the battle of Steenkirk in 1692, but he died the next year in early August from wounds received at the battle of Landen. His name and his deeds, particularly at Ballyneety, were later immortalized by Jacobite sympathizers and nineteenth-century nationalists. His role in the Williamite War achieved a posthumous significance that might have surprised his contemporaries.

SEE ALSO Jacobites and the Williamite Wars

Bibliography

Irwin, Liam. "Sarsfield: The Man and the Myth." In *The Last of the Great Wars,*" edited by Bernadette Whelan. 1995.

Wauchope, Piers. *Patrick Sarsfield and the Williamite War.* 1992.

James McGuire

~

Sculpture, Early and Medieval

The eighth-century Kilnasaggart pillar in County Armagh is probably the earliest stone sculpture in Ireland datable by inscription, though the country, of course, preserves much older decorated stones from as far back as the Neolithic period around 3000 B.C.E. But the crosses inscribed on the Kilnasaggart stone were presumably preceded by other similar Christian symbols on slightly earlier slabs (many doubtless grave markers), which continued to be produced with multiple variations until at least the twelfth century at sites like Clonmacnoise, Co. Offaly. Human figures in relief on upright monuments may not have appeared until the eighth century at the earliest, as on the pedimented stele with Pictish affinities at Fahan, Co. Donegal, while illustrations of the Crucifixion on island slabs at Inishkea North and Duvillaun More off the west coast of Mayo, and representations of pilgrims(?) at Killadeas, Co. Fermanagh, and Ballyvourney, Co. Cork, may well be somewhat later. Pilgrimage, indeed, could have been indirectly responsible in some way for the creation of two pillars carved in stylized fashion on all four sides at Carndonagh, Co. Donegal, and the unique high-relief figures with a variety of attributes on White Island, Fermanagh (not far from the twin-headed Boa Island statue, which may well be a Christian rather than a pagan monument).

The dawn of the ninth century saw a further heightening appreciation of a sense of monumentality in sculptured stonework with the appearance of free-standing pillars carved in relief, with horsemen, lions, and interlace, at Clonmacnoise and Banagher, Co. Offaly. From there it was but a short step to the development of the great scripture crosses (High Crosses), which represent the greatest corpus of religious sculpture to survive anywhere in Europe from the Carolingian period. In contrast to the stylized figures common in early Irish art, and as seen on the wonderfully graphic panels of the cross at Moone, Co. Kildare, many of the major scripture crosses have unusually naturalistic relief figures, often squat and grouped in threes, which may have been inspired by late classical and Carolingian models. The phasing-out of these crosses during the tenth century was followed by a hiatus lasting into most of the eleventh.

However, the sculpting of religious imagery picks up again in the twelfth century with the later group of High Crosses, portraying Christ and ecclesiastical figures on a large scale and in high relief, and the appearance—rare in Europe—of crowded Crucifixion scenes on church lintels, as at Maghera, Co. Derry, and Raphoe,

Carved figures from Jerpoint Abbey, Co. Kilkenny (late twelfth century), examples of Romanesque sculpture. © RICHARD CUMMINS/ CORBIS. REPRODUCED BY PERMISSION.

Co. Donegal. Other attractive manifestations of religious subjects in twelfth-century architectural sculpture include those in the chancel arch at Kilteel, Co. Kildare, and the wrongly reassembled stones on the exterior east gable of the cathedral at Ardmore, Co. Waterford.

As elsewhere in Europe, the twelfth century marks a high point in carved figures and strange beasts inhabiting a world of mysterious symbolism, encountered in Ireland largely on the portals and chancel arches of Romanesque churches—and even on Round Towers, as instanced by the doorway at Timahoe, Co. Laois. Munster first introduced the fashion in structures such as Cormac's Chapel on the Rock of Cashel in County Tipperary, consecrated in 1134, which is richly decorated with human heads, both single and on capitals, as well as having a centaur in relief firing an arrow at a large animal. Roughly contemporary are the fine voussoir heads preserved in Saint Fin Barre's Cathedral in Cork, but the most bizarre collection of heads, mandarin and west-

ern—some with beards and typically high ears—appears on the disjointed doorway at Dysert O'Dea, Co. Clare, close to one of the finest examples of the later group of High Crosses. Chevrons (of Norman derivation) and floral ornament are frequently also included in the integrated program of designs on the Irish Romanesque doors and chancel arches, as at Killeshin, Co. Laois (where a fragmentary inscription suggests the patronage of Dermot Mac Murrough); Monaincha, Co. Tipperary; and in the two County Galway cathedrals of Tuam and Clonfert. The high quality of these later twelfth-century carvings continued west of the Shannon into the first quarter of the thirteenth century at locations such as Cong and Ballintober in County Mayo and Boyle in County Roscommon. Romanesque carving also included the stone sarcophagus at Clones, Co. Monaghan (copying a wooden and metal shrine), and probably also items such as the sundial at Kilmalkedar, Co. Kerry.

By the early thirteenth century stylized Gothic foliage capitals were being used by the recently arrived Normans in styles that they introduced from their west of England homelands, while at the same time the Cistercians were incorporating very early naturalistic plant capitals with recognizable species into their abbey church at Corcomroe, Co. Clare. It was the Normans, too, who introduced the practice of placing effigies above tombs, and these can represent knights clad in armor of the period, ecclesiastics, or male and female civilians wearing long-draped garments. They were largely modeled on fashions current at the time in England, and some examples may even have been imported already carved, including a layman at New Ross, Co. Wexford, and possibly also the superb knight at Kilfane, Co. Kilkenny.

This flowering of Anglo-Norman sculpture was brought to a sudden end by the Black Death of 1347 to 1350. It was the Franciscan friaries of the west of Ireland that helped to revive the craft early in the fifteenth century, and the friary at Ennis shows how Irish master sculptors successfully adapted English alabaster panels to the much harder Irish limestone. The Dominicans responded with delicate and lively tomb- and altar-frontals at Strade, Co. Mayo.

Yet it was in the eastern counties dominated by the hibernicized Anglo-Norman lords that sculpture was most widely practiced in the fifteenth century. The Plunketts in Meath set up fine box-tombs with apostles as "weepers" supporting the effigy of lord and lady, and the crosses with religious figures in ogee-headed niches which they erected were a custom also practiced in towns such as Dublin, Kilkenny, and Athenry. The Plunketts' example was followed in the Ossory lands to

So-called tomb of Strongbow (c. 1340), Christ Church Cathedral, Dublin. COURTESY OF FAILTE IRELAND. REPRODUCED BY PERMISSION.

the south, where the Butlers—who had probably provided employment for the "Gowran master," sculptor and architect in the thirteenth century—were to act as patrons for the cloister at Jerpoint, Co. Kilkenny, with its gallery of figures from varied walks of life. They also set up their own effigial tombs in Kilkenny and elsewhere well into the sixteenth century, employing one anonymous workshop of masons in the area rivaled by another run by the O'Tunney family. The Butlers were also involved in commissioning high-quality architectural sculpture at Holy Cross Abbey in the fifteenth century, which is roughly contemporary with the fine Gothic doorways in Clonmacnoise Cathedral and at Clontuskert, Co. Galway, in the decades surrounding 1470.

Most of the native wooden statuary that furnished later medieval churches in Ireland must have been ignominiously confined to the flames by zealots during the Reformation period, but the few pieces that survive show craftsmen at work competently providing Irish versions of styles prevalent elsewhere.

SEE ALSO Arts: Early and Medieval Arts and Architecture; High Crosses; Metalwork, Early and Medieval

Bibliography

Harbison, Peter. *The High Crosses of Ireland.* 3 vols. 1992.

Henry, Françoise. *Irish Art.* 3 vols. 1966–1970.

Hunt, John. *Irish Medieval Figure Sculpture, 1200–1600.* 2 vols. 1974.

O'Brien, Jacqueline, and Peter Harbison. *Ancient Ireland.* 1996.

Rae, Edwin C. "Architecture and Sculpture, 1169–1603." In *A New History of Ireland,* vol. 2, *Medieval Ireland, 1169–1535,* edited by Art Cosgrove. 1987.

Peter Harbison

Second Reformation from 1822 to 1869

Following the revolutionary decade of the 1790s, the growth of an evangelical movement based on biblical morality was symptomatic of the growing belief that religion afforded the best protection against the destabilizing influences of the recent democratic revolutions in America and France. Convinced that the first Reformation had failed to take root in Ireland, supporters of the evangelical movement in the early decades of the nineteenth century sought to generate a "New," or "Second," Reformation. Promoters of the movement sought to effect a moral revolution among the upper classes that would make them more conscious of their duties as social and moral exemplars. They also attempted to introduce the principles of the Protestant faith to the Catholic population in the belief that this would secure Catholic acceptance of the existing social and political order. Initially, the movement was interdenominational in character and was dominated during its early years by Methodists and Congregationalists. During the second decade of the century, however, faced with the challenge launched by the Dissenting evangelicals, the Church of Ireland took the lead in the reformation campaign, especially in its outreach to the Catholic population.

The contemporary burgeoning demand for education among the poor was the most obvious and convenient avenue to control of the hearts and minds of the rising generation of Catholics. Through a variety of voluntary organizations (the Association for Discountenancing Vice, the London Hibernian Society, the Hibernian Bible Society, etc.) devoted to Bible distribution and education, the movement began to make serious progress in the 1820s, with increasing support from the landed classes and financial assistance from Parliament. When government funds went to agencies that were considered to be overtly engaged in proselytism,

Catholic leaders began to publicly condemn the movement. In 1819 and 1820, following a letter from the head of the Propaganda Fidei about the dangers of Bible schools, the Reverend John MacHale and Daniel O'Connell openly accused the schools of proselytism and attempting to subvert the Catholic religion as well as the movement for emancipation. This criticism was the opening shot in a rivalry that persisted through the 1820s against a backdrop of rising sectarian tension that was worsened by economic crisis and agrarian rebellion. It broke into open conflict following a famous sermon delivered at Saint Patrick's Cathedral in Dublin in October 1822 in which the newly appointed Archbishop William Magee called for a "glorious Second Reformation" that would establish the Church of Ireland as the church of the majority population. Magee argued that the Church of Ireland was the only legitimate ecclesiastical body in the country, deriving its legitimacy from apostolic succession and its descent from the ancient Celtic church of Saint Patrick. This claim provoked a reply from Bishop James Warren Doyle of Kildare and Leighlin, an outspoken defender of the rights of the Catholic poor. Doyle's response to Magee was immediately recognized as the first expression of a strident assertiveness on the part of Catholic leaders, particularly the hierarchy, which quickly coalesced behind the Catholic Association, and it marked the beginning of a new phase of politicization for Catholics. Magee's sermon and Doyle's reply prompted an all-out ideological conflict in newspapers, pamphlets, and public debates—a conflict that accompanied the spread of the Catholic Association and the intensification of the controversy over Bible-based education. The controversy also promoted the institutionalization of the Second Reformation movement at the local level, where the campaign was supported especially by evangelical landed aristocrats such as Lord Farnham. Damaging criticism from the Catholic side was leveled against what was perceived to be coercion in the drive to make converts. Allegations surfaced that landlords were forcing Catholic tenants to send their children to evangelical schools on pain of eviction, and providing food and work as incentives to switch denominational allegiance. Although there were certainly some conversions, they never reached large numbers. Of far greater significance were the polarization that ensued between the two denominations (widened by the success of the Catholic Association) and the efforts by the government to solve the educational problem by setting up the National Board of Education in 1831. This last measure had severe implications for the Second Reformation movement, which focused its energies on the educational needs of the poor. During the 1830s, faced with the challenge of the schools of the National Board, the promoters of the Second Reformation shifted their attention to the west of Ireland, where the scarcity of Catholic religious education and the predominance of Irish-speakers were elements that could be exploited in the drive for conversions. During the 1830s and 1840s the foundations were put in place for a new missionary offensive that reached its highest point during the years of the Great Famine, when thousands of converts were reported. The charge of "souperism" (the use of food to attract converts) became widespread, especially in the western counties. Overall, the legacy of the Second Reformation movement hardened the attitudes of the Catholic hierarchy regarding Protestant influence in Catholic affairs, particularly those relating to education and philanthropy.

SEE ALSO Church of Ireland: Since 1690; Evangelicalism and Revivals; Methodism; Presbyterianism

Bibliography

Bowen, Desmond. *The Protestant Crusade in Ireland, 1800–70: A Study of Protestant-Catholic Relations between the Act of Union and Disestablishment.* 1978.

Brown, Stewart J. "The New Reformation Movement in the Church of Ireland, 1801–29." In *Piety and Power in Ireland, 1760–1960: Essays in Honour of Emmet Larkin,* edited by Stewart J. Brown and David W. Miller. 2001.

Whelan, Irene. "The Stigma of Souperism." In *The Great Irish Famine,* Cathal Póirtéir. 1995.

Irene Whelan

Secularization

Secularization is a process in which religious belief and practice declines, people become less oriented toward the supernatural, and churches no longer have the same power within civil society, particularly over the state. It is sometimes difficult, however, to distinguish secularization from personalization, in which religion becomes more private and less formal and institutionalized. The fact that Catholics in Ireland in 2000 were going to mass less often than in 1950 and were disobeying church teachings, especially on sexual morality, could be seen as a sign of personalization more than secularization. Indeed, it could be argued that at the end of the twentieth century Irish Catholics were returning to a type of relationship with the institutional church that was prevalent before the Great Famine. Nevertheless, whatever the process of change that is taking place, Irish Catholics are still very religious by Western standards.

Three-quarters of the people on the island of Ireland are Roman Catholic—over 90 percent of people in the Irish Republic and almost 40 percent in Northern Ireland. This is not just some nominal affiliation. Being Catholic or Protestant is central to personal identity—to how people see and understand themselves. In Northern Ireland, but less so in the Republic, religious identity is closely tied to social and political identity. But this does not seem to make Northern Catholics more religious. There is very little difference between Northern and Southern Catholics when it comes to mass attendance. However, given the specific context of Northern Ireland, and the lack of comparable data, this analysis of secularization focuses on the Republic of Ireland.

BEING RELIGIOUS

The level of orthodox Catholic belief in the Republic of Ireland is high. The majority (around eight in ten) of Irish Catholics accept the fundamental principles of their faith, such as belief in God, the divinity of Christ, and, in relation to Our Lady, the immaculate conception and her assumption into heaven. Similarly, over three-quarters (78%) believe in life after death, and seven in ten believe in miracles.

But what makes Ireland unique is the extent to which religious belief is put into practice. More than six in ten (63%) go to mass once a week. This is the one of the highest levels in the West, easily surpassing, for example, U.S. Catholics (43%), Poles (42%) and Italians (29%). There are also high levels of prayer (72% at least once a day) and reception of Holy Communion (42% receive once a week). There have, however, been changes in religious practice in recent years. The proportion attending mass once a week has decreased from 91 percent in 1973.

Another aspect that makes the Catholic Irish unique is the level of engagement in traditional religious devotions. Each year tens of thousands make pilgrimages to religious sites such as Knock, Croagh Patrick, and Lough Derg. Similar numbers participate in nine-day novenas to Our Lady in different churches throughout the country.

The Catholic Church still has a monopoly over the meaning of life in Ireland, particularly when it comes to life transitions. Young people may not be going to mass as often as they once did, but the vast majority of Irish Catholics are baptized, make their first Holy Communion, are confirmed (as Catholics), married, and buried

Pope John Paul II in Galway, September 1979. The visit attracted enormous crowds, but there is no evidence that it helped to arrest the declining influence of the Catholic Church. © VITTORIANO RASTELLI/ CORBIS. REPRODUCED BY PERMISSION.

within the church. These are still major social as well as religious occasions in Ireland.

BECOMING SECULAR

To understand the process of secularization, one must look beyond formal belief and practice to the extent to which people are oriented toward the supernatural and transcendental in their everyday life. There is plenty of evidence that the symbols and language of Catholicism—the statues, holy pictures, medals, greetings, and prayers around which daily life was once formed—are fading away. They do not have the same place in the rational lifestyle of modern bureaucratic society.

If being spiritual is one-half of the religious life, the other half is being ethical. Throughout the nineteenth and twentieth centuries the Catholic Church developed a monopoly over the rules and regulations of what constituted a good life and, thereby, how to attain salvation. What changed during the last half of the twentieth century was the nature of belief in the afterlife, the kind of behavior that was considered right and wrong, and the role of the church as a moral guardian.

Hellfire sermons have become a thing of the past. Only half of Irish Catholics believe in the devil and hell—in contrast to 85 percent who believe in heaven. There has also been a decline in acceptance of traditional church teaching, particularly in relation to sexuality. The proportion of people who believe that premarital sex is always wrong (30%) continues to decline. Less than half (42%) feel that the church gives adequate answers to moral problems and the needs of individuals.

For many years now there has been a decline in confession. In the 1970s almost half (47%) of Irish Catholics went at least once a month. This has declined to 9 percent. The change can be linked to Catholics distancing themselves from church teaching, particularly in relation to sexual morality. Young Catholics may be informed by church teaching, but they are increasingly making up their own minds about what is right and wrong.

While the church still has a monopoly over the religious field, it is rapidly losing its power in other social fields. Control of education has been crucial to passing on the faith from one generation to the next. Parents who had lapsed in their youth and early adult life were in the past easily persuaded to return to the fold once they had children. The development of multidenominational schools at primary level, and of community and comprehensive schools at secondary level, has facilitated disaffiliation from the church.

Health and hospital care is another field in which the church has lost its influence. In the past, people were often forced to use Catholic hospitals, or state hospitals whose medical ethics were essentially Catholic. It is becoming easier for Catholics to gain access to procedures such as sterilization and in vitro fertilization. A similar process is taking place in the administration of social welfare services. The state rather than the church now cares for the poor, the marginalized, and the disabled members of society. Social welfare is being disentangled from religious welfare.

The main reason for the decline in the church's influence in education, health, and social welfare has been the dramatic drop in vocations. In the 1960s the church could count on 1,400 new recruits to all forms of religious life each year. Now it has less than 100. There are still nearly 15,000 priests, nuns, and brothers, but they are aging rapidly. It is in this very real sense that the Catholic Church in Ireland is dying.

The church may have won the battle with the state over the Mother and Child Scheme in 1951, but it lost the war. The state has gained control of health and social welfare. It is slowly gaining control of education. Politicians gradually became less dependent on the sym-bolic authority of the church. The state pursued a different vision of Irish society based on materialism, consumerism, and liberalism. It has encroached increasingly into the family and sexuality, previous strongholds of the church.

The church has also lost most of the control that it once had over the media. At the heart of the modern mass media is a philosophy of liberal individualism that stands in stark contrast to the message of piety, humility, and self-denial which are the traditional hallmarks of being a good Catholic. The media have been to the forefront in leading Irish Catholics to see, read, and understand their world differently. There is a new self-confidence in Irish people, particularly among women. They no longer accept the traditional church image of them as virgins, servants, housewives, or chaste mothers. If there has been one major cause for the decline in the power of the Catholic Church in Ireland, it was the demise of the Irish Catholic mother. She was once the lynchpin in passing on the faith from one generation to the next. Now, like many others throughout the world, she is busy going out to work and consuming.

SEE ALSO Divorce, Contraception, and Abortion; Gaelic Catholic State, Making of; McQuaid, John Charles; Marianism; Mother and Child Crisis; Religion: Since 1690; Roman Catholic Church: Since 1891; Social Change since 1922

Bibliography

Flannery, Tony. *The Death of Religious Life.* 1997.

Greeley, Andrew, and Conor Ward, "How 'Secularised' Is the Ireland We Live In?" *Doctrine and Life* 50, no. 1 (2000): 581–603.

Hornsby-Smith, Michael, and Christopher T. Whelan. "Religious and Moral Values." In *Values and Social Change*, edited by Christopher T. Whelan. 1994.

Inglis, Tom. *Moral Monopoly.* 1998.

Kenny, Mary. *Goodbye to Catholic Ireland.* 1997.

Tom Inglis

Shipbuilding

In the seventeenth and eighteenth centuries wooden sailing ships were built at various locations around the

The Titanic *and her sister ship the* Olympic *before launch in Harland and Wolff shipyard, Belfast, 1910.* PHOTOGRAPH REPRODUCED WITH THE KIND PERMISSION OF THE TRUSTEES OF THE NATIONAL MUSEUMS AND GALLERIES OF NORTHERN IRELAND, M10-46-124.

coast of Ireland, including Belfast Lough. Belfast's first significant shipbuilding firm was established in 1791 by William Ritchie, a shipbuilder from Saltcoats on the west coast of Scotland. After 1850, product and process innovation, with the development of iron and later steel steamships together with scale economies, led to larger establishments and firms and to regional concentration in the shipbuilding industry throughout the United Kingdom. By the late nineteenth century most U.K. merchant tonnage was launched on the River Clyde in Scotland, the northeast coast of England, and the River Lagan in Belfast. The industry in Belfast consisted of two firms: Harland and Wolff and Workman, Clark and Company. In the years from 1906 to1914 they produced 10 percent of the United Kingdom's output and 6 percent of the world's output.

Harland and Wolff was formed in 1861 by Edward Harland, an engineer and shipbuilder from the northeast of England, and Gustav Wolff, an English-trained engineer from Hamburg. The partnership acquired a

small yard on Queen's Island, which Harland had started to manage for Robert Hickson in 1854 and then purchased four years later. The Belfast Harbour Commissioners played an important role in the creation of this yard and in the subsequent development of shipbuilding on the River Lagan. Workman, Clark, and Company was formed in 1880 by Frank Workman and George Clark. Both men had served as apprentices with Harland and Wolff. The new company's yards were located mainly on the northern shore of the Lagan.

As with other U.K. firms, close links with shipping-line customers allowed the Belfast firms to maintain a high level of output and hence capacity utilization and also to develop product specialization, thereby enabling them to sustain unit-cost advantages over competitors. Under the leadership of William Pirrie, Harland and Wolff was one of a small number of yards equipped to construct the largest vessels, including the luxury liners *Olympic* (1911), and *Titanic* (1912). Workman Clark specialized in medium-sized cargo boats and combined cargo and passenger vessels; the firm pioneered the development of the Parsons turbine engine and the construction of refrigerated meat- and fruit-carrying vessels.

Employment at Harland and Wolff increased from 500 in 1861 to 2,200 in 1871, and from 9,000 in 1900 to 14,000 in 1914. Altogether 20,000 were employed in shipbuilding in Belfast in 1914, and an all-time peak of nearly 30,000 held such jobs in 1919. Belfast did not have a large reserve of skilled labor. Skilled workers from Scotland and England were attracted and retained by offering them a premium on regional rates of pay: markets for skilled labor were interregional. These premiums did not apply to unskilled labor, which was in plentiful local supply. Because of their relative scarcity the skilled shipyard workers had considerable bargaining power and, as in Great Britain, were able to exercise a traditional right to select apprentices for their crafts. This informal labor market meant that recruitment frequently came from within the established local communities, often from within family groups. These employment practices continued into the twentieth century and help to explain the religious mix of the shipyard labor force. Serious sectarian incidents occurred in the shipyards in 1886, when there was a sharp downturn in shipbuilding output and employment, and in 1920, at the beginning of another major downturn for the Belfast yards. Each of these episodes took place at a time of heightened political tension over the national question: In 1886 and 1920 riots occurred during the first Home Rule crisis and as the Anglo-Irish War edged into the north, respectively.

In the 1920s and 1930s U.K. shipbuilders confronted the problems of slow growth in demand for shipping services, excess capacity, and increased foreign competition. Both Belfast firms experienced severe financial difficulties. Harland and Wolff responded by entering the market for oil tankers in the 1920s and diversified in 1936 by entering into partnership with Short Brothers to produce aircraft. Workman Clark did not survive the world depression that began in 1929 and launched its last ship in 1934.

The outbreak of World War II, like the previous world war, caused a boom in output; Harland and Wolff's contribution made the shipyard a target for German bombs in 1941. The long postwar boom saw an increase in demand for oil tankers and bulk carriers. Despite a decline in the U.K. shipbuilding industry's share of world output, tonnage launched by Harland and Wolff reached a historical high in the 1970s. However, the firm was in receipt of government financial support from 1966, and in 1975 the Northern Ireland

government became the sole shareholder in the company.

In 1989 Harland and Wolff was returned to the private sector as Harland and Wolff Holdings after a management and employee buyout in partnership with companies associated with the Norwegian shipowner Fred Olsen. Following privatization, the company diversified its product mix to include not just oil tankers and bulk carriers but also offshore production vessels for the oil and gas industry. After further restructuring in the late 1990s the dominant shareholder in the twenty-first century is Fred Olsen Energy. Diversification continues: Recalling the glory days at the start of the twentieth century the company is developing a research and tourism area on Queen's Island called Titanic Quarter. However, its shipbuilding days may have come to an end with the launch on 17 January 2003 of *Anvil Point*, a roll-on, roll-off ferry built for service with the U.K. Ministry of Defence.

SEE ALSO Belfast; Industrialization; Industry since 1920; Transport—Road, Canal, Rail

Bibliography

Geary, F., and W. Johnson. "Shipbuilding in Belfast, 1861–1986." *Irish Economic and Social History* 16 (1989): 42–64.

Moss, Michael, and John R. Hume. *Shipbuilders to the World: 125 Years of Harland and Wolff, Belfast, 1861–1986.* 1986.

Frank Geary and Walford Johnson

Sidney, Henry

The Elizabethan administrator, diplomat, and courtier Sir Henry Sidney (1529–1586) was lord deputy of Ireland from 1565 to 1571 and from 1575 to 1578. Having made a promising beginning as one of the principal gentlemen of the privy chamber in 1550, and enjoying a particularly close relationship with King Edward VI, Sidney was one of a number of ambitious courtiers whose career declined steadily during the reign of Elizabeth through loss of favor, for which he himself believed his Irish service to have been primarily responsible.

Sidney's service in Ireland began in 1556 when he came to serve under his brother-in-law Thomas Rad-

Sir Henry Sidney (the lord deputy) setting out on a state progress through Ireland. The heads of several rebels are shown on poles over the gate of Dublin Castle. FROM JOHN DERRICKE'S *THE IMAGE OF IRELANDE* (1581).

cliffe, earl of Sussex, as vice-treasurer and treasurer-at-war. His first years in Ireland (1556–1559) were especially successful, and his careful administration of the army's finances made him popular with both the soldiers and the community of the Pale upon whom they were billeted. During two short terms as governor in Sussex's absence, Sidney established his reputation both as an effective commander and as a skillful diplomat, particularly in regard to his handling of affairs in Ulster. His success in Ireland secured him promotion in 1560 as lord president of Wales, a post he was to hold along with several other commissions until his death.

The collapse of Sussex's administration in 1564 to 1565 made Sidney a highly popular choice as the new governor in Ireland. But from the outset Sidney's first term in office was marred by the bitter court rivalries that attended on his appointment and by his perceived dependence on the powerful but deeply mistrusted favorite, Robert Dudley, earl of Leicester. Sidney sought to overcome such prejudices against him by devising a broad program of political and religious reform that incorporated the most orthodox prescriptions in every area. His attempts to implement it were obstructed by two imperatives that Elizabeth imposed on him: the reduction of the over-mighty Ulster lord, Shane O'Neill (1530–1567), and the resolution of the conflict between the great feudal lords of Ormond and Desmond. After a failed military expedition Sidney enjoyed unexpected

success in Ulster when O'Neill was assassinated by the MacDonalds of Antrim, probably with Sidney's connivance. But his perceived sympathy for Desmond and hostility toward Ormond marred this achievement, and when Sidney sought permission to commence the implementation of his reform program, he was ordered to bring both Desmond and his brother Sir John as prisoners to court. Delay ensued, and by the time Sidney returned to Ireland (August 1568) with power to inaugurate reform, this time under the auspices of an Irish parliament, Munster was in a state of open rebellion, and a new O'Neill overlord (Turlough Luineach, 1530?–1595) had risen to prominence in Ulster. While suppressing the rebellion in Munster (in an increasingly bloody manner) and containing disorder in Ulster, Sidney's reformist ambitions were again frustrated. His efforts to provide a new statutory basis for tenurial reform in the Gaelic lordships failed to bear fruit, and his attempt to establish a conventional provincial council in Connacht ended in fiasco.

The disasters of 1568 to 1571 taught him a lesson, however, and in the early 1570s Sidney, in collaboration with his adviser Edmund Tremayne, developed a radically new strategy that was to form the basis of his last administration in Ireland. He termed it simply "composition" (in effect, a deal). Accepting the failure of conventional legal and administrative means of bringing about change, composition posited that only the threat of superior force would persuade the great lords to abandon their own methods of intimidation and protection. Thus a great army was to be introduced into Ireland, not to attempt conquest or dispossession but to enforce a series of permanent financial settlements between the lords and their vassals and between both sides and the Crown. These settlements would form the basis for transforming a social structure predicated on obligation and service into one predicated on rent.

The risks inherent in the radical nature of the new policy were deepened by a number of concessions in cost and duration that Sidney was required to make in order to regain office. But the most serious opposition to composition arose not in the Irish provinces where, though controversial, it made considerable progress, but within the English Pale, where it was seen, quite rightly, to entail dangerous implications of taxation without parliamentary consent. The Irish chancellor's acknowledgment that this was so, and Elizabeth's ultimate unwillingness to countenance an extension of the royal prerogative, caused the abandonment of the policy and Sidney's recall under the charge that he had sought "to take the land of Ireland to farm." Sidney's readiness to envisage an annual tax to be assessed and collected by royal provincial administrators with the support of the local nobility, who were to enjoy exemptions as the reward for their complaisance, is strongly redolent of the system that was to emerge in continental Europe under the ancien régime; it is tempting to speculate that in his thinking about Ireland, Sidney was less influenced by Spanish notions of colonization (as has sometimes been suggested) than by certain aspects of contemporary French constitutional thought. Such speculation in the absence of hard evidence must remain inconclusive, and it is equally arguable that in reaching his conclusions, Sidney was drawing simply on his own experience in Ireland.

SEE ALSO Desmond Rebellions; English Political and Religious Policies, Responses to (1534–1690); Land Settlements from 1500 to 1690; Old English

Bibliography

Brady, Ciaran. *The Chief Governors: The Rise and Fall of Reform Government in Tudor Ireland, 1536–1588.* 1994.

Brady, Ciaran, ed. *A Viceroy's Vindication? Sir Henry Sidney's Memoir of Service in Ireland.* 2002.

Canny, Nicholas. *The Elizabethan Conquest of Ireland: A Pattern Established, 1565–76.* 1976.

Crawford, Jon G. *Anglicising the Government of Ireland: The Irish Privy Council and the Advancement of Tudor Rule, 1556–1578.* 1993.

Ciaran Brady

Sinn Féin Movement and Party to 1922

The Sinn Féin Party dominated Irish nationalism between 1917 and 1922, but for many years it had been a marginal group in Irish politics. It was effectively the creation of Arthur Griffith, a brilliant and acerbic journalist who in 1907 formed a united party out of competing and overlapping groups. Under his influence its policy was to restructure the United Kingdom by establishing a dual monarchy similar to that of Austria-Hungary: Irish MPs were to abstain from the House of Commons and form a separate parliament in Dublin. By the standards of Irish nationalists he was obsessively concerned with economic issues, arguing in favor of industrialization and the protection of Irish products against foreign (specifically British) competition.

Griffith's first Sinn Féin Party made little impact. It was Dublin-centered, had no more than 128 branches at its greatest extent, and fought (unsuccessfully) only one by-election. Its inability to contest any seats in either of the general elections of 1910 illustrated its weakness, and it was moribund long before the outbreak of World War I.

However, Griffith remained an influential propagandist and, using the name of his party as that of his weekly newspaper, proved Sinn Féin to be popular and adaptable. When the paramilitary Irish Volunteers were formed in 1913, they were called the Sinn Féin Volunteers, often to the members' disgust. The Easter Rising, which was carried out largely by Volunteers, was similarly mistitled. The result was that an insignificant political party became closely identified with a heroic and romantic insurrection. As the rising acquired a retrospective popularity, Sinn Féin was able to benefit from the swing in public opinion against the British government and the Home Rule Party.

In early 1917 the Irish Volunteers, including former rebels who viewed politics with suspicion or disdain, realized that there was no possibility of another rebellion in the near future. Many of them drifted into political activity, often by chance or for lack of something better to do, and combined forces with the more moderate elements associated with Griffith. Together they led a grouping that in the course of the year became the second Sinn Féin Party.

THE SECOND SINN FÉIN PARTY

Even more than its prewar predecessor, this body was an alliance of political and military elements, of moderates and extremists. Some of its members believed strongly in democracy and political activity, while others regarded the tasks of contesting elections and converting public opinion as no more than an unwelcome prelude to another rising. But the members were able to cooperate effectively and to overcome differences that threatened to disrupt their efforts. They won a series of by-elections, thereby providing the movement with publicity and self-confidence. The new party was fashionable, acquired the glamour of success, and spread rapidly. By the end of 1917 it had more than 1,200 branches and probably over 120,000 members. Most of its supporters were former Home Rulers, with the result that the party inherited many of the skills and habits of its rival. Sinn Féin's constitution was changed so that it became a republican movement, abandoning the old policy of a dual monarchy, and Griffith was replaced as president by Eamon de Valera, the senior surviving leader of the Easter Rising.

In early 1918, Sinn Féin experienced three successive by-election defeats at the hands of the Irish Parliamentary Party, but it was able to play the principal role in organizing resistance to British plans for imposing conscription on Ireland. Irish nationalists flocked to join Sinn Féin and the Irish Volunteers. The arrest of de Valera, Griffith, and other prominent members of the party gave it the aura of martyrdom while also confirming the general belief that the Sinn Féin movement provided the only effective organized civilian resistance to conscription.

Despite the imprisonment of most of its leaders, Sinn Féin was able to wage a formidable campaign when a general election was held in December 1918. The Labour Party stood aside, and Home Rulers were so demoralized that they did not contest twenty-five nationalist constituencies. Sinn Féin won a total of seventy-three seats, the Parliamentary Party six, and the unionists twenty-six. One Sinn Féin candidate, Countess Markievicz, was the first woman to be elected to Parliament, although her resolve to abstain from Westminster guaranteed that she would not take her seat. Sinn Féin's political supremacy in nationalist Ireland was comparable to that of Charles Stewart Parnell in the late 1880s.

THE DECLINE OF SINN FÉIN

In January 1919 Sinn Féin MPs met in Dublin, proclaimed themselves Dáil Éireann (the Irish Parliament), and re-proclaimed the republic of Easter 1916. De Valera was later elected president, a cabinet was approved, and the new government attempted to take over the administration of the country. Ironically these actions, implementing Sinn Féin policies, which Griffith had outlined for almost twenty years, were among the factors that brought about the party's dramatic decline. Most of its aims had already been achieved; in particular, it had educated and organized Irish nationalism, defeated the Home Rule Party, and implemented a policy of abstention from Westminster. Its remaining objectives could better be achieved by the Dáil government or by its army—the Volunteers, who were now more widely called the Irish Republican Army (IRA).

As Ireland was polarized by the Anglo-Irish War of 1919 to 1921, the party often seemed to be superfluous, its members' enthusiasm dwindled, and it was banned by the British authorities. In many parts of the country it faded away, although it could be revived for basic electoral purposes. It was able to fight local elections in 1920 and a general election in 1921 (when seats were contested only in the newly created Northern Ireland and all its candidates were returned unopposed in the south). Only with the truce of July 1921 could Sinn Féin reemerge and resume its normal activities. In the course of the following months it was reconstituted. It enjoyed a brief Indian summer and became more popular than ever before.

This pattern was short lived. When the Anglo-Irish Treaty was signed in December 1921, the party split in two—like the rest of nationalist Ireland. The uneasy compromise between moderates and extremists negotiated in 1917 could not survive the compromises that were imposed by an agreement with Britain. Rival factions tried to seize control of Sinn Féin's machine, its assets, and its image. The party was patched together unconvincingly in May 1922 as part of the Collins–de Valera pact, under which pro- and antitreaty candidates were supposed to bury their differences and campaign together as a "panel." In theory Sinn Féin candidates won more than 60 percent of the vote, but the reality was that the electors' loyalties lay with either Michael Collins's provisional government or with the antitreaty republicans. Sinn Féin served only as a platform that could be used by the two "real" parties. Within weeks open warfare had broken out between the government and its republican opponents, and the second Sinn Féin Party promptly disintegrated. Its name was later appropriated by a series of minority republican groupings.

The party's ignominious end should not distract attention from its considerable achievements—above all its mobilization and radicalization of Irish nationalism and its maintenance of political traditions and values in the midst of what was largely a military revolution. The rapid consolidation of democracy in independent Ireland was eased by the activities of the Sinn Féin Party in the years after the Easter Rising.

SEE ALSO Civil War; Collins, Michael; Cumann na mBan; de Valera, Eamon; Electoral Politics from 1800 to 1921; Gonne, Maud; Great War; Griffith, Arthur; Home Rule Movement and the Irish Parliamentary Party: 1891 to 1918; Markievicz, Countess Constance; Pearse, Patrick; Politics: 1800 to 1921—Challenges to the Union; Redmond, John; Struggle for Independence from 1916 to 1921; **Primary Documents:** Address at the First Annual Convention of the National Council of Sinn Féin (28 November 1905); Resolutions Adopted at the Public Meeting Following the First Annual Convention of the National Council of Sinn Féin (28 November 1905); Proclamation of the Irish Republic (24 April 1916); Declaration of Irish Independence (21 January 1919); The "Democratic Programme" of Dáil Éireann (21 January 1919); Government of Ireland Act (23 December 1920); Proclamation Issued by IRA Leaders at the Beginning of the Civil War (29 June 1922)

Bibliography

Boyce, D. G., ed. *The Revolution in Ireland, 1879–1923.* 1988.

Davis, Richard. *Arthur Griffith and Non-Violent Sinn Féin.* 1974.

Feeney, Brian. *Sinn Féin: A Hundred Turbulent Years.* 2002.

Glandon, Virginia E. *Arthur Griffith and the Advanced-Nationalist Press: Ireland, 1900–1922.* 1985.

Laffan, Michael. *The Resurrection of Ireland: The Sinn Féin Party, 1916–1923.* 1999.

Maye, Brian. *Arthur Griffith.* 1997.

Michael Laffan

Smith, Erasmus

Erasmus Smith (1611–1691), merchant and educational philanthropist, was born at Husbands Bosworth in Leicester, England, where he was baptized on 8 April. Admitted to the Grocers Company in London in 1635, his business was trade with Turkey, but he became involved in the supply of provisions to the Commonwealth armies in Ireland and Scotland in the early 1650s. His interest in Irish land began in 1643 when his father, Sir Roger, assigned to him the benefit of a 300-pound investment under the Adventurers' Act and the Sea Ordnance, which raised money for the suppression of the Irish rebellion on the security of land that would be forfeited as a result of it. After the war ended in 1653, Smith's speculative purchases of adventurers' shares at a discount raised his nominal investment to 2,995 pounds, for which he received 10,404 acres in Armagh, Down, and Tipperary. Subsequent acquisitions in the 1650s and thereafter extended his holdings to some 45,000 acres spread over nine counties.

In June 1655, Smith announced his intention to set up schools on his estates so that children could be raised "in the Fear of God and good literature and to speak the English tongue" (Barnard 1975 [2000], p. 191). In 1657 he vested 3,000 acres in trustees charged with establishing five schools and with providing for suitable students to receive scholarships to Trinity College, Dublin. The scheme was not implemented before the restoration of the monarchy in 1660, but in 1667 a modified proposal was authorized by letters patent that envisaged free grammar schools at Drogheda, Galway, and Tipperary, added an apprenticeship scheme, and required the trustees to pay 100 pounds each year to Christ's Hospital (the charity or "Bluecoat" school for orphans in London). Two years later, on Smith's petition, a royal charter confirmed the lands and the trust and appointed thirty-two governors, including the archbishops of Dublin and Armagh. Smith, whose original arrangements had favored nonconformist ministers as trustees and required the use of the Presbyterian 1646 Westminster catechism, had trimmed his sails.

Little else is known of Smith's life. He was briefly a London alderman in 1657 but withdrew after three weeks; he played an active part in the Adventurers' Committee in the late 1650s, when he visited Ireland; and he was elected to the Irish parliament for Ardee in 1665 but never attended. His trust prospered, and in 1723 an act of Parliament empowered it to use its considerable surplus income to found additional schools and to endow professorships and fellowships in Trinity College, Dublin.

SEE ALSO Education: 1500 to 1690; Restoration Ireland

Bibliography

Barnard, Toby C. *Cromwellian Ireland: English Government and Reform in Ireland, 1649–1660*. 1975. Reprint, 2000.

Bottigheimer, Karl S. *English Money and Irish Land: The "Adventurers" in the Cromwellian Settlement of Ireland*. 1971.

Ronan, Myles V. *The Erasmus Smith Endowment*. 1937.

Aidan Clarke

Social Change since 1922

Ireland was divided into two separate states in 1922. The Irish Free State was overwhelmingly rural, agrarian, and Catholic; Northern Ireland was more industrialized, and two-thirds of the population were Protestant. Political change was not followed by a social revolution; rather, the social revolution predated it. In the decades between the Great Famine and World War I, Ireland experienced a long-term decline in population, mass emigration, a fall in the marriage rate; the near-extinction of both the landlords and the agricultural laborers; and the consolidation of a powerful farming class. The conservative values of these church-going small property-owners exercised an important influence on Irish society, North and South. Although they differed in politics and religion, the two Irelands had a common suspicion of change, modernity, and the outside world. The Irish Free State aspired to remain a Catholic, rural, and backward-looking Gaelic society, and for this reason it imposed a stringent code of censorship on film and printed materials that might expose its citizens to the values of a modern, secular, and urban society. Although the Northern Ireland state was less explicit about its cultural values, its ethos was likewise insular and conservative.

POPULATION, FAMILY, AND SOCIAL LIFE BEFORE 1960

The Irish population fell by almost half between 1841 and 1911, but in Northern Ireland the fall in population was reversed in 1891. In the Irish Free State the population continued to fall until 1961, because of a continuing high rate of emigration, which reached a twentieth-century peak during the 1950s when more than 400,000 people left the state. More than half of those who were born during the 1930s had emigrated by the 1960s. The rate of emigration from Northern Ireland was substantially lower because there were more jobs available outside farming.

By 1911 the Irish marriage rate was the lowest in Europe; one adult in four never married, and although the marriage rate was higher in Northern Ireland, it was also exceptionally low by international standards. Irish couples married at a later age than elsewhere, too, but families were large. In 1911 a woman whose marriage lasted twenty to twenty-five years had given birth to five or six children. Professional couples and Protestants had smaller families, indicating the beginnings of fertility control, but the decline in family size was one of the slowest in Europe. Marriages became more common during the 1940s and 1950s, in a faint reflection of the American and European marriage boom, but the Irish marriage pattern remained so out of line with that of Europe and the United States that it was regarded as eccentric and abnormal. This was attributed to sexual repression or other psychological pathologies, or to the power of the Catholic Church, but marriage statistics from Northern Ireland were not dramatically different.

Late marriages and permanent celibacy were most pronounced in farming households. Sons or daughters who worked on the family farm had no independent income, and they could not contemplate marriage unless their parent(s) gave them some security, by transferring ownership of the farm to a son or providing a dowry for a daughter; parents also had an effective veto over their child's choice of partner. But nonfarming families were much the same: in 1926 the percentage of Irish male teachers, clerks, and skilled workers who were married by the age of thirty was significantly lower than in England and Wales. Large families served to postpone and perhaps to prevent marriages. Farmers commonly delayed the marriage of the heir until all the remaining children had been provided for. Given the late age at which men and women married, it is not surprising that in 1926, 12 percent of children under fifteen in the Irish Free State had lost one or both parents; the figure was 10 percent in Northern Ireland. Older children commonly found themselves having to support widowed mothers, ailing fathers, and younger siblings, and many had to defer marriage until these responsibilities were at an end. Children were required to attend school until the age of fourteen, but only the children of prosperous parents and a tiny number of scholarship students attended secondary school or university. By the age of fourteen and often earlier, most children were expected to contribute to family income as farm laborers, domestic servants, messenger boys, or factory workers. Many teenage girls and older women, married and single, worked in textile and clothing plants in Belfast, Derry, and other Northern Ireland towns, but the most common employment for women in independent Ireland until the 1960s was domestic service. Jobs were scarce and many parents sent teenage sons or daughters

In the west of Ireland traditional thatched cottages have given way to modern houses, funded through generous government loans and grants. COURTESY OF THE DEPARTMENT OF AGRICULTURE AND FOOD, IRELAND.

to England, some as young as fifteen years, with instructions to send money home; some fathers worked in England for part or all of the year, leaving their family in Ireland. Emigration eased the consequences of large families for both parents and Irish society.

Married women busied themselves raising large families, helping to run family farms or the pubs, groceries, and other businesses that dominated provincial Irish towns; it was highly unusual for married women to work outside the home, except in the Ulster textile towns. Housekeeping was onerous; most rural homes lacked electricity until the mid-1950s. Running water, bathrooms, and other modern amenities reached the Irish countryside only during the 1960s, but middle-class families, even those on modest incomes, commonly employed a domestic servant until the 1950s, when such workers emigrated en masse to England. By the 1930s the typical Irish family lived in a house with three to four rooms, but thousands of Dublin families continued to live in one-room tenements until after World War II. Housing standards in Belfast were significantly better, with most working-class families occupying a three- or four-room terraced house, supplied with gas and cold water.

Social life revolved around the home or the church; in rural areas the most common social activity was the *cuaird* or *céilí*—visiting a neighboring house in the evening to gossip, play cards, or listen to music. These visits were made only by men; women, married or single, stayed at home unless there was a more formal social event such as a dance, a wedding, or a funeral. A lot of socializing was single-sex. Sport was extremely important. Every Catholic parish had a Gaelic football team and perhaps a hurling team; soccer was the sport of the urban working class; rugby was supported by professional men. Horse racing was popular with all classes; local race meetings were major social events. The pub was important for certain occasions—fair days and trips to the town—and it was the place where matchmaking and dowries were commonly negotiated. But for most people the pub did not form part of everyday life, because they could not afford it.

Religion had an important place in the lives of most Irish people, both Catholic and Protestant, uniting them and dividing them. Schools, charitable services, and many hospitals were denominationally based. Church attendance was almost universal, and in contrast to continental Europe, men and women were equally devout. The practice of religion commonly went far beyond attending church on Sunday; it involved additional devotions or charitable work. Sporting clubs, musical societies, bands, dramatic groups, and scout troops were based around the church; so too were seaside outings, weekly dances, and even foreign travel. Most Irish Catholics first traveled to Europe on a pilgrimage to Rome or Lourdes. Social activities strengthened religious divisions, as did attitudes toward the Sabbath. Catholics went to church on Sundays, but they also danced and traveled to Gaelic Athletic Association matches; they did not dance on Saturday nights. Protestant Sabbatarianism ruled out social activities on Sundays.

SOCIAL CHANGE

While it would be incorrect to assume that nothing changed between the 1920s and the 1950s, nevertheless the pace of change was slow because of the lack of economic development and because Ireland, both North and South, was less affected by World War II than other European countries. In 1926 a majority of men (571 out of every 1,000) earned their living in farming; in 1961 the figure was 426. During the mid-1950s, soaring emigration forced a rethinking of economic policy and an acceptance that industrial development was essential to national survival. Although emigration may have reduced the pressures for change—by removing the discontented and the unemployed and by relieving the Irish state of the need to provide for the offspring of large families—it had a critical influence on aspirations and tastes. Reports of large pay packets, paid holidays, and a lively social life created dissatisfaction among servant girls who worked long hours in Irish homes for little more than their keep, and among farmers' adult sons who had to ask a parent for the price of a packet of cigarettes or admission to the cinema. Ireland was English-speaking, and British and American films were extremely popular. Thus, despite strict censorship, jazz and the fashions set by Hollywood permeated all parts of Ireland. British television reached Northern Ireland and its hinterland in 1955, but the remainder of the island remained a television-free zone until an Irish state service opened on 31 December 1961. The timing reinforces the sense that the 1960s was a decade of major change in Irish society.

EMPLOYMENT AND CLASS

During the 1960s the Irish Republic changed from a predominantly agrarian economy to a mainly industrial economy. By 1986 only one-fifth of male workers were engaged in farming; it has been predicted that by 2010 there will be only 20,000 full-time farmers. There has been a steady growth in the numbers employed in factory or service jobs in foreign multinational companies, and in government service. The proportion of the population in professional, white-collar, and skilled jobs has risen sharply, and there has been a corresponding fall in the numbers employed in family businesses. Recruitment is now primarily by merit; in the past it was commonly on the basis of kinship, family, or church connections. The traditional prejudice in farming families against factory jobs, especially for women, has been eroded by good pay and working conditions, while the

needs of multinational companies and equality legislation have forced the Irish government to abandon its policy of giving preference to industries that recruited men. Between 1971 and 1991 the number of women in paid employment in the Irish Republic increased by 40 percent. In the 1990s the participation of women in the labor force soared, and the proportion of married women at work is now close to the European Union (EU) average. In Northern Ireland the number of farmers has likewise fallen, but so too have the numbers employed in manufacturing industry, with the loss of jobs in traditional textile and shipbuilding plants. Public service is now the largest employer; the proportion of women in paid employment remains above that of the Irish Republic, although the gap is closing.

Irish voters have traditionally voted on the basis of religion and nationalism, not class. In 1920, Belfast was the only Irish city with a significant number of factory workers, but religious differences generally transcended class interests; workplaces and occupations were often demarcated by religion, and the trade-union movement in Northern Ireland has failed to establish itself as an effective alternative to the sectarian groupings. In Dublin and other Irish cities the working class was mainly employed in transportation and other service industries, and the dispersed and casual nature of the work worked against the emergence of a strong labor movement. Emigration, a common response to economic depression, also weakened workers' clout. Access to many skilled crafts was restricted to family members, further dividing the working class. There has been a substantial rise in trade-union membership since the 1960s, particularly among white-collar and public-service workers, but trade-union power has been reflected in quasi-corporatist bargaining with government and employers, not through the electoral process. This system began in the 1960s with the negotiation of national pay rounds. Since the late 1980s, "social partnership" involving government, employers, trade unions, and voluntary organizations has played a central role in determining policy on pay, healthcare, taxes, and welfare.

POPULATION

A sharp fall in the rate of emigration during the 1960s brought a century of population decline in the Irish Republic to an end. By the early 1970s returning emigrants outnumbered those who were leaving. The 1960s also brought a marriage boom and a fall in the age of marriage; family limitation became the norm, with many women using the contraceptive pill. The number of births peaked in 1980, twenty years later than in other developed countries; until then the decline in family size was offset by the increase in the number of marriages. In 1980 the Irish birthrate was double the European average, but fertility fell sharply during that decade; in 1991 it was below replacement level and it remains so today. Throughout this time fertility in Northern Ireland was lower than in the Irish Republic, and this remains so.

Ireland is no longer out of line with European demographic trends: The birthrate is below replacement level in both parts of Ireland, although it is one of the highest in Europe; almost one-third of babies are born outside marriage. The Irish remain rather reluctant to marry; the marriage rate is below the EU average, and a growing number of marriages end in separation or divorce. Male and female life expectancy, both North and South, remains slightly below the EU average. Until the 1950s Irish women were almost unique in Europe in having a lower life expectancy than men, but this has been reversed. Since the 1990s the Irish Republic, traditionally a country of net emigration, has begun to attract increasing numbers of immigrants, both returning emigrants and migrants from eastern Europe and the Third World; immigration into Northern Ireland is now lower than into the Republic. The major distinction between Ireland and its EU partners is in the average age of the population; Ireland's belated baby boom, together with the high rate of emigration during the 1950s, means that the proportion of the population of pensionable age is well below the EU average.

CHURCH AND STATE

The influence of the Catholic Church on Irish society probably peaked during the 1960s. At that time there were sufficient male and female religious to staff an extensive network of schools, nursing homes, and other institutions, and a devout laity had not yet begun to question the authority of the church. But the sharp fall in the numbers entering religious life during the 1970s forced the Catholic Church to begin to withdraw from schools and other institutions. The rapid expansion in the number of men and women with second- and third-level education in the 1970s created an alternative cohort of community leaders, especially in rural Ireland, and a population that questions the views expressed by church leaders. Recent revelations of physical and sexual abuse by religious have further damaged the church's authority. The 1995 referendum permitting divorce and the defeat of the 2002 referendum that attempted to strengthen restrictions on abortion reflect a waning of the Catholic Church's influence on the electorate and on social policy. But while church attendance has fallen, it remains well above the European average, and pilgrimages or religious events, such as the 2001 tour of

the bones of Saint Thérèse of Lisieux, continue to attract large attendances.

It is more difficult to chart the changing role of the Protestant churches because their authority is more decentralized, but they too have suffered from falling church attendance and a shortage of ministers. Social life for both Protestants and Catholics no longer centers around the church. In the Republic of Ireland, where the Protestant community accounts for 3 percent to 4 percent of the population (compared with 7 percent in 1926), denominational divisions are fading, perhaps because of a growing indifference to religion. More than 5 percent of couples now opt for civil marriages, and a growing number of parents send their children to multidenominational schools. For the first time in the history of the state, no new Catholic or Protestant schools opened in 2002, although there were several new Moslem schools. In Northern Ireland religious loyalties continue to unite and divide communities, although many of those who make use of religion for political ends rarely attend church. Catholics accounted for one-third of the population of Northern Ireland in 1926, a figure that remained largely unchanged until the 1970s because a higher Catholic birthrate was offset by Catholic emigration. The proportion of Catholics has risen in recent decades, and it now stands at 43 percent to 44 percent. In 1911 Belfast housing was heavily segregated by religion, and it is even more so today. But fairemployment legislation has brought a marked reduction in segregated employment. Belfast Sundays no longer reflect the Sabbatarian strictures of the Protestant religion: Public parks, shops, and even public houses are now open.

The diminishing role of the church in Irish society has been partly filled by the state. In 1922 both Irish states provided old-age pensions for those seventy or older without means and insurance against sickness and unemployment for industrial workers. The poorest one-third of the population were provided with free medical treatment, and all children were entitled to free primary schooling. The expansion of social services in Northern Ireland was dictated by developments in Britain. The 1940s saw the introduction of a welfare state in Northern Ireland which provided universal insurance against sickness and unemployment, old-age pensions regardless of income, a health service that was available to everybody free of charge, and free secondary schooling. These developments were initially viewed with suspicion by the socially conservative politicians in Northern Ireland, who placed a high premium on selfreliance; the Catholic Church was likewise wary about the reforms in health and education. In time unionist politicians saw the superior social services as evidence of the benefits of union with Britain. The civil-rights campaign of the 1960s was prompted by Catholic demands for equal access to the benefits of this welfare state, particularly in housing and government employment.

In the Irish Free State public spending increased after 1932, when the incoming Fianna Fáil government embarked on a major housing drive and unemployment assistance (the dole) was introduced to provide a basic income for small farmers, laborers, and others who were unable to emigrate because of the international recession. Although these payments were designed to thwart social change by enabling people to survive on small plots of land, this was the first time that many smallholders had received a regular cash income, and it resulted in major changes in consumption—the increased use of shop-bought food, more tobacco, and probably more Guinness. The expansion in welfare services in Britain and Northern Ireland during the 1940s prompted demands for comparable services in the Irish Republic, but the state could not afford British-style welfare services, and the Catholic Church was opposed to "the servile state"; it believed that universal free health care would undermine the family, so the improvements were modest. Nevertheless, by the early 1950s the overwhelming majority of mothers and babies were eligible for free maternity and childcare. A major housing drive removed countless urban and rural slums (including thousands of thatched cottages), and loans and subsidies provided by the state helped to bring about one of the highest rates of homeownership in the world. Although the late 1960s saw a major extension in government funding for second- and third-level education, which were regarded as an essential element in the drive for economic growth, the Irish Republic continued to lag behind Northern Ireland. After 1973 the European Economic Community assumed the cost of farm support, and this freed up money for improved welfare services. The major changes in state support since the 1970s reflect the emergence of new problems, such as the severe rise in long-term unemployment after 1973, or the consequences of changing demography and family structures, such as the rise in the number of single parents. EU directives and national legislation guarantee an equal entitlement to benefits regardless of gender, race, or sexual orientation. The stigma that was once associated with relying on the state has largely vanished. More than one-third of the population are beneficiaries of state welfare payments; access to publicly funded healthcare, welfare, and education is regarded as a right, and there are strong pressure groups demanding that these services should be expanded. Expenditure on social protection in the Irish Republic remains below the EU average, partly because of a smaller number of pensioners and elderly dependents, but also because of a less extensive benefits system. But in the Irish Republic, and to a lesser extent in Northern Ireland, demands for better public services conflict with demands for lower taxes, and the future direction of Irish society—the choice between Boston and Berlin, between a free-enterprise society such as the United States, or one based on European social democracy—has yet to be determined.

The major change since 1922 has been the belated convergence between Ireland and other developed countries, and the emergence of a modern Irish industrial/postindustrial consumer society that is part of a wider global culture. Lauren, Chloe, Dylan, and Aaron were among the most popular names for Irish children born in 2000; Mary did not make the top twenty-five, but Patrick squeezed in at number sixteen. Irish marriage and fertility patterns are no longer exceptional; the lifestyle of most Irish families—the suburban homes, long commutes, shopping malls, foreign holidays, and multichannel televisions—resembles that of other developed countries. Statistics on educational standards, material wealth, and other indices confirm that similarity. Irish pop music, literature, and sport have become part of a global culture, but they have not been swamped by it. Indeed, the international standing of Irish popular musicians such as Van Morrison and U2 is disproportionate to Ireland's population. Traditional music and distinctively Irish sports such as hurling have adapted to the global challenge and now thrive alongside pop music and soccer, often attracting the same supporters.

Ireland resembles other developed countries in one less happy respect: economic development has not eliminated social inequality. Although the numbers in absolute poverty have fallen sharply, poorer households remain at a considerable disadvantage in such matters as health, life expectancy, and education. Some of this disadvantage, such as the high rate of adult illiteracy, is a legacy of the past—the numerous children who left school at an early age because of family pressures. Irish cities, North and South, contain substantial numbers of working-class families who have benefited little from the expansion in education and job opportunities. But despite fears about the depopulation of rural Ireland, the actual facts are positive: in 2002 the population of every county increased, some for the first time since the Great Famine. Mayo, traditionally one of the poorest counties, has the highest rate of participation in third-level education. The pace of social change in Ireland was among the fastest in Europe at the end of the twentieth century, and this seems likely to remain the case for some time.

SEE ALSO Divorce, Contraception, and Abortion; Family: Fertility, Marriage, and the Family since 1950; Farming Families; Health and Welfare since 1950, State Provisions for; Industry since 1920; Media since 1960; Migration: Emigration and Immigration since 1950; Music: Popular Music; Roman Catholic Church: Since 1891; Secularization; Sport and Leisure; Women and Work since the Mid-Nineteenth Century; Women in Irish Society since 1800

Bibliography

Arensberg, Conrad M., and Solon T. Kimball. *Family and Community in Ireland.* 1968.

Central Statistics Office. *Statistical Year-Book of Ireland.* Annual publication.

Clancy, Patrick, Sheelagh Drudy, Kathleen Lynch, and Liam O'Dowd. *Ireland: A Sociological Profile.* 1986.

Coulter, Colin. *Contemporary Northern Irish Society: An Introduction.* 1999.

Goldthorpe, J. H., and C. T. Whelan. *The Development of Industrial Society in Ireland.* 1992.

Harris, Rosemary. *Prejudice and Tolerance in Ulster: A Study of Neighbours and "Strangers" in a Border Community.* 1972.

Kennedy, Liam. *People and Population Change.* 1994.

Litton, Frank. *Unequal Achievement—The Irish Experience, 1957–1982.* 1982.

Nolan, Brian, Philip J. O'Connell, and Christopher T. Whelan. *Bust to Boom? The Irish Experience of Growth and Inequality.* 2000.

Northern Ireland Statistics Research Agency. *Annual Abstract of Statistics.* Annual publication.

Mary E. Daly

Sodalities and Confraternities

Sodalities and confraternities were associations for lay people who wished to perform religious work and achieve personal sanctification by means of special devotional practices or charitable endeavors; their overall aim was to promote religious observance under ecclesiastical direction. There was a dramatic increase in the level of popular devotion to Catholicism in the latter part of the nineteenth century attributable to the impact of the Great Famine, among other things, but given the scale of prefamine church-building, it is likely that the upsurge was in train prior to the 1840s. In 1850 the Synod of Thurles, the first national assembly of the Irish church for almost 700 years, established an up-to-date code of ecclesiastical law and consolidated reforms and discipline within the Catholic Church, making a contribution to a "devotional revolution," which was further strengthened by the appointment of the archbishop of Armagh, Paul Cullen, as archbishop of Dublin in 1852.

Politically conservative, Cullen was an upholder of Ultramontanism, or the exaltation of papal authority, and he sought to oversee a new discipline and devotion in the Irish Catholic Church. During this era the involvement of Irish Catholics in confraternities and sodalities was seen as an essential contribution to external piety, accompanied at the end of the nineteenth century by new publications with large circulations, such as the *Irish Messenger of the Sacred Heart*, the *Irish Rosary*, and the *Irish Catholic*.

The promotion of this new piety was also helped by an explosion in the numbers joining religious orders. Nuns, for example, increased eightfold between 1841 and 1901. The greatest growth was recorded by the Irish Sisters of Mercy, founded in Dublin by Catherine McAuley in the late 1820s. In 1841 there were 100 nuns in this order; by the end of the nineteenth century there were 8,000. Priests anxious to improve the spiritual practices of their flocks inaugurated confraternities and sodalities in parishes and dioceses throughout the country, including confraternities of the Holy Family and Christian Doctrine, and sodalities focusing on the Virgin Mary and the rosary. Some of these organizations also had a role to play in combating the efforts of Protestant proselytizers.

By the end of the nineteenth century there was a huge variety of sodalities and confraternities to choose from. The number often depended on the enthusiasm and organizing skill of the parish priests. Their existence was also indicative of an emphasis on "externalism" in religious practice over interior spirituality. In the absence of a scriptural tradition in scholarship or popular piety, the Catholic Church proved itself capable of organizing mass public devotion, as exemplified by the gathering of one million Catholics in Dublin city for the Eucharistic Congress of 1932.

A precursor of the widespread institutionalization of Catholic piety was the attempt to inculcate temperance undertaken by Theobald Mathew, a Capuchin monk. Father Mathew inaugurated a relentless temperance crusade, through the Cork Total Abstinence Society, beginning in 1838 and quickly spreading to the rest of the country. Initially an attempt to address the serious issue of excessive drinking, it developed into a more populist crusade based on the idea of pledging among the masses. It was, superficially at least, a phenomenal short-term success, but it declined within a decade and left no durable structures behind. Undoubtedly, the famine and the social disruption, emigration, and death toll that it left fatally undermined the temperance movement.

More successful and durable was the Pioneer Total Abstinence Association, established in Dublin in 1898 by the Wexford Jesuit James Cullen, who devised a "heroic offering" in which people pledged to abstain completely from alcohol for life. It became the country's most successful Catholic lay movement, and its Jesuit directors vigorously decried the pervasive Irish drink culture. Its golden jubilee in 1949 attracted 90,000 people to Croke Park in Dublin. Membership peaked at nearly 500,000 in the 1950s, after which it went into decline.

Popular Marian societies seemed to reach their apex in Ireland in the 1950s, after which their membership contracted dramatically. By the end of the twentieth century the Legion of Mary, which was closely associated with missionary work, had a membership of 8,000, less than one-third the membership in the late 1950s and early 1960s. Another important Marian institution was the Jesuit-led Sodality of Our Lady. In 1958 there were as many as 823 local sodalities with a total membership of 250,000, but by 1975 only 82 sodalities remained. The Jesuits' attempts to transform these old-style sodalities into Christian Life Communities failed. Other significant religious activists included the prayer groups devoted to Our Lady of Fatima, Padre Pio, and Medjugorje. In recent decades members of these prayer groups have become political lobbyists against contraception, abortion, and divorce.

The collapse in the number of vocations to the priesthood and religious life, from 34,000 in 1967 to fewer than 20,000 by the end of the century, was also notable in the context of the waning influence of sodalities and confraternities. Their decline was further fueled by Vatican II reforms, which redirected activity toward dialogue with other churches and stressed the importance of inner spirituality and devotion to Christ rather than to Mary.

SEE ALSO Ancient Order of Hibernians; Devotional Revolution; Marianism; Orange Order: Since 1800; Religion: Since 1690; Religious Orders: Men; Religious Orders: Women; Temperance Movements; Roman Catholic Church: 1829 to 1891; Roman Catholic Church: Since 1891

Bibliography

Clear, Catriona. *Nuns in Nineteenth-Century Ireland.* 1987.

Donnelly, James S., Jr. "A Church in Crisis: The Irish Catholic Church Today." *History Ireland* 8, no. 3 (autumn 2000): 12–17.

Ferriter, Diarmaid. *A Nation of Extremes: The Pioneers in Twentieth-Century Ireland.* 1999.

Keenan, Desmond. *The Catholic Church in Nineteenth-Century Ireland.* 1983.

Mac Reamoinn, Seán. *Freedom to Hope? The Catholic Church in Ireland Twenty Years after Vatican II.* 1985.

Townend, Paul. *Father Mathew, Temperance, and Irish Identity.* 2002.

Whyte, John H. *Church and State in Modern Ireland, 1923–79.* New edition, 1980.

Diarmaid Ferriter

Solemn League and Covenant

The Solemn League and Covenant was drawn up in Edinburgh by commissioners for the Scottish Covenanters and English parliamentarians in the late summer of 1643. The treaty was of fundamental military, religious, and constitutional significance for Ireland as well as Scotland and England. In the first place, the Covenanters, already victorious in Scotland, were committed to help the parliamentarians defeat the royalist cause in England and, by extension, provide potential support for Charles I in Ireland. In the second place, Presbyterianism was to be imposed as the religious establishment throughout the three kingdoms. Thus, not only episcopacy but also independent sects and, above all, Roman Catholicism, which was associated with the forces of the Antichrist, were to be swept aside. In the third place, confessional solidarity within the three kingdoms was to be underscored by the replacement of regal union, operational under the Stuart dynasty since 1603, by confederal union. The Solemn League and Covenant did result in a victory over the royalist forces in England, but it also led to an intensification of civil war in both Scotland and Ireland. This treaty of confessional confederation instigated what became the Wars for the Three Kingdoms, in which Oliver Cromwell emerged triumphant and both Scotland and Ireland were reduced to satellite states under the English republic by 1651.

The Scots provided the main ideological input for the Solemn League and Covenant, a compact based on the National Covenant of 1638, in which the Scots had justified their revolution against Charles I. There were two imperatives to which all signatories were committed. In religious terms a Presbyterian reformation was to be achieved by joining the covenant of works to that of grace for national as well as individual salvation. In constitutional terms the right to resist the Crown became a mandatory one to export revolution throughout the three kingdoms. Furthermore, the most radical aspect of the National Covenant was reiterated almost verbatim in the Solemn League and Covenant, notably in the oath of allegiance and mutual association, which upheld the corporate right of the people to resist a lawful king who threatened to become tyrannical. Monarchy limited by parliaments was non-negotiable. This concept of a coactive power, which the Scots had borrowed from the French and Dutch advocates of the right of resistance in the late sixteenth century, was maintained by the radical mainstream of the Covenanting movement throughout the 1640s.

Supported militarily and materially by Sweden, the Covenanters had created a centralized state to enforce ideological, military, and financial commitment within Scotland and to seize the political initiative throughout the three kingdoms. Having decisively won the Bishops' Wars of 1639 to 1640, the Covenanting movement insisted upon English parliamentary participation in the peace negotiations, which were eventually brought to a conclusion by the Treaty of London in August 1641. In the interim Scottish commissioners were invited by the English Long Parliament to instigate the prosecution of the lord-deputy of Ireland, Thomas Wentworth, earl of Strafford.

Ever since the first sustained appeal to British public opinion in the prelude to the Bishops' Wars, the Covenanting leadership had aimed to secure a lasting alliance by a defensive and offensive league—that is, by a confederation (not a union) between Scotland and England. These negotiations were overtaken by the outbreak of the Irish rebellion in October 1641. The return from Ireland of planters and settlers in the wake of the rebellion there in 1641 had given a British resonance to Covenanting ideology. The refugees' presence was a continuous reminder of the Catholic threat not only from Ireland but also from the Counter-Reformation in continental Europe. The Covenanting leadership was not prepared to accept Charles I's invitation to protect the plantations without the consent of the English parliament. Fears of a "popish plot," reputedly organized by the hapless Randal MacDonnell, marquis of Antrim, to bring armed assistance from Ireland to the royalist cause throughout Britain, confirmed public opinion in favor of a federative treaty between the Scottish Covenanters and English parliamentarians in 1643. Ostensibly intending to supply the Scottish army in Ireland and to review the arrears of financial reparations due under the Treaty of London, the Covenanting radicals summoned a convention of "estates" which cemented a formal alliance for armed cooperation between the Scottish estates and the English parliament on 26 August. Ireland was included within the remit of the Solemn League and Covenant only at English insistence. The Scots were reluctant to accord equal standing to a satellite kingdom whose dominant religion was manifest from the confederation which the Irish Catholics had established at Kilkenny in July 1642.

Despite the initial success of armed intervention in England, British confessional confederation was beset by difficulties. Internal divisions in the parliamentary forces between the Presbyterians and the Independents were compounded by tensions between the parliamentarians and Covenanters. These tensions in turn were aggravated by the hostility generated in the north of England by Scottish occupation. In Ireland the endeavors of the Scottish army to break out of Ulster were ended by the forces of the Catholic Confederation at Dundalk in June 1646. The British influence of the Covenanting movement had been further weakened by the outbreak of debilitating civil war at home. James Graham, marquis of Montrose, ran a brilliant guerrilla campaign for the royalists in 1644 to 1645, assisted by Alasdair Mac-Colla and forces from Ulster sponsored by the Catholic Confederation. Although their cause was crushed by 1647, the intensity of their campaigning had obliged contingents of the Covenanting army to withdraw from England. The transfer of Charles I from the custody of Covenanters to the English parliament in January of that year had revived the movement's conservative element. Under the terms of an "Engagement" that came into force in 1648, Charles I was not obliged to subscribe to the covenants or to impose Presbyterianism on England for more than a trial period of three years. This effective rescinding of the coactive power over monarchy conceded that the Covenanters had lost the political initiative within Britain. Armed intervention in renewed English civil war in the summer of 1648 ended disastrously at Preston and enabled the radicals to stage a successful revolt with support from Oliver Cromwell.

News of the execution of Charles I on 30 January 1649 sundered this collaboration of the Covenanting radicals with Cromwell. Their immediate proclamation of Charles II as king of Great Britain and Ireland reasserted the supranational identity of the house of Stuart. Charles II's subscription to the National Covenant and the Solemn League prior to his coronation on 1 January 1651 underscored the old element of confessional confederation, but also provoked the occupation of Scotland by English forces. With Cromwellian armies triumphant in all three kingdoms, enforced union was marked first by the Commonwealth and then the Protectorate of England, Scotland, and Ireland. This deliberate avoidance of a "Great Britain" was an emphatic rejection of both the Stuart dynasty and confederal union through covenanting. The Restoration of 1660 produced constitutional settlements that publicly abrogated covenanting, which a militant minority maintained as a movement of protest, but no longer of power, in Ulster as well as Scotland. Covenanting has retained a residual appeal for those intent on asserting Scottish independence of, and Ulster autonomy from, Anglican supremacy.

SEE ALSO Calvinist Influences in Early Modern Ireland; Cromwellian Conquest; Puritan Sectaries; Rebellion of 1641

Bibliography

Cowan, Edward J. "The Solemn League and Covenant." In *Scotland and England, 1286–1815*, edited by Roger A. Mason. 1987.

Dickinson, William C., and Gordon Donaldson, eds. *A Source Book of Scottish History*. Vol. 3. 1961.

Macinnes, Allan I. "Covenanting Ideology in Seventeenth-Century Scotland." In *Political Thought in Seventeenth-Century Ireland: Kingdom or Colony*, edited by Jane H. Ohlmeyer. 2000.

Morrill, John. "The Britishness of the English Revolution, 1640–1660." In *Three Nations—A Common History? England, Scotland, Ireland, and British History, c. 1600–1920*, edited by R. G. Asch. 1993.

Pocock, John. "The Atlantic Archipelago and the War of the Three Kingdoms." In *The British Problem, c. 1534–1707*, edited by Brendan Bradshaw and John Morrill. 1996.

Stevenson, David. "The Early Covenanters and the Federal Union of Britain." In *Scotland and England, 1286–1815*, edited by Roger A. Mason. 1987.

Young, John R. "The Scottish Parliament and European Diplomacy, 1641–1647: The Palatinate, The Dutch Republic and Sweden." In *Scotland and the Thirty Years' War, 1618–1648*, edited by Steve Murdoch. 2001.

Allan I. Macinnes

Special Powers Act

The act, introduced in March 1922 and enacted in April, was initially intended as an emergency measure to deal with widespread political violence. The Northern Ireland parliament debate on its introduction (attended exclusively by unionists, since nationalist MPs were boycotting the new institution) reveals widespread belief that the British regime in Ireland had failed through weak and indecisive government. The rulers of the new statelet were determined to impress their enemies with the statelet's determination to survive.

The act endowed the Northern Ireland government with most of the powers granted to the imperial government under the 1914 Defence of the Realm Act (DORA) and the 1920 Restoration of Order in Ireland Act (ROIA), except for the right to create courts-martial. It allowed "the civil authority," defined as the minister of home affairs, to "take all such steps and issue all such orders as may be necessary for preserving the peace and maintaining order"; the minister could delegate this authority, in whole or in part, to any police officer. (One later critic alleged that in theory the act authorized the minister to delegate his powers to a single police constable, who could then with perfect legality intern the whole population of Northern Ireland, including the minister.) It created courts of summary jurisdiction (composed of resident magistrates without juries) to try offenses against it. Offenses were punishable by two years' imprisonment and/or a fine of £100, with confiscation of goods or articles "in respect of which the offence has been committed." The act also allowed offenders to be flogged, which had not been provided for in its DORA or ROIA prototypes.

Thirty-five regulations contained in a schedule to the act gave the minister extensive powers, including the right to declare curfews; to prohibit or restrict assemblies; to enter, close, and take possession of property; to compel persons to supply information; to arrest and detain without warrant; to make membership of certain organizations a criminal offense; and to prohibit the circulation of any newspaper. Some of these regulations derived from DORA and ROIA and their associated regulations; others were completely new. Offences under the act were defined in extremely broad terms, which allowed almost any action to be declared illegal; most notoriously, Section 2(4) stated, "If any person does any act of such a nature as to be calculated to be prejudicial to the preservation of the peace or maintenance of order in Northern Ireland and not specifically provided for in the regulations, he shall be deemed to be guilty of an offence against the regulations."

The minister was authorized to make further regulations for the preservation of the peace and maintenance of order, and to amend existing regulations; over 100 regulations were made during the act's existence. Regulations did not require prior approval from the

Northern Ireland parliament and could not be amended or repealed by it, although a majority in either House could petition the lord lieutenant (later the governor of Northern Ireland) to annul a regulation within fourteen parliamentary days after the regulation was laid before that House. (No such petition was ever submitted.)

Regulation 23 was supplemented on 1 June 1922 to allow internment, and the minister's powers in this regard were progressively extended. Seven hundred thirty-two persons (mostly republicans) were interned in the period 1922–1924, and the regulation provided the basis for subsequent use of internment in 1938–1946, 1956–1961, and 1971–1973. Further amendments allowed the minister to impose restriction orders excluding persons from all or part of Northern Ireland. The enforcement of the act certainly contributed to the fall-off in violence from late 1922 (though this was also due to the outbreak of the Civil War in the Free State).

The act was initially to remain in force for one year. In November 1922 it was extended until 31 December 1923; thereafter it was extended annually until 1928, when it was renewed for five years. By this stage its rationale had shifted from restoring law and order to defending the state by suppressing the public expression of republican (and, to a lesser extent, communist) views; opposition to partition was equated with sedition. The act was rarely used against loyalists, though about twenty Protestant paramilitaries were interned and three were flogged in 1923. Loyalist publications and processions were never banned under the act, and its use to suppress nationalist processions and such activities as the flying of the tricolor were often justified in expressly communal and political terms.

In 1936 the British National Council for Civil Liberties issued a report criticizing the act and arguing that such powers were unnecessary in peacetime; the Northern Ireland government dismissed the report as unduly influenced by nationalists. Over ninety processions and meetings were banned under the act between 1922 and 1950 (after which the 1951 Public Order Act came into effect). In the period 1924–1971, 52 orders were issued banning over 140 publications.

The act was made permanent in 1933. In 1943 it was amended to increase penalties for offences under the act that might previously have been covered by the Treason-Felony Act (which required higher standards of evidence and, as a Westminster enactment, could not be streamlined by Stormont). The act was employed less frequently after World War II, partly because of the province's relative stability and partly because some of its functions were taken over by other legislation. However, it was used during the 1956–1962 IRA border campaign. In 1957 the powers given to the RUC under the act were extended by regulation to soldiers. (This regulation provided the legal basis for the British army's role in maintaining law and order from August 1969. In February 1972 the regulation was declared *ultra vires* by the courts on the grounds that the Northern Ireland parliament could not legislate for the army, whose control was reserved to the Westminster parliament; as a result, Westminster introduced retrospective legislation to legitimize the Army's actions.)

Abolition of the act was one of the principal demands of the civil-rights campaign of the late 1960s, and some of the act's provisions were employed against civil-rights demonstrations. The Special Powers Act was repealed in 1973, but many of its provisions survived in the 1973 Northern Ireland Emergency Powers Act and subsequent antiterrorist legislation.

Contemporary and subsequent criticism of the act centers on its selective implementation, its cession of legislative powers to the executive, its institutionalization of emergency provisions as everyday legislation, and its vague and far-reaching terms. Defenders of the act stressed the ongoing existence of an armed conspiracy against the state and pointed to the harsh emergency legislation considered necessary by the southern state (including widespread executions by summary courts-martial during the Civil War and the deployment in the 1930s and 1940s of military tribunals entitled to impose the death penalty). The controversies surrounding the Special Powers Act ultimately reflected the ethnic division within the statelet (making conflict more intractable than in the post-independence south) and the majority-rule government's equation of opposition with a threat to the state's existence.

In 1963 the future South African apartheid Prime Minster Johannes Verster told critics of his own emergency legislation that he would gladly exchange it for the Northern Ireland Special Powers Act (Bell 1993, p. 45).

SEE ALSO Irish Republican Army (IRA); Royal Ulster Constabulary (including Specials)

Bibliography

Bell, J. Bowyer. *The Irish Troubles.* 1993.

Campbell, Colin. *Emergency Law in Ireland, 1918–1925.* 1994.

Donohue, Laura K. "Regulating Northern Ireland: The Special Powers Acts, 1922–72." *Historical Journal* 41, no. 4 (December 1998): 1089–1120.

Donohue, Laura K. *Counter-Terrorist Law and Emergency Powers in the United Kingdom, 1922–2000.* 2001.

Patrick Maume

Spenser, Edmund

The poet Edmund Spenser (1552/3–1599) was a planter and provincial official in Ireland. Like much else concerning his experience in Ireland, the date of Spenser's first arrival remains uncertain and contentious. The claim that he visited there in the late 1570s has allowed for some speculation about the influence of the island on his work, but it rests on the questionable identification of Spenser with Irenius, the fictional interlocutor in his dialogue *A View of the Present State of Ireland* (1596), who claimed to have been present at an execution at Limerick datable to 1577. No other evidence for Spenser's presence exists before August 1580, when he arrived as the private secretary of Lord Deputy Grey de Wilton. The political influence he exercised in this position is indeterminate, depending upon one's assessment of his role in the composition of the state correspondence, of which he made fair copies. But independent evidence confirms his presence with Grey during the latter's bloody Munster campaigns (1580–1581), and at the massacre of the surrendered garrison at Smerwick, reported on approvingly by Irenius. Grey rewarded Spenser's service with a gift of 162 pounds and a free appointment to the lucrative post of clerk of faculties in the Irish chancery in 1581.

Spenser began early to speculate in Irish lands, acquiring and selling leases of monastic properties in County Wexford, purchasing the Dublin townhouse of the attainted Viscount Baltinglass, and leasing as his residence the substantial property of New Abbey, Co. Kildare. In the later 1580s Spenser began to invest in attainted lands in Munster, acquiring some small leases and a major estate of 3,000 (grossly underestimated) acres at Kilcolman, Co. Cork. He then resigned his chancery post, and on his appointment as clerk of the council in Munster (1588) he took up residence at Kilcolman. Spenser's investment was afflicted by organizational and tenurial troubles from the outset. An increasingly troublesome lawsuit with his Anglo-Irish neighbor David Roche caused him to visit London in 1589 to 1591 in the hope of securing a favorable outcome. But though he was granted a royal pension of fifty pounds per year, he made no progress with his suit, which was determined against him to his considerable cost in 1594. Spenser then resigned from the Munster council, and his writings during this period suggest that he had become severely embittered by his Munster experience.

Still, the depth and duration of his disillusion should not be overstated. His marriage to Elizabeth Boyle, niece of the rising Munster planter Richard Boyle, is an indication of his determination to stay in Ireland and a sign that he was acquiring powerful friends in the region. By 1597 he was again investing in leases, and in 1598 he accepted appointment as sheriff of Cork. Within a month of his taking office, however, the entire plantation was overthrown in a massive rebellion fueled by the successes of the Ulster lords against the English government. Kilcolman was burned and Spenser was forced to take refuge in Cork city. Ben Jonson's claim that Spenser had lost a son in the fire, though possible, lacks corroboration. In December he was despatched to London by Lord President Norris with reports on the state of the rebellion on the understanding that he would return with instructions. But within weeks of his arrival in London he died, on 16 January 1599.

The importance of his Irish experience to Spenser's literary work is certain but difficult to evaluate. The greater part of Books II through VI of *The Faerie Queene* was composed in Ireland, and references to the country abound throughout the poem. The severe political and social attitudes struck in Book V have frequently been accounted for in relation to events in Ireland. But the complexities of his multilayered poem continue to defy reductionist interpretation. More readily explicable is Spenser's *View*. The radicalism of his analysis of the Irish problem (that no ordinary English policy could resolve it) and the ruthlessness of his proposed solution (cultural trauma through mass starvation) is undisputed (except by those who maintain that he never wrote it at all). But the internal coherence, representative character, and influence over contemporaries of a text that, though circulating in manuscript, remained unprinted until 1633 continues to stimulate scholarly debate.

SEE ALSO Colonial Theory from 1500 to 1690; Desmond Rebellions; English Writing on Ireland before 1800; **Primary Documents:** From *A View of the Present State of Ireland* (1596)

Bibliography

Coughlan, Patricia, ed. *Spenser in Ireland: An Interdisciplinary Perspective.* 1989.

Hadfield, Andrew. *Spenser's Irish Experience: Wilde Fruit and Salvage Soyle.* 1997.

Judson, A. C. *The Life of Edmund Spenser.* 1945.

Spenser, Edmund. *A View of the Present State of Ireland: From the First Printed Edition (1633).* Edited by Andrew Hadfield and Willy Maley. 1997.

Ciaran Brady

Sport and Leisure

Early Irish sporting rituals sit easily within a broad human heritage: The stories in myth and legend, the etchings of ball and stick on tombstones and elsewhere, and the rough-and-tumble football matches of village against village find echoes across the world. The eventual organization of communal, casual sports into the highly regulated sporting bodies that now dominate the Irish sporting world was also part of a global phenomenon, although the distinctive regional variations offer a unique perspective on sporting traditions.

For centuries sport in Ireland has been influenced by divisions of class. Conspicuous displays of leisure were an integral part of the lives of the aristocracy. Often, these rituals involved bloodsports including foxhunting, which was introduced from England in the eighteenth century, though the sport hunting of other animals was already long established in Ireland. Later sports such as tennis and polo were somewhat more genteel and were as much about courtship ritual as competitive endeavor. Among the peasantry sporting activity often took place in tandem with fairs and markets. Drink and gambling were an ever present feature at almost all sporting activities. Bullbaiting and cockfighting were popular (the latter until the twentieth century), as were feats of strength and athletic prowess, which play an important part in Irish folklore. Throwing weights, in particular, was a favored pastime of the rural poor. Irish throwers won numerous throwing and running contests at British championships and at the Olympics before 1920, and local competitions often drew huge crowds to see amateur and professionals compete. Later, Irish athletes enjoyed occasional international success, but limited resources and the inability of athletic organizations to cooperate has ensured that success has been borne of individual brilliance rather than systematic design; most leading Irish athletes sought to progress through the U.S. collegiate system.

There has also been a huge interest in boxing, with fighters such as Dan Donnelly in the early nineteenth century and Jack Doyle in the mid-twentieth century earning mythological status, owing more to bluff than to brilliance. Often, contests were organized secretly to avoid suppression by the police. Amateur boxing still retains a strong hold in various towns and cities, bareknuckle fighting is sponsored by the Traveller community (a separate ethnic group with a distinctive migrant lifestyle), and occasionally Ireland produces a world professional champion.

In sports such as horse racing the interests of all classes merged. The foundation by the wealthier classes of the Turf Club in 1790 was predated by steeplechase racing, which began in Cork in 1752. Permanent courses were built across the country, and Irish-bred horses have enjoyed success in England and continental Europe. The sport has a large popular following among all social classes, and it is both a major employer and a revenue earner for the state.

Before the late nineteenth century even sports organized by the gentry were unstructured. This was altered profoundly in the Victorian era. Widespread changes in popular leisure were most pronounced in sport, and the intimate links between English and Irish society were crucial to this process. Many games were brought to Ireland from England. Cricket was the most widely played sport in Victorian Ireland. The first recorded game in the country was in August 1792. Although it was spread mainly by army officers, public schoolboys, and the upper classes, cricket was also adopted by the peasantry. Irish teams played international matches beginning in the 1880s and toured Britain and the United States. The game declined in popularity with the spread of football games and the opposition of the Gaelic Athletic Association (GAA). Following the partition of Ireland in 1921, cricket was confined largely to the North and to middle-class enclaves in Dublin, although by the end of the twentieth century there were more than 100 active clubs.

Golf, on the other hand, has been popularized since its initial status as an elite sport. The first Irish club was established in Belfast in 1881, and although there were more than 150 courses by 1950, membership was limited by the costs involved. Increased average wealth and a proliferation of clubs to more then 350 by the year 2000 changed the golfer's profile—this was emphasized by the number of golf societies based in public houses. The huge volume of golfing tourists in the country is a testament to the quality of the courses.

Although there is little documentary evidence, most scholars agree that hurling and (Gaelic) football games were played across Ireland through the early modern era. Hurling was mentioned in twelfth-century manuscripts, the Statutes of Kilkenny, and the Sunday Observance Act of 1765. It received patronage from the gentry at least until the early nineteenth century but then fell into decline. Its early playing style was similar to that of hockey, and both games have enjoyed a presence on the island in their modern forms since the 1880s. Similarly, what has evolved as Gaelic football shared similar roots to other football games, including soccer, rugby, and Australian football.

Besides introducing games, the English influence was profound in terms of the organization of sports. The codification of field games in England in the latter half of the nineteenth century was replicated in Ireland. Between 1863 and 1875 soccer, rugby, and hockey associations were established in Britain; this formal organization was enmeshed in notions of education, puritanism, and the prosecution of war, all of which brought a justificatory philosophy, at least in theory, to the playing of sports. These ideas spread across Europe and the Americas in the second half of the nineteenth century as sports were codified, and Ireland was inevitably bound into this revolution of games. Associations similar to those in England were established in Ireland between 1870 and 1890. The GAA was established in 1884, initially focusing on athletics but later concentrating on field games. In an important move, the GAA developed sets of rules that enabled the traditional Irish games of hurling and Gaelic football to be played in enclosed fields and in urban areas. By providing open, fast-moving team sports to the masses, the GAA prospered and by 1910 was drawing 25,000 people to its national finals. Rugby and soccer also drew large crowds. The Irish Rugby Football Union (IRFU) had been founded in 1879, provincial and interprovincial competitions were established, and internationals were played from 1875 on. Soccer matches were played in the north of the country from the 1860s, and the Irish Football Association (IFU) was founded in Belfast in 1880. Within two years a cup competition had been established and international games were being played. Following the spread of the game to Dublin, a league was established in the 1890s, and teams from all the provinces were represented in competition, though the game was largely restricted to urban areas.

The GAA, the IRFU, and the IFA did not enjoy harmonious relations. Interpretations of this have invariably focused on the supposed split of these associations along political lines—a split that, crudely put, sees Gaelic games as national and Irish, and all other field sports lumped into the category of "foreign games." This is a gross simplification of matters. The GAA was not as intimately involved in the struggle for independence as is often suggested, and its role in preindependence Ireland was often similar to that of other sporting bodies. Furthermore, the development of the various sporting organizations in preindependence Ireland was more profoundly shaped by social and economic factors than by political ones.

Notwithstanding this, the partition of Ireland did have a significant impact on Irish sports. After unsuccessful attempts to remain united, soccer divided along the border, with separate domestic competitions and national teams representing North and South. Soccer enjoyed greater international success in the North—Northern Ireland reached the quarterfinals of both the 1958 and the 1982 World Cups (and thereafter fell into a slump). Its domestic league suffers from the tradition of players emigrating to play professionally in the English and Scottish leagues because local bodies are unable to maintain well-paid professional clubs. The domestic league in the South suffered from a similar inability to provide for squads of full-time professionals, though this began to change in the 1990s. The Republic of Ireland qualified for the World Cup for the first time in 1990 and reached the quarterfinals, then also qualified for the 1994 and 2002 competitions. In North and South, the Irish game has traditionally suffered in comparison to the English league, whose clubs enjoy huge support across Ireland. Every weekend, thousands of fans cross the Irish Sea to support English teams. A further dimension is added with support for Rangers and Celtic in Glasgow, given their traditional associations with Irish Protestant and Catholic emigrants, respectively.

Rugby sides continued to represent Ireland on an island-wide basis, but with the exception of Limerick city, it remained a minority sport for the middle classes. This lack of a broad playing base undoubtedly contributed to Ireland's failure to win more than the one grand slam it has achieved in the Five (now Six) Nations Championship. Although rugby internationals emerged as a popular social outing, it is only since the mid-1990s with the advent of professionalization that the game has come to enjoy widespread support through the involvement of the provinces in the European Cup.

Gaelic games (hurling and Gaelic football) were organized on thirty-two–county basis, but in the North they remained the preserve of the Catholic minority. In the South such games were intimately associated with notions of an Irish Ireland, and the GAA was cited alongside the Catholic Church and Fianna Fáil as part of the Holy Trinity of orthodoxy in independent Ireland. It is the largest sporting organization in the country and has a presence in almost every parish. For many its value is as much social as sporting, and for many decades it offered one of the very few leisure opportunities in rural Ireland. The GAA was prominent in the Tailteann Games,, "the Irish Olympics," held in 1924, 1928, and 1932. These were the first official events organized by the Irish Free State, embracing sports from Gaelic games and athletics to shooting and handball. Conceived as a celebration of the Irish spirit and physique, they attracted foreign competitors before being abandoned because of lack of finance.

There are many sports which enjoy significant minority support in Ireland. Handball has been played in Ireland for more than 200 years and was exported by Irish emigrants, particularly to Australia and the United

States. At one point it was the subject of large wagers and had many professional players, but now it is an amateur sport played by more than 3,000 players. From 1968 on, the purpose-built Mondello Park in County Kildare offered a focal point for motor-racing enthusiasts. In the North, motorcycle racing enjoys huge popularity; the country's roads host the Circuit of Ireland car rally. Greyhound racing began in Ireland in 1927 and marks the adaptation of coursing to urban life. Tracks have been established across the country, and betting and breeding represents a significant industry.

The Victorian sports revolution and its aftermath are perceived as a mostly male affair, but as sports were codified, women became involved at various levels, and in the 1890s Ireland won several Wimbledon titles through Lena Rice. As tennis was traditionally associated with the wealthier classes, this suggests middle- or upper-class involvement. Similarly, women of those classes were involved in hunting and horse-riding, and in hockey, tennis, swimming, and camogie (hurling) clubs. Often, sporting activities for women were connected to schools, and female participation frequently ended at school-leaving age. In the latter decades of the twentieth century women's participation in sport grew enormously. Women's Gaelic football was the fastest growing of the field games, with soccer and rugby in close pursuit. Women's hockey also attracts many players, especially in Dublin, Cork, and the North. The Irish Ladies' Hockey Union was formed in 1894. In track and field Sonia O'Sullivan won a number of international titles, as well as a silver medal at the 2000 Olympics.

Just as in England, so too in Ireland, the understanding of sport has evolved from a narrow range of the bloodsports of the elite to an ever-expanding, eclectic assembly of pastimes. The number of sports organized in the country is growing, while traditional sports have largely retained their hold. Everything from ballroom dancing to bobsledding falls under the umbrella of sport, and the economic importance of sport—apart altogether from its emotional hold—continues to grow. Its symbiotic relationship with all forms of media gives it a central role in modern Irish life and expands its meaning and importance.

SEE ALSO GAA "Ban"; Gaelic Revivalism: The Gaelic Athletic Association; Transport—Road, Canal, Rail

Bibliography

Cronin, Mike. *Sport and Nationalism in Ireland.* 1999.

Dagg, T. S. C. *Hockey in Ireland.* 1956.

D'Arcy, Fergus. *Horses, Lords and Racing Men: The Turf Club, 1790–1990.* 1991.

de Búrca, Marcus. *The GAA: A History.* 1999.

Garnham, Neal. *The Origins and Development of Football in Ireland.* 1989.

Holt, Richard. *Sport and the British.* 1989.

Judge, Yvonne. *Chasing Gold: Sportswomen of Ireland.* 1995.

Van Esbeck, Edmund. *One Hundred Years of Irish Rugby: The Official History of the Irish Rugby Football Union.* 1974.

Paul Rouse

State Enterprise

In 1957 over 5 percent of Irish workers were employed by state-owned companies, a situation which was common in western Europe. Elsewhere in Europe the growth in the number of state-owned companies was primarily due to the nationalization of declining heavy industries, such as coal and steel, and to the ideological wishes of socialist governments. In Ireland such companies emerged as a pragmatic response to economic and political circumstances. During the 1920s, former Sinn Féin members formed the Cumann na nGaedheal government, which espoused a noninterventionist economic philosophy and created the Electricity Supply Board, and an investment bank, the Agricultural Credit Company, to provide long-term capital for farmers. After 1932 when Fianna Fáil, the new party of Eamon de Valera, came to power, state enterprises played a critical role in the drive for economic self-sufficiency: producing sugar from Irish-grown sugar beet; providing capital for newly established industries; developing Ireland's peat bogs as an alternative to imported coal and oil, and making Irish steel. Irish Shipping was founded in 1941 to keep neutral Ireland supplied with essential imports during World War II.

The postwar years saw the formation of a state tourism board, Bord Fáilte; an export board, Córas Tráchtála; the Industrial Development Authority to encourage foreign investors; and companies to promote development at Shannon Airport and in Irish-speaking areas. State enterprises helped to transform the Irish economy in the 1960s: they were more dynamic and more flexible than the civil service; state investment was a means of overcoming the lack of private investment within Ireland; and these companies encouraged a new,

The blessing of the aircraft St. Patrick *before the first transatlantic flight by an Irish airline, 1958. State companies like Aer Lingus played an important role in developing the Irish economy until recent times.* COURTESY OF AER LINGUS.

meritocratic class of businessmen at a time when most private businesses were conservative and family controlled. But in time the benefits of state ownership were increasingly offset by the drawbacks: decisions on employment and investment were often determined more by political than economic considerations, and the security of state ownership encouraged militant demands from workers and a resistance to change. By the 1980s losses in state companies were a major drain on state finances, and, spurred on by the example of Thatcher's Britain, the Irish government began a gradual process of privatization, disposing of the Irish Sugar Company, Irish Steel, two investment banks, and the state telephone service. The privatization of others is under consideration. Irish state enterprises may well be entering the twilight years; early-twenty-first-century thinking favors either private enterprise or partnership between government and private business (public-private partnerships).

SEE ALSO Investment and Development Agency (IDA Ireland); Lemass, Seán; Tourism

Bibliography

FitzGerald, Garret. *State-Sponsored Bodies.* 1963.

Manning, Maurice, and Moore McDowell. *Electricity Supply in Ireland: The History of the ESB.* 1984.

Mary E. Daly

Stephens, James

Founder of the Irish Republican Brotherhood (IRB) and a key figure in the creation of the transatlantic Irish revolutionary republican movement, James Stephens (1824–1901) was born in Kilkenny in 1825. Early in his life, Stephens worked as a civil engineer on the Limerick and Waterford railway and later served as aide-de-camp to William Smith O'Brien in the 1848 insurrection, a brief and somewhat halfhearted attempt to secure Irish independence. After this unsuccessful rising Stephens escaped to Paris, where he lived with fellow '48 veteran John O'Mahony amid large numbers of exiles from other failed revolutions across Europe.

In 1856 and 1857 Stephens toured Ireland to gauge public opinion on a new uprising. Convinced that he could build a substantial following, in 1858 Stephens founded the IRB, a secret, oath-bound organization dedicated to establishing an independent Irish republic through armed force. Shortly thereafter, O'Mahony founded a sister organization in the United States, the Fenian Brotherhood, which eventually lent its name to the entire international movement. From its earliest days, Fenianism wanted more for money and arms than for recruits. The movement was strongest in urban areas, though it had members in every part of Ireland as well as within the British army.

In 1863 Stephens launched the *Irish People*, a popular newspaper that featured political writings and nationalistic ballads, in an effort to raise money for the movement and unite the U.S. and Irish organizations. The movement peaked in terms of manpower and morale in 1865, which Stephens promised would be the "Year of Irish Liberty." But before any rising could take place, the offices of the *Irish People* were raided and several leading Fenians, including Stephens, were arrested. Stephens was briefly imprisoned but escaped in a dramatic rescue operation and then made his way to the United States, where the movement was beginning to fracture. In the United States Stephens declared that 1866 would be the year of Ireland's freedom, but took few concrete steps to fulfill this promise. Irish-American Fenians, now led principally by veterans of the Civil War, became convinced that Stephens was no longer willing to risk open revolt and imprisonment. At a turbulent meeting in December 1866 the founder of the Fenians was removed as head of his own organization.

While Stephens continued to remain involved in Irish revolutionary circles, he no longer wielded any influence. After years of exile in Paris, he returned to Ireland in 1891 and died on 29 March 1901. Stephens is often remembered for reviving the tradition of Irish revolutionary republicanism, but his most important contribution was harnessing the resources and Anglophobia of postfamine Irish America.

SEE ALSO Fenian Movement and the Irish Republican Brotherhood; Newspapers; **Primary Documents: Two Fenian Oaths (1858, 1859)**

Bibliography

Comerford, R. V. *The Fenians in Context: Irish Politics and Society, 1848–82.* 1985.

Ryan, Desmond. *The Fenian Chief.* 1967.

Michael W. de Nie

Stone Age Settlement

Because of its length the European Stone Age is usually divided into three stages. The Paleolithic period represents the archaeology of Stone Age hunter-gatherer communities in the Pleistocene period (often popularly referred to as the Ice Age). In Europe the Paleolithic may have lasted for a million years until the planet finally warmed up about 11,000 years ago. The Mesolithic period began after the end of the Pleistocene and continued until farming was introduced. In the Neolithic period it is generally accepted that Stone Age communities relied on a mixture of arable farming and domesticated animals. Many of these communities used pottery.

In northern Europe there was no continuous settlement, especially during some of the colder stages of the Pleistocene, but at various points in time, perhaps as far back as 700,000 years, human settlement took place in Britain. But in Ireland the earliest known settlement dates to only about 10,000 years ago, to the Mesolithic period. The absence of an Irish Paleolithic is often explained by the fact that Ireland was usually isolated as an island, thus inhibiting initial settlement, while numerous phases of extensive glaciation would have destroyed any of the ephemeral traces of Paleolithic settlement. In the last 40,000 years, however, many other mammals managed to get to Ireland and successfully lived there. They include a diverse range of species such as reindeer, mammoth, red deer, and horse, which raises the possibility that one day traces of an Irish Paleolithic will turn up.

MESOLITHIC PERIOD

The earliest known evidence of human settlement in Ireland dates from about 8000 B.C.E. The Irish Stone Age ended probably just after 2500 B.C.E., which means that it represents half of the known human history of Ireland. The earliest reliable evidence is based on excavations at Mount Sandel, where remnants of several small huts were recovered on the edge of an escarpment overlooking the estuary of the river Bann. Ireland may have been an island for the last 13,000 years, so only a limited range of mammals, freshwater fish, and plants appear to have existed on the island in the early part of the post-glacial period. Fortunately at Mount Sandel traces of the burned remains of food refuse occasionally survived in fireplaces and pits, and from their examination it was possible to see that these people lived by catching fish such as salmon and eels, hunted animals such as wild boar, trapped hares, and in season gathered berries and hazelnuts. The site at Mount Sandel suggests that rather than following a migratory lifestyle, the people appear to have chosen to live at a spot where, as the seasons changed, they could obtain different sources of food, and they may also have stored some food for leaner times of the year.

At this period most Mesolithic communities lived in a forested environment and would have made extensive use of wood and bark for a range of utensils and weapons. In Ireland very little of this material survives, and as a result, much greater reliance has to be placed on the stone tools and manufacturing debris they discarded. The most common form of stone artifacts found at Mount Sandel are the small, geometrically shaped pieces of flint called microliths. These would have been inserted in wood or bone to act as edges on knives or barbs on arrow shafts. A range of axes, including some polished stone axes, shows how much they relied on woodworking. Many of these distinctive tool types have been found throughout Ireland, as far away as on the banks of the Shannon in County Limerick or the Blackwater in County Cork. As this early technology only lasted about a thousand years, this suggests that Mesolithic peoples spread very rapidly throughout Ireland.

Sometime after 7000 B.C.E., the stone-tool technology based on the use of microliths was abandoned and replaced by a local development using large flakes and blades of stone as knives and woodworking tools. The people who lived in this later part of the Mesolithic period continued to follow a somewhat similar lifestyle, with many of their tools being found on lake and river bottoms and banks. Numerous sites have also been found along the seashore, where sea fish, sea mammals, birds, and shellfish were exploited. A good example of this type of settlement was excavated at Ferriter's Cove on the Dingle peninsula in County Kerry.

Unfortunately the Irish Mesolithic period has not produced any art objects or examples of personal ornament, although these items have been found elsewhere in Europe. Usually, human remains are represented only by a scattering of bones and teeth, but a recent excavation at Hermitage in County Limerick has uncovered a number of pits containing human cremations, two of which had substantial posts also placed in the grave and one contained a large polished stone axe.

BEGINNING OF THE NEOLITHIC PERIOD

The Irish Later Mesolithic period saw a very successful local adaptation to insular conditions, one that reflected a slightly different way of life from that in the rest of Europe. There is, for example, very little evidence that the uplands were used at this time. This way of life might have continued indefinitely were it not for the introduction of farming. By about 5000 B.C.E. an economy that had originated in Southwest Asia, evolving as it spread across Europe, appeared along the western edge of Europe. This economy, usually associated with the Neolithic period, was based on the keeping of domesticated cattle, sheep, and pigs as well as the planting of crops such as wheat and barley. By 4000 B.C.E., at the latest, a variant of this economy was present in Ireland. How it got there is still the subject of debate. Was it brought in by small bands of farmers looking for new lands? Or did indigenous communities see advantages in this new way of life and adapt it to Irish circumstances? This change in lifestyle and equipment (material culture) was so great that most Irish archaeologists believe that the change would have necessitated some movement of people.

Besides bringing in a new lifestyle, these first farmers brought in the first ceramics and a new range of tools including carefully made, piercing arrowheads. Much more attention was paid to the manufacture of polished stone axes, and many of the axes made during the Neolithic period in Ireland used materials that had been extracted from sources of metamorphosed rock found at two locations in northeast Antrim, Tievebulliagh near Cushendall, and Brockley on Rathlin Island. These products were distributed throughout Ireland and even into parts of Britain. Besides being used for everyday purposes such as chopping down trees and building timber structures, some large, highly polished axes may also have been made for prestige and ritual purposes. The most famous of these is the hoard of eighteen axes found on the Malone Ridge in Belfast. These are all nearly 300 millimeters in length.

Neolithic Way of Life

Shortly after 4000 B.C.E. little farmsteads were springing up across Ireland. It is impossible to be sure if these houses were grouped together in small villages, but it is possible that a number of houses were built in the same general area. The members of several households probably worked together to clear forests or build monuments. Many of the houses were large rectangular timber structures around 6 meters in width and often more than 10 meters in length. In some cases walls were made of vertically set split-oak planks; in others the roof was supported on a framework of large posts.

The landscape that these first farmers would have faced was mostly covered with forests, so any cultivation of crops required an initial opening up of the woodlands. Traces of these activities show up in many parts of Ireland. It is thought that areas adjacent to the farmsteads were cleared of trees by chopping down the smaller trees, ring-barking larger ones, and burning the remaining scrub. In these clearings wheat and then barley would have been planted.

In Ireland, however, it is probable that the keeping of cattle may have been more important than growing crops. Cattle and sheep then were much smaller than modern breeds and kept mainly for their meat. Specialized dairying, for example, did not begin until perhaps the first millennium C.E., while the weaving of wool does not appear to have begun until the Bronze Age. Of course, these peoples continued to fish and to gather wild plants and shellfish, but the core of their diet was provided through one or another form of farming.

There was obviously a period of pioneering farming, but Neolithic farmers were not primitive, shifting agriculturists, and some areas were used for periods of 300 to 500 years. One area that shows clear indications of sedentary Neolithic farming is Céide Fields in coastal north Mayo, where Professor Séamus Caulfield has explored a landscape buried beneath the blanket peat bog that had developed before the end of the Neolithic period. Here an organized series of field boundaries was laid out, covering an area that may have been 2 by 2 kilometers. A series of strips of fields ran from the coast up onto higher ground. Within or associated with most of these strips was a stone circular enclosure that would have surrounded a circular farmhouse. Some megalithic tombs were also incorporated within this field system. Although there is some indication of arable farming, these fields were mostly used for pasture—probably for grazing cattle.

It would be quite wrong to think of these societies as idyllic and peaceful. There is evidence in Ireland and elsewhere that violent death was common during the Neolithic period. The fact that some of the burned Neolithic houses have a number of arrowheads associated with them suggests that violence often occurred.

Megalithic Tombs

During the Neolithic period a significant amount of energy was devoted to the construction of megalithic tombs. The term itself—mega (large) and lithos (stone)—refers to the use of large stones, some weighing many tons, particularly as structural members (orthostats) or capstones in the building of the tombs. Megalithic tombs can be found concentrated in certain parts of western Europe from the Iberian peninsula to central Sweden, and a particularly large concentration (more than 1,500) has been found in Ireland. Some cannot be classified, but three different types are known to have been built in the Neolithic period: passage tombs (230), court tombs (more than 400), and portal tombs (roughly 175). More than 500 other tombs fall into the wedge tomb class that may have been built just after the end of the Stone Age.

Normally megalithic tombs were built out of locally available stone and used in an unaltered state. Some feature massive stones, such as the capstone at Brownshill in County Carlow, which is estimated to weigh up to 100 tons. Others were built using dry stone-walling techniques. The size of the tombs varies from almost 100 meters in diameter (such as those at Newgrange and Knowth) to others only 10 meters across. In some cases these stone monuments postdate timber structures and continued to be used after the Neolithic period. On occasion, material was placed within them later, and recognition of their significance at a much later time can be seen in the fact that they often have names like the Druid's Alter or Ossian's Grave. The term tomb might suggest that these structures were simply monumental graves, but their positioning, the manner in which human bones were placed within the burial chambers, and evidence of other activities having taken place around the tomb suggest that these structures should best be seen as "tombs for the living." They were used for burying only a tiny proportion of the population, and burial rites often entailed placing inside a small handful of cremated bone or some individually selected unburned bones inside. Few complete skeletons were placed in megalithic tombs during the Neolithic period.

Passage tombs are the most spectacular examples of megalithic tombs. In this type of tomb the burial chamber is usually accessed by a passage that runs in from the edge of the cairn or mound. The mounds are usually curvilinear, with their edges defined by a kerb of orthostats. Passage tombs are often found in groups or

Central chamber from Newgrange, Co. Meath (c. 3000 B.C.E.). Note the spirals and other carved ornamentation on the stone surfaces, possibly solar symbols. © DEPARTMENT OF ENVIRONMENT, HERITAGE & LOCAL GOVERNMENT. REPRODUCED BY PERMISSION.

cemeteries. They are frequently placed apart and on higher ground. About 60 percent of the passage tombs in Ireland occur in four cemeteries: the Carrowmore and Carrowkeel cemeteries in County Sligo, and at the Loughcrew and Bend of the Boyne cemeteries in County Meath. The last of these is centered on the three large mounds of Knowth, Dowth, and Newgrange. Newgrange is 85 meters across, with a 30-meter-long passage leading into a cruciform burial chamber made up of a central chamber 6 meters in height and three ancillary cells. In the case of Knowth, where the main mound is of a similar size, a passage running from the western edge terminates in a simple chamber, but another passage that runs from the eastern edge finishes in a cruciform chamber similar to that of Newgrange. Knowth is surrounded by a series of other smaller tombs, some of which may have been built before the main mound was

constructed. In the inner chambers of a number of tombs there are large stone basins. One particularly fine example from the eastern chamber at Knowth 1 is highly decorated. The burial rites associated with these tombs mostly consisted of the placement of small patches of cremated bone, but this apparent simplicity is balanced by the presence of exotic "grave goods," such as a spectacular carved-flint mace head from Knowth. Many of the passage tombs have produced pendants, long pins of bone and antler as well as polished stone balls made from nonlocal materials. Indeed it is even suggested that many of the raw materials used in building Newgrange were imported. The kerb stones, for example, which are greywacke, may have been brought some distance from the coast. Of course, Newgrange is famous for the fact that the passage is positioned so that as the sun rises on the day of the mid-winter solstice its

Court-cairn from Creevykeel, Co. Sligo (c. 2500 B.C.E.), a Neolithic tumulus originally covered by a wedge-shaped mound. © Michael St. Maur Sheil/Corbis. Reproduced by permission.

light passes through a box in the roof of the passage and shines into the burial chamber.

The Bend of the Boyne and to a lesser extent the Loughcrew cemetery have the largest concentration of passage tomb art in Europe. This geometric art is made up of such motifs as chevrons, lozenges, spirals, and circles, etc. It is either incised or pecked onto the surface of the orthostats. This, of course, would have been done without access to metal tools. The most famous example is the entrance stone at Newgrange, which is over 2 meters in length and covered in a coherent pattern dominated by spirals. Other stones, often in prominent positions, have this "plastic" art style, but many others have less coherent patterns that may have been built up through the placement of individual motifs.

Of the other two tomb types, the vast majority of court tombs are found north of a line from Clew Bay to Dundalk Bay, whereas portal tombs tend to occur slightly farther into the midlands and also in some numbers in the southeast of Ireland. Both these forms are usually found on their own or in very small groups.

In some areas, such as in the south of County Armagh, a portal tomb and a court tomb can be found in close proximity to each other.

Court tombs tend to have rectilinear, wedge-shaped cairns where an open court area is placed, usually, though not always, at the broad end of the wedge. Burial chambers—usually two or four—are placed one behind the other to form a gallery that runs off the court farther into the body of the cairn. Numerous variations on this theme are found throughout the northern part of Ireland. Simple examples of a court tombs are at Ballyalton, Co. Down, and at Creggandevesky, Co. Tyrone, whereas larger and more complex versions are at Creevykeel and at Deerpark in County Sligo. In the latter case the court was placed at the center of the cairn, with burial chambers running off the court in different directions. Portal tombs, also called dolmens or cromlechs, often consist of one chamber and are among the most striking prehistoric monuments in Ireland. Often the cairn that surrounded them has been removed in more recent times, although in some cases the cairn may never have been extensive. Classic examples of portal tombs are Poulnabrone, Co. Clare, and Legananny, Co. Down. In many cases a large capstone is balanced on two portal stones and on a backstone. Although some aspects of the burial rites are similar, the ritual associated with these forms usually did not include placement of the same range of exotic items found in the passage tombs.

Many other forms of ritual occurred in this period. Across the south of Ireland a number of smaller round cairns have stone boxes (cists) at their center. These usually contain one or two complete skeletons. In certain areas a number of caves have also produced both complete skeletons and scatterings of bones that can also date to the Neolithic period.

With such a proliferation of monument types there is always a tendency to put them in a chronological sequence, but it is possible that at least some of the major types were in use at the same time. Court tombs and portal tombs were in use by 3800 B.C.E., whereas the earliest convincing dates for passage tombs suggest that they may have begun to be built by 3400 B.C.E. or possibly slightly earlier.

FINAL NEOLITHIC

Sometime after 3000 B.C.E. the megalithic tomb tradition seems to have gone out of fashion, and ritual instead centered on the building of large banked enclosures ranging in size from about 50 to 180 meters across. These enigmatic structures are usually referred to as henges on the basis of their similarity to monuments of that type in Britain. Groups of henges can be found in areas that are rich in other Neolithic monuments, such as the Bend of the Boyne cemetery or at Lough Gur, Co. Limerick. In some cases, as at Newgrange or at the Giants Ring on the Malone Ridge near Belfast, there were also large circles or curvilinear enclosures of posts that may have been up to 6 meters in height.

The Stone Age did not, of course, end on a neat chronological horizon, and many of the tools used for everyday purposes continued to be made from stone. It is probable, however, that sometime after 2500 B.C.E. copper artifacts such as axes and then daggers began to be made from the rich copper sources found especially in southwest Ireland.

SUMMARY

The archaeological record shows that the Irish Stone Age is not just a marginal period lost in antiquity. Not only was farming introduced, but it may be that these peoples, representing the beginning of a continuous 10,000 years of human settlement, form the foundation of the current makeup of the people of Ireland. Stone Age peoples cleared areas of forest and opened up the landscape, perhaps bringing about for the first time significant ecological changes. Through its monuments, the Stone Age has left one of the most abiding images from Ireland's past.

SEE ALSO Prehistoric and Celtic Ireland; Bronze Age Culture

Bibliography

Eogan, George. *Knowth and the Passage Tombs of Ireland.* 1986.

O'Kelly, Michael J. *Newgrange: Archaeology, Art, and Legend.* 1983.

Ryan, Michael, ed. *The Illustrated Archaeology of Ireland.* 1991.

Wadell, J. *The Prehistoric Archaeology of Ireland.* 1998.

Woodman, Peter C. "A Mesolithic Camp in Northern Ireland." *Scientific American* 245 (August 1981): 120–132.

Woodman, P. C., E. Anderson, and N. Finlay. *Excavations at Ferriter's Cove, 1983–1995.* 1999.

Peter C. Woodman

Struggle for Independence from 1916 to 1921

The combination of Ulster loyalist resistance to Home Rule and the outbreak of the First World War brought the gun back into Irish politics, shattered John Redmond's hopes of Anglo-Irish reconciliation, and began the final collapse of British administration in Ireland. Any early enthusiasm for supporting Britain in the war had evaporated by the time that plans were made for a rising to take place at Easter 1916.

THE EASTER RISING

The Military Council of the Irish Republican Brotherhood (IRB) and the leadership of the Irish Citizen Army secretly plotted to bring about a national revolution backed by German aid. There was hopeless failure of communication between Ireland, the United States, and

To put down the Easter Rising of 1916, the British used artillery fired from a gunboat in the river Liffey. The shelling destroyed much of central Dublin and especially Sackville Street (now O'Connell Street). © UNDERWOOD & UNDERWOOD/CORBIS. REPRODUCED BY PERMISSION.

Germany, and a planned landing of arms off the Kerry coast ended in the scuttling of the German boat and the capture of Sir Roger Casement, the republican emissary to Germany. It was decided to proceed with the rising a day later than planned, that is, on Easter Monday, with virtually no expectation of any military success.

The Rising was almost entirely confined to Dublin, supported by only around 2,000 Irish Volunteers and handicapped by the decision to occupy various public buildings around the city center. The rebellion, which amounted to little more than a blood protest, accorded with nineteenth-century notions of a romantic revolution and was totally unsuited to resisting a modern army with heavy artillery and armaments. The resistance heroically held out for five days and seriously embarrassed the British administration while it was almost entirely preoccupied with European events at the height of the First World War. It was the British government's decision to execute in stages most of the Irish leaders and to intern a considerable number of the participants that

altered popular attitudes to the rebellion. Many internees told of being barracked by the populace on their way to British prisons and then being feted by big crowds on their release some months later.

The power of the events of the Rising and its aftermath therefore led to a resurgence of militant nationalism. Nonetheless, Easter 1916 had some negative consequences for Irish nationalism. Much of the leadership was either dead or temporarily removed from the scene, and many criticized the secrecy, lack of planning, and naiveté of the tactics used. The almost mystical quality of the actual proclamation of the Republic would make it very difficult to win acceptance in nationalist ranks for any necessary compromise with the British in the future.

The Rising was only one of the elements that undermined the Irish Parliamentary Party (IPP) and the British administration in 1917 and 1918. The abortive British attempts to achieve an immediate settlement, the talk of partition and of the extension of conscription to

In the 1918 general election the Sinn Féin Party routed the Home Rulers and took seventy-three seats. But instead of taking their seats at Westminster in London, the victorious Sinn Féin candidates met in Dublin and set up Dáil Éireann, thus proclaiming Irish independence. This photograph of 21 January 1919 shows those members of Dáil Éireann who were not in prison. COURTESY OF THE GRADUATE LIBRARY, UNIVERSITY OF MICHIGAN.

Ireland, the sundry acts of pin-pricking coercion—all these served to further the interests of a more advanced form of nationalism which was institutionalized by the new Sinn Féin Party and the resurgent Irish Volunteers. U.S. President Woodrow Wilson's crusade on behalf of self-determination and the rights of small nations enabled Irish nationalism to recover from the pro-German associations of 1916 and placed the British administration on the defensive. This culminated in the Sinn Féin triumph in the 1918 general election, which saw the virtual obliteration of the IPP outside the northeast.

THE WAR OF INDEPENDENCE

In accordance with Arthur Griffith's ideas Sinn Féin refused to take its seats at Westminster and set up an alternative parliament, Dáil Éireann, and counterstate. To begin with, faith was put in an appeal for international recognition to the Paris Peace Conference, and there was some hope among moderates that passive-resistance methods might achieve independence. On the same day, 21 January 1919, that the Dáil met publicly for the first time, two members of the Royal Irish Constabulary (RIC) were killed by a column of Volunteers at Soloheadbeg near Tipperary town. This coincidence of political and military action is usually seen as the start of the War of Independence. Though relationships between the political and military sides of the movement were fraught, much of the Irish success in the next two years was dependent on the impression that a mandate had been given for physical-force measures to achieve a republic.

The appeal to the Paris Peace Conference produced nothing, and the political leader Eamon de Valera's eighteen-month stay in the United States beginning in June 1919 raised considerable funds but little political support beyond sympathy resolutions in state and federal legislatures. In Ireland some success was gained in the establishment of republican courts and in local-government institutions, but the counterstate was unable to perform with any credibility owing to British opposition and lack of financial resources. The Dáil was quick to authorize the boycott of the RIC that began in local areas in 1917 and 1918.

During 1919 military actions consisted of isolated attacks on RIC men and Dublin Metropolitan Police (DMP) detectives. By the autumn of that year RIC stations were being evacuated in large parts of the rural south and west. This began the process by which the mechanisms of British rule collapsed. Beginning in 1920 the Volunteers, now the Irish Republican Army (IRA), were emboldened to attempt many attacks on barracks. In an improvised way guerrilla warfare was applied and implemented. The success of Michael Collins's intelligence network of spies, double agents, and informers was a complete turnaround from the British infiltration of nationalist movements in the nineteenth century.

By the time in July 1920 that the British government made the first wide-ranging review of Irish policy since the end of the First World War, the British writ no longer ran in most parts of the Twenty-Six Counties. The offer of separate parliaments and devolved Home Rule to Dublin and Belfast in the Government of Ireland Bill, which eventually passed in Parliament in December 1920, had no relevance to the South. From the late summer of 1920 the British government followed a coercive policy based on the militarization of the police. The notorious Black and Tans were formed from unemployed ex-servicemen recruited from the end of 1919. The Auxiliaries were another force, consisting of ex-officers sent over from July 1920. Both forces acted without an effective disciplinary code and became infamous for their association with a wave of unauthorized reprisals, burnings, and shootings in the second half of 1920. The whole character of the war then dramatically intensified with a series of defining events: the seventy-four–day hunger strike and death of Terence MacSwiney, lord mayor of Cork; the execution of the eighteen-year-old Kevin Barry on All Saints' Day; the killings of Bloody Sunday, 21 November, in Dublin; the IRA triumph against a convoy of Auxiliaries at Kilmichael a week later; and the burning of much of Cork city center on the night of 11 December by the Auxiliaries.

The conflict continued to escalate until the truce of 11 July 1921, when a military stalemate was admitted on both sides. On the Irish side it was recognized that lack of resources, chiefly arms and ammunition, prevented any outright victory, while the British realized the acute unpopularity, both at home and abroad, of their methods and the extreme difficulties of countering guerrilla warfare in the long term.

The British decision to negotiate in July 1921 with men previously dismissed as gunmen and to offer dominion status in the Anglo-Irish Treaty seems to represent a triumph for the IRA. However, the aim of an all-Ireland republic had not been achieved, and therein lies the main reason for the Civil War that followed. The continuation of the constitutional and partition issues plagued Irish politics and Anglo-Irish relations for the rest of the century.

SEE ALSO Anglo-Irish Treaty of 1921; Civil War; Collins, Michael; Connolly, James; Cumann na mBan; de Valera, Eamon; Gonne, Maud; Great War; Griffith, Arthur; Home Rule Movement and the Irish Parliamentary Party: 1891 to 1918; Markievicz, Countess Constance; Pearse, Patrick; Plunkett, Sir Horace Curzon; Politics: 1800 to 1921—Challenges to the Union; Protestant Ascendancy: Decline, 1800 to 1930; Redmond, John; Sinn Féin Movement and Party to 1922; Women in Nationalist and Unionist Movements in the Early Twentieth Century; **Primary Documents:** "What Is Our Programme?" (22 January 1916); Proclamation of the Irish Republic (24 April 1916); "Easter 1916" (1916); Declaration of Irish Independence (21 January 1919); Government of Ireland Act (23 December 1920); The Anglo-Irish Treaty (6 December 1921); Proclamation Issued by IRA Leaders at the Beginning of the Civil War (29 June 1922)

Bibliography

Fitzpatrick, David. *Politics and Irish Life, 1913–21: Provincial Experience of War and Revolution.* 1977.

Hart, Peter. *The IRA and Its Enemies: Violence and Community in Cork, 1916–1923.* 1998.

Hopkinson, Michael. *The Irish War of Independence.* 2002.

Townshend, Charles. *The British Campaign in Ireland, 1919–1921.* 1975.

Michael A. Hopkinson

Subdivision and Subletting of Holdings

Though closely connected, subdivision and subletting of lands were two different things. By the early seventeenth century, English tenure had been adopted everywhere in Ireland. The major landowners all subdivided their estates into smaller holdings, which provided them with rental income. In many cases the occupying tenants rented directly from the landowner, but some owners—especially absentees with property remote from markets or difficult to manage—preferred until the later eighteenth century to let large amounts of land to a few wealthy tenants who could guarantee them a steady income without much trouble. These middlemen, as they were called, lived by subdividing their holdings and subletting, at a higher rent per acre, to undertenants, some of whom sublet in turn to undertenants of their own. For example, the lands belonging to Trinity College had three or four layers of middlemen. Up to a point, subdivision suited both landlords and tenants and was not necessarily harmful.

Carried to extremes, however, it created on many estates a host of uneconomic small farms. Excessive subdivision of this kind had several causes, apart from careless management and the activities of middlemen. The population explosion during the late eighteenth and early nineteenth centuries, combined in the years before 1815 with high prices for agricultural produce, created an insatiable demand for land. This tempted anyone with a long lease to subdivide in order to accommodate family members or to make an easy profit. A typical eighteenth-century lease, for the life spans of three named persons and a concurrent term of years, lasted, on average, for up to half a century or more—what one landowner called "eternity in parchment." During all that time the head landlord could neither raise the rent nor easily prevent a tenant from subdividing and subletting. Some landowners themselves encouraged subdivision for political reasons, by giving small tenants the type of lease that (until 1829) qualified them to vote in parliamentary elections.

The report of the Devon commission (1845) shows the change that gradually took place after 1815. Landowners granted fewer leases, resisted subdivision, and began to reverse the process by consolidating small farms into larger units. Middlemen's leases were not renewed when they ran out. For most of the surplus population, emigration was the only answer. The Great Famine completely ruined the poorest smallholders. Actively encouraged by landlords who wanted to clear their estates, the survivors joined the exodus in huge numbers. The tenants who remained had a more cautious attitude to subdivision and subletting.

SEE ALSO Agriculture: 1690 to 1845; Agriculture: 1845 to 1921; Family: Marriage Patterns and Family Life from 1690 to 1921; Famine Clearances; Great Famine; Migration: Emigration from the Seventeenth Century to 1845; Poor Law Amendment Act of 1847 and the Gregory Clause; Population, Economy, and Society from 1750 to 1950; Population Explosion; Potato and Potato Blight (*Phytophthora infestans*); Rural Life: 1690 to 1845

Bibliography

Donnelly, James S., Jr. *The Land and the People of Nineteenth-Century Cork*. 1975. Reprint, 1987.

Dowling, Martin W. *Tenant Right and Agrarian Society in Ulster, 1600–1870*. 1999.

Maguire, W. A. *The Downshire Estates in Ireland, 1801–1845*. 1972.

W. A. Maguire

~

Sullivan Brothers
(A. M. and T. D.)

Nation editors and MPs Alexander Martin (A. M.) Sullivan (1829–1884) and Timothy Daniel (T. D.) Sullivan (1827–1914) were born and educated in Bantry, Co. Cork. After contributing to various newspapers, A. M. purchased part of the *Nation* in July 1855. When A. M. assumed complete control of this famed nationalist weekly in 1857, the poetic T. D. became his co-editor. The devoutly Catholic brothers gave the previously nonsectarian paper a decidedly Catholic tone. In 1859 A. M. established the *Evening News* and the *Morning News*, Dublin's first penny morning paper. Though popular, both papers folded in 1864 because of legal problems.

During the early 1860s the Sullivans, who were constitutional nationalists, feuded with the physical-force Fenians, but after the 1867 Fenian rising failed, the Sullivans capitalized on Fenian-inspired political excitement. The *Weekly News*, a cheap paper founded by A. M. in 1860, became the most popular Irish newspaper by running political cartoons sympathetic to the Fenians. In addition to their newspapers, the Sullivans published *Speeches from the Dock*, a collection of courtroom orations by earlier Irish nationalists and the recently convicted Fenians; the book was an instant best-seller and remained so for years. When three of the Fenian prisoners were hanged in November 1867, T. D. responded by writing "God Save Ireland," which served as the unofficial national anthem for over fifty years. The *Weekly News*'s criticism of the hangings resulted in A. M. serving three months in prison for seditious libel in 1868.

A. M. helped to found the Home Rule movement in 1870 and was elected MP for Louth in 1874. Two years later he became a lawyer and sold the *Nation* and *Weekly News* to T. D., who in 1875 had founded the literary magazine *Young Ireland*. After moving to London, A. M.

won acclaim as a parliamentary speaker and lawyer before ill health forced him to retire in 1881. Meanwhile T. D.'s newspapers promoted Charles Stewart Parnell's leadership of the Irish Parliamentary Party and supported the Land League. In 1880 T. D. joined Parnell's party as MP for Westmeath. In the next year the launch of Parnell's new weekly, *United Ireland*, severely hurt the circulation of T. D.'s papers, so in 1888 T. D. turned the floundering *Weekly News* into the *Irish Catholic*, a weekly organ of Catholic opinion. Finally, in 1890 T. D. sold all his publications. During the Parnell split in 1890 and 1891, the moralistic T. D. opposed Parnell's continued leadership of the party, and he served as an anti-Parnellite MP until 1905. The Sullivans and their papers kept constitutional nationalism alive, turned their Fenian opponents into folk heroes, and laid the basis for an explicitly Catholic Irish nationalism.

SEE ALSO Fenian Movement and the Irish Republican Brotherhood; Home Rule Movement and the Irish Parliamentary Party: 1870 to 1891; Literacy and Popular Culture; Newspapers; **Primary Documents:** "God Save Ireland" (1867)

Bibliography

Comerford, R. V. *The Fenians in Context*. 1996.

Sullivan, Alexander M. *New Ireland*. 1884.

Sullivan, Timothy D. *Recollections of Troubled Times in Irish Politics*. 1905.

Patrick F. Tally

Surrender and Regrant

The policy of "surrender and regrant" was an integral part of the "Tudor revolution" in government and religion. Its aim was to anglicize Ireland and to bring both Gaelic and Anglo-Irish lordships under English sovereignty without resorting to a military conquest. The revolt of Silken Thomas (Thomas Fitzgerald, tenth earl of Kildare) in 1534, though brutally suppressed by English forces, demonstrated that a rebellious Ireland could pose a serious threat to England's security. Though the rebellion was a reaction to efforts to limit the independence of the Irish lords, rather than an act of opposition to Henry's religious policies, the rebels' efforts to secure

assistance from Catholic Spain and the papacy added a grave new dimension to relations between the two islands. The need to bring Ireland under English control and into religious conformity with England was recognized as pressing.

Prior to the accession of Henry VII in 1485, England's involvement in Irish affairs had been minimal. Having failed to make Ireland a source of profit and not wishing to spend any more money than was absolutely necessary to maintain a semblance of order, English kings had allowed Ireland a kind of self-rule. The government was entrusted to the island's leading Anglo-Irish lords. They and their followers maintained and commanded a small military force in the Pale (the area around Dublin). In return they agreed to protect the king's subjects and enforce his law. The Anglo-Irish lords also used their position and the resources at their disposal to increase their own influence. When the powerful Butlers of Ormond fell from royal favor during the English Wars of the Roses in the late fifteenth century, they were supplanted by their rivals, the Fitzgeralds of Kildare and Desmond. By the end of the fifteenth century Garret Mor Fitzgerald (1478–1513), eighth earl of Kildare and lord deputy of Ireland, had used his office and a series of alliances with the country's most powerful Gaelic and Anglo-Irish families to make himself the de facto ruler of Ireland. Fearful of allowing so much power to rest in the hands of men whose loyalty was questionable, the monarchy appointed only Englishmen as Irish lord deputies in the aftermath of the 1534 revolt.

A major source of the tensions that plagued Ireland before and after the suppression of that rebellion (called, after its instigator, "Silken Thomas"), was that both Anglo-Irish lords and Gaelic chieftains were insecure in possession of their titles to land and in their relationships with the Crown. Warfare was endemic between the two communities, and internecine strife within the Gaelic lordships added further tension. The authority of the Gaelic chieftains was based on Brehon (i.e., Gaelic Irish) law; their titles were elective. This custom meant that more than one member of a family might claim a title, with the result that titles were often won in battle and retained only by the maintenance of an army. Many Anglo-Irish lords, though inheriting their lands by primogeniture and holding their titles in accordance with English law, were able, in the absence of a strong government presence, to rule their lands independently and to make use of Irish or English law as it suited their purposes. Others, often those descended from the first Norman settlers in Ireland, did not have legally recognized titles to their lordships and feared losing both their lands and their local influence. All resented the government's increasing interference in their affairs. These "English rebels," like the "Irish enemies," as these troublesome subjects were known to their English contemporaries, were fiercely independent and resisted any government intervention that encroached upon their privileges and lifestyles.

England's religious reformation and its growing involvement in continental politics necessitated control of Irish affairs and the submission of those lords who remained loyal to Rome. Since England could not afford costly military intervention in Ireland, diplomatic means were sought to defuse a potentially explosive situation. Following the counsel of his Irish advisors, Henry VIII sought to win over the Gaelic lords by "sober ways, politic drifts, and amiable persuasions." It was hoped that if the Irish lords were given secure titles to their lands, the protection of English law, and a role in government, they could be persuaded to abandon their uncivilized manners, customs, and language and become sober, loyal servants of the Crown. This policy of conciliation, by which Gaelic chieftains and "English enemies" alike were enjoined by consent to become part of a fully anglicized Ireland, has come to be known as "surrender and regrant."

In July 1540 Sir Anthony Saint Leger replaced the unpopular Sir Leonard Gray as lord deputy of Ireland. Under his supervision a new direction was taken to win the allegiance of the king's Irish subjects and to restore order in Ireland. In the first stage the Irish chiefs and Anglo-Irish lords whose titles and/or allegiance were in question were invited to submit to the king by signing an indenture "surrendering" their lands and title in exchange for a royal patent and an English title. The title carried with it the full weight of English law and the right to be summoned to parliament. In short, the Irish earls and barons were offered constitutional equality with their Anglo-Irish peers—both would be vassals of the English king. In addition to surrendering their lands and titles, the Irish lords agreed to practice inheritance by primogeniture rather than the customary Gaelic system of elective succession, or tanistry. They also renounced papal supremacy in favor of royal authority. The policy made a major contribution to establishing peace and security in Ireland. Equally important was the passage of the Act for the King's Title, approved by the Irish parliament in 1541. Prior to this, Henry, like all monarchs since Henry II in the twelfth century, held the title lord of Ireland, granted by Pope Adrian IV. The new act dispelled any claim that the real overlord of Ireland was the pope. Now all Irishmen, Gaelic and Anglo-Irish, owed their allegiance to the king of Ireland; gone (in theory) were the distinctions and tensions created by the existence of two separate peoples—loyal Englishmen and Irish enemies.

The Crown's program was attractive to the Gaelic chiefs for a number of reasons. They were tired of war and fearful of the Crown's power, as evidenced by the fate of the 1534 rebels. Many of the rebels had been executed and much Kildare property had been confiscated. Under English law the land of a lordship became the lord's personal estate. This offered the Irish rulers greater control of their territories, and primogeniture promised greater internal peace within Gaelic lordships. By Henry's death in 1547 forty of the important Gaelic and Anglo-Irish lords had submitted, and Ireland enjoyed a measure of peace unknown in years. Not all Irish clans, however, were willing to abandon Brehon law, and some continued to elect their chiefs in defiance of English law. A disputed succession to the earldom of Tyrone and the violence that followed revealed that Henry's program of conciliation had not been entirely successful in Ulster. Surrender and regrant would cause as many problems as it solved, and it ultimately failed to provide an inexpensive alternative to military conquest.

SEE ALSO Monarchy; Politics: 1500 to 1690

Bibliography

Bradshaw, Brendan. *The Irish Constitutional Revolution of the Sixteenth Century.* 1979.

Canny, Nicholas. *From Reformation to Restoration: Ireland, 1534–1660.* 1987.

Ellis, Steven. *Tudor Ireland, 1470–1603.* 1985.

Moody, T. W., F. X. Martin, and F. J. Byrne, eds. *A New History of Ireland,* vol. 3, *Early Modern Ireland, 1534–1691.* 1976.

Monica A. Brennan

Swift, Jonathan

Political pamphleteer, Irish patriot, dean of Saint Patrick's Cathedral (Church of Ireland) in Dublin, Jonathan Swift (1667–1745) is now remembered for writing "A Modest Proposal" and *Gulliver's Travels.* His parents were Anglo-Irish colonists, and Swift devoted himself to the interests of that class. He earned his B.A. from Trinity College in 1686, an M.A. from Oxford in 1694, and launched his career as an Anglican priest in Ulster in 1695. During the next decade he nursed his prospects in

Wood engraving from Jonathan Swift's Gulliver's Travels, *c. 1865.*
© CORBIS. REPRODUCED BY PERMISSION.

church and state. Like most of the Anglo-Irish, he was a Whig, and his first great satires, *Tale of a Tub* and *The Battle of the Books*, both published in 1704, established him as a propagandist for the Whig cause. But at his core he believed that Britain was best served by safeguarding Anglican privilege, so he switched allegiance, lending his wit, in the periodical *Examiner*, to leaders of the conservative Tory ministry, the earl of Oxford and Viscount Bolingbroke, when they rose to power in 1710. When the Tories fell in 1714, Swift was suspected of treason and was spied on. He returned to Ireland feeling himself an exile and hardly comforted by the deanship of Saint Patrick's—meager spoils of his brief political eminence.

He conducted a love affair with Esther Johnson (whom he called Stella), whom he first met when he was twenty-two and she was only eight years old. He kept the relationship secret and most likely platonic to satisfy his idiosyncratic notions of intimacy, but he may have married her clandestinely. Though they lived in separate houses, their peculiar friendship continued until her death in 1728. His letters to her comprise the famous *Journal to Stella*, which was published in 1766.

Eventually, Swift began to think of himself as an Irishman and to resist the dependency that England had imposed on Ireland. His wildly popular series of *Drapier's Letters* (1724) attacked England's deliberate corruption of Irish coinage and excited much of the Irish citizenry to national consciousness. "A Modest Proposal," written five years later, upbraided all classes of Irish for the moral and material poverty of the country. In what is probably the most famous example of irony in Irish literature, Swift's proposer suggests that the poor father their children like cattle to fill the plates of the rich. Swift's greatest work, *Gulliver's Travels* (1726), satirized not only his contemporaries but all humanity. Even as the episodes among the Lilliputians and Brobdingnagians continue to delight readers today, Gulliver's last sojourn on the island of philosophical horses and bestial humans have earned Swift the reputation of a misanthrope. Later generations of Irish writers such as James Joyce considered Swift the fountainhead of an irreverent, satirical, vital stream in Irish literary history.

SEE ALSO Arts: Early Modern Literature and the Arts from 1500 to 1800; Literature: Anglo-Irish Literary Tradition, Beginnings of

Bibliography

Ehrenpreis, Irvin. *Swift: The Man, His Works, and the Age.* 3 vols. 1962–1983.

Nokes, David. *Jonathan Swift, a Hypocrite Reversed: A Critical Biography.* 1985.

Quintana, Ricardo. *Swift: An Introduction.* 1955. Reprint, 1979.

Joseph Kelly

Táin Bó Cúailnge

Táin Bó Cúailnge (*Cattle Raid of Cooley*) is the central narrative in the Ulster cycle of tales, which depict the heyday of the Ulster kingdom and its pagan heroic culture, dated by the medieval Irish scholars to the first centuries B.C.E. and C.E. The oldest version of the tale is preserved in an early twelfth-century manuscript, *Leabhar na hUidhre* (*Book of the Dun Cow*); the tale consists largely of a ninth-century core, amplified by extensive passages in later language.

The story line of the *Táin* is deceptively simple: Ailill and Maeve, king and queen of Connaught, long-standing enemies of the Ulster people, and their rivals for political supremacy, lead an army of the other Irish provinces into Ulster to raid their cattle, and in particular to seize a prize bull. In an economy based on livestock, where political submission is expressed by the imposition of cattle tribute, this amounts to a declaration of war. The Ulstermen cannot resist, as they are suffering from a strange recurring debility, and the single-handed defense of the province falls on their youthful seventeen-year-old champion Cú Chulainn, an avatar of his divine father Lug. When the Ulstermen finally emerge from their weakness, they give battle to the invaders and ward off the danger, but at a heavy cost of life and material wealth.

If the plot is relatively straightforward, the analysis is less so, and the variety of interpretations advanced testify to the underlying complexities of the tale. Since Eugene O'Curry first introduced the *Táin* to a wider public in the mid-nineteenth century, parallels have been drawn with the Classical epics, and Cú Chulainn has been compared with the youthful heroes Achilles and Aeneas. The idea that the *Táin* originated in dispa-

rate short tales drawn together to create an Irish *Aeneid* received the support of the great Thurneysen (1921). Alternatively, the Ulster cycle in general may reflect an old inheritance, being less an imitation than a late-attested congener of the heroic literature of ancient Greece (Chadwick and Chadwick 1932).

As the supremacy of Ulster did not persist into the Christian period, it has been suggested that the tales celebrating its days of glory derive from pagan times. If this were so, much reliance could be placed on the contents as a record of events, persons, and customs, and the *Táin* would be a precious repository of information about a pre-literate society. O'Curry, for one, believed that the *Táin* was "all through founded upon authentic historical facts" (O'Curry 1861, p. 33). Yet some features of the tale, such as the role of Otherworld denizens, the extravagant behavior especially of Cú Chulainn, the flights of exaggeration, are far from realistic. A number of characters, including Maeve, Cú Chulainn, and Fergus the Ulster exile, show superhuman traits which reveal them to be semi-divine figures. The plot itself, which culminates in the fight of the Ulster bull against his Connaught counterpart, places the narrative in the realm of myth. T. F. O'Rahilly (1946, p. 271) held that tales such as the *Táin* have no historical basis whatsoever, being in origin pure mythology.

A more subtle case for historicity in the *Táin* was made by K. H. Jackson (1964). Acknowledging that the characters and events in the tales may be in part mythological, and are certainly wholly legend, he argued that the lineaments of society, the material culture and customs described therein could be a genuine record of ancient times in Ireland, as they offer impressive corroboration of the Greek and Roman accounts of the Celts of the continent and Britain. The "window on the Iron Age"—in Jackson's vivid phrase—need not be projected back too far into prehistory, since the lack of Roman occupation allowed an Iron Age La Tène culture to flourish up to the threshold of the Christian era in the fifth century. According to Jackson, tales composed at this time could have been recounted orally until captured in writing in the historical period.

The theory that Early Irish literature in general is indebted to an orally transmitted pre-Christian inheritance has since been widely challenged. Some aspects of the material culture in the Ulster tales also appear on closer scrutiny to owe more to early Christian times (Mallory 1992), suggesting that the *Táin* is at least in part a historical fiction. There is a striking discrepancy, for example, between the written and the archaeological record of the function attributed to Emain Macha: in the *Táin* it is the location of the royal residence, whereas excavation has shown no evidence of occupation, only of ritual use. Another divergence, the contrast between repeated references to chariots in the Ulster cycle and the lack of archaeological evidence in Ireland for such vehicles, is often cited against Jackson's theory, but could equally be adduced for an even greater antiquity, reaching back to the Continental Celts, for the traditions depicted in the *Táin*.

Modern approaches to early Irish tales focus less on their ultimate putative origins than on their significance for the society in which they received their final written form. An allegorical reading of the *Táin* explains the prize bull of Cúailnge as code for the wealthy monastery of Armagh, and the warring Ulster and Connaught armies as the ecclesiastical factions and families competing for its control in the ninth century (Kelleher 1971).

Themes of more general import in the *Táin* are the destructive impact of war (Radner 1982) and the dangerous potential of the practice of cattle-raiding to escalate into major conflict. A very specific contemporary relevance for the latter is perhaps indicated by the early ninth-century re-promulgation of a law against cattle-raiding (Kelly 1992). These themes could plausibly be seen as the contribution of a clerical redactor.

Notwithstanding such pacifist overtones, the *Táin* celebrates the heroic age by providing a showcase for the supreme prowess of the youthful Cú Chulainn. His glory is magnified primarily by his own spectacular exploits but also by contrast with the shortcomings of his main adversary, Queen Maeve. She is depicted throughout as a strong but headstrong woman, whose efforts to excel in male domains are ridiculed. Her military invasion is thwarted, and her army disparaged by her Ulster ally and lover Fergus as "a herd of horses led by a mare" (O'Rahilly 1976, p. 237). This animal image recalls the pagan belief in the sovereignty goddess in equine form and evokes the divine figure of which Maeve is a euhemerization. Yet her affair with Fergus does not validate any aspirations of his to kingship, as other narratives using this convention would lead us to expect; it merely exposes him to dishonour and contempt. Thus the tale thematizes not just the appropriate codes of conduct for the sexes but also the enduring literary appeal of the sovereignty-goddess trope. Here, too, in the unmistakeable misogyny, one might discern a clerical input.

The *Táin*, then, affords more than a "window on the Iron Age." In recalling or imaginatively reconstructing the heroic Ulster society of pre-Christian Ireland, it weaves together a stratum of myth and the legendary history of competing dynasties and peoples into a multi-layered tapestry of themes of local, general, timebound and timeless resonance and appeal. Its literary and artistic success may therefore be greater than is at first apparent from the disjointed form in which it has come down to us.

SEE ALSO Cú Chulainn; Emain Macha (Navan Fort); Literature: Early and Medieval Literature; Myth and Saga; Prehistoric and Celtic Ireland

Bibliography

Chadwick, Henry Munro, and Nora Kershaw Chadwick. *The Growth of Literature.* Vol. 1, *The Ancient Literatures of Europe.* 1932. Reprint, 1968.

Jackson, Kenneth Hurlstone. *The Oldest Irish Tradition: A Window on the Iron Age.* 1964.

Kelleher, John V. "The *Táin* and the Annals." *Ériu* 22 (1971): 107–127.

Kelly, Patricia. "The *Táin* as Literature." In *Aspects of the Táin*, edited by J. P. Mallory. 1992.

Mallory, J. P. "The World of Cú Chulainn: The Archaeology of *Táin Bó Cúailnge*." In *Aspects of the Táin*, edited by J. P. Mallory. 1992.

O'Curry, Eugene. *Lectures on the Manuscript Materials of Ancient Irish History.* 1861.

O'Rahilly, Cecile. *Táin Bó Cúailnge. Recension I.* 1976.

O'Rahilly, T. F. *Early Irish History and Mythology.* 1946.

Radner, Joan N. "'Fury Destroys the World': Historical Strategy in Ireland's Ulster Epic." *Mankind Quarterly* 23 (1982): 41–60.

Thurneysen, Rudolf. *Die irische Helden- und Königsage bis zum siebzehnten Jahrhundert.* 1921.

Patricia Kelly

Tandy, James Napper

A celebrated radical in Dublin politics in the 1770s and 1780s and a prominent United Irishman in the 1790s, Napper Tandy (1740–1802) was born in Dublin, the son of a merchant. He entered municipal politics in the 1770s and quickly became known for his reformist views. He was outspoken in his support of the American revolutionaries beginning in 1775 and became very active in the Volunteer movement, a movement intended initially to mobilize the general population to defend the country in the event of a French invasion during the period 1778 to 1783. Tandy was also enthusiastic about the French Revolution. He was among the founding members of the Dublin Society of United Irishmen in 1791 and its first secretary. He fled the country in 1793 for fear of being charged with taking the Defender oath, and he made his way to the United States. In 1797, with United Irish emissaries active in France, he went to Hamburg, Germany, and thence to Paris. An intense personal rivalry had developed between Tandy and Theobald Wolfe Tone; partly because of this the French government became less enthusiastic about an expedition to Ireland. At the same time Tandy's letters to his brother in Ireland led some United Irishmen there to assume that a French landing was imminent. Tandy was among the United Irishmen in France who were given commissions late in the summer of 1798 and assigned to the various small expeditions dispatched to attempt to link up with the Irish rebels. Arriving on the Donegal coast on 22 September, after both the Rising in the eastern counties and the campaign of French General Jean-Joseph-Amable Humbert in the west had come to an end, Tandy left the country a day later, realizing that all hope of success was lost. He and several comrades made their way to Hamburg, where they were arrested; they were finally handed over to British authorities in September 1799 after a diplomatic standoff involving Britain, France, Prussia, and Russia. Tandy was tried and convicted of treason in Ireland but was released by British General Charles Cornwallis as a result of French pressure. He left Ireland for the last time in 1802 and sailed to Bordeaux, where he died (of dysentery) on 24 August of that year.

SEE ALSO Defenderism; Eighteenth-Century Politics: 1778 to 1795—Parliamentary and Popular Politics; Eighteenth-Century Politics: 1795 to 1800—Repression, Rebellion, and Union; United Irish Societies from 1791 to 1803; **Primary Documents:** United Irish Parliamentary Reform Plan (March 1794); Grievances of the United Irishmen of Ballynahinch, Co. Down (1795); Speech Delivered at a United Irish Meeting in Ballyclare, Co. Antrim (1795); The United Irish Organization (1797); Statement of Three Imprisoned United Irish Leaders (4 August 1798)

Bibliography

Coughlan, Rupert J. *Napper Tandy*. 1976.

Ni Chinneide, Sile. *Napper Tandy and the European Crisis*. 1962.

Daniel Gahan

Tara

Like Dún Ailinne in Leinster, Cruachain (Rathcroghan) in Connacht, and Emain Macha (Navan) in Ulster, Tara (Old Irish *Temair*), Co. Meath (ancient *Midhe*), is one of the preeminent "royal sites" in Ireland. Today Tara is composed of a set of earthworks scattered almost 3,000 feet along a ridge rising to a maximum of about 430 feet above sea level. Some monuments are well preserved while others have long since disappeared, now being recognizable only from the air (Raftery 1991). The often fanciful names derive from an early eleventh-century text.

Dominating the ridge is a large enclosure, about fourteen and a half acres in size, known as *Rath na Ríogh* (Fort of the Kings), containing several notable monuments. An earthen rampart with an internal ditch surrounds it; this is a feature also found at Emain Macha and Dún Ailinne. Excavations in the 1950s revealed that the ditch was formed from a careful V-section cut ten feet into the bedrock. "Along its immediate inner edge was found a vertical-sided trench which must once have supported the timbers of a substantial palisade" (Raftery 1991).

Inside the enclosure is located *Dumha na nGiall* (the Mound of the Hostages), a Neolithic passage grave (ca. 3000–2500 B.C.E.). The tomb (about 13 feet × 3 feet) was subdivided into three compartments that originally contained the cremated remains of the dead along with their grave goods. Two adjacent structures, *teach Cormaic* (Cormac's house) and *forradh* (the royal seat), a pair of conjoined, high earthen banks with raised, flattened interiors, are of unknown date and purpose

The Stone of Destiny and summit of Rath na Riogh, *Tara (c. 3000–2500 B.C.E.). Tara was the inaugural site of the O'Neill high kings of Ireland during the Middle Ages.* PHOTOGRAPH REPRODUCED WITH THE KIND PERMISSION OF THE TRUSTEES OF THE NATIONAL MUSEUMS AND GALLERIES OF NORTHERN IRELAND, W29/01/32.

(Raftery 1991). The standing stone known as *Lia Fáil* (Stone of Destiny), erected on *Teach Cormaic* around 1824 to honor those who died in the 1798 skirmish at Tara, may once have stood in front of the entrance to the passage grave and may be contemporary with the tomb. According to medieval Irish tradition, when the rightful heir to the kingship sat on *Lia Fáil*, the stone would shriek.

More mounds and enclosures are found north and south of the Fort of the Kings. These include *Rath na Seanaid* (Rath of the Synods), a triple-ringed earthwork badly damaged in the early twentieth century by British Israelites who thought they would find the Ark of the Covenant there (Harbison 1979). Later excavations indicate that *Rath na Seanaid* was inhabited and used as a burial site at various times, including the first to fourth century C.E., as indicated by the discovery of Roman pottery, glass, and other items. About 245 feet north of the *Rath* is *Teach Miodhchuarta* (the Banqueting Hall), a pair of straight, parallel banks that are about 100 feet apart, extending down the slope for about 590 feet (Raftery 1991). Medieval writers viewed this as a large roofed structure; a detailed description of the seating arrangement is found in the twelfth-century *Book of Leinster*.

Clearly identified in ancient times as the "capital" of the kingdom of Brega, Tara later gained fame as the inauguration site of the High Kings of Ireland, generally members of the Uí Néill dynasty, though they did not actually reside there. Its cultural significance even in modern times is demonstrated by the fact that Daniel O'Connell held a "monster meeting" on the Hill of Tara in 1843 to reinforce his demand for repeal of the Act of Union.

SEE ALSO Cruachain; Dún Ailinne; Emain Macha (Navan Fort); Prehistoric and Celtic Ireland

Bibliography

Harbison, Peter. *Guide to the National Monuments in the Republic of Ireland*. 1979.

Macalister, R. A. S. *Tara: A Pagan Sanctuary of Ancient Ireland*. 1931.

Ó Ríordáin, S. P. *Tara: The Monument on the Hill*. 1971.

Raftery, Barry. "Tara, County Meath." In V. Kruta, et al. *The Celts*. 1991.

Swan, D. L. "The Hill of Tara, County Meath: The Evidence of Aerial Photography." *Society of the Antiquarians of Ireland* 108 (1978): 51–66.

James E. Doan

~

Temperance Movements

The government first criticized the level of whiskey consumption in Ireland as early as the 1550s, and state efforts to control the sale of drink through licensing laws began in the 1630s. By the 1790s the Irish parliament was voicing considerable concern at the quantities of illegal whiskey, known as poteen, being produced and sold in illicit drink shops, known as shebeens. Despite such long-standing complaints, an organized temperance movement did not appear in Ireland until the 1820s. Societies were established in Belfast and Dublin in 1829 by Protestant clergy, doctors, and merchants. Following the example of the influential U.S. temperance movement, these societies campaigned against drinking spirits and encouraged moderate consumption of other forms of alcohol. In 1835 total-abstinence societies reached Ireland from England, although some temperance advocates resisted this innovation.

Whether in the form of temperance or teetotalism, however, the antidrink movement at first made little headway since it was viewed in Ireland as foreign, fanatical, and a front for Protestant proselytization—which indeed to a large extent it was. But when an obscure Cork Capuchin named Father Theobald Mathew (1790–1856) joined a local teetotal society in 1838, the campaign took off spectacularly. By 1841 Mathew was claiming to have administered some five million abstinence pledges at a time when the total Irish population was a little over eight million.

Historians have debated why so many flocked to take the pledge from Mathew. H. F. Kearney, writing in 1979, suggested that the crusade was the product of modernizing, urban groups, but Elizabeth Malcolm countered in 1986 by stressing its roots in rural millenarian expectations, with Mathew being perceived as a messianic figure heralding the restoration of the Catholic ascendancy in Ireland. In 1992 Colm Kerrigan, while acknowledging that popular beliefs played a role in the crusade's success, followed Kearney in characterizing it as forward-looking rather than backward-looking. Further studies appearing in 2002 by Paul Townend and J. F. Quinn offered differing interpretations. Townend in particular saw the crusade as an indication of the prefamine Catholic Church's failure to meet the spiritual needs of the Irish people. All agreed, however, that the crusade's success was short-lived; even before the Great Famine, a serious decline had begun. Mathew's opposition to repeal, his financial and administrative incompetence, and the hostility of some of the Catholic hierarchy undermined the movement. After the Great Famine, Mathew's crusade was widely perceived, not least by the Catholic Church, to have failed. The church therefore decided to promote temperance rather than total abstinence and to do so through church organizations rather than through secular temperance societies.

Meanwhile, Protestant-dominated societies, which were especially strong in Ulster, continued to operate, but in the wake of Mathew's failure they switched from trying to curb the drinking of individuals through persuasion to imposing restrictions on society through legislation. Most favored prohibition. When it became clear that this was unlikely to be passed by the British parliament, they campaigned for measures like Sunday closing (the total closure of pubs on the Sabbath), local option (communities having the power to vote to exclude pubs from their neighborhoods), and more rigorous enforcement of the licensing laws. Some limited successes were achieved, such as the introduction of Sunday closing outside the major cities in 1878. But with the demise of the Irish Liberal Party in the 1870s, the temperance movement was deprived of a solid political base in Ireland. The Home Rule Party had close links with the drink industry, as did the British Conservative Party, with which most Ulster Unionist MPs were affiliated. As the issues of land and sovereignty came to the fore of Irish politics in the 1880s, the temperance question declined in significance.

The Catholic Church, however, revived the issue of teetotalism in the 1880s, culminating in 1898 with the establishment by the Jesuit Father James Cullen (1841–1921) of the Pioneer Total Abstinence Association of the Sacred Heart. The Pioneers quickly became the most influential temperance organization in the country, and

A medal of the type distributed during the temperance campaigns of Father Theobald Mathew during the late 1830s and 1840s. From Mr. and Mrs. Samuel Carter Hall, *Ireland: Its Scenery, Character, Etc.* (1841–1843).

they remained so throughout the twentieth century. By 1925 the Pioneers claimed to have 250,000 members in Ireland; by 1945, close to 350,000 members; and by 1960 (when the population of the Republic was less than three million), 500,000 members. At the same time there were also thousands of members in Britain, the United States, South America, Australia, and various parts of Africa. By the middle of the twentieth century the Pioneer Association was arguably the largest temperance society in the world.

The Pioneers were more than just a temperance society, and their complex character ultimately proved to be problematical. Father Cullen believed that Father Mathew had failed because his crusade did not have the support of the Catholic Church and was poorly organized. Cullen therefore laid down very precise rules for the Pioneers and structured the association as a pious sodality dedicated to the Sacred Heart rather than as a secular welfare organization. He saw the association's agenda as primarily personal and spiritual, not social and ameliorative. This made it difficult for the Pioneers to engage in political lobbying. Thus they could not persuade the new Free State to introduce more draconian licensing legislation in the 1920s (although temperance groups in Northern Ireland had considerable success in this regard), nor were they able to prevent the Fianna Fáil government from ending Sunday closing in 1959. The Pioneers' impressive growth in membership during

the 1950s was in fact outstripped by per capita alcohol consumption, which increased by 60 percent between 1948 and 1970.

By the 1960s, with the emergence of new approaches to problem drinking and new organizations, the Pioneers were beginning to appear decidedly old-fashioned. Alcoholics Anonymous reached Ireland in 1946, and the view that alcoholism was a disease, not a moral or religious failing, gained ground in the 1950s. In such a climate of opinion, prayers and hellfire sermons, pledge taking, and the display of Pioneer pins all seemed inappropriate. Some investigators of Irish drinking practices in the 1970s even went so far as to suggest that the puritanical and authoritarian nature of Irish Catholicism, which the Pioneers very much represented, promoted rather than discouraged heavy drinking. At the end of the twentieth century the Pioneer Association remained a significant and distinctive expression of traditional Irish Catholic piety, but the belief that such an organization could transform Irish drinking habits had long since evaporated.

SEE ALSO Church of Ireland: Since 1690; Evangelicalism and Revivals; Methodism; Presbyterianism; Religious Orders: Men; Roman Catholic Church: 1829 to 1891; Roman Catholic Church: Since 1891; Sodalities and Confraternities

Bibliography

Ferriter, Diarmaid. *A Nation of Extremes: The Pioneers in Twentieth-Century Ireland*. 1999.

Kearney, H. F. "Fr Mathew: Apostle of Modernisation." In *Studies in Irish History Presented to R. Dudley Edwards*, edited by Art Cosgrove and Donal McCartney. 1979.

Kerrigan, Colm. *Father Mathew and the Irish Temperance Movement, 1838–1849*. 1992.

Malcolm, Elizabeth. *"Ireland Sober, Ireland Free": Drink and Temperance in Nineteenth-Century Ireland*. 1986

Quinn, J. F. *Father Mathew's Crusade: Temperance in Nineteenth-Century Ireland and Irish America*. 2002.

Stivers, Richard. *A Hair of the Dog: Irish Drinking and American Stereotype*. 1976.

Townend, Paul A. *Father Mathew, Temperance and Irish Identity*. 2002.

Elizabeth Malcolm

Tenant Right, or Ulster Custom

The custom of tenant right, commonly referred to in Victorian Ireland as the "Ulster custom," was a practice by which rural tenants claimed property rights above and beyond their contracts with landlords, allowing departing tenants to exact a payment well in excess of the yearly rent from those who wished to replace them in their farms. In practice the payment of tenant right served two purposes: it compensated the seller for investments made in the farm, and it granted to the purchaser the "goodwill" of the seller, allowing the purchaser to enjoy the "peaceable possession" of the farm. The new tenant would of course also have an agreement with the landlord, occupying the farm under the conditions of a lease or, more commonly, at the will of the landlord. The inevitable tension between these two sets of relationships was a fundamental characteristic of rural property relations in the eighteenth and nineteenth centuries. Though leases and other contracts delimited the legal rights of tenants with regard to the occupation of land, the custom of tenant right existed anterior to these, supplementing the private property system established by the plantations. Like other earlier forms of customary tenure in Scotland and the north of England, tenant right signified the tenant's place within a community, his or her way of belonging to its history and development, and, crucially, the right of the tenant's family to continue in possession in the future. In

Ulster the custom of tenant right came to signify the place of the tenant within a troublesome colonial history, the development of a commercial economy in a new property system, and the visual transformation of the landscape.

ORIGIN

The term *tenant right* was first used in Ulster during the second half of the seventeenth century, during a period of deep uncertainty about the stability of the colonial property system and the economy that underpinned it. As the colonial land system began to gain stability in the mid-eighteenth century, the contractual agreements governing the occupation of land became more varied and complex. There were head tenants holding leases of various kinds directly from landowners, middlemen holding large tracts and letting them in turn to undertenants under a variety of different contracts, and below these the mass of smallholders who sublet farms from other tenants or held land without lease at the will of the landlord. In these circumstances, the actual occupiers of the land began to assert that the very stability that had been obtained was the result of the historic efforts of their families to occupy and improve the land. Tenant right came to represent the historical right of planters to continuous occupation. Emphasizing the continuity of their families on the land through the wars and political upheavals of the seventeenth century, the houses and fences they built and maintained, and their consistent political allegiance to their landlords, they asserted their tenant right of renewal of expired leases and the right to keep their families in continuous possession of farms. With the passing of decades and the attenuation of these historical claims in the face of more severe economic competition for land, the urgency of these claims intensified. Claims for the right of renewal in the late eighteenth and early nineteenth centuries often made reference to one's ancestor's participation in, for example, the "memorable siege of Derry" or the "wars of Ireland." These claims were occasionally renewed or updated with reminders of one's electoral allegiance to the landlord or other deferential behavior.

In addition to long histories of occupation, the custom was also strengthened and given meaning by reference to the landscape itself. The colonial estate system, based on a capitalist and individualist model of agricultural production that required clear demarcation of the boundaries of farms and of the property rights between the tenants of those farms, was clearly distinguishable from the pastoral and collective economic life of Gaelic Ulster and the rundale system of redistributing strips of tilled land among members of a community. The rapid commercialization of the eighteenth century had never-

The linen industry strengthened the economic position of tenants in east Ulster. Direct profits from flax cultivation often raised farm incomes. Such income could increase the value of the tenant right of a holding when that was sold under the "Ulster custom." Flax was harvested by hand until the 1940s and was spread on dry ground in sheaves, as in this 1859 sketch. FROM ILLUSTRATED LONDON NEWS, 24 SEPTEMBER 1859.

theless steadily eroded the old pattern, as enterprising tenants stepped out from their collectives to agree to individual contracts with their landlords, severing themselves from the variety of duties and benefits of the rural village. Tenant-right payments served to compensate former partners in rundale communities and to clarify their new status. The subsequent processes of enclosure and the "improvement" of enclosed farms became powerful justifications for the claim of tenant right.

ECONOMIC CONSIDERATIONS

In the end, one's right to occupation depended fundamentally on the ability to pay a competitive rent. Though landlords consistently preferred Protestant tenants, who were in any case granted clear privileges in law over their Catholic competitors, there remained a resilient anxiety about being displaced. In practice, the ability to compete with the native population depended on developing new outputs and strengthening markets. Participation in the diversified components of the rural linen trade was one of the keys to success. The booming linen economy of the rural north allowed for the proliferation of small but independent farms, each with a separate claim to have developed the productivity and profitability of an estate. By the early nineteenth century it

was widely understood that the expanding linen economy was deeply implicated in the growth of the custom of tenant right. Although there is scattered evidence of its use in other parts of Ireland, the custom was not to become part of the social and economic fabric of rural society outside of the north. Its unique development there is bound up with economic and demographic developments that distinguish the north from the rest of the island. These were the successful plantation of an immigrant population, the advanced development of rural industry, and the dramatic transformation of the landscape of Gaelic Ulster.

In the period after 1815 the economic landscape and the meaning and function of tenant right began to change rapidly. A century-long upward trend in farm prices began to reverse itself in the more open post-Napoleonic economy, cutting into small-farm profitability. In addition, the mechanization of flax spinning and weaving and the changing nature of demand for textiles undercut a rural industrial sector that had served as a crucial girder of the economy. Ulster rural society began a long and painful transition from the heterogeneous mixture of cottiers, small-holding weavers, and middling to large capitalist farmers to the more stratified and less densely settled pattern of the post-famine period.

Sales of tenant right in the Limavady district of Londonderry from 1873 to 1880

Date	Seller	Townland	Acreage			Rent			Buyer	Amount	Landlord
			a.	r.	p.	£	s.	d.		£	
3 Dec. 1873	John M'Loskey	Leek	41	0	0	19	10	0	James Feeny	435	Wm. Cather
15 Aug. 1873	James M'Ateer	Ballyhargan	8	0	0	3	3	0	Henry Deany	60	Mr. Wray
7 Dec. 1876	John Aull	Ballyscullin	2	1	18	1	15	6	Joseph Aull	31	Sir F. W. Heygate
11 Feb. 1878	Wm. Carlin	Ballymoney	10	0	0	6	5	0	James Kane	127	John M'Curdy
23 Jan. 1878	Jas. Douglas	Boveva	22	0	0	20	0	0	Wm. Laughlin	108	J. S. Douglass
19 Feb. 1878	Dennis Brolly	Gortnaghymore	12	0	0	9	0	0	Michael Doherty	106	John Quigley
31 Jan. 1877	Wm. Stewart	Termaquin	23	1	26	17	15	2	Robert Simpson	270	Samuel Pollock
15 Feb. 1878	Alex. Lytle	Gortgarn	16	3	9	10	0	0	Geo. Stewart	200	Lord C. Beresford
1 Sept. 1877	Paul Kane	Killywill	14	0	0	10	10	5	Wm. M'Kinney	290	Rev. Maxwell
14 Dec. 1877	Ed. Hampsy	Boley	5	0	0	6	6	0	Jas. Murray	105	Ditto
16 Nov. 1876	Robt. Ogilby	Tullyvery	14	0	0	13	8	9	Wm. Mullen	360	Ditto
31 Aug. 1876	Roseau Divine	Faughanvale	23	0	0	13	0	0	James King	500	Ditto
4 Jan. 1878	John Hargan	Muldooney	18	0	0	9	10	0	Michael Carten	210	Major Brown
24 Jan. 1877	James Kane	Margymonaghan	137	0	0	64	10	0	Edward Conn	650	Sir F. W. Heygate
23 Mar. 1876	Jas. Hutton	Derrynaflaw	54	0	0	19	8	8	Jas. Fallows	406	Mr. Boyle
25 Feb. 1875	Wm. Latten	Drumballydonaghy	9	0	0	11	3	0	John Patchell	183	Ditto
27 Jan. 1876	Tho. O'Hara	Killywill	6	0	0	4	4	0	Wm. Mullan	180	Rev. Maxwell
4 Jan. 1878	Robt. Kane	Ballymoney	9	0	0	4	12	0	Thos. Murphy	120	John M. Curdy
17 Jan. 1879	Henry Donaghy	Mulkeeragh	26	0	0	14	0	0	John Steel	520	Michael King
9 Dec. 1879	Wm. Millikin	Straw	30	0	0	23	11	0	William Dale	425	John Semple
2 July 1879	Patrick Carten	Tartnakelly	25	0	0	5	5	0	Michael Bryson	140	James Ogilby
5 Mar. 1878	Henry Deany	Feeney	13	0	0	9	13	7	Jas. M'Kendry	275	J. C. F. Hunter
6 Nov. 1878	Sarah Atkinson	Broharris	33	1	14	41	5	0	James Thompson	880	Fishmongers' Company
27 Aug. 1879	William Steel	Ballymore	7	0	23	8	0	0	James M'Clelland	120	Henry Tyler
6 Feb. 1879	Pat. Heaney	Drum	34	0	0	14	9	4	John M'Losky	450	Miss C. T. D. Nesbitt
16 Dec. 1879	James Mullen	Killywill	9	0	0	5	11	4	Jas. Donaghy	151	Rev. Maxwell
7 Feb. 1879	Samuel Young	Drumraighland	10	0	0	4	4	0	Wm. Hopkins	160	Robert Ogilby
26 Dec. 1879	Wm. M'Closkey	Kilunaght	18	0	0	10	10	0	Henry M'Closkey	270	Captain Bruce
28 June 1879	Thomas Young	Killywill	6	0	0	2	17	9	John Hara	90	Rev. Maxwell
5 Sept. 1879	John Miller	Drumraighland	Ho. & Grdn.			0	0	6	James White	54	Robert Ogilby
13 Nov. 1879	John Donaghy	Cool	26	1	30	12	0	0	John Baird	400	Fishmongers' Company
26 Apr. 1879	Susan Tower	Glack	26	0	0	14	15	0	Robt. Ferguson	775	Ditto
3 Apr. 1879	Thomas M'Closkey	Gortnaghy	7	3	0	3	13	0	John Quinn	59	Michael M'Cartney
15 Apr. 1879	Margaret Heany	Drum	17	0	0	7	4	8	James M'Cully	254	Miss C. T. D. Nesbitt
18 Jan. 1879	Eliz. Rosborough	Ballyhanedin	46	0	0	25	10	0	Edward Rea	360	Fishmongers' Company
22 Jan. 1880	Jas. Stewart	Turmacoy	24	0	0	18	10	0	John Hopkin	540	Ditto
24 Dec. 1878	Henry Mullan	Lenamore	127	0	0	28	18	0	Peter Conway	340	Marquis of Waterford
22 Feb. 1879	Ed. Rea	Ballymoney	28	0	0	14	12	0	Henry M'Closkey	320	John M'Curdy
14 Nov. 1878	John L. Horner	Burnfoot	17	3	24	16	0	0	James Connor	307	John Semple
4 Mar. 1880	Wm. Connor	Magheramore	35	0	0	13	9	0	James Holmes	366	James Ogilby
9 Apr. 1879	N. M'Kennery	Gortgarn	16	2	0	11	0	0	Neil M'Kennery, jun.	156	Marquis of Waterford
28 Feb. 1879	Nancy Heany	Templemoyle	8	0	0	5	10	0	John M'Intyre	122	T. Heany
13 Feb. 1880	John Kelly	Coolagh	20	0	0	18	4	0	Joseph Mackay	480	R. P. Maxwell
19 Jan. 1880	John M'Kinney	Boley	20	0	0	16	2	10	John Jamieson	360	Ditto
3 Jan. 1880	Jos. Ferguson	Killybleught	17	0	0	20	0	0	John Quigg	200	Jacob Jackson
23 Feb. 1880	James Ross	Killylane	54	0	0	41	0	0	Edward Coyle	805	Fishmongers' Company
24 Feb. 1880	P. Hampson	Gortnaghy	8	1	7	7	0	0	James Kane	100	Adam Wray
25 Mar. 1880	Robt. M'Elree	Moneyshinare	70	0	0	60	0	0	Robt. Jno. Nelson	970	Rev. M. M'Causland
26 Mar. 1880	Michael Kane	Terrydreen	24	0	0	6	0	0	William Evans	172	J. B. Beresford
13 Jan. 1880	Jane Magill	Moyse	43	0	0	15	15	0	Joseph Neely	310	James Ogilby
31 Aug. 1880	Jas. M'Greelis	Tyrglasson	8	2	0	3	15	0	Hugh Miller	200	Fishmongers' Company

(1) In acreage, **a.** = acres, **r.** = roods, **p.** = perches.
(2) In rent, **£.** = pound, **s.** = shilling, and **d.** = pence.

SOURCE: Adapted from Finlay Dun, *Landlords and Tenants in Ireland* (1881), pp. 130–131.

From the viewpoint of estate managers the most se-rious issues revolved around the decreasing economic viability of small-holders, their mounting debts, and their often impenetrable economic interconnections. In coming to terms with these problems, they recognized the lack of sufficiently effective managerial and legal tools. Intractable enough on their own terms, these problems were exacerbated by the existence of a customary right to property that had developed, in many cases without the knowledge of absentee or inattentive landlords, over the course of a century.

The two available legal remedies against defaulting tenants were the distraint of goods or chattels for arrears of rent and eviction for nonpayment of rent. Legislation in the 1820s that made these far more efficient and effective legal weapons notwithstanding, most estate managers still regarded distraint and eviction as blunt, overly antagonistic, expensive, and unpredictable weapons. The Hearts of Oak and Hearts of Steel rebellions of the previous century were only distant memories in the 1820s, but the threat of violent and organized resistance to blunt enforcement of contracts was constantly alive in the minds of estate managers. As agents began to discover the technicalities, difficulties, and inadequacies of distraint and eviction, they were simultaneously discovering something else: The practice of tenant right on their estates, while posing a definite threat to their property rights, held out for them the potential of more effective management. Progressive estate managers, such as James Hamilton of Strabane or Henry Miller of Draperstown, clearly saw the advantages of accepting the custom and attempting to manipulate it, rather than courting open rebellion by strictly enforcing legal contracts. By the 1850s an increasing number of estate managers had obtained some control over the tenant-right system by restricting the prices paid, by asserting a power of veto over purchasers, and by actively promoting the sale and subsequent amalgamation of farms.

LEGISLATIVE RECOGNITION

The advance of estate management opened a new era of uncertainty and tension with regard to the meaning of tenant right. The year 1835 marked a critical turning point in the history of the public understanding of tenant right. In that year the liberal County Down landlord William Sharman Crawford introduced the first of many land bills that attempted to give the custom of tenant right legal recognition. His indefatigable advocacy of tenant right was based on economic ideas that defended the continued viability of the small farm within agrarian capitalism. Also in that year the first-ever public meeting urging legislative recognition of the custom took place in Comber, Co. Down. In the following decades the meaning of tenant right was no longer only a matter for tenants, land agents, and landlords on a particular estate. It was now the subject of massive parliamentary inquiries and widely read tracts by leading political economists. In short, the custom of tenant right was rapidly becoming a nationwide question, though not yet implicated in the question of nationhood.

In the 1850s an interpretation of the meaning of tenant right that denigrated historical claims to property and allowed only for a restricted conception of "compensation for improvements" held sway at Westminster. Two acts of land legislation were passed in 1860: Caldwell's Act, which endeavored to regulate compensation for improvements, and Deasy's Act, which reiterated the very fundamental aspect of the private property system that the Ulster custom usurped, namely, that the relation of landlord and tenant be founded on contracts and contracts only. Neither of these acts accomplished the goal of clarifying the meaning and practice of customary tenure. By the late 1860s, in the wake of the Fenian rising, a change in the mentality of legislators had taken place. In his introduction to a land bill that was to become law in 1870, Prime Minister Gladstone told Parliament that the Irish people "have not generally embraced the idea of the occupation of land by contract, and the old Irish notion that some interest in the soil adheres to the tenant, even though his contract has expired, is everywhere rooted in the popular mind." The Land Act of 1870 gave ambiguous legal recognition to the Ulster custom of tenant right, and in so doing, it placed the Irish land question on a new and uncertain footing.

SEE ALSO Butt, Isaac; Land Acts of 1870 and 1881; Land Questions; Oakboys and Steelboys; Protestant Ascendancy: Decline, 1800 to 1930

Bibliography

Dowling, Martin W. *Tenant Right and Agrarian Society in Ulster, 1600–1870.* 1999.

Vaughan, William E. *Landlords and Tenants in Mid-Victorian Ireland.* 1994.

Wright, Frank. *Two Lands on One Soil: Ulster Politics before Home Rule.* 1996.

Martin W. Dowling

Textiles

See Factory-Based Textile Manufacture; Rural Industry; Women and Children in the Industrial Workforce.

Theater

See Arts: Early Modern Literature and the Arts
from 1500 to 1800; Drama, Modern.

~

Tithe War (1830–1838)

The tithe war was a popular uprising in the southern
provinces of Leinster and Munster, with widespread disturbances in Connacht and some in Ulster, against the
payment of tithes to the Protestant Established Church.
The burden of tithe—theoretically, the tenth part of
one's income given in kind or money in support of the
church—had long been a complaint in Ireland. Ever
since the sixteenth century when Henry VIII transferred
the ownership of tithes from Catholic priests and
monasteries to the reformed Protestant clergymen and
laymen, the Catholics of Ireland—the overwhelming
majority of the population—were left in the unusual
position of having to finance a church to which they did
not belong and which was in fact hostile to them. Irish
Presbyterians, who had their own church to support,
objected to the payment as well. This basic injustice was
heightened by the uneven distribution of tithes upon the
land. Grasslands, often kept by wealthy Protestant graziers, were exempt from tithes after the early eighteenth
century. Conversely, the fields of the lowly potato, an
increasingly important food for the Catholic peasantry,
were assessed at a high rate throughout the southern
half of the country, ensuring that the grasping hand of
tithes would reach all the way down to the humblest laborer's potato patch. Annual disputes over what was ti-
theable, how tithes would be valued and collected, and
the notorious misbehavior of aggressive and dishonest
tithe agents ensured that tithes would remain a constant and contentious issue in the Irish countryside.

By 1830 Ireland was primed for its biggest battle
over tithes. Parliamentary investigations into the rampant abuses and severe structural problems of the Established Church left it with few defenders, while the
ranks of tithe opponents swelled with the addition of
large farmers and graziers after legislation in 1823 increasingly extended tithes to their previously exempt
grasslands. Sectarian relations were seriously strained
in the 1820s, poisoned by the aggressively anti-Catholic
Second Reformation, and inflamed by the popular and
successful struggle for Catholic Emancipation, which
left in its wake a more politically aware Catholic people
and a cadre of experienced local middle-class Catholic

activists willing and able to handle the reins during the
tithe war.

The spark igniting the tithe war was struck in the
autumn of 1830 in Graiguenamanagh, Co. Kilkenny,
when the parish priest, Father Martin Doyle, counseled
his parishioners to withhold their tithe payment from
the unpopular Protestant curate. The strategy of passive resistance first recommended by Doyle was remarkably simple and extremely effective. If anyone's
animals were seized for nonpayment of tithes, the entire
parish should attend the resulting auction but no one
should bid for the animals, thereby thwarting the legal
process by which tithe owners were allowed to recover
their money. It was an ingenious strategy that took advantage of the large number of small sums that tithe
owners had to collect, and effectively rallied the entire
parish. Everyone was called upon to shun anyone who
dared either to bid for the animals or to assist the tithe
owners in their legal proceedings. Using these easily implemented tactics, the agitation spread quickly from its
base in Kilkenny so that by the end of 1831 the concerted refusal to pay tithes was well established throughout
most of Leinster and eastern Munster.

Increasing the effectiveness of the campaign was
the constant threat of violence against Protestant clergymen and their agents should they attempt to proceed
with the collection of tithes. Beginning in early 1831
tithe agents were routinely chased off property, frequently assaulted by large crowds, and in a number of
cases even murdered. At Newtownbarry (Bunclody) in
County Wexford, fourteen people were killed when the
police and yeomen, who were protecting three heifers
seized for tithes, fired into a stone-throwing crowd.
More worrisome for the Irish government was the brutal slaughter of a process server and twelve constables
who had been sent out to protect him while he served
tithe subpoenas at Carrickshock, Co. Kilkenny, in December 1831.

In some respects this combination of passive and violent resistance reflects the various social classes involved in the anti-tithe agitation. Tithes cast a wide net,
maddening the small farmers and laborers with potato
plots, who were prone to Whiteboy tactics of violence
and intimidation, as well as large farmers, who were
anxious to make the most of legal resistance. But it
would be wrong to assume that the tithe war was two
separate but parallel movements—a violent Whiteboy
agitation and a peaceful middle-class campaign of petitions. In truth, violence was an integral component of
the entire agitation, creating the atmosphere of intimidation needed to enforce the community sanctions
against those who profited from tithes. The dual pattern
of passive and violent resistance continued in 1832 as

Among the commonest forms of collective action during the tithe war of the 1830s was the attacking of process-servers by large crowds. These functionaries had the unenviable task of delivering notices of default and warnings of the seizure of goods to those resisting payment of tithes. During the land war after 1878, tenants who resisted the payment of the customary rents often resorted to the same tactics, as this 1881 sketch shows. FROM ILLUSTRATED LONDON NEWS, 21 MAY 1881.

the agitation infected the rest of Munster, much of Connacht in the west, and finally Ulster, where the greatest resistance appeared in the heavily Catholic counties of Donegal, Cavan, and Monaghan. The tithe war never seized hold of Ulster because the large number of Protestant payers, the exemption of potato lands, and the historically lighter rates made the injustice less pressing there.

Angry tithe owners blamed Daniel O'Connell and the Catholic bishop of Kildare and Leighlin, the Reverend James Doyle, for the loss of their incomes. In fact, O'Connell took surprisingly little interest in the agitation, preferring to highlight the tithe issue only when it could be safely harnessed to promote his causes of emancipation and repeal. Tithe owners were closer to the mark in pointing the finger of blame at Bishop Doyle. In the summer of 1831, in a blistering public letter, Doyle denounced tithes as a grinding and insulting injustice and resolutely endorsed the strategy of passive resistance. His concise exposition of the case against tithes was widely disseminated as a penny pamphlet and dutifully read to Catholic parishioners from the altar during Sunday mass. Doyle's dramatic closing line, "May their hatred of tithe be as lasting as their love of justice," became the rallying cry of the campaign. But while he provided the moral underpinning of the movement, Doyle played no role in directing it.

Dublin Castle and police officials were probably accurate in their frequent descriptions of the agitation as leaderless, for there was no one leader or national organization similar to those formed during the campaigns for emancipation and repeal. Instead, as the resistance fanned out from Kilkenny, it was warmly received by prominent local Catholic leaders who had first cut their political teeth on emancipation. Included in this group were middle to large farmers, shopkeepers, newspapermen, and many parish priests who, while condemning episodes of violence, nevertheless publicly condemned the tithe system and promoted the campaign against it.

Initially responsive to tithe owners' demand for protection during tithe collection, Dublin Castle's willingness to provide police escorts waned considerably after the murder of the constables at Carrickshock. Tithe owners were instead encouraged to accept the money offered to them by acts of Parliament in 1832 and 1833 to help defray their arrears while more substantial legislation aimed at permanently resolving the issue was under consideration. Unfortunately, parliamentary action was delayed for the next five years, leaving hardy tithe owners free to continue collecting payments under the old system with its rampant opportunities for violence, such as the murderous affray at Rathcormac in December 1834, when twelve men

were killed protecting the Widow Ryan's forty shillings against seizure. The tithe war finally quieted down after the spring of 1835 when the weapons available to tithe owners were sharply curtailed by the new Whig government and especially the new Undersecretary at Dublin Castle, Thomas Drummond, who refused to allow police escorts for tithe business. Tithe opponents resorted to holding meetings to petition Parliament to abolish tithes until the 1838 Tithe Act effectively ended the hostilities.

The tithe war marked an important intersection in the fortunes of a resurgent Catholic Church and a crumbling Protestant one that was well on its way toward disestablishment thirty years later. The tactics used during the tithe war would reappear during the land war of the late 1870s and 1880s, when passive resistance would be directed toward rent and the ostracizing of collaborators received its nom de guerre courtesy of Captain Charles Boycott.

SEE ALSO Defenderism; Irish Tithe Act of 1838; Land Questions; Oakboys and Steelboys; Protestant Ascendancy: Decline, 1800 to 1930; Whiteboys and Whiteboyism

Bibliography

Brynn, Edward. *The Church of Ireland in the Age of Catholic Emancipation.* 1982.

Macintyre, Angus. *The Liberator: Daniel O'Connell and the Irish Party, 1830–1847.* 1965.

O'Donoghue, Patrick. "Causes of the Opposition to Tithes, 1830–38." *Studia Hibernica* 5 (1965): 7–28.

O'Donoghue, Patrick. "Opposition to Tithe Payments in 1830–31." *Studia Hibernica* 6 (1966): 69–98.

O'Donoghue, Patrick. "Opposition to Tithe Payments in 1832–3." *Studia Hibernica* 12 (1972): 77–108.

Suzanne C. Hartwick

Toland, John

John Toland (1670–1722), freethinker, was born into the Irish-speaking Catholic community of Inishowen, Co. Donegal. After receiving primary education locally, he entered Glasgow University and became identified with Presbyterianism and student discontent. Graduating with an M.A. (Edinburgh) in 1690, he moved first to London and then to Leyden (1692–1693). During a year at Oxford, he began work on a never-to-be-completed Irish dictionary. In 1696 he published *Christianity Not Mysterious*, which caused great scandal, alarming even John Locke, whose influence was discernible in its argument. Toland had to cut short a visit to Dublin in 1697 when the commons ordered that his tract be burned and its author arrested. Back in London he wrote a biography of John Milton (1699) and pamphlets questioning Anglican and Tory pieties. Over the years his religious views became increasingly divorced from mainstream Christian orthodoxy. The controversy over *Christianity Not Mysterious* in 1697 was a foretaste of the dismay that his later works would cause. The term *pantheist* was apparently coined by Toland, whose developing ideas on religion can be traced in *Socinianism Truly Stated* (1705), *Adeisdaemon* (1709), and, most shocking to contemporaries, *Nazarenus* (1718) and *Pantheisticon* (1720).

A strong advocate of the Hanoverian succession, he was on the delegation to Hanover that presented the Act of Settlement (1701) to the Electress Sophia. Funded by wealthy patrons, he made his living as a Whig propagandist, though he was not to be rewarded with office or emolument after the Hanoverian succession. His only interventions in Irish affairs in the last decade of his life were expressions of anxiety about Catholic revival and criticism, in *Reasons Most Humbly Offered* (1720), of the British Parliament's Declaratory Act (6th George I). In his last years he depended on the patronage of the Whig radical Robert Molesworth, and he died in relative poverty in London on 11 March 1722. He once described himself as "avowedly a commonwealth's man" (Simms 1969, p. 312), to which might be added William Molyneux's assessment: "a candid free-thinker and a good scholar" (Simms 1969, p. 310).

SEE ALSO Church of Ireland: Since 1690

Bibliography

Harrison, Alan. *Béal eiriciúil as Inis Eoghain: John Toland (1670–1722).* 1994.

McGuinness, Philip, et al., eds. *John Toland's "Christianity Not Mysterious": Text, Associated Works, and Critical Essays.* 1997.

Simms, J. G. "John Toland (1670–1722): A Donegal Heretic." *Irish Historical Studies* 16, no. 63 (1969): 304–320.

James McGuire

Theobald Wolfe Tone (1763–1798), prominent member of the Society of United Irishmen. © HULTON ARCHIVE/GETTY IMAGES. REPRODUCED BY PERMISSION.

Tone, Theobald Wolfe

Revolutionary leader and founder of the Society of United Irishmen, Theobald Wolfe Tone (1763–1798) was born in Dublin and educated at Trinity College, Dublin. Called to the Irish bar in the summer of 1789, he grew tired of the law and soon became embroiled in radical politics. He was an ardent supporter of Catholic Emancipation and acted as an agent and then secretary of the Catholic Committee. It was during this time that his gifts as a polemicist and organizer became evident. Indeed, his pamphlet *An Argument on Behalf of the Catholics of Ireland* was considered to be one of the most influential of the 1790s.

Growing disillusioned with the pace of reform, he founded the Society of United Irishmen in 1791. This was initially an organization committed to peaceful agitation, but it became radicalized in 1794 after the British government made it illegal. With the suppression of the United Irishmen, Tone dedicated his life to overthrowing British rule in Ireland and uniting Catholics, Protestants, and Dissenters in an independent Irish republic. In 1794 he emigrated to America but found it difficult to adjust to life in that country. From there he moved to France, where he became involved in various schemes to liberate Ireland. The abortive Bantry Bay invasion of 1796 did not deter him, and he sailed to Ireland in October 1798 with a French army to take part in the 1798 rebellion. Captured at Buncrana in County Donegal on 3 November, he was taken to Dublin and charged with treason. Proudly admitting his guilt, he committed suicide in prison to avoid execution by hanging. However he botched the job and it was three days before he died on 19 November. Because of his inspirational legacy Wolfe Tone has been called the father of Irish republicanism.

SEE ALSO Catholic Committee from 1756 to 1809; Eighteenth-Century Politics: 1778 to 1795—Parliamentary and Popular Politics; Eighteenth-Century Politics: 1795 to 1800—Repression, Rebellion, and Union; United Irish Societies from 1791 to 1803; **Primary Documents:** United Irish Parliamentary Reform Plan (March 1794); Grievances of the United Irishmen of Ballynahinch, Co. Down (1795); Speech Delivered at a United Irish Meeting in Ballyclare, Co. Antrim (1795); The United Irish Organization (1797); Statement of Three Imprisoned United Irish Leaders (4 August 1798)

Bibliography

Bartlett, Thomas. *Theobald Wolfe Tone.* 1997.

Bartlett, Thomas. *Life of Theobald Wolfe Tone.* 1998.

Elliott, Marianne. *Partners in Revolution: The United Irishmen and France.* 1982.

Elliott, Marianne. *Wolfe Tone: Prophet of Irish Independence.* 1990.

P. M. Geoghegan

Tourism

For centuries the main reasons for travel to Ireland were religious and political. In the early medieval period students from Britain and continental Europe received educational training at Irish monastic foundations, and sites like Saint Patrick's Purgatory in Lough Derg were European places of pilgrimage. The political travellers followed later in the wake of the Anglo-Norman and Tudor conquests and were generally concerned in their accounts with justifying military takeover and economic expropriation. The defeat of the Jacobite army at the Battle of the Boyne in 1690 meant the end to the military threat from the native Irish, and Ireland was perceived in the eighteenth century as a safe country to visit. Improvements in the road system, the introduction of coaches, and the extension of the canal system from Dublin made traveling quicker, more comfortable, and less hazardous. Later in the century, George Taylor and Andrew Skinner's *Maps of the Roads of Ireland* (1778) and *The Compleat Irish Traveller* (1778) provided practical assistance to the foreign traveler in Ireland.

The eighteenth century saw the emergence of a form of scenic tourism in Ireland. The interest in the Irish landscape was symptomatic of a much wider romantic attentiveness to remote landscapes, which would be further strengthened in the late eighteenth century by a revival of interest in the Celtic world. This revival was fueled by the instant success of James Macpherson's *Fragments of Ancient Poetry Collected in the Highlands of Scotland and Translated from the Gaelic or Erse Language* (1760). The Celtic spirit was seen to be closely bound up with the physical setting in which the remaining speakers of Celtic languages lived. The taste for rugged, dramatic landscapes in isolated areas meant that by the 1780s and 1790s, Killarney in the southwest of Ireland had established itself as a popular scenic resort for aristocratic and well-to-do travelers. The United Irish rebellion of 1798, the Great Famine of 1845 to 1851, and the political unrest accompanying the activities of the Land League and the move toward Home Rule and eventual independence did little to favor the growth of tourism to Ireland in the nineteenth and early twentieth centuries. However, the dramatic growth in the rail network in the late 1830s did encourage the development of domestic tourism, and the century saw the emergence of notable seaside resorts such as Bray on the east coast and Kilkee on the west coast.

In 1925 the Irish Tourist Association (ITA) was established to promote the development of Irish tourism. The membership of the ITA was made up of hoteliers and prominent business people, but in the early years the association was hampered by a lack of state funding. Under the Tourist Traffic (Development) Act of 1931 the ITA was designated as an official beneficiary of finance at local-government level. In 1939 the Tourist Traffic Act allowed for the creation of an official Irish Tourist Board to provide accommodation and other amenities for visitors to Ireland. The effectiveness of the board was severely constrained by a lack of finance. The absence of adequate funding was related not only to the economic difficulties of the period and the onset of war, but also to a profound reluctance in the Irish body politic to involve the country too heavily in the tourism sector. For the veterans of the Irish War of Independence on both sides of the Treaty divide, but more particularly among members of the governing party, Fianna Fáil, tourism was perceived as a somewhat degrading activity. The connotations of subservience attached to tourism were still too vivid for those who had rebelled against the subordinate role of the Irish under the earlier imperial dispensation.

The 1940s and 1950s witnessed the development of two significant initiatives that would have far-reaching consequences for Irish tourism. First, an agreement signed by the Irish and U.S. governments ensured that all U.S. aircraft in transit over Irish territory would stop at Shannon. The Irish government hoped that such a move would not only bring tourists directly to Ireland's economically depressed western seaboard but also encourage "roots" tourists (i.e., U.S. citizens of Irish extraction) to vacation in Ireland. Second, the U.S. government through its Marshall Plan aid put pressure on the Irish government to be more proactive in the development of the tourist industry. The outcome of what was known as *The Christenberry Report*, a synthesis of six separate reports produced in Ireland and the United States in 1950, was the establishment of a new board of tourism, *Bord Fáilte*, under the 1952 Tourist Traffic Act. Though funding did not substantially increase, there was an important change in attitude to tourism: It was increasingly seen as an important factor in economic growth and job creation and as a way of strengthening rather than undermining national identity. One market that was targeted by the new board was the diasporic market, and a decision was made to organize and promote an annual festival of Irish music, dance, and other cultural activities for Irish emigrants returning as visitors, which was known as *An Tóstal* (The gathering). The festival, which was launched in 1953, was not a success and was discontinued after a number of years. The initiative was premature and emigration was too painful a reality in 1950s Ireland to be a source of celebration.

The passing of eight Tourist Traffic Acts between 1952 and 1970 did point to a new commitment to tourism development in Ireland, with the acts mainly targeting accommodation and other areas of tourist infrastructure. Tourism numbers grew in the 1960s, but Irish tourism received a serious setback with the outbreak of political unrest in Northern Ireland beginning in 1968. The violence and the negative publicity particularly affected Ireland's most important source for

tourists—Britain. To avoid overdependence on any one single market, Ireland was promoted more aggressively in North America and on the European continent. Overall, in the period from 1960 to 1987 visitor numbers rose from 941,000 to 2 million. As the 1980s saw a sharp downturn in manufacturing employment and an overall decline in agricultural fortunes, it was decided that tourism should be actively promoted as a source of job creation, particularly in less developed regions. The White Paper on Tourism (1985) set out a number of objectives for tourism development, but it was the first Operational Programme for Tourism (1989–1993) and the second Operational Programme for Tourism (1994–1999) that provided specific goals and measures for the sector. In addition, substantial funding was made available through the European Regional Development Fund and the European Social Fund. The introduction of airline competition in 1986, the impact of charter liberalization in 1988 and 1989, and the ending of the sea cartel with the privatization of the two major carriers between Ireland and Britain led to greater competitiveness, which made access more affordable for greater numbers of people. The combined effect of these different factors was an unprecedented growth in visitor numbers to Ireland. The rate of tourism growth between 1986 and 1995 was twice the average of other member countries of the Organisation for Economic Co-operation and Development (OECD). Between 1988 and 1999 tourist arrivals increased from 2.1 million to approximately 6 million. The foreign-exchange earnings from tourism in the same period rose from 841 million to 2.5 billion Irish pounds.

Rapid growth in tourist numbers and broad changes in Irish society generally pose problems for tourism development in the long run in Ireland. When tourists outnumber the inhabitants, there is not only the danger of saturation, with certain regions receiving an excessive number of tourists (particularly Kerry and Connemara), but locals may become indifferent or even hostile to a presence that is increasingly felt as intrusive. Concerns have been raised about negative environmental impact and the excessive commodification of elements of Irish culture, such as music and dance, for external consumption. Furthermore, the accelerated modernization and enrichment of Ireland at the end of the twentieth century often had negative consequences for certain aspects of Irish culture (friendliness, attitude to time, sense of history) that have traditionally attracted visitors. In an increasingly competitive tourism environment Ireland has to find the right mix between tradition and modernity to remain a preferred tourist destination for the world's travelers.

SEE ALSO Economies of Ireland, North and South, since 1920; Industry since 1920; Marshall Aid; State Enterprise

Bibliography

Deegan, James, and Donal Dineen. *Tourism Policy and Performance: The Irish Experience.* 1997.

Hadfield, Andrew, and John McVeagh, eds. *Strangers to that Land: British Perceptions of Ireland from the Reformation to the Famine.* 1994.

Kockel, Ullrich, ed. *Culture, Tourism and Development: The Case of Ireland.* 1994.

McVeagh, John. *Irish Travel Writing: A Bibliography.* 1996.

O'Connor, Barbara, and Michael Cronin, eds. *Tourism in Ireland: A Critical Analysis.* 1993.

Michael Cronin

Town Life from 1690 to the Early Twentieth Century

From the late seventeenth century to the early twentieth century Ireland had few cities or towns of real consequence, but some of them were important in their own right. By 1690 Dublin, the capital city, had already become the second largest city in the British Isles, with a population of about 50,000. As the seat of government and the law courts, it proved a social magnet for the gentry, especially during the parliamentary seasons. Its port dominated the Irish Sea region. Cork was also a considerable city, with 41,000 people by 1750. Its port serviced the Munster provision trade, victualling European fleets on the Atlantic trade routes. Other ports, notably Waterford, Limerick, and Belfast, were expanding rapidly to dominate their hinterlands. Drogheda and Galway had both been important ports in the early modern period. Kilkenny was the most influential inland city.

THE EIGHTEENTH CENTURY

Irish towns were all products of the English legal and administrative system even when they were significantly different in economy, culture, and society. Granted charters of incorporation by the English Crown, they had fallen under the control of the new Protestant landlords and merchants during the Crom-

wellian period. These landlords promoted their welfare, represented their interests in Parliament and on county grand juries, and championed them against interference from government, clergy, and neighboring landlords. To provide local government, they devised or adapted various agencies such as market juries, manor courts, and parish vestries. Many corporations, however, could not cover everyday expenses. In Ulster, for example, the town of Strabane attempted to apply fees paid by residents to become freemen (to trade in the town), quarterage (a charge on those who were not permitted to become freemen or full citizens, usually Catholics), and any other fines to provide basic services such as lighting and employing watchmen. When Catholics in many towns refused to pay quarterage, the judiciary ruled that it was not lawful, and so by the 1780s town corporations had to abandon their demand. Two decades later, Belfast was advised against raising money to finance secular projects through the local parish vestry of the Church of Ireland. In the last resort, then, the quality of town government depended on the interest of the patron in the welfare of his town and often on his generosity.

It depended also on the readiness and ability of a middle class made up of merchants, professionals, and craftsmen prepared to share some of the burden of local government. As every town needed regular supplies of provisions from the surrounding countryside, weekly markets had to be properly organized and administered by market juries and local courts, both for farm produce and for textiles. In the first half of the eighteenth century the landlords and their agents struggled to cope with bad harvests and epidemics, but in the second half of the century better harvests of cereals and potatoes (originally described as "the winter food of the poor") and improved communications by road and canal eased the supply problem. As seasonal fairs attracted dealers from a distance to purchase local surpluses, notably cattle and other farm stock, many towns provided facilities for monthly "fair days." These occasions generated excitement among the local populace, with horseracing, sport of all kinds, dancing, and faction fighting. In the county towns innkeepers relied for some of their custom on the excitement generated by the twice-yearly assizes and the quarter sessions. They provided accommodation for horses as well as for their riders, and toward the close of the eighteenth century they began to hire out not only horses but postchaises for travelers, and provided regular stops for mailcoaches. A great network of roads was constructed throughout Ireland under the supervision of the county grand juries, linking the market towns and attracting the poor to raise cabins on the town approaches.

The Irish parliament adapted reforms from London to cope with the social problems of the rapidly expanding city of Dublin. The best-known institution, which survived for almost a century, was the wide-streets commission in 1757, armed with sufficient powers and funds to drive long, straight thoroughfares through the maze of streets. In all the provincial ports gentry and merchants speculated in acquiring and developing building property. In 1786 Parliament instituted a police force of 750 men for Dublin, and in 1792 it allowed the majority of the county grand juries to form their own. These grand juries already maintained county jails. In 1765 Parliament made initial grants to three Dublin hospitals and encouraged grand juries to establish county infirmaries and dispensaries, laying the foundations for the Irish medical system. In 1772 it ordered them to erect houses of industry to provide work for the destitute. Dublin and Belfast followed the lead of Edinburgh in establishing chambers of commerce to promote their commercial policies. The middle classes, tradesmen, and craftsmen became active in founding voluntary charitable societies and community enterprises for the care of the old and sick, the provision of clean water, and the maintenance of fire brigades. The hallmarks of this urban society were the assembly room, the theater, and the Masonic lodge.

THE NINETEENTH CENTURY

By 1800 the populations of Dublin and Cork were about 180,000 and 60,000, respectively. Hearth-money returns for the same year record that Limerick, Waterford, Drogheda, and Belfast each contained about 3,000 houses and were twice the size of Kilkenny and Newry. Only ten other towns contained more than 1,000 houses each.

By the Act of Union in 1800 the London parliament had assumed responsibility for dealing with the social problems of Ireland. The removal of restrictions on the civil rights of Catholics by the Catholic Emancipation Act of 1829 involved them in politics and local government. A year previously, an act had given the middle classes in Irish towns the opportunity to elect commissioners responsible for paving, lighting, and cleaning their towns and providing a fire service and a night watch. At first, many of the smaller towns rejected it, not wishing to undergo any additional taxation, but they were finally induced to elect town commissioners and undertake improvements by an act of 1854. The London parliament, tackling poverty, sickness, ignorance, and faction fighting, gave new powers and responsibilities to the new town commissioners. It was significant that the headquarters of the new poor-law unions, the new model schools for training teachers, and the new main constabulary barracks were based in the provincial towns. Dublin and Belfast became the twin hubs of the new railway and shipping networks.

A characteristic development in many nineteenth-century Irish towns was the growth of the institutional sector of the Catholic Church, which established chapels, schools, hospitals, seminaries, and convents, especially in the diocesan centers such as Thurles, Killarney, Mullingar, and Ballina that had great new cathedrals. These institutions were staffed by members of religious orders. Many of the clergy organized religious confraternities to instruct their people in the tenets of the faith. They were active also in politics and in the Gaelic Athletic Association, whose growth paralleled the rise of non-Irish spectator sports such as soccer, rugby, and athletics.

By 1900 the towns were setting the new agenda in Irish life. They provided their communities with cheap entertainment and information in popular and local newspapers, theaters, and music halls. The poor had acquired a taste for tea with sugar, white bread, and margarine. Both Dublin and its rival, Belfast, attracted many people from the country, but their death rates matched those of any British city. The task of making them fit for their inhabitants was left to the twentieth century.

SEE ALSO American Wakes; Family: Marriage Patterns and Family Life from 1690 to 1921; Great Famine; Indian Corn or Maize; Migration: Emigration from the Seventeenth Century to 1845; Migration: Emigration from 1850 to 1960; Population, Economy, and Society from 1750 to 1950; Population Explosion; Potato and Potato Blight (*Phytophthora infestans*); Towns and Villages

Bibliography

Crossman, Virginia. *Local Government in Nineteenth Century Ireland*. 1994.

Cullen, Louis M. *The Emergence of Modern Ireland, 1600–1900*. 1981

Daly, Mary E. *Dublin: The Deposed Capital, 1860–1914*. 1984.

Harkness, David W., and Mary O'Dowd, eds. *The Town in Ireland*. 1981.

Maguire, William A. *Belfast*. 1993.

Maltby, Arthur, and Jean Maltby. *Ireland in the Nineteenth Century*. 1979.

William H. Crawford

Towns and Villages

The towns and villages spread over Ireland give the country its intimacy and charm. Any countrywide traverse will yield only a handful of larger settlements of above 1,500 inhabitants; small towns and villages are the norm.

Urban genesis in Ireland came in fits and starts, unlike the more stable evolutionary experience of continental Europe. It was closely correlated with colonization and with expansive epochs in the Irish history. Three pronounced phases of town and village creation are evident: during the heyday of Anglo-Norman settlement, in the plantation era of the late sixteenth and early seventeenth centuries, and under landlord influence in the eighteenth century. Native roots reach back to the monastic "towns" of the early Christian period. Continuity as well as change may therefore illustrate the Irish town and village tradition. Early monastic settlements that left an enduring mark include the present-day towns of Kildare, Cashel, Armagh, and Kells. The last yielded the famous *Book of Kells* as testimony to its sophistication as an early cultural hub. It developed marketplace functions and by the eleventh century had paved streets and artisan quarters, along with carefully differentiated sacred and secular sectors.

From the ninth century the Vikings brought the radically new idea of the trading station, the rationale of which was long-distance maritime trade. Thus they shifted the center of gravity away from inland locales, and their most successful settlements Dublin, Wexford, Waterford, Cork, and Limerick were all sited at the head of tidal estuaries. The trading and maritime impulses are well shown by the position of the town of Wexford (Weisfiord, "the harbor of the mudflats"). Defined by waterfront and earthen rampart, Viking Wexford was one of the principal trading stations in Ireland by 892 C.E., and was later expanded in the high medieval period.

The establishment of towns picked up decisively in the Norman period when another major innovation proved crucial. This was the town charter, bestowing a measure of autonomy within the limits of the town walls, and the rapid adoption of such charters led to a surge of urban development. The fittest of the towns survived mainly in the east and south, to furnish a well-articulated network, set in a prosperous countryside. County Kilkenny, often taken to be the Norman stereotype, provides the walled towns of Callan, Inistioge, Gowran, Thomastown, and Kilkenny. However, for a bird's eye view of a medieval town in mature form, there is no better plan than that of Kilmallock in about 1600. Several of the recurring features introduced by the Normans as part of the urban institution are evident, including tomb walls, gates, castellated houses, church, abbey, and an Irish suburb outside the walls. The plan's great boon is that it shows in close-up the spatial arrangement of these items.

In Normanized country outside the towns, small manorial villages also developed. These villages featured the nuclei of castle, church, and mill, and were most prominent in south Leinster Province and the metropolitan region about Dublin. One of the best known is Newcastle Lyons on the Dublin-Kildare borderland, which lays claim to fame as a royal manor in the medieval period. It was presided over by a village with a motte (a mound where a Norman castle might be situated), a parish church, tower houses, and long open-field strips, such as were common in the manorial villages of medieval England.

Plantation brought a vigorous phase of town and village formation. Altogether, some four hundred new settlements were established by grantees and proprietors as foci for their estates in heavily colonized parts of the Provinces of Munster, Ulster, and Leinster. Strategic considerations were paramount. Towns and villages acted as military bastions and as stimuli to infrastructural growth, market germination, and were a state and church presence. A sign of the villages' insecurity of their genesis was their frequent formation around a triangular green. Examples range from places as diverse as Donegal town, Geashill, Co. Offaly, and Dromcolliher, County Limerick. A fetching case is Malin village in the Inishowen peninsula of County Donegal.

Towns and villages continued in episodic formation. The first wave of estate towns dates to the 1660s. County Cork alone saw the germination of several new towns. Among them was Charleville, where on 29 May 1661 the earl of Orrery laid the foundation stone of a new town as the centerpiece of his estate. Other waves followed in the eighteenth century, upon the effective conquest of Ireland. Then peace and prosperity combined with fashion and a new proprietorial class to generate a more expansive and aesthetic approach to the urban project. Formally planned estate villages began to appear, as at Summerhill, County Meath, Sixmilebridge, County Clare, and Stradbally, County Laois. Wide streets and market squares now become the design foci, cast between the landlord's mansion and demesne at one end and the Anglican Church at the other. One landlord's wishes are instructive. He ordered that his new town of Kenmare, County Kerry, "may be begun by laying out two capital streets, fifty feet wide." It was to be "known by its industry and order" and its success to be predicated upon trade. Industry too contributed to new town foundation, not only in Ulster's proto-industrial region but also in the south and west where linen manufacture was the mainstay of settlements, such as Dunmanway in County Cork, Mountshannon in County Clare, and Monivea in County Galway.

The final phase saw new landlord-sponsored settlements in the far west. Roads were the enabling development; landlords provided patronage; trade did most of the rest. Examples of new growth points include Dunfanaghy in County Donegal, Louisburgh in County Mayo, Clifden in County Galway, and Cahirciveen in County Kerry. These western villages were also helped by tourism, which was developing by the time that the impetus for estate-village creation finally faded in the 1840s.

By then the network of Ireland's towns and villages had become established. Yet the overall weakness of that network must also be acknowledged. In 1841 only one fifth of the population lived in towns and villages—1,655,000 out of 8,175,000. The Irish domestic world was overwhelmingly rural, and in that world the town was at the heart of the rhythms of life in the countryside.

SEE ALSO Belfast; Cork; Dublin; Landscape and Settlement; Markets and Fairs in the Eighteenth and Nineteenth Centuries; Town Life from 1690 to the Early Twentieth Century

Bibliography

Cullen, Louis M. *Irish Towns and Villages.* 1979.

Nolan, William, and Anngret Simms, eds. *Irish Towns: A Guide to Sources.* 1998.

O'Connor, Patrick J. *Exploring Limerick's Past: An Historical Geography of Urban Development in County and City.* 1987.

O'Connor, Patrick J. *Hometown: A Portrait of Newcastle West, Co. Limerick.* 1998.

Simms, Anngret, and John H. Andrews, eds. *Irish Country Towns.* 1994.

Simms, Anngret, and John H. Andrews, eds. *More Irish Country Towns.* 1995.

Thomas, Avril. *The Walled Towns of Ireland.* 2 vols. 1992.

Whelan, Kevin. "Towns and Villages." In *Atlas of the Irish Rural Landscape*, edited by F. H. A. Aalen et al. 1997.

Patrick J. O'Connor

Trade and Trade Policy from 1691 to 1800

Overseas trade became a central component of Irish economic life in the period between the Treaty of Limerick (1691) and the Act of Union (1800) in spite of the constraints imposed on Ireland by English mercantilist policy. In 1660 the English Acts of Navigation placed English and Irish colonial trade on an equal footing. In 1663, however, a modification to the law limited Irish exports across the Atlantic to horses, victuals, servants, and (in 1705) linen. In 1671 Parliament prohibited Irish importation of certain enumerated goods (articles such as sugar, tobacco, cotton, and dyestuffs) directly from the colonies. The ban was extended in 1696 to encompass all colonial produce. Another set of acts, collectively known as the Cattle Acts, at first restricted (in 1663), then prohibited (in 1671) English imports of Irish livestock, beef, pork, and bacon, and (in 1681) mutton and cheese. Later, the Woolen Act of 1699 prohibited Ireland's export of woolens to markets other than England, where they already faced prohibitive duties. Most of this legislation was modified or reversed in the eighteenth century. An act of 1731 opened Ireland to those colonial imports not specifically prohibited in 1671; the ban on meat exports to Great Britain ended in 1758, as did that on live cattle in 1759; but the Wool Act and Glass Act (1746) remained in force until 1780, the same year that the British parliament removed restrictions on Irish colonial trade.

Contemporary politicians and pamphleteers (and a later generation of historians) exaggerated the negative impact of these laws. The regulations did limit the scope of Irish trade, but they were motivated by broad mercantilist goals rather than anti-Irish sentiment. For example, restrictions on the wool trade were balanced by encouragements to Ireland's linen industry (linen exports rose from less than 20,000 yards in 1700 to about 45 million by the mid-1790s), and the Cattle Acts fostered Ireland's preeminence in the production and marketing of Irish salted provisions (exports of salted beef reached over 200,000 barrels per year by the American Revolution, and butter exports totaled nearly 300,000 hundredweight in the same period). Limits on Irish trade were further compensated for by access to London financial services, direct and indirect entrée to colonial markets, and the protection of the Royal Navy.

The volume of Irish trade expanded dramatically between 1691 and 1800, with exports growing about fivefold and imports increasing more than sevenfold. Irish overseas trade passed through three distinct phases. The first (1691–1730) began with a promising recovery from the setbacks of the Williamite War (1689–1691), but depressed export prices and bad harvests contributed to indecisive growth in the early decades of the eighteenth century. There were difficulties as well in the second phase (1731–1775), but it was a time of broad and sustained expansion for Irish overseas trade, particularly from mid-century to the outbreak of the American Revolution. Although periods of expansion and wartime disruption characterized the third phase (1776–1800), these years were distinguished by Great Britain's increasing dominance of Irish imports and exports.

Great Britain was Ireland's largest trading partner. About half of Irish exports went to England and Scotland in the early decades of the eighteenth century, a share that rose to over 85 percent by 1800. Irish imports from Britain experienced similar growth. Before the readmission of Irish salted provisions (1758) and live cattle (1759) into the English market, exports to Britain had consisted mostly of raw wool, woolen and worsted yarn, linen cloth, and linen yarn. Exports broadened further in the final three decades of the century with increased shipments of Irish grain, flour, and oatmeal. Irish imports from Great Britain were far more varied and included coal, dyewoods, hops, sugar, rum, silk, tea, tobacco, wheat and flour (in times of harvest failure), woolens, and a variety of manufactured goods.

On the European continent Irish commodities faced high tariff barriers, but salted beef suitable for reexport to the West Indies enjoyed a virtual monopoly. Irish butter (much of it for reshipment to the Caribbean) found markets in southern Europe in exchange for wine, brandy, and cognac, as did Irish wool, an article long traded illegally outside the bounds of British commercial legislation. Much of the smuggled tea and tobacco that entered Ireland in this period, the golden age of smuggling, came via the Continent. Trade with Europe is most closely identified with Nantes, Bordeaux, Cadiz, and Lisbon, but Ireland also maintained strong ties to Amsterdam, Rotterdam, Hamburg, and Copenhagen.

In its trade with British America, Ireland sent vast quantities of beef, butter, pork, herring, and linen to the West Indies in exchange for sugar (meant for ports in Great Britain) and rum (sent directly to Ireland after 1731). Much of this trade was managed by commission houses in London associated with the sugar trade. The 1731 modification of the navigation laws that allowed Ireland direct importation of colonial barrel staves, flaxseed, iron, lumber, rum, and wheat and flour gave rise to a significant trade with the middle colonies of the North American mainland. By the time of the American Revolution, New York City, Philadelphia, and other colonial ports were sending Ireland about 300,000 bushels of flaxseed per year, or about 98 percent of its total imports of that commodity.

Overseas commerce and Irish economic development were intertwined. Foreign demand for Irish provisions, linen, and wool brought employment to the countryside, encouraged investment, and stimulated the growth of Irish seaports and inland market towns. Dublin, the second-largest city in the British Isles, was Ireland's busiest port, followed by Cork, its most cosmopolitan center of transatlantic commerce, and by mid-century, Belfast, the principal trading town of the North. London also played a vital role in Irish commerce. Besides providing a ready supply of capital, credit, and maritime insurance, London was home to a large and sophisticated Irish merchant community that managed much of Ireland's long-distance trade. Enclaves of expatriate merchants scattered throughout the British Isles, continental Europe, and British America formed a distinctly Irish commercial network held together by ties of kinship, faith, and identity.

SEE ALSO Economy and Society from 1500 to 1690; Eighteenth-Century Politics: 1690 to 1714—Revolution Settlement; Eighteenth-Century Politics: 1714 to 1778—Interest Politics; Eighteenth-Century Politics: 1778 to 1795—Parliamentary and Popular Politics; Eighteenth-Century Politics: 1795 to 1800—Repression, Rebellion, and Union; Government from 1690 to 1800

Bibliography

Cochran, L. E. *Scottish Trade with Ireland in the Eighteenth Century.* 1985.

Cullen, L. M. *Anglo-Irish Trade, 1660–1800.* 1968.

Cullen, L. M. *An Economic History of Ireland since 1660.* 1972.

Dickson, David. *New Foundations: Ireland, 1660–1800.* 1987.

James, Francis G. *Ireland in the Empire, 1688–1770.* 1973.

Truxes, Thomas M. *Irish-American Trade, 1660–1783.* 1988.

Truxes, Thomas M., ed. *Letterbook of Greg & Cunningham, 1756–57: Merchants of New York and Belfast.* 2001.

Thomas M. Truxes

Trade Unions

Trade unions in southern Ireland have undergone ten phases of development, characterized by illegality up to 1824; violent militancy; atrophy after the Great Famine; three waves of agitation influenced by new unionism from 1889, Larkinism from 1907, and syndicalism from 1917; internecine strife from 1923 to 1945; national free collective bargaining from 1946; centralized bargaining from 1970; and social partnership from 1987. The story of unions in Ulster conforms more to the British periodization.

The 1841 census enumerated 240,000 male artisans and 1.2 million male unskilled workers, the bulk of them agricultural laborers. (There were also more than one million working women, mainly in clothing and domestic service, who were not members of trade unions.) Despite the enactment of anticombination laws prescribing trade union laws beginning in 1729, journeymen artisans formed secret societies as the guilds lost their role in trade protection. With the repeal of the combination acts in 1824, local craft unions formed in the main cities. These new unions had a militant conception of their role initially, but following violent episodes and an economic slump in the late 1830s, they adopted a "moral force" strategy in the 1840s and pursued their demands through campaigns for public support. Unskilled rural laborers were afforded some protection by the Whiteboy movements that emerged in 1760 to defend tenant farmers and others. In Leinster in particular, Whiteboyism extended to unskilled urban workers through Ribbon lodges, another variant of the secret societies which used violence or intimidation to protect laborers from employers or landlords.

After the famine, unions in southern Ireland were weakened by demographic and economic decline. In the industrializing north, craft unions developed with the growth of engineering and shipbuilding. In the textiles and clothing industries, unions of skilled and semiskilled men emerged in the 1870s, and some progress was made in organizing women in the 1890s. Although unions in Ulster remained secular, victimization of Catholic workers regularly accompanied political crises from the 1860s to the 1920s.

The waves of industrial unrest between 1889 and 1923 called attention to the difficulty of building bargaining power for a movement in an undeveloped economy with a craft elite too small to take the lead in trade unionism. Though new unionism was largely crushed by 1891, it gave rise to the Irish Trade Union Congress (ITUC) in 1894. Modeled on its British namesake, the

ITUC was an inappropriate form of confederation for Ireland, as it was based on industrial organization, where labor was weak. The alternative of creating an essentially political confederation linked to the national movement was rejected. The only rationale for the ITUC format was the British example, and it reflected labor's mental colonization. British unions, often called "amalgamateds," had been extending themselves to Ireland since the 1840s. By 1900, out of some 900,000 Irish waged workers, fewer than 70,000 were organized, and 75 percent of these belonged to British unions. The ITUC provided no leadership to unions until 1918 (O Connor 1992).

Anglicization affected labor politics profoundly. From the repeal movement in the 1830s until the fall of Parnell in 1890, trade unions had endorsed successive nationalist movements in the hope that self-government and tariffs would reverse the deindustrialization that accompanied Ireland's integration into the British economy. The ITUC, however, took the view that unions should restrict themselves to purely labor politics. Despite the reverence accorded to James Connolly after his execution in 1916, labor leaders never lost the sense of socialism and nationalism as dichotomous.

Anglicization was partially reversed by the Irish Transport and General Workers' Union (ITGWU), which was founded in 1909 by James Larkin as "an Irish union for Irish workers." In addition, Larkin and Connolly encouraged the ITUC to constitute itself as a Labour Party in 1914. After traumatic defeat in the 1913 lockout, ITGWU membership mushroomed from 1917. The ITUC was radicalized by revolution at home and abroad, and Labour assisted in the struggle for Irish independence without allying with Sinn Féin, a policy variously interpreted as skillful or a wasted opportunity to shape the new Ireland. When the boom years of 1916 to 1920 yielded to a slump, Labour's radicalism was gutted in a series of major strikes. The Labour Party entered parliamentary politics in 1922 but averaged only 11.4 percent of the vote until 1987. Congress and the Labour Party separated in 1930, though many unions continued to affiliate with the party. By 1923 Irish labor had assumed its modern form: The southern movement was substantially Irish-based, and unions in the North were overwhelmingly British. By default the ITUC retained its all-Ireland jurisdiction because the British Trades Union Congress was reluctant to engage with Ulster.

Unions were not important to Irish state policy until Fianna Fáil's industrialization drive in the 1930s; henceforth, the state would be an increasingly significant determinant of trade union strategy. Interunion disputes in the 1930s led the government to press for an end to the multiplicity of unions. The ITGWU especially wanted to replace sectionalist trade unionism with industrial unionism, and blamed the ITUC's failure to reform on resistance from British-based unions. Union membership in the North grew substantially during World War II, especially among general workers and women. The ITUC redressed its neglect of the North by establishing in 1944 a Northern Ireland Committee—in effect, a regional congress. Mounting friction between Irish- and British-based unions culminated in a split in 1945, when many private-sector Irish unions formed the Congress of Irish Unions. Their expectations of a more positive relationship with the state and of legislation to eliminate the British unions were disappointed. The two congresses united as the Irish Congress of Trade Unions (ICTU) in 1959.

Nineteen forty-six marked a watershed in labor history with the introduction of the Labour Court, which enabled workers to win wage increases without first establishing bargaining power through militancy, and with the introduction of national rounds of wage bargaining. Membership rose significantly from 1946 to 1951 and again in the 1960s. Renewed industrialization, accelerating inflation, and strikes in the 1960s brought government calls for centralized bargaining, and the first National Wage Agreement was struck in 1970. During the mid-1970s the government became a partner in the agreements, turning employer-labor bipartism into tripartism. Tripartite "national understandings" followed in 1979 and 1980. The failure of tripartism to address rising unemployment, inflation, and unofficial strike actions prompted a return to free collective bargaining in 1982, but the government brokered a deeper tripartism in the Programme for National Recovery in 1987. Four more social partnership programs were signed between 1990 and 2000.

Centralized bargaining became the most controversial issue in trade unionism in the 1980s and 1990s. Craft and British-based unions usually opposed central agreements, arguing that they eroded union democracy and amounted to wage restraint. General unions, which included all grades but represented a high proportion of low paid workers with a weak bargaining power, were the most supportive, claiming that the agreements contributed to the "Celtic Tiger," the label often given to the Republic's high economic growth rates since 1994. They kept the Republic free of the anti-union policies adopted by many other European countries. While union density (the proportion of employees that belong to unions) shrank in the early 1980s, and the number of unions was reduced through mergers, density in the Republic in 2001 was relatively high, at almost 50 per-

cent. By contrast, union density in Northern Ireland fell from a peak of 61 percent in 1983 to 36 percent in 2001 (ICTU 2001; Labour Force Survey 2001).

After 1968 the Northern Ireland government's traditional suspicion of unions gave way to a friendlier understanding between the unions and the state. Partly because unions were valued as allies in the propaganda war against paramilitarism, the Conservative government's labor legislation, which weakened trade unions by, for example, making the "closed shop" and secondary picketing illegal, was not fully applied to Northern Ireland until 1993. In 1972 the ICTU decided that it would be "inappropriate" to comment on Northern Ireland's constitutional question, and in addressing the "Troubles," unions gave priority to avoiding controversy, citing the absence of serious workplace sectarian conflict to justify their stance; critics accused them of reticence on oppression and inequality. In the 1990s, the consensus behind the peace process encouraged the ICTU to become more assertive, and it campaigned for the Belfast Agreement.

SEE ALSO Celtic Tiger; Conditions of Employment Act of 1936; Connolly, James; Economies of Ireland, North and South, since 1920; Irish Women Workers' Union; Labor Movement; Larkin, James; Lockout of 1913; Political Parties in Independent Ireland; Whiteboys and Whiteboyism

Bibliography

Boyle, John W. *The Irish Labor Movement in the Nineteenth Century.* 1988.

D'Arcy, Fergus, and Ken Hannigan, eds. *Workers in Union: Documents and Commentaries on the History of Irish Labour.* 1988.

Department of Trade and Industry, London. *Labour Force Survey.* Organization for National Statistics. 2001.

Irish Congress of Trade Unions (ICTU). Web site available at http://www.ictu.ie.

McCarthy, Charles. *Trade Unions in Ireland, 1894–1960.* 1977.

Mitchell, Arthur. *Labour in Irish Politics, 1890–1930: The Irish Labour Movement in an Age of Revolution.* 1974.

Nevin, Donal, ed. *Trade Union Century.* 1994.

O Connor, Emmet. *A Labour History of Ireland, 1824–1960.* 1992.

Rumpf, E., and A. C. Hepburn. *Nationalism and Socialism in Twentieth-Century Ireland.* 1977.

Emmet O Connor

Transport—Road, Canal, Rail

By the end of the twentieth century transport infrastructure in Ireland was proving entirely inadequate for the needs of a modern economy. The country's waterways had long ceased to carry much beyond the barges and boats of tourists; the rail service had been reduced to the extent that it connected only the major urban centers and such areas fortunate enough to fall in between; and the road network was unable to cope with the volume of cars attempting to travel on it. The sense of gridlock on the country's roads was heightened by extensive roadwork in every region—the result of unprecedented amounts of EU and public funding redressing many decades of underinvestment. Although funding was also extended to reforming the rail service, transport policy essentially focused on facilitating the journeys of private car users, and public transport initiatives ran a poor second.

The primacy of the road was intimately related to patterns of population and employment. Canals and railways enjoyed their own particular golden ages, but neither gathered a hold as firmly as the road, whose antiquity stretches back across the expanse of Irish history. By the early Christian period, Ireland had primitive roads paved with large stones, linking religious and other settlements. These roads included five major routes which held the Hill of Tara, seat of the high kings of Ireland, as their focal point. The increased internal commerce of the Viking and Norman eras reshaped the road network, and a statute passed by the Irish parliament in the early seventeenth century carried enduring significance by placing responsibility for the upkeep of roads on individual parishes. The pattern which emerged consisted of numerous small roads, varied in quality, maintenance, and scale. An act of 1729 established turnpikes that provided further funding for maintenance, with users paying a toll for their travel. By the nineteenth century turnpike roads were probably the best in the country and remained operational until their demise in 1857. Even at their peak, though, turnpikes were never as prominent as in England and comprised only a small percentage of the entire road mileage on the island, which was estimated at more than 8,000 by the closing decades of the eighteenth century.

By then, canals had also extended across the countryside. Partly financed by successive governments and by progressive landowners to increase industry and commerce, by 1830 almost 500 miles of canals had been constructed in Ireland. The first undertaken was the Newry navigation connecting Carlingford Lough with the River Bann, and was intended to facilitate the transportation to Dublin of coal deposits found in Tyrone. The first section opened in 1742 and was followed by completion in 1769 of the Newry ship canal, which was capable of taking ships up to 150 tons in weight. Further canals in Ulster linking collieries, mills, and other industrial ventures included the Lagan navigation, the Tyrone navigation, and the Ulster Canal, which reached from Belfast across to the River Shannon at a cost of more than £250,000.

The principal canals constructed in the south of Ireland were the Grand and Royal canals. The Royal ran from Dublin to Mullingar, with offshoots running to the Shannon at Cloondara and to Longford. It was bankrupted before its completion around 1817 and never proved as profitable as the Grand Canal, which linked Dublin to Shannon Harbour in 1805. Together with its offshoots to Ballinasloe and Kilbeggan, the Grand Canal stimulated commerce along its routes. As well as facilitating a string of hotels, it facilitated the development of breweries, distilleries, and other industries. Initially, canals provided for more efficient transport of goods and passengers than existing modes of transport. Later, this trade would be lost to the railways, but even at their peak, Irish canals struggled due to the lack of industry in the country. While Ulster was more suited to canal usage than the rest of the country, there was a general insufficiency of passengers, little coal, and few commodities. Ultimately, canals were unable to compete with the arrival of rail and an improving road network.

That improvement was partly related to the granting of power to grand juries in 1765 to raise money for the repair or provision of roads and bridges. This set in place the basis of a system which endured until late in the nineteenth century. Roads were now mandated for construction to a certain standard. A further important feature of the road networks from the early eighteenth century until the spread of the railways in the middle of the nineteenth century was the stagecoach. By 1750 there were regular services connecting Dublin with provincial towns and cities, and by 1800 there were more than a dozen centers linked to the capital by scheduled and advertised coaches serviced by teams of horses, staged at coaching inns along the route. Coaches could carry up to twenty people, as well as mail, and were escorted by armed guards to protect against highway robbery. The importance of mail is indicative of the growth of commerce in the country. Indeed, so important was the mail service to the growth of commerce that the Post Office was given extensive powers of road design in an act of 1805. By the 1840s the journey by

This exotic horse-drawn train continued to transport passengers in 1937 from Fintona railway junction, Co. Tyrone, to the nearby town. © CORBIS. REPRODUCED BY PERMISSION.

coach to Belfast had been reduced to twelve hours, but the arrival of the railway soon undermined the viability of the service.

The first railway line had opened on 17 December 1834 when the Dublin city center station of Westland Row was linked to the coastal port of Kingstown (later renamed Dún Laoghaire), which, in turn, was served by ferry to Wales. The route was constructed and financed by William Dargan, who eventually built over 600 miles of railway before his death in 1867. Despite the success of the Dublin-to-Kingstown railway, there were merely thirty-one miles of track open or under construction in Ireland by 1842. By the end of the 1840s, that figure had risen to some 700 miles. By the end of World War I there were over 3,500 miles of railway in Ireland. This phenomenal growth was deeply influenced by a similar explosion in England, by substantial government and private funding, and by the availability of cheap land and labour. Journey times between Irish urban centers were greatly reduced, with the trip from Dublin to Belfast halved to under six hours. The landscape was transformed with the appearance of tunnels,

bridges, and tracks in the most remote of areas. The effect on Irish business was mixed. In theory, Irish agriculture and industrial products could more readily access the British market, but British manufacturers were also able to send their goods more cheaply into the stores of provincial Ireland. This benefited the consumer but not the local producer who was not always able to compete. Farmers and industrialists consistently complained that transport costs were excessive, and it is unlikely that railways greatly assisted firms already hindered by their peripheral locality to increase their export earnings. The railways enjoyed a modest prosperity, however, and became one of the biggest employers in the country.

A mutually beneficial leisure industry also developed in tandem with the railways. As the expanding middle class adopted a culture of travel and daytripping, seaside resorts grew and race meetings were established, along with a whole host of other sporting events such as regattas and galas. Daily newspapers were now able to penetrate across the country, and in addition to the railways' industrial impact, they also influenced the standardization of time. The development of railway timetables lent greater urgency to the acceptance of Dublin Mean Time following an act in 1880. Previously, clocks in Cork were eleven minutes behind those of Dublin while those in Belfast were one minute and nineteen seconds ahead.

By 1916, when Greenwich Mean Time was extended to Ireland, the decline of the railway was underway. Ireland did not hold a large enough population in its urban centers nor produce enough industrial goods to sustain its railway network. Low population density and light traffic gave road transport a comparative advantage over rail. Railways had been planned for a population of more than seven million but served only half that number. Furthermore, by 1921, there were forty-six competing railway companies in operation. Following partition, attempts were made in both north and south to rationalize railways by merging the numerous companies. Many lines and stations were shut down, and by the 1980s there were merely 1,500 miles of rail on the island. Underfunded, nationalized rail companies in both jurisdictions lurched through a series of financial crises, but were largely unable to compete with their nemesis—the motor car.

The spread of private motor cars, of buses, and of haulage firms transformed Irish society. Since the First World War, and particularly since the Second World War, cars and buses have underpinned the growth of suburban Ireland. Commuters increasingly travel large distances to work, most usually from provincial towns to Dublin. The upgrading of roads to dual-carriageways and, by the last decades of the century, to motorways, has radically altered the countryside. Roads in the north have traditionally been of a higher standard than those in the south as a result of greater investment. In the south the establishment of the National Roads Authority in the 1990s signaled the pursuit of a hugely ambitious program of road building that, if completed, would transform the Irish road network. This was welcomed by the commercial interests of provincial Ireland, which has undoubtedly suffered through the overconcentration of industry in the Dublin area. Nonetheless, a growing movement opposes the building of roads as excessively damaging to the environment through its destruction of green-field sites and its attendant pollutants. For all the opposition, and despite the relatively high cost to buy and to run, car numbers in Ireland continue to grow. Patterns of settlement and public-transport policy suggest that this growth will continue unchecked for the foreseeable future.

SEE ALSO Agriculture: 1690 to 1845; Agriculture: 1845 to 1921; Agriculture: After World War I; Bank-ing and Finance to 1921; Brewing and Distilling; Industrialization; Industry since 1920; Rural Industry; Shipbuilding; Sport and Leisure

Bibliography

Collins, Michael. *Road Versus Rail in Ireland, 1900–2000.* 2000.

Daly, Mary E. *The Buffer State: The Historical Roots of the Department of the Environment.* 1997.

Delany, V. T. H., and D. R. Delany. *The Canals of the South of Ireland.* 1966.

McCutcheon, W. A. *The Canals of the North of Ireland.* 1965.

Meenan, James. *The Irish Economy since 1922.* 1970.

Nowlan, Kevin B., ed. *Travel and Transport in Ireland.* 1973.

O'Connor, Kevin. *Ironing the Land: The Coming of the Railways to Ireland.* 1999.

Ó Gráda, Cormac. *A Rocky Road: The Irish Economy since the 1920s.* 1997.

Turnock, David. *An Historical Geography of Railways in Great Britain and Ireland.* 1998.

Paul Rouse

Trimble, David

Born on 15 October 1944, the politician David Trimble was educated at Bangor Grammar School and the Queen's University of Belfast, where he read law, and subsequently lectured in that subject. His early political activity was with Vanguard (a short-lived unionist party founded to oppose Terence O'Neill), which strongly distrusted British machinations—to the point of considering independence for Northern Ireland. Trimble played an important part in organizing the successful loyalist strike against the Sunningdale Agreement in 1974.

Trimble was no mere naysayer, however, and followed Willam Craig, Vanguard's leader, in advocating voluntary coalition with the SDLP. The organization split on this issue, however, and rapidly declined. Trimble rejoined the Ulster Unionist Party mainstream in 1978. From 1990 he was reactive in politics, winning the Upper Bann Westminster constituency and in 1995 catching attention by provocative coat-trailing following the forced passage of Orangemen down the Catholic Garvaghy Road in Portadown.

Mostly by virtue of his flinty reputation, Trimble won the leadership of the UUP in 1995 when James

Molyneaux resigned. To general surprise he now showed considerable tactical flexibility. He was particularly concerned not to lead unionists out of the political process for fear that the British and Irish governments would then impose a settlement influenced by nationalist lobbying. Realizing that Britain would not accept unionist stonewalling, he and his party agreed to sign the Good Friday Agreement of 1998. This, he believed, secured the principle that Northern Ireland's constitutional status could not be changed without majority consent in the province. Evidently he found many other changes objectionable, notably toleration for the continued existence of paramilitaries, but thought them best dealt with by subsequent pressure.

In 1998 Trimble won election to the post of first minister of the new devolved government. As leader of the single largest party he experienced a slippage of votes to anti-agreement parties, but this only added to his determination to highlight the IRA's violation, as he saw it, of the spirit of the agreement. He was accused of failing to sell the agreement's positive virtues with sufficient enthusiasm.

At first the "de-commissioning" of paramilitary weapons was Trimble's touchstone, and in fall of 2001 the IRA conceded a token act of decommissioning. Attention now focused on alleged violations of the IRA's ceasefire, and Trimble increasingly pressed for a form of IRA disbandment. In the fall of 2002 he prevailed upon the British to suspend the devolved government. Trimble's primary concern now was to preserve the UUP vote against anti-agreement rivals in subsequent elections.

SEE ALSO Adams, Gerry; Hume, John; Northern Ireland: Constitutional Settlement from Sunningdale to Good Friday; Northern Ireland: The United States in Northern Ireland since 1970; O'Neill, Terence; Ulster Politics under Direct Rule

Bibliography

Hennesey, Thomas. *The Northern Ireland Peace Process: Ending the Troubles?* 2000.

McDonald, Henry. *Trimble*. 2000.

Maille, Eamonn, and David McKittrick. *Endgame in Ireland.* 2001.

Marc Mulholland

~

Trinity College

Trinity College, Dublin, the only college of the University of Dublin, was the first Irish university, founded in 1592. From medieval times there had been repeated efforts to establish an Irish university—an obvious need in a land devoid of higher education—but in a divided island it proved difficult to agree on a site or secure financial backing. During the sixteenth century there were a number of "paper universities" proposed that never got beyond the drawing board. It was not until the end of the sixteenth century that a proposal was finally successful, when the combined efforts of the Protestant archbishop of Dublin, Adam Loftus, some prominent Dublin aldermen, and the support of the English authorities led to the foundation of Trinity College on the site of an old monastery, Old Hallows.

The long delay had an influence upon the nature of the new university. Some of the earlier proposals had envisaged a broadly-based humanist institution. But by the time it came to be founded, the divisions between Protestant and Catholic had eliminated any broad consensus on educational progress in Ireland. Loftus and his allies among the Dublin aldermen were committed to the Reformation, and the university that they established was firmly Protestant, even Calvinist. Its appeal to the Irish population was therefore limited to those willing to conform to the state religion; indeed, it became the sole native seminary for the Church of Ireland. This essentially Protestant orientation was not finally lost until the late twentieth century.

After a difficult start, when the destruction of the Nine Years War (1593–1603) severely curtailed its income, Trinity found its feet in the early seventeenth century. Under the watchful eye of its first professor of theological controversies, James Ussher (1581–1656), Trinity built up its library and had by 1620 about eighty undergraduate students. Its theology was decidedly Calvinist and strongly anti-Catholic. The first three provosts—Walter Travers (1594–1598), William Alvey (1599–1609), and William Temple (1609–1626)—were all English Puritans, and the first two professors of theology, Ussher and Joshua Hoyle, spent much of their time in their lectures rebutting the claims of the great Jesuit controversialist Robert Bellarmine. As Hoyle put it, the purpose of his lectures was to "love God and hate the pope."

The character of Trinity changed dramatically in the 1630s with the appointment of a new chancellor, Archbishop William Laud in 1633, and a new provost, William Chappell, in 1634. Chappell was an Arminian—that is, theologically opposed to the narrow Calvinist system of double predestination—and was specially chosen by Laud to reform Trinity and bring it under closer control. New statutes passed in 1636 fixed the constitution of the college and reinforced the authority of the provost. Under Chappell the college expanded considerably, with the addition of new buildings and the appointment of medical and legal fellows, broadening its previously exclusively theological bent. The Irish rising of 1641, which destroyed many of the college's estates and greatly reduced its income, brought a dramatic fall in student numbers, and it was not until the Cromwellian reconquest and settlement (1649–1660) that Trinity regained its equilibrium under the leadership of the Independent, Samuel Winter.

The restoration of the monarchy in 1660 saw Trinity returned to firmly Anglican hands, and under the leadership of provosts such as Narcissus Marsh (1678–1683) the college began a long period of expansion. This was briefly interrupted by the arrival of James II in Ireland in 1689, when Trinity was occupied by royal troops and a Catholic was appointed provost of the college. But the victory of William in 1690 restored the status quo, and Trinity during the long eighteenth century, and throughout the nineteenth, became the bastion of the Protestant Ascendancy.

It was during the eighteenth century that the impressive architectural shape of the modern university was created with the help of generous parliamentary grants which led to the opening of the new library in 1732 and the completion of the examination hall in 1791 and new chapel in 1798. As the largest library in Ireland and chief seat of learning, Trinity played a vital role in the development of Irish culture, producing such notable graduates as Jonathan Swift and Edmund Burke. Though Catholics were allowed to earn degrees at Trinity beginning in 1793, the college's Divinity School was the seminary for the Church of Ireland, and the prevailing ethos of the college remained firmly Protestant. Even after all religious tests were abolished in 1873, many Catholics were reluctant to send their children to Trinity. One area where Trinity was in the vanguard of change was in relation to female students—in 1904 it became the first of the older universities in Britain and Ireland to admit women.

During the first half of the twentieth century Trinity struggled to come to terms with the rapid changes in Irish society, as the Protestant Ascendancy disintegrated and the Twenty-Six Counties became an independent Irish state. From the 1970s onwards, however, the university changed dramatically, developing as a modern center for research in the arts and sciences, with an extensive building program that saw the college grow be-

yond its original site to occupy forty-seven acres. The turning point was probably the lifting by the Catholic hierarchy in 1970 of its former ban on Catholic students attending Trinity. By the end of the century its student body reflected the composition of modern southern Irish society, with 550 full-time academic staff and almost 15,000 students, both of varied religious backgrounds.

SEE ALSO Bedell, William; Church of Ireland: Elizabethan Era; Church of Ireland: Since 1690; Dublin Philosophical Society; Education: 1500 to 1690; Education: University Education; Education: Women's Education; Maynooth; Ussher, James

Bibliography

Holland, C. H., ed. *Trinity College Dublin and the Idea of a University.* 1991.

McDowell, R. B., and D. A. Webb. *Trinity College, Dublin, 1592–1952.* 1982.

Mahaffy, J. P. *An Epoch in Irish History: Trinity College, Dublin, Its Foundation and Early Fortunes, 1591–1660.* 1903.

Alan Ford

∼

Troy, John

John Thomas Troy (1739–1823), Roman Catholic archbishop of Dublin, was born on 12 July 1739 near Dublin. In 1755 he joined the Dominican Order, leaving Ireland to pursue his studies at Rome. Troy remained in Rome and served as prior of San Clemente from 1772 until his appointment as bishop of Ossory in 1776.

Troy's return to Ireland coincided with the start of the dismantling of the penal laws in 1778, and the bishop was to play a pivotal role in the revival of Irish Catholicism. From the outset he enjoyed the confidence of the Holy See, and he led the attempt to bring the Irish church into line with Roman discipline and practice. In this way he initiated the process that is often erroneously attributed to Paul Cullen in the following century. In Kilkenny first, and subsequently in Dublin, where he served as archbishop from 1786, Troy advanced this renewal through diocesan visitations, regular clerical conferences, catechesis, the publication of comprehensive pastoral instructions, chapel building, and education. He was instrumental in the establishment of an episcopal conference, which began to meet regularly in the context of the foundation of Maynooth College in 1795.

Politically Troy has been represented as a reactionary at odds with the aspirations of his people. Such characterizations are without nuance. Certainly Troy excommunicated all the radical organizations of his time (including the Whiteboys, Rightboys, Defenders, and United Irishmen), but there is no evidence that he did not support the legitimate demands of Irish Catholics for emancipation. Troy followed the advice of Edmund Burke, political mentor of the episcopate, when he counseled the hierarchy to show themselves to be dutiful subjects of the Crown and to meddle as little as possible in politics. Troy supported the Act of Union in the belief that Pitt's promised emancipation, barred by the Protestant Ascendancy, would follow. Troy died in May 1823 and was interred in the vault of Saint Mary's Pro-Cathedral, the great neoclassical monument to his achievement.

SEE ALSO Roman Catholic Church: 1690 to 1829

Bibliography

Keogh, Dáire. *The French Disease: The Catholic Church and Radicalism in Ireland, 1790–1800.* 1993.

McNally, V. J. *Reform, Revolution and Reaction: Archbishop John Thomas Troy and the Catholic Church in Ireland, 1787–1818.* 1995.

Dáire Keogh

U

Uí Néill High Kings

The Uí Néill were descended from the protohistoric Niall Noígiallach, who may have been a real person; however, the way the genealogists and saga writers depict his ancestors and the relationships among his descendents is schematic and unhistorical. Diarmait mac Cerbaill, his grandson (d. 565), was an ancestor of the Southern Uí Néill, who were based in Meath and the east midlands. These divided into two hostile branches, Síl nAeda Sláine and Clann Cholmáin. The real establishment of Uí Néill power in the midlands may have been the work of Áed Sláne (d. 604) and his immediate successors, who provided some eight overkings of Uí Néill. Their rivals to the west, Clann Cholmáin (descendents of Áed Sláne's brother, Colmán Már, in the genealogies) became overkings of Uí Néill only in 743, and thereafter, with one exception, that of Congalach Cnogba (944–956), completely excluded their cousins from that office. Other branches of the Uí Néill of the midlands, if they ever held the overkingship, were soon excluded and survived as the political subordinates of their kinsmen.

Niall is also represented as father of Conall and Eógan, ancestors of Cenél Conaill and Cenél Eogain, the dominant dynasties in the northwest, known collectively as Northern Uí Néill. Cenél Conaill was more powerful than Cenél Eogain from the late sixth to the mid-seventh centuries. Two Cenél Conaill overkings of Uí Néill, Domnall mac Áeda (d. 642) and Longsech mac Óengusso (d. 704), are called *rex Hiberniae* (king of Ireland) in the annals. The last of their kings to hold the overkingship, Flaithbertach mac Longsig, abdicated in 734. After 789 Cenél Eogain dominated the north and expanded slowly southeastwards over central Ulster and eventually got control of County Armagh.

From the 840s the overkingship of Uí Néill, usually called the kingship of Tara, alternated regularly between Clann Cholmáin in the south and Cenél Eogain in the north. The overking of Uí Néill was usually the most powerful king in Ireland, and claimed to be king of Ireland—a claim realized for a period by Mael Sechnaill mac Mael Ruanaid (846–862). The meteoric rise of Brian Boru, king of Munster (978–1014) and king of Ireland (1002–1014), broke the Uí Néill supremacy and began an intense and violent struggle between powerful provincial kings for the kingship of Ireland, a struggle in which the northern Uí Néill remained key players.

SEE ALSO Dál Cais and Brian Boru; Norse Settlement; O'Connors of Connacht

Bibliography

Bhreathnach, Edel. "Temoria: Caput Scotorum?" *Ériu* 47 (1996): 67–88.

Byrne, Francis John. *The Rise of the Uí Néill and the High-Kingship of Ireland.* 1970.

Byrne, Francis John. *Irish Kings and High-Kings.* 1973.

Donnchadh Ó Corráin

Ulster Politics under Direct Rule

Direct rule was imposed by a Conservative government in late March 1972 as a very last resort, and for the first time in fifty-one years Northern Ireland was governed solely from London. It had been an option since 1969, but successive governments balked at taking over control of Northern Ireland because they were uncertain of how the indigenous security forces and civil servants would react. Prime Minister Edward Heath introduced direct rule only after international outrage at the events of Bloody Sunday and because there was growing uncertainty over the division of control in security matters between the army and the police. The government and parliament of Northern Ireland were prorogued, and henceforth the region was to be ruled like any other part of the United Kingdom so that Northern Ireland policy and legislation harmonized with the rest of the United Kingdom. But the measure was meant to be temporary while local politicians reached a political accommodation.

ADMINISTRATION, POLITICS, LEGISLATION

Northern Ireland Office (NIO) was established to administer the new regime, and William Whitelaw was appointed as the first secretary of state for Northern Ireland. He took political control with the support of a small ministerial team. From the outset he faced massive administrative and political problems. Administration was partially a question of structure: two locations, Belfast and London, which meant two sets of departments and two civil services coexisting within one ministry. By 1982 the head of the Northern Ireland civil service was responsible for the coordination of the work of the then six Northern Ireland departments, and the Belfast end of the NIO concerned itself mainly with the administration of reserved and excepted matters, especially law and order. The NIO in London looked after political and constitutional matters as well as security and acted as liaison between the Belfast and Whitehall departments. Politically the imposition shocked the whole of the unionist community and failed to assuage the IRA. Unionist political leaders supported a two-day general strike, and there was a huge increase in the numbers joining the paramilitary Ulster Defence Association (UDA). In anticipation of direct rule, Ulster Vanguard had been formed at the beginning of 1972 as a pressure group within unionism to transcend the weakness of party division. The year 1972 was to be the worst for political violence in the history of the "Troubles."

The government was aware that direct rule imposed a democratic deficit on Northern Ireland. It was to be governed under a Temporary Provisions Act—made more permanent by the Northern Ireland Act (1974)—that had to be renewed annually. In addition, William Whitelaw established an eleven-person advisory commission composed of local notables. It met until an assembly was elected more than a year later; in any case, it made little impact. Northern Ireland legislation was now processed by way of Orders in Council that could not be amended on the floor of the Commons. Direct rule also saw an increase in the power and growth of *quangos:* one study traced almost 150 such bodies with members being appointed by ministers. To address these deficits, a new Northern Ireland Committee was set up at Westminster in 1975, and a Speaker's Conference in 1978 accepted the case for extra Northern Ireland representation at Westminster. This pleased the Ulster Unionist Party (UUP) because they believed that it brought Northern Ireland more closely into being wholly integrated into the United Kingdom. As a result of unionist demands, a Northern Ireland Affairs Select Committee was appointed in 1994.

Direct rule may have brought institutional stability, but it imposed constitutional uncertainty. All attempts to restore power to local politicians failed. An elected constitutional convention in 1974–1975 could not muster the requisite cross-community support and thus collapsed. The most intriguing constitutional innovation was the attempt at "rolling devolution" after the election of a new Northern Ireland assembly in October 1982. The seventy-eight-seat body was to have a consultative and scrutinizing role. It could discuss local legislation and set up scrutiny committees for each of the six Northern Ireland departments. It was to be governed under the use of a weighted majority, whereby power could be devolved to any department that exercised cross-community agreement in which 70 percent or fifty-five members agreed. But the assembly failed from the outset because nationalists boycotted its proceedings. Instead it became the instrument of the unionist parties (with the reluctant assistance of the smaller Alliance Party), and it was converted into a platform of protest after the Anglo-Irish Agreement was signed in November 1985. The assembly was dissolved in June 1986.

ANGLO-IRISH AGREEMENT AND BELFAST AGREEMENT

The dissolution of the assembly showed how the nature of direct rule had changed. Initially direct rule had been imposed to create an internal political settlement, but by the 1980s the Northern Ireland problem had become internationalized, as was evident in the Anglo-Irish Agreement and the growing concerns of successive U.S. administrations. The British government had moved from a managerial phase to one of exasperation and admonition. It accepted that the failures of the 1974 power-sharing government, the 1975–1976 constitutional convention, and the 1982–1986 Northern Ireland Assembly made it less likely that local politicians would cooperate across the sectarian divide. It recognized too that there would be no security solution without the closest support of the Irish government. The first fruit of this policy was the 1985 Anglo-Irish Agreement. It fundamentally challenged unionist certainty about its place inside the United Kingdom and the IRA's invincibility. When that agreement was reviewed and confirmed in 1989 some of the protagonists began to review their own mindsets. Unionists, who had retreated to a form of internal exile after 1986, began to engage with the secretary of state. Republicans entered into a dialogue with the Social Democratic and Labour Party (SDLP) in 1988 and began to participate more fully in electoral politics. The result was the growth of attitudinal change in both communities.

Such change was not apparent for some time. The Conservative government at Westminster was increasingly reliant on UUP support to maintain its majority, and the international community did not pay sustained attention to the Northern Ireland problem until William Jefferson Clinton became U.S. president in 1992. He used the weight of his office to mobilize the political actors into taking risks for peace. The first result was the republican and loyalist cease-fires of 1994. The second was to engage in a twin-track process of moving the political process forward while dealing simultaneously with the issue of arms decommissioning. The outcome was elections to a Northern Ireland Forum in May 1996, which allowed for a more inclusive process. This was stimulated by the return of a Labour government, led by Tony Blair, in May 1997. With an overwhelming parliamentary majority of 179, Blair was not beholden to any Northern Ireland party. The IRA responded by calling a complete cessation of violence on 20 July 1997, and less than three months later Tony Blair became the first prime minister since 1921 to enter into negotiations with Sinn Féin. This led to a period of intense discussions (under the tutelage of Senator George Mitchell) that culminated in the signing of the Belfast Agreement on 10 April 1998. It was endorsed in referendums in both parts of Ireland in May and entered into law as the Northern Ireland Act in November. In the meantime, a new assembly met in July and elected David Trimble (UUP) and Seamus Mallon (SDLP) as, respectively, first minister and deputy first minister.

Direct rule remained in operation in 2003 because the parties had not dealt successfully with all aspects of the 1998 agreement, especially that of decommissioning. But the fact remained that the nature of direct rule had changed fundamentally. Whereas once it was concerned solely with Northern Ireland, it now recognized that three strands of the problem had to be dealt with in parallel: relations within Northern Ireland, relations among the people of Ireland, and relations among the United Kingdom and Irish governments.

SEE ALSO Adams, Gerry; Anglo-Irish Agreement of 1985 (Hillsborough Agreement); Faulkner, Brian; Hume, John; Hunger Strikes; Irish Republican Army (IRA); Loyalist Paramilitaries after 1965; Paisley, Ian; Trimble, David; **Primary Documents:** Anglo-Irish Agreement (15 November 1985); The Belfast/Good Friday Agreement (10 April 1998)

Bibliography

Arthur, Paul. *Special Relationships: Britain, Ireland, and the Northern Ireland Problem.* 2001.

Wilford, Rick, ed. *Aspects of the Belfast Agreement.* 2001.

Paul Arthur

≈

Ulster Unionist Party in Office

The Northern Ireland government came into official existence on 22 December 1920. The first election saw a convincing unionist mandate. Sir James Craig, leader of the Ulster Unionists, was the first prime minister. Though limited in power, the new government controlled both the Royal Ulster Constabulary (RUC) and an emergency police auxiliary—the A, B, C Specials—in which by December 1921 over 34,000 Protestants were enrolled. This ensured both unionist insulation from British pressure to come to an all-Ireland settlement and unionist victory in a mini-sectarian civil war that killed hundreds between 1919 and 1921.

1920S THROUGH WORLD WAR II

To secure the political domination of contested border regions—often Catholic and nationalist—the 1922 Local Government Act (N.I.) abolished proportional representation for local elections, and constituency boundaries were redrawn. About one-fifth of Catholics found themselves underrepresented in gerrymandered constituencies.

Ironically, by the middle of the 1920s stabilization led to a weakening through fragmentation of the unionist vote. Again, the government tweaked the electoral system. In 1929 proportional representation was abolished for elections to the parliament of Northern Ireland. This had the desired effect in consolidating the voting blocs. Unionist seats bounced back up from thirty-two in 1925 to 37.

Nevertheless, unionist concerns were reignited with the election in February 1932 of a republican Fianna Fáil government in the Irish Free State. To add to unionist concern, in October 1932 unemployed workers, both Catholic and Protestant, rioted against niggardly relief. The opening the following month of Stormont, the grand neoclassical parliamentary building complex in east Belfast, only served to highlight the hauteur of the unionist elite.

Unionists reacted with rhetorical chauvinism. In April 1934 James Craig, now Lord Craigavon, described Stormont as "a Protestant parliament for a Protestant people." It was in an atmosphere of unionist hyperbole and suspicion that severe rioting broke out during Orange processions of 12 July 1935. Nine were killed and 514 Catholics driven from their homes.

World War II at first discomfited unionists. The government spurned periodic pressure from Britain to surrender partition so as to entice the neutral South into the war. It was slow to mobilize its productive capacity. Air-raid precautions were utterly inadequate, and the government was slow to remedy the situation. But in the long run, Northern Ireland's loyalty contrasted with southern Ireland's neutrality. Thus funding was made available from Britain to permit the postwar extension of the welfare state to Northern Ireland.

POSTWAR POLITICS, CIVIL RIGHTS, BLOODY SUNDAY

In the 1950s Prime Minister Lord Brookeborough patched up traditional Protestant-dominated industries (shipbuilding, engineering) with special packages from Britain. Britain, however, increasingly insisted that further aid be linked to new employment opportunities. Under pressure from the Northern Ireland Labour Party (NILP), Captain Terence O'Neill had the technocratic reputation to front a new modernizing unionism. He succeeded Brookeborough as prime minister in March 1963.

O'Neill concentrated on developing a grand plan for transforming Northern Ireland's infrastructure and thus attracting inward investment. His championing of innovation met and repulsed the NILP threat but equally unsettled established sectarian relations.

On 14 January 1965 O'Neill made history by receiving Seán Lemass, taoiseach of the Republic of Ire-

land, at Stormont. Many unionists, and not only those sympathetic to the Reverend Ian Paisley, a firebrand who rallied loyalist opinion against the government, were suspicious of O'Neill's temporizing ambitions.

Catholics, in contrast, thought O'Neill's modernization too halfhearted, even hypocritical. A civil-rights demonstration held in Derry on 5 October developed into a battle with the RUC in which the police showed little restraint. This sparked the civil-rights movement. On 22 November, O'Neill announced a series of reforms, including the abolition of the gerrymandered Londonderry Corporation and an ambition to elevate public housing above accusations of sectarian patronage. Disorder continued, however, and within the Unionist Party there was much discontent with O'Neill's inability to maintain order.

At the "Crossroads Election" held on 24 February 1969, O'Neill failed to win a convincing mandate for his reform unionism. Severe rioting in April finally forced O'Neill's resignation. James Chichester-Clarke became unionist leader and prime minister.

Sectarian disorder continued, and on 12 August the Apprentice Boys' march in Derry triggered three days of rioting between police and Catholic inhabitants in the Battle of the Bogside. Rioting in Derry ended only with the arrival of British army troops on 14 August. Rioting spread to Belfast and many Catholics were burned out. On 16 August British troops were welcomed into Catholic areas of Belfast. Overall, ten died in the violence, mostly Catholics. On 19 August the Downing Street Declaration issued by the British and Northern Irish governments announced that reforms would be encouraged and overseen by the British government.

The RUC was disarmed for normal duties; the B-Specials were disbanded and replaced by the Ulster Defence Regiment under British army control and discipline. Electoral reforms followed to eliminate voting irregularities and gerrymandering. Loyalists reacted with rioting and, more importantly, the steady march of political "extremism." In by-elections official unionists were defeated by the militants Ian Paisley and William Beattie.

The drift to the right among Protestants only served to undermine attempts to conciliate Catholics; they remained anxious that another "pogrom" of the style of August 1969 would be launched against Catholic enclaves. Nationalists turned to their own resources to clandestinely arm. Inevitably this became dominated by the organized IRA, particularly its traditional and militarist "Provisional" wing.

On 18 June 1971 the United Kingdom general election returned a Conservative administration. This heralded a new security approach designed to placate unionists by aggressively dismantling the IRA. Within days serious rioting broke out as Catholic ghettos resisted what they saw as an attempt to disarm otherwise undefended communities. The IRA was able to pose as a resistance group and validate its demonization of the traditional British enemy.

The Provisional IRA switched to an outright offensive against the British army in early 1971. Chichester-Clark, unable to persuade Britain to provide the level of troop commitment he considered necessary, resigned as prime minister on 20 March. Brian Faulkner succeeded to the premiership.

Faulkner was elected as a security hard-liner. However, he was aware of the necessity for political reform. He offered opposition MPs a system of parliamentary committees to oversee the executive. But the nationalist Social Democratic and Labour Party (SDLP) was under pressure to eschew any involvement with the Stormont government. On 16 July the party withdrew from Stormont in protest at the refusal of the British army to hold an inquiry into the shooting deaths of two men by troops in Derry.

Catholic alienation was boosted with the introduction of internment on 10 August. This was met by severe rioting in which two soldiers and ten civilians were killed. Altogether, 340 nationalist or republican dissidents, mostly Catholics, were picked up. By December 1971 there were 1,576 men behind the wire. Before long, allegations of the torture of prisoners emerged.

Catholic alienation reached a peak with the Bloody Sunday debacle on 30 January 1972. Fourteen demonstrators were fatally shot by the First Parachute Regiment following a banned civil-rights march in Derry. Outrage was universal in nationalist Ireland. Republican violence became notably more brutal.

On 22 March 1972 Brian Faulkner and his ministers were told by the British prime minister, Edward Heath, that they had to accept either the transfer of security responsibility to London or the complete suspension of Stormont. Faulkner refused to dilute devolution, and direct rule from London was introduced. On 1 April William Whitelaw took office as secretary of state for Northern Ireland.

SEE ALSO Brooke, Basil Stanlake, First Viscount Brookeborough; Craig, James, First Viscount Craigavon; Faulkner, Brian; Politics: Nationalist Politics in Northern Ireland; Northern Ireland: Discrimination and the Campaign for Civil Rights; O'Neill, Terence; Parker, Dame Dehra; **Primary Documents:** On "A

Protestant Parliament and a Protestant State" (24 April 1934); On Community Relations in Northern Ireland (28 April 1967); "Ulster at the Crossroads" (9 December 1968)

Bibliography

Buckland, Patrick. *The Factory of Grievances: Devolved Government in Northern Ireland, 1921–39.* 1979.

Harbinson, John F. *The Ulster Unionist Party, 1882–1973: Its Development and Organisation.* 1973.

Jackson, Alvin. *Ireland, 1798–1998.* 1999.

Mulholland, Marc. *Northern Ireland at the Crossroads: Ulster Unionism in the O'Neill Years, 1960–9.* 2000.

Marc Mulholland

Union, Act of

See Act of Union.

Unionism from 1885 to 1922

The notion of a constitutional union between Great Britain and Ireland was first mooted in the seventeenth century and later, although there was no continuous unionist political tradition, became a legislative reality in 1800. Until the late nineteenth century the union was tacitly accepted by most Irish constitutional politicians. (Daniel O'Connell was an important—though not singular—exception.) But with the gradual democratization of Irish electoral politics after 1850 and the mobilization of the rural Catholic population in the 1870s and 1880s, support for devolved government ("Home Rule") grew and was more effectively represented at Westminster. In eastern Ulster a concentration of Protestants, relatively harmonious landlord-tenant relations, and the spread of an industrial economy helped to sustain support for the union with Britain. But the remarkable growth of Parnellism in the early 1880s, combined with the franchise extensions of 1884 to 1885, effectively increased the political pressure for constitutional change, and in 1886 the Liberal government of W. E. Gladstone (hitherto a supporter of the union) formulated a measure for the better government of Ireland. This, the first Home Rule bill, was defeated in

The attempt by British Liberal and Irish Nationalist MPs to pass a Home Rule bill in 1886 galvanized opposition among unionists. No organization lent more fervor to the unionist cause after 1885 than the Orange Order, with its marches and its bands. This 1888 photograph shows the Order marching in Belfast on 12 July to commemorate the Battle of the Boyne in 1690. PHOTOGRAPH REPRODUCED WITH THE KIND PERMISSION OF THE TRUSTEES OF THE NATIONAL MUSEUMS AND GALLERIES OF NORTHERN IRELAND, W10/29/50.

the House of Commons in June 1886; a second Home Rule bill, again the work of Gladstone, was defeated in the House of Lords in September 1893.

PARLIAMENTARY UNIONISM

In these contexts a movement was created to mobilize the (hitherto largely passive) unionism evident within all classes of Irish Protestantism and also (to a lesser extent) within some propertied sections of Catholic society. An important early geographical focus for these endeavors was south Ulster. In social terms landlords, the Presbyterian entrepreneurial classes, and the Orange Order were all central to the early success of organized unionism. The institutional core of the new movement lay with a distinct Irish unionist parliamentary grouping formed in 1885 to 1886 that united Irish Conservatives with those Irish Liberals who had rejected Gladstone's Home Rule initiative (the Liberal Unionists).

Different popular bodies were also important vehicles for the new cause, particularly the Irish Loyal and Patriotic Union (later renamed the Irish Unionist Alliance), which was founded in Dublin in 1885.

Until the early Edwardian period unionism retained a parliamentary focus and, at least nominally, an all-Ireland organizational scope. At this time the movement faced a variety of external and internal challenges that helped to stimulate several key organizational and strategic revisions. Irish unionism had thrived in the 1880s and 1890s partly on the basis of a strong political relationship with British Conservatism, and partly too on the strength of the Protestant social alliance. But the bond with Toryism was shaken by the conciliatory measures pursued by several British governments toward the Home Rule movement, and the class alliance upon which Irish unionism was based was rocked by the protests of northern Protestant farmers, particularly after 1900. Unionist leaders responded to these challenges with an organizational reform of the northern movement that culminated in the creation of an Ulster Unionist Council in 1905. This, combined with a more conciliatory attitude toward land reform and with the renewal of the Home Rule threat after the Liberals' electoral victory in 1906, provided the basis for some unionist political consolidation.

On the other hand, these developments also brought about the relative diminution of an all-Ireland unionism. Unionism in the three southern provinces was rich but numerically weak, and given the bias toward property ownership in the British constitution at the time, it was overrepresented in the both the House of Commons and particularly in the House of Lords. Southern unionism thus benefited from the parliamentary focus of the late Victorian and Edwardian movement. With the creation of a strong local and regional organization in the north, this focus was blurred, and the corresponding benefits for the south and west were diminished.

MILITARIZATION

The organization of Ulster unionism after 1905 provided the foundation for a popularly regimented northern resistance when a renewed British effort was made in 1912 to pass a Home Rule measure for Ireland. Unionist strategies and institutions were evolving rapidly at this time. Ulster unionists had been alienated from British parliamentary politics in the later Edwardian period, and by 1911, with the reform and weakening of the strongly Conservative House of Lords, they believed that the constitution was now stacked against them. This sense of exclusion underlay an increasing radicalization in Ulster unionist politics after about 1910 that led to the importation of weapons and the creation in early 1913 of the Ulster Volunteer Force, a citizens' militia organized along British military lines. The Ulster unionist leadership attempted to use extraconstitutional endeavors to win concessions inside the parliamentary arena, but they were unsuccessful and were gradually compelled into ever more militant tactics. These efforts culminated on 24 and 25 April 1914, when 25,000 rifles and three million rounds of ammunition were smuggled into eastern Ulster by unionist hawks.

At this time unionist goals shifted in keeping with the organizational and strategic redefinition of the movement. Unionism from 1912 to 1914 was overwhelmingly northern in its roots and focus; unionism in the south and west of Ireland was relatively unimportant in the context of the popular mobilization that was occurring in Ulster. This geographical imbalance had wide implications. Ulster unionists had originally defended the retention of the entire island of Ireland within the union settlement, but they gradually moved toward a demand for the exclusion of all, or part, of the northern province from Home Rule. At first, this seems to have been a tactical ploy that was designed to separate British Liberals from Irish nationalists, but it is clear that by 1913 exclusion or partition was being considered as a substantive goal. By 1914 the Ulster unionists had settled on the permanent exclusion of the six northeastern counties (Antrim, Armagh, Down, Fermanagh, Londonderry, and Tyrone) as their minimum terms for a settlement. However, this would cause both the political division of the island, which was hateful to Irish nationalists, and the disintegration of an all-Ireland unionism, which would render the loyalists of the south and west politically isolated and vulnerable. The polarization of Irish unionism into (in the end) mutually repellent northern and southern elements may be dated to this time.

PARTITION

The outbreak of the First World War in August 1914 helped to consolidate Ulster unionism and the partitionist demand. The Ulster Volunteer Force was largely incorporated into the British army as its 36th (Ulster) Division, and was badly mauled on the Somme in 1916 and at Passchendaele in 1917. This sacrifice to the British cause reinforced Ulster unionists' political identity and cemented their belief that the British state was politically indebted to them. Ulster unionists called for the permanent exclusion of the six northeastern counties from Home Rule in June 1916 during negotiations chaired by David Lloyd George, and they repeated this demand at the Irish Constitutional Convention, which met during the winter of 1917 to 1918. The distance that now separated them from southern unionism was compounded by the mythology that was developing around the military exploits of the 36th (Ulster) Division and by the very different public positions that the two unionisms were adopting. By 1917 some southern unionists, led by Lord Midleton and frightened by the swift radicalization of Irish nationalism, were at last prepared to accept a unitary Home Rule settlement. But southern unionism fractured under the pressure of Midleton's conversion, and Ulster unionists were able to pursue their own particularist agenda unburdened by any coherent opposition from southern loyalists.

In the long term the war helped to subvert Ulster unionism by destabilizing the industrial economy of the region and by robbing the movement of youthful talent, drive, and ability. In the short term, however, Ulster unionism was politically strengthened: Its political identity had been sharpened and its ranks were now filled with battle-hardened military veterans, while its allies, the British Conservatives, were the predominant partner in the coalition government returned to power in 1918. Moreover, the war had also seen the consolidation of a revolutionary Irish nationalist movement that was not prepared to be represented in British Parliament. This meant that Ulster unionists were able to exercise a disproportionate influence within British high politics. This influence was clear in the Government of Ireland Act (1920), through which the British sought to partition Ireland and to endow its two parts with Home Rule administrations. The measure met Ulster unionist demands in defining a six-county territory that was beyond the authority of a Dublin parliament, but the Belfast administration that was created under the act was less a result of Ulster unionist pressure than of the British desire to disengage from all aspects of Irish government. Ulster unionists had sought to exclude six counties from the operation of Home Rule entirely, but they swiftly came to see that a government in Belfast offered greater constitutional security than was possible within a British parliament.

The victims within these new arrangements were the substantial minority of nationalists within Northern Ireland, the unionists of outer Ulster (Cavan, Donegal, and Monaghan) who were excluded from the new polity, and the scattered unionists of the south and west. Northern nationalists suffered bloody and disproportionate losses in the intercommunal violence of the early 1920s. Southern unionists were broken by World War I, divided in its aftermath, and suffered heavily in the cross fire of the Anglo-Irish struggle (1919–1921). They were able to sustain their distinctive identity for a while in certain Protestant enclaves (south Dublin, for example), but in the end those who remained were mostly assimilated within the Catholic national tradition.

Ulster unionists, for their part, helped to create a state that institutionalized the struggles of the Home Rule and revolutionary eras. It would prove, as a later leader of the Ulster unionists would concede, "a cold house for Catholics" (McDonald 2000, p. 280).

SEE ALSO Act of Union; Anglo-Irish Treaty of 1921; Carson, Sir Edward; Craig, James, First Viscount Craigavon; Plunkett, Sir Horace Curzon; Politics: 1800 to 1921—Challenges to the Union; Protestant Ascendancy: Decline, 1800 to 1930; Redmond, John; Women in Nationalist and Unionist Movements in the Early Twentieth Century; **Primary Documents:** On the Home Rule Bill of 1886 (8 April 1886); Declaration against Home Rule (10 October 1911); "Solemn League and Covenant" Signed at the "Ulster Day" Ceremony in Belfast (28 September 1912); Address on the Ulster Question in the House of Commons (11 February 1914)

Bibliography

Buckland, Patrick. *Irish Unionism I: The Anglo-Irish and the New Ireland, 1885–1922.* 1972.

Buckland, Patrick. *Irish Unionism II: Ulster Unionism and the Foundations of Northern Ireland, 1886–1922.* 1973.

Jackson, Alvin. *The Ulster Party: Irish Unionists in the House of Commons, 1884–1911.* 1989.

Jackson, Alvin. *Colonel Edward Saunderson: Land and Loyalty in Victorian Ireland.* 1995.

McDonald, Henry. *Trimble.* 2000.

McDowell, R. B. *Crisis and Decline: The Fate of Southern Unionism.* 1997.

Stewart, A. T. Q. *The Ulster Crisis: Resistance to Home Rule, 1912–14.* 1967.

Alvin Jackson

United Irish League Campaigns

The United Irish League was founded on 23 January 1898 at a meeting in Westport, Co. Mayo. Its principal architect was William O'Brien, a member of Parnell's Parliamentary Party in the 1880s and of the anti-Parnellite majority faction after 1891. After withdrawing from his parliamentary seat in 1895, O'Brien worked locally in west Mayo in facilitating and influencing the development of a new agrarian agitation focused on the plight of evicted tenants, on hostility to "land grabbers," and against the graziers occupying land that would otherwise have been available for tillage farming. With the help of others, especially the Parnellite MP T. C. Harrington and the veteran founder of the Land League, Michael Davitt, O'Brien directed his energies toward "a great accumulation of national strength" (O'Brien 1910, p. 89).

The organization that resulted, the United Irish League, had three interconnected objectives. The first, and most incidental, of these was to capture an initiative on the celebrations of the centenary of the 1798 United Irishmen's rebellions, then at risk of passing to the advocates of physical force. The second objective was to infuse into national politics an enthusiasm that, "draw-

The last phase of the land war began in 1898 under the United Irish League. This phase often pitted the small tenants of Connacht against the land-monopolizing graziers or ranchers. The conflict again underlined the long-standing land hunger of western smallholders, whose hard-scrabble lives and potato dependency are captured in this 1880 illustration of a bog village in County Roscommon. FROM ILLUSTRATED LONDON NEWS, 15 MAY 1880.

ing an irresistible strength and reality from the conditions in the west," would make impossible continuation of dissension and factionalism between Parnellites and anti-Parnellites. And the third, most tangible and practical objective, was to secure from Parliament a measure enabling tenant farmers to acquire ownership of their land from the landlords by means of the government's powers of compulsory purchase. This last objective provided the central focus for the League's expansion between 1898 and 1900 across the whole of Ireland, attaching to the cause of the poor western farmers the commitment of strong and prosperous farmers in the rest of the country for whom the ownership of their farms was an urgent priority. This demand also established the basis for an alliance with the Ulster Presbyterian farmers, who had been organized in 1900 into a popular agitation for compulsory land purchase by the parliamentarian T. W. Russell.

All these objectives were achieved, in one way or another, between 1898 and 1903. The new organiza-

tion served as an embodiment, rather than a sentimental reminder, of the "spirit of '98," establishing a basis for the advocates of parliamentary politics to retrieve their nationalist credentials from the damaging factionalism of the 1890s. The zest with which the new agitation was taken up by grassroots nationalists in the countryside made it impossible for even the most obdurate to maintain a factionalist position in the face of widespread involvement of ordinary Parnellites and anti-Parnellites. This did not find expression, however, as the League leaders had hoped, in a rejuvenation of parliamentary representation with new, younger, and more robust League activists, but in a largely defensive action by the existing parliamentarians to protect their positions against the reforming zeal of the popular organization. The warring factions were reconciled in January 1900 in a party that O'Brien described as "re-unified, rather than reformed," thus averting challenges to sitting members in the general election later that year. The power of the League was manifest, nonetheless, in the place it was given organizationally in relation to the Parliamentary Party. The third and focal objective of the League, a comprehensive measure of land purchase, was also achieved, although not by compulsory purchase. A conference of representatives of landlords and tenants agreed in January 1903 on the essential elements of a scheme of purchase in which the incentives for the landlords to sell and for the tenants to buy were provided by subsidies from the British exchequer. These provisions formed the basis of the Wyndham Land Act of 1903.

The agitational methods of the United Irish League followed the pattern of the Land League between 1879 and 1881. Conflict with authority over the moral pressure—alternatively described as intimidation—applied to those who offended against the League-endorsed land code drew irresistibly to the agitation the support of an ever-expanding cross-section of nationalists. In the circumstances of the late 1890s this meant first and foremost the rank-and-file Parnellites for whom such conflict evoked powerful memories, but it also attracted many Fenians for whom the associated theater of action presented a public role long denied them. Their presence in the organization had the effect of frightening Catholic bishops, who had previously opposed the League, into encouraging the clergy to participate. For the leadership this had multiple benefits: The organization became church-sanctioned, thereby further facilitating its spread; both clergy and Fenians were valuable organizational assets; and the clerical presence helped to balance more extreme propensities that might have damaged the agitation's credibility.

The two peaks of agitation occurred during 1898 and 1899 and 1901 and 1902. In the latter years conflict became intense, with thirteen MPs and many League organizers and newspapermen imprisoned at various times. The techniques used—boycotting, league courts, use of local-government authority, and resistance to injunctions, jury-packing (exclusion of those assumed to be too sympathetic to the accused), and other governmental departures from the ordinary law—constituted an unprecedented level of passive resistance. These methods consolidated in the public consciousness patterns of popular action endemic in Irish political culture that would be reactivated in a more charged context between 1916 and 1921. This campaign in the countryside, however, faced significant opposition privately from several leading nationalists, including John Redmond and John Dillon, on the two grounds that it might offend Liberal opinion in Britain and could lead to imprisonment of political leaders.

The Land Act of 1903, and in particular the process of conference and conciliation between landlords and tenants by which it was brought about, had far-reaching implications for Irish nationalism in general and for the United Irish League in particular. The organization, under O'Brien's leadership and with the support of the parliamentary leader, John Redmond, adopted a policy of extending the cooperation between the nationalist movement and the landlord class into other areas of Irish life. This reflected both the removal of land as a central economic issue shaping landlord attitudes and a desire to heal the sectarian divisions that had been an inescapable product of the land war. Initially successful in attracting widespread support among nationalists, this new conciliation policy faced concerted opposition from a group of political leaders for whom it represented the abrogation of long-held political habits. In particular, John Dillon, Michael Davitt, and Thomas Sexton (who controlled the nationalist *Freeman's Journal*), set out to secure a return to traditional, if increasingly redundant, postures. In protest at Redmond's failure to assert his leadership against these critics, O'Brien resigned from Parliament and from his positions in the League. His hope that this would force a constructive debate proved vain; instead, its effect was to hand control of the movement to those who had opposed the new policy, with significant consequences for the future of the United Irish League.

With the removal of its founder from the helm of the organization, the United Irish League lost its role as a political initiator and became increasingly the electoral and patronage machine for the parliamentary Nationalist Party. While the principal policy issue around which it had been founded was substantially removed by the Land Act of 1903, those who now took responsibility for the organization had committed themselves to a continuation of land agitation. The effect of this was that the League took up residual issues left unresolved by the 1903 Land Act, principally the related issues of the evicted tenants and the congested (or overpopulated) districts. Land for the tenants evicted during the land war and more viable farms for small-holders through breaking up the grazing ranches now became the focus of the United Irish League's agitational strategy. The ensuing "ranch war" proved deeply divisive, its main tactic of "cattle driving" deeply offending many elements of rural society. More specifically, it soon became evident that many substantial farmers were more interested in securing redistributed land for themselves or their sons than in having outsiders take it up. Moreover, not only was grazing a highly profitable component of the Irish agricultural economy, but—as had always been the case—the graziers themselves were often very important local supporters of the Nationalist Party. Thus, whereas in the nineteenth century the land issue had been a struggle between native occupiers and the descendants of conquerors, this new campaign for land redistribution was based on a competition between different elements of the nationalist community. Its only achievement was the appointment in 1906 by a Liberal government of a royal commission on congestion, an exercise in buying time for a government unable to deliver much else to its Irish allies and a Nationalist Party desperate to show that the Liberal alliance could produce something. The Dudley Commission formulated no way forward. Ironically, it was the revolutionary Dáil Éireann in 1920 that issued a decree against claimants for land redistribution, describing their actions as a "stirring up of strife amongst our fellow countrymen." The United Irish League's campaign for landownership for Irish farmers and its subsequent appeal for conciliation between rival landed classes had built on nationalist ideals of the past, but its post-1903 strategies largely undermined its credibility as an innovative political force.

SEE ALSO Congested Districts Board; Home Rule Movement and the Irish Parliamentary Party: 1891 to 1918; Land Purchase Acts of 1903 and 1909; Land Questions; Land War of 1879 to 1882; Plan of Campaign; Protestant Ascendancy: Decline, 1800 to 1930; Redmond, John

Bibliography

Bew, Paul. Conflict and Conciliation in Ireland, 1890–1910: Parnellites and Radical Agrarians. 1987.

Bull, Philip. "The Reconstruction of the Irish Parliamentary Movement, 1895–1903: An Analysis with Special Reference to William O'Brien." Ph.D. diss., University of Cambridge, 1972.

Bull, Philip. "The United Irish League and the Reunion of the Irish Parliamentary Party, 1898–1900." Irish Historical Studies 26 (May 1988): 51–78.

Bull, Philip. "The Significance of the Nationalist Response to the Irish Land Act of 1903." Irish Historical Studies 28 (May 1993): 283–305.

Bull, Philip. Land, Politics, and Nationalism: A Study of the Irish Land Question. 1996.

Higgins, Michael D., and John P. Gibbons. "Shopkeeper-Graziers and Land Agitation in Ireland, 1895–1900." In Ireland: Land, Politics and People, edited by P. J. Drudy. 1982.

Jones, David S. Graziers, Land Reform, and Political Conflict in Ireland. 1995.

O'Brien, William. An Olive Branch in Ireland and Its History. 1910.

Philip Bull

~

United Irish Societies from 1791 to 1803

The Society of United Irishmen was founded in 1791 in Belfast and Dublin to promote radical parliamentary reform, Catholic Emancipation (or the abolition of all religious disqualifications in civic life), and a union of Catholic and Protestant to achieve them both. Within the first year of its formation the United Irishmen succeeded in extending its organization into three of the four provinces of Ireland (Ulster, Leinster, and Munster), but outside Ulster the number of associated clubs was insignificant. The purpose of the society was not initially to replicate itself throughout the countryside; rather, it was largely propagandist—to disseminate political information and to coordinate whenever possible the activities of other like-minded reform groups. These secular radicals were content to keep their own numbers relatively small as long as they could use the Volunteer corps, the Catholic Committee, Masonic lodges, Presbyterian congregations, and town, parish, and county meetings to pronounce critically on current political arrangements. The Dublin Society of United Irishmen, which had a peak membership of more than 400 professionals, merchants, and tradesmen, took the lead in publicizing the organization's aims through the distribution of a wide array of publications. The United Irishmen in Belfast supported this political-education project by publishing their highly successful newspaper, the Northern Star.

The aims and ideology of the United Irishmen drew on several vibrant political languages current in the late eighteenth century—civic humanism or classical republicanism, Lockean contractualism, British constitutionalism, Presbyterian radicalism, and the language of reason and the rights of man emanating from the American and French revolutions. Their aim was to make every man a citizen, and to throw the weight of an enlarged public opinion behind radical reform based on universal manhood suffrage and Irish legislative sovereignty to counter British influence in Ireland.

In April 1793 Britain and Ireland entered the war against revolutionary France, and the United Irishmen, with their pro-French sympathies, were easily identified by the state as the enemy within. Government harassment of the radical press, the arrest of the leaders, and the constriction of opportunities to express public opinion culminated in the suppression of the Dublin Society of United Irishmen in 1794. The recall of a popular, reforming viceroy, Earl Fitzwilliam, in April 1795 signaled unambiguously Britain's determination to stand

United Irishmen in Training, *a caricature by J. Gillray, published in London during the 1798 rebellion.* COPYRIGHT THE BRITISH MUSEUM. REPRODUCED BY PERMISSION.

by an unreformed Irish government. All hopes of peaceful reform having thus been dashed, the United Irishmen reorganized themselves as an underground paramilitary organization (to force a new government) grafted onto an expandable civil one (to form a new government), determined to separate Ireland from Britain and to create a secular, democratic republic with assistance from republican France. Their goal now was to make not only every man a citizen, but every citizen a soldier duly sworn into the United Irish organization. By 1798 the republicans would claim 300,000 such citizen-soldiers.

The reorganized republican movement was overwhelmingly Presbyterian at its birth, reflecting the confessional demographics of its stronghold in the northeast. The primary task of the United Irishmen, then, was to shore up and organize this base while preparing for a general insurrection to be coordinated with an expected French invasion of Ireland. Organizational zeal and assiduous propaganda accounted for the group's growth, but equally important was the appearance of the first fruits of the United Irish alliance with revolu-

tionary France—the arrival of the French fleet in Bantry Bay in Cork in December 1796. Although the invasion attempt failed, it dramatically proclaimed French resolve to assist an Irish insurrection and lent the United Irish project an aura of inevitability, creating a bandwagon effect. From October 1796 to February 1797, United Irish membership in Ulster nearly doubled from 38,567 to 69,190, and then nearly doubled again from February to May 1797, when the northern republicans boasted 117,917 comrades. Furthermore, the revival of sectarian warfare after 1795 between the Catholic Defenders and the newly formed Loyal Orange Order led the Catholics into an alliance with, and in many cases absorption into, the republican organization. Merchants, ministers, and professionals tended to dominate the higher ranks of the movement, while the ranks were rapidly filling with farmers, artisans, and weavers.

A mass-based secret society, democratic and inclusive in impulse, the United Irish movement was extremely porous to infiltration and detection. Just as the movement was expanding significantly from Ulster into Leinster in the spring of 1797, the government launched a vigorous counter-insurrectionary campaign in the northeast designed to deprive the republicans of both their arms and their leaders through the imposition of martial law and extraordinary legal measures. This "dragooning of Ulster" did not break the northern organization, but it did subdue it as the United Irishmen chose to wait for the ever-promised French invasion. The leadership was now centered in Dublin, torn between French delays and ruthless government repression. The eventual decision to rise without French assistance led a series of partial, failed risings after May 1798.

Bands of republican resisters persisted after the failed risings of 1798, politicized further by the bloody suppression of the rebellion. Most of the national leaders had been either executed or exiled, and there was no central coordination of the local bands of rebels. This was in fact conscious policy, a reaction to what was perceived as the main flaw of the pre-1798 republican organization—its mass, open, democratic character that was so vulnerable to government penetration. The post-1798 organization assumed, with good cause, that there were sufficient United Irishmen in the country that could be rallied when needed, and focused its energies instead on an elusive directory engaged in a tight conspiracy to maintain the French alliance and trigger the rebellion at home. Robert Emmet's plan to seize Dublin in July 1803, thus sparking a national insurrection, was only accidentally discovered by the authorities, and thus a well-conceived strategy was transformed into a street brawl, with only minor ripples in the rest of the country. This conspiratorial model of a revolutionary republican organization set forth by the post-1798 United Irishmen constituted a significant legacy to subsequent militant separatist movements.

SEE ALSO Eighteenth-Century Politics: 1778 to 1795—Parliamentary and Popular Politics; Emmet, Robert; Fitzgerald, Lord Edward; Keogh, John; Neilson, Samuel; Tandy, James Napper; Tone, Theobald Wolfe; **Primary Documents:** United Irish Parliamentary Reform Plan (March 1794); Speech Delivered at a United Irish Meeting in Ballyclare, Co. Antrim (1795); Grievances of the United Irishmen of Ballynahinch, Co. Down (1795); The United Irish Organization (1797); Statement of Three Imprisoned United Irish Leaders (4 August 1798); Speech from the Dock (19 September 1803)

Bibliography

Curtin, Nancy J. *The United Irishmen: Popular Politics in Ulster and Dublin, 1791–1798.* 1994.

Dickson, David, Kevin Whelan, and Daire Keogh, eds. *The United Irishmen: Republicanism, Radicalism, and Rebellion.* 1993.

Elliott, Marianne. *Partners in Revolution: The United Irishmen and France.* 1982.

Gough, Hugh, and David Dickson, eds. *Ireland and the French Revolution.* 1990.

O'Donnell, Ruán. *Aftermath: Post-Rebellion Insurgency in Wicklow, 1799–1803.* 2000.

Smyth, Jim. *The Men of No Property: Irish Radicals and Popular Politics in the Late Eighteenth Century.* 1992.

Thuente, Mary Helen. *The Harp Re-Strung: The United Irishmen and the Rise of Irish Literary Nationalism.* 1994.

Whelan, Kevin. *The Tree of Liberty: Radicalism, Catholicism, and the Construction of Irish Identity, 1760–1830.* 1996.

Nancy J. Curtin

United Nations

Irish diplomacy at the United Nations (UN) constitutes a compelling chapter in the history of Irish foreign policy. Ireland entered the organization as part of a sixteen-nation package deal in 1955 after being denied membership for nearly a decade by the Soviet Union's veto in the Security Council. Led by an array of distinguished diplomats, including Frank Aiken, Ireland's minister for external affairs from 1957 to 1969, Frederick H. Boland, permanent representative to the UN from 1956 to 1963, Liam Cosgrave, Conor Cruise O'Brien, Tadhg O'Sullivan, Máire Mhac an tSaoi, and Sean Ronan, the Irish delegation assumed a prominent role in the General Assembly throughout the late 1950s and 1960s. It mitigated Cold War tensions, promoted decolonization throughout Africa and Asia, mediated disputes in South Tyrol and Kashmir, and participated in numerous peacekeeping operations.

PROMOTING NATIONAL INTERESTS

Two themes have consistently underpinned Irish policy at the United Nations: national interests and the international order. With regard to the former, Irish governments have usually assigned priority to one of the many interests they have pursued at the UN. For instance, in 1956 John Costello's interparty government determined that Western victory in the Cold War was the primary interest to be furthered at the United Nations, and so the Irish delegation consistently supported the United States and its allies in the General Assembly. The cardinal aim of Eamon de Valera, who was taoiseach during the Twelfth General Assembly in 1957 and the Thirteenth Assembly in 1958, was the reduction of international tension generated by the Cold War, support for movements for self-determination across the Southern Hemisphere, and the interaction of these two world-historical forces. For de Valera's successor, Seán Lemass, as well as for Irish leaders over the past several decades, the paramount interest pursued at the UN has been the promotion of a stable international system within the framework of Ireland's equally pressing national objective, namely, economic development. At the same time, all Irish governments, regardless of their particular priorities, have uniformly acted upon a genuine community of Irish national interests at the United Nations. Irish diplomats have advocated the primacy of the rule of law in international affairs, ardently defended small nations invaded by their larger neighbors, championed human rights across the globe, particularly in Tibet and South Africa, and supported the political aspirations of national minorities.

PROMOTING INTERNATIONAL ORDER

The accumulated effect of these diplomatic endeavors signals the second theme of Ireland's policy at the United Nations: It has consistently upheld the integrity of the international order. The Irish delegation's efforts in this regard began in earnest at the Twelfth General Assembly, when it established an overtly independent identity with its infamous "China vote." In a sharp departure from the majority of other Western European nations, and its own position in the previous year, Ireland voted in favor of a discussion of which government should represent China in the UN, the communists in Beijing or the nationalists on Taiwan. This vote is often misunderstood: it was a procedural one in favor of a debate on that question only, not a ballot in favor of Beijing representing China (Ireland actually voted against just such a motion in 1961). Still, the vote certainly roused the ire of the United States, and in so doing earned Ireland the respect of many other members of the General Assembly, especially within the growing Afro-Asian bloc, but also among Western European delegations who privately concurred with its position.

With the Irish delegation's independent reputation now established, it assumed a prominent role among the middle powers, or mediators, in the General Assembly (Sweden, Denmark, Malaysia, Yugoslavia, and others), which thus enabled it to propose initiatives designed to reduce international friction. In 1957 Frank Aiken outlined a complex troop-withdrawal plan for Central Europe, whereby NATO and Warsaw Pact forces would simultaneously retreat equal distances from various flash points along the Iron Curtain. Aiken

asserted that his blueprint sought "to diminish political tension in Europe and to avert the danger of war, which is all the greater as long as soldiers of opposing armies stand face-to-face." It was not taken up by either side in the Cold War, but the following year Aiken did develop his nascent conception of neutralized spaces between warring parties into a formal "areas of law" proposal and applied it to the Middle East and other hotspots across the globe.

Ireland's most striking effort to ameliorate international tension was its nuclear nonproliferation initiative. Starting at the Thirteenth General Assembly in 1958, Frank Aiken, with the tireless assistance of the Irish diplomatic service, pushed nuclear nonproliferation to the top of the UN's agenda. In 1961 the General Assembly adopted an Irish-sponsored resolution whose operative clause laid the foundation for the Nuclear Nonproliferation Treaty of 1968. Aiken told the General Assembly that the fundamental purpose of a nuclear nonproliferation convention was "to prevent the danger of nuclear war becoming greater during the period of time it must take to evolve and strengthen a generally accepted system of world security based on international law and law enforcement." A treaty, in other words, would buy time "for the gradual evolution of a stable world order."

IRELAND AS A MEMBER OF THE EUROPEAN UNION

During the 1970s the General Assembly underwent a gradual radicalization due to the emergence of a confident Afro-Asian bloc. This process, combined with an American-led retreat to the Security Council, meant Ireland's high profile in the National Assembly dimmed. At the same time Ireland had to reconcile its own policy at the United Nations with those of the other members of European Economic Community (EEC), a process that accelerated after Ireland joined the EEC in 1973 and gathered momentum in the 1980s and 1990s as the EEC evolved first into the European Community and then into the European Union, while eventually embracing a Common Foreign and Security Policy (CFSP). Still, the Irish delegation quietly continued with its constructive work at the United Nations, especially in the field of peacekeeping. This noteworthy Irish tradition began with missions in 1958 (the Observer Group in Lebanon, or UNOGIL) and in 1959 (the Truce Supervision Organization along the Israeli-Egyptian border, or UNTSO) and was consolidated by Ireland's substantial contribution to the UN's peacekeeping operation in the Congo, Force de l'Organisation des Nations Unis en Congo (ONUC), which lasted from 1960 to 1964. Just as ONUC was ending in June 1964, Irish troops shipped out to the UN Force in Cyprus (UNFICYP), where they still remain. Irish soldiers have served in Kashmir, Lebanon, the Golan Heights, Afghanistan, Iraq, Namibia, Central America, Cambodia, the former Yugoslavia, and elsewhere. Ireland has participated in more than twenty-five UN missions, plus several European Union operations. Through these efforts Ireland has backed up its rhetoric at the UN. Indeed, along with nuclear non-proliferation, peacekeeping has been one of Ireland's most significant contributions to the international order.

Ireland's peers in the General Assembly have recognized its important contribution by electing it to important UN bodies: the Committee on South West Africa, the Congo Advisory Committee, the Security Council on three occasions (1962, 1981–1982, and 2001–2002). Likewise, Irish representatives have assumed prominent leadership roles: Frederick Boland was named chairman of the Fourth, or Trusteeship, Committee in 1958 and president of the General Assembly in 1960; Eamon Kennedy was appointed as rapporteur of the Committee on South West Africa in 1959; Conor Cruise O'Brien was selected as Dag Hammarskjold's personal representative in Katanga in 1961; General Sean McKeown commanded the UN peacekeeping force in the Congo (ONUC); and Sean MacBride served as UN commissioner for Namibia. Continuing this tradition, in 1997 Kofi Annan, the secretary-general of the UN, appointed Mary Robinson, the former president of Ireland, as the United Nations high commissioner for human rights.

SEE ALSO European Union; Lemass, Seán; Neutrality; Politics: Independent Ireland since 1922

Bibliography

Kennedy, Michael. *Ireland and the League of Nations.* 1996.

Keogh, Dermot. *Twentieth-Century Ireland.* 1994.

O'Brien, Conor Cruise. *To Katanga and Back: A UN Case Study.* 1962.

O'Brien, Conor Cruise. *Memoir: My Life and Themes.* 1998.

Skelly, Joseph Morrison. *Irish Diplomacy at the United Nations, 1945–1965: National Interests and the International Order.* 1997.

Joseph M. Skelly

~

Urban Life, Crafts, and Industry from 1500 to 1690

At the outset of the sixteenth century the town was the center of economic activity in Ireland. There were about fifty towns of some size in Ireland around 1500, and they contained roughly 10 percent of the island's population. But the principal towns that supported small-scale manufacture of crafts and goods for export numbered no more than a dozen. Chief among them was Dublin, Ireland's only true city. In Dublin was concentrated the governing apparatus of the Tudor state in Ireland linking the regional capitals of Waterford, Galway, Cork, Limerick, and Carrickfergus—and other large country and market towns—to England. The majority of these towns were located on sites that had originally been settled centuries earlier by the Vikings, and they were situated at the head of important estuaries or bays. These ports, in marked contrast to the dispersed settlements common in old Gaelic districts, came to be modeled on the towns of southeast England and maintained a recognizably English form of political, social, economic, and municipal culture. Thus the early Tudors relied heavily on the Irish towns both as trading posts and as cultural and military bastions of Englishness against the independent Gaelic lordships that dominated the rural hinterland beyond the protective walls and fortifications that surrounded all major Irish towns.

URBAN LIFE UNDER THE TUDORS

Most town dwellers in sixteenth-century Ireland were English subjects and of English extraction. In an effort to create a stable economic environment and to stimulate trade and manufacture, however, the Crown had devolved considerable powers to its subjects in the major urban centers. The Crown's confidence in its urban-dwelling subjects reached its highest form of expression in the royal charters that granted an unusual degree of political autonomy to certain towns. A two-tiered system of municipal government, varying in scale and complexity according to the size of the town or city, was thus allowed to develop. In Dublin the first, or upper, tier consisted of a mayor, two sheriffs, and twenty-four aldermen, and the lower tier comprised forty-eight so-called sheriffs piers along with a further ninety-six nominees of the city's influential merchant and craft guilds. Political power and influence in Ireland's towns were concentrated in those men who occupied the limited number of high offices of municipal government and the most prosperous merchant families dominated these key positions.

In the larger urban centers political power was shared between a large number of families, but in the smaller towns, such as Galway or Cork, only a dozen or so families had the necessary wealth to occupy what were unpaid municipal posts. Fifteen wealthy merchant families known colloquially as the "tribes," for instance, governed Galway for centuries. And a sixteenth-century observer noted that in Cork the ruling elite "trust not the country adjoining, but match in wedlock among themselves only, so that the whole city is well nigh linked one to another in affinity" (Sheehan, p. 103). Such clannishness, however, was not solely because of a provincial desire to concentrate power among a privileged and established few. Rather, it resulted from the wider difficulties facing the urban population in Ireland. Citizenship of a town was a much sought-after distinction and might be obtained only through apprenticeship in the guilds, marriage to a daughter of a citizen, heredity, or a special dispensation of the city council. People of Gaelic origin and women were restricted from becoming citizens, and Irish towns, particularly those furthest removed from England, often found it difficult to attract sufficient numbers of English immigrants either to enrich or to sustain their populations. Self-government was thus firmly entrenched in Ireland's large towns but was the exclusive domain of the rich. The ruling merchant families of Ireland's smaller towns had little recourse but to become closed and self-perpetuating entities in order to maintain uninterrupted self-government.

A testament to the effectiveness of self-government was the lack of internal challenges to the political and social hierarchy in the towns as the sixteenth century progressed. When external forces threatened the towns' autonomy—as happened during the Kildare rebellion (1534) and the Munster and Leinster rebellions (1579–1583)—the majority of Ireland's urban dwellers remained steadfastly loyal to the Crown. Behind their imposing walls the larger towns were mostly insulated from the political turmoil that characterized the extension of Tudor rule in Ireland, and urban life continued to revolve around the twin pursuits of religion and economic activity. The religious calendar dominated urban life with dramas and festivals staged to mark the passing of important religious occasions. These festivals nurtured a visible form of communal cultural identity that also manifested itself in the establishment of almshouses and hospitals as well as in the construction of primary and secondary schools. Significant advances in architecture under the early Tudors broke up the narrow, dark, and curving medieval streets that were common features of early Irish towns. Important religious sites, such as Saint Nicholas's Church in Galway, and secular buildings, such as the belfry tower and the city gates in Kilkenny, were either extended or re-edified in a more elaborate style known as late Irish Gothic (a subcategory of English Gothic).

It was economic activity, however, that most dominated the lives of Irish urban dwellers. Towns, but particularly the port towns, served as markets through which the raw materials produced in the hinterland might be exported to foreign markets. The export trade was an important source of income, and most towns held at least one fair annually. Not surprisingly, the power and influence of the merchant guilds increased sharply during the sixteenth century through the concurrent exploitation of the economic and political liberties that were enshrined in the royal charters, the flow of raw materials from the countryside, and the appetite for Irish raw materials in foreign markets.

On the other hand, the rapid rise in exports and the resulting growth of the merchant guilds tended to undermine urban manufacturing. Craftsmen represented by the guilds simply could not compete with a robust export market that sought only unfinished goods. Thus millers, tailors, shoemakers, carpenters, brewers, distillers, and other craftsmen produced their products for mostly local consumption. The demand for hats, gloves, household pottery, wooden tableware, or luxury items such as looking-glasses and playing cards was met through imports from England or the Continent.

In the late 1560s the government of Sir Henry Sidney attempted to curb the export of Irish raw materials and the reliance on foreign imports through the imposition of heavy duties on exports in order to stimulate the growth of an indigenous manufacturing sector. Sidney believed the towns to be the cornerstones of English rule in Ireland. He reasoned that the export of Irish materials to foreign markets ultimately limited the potential of Ireland's urban centers and unnecessarily strengthened the economies of rival countries, where unfinished Irish goods were processed before being re-exported to Ireland (at much higher prices) as luxury items. But because of nearly continuous Gaelic resistance to the imposition of Tudor rule, coupled with the outbreak of more serious rebellions in the early 1580s and late 1590s, the Crown sought to avoid alienating Ireland's loyal urban towns. The government's half-hearted efforts to reverse this economic trend failed to bolster the craft guilds, and the export of raw materials and the import of finished goods remained the dominant feature of urban life into the late sixteenth century. The nature of Tudor rule in Ireland, however, was changing: tensions had begun to develop between the large number of Protestant "New English" immigrants who dominated the increasingly centralized Tudor administration in Ireland

and the preponderantly Catholic urban hierarchy that controlled municipal government and the export trade.

THE SEVENTEENTH CENTURY: A PERIOD OF TRANSITION

Unlike their Tudor predecessors, the Stuarts inherited a fully conquered Ireland in 1603 and were less willing to acquiesce in a quasi-autonomous English urban population. Lord Deputy Mountjoy set the tone for this new relationship in 1603 when a delegation from Waterford refused him and his troops entry into the town, citing the municipal privilege enshrined in Waterford's centuries-old foundation charter. Mountjoy rudely responded that "he would cut King John's charter in pieces with King James's sword and if he entered the town by force, he would ruin it, and strew salt upon the ruins" (Sheehan, p. 110). The preponderantly Catholic inhabitants of many of Ireland's towns—with the notable exception of Dublin—had vainly adhered to the hope that James VI's accession to the English throne would see their political autonomy respected and Catholicism restored. But it quickly became clear that the Jacobean government intended no such thing. The Crown began legal proceedings against Dublin, Drogheda, Waterford, and Limerick in 1607 to review the rights enshrined in their respective charters, and the result was the levy of government taxes on all the towns' exports, together with the appointment of royal officers to most ports by 1612. Efforts were also made, particularly in the newly opened districts such as Ulster, to loosen the grip of the established urban hierarchy through both the development of new urban centers, populated by new English Protestants, and the encouragement of indigenous manufacture.

The Crown's attempts to transform urban areas into loyal but politically and economically subordinate bastions of Protestantism were largely unsuccessful. The hope that the planted urban population in Ulster would replicate the cultural and economic successes that had developed naturally over centuries in the older towns was dashed as the tide of new English settlers gravitated toward the more lucrative rural areas. Craftsmen too were drawn to the abundance of cheap land and readily adopted the novel status of landowner. Thus the newly created towns struggled both to attract a sustainable population and to promote manufacturing; the established urban hierarchy in the older urban centers, meanwhile, maintained a measure of municipal control and continued to dominate the booming export trade that had lately come to rely more heavily on cattle. In Dublin, however, the long-standing urban hierarchy had been consistently losing ground to new English interests for decades. And as the city entered a period of rapid expansion in the early seventeenth century, it was the sizeable Protestant mercantile community that came to dominate urban life. This religious and cultural divide between Dublin and Ireland's other major towns was brought into sharp relief during the Confederate Wars of the 1640s, when much of the urban population outside Dublin supported the Catholic Confederates.

From 1649 to 1660 the Catholic urban population lost control of municipal government and, crucially, was no longer permitted to engage in trade. During the rebellion of 1641 gold, armor, arms, and other provisions had passed through the port towns to the rebels from Europe. In many urban centers the Protestant population had suffered intimidation, and in Wexford bibles were publicly burned. The Cromwellian council at Dublin in 1656 took measures to ensure that this would not happen again and ordered that all "Irish Papists" were to be removed from port towns and not to be allowed to reside within two miles of any town. But in the absence of sufficient numbers of Protestants to replace the Catholic population (particularly in the more remote towns), such proclamations proved impossible to enforce and many Catholics remained. Urban life, however, had been utterly transformed as new English Protestants occupied the key offices of municipal government and set about changing the physical and cultural environment of Ireland's urban centers.

This transformation was most obvious in Dublin, where the rapidly expanding population, two-thirds of which were estimated to have been Protestant by 1685, soared to 60,000. Inhabiting a bustling center of manufacture and trade and the seat of national government, the population of Dublin in the late seventeenth century had access to a university, a second cathedral, a college of physicians, a theater, and a philosophical society. But change was not limited to Dublin. Unfettered from the constraints of stone-built defensive fortifications, the new urban dwellers constructed more uniform towns with houses situated on streets that were wider, straighter, and less densely populated. The transformation of the physical environment in Irish urban centers mirrored the cultural changes consequent on the arrival of large numbers of Protestant immigrants in the mid-seventeenth century. By the end of the seventeenth century urban life in Ireland had been brought more closely into line with urban culture in England, and these once independent hubs of economic activity had become wholly subordinated to an expanding British commercial market.

SEE ALSO Economy and Society from 1500 to 1690; Protestant Immigrants

Bibliography

Andrews, J. H. "Land and People, c. 1685." In *A New History of Ireland*. Vol. 3, *Early Modern Ireland, 1534–1691*, edited by T. W. Moody, F. X. Martin, and F. J. Byrne. 1976.

Butlin, R. D., ed. *The Development of the Irish Town.* 1977.

Clarke, Aidan. "The Irish Economy, 1600–60." In *A New History of Ireland*. Vol. 3, *Early Modern Ireland, 1534–1691*, edited by T. W. Moody, F. X. Martin, and, F. J. Byrne. 1976.

Clarke, Howard B., ed. *Irish Cities.* 1995.

Gillespie, Raymond. *The Transformation of the Irish Economy, 1550–1700.* 1991.

Harkness, David, and Mary O'Dowd, eds. *The Town in Ireland: Historical Studies xiii.* 1981.

Sheehan, Anthony. "Irish Towns in a Period of Change, 1558–1625." In *Natives and Newcomers: Essays on the Making of Irish Colonial Society, 1534–1641*, edited by C. Brady and R. Gillespie. 1986.

Christopher Maginn

~

Ussher, James

James Ussher (1581–1656), bishop of Meath (1621–1625) and archbishop of Armagh (1625–1656), was born on 4 January 1581 in Dublin, the fifth child of Arland Ussher and his wife, Margaret (née Stanyhurst). He was educated at the newly founded Trinity College, which he entered in 1594 as one of its first students. Ussher's early career was as an academic at Trinity, where he was appointed Professor of Theological Controversies in 1607 and published his first book in 1613 on the succession of the true Christian church. His scholarly efforts and his regular trips to England brought him to the notice of King James, who made him bishop of Meath in 1621 and archbishop of Armagh in 1625. As a bishop, Ussher tried to combine the role of scholar and ecclesiastical politician. A firm Calvinist, he published works of anti-Catholic controversial theology and also a highly influential account—*A Discourse of the Religion Anciently Professed by the Irish and British*—of the historical origins of the Church of Ireland, which by tracing its descent back to the Celtic church, provided Irish Protestants with a crucial sense of their Irish roots.

As a politician, Ussher became a member of the Irish Privy Council and leader of the Church of Ireland. Strongly antipapal, he used his influence in 1626 and 1627 to oppose the granting of toleration to Irish Catholics. But the arrival of Lord Deputy Wentworth in 1633 greatly diminished Ussher's role, as Archbishop Laud of Canterbury and his ally in Ireland, Bishop Bramhall of Derry, sought to reshape the Church of Ireland by driving out Calvinists and Presbyterians and bringing it into closer alignment with the Church of England. Ussher retreated to his study, working on his great historical investigation of the origins of Christianity in Britain and Ireland, published in 1639 as *Britannicarum ecclesiarum antiquitates*. In 1640 Ussher went to England where, following the outbreak of the Irish rising in 1641, he was to remain. As a highly respected scholar with an international reputation, Ussher was courted by both king and Parliament in 1641 and 1642. Despite his firm Calvinism and deep hostility to Catholicism, Ussher remained loyal to the king. After the defeat and execution of Charles, Ussher returned to London, where he concentrated on patristic and biblical scholarship, publishing in the 1650s his account of biblical chronology which dated the creation of the world to 23 October 4004 B.C.E. He married Phoebe Challoner in 1613 and had one daughter, Elizabeth.

SEE ALSO Bedell, William; Calvinist Influences in Early Modern Ireland; Trinity College

Bibliography

Ford, Alan. "James Ussher and the Creation of an Irish Protestant Identity." In *British Consciousness and Identity*, edited by B. I. Bradshaw and Peter Roberts. 1998.

Knox, R. B. *James Ussher, Archbishop of Armagh.* 1967.

Alan Ford

Veto Controversy

A key ingredient in securing Catholic support for passage of the Act of Union was the promise that it would be followed by legislation that would grant Emancipation, or the right of Catholics to take seats in Parliament. In the years immediately following the union, a powerful conservative lobby organized to prevent the passage of such an act, on the grounds that complete political freedom for Catholics was incompatible with the Protestant constitution and that Catholicism was a subversive force inimical to the future safety of Protestantism in Ireland. This sentiment was greatly assisted by propaganda linking the Catholic Church and its clergy to the atrocities of 1798, and it breathed new life into the doctrine of Protestant Ascendancy first enshrined by Bishop Richard Woodward of Cloyne in the 1780s. The strength of the anti-Catholic sentiment ensured the defeat of the first relief bill in 1807, after which the prime minister resigned and the government fell. Following this setback, in an attempt to appease Protestant fears of an accommodation granting political equality to Catholics, liberal supporters of Emancipation proposed that certain "securities" be attached to the legislation that would allow the government a measure of control over the workings of the Catholic Church. Chief among these was a government veto on the appointment of Catholic bishops, which was seen as a measure that would curtail the influence of Rome. Additional proposals included state payment of the clergy and the right of inspectors to scrutinize correspondence with the papacy.

It was a common feature of European political life at this time for the state to have a role in the appointment of bishops, and the Catholic hierarchy was initially willing to acquiesce in these demands. As opposition to Emancipation heightened with each passing year, however, a powerful group of lay Catholics led by Daniel O'Connell began to question openly the implications of the veto. For O'Connell and his followers the issue of who should have the final decision in the filling of vacant episcopal sees was directly related to the independence of the clergy and the amount of autonomy that Catholics could exercise in the regulation of their own affairs. The matter was especially tense because of the unique position of power and influence that bishops and priests held at all levels of Catholic society in Ireland. At a time when the demand for education and the spread of the English language indicated that ordinary Catholics were going through a process of "modernization," with all that this implied for their future role in politics, the role of the clergy as arbiters of public morality (and consequently political behavior) could hardly be denied. O'Connell perceived a hierarchy appointed at the will of Westminster as an agency of corruption, one that would hold the clergy, and consequently the entire Catholic population, in line with the demands of an imperial parliament and the forces of Protestant Ascendancy in Ireland. In opposing the veto, O'Connell cast his lot with the popular anti-establishment opinion and against the more traditional upper-class elements of the Irish Catholic world, including several peers and members of the hierarchy.

The showdown between the populist anti-veto elements led by O'Connell and the pro-veto campaigners came with a second attempt at securing passage of a relief bill in 1814. This new bill, which included a veto, was prepared by Henry Grattan in 1813 and was introduced by Canning in the following year. The bill was passed by the House of Commons and agreed upon by the Catholic Board. It also won the approval of the aristocratic elite of the Catholic Committee in Ireland, but it was rejected outright by O'Connell and his followers. In an attempt to thwart O'Connell's domination of Irish opinion on the matter, the English Catholic Board submitted the matter to Rome. Because of the threat from Napoleon the papacy was still beholden to the British government, and a conciliatory response was anticipated. The outcome was predictable. A famous rescript was delivered by the secretary of the Propaganda Fidei, Dr. Quarantotti, with a definitive recommendation that it be adopted. The Quarantotti rescript caused turmoil in Ireland. When it was rumored that the more conservative members of the hierarchy and the Catholic Committee were willing to accept the rescript, O'Connell threatened to take his campaign to the streets, warning the clergy that if they accepted the state veto, they would risk desertion by their congregations. This was the first occasion on which O'Connell showed his skill as a politician. His manipulation of the popular press to educate his followers about the veto and his fearless playing to the gallery of public opinion was the first indication of what such methods might achieve. As a result of O'Connell's imposing opposition, the controversial rescript was withdrawn for further consideration by the pope. Its successor, however, which appeared in May 1815, was still supportive of the original demand for a veto and state payment of the clergy. This time O'Connell was joined in his rejection by the hierarchy, whose members had now publicly embraced the popular position.

The rejection of the 1815 bill produced a paralyzing impasse between the pro-veto and anti-veto forces and led to the temporary collapse of the Catholic-led Emancipation movement. The consequences of this were twofold. First, the failure of Quarantotti to impose the demands of Rome on the Irish Catholic body meant that O'Connell's leadership was now authoritative, and little progress could be made without his support. Second, the demise of the Catholic-led effort opened the door for Protestant liberals to step into the breach and assume leadership of the movement. The future looked particularly bright when, following the death of Henry Grattan in 1820, the young and dynamic William Conyngham Plunket took his place as leader of the campaign. High hopes were attached to the bill that Plunket was preparing to introduce in 1822, particularly because prominent leaders of public opinion in England were willing to support the measure with the securities attached, and many in Ireland (especially among the hierarchy) would have accepted the veto as a last resort.

But the very prospect of Plunket's bill being successful had a galvanizing effect on the conservatives, who put their anti-Catholic campaign into high gear once again. Preparations for the submission of Plunket's bill in 1822 were marked by a rising tide of sectarianism in Ireland, intensified by the agrarian crisis, the Rockite movement, and verbal saber-rattling in public debate. Had Plunket's bill passed, it would undoubtedly have been accepted along with the securities. After the Commons approved the measure, however, it was ignominiously defeated by the House of Lords. This persuaded the Catholic body that they would never make any progress with the Emancipation question if they remained disunited. They were also convinced that the House of Lords would have no more respect for the bill with the veto than for one without it, and that they might just as well seek "complete emancipation."

The failure of Plunket's bill of 1823 was the last time that the veto was an issue in the Emancipation campaign. Following the events of 1821–22, the movement entered a new phase with the founding of the Catholic Association in January 1823. The aim of the association was not immediately to pursue Emancipation but to build a popular movement on the twin pillars of Catholic grievances and a powerful organization featuring mass participation in the political process. In the pursuit of both objectives O'Connell's success was phenomenal. By 1828 he had fashioned a movement that had succeeded in breaking the hold of the landlords on the electoral process and cleared the way for his own election as MP for Clare in 1828. O'Connell's tactics for securing these victories were first tested during the veto controversy of 1813–1814, which may in retrospect be seen as a trial run for the political revolution of the 1820s that ended with passage of the Catholic Relief Act in 1829.

SEE ALSO Catholic Emancipation Campaign; O'Connell, Daniel; Politics: 1800 to 1921—Challenges to the Union

Bibliography

Bartlett, Thomas. *The Fall and Rise of the Irish Nation: The Catholic Question, 1690–1830.* 1992.

MacDonagh, Oliver. *O'Connell: The Life of Daniel O'Connell, 1775–1847.* 1991.

O'Ferrall, Fergus. *Catholic Emancipation: Daniel O'Connell and the Birth of Irish Democracy, 1820–30.* 1986.

Irene Whelan

Jack B. Yeats, The Liffey Swim, *early twentieth century. A day in the life of Dublin shown with Yeats's sensitivity to detail.* COURTESY OF THE NATIONAL GALLERY OF IRELAND, CAT. NO. 941. © 2004 ARTISTS RIGHTS SOCIETY (ARS), NEW YORK/DACS, LONDON. REPRODUCED BY PERMISSION.

Visual Arts, Modern

The visual arts in Ireland have seen striking developments in the twentieth century, from the emergence of a distinctive school of Irish landscape painting, to the ascendancy of modernism and an international outlook that has dominated since the 1960s. The century also saw the establishment of art institutions that provided new venues for the display of art, and the formation in 1951 of the Arts Council, which provided an important measure of government's growing commitment to the arts.

At the beginning of the century, Irish painters who studied abroad continued to produce innovative work. William Leech (1881–1968), for instance, spent time in Brittany where, enriched by contacts with avant-garde art, he produced a series of dazzling painterly works. Roderic O'Conor (1860–1940) spent much of his career in France, and the early advances of modernism are detectable in his art. The first twentieth-century artist who made Ireland his subject matter, though, was Jack

B. Yeats (1871–1957). Yeats spent time traveling around the country painting images of Irish life and landscape, particularly the people and places he encountered as a boy in Sligo. Unlike his earlier art, which was grounded in the physical reality of the world around him, his later work is dominated by themes based on memory and past experiences. In these, Yeats's use of color and impasto and his dynamic, expressive brushwork, produce images and moods that make him unique in the Irish art world. Two other artists who were inspired by the west of Ireland in their choices of subject matter are Paul Henry (1876–1958) and Seán Keating (1889–1978). Henry spent nearly ten years in Achill, Co. Mayo; his paintings depict the cloudy skies, thatched cottages, and blue and purple mountains characteristic of the west of Ireland. His realistic interpretation of landscape inspired many eager followers such as James Humbert Craig (1878–1944), Letitia Mary Hamilton (1878–1964), and Maurice MacGonigal (1900–1979). Seán Keating was a student of William Orpen (1878–1931), whose teaching influenced a whole generation of Irish artists, and whose own superb portraits are magnificent in both tone value and color. Keating is

Paul Henry, Launching the Currach *(c. 1912–1919). The realism yet grandeur of Henry's paintings reveal much of Connemara scenery and life.* NATIONAL GALLERY OF IRELAND, CAT. NO. 1869. REPRODUCED BY PERMISSION.

known for his strong, dramatic compositions of life on the Aran Islands.

In 1920 Henry, Yeats, and others who were interested in modernist ideas set up the Society of Dublin Painters, which provided a communal focus for artists looking beyond Ireland's shores for inspiration. The Society was synonymous with the best of avant-garde Irish painting; in this milieu artists could experiment with new ideas. Among the pioneers of Irish modernism were Mainie Jellett (1897–1944), who first exhibited her cubist and abstract paintings at the society, Evie Hone (1894–1955), and Mary Swanzy (1882–1978).

Another important development in the interwar years was a desire by artists, both academic and avant-garde, to create a distinctive school of Irish art. Although this aspiration originated in the nineteenth century, it gained momentum following Ireland's political independence from Great Britain in 1922. What emerged in painting was a distinct vision of landscape, principally in the works of Henry, Craig, and MacGonigal. Unlike the earlier idyllic scenes, the new style offered realistic representations of the bleak, stark nature of the landscape and its inhabitants. In sculpture, artists

like Oliver Sheppard (1864–1941), Albert Power (1881–1945), and Oisín Kelly (1915–1981) tried to produce a recognizably Irish art: Sheppard through his choice of Irish themes, Power through a conscious selecting of Irish stone wherever possible, and Kelly through use of themes from Celtic folklore. At the same time, artists of the Arts and Crafts movement brought about a Celtic Revival, and much use was made of Celtic patterns in the manufacture of furniture, jewelry, and other ornamental and embroidery goods. With the great increase in church building, stained glass was much in demand, too; its two main exponents were Harry Clarke (1889–1931) and Evie Hone (1894–1955).

A growing dissatisfaction with the conservatism of the Royal Hibernian Academy prompted more adventurous artists to establish the Irish Exhibition of Living Art (IELA) in 1943. It marked an important watershed in the visual arts, becoming a significant annual event and representing the interests of those influenced by international trends. One of its most gifted members is Louis le Brocquy (b. 1916), whose best-known paintings are a series of highly original head images from the 1950s collectively known as "presences"; Brocquy used

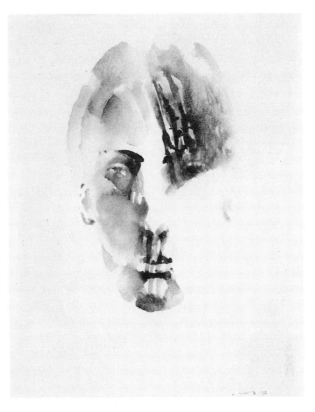

Louis le Brocquy, Study towards an Image of W. B. Yeats *(1975). Fascinated by the human image, le Brocquy's faces of great literary men, such as Yeats, Joyce, and Lorca, stare out at us from the canvas via his brilliant, built-up brushstrokes.* PHOTOGRAPH REPRODUCED WITH THE KIND PERMISSION OF THE TRUSTEES OF THE NATIONAL MUSEUMS AND GALLERIES OF NORTHERN IRELAND, U 2386.

Mainie Jellett, Decoration *(1923). Jellett is one of the few Irish artists influenced by the European avant-garde movements, specifically Cubism.* COURTESY OF THE NATIONAL GALLERY OF IRELAND, CAT. NO. 1326. REPRODUCED BY PERMISSION OF THE ESTATE FOR MAINIE JELLETT.

the face as a means of penetrating the essence of his subject. Other prominent artists involved with the IELA included Nano Reid (1900–1981) and Patrick Collins (1911–1994), whose diverse styles (the former powerfully expressionistic, the latter interpreting subject matter in a lyrical, poetic way) attest to the individualism of Irish artistic creativity throughout the century.

The most obvious feature of the visual arts since the 1960s is that it has become truly international in outlook. A genuinely original style of architecture has emerged. Its variety of modernist and postmodernist styles has dramatically changed the skyline of Ireland's capital city, Dublin. The establishment in 1967 of the international exhibition *ROSC* (an old Irish word meaning the poetry of vision) brought current works by out-

standing artists from all over the world to Dublin every two to four years. These influences have changed the character of Irish painting and sculpture, introducing a range of styles including abstraction in all its forms as well as diverse stylistic variations of figurative art. Sean Scully's (b. 1945) abstract paintings are in sharp contrast to the academic precision of Robert Ballagh's (b. 1943) figurative work and his later mulitmedia landscapes. At the end of the twentieth century political themes emerged: the "Troubles" in Northern Ireland, in the work of painters such as Rita Duffy (b. 1959) and Dermot Seymour (b. 1956), and in the photograhic work of Willie Doherty (b. 1959; and feminism, which has led to a reinterpretation of the female in painting and sculpture. Kathy Prendergast's (b. 1958) *Body Map Series* makes women's bodies a cultural site; Eithne Jordan's (b. 1954) painting within the new-expressionist wave articulates images of female and familial relationships in unusual configurations. Dorothy Cross (b. 1956), through her assemblages and installations, calls into question issues of gender and authority. In contrast, the sculpted work of Alice Maher (b. 1956) is often straightforwardly feminist.

The exhibition *L'Imaginaire Irlandais*, held in France in 1996, was a useful barometer of the state of the visual arts in Ireland at the end of the century. In providing an international arena for the concerns of contemporary Irish artists and their examination of politics, myths, and traditions, the exhibition included a cross section of work in a range of media, from photography and video to language and conceptual installations.

SEE ALSO Arts: Modern Irish and Anglo-Irish Literature and the Arts since 1800

Bibliography

Kennedy, S. B. *Irish Art and Modernism, 1880–1950.* 1991.

Walker, Dorothy. *Modern Art in Ireland.* 1997.

Síghle Bhreathnach-Lynch

W–Z

Walsh, William Joseph

Roman Catholic archbishop of Dublin, William Joseph Walsh (1841–1921) was born in Dublin on 30 January 1841. An only child, he attended John Henry (Cardinal) Newman's Catholic University of Ireland. In 1858 he entered Saint Patrick's College, Maynooth, Ireland's national seminary, and was ordained a priest in 1866. A brilliant student, he was soon appointed professor of dogmatic and moral theology at Maynooth. Further advancement came when he was appointed vice-president of the college in 1878 and president two years later.

Walsh first came to national prominence when he appeared as an expert witness on canon law in the celebrated O'Keefe law case in 1875. Following the death of Cardinal Edward McCabe in February 1885, Walsh was elected vicar capitular of the Dublin archdiocese. Pope Leo XIII appointed him archbishop of Dublin on 23 June of that same year. Irish nationalists viewed his elevation as a triumph over the British government, which had lobbied against the appointment of anyone with such pronounced nationalist sympathies.

Though an energetic diocesan administrator, Walsh also devoted much time to political matters. He worked to forge an enduring alliance between the Catholic Church in Ireland and the main force of Irish nationalism. He was an outspoken advocate of agrarian reform, lending his support to the Plan of Campaign in 1888. His greatest accomplishments, however, were in the sphere of education where he proved a vigorous and able champion of Catholic interests. He served on the National Education Board (1895–1901), the Intermediate Education Board (1892–1909), and the senates of the Royal University of Ireland (1883–1884) and the National University of Ireland (1908–1921). In 1908 he

was appointed the first chancellor of the National University. He died on 9 April 1921.

SEE ALSO Roman Catholic Church: 1829 to 1891; Roman Catholic Church: Since 1891

Bibliography

Larkin, Emmet. *The Roman Catholic Church and the Plan of Campaign, 1886–88.* 1978.

Larkin, Emmet. *The Roman Catholic Church in Ireland and the Fall of Parnell, 1888–91.* 1979.

Miller, David W. *Church, State, and Nation in Ireland, 1898–1921.* 1973.

Morrissey, Thomas. *William Joseph Walsh: Archbishop of Dublin, 1841–1921.* 2000.

David C. Sheehy

Wentworth, Thomas, First Earl of Strafford

Thomas Wentworth, first earl of Strafford (1593–1641), lord deputy and subsequently lord lieutenant of Ireland, was born on Good Friday 1593 (13 April) in London. In the 1620s he sat in every English parliament except during the 1626 session. In June 1627 he was imprisoned for having refused the forced loan, a fiscal device that the king used to raise money for warfare without parliamentary consent. One year later, howev-

Sir Thomas Wentworth, first earl of Strafford, baron of Raby (1593–1641). Engraving by F. Holl after a painting by Anthony Van Dyk, c. 1635. © HULTON ARCHIVE/GETTY IMAGES. REPRODUCED BY PERMISSION.

er, he made his peace with the king and was elevated to the peerage, and in December 1628 Charles I appointed him lord president of the north. He actively sought advancement, and on 12 January 1632 he was appointed lord deputy of Ireland. Wentworth mistrusted the class of Protestant officeholders and planters (the "New English") whom he found in power when he came to Ireland about one year later, and he was prepared to be temporarily tolerant toward Catholics until church and state had been sufficiently strengthened to enforce the official religious settlement. In 1634 and 1635 he deliberately played Protestants off against Catholics and vice versa in the Irish parliament, with considerable success. Armed with new statutes, Wentworth and Bishop Bramhall of Derry pursued a campaign for the reendowment of the Protestant Church of Ireland that affected primarily Protestant landowners. Wentworth's plans to confiscate vast tracts of land in areas that had not yet been planted, however, threatened Catholic proprietors, Gaelic and Old English alike, much more than Protestant ones. Although plantation plans for Connacht and other areas could not—in the end—be fully realized before 1640, they created a general feeling of insecurity among landowners. Other measures seen as arbitrary and vindictive by both Protestants and Catholics also contributed to Wentworth's increasing unpopularity. In 1638 the crisis in Scotland began to undermine his position in Ireland. Having refused to support the earl of Antrim's plan for an invasion of Scotland in 1639, he recruited an army of Catholic soldiers in Ireland himself—to be used against the Covenanters who had risen against Charles I to defend the Scottish church and its Calvinist traditions against English interference—in 1640. In January 1640 Wentworth was elevated to the position of lord lieutenant and made an earl, taking the title of Strafford. His attempt to save the king's cause in the fight against the Scots in the summer of 1640 failed, and after the long parliament had met, he was impeached by the English House of Commons. The majority of the more serious charges against Wentworth during the impeachment related to his period of office in Ireland. With great skill Strafford took apart most of the charges raised against him, but he was nevertheless condemned by bill of attainder and executed on 12 May at Tower Hill, London.

SEE ALSO Bedell, William; Graces, The; Monarchy; Rebellion of 1641

Bibliography

Kearney, Hugh. *Strafford in Ireland: A Study in Absolutism.* 1959. 2d edition, 1989.

Merritt, J. F., ed. *The Political World of Thomas Wentworth, Earl of Strafford, 1621–1641.* 1996.

Wedgwood, Cicely V. *Thomas Wentworth, First Earl of Strafford, 1593–1641: A Revaluation.* 1964.

Ronald G. Asch

Whiteboys and Whiteboyism

The Whiteboys were agrarian rebels based in Munster and south Leinster who engaged in two major struggles in the mid-eighteenth century with local gentry, Church of Ireland clergy, and other enemies. The term *Whiteboyism* was later used as shorthand for describing what seemed like endemic violence in the Irish countryside. Some modern historians have even extended this usage to refer to prefamine agrarian rebellion in Ireland. The Whiteboy rebellions occurred between 1761 and

1765 and between 1769 and 1776, centering on Tipperary and Kilkenny, with other troubled counties including Cork, Limerick and Waterford and, later, Wexford, Queen's County, Carlow, and Kildare. There were peaks of violence in the spring of 1762, the winter of 1763 to 1764, and especially in 1772 and 1775.

THE TWO OUTBREAKS

The first signs of Whiteboy trouble appeared in November 1761 when protests against the tithe collected on potatoes occurred in southeast Tipperary. In the following months the protests rapidly spread into the parishes nearby in counties Cork and Waterford and eventually into Kilkenny and Limerick by early 1762. The protests entered the wider public consciousness in 1762, especially after hedges on the property of the duke of Devonshire were leveled and threatening letters were sent to Protestant gentry in Tallow demanding that their horses be handed over and that the jail be opened. The response of Dublin Castle to such actions was swift, with regiments of dragoons and light infantry being sent to the affected areas. The Whiteboys seemed to retreat into silence, yet they reemerged a year later in Tipperary and Kilkenny, now the worst affected counties. This second upsurge of protests against tithes on potatoes, conacre rents, and the enclosure of common lands met with much more severe repression, and by 1765 it was confined to occasional violence in Kilkenny.

Four years later, counties Kilkenny and Tipperary were again the center of the revived Whiteboy movement. This time Dublin Castle responded much more slowly, owing to the quiet building of Whiteboy momentum up to 1772 and to the much more threatening Steelboy violence in northeast Ulster. By 1772 the Whiteboy troubles had spread beyond their original focus, and all the counties of south Leinster were gripped over the next three years by a spiral of violence.

The two Whiteboys outbreaks had differences in their causes and the composition of their members. The first Whiteboys outbreak saw large-scale mobilization of hundreds of Whiteboys over regions, which had much to do with the initial rapid spread of the rebellion. In the later outbreak the Whiteboys in smaller numbers still traveled considerable distances, but this time to punish wrongdoers or seize arms and horses rather than to mount large-scale attacks on property or spread the rebellion. There was continuity in what was becoming the format of the classic Irish agrarian rebellion. The Whiteboys employed symbolism, most famously in the wearing of white shirts or overgarments from which the rebels got their name, but also in taking as aliases the names of Queen Sive or Captain Firebrand, figures from folklore. Theatricality accompanied real violence, with graves being dug, mock gallows erected, and anonymous threatening letters sent, alongside property destruction, murders, and maimings.

Violence of the personal sort increased over time. This may have stemmed from the severity of the repression of the first Whiteboys, especially in Tipperary where a popular priest, Father Nicholas Sheehy of Clogheen, was persecuted and eventually executed by the Protestant gentry of that county in 1766. The later Whiteboys gave less quarter, particularly to informers and zealous magistrates. The violence of the later outbreak was also owing to increasing clashes with anti-Whiteboy associations and regular troops.

The Whiteboys swore in entire communities and parishes as conspirators. The organization had a military tinge, suggesting the role of those who had served in the French or Spanish armies, whose influence was reflected in marching and the confident use of arms. In the later outbreak, involvement of farmers and their sons—members of a higher social stratum—was shown in the greater numbers of horses used and in the causes of that rebellion. Beyond the local particularities of the symbolic names used or the tunes played to mobilize supporters, little distinguishes these southern disturbances from the Ulster agrarian outbreaks of the time.

CAUSES

With regard to causes, contemporaries, especially the Protestant elite in Ireland, were quick to see irredentist Catholic rebelliousness. The 1761 to 1765 outbreak, at least in its first three years, coincided with the Seven Years' War, which summoned up fears of French or Spanish invasion and boosted the activities of recruiters for those armies and the survival of at least some form of Jacobitism in Munster and the Butler heartland of Kilkenny. Such claims were less a feature of the second outbreak, perhaps owing to the absence of war, but there was some Protestant rallying of exclusive local militias. Political causes were probably incidental, but observers considered as important the near electoral success of the convert Mathew family in Tipperary in 1761 and the continuing strength of Catholic organization in the Blackwater valley in Munster.

Mid-century economic changes and their consequences were just as crucial. The first Whiteboy outbreak focused on the tithe on potatoes collected by the local Anglican clergy, enclosures by landlords and farmers keen to cash in on the rising demand for Irish cattle and wool, and other burdens suffered in the main by those on the worst tenures—agricultural laborers, woolen workers, and others in the towns of the region.

Part of this was resistance to landlords, clergy, and farmers who were profiting from war and economic growth and sought higher tithes or rents to meet their rising expectations. There was a hearkening back to better times or anger at not doing well economically in a period of growth.

The second outbreak also had an economic context, though this was more the effect of a crisis caused by bad grain harvests between 1769 and 1771 and in 1773 and the slump in both the linen and woolen trades between 1772 and 1774. More so than in the earlier troubles, these harsh facts are secondary to the major cause of the 1769 through 1776 protests: the tithe on corn. This grievance explains the geographical shift to south Leinster from the pastures of Munster, but it also reveals that the later Whiteboys, from the higher social stratum of farmers, were much more concerned with defending gains they had made in the 1760s from the bounties paid on corn sent to Dublin. Their targets reflected their priorities: tithe proctors and tenants who offered higher rents, especially Waterford dairymen, were chosen for attack by these Whiteboys. This was less an outbreak of nostalgia and more of a sophisticated resistance to any erosion of newfound wealth.

AUTHORITIES' RESPONSE

The response of the authorities, particularly at the local level, hardened over time. In the first outbreak, officials at Dublin Castle were very critical of magistrates who were too timid to act on their own initiative but quick to summon troops. By 1763 more local gentry in Tipperary and Kilkenny formed associations, some of which sprang back into life in the early 1770s to deal with the revived Whiteboy threat. In fact militias and Volunteers appeared in these counties even before the impetus provided later by the American war and the Patriot politicians. At this local level, rewards were subscribed to for the worst crimes, notably the killing of the Tipperary magistrate Ambrose Power in 1775. As in Ulster, there were active magistrates ready to pursue and capture Whiteboys, and some, like Power or Lord Carrick, gained a reputation for their actions and their readiness to both summon and use troops.

A similarly mixed response and change over time occurred at the central level. The earl of Halifax, viceroy in the years 1761 to 1763, was criticized in London for leniency and readiness to dismiss accusations of French plots in Munster. There is no doubt that Halifax did lean to the view that local Protestant landlords had brought this crisis on themselves, and his legal officials did stop the judicial bloodletting desired by some of the gentry. Later viceroys, notably the earl of Hertford, proved to

be more vacillating in the face of local pressure, as seen for example in the trial and execution of Father Nicholas Sheehy.

In a sign of hardening attitudes, tougher laws were enacted in 1765 and 1776. The first Whiteboy act made crimes against property by a group of more than five persons, the tendering of oaths, and the rescuing of prisoners all punishable by death; these felonies were added to by the 1775 act. In addition the 1765 law made it possible to exact compensation from a disturbed barony for property crimes committed there. In frustration at the Whiteboys, the Catholic hierarchy issued condemnations of the agrarian rebels and in 1779 threatened to excommunicate offenders.

SEE ALSO Defenderism; Irish Tithe Act of 1838; Land Questions; Oakboys and Steelboys; Tithe War (1830–1838); Trade Unions; **Primary Documents:** On the Whiteboys (1769)

Bibliography

Donnelly, James S., Jr. "The Whiteboy Movement, 1761–1765." *Irish Historical Studies* 21 (1978): 20–54.

Donnelly, James S., Jr. "Irish Agrarian Rebellion: The Whiteboys of 1769–1776." *Proceedings of the Royal Irish Academy* 83c (1983): 293–331.

Eoin Magennis

Wilde, Oscar

Oscar Wilde (1854–1900), essayist, poet, novelist, and dramatist, was born on 16 October 1854 at 15 Westland Row, Dublin. He was the second son of Sir William Wilde, a noted eye surgeon and folklorist, and Jane Francesca Wilde, who as "Speranza" had penned inflammatory nationalist verse in her youth. Educated at Portora Royal School, Trinity College, Dublin, and Magdalen College, Oxford, Wilde first made his name as a self-appointed "Professor of Aesthetics," touring the United States in the early 1880s and lecturing on such subjects as the "House Beautiful" and, in San Francisco, on his Irish nationalist sympathies. His first literary success was with the Gothic novel *The Picture of Dorian Gray* (1891), which was swiftly followed by a series of society comedies that simultaneously flattered and satirized Wilde's fashionable West End audiences: *Lady Windermere's Fan* (1892), *A Woman of No Importance* (1893), *An Ideal Husband* (1895), and *The Importance of Being Earnest* (1895). A noted wit and dandy, Wilde gave an outsider's informed, fascinated, yet skeptical view of the workings of the Victorian aristocracy—with its casual cruelties and sexual double standard—and of the pragmatism undermining the high-sounding sentiments of imperialist politics. Wilde, as an Irishman and a married homosexual, was doubly estranged from the conventional English society that he both commented upon and courted. As his celebrity grew, his double life became ever more precarious, and he began to conduct a semipublic affair with Lord Alfred Douglas ("Bosie"), the dangerously unstable son of the Marquess of Queensberry. At the apex of his fame—with *An Ideal Husband* and *The Importance of Being Earnest* both playing to packed audiences in the West End—Wilde took out a libel action against Queensberry (who had accused him of "posing as a Somdomite [sic]"), provoking his own subsequent trial and conviction for gross indecency. His friend Frank Harris believed that Wilde was put on trial not just for his sexuality but for his nationality as well, claiming that in front of an English judge and jury Wilde had as much chance of being found innocent as one of the Invincibles, the group responsible for the Phoenix Park murders in 1882. Wilde died virtually penniless in Paris after serving two years of hard labor, and was written out of literary and cultural history until his recuperation in the 1980s as a contemporary gay icon and his reevaluation as one of the most important figures of the Irish literary renaissance.

This recuperation has involved a rediscovery of Wilde's importance as an art theorist as well as a writer. The aesthetic theories that he outlined in his essays, collected as *Intentions* (1891), anticipate to a surprising degree some of the central tenets and assumptions of both modernism and contemporary cultural theory, such as the ideas of the dispersed and decentered nature of human identity and of language being "the parent and not the child of thought" (*Complete Works*, p. 1,023). At the same time, Wilde's studied nonchalance is now seen as a mask for the seriousness of his artistic ambitions: Much critical work has concentrated on him as a professional writer in a recognizably modern context, collaborating with other theatrical practitioners, polishing and revising his work through composition and rehearsal into performance.

SEE ALSO Arts: Modern Irish and Anglo-Irish Literature and the Arts since 1800; Literature: Anglo-Irish Literature in the Nineteenth Century

Bibliography

Ellmann, Richard. *Oscar Wilde.* 1987.

Holland, Merlin, ed. *The Complete Letters of Oscar Wilde.* 2000.

Sammells, Neil. *Wilde Style: The Plays and Prose of Oscar Wilde.* 2000.

Wilde, Oscar. *The Complete Works of Oscar Wilde.* New edition, 1966.

Neil Sammells

Wild Geese—The Irish Abroad from 1600 to the French Revolution

There are several interpretations of the term *Wild Geese.* Traditionally it referred to a relatively small number of the Catholic landed elites who, in the face of English and Protestant oppression, fled Ireland after the Treaty of Limerick in 1691 and precipitated the final collapse of Gaelic resistance to English rule in Ireland. The definition, however, has been considerably broadened by historians to include all those who left Ireland to serve in the armies of continental Europe from the sixteenth to the eighteenth centuries, including the wives, families, and dependents of soldiers. In popular writings the interpretation has been further extended to include all Irish emigrants of whatever period and character and even their descendants now living abroad.

THE MILITARY COMMUNITY IN EUROPE

One of the largest identifiable groups of people to leave Ireland in the period 1600 to 1789 is that of the Irish who went to serve in the huge continental armies of seventeenth- and eighteenth-century Europe. Although enclaves of Irish could be found in regiments of the Baltic states, Russia, and Poland, the vast majority of Irish soldiers served in the armies of Spain in the sixteenth and early seventeenth centuries (including in South America) and in France and later Austria in the second half of the seventeenth and the eighteenth centuries.

Overall figures indicate that foreign military service represented a mass movement of people out of Ireland. In 1635 there were an estimated 7,000 Irishmen enlisted in the Army of Flanders in the Spanish Netherlands. Following the collapse of the Irish Confederate Army, 22,531 Irish troops were delivered to Spain between 1641 and 1654. Between 1634 and 1660 more than

30,000 Irishmen were recruited into the French army. Following the Williamite war (1689–1691) an estimated 30,000 soldiers left Ireland to fight in Irish brigades for France.

This military group consisted mainly of family and kin groupings who tended to form clusters of Irish settlements in specific parts of cities or towns. Galicia in Spain, Brittany, Belgium, and the southwest of France were particularly popular destinations. Irish officers intermarried with Irish merchant families, and the military group was closely connected both by family and political ties to the various political and religious exile groups in Catholic Europe. Each Irish company in the Catholic armies of France and Spain was assigned a chaplain, which helped to cement links between the military and the numerous Irish religious colleges in Europe. Clerical assistance in the handling of investments and legal documentation was to prove crucial to the survival of Irish communities in Europe before the French Revolution.

THE MERCHANT COMMUNITY IN EUROPE

By 1600 there was already an extensive trade network between Ireland and the Atlantic seaboard of Europe, including particularly the ports of France, Spain, the Low Countries, and Britain. The seventeenth century witnessed a huge upsurge in this trade, and transient Irish merchants were replaced by Irish merchants residing abroad. Family groupings were so evident in the resulting merchant communities that certain surnames could easily be identified with specific towns. The Stritches and Arthurs of Limerick, for example, settled in Nantes, while the Martin, Lynch, and Kirwan families of Galway went to Saint-Malo. Most merchants were initially Old English, but Gaelic families became much more prominent in trading circles as the seventeenth century progressed. This led to tensions between Old English and Gaelic families in both merchant and military circles. In general, Irish communities in large ports were mainly Old English, and smaller or inland towns were associated with Gaelic names. There was a remarkable degree of integration between these Irish families and their local communities by the second generation in terms of social position, intermarriage, and language. Because these families were Catholic, both France and Spain allowed them a legal status that was almost on a par with that of their own citizens; such status was not generally open to members of other nationalities.

Most Irish communities that emerged in early modern Europe became immersed in both the culture and the politics of the Catholic Counter-Reformation. They subsequently produced a cultural ideology that saw Catholicism as the inherent factor that united those of Norman and Gaelic descent into one nation and identified Protestant England as the enemy of the nation. This ideology and the literature that stemmed from it ultimately helped to create an Irish identity that equated Irishness with Catholicism and did much to promote the belief that Protestant oppression was the main reason why so many left Ireland.

THE NEW WORLD

Irish men and women also became colonizers. In the seventeenth century some 50,000 to 100,000 men and women left Ireland for the West Indies and North American colonies, and another 250,000 to 400,000 departed in the years 1700 to 1776. Apart from those forced under various government schemes to go to the New World, there were four categories of Irish people attracted to the Americas: English and Scottish tenants and laborers who had come over to plantations in Ireland where they were now dissatisfied; vagrants who sought employment overseas; Old English and some Gaelic landowners deprived of land by confiscation; and a small group of Irish landowning entrepreneurs who hoped to acquire further lands in the new colonies. The majority went as indentured servants, working as servants to planters for a period of three to seven years in return for their passage out. If a servant survived the period of service, he or she could become a paid laborer or even a small planter.

Irishmen were involved in the short-lived colonies in Virginia in the 1580s. A colony of Irish adventurers was established at the mouth of the Amazon by Sir Thomas Row in 1612. The Caribbean also was a popular destination. There was a remarkable growth in the number of Irish Catholic laborers in the Leeward Islands and Barbados from the 1630s. Nevis and Montserrat became almost exclusively Irish colonies. By 1669 there were an estimated 12,000 Irish living in the West Indies. In North America an Irish settlement was established in Newfoundland in the 1620s. With the collapse of several Irish colonies in the Caribbean following the importation of Negro slaves, more Irish migrated to colonies such as Virginia, Maryland, and the Carolinas. Most of those who emigrated from Ireland in the seventeenth century were Catholic, and they went as individuals rather than in family groupings. This and the pervasive anti-Catholic sentiments in many colonies ensured that they did not form ethnic communities but were absorbed instead into Protestant colonial networks. Few settled in New England or Massachusetts, where in general Catholics were frowned upon by the local authorities.

PATTERNS OF MIGRATION

The conquest of Ireland led to a level of economic, social, and political dislocation that undoubtedly resulted in waves of mass migration from Ireland during the early modern period. Thousands of Irish left for Spain after the defeat of the predominantly Gaelic forces at the Battle of Kinsale. The entire Catholic merchant class of Waterford went abroad in the 1650s following Cromwellian measures that precluded them from trade. Vagrants and convicts were sent to Virginia as early as the 1620s by English government officials. And between 1652 and 1656 an estimated 35,000 priests, soldiers, and soldiers' wives and children, together with widows and orphans of those who were killed in the wars, were deported to the West Indies.

Early modern migration cannot be simply defined as a response to political crises in Ireland because economic factors played a part as well. The migration of poorer Irish in the late 1620s and early 1630s to Britain and the Continent was caused by food shortages and plague. Wider European politics in the form of state buildings and confessionalization constituted another key factor in the movement of Irish people. The need for manpower during the Thirty Years' War resulted in the recruitment of over 100,000 men from Ireland. The stabilization of Irish immigrant groups from the 1660s and the establishment of major Irish colleges such as Paris and Nantes in the 1670s and 1680s reflected the increasing level of organization of the absolutist French state under Louis XIV. Increasing social regulation of the poor during this period created a distinction between the deserving and undeserving poor, which prompted legislation in most European countries to define begging without a license as a crime. This forced many poorer people to leave their localities or countries. It was a particular feature of Ireland, where poor-law relief was virtually nonexistent owing to the weak infrastructure of both the Established Church and the state at the local level.

SEE ALSO Colonial Theory from 1500 to 1690; Irish Colleges Abroad until the French Revolution; Land Settlements from 1500 to 1690; O'Mahony, Conor, S. J.

Bibliography

Anderson, Malcolm, and Eberhard Bort, eds. *If the Irish Ran the World—Montserrat, 1630–1730.* 1997.

Bishop, Patrick. *The Irish Empire.* 1999.

Coogan, Tim P. *Wherever Green Is Worn.* 2001.

Henry, Gráinne. *The Irish Military Community in Spanish Flanders, 1586–1621.* 1992.

O'Connor, Thomas, ed. *The Irish in Europe, 1580–1815.* 2001.

O'Sullivan, Patrick. *The Irish World Wide: History, Heritage, Identity.* 6 vols. 1992.

Quinn, David B. *Ireland and America: Their Early Associations, 1500–1640.* 1991.

Silke, John J. "The Irish Abroad, 1534–1691." In *A New History of Ireland.* Vol. 3. 3d edition, 1991.

Stradling, R. A. *The Spanish Monarchy and Irish Mercenaries.* 1994.

Gráinne Henry

Williamite Wars

See Jacobites and the Williamite Wars.

Women and Children in the Industrial Workforce

Beginning at the end of the seventeenth century, women and children played a central role in the burgeoning Irish textile industry. Explanation of their extensive presence requires attention to the intersection of class and gender stratification and the accumulation of profit. Since women and children were culturally defined as dependent on adult males, their labor was paid less than men's, and the cheap labor pool they supplied both increased employers' profits and frequently retarded technological innovations.

THE PROTO-INDUSTRIAL PERIOD, 1690–1825

Between 1690 and 1825 the Irish textile industry gained prominence. Although debate exists about the consequences of the British Woolen Act of 1698 that prohibited the export of Irish woolen goods to foreign ports, the production of frieze and old drapery expanded in many southeastern Irish towns. The division of labor in domestic wool production was typical of the Irish textile industry: Men wove cloth, women carded and washed raw wool and spun yarn, and children picked the wool, wound bobbins, and filled shuttles. A few women, mostly widows, were clothiers responsible for the organization of production and the marketing of cloth. L. A. Clarkson's evidence from Carrick-on-Suir, Co. Tipperary, shows that in 1799, 65 percent of em-

Female workers in Chartres's linen mill, Belfast, c. 1840. FROM MR. AND MRS. SAMUEL CARTER HALL, *IRELAND: ITS SCENERY, CHARACTER, ETC.* (1841–1843).

ployed females produced textiles, compared with 24 percent of employed males.

Narrow or bandle linen had been produced by women for centuries. However, linen's rapid commercial expansion after 1696 was dependent on duty-free access to English markets. In the proto-industrial period linen yarn and cloth were produced by a stratified class of tenant farmers who combined the production of yarn and cloth with small-scale farming. The male household head worked the land while his sons wove cloth and helped during harvest season. If a household lacked sons, journeymen, apprentice weavers, or extended kin were employed. Women and children helped to harvest and prepare the flax, spun it into yarn to be woven or sold, and wound yarn onto bobbins. Women were responsible for domestic tasks such as childcare, cooking and cleaning, and spun when they had spare time. Spinning was so important that often kin or itinerant spin-

ners were hired to spin for a weaver in return for board, lodging, or a small wage.

Technological innovations in this period affected the sexual division of labor. Early in the eighteenth century women bleached linen cloth, but in the 1730s bleaching and finishing were the first processes to be centralized by capitalists who invested in time-saving technology that came to be used by men. Although male children were employed at open-air bleachgreens, relatively few women were. Similarly, seasonal water-powered flax-scutching mills multiplied in the late eighteenth century; women and children often performed ancillary tasks such as bruising, rolling, and stricking of flax for male scutchers. Such tasks posed persistent dangers owing to dust and unfenced machinery. Finally, after the introduction of the flying shuttle in 1808, women (typically, young daughters) increasingly turned to linen weaving.

Yarn spinning always had a commercial side linked to demands for yarn by weavers in the northeast of Ireland and for warp by cotton weavers in Lancashire, England. Although women's earnings helped to pay the family's rent or to lease larger plots of land, spinning was poorly remunerated and of lower status than weaving. Spinners earned from three to six pence per day, and weavers earned from one to five shillings, depending on demand and the type of cloth. Labor in Ireland was cheap because agrarian households absorbed part of the cost of reproducing their labor by leasing land to grow food and flax. Jane Gray (1993) argues that the cheap labor of spinners was integral to uneven capitalist development because merchants profited from buying cheap yarn in the western counties and selling it to manufacturers in northeast Ulster.

In the 1770s and 1780s the semiautonomous Irish Parliament acted to encourage and protect the cotton manufacture that had expanded in the Belfast vicinity. From its inception, cotton-yarn spinning was located in factories, with machinery powered by water or steam, and relied on cheap female and child labor. The Irish cotton industry was more heavily dependent on female labor than was the English industry: the male-to-female ratio in Belfast was 1:2, and in Lancashire, 1:1. The wages of women and children were also lower—in 1833 wages were 72 percent of those in Lancashire (O'Hearn 1994).

The lower cost of labor in the agrarian protoindustrial system deterred technological innovations in cotton, and cloth was produced by rural handloom weavers until the mid-nineteenth century. Although cotton handloom weavers were typically male, cotton was easier to weave than linen, and as mechanized cotton spinning declined in the 1820s and 1830s, handloom weavers' wages fell. These circumstances attracted women to cotton weaving; they comprised 31 percent of cotton weavers by 1851 in counties Antrim, Armagh, and Down.

FACTORY PRODUCTION OF TEXTILES, 1825 TO THE PRESENT

The prevalence of children's working long hours in unhealthy conditions in British textile factories led to state efforts, beginning in 1819, to limit their working hours and ages. In 1844 factory children were required to attend school for a partial day (as "halftimers"). The minimum age of employment was raised from nine in 1819 to ten in 1879; in 1891 the minimum age was again raised to eleven. However, the conflicting interests of working-class parents who needed their children's wages, and the accumulation of profits by factory owners, negatively affected working-class children's schooling.

Cheap labor also retarded technological innovations in the linen industry, which resumed its dominance after cotton's collapse. In 1825 the wet-spinning process enabled fine linen yarn to be produced more quickly and cheaply by workers, thus eliminating handspinning. Thereafter, displaced handspinners were workers in spinning mills, wound yarn for handloom weavers, wove linen cloth on handlooms, or were absorbed into the sewing industry. Although periodic investigations of working conditions in spinning mills were conducted, dust and moist heat persistently compromised workers' health.

Until the 1860s linen weaving remained unmechanized and largely decentralized. Handloom weavers working in factories were typically men, but in weaving households low wages intensified the reliance on child labor for long hours. During the 1860s and 1870s the number of powerlooms expanded. In powerloom factories winders and weavers were women because factory discipline and deskilling were distasteful to skilled male handloom weavers. Poor working conditions in weaving factories resulted in these occupations, as well as those in spinning mills, being classified as dangerous trades.

The flexibility of production in the sewing industry generated an intricate division of labor between relatively high-status female factory operatives and sweated homeworkers or outworkers. The major difference between indoor factory work and outdoor or home work was the failure to regulate the ages and working conditions of home workers under the Factory Acts. Despite long hours of labor by women and children, the work was considered intermittent and supplemental. Problems involved in regulation proved insurmountable since inspectors could not visit all homes and lists of outworkers were often incomplete. In the 1820s and 1830s Irish firms dealing in sewn muslin established warehouses where young girls from age ten were employed as apprentices. Larger numbers of children and women were employed as sewers at home; Brenda Collins estimates the number at 125,000 in 1851 (1988). Embroidery and laces were produced in factories, convents, and homes, taking advantage of surplus female labor in the northern counties. In the making-up branch of the linen industry, handkerchiefs were produced in hemstitching factories and homes around Lurgan, Co. Armagh, and the production of underclothing and shirts employed large numbers of women from the 1840s in Derry, Donegal, and Tyrone. By 1875 there were 4,000 to 5,000 indoor workers and 12,000 to 15,000 outdoor workers in these counties (Collins

1988). Donegal was also the center for the machine and hand-knitting industries. This and the Irish homespun-tweed industry, concentrated in counties Mayo, Kerry, and Donegal, were poorly paid occupations for women.

Although northeast Ireland was the world's leading producer of linen until World War I, thereafter the industry declined, creating massive female unemployment. Between 1942 and 1983 rayon production assumed importance, and the cheap, skilled, and unorganized pool of female labor was a strong attraction for capitalists.

Thus the Irish textile industry consistently depended on the cheap labor of women and children. The prevalence of young women and children generated camaraderie and vibrant shop-floor cultures that are well documented in studies of the linen industry. However, the rate of trade-union organization for women was low relative to men because women were not identified as autonomous agents, and wage and occupational discrimination was prevalent, limiting women's livelihoods. Today, in the small number of surviving textile firms, wages for women remain low, despite fair employment laws that eliminate gender-based discrimination.

SEE ALSO Factory-Based Textile Manufacture; Industrialization; Rural Industry; Women and Work since the Mid-Nineteenth Century

Bibliography

Clarkson, L. A. "Love, Labour, and Life: Women in Carrick-on-Suir in the Late Eighteenth Century." *Irish Economic and Social History* 20 (1993): 18–34.

Cohen, Marilyn. *Linen, Family, and Community in Tullylish, County Down, 1690–1914.* 1997.

Cohen, Marilyn, ed. *The Warp of Ulster's Past: Interdisciplinary Perspectives on the Irish Linen Industry, 1700–1920.* 1997.

Collins, Brenda. "Sewing and Social Structure: The Flowerers of Scotland and Ireland." In *Economy and Society in Scotland and Ireland, 1500–1939*, edited by Rosalind Mitchison and Peter Roebuck. 1988.

Crawford, W. H. "Women in the Domestic Linen Industry." In *Women in Early Modern Ireland*, edited by Margaret MacCurtain and Mary O'Dowd. 1991.

Daly, Mary E. *Women and Work in Ireland.* 1997.

Gray, Jane. "Rural Industry and Uneven Development: The Significance of Gender in the Irish Linen Industry." *Journal of Peasant Studies* 20 (1993): 590–611.

Messenger, Betty. *Picking Up the Linen Threads.* 1980.

Neill, Margaret. "Homeworkers in Ulster, 1850–1911." In *Coming into the Light: The Work, Politics, and Religion of Women in Ulster, 1840–1995*, edited by Janice Holmes and Diane Urquhart. 1994.

O'Hearn, Denis. "Innovation and the World-System Hierarchy: British Subjugation of the Irish Cotton Industry, 1780–1830." *American Journal of Sociology* 100 (November 1994): 587–621.

Marilyn Cohen

∼

Women and Work since the Mid-Nineteenth Century

Understanding women and work requires an awareness of the nature of women's work and how it is measured. Housework, paid and unpaid, has been central to the lives of women, but services provided by women on a voluntary basis at home are not counted as "work" in economic terms. Over the past one hundred and fifty years there has been a steady decline in paid domestic service and a growth, then eventual decline, in the number of full-time "housewives." These trends have been accompanied by an increase in the productivity of housework as a result of mechanization. In contrast with single women and widows, the classification of married women has posed problems that signal the need for vigilance in interpreting trends in labor-force participation.

At the 1841 census the Irish census commissioners devised a classification of occupations comprising nine categories or orders. Every adult was classified according to his or her occupation or "chief business in life." Wives who had a specified occupation (for example, dressmaking) were counted as such and included under the appropriate order (in this case, clothing). Changes in classification methods ordered by the British census commissioners in 1871 led to the disappearance of many wives from recorded occupations, notwithstanding their continued unrecorded involvement. At the 1871 census 47 percent of wives and just over 60 percent of widows had specified occupations. The recorded married women included 55 in civil service occupations, 205 midwives, 1 author, 29 actresses, 1,146 teachers, 5,883 general domestic servants, 31 pawnbrokers, 3,174 unspecified dealers, 5,858 shopkeepers, and more than 13,000 seamstresses. The largest number—more than 250,000—were agriculturists, generally graziers' wives.

By the time of the 1926 census, the first in the Irish Free State, only 8 percent of wives and 40 percent of widows were recorded as "gainfully occupied." In Northern Ireland the proportion of women in factory employment and domestic industry—many of them married—was higher than in the South, reflecting the importance of the textile and clothing industries in the North. At the 1926 census household-based economic activities of a subsistence nature continued to be significant. Two-thirds of all the women recorded at work in 1926 were in three occupations—farm proprietors (chiefly widows), workers on family farms (mainly single women), and domestic servants (also predominantly single women). Women's occupations were not exclusively traditional, however: One female chimney sweep was recorded.

At this remove it is difficult to determine how many women who were classified as in "home duties" were in effect "at work" in a domestic agricultural context. All that can be said is that intertemporal comparisons that indicate an increase in the labor-force participation of married women may be exaggerated to the extent that participation went unrecorded in earlier decades. As the twentieth century progressed, and as the relative importance of agriculture declined, more women who worked "went out to work."

The underestimation of the labor-force participation of married women was continued in the 1920s and in particular the 1930s by a deliberate policy to curtail the participation of all women. The move to exclude women—especially married women—from the workplace had its roots in nineteenth-century Britain, continental Europe, and the United States in the struggle of working-class men for a "family wage" adequate to support a wife and children and to keep them out of the mines and "satanic mills." During the 1930s, the era of the Great Depression and of the Economic War with Britain, jobs for men were given priority. Gradually, restrictions were introduced that limited the sphere of women's work outside the home. These restrictions remained in force for the most part until Ireland joined the European Community in the early 1970s.

For sixty years from 1926 to 1986 there was scarcely any change in the number of women recorded in the workforce as a proportion of all women—the share, standing at 31 percent in 1986, was marginally lower than the 32 percent share recorded in 1926. Accordingly, the share of those not in the labor force (i.e., on "home duties," "at school/students," and "others") was also static. It should be recalled, however, that married women working in agriculture on family farms were counted out of the picture.

By 1981 over 40 percent of married women were in the labor force in Northern Ireland, more than double the percentage in the Republic. The participation rate in the Republic did not rise to 40 percent until the mid-1990s. Between 1995 and 2000 female participation in

the Republic's labor market increased from 40 percent of all females aged fifteen and above to 47 percent. In contrast, the broadly corresponding Northern Ireland proportion remained stable at 48 percent.

The marital status of those in the labor force has changed significantly. In 1926, 77 percent of the female labor force were single, 7 percent were married, and 16 percent were widowed. By 1986 the single share had dropped to 62 percent and the widowed share to 4 percent, while the share of married rose to 34 percent. Over the same period the rise in the participation rate of married women increased from under 6 percent to over 21 percent.

These trends continued in the closing years of the twentieth century. In 1991 the share of women engaged in home duties dipped below 50 percent for the first time, falling to 41 percent by 1996. By 1996 over half (51%) of the female workforce was married, while 47 percent were single and just over 2 percent were widowed. Although most married women who are working in Ireland are working full-time, difficulties exist in interpreting the data because of part-time work by women. As the labor-force participation rate of married women has risen, family size has declined. In the decade 1987 to 1997 the number of mothers in the workforce almost doubled, rising to 235,000.

Strikingly, more than three-quarters of women at work are in agriculture and industry. The share of women in industry (19% in 1996) was slightly less than their share in 1926, while their share in agriculture has fallen from 21 percent to 3 percent, reflecting the relative decline in the importance of agriculture in the economy.

Prior to the School Attendance Act of 1926, which required every child to attend school from the age of six to fourteen years, girls and boys frequently entered the workforce as young as twelve years of age. At the 1926 census one-quarter of all young persons fourteen and fifteen years old were in occupations. Many young women worked in domestic service and factories, including confectionery, jam-making, and clothing factories. By the late twentieth century, following the expansion of second-level education from the late 1960s and third-level education a decade later, women and men rarely entered the workforce before the age of eighteen.

The path of women and work over the past 150 years might be described as wending its way from a domestic economy where life and work intertwined in a predominantly agricultural setting, to working life in factories and economic services, including office and clerical work, which absorbed much of the labor of single women. Beginning in the 1950s the path broadened in the direction of clerical work, especially in the public service and large corporations such as the Guinness brewery and commercial banks. The expansion at first accommodated single women and, from the mid-1970s, married women as well. By the end of the century the information-technology revolution saw the work path turning once more, at least to some degree, toward the home, as "home-working" took on a fresh meaning.

SEE ALSO Celtic Tiger; Conditions of Employment Act of 1936; Education: Women's Education; Equal Economic Rights for Women in Independent Ireland; Farming Families; Irish Women Workers' Union; Women and Children in the Industrial Workforce; Women in Irish Society since 1800

Bibliography

Central Statistics Office and Northern Ireland Statistics and Research Agency. *Ireland North and South A Statistical Profile 2000*. 2001.

Daly, Mary, E. *Women and Work in Ireland*. 1997.

Fahey, Tony. "Measuring the Female Labour Supply: Conceptual and Procedural Problems in Irish Official Statistics." *The Economic and Social Review* 21 (1990): 163–191.

Fahey, Tony. "Housework, the Household Economy, and Economic Development in Ireland since the 1920s." *Irish Journal of Sociology* 2 (1992): 42–69.

Kennedy, Finola. *Cottage to Crèche: Family Change in Ireland*. 2001.

Walsh, Brendan M. *Some Irish Population Problems Reconsidered*. 1968.

Walsh, Brendan M. "Aspects of Labour Supply and Demand with Special Reference to the Employment of Women in Ireland." *Journal of the Statistical and Social Inquiry Society of Ireland* 22 (1970–1971): Pt. 3.

Walsh, Brendan M. "Labour Force Participation and the Growth of Female Employment in Ireland, 1971–91." *The Economic and Social Review* 24, no. 4 (1993): 369–400.

Finola Kennedy

Women in Irish Society since 1800

Three distinct trajectories of change can be traced in the lives of women in Ireland over these two centuries. The first and most important area of change, as far as numbers were concerned, is the shifting relationship of women to the house as a site of unpaid or paid work. The second area encompasses the occupational and educational changes that began in the early nineteenth century. The third relates to women's involvement in movements for political change, including the feminist movement. All of these areas were interrelated, but for clarity's sake an attempt will be made here to deal with them separately.

WOMEN, HOUSE, AND HOME

The sharp decline of the home-based textile industry after 1815 all over Europe left families bereft of an important source of income, however small. It was only in geographically contained industrial areas of Europe—the midlands and north of England, northeastern Ireland, the industrialized areas of France, the low countries, and parts of modern-day Italy and Germany—that factory work replaced home-based work for women. The devastating vulnerability of Irish women and men to famine in the late 1840s was an extreme version of the malnutrition and underemployment all over Europe in that decade. The Great Famine grimly removed the poorest and most vulnerable 10 percent of the population, including a good percentage of the women who had depended on textile earnings. The only way that famine changed the lives of women who survived it was by convincing them that home-based textile earnings were, in most of the country, gone for good.

On big and on small farms women did farm work as well as housework, and a holding of forty or fifty acres needed a family of at least six children to work it effectively. Because of rising levels of literacy and politicization, the postfamine decades brought expectations of a higher standard of living. For many people these could be fulfilled only by emigration. All of Europe supplied emigrants to North America and Australia; what was unusual about Ireland was the comparatively high proportion of young, single women emigrants, traveling alone or with their peers. More women than men emigrated from the midlands and the west of the country; elsewhere the numbers were about equal. Whether these women were independent, forward-looking individuals forging their own destinies, or lonely involuntary exiles who were of more use to their families when working abroad than when idle at home, their freedom of movement and ability to act outside of parental and paternal supervision should be noted. The same freedom-within-family contributed to the high rate of permanent celibacy (outside of the religious life) among women in Ireland until the 1960s. Rates of permanent celibacy were highest in the prosperous agricultural areas. Dowried women of the well-to-do agricultural class might not have been free to chose their own mates, but they could reject those chosen for them, even though this meant living the rest of their lives with their parents or siblings.

The developments in household technology that occurred in rural and small-town areas from the 1880s and 1890s—better-built fires with cranes for pots, mantelpieces, chimneys, flagged rather than earthen floors—were partly made possible by the easing of population pressure on small holdings and by remittances from abroad. In the 1890s also, the Congested Districts Board and some local authorities began to build solid, slated houses for laborers and small farmers. In independent Ireland the next significant housing development was the construction, in the 1930s, of approximately 12,000 local-authority houses a year in an attempt to clear the slums. Over half of all dwellings in the Republic in 1946, however, were without piped water and electricity, and only 12 percent of rural dwellings were thus equipped in 1961. Nor was it until the 1950s and 1960s that all the inhabitants of the notorious disease-ridden tenements of Dublin and lanes of Cork and Limerick were given proper housing—at this stage defined as two- or three-bedroom houses with gardens and indoor plumbing and electricity. Such new dwellings made women's work immeasurably easier, with no water to carry in and dispose of, beds that did not have to be cleared away every day, lines upon which to hang washing, and flush toilets. In the north of Ireland the standard of working-class housing was generally somewhat better in nineteenth-century urban areas, where the "two-up, two-down" terraced house with a tap and a privy in the yard was the norm, though in rural areas the situation resembled that in the rest of the country. The sectarian housing policy of the Northern Ireland state was challenged by members of the civil-rights movement and other groups from the early 1970s.

For middle-class people in towns and cities piped water, gas, and later, electricity, were introduced in the early years of the twentieth century. Middle-class women, moreover, had their burden of housework eased by the ready availability of girls and women to toil for long hours at low pay, which they did, until the 1940s. Domestic service was, in Ireland as elsewhere in Europe, the default occupation for women from laboring and small-farming backgrounds. Pay was low, but the conditions of work varied widely and it is impossible to generalize, other than to comment that while women fled this occupation in other European countries after the First World War, they abandoned it in Ireland from about 1940, when the wartime economy in Britain provided plenty of comparatively well-paid and well-

regarded work. As late as the 1950s some middle-class people were still lamenting their departure and hoping that a new generation of women could be trained up in their place. This never happened; all women's expectations were rising in Ireland in these years, and the women who would formerly have been domestic servants were no exception.

The 1940s also saw the beginning of another wave of emigration, especially among women, this time to Britain and the plentiful, comparatively well-paid work and training available there after the war. The census occupational figures chart the first gradual, then accelerated, departure of women from "assisting relative" status in agriculture from 1926 onwards, and especially after World War II. If the postfamine female emigrants had emigrated to send money home, these women were emigrating for themselves, though their departure was heartily welcomed by young married women in Ireland who were increasingly reluctant to share living space with single sisters or sisters-in-law. To suggest that women were emigrating because they were "rejected" as marriage partners by Irish men ignores the evidence to the contrary. Every source from the 1950s confirms, with some alarm, the reluctance of Irish women to marry in Ireland. Women who were used to financial independence in white-collar or industrial or commercial work did not want to surrender it, as they were forced to do, on marriage.

Women's health in pregnancy and childbirth saw some improvement toward the end of the nineteenth century with the introduction of district nursing associations and public-health organizations such as the Women's National Health Association (1904) and the United Irishwomen (1911, later the Irish Countrywomen's Association). Maternal mortality fell whenever there was an appreciable rise in income and easing of financial pressure, together with trained midwives rather than doctors. The care given by the untrained handy-woman varied widely in quality, but it was often, up until the 1940s, the only care available to rural women in particular. Women in the cities had maternity hospitals whose services they could call on. The introduction of the National Health Service in Britain and Northern Ireland immediately after the war, and the implementation of a free-for-all maternity and infant-care system in the Republic in 1953, caused maternal and infant mortality to fall definitively all over the island and brought about a definitive improvement in women's health. This change also led to greater freedom from domesticity for single women, who were not called upon as often to rear motherless nieces, nephews, and siblings. Family size in both the Republic and Northern Ireland remained large by European standards until the

1970s, and the childbearing and infant-rearing work of a mother could span twenty years.

The subordination of women in Irish rural life is an oft-told tale. Yet the farm woman had until the 1960s a source of independent income unmatched in an urban setting: egg and butter money. Furthermore, because of the typical age difference between farmers and their brides, many a farm woman enjoyed a long and extremely powerful widowhood. The power of the widow (not only as farmer, but as shopkeeper, too) often oppressed younger women and men. The election to Dáil Éireann of widows, sisters, and daughters of dead male politicians shows both the strength of women's personalities at the local level and the considerable social authority of the older woman in Irish life. Women who married in the early 1950s increasingly rejected such authority, insisting upon living apart from the older generation if at all possible.

The social and economic changes from the 1960s to the 1990s narrowed the lifestyle gap between urban and rural women. The changes in agriculture that took place after Ireland's entry into the European Economic Community in 1973 also eased women's workload on the farm and made life on small farms easier. The proliferation of cars reduced rural isolation and facilitated off-farm employment.

In general, the greater availability of office and industrial work for women and the lifting of the marriage bar in the public service in 1973 slowed down emigration and contributed to a rise in the marriage rate. It was only when women in Ireland had a realistic prospect of paid work (within their own homes, in farms and businesses, or outside them) that they embraced domestic life heartily and in large numbers.

EDUCATION AND PAID WORK

The most important educational reform over these two centuries was the establishment of the National Board of Education in 1831. Making state money available to provide free primary education for boys and girls not only enabled parents to send daughters to school at no cost, but also provided employment opportunities as teachers for women of the nonpropertied classes. Girls' school attendance over the course of the nineteenth century gradually overtook that of boys, particularly in rural districts and urban areas of low female employment. By 1900 over half of all National teachers were women. Prior to the introduction of compulsory education in 1892, girls' attendance was highest in areas with low female employment, and lowest in the northeast, where the mill and the factory beckoned, and there was much home-based garment and textile work.

Nuns owed their rapid expansion in part to government support of the non-fee-paying schools they ran, 75 percent of which were affiliated to the National Board by 1850. Female religious vocations soared in public esteem in nineteenth-century Ireland and remained a very popular life choice for Catholic women in the Republic and Northern Ireland until the 1970s. It gave women training, authority, challenging and often innovative work, and a high social status, apart altogether from the immeasureable spiritual dimension. The vast majority of nuns worked with poor girls in schools of various kinds. This schooling was vocational and practical. There is little evidence for the oft-asserted claim that nuns "socialised" girls for "domesticity" either in fee-paying or in free schools. If they tried to do so, then they made a bad job of it, as many girls and women fled "domesticity" whenever other opportunities—the religious life included—presented themselves. (Nor were Irish women at any time during this period noted for their proficiency in the domestic arts, though it is difficult to credit the perceptions of observers with fixed ideas about the Irish, or about women, or about working-class people.) Nuns must receive part of the credit for the high female attendance at National schools, as they actively sought female pupils long before 1892.

Credit for advances in higher-level education, however, must go to Protestant women and the fee-paying schools that they set up in the 1860s in Dublin and Belfast. These colleges trained girls in the classics and mathematics, and their existence ultimately led to girls being admitted on equal terms with boys to the Intermediate school-leaving examination when it was established in 1878. It was after this that fee-paying convent schools began to prepare girls for the Intermediate examination, and in some cases, like the Protestant schools, to arrange for university extension lectures. Women began to take university degrees in Ireland in the 1880s. Until 1948 in Northern Ireland and 1966 in the Republic, however, secondary education for boys or for girls was limited to those lucky few whose parents could afford to pay for them, or who were clever and determined enough to win scholarships, or who lived near one of the few free secondary schools run by religious orders. Despite all of these obstacles, there was a steadily rising number of girls finishing secondary school from the 1940s. The university education of both sexes began to rise in Northern Ireland in the 1960s, when the first generation of university-educated working-class Catholics would form the civil-rights movement at the end of that decade. The 1970s saw university education take firm hold in the rest of Ireland. Since the 1970s female attendance at university and admission to the professions has soared.

Girls schools of all denominations, fee-paying and free, began to prepare girls also for the new "white-blouse" work opening up in the 1890s in post offices, offices in general, and the public service. Nursing also developed as a very respectable profession around this time, attracting women from a broad range of social backgrounds and subjecting them to rigorous training in work with a strong female identity. While academics and professional women might have been the leaders, it was teachers, nurses, and office and factory workers who made up the rank-and-file membership of the various political and cultural movements of the late nineteenth and early twentieth centuries.

Women's trade unionization was slow, not only because of the problems that always beset it—hostility from male trade unionists and a vulnerable workforce—but also because in the only geographical area of Ireland where women worked in industry in sufficiently large numbers—the north and northeast—workers' loyalties were crosscut by sectarian tensions. Nevertheless, some advances were made in the 1890s among textile workers, and there were some women in the new trade unions of the early twentieth century, north and south.

The early years of the Free State saw an increase in the numbers of women in factory and office work and a greater visibility of women in the public sphere. Women's working rights were systematically attacked in the 1920s and 1930s. In the Free State married women were barred from public-service employment by the end of the 1920s and from National School teaching in 1932. Employment legislation in 1936 barred women from working in certain kinds of industries and from night work. The 1940s and 1950s yielded a female landscape laid bare by emigration and economic decline, but big changes were happening unnoticed. Adult women were fleeing what had hitherto been their two most common occupations, the land and domestic service, and more girls were remaining in school. The economic and social development of the 1960s made jobs for women available in commercial, industrial, and office work; women were also admitted to the Garda Síochána (the police force), and later, in the 1980s, to the Defence Forces.

POLITICS AND ORGANIZATION

Women were granted fully equal citizenship in the Irish Free State Constitution of 1922, years ahead of their counterparts in the United Kingdom, France, Italy, Switzerland, and many other European countries. In France at this time, though women did not have the vote, they enjoyed very extensive rights in the workplace, including paid maternity leave. In Ireland the situation was the reverse—top-heavy with political equality, and with a small but very vocal and highly respected group of women in public life, but the women's organizations that existed were small and few, and they could do little or nothing to protect women workers.

Women's involvement in Irish politics began in the late 1870s and early 1880s when the land movement mobilized men and women throughout the country, and women played a key role in land agitation—resisting evictions and boycotting businesses and neighbors—up to 1903. The short-lived Ladies' Land League, founded in 1881 to take over the running of the movement while the male leaders were in prison, showed women for the first time in a leadership role in a nationalist movement. Longer-lasting women's nationalist movements were formed in the early twentieth century, though already the most lively and active of the cultural-revival organizations, the Gaelic League (founded in 1893), was admitting men and women as equal members. Cumann na mBan, the female auxiliary wing of the Irish Volunteers, was founded on a countrywide basis in 1914 and had branches throughout the country. The much smaller, Dublin-based Irish Citizen Army was already accepting men and women as equal combatants. The Proclamation of the Provisional Republican Government in the 1916 Rising addressed men and women as equal citizens and promised equal citizenship. In the north of Ireland more women than men signed the Solemn League and Covenant against Home Rule in 1912. Though the Solemn League and Covenant made no mention of gender equality, and though there was no female equivalent of Cumann na mBan in the Ulster Volunteers, the Ulster Women's Unionist Council, founded in 1911, had an average membership of about 60,000 and contained women of all classes. In 1898 women with property were given the local government franchise and allowed to sit on county councils, urban district councils, town and corporations. There had already been women Poor Law guardians since 1896, so by 1914 women—usually middle-class women, of all religions—were becoming familiar figures of authority on committees and in official capacities.

The Irish suffrage movement had begun in the 1870s as a small pressure group composed of women of mainly unionist sympathies. It was not until the early twentieth century that it grew in numbers, attracted nationalist women as well (who soon became the majority), and developed a militant wing. Surprisingly, the suffrage movement did not immediately founder on the rocks of unionist/nationalist divisions,

In May 1971 members of the Irish Women's Liberation Movement, returning from Belfast laden with contraceptives, publicize their campaign for the legalization of contraception. PHOTOGRAPH COURTESY OF THE *IRISH TIMES*.

but it was swallowed up by the more pressing political loyalties of the second decade of the twentieth century. In 1918 a new law granted the parliamentary vote to all men over twenty-one years old, and to women over thirty with certain property qualifications. The fact that the first woman to be elected to the House of Commons was Constance Markievicz, a Sinn Féin member, seems to indicate that nationalist revolutionaries were committed to gender equality. Many were not, however, as the actions of former revolutionaries anxious to dilute women's citizenship and to attack their working rights in the Free State show. Still, at the very least women were elected to and sat in both houses of the Oireachtas from 1922. This was in contrast to the Northern Ireland state, where, despite the strength of their organization and their considerable power at the local government level, unionist women were discouraged from standing for parliamentary elections in these years.

Yet women politicians in the Free State and Republic, even if they were respected as individuals, were ignored when they paid attention to women's issues. Overwhelmingly Catholic, they did not consider the

banning of contraception in 1929 and 1936 to be a feminist issue, and they were unable to do anything about the removal of women from jury service in 1927, the attacks on working women mentioned above, and the association of women with domesticity in Eamon de Valera's constitution of 1937. A small group of former suffragists, which became known in the 1940s as the Irish Housewives' Association, kept a watching brief on citizenship issues, and they campaigned, as did all feminists in Europe in these years, for better maternal and child welfare and on consumer issues. The Joint Committee of Women's Societies and Social Workers agitated for, among other things, a children's court and women gardaí (police). Feminism might have been moribund in the 1950s and 1960s, but the Irish Countrywomen's Assocation (in the Republic and in Northern Ireland) saw a big increase in its membership over these decades, showing a new ability and willingness by women to get out of the house and to organize. It was partly pressure from this organization that led to the founding of the Council for the Status of Women in 1973, though the high-profile, Dublin-based Women's

Liberation Movement of the early 1970s certainly helped. Over the succeeding decades, feminists gave high priority to the redefinition of women's legal and social relationship to the family, their access to economic resources, and their rights in the workplace and in education. Groups such as Irishwomen United (1975–1977), AIM (1972), the Women's Political Association, Irish Feminist Information, Cherish (a lobby group for single mothers), rape crisis centers, and others kept women's issues in the public view. Women won the right to retain public service work on marriage. They also secured separate welfare payments, several legal breakthroughs with regard to family law, children's allowances payable to mothers rather than to fathers, and access to contraception, divorce, and paid maternity leave.

SEE ALSO Equal Economic Rights for Women in Independent Ireland; Equal Rights in Northern Ireland; Farming Families; Social Change since 1922; Women and Work since the Mid-Nineteenth Century; **Primary Documents:** From the *Report of the Commission on the Status of Women* (1972); From the Decision of the Supreme Court in *McGee v. the Attorney General and the Revenue Commissioners* (1973); On the Family Planning Bill (20 February 1974)

Bibliography

Bourke, Joanna. *Husbandry to Housewifery: Women, Economic Change, and Housework in Ireland, 1890–1914.* 1993.

Clancy, Mary. "Some Aspects of Women's Contribution to Oireachtas Debate in Ireland, 1922–1937." In *Women Surviving: Studies in Irish Women's History in the Nineteenth and Twentieth Centuries,* edited by Maria Luddy and Cliona Murphy. 1990.

Clear, Caitriona. *Nuns in Nineteenth-Century Ireland.* 1990.

Clear, Caitriona. *Women of the House: Women's Household Work in Ireland, 1922–1961.* 2000.

Guinnane, Timothy. *The Vanishing Irish: Households, Migration, and the Rural Economy in Ireland, 1850–1914.* 1997.

Logan, John. "The Dimensions of Gender in Nineteenth-Century Schooling." In *Gender Perspectives in Nineteenth-Century Ireland,* edited by Maragaret Kelleher and James H. Murphy. 1997.

O'Sullivan, Patrick, ed. *The Irish World Wide: History, Heritage, Identity.* Vol. 4, *Irish Women and Irish Migration.* 1997.

Ward, Margaret. *Unmanageable Revolutionaries: Women and Irish Nationalism.* 1983.

Caitriona Clear

~

Women in Nationalist and Unionist Movements in the Early Twentieth Century

After several decades of campaigning, women over the age of thirty were given the right to vote in parliamentary elections and to sit as MPs in 1918. But with female exclusion from the parliamentary arena up to this date, one cannot assume that women played no political part or were politically disinterested. Although the nineteenth-century ideal was that women's so-called proper place was not public or political, but private and domestic, Irish women's political activity was extensive and varied. Even before the 1800s there are examples of women rioting in times of extreme economic distress and becoming involved in agrarian disturbances. Such activities continued into the nineteenth century. Other women exercised an informal but at times potent influence over the voting behavior of male family members, while others participated in election riots. In addition, aristocratic women had access to those in positions of political power and, using the networks of London's high society, a number of Anglo-Irish women became important political hostesses.

As the nineteenth century advanced, an increasing number of women became publicly active, although the motivations for this varied from the altruistic to the feminist and the political. For instance, a small number of women played a part in the Young Ireland movement of the 1840s, contributing articles, letters, and poems to the advanced nationalist newspaper, the *Nation*. However, women's involvement in Young Ireland was both subordinate and idealized. By comparison, female forays into later Irish nationalist campaigns, such as the Fenian movement of the late 1850s through 1860s and the Land League of 1879 to 1882, were more practically based. For example, women carried dispatches and messages between Fenian leaders, and in October 1865 a ladies' committee was inaugurated to assist the families of imprisoned Fenians. This work continued until the general amnesty of 1872. The Ladies' Land League, spearheaded by Anna Parnell and Fanny Parnell, functioned at first as a fundraising and philanthropic organization that was active in both America and Ireland in the early 1880s. However, with the imprisonment of key Land League leaders, the women's organization took over the day-to-day running of the land campaign—distributing propaganda and providing relief for evicted tenants. By adopting such a high public and political profile, they aroused widespread criticism, even from the higher echelons of the Land League itself.

The emergence of the Home Rule debate from the mid-1880s both divided Irish society and brought a new generation of Irish women into politics. Although still denied access to the vote, they formed organizations that helped men promote or oppose Home Rule, depending on their political persuasion, and developed a specifically female agenda. Women were excluded on the basis of sex from numerous late-nineteenth- and early-twentieth-century nationalist organizations, and this prompted the formation of an exclusively female nationalist body, Inghinidhe na hÉireann (Daughters of Ireland) in 1900. It was run for and by women. Under the presidency of Maud Gonne, it aimed to promote Irish independence (by armed means if necessary), and to encourage the purchase of Irish manufactures and the study of Irish language, history, literature, music, and art. Gonne wanted to prove that women were capable of political activity and could contribute positively to the campaign for Irish independence. However, Inghinidhe na hÉireann's agenda, although never radically feminist, was too belligerent to rally popular support. In essence, it remained a collection of interested individuals rather than a united body working toward a singular goal, and it was increasingly overshadowed by another female nationalist organization Cumann na mBan (Women's Council).

Cumann na mBan was set up in 1914 as a female auxiliary of the Irish Volunteers, aiming to assist the campaign for Irish independence and to counter the organizational efficiency and militancy of unionists who were preparing to resist Home Rule by armed force. Each branch of Cumann na mBan was affiliated to and took orders from a local battalion of Irish Volunteers, and members raised funds, cooked, sewed uniforms, cared for military equipment, and undertook first aid and the training of nurses. Despite this ancillary status, feminism had more of a place in Cumann na mBan's ideology than in that of Inghinidhe na hÉireann. However, nationalism remained its primary aim. This stance provoked some criticism from Irish suffragists, who opined that female nationalists' priorities were wrong. Cumann na mBan retorted that there could be no free women in an enslaved nation.

Cumann na mBan also developed specifically female rhetoric, highlighting the security of the home and the protection of children as contributions to nation building in an attempt to attract women into the organization. Yet a real surge in the popularity of Cumann na mBan occurred only in the aftermath of the 1916 Rising, an event that saw sixty members of the organization carry dispatches, nurse the wounded, and cook for the rebel forces. After 1916 there was an upsurge in republican sympathy, and by 1921 Cumann na mBan had an estimated 750 branches with approximately 4,500 members. This popularity was short lived. Moderate support waned as the organization was the first to reject the Anglo-Irish Treaty of 1921, and as its members supported the antitreaty forces during the Civil War (1919–1921 and 1922–1923).

Women were similarly active within unionism. Again, it was the political discourse over Home Rule that drew many women into politics from the time of the first Home Rule bill in 1886. Initially female involvement in the unionist campaign occurred on a local or individual basis with women petitioning, demonstrating, disseminating propaganda, canvassing, and fundraising, but this developed into more collective activity with the creation of the Ulster Women's Unionist Council (UWUC) in January 1911. Led by members of Ulster's aristocratic elite, with the majority of officeholders related by marriage or birth to leading unionist MPs and peers, this organization continued and augmented the female unionist activities of the late nineteenth century. However, the organization aimed to have both "the peeress and the peasant represented" (*Belfast News-Letter*, 24 January 1911) in its ranks, and by 1912 the UWUC had an estimated membership of between 115,000 and 200,000 members. This was easily the largest female political body that Ireland had ever seen. Female unionism was also dramatically apparent on 28 September 1912, when 16,000 more women than men signed the Women's declaration, a female equivalent of the Ulster Solemn League and Covenant. In addition, the UWUC waged a huge anti–Home Rule propaganda campaign, with more than 10,000 pro-unionist leaflets and newspapers being sent weekly to Britain by 1913.

Like Cumann na mBan, the UWUC was an auxiliary association, and following the creation of the Ulster Volunteer Force in 1913, many unionist women received instruction in nursing, signaling, intelligence work, and driving. Furthermore, while UWUC echoed the economic, religious, constitutional, and imperial objections espoused by male unionists, the organization also developed a gendered anti–Home Rule argument. Here, in parallel with Cumann na mBan, the sanctity of the home and well-being of children was emphasized, with women's political activism being depicted as an extension of maternal responsibility. In addition to the similarities between female unionist and nationalist rhetoric, their views of the Irish suffrage movement had much in common. The overwhelming majority of both unionist and nationalist women gave priority to Home Rule over the issue of female suffrage. This in effect weakened the level of support that the Irish suffrage movement could arouse. At a time of political crisis it became increasingly difficult for suffragists to maintain a neutral political position; thus, even though the early years of the twentieth century saw an unprecedented number of women working toward political ends, their views were as divided as the political climate in which they worked.

SEE ALSO Cumann na mBan; Fenian Movement and the Irish Republican Brotherhood; Gonne, Maud; Ladies' Land League; Struggle for Independence from 1916 to 1921; Unionism from 1885 to 1922; Young Ireland and the Irish Confederation

Bibliography

Luddy, Maria. *Women in Ireland, 1800–1918: A Documentary History.* 1995.

Urquhart, Diane. *Women in Ulster Politics, 1890–1940.* 2000.

Urquhart, Diane. *The Minutes of the Ulster Women's Unionist Council and Executive Committee, 1911–1940.* 2001.

Ward, Margaret. *Unmanageable Revolutionaries: Women and Irish Nationalism.* 1995.

Diane Urquhart

Women's Movement in Northern Ireland

The women's movement in Ireland, as elsewhere, was associated with second-wave feminism and the wider civil-rights movement of the late 1960s. In Northern Ireland it was affected by, and in turn influenced, broader movements for social justice in the region. While disagreement about methods and principles was not uncommon among women activists, the ongoing political and military struggle heightened existing differences and injected a sense of urgency and emotion into all proceedings.

Although women had come together before on occasion to protest (for example, against the ending of free school milk for children) or to focus attention on the issue of domestic violence, the year 1975 saw the formation of the first organized group, the Northern Ireland Women's Rights Movement (NIWRM). This group aimed "to spread a consciousness of women's oppres-

sion and mobilize the greatest possible numbers of women on feminist issues" (NIWRM Manifesto 1974). They called specifically for the extension of Britain's Sexual Discrimination Act to Northern Ireland. But in a movement that encompassed a diversity of political allegiances and aspirations, involving academics, trade-union activists, civil-rights activists, communists, unionists, and republicans, tensions were bound to surface.

Many Northern Irish women had become politicized not from ideological conviction, but as a result of their immediate experience. For the wives of interned men, for example, the battle for justice was waged not merely against men, but against the institutions and instruments of the state. So while on the constitutional question the NIWRM declared itself to be nonaligned, its attempts to distance itself from the wider struggle were met with accusations of their complicity with the state. Support for women political prisoners, all of whom were republican, was a particularly emotive and divisive issue. Those who aimed to combine their commitment to socialism with feminist and nationalist concerns formed the Socialist Women's Group in 1975; it dissolved two years later, and many members reunited in the Belfast Women's Collective. Women against Imperialism and the Relatives' Action Committee provided forums for campaigns more closely linked with the rights of political prisoners. During the 1980s they were heavily involved in support of women prisoners in Armagh jail who went on hunger strike, took part in a "no wash" protest, and were frequently subjected to strip-searching. But with the NIWRM refusing to engage in the protests, "Armagh became a metaphor for what divided women here from each other" (Ward 1991, p. 156).

The consequences of "lobbying for change in a context where the legitimacy of the legislature is contested" (Rooney 1995, p. 43) offered a potent reminder of the multiple identities and conflicting loyalties held by women everywhere. However, an overemphasis on the problems of division draws attention away from what was achieved during these years: An Equal Pay Act was passed in 1970 and a Sex Discrimination Act in 1976. The setting up of the Equal Opportunities Commission in the same year was seen as particularly helpful by those feminists and trade unionists for whom the right of women to work, and to be given equal opportunities and rewards, were considered fundamental entitlements. The establishment of women's aid refuges, rape crisis centers, and well-women clinics can also be attributed to feminist lobbying.

Perhaps one of the most distinctive and important developments in Northern Ireland, however, was the growth of local women's groups. Coming together for solidarity and mutual aid in their strife-torn communities, women learned from and built upon their own experience. Through consciousness-raising classes and educational courses in women's history, literature, and place in society, women in many areas became both more politicized and more experienced in dealing with local problems. During the 1980s and 1990s a series of meetings and conferences highlighted women's issues and sought ways to facilitate their inclusion in the political process. As a result, many women became more active in a range of political parties, and in April 1996 the Northern Ireland's Women's Coalition was formed and succeeded in winning two seats in the newly established Northern Ireland Forum. The party sought to bring a new gender perspective to national politics with the key principles of "inclusion, equality and human rights" (Fearon 1999, p. 13). But while many women viewed the party as a catalyst for change, others were uneasy, both about the party's evasion of the constitutional question and about the way in which it was assumed that "women's voice would change everything, simply by virtue of their gender" (Ward 1997, p. 151). The coalition, however, is only the most visible aspect of the undercurrents of change. Although political tensions in Northern Ireland may have prevented the emergence of an autonomous feminist movement, the experiences of working-class women and their community activism perhaps hold greater potential for fundamental change.

SEE ALSO Peace Movement in Northern Ireland

Bibliography

Evason, Eileen. *Against the Grain: The Contemporary Women's Movement in Northern Ireland.* 1991.

Fearon, Kate. *The Story of the Northern Ireland's Women Coalition.* 1999.

Northern Ireland Women's Rights Movement. Manifesto. NIWRM Archives. Linenhall Library, Belfast. 1974.

Rooney, Eilish. "Political Division, Practical Alliance: Problems for Women in Confict." In *Irish Women's Voices: Past and Present*, edited by Joan Hoff and Maureen Coulter. 1995.

Roulston, Carmel. "Women on the Margin: The Women's Movement in Northern Ireland." *Science and Society* 53, no. 2 (summer 1989): 219–236.

Ward, Margaret. "The Women's Movement in the North of Ireland: Twenty Years On." In *Ireland's Histories: Aspects of State, Society and Ideology*, edited by Sean Hutton and Paul Stewart. 1991.

Ward, Rachel. "The Northern Ireland Peace Process: A Gender Issue?" In *Peace or War? Understanding the Peace Movement in Northern Ireland*, edited by Chris Gilligan and Jan Tonge. 1997.

Myrtle Hill

Women's Parliamentary Representation since 1922

In the 1918 general election, the last all-Ireland election to Westminster (British parliament), Constance Gore-Booth (Countess Markievicz) was the first woman to be elected to Parliament. One year later, she had the distinction of being the first woman in Europe to hold government office when she was appointed minister for labor in the first Dáil. Markievicz's political success suggests that the Irish public and its political leaders viewed women's holding of high office with equanimity, but the next decades would prove otherwise. By the end of the 1930s the fourteen women (nine in the Dáil and five in the Seanad) who had entered Parliament following independence left politics, to be replaced by seven new women. In 1969 there were only three women in the Dáil, and none of them had cabinet experience. Women's presence in Parliament began to gradually improve from this point on, and in 2001 women held a modest twenty-one seats (13%) in the Dáil and eleven (18%) seats in the Seanad. Women also had made it into government office; in 2001 three women (20%) held ministerial offices and a further four (23%) were junior ministers.

Women have been similarly represented in Northern Ireland's electoral politics. Between 1921 and 1972 (when the Northern Ireland devolved parliament was suspended), nine women held seats (were members of Parliament) in the Northern Ireland Assembly and only one, Dame Dehra Parker, served in government (held ministerial office as well as being a member of Parliament). In general elections during this fifty-year period only three women won Westminster (British Parliament) seats. In the next three decades, women's absence from political life in Northern Ireland (with notable exceptions) was exacerbated by the "Troubles." The 1996 IRA cease-fire, the 1998 Good Friday Agreement, and the restoration of devolved government combined to provide women with renewed political opportunities. In the 1998 elections to the Northern Ireland Assembly, fourteen women (13%) won seats and two women (16%) were appointed ministers in Northern Ireland's power-sharing executive. This progress continued in 2001: In the local elections women's presence increased from 86 seats (14%) to 108 seats (19%), and in the general election a record three women (17%) were elected to Westminster.

INFLUENCING SUCCESS

A combination of individual and system-related factors act to support women's advancement in political life in Ireland. There are three main routes to national and regional politics: political parties, a family connection to politics, and community activism or local-government service. In addition, party ideology, the electoral system, and voter attitudes toward women as political decision-makers are important influences. Membership in an established political party is the dominant factor, because either party officials invite women community leaders to run for election on their ticket or because party notables support women activists. A family tradition of political involvement is a second important factor. Party and family interact to socialize women into politics, demystifying power and teaching women the rules of the political game. Although the power of the political dynasty has decreased over time, it is still a feature of political life in Ireland: nine (33%) of the new women elected to the Dáil in the 1990s were the daughters of former (male) politicians. Community activism, including involvement with women's groups, is the third most significant route to political life for women in the Republic and also has been a major factor in women's participation in Northern Ireland politics since 1998. As with the political-family factor, activism socializes women civic leaders to political life and encourages them to seek more political power. Careers are most likely when women contest elections under a party ticket, again reinforcing the role of party politics as the gatekeeper to political life. The majority of women, and men, begin their formal political careers in local politics, using it as a stepping-stone to higher political office.

Particular features of the political system—the ideological position of parties, a proportional-representation electoral system and a relative willingness by voters to support women candidates—are also significant in bringing women into elected politics. Parties in both the North and South that occupy centrist or left-wing ideological positions and new parties are more likely to have women representatives. In addition, a proportional-representation voting system does not disadvantage women's candidacies, while the electorate in both the North and South is quite open to voting for women candidates from their preferred party when given the opportunity to do so. It has been found that electoral systems based on proportional models are more favorable to women's representation than majoritarian systems (Norris 2000). All elections in the Republic of Ireland are conducted under a form of proportional representation—the single transferable vote—in multi-member constituencies. Voters can choose along a number of dimensions, including party and individual, and can also indicate their second, third, and further preferences. Local and regional elections in Northern Ireland are conducted under similar electoral rules as those in the south. Research indicates that the major factor influencing the gender composition of the Dáil is incumbency (Galligan, Laver, and Carney 1999). It also suggests that voters are quite happy to vote for women candidates, especially women incumbents. In both Northern Ireland and the Republic, the election of women candidates closely correlates with their proportion of total candidates; thus, in the 2001 elections in Northern Ireland, women constituted 19 percent of candidates and won 19 percent of local council seats.

IMPACT OF THE WOMEN'S MOVEMENT

The dominance of conservative sociocultural and religious attitudes that have conferred on women second-class citizenship accounts for women's absence from political life in Ireland until the 1970s. The emergence in the 1970s of the civil-rights and feminist movements in the North and South, influenced by similar developments in Britain and the United States, brought the position of women under public scrutiny and debate. However, in Northern Ireland the slide into political conflict (the "Troubles") cut short the potential of the women's movement to raise women's aspirations toward holding political office. When the possibility of a negotiated settlement to the long-running conflict emerged in 1996, the women's movement mobilized to win representation to the multiparty peace talks; this led to the formation of the Northern Ireland Women's Coalition, a feminist party with a membership drawn from both nationalist and unionist communities. In subsequent elections the presence of the Women's Coalition prompted longer-established parties to pay greater attention to women's political presence; in 2001 this resulted in the selection of a greater proportion of women candidates for the general election and, importantly, placement of women candidates in contests for winnable seats.

The women's movement in the Republic of Ireland was conscious of the need to increase women's presence in parliament, and the Women's Political Association was formed in the 1970s to achieve this end. The WPA continued to advocate for women candidates throughout the 1970s and 1980s, and in that period three women's movement leaders were successfully elected. During the 1990s arguments by party feminists for increasing women's representation in the political sphere began to have greater influence. Although the main parties stopped short of introducing quotas to boost women's presence, they tried, with varying degrees of commitment, to encourage women to run for political office. The success of the women's movement in bringing women into politics was evident with the election of Mary Robinson as president in 1990 and Mary McAleese as her successor in 1997.

THE FUTURE

The influx of women into politics in Northern Ireland since 1998 indicates the emergence of a degree of political stability in this troubled region. The risk facing women's continued political presence is a breakdown in the "peace process" and a return to the conflict of former years. In this eventuality many of the women holding assembly seats are likely to disengage from electoral politics—returning the political space to a virtual male monopoly—because a return to violence would make it difficult, indeed dangerous, for them to be politically aligned. Elected representatives and their families were (and in some areas continue to be) singled out for death threats, intimidation, and other forms of violence. Many women MLAs still speak of experiencing localized intimidation in their constituencies towards themselves and their families. If there is a return to violence, the risk to their lives and family members' lives would escalate.

Women in politics face an uncertain future in the coming years. The high turnover in women's representation in 1997 was repeated in 2002, with five (24%) established female legislators losing their seats. While this loss was offset with the election of five new women and two former women TDs regaining their seats, the overall representation of women in Parliament languishes at twenty-two (13%). The number of new women winning political office is too low to make an impact on the gender balance in the Dáil, and high levels of voter volatility suggest that parties may be less inclined to select significant numbers of women candidates.

Countering this conservatism are new legislative and policy-oriented measures adopted by the British and Irish governments to encourage the selection of more women for political office. In 2001 the House of Commons adopted the Sex Discrimination (Election of Candidates) Act providing that parties could develop positive measures for candidate selection to redress the existing gender imbalance in Westminster and the devolved legislatures. In the same year, the Irish government provided medium-term financial support to par-

ties aimed at developing capacity-building programs for potential women candidates. While the efficacy of these measures will be tested in time, they offer the possibility of a more hopeful future for women's political representation on the island of Ireland.

SEE ALSO Markievicz, Countess Constance; Parker, Dame Dehra; Political Parties in Independent Ireland; Robinson, Mary; **Primary Documents:** From the *Report of the Commission on the Status of Women* (1972)

Bibliography

Fearon, Kate. *Women's Work: The Story of the Northern Ireland Women's Coalition.* 1999.

Galligan, Yvonne. "Women in Politics." In *Politics in the Republic of Ireland*, 3d edition, edited by John Coakely and Michael Gallagher. 1999.

Galligan, Yvonne, Eilis Ward, and Rick Wilford. *Contesting Politics: Women in Ireland, North and South.* 1999.

Galligan, Yvonne, Michael Laver, and Gemma Carney. "The Effect of Candidate Gender on Voting in Ireland, 1997." *Irish Political Studies* 14 (1999): 118–122.

McNamara, Maedhbh, and Paschal Mooney. *Women in Parliament: Ireland, 1918–2000.* 2000.

Norris, Pippa. "Women's Representation and Electoral Systems." In *Encyclopaedia of Electoral Systems*, edited by Richard Rouse. 2000.

Yvonne Galligan

Woodlands

A mix of natural and human influences is evident in the woodland history of Ireland since the end of the last glacial phase about ten thousand years ago. Ireland was then a treeless tundra, which gradually became colonized by woodlands in which willows, birch, hazel, and pine were represented. By about 7000 B.P., woodland may have covered at least 80 percent of Ireland. Species emerging as dominant during a relatively stable climatic climax-phase were elm and hazel in the midlands, alder in wet habitats, oak on the more acid soils of the south and northeast, and pine on the more exposed acid soils of the northwest (Pilcher and Mac an tSaoir; Mitchell and Ryan). Some other species widespread in the postglacial forests of Britain and mainland Europe; for example, lime, sycamore, beech and horse chestnut did not establish themselves in Ireland at this time.

Map of King's and Queen's counties (Offaly and Laois), c. 1562. By the mid-sixteenth century Irish timber was very much in demand in England for use in constructing ships and buildings THE BOARD OF TRINITY COLLEGE DUBLIN. REPRODUCED BY PERMISSION.

Later species changes can be linked to climate change (notably, the wetter and cooler conditions after c. 6200 B.P.), disease, and human activity. A widespread abrupt decline in the elm population around 5900 B.P. has been attributed to the spread of disease and to the clearances of early Neolithic farmers. Wetter conditions and human activity can be readily associated with the expansion of blanket bog and the decline of the pine from about 4000 B.P.

Significant clearances of woodland for farming must have occurred throughout the Bronze and Iron Ages and in later periods, but their precise scale, extent, and phasing remains open to debate. Some pollen analyses, and the widespread distribution of over 40,000 raths (circular earthwork), suggest that large areas had been cleared by early Christian/early medieval times. References in early Christian law tracts may be interpreted as indicating that some trees then had a scarcity value. However, trees and woods feature prominently in place-names, and documentary records from late medieval times and into the seventeenth century support the local significance of extensive tracts of both oak woods and secondary "shrubby woods." Some early maps—for example, one that shows parts of the east midlands in the 1550s and Baptista Boazio's general

map of Ireland in 1599—depict a landscape where lowland woods and bogs were locally prominent, particularly in Ulster and along some river valleys.

1600–1900

Although some estimates place the proportion much lower (Pilcher and Mac an tSaoir), as much as one-eighth of Ireland may have been wooded about 1600 C.E. (McCracken). Much of this woodland was cleared over the next century. Commemorated in evocative Irish language poetry as well as in more prosaic estate and customs records, these clearances may have been on occasion for security reasons (to remove the hiding places of rebels and robbers, the "woodkerne" and "tories"), but they were mainly economically inspired, with Irish timber being used locally by tanneries and for coopering and iron-smelting, and being exported for staves and shipbuilding. By the early 1700s the timber resource had been largely exploited; woodland covered less than 2 percent of the island. Only a few pockets of older native woods (e.g., the Killarney broadleaves and the Geeragh in the Lee valley) survived.

The creation of formal avenues and gardens, and the planting (supported by nurseries and nurserymen) of fruit trees and orchards around landlord houses in the late seventeenth century promoted a range of introduced species, among them beech, sycamore, walnut, lime, and horse chestnut. These developments, and the more general planting of hedgerows, foreshadowed an interest in trees and plantations that expanded during the later eighteenth century as large demesnes in the contemporary "natural landscape" idiom were created to offset landlord big houses. Improvement-minded landlords became responsible for the introduction of an ever-wider range of new species (including various conifers and American varieties of elm and birch) and for the creation of new plantations. Their activities were boosted further by the Dublin Society (founded in 1731), which offered premiums for tree planting, and from 1698 by a series of legislative acts promoting the planting of trees. Records of tenant planting survive as the "tree registers" of over a dozen counties.

From the beginning of the nineteenth century, scientific support was being given for a program of afforestation. In the 1880s, as landlord insecurity intensified, much privately inspired planting yielded to felling and the sawmill. Coincidentally, government economic-development initiatives included a report (1883) concluding that some 2 million hectares (over 25 percent of the land area), much of it in western areas, were more suited for trees than anything else. An ill-fated planting experiment (1889–1898) failed at windswept Knockboy, Co. Galway, but in 1903, when little more than 1 percent of Ireland was under woodland, a sustained state forestry program began.

SINCE 1900

In its early decades afforestation progressed slowly. Only some 1,200 hectares had been planted by the 1921 partition, but by the late 1930s annual plantings stood at about 3,100 hectares in the south and 400 hectares north of the border. From the late 1940s, both governments set higher annual planting targets. Social needs, particularly job creation in western areas, influenced expansion, while newly introduced mechanical techniques for deep plowing facilitated site preparation. Annual planting levels of 10,000 hectares in the republic and 2,000 hectares in Northern Ireland were reached during the early 1960s.

The main focus for most of the twentieth century was to plant quick-growing species, with the result that conifers accounted for over 90 percent of all plantings. In both parts of the island, the most favored species was Sitka spruce (*Picea sitchensis*), followed, in the republic, by lodgepole pine (*Pinus contorta*), and in Northern Ireland by Norway spruce (*Picea abies*). Planting was

mainly on cheaply purchased marginal land, including cutaway and blanket bog and unenclosed hill slopes. Little attention was paid to the low-potential forest productivity of some of these areas. Although recreational possibilities were recognized and some forest parks were developed, little consideration was given to the visually obstructive and trivializing impact of forestry on areas of outstanding natural beauty.

Reappraisals of forestry policy in both parts of Ireland during the 1980s produced a more explicitly commercial orientation alongside greater environmental sensitivity. A new state company, Coillte, was formed (1988) in the Republic to manage the maturing state forests and to undertake new planting. Assigned explicitly commercial priorities, Coillte also had to consider recreational and environmental issues. Greater private participation and greater planting on agricultural land were now actively encouraged. Accompanied by a range of attractive tax and other incentives, and organized within the context of European Union operational programs, these measures generated unprecedented annual planting levels and succeeded in encouraging farmers and investment cooperatives to such an extent that from 1990 new planting by the private sector outstripped that of the state. With forestry regarded as a particularly appropriate land-use option in many western areas, private planting was particularly extensive in the counties of Clare, Kerry, and Leitrim.

At the start of the present century, some 640,000 hectares of the republic (9 percent of the total area) were devoted to forest or woodland. This was 250,000 hectares greater than in 1980—an indication of the scale of late-twentieth-century landscape change. Forest cover was most extensive in Counties Wicklow and Waterford (20 and 16 percent of the total area, respectively) and least extensive in County Meath (2 percent) and parts of the north midlands (4 percent). With over 16,000 persons employed in forestry and related activities, the spin-off effects of earlier development were evident in an active timber-processing industry. In Northern Ireland, 82,000 hectares (6 percent of the total area) were under forest, some 15,000 hectares more than in 1980.

Some attempt had been made during the 1990s to increase the proportion of broadleaf planting, yet by 2000 little more than one-fifth of all new plantings in the republic were broadleaved. Reservations about the continued emphasis on conifers had been expressed by the European Commission and others, while concerns had also been raised about the degradation of attractive landscapes, the destruction of biodiversity, and the negative impact of conifer-dominated afforestation on surface-water acidification, run-off, and flooding (Heritage

Council 1999). But government policy favored a further increase in the forest cover on account of its value as an alternative to agriculture, its appeal to rural tourism, its potential multiplier effects for employment, and its potential as a carbon store absorbing carbon dioxide.

With the aim of creating a "sustainable critical mass" of 1.2 million hectares (17 percent of the land area), by 2030, a future planting target was set for the Republic of Ireland of 20,000 hectares per annum. The agenda for the early twenty-first century was marked, in both parts of Ireland, by a state-supported commitment to sustainability guidelines and to policies involving greater diversity in the age and species of trees, more discriminatory landscaping, and felling programs, and the reversion of former old woodland to its preplantation composition. These measures will favor more broadleaf planting within more holistic landscape and ecological contexts.

SEE ALSO Bogs and Drainage; Estates and Demesnes; Landscape and Settlement

Bibliography

Heritage Council (Ireland). *Policy Paper on Forestry and the National Heritage.* 1999.

McCracken, Eileen M. *The Irish Woods since Tudor Times: Their Distribution and Exploitation.* 1971.

Mitchell, Frank, and Michael Ryan. *Reading the Irish Landscape.* 1997.

Neeson, Eoin. *A History of Irish Forestry.* 1991.

Pilcher, Jon R., and Sean Mac an tSaoir. *Woods, Trees and Forests in Ireland.* 1995.

Tomlinson, Roy. "Forests and Woodlands." In *Atlas of the Irish Rural Landscape,* edited by Frederick H. A. Aalen, Kevin Whelan, and Matthew Stout. 1997.

Arnold Horner

Yeats, W. B.

Poet, dramatist, essayist, Nobel laureate (in 1923), folklorist, mystic, and statesman, William Butler Yeats (1865–1939) was the eldest born (on 13 June 1865) of painter John Butler and Susan Mary Pollexfen Yeats. Educated in public schools in London and Dublin, he enrolled in art school (in 1884) and in the next two years cofounded the Dublin Hermetic Society and began publishing his first poetry in the *Dublin University Review* (1885–1886). A close friend of young poets such as AE (George Russell), Yeats was also a familiar of such literary friends of his father's as playwright John Todhunter, Blake scholar Edwin Ellis, and Fenian exile John O'Leary, and so became a central figure in the Irish literary revival of the late nineteenth century. As an editor of folklore and *Poems and Ballads of Young Ireland* (1888) and, with Ellis, *The Works of William Blake* (1893), Yeats grew in reputation as a man of letters as well as a poet. The first collected edition of his *Poems* (1895) began to establish a canon in its selections from *The Wanderings of Oisin and Other Poems* (1889) and from a work dedicated to Maud Gonne, *The Countess Kathleen and Various Legends and Lyrics* (1892). The love poetry of *The Wind among the Reeds* (1899) conflated Gonne with other women, the Sidhe (fairies), and Ireland personified. He collaborated with Lady Gregory on peasant comedies, including *Cathleen Ni Houlihan* (1902), and they joined with John Millington Synge to found the Abbey Theatre.

By 1908, with the publication of the eight-volume *Collected Works in Verse and Prose* to confirm his productivity as a writer, Yeats had begun to leave behind the mannerisms of the Celtic Twilight for a new combative and concrete poetic tone appropriate to the public man he had become. The shift is progressive from the poems of *The Green Helmet* (1910) and *Responsibilities* (1916) to *The Wild Swans at Coole* (1919) and *Michael Robartes and the Dancer* (1921), which brought to national attention a series of rebellion poems, including "Easter 1916," as Yeats was called to service in the Irish Free State Senate in 1922. His ideal "theatre of beauty" had given place to the realism of Synge and Sean O'Casey at the Abbey, and he began writing for private audiences several "plays for dancers" influenced by the Japanese theatre of the Noh. As the First World War erupted, Yeats emerged as the preeminent modern poet. His greatest achievements, *The Tower* (1928) and *The Winding Stair* (1933), were succeeded by a new aesthetic as he introduced the concept of "tragic joy" to conclude a life's work in *New Poems* (1938) and *Last Poems and Two Plays* (1939), published at the Cuala Press by his wife George (m. 1917) and sister Elizabeth Corbet Yeats (1868–1940). He died in France on 28 January 1939.

Taken as a whole, Yeats's influence on English-language poetry has been enormous. No other twentieth-century writer, except James Joyce, has commanded so high a place in Irish letters. As the greatest Irish poet, Yeats casts a giant shadow. For Austin Clarke (1896–1974), who was probably Yeats's nearest rival in the 1930s, Yeats remained an exemplar and obsession long after 1939. The Belfast-born poet Louis MacNeice (1907–1963) wrote one of the best seminal studies of Yeats's poetry; more recently, Derek Mahon (1941–) shows Yeats to be a salutary influence, as does Thomas Kinsella (1928–), who served as codirector of the Cuala Press during its short revival in the 1970s. Ireland's greatest living poet, Seamus Heaney (1939–), has also written usefully on Yeats's permanent value as a lyric bard of any nation, likening and preferring him to Wordsworth. Yeats's international reputation as a major poet and man of letters is therefore sustained by a legacy of emulation, though some of his political mythmaking has been challenged by revisionists in Ireland and elsewhere.

SEE ALSO Arts: Modern Irish and Anglo-Irish Literature and the Arts since 1800; Drama, Modern; Gonne, Maud; Literary Renaissance (Celtic Revival); Literature: Anglo-Irish Literature in the Nineteenth Century; Poetry, Modern; **Primary Documents:** "Easter 1916" (1916)

Bibliography

Foster, R. F. *W. B. Yeats: A Life.* Vol. 1, *The Apprentice Mage.* 1997. Vol. 2, *The Arch-Poet, 1915–1939.* 2003.

Heaney, Seamus. *Preoccupations: Selected Prose, 1969–1978.* 1980.

Heaney, Seamus. *The Redress of Poetry.* 1995.

Jeffares, A. Norman. *W. B. Yeats: A New Biography.* 1988.

McCormack, William J. *Ascendancy and Tradition in Anglo-Irish Literary History from 1789 to 1939.* 1985.

MacNeice, Louis. *The Poetry of W. B. Yeats.* 1941.

Yeats, W. B. *Autobiographies.* 1955.

Wayne K. Chapman

Young Ireland and the Irish Confederation

The Young Ireland movement had its origins in a discussion that took place in Dublin's Phoenix Park in the autumn of 1841 between three young nationalists: Thomas Davis (1814–1845), John Blake Dillon (1816–1866), and Charles Gavan Duffy (1816–1903). The three decided to establish a weekly newspaper, with Duffy as editor and proprietor, that would offer a fresh approach to Irish nationalism. They had in mind a publication that was more outspoken but less sectarian than other nationalist papers and that had a decided cultural emphasis. The result was the *Nation*, whose first edition on 15 October 1842 proclaimed its objective to be the creation of a nationality

> which will not only raise our people from their poverty by securing to them the blessings of a domestic legislation to inflame and purify them with a lofty and heroic love of country, . . . a nationality which will be come to be stamped upon our manners, our literature, and our deeds—a nationality which may embrace Protestant, Catholic, and Dissenter, Milesian and Cromwellian. (*Nation*, 15 October 1842, p. 1).

The paper was an unqualified success: within a year it was selling 10,000 copies per week, a figure that suggested an actual readership of at least 100,000. Besides providing news of national and international events, it published articles by Davis and others on Irish history, literature, language, and art, as well as poetry and ballads from the pens of James Clarence Mangan, Jane Francesca Elgee (also known as "Speranza"), and scores of other talented writers. Davis and his colleagues believed that the key to Ireland's regeneration was an educated public, so to this end they promoted the establishment of "repeal reading rooms" in towns and villages around the country. They also sponsored the publication of a series of monthly volumes on Irish themes called "The Library of Ireland" and a compilation of patriotic poetry (*The Spirit of the Nation*) that appeared in countless editions.

DIFFERENCES WITH DANIEL O'CONNELL

The Young Irelanders—the nickname was meant to reflect their affinity with Young Germany, Young England, and similar groups of the time—formed an articulate and vociferous wing of the repeal movement whose views increasingly set them apart from the O'Connellite leadership. The brand of cultural nationalism that they expressed was attuned to that of their contemporaries in other parts of Europe. It emphasized the uniqueness of the Irish "race" and its cultural heritage, especially its language; it condemned England as the source of Ireland's ills ("Ireland must be unsaxonised before it can be pure and strong," wrote Davis); it resisted what it saw as a growing identification between Catholicism and the nationalist movement; it stressed collectivism and the needs of society rather than the individual; it advocated total separatism, what it called "simple repeal," and it condemned any political or con-

The "rising" of 1848 was an inglorious failure, culminating in the violent affray (depicted here) in the Widow MacCormack's cabbage garden on Boulagh Commons near Ballingarry in Tipperary. About forty policemen got the better of about one hundred Confederates. The incident was soon derided as the "cabbage-patch rebellion." FROM ILLUSTRATED LONDON NEWS, 12 AUGUST 1848.

stitutional arrangement that retained British control over Ireland. Ideas such as these were at odds with those of Daniel O'Connell, whose opinions had been formed during an earlier era and shaped in the give-and-take of everyday politics.

Differences between the Young Irelanders and O'Connell became pronounced in 1844 and 1845 as the British government commenced a program of "killing repeal with kindness" through a series of conciliatory measures. The most controversial of these was the Queen's Colleges Bill that placed restrictions on the teaching of religion and theology in the three colleges it established at Belfast, Cork, and Galway. O'Connell and most of the Catholic bishops condemned the measure for creating "godless" institutions, but Young Irelanders applauded it for promoting secular and mixed education, a feature that they hoped would encourage a more pluralistic nationality. Davis and O'Connell clashed bitterly over the measure at a famous meeting of the Repeal Association on 26 May 1845 and though they were reconciled afterward, their debate symbolized the widening gulf between the two versions of nationalism that the men represented.

Despite his outspokenness, Davis was a moderating force within the Young Ireland movement. His unexpected death in September 1845 allowed other, more militant voices to be heard. Among them was John Mitchel, who succeeded Davis as chief editorial writer for

the *Nation*. An article that he contributed in November 1845 described how railways might be sabotaged and troops ambushed. The piece immediately brought O'Connell's wrath down upon the paper, which published a retraction of sorts, but the whole affair was a foretaste of what was to come.

The militancy of Mitchel and others needs to be seen against the backdrop of the Great Famine, which began at precisely this time and which colored many subsequent actions of the Young Irelanders. It seemed to many of them that the desperate conditions of the Great Famine called for desperate remedies and that the current crisis made the need for repeal more pressing than ever. They were openly critical of O'Connell for making overtures to the Whig party in hopes of gaining temporary concessions for Ireland on such matters as lower grain duties. This suggested to them that the older man was becoming "soft" on the issue of repeal. O'Connell responded in July 1846 by calling upon the members of the Repeal Association to adopt a resolution renouncing violence as a means of obtaining self-government for Ireland. This resulted in a series of lengthy debates that saw the Young Ireland leadership—including Mitchel, Duffy, the Protestant landowner and MP William Smith O'Brien, and a fiery young orator named Thomas Francis Meagher—walk out of the meeting and, in effect, secede from the Association.

Head of the Irish Confederation and a reluctant leader of the abortive 1848 "rising," the well-born and Cambridge-educated William Smith O'Brien (1803–1864) was arrested at the railway station in Thurles (depicted in this sketch) on 5 August 1848. Though originally sentenced to death, he was instead transported to Tasmania and remained there until his release in 1854. FROM *ILLUSTRATED LONDON NEWS*, 12 AUGUST 1848.

THE IRISH CONFEDERATION AND REBELLION

On 13 January 1847 the Young Irelanders formed a separate organization called the Irish Confederation which they hoped would become a less centralized and more democratic body than the Repeal Association. To this end they established clubs in Dublin and a number of provincial towns that were intended to give their members a sense of direct participation in national affairs. The Confederate Clubs sponsored lectures on a range of topics, created their own libraries and reading rooms, held formal classes and debates on various subjects, and provided social outlets for young men of various backgrounds. By the end of 1847 the clubs had attracted only a few thousand members. This changed in February 1848 when news arrived of the revolution that had broken out in Paris. During the next five months the number of clubs grew from around 30 to 225 and total membership rose to more than 40,000, most of it concentrated in Dublin and Munster.

Meanwhile, a split developed within the movement between Mitchel and his supporters, who advocated a French-style uprising, and those who, like Smith O'Brien and Duffy, favored a more moderate approach. The government arrested and convicted Mitchel in late May on a charge of treason-felony and sentenced him to transportation (exile) to Tasmania. With this, the other Young Ireland leaders and the clubs began to plan for an armed rising toward the end of the year, though they had few arms, little military experience, and no clear notion of what they hoped to achieve. The government forced their hand in late July by suspending habeas corpus, after which Smith O'Brien, Meagher, and a few others were arrested following a confused attempt at rebellion in south Tipperary.

The more prominent Young Irelanders suffered transportation or fled abroad, many of them going on to notable careers in politics, the law, and journalism in Australia, the United States, and elsewhere. The movement that they represented, though short-lived, had a profound impact upon Irish nationalists of the early twentieth century such as Arthur Griffith and Patrick Pearse, for it seemed to combine an exhilarating vision of Irishness and the Irish nation with heroic action.

SEE ALSO Balladry in English; Davis, Thomas; Electoral Politics from 1800 to 1921; Great Famine; Mitchel, John; Newspapers; O'Connell, Daniel; Politics: 1800 to 1921—Challenges to the Union; **Primary Documents:** Speech on the Use of Physical Force (28 July 1846)

Bibliography

Davis, Richard. *The Young Ireland Movement.* 1987.

Nation, 15 October 1842.

Nowlan, K. B. *The Politics of Repeal: A Study in the Relations between Great Britain and Ireland, 1841–50.* 1965.

Owens, Gary. "Popular Mobilisation and the Rising of 1848: The Clubs of the Irish Confederation." In *Rebellion and Remembrance in Modern Ireland*, edited by Laurence Geary. 2001.

Sloan, Robert. *William Smith O'Brien and the Young Ireland Rebellion of 1848.* 2000.

Gary Owens

List of Primary Documents

~

Primary documents furnish the basic materials with which scholars work in describing and analyzing the history and culture of any country. The editors of this encyclopedia have selected and, especially in the case of more modern texts, edited a large number of original sources relating to the history and culture of Ireland; we present them below with the aim of deepening the knowledge of interested readers on subjects of major importance.

The editors wish to acknowledge the special usefulness of the pioneering collection—Irish Historical Documents, 1172–1922—edited by the late Edmund Curtis and R. B. McDowell and published in London in 1943 by Methuen and Co. Many of the documents reproduced in this encyclopedia can be found in the Curtis and McDowell collection. In most cases it has been the practice of the encyclopedia editors to cite the original source of the documents appearing here.

Confessio (Declaration) (c. 450), by St. Patrick … 777

"Columbanus to His Monks" (c. 600), by St. Columbanus … 778

From Muirchú's Life of St. Patrick (c. 680) … 778

"To Mary and Her Son" (c. 750), by Blathmac, Son of Cú Brettan … 780

"The Vikings" (Early Ninth Century) … 781

"Writing out of Doors" (Early Ninth Century) … 781

The Bull Laudabiliter, Pope Adrian IV's Grant of Ireland to Henry II (c. 1155) … 782

Three Letters of Pope Alexander III, Confirming Henry II's Conquest of Ireland (1172) … 782

The Treaty of Windsor (1175) … 784

Grant of Prince John to Theobold Walter of Lands in Ireland (1185) … 785

From The Topography of Ireland (1188), by Giraldus Cambrensis … 786

From Expugnatio Hibernica (1189), by Giraldus Cambrensis … 788

Grant of Civic Liberties to Dublin by Prince John (1192) … 788

Magna Carta Hiberniæ (The Great Charter of Ireland) (12 November 1216) … 790

The Statutes of Kilkenny (1366) … 791

King Richard II in Ireland (1395) … 799

Declaration of Independence of the Irish Parliament (1460) … 801

Poynings' Law (1494) … 803

From Vocation of John Bale to the Bishopery of Ossorie (1553), by John Bale … 804

Act of Uniformity (1560) … 806

From Two Bokes of the Histories of Ireland (1571), by Edmund Campion … 806

From "Notes of His Report" (1576), by Sir William Gerard … 807

Letter to Elizabeth (12 November 1580), by Lord Arthur Grey de Wilton … 808

Ferocity of the Irish Wars (1580s–1590s) … 809

From The Image of Irelande (1581), by John Derricke … 810

From "The Sons of Clanricard" (1586), by John Hooker … 811

From Solon His Follie (1594), by Richard Beacon … 812

From A View of the Present State of Ireland (1596), by Edmund Spenser … 813

Tyrone's Demands (1599), by Hugh O'Neill … 818

Accounts of the Siege and Battle of Kinsale (1601) … 819

English Account of the Flight of the Earls (1607), by Sir John Davies   820

Irish Account of the Flight of the Earls (1608), by Tadhg Ó Cianáin   821

Conditions of the Plantation of Ulster (1610)   822

From A Direction for the Plantation of Ulster (1610), by Thomas Blennerhasset   823

From A New Description of Ireland (1610), by Barnaby Rich   824

From A Discovery of the True Causes Why Ireland Was Never Entirely Subdued (1612), by Sir John Davies   825

On Catholic Ireland in the Early Seventeenth Century   827

From An Itinerary (1617), by Fynes Moryson   829

From "A Discourse of Ireland" (1620), by Luke Gernon   831

From The Total Discourse of His Rare Adventures (1632), by William Lithgow   833

From Travels (1634–1635), by Sir William Brereton   834

Confederation of Kilkenny (1642)   835

Speech to the Speaker of the House of Commons (1642), by Richard Boyle   836

From A True and Credible Relation (1642)   837

From A Remonstrance . . . , Being the Examinations of Many Who Were Eye-Witnesses of the Same, and Justified upon Oath by Many Thousands (1643), by Thomas Morley   838

On the Capture of Drogheda (17 September 1649), by Oliver Cromwell   840

From The Great Case of Transplantation Discussed (1655), by Vincent Gookin   841

From The Interest of England in the Irish Transplantation Stated (1655), by Richard Lawrence   842

Treaty of Limerick (1691)   844

From The Memoirs of Edmund Ludlow (1698)   846

An Act to Prevent the Further Growth of Popery (1704)   847

The Declaratory Act (1720)   853

On the Whiteboys (1769), by John Bush   853

From A Philosophical Survey of the South of Ireland (1777), by Reverend Thomas Campbell   854

The Catholic Relief Act (1778)   857

On Irish Rural Society and Poverty (1780), by Arthur Young   858

The Catholic Relief Act (1782)   860

The Ulster Volunteer Resolutions (1782)   861

Yelverton's Act (1782)   862

The Renunciation Act (1783)   863

The Catholic Relief Act (1793)   864

United Irish Parliamentary Reform Plan (March 1794)   866

Grievances of the United Irishmen of Ballynahinch, Co. Down (1795)   867

Speech Delivered at a United Irish Meeting in Ballyclare, Co. Antrim (1795)   868

The Insurrection Act (1796)   869

The United Irishmen Organization (1797)   871

Statement of Three Imprisoned United Irish Leaders (4 August 1798)   873

Irish Act of Union (1 August 1800)   877

Speech from the Dock (19 September 1803), by Robert Emmet   880

From A Description of the . . . Peasantry of Ireland (1804), by Robert Bell   881

On Presbyterian Communities in Ulster (1810, 1812), by John Gamble   881

From Narrative of a Residence in Ireland (1817), by Anne Plumptre   884

Origin of the "Catholic Rent" (18 February 1824)   885

The Catholic Relief Act (1829)   888

Account of the Wexford Rising (1832), by Thomas Cloney   890

On Irish Catholicism (1839), by Gustave de Beaumont   892

On Irish Society before the Famine (1841–1843), by Mr. and Mrs. S. C. Hall   893

On Repeal of the Act of Union at the "Monster Meeting" at Mullingar (14 May 1843), by Daniel O'Connell   896

Letter Advocating Federalism as an Alternative to Repeal (November 1844), by William Sharman Crawford   899

On Rural Society on the Eve of the Great Famine (1844–1845), by Asenath Nicholson   900

Speech on the Use of Physical Force (28 July 1846), by Thomas Francis Meagher   902

From Narrative of a Recent Journey (1847), by William Bennett   903

Resolutions Adopted at the Tenant-Right Conference (6–9 August 1850)   904

Resolution Adopted at the Tenant League Conference (8 September 1852)   905

Two Fenian Oaths (1858, 1859)   905

"God Save Ireland" (1867)   906

Resolutions Adopted at the Home Rule Conference (18–21 November 1873)   907

Speech Advocating Consideration of Home Rule by the House of Commons (30 June 1874), by Isaac Butt   908

From Belfast Fifty Years Ago (1875), by Thomas Gaffikin   910

Establishment of the National Land League of Mayo (16 August 1879)   911

Call at Ennis for Agrarian Militancy (19 September 1880), by Charles Stewart Parnell   914

Land Law (Ireland) Act (22 August 1881)   915

On Home Rule and the Land Question at Cork (21 January 1885), by Charles Stewart Parnell   919

On Home Rule at Wicklow (5 October 1885), by Charles Stewart Parnell   920

On the Home Rule Bill of 1886 (8 April 1886), by William Gladstone   922

The Irish Parliamentary Party Pledge (30 June 1892)   925

From "The Necessity for De-Anglicising Ireland" (25 November 1892), by Douglas Hyde   925

Address at the First Annual Convention of the National Council of Sinn Féin (28 November 1905), by Arthur Griffith   927

Resolutions Adopted at the Public Meeting Following the First Annual Convention of the National Council of Sinn Féin (28 November 1905)   929

Declaration against Home Rule (10 October 1911)   930

"Solemn League and Covenant" Signed at the "Ulster Day" Ceremony in Belfast (28 September 1912)   930

Address on the Ulster Question in the House of Commons (11 February 1914), by Sir Edward Carson   931

O'Donovan Rossa Graveside Panegyric (1 August 1915), by Patrick H. Pearse   932

"What Is Our Programme?" (22 January 1916), by James Connolly   933

Proclamation of the Irish Republic (24 April 1916)   935

"Easter 1916" (1916), by William Butler Yeats   936

Declaration of Irish Independence (21 January 1919)   937

The "Democratic Programme" of Dáil Éireann (21 January 1919)   938

Government of Ireland Act (23 December 1920)   939

The Anglo-Irish Treaty (6 December 1921)   942

"Time Will Tell" (19 December 1921), by Eamon de Valera   945

Speech in Favor of the Anglo-Irish Treaty of December 1921 (7 January 1922), by Arthur Griffith   948

Proclamation Issued by IRA Leaders at the Beginning of the Civil War (29 June 1922)   949

Provisional Government Proclamation at the Beginning of the Civil War (29 June 1922)   950

Speech at the Opening of the Free State Parliament (11 September 1922), by William T. Cosgrave   950

Constitution of the Irish Free State (5 December 1922)   951

Republican Cease-Fire Order (28 April 1923)   954

Speech on Ireland's Admission to the League of Nations (10 September 1923), by William T. Cosgrave   955

Letter on the Commission on the Gaeltacht (4 March 1925), by William T. Cosgrave   956

"The End" (1926), by Tomás Ó Criomhthain   957

"Aims of Fianna Fáil in Office" (17 March 1932), by Eamon de Valera   959

"Pierce's Cave" (1933), by Maurice O'Sullivan   960

On "A Protestant Parliament and a Protestant State" (24 April 1934), by Sir James Craig   962

"Failure of the League of Nations" (18 June 1936), by Eamon de Valera   963

"Scattering and Sorrow" (1936), by Peig Sayers   965

From the 1937 Constitution   968

"German Attack on Neutral States" (12 May 1940), by Eamon de Valera   970

"National Thanksgiving" (16 May 1945), **971**
by Eamon de Valera

On the Republic of Ireland Bill (24 **975**
November 1948), by John A. Costello

Letter to John A. Costello, the Taoiseach **976**
(5 April 1951), by Archbishop John Charles
McQuaid

From the *Report of the Commission on* **978**
Emigration and Other Population
Problems, 1948–1954 (1955)

From *Economic Development* (1958) **979**

"An Irishman in Coventry" (1960), by John **983**
Hewitt

Speech to Ministers of the Governments of **984**
the Member States of the European
Economic Community (18 January
1962), by Seán Lemass

On Community Relations in Northern **987**
Ireland (28 April 1967), by Terence
O'Neill

"Ulster at the Crossroads" (9 December **989**
1968), by Terence O'Neill

Statement by the Taoiseach (13 August **991**
1969), by Jack Lynch

From the *Report of the Commission on the* **992**
Status of Women (1972)

"Towards Changes in the Republic" **993**
(1973), by Garret FitzGerald

From the Decision of the Supreme Court **1000**
in *McGee v. the Attorney General and the*
Revenue Commissioners (19 December
1973)

On the Family Planning Bill (20 February **1003**
1974), by Mary Robinson

"Punishment" (1975), by Seamus Heaney **1005**

Anglo-Irish Agreement (15 November **1005**
1985)

"Inquisitio 1584" (c. 1985), by Máire Mhac **1009**
an tSaoi

"Feis" ("Carnival") (c. 1990), by Nuala Ní **1010**
Dhomhnaill

Irish Republican Army (IRA) Cease-Fire **1012**
Statement (31 August 1994)

Text of the IRA Cease-Fire Statement (19 **1013**
July 1997)

The Belfast/Good Friday Agreement (10 **1013**
April 1998)

Primary Documents

CONFESSIO (DECLARATION)

c. 450

St. Patrick

This is one of the two fifth-century historical documents which seem to prove the existence of an historical St. Patrick. Written in the form of a self-defense of his missionary career, the Confessio sets forth his conviction that his mission has been inspired by God and hence is not subject to failure due to his personal foibles. This work also served as a basis for the subsequent lives of the saint, such as Muirchú's.

SEE ALSO Religion: The Coming of Christianity; Saint Patrick, Problem of

1. I, Patrick, a sinner, quite uncultivated and the least of all the faithful and utterly despicable to many, had as my father the deacon Calpornius, son of the late Potitus, a priest, who belonged to the town of Bannavem Taburniae; he had a small estate nearby, and it was there that I was taken captive. I was then about sixteen years old. I did not know the true God and I was taken into captivity in Ireland with so many thousands; and we deserved it, because we drew away from God and did not keep His commandments and did not obey our priests who kept reminding us of our salvation; and the Lord brought on us the fury of His anger and scattered us among many peoples even to the ends of the earth, where now I in my insignificance find myself among foreigners.

2. And there the Lord opened up my awareness of my unbelief, so that I might, however late, remember my faults and turn with all my heart to the Lord my God, who had regard for my lowly estate and took pity on my youth and ignorance and watched over me before I knew Him and before I learned sense or could distinguish between good and evil and who protected me and comforted me as a father might his son. . . .

16. But after I reached Ireland, well, I pastured the flocks every day and I used to pray many times a day; more and more did my love of God and my fear of Him increase, and my faith grew and my spirit was stirred, and as a result I would say up to a hundred prayers in one day, and almost as many at night; I would even stay in the forests and on the mountain and would wake to pray before dawn in all weathers, snow, frost, rain; and I felt no harm and there was no listlessness in me—as I now realise, it was because the Spirit was fervent within me.

17. And it was in fact there one night while asleep I heard a voice saying to me: "You do well to fast, since you will soon be going to your home country": and again, very shortly after, I heard this prophecy: "See, your ship is ready." And it was not near at hand but was perhaps two hundred miles away, and I had never been there and did not know a living soul there. And then I soon ran away and abandoned the man with whom I had been for six years, and I came in God's strength, for He granted me a successful journey and I had nothing to fear, till I reached that ship. . . .

23. And again a few years later I was in Britain with my kinsfolk, and they welcomed me as a son and asked me earnestly not to go off anywhere and leave them this time, after the great tribulations which I had been through. And it was there that I saw one night in a vision a man coming as it were from Ireland (his name was Victoricus), with countless letters, and he gave me one of them, and I read the heading of the letter, "The Voice of the Irish." and as I read these opening words

aloud, I imagined at that very instant that I heard the voice of those who were beside the forest of Foclut which is near the western sea; and thus they cried, as though with one voice: "We beg you, holy boy, to come and walk again among us"; and I was stung with remorse in my heart and could not read on, and so I awoke. Thanks be to God, that after so many years the Lord bestowed on them according to their cry. . . .

41. And how has it lately come about in Ireland that those who never had any knowledge of God but up till now always worshipped idols and abominations are now called the people of the Lord and the sons of God, and sons and daughters of Irish underkings are seen to be monks and virgins of Christ? . . .

58. And so may God never allow me to be separated from His people which He has won in the ends of the earth. I pray to God to give me perserverance and to deign to grant that I prove a faithful witness to Him until I pass on, for my God's sake. . . .

62. But I beg those who believe in and fear God, whoever deigns to look at or receive this document which the unlearned sinner Patrick drew up in Ireland, that no-one should ever say that if I have achieved anything, however trivial, or may have shown the way according to God's good pleasure, it was my ignorance at work, but consider and accept as the undeniable truth that it would have been God's gift. And this is my declaration before I die.

ST. PATRICK: HIS WRITINGS AND MUIRCHU'S LIFE, *edited and translated by A. B. E. Hood (1978), pp. 41, 44, 45-46, 50, 53, 54. © Text and translation: A. B. E. Hood, 1978. Reproduced by permission.*

~

"COLUMBANUS TO HIS MONKS"

c. 600(?)

Attributed to St. Columbanus

Born in Leinster c. 543, Columbanus (d. 615) became a member of the monastery at Bangor in Ulster, one of the most celebrated in sixth-century Ireland. In c. 590, he and a band of twelve companions set out on pilgrimage, traveling first to Britain (or Brittany), followed by Western Gaul, Burgundy, the Merovingian courts of Europe, and up the Rhine to Switzerland (when he presumably could have composed this Latin song). He ended up in Lombardy, receiving a strip of land there from the King and Queen, where he founded the monastery of Bobbio. This boat song

(which the translator, James Carney, sees as an "exhortation to his monks to persevere to the end") captures the adventurous mood and robust faith of the wandering Irish monks. His writings certainly reflect a knowledge of classical Latin (e.g., this poem in hexameters with a recurring refrain).

SEE ALSO Hiberno-Latin Culture

See, cut in woods, through flood of twin-horned Rhine
passes the keel, and greased slips over seas—
Heave, men! And let resounding echo sound our "heave."

The winds raise blasts, wild rain-storms wreak their
  spite
but ready strength of men subdues it all—
Heave, men! And let resounding echo sound our "heave."

Clouds melt away and the harsh tempest stills,
effort tames all, great toil is conqueror—
Heave, men! And let resounding echo sound our "heave."

Endure and keep yourselves for happy things;
you suffered worse, and these too God shall end—
Heave, men! And let resounding echo sound our "heave."

Thus acts the foul fiend: wearing out the heart
and with temptation shaking inmost parts—
You men, remember Christ with mind still sounding "heave."

Stand firm in soul and spurn the foul fiend's tricks
and seek defence in virtue's armoury—
You men, remember Christ with mind still sounding "heave."

Firm faith will conquer all and blessed zeal
and the old fiend yielding breaks at last his darts—
You men, remember Christ with mind still sounding "heave."

Supreme, of virtues King, and fount of things,
He promises in strife, gives prize in victory—
You men, remember Christ with mind still sounding "heave."

MEDIEVAL IRISH LYRICS WITH THE IRISH BARDIC POET, *translated by James Carney (1967), pp. 9, 11.*

~

FROM MUIRCHÚ'S *LIFE* OF ST. PATRICK

c. 680

Based on both legend and historical sources, such as St. Patrick's own Confessio, this version became the basis for subsequent Lives of the saint. Here is the account of his early life and mission to convert the Irish. Patrick's birthplace has never been satisfactorily identified, though it is generally thought to have been in western Britain.

SEE ALSO Hagiography; Religion: The Coming of Christianity; Saint Patrick, Problem of

1. Patrick, who was also called Sochet, was of British nationality, born in Britain, the son of the deacon Calpurnius, whose father, as Patrick himself says, was the priest Potitus, who came from the town of Bannavem Taburniae, not far from our sea; we have discovered for certain and beyond any doubt that this township is Ventre; and the mother who bore him was named Concessa.

At the age of sixteen the boy, with others, was captured and brought to this island of barbarians and was kept as a slave in the household of a certain cruel pagan king. He spent six years in captivity, in accordance with the Jewish custom, in fear and trembling before God, as the psalmist says (Psalms 54, 6), and in many vigils and prayers. He used to pray a hundred times a day and a hundred times a night, gladly giving to God what is due to God and to Caesar what is due to Caesar and beginning to fear God and to love the Lord Almighty; for up to that time he had no knowledge of the true God, but at this point the Spirit became fervent within him.

After many hardships there, after enduring hunger and thirst, cold and nakedness, after pasturing flocks, after visits from Victoricus, an angel sent to him by God, after great miracles known to almost everyone, after divine prophecies (of which I shall give just one to two examples: "You do well to fast, since you will soon be going to your home country," and again: "See, your ship is ready," though it was not near at hand but was perhaps two hundred miles away, where he had never been to) after all these experiences, as we have said, which can hardly be counted by anyone, in the twenty-third year of his life he left the earthly, pagan king and his words, received the heavenly, eternal God and now sailed for Britain by God's command and accompanied by the Holy Spirit in the ship which lay ready for him; with him were barbarian strangers and pagans who worshipped many false gods. . . .

8. And so, when a suitable opportunity so directed, with God's help to accompany him he set out on the journey which he had already begun, to the work for which he had long been prepared the work, that is, of the Gospel. And Germanus sent an older man with him, namely the priest Segitius, so that Patrick would have a witness and companion, since he had not yet been consecrated to the rank of bishop by the holy lord Germanus. For they were well aware that Palladius, the archdeacon of Pope Celestine, the bishop of the city of Rome who then held the apostolic see as forty-fifth in line from St. Peter the apostle, that this Palladius had been consecrated and sent to convert this island, lying as it does in frozen wintriness. But God prevented him, because no one can receive anything from this earth unless it has been given him from heaven. For these wild, uncivilised people did not take kindly to his teaching, nor did he himself want to spend time in a land which was not his own; he returned to him who sent him. But on his return journey from here, after making the first sea crossing and proceeding by land, he died in the land of the British.

9. And so, when the word came of the death of St. Palladius in Britain, since Palladius' disciples, Augustine, Benedict and the others, returned to Ebmoria with the news of his death, Patrick and his companions turned aside to a wonderful man, a very important bishop called Amator, who lived nearby. And there St. Patrick, knowing what was to happen to him, received the rank of bishop from the holy bishop Amator, as also Auxilius and Iserninus and others received lesser orders on the same day as St. Patrick was consecrated. They received the blessings, everything was performed in the customary way, and the following verse of the psalmist was also sung, especially appropriate for Patrick: "You are a priest for ever, in the manner of Melchisedek" (Psalms 109:4). Then in the name of the holy Trinity the venerable traveller went on board the ship which had been prepared and reached Britain; and as he made his way on foot he avoided all detours, except for the ordinary business of travelling (for no one seeks the Lord by idleness), and then he hurried across our sea with all speed and a favourable wind.

10. Now in the days in which these events took place in the aforesaid area there was a certain king, the fierce heathen emperor of the barbarians, who reigned in Tara, which was the Irish capital. His name was Loegaire, the son of Niall and the ancestor of the royal house of almost the whole of this island. He had had wise men, wizards, soothsayers, enchanters and inventors of every black art who were able in their heathen, idolatrous way to know and foresee everything before it happened; two of them were favoured above the rest, their names being Lothroch, also called Lochru, and Lucetmael, also known as Ronal.

These two repeatedly foretold by their magical arts that there would come to be a certain foreign practice like a kingdom, with some strange and troublesome doctrine; a practice brought from afar across the seas, proclaimed by a few, adopted by many and respected by all; it would overthrow kingdoms, kill kings who resisted, win over great crowds, destroy all their gods, and after driving out all the resources of their art it would reign for ever and ever. They also identified and foretold the man who would bring and urge this practice in the following words, often repeated by them in a sort of verse form, especially in the two or three years preceding Patrick's arrival. This is how the verse ran; the sense is less than clear because of the different character of the language:

'Adize-head shall come, with his crook-headed staff and his house with a hole in its head. He shall chant blasphemy from his table, from the eastern part of his house, and all his household will answer him: "So be it, so be it!" (This can be expressed more clearly in our own language.) "So when all these things happen, our kingdom, which is heathen, shall not stand."

And this is just as it later turned out. For the worship of idols was wiped out on Patrick's arrival, and the Catholic faith in Christ filled every corner of our land. So much for this topic; let us return to our subject. . . .

22. And St. Patrick, according to the Lord Jesus' command going and teaching all nations and baptising them in the name of the Father and of the Son and of the Holy Ghost, set out from Tara and preached, with the Lord working with him and confirming his words with the following signs.

St. Patrick: His Writings and Muirchu's Life, *edited and translated by A. B. E. Hood (1978), pp. 83, 85–86, 93. © Text and translation: A. B. E. Hood, 1978. Reproduced by permission.*

~

"To Mary and Her Son"

c. 750

Blathmac, Son of Cú Brettan

A member of the Fir Rois of modern-day County Monaghan, Blathmac was a son of the chieftain who took part in the Battle of Allen (722) and the brother of a saga character named Donn Bó (d. c. 759). His poems, in Old Irish, reflect a knowledge of Latin learning and also demonstrate that the cult of the Virgin Mary was established in Ireland by the eighth century. These verses, part of a much longer poem of 149 stanzas, use the caoineadh *(keen) as a structuring*

device, with the poet asking if he can join Mary in keening her dead son Jesus and ending with a moving invocation of Mary.

SEE ALSO Early Medieval Ireland and Christianity

Come to me, loving Mary,
that I may keen with you your very dear one;
Alas! The going to the cross of your son,
that great jewel, that beautiful champion.

That with you I may beat my two hands
for your fair son's captivity.
Your womb has conceived Jesus —
it has not marred your virginity.

You have conceived him and no sin with man,
you brought him forth without ailing wound;
without grief he strengthened you (fair grace!)
at the time of his crucifixion.

I ask: Have you heard of a son like this,
one who could do these three things?
Such has not come upon the thighs of women
and such will not be born.

The first-begotten of God, the Father, in heaven
is your son, Mary, virgin;
he was begotten in a pure conception
through the power of the septiform Spirit.

No father has found, Mary,
the like of your renowned son;
better he than prophet, wise than druid,
a king who was bishop and full sage.

His form was finer than that of other beings,
this stout vigour greater than any craftsman's,
wiser he than any breast under heaven,
juster than any judge.

More beautiful, more, pleasant, bigger than other boys
since he was in his swaddling clothes;
it was known what would come of him,
a being for the saving of multitudes.

Noble the being born from you!
You were granted, Mary, a great gift:
Christ, son of the Father in heaven,
him have you borne in Bethlehem.

May I have from you my three petitions,
beautiful Mary, little white-necked one;
get them, sun amongst women,
from your son who has them in his power.

That I may be in the world till old
serving the Lord who rules starry heaven,
and that then there be a welcome for me
into the eternal, ever-enduring kingdom.

That everyone who uses this as a vigil prayer
at lying down and at rising,
that it may protect him from blemish in the other world
like breastplate and helmet.

Everyone if any sort shall recite it
fasting on Friday night,
provided only that it be with full-flowing tears,
Mary, may he not be for hell.

When your son comes in anger
with his cross on his reddened back,
that then you will save
any friend who shall have keened him.

For you, beautiful Mary,
I shall go as guarantor:
anyone who says the full keen,
he shall have reward.

I call you with true words,
Mary, beautiful queen,
that we may have talk together
to pity your heart's darling.

So that I may keen the bright Christ
with you in the most heartfelt way,
shining precious jewel,
mother the great Lord.

Were I rich and honoured
ruling the people of the world to every sea,
they would all come with you and me
to keen your royal son.

There would be beating of hands
by women, children and men,
that they might keen on every hill-top
the king who made every star.

I cannot do this. With heartfelt feeling
I will bewail your son with you
if only you come at some time
on a visit to me.

Come to me, loving Mary,
you, head of unsullied faith,
that we may have talk together
with the compassion of unblemished heart.

MEDIEVAL IRISH LYRICS WITH THE IRISH BARDIC POET,
translated by James Carney (1967), pp. 13, 15, 17, 19, 21.

~

"THE VIKINGS"

Early Ninth Century

Anonymous

Possibly written by a monk who had escaped the Viking onslaughts in Ireland, which began in about 800, this verse indicates that stormy weather means that the poet need not fear Vikings tonight.

SEE ALSO Early Medieval Ireland and Christianity; Literature: Early and Medieval Literature

Bitter and wild is the wind to-night
tossing the tresses of the sea to white.
On such a night as this I feel at ease:
fierce Northmen only course the quiet seas.

MEDIEVAL IRISH LYRICS WITH THE IRISH BARDIC POET,
translated by James Carney (1967), p. 23.

~

"WRITING OUT OF DOORS"

Early Ninth Century

Anonymous

Found in the margin of Priscian's treatise on Latin grammar from the monastery of St. Gall near Lake Constance, Switzerland, together with the poem entitled "The Vikings," this work describes the Irish monk/scribe writing a poem under the trees. The manuscript in which these poems occur was probably copied in a Leinster monastery and brought to the continent by Irish monks in approximately 848.

SEE ALSO Early Medieval Ireland and Christianity; Literature: Early and Medieval Literature

A wall of forest looms above
  and sweetly the blackbird sings;
all the birds make melody
  over me and my books and things.

There sings to me the cuckoo
  from bush-citadels in grey hood.

God's doom! May the Lord protect me
writing well, under the great wood.

MEDIEVAL IRISH LYRICS WITH THE IRISH BARDIC POET,
translated by James Carney (1967), p. 23.

≈

THE BULL *LAUDABILITER*, POPE ADRIAN IV'S GRANT OF IRELAND TO HENRY II

c. 1155?

Although the authenticity of this document has been questioned, since the text was published only in Giraldus's Conquest of Ireland *(over thirty years after its alleged date), some such document is needed to explain why the Irish bishops at Cashel and the Irish kings at Waterford and Dublin submitted to Henry II in 1171. The famous churchman John of Salisbury claimed that he obtained it in 1155 for Henry from Adrian IV—"coincidentally" the only Englishman ever to become pope.*

SEE ALSO Norman Invasion and Gaelic Resurgence

Adrian, bishop, servant of the servants of God, to our well-beloved son in Christ the illustrious king of the English, greeting and apostolic benediction.

Laudably and profitably does your majesty contemplate spreading the glory of your name on earth and laying up for yourself the reward of eternal happiness in heaven, in that, as becomes a Catholic prince, you purpose to enlarge the boundaries of the Church, to proclaim the truths of the Christian religion to a rude and ignorant people, and to root out the growths of vice from the field of the Lord; and the better to accomplish this purpose you seek the counsel and goodwill of the apostolic see. In pursuing your object, the loftier your aim and the greater your discretion, the more prosperous, we are assured, with God's assistance, will be the progress you will make: for undertakings commenced in the zeal of faith and the love of religion are ever wont to attain to a good end and issue. Verily, as your excellency doth acknowledge, there is no doubt that Ireland and all islands on which Christ the sun of righteousness has shone, and which have accepted the doctrines of the Christian faith, belong to the jurisdiction of the blessed Peter and the holy Roman Church; wherefore the more pleased are we to plant in them the seed of faith acceptable to God, inasmuch as our conscience warns us that

in their case a stricter account hereafter be required of us.

Whereas then, well-beloved son in Christ, you have expressed to us your desire to enter the island of Ireland in order to subject its people to law and to root out from them the weeds of vice, and your willingness to pay an annual tribute to the blessed Peter of one penny from every house, and to maintain the rights of the churches of that land whole and inviolate: We therefore, meeting your pious and laudable desire with due favour and according a gracious assent to your petition, do hereby declare our will and pleasure that, with a view to enlarging the boundaries of the Church, restraining the downward course of vice, correcting evil customs and planting virtue, and for the increase of the Christian religion, you shall enter the island and execute whatsoever may tend to the honour of God and the welfare of the land; and also that the people of that land shall receive you with honour and revere you as their lord; provided always that the rights of the churches remain whole and inviolate, and saving to the blessed Peter and the Holy Roman Church the annual tribute of one penny from every house. If then you should carry your project into effect, let it be your care to instruct that people in good ways of life, and so act, both in person and by agents whom you shall have found in faith, in word, and in deed fitted for the task, that the Church there may be adorned, that the Christian religion may take root and grow, and that all things appertaining to the honour of God and the salvation of souls may be so ordered that you may deserve at God's hands the fullness of an everlasting reward, and may obtain on earth a name renowned throughout the ages.

Translated from the original Latin text in IRISH HISTORICAL DOCUMENTS, *1172–1922, edited by Edmund Curtis and R. B. McDowell (1943), pp. 17–18. Reproduced by permission of the publisher.*

≈

THREE LETTERS OF POPE ALEXANDER III, CONFIRMING HENRY II'S CONQUEST OF IRELAND

1172

Following the Anglo-Norman invasion and Henry II's own intervention, Pope Alexander III sent three letters which essentially confirmed the English conquest: one to the papal legate in Ireland and the Irish bishops reproving the "abuses" of the Irish revealed to Rome by the bishops themselves; a second to Henry urging him to continue his efforts to "reform" the Irish; and a third to the Irish princes, commending them for receiving Henry and swearing fealty to him as their king and lord.

SEE ALSO Norman Invasion and Gaelic Resurgence

Letter I

Alexander, bishop, servant of the servants of God, to the vernerable brothers Christian, bishop of Lismore, legate of the apostolic See, and Gelasius of Armagh, Donatus of Cashel, Laurence of Dublin, and Catholicus [Cadhla] of Tuam, archbishops, and their suffragans, greeting and apostolic blessing. With what shocking abuses the Irish people are infected and how, lapsed from the fear of God and reverence for the Christian faith, they follow those things which lead to the peril of their souls, has been made known to Us in a series of letters from you, and also has often come to the knowledge of the Apostolic See by the trustworthy accounts of others.

Hence it is that—understanding from your letters that our dear son in Christ, Henry, illustrious King of England, stirred by divine inspiration and with his united forces, has subjected to his dominion that people, a barbarous one uncivilized and ignorant of the Divine law, and that those evils which were unlawfully practised in your land are now, with God's help, already beginning to diminish—We are overjoyed and have offered our grateful prayers to Him who has granted to the said King so great a victory and triumph, humbly beseeching that by the vigilance and care of the same King that most undisciplined and untamed nation may in and by all things persevere in devotion to the practice of the Christian faith, and that you and your ecclesiastical brethren may rejoice in all due honour and tranquility.

Since therefore it is fitting that you should afford all your due care and support to carry on such things which have had so pious and happy a beginning, We command and enjoin upon you by these our Apostolic letters that you will diligently and manfully and as far as you are able, saving your order and office, assist the abovesaid King, so great a man and so devout a son of the Church, to maintain and preserve that land and to extirpate the filthiness of such great abominations.

And if any of the Kings, princes or other persons of that land shall rashly attempt to go against his due oath and fealty pledged to the said King and does not at your admonition promptly, as he ought, return to his allegiance, then you, trusting in the Apostolic authority and putting aside every pretext and excuse, shall lay ec-

clesiastical censure on such a one, diligently and effectively executing this our injunction so that—even as the said King, like a most Catholic and Christian prince is said to have obeyed our wishes in pious and generous fashion in restoring to you the tithes and other ecclesiastical rights and all things which belong to the liberties of the Church—you also will do, if you firmly respect those things which belong to the royal dignity and to the best of your ability make them to be respected by others.

Given at Tusculum on the 12th of the Kalends of October [September 20, 1172].

Letter 2

Alexander, bishop, servant of the servants of God, to his dear son in Christ, Henry, illustrious king of England, greeting and apostolic blessing.

By frequent report and trustworthy evidence and with much joy, we have been assured how that, like a pious king and magnificent prince you have wonderfully and gloriously triumphed over that people of Ireland, who, ignoring the fear of God, in unbridled fashion at random wander through the steeps of vice, and have renounced all reverence for the Christian faith and virtue, and who destroy themselves in mutual slaughter, and over a kingdom which the Roman emperors, the conquerors of the world, left (so we read) untouched in their time, and, by the will of God (as we firmly believe), have extended the power of your majesty over that same people, a race uncivilized and undisciplined. For, while we for the present omit other monstrous abuses which the same race, neglecting the observances of the Christian faith, irreverently practice, even as the venerable our brothers, Christian, bishop of Lismore, legate of the Apostolic See, and the archbishops and bishops of that land, have made known to us in their letters, and our dear son Ralph, archdeacon of Landaff, an intelligent and discreet man and bound by the chain of peculiar devotion to your royal majesty, who with his own eyes has seen all these things and made them known to you in person, both carefully and clearly, it appears that the aforesaid people, as perhaps has more fully come to your knowledge, marry their stepmothers and are not ashamed to have children by them; a man will live with his brother's wife while the brother is still alive; one man will live in concubinage with two sisters; and many of them, putting away the mother, will marry the daughters.

And all from time to time eat meat in Lent; nor do they pay tithes, or respect as they ought the churches of God and ecclesiastical persons.

And because (for so the said archbishops and bishops have signified to Us and the aforesaid archdeacon has more fully and expressly informed us) We understand that you, collecting your splendid naval and land forces, have set your mind upon subjugating that people to your lordship and, by the Divine grace, extirpating the filthiness of such abomination, We hold your purpose good and acceptable in all ways, and therefore render to Him from who all good proceeds, and who disposes the pious deeds of his faithful ones at his good pleasure, all our grateful prayers, beseeching the Almighty Lord with fervent prayer that, even as by your influence those evils which do wickedly are practised in that land begin already to diminish and the seeds of virtue to flourish instead, so also by you with God's aid the said people, with the stains of vice cast away, may receive the whole discipline of the Christian faith, to the glory of an unfading crown for you and the health of their souls.

And so we exhort and beseech your majesty and enjoin upon you for the remission of your sins that in this work which you have so laudably begun you will even more intently and strenuously continue, so that, even as you have to the remission of your sins undertaken so great a task as regards that people, so also for the benefit to their souls you shall be worthy of an eternal crown.

And because, owing to your majesty's greatness, the Roman Church has a different right in islands than on the mainland, We (holding this hope and trust, through the fervour of your devotion that wills not only to preserve the rights of the Church but even to increase them and, where She has no rights, feels bound to confer them upon Her) beseech and earnestly enjoin upon your majesty that you will carefully seek to preserve the rights of the see of Saint Peter for us in the abovesaid land and that, even if it has none there, you will appoint and assign those rights to the Church, so that in return we may owe your highness the fullest gratitude and that you may be seen to offer to God the first fruits of your glory and triumph.

Given at Tusculum, the twelfth of the Kalends of October.

Letter 3

Alexander, bishop, servant of the servants of God, to our dear and noble sons, the Kings and Princes of Ireland, greeting and apostolic blessing.

Whereas by common report and the assured relation of many it has been made known to us that you have received our dear son in Christ, Henry, the illustrious king of England, as your king and lord, and have sworn fealty to him, the greater is our joy in that, by God's aid and the power of the said King, there shall reign in your land greater peace and tranquility and

that the Irish people, in proportion as, through the enormity and filthiness of their vices, they have fallen away so far from the Divine law, so they shall be all the more surely moulded in it and receive all the more fully the discipline of the Christian faith.

Wherefore, in it that you have of your free will submitted to so powerful and magnificent a king and so devoted a son of the Church, we commend your wise forethought as most worthy of praise, seeing that from it great advantage can be looked for alike to you, to the Church and to the whole people of that land.

We moreover warn and admonish your noble order to strive to preserve the fealty which by solemn oath you have made to so great a king firm and unbroken with due submission towards him. And may you so show yourselves, in all humility and meekness, submissive and devoted towards him that you may be able ever to win his abundant favour and that we may be able to commend fully your prudence and foresight.

Given at Tusculum, 12th day of the Kalends of October.

Translated from the original Latin text in IRISH HISTORICAL DOCUMENTS, 1172–1922, edited by Edmund Curtis and R. B. McDowell (1943), pp. 19–22. Reproduced by permission of the publisher.

~

THE TREATY OF WINDSOR

1175

As part of the English settlement with the native Irish in October 1175, Roderic (Rory) O'Connor was left king of Connacht under Henry and over-king of the area unconquered by the English, as long as he paid an annual tribute of hides. There is no record that this tribute was ever paid. Though he continued to rule over half of Ireland until his death in 1198, he was a "shadow-king." Henry soon broke the spirit of the treaty by granting Munster and Ulster to other Anglo-Norman adventurers.

SEE ALSO English Government in Medieval Ireland; Norman Conquest and Colonization; Norman Invasion and Gaelic Resurgence

This is the agreement which was made at Windsor in the octaves of Michealmas [6 October] in the year of Our

Lord 1175, between Henry, king of England, and Roderic [Rory], king of Connaught, by Catholicus, archbishop of Tuam, Cantordis, abbot of Clonfert, and Master Laurence, chancellor of the king of Connaught, namely:

The king of England has granted to Roderic [Rory], his liegeman, king of Connacht, as long as he shall faithfully serve him, that he shall be king under him, ready to his service, as his man. And he shall hold his land as fully and as peacefully as he held it before the lord king entered Ireland, rendering him tribute. And that he shall have all the rest of the land its inhabitants under him and shall bring them to account [justiciet eos], so that they shall pay their full tribute to the king of England through him, and so that they shall maintain their rights. And those who are now in possession of their lands and rights shall hold them in peace as long as they remain in the fealty of the king of England, and continue to pay him faithfully and fully his tribute and the other rights which they owe to him, by the hand of the king of Connaught, saving in all things the right and honour of the king of England and of Roderic. And if any of them shall refuse to pay the tribute and other rights of the king of England by his hand, and shall withdraw from the fealty of the king of England, he, Roderic, shall judge them and remove them. And if he cannot answer for them by himself, the constable of the king of England in that land [Ireland] shall, when called upon by him, aid him to do what is necessary.

And for this agreement the said king of Connaught shall render to the king of England tribute every year, namely, out of every ten animals slaughtered, one hide, acceptable to the merchants both in his land as in the rest; save that he shall not meddle with those lands which the lord king has retained in his lordship and in the lordship of his barons; that is to say, Dublin with all its appurtenances; Meath with all its appurtenances, even as Murchat Ua Mailethlachlin [Murchadh O' Melaghlin] held it fully and freely [melius et plenius] or as others held it of him; Wexford with all its appurtenances, that is to say, the whole of Leinster; and Waterford with its whole territory from Waterford to Dungarvan, including Dungarvan with all its appurtenances.

And if the Irish who have fled wish to return to the land of the barons of the king of England they may do so in peace, paying the said tributes as others pay it, or doing to the English the services which they were wont to do for their lands, which shall be decided by the judgment and will of their lords. And if any of them are unwilling to return and their lords have called upon the king of Connaught, he shall compel them to return to their land, so that they shall dwell there in peace.

And the king of Connaught shall accept hostages from all whom the lord king of England has committed to him, and he shall himself give hostages at the will of the king.

The witnesses are Robert, bishop of Winchester; Geoffrey, bishop of Ely; Laurence, archbishop of Dublin; Geoffrey, Nicholas and Roger, the king's chaplains; William, Earl of Essex; Richard de Luci; Geoffrey de Purtico, and Reginald de Courtenea.

Translated from the original Latin text in IRISH HISTORICAL DOCUMENTS, 1172–1922, edited by Edmund Curtis and R. B. McDowell (1943), pp. 22–24. Reproduced by permission of the publisher.

~

GRANT OF PRINCE JOHN TO THEOBOLD WALTER OF LANDS IN IRELAND

1185

After arriving in Waterford in April 1185, Prince John, lord of Ireland, granted lands to his close companions, many of whom were destined to found great Anglo-Irish families. Here, for example, he gives Theobald Walter, ancestor of the Butlers, 5½ cantreds (or baronies) in north Tipperary, in exchange for his fealty.

SEE ALSO English Government in Medieval Ireland; Norman Conquest and Colonization

John, son of the King of England, Lord of Ireland, to all archbishops, bishops, abbots, earls, barons, justices, etc., and lieges, French, English and Irish, cleric and lay, present and to come, greeting. Know that we have enfeoffed Ranulf de Glanville and Theobald Walter, our lieges, in 5½ cantreds of land in Limerick, viz. the burgh of Kildelo [Killaloe] with half of the cantred called Truohekedmalech in which that burgh is situate; the whole cantred of Elykaruel [Ely O'Carroll]; the whole cantred of Elyhogarthi; the whole cantred of Ewermun [Ormond]; the whole cantred of Areth and Wetheni [Arra and Owney]; the whole cantred of Owethenihokathelan and Owethenihoiffernan [Owney O'Cathelan and Owney O'Hiffernan]. These five and a half cantreds I have given them for their homage and service with all their appurtenances in wood and plain, in castles and fortresses, meadows and pastures, etc.; also the donations of parish churches which are in those lands or shall be there. To hold of me and my heirs for ever to them and their heirs in fee and heritage by service of a fee of twenty-two knights for all service. In the same lands also I have given and granted them and their heirs sac and soc, toll and theam, infangenthef and all other liberties and free customs which pertain to the same lands, except crosses and donations of bishoprics and abbeys and dignities which belong to the royal Crown, which I have retained to myself. Wherefore I wish and ordain that they shall hold all the above well in peace, freely fully and entirely in all free customs, etc., as above-said. And this I have confirmed by my seal.

Witnesses: Hugh de Lacy, our constable, Bertram de Verdon, our seneschal, Gilbert Pipard, William de Wennevail, our steward John de Curcy, Alard, "camerarius," William the chaplain, Richard clerk "de camera nostra," etc., given at Waterford.

CALENDAR OF ORMOND DEEDS, *edited by Edmund Curtis (1932)*, II, *no. 426. Reprinted in* IRISH HISTORICAL DOCUMENTS, 1172–1922, *edited by Edmund Curtis and R. B. McDowell (1943), p. 24. Reproduced by permission of the publisher.*

~

FROM *THE TOPOGRAPHY OF IRELAND*

1188

Giraldus Cambrensis

One of the founding texts for English discourse on Ireland, this work was one of the most widely circulated accounts available to premodern students of Irish history. Here Giraldus, who was related to several of the Anglo-Norman invaders of Ireland, describes the "strange" character and customs of the Irish people, including his sense of their degeneration from the true faith and the way in which more recent settlers in Ireland have become infected with the same "vices."

SEE ALSO English Writing on Ireland before 1800

I have considered it not superfluous to give a short account of the condition of this nation, both bodily and mentally; I mean their state of cultivation, both interior and exterior. This people are not tenderly nursed from their birth, as others are; for besides the rude fare they receive from their parents, which is only just sufficient for their sustenance, as to the rest, almost all is left to nature. They are not placed in cradles, or swathed, nor are their tender limbs either fomented by constant bathings, or adjusted with art. For the midwives make no use of warm water, nor raise their noses, nor depress the face, nor stretch the legs; but nature alone, with very slight aids from art, disposes and adjusts the limbs to which she has given birth, just as she pleases. As if to prove that what she is able to form she does not cease to shape also, she gives growth and proportions to these people, until they arrive at perfect vigour, tall and handsome in person, and with agreeable and ruddy countenances. But although they are richly endowed with the gifts of nature, their want of civilisation, shown both in their dress and mental culture, makes them a barbarous people. For they wear but little woollen, and nearly all they use is black, that being the colour of the sheep in this country. Their clothes are also made after a barbarous fashion.

Their custom is to wear small, close-fitting hoods, hanging below the shoulders a cubit's length, and generally made of parti-coloured strips sewn together. Under these, they use woollen rugs instead of cloaks, with breeches and hose of one piece, or hose and breeches joined together, which are usually dyed of some colour. Likewise, in riding, they neither use saddles nor boots, nor spurs, but only carry a rod in their hand, having a crook at the upper end, with which they both urge forward and guide their horses. They use reins which serve the purpose both of a bridle and a bit, and do not prevent the horses from feeding, as they always live on grass. Moreover, they go to battle without armour, considering it a burthen, and esteeming it brave and honourable to fight without it.

But they are armed with three kinds of weapons: namely, short spears, and two darts; in which they follow the customs of the Basclenses (Basques); and they also carry heavy battle-axes of iron, exceedingly well wrought and tempered. These they borrowed from the Norwegians and Ostmen, of whom we shall speak hereafter. But in striking with the battle-axe they use only one hand, instead of both, clasping the haft firmly, and raising it above the head, so as to direct the blow with such force that neither the helmets which protect our heads, nor the platting of the coat of mail which defends the rest of our bodies, can resist the stroke. Thus is has happened, in my own time, that one blow of the axe has cut off a knight's thigh, although it was incased in iron, the thigh and leg falling on one side of his horse, and the body of the dying horseman on the other. When other weapons fail, they hurl stones against the enemy in battle with such quickness and dexterity, that they do more execution than the slingers of any other nation.

The Irish are a rude people, subsisting on the produce of their cattle only, and living themselves like beasts—a people that has not yet departed from the primitive habits of pastoral life. In the common course of things, mankind progresses from the forest to the field, from the field to the town, and to the social condition of citizens; but this nation, holding agricultural labour in contempt, and little coveting the wealth of towns, as well as being exceedingly averse to civil institutions—lead the same life their fathers did in the woods and open pastures, neither willing to abandon their old habits or learn anything new. They, therefore, only make patches of tillage; their pastures are short of herbage; cultivation is very rare, and there is scarcely any land sown. This want of tilled fields arises from the neglect of those who should cultivate them; for there are large tracts which are naturally fertile and productive. The whole habits of the people are contrary to agricultural pursuits, so that the rich glebe is barren for want of husbandmen, the fields demanding labour which is not forthcoming.

Very few sorts of fruit-trees are found in this country, a defect arising not from the nature of the soil, but from want of industry in planting them; for the lazy husbandman does not take the trouble to plant the foreign sorts which would grow very well here. There are four kinds of trees indigenous in Britain which are wanting here. Two of them are fruit-bearing trees, the chestnut and beech; the other two, the *arulus* and the box, though they bear no fruit, are serviceable for making cups and handles. Yews, with their bitter sap, are more frequently to be found in this country than in any other I have visited; but you will see them principally in old cemeteries and sacred places, where they were planted in ancient times by the hands of holy men, to give them what ornament and beauty they could. The forests of Ireland also abound with firtrees, producing frankincense and incense. There are also veins of various kinds of metals ramifying in the bowels of the earth, which from the same idle habits, are not worked and turned to account. Even gold, which the people require in large quantities, and still covet in a way that speaks their Spanish origin, is brought here by the merchants who traverse the ocean for the purposes of commerce. They neither employ themselves in the manufacture of flax or wool, or in any kind of trade or mechanical art; but abandoning themselves to idleness, and immersed in sloth, their greatest delight is to be exempt from toil, their richest possession the enjoyment of liberty.

This people, then, is truly barbarous, being not only barbarous in their dress, but suffering their hair and beards (*barbis*) to grow enormously in an uncouth manner, just like the modern fashion recently introduced; indeed, all their habits are barbarisms. But habits are formed by mutual intercourse; and as this people inhabit a country so remote from the rest of the world, and lying at its furthest extremity, forming, as it were, another world, and are thus secluded from civilized nations, they learn nothing, and practise nothing but the barbarism in which they are born and bred, and which sticks to them like a second nature. Whatever natural gifts they possess are excellent, in whatever requires industry they are worthless. . . .

The faith having been planted in the island from the time of St. Patrick, so many ages ago, and propagated almost ever since, it is wonderful that this nation should remain to this day so very ignorant of the rudiments of Christianity. It is indeed a most filthy race, a race sunk in vice, a race more ignorant than all other nations of the first principles of the faith. Hitherto they neither pay tithes nor first fruits; they do not contract marriages, nor shun incestuous connections; they frequent not the church of God with proper reverence. Nay, what is most detestable, and not only contrary to the Gospel, but to every thing that is right, in many parts of Ireland brothers (I will not say marry) seduce and debauch the wives of their brothers deceased, and have incestuous intercourse with them; adhering in this to the letter, and not to the spirit, of the Old Testament; and following the example of men of old in their vices more willingly than in their virtues. . . .

Thus it appears that every one may do just as he pleases; and that the question is not what is right, but what suits his purpose; although nothing is really expedient but what is right. However, the pest of treachery has here grown to such a height—it has so taken root, and long abuse has so succeeded in turning it into a second nature—habits are so formed by mutual intercourse, as he who handles pitch cannot escape its stains—that the evil has acquired great force. A little wormwood, mixed with a large quantity of honey, quickly makes the whole bitter; but if the mixture contains twice as much honey as it does wormwood, the honey fails to sweeten it. Thus, I say, "evil communications corrupt good manners"; and even strangers who land here from other countries become generally imbued with this national crime, which seems to be innate and very contagious. It either adopts holy places for its purposes, or makes them; for, as the path of pleasure leads easily downwards, and nature readily imitates vice, who will doubt the sacredness of its sanctions who is predisposed and foretaught by so many sacrilegious examples, by so many records of evil deeds, by such frequent forefeitures of oaths, by the want of all obligations to honesty?

STRANGERS TO THAT LAND: BRITISH PERCEPTIONS OF IRELAND FROM THE REFORMATION TO THE FAMINE, *edited by Andrew Hadfield and John McVeagh* (1994), *pp. 26–29.*

≈

FROM *EXPUGNATIO HIBERNICA*

1189

Giraldus Cambrensis

In Giraldus's second founding text, he presents the "five-fold" claim to Ireland, long used by the English crown to support their conquest of the island. To the mythical and legendary conquests by "Gurguntius, son of Belinus," and by Arthur, he adds Henry II's intervention and the authority of the twelfth-century popes.

SEE ALSO English Writing on Ireland before 1800

Therefore let the envious and thoughtless end their vociferous complaints that the kings of England hold Ireland unlawfully. Let them learn, moreover, that they support their claims by a right of ownership resting on five different counts, two of long standing and three of recent origin, as is revealed in the *Topography*. For the British History bears witness to the fact that when Gurguntius, son of Belinus and king of Britain, was returning in triumph from Dacia, he founded the Basque fleet in Orkney, and having provided them with guides, sent them for the first time into Ireland. It also recalls the fact that the kings of Ireland were among the rulers who paid tribute to Arthur, that famous king of Britain, and that Gillomar king of Ireland was present at his court at Caerleon along with other island kings. Besides, the city of Bayonne, which today is included in our province of Gascony, is the chief city of the territory of the Basques from which the Irish originally came. Again, while a man is always free to give up his lawful claims, in our own times all the princes of Ireland, although hitherto not subject to the domination of any overlord, freely bound themselves in submission to Henry II king of England by the firm bonds of their pledged word and oath. For although they may not hesitate to go back on their word within a very short space of time, thanks to that fickleness which comes from their innately unstable temperament, they are not therefore absolved from this bond of their pledged word and oath of fealty. For men are free to make contracts of this sort, but not to break them.

As well as this there is the added weight of the authority of the supreme pontiffs, who have responsibility for all islands by reason of their own peculiar rights, and of the princes and rulers of all Christendom. This should in itself be sufficient to perfect our case and put the finishing touch to it.

STRANGERS TO THAT LAND: BRITISH PERCEPTIONS OF IRELAND FROM THE REFORMATION TO THE FAMINE, *edited by Andrew Hadfield and John McVeagh* (1994), *pp. 25–26.*

≈

GRANT OF CIVIC LIBERTIES TO DUBLIN BY PRINCE JOHN

1192

This document provides a description of the liberties granted to the citizens of Dublin by Prince John, named lord of Ireland by his father, Henry II, along with a physical description of the city's boundaries.

SEE ALSO English Government in Medieval Ireland; Norman Conquest and Colonization

John, Lord of Ireland and Earl of Mortain, to all his men and friends, French, English, Irish, and Welsh, present and to come, greeting.

Know that I have given, granted and by this my charter confirmed to my citizens of Dublin dwelling both without the walls as within, even to the boundaries of the town: That they may have their boundaries even as they were perambulated by the oath of lawful men of the same city by command of King Henry my father, viz. from the eastern part of Dublin, and on the southern part the meadow which goes to the gate of St Kevin's church and so by the road even Kilmerecaregan and so by the boundary of land from Donnybrook to the Dodder and from the Dodder to the sea, viz. to Clarade near the sea and from Clarade even to Renniuelan [Ringsend], and in the western part of Dublin from St Patrick's by the valley even to Karnaclonegunethe [Dolphin's Barn] and thence to the boundary of Kilmainham and beyond the water (stream) of Kilmainham near Avon Liffey even to the fords of Kylmehavoc and beyond the water of Avon Liffey to the north by Ennecnegavhoc (or "ganhoc") and thence to the granges [*orrea*] of Holy Trinity and from those granges to the Forks [*furcas*] and so by the boundary between Clonliffe and Crinan even to the Tolka and thence to the church of Houstmanebi.

And that they have all liberties and customs and the undermentioned liberties.

The liberties which I have granted them to have, are as follows: that no citizen of Dublin shall plead outside the walls on any plea save for the pleas of external tenements which do not belong to the Hundred court of the town.

And that they shall be free of *murdrum* within the boundaries of the town.

And that no citizen shall make *duellum* [ordeal of Battle] in the city for any appeal [charge] which anyone may make against him, but he shall clear himself by oath of 40 lawful men of the same said city.

And that no one shall take forced quarters within the walls by assise or by order of any marshal against the will of the citizens.

And that they shall be free to toll, lastage, passage and pontage and all other duties throughout my whole land and jurisdiction.

That no one shall be put into mercy for a fine except according to the law of the Hundred [court], viz. by forfeiture of 40 for which he who falls into mercy shall be quit of half and shall give the other half as a fine, excepting the three fines for bread, ale, and the watch, which are fines of 2 6, of which one half shall be pardoned and the other paid.

That the Hundred court shall be held once in the week.

That no one shall in any plea be debarred by miskenning.

That they shall justly have their lands, tenures, pledges and debts throughout all my land and jurisdiction whosoever shall owe them, and that they may distrain their debtors by their pledges in Dublin.

That of the lands and tenures which are within the walls justice shall be done to them according to the custom of the city.

That of debts which are arranged and pledges given within the city the pleas shall be held according to the custom of the city.

And if any one anywhere in our land or jurisdiction shall take toll of the men of the city and does not return it after being summoned to do so, the reeve of the city shall take pledge therefor in Dublin and distrain for its return.

That no extern merchant shall buy within the city of any extern man corn, hides or wool save from the citizens.

That no extern merchant shall have a tavern for wine, save on a ship. But this liberty is reserved to me, that from each ship which happens to come thither with wine, my bailiff in my place shall choose two tuns of wine according as he wishes in the ship; namely, one before the mast and one behind the mast to my use, for 40; one for 20 and the other for 20; and he shall take nothing further therefrom, save at the will of the merchant.

That no extern merchant shall sell cloth in the city by cutting [*ad decisionem*].

That no extern merchant shall stay in the town with his wares, for the purpose of selling his wares, more than 40 days.

Also no Dublin citizen anywhere in my land or jurisdiction shall be pledged or distrained for any debt, unless he himself be debtor or pledge.

And that they [my citizens] may marry, both themselves, their sons, daughters and widows, without leave of their lords.

Also that none of their lords, on the ground of extern estates, shall have wardship or giving [in wardship] of their sons, daughters or widows, but only the wardship of their lands which are in their [the lords'] fee, until they come of age.

That no assise [*recognitio*] be made in the city.

Also that they shall have all their rightful gilds, as fully as the burgesses of Bristol have or are accustomed to have.

That no citizen shall be compelled to repledge anyone, unless he wishes to do so, although he may be dwelling on his land.

I have granted also all tenures within and without the walls up to the abovesaid boundaries, to be disposed of according to their will by common assent of the city, in messuages, thickets and buildings on the water [river] and elsewhere wherever they shall be in the town, to be held in free burgage, viz. by the service of land-gable which they pay within the walls.

I have granted also that the each of them may improve himself, as far as he is able, in making buildings wherever he shall wish upon the water [river], without damage however to the citizens and the town.

Also that they may have and possess all vacant lands and plots which are contained within the said boundaries; to build on at their will.

Also that neither Templars nor Hospitallers shall have any man or any messuage free of the common duties of the city, within the said boundaries, save one only.

All these things I have granted, saving the tenures and lands of all those who have lands and tenures by charter from me outside the walls up to the said boundaries, so that the city may not dispose of these as it may of others, but let them all obey all the customs of the city like other citizens. Of those however I say this, who had my charter for any lands within the same boundaries outside the walls, before We granted to the city the aforesaid liberties and this charter.

Wherefore I well and firmly command, that my abovesaid citizens of Dublin and their heirs after them shall have and hold all the abovesaid liberties and free customs, as is written above, of me and my heirs as fully entirely and well as they ever had them, in peace and honourably, without any impediment or hindrance which anyone may make against them.

Witnesses: Stephen Ridell, my chancellor; William de Kahaignes, my seneschal, Theobald Walter, my butler, Hamo de Valognes, etc.

Translated from the original Latin text in IRISH HISTORICAL DOCUMENTS, 1172–1922, *edited by Edmund Curtis and R. B. McDowell (1943), pp. 24–27. Reproduced by permission of the publisher.*

~

MAGNA CARTA HIBERNIÆ (THE GREAT CHARTER OF IRELAND)

12 November 1216

Drawing from the English Magna Carta promulgated by King John in 1215, this document was executed by his nine-year-old son, Henry III, in the first year of his reign, then under the regency of William the Marshall (d. 1219) and Hubert de Burgh until 1232. "The Great Charter of Ireland" grants the same rights and liberties to the Anglo-Irish settlers as to their English counterparts. Note particularly the references to the freedom of the Irish Church, probably in reference to the papal grants of 1155 and 1172.

SEE ALSO English Government in Medieval Ireland

Henry, by the grace of God, King of England, Lord of Ireland, etc., to all his archbishops, bishops, abbots, earls, barons, justices, sheriffs, reeves, ministers, etc., and to all his faithful people, greeting.

Know that to the honour of God, the exaltation of Holy Church, and the amendment of our kingdom, by advice of Gualo, cardinal priest of St. Martin's, Legate

of the Apostolic See, Peter, bishop of Winchester [and ten other bishops], William the Marshall, earl of Pembroke [and other earls and nobles], Hubert de Burgh, our justiciar, and others.

Firstly, we have granted to God, and by his present charter confirmed for us and our heirs for ever, that the Irish Church shall be free, and have all her rights entire and her liberties inviolable.

We have also granted to all free men of our kingdom, for us and our heirs for ever, all the liberties underwritten, to have and to hold to them and their heirs of us and our heirs.

[The principal liberties that follow are summarized.]

If any earl, baron or other holding of us in chief by knight service die, and at the time of his death his heir is of full age and owes relief, he shall have his heritage by the old relief, viz. a hundred pounds for the whole barony of an earl, a hundred pounds for the whole barony of a baron, and a hundred shillings at most for the whole knight's fee of a knight; and he who owes less shall give less, according to the ancient custom of fees.

But if the heir of any such be under age, his lord shall not have wardship of him before he take homage of him, and when he comes to age, that is to say twenty-one years, he shall have his heritage without relief or fine; provided that, if while under age he becomes a knight, nevertheless his land shall remain in the wardship of his lord up to that time.

The guardian of such an heir under age shall not take of his land aught save rightful issues, customs and services, and these without destruction of men [tenants] or goods. And if we commit the custody of such land to the sheriff or any other and he make destruction or waste of what is in his custody, we shall take amends of him, and commit the land to two lawful,and discreet men of that fee, who shall answer for the issues to us or to him to whom we assign them. And if we give or sell to anyone the custody of such land and he make destruction or waste thereof, he shall lose the custody, and it shall be committed to two lawful men of that fee, who shall likewise answer to us thereof, as aforesaid.

The guardian as long as he has custody, shall keep up the houses, parks, ponds, mills, etc. pertaining to that land out of the issues thereof, and restore to the heir when he shall have come of age, all his land stocked with ploughs etc. as fully as he received them.

And similarly with the custody of vacant archbishops, bishoprics, abbeys, priories, churches and ecclesiastical dignities, save that such custodies ought not be sold.

Heirs shall be married without disparagement. A widow, immediately on her husband's death, shall have her marriage portion and inheritance; nor shall she give anything for her dower, marriage portion, or inheritance which she and her husband held at his death. No widow shall be compelled to marry again as long as she wishes to live unmarried, provided that she give security not to marry without our assent, if she hold to us, or her lord's assent, if she hold to another.

The city of Dublin shall have all its ancient liberties and free customs. We further will and grant that all other cities, towns, boroughs and ports shall have their liberties and free customs. No one shall be distrained to do more service for a knight's fee or any other freehold than is due therefrom.

Common pleas shall not follow our court but shall be held in some certain place.

Assises of Novel Disseisin, Mort D'Ancestor and Darrein Presentment shall not be taken save in our own counties, and in this way. We, or if we are out of the realm, our Chief Justiciar, shall send two justices through each county four times in the year, who, with four knights of every county elected by the county, [court] on that day shall remain, by whom it may be competent to make judgements, according as the business shall be more or less.

No freeman shall be amerced for a small fault, but according to the measure of the fault, and for a great fault according to the magnitude of the fault, saving his tenement; and a merchant in the same way, saving his warnage, if he fall into our mercy. And none of the said amercements shall be assessed but by the oath of good and lawful men of the venue. Earls and barons shall not be amerced except by their peers, and according to the measure of their fault. No clerk shall be amerced except as aforesaid, and not according to the quantity of his ecclesiastical benefice.

No town nor individual shall be distrained to make bridges over rivers, except those who from of old and of right ought to make them.

No sheriff, constable, coroners, or other bailiffs shall hold pleas of our crown.

We shall not hold the lands of those who shall be convicted of felony, save for a year and a day, and then the lands shall be restored to the lords of the fees.

Also all weirs shall henceforth be put down through the whole of the Anna Liffey and all Ireland, except by the sea coast.

The writ which is called "precipe" from henceforth not be granted to anyone of any tenement whereby a freeman may lose his court.

There shall be one measure of wine throughout our entire kingdom, and one measure of ale, and one measure of corn, that is to say, the quarter of Dublin; and one breadth of dyed cloth, russets and habergets, that is to say, two ells within the lists.

Nothing shall henceforth be given for the writ of inquisition of life or limbs, but it shall be freely granted and not denied.

No freeman shall be taken or imprisoned or disseised or outlawed or exiled, or in any otherwise destroyed; nor will we pass upon him nor send upon him but by the lawful judgement of his peers or by the law of the land. We will sell to no man, we will deny to no man, or delay, right or justice.

All merchants, unless they were before publicly prohibited, shall have safe and secure [conduct] to depart from Ireland, and come into Ireland, and to tarry in and go through Ireland, as well by land as by water, to buy and sell, without all the evil extortions, by the old and rightful customs, except in time of war.

All men who have founded abbeys, for which they have charters of the Kings of England or ancient tenure, shall have the custody of them when they become vacant, as they ought to have, and as is above declared.

All forests which were afforested in the time of King John, our father; shall be immediately disafforested; and so let it be done in the case of rivers which were placed in defence by the said John in his time.

All those customs and liberties, aforesaid, which we have granted to be held in our kingdom, as far as to us appertains towards our men, everyone in our realm, as well clergy as laymen, shall observe, as far as appertains to them, towards other men.

Given by the hands of the aforesaid Legate and Marshall at Bristol, the twelfth day of November, in the first year of our reign [1216].

EARLY STATUTES OF IRELAND, *edited by Henry FitzPatrick Berry (1907), pp. 5–19.*

~

THE STATUTES OF KILKENNY

1366

These thirty-five acts were promulgated five years after the arrival in Ireland of Lionel, duke of Clarence and, through his marriage to Elizabeth de Burgo, also earl of Ulster and lord of Connacht. Written in Norman French, which remained the legal language of the time, they sought to create a permanent division between the native, or "mere" Irish, and the Anglo-Irish colonizers—on the basis of language, law, and customs—in an early form of "apartheid." These acts ultimately helped to create the complete estrangement of the two "races" in Ireland for almost three centuries.

SEE ALSO English Government in Medieval Ireland; Gaelic Society in the Late Middle Ages; Norman Invasion and Gaelic Resurgence

A STATUTE OF THE FORTIETH YEAR OF KING EDWARD III., ENACTED IN A PARLIAMENT HELD IN KILKENNY, A.D. 1366, BEFORE LIONEL DUKE OF CLARENCE, LORD LIEUTENANT OF IRELAND

Whereas at the conquest of the land of Ireland, and for a long time after, the English of the said land used the English language, mode of riding and apparel, and were governed and ruled, both they and their subjects called *Betaghes*, according to the English law, in which time God and holy Church, and their franchises according to their condition were maintained and themselves lived in due subjection; but now many English of the said land, forsaking the English language, manners, mode of riding, laws and usages, live and govern themselves according to the manners, fashion, and language of the Irish enemies; and also have made divers marriages and alliances between themselves and the Irish enemies aforesaid; whereby the said land, and the liege people thereof, the English language, the allegiance due to our lord the king, and the English laws there, are put in subjection and decayed, and the Irish enemies exalted and raised up, contrary to reason; our lord the king considering the mischiefs aforesaid, in the consequence of the grievous complaints of the commons of his said land, called to his parliament held at Kilkenny, the Thursday next after the day of Cinders Ash Wednesday in the fortieth year of his reign, before his well-beloved son, Lionel Duke of Clarence, his lieutenant in his parts of Ireland, to the honour of God and His glorious Mother, and of holy Church, and for the good government of the said land, and quiet of the people, and for the better observation of the laws, and punishment of evils doers there, are ordained and established by our said lord the king, and his said lieutenant, and our lord the king's counsel there, which the assent of the archbishops, bishops, abbots and priors (as to what appertains to them to assent to), the earls, barons, and others the commons of the said land, at the said parliament there being and assembled, the ordinances and articles under

written, to be held and kept perpetually upon the pains contained therein.

I. First, it is ordained, agreed to, and established, that holy Church shall be free, and have all her franchises without injury, according to the franchises ordained and granted by our lord the king, or his progenitors, by any statute or ordinance made in England or in Ireland heretofore; and if any (which God forbid) do to the contrary, and be excommunicated by the ordinary of the place for that cause, so that satisfaction be not made to God and holy Church by the party so excommunicated, within the month after such excommunication, that then, after certificate thereupon being made, by the said ordinary, into the Chancery, a writ shall be directed to the sheriff, mayor, seneschal of franchise, or other officers of our lord the king, to take his body, and to keep him in prison without enlarging him by main prize or bail, until satisfaction be made to God and holy Church, notwithstanding that the forty days be not passed; and that no prohibition from Chancery be henceforth granted in any suit against the franchise of holy Church; saving at all times the right for our lord the king, and of his crown; so that the franchises of holy Church be not overturned or injured; and in case that by suggestion of the party prohibition be granted, that as soon as the articles of franchise shall be shown by the ordinary in the Chancery, a consultation shall thereupon be granted to him without delay.

II. Also, it is ordained and established, that no alliance by marriage, gossipred, fostering of children, concubinage or by amour, nor in any other manner, be hencefoth made between the English and Irish of one part, or of the other part; and that no Englishman, nor other person, being at peace, do give or sell to any Irishman, in time of peace or war, horses or armour, nor any manner of victuals in time of war; and if any shall do to the contrary, and thereof be attainted, he shall have judgment of life and member, as a traitor to our lord the king.

III. Also, it is ordained and established, that every Englishman do use the English language, and be named by an English name, leaving off entirely the manner of naming used by the Irish; and that every Englishman use the English custom, fashion, mode of riding and apparel, according to his estate; and if any English, or Irish living amongst the English, use the Irish language amongst themselves, contrary to the ordinance, and thereof be attainted, his lands and tenements, if he have any, shall be seized into the hands of his immediate lord, until he shall come to one of the places of our lord the king, and find sufficient surety to adopt and use the English language, and then he shall have restitution of his said lands or tenements, his body shall be taken by any of the officers of our lord the king, and committed to the next gaol, there to remain until he, or some other in his name, shall find sufficient surety in the manner aforesaid: And that no Englishman who shall have the value of one hundred pounds of land or of rent by the year, shall ride otherwise than on a saddle in the English fashion; and he that shall do to the contrary, and shall be thereof attainted, his horse shall be forfeited to our lord the king, and his body shall be committed to prison, until he pay a fine according to the king's pleasure for the contempt aforesaid; and also, that beneficed persons of holy Church, living amongst the English, shall have the issues of their benefices until they use the English language in the manner aforesaid; and they shall have respite in order to learn the English language, and to provide saddles, between this and the feast of Saint Michael next coming.

IV. Also, whereas diversity of government and different laws in the same land cause difference in allegiance, and disputes among the people; it is agreed and established, that no Englishman, having disputes with any other Englishman, shall henceforth make caption, or take pledge, distress or vengeance against any other, whereby the people may be troubled, but that they shall sue each other at the common law; and that no Englishman be governed in the termination of their disputes by March law nor Brehon law, which reasonably ought not to, be called law, being a bad custom; but they shall be governed, as right is, by the common law of the land, as liege subjects of our lord the king; and if any do to the contrary, and thereof be attainted, he shall be taken and imprisoned and adjudged as a traitor; and that no difference of allegiance shall henceforth be made between the English born in born in Ireland, and the English born in England, by calling them English hobbe, or Irish dog, but that all be called by one, name, the English lieges of our Lord the king; and he who shall be found doing to the contrary, shall be punished by imprisonment for a year, and afterwards fined, at the king's pleasure; and by this ordinance it is not the intention of our Lord the king but that it shall be lawful for any one that he may take distress for service and rents due to them, and for damage feasant as the common law requires.

V. Also, whereas the liege people of our lord the king of his land of Ireland, or the wars of the same land cannot reasonably be controlled, unless the sale of victuals be reasonably regulated, it is ordained and established as to the merchandizes which are come, or shall come, to the same land by any merchants, and at whatever port, town or city they shall arrive, that before the said merchandizes be put up to sale, the mayor, sovereign, bailiff, or other officer who shall have care of the place where the said merchandizes shall be sold, do cause to come before them two of the most respectable and sufficient men of the said place, who meddle not in such merchandizes, and that the said mayor, seneschal, sovereign or bailiff; with the said two persons, do cause to come before them the merchants to whom the said merchandizes shall belong, and the sailors, and they shall be sworn truly to tell and show the amount of the first purchase prime cost of the said merchandizes, and of the expenses on them to the port, and thereupon that a reasonable price be put upon the said merchandizes by the said mayor, seneschal, bailiff or provost, and by the two discreet men aforesaid, without favour, as they may be able to vouch before our lord the king's council of these parts; and at such prices they shall be sold, without more being taken for them, upon forfeiture of the same, although the said merchandizes should have there become chargeable afterwards.

VI. Also, whereas a land, which is at war, requires that every person do render himself able to defend himself, it is ordained, and established, that the commons of the said land of Ireland, who are in the different marches at war, do not, henceforth, use the plays which men call hurlings, with great sticks and a ball upon the ground, from which great evils and maims have arisen, to the weakening, of the defence of the said land, and other plays which men call coiting; but that they do apply and accustom themselves to use and draw bows, and throw lances, and other gentlemanlike games, whereby the Irish enemies may be the better checked by the liege people and commons of these parts; and if any do or practise the contrary, and of this be attainted, they shall be taken and imprisoned, and fined at the will of our lord the king.

VII. Also, whereas by conspiracies, confederacies, champerties, maintainors of quarrel, false swearers, retainers, sharers of damages, the liege commons of the said land in pursuit of their rights are much disturbed, aggrieved, and deprived of their inheritance; it is ordained and established, that diligent inquiry be made of such in every county, by the Justices to hold pleas in the chief place, and of their maintainors, and that due and expeditious execution be had against those who shall be attainted thereof, according to the form of the Statute in this respect made in England, without fine or redemption to be taken of them, that others may, by such speedy execution, be deterred from doing or maintaining such horrible acts contrary to law, in grievance of the said liege commons: and that, thereupon, the archbishops and bishops of the said land, each within his diocese, shall have letters patent of our lord the king, from his chancery of Ireland, to inquire of the articles aforesaid when they think fit; and, thereupon, according to the law of holy Church to proceed against them by censures, and to certify into the said Chancery the names of those who shall be before them found guilty thereof, so that our lord the king, to the honour of God and the holy Church, the government of his laws, and the preservation of his said people, may inflict due punishment for the same.

VIII. Also, whereas, of right, no lay person whatsoever ought to meddle with tithes, or any spiritual goods, against the will of the governors of the Church, to whom tithes or such spiritual goods belong, it is ordained and established, that no man, great or little, shall interfere with or take by sale, in any other manner, manner, the tithes appertaining to holy Church or religion, by extortion or menace, nor at a less price than they may be sold at to another, against the will of him to whom the said tithes belong, and he who does to the contrary, and hereof shall be attainted, shall make restitution to him who shall be aggrieved, if he will complain, of the double of the said price, and make fine at the king's pleasure.

IX. Also, whereas persons guilty of disobedience to God and holy Church, and put out of the communion of Christians, cannot, nor ought, of right, to be received to the favour of our lord the king, or to the communion of his officers; it is ordained and established, that when the archbishops, bishops and other prelates of holy Church, have excommunicated, interdicted or fulminated the censures of holy Church against any English person or Irish, for reasonable cause, at the request of our lord the king, or ex-officio, or at the suit of the party, that after the notification of these censures shall come to our lord the king, nor into communion or alliance with his ministers, nor to maintenance in their error by any of the liege people, until they shall have made satisfaction to God and holy Church, and shall be restored as the law of holy Church requires; and if a maintainor of such excommunicated person be found and attainted against the ordinance aforesaid, he shall be taken and imprisoned, and fined at the king's will.

X. Also, whereas divers wars have often heretofore been commenced and not continued, nor brought to a good termination, but by the party taking from the enemy at their departure a small tribute, whereby the said enemies were and are the more emboldened to renew the war; it is agreed and established, that any war which shall be commenced hereafter, shall be undertaken by the council of our lord the king, by the advice of the lords, commons, and inhabitants of the marches of the county where the war shall arise; and shall be continued, and finished and supplied, by their advice and counsel; so that the Irish enemies shall not be admitted to peace, until they shall be finally destroyed, or shall make restitution fully of the costs and charges expended upon that war by their default and rebellion, and make reparation to those by whom the said charges and costs were incurred, and moreover, pay a fine for the contempt at the king's will; and in case that hostages be taken and given to our lord the king, or to his officers, for keeping the peace, by any of the Irish, that, if they shall renew the war against the form of their peace, execution of their said hostages shall without delay or favour be made, according to the ancient customs of the said land in such case used.

XI. Also for the better maintaining of peace, and doing right, as well to the Irish enemies being at peace as to the English, it is ordained and established, that if any Irishman, being at peace, by borrowing, or purchase of merchandize, or in any other manner, become debtor to an English, or Irishman being at peace, that for this cause no other Irish person belonging to him, under him, or in subjection to him, nor his goods, shall be seized nor ransomed for such debt; but his remedy shall be against the principal debtor, as the law requires. Let him be well advised to give his merchandise to such person as he can have recovery from.

XII. Also, it is ordained and established, that in every peace to be henceforth made, between our lord the king and his liege English of the one part, and the Irish of the other part, in every march of the land, there shall be comprised the point which follows, that is to say, that no Irishman shall pasture or occupy the lands belonging to English, or Irish being at peace, against the will of the lords of the said lands; and if they so do, that it shall be lawful for the said lords to lead with them to their pound the said beasts so feeding or occupying their said lands, in name of a for their rent and their damages, so that the beasts be not divided nor scattered as heretofore has been done; but that they be kept altogether as they were taken, in order to deliver them to the party in case that he shall come to make satisfaction to the lords of the said lands reasonably, according to their demand; and in case any one shall divide or separate from each other the beasts so taken, he shall be punished as a robber and disturber of the peace of our lord the king; and if any Irish rise by force to the rescue of those reasonably taken, that it is lawful for the said English to assist themselves by strong hand, without being impeached in the court of our lord the king on this account; and that no Englishman do take any distress upon any Irishman of any part between this and the Feast of St. Michael next to come; so that the Irish of every part may be warned in the meantime.

XIII. Also, it is ordained that no Irishman of the nations of the Irish be admitted into any cathedral or collegiate church by provision, collation, or presentation of any person, nor to any benefice of Holy Church, amongst the English of the land; and that if any be admitted, instituted or inducted, into such benefice, it be held for void, and the king, shall have the presentation of the said benefice for that avoidance, to whatever person the advowson of such benefice may belong, saving their right to present or make collation to the said benefice when it shall be vacant another time.

XIV. Also, it is ordained and established that no religious house which is situate amongst the English be it exempt or not, shall henceforth receive any Irishmen to their profession, but may receive Englishmen without taking into consideration whether they be born in England or in Ireland; and that any that shall act otherwise, and thereof shall be attainted, their temporalties shall be seized into the hands of our lord the king, so to remain at his pleasure; and that no prelates of holy Church shall receive any . . . to any orders without the assent and testimony of his lord, given to him under his seal.

XV. Also, whereas the Irish agents who come amongst the English, spy out the secrets, plans, and policies of the English, whereby great evils have often resulted; it is agreed and forbidden, that any Irish agents, that is to say, pipers, story-tellers, babblers, rimers, mowers, nor any other Irish agent shall come amongst the English, and that no English shall receive or make gift to such; and that shall do so, and be attainted, shall be taken, and imprisoned, as well the Irish agents as the English who receive or give them any thing, and after that they shall make fine at the king's will; and the instruments of their agency shall forfeit to our lord the king.

XVI. Also, it is agreed and assented, that no man's escape henceforth shall be adjudged against any, by any inquest of office, before the party against whom the escape ought to be adjudged, be himself put to answer or acknowledge the fact, or plea of record, although heretofore, it has been otherwise practised.

XVII. Also it is agreed and assented that no man, of what estate or condition he be, upon forfeiture of life or of members, shall keep kerns, hoblers nor idlemen in land at peace, to aggrieve the loyal people of our lord the king; but that he who will have such shall keep them in the march at his own expense, without taking anything from any person against his will: and if it happen that any man, whether a kern or any other, shall take any manner of victuals or other goods of any other against his will, hue and cry shall be raised against him, and he shall be taken and committed to gaol if he will surrender himself; and if not, but he rise to make resistance by force, so that he will not suffer the attachment, it shall be done to him as to open robbers; and such

manner of taking shall be considered a robbery; and in case such malefactors fly from the attachment, so that no man can take them, then his lord or leader shall answer for him, and shall make satisfaction to the party who has been damaged; and if he shall have made satisfaction to the party, the king shall end the flight against him as well for himself as for the party; and those who do not rise at such hue and cry shall be holden and punished as maintainors of felons; and if any man keep or maintain kerns, hoblers, or idlemen, otherwise than is abovesaid, he shall be in judgment of life and members, and his lands and tenements shall be forfeited.

XVIII. Also, that it shall be proclaimed that all those who are now idlemen, and are willing to take land of the king, shall come to the Lord duke, lieutenant of our lord the king of Ireland, the chancellor or treasurer of the king, and shall take waste lands of the king, in fee or to farm, and if they wish to take of other lords, they shall come to them, or to their seneschal, in like manner. And that no marcher, or other shall hold parley or alliance with any Irish or English who shall be against peace, without leave of the Court, or in the presence of the sheriff of our lord the king, or the wardens of the peace, that they may see that such parley or alliance is for common and not for particular benefit; and he who does to the contrary, shall be imprisoned, and make fine at the kings will.

XIX. Also, it is ordained and established, that if any of the lineage, or of the adherents or retainers of any chieftain of English lineage, within the land of Ireland, whom the said chieftain can correct, shall commit any trespass or felony, the said chieftain, after he shall have had notice thereof; shall cause the said malefactor to be taken and commit him to the next gaol, there to remain until he shall be delivered by law; and if the said chieftain shall not do so, that his body shall be taken for the said malefactor, and detained in prison until the body of the malefactor be given up to the court of our lord the King, to be amenable to justice as is above said; and nevertheless the said chieftain for the contempt shall be fined at the king's will, and make satisfaction to the party so aggrieved.

XX. Also, it is agreed and assented that one peace and war be throughout the entire land, so that if any Irish or English shall make a hostile inroad in any county, the counties surrounding them shall make war and harrass them in their marches, so soon as they shall be warned by the wardens of the peace of the said county, or by the sheriff where the war shall arise; and if they shall not so do, they shall be held as maintainors of felons; and if they of the country where the war arises, suffer their marches to be laid waste by the enemy, and will not rise to check the malice of the enemy after they shall be reasonably warned by the wardens of the peace, or by the sheriff, or proclamation has been made publicly throughout the said county, that then they shall be considered as maintainors of felons.

XXI. Also, whereas divers people commit divers robberies and felonies in franchises, and fly with their goods into guildable lands, so that the officers of the franchises are unable to execute their office there, or to take the felons or their goods, but they are there with their goods received; and in like manner divers people who commit divers robberies and felonies in guildable lands, fly with their goods into franchises, so that the officers of our lord the King cannot there execute their office, nor take the felons with their goods, but they are there with their goods received: it is agreed and assented that if any officer of a franchise make pursuit after any such felon into guildable land, that those of the guildable land shall assist to take such felon, and to deliver him to said officer, together with the goods found with him, and thereupon deliver up both his body and goods to the said officer to do that which to law appertains; and that those of a franchise shall act in like manner towards the sheriff of our lord the king, or his officers that shall make pursuit after such felons, who commit felonies and fly with their goods into franchises; and if any man commit felony in one county, and fly into another county, or into a franchise, and shall remain there, that the sheriff of that county where the felony was committed shall have power to order by his precepts, the sheriffs or seneschals of the parts where the said felon remains, as well within franchises as without, to take the body of the said felon, and to send it back; and that the said sheriffs and seneschals shall be obedient each in such case to the order of the other. And if any person of guildable land or of franchise shall rise in aid of such misdoers, so that the officers cannot excecute their office on them, that they shall be considered as notorious felons as those who commit the robberies, and be punished in the same manner. And if the officers aforesaid be remiss in the execution of the orders aforesaid, and thereof be attainted, that they shall be condemned to prison, and make fine at the king's will. And it is not the intention of the King nor of the council, that, by such entry into a franchise, or order to the seneschal, the franchise shall be injured.

XXII. Also, whereas divers people enfeof their children or other strangers of their lands, and give their goods and chattels by fraud and collusion, in order to bar and delay our lord the King of his debt, and parties of their action; and also make many feofments of their lands and tenements, in order to have divers vouchers, and abate writs; it is agreed and assented that if such alienors or feoffors take the profit of the said lands and tenements after such alienations or enfeofments made, that they, notwithstanding the said feigned alienations or feofments made, shall be adjudged tenants to all the writs purchased, and that they shall not vouch any of the persons so enfeofed; and that our lord the King, and the parties, shall have execution and recovery of the lands, goods and chattels so aliened, as well as of the proper goods and chattels of the said alienors; and if it happen that any man, in purposing to levy war against the king, or to commit any felony, do enfeof any person of his land, in order to commit such felonies and treasons after the enfeofment, and if afterwards he be attainted of the treasons or felonies abovesaid, that the lands aforesaid, into whatever hands they shall come, shall be forfeited, notwithstanding the feofment, as if they were in his hand the very clay of the felony committed: and this ordenance shall have place in respect to feofments on this account, as well heretofore made as hereafter to be made.

XXIII. Also, in every county there shall be appointed four of the most substantial men of the county, to be wardens of the peace, who shall have full power to assess horsemen-at-arms, hoblers and footmen, each according to the value and quantity of his lands, goods and chattels, so that they shall be ready whensoever there shall be occasion for them, to arrest the malice of the enemy, according, to what they shall be assessed by the wardens aforesaid; and that the said wardens, after array made in manner aforesaid, shall review the said men-at-arms, hoblers, and footmen, from month to month, in a certain place in the county, where they shall see best to do the same in ease of the people: and if the said wardens shall find any rebel who will not obey their commands, they shall have power to attach them, and commit them to the next gaol, there to remain until the law shall take its course respecting them. And if the wardens of the peace shall be remiss or negligent in performing their duty, and thereof be attainted, that then they shall be taken and imprisoned, and make fine at the king's will. And if any one so chosen a warden shall refuse to receive the king's commission, he shall be taken and imprisoned, and his lands seized into the hands of our lord the king, and so shall remain until the king shall have otherwise ordained concerning him; and the said wardens shall make oath legally to perform their duty in the manner abovesaid.

XXIV. Also, it is ordained that the marshals of the one bench, and of the other, and within franchises do not henceforth take for their fee more than they take in England; that is to say five pence, as it has been proved to the council that they do in England, according to the Statute in England in this behalf provided; and this after a man shall be acquitted or convicted, and finally delivered out of the court, and not before; and if they do to the contrary, and thereof be attainted, their bailiwicks, shall be seized into the king's hand at the complaint of him who shall be aggrieved contrary to this Statute, and shall moreover make satisfaction to those who shall be so damaged by them, and be detained in prison until their satisfaction be made. Also, that the marshal of the Exchequer shall only take half a mark every term while a man remains in his custody for arrears of account or for the king's debt; and he who does to the contrary, and thereof shall be attainted, shall suffer as is above-said. And that no constable of castles, within franchise or without, shall take of any prisoner put into his cus-tody for his fee but only five pence, except the constable of the Castle of Dyvelin, which is the king's chief castle in Ireland, by reason that it has been proved to the coun-cil that he is entitled to take more, and from ancient time has done so; and he who does otherwise, and thereof shall be attainted, his office of constable shall be seized into the hands of the king, and he who shall have acted so shall be taken and imprisoned until he make satisfac-tion to the party, and pay a fine to the king. And that the marshals or constables aforesaid within franchises or without, shall not put the prisoners which they have in their custody to distress and severity of punish-ment, for the purpose of obtaining individual profit or suit; and if they shall do so they shall be taken and detained in prison until they shall have rendered double to him from whom they have received such wrong-ful profit, and shall moreover pay a fine to the king. And hereupon writs shall be issued to every place of the land where there is a marshal or constable, as well within franchise as without, commanding the justice of each place, and also the treasurer and barons of the Exchequer, to cause charge to be given to the marshal of their place, that they do not take of any person otherwise than as aforesaid; and to inquire from them from time to time respecting those who do the contrary, and to punish them in the form abovesaid.

XXV. Also, it is ordained and established that if any man commit felony, and shall fly, or be attainted by outlawry, or in any other way, whereby his goods and chattels shall be forfeited to the king, that the sheriffs of the same county where the said felonies are commit-ted shall seize the said goods and chattels into the king's hands, into whatever hands they may have afterwards come; and that our lord the king shall be answered in respect thereof in their accounts; and if they put such goods and chattels into any custody, they shall put them into such custody, that they will be able to answer for them, and that such shall not be exchanged, as it has been practised before this time.

XXVI. Also it is ordained that if truce or peace be made by the justices, or wardens of the peace, or the sheriff, between English and Irish, and they shall be bro-ken by any English, and thereof be attainted, he shall be taken and put in prison until satisfaction be made by him to those who shall be disturbed or injured by that occasion, and he shall moreover make fine at the King's will; and if there is not wherewith to make restitution to those who shall be injured, he shall remain in perpet-ual confinement. And such wardens and sheriffs shall have power to inquire concerning those who shall have broken the peace.

XXVII. Also, it is ordained that if dispute shall arise between English and English, whereby the English on one side and on the other shall gather to to themselves English and Irish being at peace, there to remain to make war upon and aggrieve the other, to the great damage and destruction of the King's liege people; it is agreed and assented that no English shall be so daring as to make war with each other, or henceforward to draw away any English or Irish at peace for such purpose, and if they shall so do, and thereof be attainted, there shall be judgement of life and members, and their goods forfeited.

XXVIII. Also, it is agreed that no man of what state or condition he be, shall make any manner of distur-bance against any of the officers of our Lord the King, whereby he may be unable to execute his office; and he who so does, and thereof shall be attainted, shall be taken and imprisoned, and make fine at the King's plea-sure.

XXIX. Also it is ordained that no English, being common malefactors, or common robbers or barrators, shall be maintained by any of the King's court, nor by the great or little of the land, upon the peril that awaits it, that is to say, that if he be a lord of the franchise, he shall lose his franchise, and if any other person, he shall be taken and make fine at the King's pleasure.

XXX. Also, it is ordained that the chief serjeants of fees, and their attorneys, do duly execute the writs of the King, and of his sheriffs, as they ought to do; and if they shall not so do, and thereof be attainted, their bailiwicks shall be seised into the King's hands, and their bodies be sent to prison: and that henceforth they shall not lease their bailiwicks at a higher rent than anciently it was, according to what by the Statute thereupon made in England is ordained.

XXXI. Also, whereas the summonses of the Exche-quer of our Lord the King, of Ireland, come to divers sheriffs and seneschals of franchise, to levy the debts of our Lord the King off divers persons in their bailiwicks; the which sheriffs and seneschals, together with the serjeants of counties and franchises do accordingly levy divers sums of the said debts off divers persons of counties and franchises, and do not discharge them in their accounts at the Exchequer, but excuse themselves by the serjeants of fee and their deputies, whereby the payment of the debts of our Lord the King is so retarded and delayed, and the people greatly injured, in this respect, that they are not discharged of the money that they have paid; it is agreed and assented, that when the sheriffs and seneschals of Louth, Meath, Trim, Dublin, Kildare, Catherlogh, Kilkenny, Wexford, Waterford, and Tipperary, shall come to render up their accounts before the treasurer and barons, of the issues of their bailiwicks, that the serjeants of the fee that shall be present, and the deputies of those that shall be out of the land, shall be distrained to come into the Exchequer, and there remain with the said sheriffs and seneschals, until the said sheriffs and seneschals shall have fully accounted; and if it shall so be, that the said sheriffs and seneschals can charge the said serjeants or their deputies, that they have received the King's money of any one, and have not made payment to the said sheriffs or seneschals, and they thereupon shall be attainted, their bodies shall remain in custody of the marshal, until satisfaction be made to our Lord the King, for his money, in discharge of the debtors of our Lord the King, or of the said sheriffs or seneschals, if they have wherewithal, and if not, that they shall remain in prison until they be delivered by the council, and nevertheless the sheriff and seneschals shall be charged therewith in their accounts as before. And that all debts levied by the serjeants be paid to the sheriffs by indenture made between them; so that when the said serjeants shall come on the account of the sheriff in the Exchequer, they may show their indenture, and prove from whom they have received the King's money, and from whom not. And whereas the counties of Connaught Kerry, Cork, and Limerick, are so far from the court, that the serjeants of the said counties cannot conveniently come to the said Exchequer, to be present on the accounts of the sheriffs and seneschals of the said counties, as other serjeants do, it is agreed and assented that when one of the barons, or a clerk assigned by the treasurer and baron, shall come by the commission of the Exchequer to the parts aforesaid, in order to examine the truth, and to deny the debt of our Lord the King, the serjeants of the said counties or their deputies shall then remain with the said baron or clerk, as long as the said sheriffs and seneschals shall remain, and if it shall happen that they shall have received any part thereof from any person, without making payment to the said sheriffs or seneschals, in the manner aforesaid, that then they shall be arrested, and suffer the punishment aforesaid.

XXXII. Also, whereas the fees of sheriffs are settled by statute, and the sheriffs in the land of Ireland take in their tourns of every barony in their bailiwick, one mark yearly, and of every market town at a time, twenty shillings, ten shillings, and half a mark, to the great oppression of the people; it is agreed and assented that the aforesaid sheriffs shall hold their tourns twice in the year, that is to say, after the feast of Saint Michael, and after Easter; and that they shall take only forty pence off every barony at each tourn, however numerous the market towns or boroughs may be within the said barony: and if he be so paid by the lord of the barony, unless he be requested or invited to eat he shall take nothing; and that no clerks of the sheriffs on account of such tourn shall take any thing; and also, that from henceforth no money shall be levied out of any ploughland, nor in any other manner, on account of executing this office, except half a mark yearly as is aforesaid; and if any person shall act contrary to the ordinance aforesaid, and thereof be attainted, he shall be committed to prison, and moreover, shall render to those from whom he shall have taken any thing of this account against the said ordinance, double thereof if they will complain, and shall moreover make fine at the King's will. And that no sheriffs of franchises, who of reason ought to have certain fees from the lords of the said franchise for executing their office, shall take any thing for their tourns from the people of their bailiwicks, but shall consider themselves paid by what they shall receive from the said lords of franchises; and if they do so, and thereof be attainted, they shall suffer the same punishment.

XXXIII. Also, whereas the commons of the said land complain that they are in divers ways distressed by want of servants, whereof the justices appointed for labourers, are a great cause, by reason that the common labourers are for the greatest part absent, and fly out of the said land; it is agreed and assented, that, because living and victuals are dearer than they were wont to be, each labourer in his degree, according to the discretion of two of the most substantial and discreet men of the city, town, borough, village, or hamlet, in the country where he shall perform his labour, shall receive his maintenance reasonably, in gross or by the day, and if they will not do so, nor be obedient, they shall be taken before the mayor, seneschal, sovereign, provost or bailif of the cities or towns where they are, or by the sheriff of the county, and put in prison, until the coming of the justices assigned, who will come twice in the year into every county and the justice of the chief place, who shall award due punishment for the same, and right to the parties who shall feel themselves aggrieved thereby. And that no labour shall pass beyond sea; and in case that he shall do so and shall return, he shall be taken and put in prison for a year, and afterwards make fine at the King's will. And moreover, writs shall be issued to the sheriffs, mayors, seneschals, sovereigns, and bailiffs, of counties, cities and towns throughout the land where the sea reaches, commanding them that they do not suffer any such passage of labourers. And it is also agreed that the commissions issued to justices of labourers in every county he repealed, and that henceforth none such be granted.

XXXIV. Also, it is agreed and established, that in maintenance of the execution of the Statutes aforesaid, two prudent men, learned in the law, having with them two of the most substantial men of the county, by the King's council associated, be assigned by commission to iquire twice a year in every county respecting, those who shall break the articles aforesaid, and to hear and determine such cases thereunder as shall come before them by indictment, or at the suit of the party, and of the different other articles which shall be contained in the said commission, according to the penalties thereof in the said statutes contained, without doing favour to any one, and to certify unto the Chancery from time to time that which by them shall have been done therein.

XXXV. Also, our lord the duke of Clarence, lieutenant of our lord the King, in Ireland, and the council of our said lord the King there, the earls, barons and commons of the land aforesaid, at this present Parliament assembled, have requested the archbishops and bishops, abbots, priors and other persons of religion, that they do cause to be excommunicated, and do excommunicate the persons contravening the statutes and ordinances aforesaid, and the other censures of holy church to fulminate against them, if any, by rebellion of heart, act against the statutes and ordinances aforementioned. And we, Thomas archbishop of Duvelin Dublin, Thomas archbishop of Cashel, John archbishop of Thueme Tuam, Thomas bishop, of Lismore and Waterford, Thomas bishop of Killalo, William bishop of Ossorie, John bishop of Leighlin, and John bishop of Clon, being present in the said parliament, at the request of our said most worthy lord the Duke of Clarence, lieutenant of our lord the King, in Ireland, and the lords and commons aforesaid, against those contravening the Statutes and ordinances aforesaid, passing over the time preceding, do fulminate sentence of excommunication, and do excommunicate them by this present writing, we and each of us reserving absolution for ourselves and for our subjects if we should be in peril of death.

CELT: *The Corpus of Electronic Texts, University College Cork, available at www.ucc.ie/celt. Reproduced by permission.*

KING RICHARD II IN IRELAND

1395

As part of the effort to shore up the decaying English lordship in Ireland, Richard II arrived in Waterford in October 1394. Between January and May 1395, Richard received the homage and submission of eighty paramount chiefs in Dublin or other centers. An example of these is the treaty with Niall Oge O'Neill, who submitted to the king in the name of his father, "prince of the Irish of Ulster." The situation with the Leinster chiefs was somewhat different, reflected in Art Mac Murrough's pledge to quit Leinster and go conquer lands elsewhere occupied by rebels and the king's enemies, thereby releasing his hereditary lands for English settlement and creating an extension of the English "Pale" in Ireland.

SEE ALSO English Government in Medieval Ireland; Norman Invasion and Gaelic Resurgence; Richard II in Ireland

TREATIES WITH IRISH CHIEFS

(1) With Niall Oge O'Neill

On the 16th day of March 1395, in a room of the Friars Preachers in Drogheda, in the presence of King Richard, Nellanus *juvenis* O Nel [Niall Oge O'Neill] in person, captain of his nation, removing his girdle, dagger and cap, and on bended knee, fell at the feet of our said lord the King and, raising his two hands with the palms together and hold them between the hands of the King, took these words in the Irish language, which were rendered into English by Thomas O Locheran, interpreter, in the presence of many well understanding the Irish language, viz.

I, Niall junior O'Neill, captain of my nation, swear to be faithful liegeman of my Lord Richard, King of England and France and Lord of Ireland, my sovereign lord, and of his heirs and successors, being kings of England, from this day henceforth in life, limb, and earthly honour, so that he and they shall have over me power of life and death, and I will be faithful to the same and his heirs for ever in all things and will help to defend him and his heirs against all worldly enemies whatsoever, and will be obedient to the laws, commands, and ordinances of the same or any of them according to my power and that of all mine; and I will come to the said lord my King and his heirs, being kings of England, and to his or their parliament and council or otherwise whensoever he or they shall send for me or whenever I shall be required, called, or summoned on his or their part or the part of their lieutenants: and I will well and faithfully come to said Lord King, his heirs and their lieutenants, or to any of them, to give counsel, and I will do in all singular that which a good and faithful liegeman ought to do and is bound to do to his natural liege lord, so help me God and these God's holy Gospels.

For the observing of which allegiance and fealty to the Lord our King etc., he bound himself if he should violate the said oath in whole or part that he would pay to the Papal Curia 20,000 marks of English money. Whereupon the King admitted him to the kiss of peace as his liege, and Niall requested the notary to make a public instrument thereof.

Witnesses being, Thomas, archbishop of York, John of Armagh, Primate of all Ireland, the bishops of London, Chichester and Llandaff, Thomas Mowbray, Earl of Nottingham, Thomas Percy, Marshal of the Household, and William Scrope, the King's Chamberlain.

(2) With Art Oge MacMurrough Kavanagh

This indenture, made on Thursday the 7th day of January, in the 18th year of King Richard (1395), in a field between Tullow and Newcastle, between the noble lord Thomas, Earl of Nottingham and Marshal of England, etc., on one part, and Art MacMurrough, born liege Irishman of our said lord the King, for himself and his men on the other, witnesses: that at the instance and supplication of the said Art our lord the King received the said Art to his grace and peace under the form which follows, viz. that the said Art has sworn by the holy Cross and on the holy Gospels, touched by him, to keep fealty for ever to our lord the King, his heirs, and successors, being kings of England, and that he will deliver to our lord the King, or any of his deputies, or any whom he shall depute, full possession of all lands, tenements, castles, fortresses, woods, and pastures with all their appurtenances, which have been of late occupied by the said Art of his allies, men, or adherents within the land of Leinster, without any reservation to himself made or to be made in any manner and without fraud or guile; and that the said Art has sworn and promised as for himself and all his, that all his subjects and tenants of any condition whatsoever in the lands and places aforesaid shall likewise swear to keep fealty for ever to the Lord King and his successors and deputies, or those whom he shall depute, as above, and that they will stand to and obey the laws, commands, and ordinances of the King and his successors; and that the said Art has

likewise sworn that by the first Sunday of Lent next (28 February), he will leave the whole country of Leinster to the true obedience, use, and disposition of the King, his heirs, and successors, as above, saving and excepting always to him (Art) all his movable goods, and that for greater security of observance of the above fealty the said Art shall deliver to the said Lord our King and to his deputies or those whom he shall depute the son of Thomas Carragh Kavanagh his brother, as a true hostage within the next fortnight following after the date of these presents and sooner, if he can, without fraud or guile, and that, the said hostage thus received, our Lord the King shall of special grace kindly treat the said Art as his true liege, and that he will grant to the said Art to go and return well and peacefully in security; and that the Lord our King after these things are done shall generously make provision for the said Art and will grant to him and his heirs eighty marks yearly for ever, together with the heritage of the said Art's wife in the barony of Norragh with its appurtenances; and that all the armed men, warriors, or fighting men of the following, household, or nation of the said Art shall quit the whole land of Leinster aforesaid and shall go with him and shall have fitting wages from the King, for the time being, to go and conquer other parts occupied by rebels of the said Lord King, and that Art and all his men aforesaid shall have all lands which they may thus acquire and hold them of the Lord King, his heirs, and successors as above, and as his true lieges and obedient and subject to his laws, by liege homage and befitting duty done therefor as above to the King, his heirs, and successors, and that they shall enjoy them in perpetuity and by hereditary descent. Also subsequently by the above indenture it was understood and agreed between the Earl Marshal on one hand and O'Byrne, O'More, O'Nolan, O'Morchoe, MacEochaidh [Keogh], O'Dunn, Mackerelt, David Moore MacManus, and all those of Hy Kinsella on the other, that all the aforesaid O'Byrne, etc., and all of Hy Kinsella have sworn by the holy Cross and on the holy Gospels that they and all their armed upon men, warriors, and fighting men shall deliver all their possessions in Leinster to the said Lord King, his heirs, and successors, his deputies and those whom he may depute, and quit that country, saving however their movable goods always to themselves. And that when that is done the Lord King shall maintain those captains at expense of his Household at good and fitting wages, fees, or salaries, payable yearly from the King's Treasury to all and sundry these captains for the term of their lives, and that the Lord King will give to them and their fighting men aforesaid fitting wages to go, attack, and conquer other parts occupied by rebels of the King. And he will give to them all lands which they shall so acquire and they shall hold them of our Lord the King, his heirs and successors, by liege homage and befitting the duty, as his true lieges, obedient and subject to his laws. And that they shall deliver hostages to the said King, his deputies and those whom he shall depute, for the fulfilment on their part of all the above as they have sworn it. And that the peace of all the aforesaid shall be publicly proclaimed in the said field by the said Earl in the name of the King, and that likewise it is understood that all the aforesaid Irishmen, so sworn, shall abide in peace in their places even to the first Sunday of Lent abovenamed, nor shall they permit any rebels of our Lord the King or evil-doers to be received in their localities, but shall expel them to the best of their power from their borders. And in case, which God forbid, that any mischance shall happen between the date of these presents and the first Sunday of Lent aforesaid against these conventions through any of the aforesaid parties or their adherents, the peace shall not on account of that be broken, but within a fortnight after due notice made it shall be amended and fittingly restored without guile or fraud. And that the said Art has sworn and promised that if any of the aforesaid who have thus sworn shall rashly presume to go against the said conventions, he will make war on them according to his power as his deadly and capital enemies. And so that all these conventions shall be faithfully observed by the aforesaid parties, the said Earl Marshal of England swore by the holy Cross on the holy Gospels and likewise the said Art and all the others for their part swore by the holy Cross and on the holy Gospels.

In witness whereof for his part of the indenture the said Earl affixed his seal in presence of the said Art MacMurrough, and for their part of the indenture the said Art and O'Byrne affixed their seals, in presence of the said Earl Marshal.

> *Witnesses: John Griffin, bishop of Leighlin, John Golafre, Lawrence Verkerell, lord of Coytyf, John Greyly of Gascony, etc., Brother Edmund Vale, Master of the Hospital of Kyllergy, and many others.*

Which indenture, sealed with two seals in red wax, the notary saw, read, and has faithfully turned into a public deed. Whereupon the said Irishmen requested him to make them public instruments.

> *Witnesses: John Golafre and other knights.*

RICHARD II IN IRELAND, 1394–5, *edited by Edmund Curtis (1927), pp. 159–160, 169–173.*

~

DECLARATION OF INDEPENDENCE OF THE IRISH PARLIAMENT

1460

By the mid-fifteenth century the English colony in Ireland was clearly on the defensive. They were looking to King Henry VI to shore up the Pale, and when he appointed Richard, duke of York, lieutenant of Ireland in 1447, the Anglo-Irish hoped that this would improve their fortunes. However, in October 1459 the Yorkist forces in England were defeated by the Lancastrians, and the duke of York fled to Ireland. This "Declaration of Independence" was passed by the Irish parliament in Drogheda in the following winter to ensure support for York, confirming him in his office and making it a treasonable offense for anyone to challenge his authority. However, the document also reaffirmed the separateness of the Anglo-Irish colony, and even if its validity was later questioned, its very existence is memorable.

SEE ALSO English Government in Medieval Ireland

Statutes, ordinances and acts published in a parliament of the Lord King at Drogheda on Friday next after the feast of St. Blaise in the 38th year of King Henry VI [7 February 1460], held before Richard, Duke of York, Lieutenant of Lord King, and thence adjourned to Dublin on Saturday next before the feast of St. Matthias, Apostle, next following [22 February], until Monday next after the feast of St. David next following; and there on Friday next after the feast of St. David until Monday next before the feast of the apostles Philip and James next following prorogued. And from that Monday to Monday next after the feast of Holy Trinity next following prorogued. And on Wednesday next before the feast of Corpus Christi next following to Monday next after the feast of St. Margaret, Virgin [21 July 1460] next following prorogued, and there ended and terminated in the form which follows:

I. Firstly it is ordained and agreed that Holy Church be free and have and enjoy all her franchises, liberties, and free usages without any infringement, as it has been used heretofore.

II. Also it is ordained and agreed that the land of Ireland have and enjoy all its franchises, good usages and customs as it has been used heretofore.

III. Also it is ordained and established that the cities of Dublin, Waterford and the town of Drogheda and all the other cities and good towns in the said land of Ireland have and enjoy all their good customs, liberties, franchises, privileges and usages as they have had and used heretofore.

IV. Also at the request of the Commons: That whereas the King our sovereign lord by his latters patent given at Coventry the 6th day of March in the 35th year of his reign [1457] ordained and constituted his well-beloved cousin Richard, duke of York, his lieutenant of his land of Ireland to have and to hold [the same] office from the 8th day of December next following, in manner and form as is more fully specified and declared in the said letters patent enrolled of record in the rolls of the Chancery of the said land that it may be ordained, established and enacted in the said Parliament that by authority of the said Parliament the said letters patent be confirmed ratified and approved and that the said Duke may have occupy and enjoy the office and all things contained in the said letters patent according to the tenor form and effect thereof from the said eighth day to the end of the said ten years. Whereupon the premises considered: It is ordained established and enacted in the said Parliament that the said letters patent be confirmed ratified and approved and that the said Duke may have occupy and enjoy the said office and all things contained in the said letters patent, according to the tenor form and effect thereof from the said 8th day to the end of the said ten years.

V. Also at the request of the Commons: That, whereas the King of sovereign lord has constituted and appointed his well-beloved cousin Richard duke of York lieutenant and governor of his land of Ireland, wherein he represents in the absence of our said sovereign lord out of the same land his right noble person and estate; and that to the said lieutenant and governor in the said absence such reverence, obedience and fear ought to be given in the said land as to our sovereign lord whose estate is thereby honoured feared and obeyed. Whereupon, the premises considered, it is ordained, established and enacted in the said Parliament and by authority of the same that if any person or persons imagine, compass, excite or provoke the destruction or death of the said lieutenant and governor, or to that intent confederate or assent with the Irish enemies of our said sovereign lord or with any other persons, or provoke any rebellion or disobedience towards the said lieutenant and governor or by any statute made in the said parliament be proved a rebel to our said sovereign lord, that the said person or persons upon whom such imagining, compassing, excitement or provocation, confederacy, assent or rebellion is lawfully proved be and stand as attainted of high treason committed against the high person of our said sovereign lord. And it is ordained established

and enacted in the said Parliament . . . that if any person or persons shall hereafter listen to the said imagining, compassing, etc. and assent to them, they be attainted of rebellion. And that thereupon the King shall send his writ to any sheriff of any county of the said land, any mayor, bailiff and commonalty, any mayor, sheriff and commonalty, any mayor and commonalty, or any sovereign portreeve and commonalty of any city or town or any other his subject of his said land to assist his said lieutenant and governor in resistance to the said person or persons in their said intention; and to chastise, punish, and subdue them as law requires, and that every of the said mayor, bailiff, sheriff, sovereign, portreeve, commonalty and subject shall put himself with all his force and power into due and immediate [readiness] for obedience to the said writ. And if any mayor ,bailiff and commonalty, etc. [as before] herein disobey or harbour, receive, aid or favour the person or persons in the said writ specified, that they shall forfeit all such profits and commodities or other things as they have of the grant of the King or of any of his noble progenitors and moreover a thousand pounds to the King. And if any of the sheriffs of any county of the said land or any of the said subjects do contrary [to this Act] that then they so doing shall forfeit one thousand pounds, one moiety to the King for the defence of the said land and the other moiety to the party who in that case will sue a writ of "scire facias" upon this act. Provided that this act be not prejudicial to the franchises of any city or town of the said land granted to the same city or town by our said sovereign lord of any of his progenitors. This to continue so long as the said lieutenant and governor shall be resident in his own person in the said land.

VI. Also at the request of the Commons: That, whereas the land of Ireland is, and at all times has been, corporate of itself by the ancient laws and customs used in the same, freed of the burthen of any special law of the realm of England save only such laws as by the lords spiritual and temporal and the commons of the said land had been in Great Council or Parliament there held, admitted, accepted, affirmed and proclaimed, according to sundry ancient statutes thereof made. And whereas also of ancient custom, privilege, and franchise of the said land there is, and at all times has been, the seal of the King current by which the laws there and also the King's subjects of the same land are guided and directed, which seal is called the seal of the said land to which all the said subjects ought to do lawful obedience. And it has not been seen or heard that nay person or persons inhabiting or resident in any other Christian land so corporate of itself ought to obey any mandate within the same land given or made under any other seal than the proper seal of the same by which any person should be had or compelled to go by any such mandate out of the said land. And if such mandate were obeyed in the said land of Ireland very great prejudice and derogation and very perilous inconveniences would result to the same contrary to the franchises, liberties and ancient customs thereof and to the very great and immeasurable vexations of the said subjects of the same, of which many instances have been in late days seen and experienced. And moreover, whereas in no realm or land which has within itself a Constable and Marshal of the same ought any person of that realm or land to sue or prosecute any appeal or other matter determinable before the said Constable and Marshal, before the Constable and Marshal of any other land where such appeal or matter took [can take] no foundation or effect. And this notwithstanding, that although there are in the said land, and of ancient custom have been, a Constable and Marshal, yet divers persons of the same land have oftentimes heretofore sued and procured of great malice many of the King's subjects of the same to be sent for to come into England by colour of such appeals in great derogation and prejudice of the said liberty and franchise. Whereupon, the premises considered: It is ordained, enacted and established in the said Parliament and by authority thereof that henceforth no person or persons being in the said land of Ireland shall be, by any command given or made under any other seal than the said seal of the same land, compelled to answer to any appeal or any other matter out of the said land. And that no officer or minister of the same land to whom any such command comes shall put that command or any proclamation or any other thing contrary or prejudicial to the said ancient, custom, privilege or franchise in execution, on pain of the forfeiture of all the lands and goods which he or any other to his use has in the said land, as well as [a fine] of a thousand marks, the one moiety to the King, and the other moiety to the party who will sue in this case against the said officer or minister by writ of "scire facias" or by any other action at the law proper in this behalf. It is also ordained by the said authority that any appeal of treason taken in this land shall be determined before the Constable and the Marshal of the said land for the time being and within the said land in no other place. And if any person shall hereafter appeal any other person in the said land, and the matter of said appeal shall be found and proved not true, that then such person taking or commencing such appeal for the same shall be adjudged to death, and that no pardon shall serve him in such case.

VII. Also at the request of the Commons: That, whereas the defence of the English nation of this land from the danger and malice of the Irish enemies of the same land rests and depends on English bows, which give to the said enemies the greatest resistance and terror of any weapon of war used in the said land [which is] now very nearly destitute of any great number of the said bows which are not in these days employed in the exercise of the occupation of archery, whereby the said enemies have grown into such great hardihood and audacity as to ride upon the King's subject of the said land by night, so that they suffer from the said enemies very great and hard rebuke, spoliations and robberies, to their outrageous injury and loss. Whereupon, the premises considered: It is ordained in the said Parliament and by authority thereof that every of the said subjects, for and upon every twenty pounds of lands, tenements, rents, fees, annuities or other livelihood and possessions with their appurtenances which he has in the said land of yearly rent, shall provide in his house one archer mounted and arrayed defensively with bow and arrows fit for the war according to the English fashion, to be ready at all times upon warning for the defence of he said land in manner and form as heretofore it has been accustomed, so long as the most high puissant prince the Duke of York may remain in the said land. And that in every county of the said land the archers, mounted and arrayed as above with the said bows and arrows according to the assessment of their said yearly possessions, shall every quarter make their musters in the same county before the justices or wardens of the peace having authority and power to enquire in their sessions b those to whom [the power] is given. And that by this act the same justices or wardens shall have power and authority to enquire in their sessions from time to time the value of the possession of every man within the same, and also the amerce in the same sessions according to their discretions such person and persons as ought to find the said archers and who therein make default contrary to the intent and tenor of the said act, Holy Church excepted.

STATUTE ROLLS, IRELAND, HENRY VI, *edited by* Henry *Fitzpatrick Berry* (1910), *pp.* 639–649.

~

POYNINGS' LAW

1494

To render the Dublin parliament harmless as an instrument of the king's enemies and as a Yorkist center (opposed to the Tudor succession), this law indicated that henceforth Irish law would be subject to approval by the English parliament. Poynings' Law was to have a long and interesting history until overthrown by the Irish parliament in 1782.

SEE ALSO English Government in Medieval Ireland

AN ACT THAT NO PARLIAMENT BE HOLDEN IN THIS LAND UNTIL THE ACTS BE CERTIFIED INTO ENGLAND

Item, at the request of the commons of the land of Ireland, be it ordained, enacted and established, that at the next Parliament that there shall be holden by the King's commandment and licence, wherein amongst other, the King's grace intendeth to have a general resumption of his whole revenues fith [since] the last day of the reign of King Edward the second, no Parliament be holden hereafter in the said land, but at such season as the King's lieutenant and council there first do certify the King, under the great seal of that land, the causes and considerations, and all such acts as them seemeth should pass in the same Parliament, and such causes, considerations, and acts affirmed by the King and his council to be good and expedient for that land, and his licence thereupon, as well in affirmation of the said causes and acts, as to summon the said parliament under his great seal of England had and obtained; that done, a Parliament to be had and holden after the form and effect afore rehearsed: and if any parliament be holden in that land hereafter, contrary to the form and provision aforesaid, it be deemed void and of none effect in law.

THE STATUTES AT LARGE, PASSED IN THE PARLIAMENTS HELD IN IRELAND: FROM THE THIRD YEAR OF EDWARD THE SECOND, . . . (1786–1804), p. 44.

≈

FROM *VOCATION OF JOHN BALE TO THE BISHOPERY OF OSSORIE*

1553

John Bale

John Bale (1495–1563) was the Cambridge University-educated Protestant cleric who served briefly (1552–1553) as bishop of Ossory (a diocese in and around Waterford). A determined reformer, he was vexed and frustrated by the deep-seated resistance he encountered among the Irish, and he bitterly denounced it after the accession of the Catholic

Queen Mary cut the ground out from under him and forced him to return to England.

SEE ALSO English Writing on Ireland before 1800

Upon the xxi. daye of January we entered into the shippe; I, my wyfe, and one servaunt; and beinge but ii. nyghtes and ii. dayes upon the sea, we arryved most prosperously at Waterforde, in the coldest time of the yeare, so mercifull was the Lorde unto us.

In beholdynge the face and the ordre of that cytie, I see many abhomynable ydolartryes mainteined by the Epicurysh prestes, for their wicked bellies sake. The Communion, or Supper of the Lorde, was there altogyther used lyke a popysh masse, with the olde apysh toyes of Antichrist, in bowynges and beckynges, knelinges and knockinges, the Lordes death, after S. Paule's doctrine, neyther preached nor yet spoken of. There wawled they over the dead, with prodigyouse howlynges and patterynges, as though their sowles had not bene quyeted in Christe and redemed by hys passion, but that they must come after and helpe at a pinche with Requiem Eternam, to delyver them out of helle by their sorrowfull sorceryes. Whan I had beholden these heathenysh behavers, I seyd unto a Senatour of that citye, that I wele perceyved that Christe had there no Bishop, neyther yet the Kynges Majestie of England any faythful officer of the mayer, in suffering so horrible blasphemies. . . .

Upon the assension daye, I preached again at Kikennie, likewyse on Trinite sondaye, and on S. Peters Daye at midsomer than followinge.

On the xxv daye of July, the prestes were as pleasauntly disposed as might be, and went by heapes from taverne to taverne, to seke the best Rob Davye and aquavite, which are their speciall drinkes there. Thei cawsed all their cuppes to be filled in, with Gaudeamus in dolio, the misterie therof only knowne to them, and, at that time, to none other els.

Which was, that Kynge Edwarde was dead, and that they were in hope to have up their maskynge masses againe . . . For ye must consydre that the prestes are commenly the first that receive suche news. The next day folowinge, a very wicked justice called Thomas Hothe, with the Lorde Mountgarret, restored to the Cathedrall churche, requyrynge to have a communion, in the honour of S. Anne. Marke the blasphemouse blyndnesse and wylfull obstinacye of thys beastly papyst. The prestes made hym answere, That I had forbydden them that celebracion, savynge only upon the Sondayes. As I had, in dede, for the abhomynable ydolatries that I had seane therein. I discharge you (sayeth he) of obedience to your Bishop in this point, and commaunde yow to do as ye have done heretofore, which was, to make of Christes holy communion an ydolatrouse masse, and to suffre it to serve for the dead, cleane contrarye to the Christen use of the same.

Thus was a wicked justice not only a vyolatour of Christes institucion, but also a contempner of his princes earnest commaundement, and a provoker of the people by his ungraciouse example to do the lyke. Thys coulde he do whith other mischefes more, by his longe beynge there by a whole monthe's space, but for murthers, theftes, ydolatryes, and abhominable whoredomes, wherewith all that nacion haboundeth, for that time he sought no redresse, neyther appointed any correction. The prestes thus rejoycing that the Kinge was dead, and that they had bene that daye confirmed in their supersticiouse obstinacie, resorted to the forseyd false justice the same night at supper, to gratifye him with Rob Davye and Aqua vite; for that he had bene so frendly unto them, and that he might styll continue in the same. The next daye after was the Layde Jane Gylforde proclaimed their Quene, with solemnite of processions, bonefyres, and banquettes, they seyd justice, as I was infourmed, sore blamynge me for my absence that daye; for, in dede, I muche doubted that matter.

So sone as it was there rumoured abrode that the kynge was departed from this lyfe, the ruffianess of that wilde nacyon, not only rebelled against the English captaines, as their lewde custome, in suche chaunges, hath bene alwayes, chefly no English deputye beinge within the lande, but also they conspired into the very deathes of so many English men and women, as were left therein alyve: Myndinge, as they than stoughtly boasted it, to have set up a kinge of their owne. And to cause their wilde people to beare the more hate to our nacion, very subtily, but yet falsely, they caused it to be noysed over all, that the younge Earl of Ormonde, and Barnabe, the Barne of Upper Osssorie's sonne, were both slaine in the court at London.

Upon the wylye practise of myschefe, they raged without ordre, in all places, and assaulted the English fortes every where.

And at one of them, by a subtyle trayne, they got out ix our men, and slew them. . . .

On the xx. daye of August, was the ladye marye with us at Kylkennye proclaymed Quene of Englande, Fraunce, and Irelande, with the greatest solempnyte, that there coulde be devysed, of processions, musters and disgysinges, all the noble captaynes and gentilmen there being present. What-a-do I had that daye with the prebendaryes and prests abought wearinge the cope, croser, and myter in procession, it were to muche to write.

I tolde them earnestly, whan they wolde have compelled me thereunto, that I was not Moyses minister but Christes, I desyred them that they would not compell me to his denyall, which is (S. Paule sayth) in the repetinge of Moyses sacramentes and ceremoniall schadowes Gal. v. With that I toke Christes Testament in my hande, and went to the market crosse, the people in great nombre followinge. There toke I the xiii. chap. of S. Paule to the Romanes, declaringe to them brevely, what the autoritie was of the worldly powers magistrates, what reverence and obedience were due to the same. In the meane tyme, had the prelates goten ii. disgysed prestes, one to beare the myter afore me, and an other the croser, makinge iii. procession pageauntes of one. The yonge men, in the forenone, played a Tragedye of Gods Promyses in the olde lawe at the market crosse, with organe plainges and songes very aptely. In the after none agayne they played a Commedie of sanct Johan Baptiste's Preachinges, of Christe's baptisynge, and of his temptacion in the wildernesse; to the small contentacion of the prestes and other papistes there. . . .

Some men peradventure will marvele, that I utteringe matters of Irelande, shulde omitt in this treatise, to write of Coyne and lyverie. Which are so cruell pillages and opressions of the poor commens there, as are no where els in this whole earthe, neither undre wicked Saracene nor yet cruell Turke, besides all prodigiouse kindes of lecherie and other abhominacions therin committed. Thre causes there are, which hath moved me not to expresse them here. One is, for so muche as they pertaine nothinge to the tyttle of this boke, which all concerneth religion. An other is for that the matter is so large, as requireth a muche larger volume. The third cause is, for that I have known ii worthie men, whome, I will not nowe name to have done that thinge so exactly, as noman (I suppose) therein can amende them. But this I will utter brevely, that the Irishe lords and their undrecaptaines, supporting the same, are not only companions with theves, as the prophete reporteth, Esa. 1, but also they are their wicked maisters and maintainers. So that they both coupled togyther, the murtherer with his maistre, and the thefe with his maintainer, leyve nothinge undevoured behinde them that fertile region; no more than ded the devouringe locustes of Egypt, Exo. 10. Anon after their harvestes are ended there, the Kearnes, the Gallowglasses, and the other brechelesse souldiers, with horses and their horse-gromes, sumtyme iii waitinge upon one jade, enter into the villages with much crueltie and fearceness, they continue there in great ravine and spoyle, and, when they go thens, they leave nothinge els behinde them for payment, but lice, lecherie, and intollerable penureie for the yeare after. Yet set the rulers thereupon a very fayre colour, that is for defence of the English pale. I besiche God to sende such protection a shorte ende, and their lordes and Captaines also, if they see it not sone amended. For it is the utter confusion of that lande, and a maintenaunce to all vices.

Thre peoples are in Irelande in these dayes, prestes, lawyers, and kearnes, which will not suffre faythe, truthe and honestye, to dwell there. And all these have but one God their Bellye, and glory in that wicked feate to their shame, whose ende is dampnation, Phil. 3. I speake only of those which are bredde and borne there, and yet not of them all. These for the more part, are sworne bretherne together in myschefe, one to maintaine an others maliciouse cause, by murther previly procured. And, to bringe their conceyved wickednesse to passe, they can do great miracles in this age, by vertue of transubstanciation belyke, for therein are they very conninge. For they can very wittely make, of a tame Irishe, a wilde Irishe for nede, so that they shall serve their turne so wele as though were of the wilde Irish in dede.

Reprinted in STRANGERS TO THAT LAND: BRITISH PERCEPTIONS OF IRELAND FROM THE REFORMATION TO THE FAMINE, *edited by Andrew Hadfield and John McVeagh (1994), pp. 31–35.*

~

ACT OF UNIFORMITY

1560

After the brief (1553–1558) reign of the Catholic Queen Mary, the Protestant Reformation slowly resumed its progress under Mary's successor and half-sister, Elizabeth I. The Act of Uniformity of 1560, passed through an Irish parliament that was becoming heavily Protestant in its composition, extended to Ireland a variation of the Protestant (or "Anglican") faith that was being re-established in England.

SEE ALSO Burial Customs and Popular Religion from 1500 to 1690; Church of Ireland: Elizabethan Era; Family: Marriage Patterns and Family Life from 1500 to 1690

AN ACT FOR THE UNIFORMITIE OF COMMON PRAYER AND SERVICE IN THE CHURCH, AND THE ADMINISTRATION OF THE SACRAMENTS

Where at the death of our late soverain lord King Edward the 6, there remained one uniforme order of common service, prayer and the administration of sacraments, rites and ceremonies in the church of England, which was set forth in one book, intituled, "The Book of Common Prayer, and administration of Sacraments" which was repealed and taken away by act of Parliament in the said realm of England in the first year of the raign of our late soveraign lady Queen Mary, to the great decay of the true honour of God, and discomfort to the professors of the truth of Christ's religion. Be it therefore enacted by the authoritie of this present Parliament. That the said book with the order of service, and of the administration of sacraments, rites and ceremonies, with the alterations and additions therein added and appointed by this estatute, shall stand and bee from and after the feast of Pentecost, next ensuing, in full force and effect, . . .

II. And further be it enacted . . . that all and singular ministers in any cathedrall or parish church, or other place within this realm of Ireland, shall from and after the feast of Saint John Baptist, then next ensuing, be bounded to say and use the mattens, evensong, celebration of the Lord's supper, and administration of each of the sacraments, and all their common and open prayer, in such order and form as is mentioned in the said book. . . .

STATUTES AT LARGE, IRELAND, *vol. 1, pp. 284–290; 2 Eliz. I, c. 2.*

~

FROM *TWO BOKES OF THE HISTORIES OF IRELAND*

1571

Edmund Campion

Edmund Campion, executed as a Jesuit in 1581, was English-born, but a guest of leading Old English families in Dublin in 1570–1571. His "Histories of Ireland," not published until 1633, glorified the Old English (as against the Gaelic Irish), and in manuscript form influenced Richard Stanihurst (who contributed the Irish portions of

Holinshead's famous chronicles), and others among his contemporaries.

SEE ALSO English Writing on Ireland before 1800

The people are thus enclyned: religious, francke, amorous, irefull, sufferable of paynes infinite, veary glorious, many sorserers, excellent horsemen, delighted with warres, great almesgevers, passing in hospitalitie. The lewder sorte, bothe clerkes and laye, are sensuall and loose to leacherye above measure. The same being vertuously brede up or refourmed, are suche myrrors of holynes and austeritie that other nations retaine but a shadoe of devotion in comparison of them. As for abstinence and fastynge, which theis daies make so dangerous, this is to them a familiare kinde of chastisment. In which vertue and diverse other how farr the best excell, so farr in glotonie and other hatefull crymes the vitious theie are worse than to bad. Theie folowe the deade course to grave with howling and barbarous owtcries, pitiful in apparance, whereof grewe as I suppose the proverbe to weepe Irishe. The unplandishe are lightly abused to beleeve and avouche idle miracles and revelations vaine and childishe. Greedie of praise theie be, and fearfull of dishonour. And to this ende they esteeme theire poetes, who wright Irishe learnedly, and penne therein sonettes heroicall, for the which they are bountefully rewarded: yf not, they sende owt lybells in dispraise, whereof the gentlemen, specially the meere Irishe, stand in greate awe. They love tenderly theire foster children and bequeathe to them a childes portyon, whereby they nourishe sure frendship, so beneficiall every waie that commonly five hundred kyne and better are geven in reward to wynne an noblemans childe to forster. They are sharpe witted, lovers of learning, capable of any studie whereunto they bende themselves, constant in travaile, aventurous, intractable, kynde hearted, secreate in displeasure.

Hitherto the Irishe of bothe sortes, meere and Englishe, are affected mutche indifferently, save that in theis by good order and breaking the same vertues are farr more pregnant, in those other by licencious and evill custome the same faultes are more extreame and odious. I saie by lycentiousnes and evil custome, for that there is daily triall of good natures among them; howe sone they be reclaymed and to what rare giftes of grace and wisdome they doe and have aspired, againe the veary Englishe of birthe conversant with the brutishe sorte of that people become degenerate in short space, and are quite altered into worst ranke of Irish rooges. Such a force hathe education to make or marre.

Reprinted in STRANGERS TO THAT LAND: BRITISH PERCEPTIONS OF IRELAND FROM THE REFORMATION TO THE FAMINE, *edited by Andrew Hadfield and John McVeagh* (1994), *pp.* 38–39.

≈

FROM "NOTES OF HIS REPORT"

1576

Sir William Gerard

The English-born Sir William Gerard was lord chancellor of Ireland in 1576. The notes of his report constitute part of the swelling Elizabethan ethnography of the Irish. He distinguishes between the ungovernable Irish, the sometimes governable Old English, and the "degenerate" Old English who have become almost as troublesome (from the government's point of view) as the Gaelic Irish.

SEE ALSO Colonial Theory from 1500 to 1690; English Writing on Ireland before 1800

It is necesarye to understand whoe be the Irishe enymies and howe they annoye the state, and also whoe ar they so termid Englishe rebells, and howe they woorke harme, and then to thinke of the desire to reforme, and whether one lyke and one same course & waye to subdue bothe be to be followed.

The Irishe is knowen by name, speache, habitt, feadinge, order, rule, and conversacion. He accompteth him self cheife in his owne country and (whatsoever he saye or professe) lykethe of noe superior. He mortally hatethe the Englishe. By will he governethe those under him, supplyinge his and their wantes by prayinge and spoylinge of other countryes adjoyninge. Theise lyve as the Irishe lyved in all respects before the conqueste.

In twoe sortes, theise ar to be dealte with: The one, totallye to conquere theim, and that muste be by force of the swoord, for so were the other of the Irishe subdued before the Englishe were setled: the other waye is by suche pollecye to keepe theim quiett as with smalleste force, and by consequent with least chardge they may be defended from harminge the Englishe. Whiche pollecyes I finde by those recordes from age to age putt in use in that governmente.

The Englishe rebells ar people of our owne nacion, suche whose auncestors and theim selves after the expultion of the Irishe, ever sithence Henrye the secondes tyme, some of longer, some of shorter tyme, have there contynued. Theise Englishe rebells may be devided into twoe kindes: the one, soche as enter into the field in open hostilitie and actuall rebellion agaynste the Prince, comparable to the rebellinge in England. To suppresse those, the swoord muste also be the instrument. Thother sorte of Englishe rebells are suche as refuzinge Englishe nature growe Irishe in soche sorte as (otherwise then in name) not to be discerned from the Irishe.

All the force of the Irishe with all the helpe they had of anye actuall Englishe rebell harmed not (as the recordes verifie) untill this degeneratinge fell, which beganne about the xxxth yeare of the sayd Kinge Edwarde the third his reigne.

The cawsies which move theise recordes to call theim Englishe degenerates apearethe in the same.

Theye (saye theise recordes) speake Irishe, use Irishe habitt, feadinge, rydinge, spendinge, coysheringe, coyninge; they exacte, oppresse, extorte, praye, spoyle, and take pledges and distresses as doe the Irishe. They marrye and foster with the Irishe, and, to conclude, they imbrace rather Irishe braghan lawes then sweete government by justice.

Soche as affirme the swoord muste goe before to subdue theise, greatly erre. For can the swoord teache theim to speake Englishe, to use Englishe apparell, to restrayne theim from Irishe exactions and extortions, and to shonne all the manners & orders of the Irishe. Noe it is the rodd of justice that muste scower out those blottes. For the sword once wente before, and setled their auncestors, and in theim yet resteth this instincte of Englishe nature, generally to feare justice. . . .

I told their Honnors that so long as the Englishe kepte under the government of Englishe lawes they prospered, and when they fell to be Irishe and embraced the Irishe orders, customs and lawes they decayed, so as to restore theim to former Englishe civilitie lawes had from tyme to tyme still bene made restrayninge the Englishe from the Irishe; forbiddinge theim under a payne to foster or marrye with theim or to use or followe anye their Irishe lawes or customs; to use or weare anye their habitt or apparell, to receive or seeke for judgement by anye of their lawes: forbiddinge all captens and marchers to retayne anye Kerne or idell followers, and under payne of deathe to take no prayes. . . .

I sayd to their Honnors all those lawes notwithstandinge the race of the Englishe throughout the pale were in everye forbidden respecte grown more Irishe then before and so the wound greater at this daye then ever before. I sayd if Irishe speache, habit and conditions made the man Irishe, the most parte of the Englishe were Irishe.

Reprinted in STRANGERS TO THAT LAND: BRITISH PERCEPTIONS OF IRELAND FROM THE REFORMATION TO THE FAMINE, edited by Andrew Hadfield and John McVeagh (1994), pp. 39–41.

~

LETTER TO ELIZABETH

12 November 1580

Lord Arthur Grey de Wilton

Lord Arthur Grey de Wilton (1536–1593) was lord deputy of Ireland from 1580 to 1582. Zealously Protestant, he defeated and then slaughtered some six hundred Spanish and Italian soldiers who had been sent by the pope to aid a Catholic rebellion in Munster, and who landed in Smerwick harbor on County Kerry's Dingle peninsula. Grey's letter makes clear the ferocity of his actions.

SEE ALSO English Writing on Ireland before 1800

There was presently sent unto me one Alexandro, their campmaster; he told me that certain Spaniards and Italians were there arrived upon fair . . . speeches and great promises, which altogether vain and false they found, and t[hat] it was no part of their intent to molest or take any government from your Majesty, for proof that they were ready to depart as they came, and deliver in [to] my hands the fort. Mine answer was, that for that I perceived their people to stand of two nations, Italian and Spanish, I would give no a[nswer] unless a Spaniard were likewise by. He presently went and returned [with] a Spanish captain. I then told the Spaniard that I knew their nation [to] have an absolute Prince, one that was in good league and amity with your Majesty, which made me marvel that any of his people should be found associate . . . them that went about to maintain rebels against you and to disturb . . . any your Highness' governments, and taking it that it could not be his Kings' will, I was to know by whom and for what cause they were sent. His reply was, that the King had not sent them, but that one John Martinez de Ricaldi, Governor for the King, at Bilboa, had willed them to levy a band and to repair with it to St. Andrews, and there to be directed by this their colonel here, whom he followed as a blind man, not knowing whither. The other avouched that they were all sent by the Pope for the defence of the Catholica fede. My answer was, that I would not greatly have marvelled if men being commanded by natural and absolute princes did sometimes take in hand wrong actions, but that men, and that of account as some of them made show of, should be carried into unjust, desperate, and wicked actions by one that neither from God nor man could claim any princely power or empire, but indeed a detestable shaveling, the right Antichrist and general ambitious tyrant over all right principalities, and patron of the diabolica fede, I could not but greatly rest in wonder, their fault therefore, far to be aggravated by the vileness of the commander, and that at my hands no condition of composition they were to expect, other than that simply they should render me the fort, and yield their selves to my will for life or death.

With this answer he departed, after which there was one or two courses to and fro more, to have gotten a certainty for some of their lives, but finding that it would not be, the colonel himself about sunsetting came forth and requested respite with surcease of arms till the next morning, and then he would give a resolute answer.

Finding that to be but a gain of time for them and loss of the same for myself, I definitely answered, I would not grant it, and therefore presently either that he took my offer or else return, and I would fall to my business. He then embraced my knees simply putting himself to my mercy, only he prayed that for that night he might abide in the fort, and that in the morning all should be put into my hands. I asked hostages for the performance; they were given. Morning come; I presented my companies in battle before the fort, the colonel comes forth with 10 or 12 of his chief gentlemen, trailing their ensigns rolled up, and presented them unto me with their lives and the fort. I sent straight, certain gentlemen in, to see their weapons and armours laid down, and to guard the munition and victual there left for spoil. Then put I in certain bands, who straight fell to execution. There were 600 slain.

Reprinted in STRANGERS TO THAT LAND: BRITISH PERCEPTIONS OF IRELAND FROM THE REFORMATION TO THE FAMINE, *edited by Andrew Hadfield and John McVeagh (1994), pp. 102–104.*

～

FEROCITY OF THE IRISH WARS

The following are accounts of the cruelty and savagery of the Irish wars of the 1580s and 1590s. Captain Woodhouse's letter describes the annihilation by Sir William Bingham's forces of some 1,100 Scots who were allied with the Irish Burkes in their rebellion. O'Sullivan Beare's account is from a Catholic perspective. Chief Justice Saxey reports atrocities committed on English settlers in Munster.

SEE ALSO Nine Years War; O'Neill, Hugh, Second Earl of Tyrone; Politics: 1500 to 1690

Defeat of the Scots by Sir Richard Bingham in Connacht (Captain Thomas Woodhouse to Geoffrey Fenton, 23 September 1586)

It pleased God that the Governor this day met with James MacDonnell's sons and all their forces, and with the number of about four score horsemen, he, like a brave gentleman, charged them. I was as near him as I could, and so cut off their wings, and they presently were like cowardly beggars, being in number, as we did judge, about 1,300 in that place, hard by their camp, William Burke's town, called Ardnaree. About one of the clock we did join the battle, and they did set their backs to the great river called the Moy, and the Governor and we that were but a small number did with him, who I protest in God like as brave a man, charge them before our battle came in [*sic*], and kept a narrow strait in our charging of them, so as they could not pass our foot battle, and there, God be thanked, we did drown and kill, as we all did judge, about the number of a thousand or eleven hundred, for there did, by swimming, about a hundred escape, and as the country saith on the other side the water, they have killed them, for we cannot this day get over this water into Tirawley to them for want of boats, but truly I was, never since I was a man of war, so weary with killing of men, for I protest to God, for as fast as I could I did but hough them and paunch them, sometimes on horseback, because they did run as we did break them, and sometimes on foot, and so in less space than an hour this whole and good field was done.

O'Donnell Attacks the English of Connacht (Philip O'Sullivan Beare, Historiæ Catholicæ Iberniæ Compendium, 1621)

[1595] O'Donnell, remembering the cruelty with which the English had thrown women, old men and children from the Bridge of Enniskillen, with all his forces invaded Connacht, which Richard Bingham was holding oppressed under heretical tyranny. In his raids extending far and wide he destroyed the English colonists and settlers, put them to flight, and slew them, sparing no male between fifteen and sixty years old who was unable to speak Irish.

He burnt the village of Longford in Annaly, which Browne an English heretic had taken from O'Farrell. He then returned to Tyrconnel laden with the spoils of the Protestants. After this invasion of Connacht, not a single farmer, settler or Englishman remained, except those who were defended by the walls of castles and fortified towns, for those who had not been destroyed by fire and sword, despoiled of their goods, left for England, heaping curses upon those who had brought them to Ireland.

Massacre of Munster Settlers, 1598 (William Saxey, Chief Justice of Munster, to Sir Robert Cecil Concerning the State of That Province, 26 October 1598)

About the 5th Oct., some 3,000 rebels came into the county of Limerick, sent from the archtraitor Tyrone, under the leading of John FitzThomas . . . elder brother to the last attainted Earl of Desmond . . . and burnt and spoiled most of the towns and villages there. . . . These combinations and revolts have effected many execrable murders and cruelties upon the English, as well in the county of Limerick, as in the counties of Cork and Kerry, and elsewhere; infants taken from the nurses' breasts, and the brains dashed against the walls; the heart plucked out of the body of the husband in the view of the wife, who was forced to yield the use of her apron to wipe off the blood from the murderer's fingers; [an] English gentleman at midday in a town cruelly murdered, and his head cleft in divers pieces; divers sent into Youghal amongst the English, some with their throats cut, but not killed, some with their tongues cut out of their heads, other with their noses cut off; by view whereof the English might the more bitterly lament the misery of their countrymen, and fear the like to befall to themselves.

IRISH HISTORY FROM CONTEMPORARY SOURCES, *edited by Constantia Maxwell (1923), pp. 210–212.*

~

FROM *THE IMAGE OF IRELANDE*

1581

John Derricke

Little is known of John Derricke, who was apparently connected to Sir Henry Sidney, and possibly a friend of his son Philip, to whom this work is dedicated. It lavishes considerable praise on Sir Henry's abilities and may have been intended to win him favor at court. In this poem he describes the Irish woodkern (here "Karne") or soldier, *though it probably represents his view of the native, or "wild," Irish.*

SEE ALSO English Writing on Ireland before 1800

From Part One.

of feathered foules,
there breeds the cheef of all:
A mightie foule, a goodlie birde,
whom men doe Eagle call.
This builde her nast in highest toppe,
of all the Oken tree:
Or in the craftiest place, whereof
in Irelande many bee.
Not in the bounds of Englishe pale,
whiche is a ciuill place:
But in the Deuills Arse, a Peake,
where Rebells moste imbrace.
For as this foule and all the reste,
are wilde by Natures Kinde:
So do thei kepe in wildest nokes
and there men doe them finde.
For like to like the Proverbe saith,
the Leopard with the Beare:
Doth live in midst of desarts rude
and none doeth other feare.
For as the Irishe Karne be wilde,
in manners and in fashion:
So does these foules enhabite, with
that crooked generation.
Yet when as thei are taken yong,
(though wilde thei be by kinde:)
Entrusted through the fauconers lure,
by triall good I find.
That thei come as twere at becke,
and when as thei doe call:
She scarce will stint on twige or bowe,
till on his fiste she fall.
Thus thei obey their tutors hestes
and doe degenerate:
from wildnesse that belonged to,
their fore possessed state.
But Irishe Karne unlike these foules,
in burthe and high degree:
No chaunglyngs are thei love nowhit,
In civil state to bee.
Thei passe not for ciuilitie,
Nor care for wisdomes lore:
Sinne is their cheef felicitie,
whereof thei have the store.
And if perhappes a little Ape,
be taken from the henne:
And brought from Boggs to champion ground,
such thyngs happe now and then.
Yea though thei were in Courte trained up,

and yeres there lived tenne:
Yet doe thei loke to shaking boggs,
scarce provying honest menne.
And when as thei have wonne the Boggs,
suche vertue hath that grounde:
that they are wurse than wildest Karne,
And more in sinne abounde.

From Part Two.

Though that the royall soyle,
and fertill Irishe grounde:
With thousande sondrie pleasaunt thynges,
moste nobly doe abounde.
Though that the lande be free,
from vipers generation:
As in the former parte I made,
a perfecte declaration.
Though that the yearth I saie,
be bliste with heauenly thyngs:
And though tis like the fragrant flowre,
in pleasante Maie that springs.
Yet when I did beholde,
those whiche possesse the same:
Their manners lothsome to be told,
as yrksome for to name.
I mervuailede in my mynde,
and thereupon did muse:
Too see a Bride it is the Soile,
the Bridegrome is the Karne.

Reprinted in STRANGERS TO THAT LAND: BRITISH PERCEPTIONS OF IRELAND FROM THE REFORMATION TO THE FAMINE, edited by Andrew Hadfield and John McVeagh (1994), pp. 41–43.

≈

FROM "THE SONS OF CLANRICARD"

1586

John Hooker

This English account describes some of the travails of Sir William Fitzwilliam (1526–1599), lord deputy of Ireland from 1571 to 1575 and 1588 to 1594.

SEE ALSO English Writing on Ireland before 1800

And then his lordship [Fitzwilliam] prepareth to take a journie towards Waterford. . . . But when he was passed a daies journey, word was brought unto him from the bishop of Meth, who laie then upon the confines of Meth and Connagh for ordering of matters in these parties; and the like from the maior of Gallewaie, and from diverse others, who affected well the state, crieng out with trembling termes and dolefull reports, that the earle of Clanricard his sonnes that basterlie brood, which not scarse two moneths past had humbled themselves to the lord deputie, confessed their faults, and craved pardon, and had most firmelie protested and sworne and most dutifull and continuall obedience.

These (I saie) not without the counsell and consent of their father, were on a night stollen over the river of Shennon, and there cast awaie their English apparell, and clothed themselves in their old woonted Irish rags, and sent to all their old friends to come awaie to them, and to bring the Scots whom they had solicited, and their Gallowglasses, and all their forces with them. Who when they met togither, they forthwith went to the towne of Athenrie, and those few houses were newlie builded, they sacked, set the new gates on fire, beat awaie the masons and labourers which were there in working, brake and spoiled the queenes armes, and others, there made and cut to be set up. Bad and wicked they were before, but now ten times worse than ever they were; being come, even as it is said in the scriptures, that the wicked spirit was gone out of the man, and wanting his woonted diet, returneth unto the house from whense he came, and finding the same swept cleane, he goeth and seeketh out other seven wicked spirits, and entreth and dwelleth where he did before, and the last state of that man is woorse than the first. And if a man should aske of these bastardlie boies, and of their sier, what should be the cause that they should thus rage, and so wickedlie and suddenlie revolve, as dogs to their vomits, so they to their treasons and treacheries, having beene so courteouslie used, so gentile interteined, so friendlie countenanced, so fatherly exhorted, so pithilie persuaded, & so mercifullie pardoned in hope of amendment: surelie nothing can they answer, but that they would not be honest, nor in anie part satisfie a little of infinite the robberies, thefts, and spoiles which they had made. For bastardlie slips cannot bring forth better fruits, neither can thornes bring foorth grapes.

Reprinted in STRANGERS TO THAT LAND: BRITISH PERCEPTIONS OF IRELAND FROM THE REFORMATION TO THE FAMINE, edited by Andrew Hadfield and John McVeagh (1994), pp. 97–98.

~

FROM *SOLON HIS FOLLIE*

1594

Richard Beacon

The late sixteenth and early seventeenth centuries saw a profusion of English tracts on what would later be called the "Irish Problem." Most were couched, or even camouflaged, in the terms of antiquity where—among the ancient Greeks and Romans—colonies and colonial relationships were well-established and much discussed subjects. Richard Beacon's Solon His Follie *was one of the earliest of these. Solon was the legendary reformer of sixth-century B.C. Athens.*

SEE ALSO Colonial Theory from 1500 to 1690; English Political and Religious Policies, Responses to (1534–1690); Land Settlements from 1500 to 1690; Politics: 1500 to 1690

EPIMENIDES: There remaineth now that we deduct colonies, which is the last, but not the least meanes to suppresse this distemperature, which of all others is the most beneficiall for the containing of a nation conquered in their duty and obedience; wherein foure matters are worthily considered: first the necessitie of deducting colonies; secondarily the benefite that redoundeth thereby unto common-weales; thirdly what order and manner in deducting colonies is to bee used and observed; lastly, the impedimentes which are usuallie given unto the deducting of colonies.

SOLON: Shew us the necessitie of collonies.

EPI: A nation conquered may not be contained in their obedience without the strength of colonies or garrisons: for may we be induced to beleeve, that that people or nation, who daily bewaileth & accuseth his present state and condition, may persist therein longer then they be pressed therunto by necessitie? and more than this in the act of Absentes, the meere native borne people of Salamina, are tearmed to be mortall and naturall enemies unto their conquerer and all his dominions . . . for how many waies did this people incite the French King, how oft have they provoked the Pope to invade this lande of Salamina? Againe the Emperour and all other Princes and Potentates, what fortes and holdes have they not taken, and how many of our garrisons have they most cruelly slaine and murdered, the same, in the several actes of Attainder of Shane Oneile, Garralde Fitz Garralde, James of Desmond, and by severall other recordes, may appeare at large. Neither doth this forme of government drawe with it a perpetuall discontentment onelie, but also an infinite and continuall charge in maintaining these severall garrisons, as well to the Prince, as to the subject; for so in the act of subsidie and other recordes it may appeare. Neither be these all the discommodities that perpetual garrisons drawe with them, for these notwithstanding, we have beene forced to send at sundry times armies roiall to suppresse disorders and rebellions, as the same more at large may appeare in the act of restraining of tributes; so as wee may conclude, that where colonies are not strongly and faithfully deducted, there the ende of the first warres, is but a beginning of the second more dangerous than the first; the which maie appeare by the recordes of Salamina: for no sooner were the people or sects, called Omores, Odempsies, Oconores, and others, expelled by great forces and strengthes, to our great charges, out of the severall countries of Liece, Slewmarge, Irry, Glimnarliry, and Offalie, but eftsones for that we deducted not colonies, they traiterouslie entered the said countries by force, and long detained the same, untill they were with greater forces expelled, all which more at large may appeare in the act made for the deviding of countries, into shire groundes, so as we may conclude, that it is not for wise Princes to persevere in that course of government, which doth nourish as it were a perpetuall interest in troubles, charges, and expenses: for the which causes chiefely did the Venetians willingly abandon the government of Bybienna and Pisa, and wee of Athens, Salamina, the which did chiefly arise unto us, for that in steede of planting colonies, we placed garrisons. . . . [L]et us loose no opportunity of deducting of colonies, for they be deducted and maintained with small or no charges, & with no great offence, but onely to such whose landes and houses they possesse, the which remaine for the most part pacified, in that they enjoy their life which stoode in the hands of the Prince, as well as their landes to dispose, for their offences: and if they should remaine discontented, for that having respect to the whole kingdome they be but a handfull, and also dispersed and poore, they may never be able to hurt or disturbe the state, & all others which finde themselves free from their losses, shall rest pacified, partly fearing, least they commit any thing rashly or foolishly, and partly doubting, least the like befalleth them as to those which remaine spoyled for their offences. . . .

SOL: Nowe sith the necessity of colonies doeth manifestly appeare by unfallible proofs and examples, let us proceede unto the profite and benefite that groweth thereby.

EPI: The benefites that hereby arise to the common-weale, are sundry and diverse: first the people poore and seditious which were a burden to the common-weale, are drawn forth, whereby the matter of sedition is remooved out of the Cittie; and for this cause it is said, that Pericles sent into the country of Cherronesus, a thousand free men of his Cittie there to dwell, and to devide the landes amongst them; five hundreth also into the Ile of Naxus, into the Ile of Andros others, some he sent to inhabite Thracia, and others to dwell with the Bisaltes; as well thereby to ridde the Cittie of a number of idle persons, who through idlenes began to be curious and to desire a change of thinges, as also to provide for the necessity of the poore towns-men that had nothing, which being naturall Citizens of Athens served as garrisons, to keepe under those which had a desire to rebell, or to attempt any alteration or change: secondly by translating of colonies, the people conquered are drawn and intised by little and little, to embrace the manners, lawes, and government of the conquerour: lastly the colonies being placed and dispersed abroade amongest the people, like Beacons doe foretell and disclose all conspiracies. . . . lastly, they yeelde a yearely rent, profite, or service unto the crowne for ever.

Reprinted in STRANGERS TO THAT LAND: BRITISH PERCEPTIONS OF IRELAND FROM THE REFORMATION TO THE FAMINE, *edited by Andrew Hadfield and John McVeagh (1994), pp. 109–111.*

~

FROM *A VIEW OF THE PRESENT STATE OF IRELAND*

1596

Edmund Spenser

The great Elizabethan poet Edmund Spenser witnessed some of the worst of the Irish wars as secretary to Arthur Grey, Lord Grey de Wilton, lord deputy of Ireland in the 1580s, and subsequently as a resident planter at Kilcolman in County Cork. In his View of the Present State of Ireland,

he advocated the unrelenting application of martial law, but the tract takes the form of a mock-classical dialogue between a proponent of force and a proponent of conciliation.

SEE ALSO English Writing on Ireland before 1800

EUDOX.: But yf that countrey of Ireland, whence you lately came, be soe goodly and commodious a soyle, as ye report, I wonder that noe course is taken for the tourning thereof to good uses, and reducing of that savadge nation to better government and civilitye.

IREN.: Marry, soe there have beene divers good plottes devised, and wise counsells cast allereadye about reformation of that realme; but they say, it is the fatall desteny of that land, that noe puposes, whatsoever are meant for her good, will prosper or take good effect . . .

IREN.: I will then, according to your advisement, beginne to declare the evills, which seeme to me most hurtfull to the common-weale of that land: and first, those which I sayd were most auncient and long growen. And they allso are of three kindes; the first in the Lawes, the second in Customes, and the third in Religion. . . . It is a nation ever acquaynted with warres, though but amongest themselves, and in theyre owne kind of mylitary discipline, trayned up ever from theyr youthes; which they have never yet beene taught to lay aside, nor made to learne obedience unto lawe, scarcely to know the name of lawe, but insteede therof have always preserved and kept theyr owne lawe, which is the Brehoone lawe.

EUDOX.: What is that which ye call the Brehoone Lawe? It is a word to us altogither unknowen.

IREN.: It is a certayne rule of right unwritten, but delivered by tradition from one to another, in which oftentimes there appeareth great shewe of equitye, in determining the right betweene party and partye, but in many thinges repugning quite both to God and mans lawe: as for example, in the case of murder, the Brehoon, that is theyr judge, will compound betweene the murderer and the frendes of the party murthered, which prosecute the action, that the malefactor shall give unto them, or to the child or wife of him that is slayne, a recompence, which they call a Breaghe; by which bi lawe of theyrs, many murders are amongest them made up and smoothered. . . . There be many wide countryes in Ireland in which the lawes of England were never established nor any acknowledgment of subjection made; and also even in those that are subdued, and seeme to acknowledge subjection, yet the same Brehoone lawe is practised amongst themselves by reason, that dwelling as they doe, whole nations and septs of the Irish togither, without any Englishman amongest them, they may doe what they list . . .

EUDOX.: What is this that you call Tanistih and Tanistrye? They be names and termes never hard of nor knowen to us.

IREN.: It is a custome among all the Irish, that presently after the death of any theyr chief Lordes or Captaynes, they doe presently assemble themselves to a place, generally appoynted and knowen unto them, to choose another in his steede; where they doe nominate and elect, for the most part, not the eldest sonn, nor any of the children of theyre Lord deceased, but the next to him of blood, that is the eldest and woorthyest; as commonly the next brother to him yf he have any, or the next cossin germayne, or soe foorth, as any is elder in that kinred or sept, and then next to him they choose the next of bloud to be Tanistih, whoe shall next succeede him in the sayd Captaynrye, yf he live thereunto. . . . when the Earle Strangbowe, having conquered that land, delivered up the same unto the handes of Henry the second, then King, whoe sent over thither great store of gentellmen, and other warlick people, amongst whom he distributed the land, and settled such a strong colonye therin, as never since could, with all the subtill practises of the Irish, be rooted out, but abide still a mighty people, of soe many as remayne English of them.

EUDOX.: What is this that you say, of soe many as remayne English of them? Why are not they that were once English abiding English still?

IREN.: Noe, for the most part of them are degenerated and growen allmost meere Irish yea and more malicious to the English then the very Irish themselves.

EUDOX.: What heare I? And is it possible that an Englishman, brought up naturally in such sweete civilitye as England affoordes, can find such liking in that barbarous rudeness, that he should forgett his owne nature, and forgoe his owne nation? . . .

IREN.: . . . there is one use amongst them [the Irish], to keepe theyr cattell, and to live themselves the most part of the yeare in bolyes, pasturing upon the mountayn, and wast wild places; and removing still to fresh land, as they have depastured

the former. The which appeareth playne to be the manner of the Scythians, as you may reade in Olaus Magnus, and Jo. Bohemus, and yet is used amongst all the Tartarians and the people about the Caspian Sea, which are naturally Scythians, to live in heardes as they call them, being the very same that the Irish bolyes are, driving theyr cattell continually with them, and feeding onely upon theyr milke and white meates.

EUDOX.: What fault can ye find with this custome? For though it be an old Scythian use, yet it is very behoofull in that countrey of Ireland, where there are greate mountaynes, and wast desartes full of grasse, that the same should be eaten downe, and nourish many thousand of cattell for the good of the whole realme, which cannot (me thinkes) be well any other way, then by keeping those Bolyes there, as ye have shewed.

IREN.: But by this custome of bolyes there growe in the meane time many great enormityes unto that Common-wealth. For first, yf there be any out-lawes, or loose people, (as they are never without some) which live upon stealthes and spoyles, they are evermore succoured and find relief onely in those Bolyes, being upon the wast places, wheras els they should be driven shortly to starve, or to come downe to the townes to steale relief, where, by one meane or other, they would soone be caught. Besides, such stealthes of cattell as they make, they bring commonly to those Bolyes, where they are received readilye, and the theif harboured from daunger of lawe, or such officers as might light uppon him. Moreover, the people that thus live in those Bolyes growe therby the more barbarons, and live more licentiously then they could in townes, using what meanes they list, and practising what mischeives and villanyes they will, either agaynst the government there, by theyr combinations, or agaynst privat men, whom they maligne, by stealing theyr goodes, or murdering themselves. For there they thinke themselves halfe exempted from lawe and obedience, and having once tasted freedome, doe, like a steere that hath bene long out of his yoke, grudge and repyne ever after to come under rule agayne.

EUDOX.: By your speache, Irenæus, I perceave more evills come by this use of bolyes, then good by theyr grazing; and therfore it may well be reformed: but that must be in his due course . . .

IREN.: They have another custome from the Scythians, that is the wearing of Mantells and long glibbes, which is a thick curled bush of heare, hanging downe over theyr eyes, and monstrously disguising them, which are both very badd and hurtfull. . . .

EUDOX.: Sith then the necessitye therof is soe comodious, as ye alleage, that it is insteede of howsing, bedding, and clothing, what reason have ye then to wish so necessary a thing cast of?

IREN.: Because the comoditye doth not countervayle the discomoditie, for the inconveniences that therby doe arise are much more many; for it is a fitt howse for an outlawe, a meete bedd for a rebell, and an apt cloke for a theif. First the outlawe being for his many crimes and villanyes bannished from the townes and howses of honest men, and wandring in wast places, furr from daunger of lawe, maketh his mantell his howse, and under it covereth himself from the wrath of heaven, from the offence of the earth, and from the sight of men. When it rayneth it is his penthowse; when it blowes it is his tent; when it freezeth it is his tabernacle. In Sommer he can weare it loose, in winter he can weare it close; at all time he can use it; never heavy, never combersome. Likewise for a rebell it is as serviceable; for in his warre that he maketh (yf at least it besemeth the name of warr) when he still flyeth from his foe, and lurketh in the thick woodes and straite passages, wayting for advantages, it is his bedd, yea, and allmost his howsehold stuff. For the wood is his howse agaynst all weathers, and his mantell is his cave to sleepe in. Therin he wrappeth himself rounde, and encloseth himself strongly agaynst the gnattes, which in that countrey doe more annoye the naked rebelles, whilest they keepe the woodes, and doe more sharply wound them then all theyr enemyes swoordes or speares, which can come seldome nigh them: yea, and oftentimes theyr mantell serveth them when they are neere driven, being wrapt about theyr left arme in steede of a Targett, for it is as hard to cutt through it with a swoord; besides it is light to beare, light to throwe away, and, being (as they then commonly are) naked, it is to them all in all. Lastly, for a theif it is soe handsome, as it may seeme it was first invented for him; for under it he can cleanly convay any fitt pillage that cometh handsomely in his way, and when he goeth abrode in the night on free-booting, it is his best and surest frend; for lying, as they often doe, two or thre nightes togither abrode to watch for theyr bootye, with that they can pretelye shrowde themselves under a bush or bankes side, till they may conveniently doe theyr errand: and when all is done, he can in his mantell pass through any towne or company, being close hooded over his head, as he useth, from knowledge of any to

whom he is endaungered. Besides all this, yf he be disposed to doe mischeif or villanye to any man, he may under his mantell goe privilye armed without suspicion of any, carrying his head-peece, his skeane, or pistoll yf he please, to be allwaye in readiness. Thus necessarye and fitting is a mantell for a badd man, and surely for a badd howsewife it is noe less convenient, for some of those that be wandring women, there called of them Beantoolhe, it is half a wardrobe, for in Sommer you shall have her arrayed commonlye but in her smocke and mantel, to be more readye for her light services; in Winter, and in her travell, it is her best cloke and safegard, and also a coverlett for her lewde exercise. And when she hath filled her vessell, under it she can hide both her burden and her blame; yea, and when her bastard is borne it serves insteede of a craddle and all her swadling cloutes. And as for all other good women which love to doe but litle woorke, howe handsome it is to lye and sleepe, or to lowze themselves in the sunnshine, they that have bene but a while in Ireland can well witness. Sure I am that ye will thinke it very unfitt for good howsewives to stirre in, or to busy them selves about theyr howse-wiverye in such sort as they should. These be some of the abuses for which I would thinke it meete to forbidd all mantells.

EUDOX.: O evill mynded man, that having reckned up soe many uses of a mantell, will yet wish it to be abandoned! . . .

IREN.: I suppose that the cheifest cause of the bringing in of the Irish language, amongst them, was specially theyr fostring, and marrying with the Irish, the which are two most daungerous infections: for first the child that sucketh the milke of the nurse, must of necessitye learne his first speache of her, the which being the first that is enured to his tongue, is ever after most pleasing unto him, in soe much as though he afterward be taught English, yet the smacke of the first will allwayes abide with him; and not onely of the speache, but also of the manners and conditions. . . . Therfore are these evill customes of fostering and marrying with the Irish most carefully to be restrayned; for of them two, the third evill, that is the custome of language (which I speake of) cheifly proceedeth. . . . There is amongst the Irish a certayne kind of people called Bards, which are to them insteede of poetts, whose profession is to sett foorth the prayses and disprayses of men in theyr poems and rimes; the which are had in soe high request and estimation amongst them, that none dare to displease them for feare of running into reproche through theyr offence, and to be made infamous in the mouthes of all men. For theyr verses are taken up with a generall applause, and usually songe at all feasts and meetinges, but certayne other persons, whose proper function that is, which also receave for the same greate rewardes and reputation besides. . . It is most true that such Poetts, as in theyr writings doe laboure to better the manners of men, and through the sweete bayte of theyre numbers, to steale into yonge spiritts a desire of honour and vertue, are worthy to be had in great respect. But these Irish Bards are for the most part of another mynd, and soe farr from instructing yong men in mor-all discipline, that they themselves doe more de-sarve to be sharpely disciplined; for they seldome use to choose unto themselves the doinges of good men for the ornamentes of theyr poems, but whomsoever they find to be most licentious of life, most bold and lawless in his doinges, most daungerous and desperate in all partes of disobedience and rebellious disposition, him they sett up and glorifye in theyr rimes, him they prayse to the people, and to yong men make an example to followe. . . . such lycentious partes as these, tending for the most parte to the hurte of the English, or mayntenaunce of theyre owne lewde libertye, they themselves, being most de-sirous therof, doe most allowe. Besides this, evill thinges being decked and suborned with the gay attyre of goodly woordes, may easely deceave and carrye away the affection of a yong mynd, that is not well stayed, but desirous by some bold adventure to make proofe of himself; for being (as they all be brought up idlely without awe of parentes, without precepts of masters, without feare of offence, not being directed, or employed in any course of life, which may car-rye them to vertue, will easely be drawn to fol-lowe such as any shall sett before them: for a yong mynd cannot rest; and yf he be not still busyed in some goodness, he will find himself such busines as shall soone busye all about him. In which yf he shall finde any to prayse him, and to give him encouragement, as those Bards and rimers doe for a litle reward, or a share of a stollen cowe, then waxeth he most insolent and half madd with the love of himself, and his owne lewde deedes. And as for woordes to sett foorth such lewdness, it is not hard for them to give a goodly glose and paynted shewe thereunto, bor-rowed even from the prayses which are proper to vertue itself. . . .

EUDOX.: . . . But tell me (I pray you) have they any arte in theyr compositions? Or be they any thing wittye or well savoured, as Poems should be?

IREN.: Yea truly; I have caused diverse of them to be translated unto me that I might understand them; and surely they savoured of sweete witt and good invention, but skilled not of the goodly ornamentes of Poetrye: yet were they sprinckled with some pretty flowers of theyr owne naturall devise, which gave good grace and comliness unto them, the which it is greate pittye to see soe abused, to the gracing of wickedness and vice, which would with good usage serve to beautifye and adorne vertue. This evill custome therfore needeth reformation. . . . Nowe we will proceede to other like defectes, amongst which there is one generall inconvenience which raig-neth allmost throughout all Ireland: that is, of the Lordes of landes and Free-holders, whoe doe not there use to sett out theyr landes to farme, or for terme of yeares, to theyr tenauntes, but only from yeare to yeare, and some during plea-sure; neither indede will the Irish tenaunt or hus-bandman otherwise take his land then soe longe as he list himselfe. . . . Marye! the evills which cometh thereby are greate, for by this meane both the land-lord thinketh that he hath his tenaunte more at comaunde, to followe him into what action soever he shall enter, and also the tenaunte, being left at his libertye, is fitt for ev-erye occasion of chaunge that shal be offred by time; and soe much also the more readye and willing is he to runne into the same, for that he hath noe such estate in any his holding, noe such building upon any farme, noe such costes imployed in fencing and husbandring the same, as might with-hold him from any such willfull course, as his lordes cause, or his owne lewde disposition may carry him unto. All which he hath forborne, and spared so much expence, for that he had noe firme estate in his tenement, but was onely a tenaunt at will or litle more, and soe at will may leave it. . . . Therfore the faulte which I finde in Religion is but one, but the same is universall throughe out all the countrey; that is, that they are all Papistes by theyr profession, but in the same soe blindely and brutishly enfor-med, (for the most parte) as that you would rather thinke them Atheistes or Infidells for not one amongst an hundred knoweth any grounde of religion, or any article of his faythe, but can perhaps say his Pater noster, or his Ave Maria, without any knowledge or understanding what one woorde therof meaneth. . . . yet what good shall any English minister doe amongst them, by preaching or teaching, which either cannot understand him, or will not heare him? Or what comforte of life shall he have, when all his pa-rishioners are soe unsociable, soe intractable, so ill-affected-unto him, as they usually be to all the English? . . . all chaunge is to be shunned, where the affayres stand in such state as that they may continue in quietness, or be assured at all to abide as they are. But that in the realme of Ireland we see much otherwise, for everye day we perceave the troubles to growe more upon us, and one evill growing upon another, insoemuch as there is noe parte sounde nor ascertayned, but all have theyr eares upright, wayting when the watch-woord shall come that they should all rise generally into rebellion, and cast away the English subjection. To which there nowe litle wanteth; for I thinke the woorde be allreadye given, and there wanteth nothing but opportunitye, . . . But all the realme is first to be reformed, and lawes are afterwardes to be made for keeping and conteyning it in that reformed estate.

EUDOX.: Howe then doe you thinke is the reformation therof to be begunne, yf not by lawes and ordinaunces?

IREN.: Even by the swoorde; for all those evills must first be cutt away with a strong hand, before any good can be planted . . . by the swoorde I meane the royall power of the Prince, which ought to stretche it self foorthe in the cheifest strength to the redressing and cutting of of those evills, which I before blamed . . . The first thing must be to send over into that realme such a stronge power of men, as that shall perforce bring in all that rebellious route of loose people, which either doe nowe stande out in open armes, or in wandring companyes doe keepe the woodes, spoyling the good subject.

EUDOX.: You speake nowe, Irenæus, of an infinite charge to her Majestie, to send over such an armye as should treade downe all that standeth before them on foote, and laye on the grounde all the stiff-necked people of that lande; for there is nowe but one outlawe of any greate reckning, to weete, the Earle of Tyrone, abrode in armes, agaynst whom you see what huge charges she hath bene at, this last yeare, in sending of men, providing of victualls, and making head agaynst him: yet there is litle or nothing at all done, but the Queenes treasure spent, her people wasted, the poor countrey troubled, and the enemye nevertheless brought unto noe more subjection then he was, or list outwardly to shewe, which in effect is none, but rather a scorne of her power, and an emboldening of a proude rebell, and an encouradgement unto all like lewde disposed traytors that shall dare to lift up theyr heeles agaynst theyr Soveraigne Ladye. . . .

EUDOX.: Surely of such desperat persons as will willfully followe the course of theyr own follye, there is noe compassion to be had, and for others ye have propose da mercifull meanes, much more then they have deserved: but what then shalbe the conclusion of this warre? For you have prefixed a shorte time of the continuance therof.

IREN.: The end (I assure me) wil be very shorte and much sooner then can be (in soe greate a trouble, as it seemeth) hoped for allthough there should none of them fall by the swoorde, nor by slayne by the souldiour, yet thus being kept from manuraunce, and theyr cattell from running abroade, by this harde restraynte they would quickly consume themselves, and devoure one another. The proof wherof I sawe sufficiently ensampled in those late warres in Mounster; for notwithstanding that the same was a most riche and plentifull country, full of corne and cattell, that you would have thought they would have bene able to stand long, yet ere one yeare and a halfe they were brought to such wretchedness, as that any stonye harte would have rued the same. Our of every corner of the woodes the glinnes they came creeping foorthe upon theyr handes, for theyr legges could not beare them; they looked like anatomyes of death, they spake like ghostes crying out of theyr graves; they did eate of the dead carrions, happy were they yf they could finde them, yea, and one another soone after, insoemuch as the very carcasses they spared not to scrape out of theyr graves; and yf they founde a plotte of water-cresses or shamrokes, there they flocked as to a feast for the time, yet not able long to continue therewithall; that in shorte space there were none allmost left, and a most populous and plentifull countrey suddaynly made voyde of man or beast. . . .but all the landes I will give unto Englishmen whom I will have drawen thither, who shall have the same with such estates as shal be thought meete, and for such rentes as shall eft-sones be rated: under everye of these Englishmen will I place some of the Irish to be tenauntes for a certayne rente, according to the quantitye of such land, as everye man shall have allotted unto him, and shalbe founde able to weelde, wherin this speciall regarde shal be had, that in noe place under any land-lorde there shall remayne manye of them planted togither, but dispersed wide from theyr acquayntaunce, and scattred farre abrode through all the countreye: For that is the evill which I nowe finde in all Ireland, that the Irish dwell togither by theyr septs, and severall nations, soe as they may practize or conspire what they will; whereas yf there were English shedd amongest them and placed over them, they should not be able once to styrre or murmure, but that it shoulde be knowen, and they shortened according to theyr demerites.

THE WORKS OF EDMUND SPENSER, *edited by* R. Morris (1895), *pp. 609, 610, 611, 629, 630, 631–632, 638, 640–641, 644, 645, 647, 650, 654, 663.*

TYRONE'S DEMANDS

1599

Hugh O'Neill

This document articulates the demands of Hugh O'Neill, earl of Tyrone, for a Catholic Ireland and for the domination of the Catholic Irish within it. Note that they do not renounce loyalty to the Protestant Queen Elizabeth but attempt to impose qualifications or preconditions on it. O'Neill was ultimately defeated and the demands were never achieved. Had they been, Ireland's development as a Catholic kingdom under the British crown would have been very different.

SEE ALSO Nine Years War; O'Neill, Hugh, Second Earl of Tyrone

ARTICLES INTENDED TO BE STOOD UPON BY TYRONE

1. That the Catholic, Apostolic, and Roman religion be openly preached and taught throughout all Ireland, as well in cities as borough towns, by Bishops, seminary priests, Jesuits, and all other religious men.

2. That the Church of Ireland be wholly governed by the Pope.

3. That all cathedrals and parish churches, abbeys, and all other religious houses, with all tithes and church lands, now in the hands of the English, be presently restored to the Catholic churchmen.

4. That all Irish priests and religious men, now prisoners in England or Ireland, be presently set at liberty, with all temporal Irishmen, that are troubled for their conscience, and to go where they will without further trouble.

5. That all Irish priests and religious men may freely pass and repass, by sea and land, to and from foreign countries.

6. That no Englishman may be a churchman in Ireland.

7. That there be erected an university upon the Crowns rents of Ireland, wherein all sciences shall be taught according to the manner of the Catholic Roman Church.

8. That the Governor of Ireland be at least an Earl, and of the Privy Council of England, bearing the name of Viceroy.

9. That the Lord Chancellor, Lord Treasurer, Lord Admiral, the Council of State, the Justices of the laws, Queen's Attorney, Queen's Serjeant, and all other officers appertaining to the Council and law of Ireland, be Irishmen.

10. That all principal governments of Ireland, as Connaught, Munster, etc., be governed by Irish noblemen.

11. That the Master of Ordnance, and half the soldiers with their officers resident in Ireland, be Irishmen.

12. That no Irishman's heirs shall lose their lands for the faults of their ancestors.

13. That no Irishman's heir under age shall fall in the Queen's or her successors' hands, as a ward, but that the living be to put to the heir's profit, and the advancement of his younger brethren, and marriages of his sisters, if he have any.

14. That no children nor any other friends be taken as pledges for the good abearing of their parents, and, if there be any such pledges now in the hands of the English, they must presently be released.

15. That all statutes made against the preferment of Irishmen as well in their own country as abroad, be presently recalled.

16. That the Queen nor her successors may in no sort press an Irishman to serve them against his will.

17. That O'Neill, O'Donnell, the Earl of Desmond, with all their partakers, may peaceable enjoy all lands and privileges that did appertain to their predecessors 200 years past.

18. That all Irishmen, of what quality they be, may freely travel in foreign countries, for their better experience, without making any of the Queen's officers acquainted withal.

19. That all Irishmen may freely travel and traffic all merchandises in England as Englishmen, paying the same rights and tributes as the English do.

20. That all Irishmen may freely traffic with all merchandises, that shall be thought necessary by the Council of State of Ireland for the profit of their Republic, with foreigners or in foreign countries, and no Irishman shall be troubled for the passage of priests or other religious men.

21. That all Irishmen that will may learn, and use all occupations and arts whatsoever.

22. That all Irishmen may freely build ships of what burden they will, furnishing the same with artillery and all munition at their pleasure.

CALENDAR OF STATE PAPERS RELATING TO IRELAND, 1599–1600 (1899), 279–281; reprinted in IRISH HISTORICAL DOCUMENTS, 1172–1922, edited by Edmund Curtis and R. B. McDowell (1943), pp. 119–120.

≈

ACCOUNTS OF THE SIEGE AND BATTLE OF KINSALE

1601

The Battle of Kinsale (24 December 1601) effectively ended the challenge of Hugh O'Neill and Red Hugh O'Donnell in the Nine Years War (1594–1603). The English commander Charles Blount, Lord Mountjoy (1563–1606), besieged a small Spanish naval force which had taken the town in support of the Irish insurgency. The Ulster earls marched south to relieve the siege but were overwhelmed by Mountjoy before they could raise the siege and unite with their foreign allies.

SEE ALSO *Annals of the Four Masters;* Nine Years War; O'Neill, Hugh, Second Earl of Tyrone

From a Majesty's Soldier's Letter to a Friend in London (1602)

Those of the battle were almost all slain, and there were (of Irish rebels only) found dead in the place, about twelve hundred bodies, and about eight hundred were hurt, whereof many died that night; and the chase continuing almost two miles, was left off, our men being tired with killing. The enemy lost two thousand arms brought to reckoning, besides great numbers embezzled, all their powder, and drums, and eleven ensigns, whereof six Spanish. Those of the Irish that were taken prisoners, being brought to the camp, though they offered ransom, were all hanged. . . . And thus were they utterly overthrown, who but the very night before, were so brave and confident of their own good success, as that they reckoned us already theirs, and as we since have understood, were in contention whose prisoner the Lord Deputy should be, whose the Lord President, and so of the rest. The Early of Clanrickarde carried himself

this day very valiantly, and after the retreat sounded, was knighted by the Lord Deputy, in the field amongst the dead bodies. So did all the rest of the captains, officers and soldiers . . . and especially the Lord Deputy himself, who brake, in person, upon the flower of the army [of] the Spaniards, and omitted no duty of a wise diligent conductor and valiant soldier. Upon the fight ended, he presently called together the army, and with prayers gave God thanks for the victory. A victory indeed given by the God of Hosts, and marvellous in our eyes, if all circumstances be duly considered, and of such consequence for the preservation and assurance to her Majesty, of this deeply endangered Kingdom, as I leave to wiser consideration.

From the Annals of the Four Masters (1632–1636)

Manifest was the displeasure of God, and misfortune to the Irish . . . on this occasion; for, previous to this day, a small number of them had more frequently routed many hundreds of the English, than they had fled from them, in the field of battle, in the gap of danger (in every place they had encountered), up to this day. Immense and countless was the loss in that place, although the number slain was trifling, for the prowess and valour, prosperity and affluence, nobleness and chivalry, dignity and renown, hospitality and generosity, bravery and protection, devotion and pure religion, of the Island, were lost in this engagement. The Irish forces returned that night with O'Neill and O'Donnell to Inishannon (Co. Cork). Alas! The condition in which they were that night was not as they had expected to return from that expedition, for there prevailed much reproach on reproach, moaning and dejection, melancholy and anguish, in every quarter throughout the camp. They slept not soundly, and scarcely did they take any refreshment. When they met together their counsel was hasty, unsteady and precipitate, so that what they at length resolved upon was, that O'Neill . . . with subchieftains and the chiefs of Leath-Chuinn in general, should return back to their countries, to defend their territories and lands against foreign tribes, [and] that O'Donnell (and others) should go to Spain to complain of their distress and difficulties to the King of Spain.

From Thomas Stafford's Pacata Hibernia (1633)

Now are we come to the siege of Kinsale, a place ordained, wherein the honour and safety of Queen Elizabeth, the reputation of the English nation, the cause of religion, and the Crown of Ireland must be by arms disputed; for upon the success of this siege, these great and important consequences depended. And here the malice of Rome and Spain (if they had prevailed) would not have ceased, for their purpose did extend itself (Ireland having been conquered), to make it their bridge to have invaded England, the conquest and ruin whereof was the main mark whereat they aimed. . . .Tyrone . . . with the choice force, and, in effect, all the rebels of Ireland, being drawn into Munster, and joined with Spaniards that landed at Castlehaven, who brought to Tyrone's camp six ensigns of Spaniards, and the greatest part of the Irish of Munster . . . resolved to relive the town of Kinsale, and to that purpose sat down, the one-and-twentieth of December, a mile and a half from the town, between the English camp and Cork, and on that side of the army, kept from them all passages and means for forage; the other side, ovver the River of Ownyboy, being wholly at their disposition, by reason of the general revolt of these parts. It seemed they were drawn so far by the importunity of Don Juan Del Aquila, as we perceived by some of his letters intercepted, wherein he did intimate his own necessity, their promise to succour him, and the facility of the enterprise. . . . During the abode of the rebels in that place, we had continual intelligence of their purpose to give alarms from their party, and sallies from the town, but to little other effect than to weary our men, by keeping them continually in arms, the weather being extremely tempestuous, cold, and wet.

IRISH HISTORY FROM CONTEMPORARY SOURCES, *edited by Constantia Maxwell* (1923), *pp. 195–197.*

~

ENGLISH ACCOUNT OF THE FLIGHT OF THE EARLS

1607

Sir John Davies

To most Protestant observers, including Sir John Davies (attorney general for Ireland, 1606–1619), the flight of the earls to Catholic Europe in 1607 was both good riddance and implicit evidence of their complicity in continuing outbreaks of rebellion in the north.

SEE ALSO O'Neill, Hugh, Second Earl of Tyrone

It is true that they are embarked and gone with the most part of that company of men, women and children, who are named the proclamation: it is true they took shipping the 14th of this present September; that the

Saturday before the Earl of Tyrone was with my Lord Deputy at Slane . . . that from thence he went to Mellifont, Sir Garret Moore's house, where he wept abundantly when he took his leave, giving a solemn farewell to every child and every servant in the house, which made them all marvel, because it was not his manner to use such compliments. From thence, on Sunday, he went to Dundalk; on Monday he went to Dungannon, where he rested two whole days; on Wednesday night, they say, he travelled all night with his impediments, that is, his women and children; and it is likewise reported that the Countess, his wife, being exceedingly weary, slipped down from her horse, and, weeping, said she could go no farther; whereupon the Earl drew his sword, and swore a great oath that he would kill her in the place, if she would not pass on with him, and put on a more cheerful countenance withal. Yet, the next day, when he came near Lough Foyle, his passage that way was not so secret but the Governor there had notice thereof, and invited him and his son to dinner; but their haste was such that they accepted not that courtesy, but they went on, and came that Thursday night to Rathmullan, a town on the west side of Lough Swilly, where the Earl of Tyrconnel and his company met him. . . .

It is certain that Tyrone, in his heart, repines at the English government in his country, where, until his last submission, as well before his rebellion as in the time of his rebellion, he ever lived like a free prince, or rather like an absolute tyrant there. But now the law of England, and the ministers thereof, were shackles and handlocks unto him, and the garrisons planted in his country were as pricks in his side; besides, to evict any part of that land from him, which he has hitherto held after the Irish manner, making all the tenants thereof his villeins . . . this was a grievous unto him as to pinch away the quick flesh from his body. Those things, doubtless, have bred discontentment in him; and now his age and his burdened conscience . . . have of late much increased his melancholy, so that he was grown very pensive and passionate; and the friars and priests perceiving it, have wrought nightly upon his passion. Therefore it may be he has hearkened unto some project of treason, which he fears is discovered, and that fear has transported [him] into Spain. . . . As for them that are here, they are glad to see the day wherein the countenance and majesty of the law and civil government hath banished Tyrone out of Ireland, which the best army in Europe and the expense of two millions of sterling pounds did not bring to pass. And they hope His Majesty's happy government will work a greater miracle in this Kingdom than ever St. Patrick did, for St. Patrick only banished the poisonous worms, but suffered the men full of poison to inhabit the land still; but His Majesty's blessed genius will banish all those generations of vipers out of it, and make it, ere it be long, a right fortunate island.

IRISH HISTORY FROM CONTEMPORARY SOURCES, *edited by* Constantia Maxwell (1923), pp. 203–204.

∼

IRISH ACCOUNT OF THE FLIGHT OF THE EARLS

1608

Tadhg Ó Cianáin

In contrast to Sir John Davies's account, Tadhg Ó Cianáin, a Gaelic chronicler of the Maguires who accompanied the earls into exile, describes the event less as a flight than as a noble progress through a Catholic Europe which welcomed and celebrated these aristocratic Irish visitors.

SEE ALSO O'Neill, Hugh, Second Earl of Tyrone

About the middle of the same night they hoisted their sails. . . . They went out a great distance in the sea. The night was bright, quiet and calm, with a breeze from the south-west. . . . An exceeding great storm and very bad weather arose against them, together with fog and rain, so that they were driven from proximity to land. . . . Afterwards, leaving Tyrconnel on the left, they direct their course past the harbour of Sligo, straight ahead until they were opposite Croagh Patrick in Connacht. Then they feared that the King's fleet, which was in the harbour of Galway, would meet with them. They proceeded out into the sea to make for Spain straight forward if they could. After that they were on the sea for thirteen days with excessive storm and dangerous bad weather. A cross of gold which O'Neill had, and which contained a portion of the Cross of the Crucifixion and many other relics, being put by them in the sea trailing after the ship, gave them great relief.

On Sunday, the thirtieth of September, the wind came right straight against the ship. The sailors, since they could not go to Spain, undertook to reach the harbour of Le Croisic in Brittany at the end of two days and nights. The lords who were in the ship, in consequence of the smallness of their food supply, and also because of all the hardship and sickness of the sea they had received up to that gave it as their advice that it was right for them to make straight ahead towards France. . . .

On the next day, the fifteenth of October, they left Rouen with thirty-one on horseback, two coaches, three

wagons, and about forty on foot. The Governor of Quilleboeuf and many of the gentry of the town came to conduct them a distance from the city. . . .

On Monday, the twenty-second of the same month, they bade farewell to the people of the city (Arras). They proceeded five more leagues to a famous city called Douai. The people there received them with great respect. They alighted at the Irish College, which was supported by the King of Spain in the town. They themselves stayed in the College, and they sent the better part of those with them through the city. They remained there until the following Friday. . . . Assemblies of the colleges received them kindly and with respect, delivering in their honour verses and speeches in Latin, Greek and English. . . .

The thirty-first of October, O'Neill's son (Henry), the Colonel of the Irish [regiment] came to them with a large well-equipped company of captains and of noblemen, Spanish and Irish and of every other nation. On the following Saturday the Marquis Spinola, the commander-in-chief of the King of Spain's army in Flanders, came to them from Brussels with a large number of important people and welcomed them. He received them with honour and gave them an invitation to dinner on the next day in Brussels. . . .

Early the next morning they went to Brussels. . . . Colonel Francisco, with many Spanish, Italian, Irish and Flemish captains, came out of the city to meet them. They advanced through the principal streets of the town to the door of the Marquis's palace. The Marquis himself, the Papal Nuncio, the Spanish Ambassador, and the Duke of Ossuna came ot take them from their coaches. . . . Afterwards they entered the apartment where the Marquis was accustomed to take food. He himself arranged each one in his place, seating O'Neill in his own place at the head of the table, the Papal Nuncio to his right, the Earl of Tyrconnel to his left, O'Neill's children and Maguire next [to] the Earl, and the Spanish Ambassador and the Duke of Aumale on the other side, below the Nuncio. . . . The excellent dinner which they partook of was grand and costly enough for a king. . . .

On Sunday, the twenty-third March, they proceeded to the great remarkable famous city Milan. . . . A great respected earl, Count de Fuentes by name, was chief governor and representative of the King of Spain over that city and over all Lombardy. He sent the King's ambassador at Lucerne, who happened to be in the city, to welcome them and to receive them with honour. On Wednesday the nobles went in person into the presence of the earl. He received them with honour and respect. There were many noblemen and a very great guard on either side of him. They remained three full weeks in the city. During that time the earl had great honour shown them. . . . The lords took their leave of Count de Fuentes on the twelfth of April. . . . He gave them as a token of remembrance a collection of rapiers and fine daggers, with hilts of ornamented precious stones, all gilt, and belts and expensive hangers. . . .

Peter Lombard, the Archbishop of Armagh and Primate of Ireland, came . . . having a large number of coaches sent by cardinals to meet them to that place. . . . Then they proceeded in coaches (and) went on . . . through the principal streets of Rome in great splendour. They did not rest until they reached the great church of San Pietro in Vaticano. They put up their horses there and entered the church . . . afterwards they proceeded to a splendid palace which his Holiness the Pope had set apart for them in the Borgo Vecchio [and in the Borgo] Santo Spiritio. . . .

On the Thursday of Corpus Christi an order came from the holy Father to the princes that eight of their noblemen should go in person to carry the canopy over the Blessed Sacrament while it was being borne solemnly in the hands of the Pope in procession from the great Church of San Pietro in Vaticano to the Church of St. James in Borgo Vecchio and from there back to the Church of Saint Peter. . . . They carried the canopy over the Blessed Sacrament and the Pope, and never before did Irishmen receive such an honour and privilege. The Italians were greatly surprised that they should be shown such deference and respect, for some of them said that seldom before was any one nation in the world appointed to carry the canopy. With the ambassadors of all the Catholic kings and princes of Christendom who happened to be then in the city it was an established custom that they, in succession, every year carried the canopy in turn. They were jealous, envious and surprised, that they were not allowed to carry it on this particular day. The procession was reverent, imposing and beautiful, for the greater part of the regular Order and all the clergy and communities of the great churches of Rome were in it, and many princes, dukes and great lords. They had no less than a thousand lighted waxen torches. Following them there were twenty-six archbishops and bishops. Next there were thirty-six cardinals. The Pope carried the Blessed Sacrament, and the Irish lords and noblemen to the number of eight, bore the canopy. About the Pope was his guard of Swiss soldiers, and on either side of him and behind him were his two large troops of cavalry. The streets were filled with people behind. It was considered by all that there were not less in number than one hundred thousand.

Edited and translated from the Irish by the Reverend Paul Walsh and printed as an appendix to ARCHIVIUM HIBERNICUM

(*Catholic Record Society of Ireland, 1916*). *Reprinted in* IRISH HISTORY FROM CONTEMPORARY SOURCES, *edited by Constantia Maxwell (1923), pp. 205–208.*

≈

CONDITIONS OF THE PLANTATION OF ULSTER

1610

What the English and Scottish planters understandably desired was to get rich on Irish land with the least risk, inconvenience, or discomfort. What the government desired was that English and Scottish settlers should be numerous, hard-working, public-spirited, and attentive to the conditions of plantation which they had accepted in return for Irish land. These two sets of desires were immediately and enduringly in conflict.

SEE ALSO Land Settlements from 1500 to 1690

Conditions to Be Observed by the British Undertakers of the Escheated Lands in Ulster, etc.

1. What the British Undertakers Shall Have

First, the lands to be undertaken by them, are divided into sundry precincts of different quantities.

Every precinct is subdivided into proportions of three sorts, great, middle, and small.

The great proportion containeth 2000 English acres at the least.

The middle proportion containeth 1500 acres at the least.

The small proportion containeth 1000 acres at the least.

Unto every of which proportions such bog and wood shall be allowed, as lieth within the same, for which no rent shall be reserved.

The precincts are by name distinguished, part for the English, and part for the Scottish, as appeareth by the table of distribution of the precincts.

Every precinct shall be assigned to one principal undertaker and his consort, as will appear by the table of assignation of the precincts.

The chief undertakers shall be allowed two middle proportions if they desire the same; otherwise no one undertaker is to be allowed above one great proportion.

They shall have an estate in fee simple to them their heirs.

They shall have power to create manors, to hold courts baron twice every year and not oftener, and power to create tenures in socage to hold of themselves. . . .

2. What the Said Undertakers Shall for Their Parts Perform

They shall yearly yield unto his majesty for every proportion of 1000 acres, five pound six shillings eight pence English, and so rateably for the great proportions; the fist half year's payment to begin at Michaelmas 1614.

Every of said undertakers shall hold the lands so undertaken in free and common socage, as of the castle of Dublin, and by no greater service.

Every of the said undertakers of a great proportion, shall within 3 years to be accounted from Easter next, build there-upon a stone house, with a strong court or bawn about it; and every undertaker of a middle proportion shall within the same time build a stone or brick house thereupon, with a strong court or bawn about it; and every undertaker of a small proportion, shall within the same time make thereupon a strong court or bawn at least.

Every undertaker shall within three years, to be accounted from Easter next, plant or place upon a small proportion, the number of 24 able men of the age of 18 years or upwards, being English or inland Scottish; and so rateably upon the other proportions; which numbers shall be reduced into 10 families at least, to be settled upon every small proportion, and rateably upon the other proportions, in this manner, viz. the principal undertaker and his family to be settled upon a demesne of 300 acres, two fee-farmers upon 120 acres a piece, three leaseholders for three lives or 21 years upon 100 acres a piece, and upon the residue being 160 acres, four families or more of husbandmen, artificers or cottagers, their portions of land to be assigned by the principal undertaker at his discretion.

Every of the said undertakers shall draw their tenants to build houses for themselves and their families, not scattering, but together, near the principal house or bawn, as well for their mutual defence and strength, as for the making of villages and townships.

The said undertakers, their heirs and assigns, shall have ready in the houses at all times, a convenient store of arms, wherewith they may furnish a competent number of men for their defence, which may be viewed and mustered every half year according to the manner of England.

Every of the said undertakers before he be received to be an undertaker, shall take the oath of supremacy . . . and shall also conform themselves in religion according to his majesty's laws; and every of their undertenants being chief of a family, shall take the like oath. . . . And they and their families shall also be conformable in religion, as aforesaid. . . .

The said undertakers, their heirs and assigns, shall not alien or demise their portions or any part thereof to the mere Irish, or to such persons as will not take the said oath of supremacy. . . .

Reprinted in IRISH HISTORICAL DOCUMENTS, 1172–1922, *edited by Edmund Curtis and R. B. McDowell (1943), pp. 128–131.*

~

FROM *A DIRECTION FOR THE PLANTATION OF ULSTER*

1610

Thomas Blennerhasset

After the defeat of the Ulster earls in the Nine Years War (1594–1603) and their subsequent flight to the European mainland, six of Ulster's nine traditional counties were thrown open to English and Scottish "plantation." Thomas Blennerhasset (c. 1550–c. 1625) became one of these planters or "undertakers" and urged careful attention to fortification and military preparedness in an area where great hostility and resistance from the displaced Irish could reasonably be expected.

SEE ALSO Colonial Theory from 1500 to 1690; English Political and Religious Policies, Responses to (1534–1690); Land Settlements from 1500 to 1690; Politics: 1500 to 1690

For these undertakers to plant themselves so in this time of quiet, I doe verilie beleeve it would be to small availe, and not the best way to secure themselves with their goods, and that wilde country to the Crowne of England; for although there be no apparent enemy, nor any visible maine force, yet the wood-kerne and many other (who now have put on the smiling countenance of contentment) doe threaten every houre, if opportunitie of time and place doth serve, to burne and steale whatsoever: and besides them there be two, the chief supporters of al their insolencie, the inaccessable woods, & the not passible bogs: which to subject to our desires is not easie, and that not performed, it is not possible to make a profitable improvement, no not by any meanes in any place.

Moreover the frowning countenance of chance and change, (for nothing so certaine as that all thinges are moste uncertaine doth also incite a provident undertaker to lay such a foundation, as it should be rather a violent storme than a fret of foule weather that should annoy him. A scattered plantation will never effect his desire: what can the countenance of a Castle or Bawne with a fewe followers doe? even as they at this present doe: which is nothing to any purpose.

What shall we then say? or to what course shall we betake ourselves? surely by building of a wel fortified Towne, to be able at any time at an houres warning with five hundred men well armed, to encounter all occasions: neither will that be sufficient, except that be seconded with such another, and that also (if it may be, as easily it may) with a third: so there will be helpe on every side, to defend, & offend: for as in England, if a privy watch be set, many malefactors are apprehended, even amongst their cuppes: so there when the spaces in the Woods be cut out, and the bogges be made somewhat passible, then these new erected townes intending a reformation, must ten times at the first set a universall great hunt, that a suddaine search may be made in all suspitious places, for the Woolfe and the Wood-Kerne, which being secretly and wisely appointed by the governors, they with the helpe of some Irish, well acquainted with the holes and holdes of those offenders, the generalitie shall search every particular place. . . .

Throughout all Ireland where there be Fortes and garrisons in paye, if all those places were planted with this kinde of undertaking, & the old worthy Soldiers, who in those places have garrisons in pay, with every one of their Soldiers, if they were rewarded with the fee simple thereof, to them & to their heires, paying after one life yearly unto his Majestie a fee farme, as the other undertakers doe: but these Captaines and Soldiers would have their pay continued, otherwise, they shall not be able to procede with the charge of planting, and then other lands there next adjoining laide also to such places, that many might joine with them to erect corporations: which may be performed now ten times better cheape then it will be hereafter: their security would be much better and the societye farre excell, & so the charge of the garrisons might be withdrawne, the olde worthy warriour who hath gone already through with the brunt of that busines, shall with a good satisfaction be rewarded, and all Ulster a whole hundred times better secured unto the Crowne of England: for the generation of the Irish, (who doe at this time encrease ten to one more then the English, nay I might say twenty) will never otherwise be sufficiently brideled. . . .

The Conclusion, contayning an exhortation to England.

Fayre England, thy flourishing sister, brave Hibernia, (with most respective terms) commendeth unto thy due consideration her youngest daughter, depopulated Ulster: not doubting (for it cannot but come into thy understanding) how the long continuance of lamentable warres, have raced & utterly defaced, whatsoever was beautiful in her to behold, and hath so bereaved all her royalties, goodly ornaments, & well beseeming tyers, as there remaineth but onely the Majesty of her naked personage, which even in that plite is such, as whosoever shall seeke and search all Europe's best Bowers, shal not finde many that may make with her comparison. Behold the admirable worth of her worthiness! even now shee gives to the world to understand by testimoniall knowne sufficiently to all that knowne her, that if thou wilt now but assist her with meanes to erect her ruynes, she well nourish thee with much dainty provision, and so furnish thee, as thou shall not neede to send to thy neighbour-kingdomes for corne, nor to the Netherlands for fine Holland: shee will in requitall of thy kindnesse provide those thinges, with some other, such as thy heart most desireth. Art thou overcharged with much people? Ulster her excellency will imbrace that thy overplus in her amourous sweete armes: she will place them as it were Euphrates, and feed them with better Ambrosia then ever Jupiter himselfe knew.

Reprinted in Strangers to That Land: British Perceptions of Ireland from the Reformation to the Famine, *edited by Andrew Hadfield and John McVeagh (1994), pp. 112–114.*

≈

FROM *A NEW DESCRIPTION OF IRELAND*

1610

Barnaby Rich

A military man and vehement Protestant, Barnaby Rich served in the Dutch wars until 1573, when he joined the first earl of Essex's first expedition to colonize Ulster. After serving as a spy in Ireland, he was forced to return to England. In 1599 he fought with the second earl of Essex's army against Hugh O'Neill and later participated in Mountjoy's campaign. He tried unsuccessfully to obtain lands in Ulster after 1607, remaining in Dublin until his death in 1617 or 1618. This extract comes from his longest published treatise on Ireland. Here he describes the Irish, noting their physical appearance and temperament as different from the English.

SEE ALSO English Writing on Ireland before 1800

To speake now of the Irish more at large, for to them my talke doth especially belong, I say they are beholding to Nature, that hath framed them comly personages of good proportion, very well limbed, & to speak truly, the English, Scottish and Irish are easie to be discerned from all the Nations of the world: besides, aswel by the excellency of their complexions, as by the rest of their lineaments, from the crown of the head, to the sole of the foot. And although that in the romote places, the uncivill sort so disfigure themselves with their Glybs [forelocks], their Trowes [trousers], and their misshappen attire, yet they appear to every mans eye to be men of good proportion, of comly stature, and of able body. Now to speak of their dispositions, whereunto thay are adicted and inclined. I say, besides they are rude, uncleanlie, and uncivill, so they are very cruell, bloodie minded, apt and ready to commit any kind of mischiefe. I do not impute this so much to their naturall inclination, as I do to their education, that are trained up in Treason, in Rebellion, in Theft, in Robery, in Superstition, in Idolatry, and nuzeled [nursed, educated] from their Cradles in the very puddle of Popery.

This is the fruits of the Popes doctrine, that doth preach cruelty, that doth admit of murthers and bloudy executions; by poisoning, stabbing, or by any other manner of practice howsoever: the pope teacheth subjects to resist, to mutinie, and to rebel against their Princes.

From hence it proceedeth, that the Irish have ever beene, and still are, desirous to shake off the English government.

From hence it doth proceed, that the Irish can not endure to love the English, bicause they differ so much in Religion.

From hence it proceedeth, that as they cannot indure to love the English, so they cannot be induced to love anything that doth come from the English: according to the proverb, love me, and love my dog: so contrariwise, he that hateth me, hateth in like manner all that commeth from me.

From hence it is, that the Irish had rather stil retaine themselves in their sluttishnesse, in their uncleanli-nesse, in their rudenesse, and in their inhumane loathsomenes, then they would take any example from the English, either of civility, humanity, or any manner of Decencie.

We see nowe the author of this enmity, is hee that never did other good, where hee had to doe with mens consciences.

There is yet a difference to bee made, of those that do proceed from our malice: and the Irish in this are the more to be pittied, that are no better taught; whose educations, as they are rude, so they are blinded with ignorance, and I thinke for devotions sake, they have made a vow to be ignorant.

But although the vulgar sort, through their dul wits, and their brutish education, cannot conceive what is profitable for themselves, and good for their Countrey, yet there bee some other of that Countrey birth, whose thoughts and mindes being inriched with knowledge and understanding, that have done good in the Country, and whose example hereafter may give light to many others: For I thinke, that if these people did once understand the pretiousnesse of vertue, they would farre exceed us; notwithstanding, our long experience in the Soveraignty of vertue.

Reprinted in STRANGERS TO THAT LAND: BRITISH PERCEPTIONS OF IRELAND FROM THE REFORMATION TO THE FAMINE, *edited by Andrew Hadfield and John McVeagh (1994), pp. 45–47.*

≈

FROM *A DISCOVERY OF THE TRUE CAUSES WHY IRELAND WAS NEVER ENTIRELY SUBDUED*

1612

Sir John Davies

Sir John Davies was a lawyer whose poetry also served to make him famous. Under James I he was appointed solicitor-general for Ireland (1603) and later attorney general (1606). In the latter capacity he inspected the courts in the country and helped to establish the Ulster Plantation. In 1613 he became speaker of the Irish House of Commons. In this treatise, one of the most important on Ireland from the Jacobean period, Davies seeks to show that failure to sweep away Irish laws and customs has resulted in a division of the country. This extract deals with Irish customs, social conventions, and institutions.

SEE ALSO Brehon Law; Colonial Theory from 1500 to 1690; English Writing on Ireland before 1800; Legal Change in the Sixteenth and Seventeenth Centuries

For, if we consider the Nature of the Irish customes, wee shall finde that the people which doth use them must of necessitie be rebels to all good government, destroy the commonwealth wherein they live, and bring Barbarisme and desolation upon the richest and most fruitful Land of the world. For, whereas by the just and Honourable Law of England, & by the Lawes of all other well-governed Kingdomes and Commonweals, Murder, Manslaughter, Rape, Robbery, and Theft are punished with death; By the Irish Custome, or Brehon Law, the highest of these offences was punished only by Fine, which they call an Ericke [Mod. Ir. *éiric*]. Therefore, when Sir William Fitzwilliams, being Lord Deputy, told Maguyre that he was to send a sheriffe into Fermanaugh, being lately before made a County, Your sheriffe (sayde Maguyre) shall be welcome to me; but let me knowe his Ericke, or the price of his head, aforehand; that if my people cut it off I may cut the Ericke upon the Countrey. As for the Oppression, Extortion, and other trespasses, the weaker had never anie remedy against the stronger: whereby it came to passe that no man coulde enjoy his Life, his Wife, his Lands, or Goodes in safety if a mightier man than himselfe had an appetite to take the same from him. Wherein they were little better than Canniballes, who doe hunt one another, and hee that hath most strength and swiftnes doth eate and devoure all his fellowes.

Againe, in England and all well ordered Commonweales men have certaine estates in their Lands & Possessions, and their inheritances discend from Father to Son, which doth give them encouragement to builde and to plant and to improove their Landes, and to make them better for their posterities. But by the Irish Custom of Tanistry the cheefetanes of every Countrey and the chiefe of every Sept had no longer estate then for life in their Cheeferies, the inheritance whereof did rest in no man. And these Cheeferies, though they had some portions of land alloted unto them, did consist chiefly in cuttings and Cosheries, and other Irish exactions, whereby they did spoyle and impoverish the people at their pleasure: And when their chieftanes were dead their sonnes or next heires did not succeede them, but their Tanistes, who were Elective and purchased their elections by strong hand; And by the Irish Custome of gavellkinde, the inferior Tennantries were partible amongst all Males on the Sept, both Bastards and Legittimate; and after partition made, if any one of the Sept had died, his portion was not divided among his Sonnes, but the cheefe of the Sept made a new partition of all Lands belonging to that Sept, and gave evere one his part according to his antiquity.

These two Irish Customes made all their possessions uncertain, being shuffled, and changed, and removed so often from one to another, by new elections and partitions, which uncertainty of estates hath bin the true cause of such Desolation & Barbarism in this land, as the like was never seen in any Countrey that professed the name of Christ. For though the Irishry be a Nation of great Antiquity, and wanted neither wit nor valour, and though they had received the Christian Faith, above 1200 years since; and were Lovers of Musicke, Poetry, and all kind of learning, and possessed a land abounding with all thinges necessary for the Civill life of man; yet (which is strange to be related) they did never build any houses of Brick or stone (some few poor Religious Houses excepted) before the reign of King Henrie the second, though they were Lords of this Island for many hundred yeares before, and since the Conquest attempted by the English: Albeit, when they sawe us builde Castles upon their borders, they have only in imitation of us, erected some few piles for their Captaines of the Country: yet I dare boldly say, that never any particular person, eyther before or since, did build any stone or bricke house for his private Habitation; but such as have latelie obtained estates, according to the course of the Law of England. Neither did any of them in all this time, plant any Gardens or Orchards, Inclose or improve their Lands, live together in setled villages or Townes, nor made any provision for posterity, which, being against all common sense and reason, must needes be imputed to those unreasonable Customes which made their estates so uncertain and transitory in their possessions.

For who would plant or improove, or build upon that Land, which a stranger whom he knew not, should possesse after his death? For that (as Solomon noteth) is one of the strangest Vanities under the Sunne. And this is the true reason Ulster and all the Irish Countries are found so wast and desolate at this day, and so would they continue till the worlds end if these Customes were not abolished by the Law of England.

Again, that Irish custom of Gavell-kinde did breed another michiefe, for thereby every man being borne to Land, as well Bastard as Legitimate, they al held themselves to be Gentlemen. And though their portions were never so small, and them-selves never so poor (for Gavelkind must needs in the end make a poor Gentility) yet did they scorne to discend to Husbandry or Merchandize, or to learn any Mechanicall Art or Science. And this is the true cause why there were never any Corporate Towns erected in the Irish Countries. As for the Maritine

Citties and Townes, most certaine it is that they were peopled and built by Ostmen or Easterlings [i.e., the Vikings]; for the natives of Ireland never perfourmed so good a worke as to build a City. Besides, these poor Gentlemen were so affected unto their small portions of Land, as they rather chose to live at home by Theft, Extortion, and Coshering, than to seek any better fortunes abroad, which increased their Septs or Syrnames into such numbers, as there are not to bee found in any Kingdome of Europe, so many gentlemen of one Blood, Familie, and Surname as there are of the O'Nealles in Ulster; of the Bourkes in Conaght, of the Geraldines, and Butlers, in Munster & Leinster. And the like may be saide of the Inferiour Bloodes and Families; whereby it came to passe in times of trouble & Dissention, that they made great parties and factions adhering one to another, with much constancie because they were tyed together Vinculo Sanguinis ["by the chain of blood"]; whereas Rebels and Malefactors which are tyed to their Leaders by no band, either of Dutie or Blood, do more easily breake and fall off one from another: And besides, their Coe-habitation in one Countrey or Territory, gave them opportunity suddenly to assemble, and Conspire, and rise in multitudes against the Crowne. And even now, in the time of peace, we finde this inconvenience, that ther can hardly be an indifferent triall had between the King & the Subject, or between partie and partie, by reason of this generall Kindred and Consanguinity.

But the most wicked and mischeevous Custome of all others was that of Coigne and livery, often before mentioned; which consisted in taking of Man's meat, Horse meat & Money of all the inhabitants of the Country, at the will and pleasure of the soldier, who as the phrase of Scripture is, "Did eat up the people as it were bread," for that he had no other entertainment. This Extortion was or originally Irish, for they used to lay Bonoght [military service] upon their people, and never gave their Soldier any other pay. But when the English had Learned it, they used it with more insolency, and made it more intollerable; for this oppression was not temporary, or limited either to place or time; but because there was everywhere a continuall warre, either Offensive or Defensive; and every lord of a Countrey and every Marcher made war and peace at his pleasure, it became Universall and Perpetuall; and was indeed the most heavy oppression that ever was used in any Christian of Heathen Kingdom. And therefore, Vox Oppressorum ["the voice of the oppressed"], this crying sinne did draw down as great, or greater plagues upon Ireland, then the oppression of the Isrelites, did draw upon the land of Egypt. For the plagues of Egypt, though they were griveous, were but of a short continuance. But the plagues of Ireland, lasted 400 years together. This extortion of Coigne and Livery, did produce two notorious

effects, First, it made the Land waste; Next, it made the people, ydle. For, when the Husbandman had laboured all the yeare, the soldier in one night, did consume the fruites of all his labour, *Longique perit labor irritus anni* ["The labor of a long year perishes barren"]. Head hee reason then to manure the Land for the next year? Or rather might he not complaine as the Shepherd in "Virgil": —

Impuris haec tam culta novalia miles habebit? Barbarus has segetes? En quo discordia Cives Perduxit miseros! En quies conservimus agros! [Did we for these barbarians plant and sow? On these, on these, our happy lands bestow? Good heaven, what dire effects from civil discord flow.] (Virgil, *Eclogue* 1, ll. 97–99, translated by John Dryden)

And hereupon of necessity came depopulation, banishment, & extirpation of the better sort of subjects, and such as remained became ydle and lookers on, expecting the event of those miseries and evill times: So as this extreame extortion and Oppression, hath been the true cause of the Idleness of the Irish Nation; and that rather the vulgar sort have chosen to be beggars in forraigne Countries, than to manure their own fruitful Land at home.

Reprinted *in* STRANGERS TO THAT LAND: BRITISH PERCEPTIONS OF IRELAND FROM THE REFORMATION TO THE FAMINE, *edited by Andrew Hadfield and John McVeagh (1994), pp. 77–80.*

≈

ON CATHOLIC IRELAND IN THE EARLY SEVENTEENTH CENTURY

The following documents are contemporary reports of the fidelity of the Irish (Gaelic and Old English alike) to the Roman Catholic faith, and also of the oppressions that they suffered because of this under Protestant English rule in their homeland.

SEE ALSO Politics: 1500 to 1690; Religion: 1500 to 1690

Italian Report (1613)

Sufficiency of priests in Ireland.—The population Catholic, nearly all openly professing their religion.—The English penal laws not enforced.—A comparatively small number infected with heresy in the cities.—The rural population ignorant to a large extent in matters of faith.—The nobility and gentry nearly all Catholic; hence the possibility of a large number of priests.—Estimated number of the clergy in Ireland: 800 seculars, 130 Franciscans, 20 Jesuits, a few Benedictines and Dominicans. The Franciscans always held in great esteem.—Greater learning and acquirements desirable in many of the secular clergy, the best being those educated in the Continental seminaries: at Douai, Bordeaux, Lisbon, and Salamanca.—The people have preserved the faith because naturally inclined to it; always attached to the Holy See; always hating the English; always opposed to novelty and tenacious of old customs.—Heresy introduced by violence and against their wish; externally Protestantism is in the ascendancy, all the archbishoprics and bishoprics being in the hands of the heretics.—Ireland counted 4 archbishops and 37 bishops; 9 under Armagh, 5 under Dublin, 12 under Cashel, 11 under Tuam.—No factions among the clergy.

[Original in Italian.]

Memorial Presented to the King of Spain on Behalf of the Irish Catholics (1619)

Conditions of the Catholics in Things Spiritual

Every Catholic is condemned to pay 12*d.* Irish if he does not attend the Protestant service—which is held in one of his own violated churches. Four times a year the judges going on circuit enquire from the parson the names of all such Catholics as do not obey this law, in order to punish them severely. . . .

No Catholic is permitted to teach anything, even grammar. The schoolmaster must be a Protestant, in order to bring the children up in heresy. If, contrary to the command of the Viceroy and Privy Council, a Catholic dare to teach Catholic children, he is fined heavily and kept in prison during the pleasure of the Viceroy; then on pretence of restoring him to liberty they banish him out of the Kingdom. Thus they force Catholics either not to teach or else to quit the country.

They forbid a Catholic, unless he has leave from the Viceroy and the Privy Council, under penalty of imprisonment for life, to go to Spain for the purpose of education; and in case anyone does go, even without the leave of his parents, they confiscate their property and imprison them until they give bail that they will bring him back and not let him go again. . . . Besides fining Catholics for not going to church, the pseudo-archbishops and bishops of Ireland excommunicate them. If after the third warning they do not conform, they are imprisoned and cruelly treated. They get no food, and if they are not to die of hunger must incur great expenses. At the present day there are many of them in prison throughout Ireland, and especially in Dublin Castle there are many gentlemen and respectable merchants who have been confined for years. . . .

When the Lord Deputy and Council have arrested a Catholic, either a layman or an ecclesiastic, they ask him whether the Pope can depose the King for his disobedience, deprive heretics of their possessions, etc., and they suggest and affirmative answer, in order to condemn him to death and to confiscate his property. . . .

Every Protestant justice of the peace has authority to arrest priests and to search for them in any house, and the fact of having such authority is publicly announced over and over again: last year (1617), a Proclamation to this effect was posted up everywhere. . . .

If a Catholic is convicted of having heard Mass; for the first offence he is fined 200 crowns and imprisoned for 6 months, for the second he is fined 400 crowns and imprisoned for a year, for the third he is fined 800 and imprisoned for life. The imprisonment may be escaped by bribery, but there is no chance of escaping the fines. . . .

No Irish Catholic can get any title or honourable employment, unless he takes the Oath of supremacy, goes to church, and swears to bring up his children Protestants: if he fails to do so, he loses his title or office and his property is confiscated.

Some cities and towns in Ireland have lost their ancient privileges because they would not elect a Protestant to be mayor or because the Catholic whom they elected would not take the Oath of Supremacy and go to church. This is the case at the present day in Waterford, where though all the Irish are Catholics, the civic offices are conferred on Protestants by the government. . . .

The Protestants have broken up all the stone altars that were in our churches and have altered the arrangement of the churches, in order that the marks of their original destination should disappear. And they compel the unfortunate Catholic inhabitants of the parish to contribute towards defraying the cost of altering the churches and of providing a wooden table and 2 silver cups for what they call Communion. . . .

No Catholic merchant, etc., can share in the rights or privileges of his town, unless he takes the Oath of Supremacy. . . .

The Protestants have taken possession of all the religious houses and of the property belonging to them; some monasteries have been thrown down in order to furnish materials for building palaces and houses; other monasteries are occupied by families; other monasteries are used as law courts where ecclesiastics are condemned to death. And the churches of the monasteries are turned into stables. . . .

Conditions of the Catholics in Things Temporal

All the government officials are English or Scotch heretics.

No Irish Catholic, however learned he may be, is permitted to plead as advocate in court, unless he first takes the Oath of Supremacy. . . . In the civil and criminal cases where Catholics are in question, some of those appointed to serve on the juries are Catholics, and if they do not act against their consciences and join the Protestant jurymen in injuring the Catholics, they are fined and imprisoned. . . .

When the officials are going on the King's business, they live luxuriously at the expense of the poor Catholics. If a Catholic refuses to admit them into his house and to supply them with food and money, they take it by force and then fine and imprison him. For these wrongs there is no hope of redress. The plantation of Ireland with English and Scottish heretics which is going on at present is effected in this way. The King commands the Catholics because they are Irish to quit their lands, and if he does give them a little land elsewhere, it is at a great distance from their old homes, in order that their very names may be forgotten there.

The Catholics whom the King dispossesses in this way are confined in prison until they give large sums of money as security that they will not sue or otherwise molest the heretics to whom their lands have been granted. . . . The above mentioned plantation of Ireland with Scotch heretics has for its object to create discord between the Irish and Scotch who from ancient times were on most friendly terms, and to prevent the Scotch from joining the Irish against the King, and to unite the Scotch and English against the Irish. . . .

Any government official may with impunity extort money from the Catholics or inflict suffering on them. If a Catholic complains to the Lord Deputy of these extortioners and persecutors, they accuse him of some crime, and the consequence is that he loses everything he possessed. . . .

If through inadvertence a Catholic say the least thing against an act of the King, either in spirituals or in temporals, it is high treason punished by death and confiscation.

It is forbidden to sell Catholic books, under pain of imprisonment.

[Original in Spanish.]

Fidelity of Ireland to the Catholic Faith (*John Lynch*, Cambrensis Eversus, 1662)

Of all the countries of Europe subject to heretical kings, there is not one in which a greater number of subjects have persevered in the old faith, and in obedience to the sovereign pontiff, than in Ireland. Cardinal Bentivoglio has truly observed, that the Irish would seem to have sucked in the Catholic faith with their mother's milk. In other countries smitten with heresy, the majority followed the example of the king or other governing power of the State, and renounced the old faith and supremacy of the Pope; but in Ireland, I do not hesitate to assert, that not the tenth, nor the hundredth, no nor the thousandth part, revolted from the faith of their fathers to the camp of the heretics. Orlandinus might say with perfect truth "that the Irish had preserved in heart and soul the Catholic faith in all its integrity and the most devoted obedience to the Roman pontiff." And Bozius also: "as far as we can judge from history, not one of all the northern nations has been more constant in the profession of the one faith."

IRISH HISTORY FROM CONTEMPORARY SOURCES, *edited by Constantia Maxwell* (1923), *pp.* 154–158.

~

FROM *AN ITINERARY*

1617

Fynes Moryson

Secretary to Lord Deputy Mountjoy, Fynes Moryson (1566–1617) in his Itinerary *celebrated the lord deputy's victories in the closing phases of the Nine Years War (1594–1603). The exception to his general disdain for Ireland was his high regard for Irish whiskey.*

SEE ALSO English Writing on Ireland before 1800

Touching the Irish dyet, Some Lords and Knights, and Gentlemen of the English-Irish, and all the English there abiding having competent meanes, use the English dyet, but some more, some lesse cleanly, few or none curiously, and no doubt they have as great and for their part greater plenty then the English, of flesh, fowle, fish, and all things for food, if they will use like Art of Cookery. Alwaies I except the Fruits, Venison, and some dainties proper to England, and rare in Ireland. And we must conceive, that Venison and Fowle seeme to be more plentiful in Ireland, because they neither so generally affect dainty foode nor so diligently search it as the English do. Many of the English-Irish, have by little and little been infected with the Irish filthiness, and that in the very cities, excepting Dublyn, and some of the better sort in Waterford, where, the English continually lodging in their houses, they more retain the English diet. The English-Irish, after our manner serve to the table joynts of flesh cut after our fashion, with Geese, Pullets, Pigges, and like rosted meats, but their ordinary food for the common sort is of Whitmeates, and they eate cakes of oates for bread, and drinke not English Beere made of Mault and Hops, but Ale. At Corck I have seene with these eyes, young maides starke naked grinding of Corne with certaine stones to make cakes thereof, and striking of into the tub or meale, such reliques thereof as stuck on their belly, thighes and more unseemly parts.

And for the cheese and butter commonly made by the English Irish, an English man would not touch it with his lippes, though hee were halfe starved; yet many English inhabitants make very good of both kindes. In Cities they have such bread as ours, but of sharpe savour, and some mingled with Annisseeds, and baked like cakes, and that onely in the houses of the better sort.

At Dublyn and in some other Cities, they have taverns, wherein Spanish and French Wines are sold, but more commonly the Merchants sell them by pintes and quartes in their owne Cellers. The Irish Aquavitæ, vulgarly called Usquebagh, is held the best in the World of that kind; which is made also in England, but nothing so good as that which is brought out of Ireland. And the Usquebagh is preferred before our Aquavitæ, because the mingling of Raysons, Fennell seede, and other things, mitigating the heate, and making the taste pleasant, makes it lesse inflame, and yet refresh the weake stomake with moderate heate, and a good relish. These Drinkes the English-Irish drink largely, and in many families (especially at feasts) both men and women use excesse therein. And since I have in part seene, and often heard from others experience, that some Gentlewomen were so free in this excesse, as they would kneeling upon the knee, and otherwise garausse health after health with men; not to speake of the wives of Irish Lords, or to referre it to the due place, who often drinke till they be drunken, or at least till they voide urine in full assemblies of men, I cannot (though unwilling) but note the Irish women more specially with this fault, which I have observed in no other part to be a woman's vice, but onely in Bohemia: Yet, so accusing them, I meane not to excuse the men, and will also confesse that I have seen Virgins, as well Gentlewomen as Citizens, commanded by their mothers to retyre after they had in curtesie pledged one or two healths. . . .

The wild and (as I may say) meere Irish, inhabiting many and large Provinces, are barbarous and most filthy in their diet. They skum the seething pot with an handfull of straw, and straine their milk taken from the Cow through a like handful of straw, none of the cleanest, and so cleanse, or rather more defile the pot and milke. They devoure great morsels of beefe unsalted, and they eat commonly Swines flesh, seldom mutton, and all these pieces of flesh, as also the intralles of beasts unwashed, they seeth in a hollow tree, lapped in a raw Cowes hide, and so set over the fier, and therewith swallow whole lumps of filthy butter. Yea (which is more contrary to nature) they will feede on Horses dying of themselves, not only upon small want of flesh, but even for pleasure. For I remember an accident in the Army, when the Lord Mountjoy, the Lord Deputy, riding to take the ayre out of the Campe, found the buttocks of dead Horses cut off, and suspecting that some soldiers had eaten that flesh out of necessity, being defrauded of the victuals allowed them, commanded the men to bee searched out, among whom a common soldier, and that of the English-Irish, not of the meere Irish, being brought to the Lord Deputy, and asked why hee had eaten the flesh of dead Horses, thus freely answered, Your Lordship may please to eate Pheasant and Patridge, and much good doe it you that best likes your taste; and I hope it is lawfull for me without offence, to eate this flesh that likes me better then Beef. Whereupon the Lord Deputy perceiving himself to be deceived, & further understanding that he had received his ordinary victuals (the detaining whereof he suspected, and purposed to punish for example), gave the souldier a piece of gold to drinke in Usquebagh for better digestion, and so dismissed him.

The foresaid wilde Irish doe not thresh their Oates, but burne them from the straw, and so make cakes thereof, yet they seldome eate this bread, much lesse any better kind, especially in the time of warre, whereof a Bohemian Baron complained, who having seen the Courts of England and Scotland, would needes out of his curiosity returne through Ireland in the heate of the Rebellion; and having letters from the King of Scots to the Irish lords then in Rebellion, first landed among them, in the furthest North, where for eight dayes space hee had found no bread, not so much as a cake of Oates, till he came to eate with the Earl of Tyrone, and after obtaining the Lord Deputies Passe to come into our Army, related this their want of bread to us for a miracle, who nothing wondred thereat. Yea, the wilde Irish in time of greatest peace impute covetousnesse and base birth to him, that hath any Corne after Christmas, as if it were a point of Nobility to consume all within those Festivall dayes. They willingly eate the hearb Schamrock, being of a sharpe taste, which as they runne and are chased to and fro, they snatch like beasts out of the ditches. . . .

Many of these wilde Irish eate no flesh, but that which dyes of disease or otherwise of it selfe, neither can it scape them for stinking. They desire no broath, nor have any use of a spoone. They can neither seethe Artichokes, nor eate them when they are sodden. It is strange and ridiculous, but most true, that some of our carriage Horses falling into their hands, when they found Sope and Starch, carried for the use of our Laundresses, they thinking them to bee some dainty meates, did eate them greedily, and when they stuck in their teeth, cursed bitterly the gluttony of us English churles, for so they terme us. They feede most on Whitmeates, and esteem for a great daintie sower curds, vulgarly called by them Bonaclabbe. And for this cause they watchfully keep their Cowes, and fight for them as for religion and life; and when they are almost starved, yet they will not kill a Cow, except it bee old, and yeeld no Milke. Yet will they upon hunger in time of warre open a vaine of the Cow, and drinke the bloud, but in no case kill or much weaken it. A man would thinke these men to bee Scythians, who let their Horses bloud under the eares, and for nourishment drinke their bloud, and indeed (as I have formerly said), some of the Irish are of the race Scythians, comming into Spaine, and from thence into Ireland. The wild Irish (as I said) seldome kill a Cow to eate, and if perhaps they kill one for that purpose, they distribute it all to be devoured at one time; for they approve not the orderly eating at meales, but so they may eate enough when they are hungry, they care not to fast long. And I have knowne some of these Irish footemen serving in England, (where they are nothing lesse than sparing in the foode of their Families), to lay meate aside for many meales, to devoure it all at one time. . . .

These wild Irish never set any candles upon tables; What do I speak of Tables? since indeede they have no tables, but set their meate upon a bundle of grasse, and use the same Grasse for napkins to wipe their hands. But I meane that they doe not set candles upon any high place to give light to the house, but place a great candle made of reedes and butter upon the floure in the middest of a great roome. And in like sort the chiefe men in their houses make fiers in the middest of the roome, the smoake whereof goeth out at a hole in the top thereof. An Italian Frier comming of old into Ireland, and seeing at Armach this their diet and the nakedness of the women . . . is said to have cried out,

Civitas Armachana, Civitas vana
  Carnes crudæ, mulieres nudæ.

Vaine Armagh City, I did thee pity,
  Thy meates rawness, and womens nakedness.

I trust no man expects among these gallants any beds, much lesse fetherbeds and sheetes, who like the Nomades removing their dwellings, according to the commodity of pastures for their Cowes, sleepe under the Canopy of heaven, or in a poore house of clay, or in a cabbin made of the boughes of trees, and covered with turffe, for such are the dwellings of the very Lords among them. And in such places, they make a fier in the middest of the roome, and round about it they sleepe upon the ground, without straw or other thing under them, lying all in a circle about the fier, with their feete towards it. And their bodies being naked, they cover their heads and upper parts with their mantels, which they first make very wet, steeping them in water of purpose, for they finde that when their bodies have once warmed the wet mantels, the smoake of them keepes their bodies in temperate heate all the night following. And this manner of lodging, not only the meere Irish Lords, and their followers use, but even some of the English Irish Lords and their followers, when after the old but tyranicall and prohibited manner vulgarly called Coshering, they goe (as it were) on progresse, to live upon their tenants, til they have consumed all the victuals that the poore men have or can get. To conclude, not only in lodging passengers, not at all or most rudely, but even in their inhospitality towards them, these wild Irish are not much unlike to wild beasts, in whose caves a beast passing that way, might perhaps finde meate, but not without danger to be ill intertained, perhaps devoured, of his insatiable host.

Fynes Moryson, AN ITINERARY (1898), pp. 196–203.

~

FROM "A DISCOURSE OF IRELAND"

1620

Luke Gernon

Little is known of Luke Gernon's early life, but he may have been from Hertfordshire, and he was appointed second justice of Munster in 1619. He lived in Limerick until the Rebellion of 1641 when, like many English settlers in Ireland, he lost most of his possessions. He was well connected, probably friends with Richard Boyle, the Great earl of Cork, and his wife seems to have known Archbishop Ussher. He died sometime before 1673. His "Discourse," a long letter written to an unnamed friend in which he gives his impressions of the country to which he has recently moved, probably dates from the winter of 1620. In this section he describes the appearance and dress of Irish men and women.

SEE ALSO English Writing on Ireland before 1800

Lett us converse with the people. Lord, what makes you so squeamish—be not affrayed. The Irishman is no Canniball to eate you up nor no lowsy Jack to offend you.

The man of Ireland is of a strong constitution, tall and bigg limbed, but seldom fatt, patient of heate and colde, but impatient of labour. Of nature he is prompt and ingenious, but servile crafty and inquisitive after newes, the simptomes of a conquered nation. Theyr speech hath been accused to be a whyning language, but that is among the beggars. I take it to be a smooth language, well commixt of vouells and of consonants, and hath a pleasing cadence.

The better sorte are apparelled at all poynts like the English onely they retayne theyr mantle which is a garment not indecent. It differs nothing from a long cloke, but in the fringe at the upper end, which in could weather they weare over their heades for warmth. Because they are commanded at publicke assemblies to come in English habit, they have a tricke agaynst those times, to take off the fringe, and to putt on a cape, and after the assembly past, to resume it agayne. If you aske an Irishman for his cloke, he will tell you it is in his pockett and show you his cape. The churle is apparelled in this maner. His doublett is a packe saddle of canvase, or coarse cloth without skirtes, but in winter he weares a frise cote. The trowse is a long stocke of frise, close to his thighes, and drawne on almost to his waste, but very scant, and the pryde of it is, to weare it so in suspense, that the beholder may still suspecte it to be falling from his arse. It is cutt with a pouche before, whiche is drawne together with a string. He that will be counted a spruce ladd, tyes it up with a twisted band of two colours like the string of a clokebagge. An Irishman walking in London a cutpurse took it for a cheate, and gave him a slash. His broges are single soled, more rudely sewed then a shoo but more strong, sharp at the toe, and a flapp of leather left at the heele to pull them on. His hatt is a frise capp close to his head with two lappetts, to button under his chinne. And for his weapon he weares a skeyne which is a knife of three fingers broad of the length of a dagger and sharpening towards the poynt with a rude wodden handle. He weares it poynt blanke at his codpiece. The ordinary kerne seldome weares a sword. They are also wedded to theyr mantle, the plow, they ditch, they thressh with theyr mantles on. But you look after the wenches.

The weomen of Ireland are very comely creatures, tall, slender and upright. Of complexion very fayre & cleare-skinned (but frecled), with tresses of bright yellow hayre, which they chayne up in curious knotts, and devises. They are not strait laced or plated in theyr youth, but suffred to grow at liberty so that you shall hardly see one crooked or deformed, but yet as the proverb is, soone ripe soone rotten. Theyr propensity to generation causeth that they cannot endure. They are wemen at thirteene, and olde wives at thirty. I never saw fayrer wenches nor fowler calliots, so we call the old wemen. Of nature they are very kind and tractable. At meetings they offer themselves to be kiste with the hande extended to embrace you. The yong wenches salute you, conferre with you, drinke with you without controll. They are not so reserved as the English, yett very honest. Cuckoldry is a thing almost unknowne among the Irish. At solemne invitements, the Benytee, so we call the goodwife of the house meets at the hall dore with as many of her femall kindred as are about her all on a row; to leave any of them unkist, were an indignity though it were done by the lord president.

I come to theyr apparrell. About Dublin they weare the English habit, mantles onely added thereunto, and they that goe in silkes, will weare a mantle of country making. In the country even among theyr Irish habitts they have sundry fashions. I will beginne with the ornament of theyr heads. At Kilkenny they weare broad beaver hatts coloured, edged with a gold lace and faced with velvett, with a broad gould hatt band. At Waterford they weare capps, turned up with furre and laced with gold lace. At Lymerick they weare rolles of lynnen, each roll contayning twenty bandles of fyne lynnen clothe (A Bandle is half an ell), and made up in forme of a myter. To this if it be could weather, there is added a muffler over theyr neck and chinne of like quantity of linnen; being so muffled, over all they will pinne on an English maske of blacke taffety, which is most rarely ridiculous to behold. In Connaught they weare rolles in forme of a cheese. In Thomond they weare kerchiefs, hanging downe to the middle of theyr backe. The maydes weare on the forepart of theyr head about foure yards of couloured ribbon smoothly layd, and theyr owne hayre played behind. In other places they weare theyre hayre loose and cast behind. They weare no bands, but the ornament of theyr neckes is a carkanett of goldsmyths worke besett with precious stones, some of them very ritch, but most of them gawdy and made of paynted glasses and at the end of them a crucifixe. They weare also braceletts, and many rings. I proceed to theyr gowns. Lend me your imaginacion, and I will cutt it out as well as the tayler. They have straight bodyes, and longe wasts, but theyr bodyes come no closer, but to the middle of the ribbe, the rest is supplied with lacing, from the topp of their breasts, to the bottome of theyr plackett, the ordinary sort have only theyr smockes between, but the better sort have a silk scarfe about theyr neck, which they spread and pinne over theyre breasts. On the forepart of those bodyes thay have a sett of broad silver buttons of goldsmiths worke sett round about. A sett of those buttons will be worth 40s, some are worth £5. They have hanging sleeves, very narrow, but no arming sleeves, other then theyre smocke sleeves, or a wastcoate of stripped stuffe, onely they have a wrestband of the same cloth, and a lyst of the same to joyne it to theyr winge, but no thing on the hinter part of the arme least they should weare out theyr elbowes. The better sort have sleeves of satten. The skyrt is a piece of rare artifice. At every bredth of three fingers they sew it quite through with a welte, so that it seemeth so many lystes putt together. That they do for strength, they girde theyr gowne with a silke girdle, the tassell whereof must hang downe poynt blanke before to the fringe of theyr peticotes, but I will not descend to theyr peticotes, least you should thinke that I have bene under them. They beginne to weare knitt stockins coloured, but they have not disdayned to weare stockins of raw whyte frise, and broges. They weare theyr mantles also as well with in doors as with out. Theyr mantles are commonly of a browne blew colour with the fringe alike, but those that love to be gallant were them of greene, redd, yellow, and other light colours, with fringes diversified. An ordinary mantle is worth £4, those in the country which cannot go to the price weare whyte sheets mantlewise. I would not have you suppose that all the Irish are thus strangely attyred as I have described. The old women are loath to be shifted out of theyr auncient habitts, but the younger sort, especially in gentlemens houses are brought up to resemble the English, so that it is to be hoped, that the next age will weare out these disguises. Of theyr cleanlynes I will not speak.

Reprinted in STRANGERS TO THAT LAND: BRITISH PERCEPTIONS OF IRELAND FROM THE REFORMATION TO THE FAMINE, *edited by Andrew Hadfield and John McVeagh (1994), pp. 81–83.*

≈

FROM *THE TOTAL DISCOURSE OF HIS RARE ADVENTURES*

1632

William Lithgow

This text by William Lithgow is a contribution to the bizarre (although occasionally accurate) ethnography of the Irish which was begun by Gerald of Wales in the twelfth century. Wild and woolly descriptions of the highly unlikely are mixed with true reports, such as of the Irish practice of "plowing by the tail," a technique which has its agricultural defenders.

SEE ALSO Agriculture: 1500 to 1690; English Writing on Ireland before 1800

And this I dare avow, there are more Rivers, Lakes, Brookes, Strands, Quagmires, Bogs, and Marishes, in this Countrey, then in all Christendome besides; for Travelling there in the Winter, all my dayly solace, was sincke down comfort; whiles Boggy-plunging deepes kissing my horse belly; whiles over-mired Saddle, Body, and all; and often or ever set a swimming, in great danger, both I, and my Guides of our Lives: That for cloudy and fountayne-bred perils, I was never before reduced to such a floting Laborinth. Considering that in five monethes space, I quite spoyled six horses, and my selfe as tyred as the worst of them. . . .

I remember I saw in Irelands North-parts, two remarkable sights: The one was their manner of Tillage, Ploughes drawne by Horsetayles, wanting garnishing, they are only fastned, with straw, or wooden Ropes to their bare Rumps, marching all side for side, three or foure in a Ranke, and as many men hanging by the ends of that untoward Labour. It is as bad a Husbandry I say, as ever I found among the wildest Savages alive; for the Caramins, who understand not the civill forme of Agriculture; yet they delve, hollow, and turne over the ground, with manuall and Wooden instruments: but they the Irish have thousands of both Kingdomes daily labouring beside them; yet they can not learne, because they wil not learn, to use garnishing, so obstinate they are in their barbarous consuetude, unlesse punishment and penalties were inflicted; and yet most of them are content to pay twenty shillings a yeare, before they wil change their Custome.

The other as goodly sight I saw, was women travayling the way, or toyling at home, carry their Infants about their neckes, and laying the dugges over their shoulders, would give sucke to the Babes behinde their backes, without taking them in their armes: Such kind of breasts, me thinketh were very fit, to be made money bags for East or West-Indian Merchants, being more than halfe a yard long, and as wel wrought as any Tanner, in the like charge, could ever mollifie such Leather.

Reprinted in STRANGERS TO THAT LAND: BRITISH PERCEPTIONS OF IRELAND FROM THE REFORMATION TO THE FAMINE, *edited by Andrew Hadfield and John McVeagh (1994), pp. 59–60.*

FROM *TRAVELS*

1634–1635

Sir William Brereton

Sir William Brereton (1604–1661), an Englishman, later became an officer in the army of the English parliament. But in the 1630s he was an energetic tourist in Britain, Ireland, and on the Continent. Here he reports his observations during a progress south from eastern Ulster through Newry, Dundalk, and Drogheda.

SEE ALSO English Writing on Ireland before 1800

Jul. 7—We left Dromemoore and went to the NEWRIE, which is sixteen miles. This is a most difficult way for a stranger to find out. Herein we wandered, and being lost, fell amongst the Irish towns. The Irish houses are the poorest cabins I have seen, erected in the middle of fields and grounds, which they farm and rent. This is a wild country, not inhabited, planted, nor enclosed, yet it would be good corn if it were husbanded. I gave an Irishmen to bring us into the way a groat, who led us like a villain directly out of the way and so left us, so as by this deviation it was three hour before we came to the Newrie. Much land there is about this town belonging to Mr. Bagnall, nothing well planted. He hath a castle in this town, but it is for most part resident at Green Castle; a great part of this town is his, and it is reported that he hath a £1000 or £1500 per annum in this country. This is but a poor town, and is much Irish, and is navigable for boats to come up unto with the tide. Here we baited at a good inn, the sign of the Prince's Arms. Hence to Dundalke is eight mile; stony, craggy, hilly, and uneven, but a way it is nothing difficult to find. Before you come to Dundalke you may discern four or five towers or castles seated upon the sea side.

This town of DUNDALKE hath been a town of strength, and is still a walled town, and a company of fifty soldiers are here in garrison under the command of Sir Faithful Fortesque. This town is governed by two bailiffs, sheriffs, and aldermen; the greatest part of the inhabitants of the town are popishly affected, and although my Lord Deputy, at the last election of burgesses for the Parliament, commended unto them Sir Faithful Fortesque and Sir Arthur Teringham, yet they rejected both, and elected a couple of recusants. One of the present baliffs is popish. Abundance of Irish, both gentlemen and others, dwell in this town, wherein

they dare to take the boldness to go to mass openly. This town seated upon the sea so as barks may come within a convenient distance with the flood; much low, level, flat land hereabouts, which is often overflowed in the winter, and here is abundance of fowl, and a convenient seat. Here we lodged at one Mris. Veasie's house, a most mighty fat woman; she saith she is a Cheshire woman, near related in blood to the Breretons; desired much to see me; so fat she is, as she is so unwieldy, she can scarce stand or go without crutches. This reported one of the best inns in north of Ireland; ordinary 8d. and 6d., only the knave tapster over-reckoned us in drink.

Jul. 8—We left Dundalke and came to TREDAUGH [Drogheda], which is accounted sixteen mile, but they are as long as twenty-two mile. About five mile hence we saw Sir Faithful Fortesque's house or castle, wherein for most part he is resident, which he holds by a long lease upon a small rent under my Lord Primate of Armath. This is a dainty, pleasant, healthful, and commodious seat, and it is worth unto him about [gap in MS]. During ten miles riding from this town, much rich corn land, and the country as well planted; the other six miles towards Tredaugh, until you come near unto it, not so rich land, nor so well husbanded.

This town, as it is the largest and best built town I have yet seen in Ireland, so it is most commodiously seated upon a good navigable river, called Boyne, whereinto flows the sea in so deep a channel (though it be very narrow) as their ships may come to their doors. This river is built on both sides, and there is on either side convenient quay; a stone wall built along the river, so as a ship may lie close unto this quay, and may unload upon her. It is like the quay of Newcastle, and those channels I have seen in Holland in their streets. This town commodiously also situated for fish and fowl. It is governed by a mayor, a sheriffs, and twenty-four aldermen; most of these, as also the other inhabitants of the town, popishly affected, insomuch as those that have been chosen mayors, who for the most part have been recusants, have hired others to discharge that office. One man (it is said) hath been hired by deputation to execute that place thirteen times; the present mayor also is but a deputy, and the reason why they make coy to execute that office is because they will avoid being necessitated to go to church.

I observed in this city divers fair, neat, well built houses, and houses and shops well furnished, so as I did conceive this to be a rich town; the inhabitants civilized and better apparelled. . . .

We came to the city of DUBLIN, July 9, about 10 hour. This is the metropolis of the kingdom of Ireland, and is beyond all exception the fairest, richest, best built city I have met with in this journey (except York and Newcastle). . . .

This city of Dublin, is extending his bound and limits very far; much additions of buildings lately, and some of those very fair, stately and complete buildings; every commodity is grown very dear. You must pay also for an horse hire 1s. 6d. a day: here I met with an excellent, judicious and painful smith. Here are divers commodities cried in Dublin as in London, which it doth more resemble than any town I have seen in the king of England's dominions.

Jul. 14—Upon Tuesday, July 14, I left Dublin and came to HACQUETTS TOWN, about eleven hour at night. It is accounted twenty-seven miles, but it is as long as thirty-seven. After you pass four miles from Dublin, you travel through the mountains, which are dry land, and some of them good pasture for cattle that are young, and sheep, but these are not sufficiently stocked. Towards evening we passed through troublesome and dangerous ways and woods, and had wandered all night, had we not hired an Irish guide, by whose directions we arrived at eleven hour at Hacquett's Town, where we lodged in a little, low, poor, thatched castle. Here Mr. Wattson, a Lanarkshire man, hath a plantation. As we passed this way, I observed the head of the river Liffe, which comes under the bridge at Dublin, whence it is made navigable by the flood, which goeth a mile above the bridge, and little further; I passed also, about eighteen miles from Dublin, by the head of the Slane, which runs to Waxford, and is there navigable, and twenty miles above Waxford.

Reprinted in Strangers to That Land: British Perceptions of Ireland from the Reformation to the Famine, *edited by Andrew Hadfield and John McVeagh (1994), pp. 60–62.*

≈

CONFEDERATION OF KILKENNY

1642

In the aftermath of the 1641 Rebellion representatives of both the Gaelic Irish and the Old English met in Kilkenny in June 1642 and there constituted a protonationalist entity termed the Confederate Catholics of Ireland. Dominated by the conservative Old English, the Confederates acquired a royalist tinge. Eventually, in 1648, they split, with the more radical Gaelic Irish ending any continuing pretense of loyalty to the Protestant Charles I.

SEE ALSO Confederation of Kilkenny; O'Neill, Owen Roe; Rebellion of 1641; Religion: 1500 to 1690

Orders made and established by the lords spiritual and temporal, and the rest of the general assembly for the kingdom of Ireland, met at the city of Kilkenny, the 24th day of October, Anno Domini 1642, and the eighteenth year of the reign of our sovereign lord, King Charles, by the grace of God, of Great Britain, France and Ireland, etc.

I. Imprimis that the Roman Catholic church in Ireland shall and may have and enjoy the privileges and immunities according to the great charter, made and declared within the realm of England, in the ninth year of King Henry III, sometime king of England, and the lord of Ireland, and afterwards enacted and confirmed in this realm of Ireland. And that the common law of England, and all the statutes of force in this kingdom, which are not against the Roman Catholic religion, or the liberties of the natives, and other liberties of this kingdom, shall be observed throughout the whole kingdom, and that all proceedings in civil and criminal cases shall be according to the same laws.

II. Item, that all and every person and persons within this kingdom shall bear faith and true allegiance unto our sovereign lord King Charles . . . his heirs and lawful successors, and shall uphold and maintain his and their rights and lawful prerogatives, . . .

III. Item, that the common laws of England and Ireland, and the said statutes, called the greater charter, and every clause, branch and article thereof, and all other statutes confirming, expounding or declaring the same, shall be punctually observed within this kingdom, so far forth as the condition of the present times, during these times, can by possibilities give way thereunto, and after the war is ended the same to be observed without any limitations, or restriction whatsoever.

IV. . . . For the exaltation therefore of the holy Roman Catholic church, for the advancement of his majesty's service, and the preservation of the lives, estates, and liberties of his majesty's true subjects of this kingdom against the injustice, murders, massacres, rapes, depredations, robberies, burnings, frequent breaches of public faith and quarters, and destruction daily perpetrated and acted upon his majesty's said subjects, and advised, contrived, and daily executed by the malignant party, some of them managing the government and affairs of state in Dublin, and some other parts of this kingdom, to his majesty's greatest disservice, and complying with their confederates, the malignant party in England and elsewhere, who (as it is manifest to all the world) do complot, and practise to dishonour and destroy his majesty, his royal consort the queen, their issue, and the monarchial government, which is of most dangerous consequence to all the monarchs and princes of Christendom, the said assembly doth order and establish a council by name of a supreme council of the confederate Catholics of Ireland, who are to consist of the number of four and twenty to be forthwith named, whereof twelve at the least, to be forthwith named, shall reside in this kingdom, or where else they shall think expedient, and the members of the said council shall have equal votes, and two parts of three or more concurring present votes, to conclude, and not fewer to sit in council than nine, whereof seven at least are to concur; and of the four and twenty a president shall be named by the assembly, to be one of the said twelve resident. . . . And the said council shall have the power and pre-eminence following, viz. the lords general and all other commanders of armies, and civil magistrates and officers in the several provinces shall observe their orders and decrees, and shall do nothing contrary to their directions, and shall give them speedy advertisement and account of their proceedings. . . .

That the said council shall have power and authority to do and execute all manner of acts and things conducing to the advancement of the Catholic cause, and good of this kingdom, and concerning the war, as if done by the assembly, and shall have power to hear and determine all matters capital, criminal or civil, excepting the right or title of land. . . .

V. Item, it is further ordered and established, that in every province of this kingdom there shall be a provincial council, and in every county a county council. . . .

XII. Item, it is further ordered, that whosoever hath entered since the first day of October, 1641, or shall hereafter during the continuance of the war in this kingdom, enter into the lands, tenements, or hereditaments, at or immediately before the first day of October. . . . shall immediately restore upon demand, the said possession to the party or parties so put out . . . provided, and so it is meant, that if any of the parties so put out, be declared a neuter or enemy by the supreme or provincial council, then the party who gained the possession as aforesaid shall give up the possession to such person or persons, as shall be named either by the said council provincial, or supreme council, to be disposed of towards the maintenance of the general cause, . . .

XIV. Item, for the avoiding of national distinction between the subjects of his Majesty's dominions, which this assembly doth utterly detest and abhor, which ought not to be endured in a well-governed common-

wealth, it is ordered and established, that, upon pain of the highest punishment, which may be inflicted by authority of this assembly, that every Roman Catholic, as well English, Welsh, as Scotch, who was of that profession before the troubles, and who will come and please to reside in this kingdom and join in the present union, shall be preserved and cherished in his life, goods, and estates, by the power, authority, and force (if need require it) of all the Catholics of Irelands, as fully and as freely as any native born therein, and shall be acquitted and eased of one third part (in three parts to be divided) of public charges or levies raised or to be raised for the maintenance of this holy war.

XV. Item, and it is further ordered and established, that there shall be no distinction or comparison made betwixt Old Irish, and Old and New England or betwixt septs or families, or betwixt citizens and townsmen and countrymen, joining in union, upon pain of the highest punishment that can be inflicted by and of the councils aforesaid, according to the nature and quality of the offences, and division like to spring thence. . . .

XXVI. Item, it is ordered and established, that the possession of Protestant archbishops, bishops, deans, dignitaries, and parsons, in right of their respective churches, or their tenements in the beginning of these troubles, shall be deemed, taken, and construed as the possession of the Catholic archbishops, bishops, deans, dignitaries, pastors and their tenements respectively. . . .

Reprinted in IRISH HISTORICAL DOCUMENTS, 1172–1922, *edited by* Edmund Curtis *and* R. B. McDowell (1943), *pp. 148–152.*

~

SPEECH TO THE SPEAKER OF THE HOUSE OF COMMONS

1642

Richard Boyle

Richard Boyle, first earl of Cork (1566–1643), was the greatest and richest of the "new English" (i.e., Protestant) magnates in Ireland. Born in Essex, he went to Ireland in the 1580s and assembled vast holdings of confiscated land in Munster. By instinct he was a royalist and supporter of Charles I on the eve of the English civil wars (1642–1648), but the king was implicated in the Ulster Rebellion of 1641, and more sympathy and support for Protestants in Ireland was to be expected from the king's developing adversary, the English parliament.

SEE ALSO Rebellion of 1641

Sir, I pray ["let" erased] give me leave to present unto your selfe and that honourable house, that this great and generall rebellion brake forth in October last, at the very instant when I landed here out of England; and though it appeared first in Ulster, yet I who am 76 yeares of age, and have eate most parte of my bread in Ireland these 54 yeares, and by reason of my severall employments and commands in the government of this province and kindgome could not [but suspect] that the infection and contagion was generall and would by degrees quickly creep into this province, as forthwith it did. And soe that I found to my great griefe that by the course the late Earle of Strafford had taken, all or the greatest part of the English and Protestants in this province, were deprived ["debarred" erased] of their Armes, and debarred from having any powder in their houses, and the King's Magazines in ["this province" erased] heer, being soe ["very" erased] weakly furnished as in a manner they were empty. I without delay furnished all my Castles in these two Counties with such Ammunition as my owne poore Armory did afford, and sent 300li. ster. into England to bee bestowed in Ammunition for my selfe and [my] tenants, and putt in sufficient guards, and 9 monethes victualls into every of my ["victuall" erased] Castles; all which I thanke God, I have hitherto preserved and made good, not without giving great annoyance out of those Castles to the rebels. And for that the late Lord President did judiciously observe that the preservation of this important Towne and harbour of Yoghall, was of principall consequence to bee maintayned and kept for the service of the Crowne, and presuming that noe man did exceed me in power and abilitie to make it good, hee prevayled [with mee] soe farre, for the advancement of his Majestie service and securing of this considerable towne and harbour, as to leave my owne strong and defensible house of Lismore (which was well provided of Ordnance and all things fitting for defence) to the guard of my sonn Broghill with 100 horse and 100 foot, and to retyre hither; whither I brought two foot Companies of 100 a peece, all compounded of English Protestants and well disciplined, and these at my chardges armed, being men experienced and formerly seasoned with the ayre of this Countrey, wherein they are good guides. And hitherto I doe thanke my God, this Towne and harbour, are made good and is a receptacle not onely for all shipping but also for multitudes of distressed English, which have been

["strip" erased] dispossessed and stript by the rebells, and found succour and saftie heere.

Reprinted in STRANGERS TO THAT LAND: BRITISH PERCEPTIONS OF IRELAND FROM THE REFORMATION TO THE FAMINE, *edited by Andrew Hadfield and John McVeagh (1994), pp. 121–122.*

~

FROM *A TRUE AND CREDIBLE RELATION*

1642

Anonymous

The rebellion of October 1641 was to have begun with a carefully organized plot to seize Dublin Castle, the seat of English government and administration in Ireland. The plot was foiled, but a major uprising took place, directed at first against the English and then the Scottish settlers in Ulster. Later in the year and early the next it spread slowly to the rest of Ireland.

SEE ALSO Rebellion of 1641

Their Cruell and Damnable Design was first to have surprised the Castle of Dublin upon the 23. day of October Anno predicto, upon a Saturday; the same night all the Popish houses were to be marked with a Crosse to be knowne from the Protestant houses, their intent being upon the Sunday following to have surprised all the Protestants and to have stript them naked, as they did many thousands of men, women and children in other parts of the kingdome of Irelande upon the same day, and also to have surprised all the English shipping, riding at Anchor at a Harbour commonly called the Rings End, about a mile distant from the City of Dublin. But God that saw the bloudy intent discovered their practice by one of their owne faction suffering them to run in their owne wicked hope and cruell imagination, untill the night before their practise should have been put in execution, for the same night the Lord Mack-Gueere an Irish man, and Captaine Mack-Mahowne also an Irish man (who confessed the whole plot) were apprehended, the one in Cookstreet within the City of Dublin, the other neere Dublin in Saint Mary Abbey in the suburbes of the same City, both which have been ever since imprisoned in the Castle of Dublin, and doe still remaine there. . . .

It is too manifest thet the Jesuits those firebrands of hell, and Popish priests were the plotters of this and other Treasons, which can at their pleasure absolve subjects of their obedience to their princes and give power to murther and depose kings, neither could they worke upon a more rebellious and forward nation to doe mischiefe. . . .

It is too well knowne (the more is the pittie and to be lamented) that they have murthered, and starved to death of the English in the province of Ulster and other provinces where they are risen up in (re)bellion of men, women and children alone 20,000.

Their manner is and hath beene, cowardly and treacherously to surprise them upon great advantages, and without respect of persons, to rob them of all they have, but being not content therewith (but as insatiable of bloud) hunting after their pretious lives, stript ladies and gentlewomen, Virgins and Babies, old and young, naked as ever they were borne, from their clothes, turning them into open fields, (where having first destroyed the husbands and the Parents, before their wives and childrens faces) many hundreds have beene founde dead in ditches with cold for want of food and rayment, the Irish having no more compassion of their age or youth, then of Doggs.

As for the Protestant Ministers, those they take (which have been many) they use them with such cruelty, as it would make any heart so melt into teares that doth but heare this relation; Their manner is first to hang them up, and then they cut off their heads, after they quarter them, then they dismember their secret parts, stopping their mouthes therewith, a thing indeed for modestie sake, more fit to bee omitted then related.

Many of their wives, they have ravished in their sights before the multitude, stripping them naked to the view of their wicked Companions, taunting and mocking them with reproachful words, sending them away in such a shamefull or rather shameless manner that they have (most of them) either dyed for griefe, or starved with want and cold, such cruelty was never knowne before. . . .

As for the murder of Rebels, it is not certainly knowne; but without question there is a great many of them, but not the third part of them armed, and those armes they have, they have taken from the English, in surprising and murthering them cowardly and treacherously, and some of them under pretence of being rob'd by the Rebells, have deceiptfully gotten Armes to goe fight against them, and then have run away from their Captaines to the Rebells, are indeed there is no trust nor confidence to be put in them, they are so treacherously perfidious.

It is supposed that the chief Rebells doe intend to steale away by Sea (having gotten a great estate from the English Plantators whom they have robbed and murthered) and so leave the ignorant rabble of Irish in the lurch. . . .

It is to be beleeved that the Rebells will never give a Battell, and that in short time they will be starved for want of food, for they have gotten in most parts from the English all they can get, and they wast and devoure that plenty they have, and there is neither plowing nor sowing in those parts, so that it will be impossible for them to subsist long. . . .

They report and allege that Religion is the cause of their war, but that is false for they have had too much liberty and freedome of conscience in Ireland, and that hath made them Rebell. I hope that God that hath discovered their bloudy practice, will confound their devices, and bring them to confusion. To the which God be all honour, praise and Glory for ever.

Reprinted in STRANGERS TO THAT LAND: BRITISH PERCEPTIONS OF IRELAND FROM THE REFORMATION TO THE FAMINE, edited by Andrew Hadfield and John McVeagh (1994), pp. 118–120.

~

FROM A REMONSTRANCE . . . , BEING THE EXAMINATIONS OF MANY WHO WERE EYE-WITNESSES OF THE SAME, AND JUSTIFIED UPON OATH BY MANY THOUSANDS

1643

Thomas Morley

After the rebellion of October 1641, in which thousands of Protestant planters and their families were driven off their properties in Ulster amidst allegations of numerous atrocities, elaborate efforts were made to document and publicize the widespread destruction and pillage of English and Scottish settlers' property. This account by Thomas Morley relates to the county of Monaghan.

SEE ALSO Rebellion of 1641

In the County of Monaghan M. Blany a Justice of the peace and Knight of the shire, and Committee for the Subsidies, hanged up, stript and buried in a ditch by the rebels (in The County of Monaghan), because he would not turne and goe to masse; and the next night one Luke Ward hang'd and throwne into a ditch; and they and divers others were robbed, and the rest kept in prison, without reliefe from them that robd them. . . .

A man who had severall young children borne and alive, and his wife neere her time of delivery of another, was most cruelly murthered by the rebels, his wife, flying into the mountaines, the rebels, hastily pursued her and her little children, and found her newly delivered of her child there; they pittying no such, nor any distresse, presently murthered her and her other children which runne with her thither, and in most inhumane and barbarous manner suffered their dogs to eate up and devoure the new borne child. . . .

The rebels would send their children abroad in great troopes, especially neere kindred, armed with long wattles an whips, who would therewith beate mens privy members until they beat or rather threshed them off, and then they would returne in great joy to their parents, who received them for such service, as it were in triumph

If any women were found dead, lying with their faces downward, they would turne them upon their backes, and in great flockes resort unto them, censuring all the parts of their bodies, but especially such as are not to be named; which afterwards they abused so many waies and so filthily, as chaste cares would not endure the very naming thereof. . . .

The rebels themselves confessed and told it to Dr. Maxwell while he was prisoner among them, that they killed 954 in one morning in the County of Antrim, and that besides them they supposed they had kild 1100 or 1200 more in that County. . . .

Reference being had to the number in grosse which the Rebels themselves have upon enquiry found out and acknowledged, which notwithstanding will come farre short of all those that have been murthered in Ireland, there being above one hundred fifty four thousand wanting of British within the very precincts of Ulster in March 1641 as by their monethly bills brought in and made by their Priests by speciall direction appeareth.

It is proved by divers witnesses that after the drowning of many Protestants at Portadowne, strange visions and apparitions have been seen and heard there upon the water; sometimes a spirit assuming the shape of a man hath been seen there with his hands held up and closed together; and sometimes in the likenesse of a woman, appearing waste high above the water, with the haire disheveled, eyes twinkled, elevated and clasped hands, crying out, revenge, revenge, &c. and appearing, and crying so many nights together. Other visions and strange voices, and fearful scritchings have been heard where they have drowned the English at other places, as at Beltubat river in the County of Cavan; a lough near

Loghgall in the County of Armagh, which have also deterred and affrighted the Irish soldiers and others, that they durst not stay neere the place, but fled away.

In the Countie of Armagh, it was ordinary and common for the rebels to expose the murthered bodies of the British so long unto publique view and censure, that they began to stinke and infect the ayre, (which being a thing very strange) would not sometimes happen untill foure or five weekes after the murther committed. Then at length they would permit some of their bodies to be recovered and cast into ditches, but so as they must be laid with their faces downward. The reason they gave for the same was, that they so placed them to the intent they might have a prospect and sight of Hell onely. And therefore when they kild any of the Protestants they used alwaies these words, Aurius Dewll, which is, thy sole to the divell. . . .

They tooke [a] Scotchman and ripped up his belly, that they might come to his small guts. The one end whereof they tied to a Tree and made him go round untill he had drawne them all out of his body. Then they saying, they would try whether a dog, or a Scotchman's guts were longer. . . .

In the County of Cavan, James O'Rely, Hugh Brady, and other rebels often tooke the Protestant Bibles and wetting them in puddle water, did five or six severell times dash the same in the face of the Protestants, saying, come I know you love a good lesson, here is a most excellent one for you, and come tomorrow and you shall have as good a Sermon. And as the Protestants were going to the Church the rebels tooke and dragged them into the Church by the haire of the head; where they whipt, rob'd, stript, and most cruelly used them, saying, that tomorrow you shall heare the like sermon.

That Rory MacGuire, Sir Phelim O'Neale, and the Northern Rebells in the Counties of Monaghan, Armagh, Lowth, Cavan, Meath and other places where they came, burnt, tore, or otherwise trampled under their feete, and spoyled all the Protestants Bibles, and other good Bookes of the Protestants. . . .

The Generall cruelty to Ministers against Protestants and that religion duly exercised by the Papist-rebells scornfull malicious and contemptuous words and blasphemies, are so many and frequently used, and by too wofull experience found and proved by a multitude of witnesses.

Reprinted in STRANGERS TO THAT LAND: BRITISH PERCEPTIONS OF IRELAND FROM THE REFORMATION TO THE FAMINE, *edited by Andrew Hadfield and John McVeagh (1994), pp. 116–118.*

ON THE CAPTURE OF DROGHEDA

17 September 1649

Oliver Cromwell

Because of the intervening English civil wars, the Irish Rebellion of 1641 went unrepressed and unavenged for more than eight years. In the late summer of 1649, Oliver Cromwell finally brought over a large English army and a train of artillery. The siege and conquest of the walled town of Drogheda (forty miles north of Dublin) was one of his first and most celebrated triumphs. The defeated, including many hundreds of civilian men, women, and children, were slaughtered. Cromwell wrote that it was just retribution for the atrocities committed against Protestants and their families in 1641 and after.

SEE ALSO Cromwellian Conquest; Rebellion of 1641

For the Honourable William Lenthall, Esquire, Speaker of the Parliament of England: These

Sir, . . .

Your Army came before the town upon Monday following, where having pitched, as speedy course was taken as could be to frame our batteries, which took up the more time because divers of the battering guns were on shipboard. Upon Monday the 9th [10th] of this instant, the batteries began to play. Whereupon I sent Sir Arthur Ashton, the then Governor, a summons, To deliver the town to the use of the Parliament of England. To the which I received no satisfactory answer, but proceeded that day to beat down the steeple of the church on the south side of the town, and to beat down a tower not far from the same place, . . .

The enemy retreated, divers of them, into the Mill-Mount: a place very strong and of difficult access, being exceedingly high, having a good graft, and strongly palisadoed. The Governor, Sir Arthur Ashton, and divers considerable Officers being there, our men getting up to them, were ordered by me to put them all to the sword. And indeed, being in the heat of action, I forbade them to spare any that were in arms in the town, and, I think, that night they put to the sword about 2,000 men, divers of the officers and soldiers being fled over the Bridge into the other part of the Town, where about one hundred of them possessed St. Peter's church-steeple, some the west gate, and others a strong round tower next the gate called St. Sunday's. These being summoned to yield to mercy, refused, wherupon I or-

dered the steeple of St. Peter's Church to be fired, where one of them was heard to say in the midst of the flames: "God damn me, God confound me; I burn, I burn."

The next day, the other two towers were summoned, in one of which was about six of seven score; but they refused to yield themselves, and we knowing that hunger must compel them, set only good guards to secure them from running away until their stomachs were come down. From one of the said towers, notwithstanding their condition, they killed and wounded some of our men. When they submitted, their officers were knocked on the head, and every tenth man of the soldiers killed, and the rest shipped for the Barbadoes. The soldiers in the other tower were all spared, as to their lives only, and shipped likewise for the Barbadoes.

I am persuaded that this is a righteous judgment of God upon these barbarous wretches, who have imbrued their hands in so much innocent blood; and that it will tend to prevent the effusion of blood for the future, which are the satisfactory grounds to such actions, which otherwise cannot but work remorse and regret. . . .

And now give me leave to say how it comes to pass that this work is wrought. It was set upon some of our hearts, That a great thing should be done, not by power or might, but by the Spirit of God. And is it not so clear? That which caused your men to storm so courageously, it was the Spirit of God, who gave your men courage, and took it away again; and gave the enemy courage, and took it away again; and gave your men courage again, and therewith this happy success. And therefore it is good that God alone have all the glory.

It is remarkable that these people, at the first, set up the mass in some places of the town that had been monasteries; but afterwards grew so insolent that, the last Lord's day before the storm, the Protestants were thrust out of the great Church called St. Peter's, and they had public mass there: and in this very place near one thousand of them were put to the sword, fleeing thither for safety. I believe all their friars were knocked on the head promiscuously but two; the one of which was Father Peter Taaff, (brother to the Lord Taaff), whom the soldiers took, the next day, and made an end of: the other was taken in the round tower, under the repute of lieutenant, and when he understood that the officers in that tower had no quarter, he confessed he was a friar; but that did not save him. . . .

Your most humble servant,
Oliver Cromwell

Oliver Cromwell, THE LETTERS AND SPEECHES OF OLIVER CROMWELL, WITH ELUCIDATIONS BY THOMAS CARLYLE (1904), pp. 466, 467, 468–469, 470–471, 472.

FROM *THE GREAT CASE OF TRANSPLANTATION DISCUSSED*

1655

Vincent Gookin

After his military victories of 1649–1650, Oliver Cromwell called for the transplantation of virtually all the Catholic Irish to areas west of the Shannon, principally in the agriculturally poorest province, Connacht. An Irish Protestant, Vincent Gookin, who served as surveyor general of Ireland, in 1655 published this pamphlet arguing against this draconian and impractical, not to say unjust, scheme.

SEE ALSO Cromwellian Conquest; Land Settlements from 1500 to 1690

For future Inhabitants, Adventurers, Souldiers, and such others as shall engage in the planting of Ireland. The first and chiefest Necessaries to the settlement and advancement of a Plantation, are those natural riches of Food, Apparel, and Habitations. If the first be regarded, there are few of the Irish Commonality but are skilfull in Husbandry, and more exact that any English in the Husbandry proper to that Country. If the second, there are few of the Women but are skilfull in dressing Hemp and Flax, and making of Linnen and Woollen Cloth. If the third, it is believed, to every hundred Men there are five or six Masons and Carpenters at least of that Nation, and these more handy and ready in building ordinary Houses, and much more prudent in supplying the defects of Instruments and Materials, than English Artificers. Since then 1000 Acres of Land (Plantation measure) being but of indifferent goodnes, with the rest of the Lands in Ireland, shall require as much Stock as whose original price and charge of transporting will amount to 1500 or 2000l. Since likewise Husbandmen and Tradesmen that are laborious, can subsist by their Labours and Trades comfortably in England, and most will not probably leave their native soyl on any terms; and those who will, on extraordinary terms. It is necessary consequent, that the transplantation of the Irish doth not onely deprive the Planter of those aforementioned advantages, but also so exceedingly aggravates his charge and difficulty in planting (by his irredeemable want of whatever he brings not with him out of England) that his charge will manifestly appear to be more than his profit; and it is not easily conceivable how or when five or six Millions of Acres are like to be planted or inhabited upon so clear an account of expence and loss.

Objection. Against all these advantages it is onely objected, that the English may degenerate, and turn Irish, unless a separation by transplanting the one from the other be observed; and to this purpose experience of former ages is urged.

Answer. Of future contingents no man can pass a determinate judgement; but if we speak morally, and as probably may be, it may much rather be expected that the Irish will turn English. Those Topicks before instanced concerning Religion do infer it as very probable, that with the Religion professed by the English, it is likely they may receive their Manners also. And this is confirmed by experience of all that Nation who embraced the Protestant Religion. And as to the former experience, even that likewise seems to add weight to this expectation, because whatever inducements perswaded the English formerly to turn Irish, the same more strongly invite the Irish now to turn English.

1. When England was reformed from Popery, no care was took, nor endeavours used to spread the reformation in Ireland; by which means the English Colonies there continued still Papists, and so in Religion were alienated from the English, and fastened to the Irish: But now it being most probable that most of the Irish will embrace the Protestant Profession, it is upon the same grounds most probable that they will embrace the English Manners.

2. Former Conquests of Ireland were either the undertakings of some private persons, or so managed by publick persons, that the power and profitable advantages of the Land remained in the hands of the Irish: But as in the present Conquest the Nation of England is engaged, so is the power and advantage of the Land in the hands of the English. For instance.

   1. The Irish were the Body of the People, and too potent for the English (especially at such times as the troubles of England caused the Armies to be called thence, which Historians observe to have been the times of degeneration, as a means to self-preservation.

   2. The Irish were the general Proprietors of Land, and an English Planter must be their Tenant; and the temptation of this relation and dependence is very prevelant (at least) to bring the Posterity to a complyance, and that to a likeness, and that to a sameness.

   3. The Irish were the chiefly estated, and the intermarriages with them were accompanied with greater Friends and Fortunes than with the En-

glish, who were not onely Strangers, but for the most part (till of late years) comparatively poor.

4. The Lawyers were Irish, the Jurors Irish, most of the Judges Irish, and the major part of their Parliament Irish; and in all Disputes between Irish and English, the Irish were sure of the favour.

But now the condition of Ireland is (through Gods goodness) so altered, that all these Arguments are much more forcibly perswasive, that the Irish will turn English.

3. The frequent use of the Irish Language in all commerce, and the English habituating themselves to that Language, was one great means of Irishying the English Colonies: But now the Language will be generally English; and if the Irish be mingled with the English, they will probably learn and be habituated to the English Tongue, which is found by experience to be suddenly learn'd by the Irish; whereas if they be transplanted into Connaught, the distinction of the English and Irish tongue will not onely be continued, but also the Irish left without means of learning English.

Concerning the Security of the English, and Their Interests

1. For the present, This Plantation will necessarily make many Tories. For,

1. Many inhabitants, who are able to subsist on their Gardens in their present Habitations, are unable to subsist in travelling to Connaught, and for the present to derive subsistence from the wast Lands of Connaught, when they come thither; and therefore will rather choose the hazard of Torying, than the apparent danger of starving.

2. Many Irish Masters will disburthen themselves of their attendants and servants on this occasion, in regard the charge of retaining them will be greater, and their imployment of them less, both in the journey, and journeys end; and these servants, however disposed to honest labour and industry, yet being thus secluded from the means of subsistence, necessity will enforce to be Tories.

3. The range of the Tories will be so great, and advantages thereby of securing themselves and Cattel so much, that until the whole Land be otherwise planted, it will not be probable that our Armies should either have intelligence of their places of abode in their fastnesse, or be enabled to find them, those who are acquainted with the service of Tory hunting, know how much of this difficulty. And impossible it is, that those parts of the Land which adjoin to those Fastnesses, should

be planted in many ages, if Tories (secured in them) make incursions on such as shall plant.

4. The Irish numbers (now abated by Famin, Pestilence, the Sword, and Forein Transportations) are not like to overgrow the English as formerly, and so no fear of their being obnoxious to them hereafter: but being mixed with, they are likelyer to be swallowed up by the English, and incorporated into them; so that a few Centuries will know no difference present, fear none to come, and scarce believe what were pas'd. The chiefest and eminentest of the Nobility, and many of the Gentry, have taken Conditions from the King of Spain, and have transported at several times 40000 of the most active spirited men, most acquainted with danger and discipline of War, and inured to hardness; the Priests are all banished; the remaining part of the whole Nation are scarce the sixth part of what were at the beginning of the War, so great a devastation has God and Man brought upon that Land, and so far are they from those formidable numbers they are (by those that are strangers to Ireland) conceived to be; and that handfull of Natives left, are poor laborious usefull simple Creatures, whose design is onely to live, and their Families, the manner of which is so low, that it is design rather to be pitied, than by any body feared, envyed, or hindered.

Reprinted in STRANGERS TO THAT LAND: BRITISH PERCEPTIONS OF IRELAND FROM THE REFORMATION TO THE FAMINE, *edited by* Andrew Hadfield *and* John McVeagh (1994), *pp.* 124–127.

~

FROM *THE INTEREST OF ENGLAND IN THE IRISH TRANSPLANTATION STATED*

1655

Richard Lawrence

Richard Lawrence was a colonel in the Cromwellian army in Ireland from 1651 to 1659. He published a pamphlet in answer to Vincent Gookin's Great Case of Transplantation Discussed and argued in favor of the plan to move the Irish west of the Shannon. The plan was virtually impossible to implement, and after King Charles II was restored to the throne in 1660, it was abandoned.

SEE ALSO Cromwellian Conquest; Land Settlements from 1500 to 1690; Rebellion of 1641

Therefore consider what punishment it was they did incur by their offence, which will be the better done, First, by considering the offence it self, which was the most horrid causless Rebellion, and bloudy Massacre that hath been heard of in these last Ages of the world, and the Offenders not particular persons or parties of the Irish Nation (for that had been another case) but the whole Irish Nation it self consisting of Nobility, Gentry, Clergy, and Commonality, are all engaged as one Nation in the Quarell, to root out and wholly extirpate all English Protestants from amongst them, who had (for the most of them) as legal and just right to their Estates and interest in Ireland, as themselves, many of them possessing nothing, but what they had lawfully purchased, and dearly paid for, from the Irish, and others of them possessing by right of grant from the Crown of England, time out of minde what they did enjoy, and the Irish Nation enjoying equal privileges with the English, if not much more . . . so that they were under no provocation, nor oppression, under the English government at that time when the bloudy Rebells in 1641 committed that inhumane Massacre upon a company of poor, unarmed, peaceable, harmless people living quietly amongst them, wherein neither Age nor Sex were spared . . . in which rebellious practices and cruel War they persisted to the ruining of that flourishing Nation, and making of it near a waste Wilderness, thereby necessitating England (in the time of its own Trouble) to maintain an Army in Ireland, to preserve a footing there, and at last forced them to send over and maintain a potent Army, greatly exhausting their Treasure and People to recover their Interest out of the hands of this bloudy Generation, and bring the Offenders to condign punishment . . . Ireland having cost England more money and men to recover it, than it is or ever is like to be worth to them many a time over, and for England now at the close of all to heal up this wound slightly, and to leave the Interest and People of England in Ireland at as eminent uncertainties as ever, (whereby the posterity of this present Generation (if not themselves) shall after a few years to come to be at the mercy and disposition of the bloudy people again (except a few inwalled Towns and Garisons) if it may be any lawfull and prudent means prevented) I judg those who are wise and ingenious of the Irish themselves would acknowledg it a weakness, and great neglect in those in whose hand God hath placed the power, much more all true hearted Englishmen who are so much concerned therein.

And therefore it remains now to prove that the work of Transplantation (at least so far as it is at present declared and intended) is the most probable means to secure the present English Interest in Ireland, and obtain one there able to secure it self without such immediate dependence upon England (as hitherto hath been) for men and money to effect the same.

And for the better making out of this:

First, confident wherein the advantage of the Irish above the English consisted at the first breaking out of the late horrid Rebellion, whereby the many thousands of English People then inhabiting in that Countrey became so inconsiderable either as to the preservation of their own Lives and Estates, or the publick Interest of England there; which chiefly proceeded from their not being imbodied, or from their not cohabiting together, whereby they might have been in a capacity to imbody, they being scattered up and down the whole Nation, here and there, a few families, being thereby wholly subjected to the mercy of the Rabble Irish, to the general destruction and ruine of them, before the Enemy had either Army, Arms, or Ammunition, more than Skeanes and Stayes, whereas had those English that were then in Ireland been cohabiting together in one entire Plantation, or in several Plantations, so they had been but entire Colonies of themselves, and Masters of the Countrey in which they lived, the Irish would hardly have had confidence to have attempted a War, much less a Massacre upon them . . . Whereas by their promiscuous and scattered inhabiting among the Irish, who were in all places far the greatest number and in most a hundred to one, they were even as sheep prepared for the slaughter, that the very Cripples and Beggars of several of the Countreys where they lived (if they toke against them) were able to destroy them. . . .

And therefore I would propose (as essential to the security of the English interest and People in Ireland) that the England inhabiting in that Nation should live together in distinct Plantations or Colonies, separated from the Irish, and (so far as the natural advantage of the Countrey, or their own ability will afford it) to maintain frontier Garrisons, upon Lines or Passes, for the security of ever Plantation, and to admit no more Irish Papists (that they had not eminent grounds to believe were or would be faithful to the English interest) to live within them . . . it is my judgement it would not be safe to admit in any English Plantation, above the fifth part to be Irish Papists, either in the capacity of Tenants or Servants, unless in such cases where two Justices of the Peace, with two godly Ministers of that English Plantation should receive satisfaction of their being converted to the Protestant Religion, and English Civil Manners and Customs.

For though the Lord hath been pleased so far to own the English Cause and Interest in the late War, that they have been able to engage them with far less numbers, that one hath put ten, and ten one hundred to flight, yet in the work or surprisings and unexpected assaults and inroads upon the English, the Irish have been usually more expect and vigilant, for the Irish are naturally a timorous, suspicious, watchfull People; and on the other hand, the English are a confident, credulous, careless People, as our daily experience in Ireland teacheth us. And therefore if their numbers should be equal, that advantage which they would have of their Irish Neighbors to correspond with them, and fall into their assistance, would much add to their encouragement to attempt mischief upon the English, with or among whom they lived, though they were far less numbers. And if this be not admitted, that it is essential in order to the safety of the English interest and people, that their Plantation should consist of many more English than Irish (as above), then there is a necessity (in order thereto) that some of the Irish should be removed out of some parts of Ireland, to make way for the English Plantations, and if so, then a Plantation must be admitted to be essential in order to the security of the English interest and People there. . . .

[A]s to that concerning Religion, where he [Gookin] endeavoureth to hold forth that the not transplanting of the Irish, would no ways hazard the perverting of the English, and would be much in order to the converting of the Irish, which the Transplantation (saith he) will wholly prevent . . . I do not judge the Discussor can suppose that the continuing of the popish, superstitious Souldier and Proprietor among and over the common people will be a means to make way for their conversion to the Protestant Religion, more than to continue their Priests, but it is so evident it will much rather tend to the contrary, even shutting that door of hope, that may otherwise be opened to that work, that to spend time about arguing of it would not be to profit, and besides require more Lines than I am willing to swell this paper into, it being much larger already than I intended it.

Reprinted in STRANGERS TO THAT LAND: BRITISH PERCEPTIONS OF IRELAND FROM THE REFORMATION TO THE FAMINE, *edited by Andrew Hadfield and John McVeagh (1994), pp. 128–131.*

~

TREATY OF LIMERICK

1691

These articles were the terms under which the garrison of Limerick, the last significant stronghold of troops loyal to the Catholic King James II, surrendered in 1691. His Protestant adversary, William III, was willing to make a generous settlement in the interest of larger geopolitical

considerations, but William's Irish Protestant supporters were outraged. Not until 1697 did the Irish parliament ratify the treaty, and then only without the first article and the inadvertently omitted wording to protect the retainers of the Catholic leaders who were surrendering. For generations, Catholics complained bitterly, and understandably, about these omissions, but the treaty did successfully protect from confiscation the properties of hundreds of Catholic gentry in the west and southwest.

SEE ALSO Jacobites and the Williamite Wars

THE CIVIL ARTICLES OF LIMERICK

Articles agreed upon the third of October 1691 between the Right Honourable Sir Charles Porter knight and Thomas Conningsby Esq., lords justices of Ireland, and his excellency the Baron De Ginckle, lieutenant-general, and commander-in-chief of the English army, on the one part, and the Right Honourable Patrick earl of Lucan, Piercy Viscount Gallmoy, Colonel Nicholas Purcel, Colonel Nicholas Cusack, Sir Toby Butler, Colonel Garret Dillon, and Colonel John Brown, on the other part, in the behalf of the Irish inhabitants in the city and county of Limerick, the counties of Clare, Kerry, Cork, Sligo, and Mayo.

In consideration of the surrender of the city of Limerick and other agreements made between the said Lieutenant-General Ginckle, the governor of the city of Limerick, and the generals of the Irish army, bearing date with these presents, for the surrender of the said city, and submission of the said army, it is agreed, that:

1. The Roman Catholics of this kingdom, shall enjoy such privileges in the exercise of their religion, as are consistent with the laws of Ireland, or as they did enjoy in the reign of King Charles II, and their majesties, as soon as their affairs will permit them to summon a parliament in this kingdom, will endeavour to procure the said Roman Catholics such farther security in that particular, as may preserve them from any disturbance upon the account of their said religion.

2. All the inhabitants or residents of Limerick, or any other garrison now in the possession of the Irish, and all officers and soldiers, now in arms, under any commission of King James, or those authorized by him to grant the same in the several counties of Limerick, Clare, Kerry, Cork, and Mayo, or any of them, and all the commissioned officers in their majesties' quarters, that belong to the Irish regiments, now in being, that are treated with, and who are not prisoners of war or have taken protection, and who shall return and submit

to their majesties' obedience, and their and every of their heirs, shall hold, possess and enjoy all and every their estates of free-hold, and inheritance, and all the rights, titles, and interests, privileges and immunities, which they, and every, or any of them held, enjoyed, or were rightfully and lawfully entitled to in the reign of King Charles II, or at any time since, by the laws and statutes that were in force in the said reign of King Charles II, and shall be put in possession, by order of the government, of such of them as are in the king's hands or the hands of his tenants, without being put to any suit or trouble therein; and all such estates shall be freed and discharged from all arrears of crown-rents, quit-rents, and other public charges incurred and become due since Michael-mas 1688, to the day of the date hereof. And all persons comprehended in this article, shall have, hold, and enjoy all their goods and chattels, real and personal, to them, or any of them belonging, and remaining either in their own hands, or the hands of any persons whatsoever, in trust for or for the use of them, or any of them; and all, and every the said persons, of what profession, trade, or calling soever they be, shall and may use, exercise and practise their several and respective professions, trades and callings, as freely as they did use, exercise and enjoy the same in the reign of King Charles II, provided, that nothing in this article contained, be construed to extend to or restore any forfeiting person now out of the kingdom, except what are hereafter comprised. Provided also, that no person whatsoever shall have or enjoy the benefit of this article, that shall neglect or refuse to take the oath of allegiance made by act of parliament in England, in the first year of the reign of their present majesties, when thereunto required.

3. All merchants, or reputed merchants of the city of Limerick, or of any other garrison, now possessed by the Irish, or of any town or place in the counties of Clare, or Kerry, who are absent beyond the seas, that have not bore arms since their majesties' declaration in February 1688, shall have the benefit of the second article, in the same manner as if they were present, provided such merchants, and reputed merchants, do repair into this kingdom within the space of eight months from the date hereof.

4. The following officers, viz. Colonel Simon Lutterel, Captain Rowland White, Maurice Eustace of Yermanstown, Chievers of Maystown, commonly called Mount-Leinster, now belonging to the regiments in the aforesaid garrisons and quarters of the Irish army, who were beyond the seas, and sent thither upon affairs of their respective regiments, or the army in general, shall have the benefit and advantage of the second article, provided they return hither within the space of eight months from the date of these presents, and submit to their majesties' government, and take the above-mentioned oath.

5. That all and singular, the said persons comprised in the second and third articles, shall have a general pardon of all attainders, outlawries, treasons, misprisions of treason, praemunires, felonies, trespasses, and other crimes and misdemeanours whatsoever, by them or any of them committed since the beginning of the reign of King James II; and if any of them are attained by parliament, the lords justices and general, will use their best endeavours to get the same repealed by parliament, and the outlawries to be reversed gratis, all but writing-clerks' fees.

6. And whereas these present wars have drawn on great violences on both parts, and that if leave were given to the bringing all sorts of private actions, the animosities would probably continue, that have been too long on foot, and the public disturbances last; for the quieting and settling therefore of this kingdom, and avoiding those inconveniences which would be the necessary consequence of the contrary, no person or persons whatsoever, comprised in the foregoing articles, shall be sued, molested, or impleaded at the suit of any party or parties whatsoever, for any trespasses by them committed, or for any arms, horses, money, goods, chattels, merchandises, or provisions whatsoever, by them seized or taken, during the time of the war. And no person or persons whatsoever, in the second or third articles comprised, shall be sued, impleaded, or made accountable for the rents or mean rates of any lands, tenements, or houses by him or them received or enjoyed in this kingdom, since the beginning of the present war, to the day of the date hereof, nor for any waste or trespass by him or them committed in any such lands, tenements, or houses; and it is also agreed, that this article shall be mutual, and reciprocal, on both sides.

7. Every nobleman and gentleman, comprised in the said second and third article, shall have liberty to ride with a sword, and case of pistols, if they think fit, and keep a gun in their houses, for the defence of the same or for fowling.

8. The inhabitants and residents in the city of Limerick, and other garrisons, shall be permitted to remove their goods, chattels, and provisions, out of the same, without being viewed and searched, or paying any manner of duties, and shall not be compelled to leave the houses or lodgings they now have, for the space of six weeks next ensuing the date hereof.

9. The oath to be administered to such Roman Catholics as submit to their majesties' government, shall be the oath abovesaid, and no other.

10. No person or persons, who shall at any time hereafter break these articles, or any of them, shall

thereby make, or cause any other person or persons to forfeit or lose the benefit of the same.

11. The lords justices and general do promise to use their utmost endeavours, that all the persons comprehended in the above-mentioned articles, shall be protected and defended from all arrests and executions for debt or damage, for the space of eight months, next ensuing the date hereof.

12. Lastly, the lords justices and general do undertake, that their majesties will ratify these articles within the space of eight months, or sooner, and use their utmost endeavours, that the same shall be ratified and confirmed in parliament.

13. And whereas Colonel John Brown stood indebted to several Protestants, by judgments of record, which appearing to the late government, the Lord Tyrconnel, and Lord Lucan, took away the effects the said John Brown had to answer the said debts, and promised to clear the said John Brown of the said debts, which effects were taken for the public use of the Irish and their army, for freeing the said Lord Lucan of his said engagement, passed on their public account, for payment of the said Protestants, and for preventing the ruin of the said John Brown and for satisfaction of his creditors, at the instance of the Lord Lucan, and the rest of the persons aforesaid, it is agreed, that the said lords justices, and the said baron de Ginckle, shall intercede with the king and parliament, to have the estates secured to Roman Catholics, by articles and capitulation in this kingdom, charged with, and equally liable to the payment of so much of the said debts, as the said Lord Lucan, upon stating accounts with the said John Brown, shall certify under his hand, that the effects taken from the said Brown amount unto; which account is to be, stated, and the balance certified by the said Lord Lucan in one and twenty days after the date hereof:

For the true performance hereof, we have hereunto set out hands,

Char. Potter, Tho. Coningsby, Bar. De. Ginckle. Present, Scravemore, H. Maccay, T. Talmash.

And whereas the said city of Limerick hath been since, in pursuance of the said articles, surrendered unto us. Now know ye, that we having considered of the said articles are graciously pleased hereby to declare, that we do for us, our heirs, and successors, as far as in us lies, ratify and confirm the same, and every clause, matter and thing therein contained. And as to such parts thereof, for which an act of parliament shall be found to be necessary, we shall recommend the same to be made good by parliament, and shall give our royal assent to any bill or bills that shall be passed by our two houses of parliament to that purpose. And whereas it appears unto us, that it was agreed between the parties to the said articles, that after the words, "Limerick, Clare, Kerry, Cork, Mayo," or any of them in the second of such articles, the words following; viz. "And all such as are under their protection in the said counties," should be inserted, and be part of the said articles. Which words having been casually omitted by the writer, the omission was not discovered till after the said articles were signed, but was taken notice of before the second town was surrendered; and that our said justices, and general or one of them, did promise that the said clause should be made good, it being within the intention of the capitulation, and inserted in the foul draught thereof. Our further will and pleasure is, and we do hereby ratify and confirm the said omitted words, viz. "and all such as are under their protection in the said counties" hereby for us, our heirs and successors, ordaining and declaring, that all and every person and persons therein concerned, shall and may have, receive, and enjoy the benefit thereof, in such and the same manner, as if the said words had been inserted in their proper place, in the said second article, any omission, defect, or mistake in the said second article, in any wise notwithstanding. Provided always, and our will and pleasure is, that these our letters patents shall be enrolled in our court of chancery in our said kingdom of Ireland, within the space of one year next ensuing. In witness, etc. Witness Ourself at Westminster, the twenty-fourth day of February, Anno Regni Regis and Reginae Guilielmi and Mariae Quarto per breve de privato sigillo. . . .

Reprinted in IRISH HISTORICAL DOCUMENTS, 1172–1922, edited by Edmund Curtis and R. B. McDowell (1943), pp. 171–175.

≈

FROM *THE MEMOIRS OF EDMUND LUDLOW*

1698

Edmund Ludlow was a regicide (one of those held responsible for the trial, conviction, and execution of Charles I) and a republican associate of Cromwell who broke with him when, in 1655, he became lord protector. He was a lieutenant general of horse in Ireland and a commissioner for civil government from 1650 to 1655. At the Restoration he escaped to Switzerland. His memoirs, published in 1698, describe, among other things, the way confiscated Irish land was parceled out in the 1650s to repay soldiers for their services and investors (called "adventurers") for their loans to finance the campaign to reconquer Ireland.

SEE ALSO Cromwellian Conquest; Land Settlements from 1500 to 1690

The Commissioners also by order of the Parliament published a declaration to inform the publick, and particularly the adventurers, who had advanced money upon the Irish lands, that the war in Ireland was concluded. This they did as well that the said adventurers might have what was justly due to them, as that the poor wasted country of Ireland might have the assistance of their own purses and labour, to recover the stock and growth of the land; the Irish having all along eaten out the heart and vigour of the ground, and of late much more than ever, being in daily apprehension of being removed.

All arrears due to the English army in Ireland were satisfied by the Parliament out of the estates forfeited by the rebels, which were delivered to them at the same rates with the first adventurers. In this transaction those of the army shewed great partiality, by confining the satisfaction of arrears only to such as were in arms in August 1649, which was the time when the English army commanded by Lieutenant-General Cromwel arrived in Ireland; and tho the hardships endured by those who were in arms before had been much greater, yet nothing could be obtained but such a proportion of lands in the county of Wicklo, and elsewhere, as was not sufficient to clear the fourth part of what was due to them. Those who solicited the affairs of the army in Ireland with the Parliament, having perswaded the adventurers that there were forfeited lands enough in one moiety of nine principle counties, they accepted of them for their satisfaction, and the other moiety was assigned by the Act for the satisfaction of the souldiers; the rest of Ireland was also disposed of, only the province of Connaught was reserved for the Irish under the qualifications agreed upon by the Parliament; according to which they were to be put into possession of the several proportions of land which had been promised them in the said province; that so the adventurers, souldiers, and others to whom the Parliament should assign their lands, might plant without disturbance, or danger of being corrupted by intermixing with the natives in marriages or otherwise, which by the experience of former times the English had been found to be, rather than to have bettered the Irish either in religion or good man-

ners: and that the natives being divided by the River Shannon from the other provinces, and having garisons placed round and amongst them in the most proper and convenient stations, they might not have those opportunities to prejudice the English as formerly they had. An Act being drawn up to this purpose, the parliament passed it, reserving the counties of Dublin, Kildare, Carlo and Cork, (together with the remaining part of the lands formerly belonging to the Bishops, Deans and Chapters of Ireland, whereof some had been already applied, to augment the revenues of the College of Dublin) to be disposed of as the Parliament should think fit.

The forfeited lands were divided between the adventurers and souldiers by lot, according to an estimate taken of the number of acres in the respective counties, in conformity to an order from the Commissioners of Parliament; by whom were appointed sub-commissioners to judg of the qualifications of each person, and others, who upon certificate from the sub-commissioners for determining qualifications, were required to set out so much land in the province of Connaught as belonged to every one by virtue of the said Act. They also established a committee to sit at Dublin to receive and adjudg all claims of English and others to any lands, limiting a time within which they were obliged to bring in and make appear their respective claims to be legal; to the end that the adventurers, souldiers, and others, might be at a certainty, and after such a time free from any molestation in the possession of their lands; and that none through ignorance or absence might be surprized, they prorogued the said time twice or thrice to a longer day.

Reprinted in STRANGERS TO THAT LAND: BRITISH PERCEPTIONS OF IRELAND FROM THE REFORMATION TO THE FAMINE, *edited by Andrew Hadfield and John McVeagh* (1994), *pp. 131–133.*

∽

AN ACT TO PREVENT THE FURTHER GROWTH OF POPERY

1704

This statute is the most important of the so-called penal laws that were enacted against Catholics beginning in 1695. Its elaborate provisions concerning the disposition of land that had not been confiscated from Catholics during the upheavals of the seventeenth century reflect the fact that propertied Catholics were the principal target of such legislation. Property was the key to political power in this period.

SEE ALSO Catholic Merchants and Gentry from 1690 to 1800; Council of Trent and the Catholic Mission; Eighteenth-Century Politics: 1690 to 1714—Revolution Settlement; Penal Laws; Politics: 1690 to 1800—A Protestant Kingdom; Religious Orders: Men; Religious Orders: Women; Religion: Since 1690; Roman Catholic Church: 1690 to 1829

AN ACT TO PREVENT THE FURTHER GROWTH OF POPERY

I. Whereas divers emissaries of the church of Rome, popish priests, and other persons of the persuasion, taking advantage of the weakness and ignorance of some of her Majesty's subjects, or the extreme sickness and decay of their reason and senses, in the absence of friends and spiritual guides, do daily endeavour to persuade and pervert them from the Protestant religion, to the great dishonour of Almighty God, the weakening of the true religion, by his blessing so happily established in this realm, to the disquieting the peace and settlement, and discomfort of many particular families thereof: and in further manifestation of their hatred and aversion to the said true religion, many of the said persons, so professing the popish religion in this kingdom, have refused to make provisions for their own children for no other reason but their being of the Protestant religion; and also have by cunning devices and contrivances found out ways to avoid and elude the intents of an act of Parliament, made in the ninth year of the reign of the late King William the third for preventing Protestants inter-marrying with papists; and of several other laws made for the security of the Protestant religion; and whereas many persons so professing the popish religion have it in their power to raise divisions among Protestants, by voting in elections for members of Parliament, and also have it in their power to use other ways and means tending to the destruction of the Protestant interest in this kingdom; for remedy of which great mischiefs, and to prevent the like evil practices for the future, be it enacted by the Queen's most excellent Majesty, by and with the advice and consent of the lords spiritual and temporal and commons in this present Parliament assembled, and by authority of the same, that if any person or persons from and after the twenty-fourth day of March, in this present year of our Lord one thousand seven hundred and three, shall seduce, persuade, or pervert any person or persons professing, or that shall profess, the Protestant religion, to renounce, forsake, and abjure the same, and to profess the popish religion, or reconcile him or them to the church of Rome, then and in such case every such person and persons so seducing, as also every such Protes-

tant and Protestants, who shall be so seduced, perverted, and reconciled to popery, shall for the said offences, being thereof lawfully convicted, incur the danger and penalty of premunire, mentioned in the statute of premunire made in England in the sixteenth year of the reign of King Richard the second; and if any person or persons being a papist, or professing the popish religion, shall from and after the said twenty-fourth day of March send, or cause, or willingly suffer, to be sent or conveyed any child under the age of one and twenty years, except sailors, ship-boys, or the apprentice or factor of some merchant in trade of merchandise, into France, or any other parts beyond the seas, out of her Majesty's dominions, without the special license of her Majesty, her heirs or successors, or of her or their chief governor or governors of this kingdom, and four or more of her or their privy council of this realm, under their hands in that behalf first had and obtained, he, she, and they, so sending or conveying or causing to be sent or conveyed away, such child, shall incur the pains, penalties, and forfeitures mentioned in an act made in the seventh year of his late Majesty King William, entitled *An Act to restrain foreign education.*

III. And to the end that no child or children of popish parent or parents, who have professed or embraced, or who shall profess or embrace, the Protestant religion, or are or shall be desirous or willing to be instructed and educated therein, may in the life time of such popish parent or parents, for fear of being cast off or disinherited by them, or for want of a fitting maintenance or future provision, be compelled and necessitated to embrace the popish religion, or be deterred or withheld from owning or professing the Protestant religion; be it further enacted by the authority aforesaid, That from and after the said twenty-fourth of March, one thousand seven hundred and three, upon complaint in the high court of Chancery by bill founded on this act against such popish parent, it shall and may be lawful for the said court to make such order for the maintenance of every such Protestant child, not maintained by such popish parent suitable to the degree and ability of such parent, and to the age of such child, and also for the portion of every such Protestant child, to be paid at the decease of such popish parent, as that court shall adjudge fit, suitable to the degree and ability of such parent; and in case the eldest son and heir of such popish parent shall be a Protestant, that then from the time of the enrollment in high court of Chancery of a certificate of the bishop of the diocess, in which he shall inhabit, testifying his being a Protestant, and conforming himself to the church of Ireland as by law established, such popish parent shall become, and shall be, only tenant for life of all the real estate, whereof such popish parent shall be then seized in fee-tail or fee-simple, and the reversion in fee shall be vested in such eldest son being a Protestant; subject nevertheless to all such debts and real incumbrances at the time of the enrollment of such certificate charging such estate, and subject also to such maintenances and portions for the other children, as well Protestants as papists of such popish parents then born, or after to be born, as the said court of Chancery in manner aforesaid shall order for them respectively; such portions not to exceed the value of one-third part of the inheritance of such estate, which shall be held and enjoyed accordingly, discharged of all voluntary settlements made by such parent, and also of all sales and incumbrances made by him after such enrollment of such certificate: and the said court of Chancery is hereby required to take care that distinct rolls be kept for enrollment of such certificates, which shall publicly hang up or lie in some public office or place belonging to the said court, for the purpose by the said court to be appointed, where all persons may at all seasonable times resort to and peruse the same without fee or reward; and for the enrollment of each and every such certificate the sum of six pence, and no more, shall be paid.

IV. And that care may be taken for the education of children in the communion of the Church of Ireland as by law established; be it enacted by the authority aforesaid, that no person of the popish religion shall or may be guardian unto, or have the tuition or custody of, any orphan, child or children, under the age of twenty-one years; but that the same, where the person having or entitled to the guardianship of such orphan, child or children, is or shall be a papist, shall be disposed of by the high court of Chancery to some near relation of such orphan, child, or children, being a Protestant, and conforming himself to the Church of Ireland as by law established, to whom the estate cannot defend, in case there shall be any such Protestant relation fit to have the education of such child; otherwise to some other Protestant conforming himself as aforesaid, who is hereby required to use his utmost care to educate and bring up such child or minor in the Protestant religion until the age of twenty one years: and the said court of Chancery is hereby empowered and required, and by virtue of this act it shall and may be lawful for the said court, to make such order for the educating in the Protestant religion the child and children of any papist, where either the father or the mother of such child or children is or shall be a Protestant till the age of eighteen years of every such child, as to that court shall seem meet; and in order thereto to limit and appoint where, and in what manner, and by whom, such child or children shall be educated; and the father of such child or children shall pay the charges of such education as shall be directed by the said court; and such child or children shall and may be taken from such popish parent for education according

to such order: and if any person or person, being a papist or professing the popish religion, shall take upon him or them the guardianship or tuition of any orphan, child, or child, contrary hereunto, he and they, so taking upon him or them the guardianship or tuition of any such child, shall forfeit the sum of five hundred pounds to be recovered by action of debt, bill, plaint or information, wherein no protection, essoigne, or wager of law shall be allowed, or but one imparlance; the whole benefit of the said forfeitures to be, and is hereby, given to the Blue-Coat Hospital in the city of Dublin.

VI. And be it further enacted by the authority aforesaid, that every papist, or person professing the popish religion, shall from and after the said twenty-fourth day of March be disabled, and is hereby made incapable, to buy and purchase either in his or their own name, or in the name of any other person or person to his or her use, or in trust for him or her, any manors, lands, tenements or hereditaments, or any rents or profits out of the same, or any leases or terms thereof, other than any term of years not exceeding thirty-one years, whereon a rent not less than two-thirds of the improved yearly value, at the time of the making such leases of the tenements leased, shall be reserved and made payable during such term; and that all singular estates, terms, or any other interests or profits whatsoever, other than such leases, not exceeding thirty-one years as aforesaid, of, in, or out of such lands, tenements, or hereditaments, from and after the said twenty-fourth day of March, to be bought and purchased by or for the use or behoof of any such papist, or person or persons professing the popish religion, or upon any trust or confidence mediately or immediately to or for the benefit, use, or advantage of any such person or persons professing the popish religion, shall be utterly void and of none effect to all intents, constructions, and purposes whatsoever.

VII. And be it further enacted by the authority aforesaid, that from and after the first day of February, in this present year of our Lord one thousand seven hundred and three, no papist, or person professing the popish religion, who shall not within six months after he and she shall become entitled to enter, or to take, or have the profits by descent, or by virtue of any devise or gift, or of any remainder already limited, or at any time hereafter to be limited, or by virtue of any trust of any lands, tenements, or hereditaments, whereof any Protestant now is, or hereafter shall be, seized in fee simple absolute, or fee-tail, or in such manner that after his death, or the death of him and his wife, the freehold is to come immediately to his son or sons, or issue in tail, if then of the age of eighteen years, or if under, within six months after he shall attain that age, until which time from his being so entitled he shall be under the care of such Protestant relation or person conforming himself as aforesaid, as shall for that purpose be appointed by the high court of Chancery for his being educated in the Protestant religion, become a Protestant, and conform himself to the church now established in this kingdom, shall take any benefit by reason of such descent, devise, gift, remainder, or trust, but from thenceforth during the life of such person, or until he or she do become a Protestant, and conform as aforesaid, the nearest Protestant relation or relations, or other Protestant or Protestants, and his and their heirs, being and continuing Protestants, who shall and would be entitled to the same in case such person professing the popish religion, and not conforming as aforesaid, and all and other intermediate popish relations and popish persons were actually dead; and his and their heirs shall have and enjoy the said lands, tenements, and hereditaments, without being accountable for the profits to be received during such enjoyment thereof; subject nevertheless to such charges, other than such as shall be made by such disabled person, and in such condition as the disabled person would have held and enjoyed the same; the children of papists being to be taken to be papists, till they shall by their conformity to the established church appear to be Protestants; and also subject to such maintenance as the Lord Chancellor, Lord Keeper, or Commissioners of the Great Seal of Ireland, for the time being shall think fit to allow to the children of such papist, until such children attain their respective ages of eighteen years.

X. And be it further enacted by the authority aforesaid, that all lands, tenements, or hereditaments, whereof any papist now is, or hereafter shall be, seized in fee-simple or fee-tail, shall from henceforth, so long as any papist shall be seized of or entitled to the same in fee-simple or fee-tail, be of the nature of gavelkind; and if not sold, aliened, or disposed of by such papist in his life time for good and valuable consideration of money really and bona fide paid, shall for such estate from such papist descend to, and be inherited by, all and every the sons of such papist any way inheritable to such estate, share and share alike, and not descend on or come to the eldest of such sons only, being a papist, as heir at law; and shall in like manner from such respective sons, being papists, descend to and be inherited by all and every the sons of such sons, share and share alike, and not descend to the eldest of such sons, being a papist, as heir at law only; and that for want to issue male of such papist, the same shall descend to all his daughters any way inheritable to such estate in equal proportions; and for want for such issue, among the collateral kindred of such papist, of the kin of his father, any way inheritable to such estate in equal degree; and for want of such kindred, to the collateral kindred of

such papist of the kin of his mother, any way inheritable to such estate, and not otherwise; notwithstanding any grant, settlement, or disposition by will or otherwise, that shall be made by such papist, otherwise than such sale, alienation, or disposition, to be made by such papist as aforesaid; subject nevertheless to all such debts and real incumbrances at the time of the decease of such papist charging such estate.

XI. Provided nevertheless, it shall and may be lawful to and for such papist to charge such his estate with reasonable maintenances and portions for his daughters, to be raised and paid in such manner as he shall direct.

XII. Provided always, that if the eldest son or heir at law of such papist shall be a Protestant at the time of the decease of such papist, whose heir he shall be, such certificate of such eldest son, being a Protestant, not having been enrolled in the life of such papist, the lands, whereof such papist shall be so seized, shall descend to such eldest son or heir at law according to the rules of the common law of this realm, so as such certificate of the bishop's as aforesaid, be enrolled within three months after the decease of such papist in the said court of Chancery; subject nevertheless to such debts and real incumbrances at the time of the decease of such papist charging such estate: and if the eldest son or heir at law of any such papist, who shall at the time of decease of such papist, whose heir he is, be of the age of one and twenty years, shall become a Protestant and conform himself to the church of Ireland, as by law established, within one years after such decease of such papist, or being then under the age of one and twenty years, shall within one year after he shall attain that age become a Protestant, and conform himself as aforesaid, that then from the time of the enrollment in the court of Chancery of the certificate of the bishop of the diocese, in which he shall inhabit, testifying his being a Protestant, and conforming as aforesaid, in manner aforesaid, such enrollment being made within such year, he shall be entitled to, and shall have, and enjoy from thenceforth the whole real estate of such papist, as he might have done if he had been a Protestant at the time of the decease of such papist, whose heir he is; notwithstanding any grant, settlement, or disposition by will or otherwise, that shall be made by such papist, other than such sale, alienation, or disposition, to be made by such papist as aforesaid; subject nevertheless to such debts and real incumbrances at the decease of such papist charging such estate: and in every case where such eldest son shall be entitled as aforesaid by reason of his being a Protestant, such real estate shall be chargeable and charged with such sum and sums of money for the maintenance and portions of the daughters and younger sons of such papist, as the court of Chancery shall direct and appoint to be raised for them, and shall be raised and paid according to such direction; such portions not to exceed the value of one third part such estate.

XV. Provided always, that no person shall take benefit by this act as a Protestant within the intent and meaning hereof, that shall not conform to the Church of Ireland as by law established, and subscribe the declaration, and also take and subscribe the oath of abjuration following, viz.

I A.B. do solemnly and sincerely, in the presence of God, profess, testify, and declare, that I do believe, that in the sacrament of the Lord's-Supper, there is not any transubstantiation of the elements of bread and wine into the body and blood of Christ, at or after the consecration thereof, by any person whatsoever; and that the invocation or adoration of the Virgin Mary, or any other saint, and the sacrifice of the mass, as they are now used in the church of Rome, are superstitious and idolatrous. And I so solemnly, in the presence of God, profess, testify, and declare, that I do make this declaration, and every part there of, in the plain and ordinary sense of the words read unto me, as they are commonly understood by Protestants, without any evasion equivocation, or mental reservation whatsoever; and without any dispensation already granted me for this purpose by the Pope, or any other authority or person whatsoever, or without any hope of dispensation from any person or authority whatsoever, or without believing that I am, or can, be acquitted before God or man, or absolved of this declaration, or any part thereof, although the Pope or any other person or persons, or power whatsoever should dispense with or annul the same, or declare that it was null and void from the beginning.

I A.B. do truly and sincerely acknowledge, profess, testify, and declare in my conscience, before God and the world, that our Sovereign Lady Queen Anne is lawful and rightful Queen of this realm, and of all other her Majesty's dominions and countries thereunto belonging. And I do solemnly and sincerely declare, that I do believe in my conscience, that the person pretended to be Prince of Wales, during the life of the late King James, and since his decease, pretending to be, and taking upon himself the style and title of King of England, by the name of James the third, hath not any right or title whatsoever to the crown of this realm, or any other the dominions thereto belonging: and I do renounce, refuse, and abjure, any allegiance or obedience to him. And I do swear, that I will bear faith and true allegiance to her Majesty queen Anne, and her will defend to the utmost of my power against all traitorous conspiracies and attempts whatsoever, which shall be made against her

person, crown, or dignity. And I will do my best endeavour to disclose and make known to her Majesty, and her successors, all treasons and traitorous conspiracies, which I shall know to be against her or any of them. And I do faithfully promise to the utmost of my power to support, maintain, and defend the limitation and succession of the crown against him the said James, and all other persons whatsoever, as the same is and stands limited by an act, entitled *An act declaring the rights and liberties of the subject*, and settling the succession of the crown, to her present Majesty, and the heirs of her body being Protestants: and as the same by one other act entitled *An act for the further limitation of the crown*, and better securing the rights and liberties of the subject, is and stands limited, after the decease of her Majesty, and for default of issue of her Majesty, to the princess Sophia, Electoress and Duchess of Hanover, and the heirs of her body being Protestants. And all these things I do plainly and sincerely acknowledge and swear, according to these express words by me spoken, and according to the plain and common sense and understanding of the same words, without any equivocation, mental evasion, or secret reservation whatsoever. And I do make this recognition, acknowledgment, abjuration, renunciation, and promise, heartily, willingly, and truly, upon the true faith of a Christian.

So help me God.

XVII. And be it further enacted by the authority aforesaid, that all and every person and persons, that shall be admitted, entered, placed, or taken into any office or offices, civil or military, or shall receive any pay, salary, fee, or wages belonging to or by reason of any office or place of trust, by reason of any patent or grant from her Majesty, or shall have command or place of trust from or under her Majesty, or any of her predecessors or successors, or by her or their authority, or by authority derived from her or them, within this realm of Ireland, after the first day of Easter-term aforesaid, shall take the said oaths and repeat the said declaration, and subscribe the said oaths and declaration, in one of the said respective courts in the next term, or at the general quarter-sessions for that county, barony, or place, where he or they shall reside, next after his or their respective admittance or admittances into any such office or offices as aforesaid, after such his or their admittance or admittances into the said office or offices, employment or employments aforesaid, between the hours aforesaid, and no other; during which time all proceedings shall cease aforesaid: and that all and every such person or persons to be admitted after the said first day of Easter-term as aforesaid, not having taken the said oaths in one of the said courts, and subscribed the same and the said declaration as aforesaid, shall in the next term, or at the general quarter-sessions for that county, barony, or place, where he or they shall reside, next after such his or their respective admittance or admittances into any of the said respective offices or employments aforesaid, after such his or their admittance or admittances into the said office or offices, employment or employments aforesaid, take the said several and respective oaths, and make and repeat the said declaration, and subscribe his name, or make his mark, under the said oaths and declaration, in one of the respective courts aforesaid, between the hours aforesaid, and no other; during which time all proceedings shall cease as aforesaid: and all and every such person and persons, so to be admitted as aforesaid, shall also receive the sacrament of the Lord's Supper according to the usage of the Church of Ireland, within three months after his or their admittance in or receiving their said authority and employments in some public church, upon the Lord's-day commonly called Sunday, immediately after divine service and sermon: and every of the said respective persons, touching whom the said several provisions are here before made, in the respective court, where he or she takes the said oaths, shall first deliver a certificate of such his or her receiving the said sacrament as aforesaid, under the hands of the respective minister and churchwardens; and shall then make proof of the truth thereof by two credible witnesses at the least, upon oath: all which shall be enquired of and put upon record in their respective courts.

XVIII. And be it further enacted, that all and every the person or persons aforesaid, who do or shall refuse or neglect to take the said oaths and sacrament, and to deliver such a certificate of his receiving the sacrament as aforesaid, or to subscribe the said declaration as aforesaid, in one of the said courts and places, and at the respective times aforesaid, shall be ipso facto adjudged incapable and disabled in law to all intents and purposes whatsoever to have, occupy, or enjoy the said office or offices, employment or employments, or any part of them, or any matter or thing aforesaid, or any profit or advantage appertaining to them, or any of them; and every such office and place; employment and employments shall be void, and is hereby adjudged void; and that all and every such person or persons, that shall neglect or refuse to take the said oaths or the sacrament as aforesaid, and make and subscribe such declaration, and deliver such certificate of his receiving the sacrament as aforesaid, within the times and in the places aforesaid, and in the manner aforesaid, and yet after such neglect or refusal shall execute any of the said offices or employments after the said times expired, wherein he or they ought to have taken the said oaths, and made and subscribed the said declaration, and being thereupon lawfully convicted in or upon any information, presentment, or indictment in any of her Majesty's courts in Dublin, or at the assizes, every such person and persons shall be disabled from thenceforth to sue or use any action, bill, plaint, or information, in court of law, or to prosecute in any suit in any court of equity, or to be guardian of any child, or executor or administrator of any person, or capable of any legacy or deed or gift, or to bear any office within this realm, and shall forfeit the sum of five hundred pounds, to be recovered by him or them that shall sue for the same; to be prosecuted by any action of debt, suit, bill, plaint, or information in any of her Majesty's said courts in Dublin, wherein no essoign, protection, or wager of law shall lie.

XXIV. And for the preventing Papists having it in their power to breed dissention amongst Protestants by voting at elections of members of Parliament; be it further enacted by the authorities aforesaid, that from and after the twenty-fourth day of March one thousand seven hundred and three, no freeholder, burgess, freeman, or inhabitant of this kingdom, being a Papist or professing the Popish religion, shall at any time hereafter be capable of giving his or their vote for the electing of knights of any shires or counties within this kingdom, or citizens or burgesses to serve in any succeeding Parliament, without first repairing to the general quarter-sessions of the peace to be holden for the counties, cities, or boroughs wherein such Papist do inhabit and dwell, and there voluntarily take the oath of allegiance in the words following, viz.

I A.B. do sincerely promise and swear, that I will be faithful and bear true allegiance to her Majesty Queen Anne.

So help me God, &c.

And also the oath of abjuration aforesaid: and after the taking of the said several oaths aforesaid, the clerk of the peace, officiating in the sessions, shall and is by this act directed to enter the same upon record in the rolls of the said sessions; and is hereby empowered and required to give and deliver to such person or persons, so taking the said oaths, a certificate of such persons so taking and subscribing the same, for which certificate the sum of one shilling, and no more, shall be paid; which said certificate being produced to the high sheriff of the said county, or any of his deputies at any such elections for knights of the shire, and to the respective chief officer or officers of any city, town corporate, or borough in this kingdom, to whom the return of any citizen or burgess to serve in Parliament doth or shall respectively belong, he or they shall be permitted to vote as amply and fully as any Protestant freeholder, burgess, or freeman, or inhabitant of the said county, city, or borough; but in case any freeholder, burgess, freeman, or inhabitant, being a papist, shall appear at any such election as aforesaid, and tender himself to be polled for any candidate, who shall stand for knight of the shire, citizen, or burgess to service in any ensuing Parliament, without producing such certificate as aforesaid to the said sheriff or other officer or officers as aforesaid, the said sheriff or other officer or officers, to whom such return doth or shall respectively belong, shall reject such person, and absolutely refuse to enter his vote, as if he were no freeholder of the said county, or burgess, freeman, or inhabitant of the said city or borough; any former law, statute, or usage, to the contrary notwithstanding.

XXVI. And whereas the superstitions of Popery are greatly increased and upheld by the pretended sanctity of places, especially of a place called Saint Patrick's purgatory in the county of Donegal, and of wells, to which pilgrimages are made by vast numbers at certain seasons; by which not only the peace of the public is greatly disturbed, but the safety of the government also hazarded, by the riotous and unlawful assembling together of many thousands of papists to the said wells and other places; be it further, enacted, That all such meetings and assemblies shall be deemed and adjudged riots and unlawful assemblies, and punishable as such in all or any persons meeting at such places as aforesaid; and all sheriffs, justices of the peace, and other magistrates are hereby required to be diligent in putting the laws in force against all offenders in the above particulars in due execution.

Statutes at Large Passed in the Parliaments Held in Ireland, 1310–1800 (1786–1801), vol. 4, pp. 12–31.

≈

<h1 style="text-align:center">The Declaratory Act</h1>

1720

By the Declaratory Act the British parliament claimed the right to pass legislation binding upon Ireland. Irish patriots never accepted this claim. During the constitutional crisis of the early 1780s the British parliament repealed the act and renounced the claim to legislate for Ireland. The issue, of course, became moot in 1801 when the British and Irish parliaments were merged under the Act of Union.

SEE ALSO Politics: 1690 to 1800—A Protestant Kingdom

AN ACT FOR THE BETTER SECURING THE DEPENDENCY OF THE KINGDOM OF IRELAND ON THE CROWN OF GREAT BRITAIN

Whereas the house of lords of Ireland have of late, against law, assumed to themselves a power and jurisdiction to examine, correct and amend the judgments and decrees of the courts of justice in the kingdom of Ireland; . . . be it declared . . . that the said kingdom of Ireland hath been, is, and of right ought to be subordinate unto and dependent upon the imperial crown of Great Britain, as being inseparably united and annexed thereunto, and that the king's majesty, by and with the advice and consent of the lords spiritual and temporal, and commons of Great Britain in parliament assembled, had, hath, and of right ought to have full power and authority to make laws and statutes of sufficient force and validity to bind the kingdom and people of Ireland.

II. And be it further declared and enacted . . . that the house of lords of Ireland have not, nor of right ought to have any jurisdiction to judge of, affirm or reverse any judgment, sentence or decree, given or made in any court within the said kingdom, and that all proceedings before the said house of lords, upon such judgment, sentence or decrees, are, and are hereby declared to be utterly null and void to all intents and purposes whatsoever.

The Statutes at Large of England and of Great-Britain: From Magna Carta to the Union of the Kingdoms of Great Britain and Ireland (1811), vol. 4, p. 481.

≈

<h1 style="text-align:center">On the Whiteboys</h1>

1769

John Bush

From around 1760 there were frequent disturbances in the south of Ireland by groups calling themselves "Whiteboys." John Bush was an eyewitness to an assemblage of Whiteboys and a shrewd analyst of conflicting accounts of the movement.

SEE ALSO Land Questions; Whiteboys and Whiteboyism

You have frequently met with accounts, in the public papers, of the insurrections of the Whiteboys, as they are called in this country. From the people of fortune who have been sufferers by them, and who, too generally in this kingdom, look on the miserable and oppressed poor of their country in the most contemptible light, the accounts of these insurgents have, for the most part, been too much exaggerated to be depended on. . . . The original of their denomination of Whiteboys was from the practice of wearing their shirts without-side of their clothes, the better to distinguish each other in the night-time. It happened that we were at Kilkenny, in our road to Waterford, at the very time of the late considerable insurrection of these unhappy wretches, in the south of Kilkenny county, not far from Waterford.

I was naturally led to enquire into the cause of these insurrections and the pretensions of the insurgents themselves for creating these disturbances. From the people of easy and affluent circumstances it is natural to suppose the accounts would be very different from such as were given by those of the same class with the delinquents. By comparing these, however, with the obvious appearance of things in the country, I soon had sufficient reason to believe their disquiet arose, in general, from the severe treatment they met with from their landlords, and the lords of the manors and principally from their clergy. Our road to Waterford lay through the very midst of these unhappy insurgents, and we were, consequently, advised to take a different route. Why, whence should be the fear? We have neither deprived them of their common rights nor their potatoes. They have no quarrel with us, who have never injured them.

We rode through the country, in which they were assembled in great number, but the very day before the last considerable engagement they had with the troops quartered at the towns in the neighbourhood; but met with no molestation from any of them. The very next day after we came to Waterford, the news was brought of this engagement, about four or five miles from the town. The opinions and representations of the inhabitants of the town were various on the merits of the affair; but it was easy to distinguish the sentiments of the humane from the aggravated representations of inveterate prejudice. . . .

There are many little commons, or vacant spots of ground, adjacent to the road, upon which the inhabitants of the cabbins by the highwayside have been used, from time immemorial, to *rare*, as they express it, a pig or a goose, which they have bought very young, the sale of which has helped to furnish them with a few necessaries. Many of these have been taken into the fields or enclosures on the road side by the landlords, who have farmed or purchased them, or the lords of the manor. From an impartial view of their situation, I

could not, from my soul, blame these unhappy delinquents. They are attacked and reduced on all sides, so hardly, as to have barely their potatoes left them to subsist on.

John Bush, Hibernia Curiosa (1769). Reprinted in Ireland from the Flight of the Earls to Grattan's Parliament (1607–1782), edited by James Carty (1965), p. 125.

~

FROM *A PHILOSOPHICAL SURVEY OF THE SOUTH OF IRELAND*

1777

Reverend Thomas Campbell

Thomas Campbell (1733–1795), born in County Tyrone, became a Church of Ireland clergyman and a writer remembered chiefly for his association with Johnson and Boswell. He wrote his Philosophical Survey of the South of Ireland, *somewhat confusingly, in the fictitious persona of an English traveler.*

SEE ALSO English Writing on Ireland before 1800

Boate, who wrote about a hundred years since, arranges the Irish cities in the following order: Dublin, Galway, Waterford, Limerick, Cork and Londonderry. As to the other towns, he says, the best of them, which are Drogheda, Kilkenny, Belfast, &c., are hardly comparable to those market-towns which are to be found in all parts of England. But how greatly must this order be now deranged, when it is universally believed, that the third town, in trade and consequence, is Belfast. In extent also, it comes next to Cork, for it has 5,295 houses, Limerick but 3,859, and Waterford 2,628. It is remarkable that Newry, a town not so much as named by Boate, has now more trade, houses, and people than Galway.

Dublin. The magnitude of this city is much greater than I imagined; I conclude it to be nearer a fourth, than a fifth of that of London. Viewing it from any of its towers, it seems to be more; but from walking the streets, I should take it to be less . . . and reckoning six to a family, or twelve to a house, there will be above 160,000 souls in Dublin.

The bulk of this city is like the worst parts of St. Giles's, but the new streets are just as good as ours.

They have finished one side of a square called Merion's Square, in a very elegant style. Near it is a square called Stephen's Green, round which is a gravel walk of near a mile; here, genteel company walk in the evenings, and on Sundays, after two o'clock, as with us in St. James's Park. This square has some grand houses, and is in general well built. The great inequality of the houses instead of diminishing, does, in my opinion, add to its beauty. The situation is cheerful, and the buildings around it multiply fast. Almost all the tolerable houses and streets have been built within forty years. Since the year 1685, the increase has been amazing. . . .

The quays of Dublin are its principal beauty; they lie on each side the river, which is banked and walled in, the whole length of the city; and at the breadth of a wide street from the river on each side, the houses are built fronting each other, which has a grand effect. When these streets are paved like the streets of London, we shall have nothing to compare with them.

Yesterday I went down the North Strand, catching the sea breezes as I rode along. Before you is the sea covered with ships; on the left of the bay, is a country beautifully varied, and sufficiently dressed by art, to enrich the landskip; to the right, the conical mountains of Wicklow terminate your view. The river Liffey and part of the city compose the foreground of this exquisite piece. . . .

If you prefer the men of this country for their hospitality and the women for their beauty, you are likely to live well with them. The ladies are, I believe, full as handsome as ours, yet it was sometime before I could bring myself to think so. . . . They are said not to walk as well as with us. If the fact be so I would rather attribute it to the badness of the streets, than to any wrong conformation of limbs. . . . In another generation, when the sides of these streets are flagged, the ladies of Dublin may be as much praised for their way of walking, as those of London.

It is deemed almost a reproach for a gentlewoman to be seen walking these streets. An old lady of quality told me last night, when speaking on this subject, that for her part, truly she had not once walked over Essex Bridge, since she was a girl. Now Essex Bridge is the grand pass here, as Charing Cross is in London. If it were not for dancing, of which they are passionately fond, the poor girls must all become cripples. It is impossible they should excel in what they do not practise; but, if they walk ill, they certainly dance well. For last night, you must know, I was at a ball, and never enjoyed one more in my life. There is a sweet affability and sparkling vivacity in these girls, which is very captivating.

Cork is a city large and extensive, beyond my expectation. I had been taught to think worse of it, in all respects, than it deserves. . . . And as it is the great shambles of the Kingdom, I was predisposed to credit these reports; but is really as clean, in general, as the metropolis. The slaughter houses are all in the suburbs, and there, indeed, the gale is not untainted but in the city properly so called, all is tolerably clean and consequently sweet. . . . There are two large stone bridges, one to the north, and the other to the south, over the great branches of the Lee, besides several small ones and some draw-bridges thrown over the lesser branches or canals. There are seven churches, an exchange, a custom-house, a barrack, several hospitals, and other public structures, yet none of them worth a second look. I have not seen a single monument of antiquity in the whole town, nor heard a bell in any of the churches, too good for the dinner-bell of a country squire. But here is something infinitely better. Here is the busy bustle of prosperous trade, and all its concomitant blessings; here is a most magnificent temple, erected to plenty in the midst of a marsh. . . . Smith's history of Cork, quoting Stanihurst, reports that 120 years ago, Cork was but the third city in Munster, now it is the second in the kingdom, and therefore called the Bristol of Ireland.

Kilkenny values itself upon its superior gentility and urbanity. It is much frequented by the neighbouring gentry as a country residence, has a stand of nine sedan chairs, and is not without the appearance of an agreeable place. I went last night to their weekly assembly, and was soon given to understand, by one of my partners that Kilkenny has always been esteemed the most polite and well-bred part of the kingdom. Knowing so little of this country, I am not furnished with any arguments from either reason or authority, to dispute this pretension. My partner was so beautiful a woman and so striking an example of the doctrine she taught that she led me away an easy captive to the opinion. For which I can see the justest grounds. This was the site for the Ormond family, here the last duke kept a court, as several of his predecessors had done, in a style much more magnificent than any of the modern viceroys. The people imbibed the court manners, and manners remain long after their causes are removed.

At present the inheritor of the castle and some of the appendant manors, a Roman Catholic gentleman, affects the state of his ancestors; his wife receives company as, I am told, the old Ormond ladies used to do; she never returns visits; and people seem disposed to yield her this preeminence. The cook belonging to this inn, the Sheaf of Wheat, wears ruffles; and, though an old man, is full of vivacity as politeness. . . .

I am not singular in remarking that the peasants of this country are a most comely breed of men. They are generally middle sized, and have almost universally dark brown hair, and eyes of the same colour. The complexions are clear, their countenances grave, and their faces of that oval character, which the Italian painters so much admire.

Belfast is a very handsome, thriving, well-peopled Town; a great many new houses and good shops in it. The folks seemed all very busy and employed in trade, the inhabitants being for the most part merchants, or employ'd under 'em, in this sea-port, which stands, conveniently enough, at the very inner part of Carrick-fergus. Thro' the town there runs a small rivulet, not much better than that they call the Glibb in Dublin, which, however, is of great use for bringing their goods to the Key when the tide serves. . . . Here we saw a very good manufacture of earthenware which nearest Delft of any made in Ireland, and really is not much short of it. 'Tis very clean and pretty, and universally used in the north, and I think not so much owing to any peculiar happiness in their clay but rather to the manner of beating and mixing it up.

Limerick is a place fortified by nature; for, without the annoyance of circumjacent hills, it is built upon an island, encircled by a strong barrier, the arms of the Shannon. It is now happily dismantled, and scarce a trace of its old walls and seventeen gates are to be seen. The substitution of spacious quays and commodious houses, in place of lofty battlements and massive bastions, has given it a thorough and healthy ventilation. Limerick, like London, was formerly and frequently visited by the plague; but the effect has here also been removed by the removal of the cause. . . .

I can easily believe that the women here deserve their celebrated character for beauty; for I have seen great numbers of pretty faces in the streets and public walks. In general, the common people, too, are of a very comely personage. The streets are always crowded with them; having no staple manufacture to employ them, they walk about, like the sluggard, with their hands in their bosom. They once had a manufacture of serges, but that is nearly extinct. They are, however, famous for making gloves. . . . A few years ago the town stood on sixty-four acres of ground; now it covers one hundred, equal to 160 of our measure.

And now having finished my little tour through two provinces of Ireland and ruminating upon what I have seen, I must say, and I cannot say it in words so authoritative as those of Sir John Davies:

> I have observed the good temperature of the air, the fruitfulness of the soil, the pleasant and commodious seats for habitation, the safe and large ports and havens, lying open for traffic into all western parts of the world, the long inlets of many naviggable rivers and so many great lakes and fresh ponds within the land, as the like are not to be seen in any part of Europe; and, lastly, the bodies and minds of the people endued with extraordinary abilities, of nature.

After considering all this, yet seeing at the same time that the greater, and certainly the best part of what I have seen, instead of being in a progressive state of improvement, is verging to depopulation; that the inhabitants are either moping under the sullen gloom of inactive indigence, or blindly asserting the rights of nature in nocturnal insurrections, attended with circumstances of ruinous devastation and savage cruelty, must we not conclude that there are political errors somewhere?

Cruelty is not in the nature of these people more than of other men, for they have many customs among them, which discover uncommon gentleness, kindness and affection. Nor are they singular in their hatred of labour. . . . There is no necessity for recurring to natural disposition, when the political constitution obtrudes upon us so many obvious and sufficient causes of the sad effects we complain of.

The first is, the suffering avarice to convert the arable lands into pasture. The evils arising from this custom in England were so grievous . . . so great was the discontent of the people, from poverty occasioned by decay of tillage and increase of pasturage, that they rose in actual rebellion in the reign of Edward VI and sharpened by indigence and oppression, demolished in many countries the greatest part of the inclosures.

Here you see an exact prototype of the present disturbances in Munster, carried on by the rabble, originally called *Levellers*, from their levelling the inclosures of commons, but now *White Boys*, from their wearing their shirts over their coats, for the sake of distinction in the night. There it was a rebellion, here it is only a star-light insurrection, disavowed by everybody; and the impotence of those engaged to do anything effectual, drives them into wanton and malignant acts of cruelty on individuals. Hopeless of redress, they are provoked to acts of desperation. . . . And as little wonder that insurrection should rear its head in this ill-fated country; the first landlords of which are absentees, the second either forestallers or graziers, and where the only tiller of the ground stands in a third, and sometimes in a fourth degree from the original proprietor. Something should be thought of, something done, to restore the rights of human nature, in a country almost usurped by bullocks and sheep.

Reprinted in IRELAND FROM THE FLIGHT OF THE EARLS TO GRATTAN'S PARLIAMENT (1607–1782), *edited by James Carty (1965), pp. 128–132.*

~

THE CATHOLIC RELIEF ACT

1778

The process by which the penal laws were dismantled began in 1774 with the provision of a new oath of allegiance intended to be acceptable to conscientious Catholics. This 1778 law enabled Catholics to hold land on longer and more advantageous leases and ended the process of dividing land owned by a Catholic among his sons upon his death.

SEE ALSO Catholic Committee from 1756 to 1809; Eighteenth-Century Politics: 1778 to 1795—Parliamentary and Popular Politics; Politics: 1690 to 1800—A Protestant Kingdom; Religion: Since 1690; Roman Catholic Church: 1690 to 1829

AN ACT FOR THE RELIEF OF HIS MAJESTY'S SUBJECTS PROFESSING THE POPISH RELIGION

Whereas by an act made in this kingdom in the second year of her late majesty Queen Anne, entitled, *An act to prevent the further growth of popery*, and also by another act made in the eighth year of her said reign for explaining and amending the said act, the Roman Catholics of Ireland are made subject to several disabilities and incapacities therein particularly mentioned; and whereas for their uniform peaceful behaviour for a long series of years it appears reasonable and expedient to relax the same, and it must tend not only to the cultivation and improvement of this kingdom, but to the prosperity and strength of all his majesty's dominions, that his subjects of all denominations should enjoy the blessings of our free constitution, and should be bound to each other by mutual interest and mutual affection, therefore be it enacted . . . that from and after the first day

of August 1778 it shall and may be lawful to and for any papist, or person professing the popish religion, subject to the proviso hereinafter contained as to the taking and subscribing the oath and declaration therein mentioned, to take, hold, enjoy any lease or leases for any term or term of years, not exceeding nine hundred and ninety-nine years certain, or for any term of years determinable upon any number of lives, not exceeding five, provided always, that upon every such lease a rent *bona fide* to be paid in money shall be reserved and made payable during such terms with or without the liberty of committing waste, as fully and beneficially to all intents and purposes, as any other his majesty's subjects in this kingdom, and the same to dispose of by will or otherwise as he shall think fit; and all lands tenements, hereditaments, whereof any papist or person professing the popish religion is now seized or shall be seized by virtue of a title legally derived by, from, or under such person or persons, now seized in fee simple or fee tail, whether at law or in equity, shall from and after the time aforesaid be descendable, deviseable, and transferable, as fully, beneficially, and effectually, as if the same were in the seizin of any other of his majesty's subjects in this kingdom. . . .

III. Provided, that no papist or person professing the popish religion shall take any benefit from this act, unless he or she shall on or before the first day of January 1779, or some time previous to any such lease made to or in trust for him, if he or she shall be in this kingdom, or within six months after any devise, descent, or limitation shall take effect in possession, if at that time within this kingdom, or if then abroad beyond the seas, or under the age of twenty-one years, or in prison, or of unsound mind, or under coverture, then within six months after his or her return from abroad, or attaining the age of twenty-one years, or discharge from prison, or becoming of sound mind, or after she shall become a *femme sole*, take and subscribe the oath of allegiance and the declaration prescribed by an act passed in this kingdom in the thirteenth and fourteenth years of his present majesty's reign, . . .

V. And be it enacted . . . that no maintenance or portion shall be granted to any child of a popish parent, upon a bill filed against such parent . . . out of the personal property of such papist, except out of such leases which they may hereafter take under the powers granted in this act, . . .

VI. And whereas by an act made in this kingdom in the second year of the reign of her late majesty Queen Anne, entitled, *An act to prevent the further growth of popery*, it is amongst other things enacted to the effect following; in case the eldest son and heir of a popish parent shall be a Protestant, . . . such popish parent shall become and be only tenant for life of all the real estate, whereof such popish parent shall then be seized in fee tail or fee simple, and the reversion in fee shall be vested in such eldest son, being a Protestant subject, . . . and whereas it is found inexpedient to continue any longer that part of the said recited act, be it enacted . . . that from and after the first day of November 1778 the conformity of the eldest son . . . shall no affect or alter the estate of any popish parent . . . but such popish parent shall remain seized and possessed of the same estate and interest in all and every his or her real estate, as he or she would have been, if such eldest son had not conformed, or the said act of the second year of Queen Anne had not been made.

X. Provided also that no person shall take benefit by this act who having been converted from the popish to the Protestant religion shall afterwards relapse to popery, nor any person who being a Protestant shall at any time become a papist, or shall educate or suffer to be educated, any of his children under the age of fourteen years in the popish religion.

Statutes at Large Passed in the Parliaments Held in Ireland, 1310–1800 (1786–1801), vol. 11, pp. 298–301.

∼

On Irish Rural Society and Poverty

1780

Arthur Young

Arthur Young (1741–1820), an agricultural reformer, visited Ireland in 1776 and published his findings about Irish society in 1780. In the following extracts he comments on housing, marriage, and relationships between social classes.

SEE ALSO Agriculture: 1690 to 1845; English Writing on Ireland before 1800; Family: Marriage Patterns and Family Life from 1690 to 1921; Population, Economy, and Society from 1750 to 1950; Potato and Potato Blight (Phytophthora infestans); Rural Life: 1690 to 1845

Generally speaking the Irish poor have a fair bellyful of potatoes, and they have milk the greatest part of the year. What I would particularly insist on here is the value of his labour being food not money; food not for himself only, but for his wife and children. An Irishman

loves whisky as well as an Englishman does strong beer, but he cannot go on Saturday night to the whisky house and drink out the week's support of himself, his wife and his children, not uncommon in the ale house of the Englishman. . . .

The cottages of the Irish, which are called cabins, are the most miserable looking hovels that can well be conceived; they generally consist of only one room. Mud kneaded with straw is the common material of the walls; these have only a door, which lets in light instead of a window, and should let the smoke out instead of a chimney, but they had rather keep it in. These two conveniences they hold so cheap, that I have seen them both stopped up in stone cottages built by improving landlords. The roofs of the cabins are rafters, raised from the tops of the mud walls, and the covering varies; some are thatched with straw, potato stalks, or with heath, others only covered with sods of turf. The bad repair of these roofs are kept in, a hole in the thatch being often mended with turf, and weeds sprouting from every part, gives them the appearance of a weedy dunghill, especially when the cabin is not built with regular walls, but supported on one, or perhaps on both sides by the banks of a broad dry ditch; the roof then seems a hillock, upon which perhaps the pig grazes. Some of these cabins are much less and more miserable habitations than I had ever seen in England. I was told they were the worst in Connacht, but I found it an error; I saw many in Leinster to the full as bad, and in Wicklow some worse than any in Connacht. When they are well roofed, and built not of stones ill put together, but of mud, they are much warmer, independently of smoke, than the clay or lath and mortar cottages of England, the walls of which are so thin, that a rat hole lets in the wind to the annoyance of the whole family.

The furniture of the cabins is as bad as the architecture, in very many consisting only of a pot for boiling their potatoes, a bit of a table, and one or two broken stools; beds are not found universally, the family lying on straw, equally partook of by cows, calves and pigs, though the luxury of styes is coming in in Ireland, which excludes the poor pigs from the warmth of the bodies of their master and mistress.

This is a general description, but the exceptions are very numerous. I have been in a multitude of cabins that had much useful furniture, and some even superfluous; chairs, tables, boxes, chests of drawers, earthenware, and in short most of the articles found in a middling English cottage; but upon enquiry, I very generally found that these acquisitions were all made within the last ten years, a sure sign of a rising national prosperity. I think the bad cabins and furniture the greatest instances of Irish poverty, and this must flow from the mode of payment for labour, which makes cattle so valuable to the peasant, that every farthing they can spare is saved for their purchase; from hence also results another observation, which is, that the apparent poverty of it is greater than the real; for the house of a man that is master of four or five cows will have scarce anything but deficiencies, nay I was in the cabins of dairymen and farmers, not small ones, whose cabins were not at all better furnished that those of the poorest labourer; before therefore we can attribute it to absolute poverty, we must take into the account the customs and inclinations of the people. In England a man's cottage will be filled with superfluities before he possesses a cow. I think the comparison much in favour of the Irishman; a hog is a much more valuable piece of goods than a set of tea things, and though his snout in a crock of potatoes is an idea not so poetical as—

Broken teacups, wisely kept for show,
Ranged o'er the chimney, glistened in a row.

yet will the cottier and his family at Christmas find the solidity of it an ample recompense for the ornament of the other. . . .

It must be very apparent to every traveller, through that country, that the labouring poor are treated with harshness, and are in all respects so little considered, that their want of importance seems a perfect contrast to their situation in England, of which country, comparatively speaking, reign the sovereigns. The age has improved so much in humanity, that even the poor Irish have experienced its influence, and are every day treated better and better; but still the remnant of the old manners, the abominable distinction of religion, united with the oppressive conduct of the little country gentlemen, or rather vermin of the kingdom, who never were out of it, altogether still bear very heavy on the poor people and subject them to situations more mortifying than we ever behold in England. The landlord of an Irish estate, inhabited by Roman Catholics, is a sort of despot who yields obedience, in whatever concerns the poor, to no law but that of his will. To discover what the liberty of a people is, we must live among them, and not look for it in the statutes of the realm. The language of written law may be that of liberty, but the situation of the poor may speak no language but that of slavery; there is too much of this contradiction in Ireland. A long series of oppressions, aided by very many ill-judged laws, have brought landlords into a habit of exerting a very lofty superiority, and their vassals into that of an almost unlimited submission; speaking a language that is despised, professing a religion that is abhorred, and being disarmed, the poor find themselves in many cases slaves even in the bosom of *written* liberty. Landlords

that have resided much abroad are usually humane in their ideas, but the habit of tyranny naturally contracts the mind, so that even in this polished age, there are instances of a severe carriage towards the poor, which is quite unknown in England.

A landlord in Ireland can scarcely invent an order which a servant, labourer or cottier dares to refuse to execute. Nothing satisfies him but an unlimited submission. Disrespect or anything tending towards sauciness he may punish with his cane or his horsewhip with the most perfect security; a poor man would have his bones broken if he offered to lift his hand in his own defence. Knocking down is spoken of in the country in a manner that makes an Englishman stare. It must strike the most careless traveller to see whole strings of cars whipt into a ditch by a gentleman's footman to make way for his carriage; if they are overturned or broken in pieces, no matter, it is taken in patience; were they to complain they would perhaps be horsewhipped. . . .

The cabins of the poor Irish being such apparently miserable habitations, is another very evident encouragement to population. In England, where the poor are in many respects in such a superior state, a couple will not marry unless they can get a house, to build which, take the kingdom through, will cost from £25 to £60; half the life, and all the vigour and youth of a man and woman are passed before they can save such a sum; and when they have got it, so burdensome are poor to a parish, that it is twenty to one if they get permission to erect their cottage. But in Ireland, the cabin is not an object of a moment's consideration; to possess a cow and a pig is an earlier aim; the cabin begins with a hovel, that is erected with two day's labour, and the young couple pass not their youth in celibacy for want of a nest to produce their young in.

Marriage is certainly more general in Ireland than in England. I scarce ever found an unmarried farmer or cottier; but it is seen more in other classes, which with us do not marry at all; such as servants. The generality of footmen and maids, in gentlemen's families, are married, a circumstance we very rarely see in England.

Another point of importance, is their children not being burdensome. In all the enquiries I made into the state of the poor, I found their happiness and ease generally relative to the number of their children, and nothing considered as great a misfortune as having none. Whenever this is the fact, or the general idea, it must necessarily have a considerable effect in promoting early marriages, and consequently population.

The food of the people being potatoes is a point not of less importance; for when the common food of the poor is so dear as to be an object of attentive economy, the children will want that plenty which is essential to rearing them; the article of milk, so general in the Irish cabins, is a matter of the first consequence in rearing infants. The Irish poor in the Catholic parts of that country are subsisted entirely upon land, whereas the poor in England have so little to do with it, that they subsist almost entirely from shops, by a purchase of their necessaries. In the former case it must be a matter of prodigious consequence, that the product should be yielded by as small a space of land as possible; this is the case with potatoes more than with any other crop whatever. . . .

Arthur Young, A Tour in Ireland with General Observations on the Present State of That Kingdom Made in the Years 1776, 1777 and 1778, *selected and edited by* Constantia Maxwell (1925), *pp. 184, 187–191, 199–200.*

The Catholic Relief Act

1782

In 1782 the right to purchase land was restored to Catholics, and a number of restrictions on the Catholic clergy were relaxed, though various limits placed upon these concessions reflect the continuing unease among Protestants over granting full civil and political liberty to Catholics.

SEE ALSO Catholic Committee from 1756 to 1809; Eighteenth-Century Politics: 1778 to 1795—Parliamentary and Popular Politics; Politics: 1690 to 1800—A Protestant Kingdom; Religion: Since 1690; Roman Catholic Church: 1690 to 1829

AN ACT FOR THE FURTHER RELIEF OF HIS MAJESTY'S SUBJECTS OF THIS KINGDOM PROFESSING THE POPISH RELIGION

I. Whereas all such of his majesty's subjects in this kingdom, of whatever persuasion, as have heretofore taken and subscribed, or shall hereafter take and subscribe, the oath of allegiance and declaration prescribed by an act passed in the thirteenth and fourteenth years of his present majesty's reign, entitled *An act to enable his majesty's subjects of whatever persuasion, to testify their allegiance to him*, ought to be considered as good and loyal subjects to his majesty, his crown and government; and whereas a continuance of several of the laws

formerly enacted, and still in force in this kingdom, against persons professing the popish religion, is therefore unnecessary, in respect to those who have taken or shall take the said oath, and is injurious to the real welfare and prosperity of Ireland; therefore be it enacted . . . that from and after the first day of May 1782 it shall and may be lawful to and for any person or persons professing the popish religion, to purchase, or take by grant, limitation, descent, or devise, and lands, tenements, or hereditaments in this kingdom, or any interest therein (except advowsons, and also except any manor or borough, or any part of a manor or borough, the freeholders or inhabitants whereof are entitled to vote for burgesses to represent such borough or manor in parliament) and the same to dispose of as he, she, or they shall think fit, . . .

V. And be it enacted . . . that no popish ecclesiastic, who hath heretofore taken and subscribed, or who shall hereafter take and subscribe, the oath of allegiance and declaration, prescribed by an act passed in the thirteenth and fourteenth years of his present majesty's reign, entitled *An act to enable his majesty's subjects of whatever persuasion, to testify their allegiance to him*, in the manner and form as hereinafter is particularly specified and set forth, and who shall register his christian and surnames, place of abode, age, and parish, if he have a parish, and the time and place of his receiving his first, and every other popish orders, and from whom he received them, with the register of the diocese where his place of abode is (for every which registry the sum of one shilling and no more shall be paid to the register) shall, after the passing of this act, be subject to any of the penalties, incapacities, or disabilities, mentioned in an act made in the ninth year of the reign of King William the third, entitled *An act for banishing all popish papists exercising any ecclesiastical jurisdiction, and regulars of the popish clergy out of this kingdom*, or in an act made in the second year of Queen Anne, entitled *An act for registering the popish clergy*, or in an act made in the second year of Queen Anne, entitled *An act to prevent the further growth of popery*, or in an act made in the second year of Queen Anne, entitled *An act to prevent popish priests from coming into this kingdom*, or in an act made in the fourth year of Queen Anne, entitled *An act to explain and amend an act*, entitled *An act for registering popish clergy*; or in an act made in the eighth year of Queen Anne, entitled *An act for explaining and amending an act*, entitled *An act to prevent the further growth of popery*.

VI. Provided always, that no benefits in this act contained shall extend, or be construed to extend, to any regular of the popish clergy, who shall not be in this kingdom at the time of passing this act, . . .

VIII. Provided always, that no benefits in this act contained shall extend, or be construed to extend, to any popish ecclesiastic who shall officiate in any church or chapel with steeple or bell, or at any funeral in any church or church-yard, or who shall exercise any of the rites or ceremonies of the popish religion, or wear the habits of their order, save within their usual places of worship, or in private houses, or who shall use any symbol or mark of title whatsoever, . . .

IX. Provided also, that nothing in this act contained shall be construed to extend to any person or persons who shall be perverted from the Protestant to the popish religion, but that all the pains penalties and disabilities, which now subsist, according to the laws now in being, shall remain in full force against such . . .

X. Provided also, that no benefits in this act contained shall be construed to extend to any popish ecclesiastic, who shall procure, incite, or persuade any Protestant to become a papist; . . .

XII. And be it enacted . . . that so much of an act passed in the seventh year of King William III, entitled *An act for the better securing the government by disarming papists*, as subjects any papists, who shall after the twentieth day of January 1695 have or keep in his possession, or in the possession of any other person to his use or at his disposal, any horse, gelding, or mare, which shall be of the value of five pounds or more, to the penalties therein mentioned; and also so much of an act passed in the eighth year of Queen Anne, entitled *An act for explaining and amending an act*, entitled *An act to prevent the further growth of popery*, as enables the lord lieutenant or other chief governors of this kingdom, to seize and secure any horse, mare or gelding belonging to any papist, or reputed papist, upon any invasion likely to happen, or in case of intestine war broke out, or likely to break out, shall be, and is, and are hereby repealed.

XIII. And be it enacted . . . that so much of an act passed in the ninth year of King George the second, entitled *An act for continuing and amending several statutes now near expiring*, as enables the grand jury to present for the reimbursing such persons who have been robbed by privateers in time of war, for such losses as they shall respectively sustain thereby and for applotting and levying the same on the lands, tenements and hereditaments, goods, and chattels of all the popish inhabitants of the county where such robbery shall committed, shall be, and is hereby repealed.

XIV. And be it enacted . . . that so much of an act passed in the sixth year of King George the first, entitled *An act for the better regulating the parish watches, and amending the highways in this kingdom, and for prevent-*

ing the misapplication of public money, as subjects such papist or papists who shall not provide a Protestant watchman to watch in their turn, to the penalties therein mentioned, shall be, and is hereby repealed.

XVI. Provided also, that no benefit herein contained shall extend or be construed to extend, to any person who hath not heretofore, or who shall not hereafter before the accruing of such benefit to such persons or persons, being of the age of twenty-one years, or who being under the age of twenty-one years, shall not within six months after he or she shall attain the age of twenty-one years, or being of unsound mind, or in prison, or beyond the seas, or under coverture, then within six months, after such disability removed, take, and subscribe the oath of allegiance and declaration prescribed by an act passed in the thirteenth and fourteenth years of his present majesty's reign, entitled *An act to enable his majesty's subjects of whatever persuasion, to testify their allegiance to him,* . . .

STATUTES AT LARGE PASSED IN THE PARLIAMENTS HELD IN IRELAND, 1310–1800 (1786–1801), *vol. 12, pp. 237–242.*

⤳

THE ULSTER VOLUNTEER RESOLUTIONS

1782

The raising of "volunteer" military units, which might (or might not) be subsequently recognized by the government as militia units, was a familiar practice among Protestants when there was danger of popular disturbance or French invasion. Alarm over possible invasion during the French-supported insurrection in the American colonies was the occasion for an especially widespread wave of volunteering. This time the exercise coincided with an acute confrontation within the Irish polity between supporters of the government and "Patriots." Volunteer support for Patriot demands that the Irish parliament be granted greater autonomy culminated in a February 1782 convention of delegates from Ulster Volunteer units in Dungannon which adopted the following resolutions.

SEE ALSO Military Forces from 1690 to 1800

Whereas it has been asserted, "That volunteers, as such, cannot with propriety, debate or publish their opinions on political subjects, or on the conduct of parliament or public men."

Resolved unanimously, That a citizen, by learning the use of arms, does not abandon any of his civil rights.

Resolved unanimously, That a claim of any body of men, other than the king, lords, and commons of Ireland to make laws to bind this kingdom, is unconstitutional, illegal, and a grievance.

Resolved (with one dissenting voice only), That the powers exercised by the privy council of both kingdoms, under, or under colour or pretence of the law of Poynings,' are unconstitutional and a grievance.

Resolved unanimously, That the ports of this country are, by right, open to all foreign countries, not at war with the king, and that any burden thereupon, or obstruction thereto, save only by the parliament of Ireland, are unconstitutional, illegal, and a grievance.

Resolved (with one dissenting voice only), That a mutiny bill, not limited in point of duration from session to session, is unconstitutional, and a grievance.

Resolved unanimously, That the independence of judges is equally essential to the impartial administration of justice in Ireland, as in England, and that the refusal or delay of this right to Ireland, makes a distinction where there should be no distinction, may excite jealously where perfect union should prevail, and is, in itself, unconstitutional, and a grievance.

Resolved (with eleven dissenting voices only), That it is our decided and unalterable determination, to seek a redress of those grievances; and we pledge ourselves to each other and to our country, as freeholders, fellow-citizens, and men of honour, that we will at every ensuing election, support those only, who have supported, and will support us therein, and we will use all constitutional means to make such pursuit of redress speedy and effectual.

Resolved (with one dissenting voice only), That the right honourable and honourable the minority in parliament, who have supported these our constitutional rights, are entitled to our most grateful thanks, and that the annexed address be signed by the chairman, and published with these resolutions.

Resolved unanimously, That four members from each county of the province of Ulster, eleven to be a quorum, be, and are hereby appointed a committee till next general meeting, to act for the volunteer corps here represented, and as occasions shall require, to call general meetings of the province. . . .

Resolved unanimously, That said committee do appoint nine of their members to be a committee in Dublin, in order to communicate with such other volunteer associations in the other provinces as may think proper to come to similar resolutions, and to deliberate with

them on the most constitutional means of carrying them into effect.

Resolved unanimously, That the committee be, and are hereby instructed to call a general meeting of the province, within twelve months from this day, or in fourteen days after the dissolution of the present parliament, should such an event sooner take place.

Resolved unanimously, That the court of Portugal have acted towards this kingdom (being part of the British empire) in such a manner as to call upon us to declare and pledge ourselves to each other that we will not consume any wine of the growth of Portugal, and that we will, to the extent of our influence, prevent the use of said wine, save and except the wine at present in this kingdom, until such time as our exports shall be received in the kingdom of Portugal, as the manufactures of part of the British empire.

Resolved (with two differing voices only, to this and the following resolution), That we hold the right of private judgment in matters of religion, to be equally sacred in others as in ourselves.

Resolved therefore, That as men and as Irishmen, as christians and as Protestants, we rejoice in the relaxation of the penal laws against our Roman Catholic fellow-subjects, and that we conceive the measure to be fraught with the happiest consequences to the union and prosperity of the inhabitants of Ireland.

Reprinted in IRISH HISTORICAL DOCUMENTS, 1172–1922, edited by Edmund Curtis and R. B. McDowell (1943), pp. 233–235.

⁓

YELVERTON'S ACT

1782

Under Poynings' Law (1494), as it had been operationalized since the seventeenth century, legislation initiated by the Irish parliament was transmitted in draft form ("head of bills") to the privy council in England. The council might reject such a draft altogether, or it might return it to the Irish parliament either as received or with amendments. If the bill was returned, the Irish parliament could only accept or reject it with whatever amendments had been made. Yelverton's Act, enacted with government support in a quasi-revolutionary situation, eliminated this frustrating mechanism and initiated an era of "legislative independence." Although the English privy council retained the power to withhold the royal assent, it used this power cautiously during the remaining eighteen years until the Act of Union rendered the issue moot.

SEE ALSO Government from 1690 to 1800; Politics: 1690 to 1800—A Protestant Kingdom

AN ACT TO REGULATE THE MANNER OF PASSING BILLS, AND TO PREVENT DELAYS IN SUMMONING OF PARLIAMENTS

Whereas it be expedient to regulate the manner of passing bills in this kingdom, be it enacted . . . that the lord lieutenant, or other chief governor or governors and council of this kingdom for the time being, do and shall certify all such bills, and none other, as both houses of parliament shall judge expedient to be enacted in this kingdom, to his majesty his heirs and successors, under the great seal of his majesty his heirs and successors, under the great seal of this kingdom without addition, diminution, or alteration.

II. And be it further enacted . . . that all such bills as shall be so certified to his majesty, his heirs and successors, under the great seal of this kingdom, and returned into the same under the great seal of Great Britain, without addition, diminution, or alteration, and none other shall pass in the parliament of this kingdom; any former law, statute, or usage to the contrary thereof in anywise notwithstanding.

III. And be it further enacted, that no bill shall be certified into Great Britain, as a cause or consideration for holding a parliament in this kingdom, but that parliaments may be holden in this kingdom, although no such bill shall have been certified previous to the meeting thereof.

IV. Provided always, that no parliament shall be holden in this kingdom until a licence for that purpose shall be first had and obtained from his majesty, his heirs and successors, under the great seal of Great Britain.

STATUTES AT LARGE PASSED IN THE PARLIAMENTS HELD IN IRELAND, 1310–1800 (1786–1801), vol. 12, pp. 356.

≈

THE RENUNCIATION ACT

1783

In the Declaratory Act of 1719 the British parliament had asserted the right to legislate for Ireland. Repeal of that act was part of the constitutional settlement of 1782. During the following year, in response to continuing Patriot complaints that repeal of offensive legislation was not abandonment of the claims made therein, the British parliament went further and renounced the right to make laws binding on Ireland.

SEE ALSO Politics: 1690 to 1800—A Protestant Kingdom

AN ACT FOR PREVENTING AND REMOVING ALL DOUBTS WHICH HAVE ARISEN, OR MIGHT ARISE, CONCERNING THE EXCLUSIVE RIGHTS OF THE PARLIAMENT AND COURTS OF IRELAND, IN MATTERS OF LEGISLATION AND JUDICATURE; AND FOR PREVENTING ANY WRIT OF ERROR OR APPEAL FROM ANY OF HIS MAJESTY'S COURTS IN THAT KINGDOM FROM BEING RECEIVED, HEARD AND ADJUDGED, IN ANY OF HIS MAJESTY'S COURTS IN THE KINGDOM OF GREAT BRITAIN

Whereas, by an act of the last session of the present parliament, entitled *An act to repeal an act made in the sixth year of his late majesty, King George the first, entitled, An act for the better securing the dependency of the kingdom of Ireland upon the Crown of Great Britain*, it was enacted, that the last mentioned act, and all the matters and things therein contained, should be repealed: And whereas doubts have arisen whether the provisions of the said act are sufficient to secure to the people of Ireland the rights claimed by them to be bound only by laws enacted by his majesty and the parliament of that kingdom, in all cases whatever, and to have all actions and suits at law or in equity, which may be instituted in that kingdom, decided in his majesty's courts therein finally, and without appeal from thence: therefore, for removing all doubts respecting the same, . . . be it declared and enacted . . . that the said right claimed by the people of Ireland, to be bound only by laws enacted by his majesty and the parliament of that kingdom, in all cases whatever, and to have all actions and suits at law or in equity, which may be instituted in that kingdom, decided in his majesty's courts therein finally, and without appeal from thence, shall be, and is hereby declared to be established and ascertained for ever, and shall at no time hereafter be questioned or questionable.

II. And be it further enacted . . . that no writ of error or appeal shall be received or adjudged, or any other proceeding be had by or in any of his majesty's courts in this kingdom, in any action or suit at law or in equity, instituted in any of his majesty's courts in the kingdom of Ireland; and that all such writs, appeals or proceedings, shall be, and they are hereby declared, null and void to all intents and purposes; and that all records, transcripts of records or proceedings, which have been transmitted from Ireland to Great Britain, by virtue of any writ of error or appeal, and upon which no judgment has been given or decree pronounced before the first day of June one thousand seven hundred and eighty two, shall, upon application made by or in behalf of the party in whose favour judgment was given or decree pronounced, in Ireland, be delivered to such party, or any person by him authorised to apply for and receive the same.

THE STATUTES AT LARGE OF ENGLAND AND OF GREAT-BRITAIN: FROM MAGNA CARTA TO THE UNION OF THE KINGDOMS OF GREAT BRITAIN AND IRELAND (1811), *vol.* 8, *p.* 226.

~

THE CATHOLIC RELIEF ACT

1793

The onset of the French Revolution made it more urgent to redress Catholic grievances. In 1793 the government pressured the Irish parliament to pass this legislation, extending the right to vote to Catholics otherwise qualified to do so. The right to sit in parliament and to hold a number of other public offices was withheld until 1829.

SEE ALSO Catholic Committee from 1756 to 1809; Eighteenth-Century Politics: 1778 to 1795—Parliamentary and Popular Politics; Politics: 1690 to 1800—A Protestant Kingdom; Religion: Since 1690; Roman Catholic Church: 1690 to 1829

AN ACT FOR THE RELIEF OF HIS MAJESTY'S POPISH, OR ROMAN CATHOLIC SUBJECTS OF IRELAND

Whereas various acts of parliament have been passed, imposing on his majesty's subjects professing the popish or Roman Catholic religion many restraints and disabilities, to which other subjects of this realm are not liable, and from the peaceful and loyal demeanour of his majesty's popish or Roman Catholic subjects, it is fit that such restraints and disabilities shall be discontinued; be it therefore enacted . . . that his majesty's subjects being papists, or persons professing the popish or Roman Catholic religion, or married to papists, or persons professing the popish or Roman Catholic religion,

or educating any of their children in that religion, shall not be liable or subject to any penalties, forfeitures, disabilities, or incapacities, or to any laws for the limitation, charging, or discovering of their estates and property, real or personal, or touching the acquiring of property, or securities affecting property, save such as his majesty's subjects of the Protestant religion are liable and subject to; and that such parts of all oaths as are required to be taken by persons in order to qualify themselves for voting at elections for members to serve in parliament, as import to deny that the person taking the same is a papist or married to a papist, or educates his children in the popish religion, shall not hereafter be required to be taken by any voter, but shall be omitted by the person administering the same; and that is shall not be necessary, in order to entitle a papist, or person professing the popish or Roman Catholic religion to vote at an election of members to serve in parliament, that he should at, or previous to his voting, take the oaths of allegiance and abjuration, . . .

VI. Provided also, that nothing herein contained, shall extend to authorize any papist, or person professing the popish or Roman Catholic religion, to have or keep in his hands or possession any arms . . . or to exempt such person from any forfeiture, or penalty inflicted by any act respecting arms, armour, or ammunition, in the hands or possession of any papist, or respecting papists having or keeping such warlike stores, save and except papists, or persons of the popish or Roman Catholic religion seized of a freehold estate of one hundred pounds a year, or possessed of a personal estate of one thousand pounds or upwards, who are hereby authorized to keep arms and ammunition as Protestants now by law may; and also save and except papists or Roman Catholics, possessing a freehold estate of ten pounds yearly value, and less than one hundred pounds, or a personal estate of three hundred, and less than one thousand pounds, who shall have at the session of the peace in the county in which they reside, taken the oath of allegiance prescribed to be taken by an act passed in the thirteenth and fourteenth years of his present majesty's reign, entitled *An act to enable his majesty's subjects, of whatever persuasion, to testify their allegiance to him.* . . .

VII. And be it enacted, that it shall and may be lawful for papists, or persons professing the popish or Roman Catholic religion, to hold, exercise, and enjoy all civil and military offices, or places of trust or profit under his majesty, his heirs and successors, in this kingdom; and to hold or take degrees or any professorship in, or be masters, or fellows of any college, to be hereafter founded in this kingdom, provided that such college shall be a member of the university of Dublin, and shall not be founded exclusively for the education of papists or persons professing the popish or Roman Catholic religion, nor consist exclusively of masters, fellows, or other persons to be named or elected on the foundation of such college, being persons professing the popish or Roman Catholic religion, or to hold any office or place of trust, in, and to be a member of any lay-body corporate, except the college of the holy and undivided Trinity of Queen Elizabeth, near Dublin, without taking and subscribing the oaths of allegiance, supremacy, or abjuration, or making or subscribing the declaration required to be taken, made and subscribed, to enable any person to hold and enjoy any of such places, and without receiving the sacrament of the Lord's supper, according to the rites and ceremonies of the church of Ireland, any law, statute, or bye-law of any corporation to the contrary notwithstanding; provided that every such person shall take and subscribe the oath appointed by the said act passed in the thirteenth and fourteenth years of his majesty's reign, entitled *An act to enable his majesty's subjects, of whatever persuasion, to testify their allegiance to him*; and also the oath and declaration following, that is to say, I A.B. do hereby declare, that I do profess the Roman Catholic religion. I A.B. do swear, that I do abjure, condemn, and detest, as unchristian and impious, the principle that it is lawful to murder, destroy, or any ways injure any person whatsoever, for or under the pretence of being a heretic; and I do declare solemnly before God, that I believe, that no act in itself unjust, immoral, or wicked, can ever be justified or excused by or under pretence or colour, that it was done either for the good of the church, or in obedience to any ecclesiastical power whatsoever. I also declare, that it is not an article of the Catholic faith, neither am I thereby required to believe or profess that the pope is infallible, or that I am bound to obey any order in its own nature immoral, though the pope or any ecclesiastical power should issue or direct such order, but on the contrary, I hold that it would be sinful in me to pay any respect or obedience thereto. I further declare, that I do not believe that any sin whatsoever, committed by me, can be forgiven at the mere will of any pope, or of my priest, or of any person or persons whatsoever, but that sincere sorrow for past sins, a firm and sincere resolution to avoid future guilt and to atone to God, are previous and indispensible requisites to establish a well-founded expectation of forgiveness, and that any person who receives absolution without these previous requisites, so far from obtaining thereby any remission of his sins, incurs the additional guilt of violating a sacrament; and I do swear that I will defend to the utmost of my power the settlement and arrangement of property in this country, as established by the laws now in being; I do hereby disclaim, disavow and solemnly abjure any in-

tention to subvert the present church establishment for the purpose of substituting a Catholic establishment in its stead; and I do solemnly swear, that I will not exercise any privilege to which I am or may become entitled, to disturb and weaken the Protestant religion and Protestant government in this kingdom. So help me God! . . .

IX. Provided always, and be it enacted, that nothing herein contained shall extend, or be construed to extend to enable any person to sit or vote in either house of parliament, or to hold, exercise, or enjoy the office of lord lieutenant, lord deputy, or other chief governor of this kingdom, lord high chancellor or keeper, or commissioner of the great seal of this kingdom, lord high treasurer, chancellor of the exchequer, chief justice of the court of king's bench, or common pleas, lord chief baron of the court of exchequer, judge of the high court of admiralty, master or keeper of the rolls, secretary, vice-treasurer, teller and cashier of the exchequer, or auditor-general, lieutenant or governor, or custos rotulorum of counties, secretary to the lord lieutenant, lord deputy, or other chief governor or governors of this kingdom, member of his majesty's most honourable privy council, prime serjeant, attorney-general, solicitor-general, second and third serjeants-at-law, or king's counsel, masters in chancery, provost, or fellow of the college of the Holy and Undivided Trinity of Queen Elizabeth, near Dublin, postmaster-general, master and lieutenant-general of his majesty's ordnance, commander-in-chief of his majesty's forces, generals on the staff, and sheriffs and sub-sheriffs of any county in this kingdom or any office contrary to the rules, orders and directions made and established by the lord lieutenant and council, in pursuance of the act passed in the seventh and eighteenth years of the reign of King Charles the Second, entitled *An act for the explaining of some doubts arising upon an act, entitled, An act for the better execution of his majesty's gracious declaration for the settlement of his kingdom of Ireland,* . . . unless he shall have taken, made, and subscribed the oaths, and declaration, and performed the several requisites which by any law heretofore made, and now of force, are required to enable any person to sit or vote, or to hold, exercise, and enjoy the said offices respectively. . . .

XII. Provided also, and be it enacted, that nothing herein contained, shall be construed to extend to authorize any popish priest, or reputed popish priest, to celebrate marriage between Protestant and Protestant, or between any person who hath been, or professes himself or herself to be a Protestant at any time within twelve months before such celebration of marriage, and a papist, unless such Protestant and papist shall have been first married by a clergyman of the Protestant religion; and that every popish priest, or reputed popish priest, who shall celebrate any marriage between two Protestants, or between any such Protestant and papist, unless such Protestant and papist shall have been first married by a clergyman of the Protestant religion, shall forfeit the sum of five hundred pounds to his majesty, upon conviction thereof.

XIII. And whereas it may be expedient, in case his majesty, his heirs and successors, shall be so pleased so to alter the statutes of the college of the Holy and Undivided Trinity near Dublin and of the university of Dublin, as to enable persons professing the Roman Catholic religion to enter into, or to take degrees in the said university, to remove any obstacle which now exists by statute law; be it enacted, that from and after the first day of June 1793 it shall not be necessary for any person upon taking any of the degrees usually conferred by the said university, to make or subscribe any declaration, or to take any oaths of allegiance and abjuration, . . .

XIV. Provided always, that no papist or Roman Catholic, or person professing the Roman Catholic or popish religion, shall take any benefit by, or under this act, unless he shall have first taken and subscribed the oath and declaration in this act contained and set forth, and also the said oath appointed by the said act passed in the thirteenth and fourteenth years of his majesty's reign, entitled *An act to enable his majesty's subjects of whatever persuasion to testify their allegiance to him*, in some one of his majesty's four courts in Dublin, or at the general sessions of the peace, or at any adjournment thereof to be holden for the county, city, or borough wherein such papist or Roman Catholic, or person professing the Roman Catholic or popish religion, doth in habit or dwell, or before the going judge or judges of assize, . . .

STATUTES AT LARGE PASSED IN THE PARLIAMENTS HELD IN IRELAND, 1310–1800 (1786–1801), *vol. 16, pp. 685–692.*

~

UNITED IRISH PARLIAMENTARY REFORM PLAN

March 1794

In many cases, a seat in the Irish House of Commons represented a borough whose elections could be easily controlled by the government or a wealthy landlord. Reform of this corrupt system was one of the principal objectives of the United Irish movement from its foundation in 1791. In this document the Dublin Society of United Irishmen set forth a detailed plan for such reforms. The plan would have extended the vote to all adult males "of sound mind" but stopped short of enfranchising women.

SEE ALSO Eighteenth-Century Politics: 1795 to 1800—Repression, Rebellion, and Union; Neilson, Samuel; Tandy, James Napper; Tone, Theobald Wolfe; United Irish Societies from 1791 to 1803

A PLAN OF AN EQUAL REPRESENTATION OF THE PEOPLE OF IRELAND IN THE HOUSE OF COMMONS

Prepared for Public Consideration by the Society of United Irishmen of Dublin

I. That the nation, for the purposes of representation solely, should be divided into 300 electorates, formed by combination of parishes, and as nearly as possible equal in point of population.

II. That each electorate should return one representative to parliament.

III. That each electorate should, for the convenience of carrying on the elections at the same time, be subdivided into a sufficient number of parts.

IV. That there should be a returning officer for each electorate, and a deputy returning officer for each subdivision, to be respectively elected.

V. That the electors of the electorate should vote, each in the subdivision in which he is registered, and has resided after specified.

VI. That the returning officers of the subdivisions should severally return their respective polls to the returning officer of the electorate, who should tot up the whole, and return the person having a majority of votes, as the representative in parliament.

VII. That every man possessing the right of suffrage for a representative in parliament, should exercise it in his own person only.

VIII. That no person should have a right to vote in more than one electorate at the same election.

IX. That every male of sound mind, who has attained the full age of 21 years, and actually dwelt, or maintained a family establishment in any electorate for six months of the twelve immediately previous to the commencement of the election (provided his residence or maintaining a family establishment be duly registered) should be entitled to vote for the representative of the electorate.

X. That there should be a registering officer, and a registry of residence in every subdivision of each electorate; and that in all questions concerning residence, the registry should be considered as conclusive evidence.

XI. That all elections in the nation should commence and close on the same day.

XII. That the votes of all electors should be given by voice and not by ballot.

XIII. That no oath of any kind should be taken by an elector.

XIV. That the full age of 25 years should be a necessary qualification to entitle any man to be a representative.

XV. That residence within the electorate should not, but that residence within the kingdom should be a necessary qualification for a representative.

XVI. That no property qualification should be necessary to entitle any man to be a representative.

XVII. That any person having a pension, or holding a place in the executive or judicial departments, should be thereby disqualified from being a representative.

XVIII. That representatives should receive a reasonable stipend for their services.

XIX. That every representative should, on taking his seat, swear that neither he, nor any person to promote his interest, with his privity, gave or was to give any bribe for the suffrage of any voter.

XX. That any representative convicted by a jury, of having acted contrary to the substance of the above oath, should for ever be disqualified from sitting or voting in parliament.

XXI. That parliaments should be annual.

XXII. That a representative should be at liberty to resign his delegation upon giving sufficient notice to his constituents.

XXIII. The absence from duty for should vacate the seat of a representative.

Reprinted in IRISH HISTORICAL DOCUMENTS, 1172–1922, *edited by* Edmund Curtis *and* R. B. McDowell (1943), *pp. 237–238.*

~

GRIEVANCES OF THE UNITED IRISHMEN OF BALLYNAHINCH, CO. DOWN

1795

This manifesto by a United Irish society about fourteen miles south of Belfast reflects an amalgam of traditional agrarian grievances and the newer radicalism fostered by the French Revolution.

SEE ALSO Eighteenth-Century Politics: 1795 to 1800—Repression, Rebellion, and Union; Neilson, Samuel; Tandy, James Napper; Tone, Theobald Wolfe; United Irish Societies from 1791 to 1803

What evils will be removed and what advantages gained by a reform in Parliament.

1st. Tithes will be abolished and every man will pay his own clergy.

2nd. Hearth-money—that abominable badge of slavery and oppression to the poor—will cease.

3rd. We will not thereafter be taxed to pay pensioners and sinecure placemen to vote against us. The consequence of this will be that tobacco for which we now pay 10d. per lb. will then be had for 4d.—Aye for 4d.—and every other article of imported goods cheap in proportion.

4th. We shall have no excise laws: the merchant and shopkeeper will get to leave to carry on his business quietly, without the intrusion of plundering revenue officers.

5th. The expense and tediousness of the law will give place to prompt and equal justice—Gratis.

6th. County cesses would not be squandered in jobs among the parasites of agents; and 23 gentlemen sitting in a Grand Jury room, would cease to impose £10 or 12 thousand per annum, upon the inhabitants of a county without their consent. Is it not astonishing that Irishmen patiently suffer themselves to be assessed annually to the amount of £400,000 by 750 esquires nominated by an officer of the Crown? If this abuse was reformed we would have good roads and low cesses.

7th. Church cesses would be no more for every profession would support its own houses of worship as well as its own clergy.

8th. Custom at fairs would be abolished and a free passage to and from them would be had without having the sanctity of an oath profaned by scoundrel bailiffs.

9th. The press would be unshackled and a man might publish his sentiments without the terror of a Bastille; every man would have an opportunity of knowing his rights for a newspaper which now costs 2d. would then be sold for a half-penny.

10th. The honest farmer would be protected in the enjoyment of all his appurtenances against the intrusions of moss-bailiffs and bog-trotters, the present ridiculous idea of obligation to a landlord would be done away and the contract would then appear as it really is mutual.

Irishmen are these objects of any importance? perhaps not. Here one single consequence then worth ten thousand of them all. THE LAWS will be made by YOURSELVES, or in other words YOU WILL BE FREE—unite then, associate, resolve and carry your resolve into execution.

A.D. 1795
Signed, Thos. Smyth
True Copy

Endorsement: Thomas Smyth who signed the within was secretary to a committee of United Irishmen near Ballynahinch. He was arrested in his own house by the Rev. Mr. Clewlow and Captain Price where 70 or 80 copies of the within were found all signed by him. He is now in Down Jail. 29 January 1797.

Public Record Office of Northern Ireland, Roden MSS, Mic. 147/9, pp. 57–60; reprinted in ASPECTS OF IRISH SOCIAL HISTORY, 1750–1800, edited by W. H. Crawford and B. Trainor (1969), pp. 181–182.

~

SPEECH DELIVERED AT A UNITED IRISH MEETING IN BALLYCLARE, CO. ANTRIM

1795

This speech, apparently delivered by a United Irish organizer but transcribed by a marginally literate informer, reflects the millenarian enthusiasm of the 1790s. Ballyclare was a Presbyterian village not far from Catholic territory in the Glens of Antrim, and the speaker is careful to recommend reading matter compatible with his apocalyptic message from both traditions: "the Old Irish Chronicle" (probably the so-called prophecy of St. Columbkille, circulated among Catholics in Irish-language manuscripts) and "the Scotch Prophecy" (probably a printed pamphlet on the life of Alexander Peden, a seventeenth-century Covenanter).

SEE ALSO Eighteenth-Century Politics: 1795 to 1800—Repression, Rebellion, and Union; Neilson, Samuel; Tandy, James Napper; Tone, Theobald Wolfe; United Irish Societies from 1791 to 1803

I speak to you who are bound Under the hand of Disipotisim I tell you again who now has no recowrce left you only as steddy Union and faithfull Affection one till the other you see by the times that all Yourop is in a blaze you see that the whole Kingdom are Uniting in steddy Affection and stronge tyes one till the other to have that what the have longe been seeking in Vean to have the whole people fearly Represented in parlement and to hav[e] a full Manapisition of all Peop[l] of Ireland———

My Brithrin I Excort you to look to the Spirit of Freedom hou it Rouses to Arms and Strenthens the feeble and Elivates the brave. in her hand there is such Suckcess and all dispots that must bow and fall Prostrated before her the time calls for your spedy Eade and when dun you only Joyins with the Coming Cause of the Irish Neation A Neation robed and Distressed Crushed Plundred Debaised moked and Cruley distressed by the dispots of England who holds all the Monny and treasure of the Neation wh[o]se Text-seting has no end who[s] Brutish appetide Cannot be sadisfied Eving with teaking all but lays on the havey, B[ur]thons like Phara in Eigepet, how says, that you shall give in the full-tole of Breek and still with holds the Straw but thanks to Provadance the time of Deleverance is come and a Mighty Salvition is sprung up in France the Taror of yourop who has bound her self to send to your Existance fifty Thousand of well Diciplited Troops with pleanty of Arms and Aminition which when Joyned by one Milion and five Thousand all reaty United by oath[s], and who can say again so great a People besides you may Depend on the Greatiest part of the Army ho is now and will bee selisited by thier frends, not to set against thier frends and Releations I will not take up your time in this Idle manner I Recomend the Reeding of the Old Irish Cronical or the Scotch Proficay with manny others at this time is a fullfiling, I beg you will aweak it is freedom and Honnour that Cals you, see what a Progress it has maid and tis still a making this three weeks past has aded to our strenth in Three Miles of this Town one Hundred and fifty Recruits all Duley Tested———

Delevred at our Convention at Bellyclair between the 19th and 20th of this Instant May 1795———

T: F Presedent
G: C Sacry

National Archives of Ireland, Rebellion Papers, 620/22/7, enclosure in R. Johnston, Belfast, to John Lees, 26 May 1795. Reproduced by permission.

~

THE INSURRECTION ACT

1796

By 1796 the organizing activities of the United Irishmen and the Defenders in the countryside were causing serious alarm in official and propertied circles. The Insurrection Act was intended to empower the authorities to stamp out such agitation.

SEE ALSO Eighteenth-Century Politics: 1795 to 1800—Repression, Rebellion, and Union

AN ACT MORE EFFECTUALLY TO SUPPRESS INSURRECTIONS, AND PREVENT THE DISTURBANCE OF THE PUBLIC PEACE

Whereas traitorous insurrections have for some time past arisen in various parts of this kingdom, principally promoted and supported by persons associating under the pretended obligation of oaths unlawfully administered . . . be it enacted . . . that any person or persons who shall administer, or cause to be administered, or be present, aiding and assisting at the administering, or who shall by threats, promises, persuasions, or other undue means, cause, procure, or induce to be taken by any person or persons, upon a book, or otherwise any oath or engagement, importing to bind the person taking the same, to be of any association, brotherhood, society, or confederacy formed for seditious purposes, or to disturb the public peace, or to obey the orders or rules, or commands of any committee, or other body of men, not lawfully constituted, or the commands of any captain, leader, or commander (not appointed by his majesty, his heirs and successors) or to assemble at the desire or command of any such captain, leader, commander or committee, or of any person or persons not having lawful authority, or not to inform or given evidence against any brother, associate, confederate, or other person, or not to reveal or discover his having taken any illegal oath, or done any illegal act, or not to discover any illegal oath or engagement which may be tendered to him, or the import thereof, whether he shall take such oath, or enter into such engagement, or not, being by due course of law convicted thereof, shall be adjudged guilty of felony, and suffer death without benefit of clergy, and every person who shall take any such oath or engagement, not being thereto compelled by inevitable necessity, and being by due course of law thereof convicted, shall be adjudged guilty of felony and be transported for life. . . .

VI. And be it further enacted, that all persons who shall have arms in their possession at any time after the passing of this act, shall on or before the first day of May 1796, or immediately after they shall have possession of such arms, deliver to the acting clerk of the peace in the county, town, or city in which he resides . . . a written notification, signed by him or her, specifying therein . . . the place or places where the same are usually kept, accompanied by an affidavit, sworn by the person signing such notification, that the notification is true, and the he believes he is by law entitled to keep arms. . . .

VIII. And be it enacted, that any person having arms, and not making such registry as aforesaid, shall upon being convicted thereof, on the testimony of two credible witnesses on oath before any magistrate, for the first offence forfeit the sum of ten pounds . . . or be imprisoned by such magistrate for the space of two months, and for the second and every other offence shall in like manner forfeit the sum of twenty pounds, or be imprisoned for the space of four months. . . .

X. And be it further enacted, that it shall and may be lawful for any justice of the peace, or for any person authorized thereto by warrant under the hand of any justice of the peace, to search for arms in the houses or grounds of any person not having made such notification as aforesaid, and whom he shall have reasonable ground to suspect of having arms, and also in the houses or grounds of any person who having made such notification, shall refuse or neglect to deliver such list or inventory, or whom he shall have reasonable ground to suspect to have delivered a false list or inventory, and in case of refusal of admission, to break into such house and every part thereof by force, and if any arms shall be found in the possession of any such person respectively, to seize and carry away the same for the use of his majesty. . . .

XII. And whereas in several instances persons who have given information against persons accused of crime have been murdered before trial of the persons accused, in order to prevent their giving evidence and to effect the acquittal of the accused, and some magistrates have been assassinated for their exertions in bringing offenders to justice, be it declared and enacted, that if any person who hath given or shall give information or examinations upon oath against any person or persons for any offence against the laws, shall after the twentieth day of February 1796 and before the trial of the person or persons against whom such information or examination hath been or shall be given, be murdered or violently put to death, or so maimed or forcibly carried away and secreted as not to be able to give evidence on the trial of the person or persons against whom such information or examinations were given, the information or examination of such person or persons so taken on oath, shall be admitted as evidence on the trial of the person or persons against whom such information or examinations were given. . . .

XV. And be it further enacted, that it shall and may be lawful for any justice of the peace to arrest and bring before him, or cause to be arrested or brought before him, any stranger sojourning or wandering, and to examine him on oath respecting his place of abode, the place from whence he came, his manner of livelihood, and his object or motive for remaining or coming into the county, town or city, in which he shall be found, and unless he shall answer to the satisfaction of such magistrate, such magistrate shall commit him to gaol or the house of correction, there to remain until he find surety for his good behaviour.

XVI. And in order to restore peace to such parts of the kingdom as are or may be distributed by seditious persons, be it further enacted, that it shall and may be lawful to and for any two justices of the peace . . . to summon a special session of the peace . . . to consider the state of the county . . . and that the justices assembled in consequence, not being fewer than seven, or the major part of them, one of whom to be of the quorum, or if in a county of a town or city, not being fewer than three, shall and may if they see fit . . . signify by memorial signed by them to the lord lieutenant or other chief governor or governors of this kingdom, that they consider their county or any part thereof, to be in a state of disturbance or in immediate danger of becoming so, and praying that the lord lieutenant and council may proclaim such county, or part thereof, to be in a state of disturbance or in immediate danger of becoming so, and thereupon it shall and may be lawful to and for the lord lieutenant or other chief governor or governors of this kingdom, by and with the advice of his majesty's privy council by proclamation to declare such county, or any part of such county, to be in a state of disturbance or in immediate danger of becoming so, and also such parts of any adjoining county or counties as such chief governor or governors and council shall think fit, in order to prevent the continuance or extension of such disturbance.

XVII. And be it further enacted, that within three days after such proclamation made, or as soon after as may be, every clerk of the peace of every part of the district proclaimed, shall respectively in his county, give notice of holding within two days, or as soon after as may be, a petty session of the peace, and the justices of the peace shall pursuant to such notice assemble . . . and the said justices at said first meeting shall order and direct a notification signed by them to be made through-

out the district so proclaimed, that such district has been so proclaimed, and commanding in inhabitants to keep within their dwellings at all unseasonable times between sun-set and sun-rise, and warning them of the penalties to which a contrary conduct will expose them. . . .

XVIII. And be it further enacted, that it shall and may be lawful to and for any magistrate or other peace officer within such district, after such notification shall be made as aforesaid, to arrest or cause to be arrested any person who shall within such district be found in the fields, streets, highways, or elsewhere out of his dwelling or place of abode, at any time from one hour after sun-set until sun-rise and to bring before two justices of the peace . . . and unless he can prove to their satisfaction that he was out of his house upon his lawful occasions, such person shall be deemed an idle and disorderly person, and shall be transmitted by the warrant of such justices to the officer at some port appointed to receive recruits for his majesty's navy, by which officer such person shall be received as a recruit for his majesty's navy, and transmitted to serve on board his majesty's navy.

XIX. Provided always, that it shall and may be lawful to and for every such person so arrested, to appeal to the next sessions of the peace. . . .

XXII. And be it enacted . . . that persons who cannot upon examination prove themselves to exercise and industriously follow some lawful trade or employment as a labourer or otherwise, or to have some substance sufficient for their support or maintenance, shall be deemed idle and disorderly persons, and shall be dealt with according to what is herein before directed respecting persons out of their dwellings at unreasonable hours aforesaid. . . .

XXIX. And be it further enacted, that it shall and may be lawful for any justice of the peace, or any persons authorized by the warrant of such justice in any district so proclaimed and whilst such proclaimation shall remain in force, to call upon every person who has registered arms within such district to produce or account for the same, and to enter any house or place whatever, and search for arms and ammunition, and to take and carry away all arms and ammunition which they may think necessary to take possession of, in order to preserve or restore the public peace. . . .

XXXI. And be it further enacted, that all person found assembled in any proclaimed district, in any house in which malt or spirituous liquors are sold, not being inmates thereof or travellers, whether licensed or unlicensed, after the hours of nine at night and before six in the morning, shall be liable to be deemed idle and disorderly persons within the meaning of this act. . . .

XXXII. And be it further enacted, that if any man or boy shall, in any district so proclaimed, hawk or disperse any seditious handbill, paper or pamphlet, or paper by law required to be stamped and not duly stamped, such man or boy shall be deemed an idle and disorderly person, and dealt with accordingly, and as is herein before directed; and if any woman shall hawk or disperse any seditious hand-bill, paper, or paper not duly stamped, such woman being convicted thereof by the oath of one witness before two justices of the peace, one of whom to be of the quorum, such woman shall by the warrant of such two justices be committed to the gaol of the county, there to remain for three months, unless she shall sooner discover the person or persons from whom she received or by whom she was employed to sell, hawk or disperse such papers or pamphlets, provided always, that such woman may appeal from such adjudication to the next sessions of the peace. . . .

XXXVII. Provided always . . . that when verdict shall be given for the plaintiff in any action to be brought against any justice of the peace, peace officer or other person, for taking or imprisoning or detaining any person, or for seizing arms or ammunition, or entering houses under colour of any authority given by this act, and it shall appear to the judge or judges before whom the same shall be tried, that there was a probable cause for doing the act complained of in such action, and the judge or court shall certify the same on record, then in that case the plaintiff shall not be entitled to more than sixpence damages, nor to any costs of suit.

XXXVIII. Provided also, that where a verdict shall be given for the plaintiff in any such action as aforesaid, and the judge or court before whom the cause shall be tried, shall certify on the record that the injury for which such action is brought was wilfully and maliciously committed, the plaintiff shall be entitled to double costs of suit.

STATUTES AT LARGE PASSED IN THE PARLIAMENTS HELD IN
IRELAND, 1310–1800 (1786–1801), vol. 17, 978–990.

THE UNITED IRISHMEN ORGANIZATION

1797

This 1797 document reflects the changing character of the United Irish movement during the course of the 1790s. The first six paragraphs are taken from the "Declaration and Resolutions of the Society of United Irishmen of Belfast" in
October 1791 and stress the constitutional objectives of the society. From 1795, however, the movement increasingly took on the secret and military attributes of a revolutionary organization, as can be seen in the remainder of the document.

SEE ALSO Eighteenth-Century Politics: 1795 to 1800—Repression, Rebellion, and Union; Neilson, Samuel; Tandy, James Napper; Tone, Theobald Wolfe; United Irish Societies from 1791 to 1803

The Declaration, Resolutions, and Constitution of the Societies of United Irishmen

In the present era of reform, when unjust governments are falling in every quarter of Europe, when religious persecution is compelled to abjure her tyranny over conscience, when the rights of men are ascertained in theory, and theory substantiated by practice, when antiquity can no longer defend absurd and oppressive forms, against the common sense and common interests of mankind, when all governments are acknowledged to originate from the people, and to be so far only obligatory, as they protect their rights and promote their welfare, we think it our duty, as Irishmen, to come forward, and state what we feel to be our heavy grievance, and what we know to be its effectual remedy. We have no national government, we are ruled by Englishmen, and the servants of Englishmen, whose object is the interest of another country, whose instrument is corruption, and whose strength is the weakness of Ireland; and these men have the whole of the power and patronage of the country, as means to seduce and subdue the honesty of her representatives in the legislature. Such an extrinsic power, acting with uniform force, in a direction too frequently opposite to the true line of our obvious interest, can be resisted with effect solely by unanimity, decision, and spirit in the people, qualities which may be exerted most legally, constitutionally, efficaciously, by the great measure, essential to the prosperity and freedom of Ireland, an equal representation of all the people in parliament.

Impressed with these sentiments, we have agreed to form an association, to be called the Society of United Irishmen, and we do pledge ourselves to our country, and mutually to each other, that we will steadily support, and endeavour by all due means to carry into effect the following resolutions:

1st. Resolved, That the weight of English influence in the government of this country is so great, as to require a cordial union among all the people of Ireland, to maintain that balance which is essential to the preservation of our liberties, and extension of our commerce.

2nd. That the sole constitutional mode by which this influence can be opposed is by a complete and radical reform of the representation of the people in parliament.

3rd. That no reform is practicable, efficacious, or just, which shall not include Irishmen of every religious persuasion.

Satisfied, as we are, that the intestine divisions among Irishmen have too often given encouragement and impunity to profligate, audacious, and corrupt administrations, in measures which, but for these divisions, they durst not have attempted, we submit our resolutions to the nation, as the basis of our political faith. We have gone to what we conceived to be the root of the evil. We have stated what we conceive to be remedy. With a parliament thus formed, everything is easy—without it, nothing can be done—and we do call on, and most earnestly exhort our countrymen in general to follow our example, and to form similar societies in every quarter of the kingdom, for the promotion of constitutional knowledge, the abolition of bigotry in religion and politics, and the equal distribution of the rights of man throughout all sects and denominations of Irishmen. The people, when thus collected, will feel their own weight, and secure that the power which theory has already admitted as their portion, and to which, if they be not aroused by their present provocations to vindicate it, they deserve to forfeit their pretensions for ever.

1st. This society is constituted for the purpose of forwarding a brotherhood of affection, a community of rights, and a union of power among Irishmen of every religious persuasion; and thereby to obtain a complete reform in the legislature, founded on the principles of civil, political, and religious liberty.

2nd. Every candidate for admission into this society shall be proposed by one member and seconded by another, both of whom shall vouch for his character and principles. The candidate to be balloted for on the society's subsequent meeting, and if one of the beans shall be black, he shall stand rejected.

3rd. Each society shall fix upon a weekly subscription suited to the circumstances and convenience of its numbers, which they shall regularly return to their baronial by the proper officer.

4th. The officers of this society shall be a secretary and treasurer, who shall be appointed by ballot every three months: on every first meeting in November, February, May, and August.

5th. A society shall consist of no more than twelve members, and those as nearly as possible of the same street or neighbourhood, whereby they may be all thoroughly known to each other, and their conduct be subject to the censorial check of all.

6th. Every person elected a member of this society shall, previous to his admission, take the following test. But in order to diminish risk, it shall be taken in a separate apartment, in the presence of the persons who proposed and seconded him only, after which the new member shall be brought into the body of the society, and there vouched for by the same.

Test

In the awful presence of God, I, A.B., do voluntarily declare, that I will persevere in endeavouring to form a brotherhood of affection among Irishmen of every religious persuasion, and that I will also persevere in endeavours to obtain an equal, full, and adequate representation of all the people of Ireland. I do further declare, that neither hopes, fears, rewards, or punishments, shall ever induce me, directly or indirectly, to inform on, or give evidence against, any member or members of this or similar societies for an act or expression of theirs, done or made collectively or individually in or out of this society, in pursuance of the spirit of this obligation.

7th. No person, though he should have taken the test, will be considered as an United Irishman until he has contributed to the funds of the institution, or longer than he shall continue to pay such contribution.

8th. No communication relating to the business of the institution shall be made to any United Irishman on any pretence whatever, except in his own society or committee, or by some member of his own society or committee.

9th. When the society shall amount to the number of twelve members, it shall be equally divided by lot (societies in country places to divide as may best suit their local situation), that is, the names of all the members shall be put into a hat or box, the secretary or treasurer shall draw out six individually, which six shall be considered the senior society, and the remaining six the junior, who shall apply to the baronial committee, through the delegates of the senior society, for a number. This mode shall be pursued until the whole neighbourhood is organized.

Order of Business at Meetings

1st. New members read declaration and test, during which subscriptions to be collected.

2nd. Reports of committees received.

3rd. Communications called for.

4th. Candidates balloted for.

5th. Candidates proposed.

Constitution of Committees

Baronial Committees

1st. When any barony or other district shall contain from four to ten societies, the secretaries of these shall constitute a lower baronial committee, they should not exceed ten, and be numbered in the order of their formation.

2nd. An upper baronial, to consist of ten secretaries from ten lower baronials.

3rd. Baronial committees shall receive delegates from societies of a contiguous barony, provided said barony did not contain four baronial societies.

County Committees

1st. When any county shall contain four or more upper baronial committees, their secretaries shall assemble and choose deputies to form a county committee.

2nd. County committees shall receive delegates from baronial committees of adjacent counties, if said counties do not contain four baronial committees.

Provincial Committees

1st. When two or more counties shall have county committees, two persons shall be elected by ballot from each to form a provincial committee (for three months).

2nd. Delegates from county committees in other provinces will be received, if such provinces do not contain two county committees.

National Committees

That when two provincial committees are formed, they shall elect five persons each by ballot to form a national committee.

Societies first meetings in November, February, May and August to be on or before the 5th, baronial committees on or before the 8th, county committees on or before the 25th of the above months.

Baronial, county, and provincial committees, shall meet at least once in every month, and report to their constituents.

Names of committee men shall not be known by any person but by those who elect them.

Test for Secretaries of Societies or Committees

In the awful presence of God I, A.B., do voluntarily declare that as long as I shall hold the office of secretary to this I will, to the utmost of my abilities faithfully discharge the duties thereof.

That all papers or documents received by me as secretary I will in safety keep; I will not give any of them, or any copy or copies of them, to any person or persons, members or others, but by a vote of this and that I will, at the expiration of my secretaryship deliver up to this all such papers as may be in my possession. . . .

JOURNALS OF THE HOUSE OF COMMONS OF THE KINGDOM OF IRELAND, 1613–1800 (1796–1800), *vol. 17, appendix, pp. 888–889.*

~

STATEMENT OF THREE IMPRISONED UNITED IRISH LEADERS

4 August 1798

The three authors of this statement were prominent and well-to-do radicals—Emmet and O'Connor were Protestants, MacNeven was a Catholic—who joined the United Irishmen in 1796. Each had been arrested during the months preceding the 1798 rebellion. After the Wexford and northern phases of the rebellion had been suppressed, but before the French landing in Mayo, they agreed to an arrangement by which the government would cease executions in return for their disclosure of details concerning the United Irishmen and especially their dealings with France.

SEE ALSO Eighteenth-Century Politics: 1795 to 1800—Repression, Rebellion, and Union; Neilson,

Samuel; Tandy, James Napper; Tone, Theobald Wolfe; United Irish Societies from 1791 to 1803

MEMOIR OR DETAILED STATEMENT OF THE ORIGIN AND PROGRESS OF THE IRISH UNION: DELIVERED TO THE IRISH GOVERNMENT BY MESSRS. THOMAS ADDIS EMMET, ARTHUR O'CONNOR, AND WILLIAM JAMES M'NEVEN, AUGUST THE 4TH, 1798

The disunion that had long existed between the Catholics and Protestants of Ireland, particularly those of the Presbyterian religion, was found by experience to be so great an obstacle to the obtaining a reform in parliament, on any thing of just and popular principles, that some persons, equally friendly to that measure and to religious toleration, conceived the idea of uniting both sects in pursuance of the same object — a repeal of the penal laws and a reform, including in itself an extension of the right of suffrage to the Catholic.

From this originated the societies of United Irishmen in the end of the year 1791; even then it was clearly perceived that the chief support of the borough interest in Ireland was the weight of English influence; but as yet that obvious remark had not led the minds of the reformers towards a separation from England. Some individuals, perhaps, had convinced themselves that benefit would result to this country from such a measure; but during the whole existence of the society of United Irishmen of Dublin, we may safely aver, to the best of our knowledge and recollections, that no such object was ever agitated by its members, either in public debate or private conversation; nor until the society had lasted a considerable time, were any traces of republicanism to be met with there; its views were purely, and in good faith, what the test of the society avows. . . .

The discussion, however, of political questions, both foreign and domestic, and the enacting of several unpopular laws, had advanced the minds of many people, even before they were aware of it, towards republicanism and revolution; they began to reason on the subject, and to think a republican form of government was preferable to our own; but they still considered it as impossible to be obtained, in consequence of the English power and connection. This, together with its being constantly perceived that the weight of English was thrown into the scale of borough interest, gradually rendered the connection itself an object of discussion, and its advantages somewhat problematical. While the minds of men were taking this turn, the society of United Irishmen of Dublin was in the year 1794 forcibly dissolved, but the principles by which it was actuated were

as strong as ever; as hypocrisy was not of the vices of that society, it brought its destruction on itself by the openness of its discussion and publicity of its proceeding. Its fate was a warning to that of Belfast, and suggested the idea of forming societies with the same object, but whose secrecy should be their protection. The first of these societies was, as we best recollect, in the year 1795. In order to secure co-operation and uniformity of action, they organised a system of committees, baronial, county, and provincial, and even national; but it was long before the skeleton of this organisation was filled up. While the formation of these societies was in agitation, the friends of liberty were gradually, but with a timid step, advancing towards republicanism, they began to be convinced that it would be as easy to obtain a revolution as a reform, so obstinately was the latter resisted, and as the conviction impressed itself on their minds, they were inclined not to give up the struggle, but to extend their views; it was for this reason that in their test the words are "an equal representation of all the people of Ireland," without inserting the word "parliament." The test embraced both the republican and the reformer, and left to future circumstances to decide to which the common strength should be directed; but still the whole body, we are convinced, would stop short at reform. Another consideration, however, led the minds of the reflecting United Irishmen to look forward towards a republic and separation from England—this was the war with France; they clearly perceived that their strength was not likely to become speedily equal to wresting from the English and the borough interest in Ireland even a reform; foreign assistance would, therefore, perhaps become necessary; but foreign assistance could only be hoped for in proportion as the object to which it would be applied was important to the party giving it. A reform in the Irish parliament was no object to the French.—A separation of Ireland from England was a mighty one indeed! . . .

Whatever progress the United system had made among the Catholics throughout the kingdom, until after the recall of lord Fitzwilliam (notwithstanding many resolutions which had appeared from them, manifesting a growing spirit), they were considered as not only entertaining an habitual predilection for monarchy, but also as being less attached than the Presbyterians to political liberty. There were, however, certain men among them who rejoiced at the rejection of their claims, because it gave them an opportunity of pointing out that the adversaries of reform were their adversaries; and that these two objects could never be separated with any chance of success to either. They used the recall of that nobleman, and the rejection of his measures, to cement together in political union the Catholic and Presbyterian masses.

The modern societies, for their protection against informers and persecution, had introduced into their test a clause of secrecy. They did more—they changed the engagements of their predecessors into an oath; and mutual confidence increased when religion was called in aid of mutual security.

While they were almost entirely confined to the north, but increasing rapidly there, the Insurrection bill was passed in the beginning of the year 1796, augmenting the penalties upon administering unlawful oaths, or solemn obligations, even to death; but death had ceased to alarm men who began to think it was to be encountered in their country's cause. The statute remained an absolute dead letter, and the numbers of the body augmented beyond belief.

To the Armagh persecution is the Union of Irishmen most exceedingly indebted. The persons and properties of the wretched Catholics of that county were exposed to the merciless attacks of an Orange faction, which was certainly in many instances uncontrolled by the justices of peace, and claimed to be in all supported by government. When these men found that illegal acts of magistrates were indemnified by occasional statutes, and the courts of justice shut against them by parliamentary barriers, they began to think they had no refuge but in joining the Union. Their dispositions so to do were increased by finding the Presbyterians, of Belfast especially, step forward to espouse their cause and succour their distress. We will here remark, once for all, what we most solemnly aver, that wherever the Orange system was introduced, particularly in Catholic counties, it was uniformly observed that the numbers of United Irishmen increased most astonishingly. The alarm which an Orange lodge excited among the Catholics made them look for refuge by joining together in the United system; and as their numbers were always greater than that of bigoted Protestants, our harvest was ten-fold. At the same time that we mention this circumstance, we must confess, and most deeply regret, that it excited a mutual acrimony and vindictive spirit, which was peculiarly opposite to the interest, and abhorrent to the feelings of the United Irishmen, and has lately manifested itself, we hear, in outrages of so much horror.

Defenderism has been supposed to be the origin of the modern societies of United Irishmen; this is undoubtedly either a mistake or a misrepresentation; we solemnly declare that there was no connection between them and the United Irish, as far as we know, except what follows:

After the Defenders had spread into different counties, they manifested a rooted but unenlightened aversion, among other things, to the same grievances that were complained of by the Union. They were composed almost entirely of Catholics, and those of the lowest order, who, through a false confidence, were risking themselves, and the attainment of redress, by premature and unsystematic insurrection. In the north they were also engaged in an acrimonious and bloody struggle with an opposite faction, called Peep-of-day boys. The advantage of reconciling these two misguided parties, of joining them in the Union, and so turning them from any views they might have exclusively religious, and of restraining them from employing a mutually destructive exertion of force, most powerfully struck the minds of several United Irishmen. For that purpose, many of them in the northern counties went among both, but particularly the Defenders, joined with them, showed the superiority of the Union system, and gradually, while government was endeavouring to quell them by force, melted them down into the United Irish body. This rendered their conduct infinitely more orderly, and less suspicious to government.

It has been alleged against the United Irishmen that they established a system of assassination. Nothing that has ever been imputed to them, that we feel more pleasure in being able to disavow. . . .

We were none of us members of the United system until September or October in the year 1796; at that time, it must be confessed, the reasons already alleged, and the irritations of the preceding summer in the north, had disposed us to a separation and republic, principally because we were hopeless that a reform would ever be yielded to any peaceable exertions of the people. . . .

About the middle of 1796 a meeting of the executive took place, more important in its discussions and its consequences than any that had preceded it; as such we have thought ourselves bound to give an account of it with the most perfect frankness and more than ordinary precision. This meeting took place in consequence of a letter from one of the society, who had emigrated on account of political opinions: it mentioned that the state of the country had been represented to the government of France, in so favourable a point of view, as to induce them to resolve upon invading Ireland, for the purpose of enabling it to separate itself from Great Britain. On this solemn and important occasion, a serious review was taken of the state of the Irish nation at that period: it was observed that a desperate ferment existed in the public mind. A resolution in favour of a parliamentary reform had indeed been passed in 1795 by the House of Commons; but after it had been frustrated by several successive adjournments, all hope of its attainment vanished, and its friends were everywhere proscribed; the Volunteers were put down; all power of meeting by delegation for any political purpose, the mode in which it was most usual and expedient to co-operate on any object of importance, was taken away at the same time. The provocations of the year 1794, the recall of Lord Fitzwilliam, and the re-assumption of co-ercive measures that followed it, were strongly dwelt on: the county of Armagh had been long desolated by two contending factions, agreeing only in one thing—an opinion that most of the active magistrates in that county treated one party with the most fostering kind-ness, and the other with the most rigorous persecution. It was stated that so marked a partiality exasperated the sufferers, and those who sympathized in their misfor-tunes. It was urged with indignation, that notwith-standing the greatness of the military establishment in Ireland, and its having been able to suppress the Defend-ers in various counties, it was not able, or was not em-ployed, to suppress those outrages in that county, which drove 7,000 persons from their native dwellings. The magistrates, who took no steps against the Orange-men, were said to have overleaped the boundaries of law to pursue and punish the Defenders. The government seemed to take upon themselves those injuries by the In-demnity act, and even honoured the violators; and by the Insurrection act, which enabled the same magis-trates, if they choose, under colour of law, to act anew the same abominations. Nothing, it was contended, could more justly excite the spirit of resistance, and de-termine men to appeal to arms, than the Insurrection act; it punished with death the administering of oaths, which in their opinion were calculated for the most vir-tuous and honorable purposes. The power of proclaim-ing counties, and quieting them by breaking open the cabins of the peasants between sunset and sunrise, by seizing the inmates, and sending them on board tenders, without the ordinary interposition of a trial by jury, had, it was alleged, irritated beyond endurance the minds of the reflecting, and the feelings of the unthink-ing inhabitants of that province. It was contended that even according to the constitution and example of 1688, when the protection of the constituted authorities was withdrawn from the subject, allegiance, the reciprocal duty ceased, to bind; when the people were not re-dressed, they had a right to resist, and were free to seek for allies wherever they were to be found. The English revolutionists of 1688, called in the aid of a foreign re-public to overthrow their oppressors. There had sprung up in our own time a much more mighty republic, which, by its offers of assistance to break the chains of slavery, had drawn on itself a war with the enemies of our freedom, and now particularly tendered us its aid. These arguments prevailed, and it was resolved to em-ploy the proffered assistance for the purpose of separa-tion. We are aware it is suspected negotiations between

the United Irishmen and the French were carried on at an earlier period than that now alluded to, but we sol-emnly declare such suspicion is ill-founded. In conse-quence of this determination of the executive, an agent was dispatched to the French directory, who acquainted them with it, stated the dispositions of the people, and the measures which caused them. He received fresh as-surances that the succours should be sent as soon as the armament could be got ready.

About October, 1796, a messenger from the repub-lic arrived, who, after authenticating himself, said he came to be informed of the state of the country, and to tell the leaders of the United Irishmen of the intention of the French to invade it speedily with 15,000 men, and a great quantity of arms and ammunition; but neither mentioned the precise time not the place, doubting, we suppose, our caution or our secrecy. Shortly after his departure, a letter arrived from a quarter which there was reason to look on as confidential, stating that they would invade England in the spring, and positively Ire-land. The reason of this contradiction has never been ex-plained; but the consequence of it, and the messenger not having specified the place of landing, were, that when the armament arrived in December, 1796, at Ban-try bay, they came at a time and in a port we had not foreknown.

. . . In fact, no attempt or advance was made to renew the negotiation till April, 1797, when a agent was sent. In May following, the well-known proclama-tion of general Lake appeared. This very much increased the ferment of the public mind, and the wish for the re-turn of the French, to get rid of the severities of martial law. It did more—it goaded many people of the north to press the executive to an insurrection, independent of foreign aid. . . .

Sometime in the beginning of the year [1798] a let-ter was received from France, stating that the succours might be expected in April. Why the promise was not fulfilled we have never learned. We know nothing of further communications from any foreign State, nor of the future plan of operations of the French; but we are convinced they will not abandon the plan of separating this country from England, so long as the discontents of the people would induce them to support an inva-sion.

. . . The parts we have acted, have enabled us to gain the most intimate knowledge of the dispositions and hearts of our countrymen. From that knowledge we speak, when we declare our deepest conviction that the penal laws, which have followed in such doleful and rapid succession—the house burnings, arbitrary im-prisonments, free quarters, and, above all, tortures to extort confessions—neither have had, nor can have, any other effect but exciting the most lively rancour in the hearts of almost all the people of Ireland against those of their countrymen who have had recourse to such measures for maintaining their power, and against the connection with Great Britain, whose men and whose aid have been poured in to assist them.

. . . Much as we wish to stop the effusion of blood, and the present scene of useless horrors, we have not affected a change of principles which would only bring on us the imputation of hypocrisy, when it is our most anxious wish to evince perfect sincerity and good faith. . . .

Arthur O'Connor, Thomas Addis Emmet, William James Mac Neven

DOCUMENTS RELATING TO IRELAND, 1795–1804, *edited by John T. Gilbert (1893; reprint, 1970), pp. 147, 148–151, 152, 156–158, 159, 161, 162.*

~

IRISH ACT OF UNION

1 August 1800

Under the Act of Union of 1800, Ireland lost any semblance of legislative independence when the two houses of its 500-year-old parliament voted to commit political suicide and to merge the country in the United Kingdom of Great Britain and Ireland. Even though the legislative independence gained by Ireland in 1782 was rather hollow owing to pervasive political chicanery, nationalists later in the nineteenth century came to regard the extinction of the Irish parliament as a grand calamity stemming from gross corruption. But unlike the Scottish Act of Union of 1707, the Irish Act of Union did not deeply offend contemporary Irish public opinion.

SEE ALSO Act of Union; Protestant Ascendancy: Decline, 1800 to 1930

AN ACT FOR THE UNION OF GREAT BRITAIN AND IRELAND

Whereas in pursuance of his majesty's most gracious recommendation to the two houses of parliament in Great Britain and Ireland respectively, to consider of such measures as might best tend to strengthen and consolidate the connexion between the two kingdoms, the two houses of the parliament of Great Britain and the two houses of the parliament of Ireland have severally agreed and resolved that in order to promote and secure the essential interests of Great Britain and Ireland and to consolidate the strength, power, and resources of the British empire, it will be advisable to concur in such measures as may best tend to unite the two kingdoms of Great Britain and Ireland into one kingdom, in such manner and on such terms and conditions as may be established by the acts of the respective parliaments of Great Britain and Ireland.

And whereas in furtherance of the said resolution both houses of the said two parliaments respectively have likewise agreed upon certain articles for effectuating and establishing the said purposes in the tenor following:

1. That it be the first article of the union of the kingdoms of Great Britain and Ireland that the said kingdom of Great Britain and Ireland shall upon the first day of January, which shall be in the year of our Lord 1801, and forever be united into one kingdom by the name of "the United Kingdom of Great Britain and Ireland," and that the royal style and titles appertaining to the imperial crown of the said United Kingdom and its dependencies, and also the ensigns, armorial flags, and banners thereof, shall be such as his majesty by his royal proclamation under the great seal of the United Kingdom shall be pleased to appoint.

2. That it be the second article of union that the succession to the imperial crown of the said United Kingdom, and of the dominions thereunto belonging, shall continue limited and settled in the same manner as the succession to the imperial crown of the said kingdoms of Great Britain and Ireland now stands limited and settled, according to the existing laws and to the terms of union between England and Scotland.

3. That it be the third article of union that the said United Kingdom be represented in one and the same parliament, to be styled "the Parliament of the United Kingdom of Great Britain and Ireland."

4. That it be the fourth article of union that four lords spiritual of Ireland, by rotation of sessions, and twenty-eight lords temporal of Ireland, elected for life by the peers of Ireland, shall be the number to sit and vote on the part of Ireland in the House of Lords of the parliament of the United Kingdom, and one hundred commoners (two for each county of Ireland, two for the city of Dublin, two for the city of Cork, one for the university of Trinity College, and one for each of the thirty-one most considerable cities, towns, and boroughs) be the number to sit and vote on the part of Ireland in the House of Commons of the parliament of the United Kingdom. . . .

That any person holding any peerage of Ireland, now subsisting or hereafter to be created, shall not thereby be disqualified from being elected to serve if he shall so think fit, or from serving or continuing to serve if he shall so think fit, for any county, city, or borough of Great Britain in the House of Commons of the United Kingdom, unless he shall have been previously elected as above to sit in the House of Lords of the United Kingdom, but that so long as such peer of Ireland shall continue to be a member of the House of Commons, he shall not be entitled to the privilege of peerage nor be capable of being elected to serve as a peer on the part of Ireland, or of voting at any such election. . . .

That it shall be lawful for his majesty, his heirs and successors, to create peers of that part of the United Kingdom called Ireland and to make promotions in the peerage thereof after the union, provided that no new creation of any such peers shall take place after the union until the three of the peerages of Ireland which shall have been existing at the time of the union shall have become extinct, and upon such extinction of three peerages, that it shall be lawful for his majesty, his heirs and successors, to create one peer of that part of the United Kingdom called Ireland, and in like manner, so often as three peerages of that part of the United Kingdom called Ireland shall become extinct, it shall be lawful for his majesty, his heirs and successors, to create one other peer of the said part of the United Kingdom; and if it shall happen that the peers of that part of the United Kingdom called Ireland shall, by extinction of peerages or otherwise, be reduced to the number of one hundred, exclusive of all such peers of that part of the United Kingdom called Ireland as shall hold any peerage of Great Britain subsisting at the time of the union, or of the United Kingdom created since the union, by which such peers shall be entitled to an hereditary seat in the House of Lords of the United Kingdom, then and in that case it shall and may be lawful for his majesty, his heirs and successors, to create one peer of that part of the United Kingdom called Ireland as often as any of such one hundred peerages shall fail by extinction, or as often as any one peer of that part of the United Kingdom called Ireland shall become entitled by descent or creation to a hereditary seat in the House of Lords of the United Kingdom, it being the true intent and meaning of this article that at all times after the union it shall and may be lawful for his majesty, his heirs and successors, to keep up the peerage of that part of the United Kingdom called Ireland to the number of one hundred, over and above the number of such of the said peers as shall be entitled by descent or creation to an hereditary seat in the House of Lords of the United Kingdom. . . .

That if his majesty, on or before the first day of January 1801, on which day the union is to take place, shall declare under the great seal of Great Britain that it is expedient that the lords and commons of the present parliament of Great Britain should be the members of the respective houses of the first parliament of the United Kingdom on the part of Great Britain, then the said lords and commons shall accordingly be the members of the respective houses of the first parliament of the United Kingdom on the part of Great Britain, and they, together with the lords spiritual and temporal, and commons so summoned and returned as above, on the part of Ireland, shall be the lords spiritual and temporal and commons for the first parliament of the United Kingdom, and such first parliament may (in that case), if not sooner dissolved, continue to sit so long as the present parliament of Great Britain may now by law continue to sit if not sooner dissolved: provided always, that until an act shall have passed in the parliament of the United Kingdom providing in what cases persons holding offices or places of profit under the Crown in Ireland shall be incapable of being members of the House of Commons of the parliament of the United Kingdom, no greater number of members than twenty holding such offices or places as aforesaid shall be capable of sitting in the said House of Commons of the parliament of the United Kingdom. . . .

5. That it be the fifth article of union that the churches of England and Ireland, as now by law established be united into one Protestant Episcopal church, to be called "the United Church of England and Ireland," and that the doctrine, worship, discipline, and government of the said united church shall be and shall remain in full force forever, as the same are now by law established for the Church of England; and that the continuance and preservation of the said united church as the established church of England and Ireland shall be deemed and taken to be an essential and fundamental part of the union; and that in like manner the doctrine, worship, discipline, and government of the Church of Scotland shall remain and be preserved as the same are now established by law and by the acts for the union of the two kingdoms of England and Scotland.

6. That it be the sixth article of union that his majesty's subjects of Great Britain and Ireland shall, from and after the first day of January 1801, be entitled to the same privileges and be on the same footing as to encouragements and bounties on the like articles, being the growth, produce, or manufacture of either country respectively, and generally in respect of trade and navigation in all ports and places in the United Kingdom and its dependencies; and that in all treaties made by his majesty, his heirs and successors, with any foreign power, his majesty's subjects in Ireland shall have the same privileges and be on the same footing as his majes-

ty's subjects of Great Britain. That from the first day of January 1801 all prohibitions and bounties on the export of articles, the growth, produce, or manufacture of either country to the other, shall cease and determine; and that the said articles shall thenceforth be exported from one country to the other without duty or bounty on such export.

That all articles, the growth, produce, or manufacture of either country (not hereinafter enumerated as subject to specific duties) shall from thenceforth be imported into each country from the other free from duty . . . , and that for the period of twenty years from the union the articles enumerated in the schedule No. II hereunto annexed, shall be subject, on importation into each country from the other, to the duties specified. . . .

7. That it be the seventh article of union that the charge arising from the payment of the interest and the sinking fund for the reduction of the principal of the debt incurred in either kingdom before the union shall continue to be separately defrayed by Great Britain and Ireland respectively, except as hereinafter provided.

That for the space of twenty years after the union shall take place, the contribution of Great Britain and Ireland respectively towards the expenditure of the United Kingdom in each year shall be defrayed in the proportion of fifteen parts for Great Britain and two parts for Ireland, that at the expiration of the said twenty years the future expenditure of the United Kingdom (other than the interest and charges of the debt to which either country shall be separately liable) shall be defrayed in each proportion as the parliament of the United Kingdom shall deem just and reasonable upon a comparison of the real value of the exports and imports of the respective countries upon an average of the three years next preceding the period of revision, or on a comparison of the value of the quantities of the following articles consumed within the respective countries on a similar average, viz., beer, spirits, sugar, wine, tea, tobacco, and malt, or according to the aggregate proportion resulting from both these considerations combined, or on a comparison of the amount of income in each country estimated from the produce for the same period of a general tax, if such shall have been imposed on the same descriptions of income in both countries; and that the parliament of the United Kingdom shall afterwards proceed in like manner to revise and fix the said proportion according to the same rules or any of them at periods not more distant than twenty years, nor less than seven years from each other, unless previous to any such period the parliament of the United Kingdom shall have declared as hereinafter provided that the expenditure of the United Kingdom shall be defrayed indiscrimi-

nately by equal taxes imposed on the like articles in both countries. . . .

That if at any future day the separate debt of each country respectively shall have been liquidated, or if the value of their respective debts . . . shall be to each other in the same proportion with the respective contributions of each country respectively, or if the amount by which the value of the larger of such debts shall vary from such proportion shall not exceed one hundredth part of the said value, and if it shall appear to the parliament of the United Kingdom that the respective circumstances of the two countries will thenceforth admit of their contributing indiscriminately by equal taxes imposed on the same articles in each to the future expenditure of the United Kingdom, it shall be competent to the parliament of the United Kingdom to declare that all future expense thenceforth to be incurred, together with the interest and charges of all joint debts contracted previous to such declaration, shall be so defrayed indiscriminately by equal taxes imposed on the same articles in each country, and thenceforth from time to time, as circumstances may require, to impose and apply such taxes accordingly, subject only to such particular exemptions or abatements in Ireland and in that part of Great Britain called Scotland as circumstances may appear from time to time to demand.

8. That it be the eighth article of the union that all laws in force at the time of the union, and all the courts of civil and ecclesiastical jurisdiction within the respective kingdoms, shall remain as now by law established within the same, subject only to such alterations and regulations from time to time as circumstances may appear to the parliament of the United Kingdom to require, provided that all writs of error and appeals depending at the time of the union, or hereafter to be brought, and which might now be finally decided by the House of Lords of either kingdom, shall from and after the union be finally decided by the House of Lords of the United Kingdom, and provided that from and after the union there shall remain in Ireland an instance court of admiralty for the determination of causes civil and maritime only; . . . and that all laws at present in force in either kingdom, which shall be contrary to any of the provisions which may be enacted by any act for carrying these articles into effect, be from and after the union repealed.

And whereas the said articles, having by address of the respective houses of parliament in Great Britain and Ireland, been humbly laid before his majesty, his majesty has been graciously pleased to approve the same and to recommend it to his two houses of parliament in Great Britain and Ireland to consider of such measures as may be necessary for giving effect to the said articles.

In order to give full effect and validity to the same, be it enacted . . . that the said foregoing recited articles . . . be ratified, confirmed, and approved, and . . . they are hereby declared to be the articles of the union of Great Britain and Ireland, and the same shall be in force and have effect forever from the first day of January, which shall be in the year of our Lord 1801, provided that before that period an act shall have been passed by the parliament of Great Britain for carrying into effect in the like manner the said foregoing recited articles.

10. And be it enacted that the great seal of Ireland may, if his majesty shall so think fit, after the union be used in like manner as before the union, except where it is otherwise provided by the foregoing articles, within that part of the United Kingdom called Ireland, and that his majesty may, so long as he shall think fit, continue the privy council of Ireland to be his privy council for that part of the United Kingdom called Ireland.

40 Geo. III, c. 38; STATUTES AT LARGE PASSED IN THE PARLIAMENTS HELD IN IRELAND, 1310–1800 (1786–1801), vol. 20, pp. 448–487.

~

SPEECH FROM THE DOCK

19 September 1803

Robert Emmet

The widespread rebellion fomented by the United Irishmen in 1798 was put down by the Crown forces savagely and with great difficulty. The rebellion failed for a variety of reasons, including the lack of adequate French military assistance, British intelligence activity and repression, and the sectarian animosities that raged in the 1790s. The rising that Robert Emmet led in Dublin in July 1803 was suppressed with little loss of life and little difficulty. But Emmet redeemed his failure with a speech from the dock (after his conviction for high treason) that later nationalists of all stripes found ennobling and inspiring.

SEE ALSO Emmet, Robert; Politics: 1800 to 1921—Challenges to the Union; United Irish Societies from 1791 to 1803

My lords, as to why judgment of death and execution should not be passed upon me according to law, I have nothing to say; but as to why my character should not be relieved from the imputations and calumnies thrown out against it, I have much to say. I do not imagine that your lordships will give credit to what I am going to utter; I have no hopes that I can anchor my character in the breast of the court. I only wish your lordships may suffer it to float down your memories till it has found some more hospitable harbour to shelter it from the storms with which it is at present buffeted. Was I to suffer only in death after being adjudged guilty, I should bow in silence to the fate which awaits me; but sentence of the law which delivers over my body to the executioner consigns my character to obloquy. A man in my situation has not only to encounter the difficulties of fortune but also the difficulties of prejudice. Whilst the man dies, his memory lives; and that mine may not forfeit all claim to the respect of my countrymen, I seize upon this opportunity to vindicate myself from some of the charges alleged against me.

I am charged with being an emissary of France. It is false—I am no emissary. I did not wish to deliver up my country to a foreign power, and least of all to France. Never did I entertain the remotest idea of establishing French power in Ireland. . . . Were the French to come as invaders or enemies, uninvited by the wishes of the people, I should oppose them to the utmost of my strength. Yes! My countrymen, I should advise you to meet them upon the beach with a sword in one hand and a torch in the other. I would meet them with all the destructive fury of war. I would animate my countrymen to immolate them in their boats before they had contaminated the soil of my country. If they succeeded in landing, and if [I were] forced to retire before superior discipline, I would dispute every inch of ground, burn every blade of grass, and the last intrenchment of liberty should be my grave. What I could not do myself, if I should fall, I should leave as a last charge to my countrymen to accomplish, because I should feel conscious that life, even more than death, would be unprofitable when a foreign nation held my country in subjection. . . . My object and that of the rest of the Provisional Government was to effect a total separation between Great Britain and Ireland—to make Ireland totally independent of Great Britain, but not to let her become a dependent of France.

My lords, you are impatient for the sacrifice. The blood which you seek is not congealed by the artificial terrors which surround your victim; it circulates warmly and unruffled through its channels, and in a little time it will cry to heaven. Be yet patient! I have but a few words more to say—my ministry is now ended. I am going to my cold and silent grave; my lamp of life is nearly extinguished. I have parted with everything that was dear to me in this life for my country's cause, and abandoned another idol I adored in my heart—the object of my affections. My race is run—the grave opens to receive me, and I sink into its bosom. I am ready to die—I have not been allowed to vindicate my character. I have but one request to ask at my departure from this world—it is *the charity of its silence.* Let no man write my epitaph; for as no man who knows my motives dares now vindicate them, let not prejudice or ignorance asperse them. Let them rest in obscurity and peace; [let] my memory be left in oblivion, and my tomb remain uninscribed, until other times and other men can do justice to my character. When my country takes her place among the nations of the earth, then, and not till then, let my epitaph be written. I have done.

Reprinted in IRISH HISTORICAL DOCUMENTS SINCE 1800, *edited by Alan O'Day and John Stevenson (1992), pp. 15–16. © Alan O'Day and John Stevenson. Reproduced by permission.*

~

FROM *A DESCRIPTION OF THE . . . PEASANTRY OF IRELAND*

1804

Robert Bell

Most of Bell's work appeared in journal form before being published as a book. He argues that legislation for Ireland requires a truer knowledge of the country than had previously been found among English writers or officials. He rightfully notes that most accounts have been hostile, as is usual when conquerors write about the conquered.

SEE ALSO English Writing on Ireland before 1800

It must be recollected that the writers who speak of the Irish in terms of reproach, were natives of Britain, and that the hostility of mind which always existed between a conquered people and the conquerors, (and which to this hour has never been effaced in Ireland), must have thrown no weak tint of prejudice on the picture which they drew. The accounts which men give of a people whom they either fear or despise, are not to be received as authentic: and still less are they to be relied on, if it be considered that the authors, from the very nature of their situation, are unable to acquire a knowledge of those whose manners they attempt to describe. Can it be supposed that English governors or English officers going to Ireland in the character of enemies, unac-

quainted with the language of the country, and having no intercourse with the people except the ceremonial visits of perfidious Chieftains who pretended to enter into their views, were capable of giving a true description of Irish manners? Among the fragments of Irish literature which still remain, there is sufficient evidence to prove that many of the accounts of Giraldus Cambrensis are false or exaggerated. Yet this author is quoted by modern historians as an unquestionable authority.

It was not until the present enlightened era that men of liberal and philosophic minds came forward to assert the antiquity of Ireland, to examine the few records that had escaped the ravages of her invaders, and to vindicate her character from unmerited obloquy.

But whatever grounds the English historians might have had for representing the native Irish as savage and ferocious, it has been clearly ascertained that they were not so previously to the invasion of Henry II. The cause of their degeneracy must therefore be obvious to every person who has read the history of conquered countries where the dominion of the victor was only to be retained by force: and still more to those who will take the trouble of reading Dr. Leland's *History of Ireland*. It is a fact as well authenticated as most parts of ancient history, that there were many seminaries of learning in this island for four or five centuries before it was conquered by England; that numbers of persons from other countries resorted thither for instruction (the greater part of Europe being at that time in a state of deplorable ignorance); that there were Princes in the country who displayed the talents of great statesmen and generals; that the Irish were often as successful as their English neighbours in repelling Danish invasions; and that in the reign of William the Conqueror they had made a generous though unsuccessful struggle to restore the exiled family of Harold to the throne of England.

Reprinted in STRANGERS TO THAT LAND: BRITISH PERCEPTIONS OF IRELAND FROM THE REFORMATION TO THE FAMINE, *edited by Andrew Hadfield and John McVeagh (1994), pp. 151–152.*

~

ON PRESBYTERIAN COMMUNITIES IN ULSTER

1810, 1812

John Gamble

John Gamble, an Irish Protestant long resident in England, returned to Ireland three times between 1810 and 1818. His published accounts of his travels are especially valuable for their descriptions of northern Presbyterian society, in which he himself was probably raised. The first of the three selections below describes his walk through an area in Counties Down and Armagh, which had witnessed serious sectarian tensions in the 1780s and 1790s. The second relates to the mainly Presbyterian town of Belfast when it had just begun to experience Catholic migration from the countryside. In the third he writes from Strabane, a town in the west of Ulster where lowland Presbyterian settlements were overlooked by isolated mountainous areas inhabited by Irish-speaking Catholics.

SEE ALSO Belfast; Religion: Since 1690

I walked to Loughbrickland, a distance of eight miles, yesterday, before breakfast. The morning was beautiful—the hedges were blooming with the flower of the hawthorn—the air was loaded with fragrance—I could have fancied myself in Elysium, had I not met numbers of yeomen in every direction. They were in general good looking men; and were well and uniformly dressed. They all wore orange lilies. I now recollected that is was the 12th of July; (the 30th of June, old style) and of consequence the anniversary of the battle of the Boyne.

I entered into conversation with a little group who were travelling my road. They were very desirous to have my opinion of the Catholic Bill, as they called it, that is expected to be brought forward next Session of Parliament.

"Never mind acts of parliament, my lads," said I, "but live peaceably with your neighbours. I warrant you your fields will look as green, and your hedges smell as sweet this time next year, whether the bill passes or not."

"May be so," said one of them; "and may be we wouldn't be long here to smell or look at them."

I made little reply to this, for I could not expect that any thing I should urge would weaken even the rooted prejudices of their lives. What I did reply they heard with respect, though not with conviction.

"Ah, reverend Sir," said a middle-aged man, "you speak like a good man and a great scholar; but, Lord love ye, books won't make us know life."

"Tell me," said I, "why you take me for a clergyman; is it because I wear a black coat?"

"No," returned he, "but because you have a moderate face."

The lower class of people in Ireland are great physiognomists—good ones, I am bound to suppose, for my face has often received the above moderate compliment. It speaks favourably, however, of the manner of the Irish Protestant clergy that a man of mild demeanour is almost always taken for one of them.

Loughbrickland consists of one broad street. It takes its name from a lake standing near it, called Loughbrickland, or the lake of speckled trouts, with which it formerly abounded, till the spawn of pikes finding a passage into the lake, multiplied so exceedingly, that they have almost destroyed the whole breed.

That body of English forces which were quartered in this part of the north, in the year 1690, had their first rendezvous here under King William, who encamped within a mile of the town.

Nearly at the same distance from it I turned off the great road to go to Tanderagee. I passed a number of gentlemen's seats. I was struck with their uncommon neatness. I asked a countryman if he could tell me the reason. He knew no reason, he said, except that the owners were not *born* gentleman.

Much of the landed property of this part of the country has passed from the extravagant children of idleness, to the sons of the thrifty merchants of Newry and Belfast. I find, in general, they are good landlords. . . .

I came in sight of Tanderagee about two o'clock. As it is situated on a hill, I saw it at a considerable distance. The planting of the late General Sparrow's extensive demesne, which seemed to overshadow it, gave it a gay and picturesque appearance. Nor was the spectacle of the interior less radiant. Only that the bright green of nature was displaced by the deep orange of party. Tanderagee was a perfect orange grove. The doors and windows were decorated with garlands of the orange lily. The bosoms and heads of the women, and hats and breasts of the men, were equally adorned with this venerated flower. There were likewise a number of orange banners and colours, more remarkable for loyalty than taste or variety, for King William on horseback, as grim as a Saracen on a sign post, was painted or wrought on all of them.

There was much of fancy, however, in the decoration of a lofty arch, which was thrown across the entire street. The orange was gracefully blended with oak leaves, laurels, and roses. Bits of gilded paper, suited to the solemnity, were interwoven with the flowers. I passed, as well as I could, through the crowd assembled under this glittering rainbow, and proceeded to the house of an acquaintance at the upper end of the street. I had purposed spending a day with him, but he was from home. I, therefore, sat half an hour with his lady, and after having taken some refreshment, descended the hill. The people were now dancing. The music was not indifferent. The tune, however, would better have suited a minuet than a country dance. It was the (once in England) popular tune of Lillybullero, better known in this country, by the affectionate and cheering name, of the Protestant Boys.

I stopped an instant, a man came up and presented me a nosegay of orange lilies and roses, bound together—I held it in my hand, but did not put it in my hat, as he expected.

"I am no party man," I said, "nor do I ever wear party colours."

"Well, God bless you, Sir," he replied, "whether you do or not."

Nor did the crowd, who heard both the speech and reply, appear to take the slightest offence. This was the more wonderful as I stood before them rather under inauspicious circumstances. It seems, though I was then ignorant of it, the gentleman out of whose house they had seen me come, was highly obnoxious to them. He is minister of the Presbyterian congregation—a few months ago with more liberality than prudence, considering what an untractable flock he is the shepherd of, he signed his name to the Protestant petition, in favour of the Catholics. The following Sunday he found his meeting-house closed against him, nor is it yet opened, and probably never will be.

The country of Armagh Presbyterians are the very Spadassins of Protestantism. Their unhappy disputes a few years ago with the Catholics are well known. It is therefore unnecessary (and I rejoice at it) for me to touch on them here.

On quitting Tanderagee, I walked a little way on the road which I came. I then seated myself on the top of a little hill, to meditate on my future route. The world was all before me where to choose—and a most delightful world I had to choose from. Armagh is as much beautified by the industry as it has been disfigured by the passions of men. . . .

The day at length became fine, the sun shone bright, and the road soon got clear. I walked, therefore, lightly forwards—At every furlong's length, however, I met with a cross-road; luckily the people were as plenty as the roads; nor did I meet with a single cross-answer from one of them. I was overtaken by a young Scotchman on horseback. He had travelled a hundred miles in Scotland, and upwards of an hundred in Ireland, to purchase cattle, and was now returning homewards. He civilly insisted on my mounting his horse, and without giving me time to reply alighted to help me on.

"It is fitter I should be walking," said he, "than you."

I do not know that a good face is always a letter of recommendation—I have ever found that a good coat is.

I asked him what he thought of Ireland.

"It's a heaven of a place," he replied, "but they're the *devil* of a people."

I examined him as to this latter opinion, and found he had every where met with kindness and attention. He had heard it from his father, who probably had heard it from his; and in this manner are the characters of nation and individuals judged. . . .

I have now been a week in Belfast, which has rolled not unpleasantly away. In the morning I walk the streets, and frequent the libraries; and in the evening I go to card parties and concerts. I am, therefore, in some degree competent to speak of the place and people. I do it without reluctance, for I can say little of either but what is good.

Belfast is a large and well-built town. The streets are broad and straight. The houses neat and comfortable, mostly built of brick. The population, in a random way, may be estimated at thirty thousand, of which probably four thousand are Catholics. These are almost entirely working people. A few years ago there was scarcely a Catholic in the place. How much Presbyterians out-number the members of the Established Church, appears from the circumstance of there being five meeting-houses and only one church. Three of these meeting-houses are in a cluster, and are neat little buildings. Neatness and trimness, indeed, rather than magnificence, are the characteristics of all the public buildings. A large mass-house, however, to the building of which, with their accustomed liberality, the inhabitants largely contributed, is an exception. . . .

The principal library is in one of the rooms of the linen hall. I spend some hours every day in it—solitary hours; for the bustling inhabitants of this great commercial town have little leisure (I do not know that they have little inclination) for reading. Round the hall there is a public walk, prettily laid out with flowers and shrubs. I meet with as few people here, as in the library. Young women appear to walk as little as the men read. I know not whether this is a restraint of Presbyterianism, or of education; but let the cause be what it may, it is a very cruel one—young women have few enjoyments; it is a pity, therefore, to deprive them of so innocent a one as that of walking. I have conversed with them at parties, and generally found them rational and unassuming. To an Englishman, as may be easily conceived, the rusticity of their accent would at first be unpleasant. But his ear would soon accommodate itself to it, and even find beauties in it—the greatest of all beauties in a female, an apparent freedom from affectation and assumption. They seldom played cards, nor did the elderly people seem to be particularly fond of them. Music was the favourite recreation, and many were no mean proficients in it. They are probably indebted for this to Mr. Bunting, a man well known in the music world. He has an extensive school here, and is organist to one of the meeting-houses; for so little fanaticism have now the Presbyterians of Belfast, that they have admitted organs into their places of worship. At no very distant period this would have been reckoned as high a profanation as to have erected a crucifix. . . .

I write this from a farmhouse, sixteen miles from Strabane. . . .

The people with whom I am are Presbyterians. They are industrious and wealthy. Their house is what a farmhouse ought to be, comfortable and neat, without finery or fashion; it is situated in a most dreary country, and may be said to be on the very verge of civilisation in this quarter. Before my windows rise the immense mountains, which separate the county of Tyrone from the counties of Donegal and Fermanagh. The appearance of these mountains, though gloomy and forlorn, is not uninteresting: they are covered with a sort of brown heath, interspersed with scanty green rushes, and scantier blades of green grass: they are such scenes as Ossian would love to describe, and probably many of his heroes did tread those heaths over which the wind now passes in mournful gusts and moves in melancholy unison with the memory of years that are gone. . . .

These mountains are inhabited entirely by Catholics: in ancient times, they were the asylum of those unfortunate people, and they were not dispossessed of them; probably, because no other people would live in them. In these mountains, therefore, we meet with a people purely Irish, professing what may be well called the Irish religion, and retaining most of the old Irish customs, usages, opinions, and prejudices. I hold long conversations with them, as I meet them on the roads or sit with them in their own houses: hardly a day has passed since my arrival, that I have not walked from eight to ten miles, and either address, or am addressed-by, every person I meet. In almost every instance, I have been impressed with their singular acuteness of intellect, and extensive information of what is passing in the world: a London tradesman could not detail the wonderful events we are daily witnessing more correctly, and, probably, would not half so energetically. An Irish peasant, like a Frenchman, speaks with every part of his body, and his arm and countenance are as eloquent as his tongue.

John Gamble, A View of Society and Manners in the North of Ireland in the Summer and Autumn of 1812 (1813), pp. 32–39, 64–66, *and* Sketches of History, Politics, and Manners in Dublin and the North of Ireland in 1810 (1826), pp. 317–319.

⟶

FROM *NARRATIVE OF A RESIDENCE IN IRELAND*

1817

Anne Plumptre

Anne Plumptre (1760–1818) was a well-known playwright, translator, traveler, and travel writer of the early nineteenth century. After living in France between 1802 and 1805, she published an account of her residence there. Her Irish journey of 1814 to 1815 forms the basis of this narrative. Here she links the Irish with the French, both perceived as "different" from the English.

SEE ALSO English Writing on Ireland before 1800

I shall be thought, perhaps, by my own countrymen to cast the severest reflection that can be cast upon the Irish, when I say that they perpetually reminded me of the French. There is a much stronger resemblance in them to the French national character than to the English; and this resemblance is equally forcible in the lower as in the higher classes of society. Nothing is more comic than to observe the difference between an English mechanic and a French or Irish one. I once, when travelling in France, wanted something done to the lid of a trunk, which I thought in some danger of splitting in two. I did not wish, however, to be long delayed by the job; and recollecting how an English carpenter or trunk-maker would have chiselled and planed a piece of wood, and fitted and fitted it over again before he could have been satisfied to nail it upon the trunk, and how much time all this would take, I was rather afraid of submitting my wounded servant to such a process; I thought I should be *impatienté* at the *longueur*, and I tried to persuade myself that the case was not of a very pressing nature. Yet the more I examined, the more imminent the danger appeared; and at length I desired that a carpenter might be sent for, stating what I wanted. *Veni, vidi, vici* says Caesar; and so it was with the carpenter: I need not have been so much afraid of delay. He brought with him a hammer, a few nails, and a rough spline: the latter was knocked on in two minutes, and all was accomplished. It did not look quite so neat as if it had come from the hands of an English workman: it held the lid together, however, and all was well: but the rapidity with which the whole was performed was amusing and highly characteristic. The same is very much the case with the Irish: —ardent in their pursuits, rapid in their movements, they blaze brilliantly for a while, but the ardour is too apt easily to subside; while with the Englishman, who is less alive at catching fire, when the flame within him is once lighted, it burns on even and steady, nor is readily exhausted. It is perhaps extraordinary, considering the state of depression in which the Irish have been kept for such a lengthened series of years, that they still retain so much of their native wit, ardour, and vivacity; but even now an Irishman, like a Frenchman, will have his joke if it comes in his way, coûte-qui-coûte.

A very marked difference is, however, to be observed between the inhabitants of the two extremes of Ireland which I visited, the north-east or county of Antrim, and the south-west, including the counties of Cork and Kerry, strongly supporting the belief that their origin is to be traced to different sources. In the south of Ireland the people are much darker than in the north; and here was the country where the Milesians from Spain, according to all the traditions, both written and oral, were first established. Now the dark complexion, eyes and hair, have been ever, and still are, the distinguishing characteristics of all the Southern nations of Europe; as the fair complexion, blue eyes, and light hair, sometimes deviating into red, were, and are still, of the Northern. The one are bleached by colds and snows, the others darkened by the warmth of the sun. Now, every possible presumptive evidence leads to the belief that the north of Ireland, or perhaps all Ireland and Scotland, were originally peopled from the Northern nations of Europe, the parts which formed the ancient Scandinavia; while the south, if originally peopled by the same, afterwards became the settlement of an Iberian colony, whose descendants remain there to this day. A close and constant intercourse has always subsisted between the inhabitants of the north of Ireland and Scotland, so that they ever have been, as it were, one and the same people. In more than one part the coasts come so near as within eighteen miles of each other: the distance is no more between Port Patrick in Scotland and Donaghadee in Ireland, and between the Mull of Cantire in Scotland and the county of Antrim in Ireland. Indeed there can scarcely be doubt, from the name, that Port Patrick originally an establishment of the Irish. It is well known that the Irish are in ancient records called *Scots*; but at the Milesian conquest, these people coming from the land of Iberia, one of the leaders also bearing the name *Heber*, thence the name of *Hibernia*, afterwards given to the island, was derived; whilst the natives driven constantly northwards, many of them probably at that time migrating to Scotland, transferred thither with themselves the name they bore. There is besides more of the true Irish quickness and vivacity in the south of Ireland than in the north; the people of the north partake somewhat of the solemnity of their neighbours the Scots.

Reprinted in STRANGERS TO THAT LAND: BRITISH PERCEPTIONS OF IRELAND FROM THE REFORMATION TO THE FAMINE, *edited by Andrew Hadfield and John McVeagh* (1994), pp. 154–155.

~

ORIGIN OF THE "CATHOLIC RENT"

18 February 1824

The Catholic Association founded by Daniel O'Connell in May 1823 aimed to bring about "emancipation"—the admission of Catholics to seats in parliament and to the highest government offices. The new central body in Dublin had a rocky start; there was difficulty in securing a quorum at some of its early meetings. But early in 1824 the association instituted an "associate membership" that required the payment of only a penny a month (the "Catholic rent"), and as this document indicates, a plan was devised for the systematic collection of this small monthly subscription throughout Ireland. This plan became the vehicle through which a mass movement embracing the Catholic peasantry was soon created.

SEE ALSO Catholic Emancipation Campaign; O'Connell, Daniel; Politics: 1800 to 1921—Challenges to the Union; Roman Catholic Church: 1690 to 1829

The committee appointed to devise the best mode of raising a general subscription throughout Ireland beg leave respectfully to submit the following report.

The Catholics of Ireland have long been engaged in a painful and anxious struggle to attain, by peaceful and constitutional means, those civil rights to which every subject of these realms is, upon principle, and of justice entitled, and of which our forefathers were basely and perfidiously deprived, in defiance of the sacred claims of conscience and in open and indecent violation of the faith of treaties.

Your committee are impressed with the melancholy conviction that at no former period of this protracted struggle had the Catholic people of Ireland so little reason to entertain hope of immediate success. A strange combination of events has occurred to cloud our prospects and to render the expectation of redress remote and doubtful. . . .

The combination of all these untoward circumstances has almost extinguished hope; and were it forbidden to despair of the sacred cause of liberty and religion, your committee would feel it a duty to recommend a silent submission to events over which we possess, alas, no control, and a tacit acquiescence in an evil system which we want the power, or at least lawful and constitutional means, to crush, and to await, in the sullen silence of unconcealed discontent, for a more favourable opportunity and better organised resources to prove to Britain and the world—that we are men and deserve to be free.

But your committee can never recommend such a course. They do not dare to despair. They know that their cause is just and holy. It is the cause of religion and liberty. It is the cause of their country and of their God. It never can be abandoned by the Catholics of Ireland. . . .

But in order effectually to exert the energies of the Irish people, pecuniary resources are absolutely necessary. Your committee have a just and entire confidence that such resources can be procured with facility, and that it requires nothing more than a reasonable portion of exertion on the part of a few individuals to secure abundant pecuniary means to answer every legitimate object.

The purposes for which pecuniary resources are wanting should be clearly defined and distinctly understood. They should be useful in their objects and strictly legal and constitutional in all their details.

Your committee respectfully submit that the following purposes are of obvious and paramount utility; and that no doubt does or can exist of their being perfectly legal.

1st. To forward petitions to parliament, not only on the subject of Catholic emancipation but for the redress of all local or general grievances affecting the Irish people.

Under this head should be included a salary for a permanent parliamentary agent in London.

Your committee conceive that a sum of £5,000 per ann[um] would cover all the expenses under this first head.

2ndly. To procure legal redress for all such Catholics, assailed or injured by Orange violence, as are unable to obtain it for themselves, to prevent, by due course of law, Orange processions and public insults, to bring before the high courts of criminal justice all such magistrates as should participate in or countenance the illegal proceedings, processions, etc., of the Orange faction, and to arrest, by the powerful arm of the law, that career of violence by which principally in the north, but occasionally in the south, so many Catholics have been murdered by Orangemen, many of whom are intrusted with arms by the government for far different purposes—and, in fine, to prosecute the Orange murderers where we cannot prevent the murders.

There is also another head of legal relief of great importance. It is to procure for the Catholics the actual enjoyment of all such rights in the several corporations in Ireland to which they are by law entitled, and which have for thirty years past been perseveringly withheld from them by interested bigotry.

To this important object your committee would in the first years devote £15,000 per annum.

3rdly. To encourage and support a liberal and enlightened press, as well in Dublin as in London—a press which could readily refute the arguments of our enemies and expose the falsehood of their calumnies upon us and our religion—a press which would publish and explain the real principles of the Catholics, and by the irresistible force of truth, either silence or at least confound our calumniators.

For the last two centuries the British press, in all its exclusive ramifications, from the ponderous folio down to the most paltry ballad, has teemed with the most unfounded calumnies and the grossest falsehoods on the subject of the religion and principles of the Catholics. The popular writers of the present day, even those who support our claims to emancipation, affect an air of candour by joining our worst enemies in traducing our most sacred religion.

It is time that this grievous mischief should be checked; and your committee conceive that a less sum than £15,000 per annum ought not to be dedicated to this most useful purpose.

4thly. To procure for the various schools in the country cheap publications by means of which the Catholic children may attain knowledge without having their religion interfered with, or their social virtue checked by anything unchristian or uncharitable. The money given by parliament for this purpose is shamefully misapplied; and the necessity of a resource of this description is daily felt by the Catholic prelates and pastors, who have the greatest anxiety to promote the education of their flocks but are unable to afford sufficient sums of money for that purpose.

Your committee would in the first instance expend £5,000 per annum to remedy this evil; they would recommend that all the savings on the foregoing heads of expenditure (which they trust will be considerable) should be applied then to advance education.

Your committee would respectfully submit the propriety of aiding the resources of the Irish and other Catholics in North America, to procure for them a sufficient number of priests. The number of Catholics in the United States is great and daily increasing. The want of Catholic clergymen is felt as an extreme evil; and it is thought that a sum of £5,000 a year could not be better applied than in remedying in some measure this deficiency.

Besides, the Catholics in Great Britain are multiplying almost beyond hope. The French Revolution supplied the English Catholics with clergymen for many years. That resource is now gone; and it would be suited to the charity and piety of the Irish people to supply their haughty and erratic neighbours with the means of instruction in that ancient faith which, since the first days of Christianity, always was, and still is, and while the world lasts, will be the genuine source of every Christian and social virtue.

Having detailed these five distinct objects, your committee beg leave to state that as they conceive that after exhausting those purposes, there ought to remain a sum of at least £5,000 per annum at the disposal of the Association—they would recommend that such sum should be allowed to accumulate in the public funds, and that out of such accumulation the Catholic Association should from time to time be at liberty to dedicate, in fair and reasonable proportions, in contributions towards erecting schools, building Catholic churches, and erecting and furnishing dwelling-houses for the clergy in the poorer parishes, and ameliorating in other respects the condition of the Catholic clergy in Ireland.

Your committee confidently hope that if the plan which they are about to suggest be adopted, such accumulation will greatly exceed £5,000 per annum and may be five times that sum, and thereby afford means of doing great and permanent good to the most estimable, laborious, learned, and pious clergy with which it has ever pleased the eternal wisdom to bless a faithful and suffering people.

The basis of our plan is founded on the extent of the Catholic population of Ireland. We may expect a good deal of assistance from the liberal portion of our Protestant fellow countrymen, but our reliance for success must be placed upon the numbers and patriotism of the Catholic people of Ireland. . . .

The detail of the plan of your committee is this. They purpose—

1st. That a monthly subscription should be raised throughout Ireland, to be denominated "the monthly Catholic rent."

2nd. That the Association should forthwith appoint two of its members [as] a secretary and [an] assistant in order to collect such subscriptions throughout Ireland.

3rd. That such secretary and assistant should immediately open an account with each parish in Ireland and enter therein the particulars of all monies subscribed by such parish[es].

4th. That the Association should adopt the most speedy means of nominating, in conjunction with the inhabitants of each parish, and if possible with the privity of the Catholic clergyman, a number of persons not to exceed twelve, nor less than three, in order to collect the subscriptions.

5th. That monthly returns be procured from such persons or from as many of them as possible, and that a monthly report, in writing, of the progress made in each parish be given in by the [parochial] secretary for the subscriptions to the secretary of the Catholics of Ireland, to be by him laid before the Association.

6th. That care be taken to publish in, or at least as near, each Catholic chapel as may be permitted by the clergy, the particulars of the sums subscribed in such parish[es], with the names of each subscriber, unless where the individuals shall choose to insert the subscription under the head[ing of] anonymous.

7th. That accounts of subscriptions, debtor and creditor, be published annually for the satisfaction of the subscribers and the public at large.

8th. That all subscriptions be paid, as soon as transmitted to Dublin, into the hands of the treasurer to the association.

9th. That an efficient committee of 21 members be appointed to superintend and manage the collection and expenditure of the subscription money, to be styled and to act as a committee of accounts.

10th. That no monies be expended without an express vote of the Association upon a notice regularly given.

11th. That the amount expected from each individual shall not exceed one penny per month, but that each individual shall be at liberty to give any greater monthly sum he pleases, not exceeding in the entire two shillings per month.

12th. That the guinea paid by each member of the Association on his admission be deemed and taken as part of the entire of the contribution of the individual to the subscription thus proposed, and that each member be requested to allocate his guinea to some particular parish.

13th. That each subscriber be at liberty to allocate his subscription either to the fund generally or to any particular object heretofore specified, and that such allocation be in every respect, strictly and without any deviation, attended to.

14th. That Daniel O'Connell, Esq., be appointed secretary for subscriptions, and James Sugrue, Esq., [act as] his assistant.

Your committee submit that if only one million of the six millions of Catholics which this country contains will contribute the small sum of one farthing a week each, the resources of the Association will exceed the estimate of expenditures heretofore detailed. They cannot doubt the readiness with which the subscription will be raised if proper means are taken to apply for it universally.

Your committee cannot conclude without expressing their decided conviction that if this plan shall be carried into complete operation, all the difficulties in the way of our emancipation will be speedily removed—and we shall have the glory as well as the advantage of carrying into effect the Christian principle of liberty of conscience.

Daniel O'Connell, Chairman.

DUBLIN EVENING POST, *19 February 1824.*

~

THE CATHOLIC RELIEF ACT

1829

Daniel O'Connell's crusade for Catholic emancipation achieved its most notable political successes when the Catholic 40-shilling-freehold voters in certain county constituencies engaged in a "revolt" against the traditional political dictation of their landlords. The most famous such case occurred in July 1828, when O'Connell himself soundly defeated the sitting MP William Vesey Fitzgerald in the Clare by-election. The prospect of many similar Catholic victories, and the fear that the crusade might turn violent if frustrated of its goal, persuaded the Wellington-Peel government in Britain to advise George IV to concede emancipation.

SEE ALSO Catholic Emancipation Campaign; O'Connell, Daniel; Politics: 1800 to 1921—Challenges to the Union; Roman Catholic Church: 1690 to 1829; Roman Catholic Church: 1829 to 1891

AN ACT FOR THE RELIEF OF HIS MAJESTY'S ROMAN CATHOLIC SUBJECTS

Whereas by various acts of parliament certain restraints and disabilities are imposed on the Roman Catholic subjects of his majesty, to which other subjects of his majesty are not liable, and whereas it is expedient that such restraints and disabilities shall be from henceforth discontinued, and whereas by various acts certain oaths and certain declarations, commonly called the declarations against transubstantiation and the invocation of saints and the sacrifice of the mass, as practised in the church of Rome, are or may be required to be taken, made, and subscribed by the subjects of his majesty as qualifications for sitting and voting in parliament and for the enjoyment of certain offices, franchises, and civil rights, be it enacted . . . that from and after the commencement of this act all such parts of the said acts as require the said declarations, or either of them, to be made or subscribed by any of his majesty's subjects as a qualification for sitting and voting in parliament or for the exercise or enjoyment of any office, franchise, or civil right, be and the same are (save as hereinafter provided and excepted) hereby repealed.

II. And be it enacted that . . . it shall be lawful for any person professing the Roman Catholic religion, being a peer, or who shall after the commencement of this act be returned as a member of the House of Commons, to sit and vote in either house of parliament respectively, being in all other respects duly qualified to sit and vote therein, upon taking and subscribing the following oath, instead of the oaths of allegiance, supremacy, and abjuration: I, A.B., do sincerely promise and swear that I will be faithful and bear true allegiance to his majesty King George the Fourth and will defend him to the utmost of my power against all conspiracies and attempts whatever, which shall be made against his person, crown, or dignity. And I will do my utmost endeavour to disclose and make known to his majesty, his heirs and successors, all treasons and traitorous conspiracies which may be formed against him or them. And I do faithfully promise to maintain, support, and defend, to the utmost of my power, the succession of the Crown, which succession, by an act entitled *An act for the further limitation of the Crown and better securing the rights and liberties of the subject*, is and stands limited to the Princess Sophia, electress of Hanover, and the heirs of her body, being Protestants; hereby utterly renouncing and abjuring any obedience or allegiance unto any other person claiming or pretending a right to the Crown of this realm. And I do further declare that it is not an article of my faith, and that I do renounce, reject, and abjure the opinion that princes excommunicated or deprived by the pope or any other authority of the see of Rome may be deposed or murdered by their subjects or by any person whatsoever. And I do declare that I do not believe that the pope of Rome, or any other foreign prince, prelate, person, state, or potentate, hath or ought to have any temporal or civil jurisdiction, power, superiority, or pre-eminence, directly or indirectly, within this realm. I do swear that I will defend to the utmost of my power the settlement of the property within this realm as established by the laws, and I do hereby disclaim, disavow, and solemnly abjure any intention to subvert the present church establishment as settled by law within this realm, and I do solemnly swear that I never will exercise any privilege to which I am or may become entitled, to disturb or weaken the Protestant religion or Protestant government in the United Kingdom. And I do solemnly, in the presence of God, profess, testify, and declare that I do make this declaration and every part thereof in the plain and ordinary sense of the words of this oath, without any evasion, equivocation, or mental reservation whatsoever. So help me God.

V. And be it further enacted that it shall be lawful for persons professing the Roman Catholic religion to vote at elections of members to serve in parliament for England and for Ireland, and also to vote at the elections of representative peers of Scotland and of Ireland, and to be elected such representative peers, being in all other respects duly qualified, upon taking and subscribing the oath hereinbefore appointed and set forth. . . .

X. And be it enacted that it shall be lawful for any of his majesty's subjects professing the Roman Catholic religion to hold, exercise, and enjoy all civil and military offices and places of trust or profit under his majesty, his heirs or successors; and to exercise any other franchise or civil right . . . upon taking and subscribing . . . the oath herinbefore appointed. . . .

XII. Provided also, and be it further enacted that nothing herein contained shall extend or be construed to extend to enable any person or persons professing the Roman Catholic religion to hold or exercise the office of guardians and justices of the United Kingdom or of regent of the United Kingdom, under whatever name, style, or title such office may be constituted, nor to enable any person, otherwise than as he is now by law enabled, to hold or enjoy the office of lord high chancellor, lord keeper or lord commissioner of the great seal of Great Britain or Ireland, or the office of lord lieutenant, or lord deputy, or other chief governor or governors of

Ireland, or his majesty's high commissioner to the General Assembly of the Church of Scotland.

XIV. And be it enacted that it shall be lawful for any of his majesty's subjects professing the Roman Catholic religion to be a member of any lay body corporate, and to hold any civil office or place of trust or profit therein, and to do any corporate act or vote in any corporate election or other proceeding, upon taking and subscribing the oath hereby appointed and set forth, instead of the oaths of allegiance, supremacy, and abjuration, and upon taking also such other oath or oaths as may now by law be required to be taken by any persons becoming members of such lay body corporate. . . .

XVI. Provided also, and be it enacted that nothing in this act contained shall be construed to enable any persons, otherwise than as they are now by law enabled, to hold, enjoy, or exercise any office, place, or dignity of, in, or belonging to the United Church of England and Ireland, or the Church of Scotland, or any place or office whatever of, in, or belonging to any of the ecclesiastical courts of judicature of England and Ireland respectively, or any court of appeal from or review of the sentences of such courts, or of, in, or belonging to the commissary court of Edinburgh, or of, in, or belonging to any cathedral or collegiate or ecclesiastical establishment or foundation, or any office or place whatever of, in, or belonging to any of the universities of this realm, or any office or place whatever, and by whatever name the same may be called, of, in, or belonging to any of the colleges or halls of the said universities, . . . or any college or school within this realm; or to repeal, abrogate, or in any manner to interfere with any local statute, ordinance, or rule, which is or shall be established by competent authority within any university, college, hall, or school, by which Roman Catholics shall be prevented from being admitted thereto or from residing or taking degrees therein. . . .

XXIV. And whereas the Protestant Episcopal Church of England and Ireland, and the doctrine, discipline, and government thereof, and likewise the Protestant Presbyterian Church of Scotland, and the doctrine, discipline, and government thereof, are by the respective Acts of Union of England and Scotland, and of Great Britain and Ireland, established permanently and inviolably, and whereas the right and title of archbishops to their respective provinces, of bishops to their sees, and the deans to their deaneries, as well in England as in Ireland, have been settled and established by law, be it therefore enacted that if any person after the commencement of this act, other than the person thereunto authorised by law, shall assume or use the name, style, or title of archbishop of any province, bishop of any bishopric, or dean of any deanery in England or Ireland, he shall for every such offence forfeit and pay the sum of £100.

XXV. And be it further enacted that if any person holding any judicial or civil office, or any mayor, provost, jurat, bailiff, or other corporate officer, shall after the commencement of this act resort to or be present at any place or public meeting for religious worship in England or in Ireland, other than that of the United Church of England and Ireland, or in Scotland, other than that of the Church of Scotland, as by law established, in the robe, gown, or other peculiar habit of his office, or attend with the ensign or insignia, or any part thereof, of or belonging to such his office, such person shall, being thereof convicted by due course of law, forfeit such office and pay for every offence the sum of £100.

XXVI. And be it further enacted, that if any Roman Catholic ecclesiastic, or any member of any of the orders, communities, or societies hereinafter mentioned, shall, after the commencement of this act, exercise any of the rites or ceremonies of the Roman Catholic religion, or wear the habits of his order, save within the usual places of worship of the Roman Catholic religion, or in private houses, such ecclesiastic or other person shall, being thereof convicted by due courses of law, forfeit for every such offence the sum of £50.

XXXIV. And be it further enacted that in case any person shall after the commencement of this act, within any part of this United Kingdom, be admitted or become a Jesuit, or brother, or member of any other such religious order, community, or society as aforesaid, such person shall be deemed and taken to be guilty of a misdemeanour, and being thereof lawfully convicted, shall be sentenced and ordered to be banished from the United Kingdom for the term of his natural life.

XXXVII. Provided always, and be it enacted that nothing herein contained shall extend or be construed to extend in any manner to affect any religious order, community, or establishment consisting of females bound by religious or monastic vows.

10 Geo. IV, c. 7; A Collection of the Public General Statutes . . . (1829), pp. 105–115.

～

Account of the Wexford Rising

1832

Thomas Cloney

This account of the United Irish rebellion in County Wexford in 1798 was written by a relatively well-off Catholic, *Thomas Cloney. It has been powerfully argued that Cloney minimized the extent of United Irish preparation for rebellion and of his own involvement because when he wrote three decades later association with violence and conspiracy was much less acceptable among elite Catholics than it had been in the 1790s. (See L. M. Cullen, "The 1798 Rebellion in Wexford," in* Wexford: History and Society *[1987], pp. 248–295.)*

SEE ALSO Eighteenth-Century Politics: 1795 to 1800—Repression, Rebellion, and Union

I at this time was about twenty-three years of age and lived with my father, Denis Cloney, at Moneyhore, within three miles of Enniscorthy, and in a direct line from that town to Ross; he rented large tracts of land, both in the Counties of Wexford and Carlow, a good part of which his father left him in possession of, and the remainder he acquired by industry, and altogether they would, if let, produce him an interest of several hundred pounds a year. . . . I was an only son, and had three sisters, all younger than myself and unprovided for: and as my father was aged, and his health then in a very precarious state, they might be considered almost without any other protector but myself, and they were truly dear to me. . . . I was a Catholic, and that placed me in those days on the proscribed list, and under the ban of a furious Orange ascendancy, and their rapacious satellites, a blood thirsty Yeomanry, and a hireling magistracy, who looked forward to the possession of the property, not only of Catholics, but of liberal Protestants, either by plunder or confiscation; where then was the alternative for me? It became indispensable to divert their attention from those objects by meeting them in the field. . . .

On Saturday night the 26th of May, the chapel at Boolavogue and about twenty farmer's [sic] houses in that neighbourhood were burned, as also the house of the Catholic Curate, the Rev. J. Murphy. It was on that night that the first assemblage of the people took place in any part of the county of Wexford: some of the farmers and their men met a party of the Camolin Yeomen Cavalry, and in a short rencounter, killed Lieutenant Bookey, who commanded the party and one of his men. They then proceeded to rise that quarter of the county, north and east of Enniscorthy, and on Sunday morning the 27th, they appeared in considerable force on Oulart Hill, about six miles to the northeast of Enniscorthy, headed by a man hitherto the least likely of any other Priest in that county to appear in arms, a quiet inoffensive man, devoting his time and entire energies to the care and spiritual instruction of a peaceable, orderly, and industrious flock, in a parish where he was Curate, but whose resentment was so justly raised by the sanguinary persecution of his people. Expresses were soon sent from different quarters to Wexford, for a military force to check the progress of the Insurgents, and a division of the North Cork Militia, which had been for some time commanded there by Lord Kingsborough, was now led out by Lieutenant-Colonel Foote, and consisted of about 110 men, besides six officers, who, on arriving at Oulart Hill, ascended rapidly at the north side, while a body of Yeomen Cavalry appeared advancing towards it on the south. The bold and rapid advance of the North Cork Militia, struck terror for a moment in the people, and they were actually on the point of fight, when they perceived the cavalry coming too close, and found they would, by retreating into an open and level country, be exposed to immediate and certain destruction; a number of them were instantly ordered to conceal themselves behind the fences of a ditch, while others lay in ambush in a sort of trench, and allowed the military to approach within a few yards of their main body, when they rushed suddenly on them, and killed with their pikes, 106 men and their Major, Lombard, and four other Officers; Lieutenant-Colonel Foote, a Serjeant, two Privates and a Drummer, out of the whole division, only escaping to Wexford, while of the Insurgents only five were killed and two wounded. The number of the peasantry who shared in the victory, scarcely exceeded the number of the slain Militia; no doubt that the advantageous ground, the close quarters, and the formidable weapons, of which they made so good a use, contributed to their victory.

One of the Yeomen Cavalry was shot at a great distance by an Irish Rifleman, with a Strand Gun, and the rest betook themselves to an immediate and precipitate flight to Wexford. The conquerors flushed with victory, marched immediately to Carrigrue Hill, where they rested for the night, and very early on Monday morning marched upon the little town of Camolin, where they seized a quantity of arms which had been deposited there for safety. From thence they hastily proceeded to Ferns, and on to Scarawalsh Bridge, where they crossed the river Slaney; here they halted for a short time, to obtain an accession of strength, which they obtained on Ballyorrell Hill, and thence proceeded rapidly to Enniscorthy, having then a force of about 7000 men, about 1000 of which were furnished with fire arms. . . .

While the events which I have related were occurring on the 25th, 26th and 27th, the people in my quarter of the country were in perfect ignorance of those occurrences: they were in the most terror-struck and feverish anxiety, as reports were for some time industriously circulated, that the Orangemen would turn out, and commit a general and indiscriminate massacre on the Roman Catholics. The reports from different quarters of what had been already effected by the Orangemen in this way, confirmed the opinion that the Insurrection would become general. The most peaceable and well disposed fancied they saw themselves, their families, and their neighbours, involved in one common ruin, and that each approaching night might possibly be the last of their domestic happiness. No one slept in his own house—the very whistling of the birds seemed to report the approach of an enemy. The remembrance of the wailings of the women and the cries of the children awake in my mind, even at this period, feelings of deep horror. Such was the state of things in my neighbourhood, yet not one act of hostility against the Government had been even slightly indicated. The dictates of self-preservation are so implanted by an all-wise Creator in the human breast, that the savage in this respect will feel as a philosopher, though his means my be different he will have the same ends in view. . . .

The morning of the 28th having arrived, the people began to collect for mutual protection and advice—and I have often since reflected what a powerful effect mutual adversity has on our passions and prejudices; it soothes and softens down mental asperities, and reconciles the most obstinate differences, while prosperity bursts many a link in the social chain, and often severs the tenderest ties of nature. Grief and despair became now universal; such as had families consulted how they might best provide for their safety, if any one could expect to be safe, or any retreat secure against the licenced incendiary. In the midst of those gloomy forebodings, the firing commenced at Enniscorthy, and continued with little intermission for a considerable time, and was distinctly heard by us, until the town surrendered to the Insurgents; and soon after, a horseman was seen riding in full speed from Enniscorthy towards Moneyhore, the place of my father's residence. When he came within hearing he began to cheer, and continued as he galloped along, crying out "victory! victory!" Never were tidings more joyfully heard, nor more eagerly listened to. After having attended some moments to an imperfect but probably heightened account of the action, which the rude herald gave in an impassioned tone, men, whom consternation, terror, and want of resolve, had a few hours before fixed to the ground on which they stood, proceeded to the roads in groups, and in some cases prepared to search the houses of the neighbouring yeomanry for arms, dreading that the owners would return to them, and sally out at night to murder the families who were still in the ditches, and consume their habitations. This certainly could not be apprehended by any but persons devoid of all reason, as the yeomen had now a full share of those fears for their own safety, which they had been so lately prominent in creating in the minds of others. Some excesses were now committed, which were, on reflection, deeply to be regretted.

On Tuesday, the 29th of May, before day, a large body of men came to my father's house and pressed me to proceed with them to Enniscorthy. I put them off by promising to follow in a short time. Soon after another and a much more numerous party came, who were louder and more peremptory in their demands. There was now no time to be lost in deliberating. The innocent and guilty were alike driven into acts of unwilling hostility to the existing government; but there was no alternative; every preceding day saw the instruments of torture filling the yawning sepulchres with the victims of suspicion or malice; and as a partial resistance could never tend to mitigate the cruelty of their tormentors, I saw no second course for me, or indeed for any Catholic in my part of the country, to pursue. I joined the people, and took an affectionate farewell of my father and sisters, when he, as I before stated, was in a dying way, and my sisters quite unprotected. Their distraction of mind at my parting is not to be described. This was not a moment for indecision. I proceeded as a Volunteer, among many others, to Enniscorthy, without authority or command; and I believe it is a matter of rare occurrence, that those who are invested with power, willingly submit to have that power abridged, or usurped by one who had not the slightest pretensions to seek it, even did I seek for such an unenviable distinction.

Thomas Cloney, A Personal Narrative of Those Transactions in the County Wexford, in which the Author Was Engaged, during the Awful Period of 1798 . . . (1832), pp. 9–10, 11–12, 14, 15–16.

~

On Irish Catholicism

1839

Gustave de Beaumont

Gustave de Beaumont (1802–1866) is best known for his collaborations with another traveler and social observer, Alexis de Tocqueville. In this extract from Ireland: Social, Political, and Religious *(1839), he reflects on the role of the Catholic clergy in Irish society and the links between national and religious sentiment.*

SEE ALSO Roman Catholic Church: 1829 to 1891

The Catholic clergy is the most national body in Ireland; it belongs to the very heart of the country. We have elsewhere seen that Ireland, having been attacked at the same time in its religion and its liberties, his creed and his country were mingled in the heart of every Irishman, and became to him one and the same thing. Having been forced to struggle for his religion against the Englishman, and for his country against the Protestant, he is accustomed to see partisans of his faith only amongst the defenders of his independence, and to find devotion to independence only amongst the friends of his religion.

In the midst of the agitations of which his country and his soul have been the theatre, the Irishman who has seen so much ruin consummated within him and around him, believes that there is nothing permanent or certain in the world but his religion—that religion which is cœval with old Ireland—a religion superior to men, ages, and revolutions—a religion which has survived the most terrible tempests and the most dreadful tyrannies, against which Henry VIII was powerless, which braved Elizabeth, over which the bloody hand of Cromwell passed without destroying it, and which even a hundred and fifty years of continued persecution have failed to overthrow. To an Irishman there is nothing supremely true but his creed.

In defending his religion, the Irishman has been a hundred times invaded, conquered, driven from his native soil; he kept his faith, and lost his country. But, after the confusion made between these two things in his mind, his rescued religion became his all, and its influence on his heart was further extended by its taking there the place of independence. The altar at which he prayed was his country.

Traverse Ireland, observe its inhabitants, study their manners, passions, and habits, and you will find that even in the present day, when Ireland is politically free, its inhabitants are full of prejudices and recollections of their ancient servitude. Look at their external appearance; they walk with their heads bowed down to the earth, their attitude is humble, their language timid; they receive as a favour what they ought to demand as a right; and they do not believe in the equality which the law ensures to them, and of which it gives them proofs. But go from the streets into the chapels. Here the humbled countenances are raised, the most lowly heads are lifted, and the most noble looks directed to heaven; man reappears in all his dignity. The Irish people exists in its church; there alone it is free; there alone it is sure of its rights; there it occupies the only ground that has never given way beneath its feet.

When the altar is thus national, why should not the priest be so likewise? Hence arises the great power of the Catholic clergy in Ireland. When it attempted to overthrow Catholicism, the English government could not destroy the creed without extirpating the clergy. We have already seen how it tried to ruin that body. Still, in spite of the penal laws, which besides sometimes slumbered, there have been always priests in Ireland. The Catholic worship, it is true, had for a long time only a mysterious and clandestine existence; it was supposed to have no legal existence, and the same fiction was extended to its clergy. Even when the Catholic worship was tolerated, it was not authorised; it was only indirectly recognised when the parliament, in 1798, voted funds to endow a college at Maynooth for the education of Catholic priests. But now the Catholic faith exists publicly in Ireland; it has built its churches, it has organised its clergy, and it celebrates its ceremonies in open day; it counts four archbishops, twenty-one bishops, two thousand one hundred places of worship, and two thousand and seventy-four parish priests or coadjutors. The law does not thus constitute it, but the law allows it to form itself; the constitution affords it express toleration; and now the Catholic clergy, the depository of the chief national power of Ireland, exercises that power under the shield of the constitution. To comprehend this power, it is not sufficient to understand what their religion is to the Irish people, but also what their priest is to them.

Survey these immense lower classes in Ireland who bear at once all the charges and all the miseries of society, oppressed by the landlord, exhausted by taxation, plundered by the Protestant minister, their ruin consummated by the agents of law. Who or what is their only support in such suffering?—The priest—Who is it that gives them advice in their enterprises, help in their reverses, relief in their distress?—The priest—Who is it that bestows on them, what is perhaps still more precious, that consoling sympathy, that sustaining voice of sympathy, that tear of humanity, so dear to the unfortunate? There is but one man in Ireland that mourns with the poor man who has so much to mourn, and that man is the priest. Vainly have political liberties been obtained and rights consecrated, the people still suffer. There are old social wounds, to which the remedy provided by law affords only slow and tedious cure. From these deep and hideous wounds the Catholic priests alone do not turn their eyes; they are the only persons that attempt their relief. In Ireland the priest is the only person in perpetual relation with the people who is honoured by them.

Those in Ireland who do not oppress the people, are accustomed to despise them. I found that the Catholic clergy were the only persons in Ireland who loved the lower classes, and spoke of them in terms of esteem and affection

Reprinted in IRELAND FROM GRATTAN'S PARLIAMENT TO THE GREAT FAMINE (1783–1850), *edited by James Carty (1966), pp. 108–110. Reproduced by permission.*

⤳

ON IRISH SOCIETY BEFORE THE FAMINE

1841–1843

Mr. and Mrs. S. C. Hall

Mr. and Mrs. Samuel Carter Hall made five visits to Ireland between 1825 and 1841 and presented their observations in a monumental three-volume work. The following extracts deal with transportation to and within Ireland, a peasant wedding, the Irish game of hurling, and observations on social class.

SEE ALSO Literacy and Popular Culture; Population, Economy, and Society from 1750 to 1950

A voyage to Ireland is, at present, very different from what it was, within our memory, before the application of steam had made its duration a matter of certainty, and enabled the traveller to calculate without reference to wind or tide. "The sailing-packet" was a small trader—schooner, or sloop; the cabin, of very limited extent, was lined with "berths"; a curtain portioned off those that were appropriated to ladies. In the centre was a table—seldom used, the formality of a dinner being a rare event; each passenger having laid in his own supply of "sea store," to which he resorted when hungered or athirst; finding, however, very often, when his appetite returned, that his basket had been impoverished by the visits of unscrupulous voyagers who were proof against sea-sickness. The steward was almost invariably an awkward boy, whose only recommendation was the activity with which he answered the calls of unhappy sufferers; and the voyage across was a kind of purgatory for the time being, to be endured only in cases of absolute necessity. It was not alone the miserable paucity of accommodation and utter indifference to the comfort of the passengers, that made the voyage an intolerable evil. Though it usually occupied but three or four days, frequently as many weeks were expended in making it. It was once our lot to pass a month between the ports of Bristol and Cork; putting back, every now and then, to the wretched village of Pill, and not daring to leave it even for an hour, lest the wind should change and the packet weigh anchor. But with us it was "holiday time," and our case was far less dismal than that of an officer to whom we recently related it; his two months' leave of absence had expired the very day he reached his Irish home.

Under such circumstances, it is not surprising that comparatively little intercourse existed between the two countries, or that England and Ireland were almost as much strangers to each other as if the channel that divided them had been actually impassable. . . .

Machines for travelling in Ireland are, some of them at least, peculiar to the country. The stage-coaches are precisely similar to those in England, and travel at as rapid a rate. They, of course, run upon all the great roads, and are constructed with due regard to safety and convenience. The public cars of M. Bianconi have, however, to a large extent, displaced the regular coaches, and are to be encountered in every district in the south of Ireland. In form they resemble the common outside jaunting-car, but are calculated to hold twelve, fourteen, or sixteen persons; they are well horsed, have cautious and experienced drivers, are generally driven with three horses, and usually travel at the rate of seven Irish miles an hour; the fares averaging about twopence per mile. They are open cars; but a huge apron of leather affords considerable protection against rain; and they may be described as, in all respects, very comfortable and convenient vehicles. . . . His stud consists of 1300 horses—a larger number than her Majesty possesses in Ireland—[and] his cars travel, daily 3500 miles, and visit no fewer than 128 cities and towns. . . .

The cars are of three kinds: "the covered car," "the inside jaunting-car," and the "outside jaunting-car"; the latter being the one most generally in use, and the only one employed in posting. The two former, indeed, can seldom be procured except in large towns. The covered car is a comparatively recent introduction, its sole recommendation being that it is weather-proof, for it effectually prevents a view of the country, except through the two little peep-hole windows in front, or by tying back the oil-skin curtains behind. . . .

The inside jaunting-car is not often to be hired; it is usually private property, and is, perhaps, the most comfortable, as well as elegant, of the vehicles of the country.

The outside jaunting-car is that to which especial reference is made when speaking of the "Irish" car. It is exceedingly light, presses very little upon the horse, and is safe as well as convenient; so easy is it to get on and

off, that both are frequently done while the machine is in motion. It is always driven with a single horse; the driver occupies a small seat in front, and the travellers sit back to back, the space between them being occupied by "the well"—a sort of boot for luggage; but when there is only one passenger the driver usually places himself on the opposite seat "to balance the car," the motion of which would be awkward if one side was much heavier than the other. . . .

The entrance to the county of Kerry ("the kingdom of Kerry," as it was anciently called), from that of Cork, is through a tunnel, of about two hundred yards in length; a very short distance from which there are two others of much more limited extent. They have been cut through rocks—peaks to the mountain we have described as overlooking Glengariff. As the traveller emerges from comparative darkness, a scene of striking magnificence bursts upon him—very opposite in character to that which he leaves immediately behind; for while his eye retains the rich and cultivated beauty of the wooded and watered "glen," he is startled by the contrast of barren and frightful precipices, along the brinks of which he is riding, and gazes with a shudder down into the far off valley, where a broad and angry stream is diminished by distance into a mere line of white. Nothing can exceed the wild grandeur of the prospect; it extends miles upon miles; scattered through the vale and among the hill slopes, are many cottages, white always and generally slated; while to several of them are attached the picturesque lime-kilns; so numerous in all parts of the country. . . .

We had scarcely passed the tunnel, and entered the county of Kerry, when we encountered a group that interested us greatly; on enquiry we learned that a wedding had taken place at a cottage pointed out to us, in a little glen among the mountains, and that the husband was bringing home his bride. She was mounted on a white pony, guided by as smart looking and well dressed a youth as we had seen in the country; his face was absolutely radiant with joy; the parents of the bride and bridegroom followed; and a little girl clung to the dress of a staid and sober matron—whom we at once knew to be the mother of the bride, for her aspect was pensive, almost to sorrow; her daughter was quitting for another home the cottage in which she had been reared—to become a wife. . . .

Postponing, for a while, our descriptive details of the wildest but perhaps most picturesque of the Irish counties, we shall take some note of the games in favour with the peasants of the county . . .

But the great game in Kerry, and indeed throughout the South, is the game of "Hurley"—a game rather rare, although not unknown in England. It is a fine manly exercise, with sufficient of danger to produce excitement; and is indeed, par excellence, *the* game of the peasantry of Ireland. To be an expert hurler, a man must possess athletic powers of no ordinary character; he must have a quick eye, a ready hand, and a strong arm; he must be a good runner, a skilful wrestler, and withal patient as well as resolute. . . .

The forms of the game are these:—The players, sometimes to the number of fifty or sixty, being chosen for each side, they are arranged (usually bare-foot) in two opposing ranks, with their hurleys crossed, to await the tossing up of the ball, the wickets or goals being previously fixed at the extremities of the hurling-green, which, from the nature of the play, is required to be a level extensive plain. . . . A person is chosen to throw up the ball, which is done as straight as possible, when the whole party, withdrawing their hurleys, stand with them elevated, to receive and strike it in its descent; now comes the crash of mimic war, hurleys rattle against hurleys—the ball is struck and re-struck, often for several minutes, without advancing much nearer to either goal; and when some one is lucky enough to get a clear "puck" at it, it is sent flying over the field. It is now followed by the entire party at their utmost speed; the men grapple, wrestle, and toss each other with amazing agility, neither victor nor vanquished waiting to take breath, but following the course of the rolling and flying prize; the best runners watch each other, and keep almost shoulder to shoulder through the play, and the best wrestlers keep as close on them as possible, to arrest or impede their progress. The ball must not be taken from the ground by the hand; and the tact and skill shown in taking it on the point of the hurley, and running with it half the length of the field, and when too closely pressed, striking it towards the goal, is a matter of astonishment to those who are but slightly acquainted with the play. At the goal, is the chief brunt of the battle. The goal-keepers receive the prize, and are opposed by those set over them; the struggle is tremendous,—every power of strength and skill is exerted; while the parties from opposite sides of the field run at full speed to support their men engaged in the conflict; then the tossing and straining is at its height; the men often lying in dozens side by side on the grass, while the ball is returned by some strong arm again, flying above their heads, towards the other goal. Thus for hours has the contention been carried on, and frequently the darkness of night arrests the game without giving victory to either side. It is often attended with dangerous, and sometimes with fatal, results. . . .

The pecularities of the old Irish gentry are all but extinct; the originals of the past century bear but a very

remote resemblance to their successors;—the follies and vices—the drinking, duelling, and "roistering," in former times considered so essentially "Irish," belong exclusively to the ancestors of the present race. Such anecdotes as that told, upon good authority, of the father of Toler—afterwards Lord Norbury—who provided for his son by giving him, at his outset in the world, "a hundred guineas and a pair of duelling-pistols," no more illustrate the Ireland of to-day, than the Smithfield fires do the justice of England. The habits once fashionable are no longer tolerated; and the boasts and glories of a past age are scorned and execrated in this. It was, indeed, always acknowledged, that although the "Irish gentleman" was often an object of suspicion, the "gentleman from Ireland" was ever an example of courtesy, good breeding, honour, and intelligence.

In higher society, therefore, little of distinctive character will be perceived, except in that ease and cheerfulness of manner which make a stranger feel instantly "at home," and the peculiar *tone* of the Irish voice. We do not mean that the better educated have what is understood by "the brogue"; but there is an intonation that belongs to Ireland which is never lost, and cannot be disguised.

The society of the middle class, or rather of the grade above it—the members of the learned professions, and persons on a par with them—is unquestionably agreeable and invigorating in the provinces, and equally so, but more instructive and refined, in the capital and the larger towns. It is everywhere frank and cordial, tempered by playful good-humour and a keen relish for conversation; and is always distinguished by the cheerfulness that borders upon mirth, and the harmony produced by a universal aptness for enjoyment.

The women of Ireland—from the highest to the lowest—represent the national character better than the other sex. In the men, very often, energy degenerates into fierceness, generosity into reckless extravagance, social habits into dissipation, courage into profitless daring, confiding faith into slavish dependence, honour into captiousness, and religion into bigotry; for [in] no country of the world is the path so narrow that marks the boundary between virtue and vice. But the Irish women have—taken in the mass—the lights without the shadows, the good without the bad—to use a familiar expression, "the wheat without the chaff." Most faithful; most devoted; most pure; the best mothers; the best children; the best wives;—possessing, preeminently, the beauty and holiness of virtue, in the limited or the extensive meaning of the phrase. They have been rightly described as "holding an intermediate space between the French and the English"; mingling the vivacity of the one with the stability of the other; with hearts more *naturally* toned than either: never sacrificing delicacy, but entirely free from embarassing reserve; their gaiety never inclining to levity, their frankness never approaching to freedom; with reputations not the less securely protected because of the absence of suspicion, and that the natural guardians of honour through present are unseen. . . .

In Ireland, as yet, the aristocracy of wealth has made little way; and to be of "good family" is a surer introduction to society, than to be of large fortune. The prejudice in favour of "birth" is, indeed, almost universal, and pervades all ranks. Consequently, classes are to the last degree exclusive; and their divisions are as distinctly marked and recognised as are those determined by the etiquette of a court. Hence arises that perpetual straining after a higher station, to which many worthy families have been sacrificed: persons in business rarely persevere until they have amassed fortunes, but retire as early as possible after they have acquired competence; and the subdivisions which their properties necessarily undergo, when junior branches are to be provided for, creates a numerous class—almost peculiar to Ireland—of young men possessing the means of barely living without labour; disdaining the notion of "turning to trade"; unable to acquire professions, and ill-suited to adorn them if obtained; content to drag on existence in a state of miserable and degrading dependence, doing nothing—literally "too proud to work, but not ashamed to beg." This feeling operates upon the various grades of society; and the number of "idlers" in the busy world is fearfully large; from "the walking gentleman" of the upper ranks, to the "half-sir" of the middle, and "the jackeen" of the class a little above the lower; the walking gentleman being always elegantly attired, of course always unemployed, with ample leisure for the studies which originate depravity; the "half-sir" being, generally, a younger brother, with little or no income of his own, and so educated as to be deprived, utterly, of the energy and self-dependence which create usefulness; the "Masther Tom," who broke the dogs, shot the crows, first backed the vicious horse, and, followed by a half-pointer, half-lurcher, poached, secretly, upon his elder brother's land, but more openly upon the lands of his neighbours; the "jackeen" being a production found everywhere, but most abundantly in large towns. Happily, however, the class is not upon the increase. . . .

Mr. and Mrs. S. C. Hall, IRELAND: ITS SCENERY, CHARACTER, &c., 3 vols. (1841–1843), vol. 1, pp. 1–2, 63, 64–65, 161–162, 163, 256–258; vol. 2, pp. 314–316.

ON REPEAL OF THE ACT OF UNION AT THE "MONSTER MEETING" AT MULLINGAR

14 May 1843

Daniel O'Connell

The central tactic in Daniel O'Connell's campaign for repeal of the Act of Union in 1843 was the holding of a series of about forty "monster meetings" (a term first used in derision by The Times *of London). At these meetings O'Connell was always the featured speaker, and as at Mullingar on 14 May 1843, he explained why he wanted Ireland to have its own parliament and what reforms he thought such a parliament should adopt. The tactic, designed to overawe British opposition to Repeal, failed when the government banned the "monster meeting" scheduled for Clontarf in October and O'Connell called it off.*

SEE ALSO O'Connell, Daniel; Repeal Movement

My first object is to get Ireland for the Irish (loud cheers). I am content that the English should have England, but they have had the domination of this country too long, and it is time that the Irish should at length get their own country—that they should get the management of their own country—the regulation of their own country—the enjoyment of their own country—that the Irish should have Ireland (great cheers). Nobody can know how to govern us as well as we would know how to do it ourselves—nobody could know how to relieve our wants as well as would ourselves—nobody could have so deep an interest in our prosperity or could be so well fitted for remedying our evils and procuring happiness for us as we would ourselves (hear, hear). Old Ireland and liberty! (loud cheers). That is what I am struggling for (hear, hear). If I was to tell the Scotch that they should not have Scotland—if I was to tell the English that they should not have England—if I was to tell the Spaniards that they should not have Spain—or the French that they should not have France, they would have a right to laugh at, to hate, to attack, or to assail me in whatever manner they chose. But I do not say any such thing. What I say is that as all these people have their own countries, the Irish ought to have Ireland (hear, and cheers). What numberless advantages would not the Irish enjoy if they possessed their own country? A domestic parliament would encourage Irish manufactures. The linen trade and the woollen [trade] would be spreading amongst you. An Irish parliament would foster Irish commerce and protect Irish agriculture. The labourer, the artizan, and the shopkeeper would be all benefited by the repeal of the union; but if I were to describe all the blessings that it would confer, I would detain you here, crowding on each other's backs, until morning before I would be done (laughter). In the first place, I ask, Did you ever hear of the tithe rent-charge (groans)? Are you satisfied to be paying parsons who do not pray for you (no, no)? It is time, therefore, that they should be put an end to (hear, hear). The people of England do not pay for the church of the minority.

A voice: "No, nor the people of Scotland either."

You are quite right, though I think I heard the remark before (laughter). But carry home my words with you and tell them to your neighbours. I tell you, the people of Ireland will not be much longer paying them (hear, hear, and cheers). I next want to get rid of the poor rates (cheers). England does charity in the way a person will throw a bone to a dog, by slashing it in between his teeth (hear, hear). That is the poor law charity, the charity of the commissioners and assistant-commissioners, and all concerned under them except the poor themselves, and when they do give relief, they take up the poor as if they were criminals, or as if poverty were a crime to be punished by perpetual imprisonment (hear and cheers). . . . I know it will be said that I want to leave the poor destitute. I do not want to do any such thing. Would I not have the tithe rent-charge and the ecclesiastical revenues to apply for their relief? And would I not with their aid be able to maintain hospitals for the sick, the lame, the impotent, the aged, and all those who are real objects of charity, and for whom the doors would be open at every hour of the day and during a part of the night, so that anybody who did not like to remain might go out when they liked (hear, hear, and cheers)? I would thus do you two pieces of service by the repeal of the union. I would relieve the poor without the imposition of poor rates, and I would prevent you from paying any clergy but your own (loud cheers). I should not have used the word prevent, because if any of you wished to pay both, you might do it if you pleased (laughter). I often asked Protestants how would they like to pay for the support of the Catholic clergy by force, and they always said they would not like it at all; and why should the Catholics like it one bit the better (hear)? [William] Cobbett had a phrase for it. He used to say, "What's sauce for the goose is sauce for the gander" (laughter). The next thing that the repeal would abolish is the grand jury cess (cheers). I believe it grinds some of you (cries of "It does so"). There

is not a more iniquitous tax in the world, for it comes on the occupier instead of on the country at large. Give me the repeal, and the national treasury will pay for the making and repairing of all the roads, bridges, and public buildings; and instead of the poor farmers and occupiers paying the money themselves, it will come from the treasury and would go in giving employment to those who now have to pay it (hear, hear). I will tell you another thing I want to do. I want that every head of a family, every married man and every householder, should have a right to vote for members of parliament. They say that I would have an interest in that because I would then have more votes; but my answer is, if I would, it is because the people know I am acting honestly by them, and everybody else who does the same will be equally supported. The landlords now persecute those who vote differently from their wishes, but I would institute the ballot-box. Every married man should have a vote, and any blackguard who could not get a wife anywhere, I would not pity him to be without the vote (cheers and laughter). The good landlord would then be sure to be supported by his tenants; but if he were a scoundrel, whether he was a Catholic, a Protestant, or a Presbyterian, he would deserve to be turned out (hear, hear). If he was serving notices to quit or holding up his head in the street and not looking his tenants in the face and speaking to them, or if he was a man who would not salute their wives and children as he passed them, or if, when he sat upon the bench, he was always fining, fining, fining (loud laughter), the tenant would always have the advantage of using the ballot-box against that fellow (hear, hear, and cheers). . . . You know that the landlords have duties as well as rights, and I would establish the fixity of tenure (loud cheers) to remind them of these duties. I will tell you what my plan is, and you can consider it among yourselves. My plan is that no landlord could recover rent unless he made a lease for twenty-one years to the tenant—no lease or no rent, say I (loud cheers). Unless he made a lease, he would have no more business looking for his rent than a dog would have barking at the moon (cheers and laughter). It may be said that the landlords would in that case put too high a rent on their lands, but I have a remedy for that too in my plan (laughter, and cries of "more power"). At present, if a man goes to register his vote, he must prove on oath what a solvent tenant could pay to his landlord for his holding, and in the same manner I would give the tenant an opportunity of proving what a solvent tenant ought to give for his land in order to fix the amount of rent he would have to pay (cheers). I would give the poor man the benefit of a trial by jury in such case, so that it would be impossible for a landlord to get more than the fair value of his land. It may be said that the poor man would be turned out of his holding at the expiration of his lease, and his land given to another, but I have a cure for that also (cheers). I would allow the tenant by law every year to register, as he can now register trees that he plants, all the improvements that he makes on his holding, and if the landlord did not pay him the full value of these improvements, he could not turn him out, but would be obliged to give him a new holding. Every tenant would be then building a better house for his pigs than he now inhabits himself, as he would be sure to get every farthing he laid out on his holding before he could be deprived of possession at the end of his lease (hear, hear, and cheers). Is it not, I ask you, worthwhile to look for a repeal of the union for that alone (cheers)? Would it not do more to produce happiness and prosperity in the country and put an end to the horrible wholesale murders of the landlords who now send their tenants to die by twenties in the ditches, and the fearful retaliations by assassination that so frequently take place on the other side (hear). But that is not all. Every year since the union nine millions of money has been sent out of Ireland after being raised from the produce of the soil (cries of "Oh, murder, murder"). It is no wonder you should cry "murder," for there is no country in the world where such a system would exist that must not be poor. The only countries except Ireland where anything like it occurs are Sicily and Sardinia, and both of these, from having absentee landlords, are miserably poor. There is not, however, a country in the world so impoverished as Ireland, where it has been found that there are 2,300,000 persons in a state of destitution every year. . . . For the last ten years, no less than ninety millions have been drawn out of Ireland, but if we get the union [repealed], there will be ninety millions spent in Ireland that would otherwise be taken from her (hear, hear, and cheers). This will leave an average of £750,000 a month, or £125,000 a week of six days, to be spent in wages in giving employment to the people (cheers). I have all this within my grasp if the people join me. Now, what is there in all this that Wellington should stammer at in his old age, and that Peel should bluster and get very angry about it (groans)? . . . They say we want separation from England, but what I want is to prevent separation taking place, and there is not a man in existence more loyally attached than I am to the queen—God bless her. The present state of Ireland is nearly unendurable, and if the people of Ireland had not some person like me to lead them in the paths of peace and constitutional exertion, I am afraid of the result (hear). While I live, I will stand by the throne (hear, hear). But what motive could we have to separate if we obtain all those blessings and advantages I have been enumerating? They would all serve as solid golden links of connexion with England. But I would be glad to know what good did the union do (hear, hear)? What I want you to do is for every one of you to join me in looking for repeal. As many of you as are willing to do so, let them hold up their hands (here every person in the immense assemblage raised his hands aloft amidst loud continued cheers). I see you have ready hands, and I know you have stout hearts too. But what do I want you to do? Is it to turn out into battle or war (cries of no, no)? Is it to commit riot or crime (cries of no, no)? Remember, "Whoever commits a crime gives strength to the enemy" (hear, hear, and cheers). . . . I want you to do nothing that is not open and legal, but if the people unite with me and follow my advice, it is impossible not to get the repeal (loud cheers and cries of "we will"). And our country deserves that we should exert ourselves for her. Other countries changed their religious opinions at the fantasy of their governors, but Ireland is the only country that for centuries set her governors at defiance, and she is also the only country that was converted to Christianity in the short space of four years (hear, hear, hear). . . .

But nothing could be more true [than] that there was no pursuit of Roman Catholic interests as opposed to Protestant, and that the object in view was to benefit the whole nation; and because it was a national movement, it should never be abandoned until justice was done to the nation (loud cheers). Even their enemies should admit the progress they had made; and let him have but three millions of Repealers, and then he would make his arrangements for obtaining repeal. He would have the Repealers send up three hundred gentlemen, chosen from various parts of the country, each entrusted with £100, [and] that would be £30,000. They should meet in Dublin to consult upon the best means of obtaining legislative independence. They would not leave Dublin till they would agree to an act of parliament to establish a domestic legislature, household suffrage, vote by ballot, fixity of tenure, and a law against absentees having estates in the country. Many estates would then be sold in lots and purchased by those who would become small proprietors; and it was a fact well ascertained that in proportion as the owners in fee were numerous in any country, so in proportion were the people prosperous (hear, hear). It was truly said by Mr Martin, their chairman, that if they had their own parliament, taxation would be diminished to almost nothing—for in five or six years they would be able to pay off their portion of the national debt—the duty upon every exciseable article would be reduced—they would have a pound of tea for little more than was now paid for a couple of ounces, and a pound of sugar at the price of a quarter of a pound, the duty on tobacco would be reduced, so that there was not an old woman in the country who might not have her pipe lighted from morning to night if she pleased (laughter). . . .

NATION, 20 May 1843.

∽

LETTER ADVOCATING FEDERALISM AS AN ALTERNATIVE TO REPEAL

November 1844

William Sharman Crawford

The Repeal movement of the early 1840s under Daniel O'Connell's leadership was dealt a notable setback in October 1843, when the British government prohibited the holding of the "monster meeting" at Clontarf and then proceeded to indict and try O'Connell and other leading Repealers for conspiracy. As the prospects of Repeal dimmed, the northern landlord and tenant-right advocate William Sharman Crawford (1781–1861) sought to promote the idea of a federal solution to the Anglo-Irish relationship in a series of public letters.

SEE ALSO Local Government since 1800; Politics: 1800 to 1921—Challenges to the Union

Sir, I have in the preceding sections [actually, in earlier letters] shown, first, the evils produced to Ireland through the want of local legislation by a local body. I have shown, secondly, that it is the principle of British policy to grant local legislative bodies to portions of the empire so circumstanced, and I have taken the constitution of Canada as an example of their construction. I now proceed to inquire on what basis a legislature could be constructed for Ireland which would secure to her these two things; 1st, protection for her rights, and 2dly, the management of her own resources—and would at the same time avoid any danger to the integrity of the empire by leaving in the hands of an imperial parliament those matters of legislation which imperial interests require.

As it is always prudent to adopt a precedent in existence when not inconsistent with the purposes sought to be obtained, I shall take as my basis the act for the constitution of Canada, already referred to in my second section [letter]. I shall suppose, then, that a legislature is constituted for Ireland, consisting of two houses—a House of Lords, which may be considered analogous to the Legislative Council of Canada, and a House of Commons, analogous to their House of Assembly. I shall not now enter into the particular details of construction; I shall at once refer to the power with which such a parliament may be invested.

1. That this parliament shall be competent (with the royal assent) to make all laws necessary for Ireland and to impose and apply all necessary taxes, subject to the limitations and regulations hereinafter stated.

2. That all bills which may be passed by the local parliament, which make any provisions with regard to religion or religious worship, or pecuniary grants or payments for the purposes of religion, or any bills which relate to [omission in original], shall be subject to the regulations contained in the 42d section of the Canada Act—viz., that before the royal assent be given to any such bills, they shall lie for thirty days on the tables of the houses of the imperial parliament, and in case the said houses shall address the sovereign to withhold the royal assent, such assent shall not be given. (Note—Upon the subject of this exception with regard to religion, I may remark that before any new political constitution can be established, I conceive that some equitable settlement with regard to the Irish church [the Anglican Church of Ireland] and its revenues must be effected; such being made, it is only a reasonable concession to the apprehension of many persons well affected to local legislation, to provide that such settlement shall not be disturbed by any act of the local legislature without the approval of the imperial parliament; and I would further add, by any act of the imperial parliament without the approval of the local parliament. It would be a matter for consideration whether any bills, regarding any other laws than those relating to religion should be made subject to the same rules.)

3. That all acts of the imperial legislature which regard the succession to the throne or the appointment of a regent (if such should be necessary) shall be binding on Ireland without being referred to the local legislature.

4. That the local parliament shall have power to impose and apply, with the assent of the Crown, all taxation necessary for the purposes of Ireland, subject to the regulations and limitations hereinafter stated.

5. That the imperial parliament shall retain a power similar to that provided by the 43rd section of the Canada Act—to impose all duties necessary for the purposes of commerce over the United Kingdom.

6. That the net produce of all duties so imposed shall—in conformity with the proviso contained in the 43rd section of the Canada Act—be paid into the Irish exchequer and placed at the disposal of the local parliament, in [the] same manner as all taxes imposed by the local authority.

7. That if any bill be passed by the local parliament, proposing to alter or repeal, with regard to Ireland, any duty which had been so imposed by the imperial parliament, or to impose any new duty on any article of foreign or colonial produce imported into Ireland, such bill shall be subjected, previous to the royal assent being declared, to the same regulations as provided under the second head with regard to certain laws to be submitted to the consideration of the imperial parliament.

8. That it be a fundamental law that no duties shall be imposed by either parliaments [sic] which would impede the perfect freedom of trade between Great Britain and Ireland.

9. That Ireland shall pay a certain quota to the military and naval establishments and other expenses of the empire, that this quota shall be a sum fixed for a certain number of years, not to be increased under any circumstances during the time specified, except by a free grant of the parliament of Ireland; that at the termination of the period specified a new arrangement of the quota may be made if both parliaments consent.

10. That Ireland shall pay the expenses of all her civil establishments and institutions out of her own revenue.

11. That no law made, nor tax imposed, by the local parliament of Ireland shall have operation beyond the limits of Ireland; and that all foreign and colonial legislation of every description shall remain under the control and authority of the imperial parliament.

12. That no law or act of the imperial parliament made after the passing of this act, and operating locally in Ireland, shall be binding on Ireland unless assented [to] by her local parliament—with the exception of those matters reserved in proposition no. 3 and the power of imposing duties reserved in no. 5.

13. That all laws and statutes now in force shall be binding on Ireland till altered or replaced according to the power given by this act.

If the above propositions be examined, I think they shall be found to define with sufficient accuracy the general powers which I would propose to vest in a local and imperial parliament. They are not powers or distinctions which are the mere creations of my imagination—they are taken from the laws of England as developed in her legislation towards her colonial possessions. . . .

I am aware that these propositions will not meet the views of those who claim for Ireland a separate national existence—they will allege that my propositions would place her rather in the position of a colony of a[nother] nation. I cannot help this; I repeat what I have often before stated—that I cannot conceive [any] . . . means of separate national existence, except by a separation of the Crown as well as of the parliament. By this I mean a perfectly independent condition, and I think this condition cannot be obtained, and if temporarily obtained, could not be preserved. I care not what name may be given to the position in which Ireland may be placed if it gives the best practical security for her rights and her interests. Ireland is now in the position of a conquered country, held only by the military power of England; I wish to redeem her from that state by founding the connexion on a just and useful basis.

FREEMAN'S JOURNAL, 15 November 1844.

~

ON RURAL SOCIETY ON THE EVE OF THE GREAT FAMINE

1844–1845

Asenath Nicholson

Asenath Nicholson (1792–1855) was a New England widow of Puritan stock who visited Ireland in the 1840s, initially for the purpose of distributing Bibles to the poor. Such efforts to convert Irish Catholics were common among evangelical Protestants in this period, but Nicholson's evangelicalism was tempered by strong reform principles. Her accounts of her Irish labors reveal a degree of empathy with suffering Catholics rarely found among her Irish co-religionists.

SEE ALSO Family: Marriage Patterns and Family Life from 1690 to 1921; Great Famine; Population, Economy, and Society from 1750 to 1950; Potato and Potato Blight (Phytophthora infestans); Rural Life: 1690 to 1845

We have had many "Pencillings by the Way," and "Conciliation Halls," and "Killarney Lakes" from the tops of coaches and from smoking dinner tables. But one day's walk on mountain or bog, one night's lodging where the pig, and the ass, and horned oxen feed,

"Like Aaron's serpent, swallows all the rest."

"Remember, my children," said my father, "that the Irish are a suffering people; and when they come to your doors, never send them empty away." It was in the garrets and cellars of New York that I first became acquainted with the Irish peasantry, and it was there I *saw* they were a suffering people. Their patience, their cheerfulness, their flow of blundering, hap-hazard, happy wit, made them to me a distinct people from all I had seen. Often, when seated at my fireside, have I said to those most dear to my heart, "God will one day allow me to breathe the mountain air of the sea-girt coast of Ireland—to sit down in their cabins, and there learn what soil has nurtured, what hardships have disciplined so hardy a race—so patient and so impetuous, so revengeful and so forgiving, so proud and so humble, so obstinate and so docile, so witty and so simple a people." . . .

And now began my cabin life. I had read with the deepest interest in the writings of Charlotte Elizabeth, that the peasantry of the county of Kilkenny were unrivalled in kindness; but burning words from graphic pens would faintly delineate what I there experienced from that interesting people. . . .

The next morning Anne again called to invite me to her house, and to say she had been sent by a few in the parish, to invite me to attend a field dance which was to be on the next day, and the Sabbath. In surprise I was about to answer, when Anne said, "I knew you would not, and told them so, but they begged I would say that they had no other day, as all were at work, and sure God wouldn't be hard upon 'em, when they had not other time, and could do nothing else for the stranger." I thanked them heartily for their kind feelings, and declined. Judge my confusion, when about sunset on Sabbath evening, just after returning from Johnstown, where I had attended church, the cabin door opened, and a crowd of all ages walked in, decently attired for the day, and without the usual welcomes or any apology, the hero who first introduced me seated himself at my side, took out his flute, wet his fingers, saying, "This is for you, Mrs. N., and what will you have?" A company were arranged for the dance, and so confounded was I that my only answer was, "I cannot tell." He struck up an Irish air, and the dance began. I had nothing to say, taken by surprise as I was; my only strength was to sit still.

This dance finished, the eldest son of my hostess advanced, made a low bow, and invited me to lead the next dance. I looked on his glossy black slippers, his blue stockings snugly fitted up to the knee, his corduroys above them, his blue coat and brass buttons, and had no reason to hope that, at my age of nearly half a century, I could ever expect another like offer. However I was not urged to accept it. Improper as it might appear, it was done as a civility, which, as a guest in his mother's house and a stranger, he thought, and all thought (as

I was afterwards told) he owed me. The cabin was too small to contain the three score and ten who had assembled, and with one simultaneous movement, without speaking, all rushed out, bearing me along, and placed me upon a cart before the door, the player at my right hand. And then a dance began, which, to say nothing of the day, was to me of no ordinary kind. Not a laugh—not a loud word was heard; no affected airs, which the young are prone to assume; but as soberly as though they were in a funeral procession, they danced for an hour, wholly for my amusement, and for my welcome. Then each approached, gave me the hand, bade me God speed, leaped over the style, and in stillness walked away. It was a true and hearty Irish welcome, in which the aged, as well as the young, participated. A matron of sixty, of the Protestant faith, was holding by the hand a grandchild of seven years, and standing by the cart where I stood; and she asked when they had retired, if I did not enjoy it? "What are these wonderful people?" was my reply. I had never seen the like. . . .

I had seen a dance, a wake, and a faction, but had never seen a fair; and being invited to occupy a seat in a chamber at Urlingford, which overlooked the field of action, I did so. "You'll not see such fun, ma'am, now," said my companion, "as you would have seen before the days of Father Matthew. Then we had a power of bloody noses, broken bones, and fine work for the police; but ye'll see fine cattle, and fat pigs; and maybe it's the bagpipes ye'd like." . . .

The fair, as a whole, was not censurable; never on any public day in any country had I heard so little profanity and noise, or seen so little disorder and disputing, the tinkers excepted. The peasants, too, were tidily dressed, and with great uniformity; the men in blue coats, corduroy breeches, and blue stockings; whilst a blue petticoat, with a printed dress turned back and pinned behind, coarse shoes, and blue or black stockings (when they have shoes), a blue cloak, with a hood to put over the head, in case of rain, constitute the dress of the women; and thus attired, a Kilkenny peasant seeks no change in storm or sunshine. The habits of cooking and eating have scarcely varied for two centuries; their cabins, their furniture, have undergone little or no change; the thatched roofs, the ground floor, the little window, the stone or mud wall, the peat fire, the clay chimney, the wooden stool, the pot, and the griddle, have probably been the inheritance of many generations. As to cleanliness, their habits are varied, as with all other people; and if few are scrupulously tidy, few are disgustingly filthy. Though every peasant in the Emerald Isle knows that he belongs to the "lower order" (for his teachers and landlords are fond of telling him so), the Kilkenny rustic, by his self-possessed manner in presence of his superior, says, "I also am a man"; and you do not see that cringing servility; you do not hear "yer honor," "yer reverence," "my lord," and "my lady" so frequently as among many of their class in other parts of Ireland. They are not so wretchedly poor as many; for though few can afford the "mate," except at Christmas or Easter, yet most of them can purchase an occasional loaf, and "the sup of tay," and all can, and all do, by "hook or by crook," get the "blessed tobacco." They are fond of dancing, and a child is taught it in his first lessons of walking. The bagpipes and fiddle are ever at their feasts, especially the latter; and the blind performer always receives a cordial "God bless you." . . .

Thirteen miles brought me to the pleasant town of Durrow, where I stopped for the night, to take passage in the morning for Dublin. Here I found an afflicted woman, whose husband had seven years before gone to New York, and she had not once heard from him. The sight of an American opened anew the channels of grief, which had already done a serious work. Kindness was here lavished without weight or measure, and when I called for my bill in the morning, "We cannot ask you anything, for you have had nothing," alluding to a straw bed which had been prepared by my request. I paid them more than the ordinary price, for they had done more than is customary to be done for lodgers.

At five, while the waning moon and twinkling stars were still looking out upon the beautiful landscape beneath them, I was upon the car, with a talkative young coachman, and rode five miles, passing the domains of the rich, whose high walls and wide-spreading lawns made a striking contrast with the thatched hovels and muddy door-yards of the wretched poor around them. Never had I ridden in Ireland when the stillness, the scenery, and the hour of the morning all so happily combined to make the heart rejoice as now. But the one dreadful, ever-living truth, like a spectre, haunts the traveller at every step; that Ireland's poor, above all others, are the most miserable, the most forgotten, and the most patient of all beings. I heed not who says the picture is too highly drawn. Let them see this picture as I have seen it, let them walk it, let them eat it, let them sleep it, as I have done. . . .

I have spoken plainly, that I might render unto Caesar the things that are Caesar's; and as I visited Ireland to see it as it is, so I report it as I found it. I have stayed to witness that which, though so heart-rendering and painful, has given me but the proof of what common observation told me in the beginning—that there must needs be an explosion of some kind or other. But awful as it is, it has shown Ireland who are her worthy ones within her, and who are her friends abroad, and it will show her greater things than these.

May God bring her from her seven-times-heated furnace, purified and unhurt, and place her sons and daughters among the brightest of the stars that shall shine for ever in the kingdom of heaven, is the sincere desire of the writer.

Asenath Nicholson, IRELAND'S WELCOME TO THE STRANGER, OR AN EXCURSION THROUGH IRELAND IN 1844 & 1845 FOR THE PURPOSE OF PERSONALLY INVESTIGATING THE CONDITION OF THE POOR (1847), pp. iii–iv, 87, 90–91, 96, 97–98, 218–219, 456.

~

SPEECH ON THE USE OF PHYSICAL FORCE

28 July 1846

Thomas Francis Meagher

Within the Repeal Association the Young Ireland group, among whom Protestants were numerous, became increasingly dissatisfied with Daniel O'Connell's leadership between 1844 and 1846. His worst sins in their eyes were his opposition to the "Godless colleges" in 1845 and his alliance with the Whigs in 1846. O'Connell tried to bring his Young Ireland critics to heel through the "peace resolutions" of July 1846, which involved a total disavowal of physical force under almost any circumstances. In this speech Thomas Francis Meagher ("Meagher of the Sword") refused to repudiate physical force to this degree, and so did numerous other Young Irelanders. The result was a split that became permanent.

SEE ALSO Young Ireland and the Irish Confederation

I will commence as my friend Mr [John] Mitchel concluded, by an allusion to the Whigs (hear, hear). I fully concur with my friend that the "most comprehensive measures" of which the Whig ministers may propose and the English parliament may adopt, will fail to lift this country up to that position which she has the right to occupy and the power to maintain (cheers). A Whig minister, I admit, may improve the province, he will not restore the nation. Franchises, "equal laws," tenant compensation bills, "liberal appointments," in a word "full justice" as they say, may ameliorate, they will not exalt (cheers). They may meet the necessities, they will not call forth the abilities of the country. The errors of the past may be repaired. The hopes of the future will not be fulfilled. . . . From the stateliest mansion down to the poorest cottage in the land, the inactivity, the meanness, the debasement, which provincialism engenders will be perceptible. These are not the crude sentiments of youth, though the mere commercial politician who has deduced his ideas of self-government from the table of imports and exports may satirise them as such. . . .

Voter's books and reports, these are the only weapons we can employ (hear). Therefore, my lord, I do advocate the peaceful policy of this association (cheers). It is the only policy we can and should adopt (cheers). If that policy be pursued with truth, with courage, with stern determination of purpose, I do firmly believe that it will succeed (loud and enthusiastic cheers). But, my lord, I dissented from the resolutions in question for other reasons (hear, hear). . . . I dissented from these resolutions, for I felt that by assenting to them, I should have pledged myself to the unqualified repudiation of physical force in all countries, at all times, and in every circumstance. This I could not do, for, my lord, I do not abhor the use of arms in the vindication of national rights (cheers).

There are times when arms will alone suffice, and when political ameliorations call for a drop of blood—(cheers)—and many thousand drops of blood (enthusiastic cheering and cries of "Oh, Oh"). Opinion, I admit, will operate against opinion. But as the hon[ourable] member for Kilkenny observed, force must be used against force (cheers and some confusion). The soldier is proof against an argument, but he is not proof against a bullet. The man that will listen to reason, let him be reasoned with, but it is the weaponed arm of the patriot that can alone avail against battalioned despotism (loud cheers). Then, my lord, I do not disclaim the use of force as immoral, nor do I believe that it is the truth to say that the God of heaven withholds His sanction from the use of arms. From the day on which in the valley of Bethulia He nerved the arm of the Jewish girl to smite the drunken tyrant in his tent, down to the hour in which He blessed the insurgent chivalry of the Belgium priests, His Almighty hand has ever been stretched forth from His throne of light to consecrate the flag of freedom, to bless the patriot's sword (loud and enthusiastic cheering). Be it for the defence or be it for the assertion of a nation's liberty, I look upon the sword as a sacred weapon ("No, No" from the Rev. Mr Hopkins). And if, my lord, it has sometimes reddened the shroud of the oppressor, like the anointed rod of the high priest, it has at other times blossomed into flowers to deck the freeman's brow (vehement applause).

Abhor the sword and stigmatise the sword? No, my lord, for in the cragged passes of the Tyrol it cut in pieces the banner of the Bavarian and won an immortality for the peasant of Innsbruck (hear). Abhor the sword and stigmatise the sword? No, my lord, for at its blow a giant nation sprung up from the waters of the far Atlantic, and by its redeeming magic the fettered colony became a daring free republic. Abhor the sword and stigmatise the sword? No, my lord, for it scourged the Dutch marauders out of the fine old towns of Belgium, back into their own phlegmatic swamps—(cheers)—and knocked their flag, and laws, and sceptre, and bayonets into the sluggish waters of the Scheldt (enthusiastic cheers).

NATION, *1 August 1846.*

~

FROM *NARRATIVE OF A RECENT JOURNEY*

1847

William Bennett

Traveling in Ireland during the height of the Great Famine with seed provision for the victims, William Bennett ascribed the sufferings which beset Ireland during the nineteenth century to a series of natural calamities rather than to the combination of political, economic, and natural events that had developed over time. Unlike most English commentators on Ireland at this time, though, he did not blame the Irish for the situation in which they found themselves.

SEE ALSO Population, Economy, and Society from 1750 to 1950; Rural Life: 1690 to 1845; Rural Life: 1850 to 1921

Take the line of the main course of the Shannon, continued north to Lough Swilly, and south to Cork. It divides the island into two great portions, east and west. In the eastern there is distress and poverty enough, as part of the same body, suffering from the same causes; but there is much to redeem. In the west it exhibits a people, not in the centre of Africa, the steppes of Asia, the backwoods of America—not some newly-discovered tribes of South Australia, or among the Polynesian Islands—not Hottentots, Bushmen, or Esquimeaux—neither Mahomedans nor Pagans—but some millions of our own Christian nation at home, living in a state and condition low and degraded to a degree unheard of before in any civilised community; driven periodically to the borders of starvation; and now reduced, by a national calamity, to an exigency which all the efforts of benevolence can only mitigate, not control; and under which *absolute thousands* are not merely pining away in misery and wretchedness, but are dying like cattle off the face of the earth, from want and its kindred horrors! Is this to be regarded in the light of a Divine dispensation and punishment? Before we can safely arrive at such a conclusion, we must be satisfied that human agency and legislation, individual oppressions, and social relationships, have had no hand in it. . . .

Is there anything inherent in the national character fatal to improvement? The Irish are accused of being lazy, improvident, reckless of human life. I doubt their being much more so than the English, the Americans, or any other nation would be under the like circumstances. The distances to which an Irish labourer will go for work, and the hardships he will submit to, are notorious; and the private correspondence of all who have entered into the subject teems with evidence of the alacrity of the poor women and peasant girls for employment of any kind, and of the teachableness and skill they exhibit. The appeal to a wider range of facts is irresistible. Who come over in such numbers to reap our harvests, dig our canals, construct our railroads, in fact wherever hard work is to be obtained? Who save up what money they can, during harvest-time, and such-like seasons of extra employment, to take back to their families at home? Who, in a country where labour is better remunerated, send over sums exceeding all that the wealthy have raised in charity, to comfort those they have left behind, or help over their poor friends and relatives to what they think that happier land? The generosity of the Irish was never questioned. Their peaceableness has been put to the severest test. In no other country, probably, could such a state of things have endured so long, and to such an extremity, without ten-fold more outrages than have been committed. They are naturally a contented and a happy race. The charge of recklessness of human life—apart from those deplorably aggravated deeds arising invariably out of natural jealousies—is answered by the perfect safety of a stranger amongst them; and it has further been placed on the right shoulders in another quarter, more fearlessly that I durst have penned it here.

Reprinted in STRANGERS TO THAT LAND: BRITISH PERCEPTIONS OF IRELAND FROM THE REFORMATION TO THE FAMINE, edited by Andrew Hadfield and John McVeagh (1994), pp. 156–157.

~

RESOLUTIONS ADOPTED AT THE TENANT-RIGHT CONFERENCE

6–9 August 1850

The clearances associated with the Great Famine, combined with a sharp downturn in agricultural prices beginning in 1849, dramatically heightened the anxieties of tenants all over the country. The formation of local tenant-protection societies soon escalated into the emergence of a national tenant-right movement, signaled by the holding of a tenant-right conference in Dublin in August 1850. This conference, which concluded with the establishment of the Irish Tenant League, embraced what became known as the "three Fs": fair rents, fixity of tenure, and free sale of the tenant's interest in his holding.

SEE ALSO Land Questions

SECTION I

1. That a fair valuation of rent between landlord and tenant in Ireland is indispensible.

2. That the tenant shall not be disturbed in his possession so long as he pays the rent fixed by the proposed law.

3. That the tenant shall have a right to sell his interest, with all its incidents, at the highest market value.

4. That where the rent has been fixed by valuation, no rent beyond the valued rent shall be recoverable by any process of law.

5. That cases of minors and other exceptional cases be considered hereafter in any measure to be introduced into parliament.

6. That it be an instruction to the [Irish Tenant] League [founded at this conference] to take into consideration, at the earliest possible period, the condition of farm labourers, and suggest some measure for their permanent protection and improvement in connection with the arrangement of the question between landlord and tenant.

SECTION II

1. That an equitable valuation of land for rent should divide between the landlord and the tenant the net profits of cultivation, in the same way as the profits would be divided between the partners in any other business where one of them is a dormant partner and the other the working capitalist who takes upon him the whole risk.

2. That nothing shall be included in the valuation or paid under the valuation to the landlord on account of improvements made by the tenant in possession or those under whom he claims, unless these have been paid for by the landlord in reduced rent or in some other way.

3. That if the landlord shall at any time have made improvements, either when the land is in his own occupation or with the consent of the tenant in occupation, or if the landlord shall have bought the tenant's improvements, the landlord shall have the right, on letting the same to a new tenant or on giving notice to the tenant in possession, to have such improvements valued for the purpose of adding to the rent.

4. That wherever in Ulster or elsewhere tenant-right custom has prevailed, the value of such right according to the local custom shall be considered in all respects as an improvement made by the tenant, and allowed for accordingly in valuing the rent.

5. That where land is held under lease, the lease shall not be disturbed unless at the request of the lessee or his assigns in possession; and if on such requests the rent be altered by the valuators, the tenant shall hold in future at the altered rent.

6. That the valuation, when once made, shall be permanent.

7. That every seven years there may and shall be a re-adjustment of the rent payable under the valuation, according to the rise or fall of the prices of agricultural produce, when the rise in prices be manifestly occasioned by the deficiency of the corps.

SECTION III

1. That the valuation shall be made by tribunals which shall unite as far as possible the advantages of *impartiality* between landlord and tenant, cheapness, accessibility, and *nomination* by the parties interested.

2. That these advantages may be secured to a reasonable degree—first, by local tribunals consisting of two valuators, one appointed by the landed proprietors and the other by the tenant farmers of the poor law union; secondly, by having valuators bound to value according to instructions embodied in the law; and thirdly, by having attached to each local tribunal a registrar or secretary whose duty it shall be to register all the proceedings of the valuators and keep them informed and reminded of the requirements of the instructions under which they act.

RULES OF THE [IRISH TENANT] LEAGUE

1. That an association to be called the Irish Tenant League be formed on the principles and subject to the rules hereafter expressed; and that such League be hereby established accordingly.

2. That the sole objects of the Tenant League are to protect the tenant and to procure a good landlord-and-tenant law by the legal co-operation of persons of all classes and of all opinions on other subjects. . . .

FREEMAN'S JOURNAL, 7–9 August 1850.

~

RESOLUTION ADOPTED AT THE TENANT LEAGUE CONFERENCE

8 September 1852

At a conference in Dublin held in September 1852 and attended by forty-one Liberal MPs, the delegates adopted a policy (set forth in the document below) of independent opposition to any government at Westminster that refused to endorse the tenant-right principles advanced by the prominent northern landlord William Sharman Crawford. The general election of July 1852 saw the return of fifty Irish MPs supposedly committed to tenant-right, but the movement disintegrated after the Independent Irish Party proved unable to preserve its cohesion.

SEE ALSO Land Questions

That in the unanimous opinion of this conference it is essential to the proper management of this cause that the members of parliament who have been returned on tenant-right principles should hold themselves perfectly independent of, and in opposition to, all governments which do not make it a part of their policy and a cabinet question to give to the tenantry of Ireland a measure fully embodying the principles of Mr [William] Sharman Crawford's bill.

FREEMAN'S JOURNAL, 9 September 1852.

~

TWO FENIAN OATHS

1858, 1859

The revolutionary organization that eventually became known as the IRB (Irish Republican Brotherhood or Irish

Revolutionary Brotherhood) was set up by James Stephens in Dublin in March 1858. Its original oath (the first one below) clearly identified it as a secret society; its members were later called Fenians. The movement was barely set on foot when in 1859 some of its members in the town and district of Skibbereen in west Cork were arrested and tried for participating in a secret conspiracy. Though the authorities dealt with these culprits leniently, the leaders of the organization decided to adopt a new form of oath (the second one below) allowing the Fenians to argue that their society was not secret.

SEE ALSO Fenian Movement and the Irish Republican Brotherhood; Politics: 1800 to 1921—Challenges to the Union; Stephens, James

I, A.B., do solemnly swear, in the presence of Almighty God, that I will do my utmost, at every risk, while life lasts, to make Ireland an independent democratic republic; that I will yield implicit obedience, in all things not contrary to the law of God, to the commands of my superior officers; and that I shall preserve inviolable secrecy regarding all the transactions of this secret society that may be confided to me. So help me God! Amen.

I, A.B., in the presence of Almighty God, do solemnly swear allegiance to the Irish Republic, now virtually established; and that I will do my very utmost, at every risk, while life lasts, to defend its independence and integrity; and, finally, that I will yield implicit obedience in all things, not contrary to the laws of God, to the commands of my superior officers. So help me God! Amen.

John O'Leary, Recollections of Fenians and Fenianism, 2 vols. (1896), vol. 1, pp. 120, 121.

～

"God Save Ireland"

1867

The following song, best known under the title of "God Save Ireland," appeared in the Nation *newspaper within a short time of the execution of the three "Manchester Martyrs" on 23 November 1867. The words were penned by the journalist, poet, and politician T. D. Sullivan, a constitutional nationalist like his more famous brother Alexander Martin Sullivan, the editor of the* Nation. *Set to*

an American Civil War tune, the song became practically the Irish national anthem for the next fifty years.

SEE ALSO Balladry in English; Fenian Movement and the Irish Republican Brotherhood; Politics: 1800–1921—Changes to the Union; Sullivan Brothers (A. M. and T. D.)

Air—"Tramp, Tramp, the Boys Are Marching"

I
High upon the gallows tree
Swung the noble-hearted Three
By the vengeful tyrant stricken in their bloom;
But they met him face to face,
With the courage of their race,
And they went with souls undaunted to their doom.
"God save Ireland!" said the heroes;
"God save Ireland!" said they all:
"Whether on the scaffold high
"Or the battle-field we die,
"Oh, what matter, when for Erin dear we fall!"

II
Girt around with cruel foes,
Still their spirit proudly rose,
For they thought of hearts that loved them, far and
 near;
Of the millions true and brave
O'er the ocean's swelling wave,
And the friends in holy Ireland ever dear.
"God save Ireland!" said they proudly;
"God save Ireland!" said they all:
"Whether on the scaffold high
"Or the battle-field we die,
"Oh, what matter, when for Erin dear we fall!"

III
Climbed they up the rugged stair,
Rang their voices out in prayer,
Then with England's fatal cord around them cast,
Close beneath the gallows tree,
Kissed like brothers lovingly,
True to home and faith and freedom to the last.
"God save Ireland!" prayed they loudly;
"God save Ireland!" said they all:
"Whether on the scaffold high
"Or the battle-field we die,
"Oh, what matter, when for Erin dear we fall!"

IV
Never till the latest day
Shall the memory pass away
Of the gallant lives thus given for our land;
But on the cause must go,
Amidst joy, or weal, or woe,

Till we've made our isle a nation free and grand.
"God save Ireland!" say we proudly;
"God save Ireland!" say we all:
"Whether on the scaffold high
"Or the battle-field we die,
"Oh, what matter, when for Erin dear we fall!"

T. D. *Sullivan*, SONGS AND POEMS (1899), *pp.* 14–15.

~

RESOLUTIONS ADOPTED AT THE HOME RULE CONFERENCE

18–21 November 1873

Despite its failure in 1867, Fenianism was a clear sign that Irish disaffection was rooted in legitimate grievances, one of which was the continuing lack of self-government. To the disaffection of Irish Catholics was added that of many Irish Protestants when in 1869 the Liberals under Gladstone disestablished the Anglican church in Ireland and then proceeded to pass legislation in 1870 benefiting Irish tenants. Thus the Home Government Association (HGA), launched by Isaac Butt in September 1870, initially attracted the support of many disenchanted Protestants as well as the backing of aggrieved Catholics. The HGA and its successor the Home Rule League (founded in November 1873) revived the idea of a federal solution to the constitutional relationship between Britain and Ireland.

SEE ALSO Butt, Isaac; Home Rule Movement and the Irish Parliamentary Party: 1870 to 1891; Politics: 1800 to 1921—Challenges to the Union

I. That as the basis of the proceedings of this conference, we declare our conviction that it is essentially necessary to the peace and prosperity of Ireland that the right of domestic legislation on all Irish affairs should be restored to our country.

II. That solemnly reasserting the inalienable right of the Irish people to self-government, we declare that time in our opinion has come when a combined and energetic effort should be made to obtain the restoration of that right.

III. That in accordance with the ancient and constitutional rights of the Irish nation, we claim the privilege of managing our own affairs by a parliament assembled in Ireland and composed of the sovereign, the Lords, and the Commons of Ireland.

IV. That in claiming these rights and privileges for our country, we adopt the principle of a federal arrangement, which would secure to the Irish parliament the right of legislating for and regulating all matters relating to the internal affairs of Ireland, while leaving to the imperial parliament the power of dealing with all questions affecting the imperial Crown and government, legislation regarding the colonies and other dependencies of the Crown, the relations of the empire with foreign states, and all matters appertaining to the defence and stability of the empire at large; as well as the power of granting and providing the supplies necessary for imperial purposes.

V. That such an arrangement does not involve any change in the existing constitution of the imperial parliament or any interference with the prerogatives of the Crown or disturbance of the principles of the constitution.

VI. That to secure to the Irish people the advantages of constitutional government, it is essential that there should be in Ireland an administration for Irish affairs, controlled, according to constitutional principles, by the Irish parliament and conducted by ministers constitutionally responsible to that parliament.

VII. That in the opinion of the conference a federal arrangement based upon these principles would consolidate the strength and maintain the integrity of the empire and add to the dignity and power of the imperial Crown.

VIII. That while we believe that in an Irish parliament the rights and liberties of all classes of our countrymen would find their best and surest protection, we are willing that there should be incorporated in the federal constitution articles supplying the amplest guarantees that no change shall be made by parliament in the present settlement of property in Ireland, and that no legislation shall be adopted to establish any religious ascendancy in Ireland or to subject any person to disabilities on account of his religious opinions.

IX. That this conference calls on the Irish constituencies at the next general election to return men earnestly and truly devoted to the great cause which this conference has been called to promote, and who, in any emergency that may arise, will be ready to take counsel with a great national conference, to be called in such a manner as to represent the opinions and feelings of the Irish nation; and that with a view of rendering members of parliament and their constituents more in accord on all questions affecting the welfare of the country, it is recommended by this conference that at the close of each session of parliament the representatives should render to their constituents an account of their stewardships.

X. That in order to carry these objects into practical effect, an association be now formed, to be called "the Irish Home Rule League," of which the essential and fundamental principles shall be those declared in the resolutions adopted at this conference, and of which the object, and only object, shall be to obtain for Ireland by peaceable and constitutional means the self-government claimed in those resolutions. . . .

PROCEEDINGS OF THE HOME RULE CONFERENCE HELD AT THE ROTUNDA, DUBLIN, ON THE 18TH, 19TH, 20TH, AND 21ST NOVEMBER, 1873 (1874), *pp.* 201–202.

~

SPEECH ADVOCATING CONSIDERATION OF HOME RULE BY THE HOUSE OF COMMONS

30 June 1874

Isaac Butt

Though the son of an Anglican clergyman and himself conservative in temperament and general political incli-nation, Isaac Butt defended the Fenians as a barrister in the 1860s, was a staunch advocate of tenant right, and founded the Home Government Association in September 1870. Butt sought to dress up Irish Home Rule as a cause that even Conservatives could support because in its federal form it would not threaten the British empire and would draw the teeth of legitimate Irish grievances. He struck these notes when commending Home Rule to the House of Commons in late June 1874. His motion was defeated by 458 to 61.

SEE ALSO Butt, Isaac; Home Rule Movement and the Irish Parliamentary Party: 1870 to 1891

The resolutions he now submitted to the House were very clear, and if they were debated, it would be seen that they were quite sufficient to guide the House to a conclusion. In the next place he would direct their atten-tion to this fact—that they involved no change in the constitution, and he was anxious that the House should clearly understand this. He proposed no change in the imperial parliament, and if his scheme were adopted, the House would meet next year just as it had done this; there would not be a single change in members or con-stituencies; there would be the members for Leeds, Glas-gow, Dublin, and Limerick; the only change would be

to take from that assembly some of the duties which it now discharged in reference to Irish business and to rele-gate them to another. That being so, he was tempted to ask whether the removal of the Irish business from that House would be regarded by the hon[ourable] members as an intolerable grievance? Some might be of opinion that it would be no great grievance if the Irish members were sent away; but the great majority, he believed, would be of opinion that if the Irish business were transacted elsewhere, more time would be left for the transaction of the legitimate business of the House. Now, he might be asked what he called Irish business; and further, if, should Irish members go into a parlia-ment of their own to transact their own business, they would still claim the power and privilege of voting on English questions in this House? He would answer the second question by saying emphatically "No." . . .

The English parliament, including the Scotch mem-bers—he would perhaps have a word to say on the last point presently—would meet to discuss purely English affairs, and when there was any question affecting the empire at large, Irish members might be summoned to attend. He saw no difficulty in the matter. The English parliament could manage English affairs as before the union; but now the English parliament undertook a duty it was unable to perform—namely, to manage the internal affairs of Ireland to the satisfaction of the Irish people. He did not seek to interfere with the right of tax-ing Ireland for imperial purposes, providing always that Ireland had a voice in imperial matters. He was asking only for a constitutional government and the benefit of those free institutions which made England great. If he succeeded in showing that Ireland had not a constitu-tional government, then he thought he could rely on the justice and generosity of the English parliament and of the Commons at large to give it to her. What was con-stitutional government? It consisted of adequate repre-sentation in parliament—a control of the administra-tion of affairs by a representative assembly of the people, so as to bring the government of the country into harmony with the feeling, the wants, and the wishes of the people. Did the representation by 103 Irish members in the English House of Commons amount to that? Could it be said that the House discharged the great function of constitutional government to Ireland? If it did not, then it followed that Ireland was deprived of that constitutional government which was its inher-ent right. He knew it might be said that this involved the question whether Ireland and England were not so blended into one nation that the same House might dis-charge the duties of a representative assembly for both. That again was a matter of fact. The House might wish that they were all West Britons, but wishes would not alter facts. . . . The two countries were not blended together, because in every department in Ireland the distinction was marked. They had a separate government, a separate lord lieutenant, separate courts of law, and exceptional laws were passed for Ireland which would never be tolerated for England. How, then, could one representative assembly act for both? Was not the consequence that the weaker country had no constitutional government? In this country there was constitutional government. The House of Commons administered the affairs of the nation in harmony with the sentiments of the English people. Statesmen in that House breathed an atmosphere of English feeling; they discussed English questions in an English assembly; they were driven of necessity to mould the administration of the government in accordance with the wants and wishes of the people. They asked the same for Ireland, and they asked for no more. . . .

As a matter of fact, the whole government of Ireland was based upon distrust of all classes in the community. Stipendary magistrates were substituted for the resident gentry of the country, and a sub-inspector of constabulary was a more influential person than the lord lieutenant of a county. The whole record of the legislation for Ireland since the union was made up of successive Arms Acts, suspensions of the Habeas Corpus Act, to Party Processions Prevention Acts and Coercion Acts, each one being more severe than its predecessor. And this record was the more gloomy because it was a record of the doings of well-intentioned parliaments. Notwithstanding all that had been done, the curfew bell of the Norman conquerors was rung in many parts of the country, and in others blood money was exacted after the example of the Saxons. Even if it were true—which he denied—that such a course of legislation had been necessary, that very fact would be its most grievous condemnation. He was therefore justified in saying that up to now the government of the country had failed, and in asking that the Irish people might have an opportunity of managing their own affairs. He was told that parliament having passed the Land Act [of 1870] and the Church [Disestablishment] Act [of 1869], the Irish people were ungrateful in coming forward and demanding Home Rule also. It was even said that such a course was an act of ingratitude towards the individual minister who had been mainly instrumental in passing those acts. All he could say was that such assertions showed the faultiness of the system under which they could be possible. Who ever spoke of the English people being grateful for the passing of a good act? . . . Was there an Englishman in the House who would not be glad to get rid of the opprobrium attaching to the government of Ireland? If the wish was really entertained, the way to get rid of it was by allowing the Irish people an opportunity of trying to govern themselves. If they

succeeded, great and glorious would be the reward of those who gave the opportunity; if they failed, theirs alone would be the blame. And where was there to be found any valid objection to granting what they asked? The imperial parliament would hold the army, the navy, and all that was connected with affairs purely imperial, and no difficulty would be found in separating from imperial questions those with which an Irish parliament might properly deal. The United States of America afforded an illustration of a successful federal government with independent state legislatures, and in some of our own colonies they found instances of people owning the imperial sway of England, but at the same time managing their own internal affairs. Even supposing that there might be some disaffected members of an Irish parliament—and this he did not admit—they would be in a miserable minority, and the fact of their disaffection being open to the light would give the strongest assurance of its speedy extinction. In two English colonies were to be found men who, driven out of Ireland because they could no longer endure the system of government existing there, had become ministers under the British crown, and were doing honour alike to the colonies in which they served and to the sovereign who had appointed them. Sir George Grey, the governor of the Cape of Good Hope, wrote strongly in favour of giving a federal parliament to Ireland, and he believed in his soul that it would be the means of effecting a complete union with England. Wrong had driven a large proportion of the Irish people into the madness of insurrection or sympathy with insurrection. It was indeed the consciousness of this fact which made him set himself earnestly to work to devise a means of stopping this miserable series of abortive insurrections and revolts by which Ireland had been torn, and some of the best and bravest of her sons driven into exile. He believed he had devised a plan which would satisfy the just demands of the people without producing a disintegration of the empire; therefore, he had asked the people to give up the madness of revolt and join with him in constitutionally and peacefully making an appeal to England. Many of the people who supported this moderate proposal would waste their lives in useless struggles against England if they saw no other redress for the sufferings of their country. . . . He believed the Irish people were essentially conservative. It was only misgovernment that had driven them into revolt. Give them fair play, and there was no people on earth who would be more attached to true conservative principles than the Irish nation. The geographical position of Ireland made it her interest to be united with England. They were allied to England by ties of kindred and ties of self-interest which bound them to maintain inviolate the connexion with this country, and the way to maintain that connexion was to give them justice in the management of their own internal affairs. . . . Give us—continued the hon[ourable] and learned gentleman—a full participation in your freedom and make us sharers in those free institutions which have made England so great and glorious. Give us our share, which we have not now, in that greatest and best of all free institutions—a free parliament representing indifferently the whole people.

HANSARD'S PARLIAMENTARY DEBATES, *third series, ccxx, cols.* 700–717.

~

FROM *BELFAST FIFTY YEARS AGO*

1875

Thomas Gaffikin

In this lecture delivered in 1875 to the Belfast Workingman's Institute, Thomas Gaffikin recollects the city of his youth in the 1820s. At that point in the development of the Belfast textile industry, cotton, not linen, was the dominant fiber. Spinning took place in mills, but the resulting yarn was still put out to handloom weavers whose looms were located in their houses in the city and its environs.

SEE ALSO Belfast

I endeavour, as briefly as possible, to convey an impression from memory of what Belfast was like in my school-boy days—now more than fifty years ago. . . . That wide and splendid thoroughfare now leading from Cromac Street to Corporation Street could then have been scarcely imagined. This brings us back to our starting point with, perhaps, the impression that few changes in Belfast are more remarkable than the gradual occupation by the town of places formerly, to a more or less extent, covered with water; and this movement has been long on foot. I have heard of old people talking of the time when the river in High Street was open, and describing when markets were held, how both sides of the street were occupied by stalls in front of the houses. . . .

The Dublin Road, like all the other approaches to the town, was paved in the centre with large boulder stones to the rising ground at Fountainville (the only roads about the town that still exhibit this old style of pavement are the Strandtown Road, near Gelston's Corner,

and the old Ballygowan Road at Gooseberry Corner). The first toll-bar on the Dublin Road was where the new Methodist Church now stands, it interrupted the progress of all vehicles except the Royal Mail Coach, which, with four fresh horses in front, and a couple of guards fully armed behind, took the hill at a canter. It was a steeper hill then than now.

The Country Down side of the harbour was called Voke's Quay, and was principally occupied by lighters, lime cobbs, or vessels undergoing repairs. This brings us back to

The old Long Bridge, some twenty feet wide,
With numerous arches for spanning the tide;
Holes made in the walls to drain off the wet,
And niches for safety where vehicles met.

About this time the population numbered some thirty-five or forty thousand. The principal trades were cotton-spinning, tanning, timber, and provisions. We had four or five cotton mills, about thirty tanyards, and extensive provision stores, in different quarters of the town. Smithfield was the principal market for miscellaneous goods, such as hides, wool, clothing, house furnishing (new and old), and every description of farm stock and produce.

We had abundance of ballad-singers and musicians, who, with the old watchmen calling the hours, striking their pikes on the pavement, or springing their rattles on the slightest disturbance or report of a fire, and sweeps, oystermen, piemen, tapesellers, cries of Ballinderry onions and Cromac water, kept up the noise from morning till night. . . . Cockeybendy was a very little bandylegged man, who knew the tune to play at every house in the locality he frequented. "Garryowen," "St. Patrick's Day," and, "the Boyne Water" were his best paying airs.

We had two competing lines to Dublin, the Mail and Fair Trader coaches. . . . In times of public excitement great crowds used to collect about the time the coach was expected, and very important looked the guard and coachman as they detailed the latest news from the metropolis. . . . A mail coach, with the English and Scottish letters, also ran daily to Donaghadee in connection with the short sea passage to Portpatrick, which Lord Castlereagh had promoted.

There had been great changes in our local trades in fifty years. While some have increased, others have diminished. The cotton spinning has not held its relative position, while coopering and tanning have almost disappeared. High Street was naturally the best business street, but its shops were very different from the elegant establishments of to-day. Instead of a whole story of plate glass reaching almost to the ground, we had low front and small windows of little panes that were cleaned perhaps once a month, and protected, or rather encumbered, with strong iron railings on the outside. . . .

A buff vest, a swallow-tailed coat, with bright buttons, a frilled shirt, with ruffled cuffs, and a large gold seal hanging from the fob completed the costume of a dandy. I cannot describe the ladies' dress with any minuteness but its tone seemed to be more severe and forbidding than later styles. The coal scuttle bonnet kept the gentlemen at a respectful distance from their faces, while in fine weather they might admire their slender waists, and sandal shoes with ankle ties, but in wet and wintry weather the ladies took their airing in sedan chairs or muffled up and mounted on pattens. The sedan chairs were kept in entries off High Street, and the measured tramp of the bearers could be heard going to and from the theatre, evening parties, or the church on Sundays. The ladies' pattens were heard even more distinctly, and on Sundays in winter the porch of the parish church would be lined during the time of Divine service with the pattens of various sizes and colours.

The population of Belfast then (1823) numbering some forty thousand was of a very mixed character, and as the females preponderated, their labour was cheap and more varied before the flax-spinning mills were established. At that time common labourers' wages were seven shillings a week, while tradesmen and skilled labourers were paid in proportion. The pay of bricklayers and carpenters was about sixteen shillings, their hours of labour being longer than at present. The pay of a foreman or one who had charge of some particular branch of the trade, was sometimes eighteen or twenty shillings. The generality of the workmen and their families appeared as comfortable then as they do now at a time when they are receiving double the pay . . .

The population began to grow rapidly as the spinning mills and weaving factories increased. The districts of Millfield, Carrick Hill, and the Pound were thickly populated by old families long connected with Belfast, and strangers coming amongst them were looked upon with suspicion for some time. In these localities the cock fights and dock fights generally originated. The principal occupation of the people was weaving, but many of them wrought at the production of various articles exposed for sale in the stalls of Smithfield. Ballymacarrett, Sandy Row, and Brown Square were the greatest weaving localities. The sound of the shuttle was heard almost in every house. . . .

The most important changes that have taken place in Belfast are—the great increase in the population, and

the price or value of land in the neighbourhood. Farms of land and town parks, which once were held at from seven to ten shillings per acre, on terminable leases, were renewed to the tenants by the late Marquis (of Donegal). . . . The people of Belfast in the present generation are principally strangers. Living examples of successful merchants who came into Belfast from the neighbouring districts are to be found in every street. . . . Long may good and enterprising men be attracted here for commercial and scientific purposes, and may our native town prosper and flourish, and extend on every side until it clambers the slopes of the beautiful green hills that encircle it.

Reprinted in IRELAND FROM GRATTAN'S PARLIAMENT TO THE GREAT FAMINE (1783–1850), *edited by James Carty (1966), pp. 36–39.*

~

ESTABLISHMENT OF THE NATIONAL LAND LEAGUE OF MAYO

16 August 1879

The Land League of Mayo was the precursor of the Irish National Land League established in Dublin in October 1879 with Charles Stewart Parnell as its president. The Mayo League grew out of a series of successful land demonstrations held in the west of Ireland in the summer of 1879 in response to a sharply deteriorating economic situation caused by bad weather, poor crops, and falling agricultural prices. Michael Davitt and other Fenians were instrumental in founding the Mayo League and its successor, the National Land League.

SEE ALSO Davitt, Michael; Land Acts of 1870 and 1881; Land War of 1879 to 1882; Parnell, Charles Stewart

A meeting in connexion with the land agitation in Mayo . . . took place at Castlebar today in Daly's Hotel and was attended by representative delegates from all parts of the county. . . . Mr Michael Davitt read a document embodying the rules and objects of the proposed association.

This body shall be known as the National Land League of Mayo and shall consist of farmers and others who will agree to labour for the objects here set forth, and subscribe to the conditions of membership, principles, and rules specified below.

Objects: The objects for which this body is organised are—

1. To watch over the interests of the people it represents and protect the same, as far as may be in its power to do so, from an unjust or capricious exercise of power or privilege on the part of landlords or any other class in the community.

2. To resort to every means compatible with justice, morality, and right reason, which shall not clash defiantly with the constitution upheld by the power of the British empire in this country, for the abolition of the present land laws of Ireland and the substitution in their place of such a system as shall be in accord with the social rights and necessities of our people, the traditions and moral sentiments of our race, and which the contentment and prosperity of our country imperatively demand.

3. Pending a final and satisfactory settlement of the land question, the duty of this body will be to expose the injustice, wrong, or injury which may be inflicted upon any farmer in Mayo, either by rack-renting, eviction, or other arbitrary exercise of power which the existing laws enable the landlords to exercise over their tenantry, by giving all such arbitrary acts the widest possible publicity and meeting their perpetration with all the opposition which the laws for the preservation of the peace will permit of. In furthernance of which, the following plan will be adopted:—a. Returns to be obtained, printed, and circulated, of the number of landlords in this county; the amount of acreage in possession of same, and the means by which such land was obtained; farms let by each, with the conditions under which they are held by their tenants and excess of rent paid by same over the government valuation. b. To publish by placard, or otherwise, notice of contemplated evictions for non-payment of exorbitant rent or other unjust cause, and the convening of a public meeting, if deemed necessary or expedient, as near the scene of such evictions as circumstances will allow, and on the day fixed upon for the same. c. The publication of a list of evictions carried out, together with cases of rack-renting, giving full particulars of same, names of landlords, agents, etc., concerned, and number people evicted by such acts. d. The publication of the names of all persons who shall rent or occupy land or farms from which others have been dispossessed for non-payment of exorbitant rents, or who shall offer a higher rent for land or farms than that paid by the previous occupier. The publication of reductions of rent and acts of justice or kindness performed by landlords in the county.

4. This body to undertake the defence of such of its members, or those of local clubs affiliated with it, who may be required to resist by law the actions of landlords or their agents who may purpose doing them injury, wrong, or injustice in connexion with their land or farms.

5. To render assistance when possible to such farmer-members as may be evicted or otherwise wronged by landlords or their agents.

6. To undertake the organising of local clubs or defence associations in the baronies, towns, and parishes of this county, the holding of public meetings and demonstrations on the land question, and the printing of pamphlets on that and other subjects for the information of the farming classes.

7. And finally, to act as a vigilance committee in Mayo, note the conduct of its grand jury, poor law guardians, town commissioners, and members of parliament, and pronounce on the manner in which their respective functions are performed, wherever the interests, social or political, of the people represented by this club renders it expedient to do so.

Conditions of membership: 1. To be a member or any local club or defence association in the county, and be selected by such club or association to represent the same on the central or county association. . . . . 3. To pay any sum not under five shillings a year towards the carrying out of the foregoing objects and the end for which this body is created—the obtaining of the soil of Ireland for the people of Ireland who cultivate it.

Declaration of principles. The land of Ireland belongs to the people of Ireland, to be held and cultivated for the sustenance of those whom God decreed to be the inhabitants thereof. Land being created to supply the necessities of existence, those who cultivate it to that end have a higher claim to its absolute possession than those who make it an article of barter to be used or disposed of for purposes of profit or pleasure. The end for which the land of a country is created requires an equitable distribution of the same among the people who are to live upon such distribution of the same among the people who are to live upon the fruits of their labour in its cultivation. Any restriction, therefore, upon such a distribution by a feudal land system embodying the laws of primogeniture and entail, the amassing of large estates, the claiming of proprietorship under penal obligations from occupiers, and preventing the same from developing the full resources of the land, must necessarily be opposed to the divine purpose for which it was created, and to the social rights, security, and happiness of the people.

"Before the conquest the Irish people knew nothing of absolute property in land. The land virtually belonged to the entire sept; the chief was little more than managing member of the association. The feudal idea, which views all rights as emanating from a head land-lord, came in with the conquest, was associated with foreign dominion, and has never to this day been recognised by the moral sentiments of the people. Originally the offspring not of industry but of spoliation, the right has not been allowed to purify itself by protracted possession, but has passed from the original spoliators to others by a series of fresh spoliations, so as to be always connected with the latest and most odious oppression of foreign invaders. In the moral feelings of the Irish people, the right to hold the land goes, as it did in the beginning, with the right to till it." These were the words of John Stuart Mill, the English political economist. . . .

The area of Ireland and the natural wealth of its soil is capable of supporting from twelve to twenty millions of inhabitants if restrictive land laws did not operate against the full development of the country's resources and the unfettered cultivation of the land. Yet a population of 8,000,000 previous to the year 1847 was reduced by death, starvation, and exile, consequent upon an artificial famine and continued impoverishment, to little over 5,000,000 at the present day. Decreased population with its concomitant absorption of small-holdings into large estates has produced no beneficial changes in the condition of the existent farming classes, who are compelled by the coercion of necessity in the absence of manufacturing industry to the acceptance of a non-alternative bargain in the shape of exorbitant rent in order to obtain the use of the soil. The dread of eviction or rack-renting must necessarily operate against the expenditure of labour and enterprise in the cultivation of the land and improvement of farm dwellings and premises which follow in every country where the fruits of the people's industry is [sic] protected by the state; hence the soil of Ireland is worse and less cultivated, and the living and habitations of its agricultural classes [are] more wretched, than in any country in the civilised world. Over 6,000,000 acres of Irish land is owned by less than 300 individuals, twelve of whom are in possession of 1,297,888 acres between them, while 5,000,000 of the Irish people own not a solitary acre. For the protection of the proprietorial rights of the few thousand landlords in the country, a standing army of semi-military police is maintained which landless millions have to support, while the conduct of the landocracy in the exercise of its legal privileges occasions almost all the evils under which our people suffer.

Thus the rights of the soil cultivators, their security from arbitrary disturbance and incentives to social advancement, together with the general well-being, peace, and prosperity of the people at large, are sacrificed for the benefit of a class insignificant in numbers and of least account in all that goes towards the maintenance

of a country, but which by the aid of existing land laws extracts some twenty million pounds annually from the soil of Ireland without conferring any single benefit in return on the same or [on] the people by whose industry it is produced.

If the land in the possession of 744 landlords in this country were divided into 20-acre farms, it would support in ease and comparative independence over two millions and a half of our people.

To substitute for such an unjust and anomalous system as the present land code—one that would show an equal protection and solicitude for the social rights and well-being of the labouring millions as that shown for those of the wealthy but non-operative few—is the principle upon which enlightened statesmanship aims at following in modern times to meet the growing necessities of that popular intelligence and awakening civilisation which demands the sweeping away of those feudal laws opposed to the social progress and ideas of the age. Sacrificing the interests of the few to the welfare of the many by the abolition of feudal land codes has laid the foundation of solid governments and secured the contentment of peoples in most European countries. The interests of the landlords of Ireland are pecuniary and can be compensated, but the interests of the people of Ireland, dependant upon the produce of the soil, is [sic] their very existence. In denouncing the existing land laws and demanding in their place such a system as will recognise and establish the cultivator of the said soil as its proprietor, we neither purpose nor demand the confiscation of the interest which the landlords now hold in the land, but ask that compensation be given them for loss of said rights when the state, for the peace, benefit, and happiness of the people, shall decree the abolition of the present system.

We appeal to the farmers of Ireland to be up and doing at once and organise themselves forthwith in order that their full strength may be put forth in behalf of themselves and their country in efforts to obtain what has brought security and comparative plenty to the farming classes of continental countries. Without an evidence of earnestness and practical determination being shown now by the farmers of Ireland and their friends in a demand for a small proprietary which alone can fully satisfy the Irish people or finally settle the great land question of the country, the tribunal of public opinion will neither credit the urgent necessity for such a change nor lend its influence in ameliorating the condition or redressing the social and political wrongs of which we complain. Let us remember, in the words of one of Ireland's greatest sons [John Mitchel], that "the land is the fund whence we all ultimately draw; and if the terms on which the land is cultivated be unfair—if the agricultural system of a country be unsound, then the entire structure is rotten and will inevitably come down. Let us never forget that mere appeals to the public to encourage native industry in other departments must be utterly futile so long as the great and paramount native industry of the farmer is neglected. In vain shall we try to rouse national spirit if the very men who make the nation sink into paupers before our face. Paupers have no country, no rights, no duties; and, in short, if we permit the small farmers to be reduced to pauperism—if we see them compelled to give up their land and throw themselves on public relief, there is an end of Ireland."

The manifesto was unanimously adopted.

FREEMAN'S JOURNAL, *18 August 1879.*

CALL AT ENNIS FOR AGRARIAN MILITANCY

19 September 1880

Charles Stewart Parnell

Boycotting, of course, was not invented by the Land League, but the League did bring boycotting to bear on the land question in innovative ways and on an unprecedented scale. The word entered the language through the name of Captain Charles Cunningham Boycott, the agent of Lord Erne's estate in County Mayo, who was targeted beginning on 24 September 1880. This was less than a week after Charles Stewart Parnell had advocated such ostracism in a speech at Ennis. On the whole, boycotting was employed to discipline recalcitrant tenant farmers more often than offending landlords or agents.

SEE ALSO Land War of 1879 to 1882; Parnell, Charles Stewart

. . . Depend upon it that the measure of the land bill of next session will be the measure of your activity and energy this winter (cheers)—it will be the measure of your determination not to pay unjust rents—it will be the measure of your determination to keep a firm grip of your homesteads (cheers). It will be the measure of your determination not to bid for farms from which others have been evicted, and to use the strong force of public opinion to deter any unjust men amongst yourselves—

and there are many such—from bidding for such farms (hear, hear). If you refuse to pay unjust rents, if you refuse to take farms from which others have been evicted, the land question must be settled, and settled in a way that will be satisfactory to you. It depends therefore upon yourselves, and not upon any commission or any government. When you have made this question ripe for settlement, then and not till then will it be settled (cheers). It is very nearly ripe already in many parts of Ireland. It is ripe in Mayo, Galway, Roscommon, Sligo, and portions of the County Cork (cheers). But I regret to say that the tenant farmers of the County Clare have been backward in organisation up to the present time. You must take and band yourselves together in Land Leagues. Every town and village must have its own branch. You must know the circumstances of the holdings and of the tenures of the district over which the League has jurisdiction—you must see that the principles of the Land League are inculcated, and when you have done this in Clare, then Clare will take her rank with the other active counties, and you will be included in the next land bill brought forward by the government (cheers). Now, what are you to do to a tenant who bids for a farm from which another has been evicted?

Several voices: "Shoot him."

Mr. Parnell: I think I heard somebody say shoot him (cheers). I wish to point out to you a very much better way—a more Christian and charitable way which will give the lost man an opportunity of repenting (laughter, and hear). When a man takes a farm from which another has been evicted, you must shun him on the roadside when you meet him—you must shun him in the streets of the town—you must shun him in the shop—you must shun him in the fairgreen and in the market place, and even in the place of worship, by leaving him alone, by putting him into a moral Coventry, by isolating him from the rest of his country as if he were the leper of old—you must show him your detestation of the crime he has committed. If you do this, you may depend on it, there will be no man so full of avarice—so lost to shame—as to dare the public opinion of all the right-thinking men in the county and transgress your unwritten code of laws. People are very much engaged at present in discussing the way in which the land question is to be settled, just the same as when a few years ago Irishmen were at each other's throats as to the sort of parliament we would have if we got one. I am always thinking it is better first to catch your hare before you decide how you are going to cook him (laughter). I would strongly recommend public men not to waste their breath too much in discussing how the land question is to be settled, but rather to help and encourage the people in making it, as I said just now, ripe for settlement (applause). When it is ripe for settlement, you will probably have your choice as to how it shall be settled, and I said a year ago that the land question would never be settled until the Irish landlords were just as anxious to have it settled as the Irish tenants (cheers).

A voice: "They soon will be."

Mr. Parnell: There are indeed so many ways in which it may be settled that it is almost superfluous to discuss them; but I stand here today to express my opinion that no settlement can be satisfactory or permanent which does not ensure the uprooting of that system of landlordism which has brought the country three times in a century to famine. The feudal system of land tenure has been tried in almost every European country and it has been found wanting everywhere; but nowhere has it brought more exile, produced more suffering, crime, and destitution than in Ireland (cheers). It was abolished in Prussia by transferring the land from the landlords to the occupying tenants. The landlords were given government paper as compensation. Let the English government give the landlords their paper tomorrow as compensation (laughter). We want no money—not a single penny of money would be necessary. Why, if they gave the Irish landlords—the bad section of them—the four or five millions a year that they spend on the police and military (groans) in helping them to collect their rents, that would be a solution of it (cheers), and a very cheap solution of it. But perhaps as with other reforms, they will try a little patchwork and tinkering for a while until they learn better (hear, hear). Well, let them patch and tinker if they wish. In my opinion the longer the landlords wait, the worse the settlement they will get (cheers). Now is the time for them to settle before the people learn the power of combination. We have been accused of preaching communistic doctrines when we told the people not to pay an unjust rent, and the following out of that advice in a few of the Irish counties had shown the English government the necessity for a radical alteration in the land laws. But how would they like it if we told the people some day or other not to pay any rent until this question is settled (cheers). We have not told them that yet, and I suppose it may never be necessary for us to speak in that way (hear). I suppose the question will be settled peaceably, fairly, and justly to all parties (hear, hear). If it should not be settled, we cannot continue to allow this [millstone] to hang round the neck of our country, throttling its industry and preventing its progress (cheers). It will be for the consideration of wiser heads than mine whether, if the landlords continue obdurate and refuse all just concessions, we shall not be obliged to tell the people of Ireland to strike against rent until this question has been settled (cheers). And if the five hundred thousand tenant farmers of Ireland struck against the ten thousand landlords, I would like to see where they would get police and soldiers enough to make them pay (loud cheers).

FREEMAN'S JOURNAL, 20 September 1880.

∽

LAND LAW (IRELAND) ACT

22 August 1881

The Land League spearheaded a campaign of violence and intimidation against the existing land system between 1879 and 1881. To this campaign the British government responded with a combination of conciliation and coercion. Conciliation took the form of the 1881 Land Act, which finally conceded the three Fs for which tenant advocates had been contending since the 1850s. To "fair rents," fixity of tenure, and free sale was added a modest provision for tenant land-purchase. The omission of leaseholders and tenants in arrears from the benefits of the Land Act, and the lack of adequate facilities for land purchase, meant that the agrarian struggle would continue in spite of these substantial concessions.

SEE ALSO Land Acts of 1870 and 1881; Land War of 1879 to 1882; Parnell, Charles Stewart

AN ACT TO FURTHER AMEND THE LAW RELATING TO THE OCCUPATION AND OWNERSHIP OF LAND IN IRELAND, AND FOR OTHER PURPOSES RELATING THERETO

Be it enacted . . . as follows:

1. The tenant for the time being of every holding, not hereinafter specially excepted from the provisions of this act, may sell his tenancy for the best price that can be got for the same, subject to the following regulations and subject also to the provisions in this act contained with respect to the sale of a tenancy subject to statutory conditions:

(1) Except with the consent of the landlord, the sale shall be made to one person only:

(2) The tenant shall give the prescribed notice to the landlord of his intention to sell his tenancy:

(3) On receiving such notice the landlord may purchase the tenancy for such sum as may be agreed

upon, or in the event of disagreement, may be ascertained by the court to be the true value thereof:

(4) Where the tenant shall agree to sell his tenancy to some other person than the landlord, he shall, upon informing the landlord of the name of the purchaser, state in writing therewith the consideration agreed to be given for the tenancy:

(5) If the tenant fails to give the landlord the notice or information required by the foregoing subsections, the court may, if it think fit and that the just interests of the landlord so require, declare the sale to be void:

(6) Where the tenancy is sold to some other person than the landlord, the landlord may within the prescribed period refuse on reasonable grounds to accept the purchaser as tenant. . . .

(7) Where the tenancy is subject to any such conditions as are in this act declared to be statutory conditions, and the sale is made in consequence of proceedings by the landlord for the purpose of recovering possession of the holding by reason of the breach of any of such conditions, the court shall grant to the landlord out of the purchase moneys payment of any debt, including arrears of rent, due to him by the tenant. . . .

(8) Where permanent improvements on a holding have been made by the landlord or his predecessors in title . . . , and the landlord . . . consents that his property in such improvements shall be sold along with the tenancy . . . , the purchase money shall be apportioned by the court. . . .

(9) When a tenant sells his tenancy to any person other than the landlord, the landlord may at any time within the prescribed period give notice both to the outgoing tenant and to the purchaser of any sums which he may claim from the outgoing tenant for arrears of rent or other breaches of the contract or conditions of tenancy. And

(a) If the outgoing tenant does not within the prescribed period give notice to the purchaser that he disputes such claims or any of them, the purchaser shall out of the purchase moneys pay the full amount thereof to the landlord; and

(b) If the outgoing tenant disputes such claims or any of them, the purchaser shall out of the purchase moneys pay to the landlord so much (if any) of such claims as the outgoing tenant admits, and pay the residue of the amount claimed by the landlord into court in the prescribed manner.

Until the purchaser has satisfied the requirements of this subsection, it shall not be obligatory on the landlord to accept the purchaser as his tenant. . . .

(11) A tenant who has sold his tenancy on any occasion of quitting his holding shall not be entitled on the same occasion to receive compensation for either disturbance or improvements; and a tenant who has received compensation for either disturbance or improvements on any occasion of quitting his holding shall not be entitled on the same occasion to sell his tenancy.

(12) The tenant of a holding subject to the Ulster tenant-right custom or to a usage corresponding to the Ulster tenant-right custom may sell his tenancy either in pursuance of that custom or usage or in pursuance of this section. . . .

4. Where the landlord demands an increase of rent from the tenant of a present tenancy . . . , or demands an increase of rent from the tenant of a future tenancy, beyond the amount fixed at the beginning of such tenancy, then,

(1) Where the tenant accepts such increase, until the expiration of a term of fifteen years from the time when such increase was made (in this act referred to as a statutory term), such tenancy shall (if it so long continues to subsist) be deemed to be a tenancy subject to statutory conditions, with such incidents during the continuance of the said term as are in this act in that behalf mentioned.

(2) Where the tenant of any future tenancy does not accept such increase and sell his tenancy, the same shall be sold subject to the increased rent, and in addition to the price paid for the tenancy, he shall be entitled to receive from his landlord the amount (if any) by which the court may, on the application of the landlord or tenant, decide the selling value of his tenancy to have been depreciated below the amount which would have been such selling value if the rent had been a fair rent. . . .

(3) Where the tenant does not accept such increase and is compelled to quit the tenancy by or in pursuance of a notice to quit, but does not sell the tenancy, he shall be entitled to claim compensation as in the case of disturbance by the landlord.

(4) The tenant of a present tenancy may, in place of accepting or declining such increase, apply to the court in manner hereafter in this act mentioned to have the rent fixed.

5. A tenant shall not, during the continuance of a statutory term in his tenancy, be compelled to pay a

higher rent than the rent payable at the commencement of such term, and shall not be compelled to quit the holding of which he is tenant except in consequence of the breach of some one or more of the conditions following (in this act referred to as statutory conditions), that is to say,

(1) The tenant shall pay his rent at the appointed time.

(2) The tenant shall not, to the prejudice of the interest of the landlord in the holding, commit persistent waste. . . .

(3) The tenant shall not, without the consent of his landlord in writing, subdivide his holding or sublet the same. . . . Agistment or the letting of land for the purpose of temporary depasturage, or the letting in conacre of land for the purpose of its being solely used . . . for the growing of potatoes or other green crops, the land being properly manured, shall not be deemed a subletting for the purposes of this act. . . .

(5) The landlord, or any persons authorised by him in that behalf (he or they making reasonable amends and satisfaction for any damage to be done or occasioned thereby), shall have the right to enter upon the holding for any of the purposes following . . .

(6) The tenant shall not on his holding, without the consent of his landlord, open any house for the sale of intoxicating liquors.

Nothing contained in this section shall prejudice or affect any ejectment for non-payment of rent instituted by a landlord, whether before or after the commencement of a statutory term, in respect of rent accrued due for a holding before the commencement of such term.

During the continuance of a statutory term in a tenancy, save as hereinafter provided, the court may, on the application of the landlord and upon being satisfied that he is desirous of resuming the holding or part thereof for some reasonable and sufficient purpose, authorize the resumption thereof by the landlord. . . .

Provided that the rent of any holding subject to statutory conditions may be increased in respect of capital laid out by the landlord under agreement with the tenant to such an amount as may be agreed upon between landlord and tenant. . . .

8. (1) The tenant of any present tenancy to which this act applies, or such tenant and the landlord jointly, or the landlord . . . may from time to time during the continuance of such tenancy apply to the court to fix the fair rent to be paid by such tenant to the landlord for the holding . . .

(3) Where the judicial rent [the rent set by the assistant land commissioners] of any present tenancy has been fixed . . . ,then, until the expiration of a term of fifteen years from the rent day next succeeding the day on which the determination of the court has been given (in this act referred to as a statutory term), such present tenancy shall (if it so long continue to subsist) be deemed to be a tenancy subject to statutory conditions. . . .

(6) Subject to rules made under this act, the landlord and tenant of any present tenancy to which this act applies, may . . . by writing under their hands agree and declare what is then the fair rent of the holding; and such agreement and declaration, on being filed in court in the prescribed manner, shall have the same effect and consequences in all respects as if the rent so agreed on were a judicial rent. . . .

10. The landlord and tenant of any ordinary tenancy and the landlord and proposed tenant of any holding to which this act applies which is not subject to a subsisting tenancy, may agree, the one to grant and the other to accept a lease for a term of thirty-one years or upwards (in this act referred to as a judicial lease), on such conditions and containing such provisions as the parties to such lease may mutually agree upon, and such lease . . . shall be substituted for the former tenancy, if any, in the holding. . . .

13. (1) Where proceedings are or have been taken by the landlord to compel a tenant to quit his holding, the tenant may sell his tenancy at any time before, but not after, the expiration of six months from the execution of a writ or decree for possession in an ejectment for non-payment or rent, and at any time before, but not after, the execution of such writ or decree in any ejectment other than for non-payment of rent; and such tenancy so sold shall be and be deemed to be a subsisting tenancy notwithstanding such proceedings, without prejudice to the landlord's rights, in the event of the said tenancy not being redeemed within said period of sixth months; and if any judgment or decree in ejectment has been obtained before the passing of this act, such tenant may within the same periods respectively apply to the court to fix the judicial rent of the holding, but subject to the provisions herein contained such application shall not invalidate or prejudice any such judgment or decree, which shall remain in full force and effect. . . .

(3) Where any proceedings for compelling the tenant of a present tenancy to quit his holding shall have been taken before or after an application to fix a judicial rent and shall be pending before such application is disposed of, the court before which such proceedings are pending shall have power . . . to postpone or suspend such proceedings until the termination of the proceedings on the application for such judicial rent. . . .

(6) A tenant compelled to quit his holding during the continuance of a statutory term in his tenancy, in consequence of the breach by the tenant of any statutory condition, shall not be entitled to compensation for disturbance. . . .

22. A tenant whose holding or the aggregate of whose holdings valued under the act relating to the valuation of rateable property in Ireland at an annual value of not less than one hundred and fifty pounds shall be entitled by writing under his hand to contract himself out of any of the provisions of this act or of the *Landlord and Tenant (Ireland) Act, 1870.*

24. (1) The Land Commission, out of moneys in their hands, may, if satisfied with the security, advance sums to tenants for the purpose of enabling them to purchase their holdings, that is to say,

  (a) Where a sale of a holding is about to be made by a landlord to a tenant in consideration of the payment of a principal sum, the Land Commission may advance to the tenant for the purposes of such purchase any sum not exceeding three fourths of the said principal sum.

  (b) Where a sale of a holding is about to be made by a landlord to a tenant in consideration of the tenant paying a fine and engaging to pay to the landlord a fee farm rent, the Land Commission may advance to the tenant for the purposes of such purchase, any sum not exceeding one half of the fine payable to the landlord. . . .

26. (1) Any estate may be purchased by the Land Commission for the purpose of reselling to the tenants of the lands comprised in such estate their respective holdings, if the Land Commission are satisfied . . . that a competent number of the tenants are able and willing to purchase their holdings from the Land Commission.

(2) The sale by the Land Commission of a holding to the tenant thereof may be made either in consideration of a principal sum being paid as the whole price . . . or in consideration of a fine and of a fee farm rent, with this qualification, that the amount of the fee farm rent shall not exceed seventy-five per cent of the rent which in the opinion of the land commission would be a fair rent for the holding.

(3) For the purposes of this section a competent number of tenants means a body of tenants who are not less in number than three fourths of the whole number of tenants on the estate, and who pay rent not less than two thirds of the whole rent of the estate. . . .

28. (1) Any advance made by the Land Commission for the purpose of supplying money for the purchase of a holding from a landlord or of a holding or parcel from the Land Commission, shall be repaid by an annuity in favour of the Land Commission for thirty-five years of five pounds for every hundred pounds of such advance, and so in proportion for any less sum. . . .

37. (1) The expression "the court" as used in this act shall mean the civil bill court of the county where the matter requiring the cognizance of the court arises. . . .

(3) Any proceedings which might be instituted before the civil bill court may, at the election of the person taking such proceedings, be instituted before the Land Commission. . . .

40. Any matter capable of being determined by the court under this act, may, if the parties so agree, be decided by arbitration, . . . and where the amount of rent is decided by arbitration, such rent shall for the purposes of this act be deemed to be the judicial rent.

41. A Land Commission shall be constituted under this act consisting of a judicial commissioner and two other commissioners. . . .

43. The lord lieutenant may from time to time, with the consent of the treasury as to number, appoint and by order in council remove assistant commissioners. . . .

44. Any power or act by this act vested in or authorised to be done by the Land Commission, except the power of hearing appeals, may be exercised or done by any one member of the Land Commission or by any sub-commission. . . .

44 & 45 Vict., c. 4; THE PUBLIC GENERAL ACTS . . . (1881), pp. 139–164.

~

ON HOME RULE AND THE LAND QUESTION AT CORK

21 January 1885

Charles Stewart Parnell

With the goal of bringing the issue of Irish Home Rule to the center of the stage at Westminster, Charles Stewart Parnell spent the years from 1882 to 1885 building up the Irish Parliamentary Party into a modern political machine. He astutely left the definition of Home Rule ambiguous, as seen in the speech below that he gave at Cork in January 1885. With a bow toward the fears of opponents on the right, he indicated that "Grattan's parliament" (itself a problematic phrase) was the most that nationalists could demand consistent with a continuing place in the British empire, but in a line that became famous, he also declared that "no man has the right to fix the boundary to the march of a nation."

SEE ALSO Home Rule Movement and the Irish Parliamentary Party: 1870 to 1891; Parnell, Charles Stewart; Politics: 1800 to 1921—Challenges to the Union

. . . At the election in 1880 I laid certain principles before you, and you accepted them (applause, and cries of "we do"). I said and I pledged myself that I should form . . . an independent Irish party to act in opposition to every English government which refused to concede the just rights of Ireland (applause). And the longer time which is gone by since then, the more I am convinced that that is the true policy to pursue so far as parliamentary policy is concerned, and that it will be impossible for either or both of the English parties to contend for any long time against a determined band of Irishmen acting honestly upon these principles and backed by the Irish people (cheers). But we have not alone had that object in view—we have always been very careful not to fetter or control the people at home in any way, not to prevent them from doing anything by their own strength which it is possible for them to do. . . . You have been encouraged to organise yourselves, to depend upon the rectitude of your cause for your justification, and to depend upon the determination which has helped Irishmen through many centuries to retain the name of Ireland and to retain her nationhood. Nobody could point to any single action of ours in the House of Commons or out of it which was not based upon the knowledge that behind us existed a strong and brave people, that without the help of the people our exertions would be as nothing, and that with their help and with their confidence we should be, as I believe we shall prove to be in the near future, invincible and unconquerable (great applause). . . . We shall struggle, as we have been struggling, for the great and important interests of the Irish tenant farmer. We shall ask that his industry shall not be fettered by rent. We shall ask also from the farmer in return that he shall do what in him lies to encourage the struggling manufacturers of Ireland, and that he shall not think it too great a sacrifice to be called upon when he wants anything, when he has to purchase anything, to consider how we may get it of Irish material and manufacture (hear, hear), even supposing he has to pay a little more for it (cheers). I am sorry if the agricultural population has shown itself somewhat deficient in its sense of duty in this respect up to the present time, but I feel convinced that the matter has only to be put before them to secure the opening up of most important markets in this country for those manufactures which have always existed, and for those which have been reopened anew as a consequence of the recent exhibitions, the great exhibition in Dublin and the other equally great one in Cork, which have been recently held (cheers). We shall also endeavour to secure for the labourer some recognition and some right in the land of his country (applause). We don't care whether it be the prejudices of the farmer or of the landlord that stands in his way (hear, hear). We consider that whatever class tries to obstruct the labourer in the possession of those fair and just rights to which he is entitled, that class should be put down, and coerced if you will, into doing justice to the labourer. . . . Well, but gentlemen, I go back from the consideration of these questions to the land question, in which the labourers' question is also involved and the manufacturers' question. I come back, and every Irish politician must be forcibly driven back, to the consideration of the great question of national self-government for Ireland (cheers). I do not know how this great question will be eventually settled. I do not know whether England will be wise in time and concede to constitutional arguments and methods the restitution of that which was stolen from us towards the close of the last century (cheers). It is given to none of us to forecast the future, and just as it is impossible for us to say in what way or by what means the national question may be settled, in what way full justice may be done to Ireland, so it is impossible for us to say to what extent that justice should be done. We cannot ask for less than restitution of Grattan's parliament (loud cheers), with its important privileges and wide and far-reaching constitution. We cannot under the British constitution ask for more than the restitution of Grattan's parliament (renewed cheers), but no man has the right to fix the boundary to the march of a nation (great cheers). No man has a right to say to his country, "Thus far shalt thou go and no further," and we have never attempted to fix the *ne plus ultra* to the progress of Ireland's nationhood, and we never shall (cheers). But, gentlemen, while we leave those things to time, circumstances, and the future, we must each one of us resolve in our own hearts that we shall at all times do everything that within us lies to obtain for Ireland the fullest measure of her rights (applause). In this way we shall avoid difficulties and contentions amongst each other. In this way we shall not give up anything which the future may put in favour of our country; and while we struggle today for that which may seem possible for us with our combination, we must struggle for it with the proud consciousness that we shall not do anything to hinder or prevent better men who may come after us from gaining better things than those for which we now contend (prolonged applause).

FREEMAN'S JOURNAL, 22 *January* 1885.

～

ON HOME RULE AT WICKLOW

5 October 1885

Charles Stewart Parnell

As a critical general election approached in the autumn of 1885, Parnell gave a speech at Wicklow openly acknowledging that a Home Rule parliament in Ireland would move to protect certain nascent Irish industries—a stance likely to scare Liberal adherents of free trade. But he also tried to turn on its head the argument of opponents that Home Rule would lead to Irish separation and complete independence. To hear him tell it, it was the current forcible yoking together of the two countries in the same British parliament that led to the extreme Irish disaffection that threatened imperial unity.

SEE ALSO Home Rule Movement and the Irish Parliamentary Party: 1870 to 1891; Parnell, Charles Stewart; Politics: 1800 to 1921—Challenges to the Union

When I last spoke in public in Ireland, I expressed my conviction that in the new parliament we should be able to form our platform of a single plank, and that plank [is] the plank of legislative independence (cheers), and that we should carry that plank to a successful issue in the same way as during the last parliament we have carried other subordinate planks, such as the extension of the franchise and so forth (cheers). My declaration has been received by the English press and by some, although not by all, the English leaders with a storm of disapproval, and they have told us that the yielding of an independent parliament to Ireland is a matter of impossibility. But nothing that has been said in this interval has in the slightest degree diminished my confidence in the near success of our efforts (loud cheers). On the contrary, very much that has been said by our enemies in reference to this claim of ours has very much increased my confidence (cheers). They practically admit that things cannot be allowed to go on as they are; that it is impossible to keep an unwilling people and unwilling representatives in forced legislative connexion with the other two kingdoms (hear, hear). They admit that there must be some change; but the two conditions that they put forward in regard to this change, and as a condition of this change, are—firstly, that the separation of Ireland from England shall not be a consequence of the grant of legislative independence to Ireland; and in the second place they claim that we shall not be allowed to protect our manufacturers at the cost of those in England. . . . To take the last point first and to deal with the question of the protection of Irish manufacturers, I have claimed for Ireland a parliament that shall have power to protect these Irish manufacturers (cheers) if it be the will of the parliament and of the Irish people that they should be protected (cheers). But it is not for me to say beforehand what the action of such a freely elected Irish assembly would be. I may have my own opinion as to the best course for that assembly to take, but I have claimed that no parliamentary assembly will work satisfactorily which has not free power over Irish affairs (applause); which has not free power to raise a revenue for the purpose of government in Ireland as shall seem fit and best to that assembly (applause). I am of the opinion . . . that it would be wise to protect certain Irish industries at all events for a time (hear, hear); that it is impossible for us to make up for the loss of the start in the manufacturing race which we have experienced owing to adverse legislation in times past against Irish industries by England, unless we do protect these industries, not many in number, which are capable of thriving in Ireland (applause). I am not of the opinion that it would be necessary for us to protect these industries very long; possibly protection continued for two or three years would give us that start which we have lost owing to the nefarious legislative action of England in times past (hear, hear). . . . I believe there are several industries which would thrive, and could be made to thrive, in Ireland. But I think that as regards many other branches of manufacture, of which we have now to seek our supply from the English markets, we should still have to go to their markets for supply on account of natural reasons which I have not time to enter into at the present moment. But I claim this for Ireland, that if the Irish parliament of the future considers that there are certain industries in Ireland which could be benefited by protection, which could be nursed by protection, and which could be placed in such a position as to enable them to complete with similar industries in other countries by a course of protection extending over a few years, the parliament ought to have power to carry out that policy (cheers). . . . I will proceed a little further, and I will deal with the claim that has been put forward, that some guarantee should be given that the granting of legislative powers to Ireland should not lead to the separation of Ireland from England. This claim is one which at first sight may seem a fair one. It may appear preposterous, and it undoubtedly would be preposterous, to ask England to concede to us an engine which we announced our intention of using to bring about either separation of the two countries, or which we accepted silently with the intention of so using it; but there is a great difference between having such an intention or announcing such an intention and giving counter guarantees against such an intention. It is not possible for human intelligence to forecast the future in these matters; but we can point to this—we can point to the fact that under 85 years of parliamentary connexion with England, Ireland has become intensely disloyal and intensely disaffected (applause); that notwithstanding the Whig policy of so-called conciliation, alternative conciliation and coercion, and ameliorative measures, that disaffection has broadened, deepened, and intensified from day to day (cheers). Am I not, then, entitled to assume that one of the roots of this disaffection and feeling of disloyalty is the assumption by England of the management of our affairs (cheers). It is admitted that the present system can't go on, and what are you going to put in its place? (Cries of "Home Rule.") My advice to English statesmen considering this question would be this—trust the Irish people altogether or trust them not at all (cheers). Give with a full and open hand—give our people the power to legislate upon all their domestic concerns, and you may depend upon one thing, that the desire for separation, that means of winning separation at least, will not be increased or intensified (cheers). Whatever chance the English rulers may have of drawing to themselves the affection of the Irish people lies in destroying the abominable system of legislative union between the two countries by conceding fully and freely to Ireland the right to manage her own affairs. It is impossible for us to give guarantees, but we can point to the past; we can show that the record of En-

glish rule is a constant series of steps of bad to worse (cheers), that the condition of English power is more insecure and more unstable at the present moment than it has ever been (applause). We can point to the example of other countries—of Austria and of Hungary—to the fact that Hungary, having been conceded self-government, became one of the strongest factors in the Austrian empire. We can show the powers that have been freely conceded to the colonies—to the greater colonies—including this very power to protect their own industries against and at the expense of those of England. We can show that disaffection has disappeared in all the greater English colonies, that while the Irishman who goes to the United States of America carries with him a burning hatred of English rule (cheers); that while that burning hatred constantly lives in his heart, never leaves him, and is bequeathed to his children, the Irishman coming from the same village, and from the same parish, and from the same townland, equally maltreated, cast out on the road by the relentless landlord, who goes to one of the colonies of Canada or one of the colonies of Australia and finds there another and a different system of English rule to that which he has been accustomed to at home, becomes to a great extent a loyal citizen and a strength and a prop to the community amongst whom his lot has been cast; that he forgets the little memories of his experience of England at home, and that he no longer continues to look upon the name of England as a symbol of oppression and the badge of the misfortunes of his country (cheers). I say that it is possible and that it is the duty of English statesmen at the present day to inquire and examine into these facts for themselves with their eyes open; and to cease the impossible task, which they admit to be impossible, of going forward in the continued misgovernment of Ireland and persisting in the government of our people by a people outside herself who know not her real wants (cheers); and if these lessons be learned, I am convinced that the English statesman who is great enough and who is powerful enough to carry out these teachings, to enforce them on the acceptance of his countrymen, to give to Ireland full legislative liberty, full power to manage her own domestic concerns, will be regarded in the future by his countrymen as one who has removed the greatest peril to the English empire (hear, hear)—a peril, I firmly believe, which if not removed, will find some day . . . an opportunity of revenging itself—(loud cheers)—to the destruction of the British empire—for the misfortunes, the oppressions, and the misgovernment of our country (loud cheers).

FREEMAN'S JOURNAL, 6 October 1885.

On the Home Rule Bill of 1886

8 April 1886

William Gladstone

The outcome of the general election of 1885, in which Irish nationalist MPs won eighty-six seats, helped to convince the Liberal prime minister William Gladstone to identify his party with Irish self-government. His speech introducing the Home Rule bill in April 1886 was designed to persuade other politicians that Ireland deserved to be governed in accordance with "Irish ideas," and that any other course would require the persistent use of coercion, which good Liberals found abhorrent. When ninety-three Liberals defected on the second reading of the bill in June, Home Rule was defeated by thirty votes.

SEE ALSO Home Rule Movement and the Irish Parliamentary Party: 1870 to 1891; Politics: 1800 to 1921—Challenges to the Union; Unionism from 1885 to 1922

I could have wished, Mr Speaker, on several grounds, that it had been possible for me on this single occasion to open to the House the whole of the policy intentions of government with respect to Ireland. The two questions of land and of Irish government are in our view closely and inseparably connected, for they are the two channels through which we hope to find access, and effectual access, to that question which is the most vital of all—namely, the question of social order in Ireland. . . .

Since the last half-century dawned, we have steadily engaged in extending as well as in consolidating free institutions. I divide the period since the Act of Union with Ireland into two—the first from 1800 to 1832, the epoch of what is still justly called the Great Reform Act; and secondly, from 1833 to 1885. I do not know whether it has been as widely observed as I think it deserves to be that in the first of those periods—32 years—there were no less than 11 years—it may seem not much to say, but wait for what is coming—there were no less that 11 of those 32 years in which our statute book was free throughout the whole year from repressive legislation of an exceptional kind against Ireland. But in the 53 years since we advanced far in the career of liberal principles and actions—in those 53 years from 1833 to 1885—there were but two years which were entirely free from the action of this special legislation for

Ireland. Is not that of itself almost enough to prove we have arrived at the point where it is necessary that we should take a careful and searching survey of our position? . . .

Well, sir, what are the results that have been produced? This result above all—and now I come to what I consider to be the basis of the whole mischief—that rightly or wrongly, yet in point of fact, law is discredited in Ireland, and discredited in Ireland upon this ground especially—that it comes to the people of that country with a foreign aspect and in a foreign garb. These coercion bills of ours, of course—for it has become a matter of course—I am speaking of the facts and not of the merits—these coercion bills are stiffly resisted by the members who represent Ireland in parliament. The English mind, by cases of this kind and by the tone of the press towards them, is estranged from the Irish people, and the Irish mind is estranged from the people of England and Scotland. I will not speak of other circumstances attending the present state of Ireland, but I do think that I am not assuming too much when I say that I have shown enough in this comparatively brief review—and I wish it could have been briefer still—to prove that if coercion is to be the basis for legislation, we must no longer be seeking, as we are always laudably seeking, to whittle it down almost to nothing at the very first moment we begin, but we must, like men, adopt it, hold it, sternly enforce it, till its end has been completely attained—with what results to peace, goodwill, and freedom I do not now stop to inquire. Our ineffectual and spurious coercion is morally worn out. . . .

Now, I enter upon another proposition to which I hardly expect broad exception can be taken. I will not assume, I will not beg, the question, whether the people of England and Scotland will ever administer that sort of effectual coercion which I have placed in contrast with our timid and hesitating repressive measures; but this I will say, that the people of England and Scotland will never resort to that alternative until they have tried every other. Have they tried every other? Well, some we have tried, to which I will refer. I have been concerned with some of them myself. But we have not yet tried every alternative because there is one—not unknown to human experience—on the contrary, widely known to various countries in the world, where this dark and difficult problem has been solved by the comparatively natural and simple, though not always easy, expedient of stripping of law of its foreign garb and investing it with a domestic character. I am not saying that this will succeed; I by no means beg the question at this moment; but this I will say, that Ireland, as far as I know, and speaking of the great majority of the people of Ireland, believes it will succeed and that experience elsewhere supports that conclusion. The case of Ireland, though she is represented here not less fully than England or Scotland, is not the same as that of England or Scotland. England, by her own strength and by her vast majority in this House, makes her own laws just as independently as if she were not combined with two other countries. Scotland—a small country, smaller than Ireland, but a country endowed with a spirit so masculine that never in the long course of history, excepting for two brief periods, each of a few years, was the superior strength of England such as to enable her to put down the national freedom beyond the border—Scotland, wisely recognised by England, has been allowed and encouraged in this House to make her own laws as freely and as effectually as if she had a representation six times as strong. The consequence is that the mainspring of law in England is felt by the people to be English; the mainspring of law in Scotland is felt by the people to be Scotch; but the mainspring of law in Ireland is not felt by the people to be Irish, and I am bound to say—truth extorts from me the avowal—that it cannot be felt to be Irish in the same sense as it is English and Scotch. The net results of this statement which I have laid before the House, because it was necessary as the groundwork of my argument, are these—in the first place, I admit it to be little less than a mockery to hold that the state of law and of facts conjointly, which I have endeavoured to describe, conduces to the real unity of this great, noble, and world-wide empire. In the second place, something must be done, something is imperatively demanded from us to restore to Ireland the first conditions of civil life—the free course of law, the liberty of every individual in the exercise of every legal right, the confidence of the people in the law, apart from which no country can be called in the full sense of the word a civilised country, nor can there be given to that country the blessings which it is the object of civilised society to attain. Well, this is my introduction to the task I have to perform, and now I ask attention to the problem we have before us.

It is a problem not unknown in the history of the world; it is really this—there can be no secret about it as far as we are concerned—how to reconcile imperial unity with diversity of legislation. Mr Grattan not only held these purposes to be reconcilable, but he did not scruple to go the length of saying this—"I demand the continued severance of the parliaments with a view to the continued and everlasting unity of the empire." Was that a flight of rhetoric, an audacious paradox? No; it was the statement of a problem which other countries have solved, and under circumstances much more difficult than ours. We ourselves may be said to have solved it, for I do not think that anyone will question the fact

that, out of the six last centuries, for five centuries at least Ireland has had a parliament separate from ours. That is a fact undeniable. Did that separation of parliament destroy the unity of the British empire? Did it destroy it in the 18th century? Do not suppose that I mean that harmony always prevailed between Ireland and England. We know very well there were causes quite sufficient to account for a recurrence of discord. But I take the 18th century alone. Can I be told that there was no unity of empire in the 18th century? Why, sir, it was the century which saw our navy come to its supremacy. It was the century which witnessed the foundation of that great, gigantic manufacturing industry which now overshadows the whole world. It was in a preeminent sense the century of empire, and it was in a sense, but too conspicuous, the century of wars. Those wars were carried on, that empire was maintained and enormously enlarged, that trade was established, that navy was brought to supremacy, when England and Ireland had separate parliaments. Am I to be told that there was no unity of empire in that state of things? Well, sir, what has happened elsewhere? Have any other countries had to look this problem in the face? The last half-century—the last 60 to 70 years since the great war—has been particularly rich in its experience of this subject and in the lessons which it has afforded to us. There are many cases to which I might refer to show how practicable it is, or how practicable it has been found by others whom we are not accustomed to look upon as our political superiors—how practicable it has been found by others to bring into existence what is termed local autonomy, and yet not to sacrifice, but to confirm imperial unity. . . .

What is the essence of the union? That is the question. It is impossible to determine what is and what is not the repeal of the union, until you settle what is the essence of union, Well, I define the essence of the union to be this—that before the Act of Union there were two independent, separate, co-ordinate parliaments; after the Act of Union there was but one. A supreme statutory authority of the imperial parliament over Great Britain, Scotland, and Ireland as one United Kingdom was established by the Act of Union. That supreme statutory authority it is not asked . . . in the slightest degree to impair. . . .

I will deviate from my path for a moment to say a word upon the state of opinion in that wealthy, intelligent, and energetic portion of the Irish community which, as I have said, predominates in a certain portion of Ulster. Our duty is to adhere to sound general principles and to give the utmost consideration we can to the opinions of that energetic minority. The first thing of all, I should say, it that if upon any occasion, by any individual or section, violent measures have been threatened in certain emergencies, I think the best compliment I can pay to those who have threatened us is to take no notice whatever of the threats, but to treat them as momentary ebullitions which will pass away with the fears from which they spring, and at the same time to adopt on our part every reasonable measure for disarming those fears. I cannot say it is otherwise when five-sixths of its lawfully-chosen representatives are of one mind in this matter. There is a counter voice; and I wish to know what is the claim of those by whom that counter voice is spoken, and how much is the scope and allowance we can give them. Certainly, sir, I cannot allow it to be said that a Protestant minority in Ulster or elsewhere is to rule the question at large for Ireland. I am aware of no constitutional doctrine tolerable on which such a conclusion could be adopted or justified. But I think that the Protestant minority should have its wishes considered to the utmost practicable extent in any form which they may assume.

Various schemes, short of refusing the demand of Ireland at large, have been proposed on behalf of Ulster. One scheme is that Ulster itself, or perhaps with more appearance of reason, a portion of Ulster, should be excluded from the operation of the bill we are about to introduce. Another scheme is that certain rights with regard to certain subjects—such, for example, as education and some other subjects—should be reserved and should be placed to a certain extent under the control of provincial councils. These, I think, are suggestions which reached me in different shapes; there may be others. But what I wish to say of them is this—there is no one of them which has appeared to us to be so completely justified, either upon its merits or by the weight of opinion supporting and recommending it, as to warrant our including it in the bill and proposing it to parliament upon our responsibility. What we think is that such suggestions deserve careful and unprejudiced consideration. It may be that free discussion, which I have no doubt will largely take place after a bill such as we purpose shall have been laid on the table of the House, may give to one of these proposals, or to some other proposals, a practical form, and that some such plan may be found to be recommended by a general or pedominating approval. If it should be so, it will at our hands have the most favourable consideration. . . .

In 1782 there were difficulties that we have now before us. At any time it might have been very fairly said that no one could tell how a separate legislature would work unless it had under its control what is termed a responsible government. We have no such difficulty and no such excuse now. The problem of responsible gov-

ernment has been solved for us in our colonies. It works very well there; and in perhaps a dozen cases in different quarters of the globe it works to our perfect satisfaction. It may be interesting to the House if I recount the fact that that responsible government in the colonies was, I think, first established by one of our most distinguished statesmen, Earl Russell, when he held the office of colonial secretary in the government of Lord Melbourne. But it was a complete departure from established tradition; and if I remember right, not more than two or three years before that generous and wise experiment was tried, Lord Russell had himself written a most able despatch to show that it could not be done; that with responsible government in the colonies you would have two centres of gravity and two sources of motion in the empire; while a united empire absolutely required that there should be but one, and that consequently the proposition could not be entertained. . . .

There is only one subject more which I feel it still necessary to detain the House. It is commonly said in England and Scotland—and in the main it is, I think, truly said—that we have for a great number of years been struggling to pass good laws for Ireland. We have sacrificed our time, we have neglected our own business, we have advanced our money—which I do not think at all a great favour conferred on her—and all this in the endeavour to give Ireland good laws. That is quite true in regard to the general course of legislation since 1829. But many of those laws have been passed under influences which can hardly be described otherwise than as influences of fear. Some of our laws have been passed in a spirit of grudging and of jealousy. . . .

But, sir, I do not deny the general good intentions of parliament on a variety of great and conspicuous occasions, and its desire to pass good laws for Ireland. But let me say that in order to work out the purposes of government there is something more in this world occasionally required than even the passing of good laws. It is sometimes requisite not only that good laws should be passed, but also that they should be passed by the proper persons. The passing of many good laws is not enough in cases where the strong permanent instincts of the people, their distinctive marks of character, the situation and history of the country, require not only that these laws should be good but [that] they should proceed from a congenial and native source, and besides being good laws, should be their own laws.

HANSARD'S PARLIAMENTARY DEBATES, *series 3, ccciv,*
cols. 1036–1085.

THE IRISH PARLIAMENTARY PARTY PLEDGE

30 June 1892 (instituted in 1885)

The careful selection of parliamentary candidates and the payment of salaries to needy members were two of the central pillars on which the Irish Parliamentary Party was erected by Parnell between 1882 and 1885. The third pillar was the party pledge, introduced in 1885, which required all members to maintain their independence of the other parties at Westminster and to vote as a compact bloc on all questions that arose in parliament. The adoption of the pledge brought the tight discipline that Home Rule MPs had often escaped in the past.

SEE ALSO Electoral Politics from 1800 to 1921; Home Rule Movement and the Irish Parliamentary Party: 1870 to 1891; Parnell, Charles Stewart; Politics: 1800 to 1921—Challenges to the Union

I pledge myself that in the event of my election to parliament, I will sit, act, and vote with the Irish Parliamentary Party ; and if at a meeting of the party, convened upon due notice, specially to consider the question, it be determined by resolution, supported by a majority of the Irish party, that I have not fulfilled the above pledges, I hereby undertake to resign my seat.

Davit MSS, Library of Trinity College, Dublin; reprinted in IRISH HISTORICAL DOCUMENTS, 1172–1922, edited by Edmund Curtis and R. B. McDowell (1943), pp. 281–282.

FROM "THE NECESSITY FOR DE-ANGLICISING IRELAND"

25 November 1892

Douglas Hyde

Among the most important of the renegades from the old traditions of the Protestant Ascendancy class in late nineteenth-century Ireland was Douglas Hyde (1863–1947), the founder of the Gaelic League in July 1893, a prolific scholar, and late in life the president of independent Ireland. He deplored the abandonment of the native tongue among those who could still speak the language if they wished. But it was not only the loss of the language that Hyde deeply lamented, but also the whole process by which Ireland was becoming ever more anglicized. His presidential address to the newly formed National Literary Society in Dublin in November 1892 became a classic pronouncement of the Gaelic Revival.

SEE ALSO Arts: Modern Irish and Anglo-Irish Literature and the Arts since 1800; Gaelic Revival; Gaelic Revivalism: The Gaelic League; Hyde, Douglas

. . . If we take a bird's-eye view of our island today and compare it with what it used to be, we must be struck by the extraordinary fact that the nation which was once, as every one admits, one of the most classically learned and cultured nations in Europe, is now one of the least so; how one of the most reading and literary peoples has become on of the *least* studious and most *un*-literary, and how the present art products of one of the quickest, most sensitive, and most artistic races on earth are now only distinguished for their hideousness.

I shall endeavour to show that this failure of the Irish people in recent times has been largely brought about by the race diverging during this century from the right path and ceasing to be Irish without becoming English. I shall attempt to show that with the bulk of the people this change took place quite recently, much more recently than most people imagine, and is in fact still going on. I should also like to call attention to the illogical position of men who drop their own language to speak English, of men who translate their euphonious Irish names into English monosyllables, of men who read English books and know nothing about Gaelic literature, nevertheless protesting as a matter of sentiment that they hate the country which at every hand's turn they rush to imitate.

I wish to show you that in anglicising ourselves wholesale, we have thrown away with a light heart the best claim which we have upon the world's recognition of us as a separate nationality. What did Mazzini say? What is Goldwin Smith never tired of declaiming? What do the *Spectator* and *Saturday Review* harp on? That we ought to be content as an integral part of the United Kingdom because we have lost the notes of nationality, our language and customs.

It has always been very curious to me how Irish sentiment sticks in this half-way house—how it continues to apparently hate the English and at the same time continues to imitate them; how it continues to clamour for recognition as a distinct nationality and at the same time throws away with both hands what would make it so. If Irishmen only went a little farther, they would become good Englishmen in sentiment also. But—illogical as it appears—there seems not the slightest sign or probability of their taking that step. It is the curious certainty that come what may, Irishmen will continue to resist English rule even though it should be for their good, which prevents many of our nation from becoming unionists upon the spot. It is a fact, and we must face it as a fact, that although they adopt English habits and copy England in every way, the great bulk of Irishmen and Irishwomen over the whole world are known to be filled with a dull, ever-abiding animosity against her, and—right or wrong—to grieve when she prospers and joy when she is hurt. Such movements as Young Irelandism, Fenianism, Land Leagueism, and parliamentary obstruction seem always to gain their sympathy and support. It is just because there appears no earthly chance of their becoming good members of the empire that I urge that they should not remain in the anomalous position they are in, but since they absolutely refuse to become the one thing, that they become the other; cultivate what they have rejected, and build up an Irish nation on Irish lines.

But you ask, Why should we wish to make Ireland more Celtic than it is—why should we de-anglicise it at all?

I answer because the Irish race is at present in a most anomalous position, imitating England and yet apparently hating it. How can it produce anything good in literature, art, or institutions as long as it is actuated by motives so contradictory? Besides, I believe it is our Gaelic past which, though the Irish race does not recognise it just at present, is really at the bottom of the Irish heart and prevents us becoming citizens of the empire, as, I think, can be easily proved.

To say that Ireland has not prospered under English rule is simply a truism; all the world admits it, England does not deny it. But the English retort is ready. You have not prospered, they say, because you would not settle down contentedly, like the Scotch, and form part of the empire. "Twenty years of good, resolute, grandfatherly government," said a well-known Englishman, will solve the Irish question. He possibly made the period too short, but let us suppose this. Let us suppose for a moment—which is impossible—that there were to arise a series of Cromwells in England for the space of one hundred years, able administrators of the empire, careful rulers of Ireland, developing to the utmost our national resources, whilst they unremittingly stamped out every spark of national feeling, making Ireland a land of wealth and factories, whilst they extinguished every thought and every idea that was Irish, and left us at last after a hundred years of good government, fat, wealthy, and populous, but with all our characteristics gone, with every external that at present differentiates us from the English lost or dropped; all our Irish names of places and people turned into English names; the Irish language completely extinct; the O's and the Macs dropped; our Irish intonation changed, as far as possible, by English schoolmasters into something English; our history no longer remembered or taught; the names of our rebels and martyrs blotted out; our battlefields and traditions forgotten; the fact that we were not of Saxon origin dropped out of sight and memory, and let me know put the question—How many Irishmen are there who would purchase material prosperity at such a price? It is exactly such a question as this and the answer to it that shows the difference between the English and Irish race. Nine Englishmen out of ten would jump to make the exchange, and I as firmly believe that nine Irishmen out of ten would indignantly refuse it.

And yet this awful idea of complete anglicisation, which I have here put before you in all its crudity, is and has been making silent inroads upon us for nearly a century.

Its inroads have been silent because, had the Gaelic race perceived what was being done, or had they been once warned of what was taking place in their own midst, they would, I think, never have allowed it. When the picture of complete anglicisation is drawn for them in all its nakedness, Irish sentimentality becomes suddenly a power and refuses to surrender its birthright.

What lies at the back of the sentiments of nationality with which the Irish millions seem so strongly leavened, what can prompt them to applaud such sentiments as:

"They say the British empire owes much to Irish hands,
That Irish valour fixed her flag o'er many conquered
    lands;
And ask if Erin takes no pride in these her gallant sons,
Her Wolseleys and her Lawrences, her Wolfes and Wellingtons.

Ah! these were of the empire—we yield them to her
    fame,
And ne'er in Erin's orisons are heard their alien name;
But those for whom her heart beats high and benedictions swell,
They died upon the scaffold and they pined within the
    cell."

Of course, it is a very composite feeling which prompts them; but I believe that what is largely behind it is the half unconscious feeling that the race which at one time held possession of more than half Europe, which established itself in Greece and burned infant Rome, is now—almost extirpated and absorbed elsewhere—making its last stand for independence in this island of Ireland; and do what they may, the race of today cannot wholly divest itself from the mantle of its own past. Through early Irish literature, for instance, can we best form some conception of what that race really was, which, after overthrowing and trampling on the primitive peoples of half Europe, was itself forced in turn to yield its speech, manners, and independence to the victorious eagles of Rome. We alone of the nations of Western Europe escaped the claws of those birds of prey; we alone developed ourselves naturally upon our own lines outside of and free from all Roman influence; we alone were thus able to produce an early art and literature, *our* antiquities can best throw light upon the pre-Romanised inhabitants of half Europe, and—we are our father's sons. . . .

What we must endeavour to never forget is this, that the Ireland of today is the descendant of the Ireland of the seventh century, then the school of Europe and the torch of learning. It is true that Northmen made some minor settlements in it in the ninth and tenth centuries, it is true that the Normans made extensive settlements during the succeeding centuries, but none of those broke the continuity of the social life of the island. Dane and Norman drawn to the kindly Irish breast issued forth in a generation or two fully Irishised and more Hibernian than the Hibernians themselves, and even after the Cromwellian plantation the children of numbers of the English soldiers who settled in the south and midlands were, after forty years' residence and after marrying Irish wives, turned into good Irishmen and unable to speak a word of English, while several Gaelic poets of the last century have, like Father English, the most unmistakably English names. In two points only was the continuity of the Irishism of Ireland damaged. First, in the north-east of Ulster, where the Gaelic race was expelled and the land planted with aliens, whom our dear mother Erin, assimilative as she is, has hitherto found it difficult to absorb, and in the ownership of the land, eight-ninths of which belongs to people many of whom always lived or live abroad, and not half of whom Ireland can be said to have assimilated.

During all this time the continuation of Erin's national life centred, according to our way of looking at it, not so much in the Cromwellian or Williamite landholders who sat in College Green and governed the country, as in the mass of the people whom Dean Swift

considered might be entirely neglected and looked upon as hewers of wood and drawers of water; the men who nevertheless constituted the real working populations, and who were living on in the hopes of better days; the men who have since made America, and have within the last ten years proved what an important factor they may be in wrecking or in building the British empire. These are the men of whom our merchants, artisans, and farmers mostly consist, and in whose hands is today the making or marring of an Irish nation. But, alas, *quantum mutatus ab illo!* What the battleaxe of the Dane, the sword of the Norman, the wile of the Saxon were unable to perform, we have accomplished ourselves. We have at last broken the continuity of Irish life, and just at the moment when the Celtic race is presumably about to largely recover possession of its own country, it finds itself deprived and stript of its Celtic characteristics cut off from the past, yet scarcely in touch with the present. It has lost since the beginning of this century almost all that connected it with the era of Cuchullain and of Ossian, that connected it with the Christianisers of Europe, that connected it with Brian Boru and the heroes of Clontarf, with the O'Neills and O'Donnells, with Rory O'More, with the Wild Geese, and even to some extent with the men of '98. It has lost all that they had—language, traditions, music, genius, and ideas. Just when we should be starting to build up anew the Irish race and the Gaelic nation—as within our own recollection Greece has been built up anew—we find ourselves despoiled of the bricks of nationality. The old bricks that lasted eighteen hundred years are destroyed; we must now set to, to bake new ones, if we can, on other ground and of other clay. . . .

Charles Gavan Duffy, George Sigerson, and Douglas Hyde,
THE REVIVAL OF IRISH LITERATURE (1894), *pp. 118–129.*

∾

ADDRESS AT THE FIRST ANNUAL CONVENTION OF THE NATIONAL COUNCIL OF SINN FÉIN

28 November 1905

Arthur Griffith

Almost every Irish nationalist leader of the late nineteenth and early twentieth centuries advocated protectionist tariffs as one major instrument in the development of Irish industry. In his speech before the first annual conference of the National Council of Sinn Féin in November 1905, Arthur Griffith declared himself a follower of the German economist Friedrich List, whose writings supported this viewpoint. The protectionist policies of independent Ireland after 1921, however, were of limited success and were eventually replaced beginning in the 1960s by free trade.

SEE ALSO Griffith, Arthur; Politics: 1800 to 1921— Challenges to the Union; Sinn Féin Movement and Party to 1922

. . . I am in economics largely a follower of the man who thwarted England's dream of the commercial conquest of the world, and who made the mighty confederation before which England has fallen commercially and is falling politically—Germany. His name is a famous one in the outside world, his works are the text books of economic science in other countries—in Ireland his name is unknown and his works unheard of—I refer to Frederick List, the real founder of the German Zollverein—. . . .

Brushing aside the fallacies of Adam Smith and his tribe, List points out that between the Individual and humanity stands, and must continue to stand, a great fact—the nation. The nation, with its special language and literature, with its peculiar origin and history, with its special manners and customs, laws and institutions, with the claims of all these for existence, independence, perfection, and continuance for the future, with its separate territory, a society which, united by a thousand ties of minds and interests, combines itself into one independent whole, which recognises the law of right for and within itself, and in its united character is still opposed to other societies of a similar kind in their national liberty, and consequently can, only under the existing conditions of the world, maintain self-existence and independence by its own power and resources. As the individual chiefly obtains, by means of the nation and in the nation, mental culture, power of production, security, and prosperity, so is the civilisation of the human race only conceivable and possible by means of the civilisation and development of individual nations. But as there are amongst men infinite differences in condition and circumstances, so there are in nations—some are strong, some are weak, some are highly civilised, some are half civilised, but in all exists as in the unit the impulse of self-preservation and the desire for improvement. It is the task of national politics to ensure existence and continuance to the nation to make the weak strong, the half civilised more civilised. It is the task of national economics to accomplish the economical development of the nation and fit it for admission into the universal society of the future. . . .

We in Ireland have been taught by our British lords lieutenant, our British educational boards, and our Barrington lecturers that our destiny is to be the fruitful mother of flocks and herds—that it is not necessary for us to pay attention to our manufacturing arm since our agricultural arm is all sufficient. The fallacy is apparent to the man who thinks—but is a fallacy which has passed for truth in Ireland. With List I reply: A nation cannot promote and further its civilisation, its prosperity, and its social progress equally as well by exchanging agricultural products for manufactured goods as by establishing a manufacturing power of its own. A merely agricultural nation can never develop to any extent a home or foreign commerce, with inland means of transport, and its foreign navigation, increase its population in due proportion to their well-being or make notable progress in its moral, intellectual, social, and political development; it will never acquire important political power or be placed in a position to influence less advanced nations and to form colonies of its own. A mere agricultural state is infinitely less powerful than an agricultural-manufacturing state. An agricultural nation is a man with one arm who makes use of an arm belonging to another person, but cannot, of course, be sure of having it always available. An agricultural-manufacturing nation is a man who has both arms of his own at his own disposal. . . . We must offer our producers protection where protection is necessary; and let it be clearly understood what protection is. Protection does not mean the exclusion of foreign competition; it means the enabling of the native manufacturer to meet foreign competition on an equal footing. It does not mean that we shall pay a higher profit to any Irish manufacturer, but that we shall not stand by and see him crushed by mere weight of foreign capital. If an Irish manufacturer cannot produce an article as cheaply as an English[man] or other foreigner, solely because his foreign competitor has had larger resources at his disposal, then it is the first duty of the Irish nation to accord protection to the Irish manufacturer. If, on the other hand, an Irish manufacturer can produce as cheaply, but charges an enhanced price, such a man deserves no support—he is in plain words a swindler. It is the duty of our public bodies in whose hands the expenditure of £4,000,000 annually is placed to pay where necessary an enhanced price for Irish manufactured articles, when the manufacturers show them they cannot produce them at the lesser price—this is protection. . . . With the development of [Ireland's] . . .

manufacturing arm will proceed the rise of a national middle class in Ireland and a trained national democracy and—I here again quote List against the charlatans who profess to see in a nation's language and tradition things of no economic value—"in every nation will the authority of national language and national literature, the civilising arts and the perfection of municipal institutions keep pace with the development of the manufacturing arm." How are we to accord protection to and procure the development of our manufacturing arm? First, by ourselves individually; secondly, through our county [councils], urban and district councils, and poor law guardians: thirdly, by taking over control of those inefficient bodies known as harbour commissioners; fourthly, by stimulating our manufacturers and our people to industrial enterprise; and fifthly, by inviting to aid in our development, on commercial lines, Irish-American capital. In the first case every individual knows his duty, whether he practises it or not—it is, unless where fraud is attempted, to pay if necessary an enhanced price for Irish goods and to use whenever possible none but Irish goods. As to our public elective bodies which annually control the expenditure of our local taxation, their duty is the same. . . .

We propose the formation of a Council of Three Hundred composed of members of the General Council of County Councils and representatives of the urban councils, rural councils, poor law boards, and harbour boards of the country to sit in Dublin and form a *de facto* Irish parliament. Associated and sitting and voting with this body, which might assemble in Dublin in the spring and in the autumn, could be the persons elected for Irish constituencies, who decline to confer on the affairs of Ireland with foreigners in a foreign city. On its assembly in Dublin this national assembly should appoint committees to especially consider and report to the general assembly on all subjects appertaining to the country. On the reports of these committees the council should deliberate and formulate workable schemes which, once formulated, it would be the duty of all county councils, rural councils, urban councils, poor law boards, and other bodies to give legal effect to so far as their powers permit, and where their legal powers fall short, to give it the moral force of law by inducing and instructing those whom they represent to honour and obey the recommendations of the Council of Three Hundred individually and collectively.

~

RESOLUTIONS ADOPTED AT THE PUBLIC MEETING FOLLOWING THE FIRST ANNUAL CONVENTION OF THE NATIONAL COUNCIL OF SINN FÉIN

28 November 1905

The journalist and politician Arthur Griffith edited the weekly newspaper Sinn Féin *beginning in 1906. He identified the term "Sinn Féin" with a set of ideas that emphasized abstention from the Westminster parliament, passive resistance to British domination, and the development of the Irish economy. The National Council of Sinn Féin, founded by Griffith in 1903, evolved into a party of sorts by 1907, but the party put forward no candidates in either of the general elections of 1910 and was generally moribund before World War I. Nevertheless, the Griffith doctrine of Irish political, economic, and cultural self-sufficiency (outlined briefly in the document below) was to have its day after the 1916 Rising.*

SEE ALSO Griffith, Arthur; Politics: 1800 to 1921—Challenges to the Union; Sinn Féin Movement and Party to 1922

1. That the people of Ireland are a free people, and that no law made without their authority or consent is or can ever be binding on their conscience. That the General Council of County Councils presents the nucleus of a national authority, and we urge upon it to extend the scope of its deliberation and action, to take within its purview every question of national interest, and to formulate lines of procedure for the nation.

2. That national self-development through the recognition of the duties and rights of citizenship on the part of the individual, and by the aid and support of all movements originating from within Ireland, instinct with national tradition and not looking outside Ireland for the accomplishment of their aims, is vital to Ireland.

DECLARATION AGAINST HOME RULE

10 October 1911

A combination of political, economic, and religious reasons motivated Irish unionists to oppose Home Rule. The tenacity and scope of their resistance increased in the aftermath of the two general elections of 1910, confirming the Liberals in government office and leading to the passage of the Parliament Act of 1911, which made Home Rule seem inevitable in the near future by abolishing the absolute veto of the House of Lords. The Protestants of Ulster dominated unionist resistance, but in general the 400,000 or so Protestants living in southern Ireland were also strenuously opposed to Home Rule, as the document below, produced during a meeting of southern Unionists in Dublin, makes clear.

SEE ALSO Politics: 1800 to 1921—Challenges to the Union; Unionism from 1885 to 1922

We, Irishmen belonging to the three southern provinces, being of all creeds and classes, representing many separate interests, and sharing a common desire for the honour and welfare of our country, hereby declare our unalterable determination to uphold the legislative union between Great Britain and Ireland.

We protest against the creation of a separate parliament for Ireland, whether independent or subordinate.

We protest against the creation of an executive dependent for its existence upon the pleasure of such a parliament.

We do so upon the following grounds: because any measure for the creation of a separate Irish parliament and a separate Irish executive would produce most dangerous social confusion, involving a disastrous conflict of interests and classes and a serious risk of civil war. Because such a measure would endanger the commercial relations between Ireland and Great Britain, and would cause in Ireland widespread financial distrust, followed by a complete paralysis of enterprise.

Because such a measure would imperil personal liberty, freedom of opinion, and the spirit of tolerance in Ireland.

Because such a measure, instead of effecting a settlement, would inevitably pave the way for further efforts towards the complete separation of Ireland from Great Britain.

Because no statutory limitations restricting the authority of an Irish legislative assembly or the power of an Irish executive could protect the freedom and the rights of minorities in this country. Because such a measure would hand over Ireland to the government of a party which, notwithstanding [its] professions, the political purpose of which is obvious, has proved itself during its long course of action unworthy of the exercise of power by its repeated defiance of the law and disregard of the elementary principles of honesty and justice.

Because the great measures enacted in recent years by the imperial parliament have resulted in such industrial, agricultural, social, and educational progress that our country has been steadily advancing in prosperity, and we view with the gravest alarm an experiment which must in large measure destroy the good work already done and hinder the progress now in operation.

Finally, regarding the question from a wider point of view than that which concerns alone the internal government of Ireland, highly prizing as we do the advantages we derive from our present imperial position, and being justly proud of the place we Irishmen have long held amongst those to whom the empire owes its prosperity and fame, having been always faithful in our allegiance to our sovereigns and upholders of the constitution, we protest against any change that will deprive us of our birthright, by which we stand on equal ground with our fellow-countrymen of Great Britain as subjects of our king and citizens of the British empire.

THE TIMES, *11 October 1911.*

"SOLEMN LEAGUE AND COVENANT" SIGNED AT THE "ULSTER DAY" CEREMONY IN BELFAST

28 September 1912

Backed by the Tory Party in Britain and deeply embittered by the passage of the Parliament Act of 1911, northern unionists staged the great "Ulster Day" ceremony on 28 September 1912 as a mass protest against the apparently imminent prospect of Home Rule. All over the province, but above all in Belfast, unionists lined up to sign the document called the "Solemn League and Covenant." Over 218,000 Ulstermen signed it on that day or shortly afterward, some doing so in their own blood. Women were not permitted to sign the document itself, but 229,000 unionist women signed a declaration of support.

SEE ALSO Politics: 1800 to 1921—Challenges to the Union; Unionism from 1885 to 1922

SEE ALSO Carson, Sir Edward; Politics: 1800 to 1921—Challenges to the Union; Unionism from 1885 to 1922

Being convinced in our consciences that Home Rule would be disastrous to the material well-being of Ulster as well as of the whole of Ireland, subversive of our civil and religious freedom, destructive of our citizenship, and perilous to the unity of the empire, we, whose names are underwritten, men of Ulster, loyal subjects of His Gracious Majesty King George V, humbly relying on the God whom our fathers in days of stress and trial confidently trusted, do hereby pledge ourselves in solemn covenant, throughout this our time of threatened calamity, to stand by one another in defending for ourselves and our children our cherished position of equal citizenship in the United Kingdom, and in using all means which may be found necessary to defeat the present conspiracy to set up a Home Rule parliament in Ireland. And in the event of such a parliament being forced upon us, we further solemnly and mutually pledge ourselves to refuse to recognise its authority. In sure confidence that God will defend the right, we hereto subscribe our names. And further, we individually declare that we have not already signed this covenant. God save the king.

Ronald McNeill, ULSTER'S STAND FOR UNION (1922), pp. 105–106.

~

ADDRESS ON THE ULSTER QUESTION IN THE HOUSE OF COMMONS

11 February 1914

Sir Edward Carson

Ulster Protestants were apparently prepared to fight to resist Irish Home Rule. The introduction of the third Home Rule bill in April 1912 helped to prompt the formation in January 1913 of the Ulster Volunteer Force, a 100,000-man Protestant army. This force succeeded in arming itself in April 1914. These events strengthened the hand of the Unionist Party leader Sir Edward Carson at Westminster, where he and his colleagues sought to extract concessions, especially the exclusion of Ulster, from Prime Minister Asquith. In this speech in February 1914, Carson suggested that violence could be avoided by excluding Ulster, though unionists would oppose the bill to the last.

. . . The speech from the throne talks of the fears of these men [the Ulster unionists]. Yes, they have, I think, genuine fears for their civil and religious liberty under the [proposed Home Rule] bill, but do not imagine that that is all that these men are fighting for. They are fighting for a great principle and a great ideal. They are fighting to stay under the government which they were invited to come under, under which they have flourished and under which they are content, and to refuse to come under a government which they loath and detest. Men do not make sacrifices or take up the attitude these men in Ulster have taken up on a question of detail or paper safeguards. I am not going to argue whether they are right or wrong in resisting. It would be useless to argue it because they have thoroughly made up their minds, but I say this: If these men are not morally justified when they are attempted to be driven out of one government with which they are satisfied and put under another which they loath, I do not see how resistance ever can be justified in history at all. There was one point made by the prime minister yesterday, and repeated by Lord Morley in another place [the House of Lords] which I should like to deal with for one moment, although it has been already referred to by my right hon[ourable] friend last night. The prime minister said, it is "as the price of peace that any suggestion we make will be put forward," . . . and he elaborated that by saying that he did not mean the mere abandonment of resistance, but that he meant that the bill, if these changes were made . . . , should as the price of the changes be accepted generally by opponents in Ireland and in the Unionist Party, so as to give, as he hoped, a good chance and send-ff to the bill. If he means that as the condition of the changes in the bill, we are to support the bill or take any responsibility whatever for it, I tell him we never can do it. Ulster looms very largely in this controversy simply because Ulster has a strong right arm, but there are unionists in the south and west who loath the bill just as much as we Ulster people loath it, whose difficulties are far greater, and who would willingly fight, as Ulster would fight, if they had the numbers. Nobody knows the difficulties of these men better than I do. Why, it was only the other day some of them ventured to put forward as a business proposition that this bill would be financial ruin to their businesses, saying no more, and immediately they were boycotted, and resolutions were passed, and they were told that they ought to understand as Protestants that they ought to be thankful and grateful for being allowed to live in peace among the people who are there. Yes, we can never support the bill which hands these people over to the tender mercies of those who have always been their bitterest enemies. We must go on whatever happens, opposing the bill to the end. That we are entitled to do; that we are bound to do. But I want to speak explicitly about the exclusion of Ulster. . . . If the exclusion of Ulster is not shut out, and if at the same time the prime minister says he cannot admit anything contrary to the fundamental principles of the bill, I think it follows that the exclusion of Ulster is not contrary to the fundamental principles of the bill. If that is so, are you really going on to these grave difficulties in the future that the gracious speech from the throne deals with, and not going to make your offer now, at once, with a view, not to our adopting the bill, but to putting an end to resistance in Ulster. Why do you hesitate? Surely, something that is not fundamental to the principles of the bill is a thing that you may readily concede, rather than face these grave difficulties which you yourselves admit to exist. I can only say this to the prime minister: If the exclusion for that purpose is proposed, it will be my duty to go to Ulster at once and take counsel with the people there; for I certainly do not mean that Ulster should be any pawn in any political game. . . .

No responsible man, whether he was a leader or follower, could possibly go to the people under any condition and say, "We are offered something," but say to them that for political purposes "you ought to prepare to fight for it rather than accept it"; and I am not going to do anything of the kind.

On the other hand, I say this, that if your suggestions—no matter what paper safeguards you put, or no matter what other methods you may attempt to surround these safeguards with for the purpose of raising what I call "your reasonable atmosphere"—if your suggestions try to compel these people to come into a Dublin parliament, I tell you I shall, regardless of personal consequences, go on with these people to the end with their policy of resistance. Believe me, whatever way you settle the Irish question, there are only two ways to deal with Ulster. It is for statesmen to say which is the best and right one. She is not a part of the community which can be bought. She will not allow herself to be sold. You must therefore either coerce her if you go on, or you must in the long run, by showing that good government can come under the Home Rule bill, try and win her over to the case of the rest of Ireland. You probably can coerce her—though I doubt it. If you do, what will be the disastrous consequences not only to Ulster but to this country and the empire? Will my fellow-countryman, the leader of the Nationalist Party, have gained anything? I will agree with him—I do not believe

he wants to triumph any more than I do. But will he have gained anything if he takes over these people and then applies for what he used to call—at all events his party used to call—the enemies of the people to come in and coerce them into obedience? No, sir, one false step taken in relation to Ulster will in my opinion render forever impossible a solution of the Irish question. I say this to my nationalist fellow-countrymen and indeed also to the government: You have never tried to win over Ulster. You have never tried to understand her position. You have never alleged, and can never allege, that this bill gives her one atom of advantage. Nay, you cannot deny that it takes away many advantages that she has as a constituent part of the United Kingdom. You cannot deny that in the past she had produced the most loyal and law-abiding part of the citizens of Ireland. After all that, for these two years, every time we came before you, your only answer to us—the majority of you, at all events—was to insult us and to make little of us. I say to the leader of the Nationalist Party, if you want Ulster, go and take her, or go on and win her. You have never wanted her affections; you have wanted her taxes.

THE PARLIAMENTARY DEBATES (OFFICIAL REPORT), HOUSE OF COMMONS, series 5, lviii, cols. 171–177.

≈

O'DONOVAN ROSSA GRAVESIDE PANEGYRIC

1 August 1915

Patrick H. Pearse

While he lived, the old Fenian Jeremiah O'Donovan Rossa (1831–1915) from Skibbereen was the very embodiment of what it meant to be an Irish revolutionary nationalist. The Irish Republican Brotherhood used his funeral in Glasnevin cemetery in Dublin to create an impressive demonstration of militancy. The keynote was the famous oration given by Patrick Pearse at his graveside. This powerful speech continued to project the spirit of Fenian revolution long after the event itself on 1 August 1915.

SEE ALSO Fenian Movement and the Irish Republican Brotherhood; Pearse, Patrick; Politics: 1800 to 1921—Challenges to the Union

It has seemed right, before we turn away from this place in which we have laid the mortal remains of [Jeremiah]

O'Donovan Rossa, that one among us should, in the name of all, speak the praise of that valiant man and endeavour to formulate the thought and the hope that are in us as we stand around his grave. And if there is anything that makes it fitting that I, rather than some other, I rather than one of the grey-haired men who were young with him and shared in his labour and in his suffering, should speak here, it is perhaps that I may be taken as speaking on behalf of a new generation that has been re-baptised in the Fenian faith, and that has accepted the responsibility of carrying out the Fenian programme. I propose to you, then, that here by the grave of this unrepentant Fenian we renew our baptismal vows; that here by the grave of this unconquered and unconquerable man, we ask of God, each one for himself, such unshakable purpose, such high and gallant courage, such unbreakable strength of soul as belonged to O'Donovan Rossa.

Deliberately here we avow ourselves, as he avowed himself in the dock, Irishmen of one allegiance only. We of the Irish Volunteers, and you others who are associated with us in today's task in brotherly union for the achievement of the freedom of Ireland. And we know only one definition of freedom: it is Tone's definition, it is Mitchel's definition, it is Rossa's definition. Let no man blaspheme the cause that the dead generations of Ireland served by giving it any other name and definition than their name and their definition.

We stand at Rossa's grave not in sadness but rather in exaltation of spirit that it has been given to us to come thus into so close a communion with that brave and splendid Gael. Splendid and holy causes are served by men who are themselves splendid and holy. O'Donovan Rossa was splendid in the proud manhood of him, splendid in the heroic grace of him, splendid in the Gaelic strength and clarity and truth of him. And all that splendour and pride and strength was compatible with a humility and a simplicity of devotion to Ireland, to all that was olden and beautiful and Gaelic in Ireland, the holiness and simplicity of patriotism of a Michael O'Clery or of an Eoghan O'Growney. The clear true eyes of this man almost alone in his day visioned Ireland as we of today would surely have her: not free merely, but Gaelic as well; not Gaelic merely, but free as well.

In a closer spiritual communion with him now than ever before or perhaps ever again, in a spiritual communion with those of his day, living and dead, who suffered with him in English prisons, in communion of spirit too with our own dear comrades who suffer in English prisons today, and speaking on their behalf as well as our own, we pledge to Ireland our love, and we pledge to English rule in Ireland our hate. This is a place of peace, sacred to the dead, where men should speak

with all charity and with all restraint; but I hold it a Christian thing, as O'Donovan Rossa held it, to hate evil, to hate untruth, to hate oppression, and hating them, to strive to overthrow them. Our foes are strong and wise and wary; but strong and wise and wary as they are, they cannot undo the miracles of God who ripens in the hearts of young men the seeds sown by the young men of a former generation. And the seeds sown by the young men of '65 and '67 are coming to their miraculous ripening today. Rulers and defenders of realms had need to be wary if they would guard against such processes. Life springs from death, and from the graves of patriot men and women spring living nations. The defenders of this realm [the British] have worked well in secret and in the open. They think that they have pacified Ireland. They think that they have purchased half of us and intimidated the other half. They think that they have foreseen everything, think that they have provided against everything; but the fools, the fools, the fools!—they have left us our Fenian dead, and while Ireland holds these graves, Ireland unfree shall never be at peace.

Collected Works of Padraic H. Pearse: Political
Writings and Speeches (1916), pp. 133–137.

〜

"What Is Our Programme?"

22 January 1916

James Connolly

After the failure of the workers' mass resistance to the famous Dublin lockout of 1913, James Connolly had the unenviable task of restoring morale to the Irish labor movement and of promoting the advanced nationalism to which he was also committed. His particular way of reconciling militant nationalism with the goals of the labor movement was made evident in the article "What Is Our Programme?" which he published in the Workers' Republic *(new series), a newspaper that he edited from May 1915.*

SEE ALSO Connolly, James; Politics: 1800 to 1921—Challenges to the Union; Struggle for Independence from 1916 to 1921

We are often asked the above question. Sometimes the question is not too politely put, but sometimes it is put in frantic bewilderment, sometimes it is put in wrathful objurgation, sometimes it is put to tearful entreaty, sometimes it is put by nationalists who affect to despise the labour movement, sometimes it is put by socialists who distrust the nationalists because of the anti-labour record of many of their friends, sometimes it is put by our enemies, sometimes by our friends, and always it is pertinent and worthy of an answer.

The labour movement is like no other movement. Its strength lies in being like no other movement. It is never so strong as when it stands alone. Other movements dread analysis and shun all attempts to define their objects. The labour movement delights in analysing, and is perpetually defining and re-defining its principles and objects.

The man or woman who has caught the spirit of the labour movement brings that spirit of analysis and definition into all his or her public acts, and expects at all times to answer the call to define their position. They cannot live on illusions, nor thrive by them; even should their heads be in the clouds, they will make no forward step until they are assured that their feet rest upon the solid earth.

In this they are essentially different from the middle or professional classes and the parties or movements controlled by such classes in Ireland. These always talk of realities but nourish themselves and their followers upon the unsubstantial meat of phrases; always prate about being intensely practical but nevertheless spend their whole lives in following visions.

When the average non-labour patriot in Ireland who boasts his practicality is brought in contact with the cold world and its problems, he shrinks from the contact; should his feet touch the solid earth, he affects to despise it as a "mere material basis" and strives to make the people believe that true patriotism needs no foundation to rest upon other than the brainstorms of its poets, orators, journalists, and leaders.

Ask such people for a programme and you are branded as a carping critic; refuse to accept their judgment as the last word in human wisdom and you become an enemy to be carefully watched; insist that in the crisis of your country's history your first allegiance is to your country and not to any leader, executive, or committee, and you are forthwith a disturber, a factionist, a wrecker.

What is our programme! We at least, in conformity with the spirit of our movement, will try and tell it.

Our programme in time of peace was to gather into Irish hands in Irish trade unions the control of all the forces of production and distribution in Ireland. We never believed that freedom would be realised without fighting for it. From our earliest declaration of policy in Dublin in 1896 the editor of this paper has held to the dictum that our ends should be secured "peacefully if possible, forcibly if necessary." Believing so, we saw what the world outside Ireland is realising today, that the destinies of the world and the fighting strength of armies are at the mercy of organised labour as soon as that labour becomes truly revolutionary. Thus we strove to make labour in Ireland organised—and revolutionary.

We saw that should it come to a test in Ireland (as we hoped and prayed it might come) between those who stood for the Irish nation and those who stood for the foreign rule, the greatest civil asset in the hand of the Irish nation for use in the struggle would be the control of Irish docks, shipping, railways, and production by unions who gave sole allegiance to Ireland.

We realised that the power of the enemy to hurl his forces upon the forces of Ireland would lie at the mercy of the men who controlled the transport system of Ireland; we saw that the hopes of Ireland a nation rested upon the due recognition of the identity of interest between that ideal and the rising hopes of labour.

In Europe today we have seen the strongest governments of the world exerting every effort, holding out all possible sort of inducement to organised labour to use its organisation on the side of those governments in time of war. We have spent the best part of our lifetime striving to create in Ireland the working class spirit that would create an Irish organisation of labour willing to do voluntarily for Ireland what those governments of Europe were beseeching their trade unions to do for their countries. And we have partly succeeded.

We have succeeded in creating an organisation that will willingly do more for Ireland than any trade union in the world has attempted to do for its national government. Had we not been attacked and betrayed by many of our fervent advanced patriots, had they not been so anxious to destroy us, so willing to applaud even the British government when it attacked us, had they stood by us and pushed our organisation all over Ireland, it would not be in our power at a word to crumple up and demoralise every offensive move of the enemy against the champions of Irish freedom.

Had we been able to carry out all our plans, as such an Irish organisation of labour alone could carry them out, we could at a word have created all the conditions necessary to the striking of a successful blow whenever the military arm of Ireland wished to move.

Have we a programme? We are the only people that had a programme—that understood the mechanical conditions of modern war, and the dependence of national power upon industrial control.

What is our programme now? At the grave risk of displeasing alike the perfervid Irish patriot and the British "competent military authority," we shall tell it.

We believe that in times of peace we should work along the lines of peace to strengthen the nation, and we believe that whatever strengthens and elevates the working class strengthens the nation.

But we also believe that in times of war we should act as in war. We despise, entirely despise and loathe, all the mouthings and mouthers about war who infest Ireland in time of peace, just as we despise and loathe all the cantings about caution and restraint to which the same people treat us in times of war.

Mark well, then, our programme. While the war lasts and Ireland still is a subject nation, we shall continue to urge her to fight for her freedom.

We shall continue, in season and out of season, to teach that the "far-flung battle line" of England is weakest at the point nearest its heart, that Ireland is in that position of tactical advantage, that a defeat of England in India, Egypt, the Balkans, or Flanders would not be so dangerous to the British empire as any conflict of armed forces in Ireland, that the time for Ireland's battle is NOW, the place for Ireland's battle is HERE.

That a strong man may deal lusty blows with his fists against a host of surrounding foes and conquer, but will succumb if a child sticks a pin in his heart.

But the moment peace is once admitted by the British government as being a subject ripe for discussion, that moment our policy will be for peace and in direct opposition to all talk or preparation for armed revolution.

We will be no party to leading out Irish patriots to meet the might of an England at peace. The moment peace is in the air, we shall strictly confine ourselves and lend all our influence to the work of turning the thought of labour in Ireland to the work of peaceful reconstruction.

That is our programme. You can now compare it with the programme of those who bid you hold your hand now and thus put it in the power of the enemy to patch up a temporary peace, turn round and smash you at his leisure, and then go to war again with the Irish question settled—in the graves of Irish patriots.

We fear that is what is going to happen. It is to our mind inconceivable that the British public should allow conscription to be applied to England and not to Ireland. Nor do the British government desire it. But that government will use the cry of the necessities of war to force conscription upon the people of England and will then make a temporary peace and turn round to force

Ireland to accept the same terms as have been forced upon England.

The English public will gladly see this done—misfortune likes company. The situation will then shape itself thus: The Irish Volunteers who are pledged to fight conscription will either need to swallow their pledge and see the young men of Ireland conscripted, or will need to resent conscription and engage the military force of England at a time when England is at peace.

This is what the diplomacy of England is working for, what the stupidity of some of our leaders who imagine they are Wolfe Tones is making possible. It is our duty, it is the duty of all who wish to save Ireland from such shame or such slaughter, to strengthen the hand of those of the leaders who are for action as against those who are playing into the hands of the enemy.

We are neither rash nor cowardly. We know our opportunity when we see it, and we know when it has gone. We know that at the end of this war England will have at least an army of one million men, or more than two soldiers for every adult male in Ireland. And these soldiers [will be] veterans of the greatest war in history.

We shall not want to fight those men. We shall devote our attention to organising their comrades who return to civil life, to organising them into trade unions and labour parties to secure them their rights in civil life.

Unless we emigrate to some country where there are men.

WORKERS' REPUBLIC, 22 January 1916.

~

PROCLAMATION OF THE IRISH REPUBLIC
24 April 1916

The Irish Republican Brotherhood (IRB) decided soon after the start of World War I that a rising should occur in Ireland to overthrow British rule before the war was over. For this enterprise the IRB sought German assistance and infiltrated the leadership of the Irish Volunteers, a military but poorly armed body whose leaders rejected the notion of fighting for Britain and wanted Home Rule or independence. The IRB Military Council eventually set Easter Sunday 1916 as the day for the rising to begin. It began a day late amid confusion over conflicting orders and without German arms. Its greatest achievement was the proclamation of an Irish republic that Patrick Pearse read in front of the General Post Office on Easter Monday.

SEE ALSO Connolly, James; Pearse, Patrick; Politics: 1800 to 1921—Challenges to the Union; Sinn Féin Movement and Party to 1922; Struggle for Independence from 1916 to 1921

POBLACHT NA H-ÉIREANN: THE PROVISIONAL GOVERNMENT OF THE IRISH REPUBLIC TO THE PEOPLE OF IRELAND

Irishmen and Irishwomen: In the name of God and of the dead generations from which she receives her old tradition of nationhood, Ireland, through us, summons her children to her flag and strikes for her freedom.

Having organised and trained her manhood through her secret revolutionary organisation, the Irish Republican Brotherhood, and through her open military organisations, the Irish Volunteers and the Irish Citizen Army, having patiently perfected her discipline, having resolutely waited for the right moment to reveal itself, she now seizes that moment, and supported by her exiled children in America and by gallant allies in Europe, but relying in the first on her own strength, she strikes in full confidence of victory.

We declare the right of the people of Ireland to the ownership of Ireland and to the unfettered control of Irish destinies to be sovereign and indefeasible. The long usurpation of that right by a foreign people and government has not extinguished the right, nor can it ever be extinguished except by the destruction of the Irish people. In every generation the Irish people have asserted their right to national freedom and sovereignty: six times during the past three hundred years they have asserted it in arms. Standing on that fundamental right and again asserting it in arms in the face of the world, we hereby proclaim the Irish Republic as a sovereign independent state, and we pledge our lives and the lives of our comrades-in-arms to the cause of its freedom, of its welfare, and of its exaltation among the nations.

The Irish Republic is entitled to and hereby claims the allegiance of every Irishman and Irishwoman. The Republic guarantees religious and civil liberty, equal rights and equal opportunities to all its citizens, and declares its resolve to pursue the happiness and prosperity of the whole nation and of all its parts, cherishing all the children of the nation equally and oblivious of the differences, carefully fostered by an alien government, which have divided a minority from the majority in the past.

Until our arms have brought the opportune moment for the establishment of a permanent national government, representative of the whole people of Ireland and elected by the suffrages of all her men and women, the Provisional Government hereby constituted will administer the civil and military affairs of the Republic in trust for the people.

We place the cause of the Irish Republic under the protection of the Most High God, whose blessing we invoke upon our arms, and we pray that no one who serves that cause will dishonour it by cowardice, inhumanity, or rapine. In this supreme hour the Irish nation must, by its valour and discipline and by the readiness of its children to sacrifice themselves for the common good, prove itself worthy of the august destiny to which it is called.

Signed on behalf of the Provisional Government: Thomas J. Clarke, Seán Mac Diarmada, Thomas MacDonagh, P. H. Pearse, Eamonn Ceannt, James Connolly, Joseph Plunkett

Reprinted in IRISH HISTORICAL DOCUMENTS, 1172–1922, edited by Edmund Curtis and R. B. McDowell (1943), pp. 317–318.

～

"EASTER 1916"

1916

William Butler Yeats

At the time of the Easter Rising, Yeats was living in England and later complained of not having been informed in advance of the plot. Maud Gonne, whose estranged husband John MacBride was one of the executed leaders, persuaded Yeats to return now that "tragic dignity had returned to Ireland." This poem was written between May and September 1916, possibly as a palinode to retract earlier statements, such as those found in the poem "September 1913," lambasting the rising Catholic middle class for their philistinism. Here Yeats presents his reflections on the revolutionaries, some of whom he had numbered among his friends, as well as his ambivalent views on nationalism and heroism.

SEE ALSO Arts: Modern Irish and Anglo-Irish Literature and the Arts since 1800; Poetry, Modern; Struggle for Independence from 1916 to 1921; Yeats, W. B.

I have met them at close of day
Coming with vivid faces
From counter or desk among grey
Eighteenth-century houses.

I have passed with a nod of the head
Or polite meaningless words,
Or have lingered awhile and said
Polite meaningless words,
And thought before I had done
Of a mocking tale or a gibe
To please a companion
Around the fire at the club,
Being certain that they and I
But lived where motley is worn:
All changed, changed utterly:
A terrible beauty is born.

That woman's days were spent
In ignorant good-will,
Her nights in argument
Until her voice grew shrill.
What voice more sweet that hers
When, young and beautiful,
She rode to harriers?
This man had kept a school
And rode our wingèd horse;
This other his helper and friend
Was coming into his force;
He might have won fame in the end,
So sensitive his nature seemed,
So daring and sweet his thought.
This other man I had dreamed
A drunken, vainglorious lout.
He had done most bitter wrong
To some who are near my heart,
Yet I number him in the song;
He, too, has resigned his part
In the casual comedy;
He, too, has been changed in his turn,
Transformed utterly:
A terrible beauty is born.

Hearts with one purpose alone
Through summer and winter seem
Enchanted to a stone
To trouble the living stream.
The horse that comes from the road,
The rider, the birds that range
From cloud to tumbling cloud,
Minute by minute they change;
A shadow of cloud on the stream
Changes minute by minute;
A horse-hoof slides on the brim,
And a horse plashes within it;
The long-legged moore-hens dive,
And hens to moor-cocks call;
Minute by minute they live:
The stone's in the midst of all.

Too long a sacrifice
Can make a stone of the heart.
O when may it suffice?

That is Heaven's part, our part
To murmur name upon name,
As a mother names her child
When sleep at last has come
On limbs that had run wild.
What is it but nightfall?
No, no, not night but death;
Was it needless death after all?
For England may keep faith
For all that is done and said.
We know their dream; enough
To know they dreamed and are dead;
And what if excess of love
Bewildered them till they died?
I write it out in a verse—
MacDonagh and MacBride
And Connolly and Pearse
Now and in time to be,
Wherever green is worn,
Are changed, changed utterly:
A terrible beauty is born.

SELECTED POEMS AND TWO PLAYS OF WILLIAM BUTLER YEATS,
edited by M. L. Rosenthal (1962), *pp.* 85–87.

༄

DECLARATION OF IRISH INDEPENDENCE

21 January 1919

Following the general election of December 1918, the victorious Sinn Féin candidates who were not in jail met in Dublin in January 1919 and established an Irish parliament which they christened Dáil Éireann. Among their very first acts was to issue a declaration of independence ratifying the Irish Republic that had been proclaimed by the leaders of the Easter Rising in April 1916.

SEE ALSO Politics: 1800 to 1921—Challenges to the Union; Sinn Féin Movement and Party to 1922; Struggle for Independence from 1916 to 1921

Whereas the Irish people is by right a free people:

And whereas for seven hundred years the Irish people has never ceased to repudiate and has repeatedly protested in arms against foreign usurpation:

And whereas English rule in this country is, and always has been, based upon force and fraud and maintained by military occupation against the declared will of the people:

And whereas the Irish Republic was proclaimed in Dublin on Easter Monday 1916 by the Irish Republican Army, acting on behalf of the Irish people:

And whereas the Irish people is resolved to secure and maintain its complete independence in order to promote the common weal, to re-establish justice, to provide for future defence, to insure peace at home and good will with all nations and to constitute a national polity based upon the people's will with equal right and equal opportunity for every citizen:

And whereas at the threshold of a new era in history the Irish electorate has, in the general election of December of 1918, seized the first occasion to declare by an overwhelming majority its firm allegiance to the Irish Republic:

Now, therefore, we, the elected representatives of the ancient Irish people in national parliament assembled, do in the name of the Irish nation ratify the establishment of the Irish Republic and pledge ourselves and our people to make this declaration effective by every means at our command:

We ordain that the elected representatives of the Irish people alone have power to make laws binding on the people of Ireland, and that the Irish parliament is the only parliament to which that people will give its allegiance:

We solemnly declare foreign government in Ireland to be an invasion of our national right which we will never tolerate, and we demand the evacuation of our country by the English garrison:

We claim for our national independence the recognition and support of every free nation in the world, and we proclaim that independence to be a condition precedent to international peace hereafter:

In the name of the Irish people we humbly commit our destiny to Almighty God, Who gave our fathers the courage and determination to persevere through long centuries of a ruthless tyranny, and strong in the justice of the cause which they have handed down to us, we ask His Divine blessing on this the last stage of the struggle we have pledged ourselves to carry through to freedom.

MINUTES OF THE PROCEEDINGS OF THE FIRST PARLIAMENT OF THE REPUBLIC OF IRELAND, 1919–1921, OFFICIAL RECORD (n.d.), pp. 15–16.

~

THE "DEMOCRATIC PROGRAMME" OF DÁIL ÉIREANN

21 January 1919

In its original radical form the "Democratic Programme" was the work of the labor leader Thomas Johnson. Even after being toned down by Seán T. O'Kelly, this idealistic document seemed to commit the independent government declared by Dáil Éireann in January 1919 to a social revolution. Though adopted in revised form by the Dáil, it was soon submerged by the more urgent necessities of revolutionary war, and after independence it was essentially forgotten by the bourgeois leaders of the new state.

SEE ALSO Politics: 1800 to 1921—Challenges to the Union; Sinn Féin Movement and Party to 1922

We declare in the words of the Irish Republican Proclamation the right of the people of Ireland to the ownership of Ireland and to the unfettered control of Irish destinies to be indefeasible, and in the language of our first president, Pádraig Mac Phiarais, we declare that the nation's sovereignty extends not only to all men and women of the nation, but to all its material possessions, the nation's soil and all its resources, all the wealth and all the wealth-producing processes within the nation, and with him we reaffirm that all right to private property must be subordinated to the public right and welfare.

We declare and we desire our country to be ruled in accordance with the principles of liberty, equality, and justice for all, which alone can secure permanence of government in the willing adhesion of the people.

We affirm the duty of every man and woman to give allegiance and service to the commonwealth, and declare it is the duty of the nation that every citizen shall have opportunity to spend his or her strength and faculties in the service of the people. In return for willing service, we, in the name of the Republic, declare the right of every citizen to an adequate share of the nation's labour.

It shall be the first duty of the government of the Republic to make provision for the physical, mental, and spiritual well-being of the children, to secure that no child shall suffer hunger or cold from lack of food, clothing, or shelter, but that all shall be provided with the means and facilities requisite for their proper education and training as citizens of a free and Gaelic Ireland.

The Irish Republic fully realises the necessity of abolishing the present odious, degrading, and foreign poor law system, substituting therefor a sympathetic native scheme for the care of the nation's aged and infirm, who shall not be regarded as a burden but rather entitled to the nation's gratitude and consideration. Likewise, it shall be the duty of the Republic to take such measures as will safeguard the health of the people and ensure the physical as well as the moral well-being of the nation.

It shall be our duty to promote the development of the nation's resources, to increase the productivity of its soil, to exploit its mineral deposits, peat bogs, and fisheries, its waterways and harbours in the interests and for the benefit of the Irish people.

It shall be the duty of the Republic to adopt all measures necessary for the creation and invigoration of our industries and to ensure their being developed on the most beneficial and progressive co-operative and industrial lines. With the adoption of an extensive Irish consular service, trade with foreign nations shall be revived on terms of mutual advantage and goodwill, and while undertaking the organisation of the nation's trade, import and export, it shall be the duty of the Republic to prevent the shipment from Ireland of food and other necessities until the wants of the Irish people are fully satisfied and the future provided for.

It shall also devolve upon the national government to seek co-operation of the governments of other countries in determining a standard of social and industrial legislation with a view to a general and lasting improvement in the conditions under which the working classes live and labour.

MINUTES OF THE PROCEEDINGS OF THE FIRST PARLIAMENT OF THE REPUBLIC OF IRELAND, 1919–1921, OFFICIAL RECORD (n.d.), pp. 22–23.

GOVERNMENT OF IRELAND ACT

23 December 1920

In the midst of the war of independence between 1919 and 1921, the British government carried into law at Westminster in London the Government of Ireland Act of 1920. Its provisions with respect to the setting up of a Home Rule parliament in southern Ireland were essentially ignored by the revolutionary nationalists, but northern unionists proceeded to implement its provisions in the Six

Counties by setting up a legislature and an executive government there. For decades afterward Protestants completely dominated these governmental institutions in Northern Ireland.

SEE ALSO Politics: 1800 to 1921—Challenges to the Union; Sinn Féin Movement and Party to 1922; Struggle for Independence from 1916 to 1921

AN ACT TO PROVIDE FOR THE BETTER GOVERNMENT OF IRELAND . . .

Be it enacted by the king's most excellent majesty, by and with the advice and consent of the lords spiritual and temporal, and commons, in this present parliament assembled, and by the authority of the same, as follows:
ESTABLISHMENT OF PARLIAMENTS FOR SOUTHERN IRELAND AND NORTHERN IRELAND AND A COUNCIL OF IRELAND.

1. (1) On and after the appointed day there shall be established for Southern Ireland a parliament to be called the parliament of Southern Ireland consisting of his majesty, the Senate of Southern Ireland, and the House of Commons of Southern Ireland, and there shall be established for Northern Ireland a parliament to be called the parliament of Northern Ireland consisting of his majesty, the Senate of Northern Ireland, and the House of Commons of Northern Ireland.

(2) For the purpose of this act, Northern Ireland shall consist of the parliamentary counties of Antrim, Armagh, Down, Fermanagh, Londonderry, and Tyrone, and the parliamentary boroughs of Belfast and Londonderry, and Southern Ireland shall consist of so much of Ireland as is not comprised within the said parliamentary counties and boroughs.

2. (1) With a view to eventual establishment of a parliament for the whole of Ireland, and to bringing about harmonious action between the parliaments and governments of Southern Ireland and Northern Ireland, and to the promotion of mutual intercourse and uniformity in relation to matters affecting the whole of Ireland, and to providing for the administration of services which the two parliaments mutually agree should be administered uniformly throughout the whole of Ireland, or which by virtue of this act are to be so administered, there shall be constituted, as soon as may be after the appointed day, a council to be called the Council of Ireland.

(2) Subject as hereinafter provided, the Council of Ireland shall consist of a person nominated by the lord lieutenant acting in accordance with instructions from his majesty, who shall be president, and forty other per-

sons, of whom seven shall be members of the Senate of Southern Ireland, thirteen shall be members of the House of Commons of Southern Ireland, seven shall be members of the Senate of Northern Ireland, and thirteen shall be members of the House of Commons of Northern Ireland.

The members of the Council of Ireland shall be elected in each case by the members of that house of the parliament of Southern Ireland or Northern Ireland of which they are members. The election of members of the Council of Ireland shall be the first business of the Senates and Houses of Commons of Southern Ireland and Northern Ireland.

A member of the council shall, on ceasing to be a member of that house of the parliament of Southern Ireland or Northern Ireland by which he was elected a member of the council, cease to be a member of the council: provided that, on the dissolution of the parliament of Southern Ireland or Northern Ireland, the persons who are members of the council elected by either house of that parliament shall continue to hold office as members of the council until the date of the first meeting of the new parliament and shall then retire unless re-elected.

The president of the council shall preside at each meeting of the council at which he is present and shall be entitled to vote in case of an equality of votes, but not otherwise.

The first meeting of the council shall be held at such time and place as may be appointed by the lord lieutenant.

The council may act notwithstanding a vacancy in their number, and the quorum of the council shall be fifteen; subject to aforesaid, the council may regulate their own procedure, including the delegation of powers to committees.

(3) The constitution of the Council of Ireland may from time to time be varied by identical acts passed by the parliament of Southern Ireland and the parliament of Northern Ireland, and the acts may provide for all or any of the members of the Council of Ireland being elected by parliamentary electors, and determine the constituencies by which the several elective members are to be returned and the number of the members to be returned by the several constituencies and the method of election.

Power to Establish a Parliament for the Whole of Ireland

3. (1) The parliaments of Southern Ireland and Northern Ireland may, by identical acts agreed to by an absolute majority of members of the House of Commons of each parliament at the third reading (hereinaf-

ter referred to as constituent acts), establish, in lieu of the Council of Ireland, a parliament for the whole of Ireland consisting of his majesty and two houses (which shall be called and known as the parliament of Ireland), and may determine the number of members thereof and the manner in which the members are to be appointed or elected, and the constituencies of which the several elective members are to be returned, and the number of members to be returned by the several constituencies, and the method of appointment or election, and the relations of the two houses to one another; and the date at which the parliament of Ireland is established is hereinafter referred to as the date of Irish union:

Provided that the bill for a constituent act shall not be introduced except upon a resolution passed at a previous meeting of the house in which the bill is to be introduced.

(2) On the date of Irish union the Council of Ireland shall cease to exist, and there shall be transferred to the parliament and government of Ireland all powers then exercisable by the Council of Ireland, and (except so far as the constituent acts otherwise provide) the matters which under this act cease to be reserved matters at the date of Irish union, and any other powers for the joint exercise of which by the parliament or governments of Southern and Northern Ireland provision has been made under this act.

(3) There should also be transferred to the parliament and government of Ireland, except so far as the constituent acts otherwise provide, all the powers and duties of the parliaments and governments of Southern Ireland and Northern Ireland, including all powers as to taxation, and unless any powers and duties are retained by the parliaments and governments of Southern Ireland and Northern Ireland under the constituent acts, those parliaments and governments shall cease to exist:

Provided that if any powers and duties are so retained, the constituent acts shall make provision with respect to the financial relations between the exchequers of Southern and Northern Ireland on the one hand and the Irish exchequer on the other.

(4) If by the constituent acts any powers and duties are so retained as aforesaid, the parliaments of Southern Ireland and Northern Ireland may subsequently by identical acts transfer any of those powers and duties to the government and parliament of Ireland, and in the event of all such powers and duties being so transferred, the parliaments and governments of Southern Ireland and Northern Ireland shall cease to exist.

Legislative Powers

4. (1) Subject to the provisions of this act, the parliament of Southern Ireland and the parliament of

Northern Ireland shall respectively have power to make laws for the peace, order, and good government of Southern Ireland and Northern Ireland, with the following limitations, namely, that they shall not have power to make laws except in respect of matters exclusively relating to the portion of Ireland within their jurisdiction or some part thereof, and (without prejudice to that general limitation) that they shall not have power to make laws in respect of the following matters in particular, namely:—

(1) The Crown or the succession to the Crown, or a regency, or the property of the Crown (including foreshore vested in the Crown), or the lord lieutenant, except as respects the exercise of his executive power in relation to Irish services as defined for the purposes of this act; or

(2) The making of peace or war, or matters arising from a state of war; or the regulation of the conduct of any portion of his majesty's subjects during the existence of hostilities between foreign states with which his majesty is at peace, in relation to those hostilities; or

(3) The navy, the army, the air force, the territorial force, or any other naval, military, or air force, or the defence of the realm, or any other naval, military, or air force matter (including any pensions and allowances payable to persons who have been members of or in respect of service in any such force or their widows or dependants, and provision for the training, education, employment, and assistance for the reinstatement in civil life of persons who have ceased to be members of any such force); or

(4) Treaties, or any relations with foreign states, or relations with other parts of his majesty's dominions, or matters involving the contravention of treaties or agreements with foreign states or any part of his majesty's dominions, or offences connected with any such treaties or relations, or procedure connected with the extradition of criminals under any treaty, or the return of fugitive offenders from or to any part of his majesty's dominions; or

(5) Dignities or titles of honour; or

(6) Treason, treason felony, alienage, naturalisation, or aliens as such, or domicile; or

(7) Trade with any place out of the part of Ireland within their jurisdiction, except so far as trade may be affected by the exercise of the powers of taxation given to the said parliaments, or by regulations made for the sole purpose of preventing contagious disease, or by steps taken by means of inquiries or agencies out of the part of Ireland within their jurisdiction for the improvement of the trade of that part or for the protection of traders of that part from fraud; the granting of bounties on the export of goods; quarantine; navigation, including merchant shipping (except as respects inland waters, the regulation of harbours, and local health regulations); or

(8) Submarine cables; or

(9) Wireless telegraphy; or

(10) Aerial navigation; or

(11) Lighthouses, buoys, or beacons (except so far at they can consistently with any general act of the parliament of the United Kingdom be constructed or maintained by a local harbour authority); or

(12) Coinage; legal tender; negotiable instruments (including bank notes), except so far as negotiable instruments may be affected by the exercise of the powers of taxation given to the said parliaments; or any change in the standard of weights and measures; or

(13) Trade marks, designs, merchandise marks, copyright, or patent rights; or

(14) Any matter which by this act is declared to be a reserved matter, so long as it remains reserved. Any law made in contravention of the limitations imposed by this section shall, so far as it contravenes those limitations, be void.

(2) The limitation on the powers of the said parliaments to the making of laws with respect to matters exclusively relating to the portion of Ireland within their respective jurisdiction shall not be construed so as to prevent the said parliaments by identical legislation making laws respecting matters affecting both Southern and Northern Ireland.

5. (1) In the exercise of their power to make laws under this act, neither the parliament of Southern Ireland nor the parliament of Northern Ireland shall make a law so either directly or indirectly to establish or endow any religion, or prohibit or restrict the free exercise thereof, or give a preference, privilege, or advantage, or impose any disability or disadvantage, on account of religious belief or religious or ecclesiastical status, or make any religious belief or religious ceremony a condition of the validity of any marriage, or affect prejudicially the right of any child to attend a school receiving public money without attending the religious instruction at the school, or alter the constitution of any religious body except where the alteration is approved on behalf of the religious body by the governing body thereof, or divert from any religious denomination the

fabric of cathedral churches, or, except for the purpose of roads, railways, lighting, water, or drainage works, or other works of public utility upon payment of compensation, any other property, or take any property without compensation. Any law made in contravention of the restrictions imposed by this subsection shall, so far as it contravenes those restrictions, be void.

(2) Any existing enactment by which any penalty, disadvantage, or disability is imposed on account of religious belief or on a member of any religious order as such shall, as from the appointed day, cease to have effect in Ireland.

6. (1) Neither the parliament of Southern Ireland nor the parliament of Northern Ireland shall have power to repeal or alter any provision of this act (except as is specially provided by this act), or of any act passed by the parliament of the United Kingdom after the appointed day and extending to the part of Ireland within their jurisdiction, although that provision deals with a matter with respect to which the parliaments have power to make laws.

(2) Where any act of the parliament of Southern Ireland or the parliament of Northern Ireland deals with any matter with respect to which that parliament has power to make laws which is dealt with by any act of the parliament of the United Kingdom passed after the appointed day and extending to the part of Ireland within its jurisdiction, the act of the parliament of Southern Ireland or the parliament of Northern Ireland shall be read subject to the act of the parliament of the United Kingdom, and so far as it is repugnant to that act, but no further, shall be void.

(3) Any order, rule, or regulation made in pursuance of, or having the force of, an act of parliament of the United Kingdom shall be deemed to be a provision of an act within the meaning of this section.

7. (1) The Council of Ireland shall have power to make orders with respect to matters affecting interests both in Southern Ireland and Northern Ireland, in any case where the matter—

(a) is of such a nature that if it had affected interests in one of those areas only, it would have been within the powers of the parliament for that area; and

(b) is a matter to affect which, it would, apart from this provision, have been necessary to apply to the parliament of the United Kingdom by petition for leave to bring in a private bill.

(2) The provisions contained in the first schedule to this act shall have effect with respect to the procedure for making such orders.

(3) Any order so made by the Council of Ireland under this section shall be presented to the lord lieutenant for his majesty's assent, in like manner as a bill passed by the Senate and House of Commons of Southern Ireland or Northern Ireland, and on such assent being given, the order shall have effect in Southern and Northern Ireland respectively, as if enacted by the parliament of Southern Ireland or Northern Ireland, as the case may be.

Executive Authority

8. (1) The executive power in Southern Ireland and in Northern Ireland shall continue vested in his majesty the king, and nothing in this act shall affect the exercise of that power. . . .

> 10 & 11 Geo. V, c. 67; reprinted in IRISH POLITICAL DOCUMENTS, 1916–1949, edited by Arthur Mitchell and Pádraig Ó Snodaigh (1989), pp. 91–96.

~

THE ANGLO-IRISH TREATY

6 December 1921

The British coalition government that negotiated the Anglo-Irish Treaty of 1921 was dominated by Conservatives, who were bound to reject recognizing Southern Ireland as a republic or allowing Ulster to be coerced into a united Ireland. Thus the treaty conceded only dominion status to Southern Ireland and left the existing Northern Ireland government intact, though it did not rule out future North-South unity (see the treaty's provisions relating to the stillborn Council of Ireland). But the treaty split the Irish political movement that had fought the war of independence together; it led to the Civil War of 1922 to 1923 and became the main touchstone of political allegiances for decades thereafter.

SEE ALSO Anglo-Irish Treaty of 1921; Collins, Michael; Griffith, Arthur; de Valera, Eamon; Struggle for Independence from 1916 to 1921

TREATY BETWEEN GREAT BRITAIN AND IRELAND: ARTICLES OF AGREEMENT

1. Ireland shall have the same constitutional status in the community of nations known as the British empire as the Dominion of Canada, the Commonwealth of

Australia, the Dominion of New Zealand, and the Union of South Africa, with a parliament having powers to make laws for the peace and good government of Ireland and an executive responsible to that parliament, and shall be styled and known as the Irish Free State.

2. Subject to the provisions hereinafter set out, the position of the Irish Free State in relation to the imperial parliament and government and otherwise shall be that of the Dominion of Canada, and the law, practice, and constitutional usage governing the relationship of the Crown or the representative of the Crown and of the imperial parliament to the Dominion of Canada shall govern their relationship to the Irish Free State.

3. The representative of the Crown in Ireland shall be appointed in like manner as the governor-general of Canada, and in accordance with the practice observed in the making of such appointments.

4. The oath to be taken by members of the parliament of the Irish Free State shall be in the following form: I   do solemnly swear true faith and allegiance to the constitution of the Irish Free State as by law established and that I will be faithful to H.M. King George V, his heirs and successors by law, in virtue of the common citizenship of Ireland with Great Britain and her adherence to and membership of the group of nations forming the British Commonwealth of Nations.

5. The Irish Free State shall assume liability for the service of the public debt of the United Kingdom as existing at the date hereof and towards the payment of war pensions as existing at that date in such proportion as may be fair and equitable, having regard to any just claims on the part of Ireland by way of set off or counter-claim, the amount of such sums being determined in default of agreement by the arbitration of one or more independent persons being citizens of the British empire.

6. Until an arrangement has been made between the British and Irish governments whereby the Irish Free State undertakes her own coastal defence, the defence by sea of Great Britain and Ireland shall be undertaken by his majesty's imperial forces, but this shall not prevent the construction or maintenance by the government of the Irish Free State of such vessels as are necessary for the protection of the revenue or the fisheries.

The foregoing provisions of this article shall be reviewed at a conference of representatives of the British and Irish governments to be held at the expiration of five years from the date hereof with a view to the undertaking by Ireland of a share in her own coastal defence.

7. The government of the Irish Free State shall afford to his majesty's imperial forces :

(a) In time of peace such harbour and other facilities as are indicated in the annex hereto, or such

other facilities as may from time to time be agreed between the British government and the government of the Irish Free State; and

(b) In time of war or of strained relations with a foreign power such harbour and other facilities as the British government may require for the purposes of such defence as aforesaid.

8. With a view to securing the observance of the principle of international limitation of armaments, if the government of the Irish Free State establishes and maintains a military defence force, the establishments thereof shall not exceed in size such proportion of the military establishments maintained in Great Britain as that which the population of Ireland bears to the population of Great Britain.

9. The ports of Great Britain and the Irish Free State shall be freely open to the ships of the other country on payment of the customary port and other dues.

10. The government of the Irish Free State agrees to pay fair compensation on terms not less favourable than those accorded by the act of 1920 to judges, officials, members of police forces, and other public servants who are discharged by it or who retire in consequence of the change of government effected in pursuance hereof.

Provided that this agreement shall not apply to members of the Auxiliary Police Force or to persons recruited in Great Britain for the Royal Irish Constabulary during the two years next preceding the date hereof. The British government will assume responsibility for such compensation or pensions as may be payable to any of these excepted persons.

11. Until the expiration of one month from the passing of the act of parliament for the ratification of this instrument, the powers of the parliament and the government of the Irish Free State shall not be exercisable as respects Northern Ireland, and the provisions of the Government of Ireland Act, 1920, shall, so far as they relate to Northern Ireland, remain of full force and effect, and no election shall be held for the return of members to serve in the parliament of the Irish Free State for constituencies in Northern Ireland unless a resolution is passed by both houses of the parliament of Northern Ireland in favour of the holding such elections before the end of the said month.

12. If before the expiration of the said month an address is presented to his majesty by both houses of the parliament of Northern Ireland to that effect, the powers of the parliament and government of the Irish Free State shall no longer extend to Northern Ireland, and the provisions of the Government of Ireland Act, 1920 (including those relating to the Council of Ireland), shall so

far as they relate to Northern Ireland, continue to be of full force and effect, and this instrument shall have effect subject to the necessary modifications.

Provided that if such an address is so presented, a commission consisting of three persons, one to be appointed by the government of the Irish Free State, one to be appointed by the government of Northern Ireland, and one, who shall be chairman, to be appointed by the British government, shall determine in accordance with the wishes of the inhabitants, so far as may compatible with economic and geographic conditions, the boundaries between Northern Ireland and the rest of Ireland, and for the purposes of the Government of Ireland Act, 1920, and of this instrument, the boundary of Northern Ireland shall be such as may be determined by such commissions.

13. For the purpose of the last foregoing article the powers of the parliament of Southern Ireland under the Government of Ireland Act, 1920, to elect members of the Council of Ireland shall, after the parliament of the Irish Free State is constituted, be exercised by that parliament.

14. After the expiration of the said month, if no such address as is mentioned in Article 12 hereof is presented, the parliament and government of Northern Ireland shall continue to exercise as respects Northern Ireland the powers conferred on them by the Government of Ireland Act, 1920, but the parliament and government of the Irish Free State shall in Northern Ireland have, in relation to matters in respect of which the parliament of Northern Ireland has not the power to make laws under the act (including matters which under the said act are within the jurisdiction of the Council of Ireland), the same powers as in the rest of Ireland, subject to such provisions as may be agreed in manner hereinafter appearing.

15. At any time after the date hereof the government of Northern Ireland and the provisional government of Southern Ireland hereinafter constituted may meet for the purpose of discussing the provisions subject to which the last foregoing article is to operate in the event of no such address as is therein mentioned being presented, and those provisions may include:

(a) Safeguards with regard to patronage in Northern Ireland.

(b) Safeguards with regard to the collection of revenue in Northern Ireland.

(c) Safeguards with regard to import and export duties affecting the trade or industry of Northern Ireland.

(d) Safeguards for minorities in Northern Ireland.

(e) The settlement of the financial relations between Northern Ireland and the Irish Free State.

(f) The establishment and powers of a local militia in Northern Ireland and the relation of the defence forces of the Irish Free State and of Northern Ireland respectively,

and if at any such meeting provisions are agreed to, the same shall have effect as if they were included amongst the provisions subject to which the powers of the parliament and government of the Irish Free State are to be exercisable in Northern Ireland under Article 14 hereof.

16. Neither the parliament of the Irish Free State nor the parliament of Northern Ireland shall make any law so as to either directly or indirectly to endow any religion or prohibit or restrict the free exercise thereof, or give any preference or impose any disability on account of religious belief or religious status, or affect prejudicially the right of any child to attend a school receiving public money without attending the religious instruction at the school, or make any discrimination as respects state aid between schools under the management of different religious denominations, or divert from any religious denomination or any educational institution any of its property except for public utility purposes and on payment of compensation.

17. By way of provisional arrangement for the administration of Southern Ireland during the interval which must elapse between the date hereof and the constitution of a parliament and government in accordance therewith, steps shall be taken forthwith for summoning a meeting of members of parliament elected for constituencies in Southern Ireland since the passing of the Government of Ireland Act, 1920, and for constituting a provisional government, and the British government shall take the steps necessary to transfer to such provisional government the powers and machinery requisite for the discharge of its duties, provided that every member of such provisional government shall have signified in writing his or her acceptance of this instrument. But this arrangement shall not continue in force beyond the expiration of twelve months from the date hereof.

18. This instrument shall be submitted forthwith by his majesty's government for the approval of parliament and by the Irish signatories to a meeting summoned for the purpose of the members elected to sit in the House of Commons of Southern Ireland, and, if approved, shall be ratified by the necessary legislation.

(Signed)
On behalf of the British delegation,
D. Lloyd George.
Austen Chamberlain.

Birkenhead.
Winston S. Churchill.
L. Worthington-Evans.
Hamar Greenwood.
Gordon Hewart.

On behalf of the Irish delegation,
Art Ó Gríobhtha (Arthur Griffith).
Mícheál O Coileáin.
Riobárd Bartún.
E. S. Ó Dugáin.
Seórsa Ghabháin Uí Dhubhthaigh.

6th December 1921.

PRIVATE SESSIONS OF THE SECOND DÁIL: MINUTES OF PROCEEDINGS, 18 AUGUST 1921 TO 14 SEPTEMBER 1921, AND REPORT OF DEBATES, 14 DECEMBER 1921 TO 6 JANUARY 1922 (*n.d.*), *pp. 312–314.*

≈

"TIME WILL TELL"

19 December 1921

Eamon de Valera

In the following speech by Eamon de Valera in Dáil Éireann against the Anglo-Irish Treaty of December 1921, de Valera was responding to a speech by Arthur Griffith in which Griffith moved that the treaty should be adopted by Dáil Éireann. De Valera argued that the treaty would not end the centuries of conflict between Britain and Ireland; he made very specific objections to the oath of allegiance. Like the majority of Dáil deputies who spoke either in favor or against the treaty, he did not mention partition.

SEE ALSO Anglo-Irish Treaty of 1921; Civil War; de Valera, Eamon; Politics: 1800 to 1921—Challenges to the Union

I think it would scarcely be in accordance with standing orders of the Dáil if I were to move directly the rejection of this Treaty. I daresay, however, it will be sufficient that I should appeal to this House not to approve of the Treaty.

We were elected by the Irish people, and did the Irish people think we were liars when we said that we meant to uphold the Republic, which was ratified by the vote of the people three years ago and was further ratified— expressly ratified—by the vote of the people at the elections last May? When the proposal for negotiation came from the British government asking that we should try by negotiation to reconcile Irish national aspirations with the association of nations forming the British empire, there was no one here as strong as I was to make sure that every human attempt should be made to find whether such reconciliation was possible. I am against this Treaty because it does not reconcile Irish national aspirations with association with the British government. I am against this Treaty, not because I am a man of war, but a man of peace. I am against this Treaty because it will not end the centuries of conflict between the two nations of Great Britain and Ireland. We went out to effect such a reconciliation, and we have brought back a thing which will not even reconcile our own people, much less reconcile Britain and Ireland.

If there was to be reconciliation, it is obvious that the party in Ireland which typifies national aspirations for centuries should be satisfied, and the test of every agreement would be the test of whether the people were satisfied or not. A war-weary people will take things which are not in accordance with their aspirations. You may have a snatch election now, and you may get a vote of the people, but I will tell you that Treaty will renew the contest, that it is going to begin the same history that the Union began, and Lloyd George is going to have the same fruit for his labours as Pitt had. When in Downing Street the proposals to which we could unanimously assent in the cabinet were practically turned down at the point of the pistol and immediate war was threatened upon our people, it was only then that this document was signed; and that document has been signed by plenipotentiaries, not perhaps individually under duress, but it has been signed, and would only affect this nation as a document signed under duress, and this nation would not respect it.

I wanted, and the cabinet wanted, to get a document we could stand by, a document that could enable Irishmen to meet Englishmen and shake hands with them as fellow-citizens of the world. That document makes British authority our masters in Ireland. It was said that they had only an oath to the British king in virtue of common citizenship, but you have an oath to the Irish constitution, and that constitution will be a constitution which will have the king of Great Britain as head of Ireland. You will swear allegiance to that constitution and to that king; and if the representatives of the Republic should ask the people of Ireland to do that which is inconsistent with the Republic, I say they are subverting the Republic. It would be a surrender which was never heard of in Ireland since the days of Henry II; and are we in this generation, which has made Irishmen famous throughout the world, to sign our names to the most ignoble document that could be signed?

When I was in prison in solitary confinement, our warders told us that we could go from our cells into the hall, which was about fifty feet by forty. We did go out from the cells to the hall, but we did not give our word to the British jailer that he had the right to detain us in prison because we got that privilege. Again, on another occasion, we were told that we could get out to a "garden party," where we could see the flowers and the hills, but we did not for the privilege of going out to garden parties sign a document handing over our souls and bodies to the jailers. Rather than sign a document which would give Britain authority in Ireland, they should be ready to go into slavery until the Almighty had blotted out their tyrants. If the British government passed a Home Rule Act or something of that kind, I would not have said to the Irish people, "Do not take it." I would have said, "Very well; this is a case of the jailer leading you from the cell to the hall," but by getting that we did not sign away our right to whatever form of government we pleased.

It was said that an uncompromising stand for a Republic was not made. The stand made by some of them [us?] was to try and reconcile a Republic with an association. [Editors' note: De Valera is here referring to his idea of the external association of Ireland with the countries making up the British Commonwealth.] There was a document presented to this House to try to get unanimity, to see whether the views which I hold could be reconciled to that party which typified the national aspirations of Ireland for centuries. The document was put there for that purpose, and I defy anybody in this House to say otherwise than that I was trying to bring forward before this assembly a document which would bring real peace between Great Britain and Ireland—a sort of document we would have tried to get and would not have agreed if we did not get. It would be a document that would give real peace to the people of Great Britain and Ireland, and not the officials [politicians?]. I know it would not be a politicians' peace. I know the politician in England who would take it would risk his political future, but it would be a peace between peoples and would be consistent with the Irish people being full masters of everything within their own shores.

Criticism of this Treaty is scarcely necessary from this point of view, that it could not be ratified because it would not be legal for this assembly to ratify it, because it would be inconsistent with our position. We were elected here to be the guardians of an independent Irish state, a state that had declared its independence; and this House could—no more than the ignominious House that voted away the colonial parliament that was

in Ireland in 1800, unless we wished to follow the example of that House and vote away the independence of our people—we could not ratify that instrument if it were brought before us for ratification. It is therefore to be brought before us not for ratification, because it would be inconsistent, and the very fact that it is inconsistent shows that it could not be reconciled with Irish aspirations, because the aspirations of the Irish people have been crystallised into the form of government they have at the present time.

As far as I was concerned, I am probably the freest man here to express my opinion. Before I was elected president at the private session, I said, "Remember, I do not take, as far as I am concerned, oaths as regards forms of government. I regard myself here to maintain the independence of Ireland and to do the best for the Irish people," and it is to do the best for the Irish people that I ask you not to approve but to reject this Treaty.

You will be forsaking the best interest of Ireland if you pretend to the world that this will lay the foundation of a lasting peace, and you know perfectly well that even if Mr Griffith and Mr Collins set up a Provisional Government in Dublin Castle, until the Irish people would have voted upon it, the government would be looked upon as a usurpation equally with Dublin Castle in the past.

We know perfectly well there is nobody here who has expressed more strongly dissent from any attacks of any kind upon the delegates that went to London than I did. There is no one who knew better than I did how difficult is the task they had to perform. I appealed to the Dáil, telling them the delegates had to do something a mighty army or a mighty navy would not be able to do. I hold that, and I hold that it was in their excessive love for Ireland they have done what they have.

I am as anxious as anyone for the material prosperity of Ireland and the Irish people, but I cannot do anything that would make the Irish people hang their heads. I would rather see the same thing over again than that Irishmen should have to hang their heads in shame for having signed and put their hands to a document handing over their authority to a foreign country. The Irish people would not want me to save them materially at the expense of their national honour. I say it is quite within the competence of the Irish people if they wished to enter into an association with other peoples, to enter into the British empire; it is within their competence if they want to choose the British monarch as their king, but does this assembly think the Irish people have changed so much within the past year or two that they now want to get into the British empire after seven centuries of fighting? Have they so changed that they now want to choose the person of the British monarch, whose forces they have been fighting against and who . . . [has] been associated with all the barbarities of the past couple of years—have they changed so much that they want to choose the king as their monarch? It is not King George as a monarch they choose: it is Lloyd George, because it is not the personal monarch they are choosing, it is British power and authority as sovereign authority in this country. The sad part of it, as I was saying, is that a grand peace could at this moment be made—and to see the difference! I say, for instance, if approved by the Irish people, and if Mr Griffith, or whoever might be in his place, thought it wise to ask King George over to open parliament, he would see black flags in the streets of Dublin. Do you think that that would make for harmony between the two peoples? What would the people of Great Britain say when they saw the king accepted by the Irish people greeted in Dublin with black flags? If a Treaty was entered into, if it was a right Treaty, he could have been brought here. Yes, he could. Why not? I say if a proper peace had been made, you could bring, for instance, the president of France, the king of Spain, or the president of America here, or the head of any other friendly nation here, in the name of the Irish state, and the Irish people would extend to them in a very different way a welcome as the head of a friendly nation coming on a friendly visit to their country, and not as a monarch who came to call Ireland his legitimate possession. In one case the Irish people would regard him as a usurper, in the other case it would be the same as a distinguished visitor to their country. Therefore, I am against the Treaty because it does not do the fundamental thing and bring us peace. The Treaty leaves us a country going through a period of internal strife just as the Act of Union did.

One of the great misfortunes in Ireland for past centuries has been the fact that our internal problems and our internal domestic questions could not be gone into because of the relationship between Ireland and Great Britain. Just as in America during the last presidential election, it was not the internal affairs of the country were uppermost; it was other matters. It was the big international question. That was the misfortune for America at the time, and it was the great misfortune for Ireland for 120 years; and if the present pact is agreed on, that will continue. I am against it because it is inconsistent with our position, because if we are to say the Irish people do not mean it, then they should have told us that they did not mean it.

Had the chairman of the delegation said he did not stand for the things they had said they stood for, he would not have been elected. The Irish people can change their minds if they wish to. The Irish people are our masters, and they can do as they like, but only the Irish people can do that, and we should give the people credit that they meant what they said just as we mean what we say.

I do not think I should continue any further on this matter. I have spoken generally, and if you wish, we can take these documents up, article by article, but they have been discussed in private session and I do not think there is any necessity for doing so.

Therefore, I am once more asking you to reject the Treaty for two main reasons: that, as every teachta [deputy] knows, it is absolutely inconsistent with our position; it gives away Irish independence; it brings us into the British empire; it acknowledges the head of the British empire, not merely as the head of an association, but as the direct monarch of Ireland, as the source of executive authority in Ireland.

The ministers of Ireland will be his majesty's ministers, the army that Commandant MacKeon spoke of will be his majesty's army. You may sneer at words, but I say words mean, and I say in a Treaty words do mean something—else why should they be put down? They have meanings and they have facts, great realities that you cannot close your eyes to. This Treaty means that the ministers of the Irish Free State will be his majesty's ministers, and the Irish forces will be his majesty's forces. Well, time will tell, and I hope it will not have a chance because you will throw this out. If you accept it, time will tell. It cannot be one way in this assembly and another way in the British House of Commons. The Treaty is an agreed document, and there ought to be pretty fairly common interpretation of it. If there are differences of interpretation, we know who will get the best of them.

I hold, and I do not mind my words being on record, that the chief executive authority in Ireland is the British monarch—the British authority. It is in virtue of that authority the Irish ministers will function. It is to the commander-in-chief of the Irish army, who will be the English monarch, they will swear allegiance, these soldiers of Ireland. It is on these grounds, as being inconsistent with our position and with the whole national tradition for 750 years, that it cannot bring peace. Do you think that because you sign documents like this you can change the current of tradition? You cannot. Some of you are relying on that "cannot" to sign this Treaty. But do not put a barrier in the way of future generations.

Parnell was asked to do something like this—to say it was a final settlement. . . . Parnell said, practically, "You have no right to ask me, because I have no right to say that any man can set boundaries to the march of a nation." As far as you can, if you take this, you are presuming to set bounds to the onward march of a nation.

SPEECHES AND STATEMENTS BY EAMON DE VALERA, 1917–73, edited by Maurice Moynihan (1980), pp. 87–91. Reproduced by permission of St. Martin's Press, LLC, and Gill & Macmillan, Dublin.

~

SPEECH IN FAVOR OF THE ANGLO–IRISH TREATY OF DECEMBER 1921

7 January 1922

Arthur Griffith

Arthur Griffith headed the delegation that negotiated the Anglo-Irish Treaty in London between October and December 1921. Though the British prime minister David Lloyd George may have outmaneuvered him at a critical stage of the negotiations, preventing Griffith from breaking off the talks on the Ulster question when he failed to secure complete independence from Britain, the Irish delegates made a bargain that a slim majority of the Dáil, and a much larger majority of the general population, considered worthy of acceptance. Griffith offered a strong defense of the treaty in the Dáil on 7 January 1922, combating the main objections from Eamon de Valera and other staunch republicans.

SEE ALSO Anglo-Irish Treaty of 1921; Griffith, Arthur; Politics: 1800 to 1921—Challenges to the Union; Politics: Independent Ireland since 1922

. . . We were sent to make some compromise, bargain, or arrangement; we made an arrangement; the arrangement we made is not satisfactory to many people. Let them criticise on that point, but do not let them say that we were sent to get one thing and that we got something else. We got a different type of arrangement from that which many wished; but when they charge us or insinuate that we went there with a mandate to demand a republic, and nothing but a republic, then they are maligning us; if we got that mandate, we would have finished up in five minutes in Downing Street. . . . We went there to London, not as republican doctrinaires, but looking for the substance of freedom and independence. If you think what we brought back is not the substance of independence, that is a legitimate ground for attack upon us, but to attack us on the ground that we went there to get a republic is to attack us on false and lying grounds; and some of those who criticise on that ground know perfectly the conditions

under which we went. "We are ready," said President de Valera, . . . "to leave the whole question between Ireland and England to external arbitration." What did that mean? Need I comment on it? Is that saying you will have a republic and nothing but a republic? . . . I have listened here for days to discussions on the oath [of allegiance to the British crown required by the Treaty]. If you are going to have a form of association with the British empire, call it what you will, you must have an oath; and such an oath was suggested and put before us and not rejected, and put before the plenipotentiaries when going back to London. The difference between these two oaths is the difference in the terms. I am not going to speak in terms of theology or terms of law about them; we have had quite a considerable discussion on that point; but what I am going to speak about is this: that in this assembly there are men who have taken oath after oath to the king of England; and I noticed that these men applauded loudly when insulting or slighting references were made to the young soldiers here on account of the oath. . . . Ah! This hypocrisy that is going to involve the lives of gallant and brave men is damnable. . . .

You say we are dishonourable men; this does not affect the fact of the Treaty which has been discussed on the basis of the failure, at least, of the plenipotentiaries, and not discussed on what was in it. It has been discussed in the way that Carlyle once described—and I have thought of this many times while listening to the criticism of the Treaty—he describes the fly that crawled along the front of the Cologne cathedral and communicated to all the other flies what a horribly rough surface it was, because the fly was unable to see the edifice. Now, as to that Treaty, an effort has been made to put us in the position of saying that this Treaty is an ideal thing; an effort has been made to put us into a false position. That Treaty is not an ideal thing; it has faults. I could draw up a treaty—any of us could draw up a treaty which would be more satisfactory to the Irish people; we could "call spirits from the vasty deep," but will they come when you call them? We have a Treaty signed by the heads of the British government; we have nothing signed against it. I could draw up a much better treaty myself, one that would suit myself; but it is not going to be passed. We are therefore face to face with a practical situation. Does this Treaty give away the interests and the honour of Ireland? I say it does not. I say it serves the interests of Ireland; it is not dishonourable to Ireland. It is not an ideal thing; it could be better. It has no more finality than that we are the final generation on the face of the earth (applause). No man is going, as we quoted here—I have used, it all my life— "No man can set bounds to the march of a nation." But we here can accept the Treaty and deal with it in good faith with the English people, and through the files of events reach, if we desire it, any further status that we desire or require after[ward]. Who is going to say what the world is to be like in ten years hence? We can make peace on the basis of that Treaty; it does not forever bind us not to ask for any more. England is going beyond where she is at present; all nations are going beyond where they are at present; and in the meantime we can move on in comfort and peace to the ultimate goal. This Treaty gives the Irish people what they have not had for centuries; it gives them a foothold in their own country; it gives them solid ground on which to stand; and Ireland has been a quaking bog for three hundred years, where there was no foothold for the Irish people. Well, reject this Treaty; throw Ireland back into what she was before this Treaty came—I am not a prophet, though I have listened to many prophets here, and I can't argue with prophets; but I know where Ireland was twenty or thirty years ago, I know where Ireland was when there was only a few dozen of us up in Dublin trying to keep the national idea alive, not trying to keep it alive, because the Irish people never deserted it, but a few of us who had faith in our people and faith in our country, stood by her—you are going to throw Ireland back to that; to dishearten the men who made the fight and to let back into Irish politics the time-servers and men who let down Ireland before, and who will, through their weakness if not through dishonesty, let down Ireland again. You can take this Treaty and make it the basis of an Irish Ireland. . . .

I have heard in this assembly statements about the people of Ireland. The people of Ireland sent us here—we have no right and no authority except what we derive from the people of Ireland—we are here because the people of Ireland elected us, and our only right to speak is to seek what they want. I am told that the people of Ireland elected us to get a republic. They elected us in 1918 to get rid of the Parliamentary Party; they elected us in 1921 as a gesture, a proper gesture of defiance to the Black and Tans; they elected us, not as doctrinaire republicans, but as men looking for freedom and independence. When we agreed to enter into negotiations with England with the object of producing a treaty, we were bound, I hold, to respect whatever the Irish people—the people of Ireland—thought of that Treaty. I have heard one deputy saying here that it does not matter what his constituents say. I tell him it does. If representative government is going to remain on the earth, then a representative must voice the opinion of his constituents; if his conscience will not let him do that, he has only one way out, and that is to resign and refuse to misrepresent them; but that men who know their constituents want this Treaty should come her and tell us that, by virtue of the vote they derive from these constituents, they are

going to vote against the Treaty—that is the negation of all democratic right; it is the negation of all freedom. . . .

IRIS DHAIL ÉIREANN, OFFICIAL REPORT: DEBATE ON THE TREATY BETWEEN GREAT BRITAIN AND IRELAND SIGNED IN LONDON ON THE 6TH [OF] DECEMBER, 1921 (n.d.), pp. 336–340.

～

PROCLAMATION ISSUED BY IRA LEADERS AT THE BEGINNING OF THE CIVIL WAR

29 June 1922

This proclamation and the following proclamation came one day after the army of the Provisional Government launched an attack on the Four Courts, which had been occupied by republican forces for several months. The attack ended months of stand-off between the pro- and antitreaty sides and sustained efforts by leaders on both sides to avert war. The republican forces were outnumbered from the beginning; the Civil War ended in May 1923 with a republican cease-fire.

SEE ALSO Irish Republican Army (IRA); Politics: 1800 to 1921—Challenges to the Union; Sinn Féin Movement and Party to 1922; Struggle for Independence from 1916 to 1921

Fellow Citizens of the Irish Republic: The fateful hour has come. At the dictation of our hereditary enemy our rightful cause is being treacherously assailed by recreant Irishmen. The crash of arms and the boom of artillery reverberate in this supreme test of the nation's destiny. Gallant soldiers of the Irish Republic stand vigorously firm in its defence and worthily uphold their noblest traditions. The sacred spirits of the Illustrious Dead are with us in this great struggle. "Death before Dishonour," being an unchanging principle of our national faith as it was of theirs, still inspires us to emulate their glorious effort. We, therefore, appeal to all citizens who have withstood unflinchingly the oppression of the enemy during the past six years, to rally to the support of the Republic and recognise that the resistance now being offered is but the continuance of the struggle that was suspended with British. We especially appeal to our former comrades of the Irish Republic to return to that allegiance and thus guard the nation's honour from the infamous stigma that her sons aided her foes in retaining a hateful domination over her. Confident of victory and of maintaining Ireland's Independence this appeal is issued by the army executive on behalf of the Irish Republican Army.

(Signed:) Comdt. Gen. Liam Mellows, Comdt. Gen. Rory O'Connor, Comdt. Gen. Jos. McKelvey, Comdt. Gen. Earnán Ó Máille, Comdt. Gen. Seumas Robinson, Comdt. Gen. Sean Moylan, Comdt. Gen. Michael Kilroy, Comdt. Gen. Frank Barrett, Comdt. Gen. Thomas Derrig, Comdt. T. Barry, Col. Comdt. F. Ó Faolain, Brig. Gen. J. O'Conor, Gen. Liam Lynch, Comdt. Gen. Liam Deasey, Col. Comdt. Peadar O'Donnell, P. Ruttledge.

28th June, 1922.

POBLACHT NA HÉIREANN WAR NEWS, *no. 2, 29 June 1922.*

But it will be constitutional liberty, and no man shall be permitted to do violence to the views of his neighbour or to the will of the majority.

Least of all will the profession of ideals and principles be permitted as an excuse of undermining the people's right to security of the person, security of property, and freedom to live their own lives in their own way, as long as they do not trespass on the rights of others.

Fellow citizens, this is what your government stands for, that is what your soldiers are fighting for. In this programme we do not hesitate to turn to you for support in any call which we may be compelled to make on you. Dishonest appeals to your emotions, founded in many cases upon deliberate falsehoods, are being circulated amongst you. Your proven steadiness and good sense will discard these appeals, and discountenence these falsehoods.

IRISH INDEPENDENT, *30 June 1922.*

PROVISIONAL GOVERNMENT PROCLAMATION AT THE BEGINNING OF THE CIVIL WAR

29 June 1922

SEE ALSO Civil War; Political Parties in Independent Ireland; Politics: Independent Ireland since 1922

For forty-eight hours the soldiers of your army have unflinchingly borne the brunt of battle against the forces of anarchy in your capital. Some of them have given their lives, and others have been wounded in the defence of your rights as citizens.

You are faced with a conspiracy, whose calculated end is to destroy the Treaty signed by your representatives, and endorsed by yourselves.

Under the Treaty, the government and control of your own country and resources have been surrendered back to you. After centuries of usurpation you are asked to reject this surrender, and to engage in a hopeless and unecssary war with Great Britain.

The people in the Four Courts say they are fighting for a Republic—in reality they are fighting to bring the British back.

Remember, we ask no man or woman to yield to any ideal or principle. Liberty will be secured to all, under constitutional guarantees.

SPEECH AT THE OPENING OF THE FREE STATE PARLIAMENT

11 September 1922

William T. Cosgrave

The Dáil or parliament of the Irish Free State held its first meeting less than three weeks after the death of Michael Collins. The decision to convene the Dáil while civil war still raged was a statement by the Provisional Government that democracy would prevail. The attendance consisted of the protreaty Sinn Féin members, members of the Labour Party, the Farmers' Party, and independents; the thirty-six antitreaty Sinn Féin members boycotted the parliament.

SEE ALSO Anglo-Irish Treaty of 1921; Cosgrave, W. T.; Politics: Independent Ireland since 1922

. . . The nation which has struggled so long against the most powerful foreign aggression will not submit to an armed minority which makes war upon its liberties, its institutions, its representation and its honour. During its long and bitter struggle Irish honour was bright and resplendent. An Irishman's word of honour was dearer than his life, and no political advantage can have any respect without honour. There must be clear thinking on this subject of peace. We demand no concessions which cannot be given without honour. We insist upon the people's rights. We are the custodians of the rights of the people and we shall not hesitate to shoulder them. We are willing to come to a peaceful understanding with those in arms, but it must be on a definite basis. We want peace with England on the terms agreed to by the country. Apart from the question of the honour of the nation we are satisfied that the nation stands to lose incomparably less from the armed internal opposition than from a reconquest. The national army is prepared to pay the price, and so are we. Last December Ireland was in a position of power and of influence of great promise for the country. Foreign nations expressed their appreciation of the settlement, and for a short period there was a boom in business. The action of the opposition destroyed that boom, lessened that power and damaged the reputation of the nation. These potentialities must be restored. Great material loss has been inflicted on the nation. It is impossible to estimate the extent of this loss, but it is easy to appreciate how much was needed to restore the country after the war with the English; war with the English in this sense meaning not the last 3 or 4 or 5 years, but the war which restricted national development, which left us a poor nation, which left us industrially and politically on the same level with the smaller nations of Europe, and the education of the country fashioned as if Ireland were a province and not a nation. Hard work lies before the parliament of the nation, and with the active and cordial cooperation of both and of the various sections making up the community it will be possible to restore the Irish nation not alone to the position in which it was at the time the treaty was signed but to the potentialities which the treaty offered and which it is possible to get out of the treaty. There is now no reason why blame should be shifted on the British or any other government blamed if we do not succeed. This parliament and this government is of the people and expects to get that support which is essential to a government and a parliament. We must realise our responsibilities not to one section or to one order of the community, and we must seek to make the administration of this country and the business of the parliament something worthy of the people. Our army and police force must be efficient; the courts must command the confidence of the people, and the parliament must resuscitate the Gaelic spirit and the Gaelic civilisation for which we have been fighting through the ages and all but lost. The nation is still full of vigour and is conscious that a mere handful of violent persons is for the moment standing athwart its upward and onward march towards the achievement of its highest hopes.

Reprinted in IRISH POLITICAL DOCUMENTS, 1916–1949, edited by Arthur Mitchell and Pádraig Ó Snodaigh (1985), pp. 144–145.

~

CONSTITUTION OF THE IRISH FREE STATE

5 December 1922

The 1922 constitution was drafted in Dublin's Shelbourne Hotel by a committee chaired by Michael Collins. The initial version was designed to win the support of opponents of the Anglo-Irish Treaty by omitting contentious clauses such as the oath of allegiance to the king, but this version was extensively altered by the British law officers to ensure that it conformed to the treaty. This constitution remained in force until 1937.

SEE ALSO Anglo-Irish Treaty of 1921; Civil War; Politics: Independent Ireland since 1922

AN ACT TO PROVIDE FOR THE CONSTITUTION OF THE IRISH FREE STATE

Whereas the house of the parliament constituted pursuant to the Irish Free State (Agreement) Act, 1922, sitting as a constituent assembly for the settlement of the constitution of the Irish Free State, has passed the measure (hereinafter referred to as "the Constituent Act") set forth in the schedule to this act, whereby the constitution appearing as the First Schedule to the Constituent Act is declared to be the constitution of the Irish Free State:

And whereas by the Constituent Act the said constitution is made subject to the following provisions, namely:—

The said constitution shall be construed with reference to the Articles of Agreement for a Treaty between Great Britain and Ireland set forth in the Second Schedule hereto annexed (hereinafter referred to as the Scheduled Treaty) which are hereby given the force of law, and if any provision of the said constitution or of any amendment thereof or of any law made thereunder is in any respect repugnant to any of the provisions of the Scheduled Treaty, it shall, to the extent only of such repugnancy, be absolutely void and inoperative and the parliament and the executive council of the Irish

Free State shall respectively pass such further legislation and do all such other things as may be necessary to implement the Scheduled Treaty.

And whereas by Article seventy-four of the said constitution provision is made for the continuance within the Irish Free State of existing taxation in respect of the current present financial year and any preceding financial year, and in respect of any period ending or occasion happening within those years, and it is expedient to make a corresponding provision with respect to taxation within the rest of the United Kingdom:

Be it therefore enacted by the king's most excellent majesty, by and with the advice and consent of the lords spiritual and temporal, and commons, in this present parliament assembled, and by the authority of the same as follows:—

1. The constitution set forth in the First Schedule to the Constitution Act shall, subject to the provisions to which the same is by the Constituent Act so made subject as aforesaid, by the constitution of the Irish Free State, and shall come into operation on the same being proclaimed by his majesty in accordance with article eighty-three of the said constitution, but his majesty may at any time after the proclamation appoint a governor-general for the Irish Free State.

2. (1) In relation to taxes and duties, so far as leviable outside the Irish Free State, the following provisions shall have effect:—

(a) The establishment of the Irish Free State shall not affect any liability to pay any tax or duty payable in respect of the current or any preceding financial year, or in respect of any period ending on or before the last day of the current financial year, or payable on any occasion happening within the current or any preceding financial year, or the amount of such liability, and all such taxes and duties as aforesaid and arrears therefore shall continue to be assessed, levied, and collected and all payments and allowances of such taxes and duties shall continue to be made in like manner in all respects as immediately before the establishment of the Irish Free State, subject to the like adjustments of the proceeds collected as were theretofore applicable, and arrears thereof shall continue to be assessed, levied, and collected and all payments and allowances of such taxes and duties shall continue to be made in like manner in all respects as immediately before the establishment of the Irish Free State, subject to the like adjustments of the proceeds collected as were theretofore applicable.

(b) Goods transported during the current financial year from or to the Irish Free State to or from any other part of the United Kingdom or the Isle of Man shall not, except in respect of the forms to be used and the information to be furnished, be treated as goods imported or exported as the case may be.

(2) If an arrangement is made with the Irish Free State for an extension of the provisions of this section as respects all or any taxes and duties to the next ensuing financial year or any part thereof, it shall be lawful for his majesty, if a resolution to that effect is passed by the Commons House of Parliament, by order in council to extend the provisions of this section so as to apply, in the case of the taxes and duties to which the arrangement relates, in respect to the next ensuing financial year or part thereof in like manner as it applies in respect of the current financial year.

(3) For the purposes of this section, the expression "financial year" means, as respects income tax (including super-tax), the year of assessment, and as respects other taxes and duties, the year ending on the thirty-first day of March.

3. If the parliament of the Irish Free State make provision to that effect, any act passed before the passing of this act which applies to or may be applied to self-governing dominions, whether alone or to such dominions and other parts of his majesty's dominions, shall apply or may be applied to the Irish Free State in like manner as it applies or may be applied to self-governing dominions.

4. Nothing in the said constitution shall be construed as prejudicing the power of parliament to make laws affecting the Irish Free State in any case where, in accordance with constitutional practice, parliament would make laws affecting other self-governing dominions.

5. This act may be cited as the Irish Free State Constitution Act, 1922 (Session 2), and shall be deemed to be the act of parliament for the ratification of the said Articles of Agreement as from the passing whereof the month mentioned in Article eleven of the said articles is to run.

SCHEDULE

Constituent Act

Dáil Éireann sitting as a Constituent Assembly in this provisional parliament, acknowledging that all lawful authority comes from God to the people and in the confidence that the national life and unity of Ireland shall thus be restored, hereby proclaims the establishment of the Irish Free State (otherwise called Saorstát Éireann) and in the exercise of undoubted right, decrees and enacts as follows:—

1. The constitution set forth in the First Schedule hereto annexed shall be the constitution of the Irish Free State (Saorstát Éireann).

2. The said constitution shall be construed with reference to the Articles of Agreement for a treaty between Great Britain and Ireland set forth in the Second Schedule hereto annexed (hereinafter referred to as "the Scheduled Treaty") which are hereby given the force of law, and if any provision of the said constitution or of any amendment thereof or of any law made thereunder is in any respect repugnant to any of the provisions of the Scheduled Treaty, it shall, to the extent only of such repugnancy, be absolutely void and inoperative and the parliament and the executive council of the Irish Free State (Saorstát Éireann) shall respectively pass such further legislation and do all such other things as may be necessary to implement the Scheduled Treaty.

3. This act may be cited for all purposes as the Constitution of the Irish Free State (Saorstát Éireann) Act, 1922.

FIRST SCHEDULE ABOVE REFERRED TO
CONSTITUTION OF THE IRISH FREE STATE
(SAORSTÁT ÉIREANN)

Article 1   The Irish Free State (otherwise hereinafter called or sometimes called Saorstát Éireann) is a co-equal member of the community of nations forming the British Commonwealth of Nations.

Article 2   All powers of government and all authority legislative, executive, and judicial in Ireland, are derived from the people of Ireland and the same shall be exercised in the Irish Free State (Saorstát Éireann) through the organisations established by or under, and in accord with, this constitution.

Article 3   Every person, without distinction of sex, domiciled in the area of the jurisdiction of the Irish Free State (Saorstát Éireann) at the time of the coming into operation of this constitution who was born in Ireland or either of whose parents was born in Ireland or who has been ordinarily resident in the area of the jurisdiction of the Irish Free State (Saorstát Éireann) for not less than seven years, is a citizen of the Irish Free State (Saorstát Éireann) and shall within the limits of the jurisdiction of the Irish Free State (Saorstát Éireann) enjoy the privileges and be subject to the obligations of such citizenship: Provided that any such person being a citizen of another State may elect not to accept the citizenship hereby conferred; and the conditions governing the future acquisition and termination of citizenship in the

Irish Free State (Saorstát Éireann) shall be determined by law.

Article 4   The national language of the Irish Free State (Saorstát Éireann) is the Irish language, but the English language shall be equally recognised as an official language. Nothing in this Article shall prevent special provisions being made by the parliament of the Irish Free State (otherwise called and herein generally referred to as the "Oireachtas") for districts or areas in which only one language is in general use.

Article 5   No title of honour in respect of any services rendered in or in relation to the Irish Free State (Saorstát Éireann) may be conferred on any citizen of the Irish Free State (Saorstát Éireann) except with the approval or upon the advice of the executive council of the state.

Article 6   The liberty of the person is inviolable, and no person shall be deprived of his liberty except in accordance with law. Upon complaint made by or on behalf of any person that he is being unlawfully detained, the high court and any and every judge thereof shall forthwith enquire into the same and may make an order requiring the person in whose custody such person shall be detained to produce the body of the person so detained before such court or judge without delay and to certify in writing as to the cause of the detention and such court or judge shall thereupon order the release of such person unless satisfied that he is being detained in accordance with the law: Provided, however, that nothing in this article contained shall be invoked to prohibit control or interfere with any act of the military forces of the Irish Free State (Saorstát Éireann) during the existence of a state of war or armed rebellion.

Article 7   The dwelling of each citizen is inviolable and shall not be forcibly entered except in accordance with law.

Article 8   Freedom of conscience and the free profession and practice of religion are, subject to public order and morality, guaranteed to every citizen, and no law may be made either directly or indirectly to endow any religion, or prohibit or restrict the free exercise thereof or give any preference, or impose any disability on account of religious belief or religious status, or affect prejudicially the right of any child to attend a school receiving public money without attending the religious instruction at the school, or make any discrimination as respects state aid between schools under the management of different religious denominations, or divert from any religious denomination or any educational institution any of its property except for the purpose of roads, railways, lighting, water or drainage works or other works of public utility, and on payment of compensation.

Article 9   The right of free expression of opinion as well as the right to assemble peaceably and without arms, and to form associations or unions is guaranteed for purposes not opposed to public morality. Laws regulating the manner in which the right of forming associations and the right of free assembly may be exercised shall contain no political, religious or class distinction.

Article 10   All citizens of the Irish Free State (Saorstát Éireann) have the right to free elementary education.

Article 11   All the lands and waters, mines and minerals, within the territory of the Irish Free State (Saorstát Éireann) hitherto vested in the state, or any department thereof, or held for the public use or benefit, and also all the natural resources of the same territory (including the air and all forms of potential energy), and also all royalties and franchises within that territory shall, from and after the date of the coming into operation of this constitution, belong to the Irish Free State (Saorstát Éireann), subject to any trusts, grants, leases or concessions then existing in respect thereof, or any valid private interest therein, and shall be controlled and administered by the Oireachtas, in accordance with such regulations and provisions as shall be from time to time approved by legislation, but the same shall not, nor shall any part thereof, be alienated, but may in the public interest be from time to time granted by way of lease or licence to be worked or enjoyed under the authority and subject to the control of the Oireachtas: Provided that no such lease or licence may be made for a term exceeding ninety-nine years, beginning from the date thereof, and no such lease or licence may be renewable by the terms thereof.

Article 12   A legislature is hereby created to be known as the Oireachtas. It shall consist of the king and two houses, the chamber of deputies (otherwise called and herein generally referred to as "Dáil Éireann") and the Senate (otherwise called and herein generally referred to as "Seanad Éireann"). The sole and exclusive power of making laws for the peace, order and good government of the Irish Free State (Saorstát Éireann) is vested in the Oireachtas.

Article 13   The Oireachtas shall sit in or near the city of Dublin or in such other place as from time to time it may determine.

Article 14   All citizens of the Irish Free State (Saorstát Éireann) without distinction of sex, who have reached the age of twenty-one years and who comply with the provisions of the prevailing electoral laws, shall have the right to vote for members of Dáil Éireann, and to take part in the referendum and initiative. All citizens of the Irish Free State (Saorstát Éireann) without distinction of sex who have reached the age of thirty years and who comply with the provisions of the prevailing electoral laws, shall have the right to vote for members of Seanad Éireann. No voter may exercise more than one vote at an election to either house and the voting shall be by secret ballot. The mode and place of exercising this right shall be determined by law.

Article 15   Every citizen who has reached the age of twenty-one years and who is not placed under disability or incapacity by the constitution or by law shall be eligible to become a member of Dáil Éireann.

Article 16   No person may be at the same time a member both of Dáil Éireann and of Seanad Éireann and if any person who is already a member of either house is elected to be a member of the other house, he shall forthwith be deemed to have vacated his first seat.

Article 17   The oath to be taken by members of the Oireachtas shall be in the following form:—

I   do solemnly swear true faith and allegiance to the constitution of the Irish Free State as by law established, and that I will be faithful to H.M. King George V., his heirs and successors by law in virtue of the common citizenship of Ireland with Great Britain and her adherence to and membership of the group of nations forming the British Commonwealth of Nations.

Such oath shall be taken and subscribed by every member of the Oireachtas before taking his seat therein before the representative of the Crown or some person authorised by him. . . .

Reprinted in Irish Political Documents, 1916–1949, *edited by Arthur Mitchell and Pádraig Ó Snodaigh (1985), pp. 150–156.*

⁓

Republican Cease-Fire Order
28 April 1923

The republican's cease-fire brought to an end a war that they had no chance of winning; the cease-fire was made possible by the death in combat of Irish Republican Army's chief of staff Liam Lynch. His successor Frank Aiken was much closer to Eamon de Valera and much more willing to agree to a cease-fire. De Valera tried to negotiate peace terms, but the government was not prepared to make any compromises, and on 24 May, Frank Aiken issued an order to "cease fire and dump arms." De Valera, Aiken, and other leaders were arrested shortly afterward.

SEE ALSO Civil War; de Valera, Eamon; Irish Republican Army (IRA); Political Parties in Independent Ireland; Politics: Independent Ireland since 1922

DÁIL ÉIREANN
GOVERNMENT OF THE REPUBLIC OF IRELAND
PROCLAMATION

The government of the Republic, anxious to contribute its shares to the movement for peace, and to found it on principles that will give governmental stability and otherwise prove of value to the nation, hereby proclaims its readiness to negotiate an immediate cessation of hostilities on the basis of the following:—

(1) That the sovereign rights of this nation are indefeasible and inalienable.

(2) That all legitimate governmental authority in Ireland, legislative, executive and judicial, is derived exclusively from the people of Ireland.

(3) That the ultimate court of appeal for deciding disputed questions of national expediency and policy is the people of Ireland—the judgment being by majority vote of the adult citizenry, and the decision to be submitted to, and resistance by violence excluded, not because the decision is necessarily right or just or permanent, but because acceptance of this rule makes for peace, order, and unity in national action, and is the democratic alternative to arbitrament by force. Adequate opportunities and facilities must, of course, be afforded for a full and proper presentation to the court of all facts and issues involved, and it must be understood that 1 and 2 are fundamental and non-judicable.

(4) That no individual or class of individuals who subscribe to these principles of national right, order, and good citizenship can be justly excluded by any political oath, test, or other device from their proper share and influence in determining national policy, or from the councils and parliament of the nation.

(5) That freedom to express political or economic opinions, or to advocate political or economic programmes, freedom to assemble in public meeting, and freedom of the press are rights of citizenship and of the community which must not be abrogated.

(6) That the military forces of the nation are the servants of the nation and, subject to the foregoing, amenable to the national assembly when freely elected by the people.

We are informed that many in the ranks of our opponents will accept these principles as we accept them. If that be so, peace can be arranged forthwith.

We hope that this advance will be met in the spirit in which we make it, and that it will be supported by all who love our country, and who desire a speedy and just ending to the present national troubles.

As evidence of our own goodwill, the army command is issuing herewith an order to all units to suspend aggressive action—the order to take effect as soon as may be, but not later than noon Monday, April 30th.

Eamon de Valera, President.
Dublin, April 27th, 1923.

Óglaigh na h-Éireann
(Irish Republican Army) . . .
General Headquarters, Dublin,
April 27th, 1923 . . .

To: O.C.'s Commands and Independent Brigades.

Suspension of Offensive

1. In order to give effect to decision of the government and army council, embodied in attached proclamation of this date, you will arrange the suspension of all offensive operations in your area as from noon, Monday, April 30th.

2. You will ensure that—whilst remaining on the defensive—all units take adequate measures to protect themselves and their munitions.

Frank Aiken, Chief of Staff.

IRISH TIMES, 28 *April* 1923.

≈

SPEECH ON IRELAND'S ADMISSION TO THE LEAGUE OF NATIONS

10 September 1923

William T. Cosgrave

Britain sought to ensure that all foreign relations between the dominions (such as the Irish Free State) and countries outside the Commonwealth would be conducted through the British Foreign Office. The decision to join the League of Nations less than a year after the establishment of the Irish Free State was an indication that the Irish government was determined to pursue an independent foreign policy.

SEE ALSO Cosgrave, W. T.; Politics: Independent Ireland since 1922

On behalf of Ireland, one of the oldest and yet one of the youngest nations, and speaking for the Irish government and the Irish delegation, I thank this assembly of the League of Nations for the unanimous courtesy and readiness with which our application to be admitted to membership of the League has been received and approved.

Ireland, in ancient times linked by bonds of culture and of friendly intercourse with every nation to which the ambit of travel could carry her far-venturing missionaries and men of learning has today formally, yet none the less practically, entered into a new bond of union with her sister nations, great and small, who are represented in this magnificent world-concourse.

With all the nations whose spokesmen form this assembly, Ireland joins today in a solemn covenant to exercise the powers of her sovereign status in promoting the peace, security and happiness, the economic, cultural, and moral well-being of the human race.

Lofty ideals have inspired the best minds who have faith in the power of good will and of joint international endeavour to operate for good through this Council of the Nations. It is our earnest desire to co-operate with our fellow-members in every effort calculated to give effect to those ideals—to mitigate, and whenever possible, to avert the ancient evils of warfare and oppression; to encourage wholesome and to discourage unwholesome relations between nation and nation; to enable even the weakest of nations to live their own lives and make their own proper contribution to the good of all, free even from the shadow and the fear of external violence, vicious penetration, or injurious pressure of any kind.

In the actual proceedings which we have witnessed, we have seen a keen appreciated of the fact that nations are interdependent in matters of economic and intellectual development. We hope that the means of closer intercourse provided or initiated through the League of Nations will be helpful to the economic and educational progress for which Ireland is looking forward and always striving.

We willingly testify that the advocacy of these ideals has strongly attracted us towards the League of Nations, and if as yet the means provided have not always proved fully effective to secure their worthy ends, we are mindful of our national proverb, "Bíonn gach tosnú lag" ("every beginning is weak"), and we trust that in time to come, adequate means and faithful use

of them will justify our common hopes. Our history and the instinct of our hearts forbid us to think that temporary or even recurrent failures can deprive a just and steadfast purpose of the assurance of success.

Ireland counts on having no enemy and on harbouring no enmity in the time to come. She counts also on bringing forth fruits worthy of liberty. *Si tollis libertatem, tollis dignitatem.* These are the words of a famous Irishman of the sixth and seventh century. Inscribed on his tomb at Bobbio in Italy, they met our eyes when, a few days ago, a happy conjuncture enabled the members of this Irish delegation to assist at the celebration of the thirteenth centenary of Saint Columbanus, pioneer of Ireland's moral and intellectual mission among the nations of Western Europe.

We shall return to our own country to take part with our own patriotic people in the enormous work of national construction and consolidation. The kind welcome, the cordial words of understanding, that have greeted us here on the part of every nation whose representatives we have met, will not be forgotten. They will cheer and sustain us in that work, and they will remind us, too, that as the life of a man is bettered and fructified beyond measure in the harmonious society of men, so must the life of nations reach a much fuller liberty and a much fuller dignity in the harmonious society of nations.

Reprinted in Documents on Irish Foreign Policy, *vol. 2, 1923–1926, edited by Ronan Fanning, Michael Kennedy, Dermot Keogh, and Eunan O'Halpin (2000), pp. 156–157.*

~

Letter on the Commission on the Gaeltacht

4 March 1925

William T. Cosgrave

The Commission on the Gaeltacht (the term used to describe the Irish-speaking areas) was one of the first commissions established by the government of the Irish Free State—an indication of the high priority given to protecting and restoring the Irish language. The cultural and political importance of the Irish language was an issue on which supporters and opponents of the treaty were in agreement, and it was seen as a unifying force in a divided society; but the Irish-language policy served to alienate the Protestant minority. This letter is included in the Report of the Commission on the Gaeltacht, *published in 1926.*

SEE ALSO Gaelic Catholic State, Making of; Gaelic Revival; Gaelic Revivalism: The Gaelic League

General Mulcahy, T.D.,

Chairman, Commission of Inquiry into the Preservation of the Gaeltacht, 6 Harcourt Street, Dublin.

A CHARA DHÍL,—The commission of which you are chairman has been formed, and its terms of reference drawn up, in the hope that proper inquiry will lead to a clear and definite national policy in respect of those districts and local populations which have preserved the Irish language as the language of their homes.

By the consitution of Saorstát Éireann, Irish is expressly recognised as the national language. Its maintenance and cultivation have always been an important element of the national policy which has led up to the establishment of a sovereign state in Ireland. Of this policy the Oireachtas and the government of Saorstát Éireann are the appointed trustees. We believe that the Irish people as a body recognise it to be a national duty, incumbent on their representatives and their government as on themselves, to uphold and foster the Irish language, the central and most distinctive factor of the tradition which is Irish nationality; and that everything that can be rightly and effectively done to that end will be in accordance with the will of the Irish people.

We recognise the facts and the factors that have militated in the past and by force of continuity still militate in large part against the very existence of the Irish language: its exclusion from most of the activities of public life, from "court and bar and business"; its exclusion for generations from nearly all our schools; how it fell under a kind of social ban and became in the minds of many a badge of poverty and backwardness. The neglect and contempt, the ignominy and the abuse to which it has been subjected, are a part of our tragic history. These very things and their unfortunate effects, instead of infecting us with their spirit and making us also contemptuous and apathetic, ought rightly to enliven our purpose to undo the damage of the past—the more so, because the possession of a cultivated national language is known by every people who have it to be a secure guarantee of the national future. Our language has been waylaid, beaten and robbed, and left for dead by the wayside, and we have to ask ourselves if it is to be allowed to lie there, or if we are to heal its wounds, place it in safety and under proper care, and have it restored to health and vigour.

We recognise also that the future of the Irish language and its part in the future of the Irish nation depend, more than on anything else, on its continuing in an unbroken tradition as the language of Irish homes. This tradition is the living root from which alone organic growth is possible. For this reason, the Irish people rightly value as a national asset their "Gaeltaeht," the scattered range of districts in which Irish is the home language.

These districts are known to coincide more or less with areas of rural Ireland which present an economic problem of the greatest difficulty and complexity. The language problem and the economic problem are in close relation to each other, and your commission is asked to consider both together.

The public will look with eager interest to the course and outcome of your inquiries, and public opinion may be expected to support any practical measures that can be instituted to safeguard the future of Irish as the home language and the economic future of the people who use Irish as their ordinary and principal language of intercourse with each other.

Mise,
Le fíor-mheas ort,
(Signed) LIAM T. MAC COSGAIR.

COIMISIÚN NA GAELTACHTA REPORT (R. 23/27), *Dublin,* 1926.

~

"THE END"

1926

Tomás Ó Criomhthain

This is the final chapter of the autobiography of Tomás Ó Criomhthain (Tomás O'Crohan), written when he was close to seventy years old, published in Irish in 1929 and translated into English by Robin Flower in 1934. The first of the Blasket Island memoirs, the book reveals the harshness of island life, with near starvation at times when the crops failed or fish were scarce, yet plenty when a storm drove a wrecked cargo onto the shore. Ó Criomhthain reveals here his shrewd, yet humorous detachment, which allowed him faithfully to depict a vanishing way of life.

SEE ALSO Arts: Modern Irish and Anglo-Irish Literature and the Arts since 1800; Blasket Island Writers

Well, I've slipped along thus far to the end of my story. I have set down nothing but the truth; I had no need of invention, for I had plenty of time, and have still a good deal in my head. It's amazing what a lot there is in an old man's head when somebody else starts him talking and puts questions to him. All the same, what I've written down are the things that meant most to me. I considered the whole course of my life, and the things that had meant most to me were the first to come back to memory.

I have brought other people besides myself into my story, for, if I hadn't, it would have been neither interesting nor complete. I never disliked any of them, and I've spent my life in their company till to-day without any trouble between us. I don't know what colour the inside walls of the court in Dingle are, old though I am.

We are poor simple people, living from hand to mouth. I fancy we should have been no better off if we had been misers. We were apt and willing to live, without repining, the life the Blessed Master made for us, often and again ploughing the sea with only our hope in God to bring us through. We had characters of our own, each different form the other, and all different from the landsmen; and we had our own little failings too. I have made no secret of our good traits or of our little failings either, but I haven't told all the hardships and the agonies that befell us from time to time when our only resource was to go right on.

This is a crag in the midst of the great sea, and again and again the blown surf drives right over it before the violence of the wind, so that you daren't put your head out any more than a rabbit that crouches in his burrow in Inishvickillane when the rain and the salt spume are flying. Often would we put to sea at the dawn of day when the weather was decent enough, and by the day's end our people on land would be keening us, so much had the weather changed for the worse. It was our business to be out in the night, and the misery of that sort of fishing is beyond telling. I count it the worst of all trades. Often and again the sea would drive over us so that we could see the land no more—a long, long night of cold like this, struggling against the sea, with often little to get, only praying from moment to moment for the help of God. It was rare, indeed, for us to get a full catch, and then often we would have to cut away the nets and let it all go with the sea. On other nights, after all the labour of the fishing, the boats would be fairly full, and we couldn't make the harbour or the land, but the swell would be rising to the green grass, the storm blowing out of the north-west, and the great waves breaking. We would have to flee then before the gale, some of us to Cuan Croumha, some to Ventry Harbour, some to Dingle.

You may understand from this that we are not to be put in comparison with the people of the great cities of the soft and level lands. If we deserved blame a little at times, it would be when a drop of drink was going round among us. The drink went to our heads the easier because we were always worn and weary, as I have described, like a tired horse, with never any rest or intermission.

It was a good life in those days. Shilling came on shilling's heels; food was plentiful, and things were cheap. Drink was cheap, too. It wasn't thirst for the drink that made us want to go where it was, but only the need to have a merry night instead of the misery that we knew only too well before. What the drop of drink did to us was to lift up the hearts in us, and we would spend a day and a night ever and again in company together when we got the chance. That's all gone by now, and the high heart and the fun are passing from the world. Then we'd take the homeward way together easy and friendly after all our revelry, like the children of one mother, none doing hurt or harm to his fellow.

I have written minutely of much that we did, for it was my wish that somewhere there should be a memorial of it all, and I have done my best to set down the character of the people about me so that some record of us might live after us, for the like of us will never be again.

I am old now. Many a thing has happened to me in the running of my days until now. People have come into the world around me and have gone again. There are only five older than me alive in the Island. They have the pension. I have only two months to go till that date—a date I have no fancy for. In my eyes it is a warning that death is coming, though there are many people who would rather be old with the pension than young without it.

I can remember being at my mother's breast. She would carry me up to the hill in a creel she had for bringing home the turf. When the creel was full of turf, she would come back with me under her arm. I remember being a boy; I remember being a young man; I remember the bloom of my vigour and my strength. I have known famine and plenty, fortune and ill-fortune, in my life days till today. They are great teachers for one that marks them well.

One day there will be none left in the Blasket of all I have mentioned in this book—and none to remember them. I am thankful to God, who has given me the chance to preserve from forgetfulness those days that I have seen with my own eyes and have borne their burden, and that when I am gone men will know what life was like in my time and the neighbours that lived with me.

Since the first fire was kindled in this Island none has written of his life and his world. I am proud to set down my story and the story of my neighbours. This writing will tell how the Islanders lived in the old days. My mother used to go carrying turf when I was eighteen years of age. She did it that I might go to school, for rarely did we get a chance of schooling. I hope in God that she and my father will inherit the Blessed Kingdom; and that I and every reader of this book after me will meet them in the Island of Paradise.

Tomás O'Crohan, The Islandman (1934), pp. 320–324.
Reproduced by permission of Oxford University Press.

~

"Aims of Fianna Fáil in Office"

17 March 1932

Eamon de Valera

Eamon de Valera took advantage of this St. Patrick's Day radio broadcast, nine days after Fianna Fáil took office for the first time, to outline his party's political aims. The peaceful transfer of power after the 1932 general election, from the winning to the losing side in the Irish Civil War, consolidated the democratic tradition in the new Irish state.

SEE ALSO de Valera, Eamon; Political Parties in Independent Ireland; Politics: Independent Ireland since 1922

This is the first occasion that I have had the opportunity of speaking at the same moment to the Irish people at home and in the United States of America.

The fifteenth centenary anniversary of the coming of St. Patrick, the year of the Eucharistic Congress, the recent election by the people of this state of the first Fianna Fáil government, all combine to make this year's celebration of the national festival one of unique interest our history.

For us here in Ireland the National Feast Day is now drawing to a close. For you who are listening to me beyond the ocean, over the plains of the United States, stretching to San Francisco, the day is still young. The changes in the hour indicate at once the vastness of the country in which so many of the children of our race have found a home and the magnitude of the dispersion of our people—a dispersion almost without parallel in the story of mankind.

Nowhere, however, is the hour too late or too early to send you all, wherever you be, my most fervent greetings and my most earnest wishes for your welfare and happiness.

The aims of the new government are simple. I know no words in which I can express them better that those of Fintan Lalor:

Ireland her own, and all therein, from the sod to the sky. The soil of Ireland for the people of Ireland, to have and hold from God alone who gave it—to have and to hold to them and their heirs forever, without suit or service, faith or fealty, rent or render, to any power under heaven.

We desire to pursue these aims without ill-feeling towards any Irishman, without injury to any Irishman, without injury to any nation.

I believe that the people of Great Britain wish to be on peaceful and friendly relations with us just as we do with them. And I believe that they desire that no obstacles should be allowed to stand which would hinder the establishment of such relations. The will of our own people must prevail in all matters concerning their sovereign rights, and as our people do not desire in any way to impose burdens or tests on the people of Great Britain, they justly feel that no burdens or tests should be imposed on them. Friendship between neighbouring countries is largely dependent on the degree to which they respect each other's freedom, and it is hardly to be supposed that a different principle can operate between ourselves and Great Britain.

In the Irish Free State, as in America, there is an economic crisis. Whatever be the causes of such a crisis in this state, it is going to call forth all the energies of both the government and the people to provide adequate remedies. Our most urgent problem is that of unemployment, and my colleagues and I intend to work without ceasing until that gravest of evils has been eliminated. The slums of our cities are still a disgrace to us. The problem of their complete elimination will be studied at once, and I hope to be able to propose definite plans at an early date.

In the interests of economy considerable sacrifices will have to be made by state servants and other sections of the population. The ministers have already decided on a considerable decrease in emoluments. I have no doubt whatever that the people who are called upon will be ready and willing to make whatever sacrifices may be required of them for the betterment of the people as a whole.

Our problems are grave and numerous, but at the moment I shall only touch on two other matters which

I think may be of special interest to you, my friends in America.

In our external relations, we intend to maintain our existing legations and to give attention to all those countries in which are large populations of Irish origin. Whenever the opportunity presents itself, we intend to uphold the principle of the equality of states and to advocate the reduction and eventual abolition of armaments and the establishment of a system of inter-state relationship in which the rule of law shall hold between nations as between individuals. As you are aware, we are in diplomatic relations with the Vatican, the United States, France and Germany. I am an earnest believer in close friendship and frequent contact between the nations—for by no other means can war be more effectively abolished than by mutual understanding. We can all learn much from each other and profit by each other's experience. This small state has to be satisfied with small beginnings in external affairs, and our machinery is now almost adequate for our present needs.

In America you are deeply interested in education, and for us here it is, in more than one sense, the most important question of all. Besides the progressively increasing use of the Irish language in our schools, we intend to develop a system of primary education more in accord with our economic life than at present exists in the Saorstát.

The system of adapting part of the curriculum to regional needs will probably be selected as one means of encouraging the young men and women to stay in the country. Our whole system of technical education must be linked up with the primary and art schools. This will lead to the rural development of small industries such as exist in Italy, and will also help toward the problem of providing employment for the children of the small farmer during the slack months of the year.

I cannot now speak to you in detail of our plans for the development of our rural industries, but I cannot let the occasion pass without urging our people at home to regard it as a matter of duty to support our existing industries.

I urge upon our people abroad to give a preference to Irish over foreign produce.

I have read with admiration the appeals made by certain European statesmen for special sacrifice and hard work amongst their people, and I have watched with even greater admiration the ready response given by whole peoples vastly greater than the population of this island. I have the utmost confidence that my appeal to the people of the Free State to make a special effort on behalf of their own industries will meet with a response no less ready.

My time is running out, but before concluding I wish to extend in advance to all our American friends who intend to come to the Eucharistic Congress a right hearty welcome. We earnestly hope that great numbers of our exiles will return for that great festival which will bring blessings and glory to our country. You may feel assured that you will find peace and harmony amongst us, and you will return to your adopted country with new and joyful hopes for the future of the motherland.

The Tailteann games are also being held this year and have our wholehearted approval. The games are of very great national value, unifying our people in sentiment and endeavour and giving them, no matter in what land they live, a just sense of pride in the spiritual ideals, the physical prowess and the intellectual achievements of the Gael.

In conclusion I wish to seize this opportunity to thank all our friends in America who helped us in our work for Ireland, whether in the more remote or the recent past. Your common desire has always been to bring about the unity and independence of this nation.

I ask all the friends of Ireland in America to regard the advent of the government in the Free State as a sign from our people that they wish to put an end to all bitterness and disunion. As my last word on our National Feast Day, I most earnestly appeal to all Irishmen at home and abroad to close their ranks and to march forward with us. Let our desire to work for our country be our common bond, and let us be content to vie with each other for the honour of serving Ireland.

SPEECHES AND STATEMENTS BY EAMON DE VALERA, 1917–73, edited by Maurice Moynihan (1980), pp. 193–196. Reproduced by permission of St. Martin's Press, LLC, and Gill & Macmillan, Dublin.

≈

PIERCE'S CAVE

1933

Maurice O'Sullivan

In this passage of his autobiography, the young Maurice O'Sullivan, accompanied by his grandfather, discovers the great Irish Renaissance poet Pierce Ferriter and learns about the history of resistance to English rule in Ireland.

SEE ALSO Arts: Modern Irish and Anglo-Irish Literature and the Arts since 1800; Blasket Island Writers

My grandfather and I were lying on the Castle Summit. It was a fine sunny day in July. The sun was splitting the stones with its heat and the grass burnt to the roots. I could see, far away to the south, Iveragh painted in many colours by the sun. South-west were the Skelligs glistening white and the sea around them dotted with fishing-boats from England.

"Isn't it a fine healthy life those fishermen have, daddo?" said I.

I got no answer. Turning round I saw that the old man was asleep. I looked at him, thinking. You were one day in the flower of youth, said I in my own mind, but, my sorrow, the skin of your brow is wrinkled now and the hair on your head is grey. You are without suppleness in your limbs and without pleasure in the grand view to be seen from this hill. But, alas, if I live, some day I will be as you are now.

The heat was very great, and so I thought of waking him for fear the sun would kill him. I caught him by his grey beard and gave it a pull. He opened his eyes and looked round.

"Oh, Mirrisheen," said he, "I fell asleep. Am I long in it?"

"Not long," said I, "but I thought I had better wake you on account of the sun. Do you see those trawlers out in the horizon? I was just saying that it's a fine healthy life they have."

"Musha, my heart," said my grandfather, "a man of the sea never had a good life and never will, as I know well, having spent my days on it, and I have gone through as many perils on it as there are grey hairs in my head, and I am telling you now, wherever God may guide you, keep away from the sea."

"Musha, it seems to me there is no man on earth so contented as a seaman."

I looked south-east to the Macgillicuddy Reeks. They looked as if they were touching the sky.

"Musha, aren't those high mountains?"

"They are indeed, if you were down at their foot."

At that moment a big bee came around murmuring to itself. My grandfather started to drive it away with his hat. "There is no place under the sun is finer than that," said he, stretching his finger south towards the harbour of Iveragh. "When you would be entering that harbour you would have the Isle of Oaks on your right hand and Beg-Inish out before your face."

"I dare say the water is very still there."

"A dead calm. The creek runs three miles up through the land of Cahirciveen. And do you see, on the east of the creek, there is another harbour? That is Cooan Una. And east again is Cooas Cromha, and east again the place they call the Rodana."

"It seems you know those places well, daddo."

"Ah, my sorrow, it is many a day I spent in them."

He put his hand in his pocket and drew out his pipe. When he had it lighted, he got up. "Come now and I will take you into Pierce Ferriter's Cave."

We moved down through the Furrows of the Garden, up to our ears in fern and dry heather.

"Look now," said he, pointing down, "do you see that ledge of rock? That's the Cave."

"Isn't it a great wonder he went down so far?"

"Sure that's the place he wanted, my boy, where he could cut down the soldiers of England."

"How?"

"Don't you see the ledge? The entrance is under the overhanging cliff. He used to be inside with a big stick. Then the first soldier would come down to the mouth of the cave, Pierce would just give him a thrust with the stick and send him over the cliff."

"Wasn't he a wonderful man?"

"Oh, he did great destruction on the English at that time."

We were down at the Cave now. My grandfather crept in on all-fours and I behind him, for the entrance was not more than two feet high. Once inside, there was room to stand up for it was above seven feet. I looked around. "Musha, isn't it a comfortable place he had, but I dare say he used never to leave it."

"Indeed he did, whenever the soldiers left the Island."

"And how would he know that?"

"The people here used to be coming to attend upon him whenever they got the chance. Look at that stone. That's where he used to lay his head."

"It was hard pillow."

"No doubt. Did you ever hear the verse he composed here when he was tired of the place, on a wild and stormy night? It is only a couple of words."

He sat down on the stone and, taking off his hat, he recited:

"O God above, dost Thou pity the way I am,
Living alone where it is little I see of the day;
The drop above in the top of the stone on high
Falling in my ears and the roar of the sea at my heels."

As he spoke the last words, the tears fell from the old man.

"Musha, daddo, isn't it a nice lonesome verse? And another thing, it is many the fine learned man the English laid low at that time."

"Ah, Mary, it is true. I tell you, Maurice, Pierce suffered here if ever a man did. Have you the verse now?" said he.

"I think I have, for it went to my heart." And I repeated it to him.

"You have every word of it."

"Isn't it wonderful the way you would keep in your head anything you would take an interest in?"

"That is very true, for when I was young like yourself there is not a word I would hear my father saying, dear God bless his soul, but it would stay in my memory. It is time for us to be making for the house now in the name of God."

I looked up at the cliff and then down where the waves were breaking angrily. "There's no doubt, daddo," said I, "but he had the roar of the waves at his heels."

The sun was fading in the west, yellow as gold, the birds singing in the heather, hundreds of rabbits out on the clumps of thrift, some of them, when they saw us, running off with their white tails cocked in the air, other with their ears up looking hard at us.

"Wait now, till you see them scatter in a moment," said my grandfather, picking up a stone. He threw it but they did not stir. "Upon my word but they are bold," said he and gave a shout, and it seemed five voices answered him with the echo in the coves below. Then I saw the rabbits running, tails up and ears back, and in a moment there was not one to be seen save an old one as grey as a badger.

"Isn't it strange the grey one didn't stir?"

"Ah, my boy, that's an old soldier at the end of his life and he is well used to that shouting."

"I wonder what length of life is appointed for them?"

"Only three years, and I assure you they work those three years for a livelihood as hard as any sinner. But here we are home again," said he as we came in sight of the village.

"You are very good at shortening the road."

"Upon my word, Mirrisheen, I would be better still if I were seated up on a horse-cart for it is hard for an old man to be talking and walking together."

Maurice O'Sullivan, Twenty Years A-Growing, translated by Moya Llewelyn Davies and George Thomson (1933), pp. 76–80.

ON "A PROTESTANT PARLIAMENT AND A PROTESTANT STATE"

24 April 1934

Sir James Craig

This phrase is often cited as "a Protestant parliament for a Protestant people." Northern Ireland prime minister Sir James Craig justified his position by asserting that the South (Irish Free State) was a Catholic state. The proportion of Catholics employed in public-service posts in Northern Ireland fell steadily throughout the 1920s and the 1930s. Craig and other Northern politicians justified excluding Catholics from both public and private employment by suggesting that they were a threat to state security.

SEE ALSO Craig, James, First Viscount Craigavon; Northern Ireland: Discrimination and the Campaign for Civil Rights; Northern Ireland: History since 1920; Ulster Unionist Party in Office

I have never yet known a country to prosper where appointments to the judiciary were made on religious grounds. (HON. MEMBERS: Hear, hear.) I think it would be a fatal mistake if whoever had an opportunity of recommending to his majesty the names for the high position of judges in this land had to take into consideration a man's religion. As long as I have anything to do with it, I say here quite frankly and openly, that that aspect will never enter into my mind. Only the best man who can be had for the position will be recommended. These matters are all readily answered, I think, to the satisfaction of any fair minded man.

I will refer next to the speech of the hon. member for West Tyrone (Mr. Donnelly). I am very glad he has admitted something along the lines of the amendment which the government has seen fit to put down to this vote of want of confidence, for that is really what it amounts to. When my colleagues have passed the resolution it will read like this:—

That in the opinion of this house the employment of disloyalists entering Northern Ireland is prejudicial, not only to the interests of law and order and the safety of the state, but also to the prior claims of loyal Ulster-born citizens seeking employment.

All through this debate the charges made by hon. members opposite have been grossly exaggerated. Since we took up office we have tried to be absolutely fair towards all the citizens of Northern Ireland. Actually, on an Orange platform, I, myself, laid down the principle, to which I still adhere, that I was prime minister not of one section of the community but of all, and that as far as I possibly could I was going to see that fair play was not meted out to all classes and creeds without any favour whatever on my part.

MR LEEKE: What about your Protestant parliament?

THE PRIME MINISTER: The hon. member must remember that in the South they boasted of a Catholic state. They still boast of Southern Ireland being a Catholic state. All I boast of is that we are a Protestant parliament and Protestant state. It would be rather interesting for historians of the future to compare a Catholic state launched in the South with a Protestant state launched in the North and to see which gets on the better and prospers the more. It is more interesting for me at the moment to watch how they are progressing. I am doing my best always to top the bill and be ahead of the South.

As I have said, there is a great deal of exaggeration in the statements made today. Are memories so short that hon. members opposite have forgotten that those who came into this Northern area at a certain period of our career came for the purpose of preventing the Ulster government from being established. We will never forget the death of our old colleague, Mr. Twaddell, and there are two hon. members of this house who bear the marks of bullets because of their loyalty in helping the government to maintain law and order. Those people, I always believe, came from outside. Is it any wonder that we should take precautions and advise our own people in this area to beware of persons of that type coming into Ulster in order to recreate all the turmoil, murder, bloodshed, and trouble from which we formerly suffered? . . .

NORTHERN IRELAND PARLIAMENTARY DEBATES, HOUSE OF COMMONS, *vol. 16, pp. 1094–1096.*

~

"FAILURE OF THE LEAGUE OF NATIONS"

18 June 1936

Eamon de Valera

Eamon de Valera gave this speech in Dáil Éireann, shortly before he traveled to Geneva to attend the reconvened 16th Assembly of the League of Nations. Ireland had supported the league in its efforts to maintain international security,

but de Valera had been very disillusioned at the league's failure to protect Abyssinia (a member) against Italian aggression. With the increasing threat of war in Europe, de Valera had become convinced that Ireland must rely on its own resources for national security.

SEE ALSO de Valera, Eamon; Politics: Independent Ireland since 1922

With regard to the League of Nations and to our policy in it, I do not know if the chair would agree if it would be appropriate at this stage to discuss the question as to whether or not we should withdraw from the League. At any rate, as far as I am concerned and as far as the government is concerned, our attitude in regard to this particular dispute is very clear. We are satisfied that this aggression occurred, and we see today that Italy has been successful in getting military supremacy in Ethiopia. I think it is equally clear that the sanctions policy of the League of Nations has failed to do what was expected of it by the founders of the League.

What we are to do in regard to the future, then, becomes a question of very great importance. As far as we are concerned, we are satisfied that the League, as it was, cannot any longer command the confidence of the ordinary people in the world. It does not command our confidence. Therefore the League of Nations, unless it is reformed, is not of advantage to us, and I do not think it would be, in its present form, of advantage to humanity in general. There were very serious obligations involved in membership of the League of Nations. If there was no doubt whatever that we would be put in positions of risk without the feeling that what we hoped to gain from the League would be secured, then I think it would be madness to continue to remain a member of it. But the probability is that the League will be changed. I think what I am saying is the feeling of most people, would be the feeling of most governments, that the League of Nations must be fundamentally changed.

The League in the past set itself an objective which clearly is not attainable in present circumstances. In my view, and it is the view I would urge upon the government as minister for external affairs if the matter had to be immediately settled, the League in future will have to set itself a humbler task, and the question of compelling other states to maintain their obligations will have to be abandoned. It is quite clear that economic sanctions alone are not sufficient and that if we are to have effective action, we must go beyond the range of mere economic sanctions and consider whether military sanctions are necessary. Anybody looking at the course of the conflict that has taken place in Ethiopia must be satisfied that, if the states really wanted to maintain the independence and integrity of Ethiopia, they should have been ready at certain stages to face the possibility of military action. It might not be military action in the first instance, but it would eventually involve military action.

Before I leave that point, perhaps I should say that I do not think nations are ready for that yet. War to prevent war is a peculiar position, and there is no doubt that, in order effectively to stop the last war, the states would have had to be ready to face even a more extended war than the war in question. You saw that there was hesitation with regard to the sanctions that would be most effective. You saw that, with regard to oil sanctions, for instance, the states were very chary about proceeding along these lines, because they were told that to do so would involve war. It is clear that if there were oil sanctions, it might have involved war, and if you are not going to meet a challenge of that sort, then you had better not make these threats or proceed along that line. It is obvious that, if the powers were really serious and were prepared to take definite measures, the closing of the Suez Canal would have been resorted to as one measure. Consequently it was obvious the League of Nations was taking half-measures which could not in the ultimate fail to be ineffective.

The question is: Are we prepared to say that the League should be reformed in the direction of imposing military sanctions if necessary? I do not think that our people would be prepared for that, and I do not think the people of any other country would be prepared either. Therefore the only practical line, it seems to me, to go upon, if the League is to be reformed, is the line of using the League in other directions, using it as a forum for the consideration of such questions as might otherwise lead to war, using it as a conciliatory machine, perhaps on occasion as an arbitration machine. But I certainly cannot see any government here that would come to the Dáil and say that we would, in our present circumstances, be prepared to enter into obligations which might necessitate our sending out expeditionary forces in order to prevent aggression somewhere else.

We are not in a position to do that, and I do not think the people in other countries are prepared to do it either. Certain countries with special interests abroad may be prepared for that because, in the main, their interests would best be served by it; but I do not think that the small nations are prepared for it or should be prepared for it; certainly our nation is not prepared for it. Consequently, if this manner comes up for consideration, our position will have to be made clear. If we are to remain members of the League, our position will

have to be considered in the light of whether we feel it would be in the interests of our country to belong to the League.

The question of the present position in regard to sanctions naturally comes up for consideration. In that matter, too, I think the position is clear enough. It would be foolish not to take cognisance of the facts of the situation. If there was any possibility of sanctions being able to perform the task that remains, if they are to be continued, then there is no doubt they should have been able to perform the easier task which was set them before, and if nations were not prepared to run the risk of war in the situation that existed up to the present, I do not think there is any likelihood of their being prepared to run the same risk in regard to the situation we have to face now. We have to remember that we cannot deal with this question without meeting the other states that have agreed to a co-ordinating committee, but our attitude in any meeting of the sort would be that the League of Nations policy up to the present has failed and that the League must be reformed. As regards sanctions, it is quite clear they have failed and that the continuance of them would serve no good purpose. These, I take it, are the principal matters on which deputies wished for an expression of opinion from the government.

With regard to the position in Europe in general, deputies know as well as I do that that position is more tense and that there are greater possibilities of war in it than at any time since the conclusion of the World War. Naturally, when you see all the smaller states spending large sums of money providing for their defences, looking to their defences, it provides food for thought. Some of them in the past relied, as events have now shown, altogether too much on the strength of the League of Nations. Turning back once more to the position of Ethiopia, I have no doubt Ethiopia suffered severely through the fact that it was a member of the League, that it expected certain results and did not get them. . . .

With regard to the position generally, the small states in Europe have begun to provide for their own defences. In the case of Ethiopia there is no doubt that its association with the League of Nations, instead of helping, hindered it. In the early stages, when it became apparent that Ethiopia was about to be attacked, she had scarcely any defences to rely on and there was dangled before the faces of those responsible the hope that the League of Nations would assist. If her will not been paralysed by the idea that if she took action early the case against Italy might not be so clear and they might not get such help as they expected, I think Ethiopia at any rate would not have waited until the last moment to try to defend herself properly. So it is with the small states. The fate of Ethiopia has warned them of the danger in which they are, and most of them are doing their utmost to make good their defences.

That naturally brings us to the position at home. Any government at the present time would have seriously to consider the question of the defences of the country. Our position is particularly complicated. If we held the whole of our territory, there is no doubt whatever that our attitude would be that which is the attitude, I think of, practically every Irishman, and that is that we have no aggressive designs against any other people. We would strengthen ourselves so as to maintain our neutrality. We would strengthen ourselves so that we might resist any attempt to make use of our territory for attack upon any other nation. I think that the average person in this country wants to make war on nobody. We have no aggressive designs. We want to have our own country for ourselves, as I have said on more than one occasion, and that is the limit of our ambition. We have no imperial ambitions of any sort. But we are in this position, that some of our ports are occupied, and, although we cannot be actively committed in any way, the occupation of those ports will give, to any foreign country that may desire a pretext, an opportunity of ignoring our neutrality. Our population in the neighbourhood of those ports are in a position in which, through no fault of theirs and through no fault of the rest of the people, they may become sufferers through retaliation of this kind as a result of the occupation of those ports.

The first thing that any government here must try to secure is that no part of our territory will be occupied by any forces except the forces that are immediately responsible to the government here. I have tried to indicate on many occasions that that is our desire and that it would work out to the advantage of Britain as well as to our own advantage. I think Britain, or at any rate the average person in Britain, wants to feel that they are not going to be attacked through foreign states that might attempt to use this country as a base. We are prepared, and any government with which I have been associated has always been prepared, to give guarantees, so far as guarantees can be given, that that will not happen. We are prepared to meet the necessary expense and to make the necessary provision to see that the full strength of this nation will be used to resist any attempt by any foreign power to abuse our neutrality by using any portion of our territory as a base. If that situation were realised, then of course the government here would have a definite task. All the uncertain elements of the present situation would disappear. We would know what to expect; in the main, we would know what to provide against. But in the present uncertain position it is very difficult to have any adequate scheme of defence or to take any adequate measures which would safeguard us against the risks which we have got to face now that our territory is within reaching distance of aeroplanes from the continent and that we are liable, on account of the occupation of certain parts of our territory, to attack by any enemy of Great Britain.

As I have said, the whole position in Europe is one of uncertainty and one of menace. We want to be neutral. We are prepared to play a reasonable part in the maintenance of peace. Unfortunately, as I said on previous occasions here, we are not a great power. We have a certain amount of moral influence, and we try to exert that in favour of peace, but when we think of the Kellogg Pact and all the other indications of goodwill, if I might put it that way, that have been given in the past, we see how hopeless and how useless all those things become when one state is satisfied that it is to its advantage that those obligations and the policy embodied in them should be set aside.

Dáil Debates, vol. 62, cols. 2655–2661, available at www.oireachtas-debates.gov.ie. Reprinted in Speeches and Statements by Eamon de Valera, 1917–73, edited by Maurice Moynihan (1980), pp. 273–277. Reproduced by permission of St. Martin's Press, LLC, and Gill & Macmillan, Dublin.

~

"Scattering and Sorrow"

1936

Peig Sayers

Coming from Peig Sayers's famous autobiography, first published in 1936 in Irish, this passage deals with the deaths or emigration to America of most of her remaining loved ones. Her son, Micheál Ó Guithín, leaves her a poem as a souvenir before departing for the United States. He eventually returned to Ireland, the last of the Blasket Island poets.

SEE ALSO Arts: Modern Irish and Anglo-Irish Literature and the Arts since 1800; Blasket Island Writers; Literature: Twentieth-Century Women Writers

Tomás dies accidentally – Pádraig and Cáit go to
America – My husband dies – Muiris, Eibhlín
and Micheál leave me one after the
other – Micheál's poetry

When a person thinks his life is going smoothly then it
changes as if he were a cat's-paw of fate; that's true
saying for it's exactly what happened to me, alas, in the
year 1920.

We had no turf on the Island that year; the fuel we
used was heather from the hill, and that was the fuel I
bought dearly! On the morning of Friday the 20th day
of April, Tomás and myself were up early. We had the
tea ready and no one else in the house had as yet risen.
While we were eating I told Tomás that Pádraig intended going to America.

"Don't let it bother you!" he said. "Isn't it time he
went?"

"It's a pity he won't stay with ye for another year,"
I said. "Ye're too young to handle a currach and as the
proverb has it, 'One year matures a child greatly,'"

He looked at me across the table. A light shone in
his grey eyes; then he stretched out his right hand.

"Afraid you'll be hungry, mother?" he asked.
"Don't be a bit in dread that this hand won't be able to
put a bite of food into your mouth!"

"I know that, but the hand is still soft and young,"
I said.

By the time we had the breakfast eaten the other
members of the family were getting up. Tomás stood in
the middle of the floor; he appeared to be pondering on
some subject, for he examined every inch of the house
carefully. Then he proceeded out the door. "I won't go
to the hill today," he said as he stood between the two
door-jambs.

"The heather is too wet and we have enough inside
for today," I said. "Let it hold over till tomorrow."

He bounced out the door and that was the last time
I saw him alive. When next I saw him he was calm and
dead, laid out on a bier before me and the gentle bright
hand he had stretched out so proudly to me in the
morning was broken, bruised and lifeless.

It appears that when he left me that time in the
morning he met other lads on their way to the hill to
gather heather and he went off with them. The poor fellow was pulling a bush of heather when it gave way
with him and he fell over the cliff top. He fell on his back
pitching from rock to rock, each rock hundreds of feet
above the sea until he crashed down at the bottom of the
ravine. And may God save hearers!

I knew nothing whatsoever about his being on the
hill that day; I thought he was rambling around the
neighbourhood with the other lads—until news of his
death reached me. God save us, my life was then completely shattered. Fear and awe seized the heart of everyone for this was something that had never before happened on the Island and this multiplied everyone's
terror. As far as I was concerned, no pen can describe
what I suffered and endured. My son was dead; for the
previous year his father had been keeping to the bed and
when he heard the news the terrifying scream of sorrow
he uttered will remain branded in my hear forever. The
poor man thought that if he could only leave the bed he
would be all right but even that much was beyond him.

That was my difficulty—how could I go away and
leave my husband there in the pains of death? Tomás
was gone to God but my husband was still alive and I
realized that it would be flying in the face of the Almighty to leave the house without having someone to
look after him. God granted me that much sense, praise
be to Him forever, that I remained behind to give him
a helping hand.

Two currachs and eight men had to go out to bring
back the body. When they came to the place where he
was they were amazed to find that instead of his being
hundreds of yards out in the broad ocean he was high
up on a hollow smooth slippery detached stone barely
the length and breadth of his body. There he was laid
out as expertly and as calmly as if twelve women had
tended him. No one knows how he landed on that table
of stone with the blue sea all around him. No one except
God alone.

When his body was brought back to the house the
rest of the family was terrified except alone Muiris. He
was more mature than the others. The neighbours had
to take Cáit and Pádraig away from me because they
were demented with shock. As for their unfortunate
sick father, I didn't know the minute he'd drop dead. Remember, you who read this, that I was in a predicament
if ever a poor woman was. The neighbours got such a
fright that they were too terrified to approach me, all
with the exception of two—Seán Eoghain and Máire
Scanlan. Seán himself is dead now, God rest his soul and
the souls of all the dead, but that same Seán—aye and
God!—came to my relief on that sorrowful afternoon.
There was hard work to be done and who would do it?
That was the problem! I was only a mother and the job
on hands was beyond me. I, who wouldn't like to see
a simple cut had to set about the task; I had to wash and
clean my fine young boy and lay him out in death. That
task was before me and there was no way out of it. I
hadn't a friend or relation beside me and I needed a heart
of stone to be able to stand it.

I prayed to the Sacred Heart and to the Holy Mother to come and assist me! And indeed, dear reader, when I returned to the place where my son was, it could have been the body of a stranger, I felt my courage so strong and my heart so lightsome! But the task I had undertaken was too much for me; when I found my heart tightening I took the statue of the Virgin and placed it on the floor beside me and from that moment forward I confess that I was but an instrument in the hands of the Virgin and her only Son.

Muiris and his uncle, together with two others had gone off to get what was needed for the wake. When they returned, Muiris was uneasy asking if he could blot out the English inscription and the breastplate of the coffin. This he succeeded in doing for the schoolmaster helped him and wrote it out again in Irish. Muiris was completely satisfied when he had done this. He then said:

"It's a great relief to my mind to know that you're the first corpse for hundreds of years to go into Ventry churchyard under an inscription in Irish."

We found times upsetting and bothersome but God always opens a gap, for Tomás was barely six weeks buried when Father Seoirse Clune came to the Island on his holidays. I admit that it was God himself and Father Clune who gave the first shred of comfort. Father Clune was with me every day for I had fluent Irish to give him; something better than that, he had sound advice and prime teaching to give me in return and that was a great help in healing a wounded heart. Scarcely a day passed that he wasn't with me and however sad I'd be on his arrival it seemed as if a ray of light accompanied him and that all my troubles would vanish. I was sorry when he left the Island, for he certainly helped me in great measure to forget my worldly troubles. This day, I wish him a long life in the service of God!

Six months after this my son Pádraig hoisted his sails and went off to America. There's no need for me to say that I was lonely after him but my hope in God was that I'd see him again some day. "Better hope from a locked door than from a grave." As soon as he had earned the passage-money Pádraig sent for his sister Cáit.

All these events were raining powerful blows on my heart, and barely five months after Cáit had gone, her father died—Lord have mercy on his soul. His heart was broken with sorrow and ill-health. His death was the worst blow I suffered and it left me poor and without anyone near me to offer me much assistance.

But while Muiris remained, I still had a man on my floor. He was an excellent son and one on whom I could depend completely. He was deeply attached to his country and to his native language and he never had any desire to leave Ireland. But that's not the way events turned out for he too had to take to the road like the others, his heart laden with sorrow.

As soon as he had turned the last sod of his father's grave he made ready to go. The day he went will remain forever in my memory because beyond all I had endured, nothing ever dealt me as crushing a blow as that day's parting with Muiris. The morning he left he was standing with his luggage and his papers on the table beside him. I was seated in the corner doing my best to be pleasant, but unknown to him I was watching him because he stood there as stiff as a poker with his two lips clamped together as if he were thinking. He rounded on me.

"Here!" he said handing me something wrapped in paper. I took it and opened it; it was the Irish flag.

"Yes," he said again with a tremor in his voice, "Put that away to keep in a place where neither moths nor flies can harm it! I have no business of it from this out." Then he got a catch of emotion in his voice.

"Son, dear," I said, "this will do me more harm than good for it will only make me lonely."

"No!" he said, and the words that jerked out of his mouth were all mixed up because of his emotion. "You'll have it to welcome the Royal Prince of the Feast yet!"

However badly I felt, I had to laugh at him but this was, as they say, "laughter from the teeth out."

"You poor silly awkward gom," I said. "You'll have to put these ideas out of your head!"

"Before God," he said, "it's true for you. And isn't this a sad day for me!"

"God is mighty and He has a good Mother," I told him. "Gather your gear and have courage for there was never a tide flowed west but flowed east again."

"Maybe in God it could happen," he said and he held my hand in a grip of steel.

I followed him down to the slip; what with all the people making their way to the haven it was like a great funeral that day.

He promised me that if things went well with him I'd never want either by day or by night and that he'd return to me as soon as he had a fair amount of money put together. True, that talk gave me courage but I knew well that in the words of the proverb: "The city has a broad entrance but a narrow exit."

"My dear son," I said "'Twould be a bad place that wouldn't be better for you than this dreadful rock.

Whatever way things go you'll be among your own equals. All around me here I see nothing on which a man can earn a living for here there's neither land nor property. I wouldn't like to make a cormorant of you, my son, and already too many are suffering misfortune. My own blessing and the blessing of God go with you. Follow your own road but heed me now, let nothing cross your path that'll lessen the love of God in your heart. Cherish your faith, avoid evil and always do good. A blessing go with you now and may God take you with him in safety."

I was very uneasy in my mind until I got a letter from him.

Micheál and Eibhlín were the last pair to leave me. Eibhlín was the youngest of all and I thought I'd never allow her to go to America. At this time she was in Dublin in Seán O'Shea's house in Dundrum and I was completely content with that. She had nothing but love and respect for Seán, but alas, her brother Pádraig paid a visit home and nothing would satisfy him but to go up to Dublin and bring her back. He took her away with him when he was returning to America.

Then Micheál was watching out for the chance to be off; he had no great mind to leave home but nevertheless, life was hard and he had nothing better to do. He too thought that if God left him his health he could put a fair share of money together and then come back home to me. A few days before he left the house he said:

"I wouldn't be a bit loath to leave, mother, if you'd promise me not be lonely."

"If I promised you that, son." I told him, "I'd promise you a lie; but I give you my word that I'll do my best not to be troubled."

He was fairly satisfied then, although he was sad and heartbroken. The second day after that, he bade me goodbye, asked God to bless me and said:

"I hope, mother, that we'll be together again."

"Maybe we will, boy," I said, "with God's help."

Then he went out the door and faced down for the landing-slip. I was absolutely desolate when he was gone.

A few days later I was tidying the little odds and ends he had left behind when I came across a scrap of paper on which he had written the following verses:

> Mother dear, don't weep for me,
> Nor for the lost one intercede;
> Lament in the Virgin's shining Son
> Your help in time of direst need.

> Lament his beauteous royal brow,
> His lime-white limbs that once were free;

> Lament the pearl was shattered sore
> On Calvary's hideous tree.

> Herdsman Who gave us clerics fair,
> To you we cry, dear Master,
> Place hatred in our hearts for sin
> The source of your disaster.

> Bless thou myself and all my kin
> At home or o'er the sea
> And by the Holy Spirit's grace
> Let me not one stray from Thee.

> For mother, Judgement Day shall come
> When mocking lie dare not intrude—
> You'll view our shining Saviour then,
> King of the multitude.

> By God's assistance, saint's and choirs',
> I'll cross the raging tide,
> And pleasant, sheltered, two as one
> Together we'll abide.

Peig Sayers, PEIG: THE AUTOBIOGRAPHY OF PEIG SAYERS OF THE GREAT BLASKET ISLAND (1974), pp. 180–187. *Copyright © 1973 by Bryan MacMahon. Copyright © 1974 by Syracuse University Press. Reproduced by permission.*

~

FROM THE 1937 CONSTITUTION

Eamon de Valera was the principal author of the 1937 constitution, designed to remove the restrictive features of the 1922 constitution. Ronan Fanning has described it as "the ultimate vindication of de Valera's brand of Irish republicanism." It was approved by referendum on 1 July 1937 by a margin 685,000 to 527,000 votes. Since then it has been subject to more than twenty amendments, including the removal of the ban on divorce and of Article 44, which recognized the special position of the Catholic Church. Articles 2 and 3 were amended in 1998 to conform to the Belfast Agreement.

SEE ALSO Declaration of a Republic and the 1949 Ireland Act; de Valera, Eamon; Gaelic Catholic State, Making of; Overseas Investment; Political Parties in Independent Ireland; Politics: Independent Ireland since 1922; Politics: Impact of the Northern Ireland Crisis on Southern Politics; Religion: Since 1690; Roman Catholic Church: Since 1891

In the name of the most holy trinity, from whom is all authority and to whom, as our final end, all actions both of men and states must be referred,

We, the people of Éire,

Humbly acknowledging all our obligations to our divine lord, Jesus Christ, who sustained our fathers through centuries of trial,

Gratefully remembering their heroic and unremitting struggle to regain the rightful independence of our nation,

And seeking to promote the common good, with due observance of prudence, justice and charity, so that the dignity and freedom of the individual may be assured, true social order attained, the unity of our country restored, and concord established with other nations,

Do hereby adopt, enact, and give to ourselves this constitution.

The Nation

Article 1　The Irish nation hereby affirms its inalienable, indefeasible, and sovereign right to choose its own form of government, to determine its relations with other nations, and to develop its life, political, economic and cultural, in accordance with its own genius and traditions.

Article 2　The national territory consists of the whole island of Ireland, its islands and the territorial seas.

Article 3　Pending the re-integration of the national territory, and without prejudice to the right of the parliament and government established by this constitution to exercise jurisdiction over the whole of that territory, the laws enacted by that parliament shall have the like area and extent of applications as the laws of Saorstát Éireann and the like extra-territorial effect.

The State

Article 4　The name of the state is Éire, or in the English language, Ireland.

Article 5　Ireland is a sovereign, independent, democratic state.

Article 6　1. All powers of government, legislative, executive and judicial, derive, under God, from the people, whose right it is to designate the rulers of the state and, in final appeal, to decide all questions of national policy, according to the requirements of the common good.

2. These powers of government are exercisable only by or on the authority of the organs of state established by this constitution.

Article 7　The national flag is the tricolour of green, white and orange.

Article 8　1. The Irish language as the national language is the first official language.

2. The English language is recognised as a second official language.

3. Provision may, however, be made by law for the exclusive use of either of the said languages for any one or more official purposes, either throughout the state or in any part thereof.

Article 9　1. 1° On the coming into operation of this constitution any person who was a citizen of Sarostát Éireann immediately before the coming into operation of this constitution shall become and be a citizen of Ireland.

2° The future acquisition and loss of Irish nationality and citizenship shall be determined in accordance with law.

3° No person may be excluded from Irish nationality and citizenship by reason of the sex of such person.

2. Fidelity to the nation and loyalty to the state are fundamental political duties of all citizens.

Article 10　1. All natural resources, including the air and all forms of potential energy, within the jurisdiction of the parliament and government established by this constitution and all royalties and franchises within that jurisdiction belong to the state subject to all estates and interests therein for the time being lawfully vested in any person or body.

2. All land all mines, minerals and waters which belonged to Saorstát Éireann immediately before the coming into operation of this constitution belong to the state to the same extent as they then belonged to Saorstát Éireann. . . .

Article 41　3. 1° The State pledges itself to guard with special care the institution of marriage, on which the family is founded, and to protect it against attack.

2° No law shall be enacted providing for the grant of a dissolution of marriage.

3° No person whose marriage has been dissolved under the civil law of any other state but is a subsisting valid marriage under the law for the time being in force within the jurisdiction of the government and parliament established by this constitution shall be capable of contracting a valid marriage within the jurisdiction during the lifetime of the other party to the marriage so dissolved. . . .

Article 44　1. 1° The state acknowledges that the homage of public worship is due to Almighty God. It shall hold his name in reverence, and shall respect and honour religion.

2° The state recognises the special position of the Holy Catholic Apostolic and Roman Church as the guardian of the faith professed by the great majority of its citizens.

3° The state also recognises the Church of Ireland, the Presbyterian Church in Ireland, the Methodist Church in Ireland, the Religious Society of Friends in Ireland, as well as the Jewish congregations and the other religious denominations existing in Ireland at the date of the coming into operation of this constitution.

BUNREACHT NA HÉIREANN (1937), pp. 2, 4–8, 138, 144.

~

"GERMAN ATTACK ON NEUTRAL STATES"

12 May 1940

Eamon de Valera

By 12 May 1940 German forces were sweeping across continental Europe and there were growing fears that Germany might mount an invasion of Britain and perhaps Ireland. In this speech Eamon de Valera emphasized that Ireland would resist an attack "from any quarter"; he also spoke about his efforts to bring about good relations with Britain—an important message at a time when a German victory appeared inevitable.

SEE ALSO de Valera, Eamon; Neutrality; Politics: Independent Ireland since 1922

We have been in danger from the moment this war began, and we will be in danger until it is over. Our duty is that every one of us in his own way should try to save himself and his neighbour, and the whole community, as best as he can from its consequences.

I was at Geneva on many occasions. When I was there, I used to particularly seek out the representatives of small nations because their problems, I thought, were in many respects like our problems. Just as I was coming in here I was going over in my mind the number of small independent nations that were represented there and the number of them that have, for the moment at any rate, disappeared. Go over in your own minds the list of small nations, and ask yourselves how many of them are now with their old independence or free from the horrors of war.

The representatives of Belgium and the representatives of The Netherlands were people that I met frequently, because we co-operated not a little with the northern group of nations. Today these two small nations are fighting for their lives, and I think I would be unworthy of this small nation if, on an occasion like this, I did not utter our protest against the cruel wrong which has been done them.

We have to see to it that, if there should be any attack of any kind upon us from any quarter, they will find us a united people ready to resist it. There is alive, thanks be to God, in this country a generation that has passed through war and that has done its part to secure the freedom that we have at the moment. I know that that generation, if it were called upon, is prepared to defend that freedom, and I know the younger people who are coming along will be not less ready to defend it if they are called upon. . . .

I have preached the national policy for many years. It is a policy which was commonly accepted—that we wanted our independence because it was our right. We proclaimed to the world that we did not want that independence to use it in any way hurtful to any other country, and particularly we did not desire it to be hurtful to Britain. We were prepared to let bygones by bygones as far as Britain was concerned, once we had our independence.

In so far as the portion of the country where we have that independence is concerned, we have pursued that policy and, as a result, as far as it was possible, established good relations between the two countries. My one regret in a time like the present is that there is still a cause of difference between the two countries. I believe, trying to look into the future, that the destiny of the peoples of these two islands off the coast of Europe will be similar in many respects. I believe that we will have many interests in common in the future as in the past. I believe these common interests would beget good relations. During the whole time I have been in public life I have sought to lay the foundation for these good relations by removing the causes of differences. Down here we have removed these causes of differences one by one, and as each one was removed, better relations ensued.

I strove to get that other cause removed, and I hoped all the time that it would be appreciated that it was necessary, in the interests of both these islands, for that cause to be removed. I will strive, and it will be the national policy to strive, in the future as in the past to secure the ending of these causes of difference between us.

SPEECHES AND STATEMENTS BY EAMON DE VALERA, 1917–73, *edited by Maurice Moynihan (1980), pp. 434–436.*

~

"NATIONAL THANKSGIVING"

16 May 1945

Eamon de Valera

Eamon de Valera made very effective use of radio as a means of communicating with Irish people at home and abroad. As the war in Europe was coming to an end, de Valera paid a highly controversial visit to the German minister in Ireland to express his condolences on the death of Hitler. In his victory broadcast, which would have been heard by many Irish people, the British prime minister Sir Winston Churchill referred to the Dublin government being left "to frolic with the German and later with the Japanese representatives to their hearts' content." De Valera's restrained response to Churchill in this speech was much admired. Joseph Lee, in his Ireland, 1912–1985: Politics and Society, *described this speech as "a magisterial performance, exquisitely tuned to the emotional needs of his flock."*

SEE ALSO de Valera, Eamon; Neutrality

Go mbeannaí Dia dhíbh, a chairde Gael. Is libhse, a Ghaelgeoirí, is ceart dom an chéad fhocal a rá. Tá an cogadh san Eoraip caite. Ba é deonú Dé, as méid A mhórthrócaire, sinn a shábháil ar an troid agus ar an doirteadh fola agus sinn a chaomhnadh ar an bhfulang atá ag céasadh furmhór tiortha na hEorpa le cúig bhliain anuas.

Níor thángamar slán ó gach cruatan ar ndóigh—is fada fairsing a théann drochiarsmaí cogaidh. Ach, nuair a chuimhnímíd ar na tíortha agus na daoine go léir mór-thimpeall orainn, is ceart dúinn ár mbuíochas croí a ghabháil go dílis dúthrachtach le Dia na Glóire as ucht sinn a chaomhnadh in am an ghábha.

An uair ba mhó a bhí an chontúirt ag bagairt orainn, d'iarras oraibhse, a Ghaela, seasamh sa mbearna bhaoil chun an náisiún a chaomhnadh. Bhí a fhios agam go mbeadh fonn ar na Gaeilgeoirí, na daoine is fearr a thuigeann céard is brí agus beatha don náisiúntacht, bheith ar tosach imeasc na bhfear a bheadh ina sciath cosanta ar thír na hÉireann.

Níor chlis sibh orm, a Ghaela. Rinne sibh bhur gcion féin den obair—an obair a rinne, faoi dheonú Dé, sinn a thabhairt slán le cúig bhliain anuas.

Caithfídh mé anois ionntó ar an mBéarla. Tá rudaí áirithe ba mhian liom a rá agus a caithfear a rá sa teanga sin.

Day of Thanksgiving

The long and fearful war which has devastated Europe has at last, mercifully, come to an end. And my first object in speaking to you tonight must be to try to express in words the gratitude to Almighty God with which all our hearts are full. I am assured that we shall be able to arrange for a day of national thanksgiving on which we may publicly express due gratitude to God for His immense mercy in our regard.

To the people of all the nations which have been directly involved in the war our thoughts go out in sympathy on their deliverance from the daily terrors in which they lived, and in sorrow that they must still endure the inevitable suffering of the aftermath. We have been spared what so many nations have had to undergo, and there lies upon us, accordingly, a duty, within our limited power, to assist in succouring those who have been less fortunate than we have been.

I have here before me the pencilled notes from which I broadcast to you on September 3, 1939. I had so many other things to do on that day that I could not find time to piece them together into a connected statement. From these notes I see that I said that, noting the march of events, your government had decided its policy the previous spring and had announced its decision to the world.

The aim of our policy, I said, would be to keep our people out of the war. I reminded you of what I had said in the Dáil, that in our circumstances, with our history and our experience after the last war and with a part of our country still unjustly severed from us, no other policy was possible.

I did not have to go into any details then as to what precisely were the circumstances to which I referred, nor had I to go into detail as to what were our experiences after the last war, nor had I to point out what a vital factor in our situation was the partition of our country. I had merely to refer to them and I felt sure you would understand. Similarly, I do not think it necessary to dwell upon them tonight.

I pointed out then that the policy adopted had the backing of practically the entire Dáil and the entire community, irrespective of any personal views which citizens held on the merits of the cause which occasioned the conflict.

The national policy then announced was thus supported by a unity rare to find amongst democratic peoples, a unity tested through two free general elections in 1943 and 1944, a unity which happily survived with us to the end. All political parties and all sections are entitled to their share of credit for what that unity has achieved. It has been a triumph of national understanding and good sense.

There were times when we stood in the gravest danger. But we have been preserved from the calamity of invasion, and such privations as we have suffered in our economic life have been by comparison very slight indeed.

The dire economic consequences which might have been anticipated were prevented by the united efforts of our people, by the co-operation of the public representatives of all parties, by hard word, by careful organisation, and by being enabled to obtain supplies from other countries, particularly Britain, the United States and Canada.

Army, Services, Thanked

I know you all feel with me the deep debt of gratitude we owe to all those who, at heavy personal sacrifice, joined the army, including the marine service, and the various auxiliary defence organisations, and helped to guard us against the most serious of all the dangers that threatened.

The officers, non-commissioned officers and men of the regular army already in service at the beginning of the war formed, with the reserve, and the volunteer force, a well-trained nucleus round which it was possible, in an incredibly short time, to build up an efficient fighting force.

Many tens of thousands of young men responded to the appeals of the government, and of the leaders of all the political parties in the Defence Conference, to join the army. Without regard to their own personal interests, these young men left their employment of the studies which they had been pursuing in preparation for professional careers.

Many thousands of others joined the local defence force and the maritime inscription and made it possible for the army to feel confident that our best-equipped striking force would be capably assisted by large bodies of well-trained men throughout the country.

The local security force, the different branches of the Air Raid Precautions Services, the Irish Red Cross Society, the St. John Ambulance Brigade, the Knights of Malta, also made themselves available to provide services without which it would not have been possible for us to face, with any degree of confidence, the dangers of the military situation outside.

To all of these, to the many other voluntary bodies who helped in the national effort and to the men of our merchant marine, who faced all the perils of the ocean to bring us essential supplies, the nation is profoundly thankful.

Trials Still Ahead

We have survived the ordeal, but I am sure you all realise that the end of the war in Europe does not mean an immediate, or even an early, ending of the period of emergency.

The world is still in a most unsettled state and what may still happen no one can prophesy. Many difficulties concerning supplies of essential goods which the war created will still continue, and there can be no relaxation of the regulations relating to the distribution or use of the commodities that have had to be kept under control.

It is indeed probable that, for a time, supplies of some important goods will be scarcer than ever. A great war is still in progress in the Far East, the requirements of which will be a first demand on the productive resources and the shipping of the countries from which, in times of peace, we were accustomed to import great quantities of goods. There is, moreover, a grave shortage of food in many European countries and a danger of famine in many parts of the continent next winter.

We cannot, therefore, safely look to other countries to make good the deficience in our own production. Not merely will international transport difficulties remain acute, but other peoples will have prior call on such supplies as may be available.

Rationing and other forms of control of the distribution and use of goods will have to be maintained so long as the scarcity continues, and can be terminated only when normal supplies are again freely available.

Must Produce All Food Possible

It is of the utmost importance, therefore, that there should be no relaxation whatever in the effort to produce all the food possible from our own soil. There is every indication that the world food situation will be very serious, not merely this year but for a considerable time to come, and that within the next few years we will have to rely on our own efforts to produce the bulk of the food required to maintain the life and the health of our people.

We must, indeed, not only reduce to a minimum our dependence on imported foodstuffs but, by increasing production, endeavor to make substantial quantities available also for peoples who have been less fortunate than ourselves.

So far as this year is concerned, the intention to provide food from our own resources to help in warding off starvation in European countries can be put into effect only by reducing the supplies available for our own consumption. This may, in fact, involve not merely the reduction for a time of the present rations of some commodities, but the extension of rationing to other commodities not now subject to control.

As to the future, there is no likelihood of any material change in the requirements in regard to compulsory tillage for the year 1946 as compared with those operations in 1945.

The difficulties which we have experienced during the past years in regard to fuel will also remain. There are no prospects whatever of any early resumption of coal imports on anything approaching a normal scale, and our domestic fuel needs and the requirements of industry must, in this coming winter, be met by turf.

The government desire to restore normal trading conditions as early as possible, and no control or regulations will be kept in force for one day longer than is strictly necessary.

The controls established by the government to prevent inflation must also be maintained for the time being. It will be remembered that it was after the end of hostilities in 1918, and because of the too early removal of the war-time checks on expenditure, that inflationary forces got out of control.

The economic disorganisation which caused so much hardship and distress in later years had its origin at that time. I know that these restrictions are irksome, but in the national interest it is for me to ask you to accept and bear them patiently until the danger is past. Again you may be certain that the government will remove them as soon as it is found safe to do so.

Reply to Mr. Churchill

Certain newspapers have been very persistent in looking for my answer to Mr. Churchill's recent broadcast. I know the kind of answer I am expected to make. I know the answer that first springs to the lips of every man of Irish blood who heard or read that speech, no matter in what circumstances or in what part of the world he found himself.

I know the reply I would have given a quarter of a century ago. But I have deliberately decided that this is not the reply I shall make tonight. I shall strive not to be guilty of adding any fuel to the flames of hatred and passion which, if continued to be fed, promise to burn up whatever is left by the war of decent human feeling in Europe.

Allowances can be made for Mr. Churchill's statement, however unworthy, in the first flush of his victo-

ry. No such excuse could be found for me in this quieter atmosphere. There are, however, some things which it is my duty to say, some things which it is essential to say. I shall try to say them as dispassionately as I can.

Mr. Churchill makes it clear that, in certain circumstances, he would have violated our neutrality and that he would justify his action by Britain's necessity. It seems strange to me that Mr. Churchill does not see that this, if accepted, would mean that Britain's necessity would become a moral code and that when this necessity became sufficiently great, other people's rights were not to count.

It is quite true that other great powers believe in this same code—in their own regard—and have behaved in accordance with it. That is precisely why we have the disastrous succession of wars—World War No.1 and World War No. 2—and shall it be World War No. 3?

Surely Mr. Churchill must see that, if his contention be admitted in our regard, a like justification can be framed for similar acts of aggression elsewhere and no small nation adjoining a great power could ever hope to be permitted go its own way in peace.

It is, indeed, fortunate that Britain's necessity did not reach the point when Mr. Churchill would have acted. All credit to him that he successfully resisted the temptation which, I have no doubt, many times assailed him in his difficulties and to which I freely admit many leaders might have easily succumbed. It is, indeed, hard for the strong to be just to the weak, but acting justly always has its rewards.

By resisting his temptation in this instance, Mr. Churchill, instead of adding another horrid chapter to the already bloodstained record of the relations between England and this country, has advanced the cause of international morality an important step—one of the most important, indeed, that can be taken on the road to the establishment of any sure basis for peace.

As far as the peoples of these two islands are concerned, it may, perhaps, mark a fresh beginning towards the realisation of that mutual comprehension to which Mr. Churchill has referred and for which he has prayed and for which, I hope, he will not merely pray but work, also, as did his predecessor [Neville Chamberlain] who will yet, I believe, find the honoured place in British history which is due to him, as certainly he will find it in any fair record of the relations between Britain and ourselves.

If England Lost Six Counties—

That Mr. Churchill should be irritated when our neutrality stood in the way of what he thought he vitally needed, I understand, but that he or any thinking person in Britain or elsewhere should fail to see the reason for our neutrality, I find it hard to conceive.

I would like to put a hypothetical question—it is a question I have to put to many Englishmen since the last war. Suppose Germany had won the war, had invaded and occupied England, and that after a long lapse of time and many bitter struggles she was finally brought to acquiesce in admitting England's right to freedom, and let England go, but not the whole of England, all but, let us say, the six southern counties.

These six southern counties, those, let us suppose, commanding the entrance to the narrow seas, Germany had singled out and insisted on holding herself with a view to weakening England as a whole and maintaining the security of her own communications through the Straits of Dover.

Let us suppose, further, that after all this had happened Germany was engaged in a great war in which she could show that she was on the side of the freedom of a number of small nations. Would Mr. Churchill as an Englishman who believed that his own nation had as good a right to freedom as any other—not freedom for a part merely, but freedom for the whole—would he, whilst Germany still maintained the partition of his country and occupied six counties of it, would he lead this partitioned England to join with Germany in a crusade? I do not think Mr. Churchill would.

Would he think the people of partitioned England an object of shame if they stood neutral in such circumstances? I do not think Mr. Churchill would.

Ireland's Lone, Long Stand

Mr. Churchill is proud of Britain's stand alone, after France had fallen and before America entered the war.

Could he not find in his heart the generosity to acknowledge that there is a small nation that stood alone, not for one year or two, but for several hundred years against aggression; that endured spoliations, famines, massacres in endless succession; that was clubbed many times into insensibility, but that each time, on returning consciousness, took up the fight anew; a small nation that could never be got to accept defeat and has never surrendered her soul?

Mr. Churchill is justly proud of his nation's perseverance against heavy odds. But we in this island are still prouder of our people's perseverance for freedom through all the centuries. We of our time have played our part in that perseverance, and we have pledged ourselves to the dead generations who have preserved intact for us this glorious heritage, that we too will strive to be faithful to the end, and pass on this tradition unblemished.

Many a time in the past there appeared little hope except that hope to which Mr. Churchill referred, that by standing fast a time would come when, to quote his own words, "the tyrant would make some ghastly mistake which would alter the whole balance of the struggle."

I sincerely trust, however, that it is not thus our ultimate unity and freedom will be achieved, though as a younger man I confess I prayed even for that, and indeed at times saw no other.

In latter years I have had a vision of a nobler and better ending, better for both our peoples and for the future of mankind. For that I have now been long working. I regret that it is not to this nobler purpose that Mr. Churchill is lending his hand rather than, by the abuse of a people who have done him no wrong, trying to find in a crisis like the present excuse for continuing the injustice of the mutilation of our country.

I sincerely hope that Mr. Churchill has not deliberately chosen the latter course but, if he has, however regretfully we may say it, we can only say, be it so.

Meanwhile, even as a partitioned small nation, we shall go on and strive to play our part in the world, continuing unswervingly to work for the cause of true freedom and for peace and understanding between all nations.

As a community which has been mercifully spared from all the major sufferings, as well as from the blinding hates and rancours engendered by the present war, we shall endeavor to render thanks to God by playing a Christian part in helping, so far as a small nation can, to bind up some of the gaping wounds of suffering humanity.

Agus anois, caithfídh mé slán a fhágáil agaibh. Nuair a bhíos ag caint libh i dtús an chogaidh, chuireas an tír agus a muintir faoi choimirce Dé agus A Mháthar Muire, agus is é mo ghuí anocht: Go raibh an choimrí chumhachtach chéanna oraibh san aimsir atá romhainn!

Radio broadcast, 16 May 1945. IRISH PRESS, 17 May 1945. Reprinted in SPEECHES AND STATEMENTS BY EAMON DE VALERA, 1917–73, edited by Maurice Moynihan (1980), pp. 471–477. Reproduced by permission of St. Martin's Press, LLC, and Gill & Macmillan, Dublin.

~

ON THE REPUBLIC OF IRELAND BILL

24 November 1948

John A. Costello

The Republic of Ireland Act marked the final stage in the undoing of the 1921 treaty insofar as that treaty restricted the independence of the Irish state. The 1937 constitution and the 1936 External Relations Act had left the British monarch with only one function—to sign the credentials of Irish diplomats. Ireland became a republic and left the Commonwealth on 18 April 1949—Easter Monday, a date chosen to signify continuity with the proclamation of a republic on Easter Monday, 1916. In his speech Costello expressed the hope that the bill would help to bring a solution to partition, but Britain responded by enacting the 1949 Ireland Act, which ensured that the status of Northern Ireland could be changed only by a majority vote of the Northern Ireland parliament.

SEE ALSO Commonwealth; Declaration of a Republic and the 1949 Ireland Act; Politics: Independent Ireland since 1922

The bill is a simple bill but it has tremendous and, I believe and hope, very beneficial results. The first section repeals the External Relations Act. I have dealt fully with that. Section Two provides: "It is hereby declared that the description of the state shall be the Republic of Ireland." That section is so obviously necessary that it requires no advocacy on my part to commend it to the Dáil. Deputies will recall that under the consitution the name of the state is Éire or, in the English language, Ireland. Now, this section does not purport, as it could not, to repeal the consitution. There is the name of the state and there is the description of the state. The name of the state is Ireland and the description of the state is the Republic of Ireland. That is the description of its constitutional and international status. Deputies are probably aware of the fact that tremendous confusion has been caused by the use of that word "Éire" in Article 4. By a misuse by malicious people of that word, "Éire," they have identified it with the twenty-six counties and not with the state that was set up under this consitution of 1937.

In documents of a legal character, such as, for instance, policies of insurance, there is always difficulty in putting in what word one wants to describe the state referred to. Section 2 provides a solution for these diffi-culties, and those malicious newspapers who want to refer in derogatory tones to this country as "Éire" and who have coined these contemptuous adjectives about it, such as "Eireannish" and "Eirish," and all the rest of it, will have to conform to the legal direction here in this bill.

Section 2 does these subsidiary things but it does more than that. It does something fundamental. It declares to the world that when this bill is passed this state is unequivocally a republic. It states that as something that cannot be controverted or argued about and we can rely, I think and I hope, on international courtesy to prevent in future this contemptuous reference to us and the name of our state being used for contemptuous purposes, as it has been, by some people and by some organs in the last few years.

Section 3 merely provides that the president, on the authority and on the advice of the government, may exercise the executive power or any executive function of the state in or in connection with its external relations. We now, and we will under this clause and under this bill, have clarified our international position. No longer will there be letters of credence sent furtively across to Buckingham Palace. Diplomatic representatives will be received by the president of Ireland, the head of the state. We now have the unambiguous position that the president is head of the state and, if there are heads of state treaties to be entered into, if he goes abroad, he will go abroad as the head of this state, the head of the Republic of Ireland.

Section 4 says:

"This Act shall come into operation on such day as the government may by Order appoint."

When this bill is enacted there will be no reason for those fears, those apprehensions which have been so assiduously set abroad by the poisonous sections of the press, but there will be certain difficulties though not of a major character. I can hardly call them difficulties because they are not difficulties but merely legal matters that have to be cleared up and which may necessitate legislation here perhaps or perhaps in Canada, Australia, or Great Britain and we must provide a time limit, a breathing space within which these matters of detail can be carried out in concord and agreement. There are no very important matters; they are matters of detail, legal technicalities, not matters of difficulty or controversy. The will take some little time. I cannot say how long it will take to have these details brought into operation and accordingly, however much we would like to see this bill come into immediate operation, we will have to have a breathing space for the various parliaments to settle up the details which require to be settled up. They are not matters of difficulty.

As I said before and now repeat, I recommend this bill to the Dáil and ask for its unanimous acceptance by the Dáil. It will, I believe, if it is passed in a spirit of goodwill, if it is passed unanimously, do and achieve what its primary purpose hopes for: to bring peace here in this part of our country and by bringing this country well on to the international stage, by lifting this problem of partition from the domestic arena and putting it on the international scene, give us not a faint hope but a clear prospect of bringing about the unity of Ireland.

I should like to say one more thing in conclusion. There have been sometimes smug, sometimes fearsome declarations by British ministers or British governments that the problem of partition is an Irish problem, that must be settled between Irishmen. That Pilate-like attitude can no longer he held by statesmen with the courage and decency to look facts in the face. This problem was created by an act of the British parliament, the Government of Ireland Act, 1920. It may be insisting on the obvious, but I have had occasion to insist very strongly on the obvious in recent months. That Act of 1920 was passed before the Treaty of 1921 and it is surprising how many people think that the partition of our country was effected by the Treaty of 1921. The problem was created by the British government and the British parliament and it is for them to solve the problem. They cannot wash their hands of it and clear themselves of responsibility for it. The Act of 1920 is a very poor title for a claim which is not based upon morality and justice. The government of the six north-eastern counties claim[s] that and assert it by virtue of a majority, a statutorily created majority, a majority created deliberately under the Act of 1920 to coerce and keep within the bounds of their so-called state masses of our Catholic people and fellow Irishmen who do no want to be there. The Act of 1920 was put on the Statute Book and brought into operation without a single vote cast in its favour by any Irish representative in the British parliament or without anybody North or South wanting it. Therefore the problem of undoing that wrong devolves upon the British government. We are doing our part down here. We are doing our part by this bill.

The whole basis of the case I make for this bill is founded on goodwill, is founded on the end of bitterness. It is founded on a sincere desire to have greater goodwill with Great Britain. We hope through the creation of that goodwill, through fostering further goodwill, that that will help materially to induce the British government and Great Britain to take a hand in the undoing of the wrong for which the predecessors were responsible in 1920. We believe that this bill, by creating conditions on which that goodwill can increase, will help towards the solution of the problem of partition.

We hold out, as I said here earlier today, the hand of friendship to the descent people of Northern Ireland and they can be assured if they come in here, end this great wrong and come into a unified Ireland, they will be doing good work for themselves, for the whole of Ireland and for that country to which they proclaim their intense loyalty, Great Britain, and the Commonwealth of Nations and be giving a lasting contribution to the peace of the world.

DÁIL DEBATES, *vol. 113, cols. 394–398, available at www.oireachtas-debates.gov.ie.*

LETTER TO JOHN A. COSTELLO, THE TAOISEACH

5 April 1951

Archbishop John Charles McQuaid

The dispute between Noël Browne, minister for health in the first interparty government from 1948 to 1951, and the Catholic hierarchy over a government medical scheme for mothers and children is one of the landmark events in the history of church-state relations in independent Ireland. Browne resigned from the cabinet, having failed to secure the support of his fellow ministers, and he released copies of the correspondence with the Catholic hierarchy to the Dublin newspapers. The episode led to the fall of the government. A reduced mother and child scheme was introduced by the Fianna Fáil government in 1953.

SEE ALSO Gaelic Catholic State, Making of; Health and Welfare since 1950, Provisions for; Language and Literacy: Irish Language since 1922; McQuaid, John Charles; Mother and Child Crisis; Political Parties in Independent Ireland; Politics: Independent Ireland since 1922; Religion: Since 1690; Roman Catholic Church: Since 1891

Dear Taoiseach,

The archbishops and bishops have considered very carefully your letter of 27th March, 1951, and the memorandum submitted by the minister for health in reply to their letter to you of 10th October, 1950.

The archbishops and bishops wish first to point out that, on 7th October, 1947, they sent to the head of government a letter in which they expressed grave disapproval of certain parts of the then recently enacted Health Act, 1947, especially those dealing with mother and child services. In sections 21–28 the public authority was given the right and duty to provide for the health of all children, to treat their ailments, to educate them in regard to health, to educate women in regard to motherhood, and to provide all women with gynaecological care. They pointed out that to claim such powers for the public authority, without qualification, is entirely and directly contrary to Catholic teaching on the rights of the family, the rights of the church in education, the rights of the medical profession and of voluntary institutions. The then taoiseach replied, deferring a fuller answer to our comments on the ground that the constitutionality of the act was being called into question.

The archbishops and bishops desire to express once again approval of a sane and legitimate health service, which will properly safeguard the health of mothers and children.

The hierarchy cannot approve of any scheme which, in its general tendency, must foster undue control by the state in a sphere so delicate and so intimately concerned with morals as that which deals with gynaecology or obstetrics and with the relations between doctor and patient.

Neither can the bishops approve of any scheme which must have for practical result the undue lessening of the proper initiative of individuals and associations and the undermining of self-reliance.

The bishops do not consider it their duty to enter into an examination of the detailed considerations put forward by the minister for health in his memorandum, save in so far as they wish to point out the fallacy of treating the proposed mother and child health scheme on a basis of parity with the provision by the state of minimum primary education, or the prevention of infectious diseases or a scheme of children's allowances.

It is to be noted that the proposed scheme fails to give clear evidence of the details of implementation. The scheme, as set forth in vague, general terms, has the appearance of conferring a benefit on the mothers and children of the whole nation.

The hierarchy must regard the scheme proposed by the minister for health as opposed to Catholic social teaching:

Firstly—In this particular scheme the state arrogates to itself a function and control, on a nationwide basis, in respect of education, more especially in the very intimate matters of chastity, individual and conjugal.

The bishops have noted with satisfaction the statement of the minister for health that he is willing to amend the scheme in this particular. It is the principle which must be amended, and it is the principle which must be set forth correctly, in a legally binding manner and in an enactment of the Oireachtas. The bishops believe that this result cannot be achieved except by the amendment of the relevant sections of the Health Act, 1947.

Secondly—In this particular scheme, the state arrogates to itself a function and control, on a nationwide basis, in respect of health services, which properly ought to be and actually can be, efficiently secured, for the vast majority of the citizens, by individual initiative and by lawful associations.

Thirdly—In this particular scheme, the state must enter unduly and very intimately into the life of patients, both parents and children, and of doctors.

Fourthly—To implement this particular scheme, the state must levy a heavy tax on the whole community, by direct or indirect methods, independently of the necessity or desire of the citizens to use the facilities provided.

Fifthly—In implementing this particular scheme by taxation, direct or indirect, the state will, in practice, morally compel the citizens to avail of the services provided.

Sixthly—This particular scheme, when enacted on a nationwide basis, must succeed in damaging gravely the self-reliance of parents, whose family-wage or income would allow them duly to provide of themselves medical treatment for their dependents.

Seventhly—In implementing this particular scheme, the state must have recourse, in great part, to ministerial regulations, as distinct from legislative enactments of the Oireachtas.

Finally, the bishops are pleased to note that no evidence has been supplied in the letter of the taoiseach that the proposed mother and child health scheme advocated by the minister for health enjoys the support of the government. Accordingly, the hierarchy have firm confidence that it will yet be possible, with reflection and calm consultation, for the government to provide a scheme which, while it affords due facilities for those whom the state, as guardian of the common good, is rightly called upon to assist, will nonetheless respect, in its principles and implementation, the traditional life and spirit of our Christian people.

We have the honour to remain, dear taoiseach,

Yours respectfully and sincerely,
(Signed on behalf of the Hierarchy of Ireland)
John C. McQuaid,
Archbishop of Dublin,
Primate of Ireland.

IRISH TIMES, *12 April 1951.*

~

FROM THE *REPORT OF THE COMMISSION ON EMIGRATION AND OTHER POPULATION PROBLEMS, 1948–1954*

1955

The Commission on Emigration and Other Population Problems was appointed in 1948 to examine various aspects of Ireland's population, but in practice it concentrated almost exclusively on emigration. Although most of its work was completed by 1950, it did not report until 1954 because the members were unable to agree on a report. The eventual report is more valuable as a historical record than as a blueprint for ending emigration; few of its recommendations were implemented.

SEE ALSO Family: Marriage Patterns and Family Life from 1690 to 1921; Migration: Emigration from 1850 to 1960; Migration: Emigration and Immigration since 1950

While the fundamental cause of emigration is economic, in most cases the decision to emigrate cannot be ascribed to any single motive but to the interplay of a number of motives. As between one person and another these motives undoubtedly differ in importance and intensity, depending on outlook, temperament, family background, education, age, sex and conjugal condition, as well as on economic, social, domestic and other circumstances. It is not possible, therefore, to attribute emigration to a single cause that would account satisfactorily for the decision to emigrate in all cases. The causes put before us in evidence were very many—principally economic, but also social, political, cultural and psychological. . . .

There has been a great demand for labour in the United States of America and more recently in Great Britain, countries which, in general, presented the Irish emigrant with no difficulties of language or barriers due to race, thus causing him a minimum of personal and social adjustment in his new environment. The existence of employment opportunities more attractive than those at home became increasingly well known—in the case of America from the family connections which have continued since the original heavy post-Famine emigration to that continent, and in the case of Great Britain because of its proximity and easy accessibility. . . .

Generally throughout the country there is a lack of opportunities for employment to absorb the natural increase of the population. . . .

The other principal reason for emigration is the desire for improved material standards together with a dissatisfaction with life on the land, whether in its economic or its social aspects. Migration from rural to urban areas is a feature common in most countries, but it does not always bring about a progressive decline in the numbers remaining on the land as in this country . . . nowadays, fewer people are satisfied with a subsistence standard of living and they find an easy alternative in emigration. Very small holdings of poor or marginal land are tending to become amalgamated. Modern technology can provide rising material standards of life more easily in urban than in rural areas and hence, the world over, life in agricultural districts is proving less attractive. In the eyes of many, particularly of those who do not own a farm, agriculture has serious disadvantages; it does not appear to provide a sufficient income, it makes great demands on time, and it involves much physical effort in return for relatively small remuneration. . . .

While the fundamental causes of emigration are economic, social amenities are also an important factor. There are differences between rural and urban areas in the standards and availability of housing as well as in services such as electricity, water supplies and transport. . . . Again, modern urban life has developed high standards of organised entertainment and a wide range of recreational facilities. By contrast, and particularly to the young mind, rural areas appear dull, drab, monotonous, backward and lonely—a view, however, many would regard as superficial. . . .

Tradition and example have also been very powerful influences. Emigration of some members of the family has almost become part of the established custom of the people in certain areas—a part of the generally accepted pattern of life. For very many emigrants there was a traditional path "from the known to the known," that is to say, from areas where they lived to places where their friends and relations awaited them. This path they followed as a matter of course without even looking for suitable employment in this country . . .

Apart from tradition and example, there is a widespread awareness of the existence of opportunities abroad and a realisation of differences between conditions at home and in other countries. This is confirmed and encouraged by the reports of emigrants who return well-dressed and with an air of prosperity, by glowing accounts in letters of high incomes and easy conditions and by practical demonstration in the remittances which are sent home. These accounts, which rarely paint any other side of the picture—and there is another side to it—are frequently exaggerated, and make a strong impression on the minds of young people. . . .

Although female emigration, like male, is the result of a variety of causes, the purely economic cause is not always dominant. For the female emigrant improvement in personal status is of no less importance than the higher wages and better conditions of employment abroad and some of the evidence submitted to us would suggest that the prospect of better marriage opportunities is also an influence of some significance. Large numbers of girls emigrate to domestic service in Great Britain because they consider that the wages, conditions of work and also the status of domestic service in this country are unsatisfactory. Many others emigrate because the opportunities of obtaining factory or office work are better than here, and in the nursing profession numbers leave the country because the remuneration, facilities for training, pension schemes and hours of work in this country are considered to be unattractive. . . .

While some emigrants have deliberately weighed the pros and cons, and have come to the conclusion that on balance they will be better off elsewhere, others emigrate for different reasons. A natural desire for adventure of change, and eagerness to travel, to see the world and share the enjoyments of modern city life, to secure financial independence by having pocket money and by being free to spend it in one's own way, to obtain freedom from parental control and a privacy not obtainable in one's home environment, to be free to choose one's own way of life—such matters affect a proportion of young people everywhere and they appeal strongly in a country where there has been, for so many years, an established tradition of emigration.

Reprinted in THE FIELD DAY ANTHOLOGY OF IRISH WRITING, *vol. 5,* IRISH WOMEN'S WRITING AND TRADITIONS, *edited by Angela Bourke et al. (2002), pp. 583–584.*

~

FROM *ECONOMIC DEVELOPMENT*

1958

Economic Development was the personal initiative of T. K. Whitaker, the secretary of the Department of Finance, as a response to the economic crisis facing Ireland in the 1950s, a crisis that led to a record level of emigration and a loss of morale. His report prompted the Irish government to draw up a program for economic expansion, which set modest targets for economic growth and outlined measures designed to transform the Irish economy from protectionism toward free trade and attracting foreign investment.

SEE ALSO *Economic Development*, 1958; Economic Relations between Independent Ireland and Britain; Economies of Ireland, North and South, since 1920

1. . . . It is well to reiterate here that the aim is not to draw up a detailed five or ten-year plan of national development. For a small country so exposed to the perpetual flux of world economic forces there would be little sense in trying to establish a rigid pattern of development. The aim is rather (a) to highlight the main deficiencies and potentialities of the economy and (b) to suggest the principles to be followed to correct the deficiencies and realise the opportunities, indicating a number of specific forms of productive development which appear to offer good long-term prospects. One must be prepared at all times to fluctuations and upsets. A readiness to adapt to changing conditions is a *sine qua non* of material progress. Nevertheless, one may reasonably hope to find some guiding principles which it would be advantageous to follow through thick and thin.

2. While planning in rigid sense is not useful in our circumstances, there can be no doubt about the wisdom of looking ahead and trying to direct national policy along the most productive lines. A year is too restricted a frame of reference for policy decisions. Their effects overflow such arbitrary boundaries. It is, of course, necessary to see parliamentary approval year by year for financial policy as indicated in the annual budget. But this yearly process, if it is to be fully effective in contributing to national development, must be set in a much broader framework. An attempt should be made to secure a more general coordination of financial and economic policy with a view to the maximum progress being made in the years

immediately ahead. Otherwise, unintended but damaging inconsistencies and conflicts can only too easily arise. . . .

4. Apart from its obvious value in making policy more long-term and logical, forward thinking is particularly urgent and necessary for other reasons. It is apparent that we have come to a critical and decisive point in our economic affairs. The policies hitherto followed, though given a fair trial, have not resulted in a viable economy. We have power, transport facilities, public services, houses, hospitals and a general "infrastructure" on a scale which is reasonable by western European standards, yet large-scale emigration and unemployment still persist. The population is falling, the national income rising more slowly than in the rest of Europe. A great and sustained effort to increase production, employment and living standards is necessary to avert economic decadence.

5. The possibility of freer trade in Europe carries disquieting implications for some Irish industries and raises special problems of adaptation and adjustment. It necessitates also a re-appraisal of future industrial and agricultural prospects. It seems clear that, sooner or later, protection will have to go and the challenge of free trade be accepted. There is really no other choice for a country wishing to keep pace materially with the rest of Europe. It would be a policy of despair to accept that our costs of production must permanently be higher than those of other European countries, either in industry or in agriculture. Our level of real incomes depends on our competitive efficiency. If that must be lower than in the rest of Europe we should have to be content with relatively low living standards. With the alternative of emigration available we are unlikely, either as a community or as individuals, to accept such a situation for long unless it is seen as an essential part of a programme of national regeneration. The effect of any policy entailing relatively low living standards here for all time would be to sustain and stimulate the outflow of emigrants and in the end jeopardise our economic independence. Any little benefit obtained in terms of employment in protected non-competitive industries would be outweighed by losses through emigration and general economic impoverishment. If we do not expand production on a competitive basis, we shall fail to provide the basis necessary for the economic independence and material progress of the community. Even a spectacular increase in efficiency and output will still leave us for a long time at a relative disadvantage to Britain and many other countries in respect of real income per head of the population. Indeed, if we are to catch up at all, our annual rate of improvement must exceed theirs.

6. Our economic progress requires that more resources be devoted to productive purposes. But there is as yet no agreement on a systematic programme of development. There is need for urgent determination of the productive purposes to which resources should be applied and of the unproductive, or relatively unproductive, activities which can, with the minimum social disadvantage, be curtailed to set free resources for productive development.

7. It is well to state that by "productive investment" in this study is meant investment yielding an adequate return to the national economy as a whole. Private investment is not normally undertaken unless there appears to be a fair prospect of financial success, that is, of the investment producing commodities saleable at competitive prices. In the case of public investment, the term "productive" cannot be limited to investments yielding an adequate direct return to the exchequer. It extends also to investment which enlarges the national income by creating a flow of goods and services which are saleable without the aid of subsidies; for this will result indirectly in revenue to pay debt charges. Whether the first test is satisfied is easy to establish, but the second is often a matter of doubt. It is clear that, where neither test is satisfied and part, if not all, of the cost of servicing the capital must be met by a levy on the taxpayer, the investment results in a redistribution rather an increase in national income. Progress in the building up of real national income depends on capital and labour being devoted to industrial and agricultural development, particularly for export, rather than to the provision of welfare services for home consumption. In an expanding economy, where real incomes are rising and the demand for goods and services is growing, opportunities for useful and continuing employment will arise automatically and, as has been shown in Germany since the war, a progressive improvement in social amenities will be possible without undue strain on the economy.

8. It should be added that there is no conflict between what are termed "socially desirable" and "economic" objectives. "Socially desirable" objectives will not be permanently realised merely by increasing "social" investment. The erection of houses, schools and hospitals—socially desirable in themselves—will, of course, provide employment but the employment ceases once the period of construction is over and the unemployed man is then left with an amenity which, if he remains unemployed, will contribute but little to his standard of living. Investment which is not productive may provide employment but it does so only for a time and at the cost of weakening the capacity of the economy as a whole to provide lasting and self-

sustaining employment. For these reasons the emphasis must be on productive investment, though not, of course, to the exclusion of all social investment. The permanent increase in employment associated with an expansion of real national output is to be preferred to the purely temporary increase which is all that non-productive investment, entailing a mere redistribution of existing incomes, can bring about.

9. Without positive action by the government, a slowing down in housing and certain other forms of so-cial investment will occur from now on because needs are virtually satisfied over wide areas of the state. This decline in building will cause a reduction in employ-ment. The continuance of large-scale investment in housing or other forms of social building would not, however, be justified merely to create artificial employ-ment opportunities. If the objective of an expanding economy is not to be jeopardised, the right course is to replace social investment by productive investment which will provide self-sustaining and permanent em-ployment. This means that no time can be lost in devis-ing a realistic long-term programme of productive in-vestment.

10. In the context of a programme of economic de-velopment extending over five years or longer, it would be easier not only to avoid inconsistencies between indi-vidual decisions but also to secure acceptance of deci-sions which, presented in isolation, might arouse strong opposition. It would be more apparent to all sections of the community that certain adjustments of present pol-icy were necessary and it would be less difficult to have efforts made and sacrifices borne if they were seen to be a necessary contribution to national welfare and were not in danger of being nullified by neglect or extrava-gance elsewhere.

11. A further reason for careful mapping of future economic policy is that we have no longer the surplus resources with which to meet deficits in external pay-ments. Our wartime accumulation of sterling reserves has been run down. Our postwar dollar borrowings have been spent. But our balance of payments remains unstable. The present state of balance is exceptional—the year 1957 being the first year since 1946 in which a deficit was not recorded—and it is insecure. The equi-librium attained is at a depressed level of domestic eco-nomic activity and is due in part to the using up of stocks. A reduction in supplies of cattle, a fall in their ex-port price, and rising money incomes and expenditures, due to wage and salary increases, are only some of the factors capable of disturbing this precarious balance and causing renewed loss of national capital. In fact, the im-port excess has been tending to increase since August 1957. It is, therefore, of the greatest importance that

policy be concentrated henceforth on the development of productive capacity, so as to sustain and strengthen our economic position and external purchasing power. To allow social services or non-productive forms of ex-penditure priority over productive projects would cause a misdirection of resources and increase the difficulties of development by raising our production costs, artifi-cially stimulating our imports and putting us in deficit again with the rest of the world.

12. There is also a sound *psychological* reason for having an integrated development programme. The ab-sence of such a programme tends to deepen the all-too-prevalent mood of despondency about the country's fu-ture. A sense of anxiety is, indeed, justified. But it can too easily degenerate into feelings of frustration and de-spair. After 35 years of native government people are asking whether we can achieve an acceptable degree of economic progress. The common talk amongst parents in the towns, as in rural Ireland, is of their children hav-ing to emigrate as soon as their education is completed in order to be sure of a reasonable livelihood. To the chil-dren themselves and to many already in employment the jobs available at home look unattractive by compar-ison with those obtainable in such variety and so readily elsewhere. All this seems to be setting up a vicious cir-cle—of increasing emigration, resulting in a smaller do-mestic market depleted of initiative and skill, and a re-duced incentive, whether for Irishmen or foreigners, to undertake and organise the productive enterprises which alone can provide increased employment oppor-tunities and higher living standards. There is, therefore, a real need at present to buttress confidence in the coun-try's future and to stimulate the interest and enthusi-asm of the young in particular. A general resurgence of will may be helped by setting up targets of national en-deavour which appear to be reasonably attainable and mutually consistent. This is an aspect of good leader-ship. But there is nothing to be gained by setting up fan-ciful targets. Failure to reach such targets would merely produce disillusionment and renew the mood of nation-al despondency. Realism also demands an awareness that, at present, and for a long time ahead, the material reward for work here may be less than that obtainable elsewhere but that there are many countervailing ad-vantages in living in Ireland. No programme of develop-ment can be effective unless it generates increased effort, enterprise and saving on the part of a multitude of indi-viduals. Its eventual success or failure will depend pri-marily on the individual reactions of the Irish people. If they have not the will to develop, even the best possible programme is useless.

13. A concerted and comprehensive programme aimed at a steady progress in material welfare, even

though supported by the churches and other leaders of opinion, could only be successful if the individual members of the community were realistic and patriotic enough to accept the standard of living produced by their own exertions here, even if it should continue for some time to be lower than the standard available abroad. Otherwise the possibility of economic progress scarcely exists.

14. For all these reasons the importance of the next five to ten years for the economic and political future of Ireland cannot be overstressed. Policies should be re-examined without regard to past views or commitments. It is desirable to remind ourselves that at all times in a nation's history decisions have to be taken; that there is no guarantee when they are taken that they will prove right; and that the greatest fault lies in pursuing a policy after it has proved to be unsuitable or ineffective. What matters above all is to understand the present position and find the best and quickest ways of improving it.

15. This study is intended to help in the preparation of a programme of economic development. Information which may be useful in this connection is assembled for ease of reference. . . . No programme of development can be regarded as realistic which is not founded on a reasonable assessment of the resources likely to be available to finance it. The closer analysis of agriculture, fisheries, industry and tourism is intended to indicate the general lines of development which can most effectively be followed over the next five years or so. . . .

16. It may, perhaps, be said here that problems of economic development are exercising the minds of statesmen, economists, scientists, and administrators all over the world. It is clear that development can be accelerated by government policy but how this can best be done is by no means obvious. It is reasonable to suppose that the solution must vary according to the circumstances of individual countries. Economists have not so far developed any general theory of economic development. . . .

18. . . . A *dynamic* has to be found and released and it is not necessarily increased capital investment, though this may be called for to support a higher rate of development once it is set in motion. It would, indeed, be a mistake to think that a faster rate of increase in output is a matter simply of stepping up the volume of home investment. It is true that there is a close relationship between output per head and the amount of capital per head but there are other conditions of economic progress no less important than increased capitalisation. The first of these is the development of a better appreciation of the dependence of material progress on in-

dividual output. Others are a raising of the general level of education, health and skill, the loosening of restrictive practices, whether of employers or employees, the practical encouragement of initiative and enterprise, the adoption of improved methods, techniques and principles of organisation and management both in agriculture and industry, and a greater readiness to apply scientific advances. Attention to matters such as these may yield even greater increases in production than direct capitalisation in the form of new plant and machinery though this does not, of course, imply that increased capitalisation is not also required. It is essential for sustained and balanced progress that an increase in productive capital should be supported not only by advances in education and technical training but also—though these are not short in Ireland—by the provision of basic utilities and amenities, including power supplies, good housing and transport services. Harmonious development calls also for suitable fiscal and monetary policies designed to increase the supply of savings and the incentive to invest in productive enterprises. As between countries, differences in climate, political institutions, educational and technical facilities, individual attitudes to work, trade union outlook and policy can be as important as differences in natural resources or in the volume of investment in causing divergent rates of development. Economic growth is, in fact, a complex process depending on social, psychological and political as well as economic and technical factors. In Ireland, the trend of population is an important factor inasmuch as dynamism and flexibility are rarely associated with a declining home population, whereas even a stable population would have good prospects of economic advance if its exports were competitive.

19. This study suggests that, given favourable public policies and private dispositions, a dynamic of progress awaits release in agriculture, fisheries, industry and tourism. It is hoped that it will be possible to set this force to work simultaneously in these major branches of the Irish economy. The opportunities of development may not be great enough to give all who are born in Ireland a standard of living they would accept—though there are advantages of living here not to be reckoned in money terms—but such as they are they should be exploited. It is not unreasonable to hope that sufficient advance can be made in the next decade not merely to consolidate our economic independence but to enable us to provide higher material standards for a rising population. . . .

21. In pressing on with this study, despite the claims of ordinary office work, it has been an inspiration to turn to the following words of the Bishop of Clonfert, Most Rev. Dr. Philbin:—

Our version of history has tended to make us think of freedom as an end in itself and of independent government—like marriage in a fairy story—as the solution of all ills. Freedom is useful in proportion to the use we make of it. We seem to have relaxed our patriotic energies just at the time when there was most need to mobilise them. Although our enterprise in purely spiritual fields has never been greater, we have shown little initiative or organisational ability in agriculture and industry and commerce. There is here the widest and most varied field for the play of the vital force that our religion contains.

This study is a contribution, in the spirit advocated by the Bishop of Clonfert, towards the working out of the national good in the economic sphere. It is hoped that, supplemented by productive ideas from other sources, it will help to dispel despondency about the country's future. We can afford our present standard living, which is so much higher than most of the inhabitants of this world enjoy. Possibilities of improvement are there, if we wish to realise them. It would be well to shut the door on the past and to move forward, energetically, intelligently and with the will to succeed, but without expecting miracles of progress in a short time.

Department of Finance, ECONOMIC DEVELOPMENT, *November 1958, pp. 1, 2–6, 7–8, 9.*

~

"AN IRISHMAN IN COVENTRY"

1960

John Hewitt

Born to an old Protestant family in Belfast in 1907, John Hewitt (d. 1987) was educated at Queen's University and served as Art Assistant at the Belfast Museum and Art Gallery from 1930 to 1957. His failure to obtain the directorship of the Ulster Museum and Art Gallery in 1953 led to depression and marital problems. He considered his appointment as director of the Coventry Art Gallery "one of the best things that happened to me," remaining in that post from 1957 to 1972, when he returned to Belfast, where he greatly influenced the subsequent generation of Ulster poets, including Seamus Heaney, Michael Longley, and Derek Mahon. His exile in Coventry led to one of his most

beautiful, and often anthologized, poems, printed here. A leftist, humanist, and essayist, he affirmed his Irish identity in his monographs on the regional painters and poets of Ulster, including Rhyming Weavers and Other Country Poets of Antrim and Down *(1974), based on his M.A. thesis.* The Planter and the Gael *(1970) grew out of a reading series that he did with the Catholic poet John Montague.*

SEE ALSO Arts: Modern Irish and Anglo-Irish Literature and the Arts since 1800; Diaspora: The Irish in Britain; Poetry, Modern

A full year since, I took this eager city,
the tolerance that laced its blatant roar,
its famous steeples and its web of girders,
as image of the state hope argued for,
and scarcely flung a bitter thought behind me
on all that flaws the glory and the grace
which ribbons through the sick, guilt-clotted legend
of my creed-haunted, godforsaken race.
My rhetoric swung round from steel's high promise
to the precision of the well-gauged tool,
tracing the logic in the vast glass headlands,
the clockwork horse, the comprehensive school.

Then, sudden, by occasion's chance concerted,
in enclave of my nation, but apart,
the jigging dances and the lilting fiddle
stirred the old rage and pity in my heart.
The faces and the voices blurring round me,
the strong hands long familiar with the spade,
the whiskey-tinctured breath, the pious buttons,
called up a people endlessly betrayed
by our own weakness, by the wrongs we suffered
in that long twilight over bog and glen,
by force, by famine and by glittering fables
which gave us martyrs when we needed men,
by faith which had no charity to offer,
by poisoned memory, and by ready wit,
with poverty corroded into malice,
to hit and run and howl when it is hit.
This is our fate; eight hundred years' disaster,
crazily tangled as the Book of Kells;
the dream's distortion and the land's division,
the midnight raiders and the prison cells.
Yet like Lir's children banished to the waters
our hearts still listen for the landward bells.

THE COLLECTED POEMS OF JOHN HEWITT, *edited by Frank Ormsby (1991), pp. 97–98. Reproduced by permission of Blackstaff Press.*

~

Speech to Ministers of the Governments of the Member States of the European Economic Community

18 January 1962

Seán Lemass

The decision to apply for membership in the European Economic Community (EEC) was an important step in Ireland's transition from isolation to closer involvement in international economic and political organizations. When French president Charles de Gaulle vetoed Britain's application for membership in January 1963, Ireland's application effectively lapsed and was not renewed until the late 1960s. Ireland eventually became a member of the EEC on 1 January 1973. Ireland was the first country to join the EEC that was not a member of NATO.

SEE ALSO Agriculture: After World War I; Economic Relations between Independent Ireland and Britain; European Union; Lemass, Seán; Neutrality; Overseas Investment; Politics: Independent Ireland since 1922

Mr. Chairman:

1. I would like, at the outset, on behalf of the government of Ireland, to thank you for your kindness in arranging this meeting. We appreciate very much the opportunity you have thus provided for an exchange of views on Ireland's application for membership of the European Economic Community with the representatives of the governments of the member states. I hope that what I shall say will be of help to you in considering our application. I am also pleased that the commission is represented at this meeting.

2. Ireland belongs to Europe by history, tradition and sentiment no less than by geography. Our destiny is bound up with that of Europe and our outlook and our way of life have for fifteen centuries been moulded by the Christian ideals and the intellectual and cultural values on which European civilisation rests. Our people have always tended to look to Europe for inspiration, guidance and encouragement.

3. It is thus natural that we in Ireland should regard with keen and sympathetic interest every genuine effort to bring the peoples of Europe closer together, so as to strengthen the foundations of our common civilisation.

We were happy at the development in the years following the last war of a strong movement towards closer European union; and we have participated actively from the outset in the two organisations established to promote cooperation between European states, the Organisation for European Economic Cooperation and the Council of Europe. While Ireland did not accede to the North Atlantic Treaty, we have always agreed with the general aim of that Treaty. The fact that we did not accede to it was due to special circumstances and does not qualify in any way our acceptance of the ideal of European unity and of the conception, embodied in the Treaty of Rome and the Bonn Declaration of 18 July last, of the duties, obligations and responsibilities which European unity would impose.

4. The Treaty of Rome, as an expression of the ideal of European unity, brought into being a more closely integrated organisation than either the Council of Europe or the Organisation for European Economic Cooperation. Political considerations, we know, played a considerable part in the motivation and the successful outcome of the negotiations for the Treaty and the aims of the European Economic Community go much beyond purely economic matters. The contracting parties in the preamble to the Treaty affirmed their determination to lay the foundations of an ever closer union between European peoples and their resolve to strengthen, by combining their resources, the safeguards of peace and freedom. Their call to other peoples of Europe to join in their effort was addressed to those "who share their ideal." In the Bonn Declaration, they reaffirmed their resolve to develop their political cooperation with a view to the union of their peoples and set in motion procedures designed to give statutory form to this union.

5. It was in full awareness of these facts and, in particular, of the importance attached by the member states to political objectives, that my government, in the letter of 31 July 1961, applying for admission to the Community under Article 237 of the Treaty, declared that we share the ideals which inspired the parties to the Treaty and accept the aims of the Community as set out therein, as well as the action proposed to achieve those aims.

6. I desire to emphasise that the political aims of the Community are aims to which the Irish government and people are ready to subscribe and in the realisation of which they wish to play an active part. As I have already said, the Irish nation has always had a strong sense of belonging to Europe. We are also very conscious of the great advantages which can accrue to all the countries concerned and to world peace from a strong and united Europe. These considerations were an important factor in the decision taken by my govern-

ment in July. That decision was discussed at the time in our national parliament and, I am happy to say, met with almost unanimous approval. But long before the formal decision was taken the European Economic Community and our position in relation to it were matters of wide public interest and debate. I can, therefore, say that our application not only represents a deliberate decision on the part of the government but also corresponds to the sentiments of our people generally.

7. My government are in full agreement with the purposes of the Community as defined in Article 2 and will most readily work with the member states in the accomplishment of these purposes by the methods prescribed in Article 3. We also agree that the achievement of the tasks entrusted to the Community be assured by the institutions set up under Article 4.

8. As regards the economic aspects of membership of the Community, I propose to deal first with agriculture, which has a particularly important place in our economy. It generates about one-quarter of the national income, employs over one-third of the gainfully-occupied population, and is responsible, directly or indirectly, for three-quarters of our exports. With the development of industry these proportions will decline, but for Ireland agriculture will always be of major importance. We are, naturally, anxious that, through membership of the European Economic Community, Ireland should be able to look forward to a balanced development of agriculture and industry.

9. We have studied with interest and attention the agricultural provisions of the Treaty of Rome and the proposals of the commission for a common agricultural policy. We agree with the aims and principles set out in the Treaty and are in sympathy with the basic features of the commission's proposals. We note that the common agricultural policy is intended, when fully implemented, to provide rational and orderly conditions of trading in a unified market, so that efficient farmers in member countries would have equal marketing opportunities under a uniform price structure. The sociological concepts which underlie the agricultural policy of the Community, and in particular the emphasis placed on the maintenance of viable family farms, also appeal to us as our rural society is based on the family farm and on ownership of the land by the occupier. The governments of the member states may, therefore, be assured that we would play a constructive and cooperative part in the evolution and implementation of the Community's agricultural policy.

10. We do not, of course, assert that we have no agricultural problems. While the average size of agricultural holding in Ireland is somewhat higher than in most continental countries and there is relatively little fragmentation of holdings, there are, as in other countries, variations in soil fertility and site of holding in different regions. In some districts where structural reorganisation has been in progress for many years it may be desirable to accelerate this activity and widen its scope in accordance with the commission's proposals. Our horticultural industry is of rather recent growth and may not find it easy to adapt itself rapidly to common market conditions. It is not our intention, however, to seek any arrangements in relation to such matters which would be inconsistent with the common agricultural policy.

11. Our principal concern in the agricultural sphere relates to the manner in which British agricultural and food import policy will be harmonised with that of the Community. As you know, a high proportion of our agricultural exports goes to the United Kingdom, and we have long-standing trade agreements which reflect our economic relations with that country. We realise that, when a common agricultural policy is in full operation in an enlarged Community including—as we hope it will—the United Kingdom and Ireland, our economic arrangements with the United Kingdom would become merged in a greater whole, but we expect that in the normal course of things the United Kingdom market will continue to provide an outlet for a considerable proportion of our agricultural exports. The nature of the arrangements which have yet to be settled in relation to the agricultural and food import policy of the United Kingdom in the context of her membership of the common market will be of vital concern to us.

12. We also export agricultural and fishery products to the present members of the European Economic Community, and in some cases this trade is the subject of bilateral agreements between Ireland and member states. We note that Article 45 of the Rome Treaty envisages the conclusion of long-term agreements or contracts between exporting and importing countries as a means of expanding trade during the transitional period, but that such arrangements must be concluded during the first stage. We recognise, however, that in general, bilateral policies are not consonant with the basic ideas and aims of the Rome Treaty. It is not, therefore, our intention, if we are admitted to the Community, to seek to extend or add to existing bilateral agreements with the other members, since we assume that the development of agricultural trade within the Community will proceed henceforth on a multilateral basis as envisaged in the Treaty of Rome and in the proposals of the commission. Should it be decided, however, in relation to the admission of any other country to membership of the Community that bilateral agricultural agreements between members should be allowed as a transi-

tional measure, then we would, of course, assume that such arrangements would be open to Ireland as well.

13. This concludes what I have to say on the subject of agriculture. In this important if difficult field, as in all others, we look forward to active and constructive collaboration with the other members in their efforts to overcome the problems arising in putting into effect a common agricultural policy in accordance with the objectives of the Treaty.

14. Turning now to the position of Irish industry, I shall begin with a few general remarks. For historical reasons, the industrial development of Ireland was retarded until well on in the present century. To hasten progress in industrialisation under our own governments it was necessary to rely on a policy of protection. Industrial capacity, though it has been steadily increasing, still makes a smaller contribution to national output and employs a smaller proportion of the working population than in the Community generally. In recent years special efforts have been made to achieve a higher degree of economic activity and better balance in the economy as between industry and agriculture. A Programme for Economic Expansion initiated in 1958, the objectives of which are entirely consistent with those of the Community, has had encouraging results. The volume increase in gross national product, which averaged only 1 percent per annum in the preceding decade, amounted to 4.5 percent in 1959, 5 percent in 1960 and not less than 5 percent, it is estimated, in 1961. The greater part of this expansion is attributable to the industrial sector. For manufacturing industry rates of growth of 6 percent and 7 percent were achieved in 1959 and 1960, respectively, and the estimate for 1961 is almost 9 percent, a rate of expansion amongst the highest in Western Europe. The economic growth of recent years has been achieved in conditions of equilibrium in Ireland's international payments.

15. These results confirm not only the considerable scope for economic development in Ireland but the capacity of Irish initiative and effort, augmented by Western European enterprise, to exploit the existing potentialities. We have an economic and social infrastructure capable of supporting a much greater degree of industrial development. We also enjoy conditions of political and social stability conducive to maintenance of the higher rate of economic growth achieved in recent years. There is, therefore, good ground for the belief that a total increase in production of 50 percent by 1970 is within the capacity of the Irish economy; in other words, that Ireland can reach the collective target recently set by the members of the Organisation for Economic Cooperation and Development.

16. The lower income per head than in highly industrialised countries, the smallness of the home market, and the hitherto downward trend in population made it all the more necessary to achieve export outlets as a condition of the continued growth of industry and of the economy generally. Government policy has been directed towards helping exporters over their initial difficulties. Domestic exports of industrial raw materials and manufactured goods have risen from £25 million in 1958 to almost £50 million in 1961. This I believe, demonstrates the growing competitive capacity of Irish industry.

17. It is, however, important that the industries thus already advancing, despite various handicaps, be enabled to consolidate their position and that those not yet fully competitive be helped to make the changes necessary to ensure progress in an increasingly competitive environment. The Irish government intend to promote energetically the adaptation of Irish industry to common market conditions. A comprehensive series of industrial surveys has been initiated to analyse the situation of particular industries and devise positive measures of adjustment and adaptation. Furthermore, the review now proceeding of our Programme for Economic Expansion will take account of the obligations which Ireland will have to assume as a member of the Community and will ensure that in the new conditions progress towards the objectives of the programme will be maintained.

18. External trade, particularly trade with Western Europe, is of great importance to Ireland's economy. Exports represent almost one-quarter of gross national product, while imports exceed one-third. In relation to gross national product, Ireland's external trade is the second highest in Europe. Four-fifths of our exports go to, and almost two-thirds of our imports come from, the United Kingdom and the present member states of the Community. As far as industrial exports are concerned, we have enjoyed for many years in the British market conditions of free entry similar to those which the Rome Treaty will have established between the member states when the common market is finally in being. These advantages we shall henceforth be sharing progressively with many continental countries. We are, therefore, disposed to look to continental Europe for new scope and opportunity for the expansion of industrial exports. As yet, our export trade in industrial products to the Continent is small. Indeed, there is at present a significant lack of balance in our general trade relations with the Community; we import from the existing members over three times as much as we export to them.

19. Having thus described the general position of the Irish economy and the present state of Ireland's industrial development, I now propose to give some general indications of our capacity to accept the obligations of the Treaty in the industrial field.

20. Approximately two-thirds of our imports from the Community enter Ireland free of any protective duty or quantitative restriction. As a general rule, we impose no duties or import restrictions on industrial raw materials or on capital goods such as plant and machinery. In respect of fiscal duties, we anticipate that we shall be able to match the reductions already made by the member states and to keep pace with them in the future. It is intended to replace industrial quantitative restrictions, as soon as possible, by tariffs of no greater, and probably less, restrictive effect. In respect of protective tariffs, the Irish government would hope that the member states would find it possible to agree to an appropriate general rhythm of tariff reductions to operate from the date of Ireland's accession to the end of the transitional period. It is only reasonable, however, to envisage that, despite their own best endeavours and state aids, some basically sound industries might find it too difficult to comply fully with this rhythm. The Irish government would hope that a solution could be found for cases of this kind either under Article 226 of the Treaty or under the provisions of a protocol dealing generally with the subject of tariff reductions. . . .

29. . . . As a country small in extent, population and production, Ireland would not represent, in terms of statistics, any considerable addition to the Community. We do feel, however, that we have a contribution to make to the accomplishment of the Community's design for a new European society. . . .

National Archives of Ireland, Government Information Services, GIS 1/216.

~

ON COMMUNITY RELATIONS IN NORTHERN IRELAND

28 April 1967

Terence O'Neill

This article by Northern Ireland prime minister Terence O'Neill was addressed to a British audience and can be read as an attempt to gain British support for his policies. By 1967, O'Neill was coming under attack from nationalists, who were dissatisfied with the slow pace of change, *whereas an increasing number of unionists were becoming uneasy about O'Neill's overtures to Dublin and to the nationalist community in Northern Ireland.*

SEE ALSO Irish Republican Army (IRA); Lemass, Seán; Northern Ireland: History since 1920; Northern Ireland: Policy of the Dublin Government from 1922 to 1969; O'Neill, Terence; Politics: Nationalist Politics in Northern Ireland; Ulster Unionist Party in Office

It is a truism that Northern Ireland has long had a divided community. The reasons for this division are rooted in the long sequence of historical events connecting the destinies of Ireland and Great Britain. However those events may be interpreted, they do demonstrate with absolute clarity the fact that Irish problems are deep-seated and not amenable to facile external solutions, however well intentioned. When, by an irony of history, the one area of Ireland which had consistently resisted home rule was the only part left to operate a home rule parliament, it was unfortunate but perhaps inevitable that opinion polarized on a religious basis. This polarisation tended to push both sides into extreme attitudes.

The majority, loyal by tradition and sentiment to its British heritage, regarded the minority as a disloyal "Trojan Horse" in its midst, intent only upon subverting the constitution and merging Ulster in an independent All-Ireland Republic. The minority, seeing in the new government merely a perpetuation of the historic Protestant ascendancy, withdrew into attitudes ranging from detachment to outright hostility. Northern Ireland simply cannot be understood unless it is appreciated that regularly over the years actual physical violence has been used as a political weapon: that as recently as 1956–62 a campaign of IRA terrorism caused six deaths, thirty-four injuries and over £1 million worth of damage to property: and that for much of the period of the state's existence a substantial minority of its people have failed clearly to dissociate themselves from such activities.

At this point the reader may well comment that all too often in any discussion of Irish affairs one becomes lost in a lengthy historical preamble, long before reaching the present day. That is not my intention. I mention this background merely to put current events in their proper setting and perspective.

What was the position when I took office in 1963? The largest opposition party attending the Northern Ireland House of Commons, the Nationalist Party, had declined the role to which its numbers clearly entitled it, leaving a four-man Northern Ireland Labour Party to discharge the role of official opposition. Throughout society the hostility and suspicion of more than three decades still persisted very widely, although beginning to break down in more educated circles. This divide within society was paralleled by another in external politics, because not since partition had a prime minister of Northern Ireland met his opposite number in Dublin.

It was clearly time for a change, and the whole basis of my political effort of the last four years—with the help and support of my colleagues in the government—has been to demonstrate that the historic divisions cannot be allowed forever to stand in the way of that community spirit without which we will never realize our full economic or social potential.

That is why I regretted so much in *The Times'* article, to cite one example, the reference to Lord Craigavon's remark about "a Protestant parliament for a Protestant people." This had some relevance in its historic setting of the troubled twenties, but it is no more representative of the present spirit of Ulster Unionist politics than the declarations of Stanley Baldwin are of conservatism in the sixties. What are the facts? By inviting the prime minister of the Irish Republic, Mr. Seán Lemass, to Stormont I ended an absurd mini cold war and made possible a whole series of useful exchanges between ministers on both sides of the border. This did not mean any weakening whatever of Ulster's determination to remain within the United Kingdom, but it was intended on my part to create a more friendly and relaxed spirit both between the two countries, and within our own community. In our domestic policies over these recent years, we have consistently tried to emphasize those aims to which all our people can make a contribution, and from which no one will be excluded. I defy anyone to detect in our last election manifesto, or in any of the speeches in which my colleagues and I sought a further mandate, even a suggestion of a sectarian approach.

Little by little one had the impression that old barriers were in fact breaking down. Sensitive observers were able to detect a new and heartening aggiornamento in our affairs. Why, then, has the current critical attitude gained momentum? Unfortunately 1966 was not an easy year for us in Northern Ireland. There were widespread celebrations of the fiftieth anniversary of the Dublin Easter Rising, undoubtedly encouraged and exploited by people of extreme Republican views who would see in any permanent easing of inter-community relations a real threat to their ultimate aims. These celebrations in Belfast and elsewhere in their turn produced a backlash from the most extreme elements of ultra-Protestant opinion which had to be met by extremely firm action on the part of the government of Northern Ireland.

These events made many people realize that harmony in a previously divided community cannot be achieved overnight, but demands a long and patient process of social and political education. *The Times* news team commented on Monday, as though I had said something rather whimsical, that I had told them that "Reform takes a long time." Perhaps this illustrates the difference between the idealism of the journalist, who can propound his theories and leave for pastures new, and the realism of the politician, who has to cope with problems on the spot.

There are two points which must be made. First, that although reform does indeed take a long time—and is in fact a process which is never at an end in any community—no one should assume that reforms in Northern Ireland are not in progress. As an example, university representation and plural voting in elections to the Northern Ireland parliament are being abolished, and we will be setting up a permanent impartial boundary commission to keep electoral boundaries under review. Ulster members at Westminster have, of course, all along been returned for constituencies fixed by the UK boundary commission and on a franchise identical with that in Great Britain. Again, a most exhaustive re-examination of the functions, areas and financing of local government is now under way, and this is likely to lead to far-reaching reforms in that area.

The second point to make is that many of the criticisms now being directed at us are demonstrably ill-founded. We have been accused, for instance, of "discrimination" in the siting of Ulster's new city and second university; yet in both these instances we were guided by the most objective expert advice—in the one case Sir Robert Matthew, and in the other a committee chaired by Sir John Lockwood, neither of whom had any connection with Northern Ireland or was influenced in any way by the Northern Ireland government.

Of course there are still some unhealthy tensions in Northern Ireland affairs, although comments equating the lot of the Ulster Catholic with that of American Negro are absurd hyperbole. But there really is no acceptable or truly democratic alternative to letting us find the solution for our own problems. Stormont is, after all, a democratically elected parliament, and no solution which is imposed upon the majority of the population could fail to provoke greater evils than it would solve.

I would like to conclude by quoting some words I used at Easter last year, when, at a time of considerable strain, I spoke to a joint conference of Protestants and Roman Catholics. I said:

It is easy to be impatient with the pace of change in 1966, but it is no answer to return to the mentality of 1926. We may not have achieved perfection in our affairs, but in the words of the song we are "forty years on," and have built up material and other assets which this generation must not squander. If we cannot be united in all things, let us at least be united in working—in a Christian spirit—to create better opportunities for our children, whether they come from the Falls Road or from Finaghy [a Roman Catholic and a Protestant area, respectively]. In the enlightenment of education, in the dignity of work, in the security of home and family there are ends which all of us can pursue. As we advance to meet the promise of the future, let us shed the burden of traditional grievances and ancient resentments. There is much we can do together. It must and—God willing—it will be done.

It is my hope that, in spite of the current clamour, my colleagues and I may be allowed to pursue the course inherent in these words. Certainly this is not the moment for an ill-judged intervention in our affairs. As I said at the beginning, the long history of Anglo-Irish relationships warns that such an intervention may produce effects which no one can foresee. What we want to do is not become involved in a profitless exchange of charge and counter-charge but to emphasize more and more those things which unite Protestant and Catholic in our community. For, in the last resort, a truly happy and stable society must depend not upon legislation by Stormont or by Westminster but upon mutual trust.

THE TIMES, 28 April 1967. Reprinted in Terence O'Neill, ULSTER AT THE CROSSROADS (1969), pp. 123–128. Reproduced by permission of Faber & Faber Ltd.

"ULSTER AT THE CROSSROADS"

9 December 1968

Terence O'Neill

Following an escalation of the civil-rights campaign in the autumn of 1968, the British government put pressure on the Northern Ireland government to introduce reforms in local government in Derry and the allocation of public housing. These concessions failed to halt the civil-rights marches, and a growing number of Ulster unionists were expressing opposition to British intervention in Northern Ireland affairs. O'Neill's speech was aimed at the silent majority and the Unionist Party. Although the televised speech attracted 125,000 letters of support, in May 1969 he resigned as prime minister, having failed to reconcile demands for further concessions from the civil-rights movement and the growing intransigence among Ulster unionists.

SEE ALSO Economic Relations between Northern Ireland and Britain; Northern Ireland: History since 1920; O'Neill, Terence; Ulster Unionist Party in Office

Ulster stands at the crossroads. I believe you know me well enough by now to appreciate that I am not a man given to extravagant language. But I must say to you this evening that our conduct over the coming days and weeks will decide our future. And as we face this situation, I would be failing in my duty to you as your prime minister if I did not put the issues, calmly and clearly, before you all. These issues are far too serious to be determined behind closed doors, or left to noisy minorities. The time has come for the people as a whole to speak in a clear voice.

For more than five years now I have tried to heal some of the deep divisions in our community. I did so because I could not see how an Ulster divided against itself could hope to stand. I made it clear that a Northern Ireland based upon the interests of any one section rather than upon the interests of all could have no long-term future.

Throughout the community many people have responded warmly to my words. But if Ulster is to become the happy and united place it could be there must be the will throughout our province and particularly in parliament to translate these words into deeds.

In Londonderry and other places recently, a minority of agitators determined to subvert lawful authority played a part in setting light to highly inflammable material. But the tinder for that fire, in the form of grievances real or imaginary, had been piling up for years.

And so I saw it as our duty to do two things. First, to be firm in the maintenance of law and order, and in resisting those elements which seek to profit from any disturbances. Secondly, to ally firmness with fairness, and to look at any underlying causes of dissension which were troubling decent and moderate people. As I saw it, if we were not prepared to face up to our problems, we would have to meet mounting pressure both *internally*, from those who were seeking change, and *externally* from British public and parliamentary opinion, which had been deeply disturbed by the events in Londonderry.

That is why it has been my view from the beginning that we should decide—of our own free will and as a responsible government in command of events—to press on with a continuing programme of change to secure a united and harmonious community. This, indeed, has been my aim for over five years.

Moreover, I knew full well that Britain's financial and other support for Ulster, so laboriously built up, could no longer be guaranteed if we failed to press on with such a programme.

I am aware, of course, that some foolish people have been saying: "Why should we bow the knee to a Labour prime minister? Let's hold out until a conservative government returns to power, and then we need do nothing." My friends, that is a delusion. This letter is from Mr. Edward Heath, and it tells me—with the full authority of the Shadow Cabinet and the expressed support of my old friend Sir Alec Douglas-Home—that a reversal of the policies which I have tried to pursue would be every bit as unacceptable to the Conservative Party. If we adopt an attitude of stubborn defiance we will not have a friend left at Westminster.

I make no apology for the financial and economic support we have received from Britain. As a part of the United Kingdom, we have always considered this to be our right. But we cannot be a part of the United Kingdom merely when it suits us. And those who talk so glibly about acts of impoverished defiance do not know or care what is at stake. Your job, if you are a worker at Short's or Harland & Wolff; your subsidies if you are a farmer; your pension, if you are retired—all these aspects of our life, and many others, depend on support from Britain. Is a freedom to pursue the un-Christian path of communal strife and sectarian bitterness really more important to you than all the benefits of the British welfare state?

But this is not all. Let me read to you some words from the Government of Ireland Act, 1920—the Act of the British parliament on which Ulster's constitution is founded.

> Notwithstanding the establishment of the Parliament of Northern Ireland . . . the supreme authority of the Parliament of the United Kingdom shall remain unaffected and undiminished over all persons, matters, and things in [Northern] Ireland and every part thereof.

Because Westminster has trusted us over the years to use the powers of Stormont for the good of all people of Ulster, a sound custom has grown up that Westminster does not use its supreme authority in fields where we are normally responsible. But Mr. Wilson made it absolutely clear to us that if we did not face up to our problems the Westminster parliament might well decide to act over our heads. Where would our constitution be then? What shred of self-respect would be left to us? If we allowed others to solve our problems because we had not the guts—let me use a plain word—the guts to face up to them, we would be utterly shamed.

There are, I know, today some so-called loyalists who talk of independence from Britain—who seem to want a kind of Protestant Sinn Féin. These people will not listen when they are told that Ulster's income is £200 million a year but that we can spend £300 million—only because Britain pays the balance.

Rhodesia, in defying Britain from thousands of miles away, at least has an Air Force and an Army of her own. Where are the Ulster armoured divisions or the Ulster jet planes? They do not exist and we could not afford to buy them. These people are not merely extremists. They are lunatics who would set a course along a road which could only lead at the end into an all-Ireland Republic. They are not loyalists but disloyalists: disloyal to Britain, disloyal to the constitution, disloyal to the Crown, disloyal—if they are in public life—to the solemn oaths they have sworn to her majesty the queen.

But these considerations, important though they are, not my main concern. What I seek—and I ask for the help and understanding of you all—is a swift end to the growing civil disorder throughout Ulster. For as matters stand today, we are on the brink of chaos, where neighbour could be set against neighbour. It is simple-minded to imagine that problems such as these can be solved by repression. I for one am not willing to expose our police force to indefinite insult and injury. Nor am I prepared to see the shopkeepers and traders of Ulster wrecked and looted for the benefit of the rabble. We must tackle root causes if this agitation is to be contained. We must be able to say to the moderate on both sides: come with us into a new era of co-operation, and leave the extremists to the law. But this I also say to all, Protestant or Roman Catholic, Unionist or Nationalist: disorder must now cease. We are taking the necessary measures to strengthen our police forces. Determined as we are to act with absolute fairness, we will also be resolute in restoring respect for the laws of the land.

Some people have suggested that I should call a general election. It would, in my view, be utterly reprehensible to hold an election against a background of bitterness and strife. I have spoke to you in the past about the groundswell of moderate opinion. Its presence was seen three years ago when we fought an election on a manifesto which would stand inspection in any Western democracy and we swept the country on a non-sectarian platform. Those who would sow the wind by having a bitter election now would surely reap the whirlwind.

And now I want to say a word directly to those who have been demonstrating for civil rights. The changes which we have announced are genuine and far-reaching changes and the government as a whole is totally committed to them. I would not continue to preside over an administration which would water them down or make them meaningless. You will see when the members of the Londonderry commission are appointed that we intend to live up to our words that this will be a body to command confidence and respect. You will see that in housing allocations we mean business. You will see that legislation to appoint an Ombudsman will be swiftly introduced. Perhaps you are not entirely satisfied; but this is a democracy, and I ask you now with all sincerity to call your people off the streets and allow an atmosphere favourable to change develop. You are Ulstermen yourselves. You know we are all of us stubborn people, who will not be pushed too far. I believe that most of you want change, not revolution. Your voice has been heard, and clearly heard. Your duty now is to play your part in taking the heat out of the situation before blood is shed.

But I have a word too for all those others who see in change a threat to our position in the United Kingdom. I say to them, Unionism armed with justice will be a stronger cause than Unionism armed merely with strength, The bully-boy tactics we saw in Armagh are no answer to these grave problems: but they incur for us the contempt of Britain and the world, and such contempt is the greatest threat to Ulster. Let the government govern and the police take care of law and order.

What in any case are these changes which we have decided must come? They all amount to this: that in every aspect of our life, justice must not only be done but be *seen* to be done to all sections of the community. There must be evident fairness as between one man and another.

The adoption of such reforms will not, I believe, lose a single seat at Stormont for those who support the Unionist cause and indeed some may be gained. And remember that it is with Stormont that the power of decision rests for maintaining our constitution.

And now a further word to you all. What kind of Ulster do you want? A happy and respected Province, in good standing with the rest of the United Kingdom? Or a place continually torn apart by riots and demonstrations, and regarded by the rest of Britain as a political outcast? As always in a democracy, the choice is yours. I will accept whatever your verdict may be. If it is your decision that we should live up to the words "Ulster is British" which is part of our creed, then my services will be at your disposal to do what I can. But if you should want a separate, inward-looking, selfish and divided Ulster then you must seek for others to lead you along that road, for I cannot and will not do it. Please weigh well all that is at stake, and make your voice heard in whatever way you think best, so that we may know the views *not* of the few *but* of the many. For this is truly a time of decision, and in your silence *all* that we have built up could be lost. I pray that you will reflect carefully and decide wisely. And I ask all our Christian people, whatever their denomination, to attend their places of worship on Sunday next to pray for the peace and harmony of our country.

Television broadcast on BBC and ITA networks, 9 December 1968. Reprinted in Terence O'Neill, ULSTER AT THE CROSSROADS (1969), pp. 140–146. Reproduced by permission of Faber & Faber Ltd.

≈

STATEMENT BY THE TAOISEACH

13 August 1969

Jack Lynch

The 12th and 13th of August 1969 are generally accepted as the beginning of the Northern Ireland "Troubles." On 12 August the annual Apprentice Boys' march in Derry resulted in violence, which spread to Belfast. At least seven people were killed and many others wounded, houses were set on fire, and many Catholic families were driven from their homes. Emotions were running high in Northern Ireland and the Republic. This speech on Irish television by the Irish prime minister Jack Lynch was a response to demands for the Irish government or the Irish army to intervene to protect Northern Catholics. Lynch's statement that "the Irish government can no longer stand by," often misreported as "can no longer stand idly by," was interpreted by many people in Northern Ireland and the Republic as a commitment to intervene; in reality it was designed to mask the impotence of the Irish government.

SEE ALSO Northern Ireland: History since 1920; Northern Ireland: Policy of the Dublin Government from 1922 to 1969; Politics: Impact of the Northern Ireland Crisis on Southern Politics

It is with deep sadness that you, Irishmen and women of goodwill and I have learned of the tragic events which have been taking place in Derry and elsewhere in the North in recent days. Irishmen in every part of this island have made known their concern at these events. This concern is heightened by the realisation that the spirit of reform and intercommunal co-operation has given way to the forces of sectarianism and prejudice. All people of goodwill must feel saddened and disappointed at this backward turn in events and must be apprehensive for the future.

The government fully share these feelings and I wish to repeat that we deplore sectarianism and intolerance in all their forms wherever they occur. The government have been very patient and have acted with great restraint over several months past. While we made our views known to the British government on a number of occasions both by direct contact and through our diplomatic representatives in London, we were careful to do nothing that would exacerbate the situation. But it is clear now that the present situation cannot be allowed to continue.

It is evident, also, that the Stormont government is no longer in control of the situation. Indeed the present situation is the inevitable outcome of the policies pursued for decades by successive Stormont governments. It is clear, also, that the Irish government can no longer stand by and see innocent people injured and perhaps worse.

It is obvious that the R.U.C. is no longer accepted as an impartial police force. Neither would the employment of British troops be acceptable nor would they be likely to restore peaceful conditions—certainly not in the long term. The Irish government have, therefore, requested the British government to apply immediately to the United Nations for the urgent despatch of a peace-keeping force to the 6 counties of Northern Ireland and have instructed the Irish permanent representative to the United Nations to inform the secretary-general of this request. We have also asked the British government to see to it that police attacks on the people of Derry should cease immediately.

Very many people have been injured and some of them seriously. We know that many of these do not wish to be treated in 6 county hospitals. We have, therefore, directed the Irish army authorities to have field hospitals established in County Donegal adjacent to Derry and at other points along the border where they may be necessary.

Recognising, however, that the re-unification of the national territory can provide the only permanent solution for the problem, it is our intention to request the British government to enter into early negotiations with the Irish government to review the present constitutional position of the 6 counties of Northern Ireland.

These measures which I have outlined to you seem to the government to be those most immediately and urgently necessary.

All men and women of goodwill will hope and pray that the present deplorable and distressing situation will not further deteriorate but that it will soon be ended firstly by the granting of full equality of citizenship to every man and woman in the 6-county area regardless of class, creed or political persuasion and, eventually, by the restoration of the historic unity of our country.

∽

FROM THE *REPORT OF THE COMMISSION ON THE STATUS OF WOMEN*

1972

The Commission on the Status of Women was established in 1970 by the Irish government in response to a directive issued by the United Nations' Commission on the Status of Women, with a mandate to "examine and report on the status of women in Irish society and to make recommendations on the steps necessary to ensure the participation of women on equal terms and conditions with men in the political, social, cultural, and economic life of the country." An interim report (1971) recommended the implementation of equal pay and the removal of the prohibition on married women in public-service employment; the final report appeared in 1972. The commission reinvigorated the Irish women's movement, and its recommendations provided a focus for later campaigns.

SEE ALSO Education: Women's Education; Equal Economic Rights for Women in Independent Ireland; Women in Irish Society since 1800; Women's Parliamentary Representation since 1922

In general . . . the picture presented of women's involvement in politics is one of relatively small participation at local level, with a progressive decline of involvement at the higher levels. This, of course, is true of women's participation in many other areas where the promotion of women comes up against serious obstacles and traditional attitudes. It is true also of practically all countries abroad. . . . There is a strong indication that women are themselves in a certain measure to blame for this situation by displaying a considerable degree of apathy. It has also been suggested that women's educational background is at fault and that even with equality of access to education the present large degree of segregated education operates to preserve a traditional division of interests between the sexes. In politics, this manifests itself in the orientation of women to believe that political power and activity is primarily for men. There is clearly a great need for really impressing on girls that they have a part to play in political life and that the general failure of women to participate more fully in political activity can only operate to their disadvantage. The United Nations Commission on the Status of Women has drawn attention to the part that education must play in this matter and has referred to the necessity for an intensive programme of civic and political training to ensure that women realise the full extent of their rights, obligations and abilities, that young people be encouraged to participate in political activity and that civic education be available at all educational levels, including adult educational institutes. . . .

In addition, the political parties themselves should make greater efforts to attract women members and to let it be seen that they welcome them. Once they become members, they should be treated equally with men and should be given posts of responsibility in the organisation on merit. Progress of women within the parties will be clearly related to their willingness to work hard and to perform uncongenial tasks where necessary. The women's organisations, also, have a part to play in providing training in public speaking and civics and encouraging a greater political and social awareness among their members even if the organisations themselves are non party-political.

Reprinted in THE FIELD DAY ANTHOLOGY OF IRISH WRITING, vol. 5, IRISH WOMEN'S WRITING AND TRADITIONS, edited by Angela Bourke et al. (2002), p. 191.

≈

"TOWARDS CHANGES IN THE REPUBLIC"

1973

Garret FitzGerald

This document illustrates the views of one thoughtful moderate nationalist on Northern Ireland and reunification in 1972, a time when the constitutional future of Northern Ireland was uncertain following the suspension of the Northern Ireland parliament and the introduction of direct rule from London. Garret FitzGerald was very conscious of the need for legislative change in the Republic of Ireland in order to accommodate the views of Ulster Protestants. In March 1973 FitzGerald became minister for external affairs, a portfolio that included Northern Ireland.

SEE ALSO Northern Ireland: Policy of the Dublin Government from 1922 to 1969; Politics: Impact of the Northern Ireland Crisis on Southern Politics

Throughout most of the past half-century the issue of Irish reunification was debated in somewhat simplistic terms. Because to both sides it appeared at first a temporary arrangement (although of course this was not publicly admitted by leaders of the majority in the North), relatively little thought was given to how it could be brought to an end, or even as to how the divergence between the two parts of Ireland could be prevented from widening. Northern Unionists were content with a "no surrender" attitude, which some of them in their hearts did not take too seriously, and the Northern minority and the bulk of the people in the rest of the country were equally content to assert a claim to unity without pursuing very far the question of how this ambition might be realised. As the years passed the attitude of many supporters of Irish reunification imperceptibly and unconsciously changed from a presumption that partition was temporary and would be brought to an early end, to an equally unconscious acceptance of it as an indefinitely continuing feature on the Irish landscape, but this underlying change of private attitudes brought no change in public policies. From time to time politicians in the Republic were moved to public statements of abhorrence of the political division of the island and at certain periods this sporadic competition in oratory developed into a campaign against partition; most notably, perhaps, in the period 1948–1949, when Mr. de Valera took advantage of a spell in opposition after sixteen years of government to launch a worldwide campaign on the subject. This campaign continued into the early 1950s, aided by a fund collected, rather tactlessly from the point of view of Northern Unionist sentiment, at the gates of Catholic churches, and punctuated by the declaration of the Republic in 1949, and by the British guarantee in the consequential Ireland Act, 1949, of the Northern Ireland parliament's right to decide the reunification issue.

The IRA border raid campaign of the years from 1956 onwards introduced a new element into the controversy, which, however, had no lasting effects, except on Northern Unionist attitudes. By the early 1960s the whole question seemed to be back where it had started, except that opinion had become accustomed to the fact of partition, and pessimistic about prospects for its disappearance in the forseeable future.

Within Northern Ireland these decades saw many fluctuations in the attitude of the minority, ranging from abstentionism to limited participation in the governmental system, and even, at certain periods, an abdication by the constitutional Nationalist Party of its role in the face of Republican determination to contest seats at elections. (Fearing that to put forward candidates as it had done for decades previously would "split the vote" and let the seats concerned go to the Unionists, the Nationalists temporarily ceded the ground to abstentionist Republicans, possibly believing that this threat to their political control of the minority would go away if left to blow itself out, as in fact eventually happened.)

The 1960s saw the emergence of a new attitude amongst the Northern minority, however. In the aftermath of the border raids and the temporary takeover of parliamentary representation by abstentionist Republicans, the mood of the minority switched back towards acceptance of a measure of involvement with the system; a willingness to try co-operation. One of the earliest protagonists of this policy was Mr. G. B. Newe, later, towards the end of 1971, to be appointed a member of the Northern Ireland Cabinet in a belated effort by Mr. Brian Faulkner to lend credibility to his government. But it received a measure of support as time went on from Nationalist politicians also, amongst them Mr. Paddy Gormley, MP, brother of Mr. Tom Gormely, who in early 1972, with two Unionist MPs, joined the Alliance Party.

It is against this background that one must see the analysis of minority attitudes in the Rose Survey, carried out in 1968. . . . This survey was undertaken just at the end of this "honeymoon" period, which had also been marked by the exchange of visits at prime minister level initiated by Mr. Seán Lemass in 1965.

But it is also against this background that one must see the emergence of the civil rights movement. The tactical approach of this movement reflected the shift in minority attitudes during the 1960s towards an attempt to work the system by concentrating on a political evolution within Northern Ireland as a preliminary to, and indeed a condition precedent of, any move towards seeking reunification by consent. Of course the civil rights movement did not accept the rather formless drift towards co-operation that had marked the years before 1968; it adopted a positive policy of non-violent demonstration in pursuit of its aims, conscious, no doubt, of the strong possibility that such a show of independence and self-confidence by those who had suffered from the system of government in Northern Ire-

land since 1920 would be likely to arouse opposition and even physical resistance by supporters of the regime.

But although its tactics were aggressive rather than passive, its strategy was similar to that which had emerged more or less haphazardly amongst the minority during the immediately preceding years: tackle the internal problems of Northern Ireland in the first instance, and leave the issue of reunification on one side for the time being, to be settled later by agreement in the light of the new and, hopefully, saner situation that would emerge following the battle for reforms.

Despite the fact that the conservatism of most Northern Protestants, and their suspicion of Republican influences in the civil rights movement, prevented that movement from mobilising significant support from the Protestant community (although many Protestants did, of course, support the reforms when they were introduced), this development nevertheless changed the character of the Northern problem. Because the civil rights movement was content to leave the partition issue to be decided at a later stage, in a, hopefully, different atmosphere created by reforms, its reform programme was much more difficult to resist than any previous opposition movement to the Northern government. The Northern government might convince a high proportion of its own supporters that the civil rights movement was, despite its new policies, only anti-partitionism under another guise; it could not so easily persuade opinion outside Northern Ireland of this thesis. Moreover because civil rights had become a fashionable issue in other countries during the 1960s, and because the campaign—and any attempt to repress it—was transmitted with all the instantaneity and impact of television, the effect of the civil rights movement on opinion outside Northern Ireland was greater than, perhaps, even its organisers had ever conceived possible. Had it been merely another stage in a long-drawn out campaign against partition, it is doubtful whether, even with the aid of television, it could have had the same effect on opinion in Britain and elsewhere. The reaction to this campaign culminated in the violence of August 1969, the intervention of the British army to prevent a pogrom, and the granting of the reforms—subject to a certain amount of subsequent delay and whittling down, referred to earlier. In retrospect one is forced to wonder whether the civil rights movement, and the politicians associated with it who later formed the Social Democratic and Labour Party, were prepared for the measure of success they achieved, and for the speed with which it was secured. The logical corollary of the anti-discrimination reform programme would have been a demand for a right on the part of the minority to participate in government, yet this demand was not made until much later, long after the minority in Belfast and Derry had come into conflict with the British army.

The extent to which the new approach—concentrating on internal changes within Northern Ireland and leaving the partition issue for later settlement—had taken deep root amongst the minority became evident during the period from August 1969 until August 1971, when internment was introduced. Throughout this period the partition issue remained in the background, despite the increasing polarisation between Protestants and Catholics. It was only after the introduction of internment that the emphasis of minority attitudes began to switch back from internal charges within North to national reunification as an immediate aim. This reversal of emphasis in the autumn of 1971 was encouraged by the Wilson proposals, which envisaged an agreement on ultimate reunification, followed by a fifteen-year transitional period. It was given further impetus by the radio and newspaper interviews with Rev. Ian Paisley towards the end of 1971, when his proposals for constitutional change in the Republic, and deliberate side-stepping of questions about his attitude to reunification if these changes were effected, hinted at a possible change of attitude on this issue.

By the beginning of 1972 there was, moreover, evidence of similar stirrings in non-Paisleyite Northern Protestant opinion. The sense of insecurity of the Northern majority, and their fear that even if this crisis were overcome, the whole cycle of violence could start again in the future, seemed to be beginning to lead some more thoughtful members of the Protestant community to ask themselves whether there might not be something to be gained by examining the question of the kind of Ireland that might emerge if the two parts of the country were eventually to be reunited. Speeches by Richard Ferguson, a former Unionist MP, from December 1971 onwards in which he addressed himself to the need to consider the possibility of a new non-sectarian united Ireland, underlined this new mood.

Thus, the failure to find a solution within the context of Northern Ireland based on the willingness of the minority in the late 1960s to leave the reunification issue on one side for the time being and to concentrate rather on internal reforms, had created by the start of 1972 a situation in which the whole question of a united Ireland had again become a live issue. Now, however, reunification seemed to have rather more prospect of realisation within a reasonable period that had seemed to exist at any time during the first forty years of the existence of Northern Ireland, when a sporadic campaign was being waged against partition. Historians will, no doubt, debate the relative contributions to this new sit-

uation of a multiplicity of factors at work during the period from 1969 onwards, and especially in the closing months of 1971. These factors will probably include the following:

1. The policy vacuum on the side of the minority after the concession of the reform programme in August and October, 1969, which, in retrospect, can be seen to have inhibited change in the political structure of the North during this period.

2. The intransigence of the Unionist government and party when the proposals for minority participation in government in Northern Ireland emerged during the course of 1971.

3. The British government's internment decision and that government's failure, influenced, no doubt, by repeated army promises of imminent victory over the IRA, to take any initiative in the closing months of 1971 to recover the ground thus lost.

4. The brutality associated with internment, and the failure of the British army authorities to prevent some of its units from behaving in a manner that alienated the goodwill of even the most moderate members of the minority.

5. The disturbing effect on Northern Protestant opinion of the IRA campaign in the period after internment, and the growing belief amongst Protestants in Northern Ireland that the British government, politicians and people neither understood their situation nor cared enough about it to sustain a prolonged campaign.

6. The reintroduction of the reunification issue into the sphere of practical politics by the Harold Wilson initiative of late 1971.

7. The emergence in the Republic of a movement favouring a more liberal and pluralist society, which for the first time offered Protestants some hope that a united Ireland would not necessarily be simply an enlarged version of what they had always seen as a Republic dominated by Roman Catholic teaching and influence.

All of these factors, and perhaps others besides that may not be evident to an observer writing early in 1972, myopically close to the events in question, no doubt played their part, for nothing less than a complex combination of many causes could account for the emergence of a willingness on the part even of a thinking minority of Northern Protestants to start giving serious consideration to a solution involving eventual reunification in some form.

The ultimate significance of this shift in opinion is unknowable in early 1972; but enough has happened to make it worth considering seriously ways in which it might prove possible to overcome the obstacles to re-unification that have been strengthened in the past half-century, reinforcing the basic inter-community hostility that initially led to partition. The shape of an eventual solution, rather than the practical path towards its negotiation, will be the theme of the concluding pages of this book. How and whether it might be possible to secure the consent, or at any rate, acquiescence, of the Northern majority to a peaceful evolution towards national unity remains an uncertain question—and reunification achieved other than peacefully would ensure lasting discord affecting the whole of Ireland, rather than anything that could properly be called national unity. All that can be said is that the prospect of reunification without violence had by the start of 1972 emerged as a possibility strong enough to warrant practical consideration and to call for serious study.

First of all, some "non-starter" solutions should, perhaps, be ruled out. Thus the proposal sometimes canvassed in Britain, and occasionally even in Ireland, for a re-partitioning of Northern Ireland should be excluded. The politico-religious geography of Northern Ireland is much too complex to make any such solution worth considering. While there is a rather higher proportion of Catholics in the West and South of Northern Ireland, than in the North and East of the area, there are, nevertheless, about 200,000 Catholics in the North-East corner of Northern Ireland—Antrim, North Down, Belfast and North Armagh. Thus even if the boundary were re-drawn to include only these parts of Northern Ireland in which there is an overwhelming Protestant majority, less than 10% of the land area of Ireland, there would remain within this enclave 200,000 Catholic hostages—well over half of them in Belfast itself. This problem could no doubt be overcome by a transfer of populations, but the hardship this would entail would be immense and the resultant all-Protestant enclave would by the standards of modern European civilisation be a political monstrosity. This kind of solution assumes that the differences between Protestants and Catholics are of a permanently irreconcilable character; that these two communities of Ulster people are so inherently different and mutually hostile that it is hopeless to conceive of their *ever* living together in peace. Even the events of the years from 1969 to 1972 do not warrant such a deeply pessimistic conclusion.

Another proposal for a boundary change—the inclusion within Northern Ireland of the three Ulster counties now in the Republic—has been put forward by the provisional Sinn Féin organisation as a means of persuading Unionists to accept reunification. This solution would, however, be highly unlikely to prove ac-

ceptable to the majority of people in the three Ulster counties in the Republic, and it is, of course, specifically designed to threaten the position of the Protestant community within the area of Northern Ireland. Protestants who might accept participation in a United Ireland if they retained their own provincial autonomy within the present territory of Northern Ireland, where they have a clear domestic majority, would not be attracted by a proposal which with the faster growth of the Catholic population of these areas, would threaten at a fairly early date their submergence as a minority in an overwhelmingly Catholic Ireland. Moreover, as the provisional Sinn Féin proposal envisages four provincial parliaments within a federal Ireland, the Ulster province, within which the Protestants would have a tenuous and impermanent majority, would at the level of the federal institutions find itself in a minority of one-in-four—whereas if the existing Northern Ireland state federated with the Republic, the balance in population terms would be only two-to-one against Northern Ireland, and Northern Ireland might reasonably hope within such a twin-state system to be accorded equal representation at, say, the level of the Upper House, as is accorded in certain other federations (e.g., the United States of America) where the lower house of parliament is constituted on the one-man-one-vote principle.

Thus there seems to be nothing to be gained by playing around with the existing boundary; for good or ill, it exists, and if a federal system is to be created, it is more likely that agreement can be reached on the basis that this boundary would be let stand, than on a basis that involved a radical change in it.

The concept of a federation of the two existing Irish political entities has its difficulties, of course. There appears to be a general sentiment in the Republic in favour of such a solution, however—at any rate, no voices have been raised to protest that a united Ireland must be a unitary state, and most discussion has either explicitly or implicitly been based on the concept of an autonomous Northern Ireland region within a unified but not unitary 32-county Irish state.

This general acceptance of the concept of an autonomous Northern Ireland region depends, however, upon agreement on a reconstitution of the system of government within that region along lines that would be acceptable to the minority and would guarantee human rights, viz. on the pattern suggested in the immediately preceding chapter. This would leave the following questions to be settled:

1. The nature of the special relationship, if any, that would exist between a united Ireland and Great Britain.

2. The guarantees that the Northern Protestant community would have for their rights within a united Ireland.

3. The kind of constitution required for a United Ireland.

4. The steps to be taken to ensure that the ending of Northern Ireland's present relationship with the United Kingdom, and its participation in a United Ireland, would not adversely affect agricultural incomes, employment in industries such as shipbuilding, social welfare benefits, or living standards generally.

5. The changes that would, in the meantime, be required within the Republic to persuade Northern Protestants that an association with the Republic within an Irish federal state could be acceptable.

The last of these points will be considered first, in the concluding pages of this chapter, leaving the other matters over to a final chapter, for the creation of sufficient goodwill within the Northern Ireland Protestant community to enable a constructive debate to start on participation by the North in a federal Irish state will certainly require concrete evidence on the part of the Republic of a willingness to establish conditions within its own territory that Northern Protestant opinion would find broadly acceptable.

A clear distinction must be made here between more immediate changes required within the Republic to create a favourable atmosphere for future discussions, and the eventual changes in the present constitution of the Republic that would be required to make it acceptable as the constitution of a federal Irish state. While some matters will come up for consideration under both headings, this distinction is an important one, which emerged clearly towards the end of 1971, in the limited public debate that surrounded the decision to establish an all-party committee in the Republic to discuss Northern Ireland policy and possible relevant constitutional changes.

The sensitivities of Northern Protestant opinion with respect to laws and practices in the Republic have been outlined earlier. At this stage the only issue is what changes are necessary to prepare the way for constructive discussions on eventual reunification. The central problem here is the influence of the Catholic Church in the Republic on social and legal issues within the political forum. This is only minimally a matter of constitutional and legal provisions: much more important to the Northern Protestant is the evidence of indirect influence wielded by the authorities of the Catholic Church, either in preventing laws being enacted, or in securing the administration of laws in a manner favourable to

what its authorities regard as the interests of the Catholic religion.

The formal constitutional and legal changes called for are, indeed, relatively few. The provisions of Articles 44.1.2—"The State recognises the special position of the Holy Catholic Apostolic and Roman Church as the guardian of the faith professed by the great majority of the citizens"—would clearly have to be repealed, but as Cardinal Conway has said that he would not shed a tear at its deletion from the constitution, and as only one member of the Dáil—a rural Labour Deputy—has criticized its proposed repeal, this creates no problem.

Secondly, it would be desirable as an indication of goodwill towards the Northern Ireland legal position on divorce, to delete also the provision of Article 41.3.2 of the constitution—which forbids the enactment of any law granting a dissolution of marriage. The making of such a constitutional change *might* suffice to meet Northern Protestant opinions on this matter, without going beyond this to introduce actual divorce legislation in the Republic, for divorce is a matter of jurisdiction and, as is evident from the legal position with respect to divorce in England and Wales and in Scotland, different divorce laws can exist within a non-federal state, and all the more so within a federal state, as Ireland on the hypothesis might in time become.

There will be those who argue that divorce is a human right, and that failure by the Republic to make provision for this "right" would make more difficult reunification on a federal basis, even if Northern Ireland could retain its own divorce law, and power to modify this law in future. But the concept of divorce as an absolute human rights is an arguable one, if for no other reason than because the divorce laws of every state are different, allowing the dissolution of marriage for widely differing reasons, and with widely different conditions attached. A human right must surely be something more precise than a vague provision of this kind, differently interpreted from state to state. Moreover, although the question of divorce is frequently raised in connection with the question of reunification, divorce is in fact disapproved of in varying degrees by all the Protestant churches in Ireland, and is frowned on by a high proportion, possibly a substantial majority, of their members; although, of course, this does not mean that they would wish their view to have the force of law. The introduction of divorce in Northern Ireland is of relatively recent origin; apart from the traditional system of divorce by act of parliament, which applied to the whole of Ireland up to and after the division of the country and the establishment of the Irish Free State, it was only in 1939 that divorce through the courts was introduced in Northern Ireland. In these circumstances it is possible that the genuine feelings of Northern Ireland people on this matter would be met if pending reunification a change in the Republic's constitution were effected that made it clear that reunion would not interfere with Northern Ireland's freedom of action in relation to divorce laws, although some will feel that Republic should go further in this matter.

Abortion, an issue sometimes raised by British commentators, and rather oddly included in Mr. Wilson's late 1971 proposals for a solution to the Irish problem, is not an issue with the bulk of Northern Protestant opinion, although there is some sensitivity about differences in obstetrical practice between Catholic and Protestant or public authority hospitals. Easier abortion has not hitherto been a significant issue within Northern Ireland, and accordingly should not create a serious problem in relation to proposals for reunification.

The Republic's laws on censorship and contraception are highly contentious issues with Northern Protestant opinion. Moreover, since unlike divorce, what is involved here is the movement of goods rather than legal jurisdiction, and as, presumably, in a united federal Ireland it would be proposed to eliminate customs controls between the two parts of the country, some solution must in any event be found to divergences in practice in these matters when a negotiated settlement is sought. It seems sensible, therefore, to initiate changes in the Republic in advance of such a settlement, as part of a programme designed to show Northern Protestant opinion that the will to reunification on an acceptable basis is genuine.

The scale of minority support in the Republic for changes in the law on contraception, demonstrated by a public opinion poll in April 1971, which posed the issue in the context of the Republic alone, without reference to the question of reunification, suggests that if the issue were re-posed as part of a "package" designed to create a favourable climate for reunification, it would have the assent of a majority; especially if safeguards and limitations on free sale, not adverted to in the poll, were spelt out.

In the case of obscene literature the contentious issue is the method of control rather than any disagreement on the need for some form of control. Perhaps because the censorship system of the Republic has applied not only to obscene printed matter but also to works "advocating" artificial methods of birth control, thus enforcing what Protestants regard as Catholic morality on this issue, it has got a bad name in Northern Ireland. It may also be that mere fact that the system of control in the Republic is different from that in the North, and is called "censorship," has helped to make it a bone of contention.

The removal of the control over books advocating artificial forms of birth control would go some way to meet Northern objections, but it may be worth considering whether the Republic's pre-censorship system is worth maintaining, in view of its controversial character, now that it is in practice virtually limited in applications to books which, by reasonable standards—such as may be shared by many Protestants in Northern Ireland—could be regarded as pornographic and thus amenable to a normal legal process. Such a process could be implemented in accordance with regional norms, but subject to some overall supervision to prevent local outbursts of excessive illiberalism from interfering with the sale of works which by the general standards of the time in Ireland, or in the relevant part of Ireland, would not be regarded as obscene.

In other words the real issue is not now so much a divergence of view between North and South as to what kind of books should be banned—local divergences of this kind can and do exist within the legal systems of unitary states such as Great Britain—but rather the method of control. A national precensorship system is objectionable in principle to many Northern Protestants, for reasons that are not necessarily entirely logical, and raises issues as between North and South which a normal police-type control on a regional or local basis would not raise. As this latter type of control could well yield similar results in the Republic to those at present achieved through pre-censorship a reversion to this latter system, employed in the independent Irish state during its early years, could well provide a solution to this problem—if accompanied by provisions to eliminate the ban on books advocating certain methods of birth control. In considering such an arrangement it must be borne in mind that the attitudes of many Northern Protestants to pornography is as close to that of Irish Catholics as to that of British public opinion, so that the problem of divergence of standards in this matter is probably less acute than the controversy over the *method* of censorship might suggest.

It is in the educational sphere, however, that the influence of the Roman Catholic Church is seen by Northern Protestants as most pervasive. At the same time the educational systems of the two parts of Ireland, despite the differences that have grown up between them in the past half-century, retain basic similarities; both have post-primary public schools operating in parallel with denominational post-primary schools; and in both areas primary education is denominational. In Northern Ireland, however, the acceptance by the Roman Catholic hierarchy of the principle that one-third of the members of the management boards of Catholic post-primary schools in receipt of 80% capital grants should be representatives of the relevant local educational authority to be nominated by the minister for education, has created a situation very different from that in the Republic.

But although Protestant fears of Roman Catholic ecclesiastical influence in education are real and run very deep, the concern of the Church of Ireland in particular, especially in the Republic, to retain its own denominational schools at both primary and post-primary level has meant that there has been relatively little pressure for a diminution of the denominational element in education. In these circumstances, it is not easy to see what precise changes in the educational system in the Republic could be initiated, or are required, in order to offer reassurance to Protestant opinion in Northern Ireland.

The other important area where a change in the present arrangements in the Republic would be regarded as an earnest of the sincerity of its people's wish for a reunited Ireland acceptable to the Protestants of Northern Ireland is that concerning the Irish language. To Protestants in Northern Ireland the refusal to grant school leaving certificates to those who do not pass in Irish, the Irish language requirement for entry to the Colleges of the National University of Ireland, and the Irish language requirements in relation to recruitment into and promotion within the public service of the Republic, appear discriminatory against people of their tradition, few of whom in past generations were Irish speaking. It can, of course, be argued (in this as in every other instance where changes are proposed in the Republic as an indication of willingness to meet the point of view of the majority in Northern Ireland) that the present arrangements in the Republic are without prejudice to quite different arrangements that might apply in the examination system or public service of a federal Irish state. But this will not appear convincing to Northern Protestants, even those with goodwill towards an eventual reunification of the country, for they see their co-religionists in the Republic as being adversely affected by these language requirements, and regard the provisions under which these requirements are imposed as penal in character vis-à-vis people who do not belong to the native Gaelic tradition, and as indicating an attitude of mind opposed to the kind of pluralist society that they would expect to find a united Ireland.

A change in policy in this matter, as in the others referred to above, seems desirable, therefore, if the Republic is to show itself to the Protestant people of Northern Ireland as liberal and open-minded, concerned to meet their reasonable requirements, and determined to treat the existing small Protestant minority in the Republic in a manner satisfactory to Protestants of the North. It is worth noting that the principal opposition party in the Republic, Fine Gael, is in fact committed to these reforms affecting the Irish language.

Summing up the specific steps that might usefully be taken in the Republic at this stage as an earnest wish of its people to seek a reunification of the country in terms that could be acceptable to Northern Protestants, the changes that seem to be most needed are the repeal by referendum of the constitutional provisions on the special position of the Catholic Church and divorce; amendment of the law banning the import and sale of contraceptives; a modification of the system of dealing with obscene printed matter, substituting a new version of the older system of control by prosecution for the existing censorship system and the removal of Irish language requirements in examinations and in recruitment for, and promotion within the public service.

Consideration should also be given to implementing in the Republic reforms introduced in Northern Ireland since 1969. Some of these reforms may be less necessary in the Republic than in Northern Ireland, but they nevertheless could have a useful part to play, and Northern Catholics and Protestants alike would be reassured to know that the Republic was keeping in step with Northern Ireland in this respect. The matters concerned include the appointment of a commissioner for complaints and a parliamentary commissioner for administration; the appointment also of a police authority; and steps to extend the impartial systems of public appointments in the Republic to posts not now covered, e.g. rate collections, sub-postmasters, etc. In these and other reforms the guiding principle should be the provision of absolute guarantees of fair and equal treatment for all citizens regardless of religion, or politics.

Finally, in all legislation dealing with matters that may be at issue between the two religious communities, the guiding principle should be the general welfare of all, rather than the moral consensus of the majority community. If that principle is followed then the problems hitherto created both North and South as a result of legislation influenced by the views of the predominant group in the area concerned, will be avoided in future.

Such a programme, if implemented generously, and if accompanied by an evident willingness on the part of the Catholic Church authorities and the political parties in the Republic to offer concrete re-assurance to Northern Protestants that a united Ireland would not, as they fear, be dominated by the church authorities, or by the teaching and influence of the church, would create conditions favourable to an eventual serious discussion of a programme of reunification. Some kind of declaration of intent by churchmen and politicians could make a great contribution here.

Pressures favouring a development of this kind have been the impact in the Republic of the implication by Rev. Ian Paisley in his December 1971 radio and newspaper interviews that changes in the Republic might affect the attitude of Northern Protestants towards the North-South relationship, and the proposals by Richard Ferguson, the former Unionist MP who since his resignation has joined the Alliance Party, for a new, non-sectarian Ireland, which in the spring of 1972 began to make a significant impact in the Republic. The refusal of the Fianna Fáil Party conference early in 1972 to accept a proposal to postpone constitutional reform until negotiations started for a united Ireland reflected the growing willingness of public opinion in the Republic to seek a solution in the form of a new kind of society, rather than by an attempt to impose the Republic's cultural values and Catholic ethos on Northern Ireland. Up to May 1972, however, this approach was still being resisted by the Fianna Fáil government which appeared, however, to be swimming increasingly against the tide of public opinion on this issue. Even if the all-party committee of the Dáil announced in December 1971, but not set up until May 1972, was envisaged by the government as a body that should concern itself with changes to be made as a part of an eventual negotiation, it is quite possible that its work will lead to proposals for interim changes in the Republic along the lines suggested above. Fresh pressure in favour of such changes will come from the proposal in the British initiative of March 24, 1972, to have regular plebiscites in Northern Ireland on the reunification issue.

Garret FitzGerald, TOWARDS A NEW IRELAND *(1973), pp. 142–157. Reproduced by permission of the author.*

~

From the Decision of the Supreme Court in *McGee v. the Attorney General and the Revenue Commissioners*

19 December 1973

Mrs. Mary McGee ordered contraceptive materials that were impounded by the Irish customs service. Her appeal against this action was supported by the Irish Family Planning Association. The appeal was dismissed by the president of the High Court, but this decision was overturned by the Supreme Court in a far-reaching decision that made it legal to import contraceptives for private use.

SEE ALSO Divorce, Contraception, and Abortion; Family: Fertility, Marriage, and the Family since 1950; Women in Irish Society since 1800

The Act of 1935, as its long title shows, is not aimed at population control but at the suppression of vice and the amendment of the law relating to sexual offences. Section 17 follows immediately on a section directed against the practice of prostitution in public and immediately precedes a section making criminal certain acts which offend modesty or cause scandal or injure the morals of the community. The section creates a criminal prohibition in an area in which the legislature has thought fit to intervene in the interests of public morality. What it seeks to do, by means of the sanction of the criminal law, is to put an end, as far as it was possible to do so by legislation, to the use of contraceptives in the state. It does not in terms make the use of contraceptives a crime, but the totality of the prohibition aims at nothing less. Presumably because contraceptives are of differing kinds and vary in the ways, internal and external, they can be used, and because of the difficulty of proving their use in the intimacy of the sexual act, the section strikes at their availability. Sub-section 1 of s. 17 of the Act of 1935 makes it an offence to sell, or expose, offer, advertise, or keep for sale or to import or attempt to import for sale any contraceptives. In effect, this makes it legally impossible to sell or buy a contraceptive in the state. Had the prohibition stopped there, it would have left the loophole that contraceptives could be imported otherwise than for sale. That loophole, however, is sealed by sub-s. 3 of s. 17 which makes contraceptives prohibited articles under the customs code so that their importation for any purpose, if effected with the intention of evading the prohibition, is an offence. . . .

Because contraceptives are not manufactured in this state, the effect of s. 17 of the Act of 1935 as a whole is that, except for contraceptives that have been imported without the intention of evading the prohibition on importation, it is not legally possible to obtain a contraceptive in this state. It is doubtful if the legislature could have taken more effective steps by means of the criminal law to put an end to their use in the state.

The dominant feature of the plaintiff's dilemma is that she is a young married woman who is living, with a slender income, in the cramped quarters of a mobile home with her husband and four infant children, and that she is faced with a considerable risk of death or crippling paralysis if she becomes pregnant. The net question is whether it is constitutionally permissible in the circumstances for the law to deny her access to the contraceptive method chosen for her by her doctor and which she and her husband wish to adopt. In other words, is the prohibition effected by s. 17 of the Act of 1935 an interference with the rights which the state guarantees in its laws to respect, as stated in sub-s. 1 of s. 3 of Article 40?

The answer lies primarily in the fact that the plaintiff is a wife and a mother. It is the informed and conscientious wish of the plaintiff and her husband to maintain full marital relations without incurring the risk of a pregnancy that may well result in her death or a crippling paralysis. Section 17 of the Act of 1935 frustrates that wish. It goes further; it brings the implementation of the wish within the range of the criminal law. Its effect, therefore, is to condemn the plaintiff and her husband to a way of life which, at best, will be fraught with worry, tension and uncertainty that cannot but adversely affect their lives and, at worst, will result in an unwanted pregnancy causing death or serious illness with the obvious tragic consequences to the lives of her husband and young children. And this in the context of a constitution which in its preamble proclaims as one of its aims the dignity and freedom of the individual; which in sub-s. 2 of s. 3 of Article 40 casts on the state a duty to protect as best it may from unjust attack and, in the case of injustice done, to vindicate the life and person of every citizen; which in Article 41 after recognising the family as the natural primary and fundamental unit group of society, and as a moral institution possessing inalienable and imprescriptible rights antecedent and superior to all positive law guarantees to protect it in its constitution and authority as the necessary basis of social order and as indispensable to the welfare of the nation and the state; and which also in article 41, pledges the state to guard with special care the institution of marriage, on which the family is founded, and to protect it against attack.

Section 17, in my judgment, so far from respecting the plaintiff's personal rights, violates them. If she observes this prohibition (which in practice she can scarcely avoid doing and which in law she is bound under penalty of fine and imprisonment to do), she will endanger the security and happiness of her marriage, she will imperil her health to the point of hazarding her life, and she will subject her family to the risk of distress and disruption. These are intrusions which she is entitled to say are incompatible with the safety of her life, the preservation of her health, her responsibility to her conscience, and the security and well-being of her marriage and family. If she fails to obey the prohibition in s. 17, the law, by prosecuting her, will reach into the privacy of her marital life in seeking to prove her guilt. . . .

If the plaintiff were prosecuted for an offence arising under or by virtue of s. 17 of the Act of 1935 . . .

there would necessarily be a violation of intimate aspects of her marital life which, in deference to her standing as a wife and mother, ought not to be brought out and condemned as criminal under a glare of publicity in a courtroom. Furthermore, if she were found guilty of such an offence, in order to have the penalty mitigated to fit the circumstances of her case, she would have to disclose particulars of her marital dilemma which she ought not to have to reveal.

In my opinion, s. 17 of the Act of 1935 violates the guarantee in sub-s. 1 of s. 3 of article 40 by the state to protect the plaintiff's personal rights by its laws; it does so not only by violating her personal right to privacy in regard to her marital relations but, in a wider way, by frustrating and making criminal any efforts by her to effectuate the decision of her husband and herself, made responsibly, conscientiously and on medical advice, to avail themselves of a particular contraceptive method so as to ensure her life and health as well as the integrity, security and well-being of her marriage and her family. (Justice Henchy)

I shall deal first with the submission made in relation to the provisions of Article 41 of the constitution which deals with the family. On the particular facts of this case, I think this is the most important submission because the plaintiff's claim is based upon her status as a married woman and is made in relation to the conduct of her sexual life with her husband within that marriage. For the purpose of this article I am of the opinion that the state of the plaintiff's health is immaterial to the consideration of the rights she claims are infringed in relation to Article 41. In this article the state, while recognising the family as the natural primary and fundamental unit group of society and as a moral institution possessing inalienable and imprescriptible rights antecedent and superior to all positive law, guarantees to protect the family in its constitution and authority as the necessary basis of social order and as indispensable to the welfare of the nation and the state. The article recognises the special position of woman, meaning the wife, within that unit; the article also offers special protection for mothers in that they shall not be obliged by economic necessity to engage in labour to the neglect of their duties in the home. The article also recognises the institution of marriage as the foundation of the family and undertakes to protect it against attack. By this and the following article, the state recognises the parents as the natural guardians of the children of the family and as those in whom the authority of the family is vested and those who shall have the right to determine how the family life shall be conducted, having due regard to the

---

rights of the children not merely as members of that family but as individuals.

It is a matter exclusively for the husband and wife to decide how many children they wish to have; it would be quite outside the competence of the state to dictate or prescribe the number of children which they might have or should have. In my view, the husband and wife have a correlative right to agree to have no children. This is not to say that the state, when the common good requires it, may not actively encourage married couples either to have larger families or smaller families. If it is a question of having smaller families then, whether it be a decision of the husband and wife or the intervention of the state, the means employed to achieve this objective would have to be examined. What may be permissible to the husband and wife is not necessarily permissible to the state. For example, the husband and wife may mutually agree to practise either total or partial abstinence in their sexual relations. If the state were to attempt to intervene to compel such abstinence, it would be an intolerable and unjustifiable intrusion into the privacy of the matrimonial bedroom. On the other hand, any action on the part of either the husband and wife or of the state to limit family sizes by endangering or destroying human life must necessarily not only be an offence against the common good but also against the guaranteed personal rights of the human life in question.

The sexual life of a husband and wife is of necessity and by its nature an area of particular privacy. If the husband and wife decide to limit their family or to avoid having children by use of contraceptives it is a matter peculiarly within the joint decision of the husband and wife and one into which the state cannot intrude unless its intrusion can be justified by the exigencies of the common good. The question of whether the use of contraceptives by married couples within their marriage is or is not contrary to the moral code or codes to which they profess to subscribe, or is or is not regarded by them as being against their conscience, could not justify state intervention. Similarly the fact that the use of contraceptives may offend against the moral code of the majority of the citizens of the state would not per se justify an intervention by the state to prohibit their use within marriage. The private morality of its citizens does not justify intervention by the state into the activities of those citizens unless and until the common good requires it. Counsel for the attorney general did not seek to argue that the state would have any right to seek to prevent the use of contraceptives within marriage. He did argue, however, that it did not follow from this that the state was under any obligation to make contraceptives available to married couples. Counsel for the [Reve-

nue Commissioners] put the matter somewhat further by stating that, if she had a right to use contraceptives within the privacy of her marriage, it was a matter for the plaintiff to prove from whence the right sprang. In effect he was saying that, if she was appealing to a right anterior to positive law, the burden was on her to show the source of that right. At first sight this may appear to be a reasonable and logical proposition. However, it does appear to ignore a fundamental point, namely, that the rights of a married couple to decide how many children, if any, they will have are matters outside the reach of positive law where the means employed to implement such decisions do not impinge upon the common good or destroy of endanger human life. It is undoubtedly true that among those persons who are subject to a particular moral code no one has a right to be in breach of that moral code. But when this is a code governing private morality and where the breach of it is not one which injures the common good then it is not the state's business to intervene. It is outside the authority of the state to endeavour to intrude into the privacy of the husband and wife relationship for the sake of imposing a code of private morality upon that husband and wife which they do not desire.

In my view, Article 41 of the constitution guarantees the husband and wife against such invasion of their privacy by the state. It follows that the use of contraceptives by them within that marital privacy is equally guaranteed against such invasion and, as such, assumes the status of a right so guaranteed by the constitution. If this right cannot be directly invaded by the state it follows that it cannot be frustrated by the state taking measures to ensure that the exercise of that right is rendered impossible. I do not exclude the possibility of the state being justified where the public good requires it (as, for example, in the case of a dangerous fall in population threatening the life or the essential welfare of the state) in taking such steps to ensure that in general, even if married couples could not be compelled to have children, they could at least be hindered in their endeavours to avoid having them where the common good required the maintenance or increase of the population. That, however, is not the present case and there is no evidence whatever in the case to justify state intervention on that ground. Similarly it is not impossible to envisage a situation where the availability of contraceptives to married people for use within marriage could be demonstrated to have led or would probably lead to such an adverse effect on public morality so subversive of the common good as to justify state intervention by restricting or prohibiting the availability of contraceptives for use within marriage or at all. In such a case it would have to be demonstrated that all the other resources of the state had proved or were likely to prove incapable to avoid this subversion of the common good while contraceptives remained available for use within marriage.

In my opinion, s. 17 of the Act of 1935, in so far as it unreasonably restricts the availability of contraceptives for use within marriage, is inconsistent with the provisions of Article 41 of the constitution for being an unjustified invasion of the privacy of husband and wife in their sexual relations with one another. The fundamental restriction is contained in the provisions of sub-s. 3 of s. 17 of the Act of 1935 which lists contraceptives among the prohibited articles which may not be imported for any purposes whatever. On the present state of facts, I am of the opinion that this provision is inconsistent with the constitution and is no longer in force. (Justice Walsh)

Reprinted in THE FIELD DAY ANTHOLOGY OF IRISH WRITING, *vol. 5,* IRISH WOMEN'S WRITING AND TRADITIONS (2002), *pp.* 335–338.

~

ON THE FAMILY PLANNING BILL

20 February 1974

Mary Robinson

Section 17 of the 1935 Criminal Law Amendment Act prohibited the sale and importation of contraceptives. By the late 1960s the restrictions on access to contraception were being challenged by the contraceptive pill, which was not covered by the 1935 act, and by the emergence of family planning clinics which supplied contraceptives in return for "voluntary" donations. In 1970 Mary Robinson, a senator elected by graduates of Trinity College Dublin, and a future president of Ireland, together with Senators Trevor West and John Horgan, elected by graduates of Trinity College and the National University of Ireland, attempted to introduce a bill to permit the import and sale of contraceptives, but it failed to get a first reading. They reintroduced this bill in the autumn of 1973, and on this occasion they secured a second reading, prompting a statement from the Catholic Church, which condemned contraception but rejected the suggestion that the state was obliged in its legislation to defend the moral teaching of the Catholic Church. Although this bill was defeated, it can be seen as the first attempt to provide a legislative framework for access to contraception; the matter was finally resolved in 1985. (See also excerpts from the decision of the Supreme Court in McGee v. the Attorney General and the Revenue Commissioners, *1973.)*

SEE ALSO Divorce, Contraception, and Abortion; Family: Fertility, Marriage, and the Family since 1950; Robinson, Mary; Women in Irish Society since 1800

This bill provides the first opportunity for a full debate in either house of the Oireachtas on the subject of family planning. It allows the Seanad to discuss the general principles involved in any changes in the law and it also allows the Seanad to consider the specific framework which Senators Horgan, West and I have put forward in this bill for such amendment. I should like to appeal to my fellow Senators: let us approach this subject with compassion rather than dogmatism and with open-minded concern rather than bigotry. Family planning involves the most intimate relationship between a man and a woman. It is a subject matter which has been discussed very broadly outside parliament in recent times. It is also a subject which was taboo for discussion for a very long time. It is now to be debated inside parliament.

It is worth noting that family planning is now supported positively by all the Christian churches. This includes the Catholic Church which is in favour of responsible parenthood, in favour of family planning. The difference between them relates only to choice of means. This bill would create the possibility of a wider choice of means of family planning and the possibility of getting full information on the subject. It is in other words an enabling bill. . . . It would not compel any person to use contraceptives, or any doctor to prescribe contraceptives, or any chemist to stock contraceptives. It would facilitate family planning by allowing choice to the individual citizens concerned.

When an attempt was made by Senators Horgan, West and me to introduce a similar bill in 1970, four years ago now, there was a significant resistance both in the Oireachtas and in the general public to any change in the law. In the intervening period no government bill was introduced either by the previous government or by this government. When we tabled this family planning bill there was a similar resistance to any change. Meanwhile however the Supreme Court has acted on one section of the law, that is subsection (3) of section 17 of the Criminal Law (Amendment) Act, 1935, and has deemed that section to be repugnant to the constitution. This was one section which we had repealed in the framework of our bill, which certain bigoted, unthinking people opposed, in a blanket form—opposed in many cases without having read the bill because they opposed any change in the law. . . .

Let us turn then to an examination of the present state of the law. As the law now stands, any person, married, or unmarried, and with no age limit, can use contraceptives, manufacture contraceptives, distribute contraceptives, and, since the judgment of the Supreme Court in the McGee case, import contraceptives. Also the pill is regarded not as a contraceptive but as a cycle regulator and therefore does not come within the legislation prohibiting the sale of contraceptives. More than 38,000 Irish women, be they married or unmarried, use the pill under a prescription every month, however none of these people can inform herself fully on the subject. As the law now stands, they cannot acquire responsible literature describing the various forms of contraceptives, warning them of the potential danger of the contraceptives which they are importing from abroad, warning them of the conditions which make it unsafe for them to use the pill and generally advising them in a full manner of the whole question of family planning and of the choices open, if the person wishes to exercise choice, in the methods of family planning. . . .

The argument is very strong that the law in so far as it regulates or controls the whole subject of family planning is not satisfactory, is no longer a coherent structure and has very real dangers built into it. I would hope that the members of the Seanad in the course of this debate, and also members of the other house, in examining either this bill or a government bill, when that is forthcoming, will have the courage to face up to this situation, because they have the advantage over their constituents. The average Irish person is not faced in the same way with the opportunity to examine the present state of the law and to consider a proposal for change. The average person may very well be confused, is obviously concerned, and rightly so, and may in consequence be resisting change. This is a very good example of where there must be leadership from the representatives of the people, and not a rather cowardly fear of the grassroots opinion and fear of change, lest it might translate into a turning away either from a particular politician or from a party.

Therefore I would submit that we ought to take this subject matter out of the realm of party politics by agreeing to the consensus view that there is a need for a law to be regularised in the public interest. We can differ perhaps on the degree to which there might be liberalisation or the degree to which there might be restrictions and controls built in. But on the fundamental proposition of need for regularisation of the position through an act of this Oireachtas, I would submit that no senator or deputy examining the position can dissent from that in good faith. . . .

There is one possible way in which the law in relation to family planning in this country could continue to be changed. We could continue to have people bringing individual cases before the High Court and Supreme Court and testing the constitutionality of the prohibition on sale of contraceptives and the constitutionality of the prohibition on being able to read about family planning in the relevant provisions of the censorship acts. We could have over a period of a number of years—because law suits take a length of time—a series of decisions which chipped away in a piecemeal fashion at our law, leaving an unregulated and unco-ordinated situation and one which gradually liberalised— probably more than many legislators would wish—the law relating to family planning.

I would submit that this would be a very sad state of the law if legislators abdicated their responsibility and left it to the courts; so that we would be dependent on individual plaintiffs bringing their single problems before the court, to gradually chip away at the existing law. We must face up to our responsibilities as members of this parliament. We must restore the balance by providing a properly planned and properly considered framework within which we regulate the whole subject matter of family planning.

Action by the Oireachtas is necessary for two reasons: first, because of the nature of the subject matter. If it becomes necessary for individuals to bring actions in the courts the results will be pragmatic, piecemeal, unco-ordinated and will result in a bad overall situation; secondly, because political scientists observe it as a weakness in the system if one leaves the legislating to the judges. It is not the function of the judiciary to legislate. It is the function of parliament. We must not abdicate to the judiciary the function of gradually finding our laws unconstitutional and, therefore, in effect legislating. We must take upon ourselves the primary responsibility. We must exercise the function of legislating without fear of the grassroots, without fear of misunderstanding and with a compassion and a concern for the human beings who are affected in their daily lives—in their intimate relationships—by the law which we pass.

This is the first task before the Oireachtas; to regularise the unacceptable nature of the existing law. The second task I believe goes further. It is to consider the objective of the proposers of this family planning bill. We seek to amend, for positive reasons, the law relating to family planning and to protect and sustain the right of individuals to use contraceptives and to plan their families and also to ensure that they have the proper access to information in this regard.

SEANAD DEBATES, *vol. 77, cols. 205–212, 20 February 1974, available at www.oireachtas-debates.gov.ie.*

"PUNISHMENT"

1975

Seamus Heaney

Born in Mossbawn, Co. Derry, in 1939, Seamus Heaney is undoubtedly the most famous Irish poet of his generation. He grew up on a small farm and was later educated at Queen's University, Belfast. After qualifying as a teacher and working at a teacher-training college, he moved to Wicklow in 1972. He subsequently taught in Dublin and at Harvard University, where he received the Boylston Chair of Rhetoric in 1981. He was Professor of Poetry at Oxford from 1989 to 1994 and received the Nobel Prize for Literature in 1995. This poem, which was published in his second poetry collection, North *(1975), draws on the image of the perfectly preserved bodies of prehistoric people found in the bogs of northern Denmark (Jutland). Here he compares the body of a woman who had been ritually strangled with her latter-day counterparts in Northern Ireland, whose heads are shaved and tarred for some infraction against the "tribal" rules.*

SEE ALSO Arts: Modern Irish and Anglo-Irish Literature and the Arts since 1800; Heaney, Seamus; Poetry, Modern

I can feel the tug
of the halter at the nape
of her neck, the wind
on her naked front

It blows her nipples
to amber beads,
it shakes the frail rigging
of her ribs.

I can see her drowned
body in the bog
the weighing stone,
the floating rods and boughs.

Under which at first
she was a barked sapling
that is dug up
oak-bone, brain-firkin:

her shaved head
like a stubble of black corn,
her blindfold a soiled bandage,
her noose a ring

to store
the memories of love.
Little adulteress,
before they punished you

you were flaxen-haired,
undernourished, and your
tar-black face was beautiful.
My poor scapegoat,

I almost love you
but would have cast, I know,
the stone of silence.
I am the artful voyeur

of your brain's exposed
and darkened combs,
your muscles' webbing
and all your numbered bones:

I who have stood dumb
when your betraying sisters,
cauled in tar,
wept by the railings,

who would connive
in civilized outrage
yet understand the exact
and tribal, intimate revenge.

Seamus Heaney, NORTH *(1975), pp. 30–31. Reproduced by permission of Farrar, Straus and Giroux in the U.S. and Faber & Faber Ltd. in the U.K.*

ANGLO-IRISH AGREEMENT

15 November 1985

This Anglo-Irish Agreement, often described as the Hillsborough Agreement, was signed by British prime minister Margaret Thatcher and Irish taoiseach Garret FitzGerald. The agreement included many elements that form part of the 1998 Belfast Agreement: a statement that the status of Northern Ireland could be changed only by a majority vote of the people of Northern Ireland; an intergovernmental conference dealing with politics, security, legal matters, and cross-border cooperation; and an acknowledgment that there were two traditions in Northern Ireland. Ulster unionists bitterly opposed the formal recognition of a role for the Irish government in Northern Ireland affairs. The agreement remained in force until it was superseded by the Belfast Agreement of 1998.

SEE ALSO Anglo-Irish Agreement of 1985 (Hillsborough Agreement); Northern Ireland: Constitutional Settlement from Sunningdale to Good Friday; Northern Ireland: The United States in Northern Ireland since 1970; Politics: Impact of the Northern Ireland Crisis on Southern Politics; Ulster Politics under Direct Rule

The government of Ireland and the government of the United Kingdom:

Wishing further to develop the unique relationship between their peoples and the close co-operation between their countries as friendly neighbors and as partners in the European community;

Recognising the major interest of both their countries and, above all, of the people of Northern Ireland in diminishing the divisions there and achieving lasting peace and stability;

Recognising the need for continuing efforts to reconcile and to acknowledge the rights of the two major traditions that exist in Ireland, represented on the one hand by those who wish for no change in the present status of Northern Ireland and on the other hand by those who aspire to a sovereign united Ireland achieved by peaceful means and through agreement;

Reaffirming their total rejection of any attempt to promote political objectives by violence or the threat of violence and their determination to work together to ensure that those who adopt or support such methods do not succeed;

Recognising that a condition of genuine reconciliation and dialogue between unionists and nationalists is mutual recognition and acceptance of each other's rights;

Recognising and respecting the identities of the two communities in Northern Ireland, and the right of each to pursue its aspirations by peaceful and constitutional means;

Reaffirming their commitment to a society in Northern Ireland in which all may live in peace, free from discrimination and intolerance, and with the opportunity for both communities to participate fully in the structures and processes of government;

Have accordingly agreed as follows:

A
STATUS OF NORTHERN IRELAND

Article 1

The two governments

(a) affirm that any change in the status of Northern Ireland would only come about with the consent of a majority of the people in Northern Ireland;

(b) recognise that the present wish of a majority of the people of Northern Ireland is for no change in the status of Northern Ireland;

(c) declare that, if in the future a majority of the people of Northern Ireland clearly wish for and formally consent to the establishment of a united Ireland, they will introduce and support in the respective parliaments legislation to give effect to that wish.

B
THE INTERGOVERNMENTAL CONFERENCE

Article 2

(a) There is hereby established, within the framework of the Anglo-Irish intergovernmental council set up after the meeting between the two heads of government on 6 November 1981, an intergovernmental conference (hereinafter referred to as "the Conference"), concerned with Northern Ireland and with relations between the two parts of the island of Ireland, to deal, as set out in this agreement, on a regular basis with

(i) political matters;

(ii) security and related matters;

(iii) legal matters, including the administration of justice;

(iv) the promotion of cross-border co-operation.

(b) The United Kingdom government accept that the Irish government will put forward views and proposals on matters relating to Northern Ireland within the field of activity of the Conference in so far as those matters are not the responsibility of a devolved administration in Northern Ireland. In the interest of promoting peace and stability, determined efforts shall be made through the Conference to resolve any differences. The Conference will be mainly concerned with Northern Ireland; but some of the matters under consideration will involve co-operative action in both parts of the island of Ireland, and possibly also in Great Britain. Some of the proposals considered in respect of Northern Ireland may also be found to have application by the Irish government. There is no derogation from the sovereignty of either the Irish government or the United Kingdom government, and each retains responsibility for the decisions and administrations of government within its own jurisdiction.

Article 3

The Conference shall meet at ministerial or official level, as required. The business of the Conference will thus receive attention at the highest level. Regular and frequent ministerial meetings shall be held; and in particular special meetings shall be convened at the request of either side. Officials may meet in subordinate groups. Membership of the Conference and of sub-groups shall be small and flexible. When the Conference meets at ministerial level an Irish minister designated as the permanent Irish ministerial representative and the secretary of state for Northern Ireland shall be joint chairmen. Within the framework of the Conference other Irish and British ministers may hold or attend meetings as appropriate: when legal matters are under consideration the attorneys general may attend. Ministers may be accompanied by their officials and their professional advisers: for example, when questions of security policy or security co-operation are being discussed, they may be accompanied by the commissioner of the Garda Síochána and the chief constable of the Royal Ulster Constabulary; or when questions of economic or social policy or cooperation are being discussed, they may be accompanied by officials of the relevant departments. A secretariat shall be established by the two governments to service the Conference on a continuing basis in the discharge of its functions as set out in this agreement.

Article 4

(a) In relation to matters coming within its field of activity, the Conference shall be a framework within which the Irish government and the United Kingdom government work together

    (i) for the accommodation of the rights and identities of the two traditions which exist in Northern Ireland; and

    (ii) for peace, stability and prosperity throughout the island of Ireland by promoting reconciliation, respect for human rights, cooperation against terrorism and the development of economic, social and cultural co-operation.

(b) It is the declared policy of the United Kingdom government that responsibility in respect of certain matters within the powers of the secretary of state for Northern Ireland should be devolved within Northern Ireland on a basis which would secure widespread acceptance throughout the community. The Irish government support that policy.

(c) Both governments recognise that devolution can be achieved only with the co-operation of consti-

tutional representatives within Northern Ireland of both traditions there. The Conference shall be a framework within which the Irish government may put forward views and proposals on the modalities of bringing about devolution in Northern Ireland, in so far as they relate to the interests of the minority community.

C
POLITICAL MATTERS

Article 5

(a) The Conference shall concern itself with measures to recognise and accommodate the rights and identities of the two traditions in Northern Ireland, to protect human rights and to prevent discrimination. Matters to be considered in this area include measures to foster the cultural heritage of both traditions, changes in electoral arrangements, the use of flags and emblems, the avoidance of economic and social discrimination and the advantages and disadvantages of a bill of rights in some form in Northern Ireland.

(b) The discussion of these matters shall be mainly concerned with Northern Ireland, but the possible application of any measures pursuant to this article by the Irish government in their jurisdiction shall not be excluded.

(c) If it should prove impossible to achieve and sustain devolution on a basis which secures widespread acceptance in Northern Ireland, the Conference shall be a framework within which the Irish government may, where the interests of the minority community are significantly or especially affected, put forward views on proposals for major legislation and on major policy issues, which are within the purview of the Northern Ireland departments and which remain the responsibility of the secretary of state for Northern Ireland.

Article 6

The Conference shall be a framework within which the Irish government may put forward views and proposals on the role and composition of bodies appointed by the secretary of state for Northern Ireland or by departments subject to his direction and control including the Standing Advisory Commission on Human Rights; the Fair Employment Agency; the Equal Opportunities Commission; the Police Authority for Northern Ireland; the Police Complaint Board.

D

SECURITY AND RELATED MATTERS

Article 7

(a) The Conference shall consider

    (i) security policy;

    (ii) relations between the security forces and the community;

    (iii) prisons policy.

(b) The Conference shall consider the security situation at its regular meetings and thus provide an opportunity to address policy issues, serious incidents and forthcoming events.

(c) The two governments agree that there is a need for a programme of special measures in Northern Ireland to improve relations between the security forces and the community, with the object in particular of making the security forces more readily accepted by the nationalist community. Such a programme shall be developed, for the Conference's consideration, and may include the establishment of local consultative machinery, training in community relations, crime prevention schemes involving the community, improvements in arrangements for handling complaints, and action to increase the proportion of members of the minority in the Royal Ulster Constabulary. Elements of the programme may be considered by the Irish government suitable for application within their jurisdiction.

(d) The Conference may consider policy issues relating to prisons. Individual cases may be raised as appropriate, so that information can be provided or inquiries instituted.

E

LEGAL MATTERS, INCLUDING THE ADMINISTRATION OF JUSTICE

Article 8

(a) The Conference shall deal with issues of concern to both countries relating to the enforcement of the criminal law. In particular it shall consider whether there are areas of the criminal law applying in the North and in the South respectively which might with benefit be harmonised. The two governments agree on the importance of public confidence in the administration of justice. The Conference shall seek, with the help of advice from experts as appropriate; measures which would give substantial expression to this aim, considering inter alia the possibility of mixed courts in both jurisdictions for the trial of certain offences. The Conference shall also be concerned with policy aspects of extradition and extra-territorial jurisdiction as between North and South.

F

CROSS-BORDER CO-OPERATION ON SECURITY, ECONOMIC AND CULTURAL MATTERS

Article 9

(a) With a view to enhancing cross-border co-operation on security matters, the Conference shall set in hand a programme of work to be undertaken by the commissioner of the Garda Síochána and the chief constable of the Royal Ulster Constabulary and, where appropriate, groups of officials, in such areas as threat assessments, exchange of information, liaison structures, technical co-operation, training of personnel, and operational resources.

(b) The Conference shall have no operational responsibilities; responsibility for policy operations shall remain with the heads of the respective police forces, the commissioner of the Garda Síochána maintaining his links with the minister for justice and the chief constable of the Royal Ulster Constabulary his links with the secretary of state for Northern Ireland.

Article 10

(a) The two governments shall co-operate to promote the economic and social development of those areas of both parts of Ireland which have suffered most severely from the consequences of the instability of recent years, and shall consider the possibility of securing international support for this work.

(b) If it should prove impossible to achieve and sustain devolution on a basis which secures widespread acceptance in Northern Ireland, the Conference shall be a framework for the promotion of co-operation between the two parts of Ireland concerning cross-border aspects of economic, social and cultural matters in relation to which the secretary of state for Northern Ireland continues to exercise authority.

(c) If responsibility is devolved in respect of certain matters in the economic, social or cultural areas currently within the responsibility of the secretary of state for Northern Ireland, machinery will need to be established by the responsible authorities in the North and South for practical co-operation in respect of cross-border aspects of these issues.

G
ARRANGEMENTS FOR REVIEW

Article 11

At the end of three years from signature of this agreement, or earlier if requested by either government, the working of the Conference shall be reviewed by the two governments to see whether any changes in the scope and nature of its activities are desirable.

H
INTERPARLIAMENTARY RELATIONS

Article 12

If will be for parliamentary decision in Dublin and in Westminster whether to establish an Anglo-Irish parliamentary body of the kind adumbrated in the Anglo-Irish Studies Report of November 1981. The two governments agree that they would give support as appropriate to such a body, if it were to be established.

I
FINAL CLAUSES

Article 13

This agreement shall enter into force on the date on which the two governments exchange notifications of their acceptance of this agreement.

In witness whereof the undersigned, being duly authorised thereto by their respective governments, have signed this agreement.

Done in two originals at Hillsborough on the 15th day of November 1985.

For the government of Ireland—Gearóid Mac Gearailt

For the government of the United Kingdom—Margaret Thatcher

Reprinted in FIELD DAY ANTHOLOGY OF IRISH WRITING, edited by Seamus Deane (1991), vol. 3, pp. 803–807.

"INQUISITIO 1584"

c. 1985

Máire Mhac an tSaoi

Born in 1922 the daughter of Seán MacEntee, deputy prime minister in the de Valera and Lemass governments, Máire Mhac an tSaoi (the Gaelic form of her surname) studied in Paris after completing her B.A. and M.A. at University College Dublin and then returned to work in Celtic Studies at the Dublin Institute for Advanced Studies. She studied for the Irish bar, entered the foreign service, and later married the Irish diplomat and journalist Conor Cruise O'Brien. A well-known Gaelic poet and scholar, she has published seven collections of poetry and several critical and historical essays. This poem, an elegy on the hanging of Sean MacEdmund MacUllick by the English in Limerick c. 1584, published in An Cion go dtí Seo (The amount to now, 1987), reveals her extensive knowledge of Irish history and the Gaelic literary tradition.

SEE ALSO Arts: Modern Irish and Anglo-Irish Literature and the Arts since 1800; Literature: Twentieth-Century Women Writers

In that year of the age of Our Lord
Fifteen hundred and eighty
Or some few short years after
Sean MacEdmund MacUllick
Hard by Shannon was hanged.

Hard by the shoals of Shannon
In Limerick, history's city,
Sean MacEdmund MacUllick
Come west from the parish of Marrhan
Who was chieftain of Balleneenig.

Treason his crime, his lands
Were given in hand of the stranger
And now around Mount Marrhan
His name is not even remembered
Nor is his kindred known there.

Undisturbed be your sleep
Sean MacEdmund MacUllick
On the banks of the mighty Shannon
When the wind blows in from the sea
From the west and from your own country.

Reprinted in IRISH LITERATURE: A READER, edited by Maureen O'Rourke Murphy and James Mackillop (1987). Reproduced by permission of the author.

"FEIS" ("CARNIVAL")

c. 1990

Nuala Ní Dhomhnaill

Born to London-Irish parents in 1952, Nuala Ní Dhomhnaill was later fostered by her aunt in the Kerry Gaeltacht. After receiving a B.A. at University College Cork, she married a Turkish geologist and lived abroad for many years. Returning to Ireland in 1980, she began to immerse herself in Irish folklore and mythology, which provides a source for much of her work, such as this poem. The Irish title, "Feis," is taken from an Old Irish verb, fo-aid (meaning "to sleep with"), and connotes the ancient Irish king's act of ritually sleeping with the goddess of sovereignty and the land. Nuala combines this with the archaeology of the Neolithic burial mound, Brú na Bóinne (Newgrange), where the sunlight illuminates the enclosed passageway at dawn on the winter solstice, symbolically fertilizing the earth. Originally published in Irish in 1991, the parallel texts in Irish and English appeared in a collection translated by Paul Muldoon in the following year. The author is one of the best known and most acclaimed Gaelic poets of the past century.

SEE ALSO Arts: Modern Irish and Anglo-Irish Literature and the Arts since 1800; Literature: Twentieth-Century Women Writers

"Feis"

1

Nuair a éiríonn tú ar maidin
is steallann ionam
seinneann ceolta sí na cruinne
istigh im chloigeann.
Taistealaíonn an ga gréine
caol is lom
síos an pasáiste dorcha
is tríd an bpoll

sa bhfardoras
is rianann solas ribe
ar an urlár cré
sa seomra iata
is íochtaraí go léir.
Atann ansan is téann i méid
is i méid go dtí go líontar
le solas órga an t-aireagal go léir.

Feasta
beidh na hoícheanta níos giorra.
Raghaidh achar gach lae i bhfaid is i bhfaid.

2

Nuair a osclaím mo shúile
ag teacht aníos chun aeir
tá an spéir
gorm.
Canann éinín aonair
ar chrann.

Is cé go bhfuil an teannas
briste
is an ghlaise
ídithe ón uain
is leacht meala leata
mar thúis
ar fuaid an domhain,
fós le méid an tochta
atá eadrainn
ní labhrann ceachtar againn
oiread is focal
go ceann tamaill mhaith

3

Dá mba dhéithe sinn
anseo ag Brú na Bóinne —
tusa Sualtamh nó an Daghdha,
mise an abhainn ghlórmhar —

do stadfadh an ghrian is an ré
sa spéir ar feadh bliana is lae
ag cur buaine leis an bpléisiúr
atá eadrainn araon.

Faraoir, is fada ó dhéithe
sinne, créatúirí nochta.
Ní stadann na ranna neimhe
ach ar feadh aon nóiméad neamhshíoraí amháin.

4

Osclaíonn rós istigh im chroí.
Labhrann cuach im bhéal.
Léimeann gearrcach ó mo nead.
Tá tóithín ag macnas i ndoimhneas mo mhachnaimh.

5

Cóirím an leaba
i do choinne, a dhuine
nach n-aithním
thar m'fhear céile.

Tá nóiníní leata
ar an bpilliúr is ar an adharta.
Tá sméara dubha
fuaite ar an mbraillín.

6

Leagaim síos trí bhrat id fhianaise:
brat deora,
brat allais,
brat fola.

7

Mo scian trím chroí tú.
Mo sceach trím ladhar tú.
Mo cháithnín faoi m'fhiacail.

8

Thaibhrís dom arís aréir:
bhíomair ag siúl láimh amuigh faoin spéir.
Go hobann do léimis os mo chomhair
is bhain greim seirce as mo bhráid.

9

Bhíos feadh na hoíche
ag tiomáint síos bóithre do thíre
i gcarr spóirt béaloscailte
is gan tú faram.
Ghaibheas thar do thigh
is bhí do bhean istigh
sa chistin.
Aithním an sáipéal
ag a n-adhrann tú.

10

Smid thar mo bhéal ní chloisfir,
mo theanga imithe ag an gcat.
Labhrann mo lámha dhom.
Caipín snámha iad faoi bhun do chloiginn
dod chosaint ar oighear na bhfeachtaí bhfliuch.
Peidhleacáin iad ag tóraíocht beatha
ag eitealaigh thar mhóinéar do choirp.

11

Nuair a dh'fhágas tú
ar an gcé anocht
d'oscail trinse ábhalmhór
istigh im ucht
chomh doimhin sin
ná líonfar
fiú dá ndáilfí
ar aon tsoitheach
Sruth na Maoile, Muir Éireann
agus Muir nIocht.

"Carnival"

1

When you rise in the morning
and pour into me
an unearthly music
rings in my ears.
A ray of sunshine comes
slender and spare

down the dark passageway
and through the gap

in the lintel
to trace a light-scroll
on the mud floor
in the nethermost
sealed chamber.
Then it swells
and swells until a golden glow
fills the entire oratory.

From now on
the nights will be getting shorter
and the days longer and longer.

2

When I open my eyes
to come up for air
the sky
is blue.
A single bird sings
in a tree.

And though the tension
is released
and the chill
gone from the air
and a honeyed breath spreads
like frankincense
about the earth
such is the depth of emotion
we share
that neither of us speaks
as much as a word
for ages and ages.

3

If we were gods
here at Newgrange —
you Sualtam or the Daghda,
myself the famous river —

we could freeze the sun
and the moon
for a year and a day
to perpetuate the pleasure
we have together.

Alas, it's far from gods
we are, but bare, forked creatures.
The heavenly bodies stop
only for a single, transitory moment.

4

A rose opens in my heart.
A cuckoo sings in my throat.
A fledgeling leaps from my nest.
A dolphin plunges through my deepest thoughts.

5

I straighten the bed
for you, sweetheart:
I cannot tell
you and my husband apart.

There are daisies strewn
on the pillow and bolster:
the sheets are embroidered
with blackberry-clusters.

6

I lay down three robes before you:
a mantle of tears,
a coat of sweat,
a gown of blood.

7

You are a knife through my heart.
You are a briar in my fist.
You are a bit of grit between my teeth.

8

I dreamt of you again last night:
we were walking hand in hand through the countryside
when you suddenly ambushed
me and gave me a lovebit on my chest.

9

I spent all last night
driving down the byroads of your parish
in an open sports car
without you near me.
I went past your house
and glimpsed your wife
in the kitchen.
I recognise the chapel
at which you worship.

10

You won't hear a cheep from me.
The cat has got my tongue.
My hands do all the talking.
They're a swimming cap about your head
to protect you from the icy currents.
They're butterflies searching for sustenance
over your body's meadow.

11

When I left you
at the quay tonight
an enormous trench opened up
in my core
so profound
it would not be filled
even if you were to pour
from one utensil
the streams of the Mull of Kintyre
and the Irish Sea and the English Channel.

Nuala Ní Dhomhnaill, THE ASTRAKHAN CLOAK, *translated by Paul Muldoon (1992), pp. 10–19. Translations © Paul Muldoon 1992. Reproduced by kind permission of the authors and The Gallery Press, Loughcrew, Oldcastle, County Mead, Ireland.*

~

IRISH REPUBLICAN ARMY (IRA) CEASE-FIRE STATEMENT

31 August 1994

The IRA cease-fire opened the way for Sinn Féin to be included in talks on the future of Northern Ireland, but these negotiations stalled because of the refusal to decommission IRA arms and Sinn Féin's suspicion about the British government's motives. The cease-fire ended on 9 February 1996 when the IRA bombed Canary Wharf in London.

SEE ALSO Irish Republican Army (IRA); Northern Ireland: Constitutional Settlement from Sunningdale to Good Friday; Northern Ireland: History since 1920; Politics: Nationalist Politics in Northern Ireland

Recognising the potential of the current situation and in order to enhance the democratic process and underlying our definitive commitment to its success, the leadership of the IRA have decided that as of midnight, August 31, there will be a complete cessation of military operations. All our units have been instructed accordingly.

At this crossroads the leadership of the IRA salutes and commends our volunteers, other activists, our supporters and the political prisoners who have sustained the struggle against all odds for the past 25 years. Your courage, determination and sacrifice have demonstrated that the freedom and the desire for peace based on a just and lasting settlement cannot be crushed. We remember all those who have died for Irish freedom and we reiterate our commitment to our republican objectives. Our struggle has seen many gains and advances made by nationalists and for the democratic position.

We believe that an opportunity to secure a just and lasting settlement has been created. We are therefore entering into a new situation in a spirit of determination and confidence, determined that the injustices which created this conflict will be removed and confident in the strength and justice of our struggle to achieve this.

We note that the Downing Street Declaration is not a solution, nor was it presented as such by its authors. A solution will only be found as a result of inclusive negotiations. Others, not the least the British government have a duty to face up to their responsibilities. It is our desire to significantly contribute to the creation of a climate which will encourage this. We urge everyone to approach this new situation with energy, determination and patience.

Reprinted in A FAREWELL TO ARMS? FROM "LONG WAR" TO LONG PEACE IN NORTHERN IRELAND, *edited by Michael Cox, Adrian Guelke, and Fiona Stephens (2000), appendix 7, p. 336.*

~

TEXT OF THE IRA CEASE-FIRE STATEMENT

19 July 1997

This second cease-fire statement by the IRA refers to "a permanent peace," a phrase that was missing from the first, although the British government had sought it. The second cease-fire opened the way for elections to the Northern Ireland forum on 30 May 1997 and the start of multi-party talks on 10 June 1997, which resulted in the 1998 Belfast Agreement.

SEE ALSO Irish Republican Army (IRA); Northern Ireland: Constitutional Settlement from Sunningdale to Good Friday; Northern Ireland: History since 1920; Politics: Nationalist Politics in Northern Ireland

On August 31, 1994 the leadership of Óglaigh na hÉireann (IRA) announced their complete cessation of military operations as our contribution to the search for lasting peace.

After 17 months of cessation in which the British government and the unionists blocked any possibility of real or inclusive negotiations, we reluctantly abandoned the cessation.

The IRA is committed to ending British rule in Ireland. It is the root cause of divisions and conflict in our country. We want a permanent peace and therefore we are prepared to enhance the search for a democratic peace settlement through real and inclusive negotiations.

So having assessed the current political situation, the leadership of Óglaigh na hÉireann are announcing a complete cessation of military operations from 12 midday on Sunday 20 July, 1997.

We have ordered the unequivocal restoration of the ceasefire of August 1994. All IRA units have been instructed accordingly.

Reprinted in A FAREWELL TO ARMS? FROM "LONG WAR" TO LONG PEACE IN NORTHERN IRELAND, *edited by Michael Cox, Adrian Guelke, and Fiona Stephens (2000), appendix 11, p. 343.*

~

THE BELFAST/GOOD FRIDAY AGREEMENT

10 April 1998

The Belfast Agreement (or Good Friday Agreement) was the outcome of marathon talks, chaired by former U.S. Senator George Mitchell, involving all the major political groups in Northern Ireland and representatives of the British and Irish governments. It was endorsed on 22 May by referenda held in both parts of Ireland, with a vote of 71 percent in favor in Northern Ireland, and over 94 percent in the Republic of Ireland. Unedited excerpts from the agreement follow.

SEE ALSO Adams, Gerry; Constitution; Decommissioning; Economic Relations between North and South since 1922; Economic Relations between Northern Ireland and Britain; Equal Rights in Northern Ireland; Northern Ireland: Constitutional Settlement from Sunningdale to Good Friday; Northern Ireland: History since 1920; Northern Ireland: The United States in Northern Ireland since 1970; Royal Ulster Constabulary (including Specials); Ulster Politics under Direct Rule

AGREEMENT REACHED IN THE MULTI-PARTY NEGOTIATIONS

Declaration of Support

1. We, the participants in the multi-party negotiations, believe that the agreement we have negotiated offers a truly historic opportunity for a new beginning.

2. The tragedies of the past have left a deep and profoundly regrettable legacy of suffering. We must never forget those who have died or been injured, and their

families. But we can best honour them through a fresh start, in which we firmly dedicate ourselves to the achievement of reconciliation, tolerance, and mutual trust, and to the protection and vindication of the human rights of all.

3. We are committed to partnership, equality and mutual respect as the basis of relationships within Northern Ireland, between North and South, and between these islands.

4. We reaffirm our total and absolute commitment to exclusively democratic and peaceful means of resolving differences on political issues, and our opposition to any use or threat of force by others for any political purpose, whether in regard to this agreement or otherwise.

5. We acknowledge the substantial differences between our continuing, and equally legitimate, political aspirations. However, we will endeavour to strive in every practical way towards reconciliation and rapprochement within the framework of democratic and agreed arrangements. We pledge that we will, in good faith, work to ensure the success of each and every one of the arrangements to be established under this agreement. It is accepted that all of the institutional and constitutional arrangements—an assembly in Northern Ireland, a North/South Ministerial Council, implementation bodies, a British-Irish Council and a British-Irish Intergovernmental Conference and any amendments to British acts of parliament and the constitution of Ireland—are interlocking and interdependent and that in particular the functioning of the assembly and the North/South Council are so closely inter-related that the success of each depends on that of the other.

6. Accordingly, in a spirit of concord, we strongly commend this agreement to the people, North and South, for their approval.

Constitutional Issues

1. The participants endorse the commitment made by the British and Irish governments that, in a new British-Irish Agreement replacing the Anglo-Irish Agreement, they will:

(i) recognise the legitimacy of whatever choice is freely exercised by a majority of the people of Northern Ireland with regard to its status, whether they prefer to continue to support the Union with Great Britain or a sovereign united Ireland;

(ii) recognise that it is for the people of the island of Ireland alone, by agreement between the two parts respectively and without external impediment, to exercise their right of self-determination on the basis of consent, freely and concurrently given, North and South, to bring about a united Ireland, if that is their wish, accepting that this right must be achieved and exercised with and subject to the agreement and consent of a majority of the people of Northern Ireland;

(iii) acknowledge that while a substantial section of the people in Northern Ireland share the legitimate wish of a majority of the people of the island of Ireland for a united Ireland, the present wish of a majority of the people of Northern Ireland, freely exercised and legitimate, is to maintain the Union and, accordingly, that Northern Ireland's status as part of the United Kingdom reflects and relies upon that wish; and that it would be wrong to make any change in the status of Northern Ireland save with the consent of a majority of its people;

(iv) affirm that if, in the future, the people of the island of Ireland exercise their right of self-determination on the basis set out in sections (i) and (ii) above to bring about a united Ireland, it will be a binding obligation on both governments to introduce and support in their respective parliaments legislation to give effect to that wish;

(v) affirm that whatever choice is freely exercised by a majority of the people of Northern Ireland, the power of the sovereign government with jurisdiction there shall be exercised with rigorous impartiality on behalf of all the people in the diversity of their identities and traditions and shall be founded on the principles of full respect for, and equality of, civil, political, social and cultural rights, of freedom from discrimination for all citizens, and of parity of esteem and of just and equal treatment for the identity, ethos, and aspirations of both communities;

(vi) recognise the birthright of all the people of Northern Ireland to identify themselves and be accepted as Irish or British, or both, as they may so choose, and accordingly confirm that their right to hold both British and Irish citizenship is accepted by both governments and would not be affected by any future change in the status of Northern Ireland.

2. The participants also note that the two governments have accordingly undertaken in the context of this comprehensive political agreement, to propose and support changes in, respectively, the constitution of Ireland and in British legislation relating to the constitutional status of Northern Ireland.

Annex A

Draft Clauses/Schedules for Incorporation in British Legislation

1. (1) It is hereby declared that Northern Ireland in its entirety remains part of the United Kingdom and shall not cease to be so without the consent of a majority of the people of Northern Ireland voting in a poll held for the purposes of this section in accordance with Schedule 1.

(2) But if the wish expressed by a majority in such a poll is that Northern Ireland should cease to be part of the United Kingdom and form part of a united Ireland, the secretary of state shall lay before parliament such proposals to give effect to that wish as may be agreed between her majesty's government in the United Kingdom and the government of Ireland.

2. The Government of Ireland Act 1920 is repealed; and this act shall have effect notwithstanding any other previous enactment. . . .

Annex B

Irish Government Draft Legislation to Amend the Constitution

Add to Article 29 the following sections:

7.

1. The state may consent to be bound by the British-Irish Agreement done at Belfast on the day of 1998, hereinafter called the Agreement.

1. Any institution established by or under the Agreement may exercise the powers and functions thereby conferred on it in respect of all or any part of the island of Ireland notwithstanding any other provision of this constitution conferring a like power or function on any person or any organ of state appointed under or created or established by or under this constitution. Any power or function conferred on such an institution in relation to the settlement or resolution of disputes or controversies may be in addition to or in substitution for any like power or function conferred by this constitution on any such person or organ of state as aforesaid.

1. If the government declare that the state has become obliged, pursuant to the Agreement, to give effect to the amendment of this constitution referred to therein, then, notwithstanding Article 46 hereof, this constitution shall be amended as follows: . . .

Article 2

It is the entitlement and birthright of every person born in the island of Ireland, which includes its islands and seas, to be part of the Irish nation. That is also the entitlement of all persons otherwise qualified in accordance with law to be citizens of Ireland. Furthermore, the Irish nation cherishes its special affinity with people of Irish ancestry living abroad who share its cultural identity and heritage.

Article 3

1. It is the firm will of the Irish nation, in harmony and friendship, to unite all the people who share the territory of the island of Ireland, in all the diversity of their identities and traditions, recognising that a united Ireland shall be brought about only by peaceful means with the consent of a majority of the people, democratically expressed, in both jurisdictions in the island. Until then, the laws enacted by the parliament established by this constitution shall have the like area and extent of application as the laws enacted by the parliament that existed immediately before the coming into operation of this constitution.

2. Institutions with executive powers and functions that are shared between those jurisdictions may be established by their respective responsible authorities for stated purposes and may exercise powers and functions in respect of all or any part of the island. . . .

'8. The state may exercise extra-territorial jurisdiction in accordance with the generally recognised principles of international law. . . .

Strand One: Democratic Institutions in Northern Ireland

1. This agreement provides for a democratically elected assembly in Northern Ireland which is inclusive in its membership, capable of exercising executive and legislative authority, and subject to safeguards to protect the rights and interests of all sides of the community.

The Assembly

2. A 108-member assembly will be elected by PR(STV) from existing Westminster constituencies.

3. The assembly will exercise full legislative and executive authority in respect of those matters currently within the responsibility of the six Northern Ireland government departments, with the possibility of taking on responsibility for other matters as detailed elsewhere in this agreement.

4. The assembly—operating where appropriate on a cross-community basis—will be the prime source of authority in respect of all devolved responsibilities.

Safeguards

5. There will be safeguards to ensure that all sections of the community can participate and work together successfully in the operation of these institutions and that all sections of the community are protected, including:

(a) allocations of committee chairs, ministers and committee membership in proportion to party strengths;

(b) the European Convention on Human Rights (ECHR) and any bill of rights for Northern Ireland supplementing it, which neither the assembly nor public bodies can infringe, together with a Human Rights Commission;

(c) arrangements to provide that key decisions and legislation are proofed to ensure that they do not infringe the ECHR and any bill of rights for Northern Ireland;

(d) arrangements to ensure key decisions are taken on a cross-community basis;

    (i) either parallel consent, i.e., a majority of those members present and voting, including a majority of the unionist and nationalist designations present and voting;

    (ii) or a weighted majority (60%) of members present and voting, including at least 40% of each of the nationalist and unionist designations present and voting.

Key decisions requiring cross-community support will be designated in advance, including election of the chair of the assembly, the first minister and deputy first minister, standing orders and budget allocations. In other cases such decisions could be triggered by a petition of concern brought by a significant minority of assembly members (30/108).

(e) an Equality Commission to monitor a statutory obligation to promote equality of opportunity in specified areas and parity of esteem between the two main communities, and to investigate individual complaints against public bodies.

Operation of the Assembly

6. At their first meeting, members of the assembly will register a designation of identity—nationalist, unionist or other—for the purposes of measuring cross-community support in assembly votes under the relevant provisions above.

7. The chair and deputy chair of the assembly will be elected on a cross-community basis, as set out in paragraph 5(d) above.

8. There will be a committee for each of the main executive functions of the Northern Ireland administration. The chairs and deputy chairs of the assembly committees will be allocated proportionally, using the d'Hondt system. Membership of the committees will be in broad proportion to party strengths in the assembly to ensure that the opportunity of committee places is available to all members.

9. The committees will have a scrutiny, policy development and consultation role with respect to the department with which each is associated, and will have a role in initiation of legislation. They will have the power to:

    consider and advise on departmental budgets and annual plans in the context of the overall budget allocation;

    approve relevant secondary legislation and take the committee stage of relevant primary legislation;

    call for persons and papers;

    initiate enquiries and make reports;

    consider and advise on matters brought to the committee by its minister.

10. Standing committees other than departmental committees may be established as may be required from time to time.

11. The assembly may appoint a special committee to examine and report on whether a measure or proposal for legislation is in conformity with equality requirements, including the ECHR/bill of rights. The committee shall have the power to call people and papers to assist in its consideration of the matter. The assembly shall then consider the report of the committee and can determine the matter in accordance with the cross-community consent procedure.

12. The above special procedure shall be followed when requested by the executive committee, or by the relevant departmental committee, voting on a cross-community basis.

13. When there is a petition of concern as in 5(d) above, the assembly shall vote to determine whether the measure may proceed without reference to this special procedure. If this fails to achieve support on a cross-community basis, as in 5(d)(i) above, the special procedure shall be followed.

Executive Authority

14. Executive authority to be discharged on behalf of the assembly by a first minister and deputy first minister and up to ten ministers with departmental responsibilities.

15. The first minister and deputy first minister shall be jointly elected into office by the assembly voting on a cross-community basis, according to 5(d)(i) above.

16. Following the election of the first minister and deputy first minister, the posts of ministers will be allocated to parties on the basis of the d'Hondt system by reference to the number of seats each party has in the assembly.

17. The ministers will constitute an executive committee, which will be convened, and presided over, by the first minister and deputy first minister.

18. The duties of the first minister and deputy first minister will include, inter alia, dealing with and coordinating the work of the executive committee and the response of the Northern Ireland administration to external relationships.

19. The executive committee will provide a forum for the discussion of, and agreement on, issues which cut across the responsibilities of two or more ministers, for prioritising executive and legislative proposals and for recommending a common position where necessary (e.g., in dealing with external relationships).

20. The executive committee will seek to agree each year, and review as necessary, a programme incorporating an agreed budget linked to policies and programmes, subject to approval by the assembly, after scrutiny in assembly committees, on a cross-community basis. . . .

Legislation

26. The assembly will have authority to pass primary legislation for Northern Ireland in devolved areas, subject to:

(a) the ECHR and any bill of rights for Northern Ireland supplementing it which, if the courts found to be breached, would render the relevant legislation null and void;

(b) decisions by simple majority of members voting, except when decision on a cross-community basis is required;

(c) detailed scrutiny and approval in the relevant departmental committee;

(d) mechanisms, based on arrangements proposed for the Scottish parliament, to ensure suitable coordination, and avoid disputes, between the assembly and the Westminster parliament;

(e) option of the assembly seeking to include Northern Ireland provisions in United Kingdom-wide legislation in the Westminster parliament, . . .

Relations with Other Institutions

. . . 32. Role of secretary of state:

(a) to remain responsible for NIO matters not devolved to the assembly, subject to regular consultation with the assembly and ministers;

(b) to approve and lay before the Westminster parliament any assembly legislation on reserved matters;

(c) to represent Northern Ireland interests in the United Kingdom cabinet;

(d) to have the right to attend the assembly at their invitation.

33. The Westminster parliament (whose power to make legislation for Northern Ireland would remain unaffected) will:

(a) legislate for non-devolved issues, other than where the assembly legislates with the approval of the secretary of state and subject to the control of parliament;

(b) to legislate as necessary to ensure the United Kingdom's international obligations are met in respect of Northern Ireland;

(c) scrutinise, including through the Northern Ireland grand and select committees, the responsibilities of the secretary of state.

34. A consultative civic forum will be established. It will comprise representatives of the business, trade union and voluntary sectors, and such other sectors as agreed by the first minister and the deputy first minister. It will act as a consultative mechanism on social, economic and cultural issues. . . .

Strand Two: North/South Ministerial Council

1. Under a new British/Irish Agreement dealing with the totality of relationships, and related legislation at Westminster and in the Oireachtas, a North/South Ministerial Council to be established to bring together those with executive responsibilities in Northern Ireland and the Irish government, to develop consultation, cooperation and action within the island of Ireland—including through implementation on an all-island and cross-border basis—on matters of mutual interest within the competence of the administrations, North and South.

2. All council decisions to be by agreement between the two sides. Northern Ireland to be represented by the

first minister, deputy first minister and any relevant ministers, the Irish government by the taoiseach and relevant ministers, all operating in accordance with the rules for democratic authority and accountability in force in the Northern Ireland Assembly and the Oireachtas respectively. Participation in the council to be one of the essential responsibilities attaching to relevant posts in the two administrations. If a holder of a relevant post will not participate normally in the council, the taoiseach in the case of the Irish government and the first and deputy first minister in the case of the Northern Ireland administration to be able to make alternative arrangements.

3. The Council to meet in different formats:

(i) in plenary format twice a year, with Northern Ireland representation led by the first minister and deputy first minister and the Irish government led by the taoiseach;

(ii) in specific sectoral formats on a regular and frequent basis with each side represented by the appropriate minister;

(iii) in an appropriate format to consider institutional or cross-sectoral matters (including in relation to the EU) and to resolve disagreement.

4. Agendas for all meetings to be settled by prior agreement between the two sides, but it will be open to either to propose any matter for consideration or action.

5. The council:

(i) to exchange information, discuss and consult with a view to co-operating on matters of mutual interest within the competence of both administrations, North and South;

(ii) to use best endeavours to reach agreement on the adoption of common policies, in areas where there is a mutual cross-border and all-island benefit, and which are within the competence of both administrations, North and South, making determined efforts to overcome any disagreements;

(iii) to take decisions by agreement on policies for implementation separately in each jurisdiction, in relevant meaningful areas within the competence of both administrations, North and South;

(iv) to take decisions by agreement on policies and action at an all-island and cross-border level to be implemented by the bodies to be established as set out in paragraphs 8 and 9 below.

6. Each side to be in a position to take decisions in the council within the defined authority of those attending, through the arrangements in place for co-ordination of executive functions within each jurisdiction. Each side to remain accountable to the assembly and Oireachtas respectively, whose approval, through the arrangements in place on either side, would be required for decisions beyond the defined authority of those attending.

7. As soon as practically possible after elections to the Northern Ireland Assembly, inaugural meetings will take place of the assembly, the British/Irish Council and the North/South Ministerial Council in their transitional forms. All three institutions will meet regularly and frequently on this basis during the period between the elections to the assembly, and the transfer of powers to the assembly, in order to establish their modus operandi.

8. During the transitional period between the elections to the Northern Ireland Assembly and the transfer of power to it, representatives of the Northern Ireland transitional Administration and the Irish government operating in the North/South Ministerial Council will undertake a work programme, in consultation with the British government, covering at least 12 subject areas, with a view to identifying and agreeing by 31 October 1998 areas where co-operation and implementation for mutual benefit will take place. Such areas may include matters in the list set out in the Annex.

9. As part of the work programme, the council will identify and agree at least 6 matters for co-operation and implementation in each of the following categories:

(i) Matters where existing bodies will be the appropriate mechanisms for co-operation in each separate jurisdiction;

(ii) Matters where the co-operation will take place through agreed implementation bodies on a cross-border or all-island level.

10. The two governments will make necessary legislative and other enabling preparations to ensure, as an absolute commitment, that these bodies, which have been agreed as a result of the work programme, function at the time of the inception of the British-Irish Agreement and the transfer of powers, with legislative authority for these bodies transferred to the assembly as soon as possible thereafter. Other arrangements for the agreed co-operation will also commence contemporaneously with the transfer of powers to the assembly.

11. The implementation bodies will have a clear operational remit. They will implement on an all-island and cross-border basis policies agreed in the council.

12. Any further development of these arrangements to be by agreement in the Council and with the specific endorsement of the Northern Ireland Assembly and Oireachtas, subject to the extent of the competences and responsibility of the two administrations.

13. It is understood that the North/South Ministerial Council and the Northern Ireland Assembly are mutually inter-dependent, and that one cannot successfully function without the other.

14. Disagreements within the council to be addressed in the format described at paragraph 3(iii) above or in the plenary format. By agreement between the two sides, experts could be appointed to consider a particular matter and report.

15. Funding to be provided by the two administrations on the basis that the council and the implementation bodies constitute a necessary public function.

16. The council to be supported by a standing joint secretariat, staffed by members of the Northern Ireland Civil Service and the Irish Civil Service.

17. The council to consider the European Union dimension of relevant matters, including the implementation of EU policies and programmes and proposals under consideration in the EU framework. Arrangements to be made to ensure that the views of the council are taken into account and represented appropriately at relevant EU meetings.

18. The Northern Ireland Assembly and the Oireachtas to consider developing a joint parliamentary forum, bringing together equal numbers from both institutions for discussion of matters of mutual interest and concern.

19. Consideration to be given to the establishment of an independent consultative forum appointed by the two administrations, representative of civil society, comprising the social partners and other members with expertise in social, cultural, economic and other issues.

Annex

Areas for North-South co-operation and implementation may include the following:

1. Agriculture—animal and plant health.
2. Education—teacher qualifications and exchanges.
3. Transport—strategic transport planning.
4. Environment—environmental protection, pollution, water quality, and waste management.
5. Waterways—inland waterways.
6. Social Security/Social Welfare—entitlements of cross-border workers and fraud control.
7. Tourism—promotion, marketing, research, and product development.
8. Relevant EU Programmes such as SPPR, INTERREG, Leader II and their successors.
9. Inland Fisheries.
10. Aquaculture and marine matters.
11. Health: accident and emergency services and other related cross-border issues.
12. Urban and rural development.

Others to be considered by the shadow North/South Council.

Strand Three: British-Irish Council

1. A British-Irish Council (BIC) will be established under a new British-Irish Agreement to promote the harmonious and mutually beneficial development of the totality of relationships among the peoples of these islands.

2. Membership of the BIC will comprise representatives of the British and Irish governments, devolved institutions in Northern Ireland, Scotland and Wales, when established, and, if appropriate, elsewhere in the United Kingdom, together with representatives of the Isle of Man and the Channel Islands.

3. The BIC will meet in different formats: at summit level, twice per year; in specific sectoral formats on a regular basis, with each side represented by the appropriate minister; in an appropriate format to consider cross-sectoral matters.

4. Representatives of members will operate in accordance with whatever procedures for democratic authority and accountability are in force in their respective elected institutions.

5. The BIC will exchange information, discuss, consult and use best endeavours to reach agreement on cooperation on matters of mutual interest within the competence of the relevant Administrations. Suitable issues for early discussion in the BIC could include transport links, agricultural issues, environmental issues, cultural issues, health issues, education issues and approaches to EU issues. Suitable arrangements to be made for practical co-operation on agreed policies. . . .

British-Irish Intergovernmental Conference

1. There will be a new British-Irish Agreement dealing with the totality of relationships. It will establish a standing British-Irish Intergovernmental Conference, which will subsume both the Anglo-Irish Intergovernmental Council and the intergovernmental Conference established under the 1985 Agreement.

2. The conference will bring together the British and Irish governments to promote bilateral co-operation at all levels on all matters of mutual interest within the competence of both governments.

3. The conference will meet as required at summit level (prime minister and taoiseach). Otherwise, govern-

ments will be represented by appropriate ministers. Advisers, including police and security advisers, will attend as appropriate.

4. All decisions will be by agreement between both governments. The governments will make determined efforts to resolve disagreements between them. There will be no derogation from the sovereignty of either government.

5. In recognition of the Irish government's special interest in Northern Ireland and of the extent to which issues of mutual concern arise in relation to Northern Ireland, there will be regular and frequent meetings of the conference concerned with non-devolved Northern Ireland matters, on which the Irish government may put forward views and proposals. These meetings, to be co-chaired by the minister for foreign affairs and the secretary of state for Northern Ireland, would also deal with all-island and cross-border co-operation on non-devolved issues.

6. Co-operation within the framework of the conference will include facilitation of co-operation in security matters. The conference also will address, in particular, the areas of rights, justice, prisons and policing in Northern Ireland (unless and until responsibility is devolved to a Northern Ireland administration) and will intensify co-operation between the two governments on the all-island or cross-border aspects of these matters.

7. Relevant executive members of the Northern Ireland administration will be involved in meetings of the conference, and in the reviews referred to in paragraph 9 below to discuss non-devolved Northern Ireland matters.

8. The conference will be supported by officials of the British and Irish governments, including by a standing joint secretariat of officials dealing with non-devolved Northern Ireland matters.

9. The conference will keep under review the workings of the new British-Irish Agreement and the machinery and institutions established under it, including a formal published review three years after the Agreement comes into effect. Representatives of the Northern Ireland administration will be invited to express views to the conference in this context. The conference will contribute as appropriate to any review of the overall political agreement arising from the multi-party negotiations but will have no power to override the democratic arrangements set up by this agreement.

Rights, Safeguards and Equality of Opportunity

Human Rights

1. The parties affirm their commitment to the mutual respect, the civil rights and the religious liberties of everyone in the community. Against the background of the recent history of communal conflict, the parties affirm in particular:

the right of free political thought;

the right to freedom and expression of religion;

the right to pursue democratically national and political aspirations;

the right to seek constitutional change by peaceful and legitimate means;

the right to freely choose one's place of residence;

the right to equal opportunity in all social and economic activity, regardless of class, creed, disability, gender or ethnicity;

the right to freedom from sectarian harassment; and

the right of women to full and equal political participation.

United Kingdom Legislation

2. The British government will complete incorporation into Northern Ireland law of the European Convention on Human Rights (ECHR), with direct access to the courts, and remedies for breach of the convention, including power for the courts to overrule assembly legislation on grounds of inconsistency.

3. Subject to the outcome of public consultation underway, the British government intends, as a particular priority, to create a statutory obligation on public authorities in Northern Ireland to carry out all their functions with due regard to the need to promote equality of opportunity in relation to religion and political opinion; gender; race; disability; age; marital status; dependants; and sexual orientation. Public bodies would be required to draw up statutory schemes showing how they would implement this obligation. Such schemes would cover arrangements for policy appraisal, including an assessment of impact on relevant categories, public consultation, public access to information and services, monitoring and timetables.

4. The new Northern Ireland Human Rights Commission (see paragraph 5 below) will be invited to consult and to advise on the scope for defining, in Westminster legislation, rights supplementary to those in the

European Convention on Human Rights, to reflect the particular circumstances of Northern Ireland, drawing as appropriate on international instruments and experience. These additional rights to reflect the principles of mutual respect for the identity and ethos of both communities and parity of esteem, and—taken together with the ECHR—to constitute a bill of rights for Northern Ireland. Among the issues for consideration by the commission will be:

the formulation of a general obligation on government and public bodies fully to respect, on the basis of equality of treatment, the identity and ethos of both communities in Northern Ireland; and

a clear formulation of the rights not to be discriminated against and to equality of opportunity in both the public and private sectors.

New Institutions in Northern Ireland

5. A new Northern Ireland Human Rights Commission, with membership from Northern Ireland reflecting the community balance, will be established by Westminster legislation, independent of government, with an extended and enhanced role beyond that currently exercised by the Standing Advisory Commission on Human Rights, to include keeping under review the adequacy and effectiveness of laws and practices, making recommendations to government as necessary; providing information and promoting awareness of human rights; considering draft legislation referred to them by the new assembly; and, in appropriate cases, bringing court proceedings or providing assistance to individuals doing so. . . .

Comparable Steps by the Irish Government

9. The Irish government will also take steps to further strengthen the protection of human rights in its jurisdiction. The government will, taking account of the work of the All-Party Oireachtas Committee on the Constitution and the Report of the Constitution Review Group, bring forward measures to strengthen and underpin the constitutional protection of human rights. These proposals will draw on the European Convention on Human Rights and other international legal instruments in the field of human rights and the question of the incorporation of the ECHR will be further examined in this context. The measures brought forward would ensure at least an equivalent level of protection of human rights as will pertain in Northern Ireland. In addition, the Irish government will:

establish a Human Rights Commission with a mandate and remit equivalent to that within Northern Ireland;

proceed with arrangements as quickly as possible to ratify the Council of Europe Framework Convention on National Minorities (already ratified by the UK);

implement enhanced employment equality legislation;

introduce equal status legislation; and

continue to take further active steps to demonstrate its respect for the different traditions in the island of Ireland.

A Joint Committee

10. It is envisaged that there would be a joint committee of representatives of the two Human Rights Commissions, North and South, as a forum for consideration of human rights issues in the island of Ireland. The joint committee will consider, among other matters, the possibility of establishing a charter, open to signature by all democratic political parties, reflecting and endorsing agreed measures for the protection of the fundamental rights of everyone living in the island of Ireland.

Reconciliation and Victims of Violence

11. The participants believe that it is essential to acknowledge and address the suffering of the victims of violence as a necessary element of reconciliation. They look forward to the results of the work of the Northern Ireland Victims Commission.

12. It is recognised that victims have a right to remember as well as to contribute to a changed society. The achievement of a peaceful and just society would be the true memorial to the victims of violence. The participants particularly recognise that young people from areas affected by the troubles face particular difficulties and will support the development of special community-based initiatives based on international best practice. The provision of services that are supportive and sensitive to the needs of victims will also be a critical element and that support will need to be channelled through both statutory and community-based voluntary organisations facilitating locally-based self-help and support networks. This will require the allocation of sufficient resources, including statutory funding as necessary, to meet the needs of victims and to provide for community-based support programmes.

13. The participants recognise and value the work being done by many organisations to develop reconcili-

ation and mutual understanding and respect between and within communities and traditions, in Northern Ireland and between North and South, and they see such work as having a vital role in consolidating peace and political agreement. Accordingly, they pledge their continuing support to such organisations and will positively examine the case for enhanced financial assistance for the work of reconciliation. An essential aspect of the reconciliation process is the promotion of a culture of tolerance at every level of society, including initiatives to facilitate and encourage integrated education and mixed housing.

Rights, Safeguards and Equality of Opportunity

Economic, Social and Cultural Issues

1. Pending the devolution of powers to a new Northern Ireland Assembly, the British government will pursue broad policies for sustained economic growth and stability in Northern Ireland and for promoting social inclusion, including in particular community development and the advancement of women in public life.

2. Subject to the public consultation currently under way, the British government will make rapid progress with:

(i) a new regional development strategy for Northern Ireland, for consideration in due course by a the assembly, tackling the problems of a divided society and social cohesion in urban, rural and border areas, protecting and enhancing the environment, producing new approaches to transport issues, strengthening the physical infrastructure of the region, developing the advantages and resources of rural areas and rejuvenating major urban centres;

(ii) a new economic development strategy for Northern Ireland, for consideration in due course by a the Assembly, which would provide for short and medium term economic planning linked as appropriate to the regional development strategy; and

(iii) measures on employment equality included in the recent White Paper ("Partnership for Equality") and covering the extension and strengthening of anti-discrimination legislation, a review of the national security aspects of the present fair employment legislation at the earliest possible time, a new more focused Targeting Social Need initiative and a range of measures aimed at combating unemployment and progressively eliminating the differential in unemployment rates between the two communities by targeting objective need.

3. All participants recognise the importance of respect, understanding and tolerance in relation to linguistic diversity, including in Northern Ireland, the Irish language, Ulster-Scots and the languages of the various ethnic communities, all of which are part of the cultural wealth of the island of Ireland.

4. In the context of active consideration currently being given to the UK signing the Council of Europe Charter for Regional or Minority Languages, the British government will in particular in relation to the Irish language, where appropriate and where people so desire it:

take resolute action to promote the language;

facilitate and encourage the use of the language in speech and writing in public and private life where there is appropriate demand;

seek to remove, where possible, restrictions which would discourage or work against the maintenance or development of the language;

make provision for liaising with the Irish language community, representing their views to public authorities and investigating complaints;

place a statutory duty on the Department of Education to encourage and facilitate Irish medium education in line with current provision for integrated education;

explore urgently with the relevant British authorities, and in co-operation with the Irish broadcasting authorities, the scope for achieving more widespread availability of Teilifís na Gaeilige in Northern Ireland;

seek more effective ways to encourage and provide financial support for Irish language film and television production in Northern Ireland; and

encourage the parties to secure agreement that this commitment will be sustained by a new Assembly in a way which takes account of the desires and sensitivities of the community.

5. All participants acknowledge the sensitivity of the use of symbols and emblems for public purposes, and the need in particular in creating the new institutions to ensure that such symbols and emblems are used in a manner which promotes mutual respect rather than division. Arrangements will be made to monitor this issue and consider what action might be required.

Decommissioning

1. Participants recall their agreement in the Procedural Motion adopted on 24 September 1997 "that the

resolution of the decommissioning issue is an indispensable part of the process of negotiation," and also recall the provisions of paragraph 25 of Strand 1 above.

2. They note the progress made by the Independent International Commission on Decommissioning and the governments in developing schemes which can represent a workable basis for achieving the decommissioning of illegally-held arms in the possession of paramilitary groups.

3. All participants accordingly reaffirm their commitment to the total disarmament of all paramilitary organisations. They also confirm their intention to continue to work constructively and in good faith with the Independent Commission, and to use any influence they may have, to achieve the decommissioning of all paramilitary arms within two years following endorsement in referendums North and South of the Agreement and in the context of the implementation of the overall settlement.

4. The Independent Commission will monitor, review and verify progress on decommissioning of illegal arms, and will report to both governments at regular intervals.

6. Both governments will take all necessary steps to facilitate the decommissioning process to include bringing the relevant schemes into force by the end of June.

Security

1. The participants note that the development of a peaceful environment on the basis of this agreement can and should mean a normalisation of security arrangements and practices.

2. The British government will make progress towards the objective of as early a return as possible to normal security arrangements in Northern Ireland, consistent with the level of threat and with a published overall strategy, dealing with:

(i) the reduction of the numbers and role of the Armed Forces deployed in Northern Ireland to levels compatible with a normal peaceful society;

(ii) the removal of security installations;

(iii) the removal of emergency powers in Northern Ireland; and

(iv) other measures appropriate to and compatible with a normal peaceful society. . . .

Policing and Justice

1. The participants recognise that policing is a central issue in any society. They equally recognise that Northern Ireland's history of deep divisions has made it

highly emotive, with great hurt suffered and sacrifices made by many individuals and their families, including those in the RUC and other public servants. They believe that the Agreement provides the opportunity for a new beginning to policing in Northern Ireland with a police service capable of attracting and sustaining support from the community as a whole. They also believe that this agreement offers a unique opportunity to bring about a new political dispensation which will recognise the full and equal legitimacy and worth of the identities, senses of allegiance and ethos of all sections of the community in Northern Ireland. They consider that this opportunity should inform and underpin the development of a police service representative in terms of the make-up of the community as a whole and which, in a peaceful environment, should be routinely unarmed. . . .

4. The participants believe that the aims of the criminal justice system are to:

deliver a fair and impartial system of justice to the community;

be responsive to the community's concerns, and encouraging community involvement where appropriate;

have the confidence of all parts of the community; and

deliver justice efficiently and effectively.

5. There will be a parallel wide-ranging review of criminal justice (other than policing and those aspects of the system relating to the emergency legislation) to be carried out by the British government through a mechanism with an independent element, in consultation with the political parties and others. . . .

Prisoners

1. Both governments will put in place mechanisms to provide for an accelerated programme for the release of prisoners, including transferred prisoners, convicted of scheduled offences in Northern Ireland or, in the case of those sentenced outside Northern Ireland, similar offences (referred to hereafter as qualifying prisoners). Any such arrangements will protect the rights of individual prisoners under national and international law. . . .

Validation, Implementation and Review

Validation and Implementation

1. The two governments will as soon as possible sign a new British-Irish Agreement replacing the 1985 Anglo-Irish Agreement, embodying understandings on constitutional issues and affirming their solemn commitment to support and, where appropriate, implement

the Agreement reached by the participants in the negotiations which shall be annexed to the British-Irish Agreement.

2. Each government will organise a referendum on 22 May 1998. Subject to parliamentary approval, a consultative referendum in Northern Ireland, organised under the terms of the Northern Ireland (Entry to Negotiations, etc.) Act 1996, will address the question: "Do you support the agreement reached in the multi-party talks on Northern Ireland and set out in Command Paper 3883?" The Irish government will introduce and support in the Oireachtas a bill to amend the constitution as described in paragraph 2 of the section "Constitutional Issues" and in Annex B, as follows: (a) to amend Articles 2 and 3 as described in paragraph 8.1 in Annex B above and (b) to amend Article 29 to permit the government to ratify the new British-Irish Agreement. On passage by the Oireachtas, the bill will be put to referendum.

3. If majorities of those voting in each of the referendums support this agreement, the governments will then introduce and support, in their respective parliaments, such legislation as may be necessary to give effect to all aspects of this agreement. . . .

Review Procedures Following Implementation

. . . 7. If difficulties arise which require remedial action across the range of institutions, or otherwise require amendment of the British-Irish Agreement or relevant legislation, the process of review will fall to the two governments in consultation with the parties in the assembly. Each government will be responsible for action in its own jurisdiction. . . .

AGREEMENT BETWEEN THE GOVERNMENT OF THE UNITED KINGDOM OF GREAT BRITAIN AND NORTHERN IRELAND AND THE GOVERNMENT OF IRELAND

The British and Irish governments:

Welcoming the strong commitment to the Agreement reached on 10th April 1998 by themselves and other participants in the multi-party talks and set out in Annex 1 to this agreement (hereinafter "the Multi-Party Agreement");

Considering that the Multi-Party Agreement offers an opportunity for a new beginning in relationships within Northern Ireland, within the island of Ireland and between the peoples of these islands;

Wishing to develop still further the unique relationship between their peoples and the close co-operation between their countries as friendly neighbours and as partners in the European Union;

Reaffirming their total commitment to the principles of democracy and non-violence which have been fundamental to the multi-party talks;

Reaffirming their commitment to the principles of partnership, equality and mutual respect and to the protection of civil, political, social, economic and cultural rights in their respective jurisdictions;

Have agreed as follows:

Article 1

The two governments:

 (i) recognise the legitimacy of whatever choice is freely exercised by a majority of the people of Northern Ireland with regard to its status, whether they prefer to continue to support the union with Great Britain or a sovereign united Ireland;

(ii) recognise that it is for the people of the island of Ireland alone, by agreement between the two parts respectively and without external impediment, to exercise their right of self-determination on the basis of consent, freely and concurrently given, North and South, to bring about a united Ireland, if that is their wish, accepting that this right must be achieved and exercised with and subject to the Agreement and consent of a majority of the people of Northern Ireland;

(iii) acknowledge that while a substantial section of the people in Northern Ireland share the legitimate wish of a majority of the people of the island of Ireland for a united Ireland, the present wish of a majority of the people of Northern Ireland, freely exercised and legitimate, is to maintain the Union and accordingly, that Northern Ireland's status as part of the United Kingdom reflects and relies upon that wish; and that it would be wrong to make any change in the status of Northern Ireland save with the consent of a majority of its people;

(iv) affirm that, if in the future, the people of the island of Ireland exercise their right of self-determination on the basis set out in sections (i) and (ii) above to bring about a united Ireland, it will be a binding obligation on both governments to introduce and support in their respective parliaments legislation to give effect to that wish;

 (v) affirm that whatever choice is freely exercised by a majority of the people of Northern Ireland, the power of the sovereign government with jurisdiction there shall be exercised with rigorous impartiality on behalf of all the people in the diversity of their identities and traditions and shall be founded on the principles of full respect for, and equality of, civil, political, social and cultural rights, of freedom from discrimination for all citizens, and of parity of esteem and of just and equal treatment for the identity, ethos and aspirations of both communities;

(vi) recognise the birthright of all the people of Northern Ireland to identify themselves and be accepted as Irish or British, or both, as they may so choose, and accordingly confirm that their right to hold both British and Irish citizenship is accepted by both governments and would not be affected by any future change in the status of Northern Ireland.

Article 2

The two governments affirm their solemn commitment to support, and where appropriate implement, the provisions of the Multi-Party Agreement. In particular there shall be established in accordance with the provisions of the Multi-Party Agreement immediately on the entry into force of this agreement, the following institutions:

(i)   a North/South Ministerial Council;

(ii) the implementation bodies referred to in paragraph 9 (ii) of the section entitled "Strand Two" of the Multi-Party Agreement;

(iii) a British-Irish Council;

(iv) a British-Irish Intergovernmental Conference.

Article 3

(1) This agreement shall replace the Agreement between the British and Irish governments done at Hillsborough on 15th November 1985 which shall cease to have effect on entry into force of this agreement.

(2) The Intergovernmental Conference established by Article 2 of the aforementioned agreement done on 15th November 1985 shall cease to exist on entry into force of this agreement.

Article 4

(1) It shall be a requirement for entry into force of this agreement that:

(a) British legislation shall have been enacted for the purpose of implementing the provisions of Annex A to the section entitled "Constitutional Issues" of the Multi-Party Agreement;

(b) the amendments to the constitution of Ireland set out in Annex B to the section entitled "Constitutional Issues" of the Multi-Party Agreement shall have been approved by referendum;

(c) such legislation shall have been enacted as may be required to establish the institutions referred to in Article 2 of this agreement.

(2) Each government shall notify the other in writing of the completion, so far as it is concerned, of the requirements for entry into force of this agreement. This agreement shall enter into force on the date of the receipt of the later of the two notifications.

(3) Immediately on entry into force of this agreement, the Irish government shall ensure that the amendments to the constitution of Ireland set out in Annex B to the section entitled "Constitutional Issues" of the Multi-Party Agreement take effect.

In witness thereof the undersigned, being duly authorised thereto by the respective governments, have signed this agreement.

Done in two originals at Belfast on the 10th day of April 1998.

For the government
of the United Kingdom of
Great Britain and Northern
Ireland
For the government
of Ireland

A full text of this document is available at the Northern Ireland Office Online at http://www.nio.gov.uk/issues/ agreement.htm.

Index

~

Page numbers in **boldface** refer to the main articles on the subject. Page numbers in *italics* refer to illustrations, tables, figures, and maps. Page numbers followed by (d) refer to primary documents.

~ A

Abbey Theatre, **1**:38, 39, 151, 388
　nationalism and, **1**:152–153
　women playwrights at, **1**:154
　Yeats and, **1**:38–39; **2**:769
ABC of Reading, **1**:84
Abernethy, John, **1**:1
abortion, **2**:631. *See also* divorce, contraception, and abortion
Absentee, The (Edgeworth), **1**:38, 392
Academical Institution, Belfast, **1**:107
Accession, Treaty of (1972), **1**:233
Acta Sanctorum Hiberniae (Colgan), **1**:21, 289
　on St. Patrick, **2**:650
Act for encouragement of Protestant strangers to settle in this kingdom of Ireland (1692), **2**:590
Act for encouraging Protestant strangers and others to inhabit and plant in the kingdom of Ireland (1662), **2**:590
Act for the King's Title (1541), **2**:689
Act of Conformity, **2**:605
Act of Explanation (1665), **2**:626
Act of Settlement (1652), **1**:370
Act of Settlement (1662), **1**:370; **2**:626
Act of Settlement (1701), **1**:203; **2**:704
Act of Supremacy (1560)
　adopted by Irish parliament, **2**:605
　Church of Ireland in, **1**:85
Act of Uniformity (1560), **2**:806 (d)
　Church of Ireland in, **1**:85

Act of Uniformity (1666), **2**:626
Act of Union (1800), **1:1–2**; **2**:544, 545
　Church of Ireland and, **1**:88
　Cork under, **1**:109
　decline of Protestant Ascendancy, **2**:585, 586
　Dublin under, **1**:156
　economic relations and, **1**:171–172
　Grattan's opposition to, **1**:280
　industrialization and, **1**:318
　Irish MPs under, **1**:209
　O'Connell and, **1**:498
　Orange Order and, **1**:508, 509–510
　passage of, **1**:208
　repeal of at "monster meeting" at Mullingar, by O'Connell, **2**:896–899 (d)
　repeal of demanded, **1**:209, 213
　Tara meeting on, **2**:694
　Troy and, **2**:719
Act to prevent the further growth of popery (1704), **1**:202; **2**:521, 847–853 (d)
Adair, Johnny, **1**:409
Adam, Robert, **1**:114
Adams, Gerry, **1:2–4**, *3*
　conversations with Hume, **1**:487
　Good Friday Agreement and, **1**:331
　IRA and, **1**:331
　and peace process, **1**:487
　visit to United States, **1**:492
Adamson, Ian, **1**:120
address at the First Annual Convention of the National Council of Sinn Féin (Griffith), **2**:927–929 (d)

address on the Ulster Question in the House of Commons (Carson), **2**:931–932 (d)
Adomnán, **1**:164
　on Columba, **1**:163, 289–290
Adrian IV (pope), **1**:446
　grant of crusader rights to Henry II, **1**:412, 471; **2**:782 (d)
　surrender and regrant policy, **2**:689
Adventurers, **1**:230
Adventurers' Act, **2**:662
Adventurers' Committee, **2**:662
advertising of Guinness, **1**:288
AE (George Russell), **1**:388
　Yeats and, **2**:769
Aer Lingus, **2**:677
afforestation, **2**:768
After Easter (Devlin), **1**:404
Agar, James, **1**:257
Agricultural Credit Company, **2**:676
agriculture
　after World War I, **1:11–15**
　American migration and, **1**:145–146
　Anglo-Irish Free Trade Agreement of 1965 and, **1**:17
　booleying system of transhumance, **1**:178; **2**:648
　Celtic Tiger and, **1**:83
　Common Agricultural Policy, **1**:81–83, **98–99**
　Congested Districts Board and, **1**:104
　contests for land between graziers and farmers, **1**:358
　depressions
　　1859 to 1864, **1**:10
　　1879 to 1882, **1**:11
　dominance of, **1**:319–320

agriculture CONTINUED
  Economic Development and,
    1:167
  EEC policies on, **1**:168–169
  enclosures, **1**:5, 364; **2**:647
    tenant right, or Ulster
      custom, **2**:698
  farming families, **1**:247–249
  innovations of New English,
    1:5
  modernization of farming in
    twentieth century, **1**:14
  Normans and, **1**:470
  in Northern Ireland, **1**:174–175
    after World War II, **1**:484–
      485
  Oakboys and Steelboys, **1**:495–
    496
  open-field system, **2**:648
  percentage of population in,
    2:644
  plantations and, **1**:368
  protectionism and, **1**:320
  railways and, **2**:715
  reduced labor due to shift from
    tillage to pasturage, **2**:645
  reform
    Horace Curzon Plunkett and,
      2:528
    Walsh and, **2**:745
  seasonal migrants, **1**:442
  Stone Age, **2**:678, 679
  subdivision and subletting of
    holdings, **2**:687
  tenant right, or Ulster custom,
    2:697–700
  three-course rotation, **1**:4
  1500 to 1690, **1:4–5**
  1690 to 1845, **1:5–8**
  1845 to 1921, **1:8–11**
Águila, Juan del, **1**:468
Ahenny group of crosses, **1**:297
Ahern, Bertie, **1**:488
Aibidil Gaoidheilge agus Caiticiosma,
  1:397
Aidan (bishop), **1**:163–164
AIDS, contraception and, **1**:149
Aiken, Frank, **1**:463, 490; **2**:734
  and Civil War cease-fire, **2**:954
  and Irish diplomacy, **2**:555,
    733
Aikenhead, Mary, **1**:452; **2**:621
Ailill
  Cruachain and, **1**:118
  Cú Chulainn and, **1**:119
  in *Táin Bó Cúailnge*, **2**:691–692
Ailill Molt (high king), **1**:347
"Aims of Fianna Fáil in Office" (de
  Valera), **2**:959–960 (d)
aisling (vision poem/song), **1**:396,
  399, 453

"Alasdrium's March," **1**:453
Alcock, Mary, **1**:390
Alcoholics Anonymous, **2**:696
Aldhelm, **1**:164
Alen, John, **1**:256
Alexander III (pope)
  and Henry II's crusader rights,
    1:471
  letters confirming Henry II's
    conquest of Ireland, **2**:782–
    784 (d)
Alexandra School and College,
  1:194, 198
  women at, **1**:199, 200
All Children Together (ACT), **1**:192
Allen, William O'Meara, **1**:252,
  252
All Hallows College, **1**:514
Alliance Party (Northern Ireland),
  1:477, 485
  Faulkner and, **1**:250
All-Ireland Fleadh Cheoil, **1**:256–
  257
All Souls (Coady), **2**:530
almanacs, **1**:385
Alo, Colmán, **1**:296
Alternative Prayer Book, **1**:89
Altus prosator (Ancient creator)
  (Columba), **1**:296
Amalgamated Society of Tailors,
  1:497
American Federation of Labor,
  1:146
American wakes, **1:15**
Amnesty Association, **1**:299
Amongst Women (McGahern), **1**:40,
  254
Ancient Order of Hibernians,
  1:15–16; 2:635
  revival by Devlin, **2**:558
Anderson, Mary, **2**:630
Andrews, J. M., **1**:64
Anglican Established Church. *See*
  Church of Ireland
Anglican-Methodist Covenant
  (2002), ecumenism and, **1**:182
anglicization of the Irish landscape,
  2:584
Anglo-Irish Agreement of 1985
  (Hillsborough Agreement), **1:16–
  17**, 479, 487; **2**:723, 1005–1009
  (d)
  Hume and, **1**:306
  Reagan's support of, **1**:492
Anglo-Irish Free Trade Agreement
  of 1965, **1:17–18**, 169, 170–171
  and agriculture, **1**:12
  economy development and,
    1:175
Anglo-Irish literature. *See* literature

Anglo-Irish Trade Agreement of
  1938
  cattle and, **1**:12
  de Valera and, **1**:136
  Fianna Fáil and, **2**:553
  and Irish neutrality, **1**:462–463
  partition discussed during talks,
    1:489
Anglo-Irish Treaty of 1921, **1:18–
  20; 2**: 550, 942–945 (d)
  and Boundary Commission,
    1:55
  Civil War as result of, **1**:91–93
  Collins and, **1**:96, 287
  Commonwealth in, **1:99–101**
  constitution and, **1**:105–106
  Cosgrave and, **1**:110
  Craig and, **1**:116
  Cumann na mBan and, **1**:121
  Griffith's support for, **1**:287
    speech, **2**:948–949 (d)
  IRA and, **1**:329; **2**:686
  and North-South boundary,
    1:483
  opposed by Markievicz, **1**:422
  Sinn Féin and, **2**:661
  speech against by de Valera,
    2:945–948 (d)
  and split in Sinn Féin, **2**:531
Anglo-Irish union. *See* Act of
  Union (1800)
Anglo-Irish War (1919–1921),
  1:92; **2**:728
  country houses in, **1**:113
  Cumann na mBan and, **1**:121
  estates burned in, **1**:232
  GAA members in, **1**:267
  shipbuilding industry and,
    2:658
  Sinn Féin in, **2**:661
Anglo-Normans. *See* Norman
  conquest and colonization
*Annála Ríoghachta Éireann. See
  Annals of the Four Masters*
annalistic tradition, **1**:396
Annals of Innisfallen, **1**:338, 472
  anti-Viking propaganda in,
    1:476
Annals of the Four Masters, **1:20–
  21**, 34, 398
  on Battle of Kinsale, **2**:819 (d)
  on High Crosses, **1**:297
  O'Donovan's edition and
    translation of, **1**:401, 500
*Annals of the Kingdom of Ireland. See
  Annals of the Four Masters*
Annals of Tighearnach, **1**:472
Annals of Ulster
  anti-Viking propaganda in,
    1:476

on theft and recovery of *Book of Kells*, **1**:417
Anne, Queen
    penal laws under, **1**:202
    union petitions to, **1**:203
Anselm, Saint, **1**:471
Anteroom, The (O'Brien), **1**:402
anti-Catholicism
    in literature, **1**:223–225
    of Methodism, **1**:429
    Orange Order, **1**:507–510
anticombination laws, **2**:712
anticommunism and Marianism, **1**:418
Anti-Discrimination (Pay) Act of 1974, **1**:227
Anti-Partition League (APL), **2**:559
"Antiphony of Bangor," **1**:164
Anti-Processions Act of 1832, Orange Order and, **1**:509
antiquarianism, **1**:22–23
    O'Donovan and, **1**:500
Antiquities of Ireland (Ledwich), **1**:23
anti-Semitism, **1**:338, 339
antiterrorist legislation, Special Powers Act, **2**:672
Antrim, Alexander McDonnell, earl of, **1**:131
Anvil Point, **2**:658
Apology for the British Government in Ireland, An (Mitchel), **1**:445
Apprentice Boys' march in Derry, **2**:724
Approaching Priests (Leland), **1**:404
Aran Islands, The (Synge), **1**:388
archaeology and the Celts, **1**:79–81
architecture
    country houses, **1**:*113*, 113–**116**
    demesnes, **1**:*231*, 232
    Dublin, **1**:156
        Georgian Dublin, **1**:273–275
    early and medieval, **1**:23–26, 27–32
    first public buildings, **1**:35
    modernist and postmodernist, **2**:743
    neoclassicism, **1**:35
    Norman-style castles, **1**:31–32
    Palladian, **1**:35, 365–366
        country houses, **1**:113
    sculpture in, **2**:651–652, *652*
    seventeenth-century, **1**:35
    stone forts of Iron Age, **1**:362
    Trinity College and, **2**:718
    Tudor, **2**:736
Ardagh Chalice, **1**:27, 427
Argentina, Irish emigration to, **1**:435

"Argument, An" (Darcy), **1**:125
Argument on Behalf of the Catholics of Ireland (Tone), **2**:704
Arians, **2**:581
    Cooke and, **1**:107
Armagh monastery
    hagiography of, **1**:289–290
    Saint Patrick and, **1**:449; **2**:649–650
Arminianism, **2**:717–718
Armory, Thomas, **1**:33
Arms and the Man (Shaw), **1**:153
Arnold, Matthew, **1**:22
"Articles of Agreement for a Treaty" (1921), **1**:99
Articles of Limerick. *See* Limerick, Treaty of
arts
    early and medieval arts and architecture, **1**:27–32
        High Crosses, **1**:297–298, *298*
    early modern literature and the arts from 1500 to 1800, **1**:32–37
    modern Irish and Anglo-Irish literature and the arts since 1800, **1**:37–42
    modern visual arts, **2**:741–744
    from 1500 to 1800, **1**:35–37
    See also architecture; literature; painting; sculpture
Arts and Crafts movement and Celtic Revival, **2**:742
art schools, **1**:36
Arts Council, **2**:741
Ashford, William, **1**:36
As Music and Splendour (O'Brien), **1**:404
Asquith, H. H., **2**:548
Assisted Passage Scheme (1947–1971), **1**:441
Association for Discountenancing Vice
    education and, **1**:187
    publications of, **1**:85
Association for the Propagation for the Faith, **1**:514
Aston, Robert, **1**:390
Astrakhan Cloak, The (Ní Dhomhnaill), **1**:41; **2**:530
"Astral Weeks" (Van Morrison), **1**:457
Asylum Road (O'Malley), **1**:41; **2**:530
Athanasius, **1**:90
athletics. *See* Gaelic Athletic Association; sport and leisure
Atkins, Humphrey, **1**:478
Atlee, Clement, **2**:559

At-Swim Two Birds (O'Brien), **1**:40, 253
Aughrim, Battle of (1691), **1**:337–338
    Orange Order and commemoration of, **1**:507
Augustinus Hibernicus, **1**:379
Auraicept na n-Éces (primer), **1**:393
Australia
    Fenian prisoners' escape from, **1**:252–253
    Irish emigration to, **1**:139–141
        in 1800s, **1**:433
        from 1850 to 1960, **1**:435
        in twentieth century, **1**:440, 441
    status argument with, **1**:129
Austria, Irish in army of, **2**:749
autobiographies from Gaeltacht, **1**:265. *See also* Blasket Island Writers
Awkward Girl, The (Callaghan), **1**:403
Aylward, Margaret, **2**:621

∾ B

Bacon, Francis, **1**:157
Bagehot, Walter, **2**:546
Bagenal, Mabel, **1**:504
Bagenal, Sir Henry, **1**:466, 504
Baggot, Mark, **1**:158
Bailegangaire (Murphy), **1**:40
Bairéad, Riocard, **1**:454
Baker, Henry, **1**:131
Bakhtin, Mikhail, **2**:617
Bale, John, **2**:593, 605
    Edwardian reform and, **1**:201
    Vocation of John Bale to the Bishopery of Ossorie, **2**:804–806 (d)
    writings of, **1**:223
Balfour, Arthur James, **2**:525
    Congested Districts Board and, **1**:104
    Home Rule and, **1**:301
    Punch cartoon, **2**:526
Balfour Declaration (1926), **1**:100
Ball, Frances, **2**:621
Ballad Poetry of Ireland, The (Duffy), **1**:159
ballads
    at American wakes, **1**:15
    in English, **1**:43–45
    Fenian, **1**:397
    and politics, **1**:385
    and publishing, **1**:386–387
    See also songs
Ballagh, Robert, **1**:41; **2**:743

Ballagh, Robert CONTINUED
    Irish pound design, **1:**327
Ballynahinch, Battle of (1798),
    1:207
Ballinamuck, Battle of, **2:**544
Ballroom of Romance, The (Trevor),
    1:40, 254
Ballymascanlon conferences,
    ecumenism and, **1:**183
Baltinglass rebellion of 1580,
    2:606
Bangor monastery, literature from,
    1:164
Banim, John, **1:**38
Banim, Michael, **1:**38
Banishment Act (1697), **2:**633
banking and finance
    to 1921, **1:45–46**
        Catholics in, **1:**78
        industrialization and, **1:**316,
            317, 318
        Huguenots in, **2:**590
        Irish pound, **1:**326–327
        and interest rates, **1:**328
Bank of Ireland, **1:**45, 46, *156*
    Irish pound and, **1:**326
Banner of Ulster (newspaper),
    1:465
Bann River Trilogy, The (Casey),
    1:41, 254
Bantry Bay invasion (1796), **2:**705
Banville, John, **1:**41, 254
    on country houses, **1:**115
Baptists, **1:**236; **2:**594, 604, 608
barántas warrant poem, **1:**399
bardic poetry
    in family poem-books
        (*duanaireadha*), **1:**396
    and manuscript tradition,
        1:400
    and Marian devotion, **1:**417
    praise poetry, **1:**66
    tradition and innovation in,
        1:396
bards, **1:**454–455
    insecurity of following the
        Flight of the Earls, **1:**398
    maintenance of literary
        language by, **1:**34
    schools, **1:**395
        apprenticeship and, **1:**185
    and Stuart dynasty, **2:**537
Bardwell, Lelan, **1:**404
Baring Brothers and Company,
    1:313
barley, **1:**4, 8
Barnacle, Nora, **1:**339
Barra, Dáibhí de, **1:**400
Barret, George, **1:**36
Barrington, Jonah, **2:**642–643

Barrington, Margaret, **1:**403
Barry, James, **1:**36
    Self-Portrait as Timarthes, **1:**36
Barry, Kevin, **2:**686
Barry, Sebastian, **1:**41, 153, 154
Barry, Spranger, **1:**33
Barrytown Trilogy (Doyle), **1:**41,
    254
Barton, Robert, **1:**18, 19
Bath, John, **1:**277
Battle of Aughrim, The (Ashton),
    1:84, 390
Battle of Ballynahinch (Robinson),
    1:207
Battle of the Books (Swift), **2:**690
Beach, Sylvia, **1:**339
Beacon, Richard, **1:**369
    colonial theory of, **1:**98
    Solon His Follie, **2:**812–813 *(d)*
Béal Bocht, An (The Poor Mouth)
    (O'Brien), **1:**40
Bealin cross, **1:**30
Beamish, **1:**61
Beamish and Crawford, **1:**315
Bean na hÉireann (Woman of
    Ireland) (newspaper), **1:**275
Beare, Donal Cam O'Sullivan,
    1:323
Beatha Aodha Ruaidh Uí Dhomhnaill
    (Life of Red Hugh O'Donnell) (Ó
    Clérigh), **1:**20
Beattie, William, **2:**724
Beaumont, Gustave de, **2:**892–893
    (d)
Beaux' Strategem, The (Farquhar),
    1:34
Becket, Mary, **1:**404
Beckett, Samuel, **1:**39–40, **47**, 153
    Hiberno-English in, **1:**295
    Joyce and, **1:**340
    Malone Dies, **1:**253
    Molloy, **1:**253
    The Unnamable, **1:**253
    Waiting for Godot, **1:**253
Bede, Venerable, **1:**450
    on Irish missionaries, **1:**164
Bedell, William, **1:47–48**
    and translation of Old
        Testament, **1:**398
Beere, Thekla, **1:**226–227
Behan, Brendan, **1:**153
Belfast, **1:48–49**
    banks in, **1:**45
    Bloody Friday (21 July 1972),
        1:486
    Chamber of Commerce, **1:**316,
        318
    civil-rights march, **1:**506
    cotton industry in, **2:**641
    Harbour Board, **1:**316

industrialization in, **1:**316–319
intercommunal rioting in,
    1:485
labor movement in, **1:**350
publishing in, **1:**387
religious geography of, **2:**619
shipbuilding in, **2:**657–658
textile production in, **1:**316–
    319
Belfast Agreement of 1998, **1:**2, 3,
    331, 409, 480, 488; **2:**723,
    1013–1026 *(d)*
    Anglo-Irish Agreement of 1985
        compared to, **2:**1005
    constitutional amendments and,
        1:107; **2:**561
    decommissioning in, **1:**129–130
    economic relations and, **1:**172
    human rights in, **1:**229–230
    Hume and, **1:**306
    Patten Commission, **2:**639
    trade unions and, **2:**713
    Trimble and, **2:**717
Belfast Bank, **1:**45, 46
Belfast Boycott, economic relations
    and, **1:**170
Belfast Confetti (Carson), **1:**41;
    2:530
Belfast Fifty Years Ago (Gaffikin),
    2:910–911 *(d)*
Belfast Harbour Commission,
    2:657–658
Belfast Harp Festival (1792), **1:**37,
    455
Belfast News-Letter (newspaper),
    1:466
Belfast Society, **1:**1
Belfast Society of United Irishmen,
    1:462
Belfast Telegraph (newspaper),
    1:465
Belfast Vindicator (newspaper),
    1:465
Belfast Woman, A (Beckett), **1:**404
Belfast Women's Collective, **2:**763
Belfast Workingman's Institute,
    2:910
Bell, Robert, **2:**881 *(d)*
Bellamy, Mrs. George Ann, **1:**34
Bellarmine, Robert, **2:**717
Belle of Belfast City (Reid), **1:**405
Bellingham, Sir Edward
    Edwardian reform and, **1:**201
    military campaigns of, **1:**219
Bellings, Richard, **1:**102, 103
Belmore Commission, **1:**190
Beloved Stranger (Boylan), **1:**404
Benburb, Battle of (1646), **1:**505
Bend of the Boyne cemetery,
    2:681–682, 683

Benedict XIV (pope), and women's orders, **2:**621

Bennett, Louie, **1:**332–333

Bennett, William, **2:**903–904 *(d)*

Beowulf, Heaney translation of, **1:**294

Beresford, John, **1:**274

Beresford, Lord George, **1:**76

Beresford, Lord John George, **1:**88

Berkeley, George, **1:**87–88

Berkeley, Sara, **1:**41; **2:**530

Bernard of Clairvaux, Saint, **1:**290, 471

Beside the Fire (Hyde), **1:**309

Betha Colaim Chille (Life of Colum Cille) (O'Donnell), **1:**34, 290, 397

Bethu Brigte, **1:**290

Beveridge Report, **1:**292

Bhean Oibre, An (The woman worker), **1:**332

Bianconi, Charles, **2:**628

Bible

New Testament

Irish translation, **1:**397

Old Testament translation, **1:**398

sponsored by Bedell, **1:**47–48

Bible Churchmen's Missionary Society, **1:**513

Bibliothèque Bleue, **1:**84

Biggar, Joseph, **1:**70

Home Rule and, **1:**299–300

Big House of Inver, The (Somerville and Martin), **1:**254

Big Houses, **1:**365; **2:**643

in literature, **1:**254, 392–393, 403

bills of exchange, **1:**316

Bingham, Sir Richard, **1:**221

capture of Granuaile, **1:**279

defeat of Scots in Connacht by, **2:**809 *(d)*

Bíobla Naomhtha, An, **1:**398

Biography of Desire (Dorcey), **1:**404

Birds of the Innocent Wood (Madden), **1:**403

Birkenhead, Lord (Frederick Edwin Smith), **1:**18, *19*

Birrell, Augustine, **1:**198

Birrell Act. *See* Land Purchase Acts of 1903 and 1909

Bishops' Banishment Act of 1697, **2:**521

Bishops' Wars (1639–1640), **2:**670

Black and Tans, **2:**686

Black Baby (Boylan), **1:**404

Black Death (1348–1350)

in Cork, **1:**108

effect on architecture, **1:**31

effect on towns and villages, **1:**263

sculpture and, **2:**652

Black Pig's Dyke, **1:**362

"black rents," **1:**179

Blackstone, William, **1:**381

Blackwood, Caroline, **1:**403

Blair, Tony, **1:**492; **2:**723

and Bloody Sunday, **1:**51, 52

and peace process, **1:**488

blanket bogs. *See* bogs and drainage

Blasket Island writers, **1:**49–51, 265

Blennerhasset, Thomas, on Ulster plantations, **2:**823–824 *(d)*

Blind Piper, The (Haverty), **1:**454

Bloody Friday (21 July 1972), **1:**486

Bloody Sunday (30 January 1972), **1:**51–52; **2:**561, 686, 725

Provisional IRA and, **1:**485–486

results of, **1:**331

Blueshirt movement, **1:**136; **2:**553

Board of Trustees of the Linen and Hempen Manufactures. *See* Linen Board

Boate, Gerard, **1:**224–225

Boazio, Baptista, **2:**767

Bodkin, Matthew, **1:**465

Bodleian Library, **1:**291

Body Map Series (Prendergast), **2:**743

bogs and drainage, **1:**52–55, 359; **362**

blanket bogs, **1:**359, *54*

raised bogs, **1:**359, *54*

diagram, **1:***53*

Bogside, Battle of the (Derry, 1969), **2:**724

Boland, Eavan, **1:**41, 403, 405; **2:**530

Kavanagh's influence on, **1:**40; **2:**529

Boland, Frederick H., **2:**733, 735

Boland, Harry, **1:**267

Bolger, Dermot, **1:**153

bone-barbell pins, **2:**577

Bones of Contention and Other Stories (O'Connor), **1:**253–254

Bonnell, James, **1:**87

Bono (U2), **1:**479

Book (Heaney), **1:**294

Book of Armagh (Ferdomnach), **1:**417; **2:***650*

Brian Boru in, **1:**123, *124*

Book of Common Prayer

Act of Uniformity on, **1:**85

in the Church of Ireland, **1:**86

Edwardian reform and, **1:**200, 201

introduction in Ireland, **2:**605

Archbishop Browne and, **2:**593

Irish translation, **1:**86, 398

revisions to, **1:**89

Book of Dimma, **1:**417

Book of Durrow, **1:**27, 29, 416

symbol of Saint Matthew, **1:***449*

Book of Evidence, The (Banville), **1:**41, 254

Book of Fenagh, **1:**396

Book of Irish Verse, A (Yeats, ed.), **1:**388

Book of Kells, **1:**23, 27, 28, 29, 166, 417

genealogy of Christ, **1:***416*

interior decoration and, **1:**114

symbols of the Four Evangelists, **1:***415*

Book of Leinster, **1:**458; **2:**694

Book of Lindisfarne, **1:**29

Book of Lismore, **1:**290

Book of the Dean of Lismore (comp. MacGregor), **1:**397

Book of the Dun Cow, **1:**119, *394*, 458

Táin Bó Cúailnge in, **2:**691–692

Book of Mulling, **1:**417

"Boolavogue" (McCall), **1:**44

booleying, **1:**178; **2:**648

Boran, Pat, **1:**41; **2:**530

Bord Fáilte, **2:**706

Bord na Móna (state peat authority), **1:**53, 361

Boru, Brian, **1:**123–124; **2:**721

and Battle of Clontarf, **1:**96, 476

church at Inish Caltra, **1:**25

on coinage, **1:**326

Boston, Irish in, **1:**143, 145

bottle night. *See* American wakes

Boucicault, Dion, **1:**38

Boundary Commission, **1:**55–56, 489; **2:**553, 559

collapse of, **2:**559

Craig and, **1:**116

Bourke, Sir Richard, **1:**139

Bourke, Ulick, earl of Clanrickard, **2:**535

Bowen, Elizabeth, **1:**40, 254, 402–403, 404

on country houses, **1:**115

Bowen's Court, Co. Cork, **1:**113

boxing, **2:**674

Boycott, Charles Cunningham, **1:**372; **2:**703, 914

boycotting by Land League, **1:**372; **2:**914

condemnation by Leo XIII, **2:**524, 635

Boyd, John, **1**:153
Boylan, Clare, **1**:403, 404
Boyle, Elizabeth, **2**:673
Boyle, Henry, **1**:204
Boyle, Richard
  estates and demesnes, **1**:230
  speech to the Speaker of the
    House of Commons, **2**:836–
    837 *(d)*
  Spenser and, **2**:673
Boyle, Robert, **1:56–57**
  on Greatorex, **1**:284
Boyle, Roger
  Cromwellian conquest and,
    1:117
  patron of Greatorex, **1**:284
Boyne, Battle of the (1690), **1:57–
  59**, *58, 202*
  European context of, **1**:337
  Huguenots at, **2**:590
  importance of, **1**:338
  Orange Order and
    commemoration of, **1**:507,
    509, 510
  tourism and, **2**:705
Boyne, Joseph, **1**:1
Bradshaw, Brendan, **2**:604
Braig, Bill, **1**:482
Bramhall, John, **2**:593, 746
  Calvinism and, **1**:72
Breathnach, Breandán, **1**:457
Brehon laws, **1:59–60**
  conquest-right justified
    eradication, **1**:380
  hunger strikes in, **1**:307
  and landed property rights,
    1:380
  reform through judicial
    resolutions, **1**:381
  surrender and regrant policy,
    2:688–689
Brendan, Saint, **1**:290
Brereton, William, **2**:834–835 *(d)*
Bretha Crólige (medico-legal tract),
  1:60
Bretha Déin Chécht (medico-legal
  tract), **1**:60
Brett, Charles, killing of, **1**:*251*;
  1:252
*Brevis synopsis provinciae Hiberniae
  FF Minorum* (O'Mahony), **1**:20
brewing, **1:61–62**
  Dublin, **1**:315
  in eighteenth century, **2**:566
  See also Guinness Brewing
    Company
Bridie Steen (Croon), **1**:403
Brief Description of Ireland (Payne),
  1:224
Brigit, Saint, **1**:161, 448

documents on, **1**:291
in hagiography, **1**:163, 289,
  290
Britain
  emigration to
    during Great Famine, **1**:*283*
    since 1950, **1**:440
    women, **1**:142; **2**:757
  responsiblity in Great Famine,
    2:568–569
  seasonal employment of Irish
    in, **1**:442
Britannia (Camden), **1**:224
*Britannicarum ecclesiarum
  antiquitates* (Ussher), **2**:738
British-Irish Council, **1**:488
British Library, **1**:291
British National Council for Civil
  Liberties, **2**:672
British Passenger Act (1803),
  1:433
British Trades Union Congress
  (TUC)
  Irish trade unions and, **1**:349;
    2:712
  support of Irish during lockout
    of 1913, **1**:407
British West Indies, Irish
  transported to, **1**:431
Broadcasting Act of 1988, **1**:425
Brockett, Oscar, **1**:151
Brockley excavations, **2**:679
Brocquy, Louis de, **1**:41
Brodrick, Alan, **1**:203
Brogan, Patricia Burke, **1**:154, 404
Bronze Age, **1:62–64**, 361;
  2:577–578, *578*
  trade, **1**:80–81
brooches, decorative, **1**:29, 427
Brooke, Basil Stanlake, First
  Viscount Brookeborough, **1:64–
  65**
  as prime minister, **2**:724
  Republic of Ireland bill and,
    1:128
Brooke, Charlotte, **1**:35, 391
Brooke, Henry, **1**:33, 391
Brooke, John, **1**:65
Brooke, Peter, **1**:487
Browne, George, **1**:419; **2**:593
Browne, Noël, **1**:413, 450, 451;
  2:555
  crusade against tuberculosis,
    1:*292*
  on repeal of External Relations
    Act, **1**:128
Brownshill megaliths, **2**:680
Bruce, Edward, **1**:65
Bruce, Robert, **1**:65
Bruce invasion (1315–1317), **1:65**,
  263, 475

Bruton, John, **1**:488; **2**:562
Buile Shuibne (Frenzy of Sweeney),
  1:460
Bunreacht na hÉireann. *See*
  constitution of independent
  Ireland: constitution of 1937
Bunting, Edward, **1**:37, 455
Burca, Mairin de, **2**:630
Burghley, Lord William Cecil,
  1:134
burial customs
  cinerary urns, **2**:578
  Cruachain, **1:118–119**
  in Early Bronze Age, **1**:62–63
  heraldic funerals in mid-
    seventeenth century, **1**:66
  megalithic, **2**:680–683
  and popular religion from 1500
    to 1690, **1:65–67**
  sarcophagi, **2**:652
  Stone Age, **2**:679
  See also tombs
Burke, Edmund, **1**:33, 36, **67–68**,
  68, 391; **2**:522
  Troy and, **2**:719
Burke, Helen Lucy, **1**:403
Burke, Honora, **2**:651
Burke, MacWilliam, first earl of
  Clanrickard, **1**:447
Burke, Richard-an-Iarainn (Iron
  Dick), **1**:279
Burnell, Henry, **1**:390
Burnett, Gilbert, **1**:48
Burton, Philip, **1**:491
Bush, John, **2**:853–854 *(d)*
Butcher Boy (McCabe), **1**:41, 254
Butler, Black Tom, **1**:133
Butler, James, twelfth earl and
  first duke of Ormond, **1:68–69**
  Confederation of Kilkenny and,
    1:102, 103
  and Huguenot community,
    2:589
Butler, John, **2**:769
Butler family
  and carving, **1**:32
  great house of, **1**:*231*
  surrender and regrant policy,
    2:688
Butt, Isaac, **1:69–70**; **2**:546
  and Home Government
    Association, **2**:907, 908
  Home Rule Party under, **1**:213,
    299–300
  Speech Advocating
    Consideration of Home Rule
    by the House of Commons,
    2:908–910 *(d)*
butter-making, **1**:*10*
  in Cork, **1**:109

exports, **1**:181
Byers, Margaret, **1**:193
Byrne, Garret, **1**:207
Byrne, Gay, **1**:424
By the Bog of Cats (Carr), **1**:154

~ **C**

Caesar on Celts, **1**:79
Cáin Adomnáin (Adomnáin's law), **1**:164
Cáin Domnaig (Law of Sunday), **1**:164
Caín Fhuithirbe, **1**:59
Cáin Phátraic (Patrick's law), **1**:164
Cáirde na Cruite, **1**:456
Caisleáin Óir (Golden castles) (Mac Grianna), **1**:265
Caldwell's Act (1860), **2**:700
Callaghan, Mary Rose, **1**:403
Callan, Battle of (1261), **1**:474
"Calre's Dragoons," **1**:453
Calvin, John, **1**:71
Calvinist influences in early modern Ireland, **1**:71–72
    Trinity College and, **2**:717–718
Cambrai Homily, **1**:297
Camden, earl of (John Jeffreys Pratt), **1**:206
Camden, William, **1**:408
    Britannia, **1**:224
    on O'Neill, **1**:503
Cameron Commission, **1**:249
Campaign for Civil Rights (Northern Ireland), **1**:480–482
Campaign for Democracy in Ulster (CDU), **1**:481
Campaign for Social Justice (CSJ), **1**:485; **2**:560
    foundation, **1**:481
Campbell, George, **1**:357
Campbell, Thomas, **1**:225; **2**:854–857 (d)
Campion, Edmund, **1**:223; **2**:806–807 (d)
Canada
    emigration to during Great Famine, **1**:283
    migration to, **1**:144, 146, 147
    Orange Order in, **1**:510
Cannon, Moya, **1**:41, 403; **2**:530
Canny, Nicholas, **2**:604
canon law
    marriage in, **1**:239
    revival of under Dowdall, **1**:419
Cantwell, Thomas de, tomb effigy of, **1**:414
Caoineadh Airt Uí Laoire (Lament for Art O'Leary) (Ní Chonaill), **1**:34, 399, 453

caoineadh (lament, keen), **1**:399, 453
Caoineadh Uí Dhomhnaill, **1**:453
Capel, Henry, **1**:201–202
Carbery, Eithne, **1**:44
Carew, George, **1**:468
    Munster under, **1**:221
Carew, Peter, **1**:368
    Butler family and, **1**:220
Carey, Hugh, **1**:492
Carey, James, **1**:44
Carleton, William, **1**:38, 392
    on country houses, **1**:115
    Traits and Stories of the Irish Peasantry, **2**:632
"Carmilla" (Le Fanu), **1**:392
Carney, James, **2**:778 (d)
Carn Fraoich, **1**:346
Carnfree, **1**:118–119
Carolan, Turlough, **1**:37, 72, 72–73, 454–455
Carr, Marina, **1**:41, 154, 403
"Carrickfergus" (MacNeice), **1**:40; **2**:529
Carrickshock, tithe war and, **2**:701, 703
Carroll, Michael, **1**:138
Carrowkeel cemetery, **2**:576, 681
Carrowmore cemetery, **2**:681
Carson, Ciaran, **1**:41; **2**:529
Carson, Sir Edward, **1**:73–74
    address on the Ulster Question in the House of Commons, **2**:931–932 (d)
    Home Rule and, **1**:304–305
Carswell, John, **1**:397
Carter, Jimmy, **1**:492
Carton, Co. Kildare, **1**:114
Cas, Cormac, **1**:123
Casement, Roger, **1**:462; **2**:684
Case of Ireland's Being Bound by Acts of Parliament in England Stated (Molyneux), **1**:33, 203, 446
Casey, Eamonn, **2**:638
Casey, Philip, **1**:41, 254; **2**:530
Cashel, Synod of (1101), **1**:89–91, 215, 471, 473
cashels, **2**:599
Cassian, John, **1**:90
Casti connubii (On Christian marriage), **1**:148
Castle, Richard, **1**:35, 366
    country houses by, **1**:113
    and Georgian Dublin, **1**:273
Castle Coole, Co. Fermanagh, **2**:643
Castle Rackrent (Edgeworth), **1**:33, 38, 115, 389, 392
Castlereagh, Robert Stewart, Lord, **1**:2, 462

Castletown, Co. Kildare, **1**:114; **2**:585, 643
Castle Ward, **1**:114, *114*
Catastrophe (Beckett), **1**:47
catechisms
    Gaelic Tridentine, **1**:222
    printed, **1**:84–85, 385
Cathach of Saint Columba, **1**:27, *162*, 415
    enshrinement of, **1**:428
Cathleen ni Houlihan (Yeats and Gregory), **1**:388, 402; **2**:769
Cath Maige Rath (Battle of Moira), **1**:460
Cath Maige Tuired (The Second Battle of Mag Tuired/Moytura), **1**:459
Catholic Association
    Catholic emancipation campaign and, **1**:75–76
    and "Catholic Rent," **2**:885–888 (d)
    Doyle and, **1**:150
    founding of, **1**:74; **2**:740
    O'Connell and, **1**:497–498
    outlawed, **1**:76
    Second Reformation and, **2**:654
    See also Catholic Committee from 1756 to 1809; New Catholic Association
Catholic Book Society, **1**:385
Catholic Church. *See* Roman Catholic Church
Catholic Committee, **2**:610
Catholic Committee from 1756 to 1809, **1**:74–75
    Catholic emancipation campaign and, **1**:75
    Defenderism and, **1**:131
    Keogh in, **1**:342
    merchants in, **1**:77
    O'Conor and, **1**:499–500
    Tone in, **2**:704
Catholic Convention of 1792, **1**:74
Catholic Defence Association of Great Britain and Ireland, **1**:311
Catholic Emancipation Act (1829), **1**:76
    Eucharistic Congress and, **1**:233
    MPs under, **1**:209
    Protestant Ascendancy and, **2**:586
    town life and, **2**:708
Catholic emancipation campaign, **1**:75–77
    Burke and, **1**:68
    O'Connell and, **1**:497–498; **2**:545
    Raiftearaí's support of, **2**:598
    repeal movement different from, **2**:623

Catholic emancipation campaign
  CONTINUED
    Tone in, **2:**704
    Troy and, **2:**718–719
Catholic Ireland in the early
  seventeenth century, documents
  on, **2:**827–829 (d)
Catholicism, restoration in Ireland,
  1:419
Catholic merchants and gentry
  from 1690 to 1800, **1:77–79**
    revolution settlement and,
      1:202–203
Catholic Relief Acts
  Catholic emancipation
    campaign and, **1:**75
  Catholic Relief Act (1778),
    2:857–858 (d)
  Catholic Relief Act (1782),
    2:860–861 (d)
  Catholic Relief Act (1793),
    2:864–866 (d)
  Catholic Relief Act (1829),
    2:740, 888–890 (d)
  Catholic Relief Bill (1821), **1:**75,
    76
  introduction at the instigation
    of British cabinet, **1:**277
  merchants and gentry under,
    1:77
"Catholic rent"
  Catholic Association and, **1:**76
  endorsed by Raiftearaí, **2:**598
  origin of, **2:**885–888 (d)
Catholics
  in Belfast, **1:**48
  Charles II and, **2:**626
  discrimination in Northern
    Ireland, **1:**480–482; **2:**962
  and Fair Employment Act (FEA)
    of 1976, **1:**228
  and Fair Employment Act (FEA)
    of 1989, **1:**228–229
  members of the Volunteers,
    2:542
  in Northern Ireland
    demand for equality in
      1960s, **2:**560
    and public service, **2:**962
  as percentage of population,
    2:618
  right to vote granted in 1793,
    2:543
  and street ballads, **1:**43
  under Stuarts, **2:**737
  survivalism, **1:**86; **2:**606
Catholic Social Service Conference,
  1:413
Catholic University, **1:**197–198
Catholic University Medical School,
  1:197–198

women at, **1:**199
cattle, **1:**4, 6
  booleying, **1:**178
  and decrease in rural labor,
    1:11
  as dowry, **1:**239–240
  exports, **1:**9, 180, 181–182
  farming families and, **1:**248
  production in 1845–1921, **1:**8
  raiding or rustling, **1:**4; **2:**599
  salted beef exports, **2:**710, 711
  Stone Age farming, **2:**679, 680
Cattle Acts (1660s)
  economic diversification and,
    1:181
  effects of, **2:**710
  and Irish economy, **1:**6
Caulfield, Séamus, **2:**680
C case (1997), **1:**150
Cecilia Street Medical School,
  1:197–198
  women at, **1:**199
Céide Fields, **1:**359; **2:**680
céili, **1:**456; **2:**664
Céitinn, Seathrún. See Keating,
  Geoffrey
Celestine I (pope), **1:**161; **2:**603
  St. Patrick and, **2:**649
celibacy, permanent, **2:**567, 570,
  646, 756
  in Belfast, **2:**571
Céli-Dé (Culdees), **1:**90, 290
Cellach, bishop of Armagh, **1:**91
Celtic languages, **1:**79
Celtic migrations, **1:79–81**
  cultural impact, **1:**361
Celtic Society, **1:**500
Celtic Tiger, **1:81–84,** 440
  Anglo–Irish relations and,
    1:169
  in Cork, **1:**109
  IDA Ireland and, **1:**322
  in the North vs. the South,
    1:176–177
  overseas investment in, **1:**512–
    513
  trade unions and, **2:**713
Celtic Twilight, The (Yeats), **1:**388
Cenél Cairpre, **1:**345, 348
Cenél Conaill, **1:**347–348; **2:**721
Cenél Eogain, **2:**721
Cenél Fiachach, **1:**345, 348
Cenél Loegaire, **1:**345, 348
Cenél nEogain, **1:**348
Cennick, John, **1:**236
censorship
  Fianna Fáil and, **2:**553
  publishing and, **1:**261
Censorship of Publications Act
  (Ireland, 1929), **1:**261

contraception in, **1:**148
censuses
  1841
    on age of marriage, **2:**567
    on housing, **2:**643–644
  1834 on religion, **2:**618
  and information on use of
    language, **1:**373, 375
  and population after Great
    Famine, **1:**281
  and recording of women's
    work, **2:**754–755
Central Association of
  Schoolmistresses and Other Ladies
  Interested in Education, **1:**198–
  199
Central Bank of Ireland, **1:**327
Central Statistics Office on farm
  wives' labor, **1:**249
Ceoltóirí Cualann (orchestra),
  1:456
Ceoltóirí Laighean (orchestra),
  1:456
ceramics
  Beaker pottery, **1:**62
  Carrowkeel ware, **2:**576
  Irish delftware, **1:**36–37
  Stone Age, **2:**679
cess
  Anglo-Irish resistance to, **2:**606
  attempts to commute in the
    1580s, **2:**535
  Oakboys and Steelboys, **1:**495–
    496
  Old English and, **1:**219, 220,
    501
Chagineau, William, **1:**33
chain migration, **1:**140
Chamberlain, Austen, **1:**18
Chamberlain, Neville, **1:**489
Chamber Music (Joyce), **1:**340
Chambers, James, **1:**113
Chambers, William, **1:**273
chapbooks and popular literature,
  1:84–85
  Duffy in, **1:**159
  Kildare Place Society, **1:**343
Chappell, William, **2:**717–718
Charabanc Theatre Company,
  1:152, 153, 154, 405
Charlemont, first earl of (James
  Caulfeild), **1:**205
Charles I, **2:**538
  Calvinism and, **1:**71–72
  Church of Ireland under, **1:**87
  Confederation of Kilkenny and,
    1:102
  and the Graces, **1:**277
  Old English and, **1:**502
  O'Mahony on, **1:**503

O'Neill and, **1:**504–505
Solemn League and Covenant, **2:**669–670
and Ulster plantations, **1:**369
Charles II, **2:**538, 626
Solemn League and, **2:**670
Charles V, **1:**255, 256
Charleville as estate town, **2:**709
Chearnley, Anthony, **1:**36
Cherish, **2:**761
Chichester, Sir Arthur, **1:**48
Chichester, Robert Spencer, **2:**518
Chichester-Clark, James, **2:**724, 725
Faulkner and, **1:**249
O'Neill and, **1:**506
Parker and, **2:**518
Chieftains, The, **1:**456, 457
child care, **1:**450–451
Childers, Erskine, **1:**18
children
family size, **1:**242
fostering, **1:**240, 272
in the industrial workforce, **2:751–754**
legitimate *vs.* illegitimate, **1:**240, 243
in manufacturing, **1:**316
medical care for, **1:**292–293
treatment in institutions, **2:**555
welfare system and, **1:**292–293
Children of Mary, **1:**418
Christ Church Cathedral (Dublin), **1:**26, *156*
sculpture in, **2:**653
Christenberry Report, The, **2:**706
Christian Brothers, **2:**620, 628, 634
overseas missions and, **1:**514
schools, **1:**195–196
Christian Brothers' schools, **1:**196
Christianity
early medieval Ireland and Christianity, **1:161–166**
Eiscir Riata sites, **1:**208
Hiberno-Latin culture and, **1:**296–297
High Crosses and, **1:**297–298, *298*
introduction in Ireland, **2:**580, **602–604**
Irish as literary language in early Christian Church, **1:**393
Christianity Not Mysterious (Toland), **2:**704
Christian Life Communities, **2:**669
Christmas Tree, The (Johnston), **1:**403
Chronicle (Prosper), **1:**161
Chronicles (Holinshed), **1:**223

"Chuilfhionn, An," **1:**455
Church Education Society, **1:**187, 189, 190
churches, **1:**366
Cistercian, **1:**31–32, 364
early
stone, **1:**23–25, 30–3'
in wood, **1:**23–24, 30
early monastic, **1:**362
Churches Together in Britain and Ireland, **1:**183
Churchill, Winston, **1:***19*
church law. *See* canon law
Church of England
building ownership by, **1:**111–112
Calvinism and, **1:**71–72
Cullen and, **1:**120
disestablishment of, **1:**120
education under, **1:**186, 188–189
Forty-Three Articles, **1:**200
Missionary Society, **1:**513
Church of Ireland, **2:**604, 606
adoption of evangelical attitudes, **2:**612
Calvinism and, **1:**71–72
catechisms published, **1:**84
Catholic landowners in, **1:**77
Charles II and, **2:**626
disestablishment of (1869), **2:**586, 614
Dublin Philosophical Society and, **1:**158
education and, **1:**185, 195
Edwardian reform and, **1:**201
Elizabethan era, **1:85–87**
as Erastian state church, **2:**613
evangelicalism and revivals, **1:**235–236
and Gaelic-language policy, **1:**260
Huguenots and, **2:**590
Irish Articles (1615), **1:**71
Irish Tithe Act and, **1:**332
King in, **1:**344
Lambeth Articles (1615), **1:**71, 72
movement to convert Catholics in the 1820s, **2:**613
and National Education Board, **2:**614
and New English, **2:**607
Oakboys and Steelboys, **1:**495–496
Old English and, **1:**500–502; **2:**607
Orange Order, **1:507–510**
preservation of, **1:**209
reform in, **1:**89–91

replacement of the 104 Irish by the 39 English Articles in 1645, **2:**608
Second Reformation and, **2:**653–654
since 1690, **1:87–89**
tithe war and, **2:**701–703
Wentworth and, **2:**608
church reform, **1:89–91**
circular enclosures, **1:**362, 449
Cirese, Alberto Mario, **2:**615
Cistercian Order, **1:**290
and architecture, **1:**26, 31, 449
arrival in Ireland, **1:**91
cists, **2:**683
Citizen Army and Easter Rising of 1916, **2:**548
civil rights, **2:**724
Campaign for Civil Rights (Northern Ireland), **1:480–482**
demonstration and Royal Ulster Constabulary, **2:**639
Hume and, **1:**306
Irish Americans and, **1:**147
Northern Ireland Civil Rights Association (NICRA), **1:**2, 481, 485; **2:**560
Hume and, **1:**306
O'Connell and, **1:**497–498
O'Neill and, **1:**505–506
Paisley's reaction to, **2:**517
social change and, **2:**667
Special Powers Act, **2:**672
Civil Service Academy, **1:**122
Civil Wars (1641–1649), **2:**538
Civil War (1922–1923), **1:91–94**; **2:**553, 942
country houses in, **1:**113
Cumann na mBan and, **1:**121
de Valera and, **1:**135
Eucharistic Congress and, **1:**233
IRA and, **1:**329
proclamations at beginning of by IRA leaders, **2:**949–950 *(d)*
by Provisional Government, **2:**950 *(d)*
as result of Anglo-Irish Treaty of 1921, **1:**18, 91–93
Special Powers Act, **2:**671–672
clachans, **1:94–95**; **2:**647
Claidheamh Soluis, An (The sword of light) (newspaper), **1:**265, 269, 465
edited by Pearse, **2:**520
Clancy Brothers, **1:**456
Clan na Gael
Clarke in, **1:**95
Devoy in, **1:**300

Clan na Gael CONTINUED
  Fenian movement and, **1**:252–253
Clann Cholmáin, **2**:721
Clann Cholmáin Móir, **1**:346, 348
Clann na Poblachta (Party of the Republic), **1**:451, 489; **2**:532, 554, 562
  Declaration of a Republic and the 1949 Ireland Act and, **1**:128
Clann na Talmhan (Party of the Land), **2**:532
Clare, Richard "Strongbow" de, lord of Pembroke and Chepstow, **1**:412–413, 468–469, 472
  tomb of, **2**:653
Clare Island Survey, The (Lysaght), **2**:530
Clark, William P., **1**:492
Clarke, Aidan, **1**:181
Clarke, Austin, **1**:40; **2**:528
  on Yeats, **2**:769–770
Clarke, Harry, **2**:742
Clarke, Kathleen, **1**:95–96, 275, 422
Clarke, Thomas, **1**:95
Clarke, Tom, **2**:548
Clarkson, L. A., **2**:751
Clifford, Conyers, **1**:467
Cline, Maggie, **1**:146
Clinton, Bill, **1**:488, 492; **2**:723
  Good Friday Agreement and, **1**:331
Cloitech, Battle of (789), **1**:348
Cloncurry, Lord (Valentine Browne Lawless), **1**:343
Cloney, Thomas, **2**:890–892 (d)
Clonfert cathedral, **2**:652
Clonmacnoise, cathedral at, **1**:25
  Eiscir Riata and, **1**:208
  sculpture at, **2**:653
Clontarf, Battle of (1014), **1**:96, 476
  Brian Boru and, **1**:123
  as dynastic war, **1**:166
Clontibret, Battle of (1595), **1**:466
  O'Neill and, **1**:504
Cnogba, Congalach, **2**:721
Coady, Michael, **1**:41; **2**:530
Codex Insulensis, **1**:290
Codex Kilkenniensis, **1**:290
Codex Salmanticensis, **1**:290
Codex Usserianus Primus, **1**:415
Coffey, Brian, **1**:40; **2**:529
Cogadh Gaedhel re Gallaibh (War of the Irish with the foreigners), **1**:96
Cogitosus, **1**:379, 448, 449
  on Saint Brigit, **1**:163, 289

cohabitation, **1**:244
Cohan, George M., **1**:146
Cohesion Fund, **1**:83
coign of vantage and livery, **1**:133, 219
Coillte, **2**:768
Coimisiún le Rincí Gaelacha (Irish Dancing Commission), **1**:456
Cold War and Irish neutrality, **1**:463–464
Coleman, Michael, **1**:456
Colgan, John, **1**:21, 291
  in education, **1**:324
Collectanea de Rebus Hibernicis (Vallancey), **1**:22
Collected Poems (Kinsella), **2**:529
Collected Poems (Liddy), **2**:529
Collected Works in Verse and Prose (Yeats), **2**:769
Collection of the Most Celebrated Irish Tunes, A (Neal and Neal), **1**:73
Colleen Bawn, The (Coucicault), **1**:38
Collège de Montaigu, **1**:323
Collège de Navarre, **1**:323
College of Saint Anthony, **1**:291
Collegians, The (Griffin), **1**:38
Collins, Brenda, **2**:753
Collins, Michael, **1**:96–97, 97, 267
  and Anglo-Irish Treaty of 1921, **1**:18, 19, 20, 55; **2**:559
  in the Civil War, **1**:92, 93–94
  Commonwealth and, **1**:100
  and constitution of the Irish Free State (1922), **1**:105; **2**:951–954 (d)
  death of, **1**:94
  IRA and, **1**:329
  and Irish Republican Brotherhood, **1**:382
  negotiations with Lloyd George, **2**:549
Collins, Patrick, **2**:743
colonial theory from 1500 to 1690, **1**:97–98
  Sidney and, **2**:659–660
Colum, Mary, **1**:121
Colum, Padraic, **1**:153
Columba, Saint, **1**:27, 415, 448
  Altus prosator (Ancient creator), **1**:296
  Cathach, **1**:162
  documents on, **1**:291
  in hagiography, **1**:161, 163, 289–290
  writings of, **1**:164
Columbans, **2**:620
Columbanus, Saint, **1**:379, 450
  exhortation to his monks, **2**:778 (d)

Hiberno-Latin culture and, **1**:296
  as pilgrim exile, **1**:163, 290
"Columbanus to His Monks" (att. to St. Columbanus), **2**:778 (d)
Colum Cille, Saint. *See* Columba, Saint
Comgall, Saint, **1**:450
Comhaltas Ceoltóirí Éireann, **1**:41, 456
Comiskey, Brendan, **2**:638
Commercial Bank, **1**:45
Commissioners of National Education, **1**:191
Commission of Ecclesiastical Causes, **1**:86
Commission of Faculties, **1**:86
Commission on Emigration and Other Population Problems, 1948–1954, Report of the, **2**:978–979 (d)
Commission on Manual and Practical Instruction, **1**:190
Commission on Social Welfare, **1**:293
Commission on the Gaeltacht. *See* Gaeltacht
Commission on the Status of Women, **1**:226–227
  1972 report, **2**:992–993 (d)
Committee on the Administration of Justice (CAJ), **1**:228–229
Common Agricultural Policy (CAP), **1**:98–99, 234
  farming families in, **1**:248
  Ireland and, **1**:83
Common Market. *See* European Economic Community
Commonwealth, **1**:99–101
  Declaration of a Republic and the 1949 Ireland Act and, **1**:127–129
community, religion and, **2**:609–611
commuters, **2**:716
Compleat Irish Traveller, The (Skinner), **2**:705
composition system, **1**:220
  Sidney and, **2**:659–660
Computer-aided design (CAD), Ordnance Survey and, **1**:511
Comyn, David, **1**:264
conacre, **2**:642
Concanen, Matthew, **1**:391
  Conchobair (king of Connacht), **1**:498
Conditions of Employment Act of 1935, **1**:101–102
  Bennett and, **1**:332
  Clarke on, **1**:95
  women in, **1**:227

Confederate Catholics, **1:**102, 103; **2:**538
    Cromwell and, **1:**117–118
    Darcy and, **1:**125
    O'Mahony and, **1:**502, 503
    Rinuccini nuncio to, **2:**629
    Solemn League and, **2:**670
    See also Confederation of Kilkenny
Confederate Clubs, **2:**772
Confederate Supreme Council, **2:**630
Confederation of Kilkenny, **1:**102–104; **2:**6–8, 600, 835–836 *(d)*
    Darcy and, **1:**125
    Old English and, **1:**502
    Old English joining in a Catholic war, **2:**608
    O'Neill in, **1:**504–505
    Solemn League and, **2:**670
Confessio (Declaration) (Saint Patrick), **1:**161, 289; **2:**603, 777–778 *(d)*
    Hiberno-Latin culture and, **1:**296
    problems regarding, **2:**649, *650*
confessional state, **2:**613, 614
confraternities. *See* sodalities and confraternaties
Congested Districts Board, **1:**104; **2:**648, 757
    Ordnance Survey and, **1:**511
    Plunkett and, **2:**528
Congregation of the Holy Ghost, **1:**514
Congress of Irish Unions, **1:**497
Congreve, William, **1:**34, 390
Conlon, Evelyn, **1:**404
Connacht
    on defeat of Scots in, **2:**809 *(d)*
    rebellion of 1641 in, **2:**600
Connaught Patriot (newspaper), **1:**465
Conn Céadchathach (king), **1:**208
Connell, Desmond, **2:**638
Connell, Kenneth H.
    The Population of Ireland, 1750 to 1845, **1:**241
    on potato and age of marriage, **2:**572–573
Conner, William, **1:**358
    and definition of the land question, **1:**356, 357
Connolly, James, **1:**104–105, *105*, 349, 378; **2:**548
    Gonne and, **1:**275
    ITUC and, **2:**712
    Markievicz and, **1:**422
    O'Brien and, **1:**497
    Pearse and, **2:**520

"What Is Our Programme?" **2:**933–935 *(d)*
Connolly, William, **1:**203; **2:**585
Conn the Hundred-Battler, **1:**165
Conry, Florence, **1:**323, 324
    Irish colleges abroad and, **1:**325
conscription, **1:**304–305
    Catholic clergy and anticonscription movement, **2:**636
    opposition to during World War I, **2:**548
Conservatives
    Ascendancy and, **2:**586
    in electoral politics, **1:**213
    Irish Parliamentary Party and, **1:**304
    temperance movement, **2:**695
constitutional nationalism
    Redmond and, **2:**601
constitution of Independent Ireland, **1:**105–107
    constitution of 1922
        Commonwealth and, **1:**99
    constitution of 1937, **1:**106–107; **2:**554, 968–970 *(d)*
        Clarke on, **1:**95
        de Valera, **1:**136
        divorce in, **1:**148
        Gaelic and Catholic state in, **1:**261–262
        IWWU and, **1:**332
        McQuaid and, **1:**413
        and presidency, **2:**582
        Jews in, **1:**339
Constructive Unionism, **1:**104
Contention of the Bards, **1:**398
contraception
    Cumann na nGaedheal and, **1:**261
    decriminalization of, **2:**557
    and *Humanae Vitae*, **2:**638
    McGee v. the Attorney General and the Revenue Commissioners (1973), **2:**1000–1003 *(d)*
    Robinson on the family planning bill, **2:**1003–1004 *(d)*
    See also divorce, contraception, and abortion
Contra Collatorem (Prosper of Aquitaine), **2:**603
Control of Manufactures Act (1932), **1:**512
Convention on the Future of Europe, **1:**235
Conversation Piece (Keane), **1:**403
Cooke, Barrie, **1:**41
Cooke, Henry, **1:**107–108, *108*; **2:**614
Cooley, Thomas, **1:**35

Cooper, Ivan, **1:**482
Coote, Sir Charles, **1:**117
copper, prehistoric mining of, **1:**62; **2:**577
Córas Tráchtála, **2:**676
Corbett, Jim, **1:**146
Corcach Mór Mumhan. *See* Cork
Cork, **1:108–110**
    cotton industry in, **2:**641
    housing in, **2:**757
    industrialization in, **1:**314–315
    under Tudors, **2:**736
    Viking settlement in, **1:**476
Cork Airport, **1:**110
Cork Butter Exchange, **1:**10
Cork Examiner (newspaper), **1:**465
Cork Total Abstinence Society, **2:**668
Cormac's Chapel (Cashel, Co. Tipperary), **1:**25, *30*, 30
    sculpture in, **2:**652
corn laws, **1:**7
    repeal of, **1:**283
Cornwallis, Charles, marquis, **1:**2
    as lord lieutenant, **1:**277
    Tandy and, **2:**693
Corrigan, Máiréad, **2:**520
Corrs, The, **1:**457
Corrymeela Community, **1:**183
Córus bésgnai, **1:**59
Cosgrave, Liam, **1:**111; **2:**733
    Fine Gael under, **2:**562
    social welfare and, **1:**227
Cosgrave, William T., **1:**56, **110–111**, 489
    Commonwealth and, **1:**100
    Eucharistic Congress and, **1:**232–233
    governments of, **2:**553
    letter on the Commission on the Gaeltacht, **2:**956–957 *(d)*
    speeches
        on Ireland's admission to the League of Nations, **2:**955–956 *(d)*
        at opening of Dáil Éireann, **2:**950–951 *(d)*
Costello, John A., **1:**451; **2:**733
    coalition government of, **2:**554
    Declaration of a Republic and the 1949 Ireland Act and, **1:**128
    McQuaid's letter to, on Mother and Child Scheme, **2:**976–978 *(d)*
    on the Republic of Ireland bill, **2:**975–976 *(d)*
cottiers, **2:**642
    housing, **2:**643
Cotton, Sir Robert, **1:**291

cotton industry, **1**:237; **2**:753
cotton-spinning mills, **2**:641
effect on linen and woollen
industries, **2**:641–642
industrialization and, **1**:316–
319
Council for the Status of Women,
2:760
Council of Trent. *See* Trent, Council
of
Counter-Reformation. *See*
Tridentine Catholicism
Countess Cathleen, The (Yeats),
1:388, 393; **2**:769
Country Boy, The (Murphy), **1**:153
Country Girls, The (O'Brien), **1**:40,
254, 403
country houses and the arts,
1:113–116, *114*
estates and demesnes, **1**:230–
232
county constabulary, **1**:405
county councils, **1**:406
county system, **1**:217
courts
Commonwealth and, **1**:99
under Henry III, **1**:215
Special Powers Act, **2**:671–672
summary jurisdiction, **2**:671–
672
courts of poetry, **1**:454
Cowan, Peadar, **1**:128
cows as symbol of wealth, **1**:272
Cox, Sir Richard, **1**:158
Crabtree, Pam, **1**:160
craft unions as friendly societies,
1:349
Craig, Sir James (Viscount
Craigavon), **1:116–117**, 483,
491; **2**:723, 724
and Anglo-Irish Treaty of 1921,
1:19, 55
on "A Protestant Parliament and
a Protestant State," **2**:962–963
(d)
Carson and, **1**:73
Craig, James Humbert, **2**:741, 742
Craig, Maurice, **1**:114
Craig, William, **1**:482
Trimble and, **2**:716
Cranmer, Thomas, **1**:200
craobhacha. See Gaelic League
Crawford, R. L., **1**:510
Crawford, William Sharman,
1:356, 357, 358
on federalism as alternative to
repeal, **2**:899–900 *(d)*
tenant movement and, **1**:311
tenant right and, **2**:700, 905
Creagh, Richard, **1**:111

Creevykeel cairn, **2**:682, *682*
Cré na Cille (Graveyard Clay) (Ó
Cadhain), **1**:40, 253
Creton, Jean, **2**:629
cricket, **2**:674
criminal biographies, **1**:84
Criminal Justice Act (1945),
abortion in, **1**:148
Criminal Law Amendment Act
(Ireland, 1935), **1**:261
and contraceptives, **1**:148–149,
261; **2**:1003
Criminal Law Amendment Bill
(1971), contraception and, **1**:148
Criminal Law and Procedure Act
(1887), **1**:301
Críth gablach, **1**:60
Crock of Gold, The (Stephens),
1:254
Croft, Sir James
Edwardian reform and, **1**:201
military campaigns of, **1**:219
Croke, Thomas, **1**:266
and Plan of Campaign, **2**:524
Croker, Thomas Crofton, **2**:617
cromlechs, **2**:682
Crommelin, Louis, **2**:590, 640
Cromwell, Henry, **2**:523, 594
Cromwell, Oliver
on capture of Drogheda, **2**:840
(d)
Jews under, **1**:338
military subjugation of Ireland,
2:538
plan of transplantation of
Catholic Irish, **2**:538, 841–844
(d)
Cromwell, Thomas, **2**:592
church and state under, **1**:218
Old English and, **1**:501
Cromwellian conquest, **1:117–**
118; **2**:538
colonization and, **1**:98
Confederation of Kilkenny and,
1:103
Council of Trent and, **1**:112
literature from, **1**:224–225
Old English and, **1**:502
O'Neill and, **1**:505
Solemn League and Covenant,
2:669, 670–671
1640s revolt and, **1**:222
Cromwellian land settlement,
2:522
Crone, Anne, **1**:403
Cronin, Anthony, **2**:529
crosiers
of Clonmacnoise, **1**:428, *428*
Inishgallen, **1**:428
of Lismore, **1**:428

O'Dea (1418), **1**:31
Cross, Dorothy, **2**:743
Crossman, Virginia, **1**:301
Cross of Cong, **1**:428
Cross of the Scriptures, **1**:*298*
"Crossroads Election" (1969),
2:724
"crowbar brigades," **1**:247
Cruachain, **1:118–119**
prehistorical, **2**:579
Crying Game, The (film, Jordan),
1:42
crypto-Catholicism. *See* Catholics:
survivalism
cuaird, **2**:664
Cú Chuimne, **1**:59
Cú Chulainn, **1:119–120**
in *Táin Bó Cúailnge*, **2**:691–692
Cuchulain of Muirthemne (Gregory),
1:39, 402
Cúirt an Mheán Oíche (The
midnight court) (Merriman),
1:34, 38, 399
Cullen, James, **2**:669
temperance movement, **2**:695–
696
Cullen, L. M., **2**:642
Cullen, Paul, **1:120–121**, *121*;
2:614, 634
devotional revolution and,
1:137
on education, **1**:190
MacHale and, **1**:411; **2**:634
and reform of the Catholic
Church, **2**:612
sodalities and confraternities,
2:668
tenant movement and, **1**:313
Troy and, **2**:718
Culliton report (1992), **1**:320–321
Cumann Ceoltóirí Éireann, **1**:256
Cumann na mBan (Women's
Council), **1:121–122**; **2**:759
Clarke in, **1**:95
Cumann na nGaedheal (Party of
the Irish)
changing name to Fine Gael,
2:554
and Civil War, **2**:553
creation of, **2**:532
government (1922–1932)
and agriculture, **1**:11
and Catholic Church, **1**:260
Commonwealth and, **1**:100
Eucharistic Congress and,
1:232–233
protectionism and, **1**:320
state enterprise and, **2**:676
Cumberland, Richard, **1**:390
Cumin, John, **1**:473

Cummian, **1**:379
  on the Easter question, **1**:296
  Paschal letter and Saint Patrick,
    2:603
Cunningham, Waddell, **1**:495
Curry, John
  Catholic Association and, **1**:74
  O'Conor and, **1**:499
Cúrsaí Thómáis (The story of
  Tomás) (MacLysaght), **1**:265
Curtis, L. Perry, Jr., **1**:301
Curtis, Tony, **1**:41; **2**:530
Curwin, Hugh, **1**:419
Cusack, Michael, **1**:**122**, 266
Cusack, Thomas, **1**:446–447
Cycle of Kings, **1**:460

⁓ D

Dáil Éireann
  Civil War and, **1**:92
  constituencies in 1923, **2**:*551*
  constituencies in 1935, **2**:*552*
  Cosgrave's speech at opening of,
    2:*950–951 (d)*
  creation, **1**:213; **2**:661, 685,
    685, 937
  "Democratic Programme,"
    2:*938–939 (d)*
  Griffith president of, **1**:287
  IRA and, **1**:329
  Jews in, **1**:339
  local councils and, **1**:406
  Markievicz minister of labour in
    first, **1**:422
Daily Nation (newspaper), **1**:465
dairying industry, **1**:*13*
  milk quotas, **1**:14
Dál Cais and Brian Boru, **1**:**123–
124**
Dalkey School Project, **1**:191
Dál nAraide, **1**:*345*, 347
Dál Riata, **1**:*345*, 347
Daly, Edward, **1**:95
Daly, James, **1**:371, 386
Daly, Kathleen. *See* Clarke, Kathleen
dance, **1**:454
  céili, **1**:456
  Cumann na nGaedheal and
    dance halls, **1**:261
  dance music, **1**:455
  GAA ban on "foreign dances,"
    1:259
  set dancing, **1**:456
  step dancing, **1**:456
Dance Hall Act (1935), **1**:456
Dancers Dancing, The (Ní
  Dhuibhne), **1**:404
Dancing at Lughnasa (Friel), **1**:154

Danelaw, **1**:166
Daniel, William, **1**:397, 398
Darcy, Patrick, **1**:**125**, *126*
Dargan, William, **2**:715
"Dark Rosaleen" (Mangan), **1**:38
Daughters of Charity of Saint
  Vincent de Paul, **2**:621
Davey, Ray, **1**:183
Davies, John, **1**:368, 380
  *A Discovery of the True Causes
    Why Ireland Was Never Entirely
    Subdued*, **1**:224; **2**:825–827 *(d)*
  on Flight of the Earls (1607),
    2:820–821 *(d)*
Davin, Maurice, **1**:266
  Cusack and, **1**:122
Davis, Thomas, **1**:38, 44, **125–
126**, 388, *445*, 464; **2**:625
  and land question, **1**:356
  Library of Ireland, **1**:159
  and *Nation*, **1**:392
  and Young Ireland, **2**:545, 770
Davitt, Michael, **1**:**126–127**, *127*,
  371, 372
  founding of the Mayo Land
    League, **2**:911
  Home Rule and, **1**:300
  proposing Ladies' Land League,
    1:351
  and United Irish League, **2**:728,
    730
Davitt, Michael (poet), **1**:41; **2**:530
Dead Kingdom, The (Montague),
  1:40; **2**:529
Deageo, **1**:288
Deane, Anne, **1**:351
Deane, Seamus, **1**:22, 23
Deasy, Timothy, and Brett trial,
  1:*251*, *252*
Deasy's Act (1860), **2**:700
Death of a Naturalist, The (Heaney),
  1:294
de Barri, Gerald. *See* Giraldus
  Cambrensis
de Barri, Robert, **1**:412
de Burgh, Hubert, **2**:790
de Burgh family, **1**:473
Declaration of a Republic and the
  1949 Ireland Act, **1**:**127–129**
Declaration of Independence of the
  Irish Parliament (1460), **2**:801–
  803 *(d)*
Declaratory Act (Britain, 1720),
  1:204; **2**:541, 853 *(d)*
  Irish parliament and, **1**:276
  repeal of, **1**:205
decommissioning, **1**:**129–130**
  Trimble and, **2**:717
de Courcy, John, **1**:469, 473;
  2:650

Decoration (Jellett), **2**:*743*
Deering, Michael, **1**:267
Deevy, Teresa, **1**:153, 402
De excidio Britanniae (The ruin of
  Britain) (Gildas), **1**:296, 379
Defence Forces, women in, **2**:759
Defence of the Realm Act (1914),
  2:671
Defenderism, **1**:**130–131**; **2**:542
  Insurrection Act and, **2**:869–
    871 *(d)*
  Irish Tithe Act and, **1**:332
  and oath-taking, **2**:543
  Orange Order and, **1**:507
  resistance to militia
    conscription, **2**:543
  Tandy and, **2**:693
  United Irishmen and, **1**:206–
    207
de Gaulle, Charles, **1**:169
de Heere, Lucas, and *Theatre de tous
  les peuples et nations de la terre
  avec leurs haibts et ornemens divers
  . . .* , **1**:471
De insulae Hiberniae commentarius
  (Commentary on the island of
  Ireland) (Lombard), **1**:408
Deirdre (AE), **1**:388
Deirdre of the Sorrows (Synge),
  1:389
de Lacy, Hugh, **1**:215
Delamain, Henry, **1**:37
Delaney, Malachy, **1**:208
Delanty, Greg, **1**:41; **2**:530
Delany, Mary, **1**:390
  writing on Ireland, **1**:225
Delany, Patrick, **1**:390
demesnes. *See* estates and demesnes
Democratic Unionist Party (DUP),
  1:485
  Paisley and, **2**:517
Dempsey, Charles, **1**:84
de Nelan (bard), **1**:255
Deoraidheacht (Exile) (Ó Conaire),
  1:265
De Origine Mali (King), **1**:344
de Paor, Louis, **1**:41
Derricke, John, **1**:35, 369
  depiction of Irish life, **2**:536
  The Image of Irelande, **1**:35, 224,
    224, 225, 272; **2**:536, 659,
    810–811 *(d)*
Derrig, Tomás, **1**:260
Derry, **1**:481–482
  Citizens' Action Committee,
    1:482
  civil-rights march of 5 October
    1968, **1**:506; **2**:560
  intercommunal rioting in,
    1:485

Derry CONTINUED
religious geography of, **2**:619
siege of, **1:131–132**, *132*
Derry Journal (newspaper), **1**:51
Derrynaflan Chalice, **1**:427
Derrynaflan Paten, **1**:427
Description of the . . . Peasantry of Ireland, A (Bell), **2**:881 *(d)*
Deserted Village (Goldsmith), **1**:33
Desiderius (Ó Maolchonaire), **1**:398
Desmond, Sir John and Sir James of, **1**:134
Desmond rebellions, **1:133–135**; **2**:537, 606
colonial theory and, **1**:98
Sidney and, **2**:659
De statu ecclesiastico (Gilbert), **1**:91
de Valera, Eamon, **1**:*135*, **135–136**, *490*; **2**:531
"Aims of Fianna Fáil in Office," **2**:959–960 *(d)*
antipartition strategy, **1**:489
arrest of, **2**:661
in the Civil War, **1**:92, 93
Clarke on, **1**:95
Collins and, **1**:96, 97
and constitution of 1937, **1**:106–107; **2**:968–970 *(d)*
Craig and, **1**:116
Cú Chulainn and, **1**:120
Declaration of a Republic and the 1949 Ireland Act and, **1**:127–128
economy and, **1**:174
Eucharistic Congress, **1**:232–233
"Failure of the League of Nations," **2**:963–965 *(d)*
and foundation of the *Irish Press*, **1**:465
"German Attack on Neutral States," **2**:970 *(d)*
IRA and, **1**:329, 330
Kennedy and, **1**:341
Lemass and, **1**:382
McQuaid's influence on, **2**:554, 636–637
"National Thanksgiving" (1945), **2**:971–974 *(d)*
and neutrality, **1**:462, 489; **2**:554
opposition to Anglo-Irish Treaty of 1921, **1**:18, 19; **2**:945–948 *(d)*
as president, **2**:582
protectionism and, **1**:320
Sinn Féin and, **2**:661
state enterprise and, **2**:676
and television, **1**:424
"Time Will Tell," **2**:945–948 *(d)*

and United Nations, **2**:733–734
in the United States, **2**:685
Devlin, Anne, **1**:154, 404
Devlin, Denis, **1**:40; **2**:529
Devlin, Joseph, **2**:558
and Ancient Order of Hibernians, **1**:16
victory over de Valera, **2**:559
Devlin, Marie, **1**:294
Devlin, Paddy, **1**:482
Devon Commission, **1**:356
subdivision and subletting of holdings, **2**:687
devotional revolution, **1:136–139**, *137*; **2**:612
American, **1**:145
Cullen's ministry and, **2**:634
secularization and, **2**:654–656
sodalities and confraternities, **2**:668
devotion to the Miraculous Medal and the Sacred Heart of Jesus, **2**:620
Devoy, John, **1**:371
and Ancient Order of Hibernians, **1**:16
Davitt and, **1**:127
Fenian escape from Australia, **1**:252–253
Home Rule and, **1**:300
Diamond, Battle of the (1795), **1**:507
Diamond, Harry, **2**:560
diaspora. *See* emigration
Dickson, R. J., **1**:432
Dicuil, **1**:297
Dillon, John, **2**:524, 636, 730
Dillon, John Blake, **1**:464
Davis and, **1**:125
and Young Ireland, **2**:770
Dineen, Frank, **1**:266
Dinneen, Patrick, **1**:265
Direction for the Plantation of Ulster, A (Blennerhasset), **2**:823–824 *(d)*
Directory of Worship (1647), **2**:593
direct rule, **2**:534, 605
Disbanding Act (England, 1699), **1**:443
"Discourse of Ireland, A" (Gernon), **1**:224; **2**:831–833 *(d)*
Discourse of the Religion Anciently Professed by the Irish and British, A (Ussher), **2**:738
Discourses on the Being and Attributes of God (Abernathy), **1**:1
Discovery of the True Causes Why Ireland Was Never Entirely Subdued, A (Davies), **1**:224, 368–369; **2**:825–827 *(d)*

Disputatio apologetica de iure regni Hiberniae pro Catholicis Hibernis adversus haereticos Anglos (Explanatory argument concerning the authority of the kingdom of Ireland on behalf of Irish Catholics against English heretics) (O'Mahony), **1**:503
Dissenters
Presbyterians as, **1**:202; **2**:581, 608, 610
Second Reformation and, **2**:653
and Test Act, **2**:594
Dissertations on the History of Ireland (O'Conor), **1**:499
distilling, **1:61–62**
in eighteenth century, **2**:566
distraint of goods, **2**:700
district councils, **1**:406
"Disused Shed in Co. Wexford, A" (Mahon), **2**:529
divorce
decriminalization of, **2**:557
effective ban in Free State, **1**:260
divorce, contraception, and abortion, **1:148–150**, *149*
family size and, **1**:242
Gaelic divorce, **1**:240
separation, **1**:244
social change and, **2**:666
Divorce Action Group, **2**:631
Dobbs, Francis, **1**:391
Docwra, Henry, **1**:468
Doherty, Willie, **2**:743
Doirse earthwork, **1**:346
Dolan, Jay, **1**:145
Dolan, Joe, **1**:456
Dolly's Brae, fight at, **1**:509
dolmens, **2**:682
domestic service, **2**:642, 757
American, **1**:146
in Australia, **1**:140
employment rates in, **2**:663
Domhnach Airgid, **1**:428
Dominicans
and education, **1**:194, 199
rosary crusades of, **2**:637
women in, **2**:621
dominion status offered to Ireland, **2**:549
Dominus Iesus, **1**:184
Don Belianis of Greece, **1**:84
donjons (keeps), **1**:26
Donnelly, Dan, **2**:674
Donoghue, Emma, **1**:254, 404
Donore Hoard, **1**:416
Donovan, Gerard, **1**:41; **2**:530
Door into the Dark (Heaney), **1**:294
Doran, Theo, **1**:41; **2**:530

Dorcey, Mary, **1:**403, 404

Douglas, David, **1:**495

Douglas, Lord Alfred, **2:**749

"Dove of Peace" (Bardwell), **1:**404

Dowdall, George, **1:**419; **2:**593
  Edwardian reform and, **1:**201
  Old English and, **1:**501

Down, Battle of (1260), **1:**474

Down by the River (O'Brien), **1:**404

Downing Street Declaration (1993), **1:**331, 479, 487; **2:**724

Downshire Protestant (newspaper), **1:**465

Down Survey, **1:**117; **2:**522
  Ordnance Survey and, **1:**500

dowries, **1:**239–240

Dowson, Ernest, **1:**388

Dowth mounds, **2:**681

Doyle, Jack, **2:**674

Doyle, James Warren, **1:150–151,** *151,* 452; **2:**634
  education and, **1:**188
  Second Reformation and, **2:**654
  tithe war and, **2:**703

Doyle, Martin, **2:**701

Doyle, Roddy, **1:**41, 254

Dracula (Stoker), **1:**38, 392

drama
  Hiberno-English and, **1:**295
  Irish depicted in, **1:**223, 225, 295
  in Irish Free State, **1:**265
  Irish productions, **1:**377
  in Middle English, **1:**431
  modern, **1:**40, 41, **151–155**
  theatre of the absurd, **1:**153, 253

Drama in Muslin, A (Moore), **1:**253

drapers, **1:**316

Drapier's Letters (Swift), **1:**33, 204; **2:**690

Drennan, William, **1:**391

Drogheda, **2:**737
  Cromwellian conquest of, **1:**117; **2:**840 *(d)*

Druid Theatre Company, **1:**154

Druma Mór, An (The big drum) (Mac Grianna), **1:**265

Drummond, Thomas, **2:**703

Drury, Susannah, **1:**36

Dublin, **1:155–157**
  architecture
    Georgian Dublin architecture, **1:273–275**
    modern, **2:**743
    neoclassical buildings, **1:**35
  Celtic Tiger and, **1:**83
  civil liberties granted by Prince John (1192), **2:**788–790 *(d)*
  cotton industry in, **2:**641

Custom House (Gandon), **1:***156,* 274
  Easter Rising, **2:**683–685, *684*
  housing in, **2:**757
  industrialization in, **1:**314, 315
  International Financial Services Centre, **1:***82,* 83
  Irish Literary Renaissance in, **1:**388
  loyalist bombing in, **2:**556
  map of, **1:***156*
  origins of, **1:**362
  publishing in, **1:**387
  under Stuarts, **2:**737
  theatre in, **1:**154
  trade in, **1:**178–179
  under Tudors, **2:**735–736
  Viking settlement in, **1:**475, 476
  Wide Streets Commission, **1:**274

Dublin Castle, **1:***156,* 275
  tithe war and, **2:**703
  United Irishmen in, **1:**206

Dublin Corporation, **1:**156
  definition of Protestant Ascendancy, **2:**584

Dubliners, The, **1:**457

Dubliners (Joyce), **1:**39, 253, 339

Dublin Gate Theatre, **1:**153

Dublin Hermetic Society, **2:**769

Dublin International Exhibition (1907), **1:**451

"Dublin Kiddies' Scheme," **1:**407

Dublin Mean Time, **2:**716

Dublin Metropolitan Police (DMP), **2:**686

Dublin Penny Journal, **1:**500

Dublin Philosophical Society, **1:157–159**
  Molyneux and foundation of, **1:**446
  Petty and, **2:***523*

Dublin Society
  foundation of, **1:**36; **2:**584
  Tandy and, **2:**693

Dublin Society of United Irishmen, **2:**731
  parliamentary reform plan (1794), **2:**866–867 *(d)*

Dublin Trades Council, **1:**497

Dublin United Tramways Company, **1:**407, 451

Dublin University, Irish MPs from, **1:**209

Dublin University Magazine, **1:**69

Dublin University Review, **1:**388
  Yeats and, **2:**769

Dudley, Robert, **2:**659

dueling, Protestant Ascendancy and, **2:**584

Duffy, Charles Gavan, **1:**464, 465
  Davis and, **1:**125–126
  Independent Irish Party and, **1:**311
  Library of Ireland, **1:**159
  tenant movement and, **1:**312–313
  and Young Ireland, **2:**770, 772

Duffy, George Gavan, **1:**18, 19

Duffy, James, **1:159,** 387

Duffy, Louise Gavan, **1:**121

Duffy, Rita, **2:**743

Duffy's Hibernian Sixpenny Magazine, **1:**159

Duffy's Irish Catholic Magazine, **1:**159

Duggan, Eamon, **1:**18

Duggan, James, **1:**455

Dún Ailinne, **1:159–160**

Dunkin, William, **1:**33, 391

Dunlevy, Anthony, **1:**325

Dunne, Catherine, **1:**403

Dunsany Co-operative Society, **2:**528

Duns Scotus, John, **1:**323, 324

Dürer, Albrecht, **1:***217*

Dury, Sir William, **1:**133

Dymmok, John, **1:**224

Dysert O'Dea, Battle of (1318), **1:**475

⁓ **E**

Eames, Robin, **1:**89

"Éamonn A'Chnuic," **1:**453

Easpuig, Gille (Gilbert), **1:**90–91
  De statu ecclesiastico, **1:**91

Easter controversy, **1:**89–90, 296

Easter Rising (1916), **2:**548, 683–685, *684*
  Catholic clergy and, **2:**636
  Civil War and, **1:**92
  Collins in, **1:**96, 97
  Connolly in, **1:**105
  Cosgrave in, **1:**110
  Cú Chulainn and, **1:**119–120
  Cumann na mBan and, **1:**121
  de Valera in, **1:**135
  fiftieth-anniversary commemorations, **2:**556
  GAA members in, **1:**267
  Home Rule and, **1:**305
  Liberals after, **1:**213
  Markievicz and, **1:**422
  Pearse and, **2:**520
  and Proclamation of the Irish Republic, **2:**935
  and Proclamation of the Provisional Republican Government, **2:**759

Easter Rising Continued
   Sinn Féin and, **2:**660, 662
"Easter 1916" (Yeats), **1:**39;
   2:769, 936–937 (d)
Ecclesiastical Titles bill, **1:**311
   Aberdeen and, **1:**312
Eccles Street Dominican School,
   1:194, 199
Echtra Nerai, **1:**118
Eclipsed (Brogan), **1:**154, 404
Economic Cooperation
   Administration (ECA), **1:**423
Economic Development (Whitaker),
   1:167, 168; **2:**979–983 (d)
   development strategy in, **1:**175
economic relations
   between Independent Ireland
      and Britain, **1:167–170**
   between North and South since
      1922, **1:170–171**
   between Northern Ireland and
      Britain, **1:171–173**
economic war
   basis of, **1:**173
   protectionism and, **1:**168
   women's economic rights and,
      1:227
economies of Ireland, North and
   South, since 1920, **1:173–178**
economy
   agriculture in, **1:**247–249
   Celtic Tiger, **1:81–84; 2:**557
   Civil War and, **1:**94
   in Cork, **1:**108–109
   and eighteenth-century
      population explosion, **2:**565–
      566, 574
   European Union and, **1:**233–
      235
   Fianna Fáil's policies, **2:**553–
      554
   newspapers and integration of
      Ireland into international
      economy, **1:**386
   in nineteenth century, **2:**570
   Normans and, **1:**470
   overseas investment in, **1:**511–
      513
   and society from 1500 to 1690,
      1:178–182
   Stone Age, **2:**679
   tenant right, or Ulster custom,
      2:698–700
ecumenism and interchurch
   relations, **1:182–184**
   opposition of McQuaid to,
      1:413
   opposition of Paisley to, **2:**517
Edgeworth, Maria, **1:**33, 38, 115,
   389, 392

Educate Together, **1:**191–192
education
   Catholic Church and, **1:**227;
      2:635, 638
      religious orders and teaching,
         2:622
   Celtic Tiger and, **1:**82, 83
   Church of Ireland and, **2:**613
   constitution on, **1:**106
   Cromwellian conquest and,
      1:118
   Doyle and, **1:**150
   economic development and,
      1:175
   Elizabethan era, **1:**86
   farm children's performance in,
      1:249
   1500 to 1690, **1:184–186**
   government funding for, **2:**667
   Irish colleges abroad, **1:**323–
      326
   and Irish language, **1:***189*, 190,
      196, 198, 260, 375
      Irish-immersion primary
         schools, **1:**377
   Kildare Place Society in, **1:**343
   monasteries
      in the Middle Ages, **1:**290–
         291
   monasteries and, **1:**163–164
      in the early Middle Ages,
         1:448
   Nagle and, **1:**461
   national-school system, **1:**383,
      385
      condemnation by MacHale,
         1:411
   nondenominational schooling,
      1:191–192, 383
   Oliver Plunkett and, **2:**527
   Pearse and, **2:**520
   primary
      national schools from 1831,
         1:188–191
      private "hedge schools" and
         other schools, **1:186–188,**
         383
      state investigations into,
         1:383
   Protestant clergy, **1:**86
   reform of, **1:**219
   secondary
      announcement of free, **2:**555
      female, **1:192–194; 2:**758
      male, **1:194–196**
   Second Reformation and,
      2:653–654
   secularization and, **2:**656
   social change and, **2:**666
   sport and leisure and, **2:**675

   for teachers, **1:**190
   university education, **1:196–
      198**
      Catholic Church and, **2:**634
      women and, **2:**758
   Walsh and, **2:**635, 745
   women and, **1:198–200;
      2:**758–759
   See also schools
Education Act (Northern Ireland,
   1923), **1:**191; **2:**559
Education Act of 1998, **1:**191
educational societies, **1:**383
   as publishers of short books,
      1:385
Edward I, annual revenue under,
   1:218
Edwardian reform, **1:200–201;
   2:**593
Edward II, Jews expelled by, **1:**338
Edward III, annual revenue under,
   1:218
Edwards, Hilton, **1:**153
Edward VI
   church and state under, **1:**219
   militarist strategy in Ireland,
      1:448; **2:**535
   reform under, **1:200–201**
   Sidney and, **2:**658
Edward VIII, de Valera and, **1:**136
eighteenth-century politics
   1690 to 1714—revolution
      settlement, **1:201–203**
   1714 to 1778—interest politics,
      1:203–204
   1778 to 1795—parliamentary
      and popular politics, **1:204–
      206**
   1795 to 1800—repression,
      rebellion, and union, **1:206–
      208**
Eighty Club (London), Parnell's
   address to, **2:**525
Eiscir Riata, **1:208–209**
   as kingdom division, **1:**346
electoral politics
   gerrymandering of
      constituencies in Northern
      Ireland, **2:**723–724
   from 1800 to 1921, **1:209–
      213**
Electricity Supply Board, **2:**676
Electric Light (Heaney), **1:**294
Elgee, Jane Francesca (Speranza),
   2:748
   and the *Nation*, **2:**770
Eliade, Mircea, **2:**616
Elizabeth I
   Church of Ireland in, **1:**85–87
   decrees prohibiting music,
      1:453

excommunication of, **1:**111
Granuaile's meeting with,
1:280
letter from Arthur Grey de
Wilton to, **2:**808–809 *(d)*
and maintenance of order in
Ireland, **2:**536
O'Neill and, **1:**504–505
reform after, **1:**219–221
and religion in Ireland, **2:**605
Protestant Reformation, **2:**806
(d)
Sidney and, **2:**658–660
Ellis, Edwin, **2:**769
Emain Macha (Navan Fort), **1:**214
in *Táin Bó Cúailnge,* **2:**692
embroidery, **1:**318
emigration
1851–1911, **1:***436*
between 1815 and 1845, **2:**567
to Australia, **1:139–141**
to Britain, **1:141–142,** *440*
constitutional amendments on,
1:107
due to Great Famine, **1:**283,
435
Irish in foreign armies, **2:**749–
750
from Irish Republic, **2:**555
and lack of Irish urbanization,
2:644
merchant community in
Europe, **2:**750
to North America, **1:142–148**
overseas missions and, **1:**513–
514
of Protestants, **2:**587
from Southern Ireland,
2:588
*Report of the Commission on
Emigration and Other
Population Problems, 1948–
1954,* **2:**978–979 *(d)*
from the seventeenth century to
1845, **1:431–435**
ship with emigrants in 1850,
1:*432*
since 1950, **1:439–442**
social change and, **2:**665
from 1850 to 1960, **1:435–
439**
from 1600 to the French
Revolution, **2:749–751**
of women, **1:**438, 441; **2:**570,
756
to Australia, **1:**140
to Britain, **1:**142; **2:**757
Emmet, Robert, **1:214–215;**
2:548, 733
Act of Union and, **1:**208

Pearse's affinity for, **2:**520
speech from the dock (1803),
2:880–881 *(d)*
Emmet, Thomas Addis, **1:**214
statement made with O'Connor
and MacNeven on United
Irishmen, **2:**873–877 *(d)*
Emnae Emain, **1:**214
Emperor of Ice Cream, The (Moore),
1:40, 254
Employers' Federation, **1:**378
employment
in Australia, **1:**140
Catholics' rights and, **1:**228–
230
family size and, **1:**244
family wage, **2:**755
in farming, **1:**248–249
female education for, **1:**193
in forestry, **2:**768
in IDA-supported companies,
1:*322*
in manufacturing, **1:**314
marriage rates and, **2:**663–664
North *vs.* South, **1:**176–177
outward-looking strategy and,
1:320–321
overseas investment and, **1:**513
seasonal in Britain and Scotland,
1:442
segregation in, **2:**666
in shipbuilding, **2:**658
social class and, **2:**665
in state enterprises, **2:**676
transport and, **2:**714
Whitaker on, **1:**167
women's economic rights in,
1:226–228
Employment Equality Act of 1977,
2:557
women's economic rights in,
1:227
encastellation, Norman policy of,
1:469, 472
enclosures. *See* agriculture
Endgame (Beckett), **1:**47
Engels, Friedrich, on Irish in
Manchester, **1:**141
English government in medieval
Ireland, **1:215–218,** *216*
English language
replacing Irish as predominant
spoken language, **1:**386
writing on Ireland before 1800,
1:223–226
English Pale, **1:**362, 364; **2:**533
defended by Kildare earls, **2:**534
economy and, **1:**178
Kildare rebellion and, **1:**256
in late medieval Ireland, **2:**605

Old English in, **1:**500–502
origin of, **1:**218
Sidney and, **2:**660
English political and religious
policies, responses to (1534–
1690), **1:218–223**
English settlement, **1:**431
in Middle Ages, **2:**533
Enlightenment, Catholic Ireland
and, **2:**631
Ennis, call for agrarian militancy
at (Parnell), **2:**914–915(d)
Ennis-friary carvings, **1:**31
Ennui (Edgeworth), **1:**38, 392
Enright, Anne, **1:**254, 404
Enterprise Ireland, **1:**83
environmental concerns
agriculture and, **1:**14
bogs and, **1:**53, 55, 361
EU and, **1:**234
Enya, **1:**457
Eóganacht, **1:**123
Eóganacht Áine, **1:***345,* 347
Eóganacht Airthir Cliach, **1:***345,*
347
Eóganachta of Munster, **1:***345,*
347
Eóganacht Caisil, **1:***345,* 347
Eóganacht Glendamnach, **1:***345,*
347
equal economic rights for women
in Independent Ireland, **1:226–
228**
Conditions of Employment Act
and, **1:**101
IWWU and, **1:**332–333
Equal Opportunities Commission
(Northern Ireland), **2:**763
Equal Pay Act (Northern Ireland,
1970), **2:**763
equal rights in Northern Ireland,
1:228–230
Eriugena, Iohannes, **1:**297
Ervine, David, **1:**409
Ervine, St. John, **1:**153
Essex, second earl of (Robert
Devereux), **1:**467
colonization under, **1:**220–221
estates and demesnes, **1:230–232,**
231, 364–365
tenant right, or Ulster custom,
2:697–700
towns around, **2:**709–710
Esther Waters (Moore), **1:**253
ethics, **2:**655
Eucharistic Congress, **1:232–233**
Fianna Fáil and, **2:**553
sodalities and confraternities,
2:668
Eugenius IV (pope), **1:**270

"Eulogy for Columba" (*Amra Choluim Chille*) (Forgaill), **1**:164
Eureka Street (Wilson), **1**:41, 254
euro, **1**:169, 176
   Irish pound and, **1**:327–329, *328*
European Central Bank, **1**:326
European Convention on Human Rights, **1**:229
European Court of Human Rights (ECHR), **1**:229
European Court of Justice (ECJ), **1**:229
European Directive on Equal Treatment for Men and Women in Social Security, **1**:293
European Economic Community (EEC)
   Catholics' rights and, **1**:228, 229
   Celtic Tiger economy and, **1**:81
   economic development and, **1**:167, 175
   economic relations and, **1**:170–171
   Equality Directive of the European Community, **1**:227
   farm support, **2**:667
   Ireland and, **1**:463; **2**:557
   Irish-British economic relations and, **1**:168–169
   Lemass's speech on membership to (1962), **2**:984–987 *(d)*
   summits, **1**:*234*
   women's economic rights in, **1**:227
   See also European Union
European Monetary System, **1**:169, 176
   Irish pound and, **1**:326
European Recovery Programme (ERP). *See* Marshall Aid
European Regional Development Fund, **2**:706
European Social Fund, **2**:706
European Union (EU), **1**:233–235
   and agriculture, **1**:13–14
   Common Agricultural Policy, **1**:83, **98–99**, 234
   Celtic Tiger economy and, **1**:81–83
   Common Foreign and Security Policy (CFSP), **1**:464; **2**:724
   Investment and Development Agency and, **1**:322
   Ireland as member of, **2**:557, 734–735
   Rapid Reaction Force (RRF), **1**:464
   welfare system and, **1**:293

See also European Economic Community
Eustace, James, Viscount Baltinglass, **1**:220
   Old English and, **1**:501–502
Eustace, Janet, **1**:240
evangelicalism and revivals, **1**:235–236
   Methodism and, **1**:430
   Presbyterianism and, **2**:581
   See also Second Reformation
Evans, Estyn, **1**:95
Evening News (newspaper), **2**:687
Evening Press (newspaper), **1**:424
evictions
   due to Poor Law Amendment Act, **2**:*563*, 564
   tenant right and, **2**:700
Examiner, Swift in, **2**:690
exchequer, **1**:217
Exiles (Joyce), **1**:340
exports
   from agriculture, **1**:9
   cattle, **1**:9, 180, 181–182
   export sales relief (ESR) and overseas investment, **1**:512
   food
      to British economy, **1**:6
      butter, **1**:181
      and economic expansion, **2**:565, 574
      during Great Famine, **1**:282
      salted beef, **2**:710, 711
   hides, **1**:4
   Irish Republic and, **2**:557
   linen trade and industry, **1**:7, 317
   textiles to United States, **1**:317–318
   woolens, **2**:641
      in Restoration Ireland, **2**:627
      under William III, **1**:202–203
Expugnatio Hibernica (Giraldus Cambrensis), **1**:223, 431, 472; **2**:788 *(d)*
External Relations Act (1936), **1**:100–101
   Declaration of a Republic and the 1949 Ireland Act and, **1**:127–129

≈ F

Faerie Queene (Spenser), **1**:224; **2**:673
Fáinne an Lae (Dawn of day) (newspaper), **1**:269
Fair Employment Act (FEA) of 1976, **1**:228

Fair Employment Act (FEA) of 1989, **1**:228–229
Fair Employment and Treatment Order (FETO) of 1998, **1**:229
fairies
   intervention in people's lives, **2**:617
   raths as homes of, **2**:599
fairs. *See* markets and fairs
faith healing. *See* Greatorex, Valentine
Fallen Patriot, The (O'Brien), **1**:391
family
   emphasis on family values in constitution of 1937, **1**:107; **2**:554
   farming, **1**:247–249
   fertility, marriage, and the family since 1950, **1**:242–244
   in Irish-American culture, **1**:145
   marriage patterns and
      from 1500 to 1690, **1**:239–241
      from 1690 to 1921, **1**:241–242
   size of, **2**:663–664
      in twentieth century, **2**:646
   social change and, **2**:663–665
Family Home Protection Act of 1976, **1**:227
Family Law (Maintenance of Spouses and Children) Act of 1976, **1**:227
"Family Likeness, A" (Lavin), **1**:404
family planning bill, Robinson on, **2**:1003–1004 *(d)*
famine clearances, **1**:*245*, **245–247**; **2**:564
Famine (O'Flaherty), **1**:254
famines
   in eighteenth century, **2**:642
   Famine of 1821 to 1822, Quakers and, **2**:622
   See also Great Famine
Fanning, Ronan
   on constitution of 1937, **2**:968
   on neutrality, **1**:463
farewell suppers. *See* American wakes
Farmers' Party, **2**:532
farming families, **1**:247–249
   marriage among, **2**:663–664
   women in, **2**:756
Farquhar, George, **1**:34, 390
Fatima, cult of, **1**:418
Faughart, Battle at (1318), **1**:65
Faulkner, Brian, **1**:249–250, 477; **2**:725

economic relations and, **1**:171
Fay, Frank, **1**:151
Fay, W. G., **1**:151
Feast of Tara, **1**:346
federalism as alternative to repeal, **2**:899–900 (d)
Federated Workers' Union of Ireland, the IWWU and, **1**:333
Feetham, Richard, **1**:55
"Feis" ("Carnival") (Ní Dhomhnaill), **2**:1010–1012 (d)
Fenian Brotherhood, **2**:546
Fenian Cycle, **1**:34, 459–460
Fenian movement, **1**:250–253
  Fenians defended by Butt, **1**:69
  Home Rule and, **1**:300
  Parnell and, **1**:300
  and press, **1**:465
  Stephens and, **2**:678
  Sullivan brothers and, **2**:687–688
  women and, **2**:761
Fenian oaths, **2**:905–906 (d)
Ferguson, Samuel, **1**:38, 388
Ferriter, Pierce, **2**:960
Ferriter's Cove Stone Age settlement, **2**:679
fertility rates, **1**:242–244; **2**:565
  Ireland and European fertility transition, **2**:570
  and population explosion, **2**:572–573
  social change and, **2**:665–666
festivals
  of Gaelic League, **1**:269
  Oireachtas (national literary festival), **1**:269, 270
    competitions, **1**:265
  in traditional popular religion, **2**:617
feudalism
  Anglo-Normans and, **1**:362
  estates and demesnes from, **1**:230
Fiachna, Dáire mac, **1**:119
Fianna, **1**:397
  founded by Markievicz, **1**:422
Fianna Fáil (Soldiers of Destiny), **2**:532, 553–554
  and agriculture platform, **1**:12
  and Catholic Church, **1**:260
  Clarke in, **1**:95
  Conditions of Employment Act and, **1**:101
  constitution and, **1**:106, 107
  Cosgrave and, **1**:110
  de Valera and, **1**:135–136
  Eucharistic Congress and, **1**:232–233
  foundation of, **1**:489; **2**:532

Lemass and, **1**:382
  hunger strikes and, **1**:308
  IRA and, **1**:329–330
  and Irish unity, **2**:561–562
  Markievicz member of, **1**:422
  members marching to Dáil Éireann, **2**:531
  oath of allegiance and, **1**:100–101
  protectionism and, **1**:320
  and public morality, **1**:261
  social change and, **2**:667
  supported by the *Irish Press*, **1**:424
  temperance and, **2**:696
  tourism and, **2**:706
  trade unions and, **2**:712–713
Fiche Blian ag Fás (Ó Súilleabháin), **1**:50, 265
Fidelity of Ireland to the Catholic Faith (Cambrensis Eversus) (John Lynch), **2**:829 (d)
Field, The (film, Sheridan), **1**:42
Field Day Anthology of Irish Writing (McCarthy et al.), **1**:389
Field Day Theatre, **1**:154
Fielding, Henry, Irish depicted by, **1**:223
fields, **1**:364
  planting of hedgerows, **1**:364; **2**:768
  See also agriculture: enclosures
Field Work (Heaney), **1**:294
filidh. See bards
films
  social change and, **2**:665
  twentieth-century, **1**:42
Finbarr, Saint, monastery of, **1**:108
Fine Gael (Family or Tribe of the Gaels), **2**:532, 533
  Cosgrave and, **1**:111
  creation of, **2**:532
  critical of Mother and Child Scheme, **1**:451
  and Irish unity, **2**:562
  move to the left, **2**:556
  on repeal of External Relations Act, **1**:128–129
  supported by the Independent Group, **1**:424
Fingal Rónáin (How Rónán killed his son), **1**:460
Finn Cycle. *See* Fenian Cycle; Fionn sagas
Finnegans Wake (Joyce), **1**:40, 253, 339–340
Finnian, **1**:296
Fionn mac Cumhaill, **1**:397
Fionn sagas, **1**:34

"First Fleet" (1788), **1**:139
First Vatican Council, Cullen and, **1**:120
Fisher, J. R., **1**:55, 56
Fisher, Jonathan, **1**:36
Fitt, Gerry, **1**:477; **2**:560
  Hume and, **1**:306
  unseated by Adams, **1**:3
Fitzgerald, Lord Edward, **1**:255
  in rebellion of 1798, **1**:207
  United Irishmen under, **1**:206
Fitzgerald, Emily, **1**:225
FitzGerald, Garret, **1**:16, 373; **2**:556, 562
  and Hillsborough Agreement, **2**:1005
  "Towards Changes in the Republic," **2**:993–1000 (d)
Fitzgerald, Garret Mor, **2**:688
Fitzgerald, Gerald, Anglo-Norman earl of Kildare, **1**:395
FitzGerald, Gerald fitz James, fifteenth earl of Desmond, **1**:135
FitzGerald, James fitz John, fourteenth earl of Desmond, **1**:447; **2**:535
FitzGerald, James Fitzmaurice, **1**:133–134; **2**:536
  Old English and, **1**:501–502
  revolt of, **1**:220–221
FitzGerald, John fitz Thomas, **1**:474
FitzGerald, Maurice, **1**:412, 474
Fitzgerald, Thomas, Tenth Earl of Kildare ("Silken Thomas"), **255–256**
  fostering of, **1**:240
  and rebellion against reformation of Henry VIII, **2**:592
  surrender and regrant policy, **2**:688
Fitzgerald, William Vesey, **2**:888
  Catholic emancipation campaign and, **1**:76
  O'Connell's victory against, **2**:545
fitz Godebert, Richard, **1**:412
Fitzmaurice, James. *See* FitzGerald, James Fitzmaurice
FitzSimon, Henry, **1**:291
fitz Stephen, Robert, **1**:412
Fitzwilliam, Sir William (lord deputy), **1**:466; **2**:811
  religious reform under, **1**:220
Fitzwilliam, second earl (William Wentworth-Fitzwilliam)
  Catholic Committee and, **1**:75
  as lord lieutenant, **1**:205
  recall of, **2**:731–732

Five Nations Championship, **2:**675
Flanagan, Sinéad, **1:**135
Flann Sinna (king), **1:**30
   and construction of cathedral at
      Clonmacnoise, **1:**25
Flaubert, Gustave, **1:**253
flax, **1:**4, 8, 316
   factory manufacture of, **1:**237–
      238
   in Ulster plantations, **2:**640
Fleadh Cheoil (festival of
   traditional music), **1:**42, **256–
   257**
Fleetwood, Charles, **2:**594
Fleming, John, **1:**264
Fleming, Patrick, **1:**291
   in education, **1:**324
Flesh–The Greatest Sin (Strong),
   1:403
Fletcher, John, **1:**33
Flight of the Earls (1607), **1:**468
   account by Davies, **2:**820–821
      (d)
   account by Ó Cianáin, **2:**821–
      822 *(d)*
   bards' insecurity following,
      1:398
   Hugh O'Neill and, **1:**504
   and Irish musical culture, **1:**453
   kingship and, **1:**344
Flood, Henry, **1:257**
   Grattan's disagreement with,
      1:205, 280
Flower, Robin, **1:**49, 50
   translation of Ó Criomhthain's
      autobiography, **2:**957
Fly on the Wheel, The (Thurston),
   1:402
Foirm na nUrrnuidheadh (Carswell),
   1:397
Foley, Donal, **1:**424
folklore movement
   Blasket Island writers and, **1:**50
   romanticism and, **615**
   See also Irish Folklore
      Commission; Irish Folklore
      Society
Folk Music and Dances of Ireland,
   1:457
Folk Music Society of Ireland,
   1:457
folk poets and musicians, **1:**454
food
   exports
      to British market, **1:**6
      and economic expansion,
         2:565, 574
      during Great Famine, **1:**282
   imports
      during Great Famine, **1:**282

processing
   in eighteenth century, **2:**566
   riots (1839–1841), **2:**568
Fool of Quality, The (Brooke), **1:**33
football, Gaelic. *See* Gaelic football
Foran, Thomas, **1:**332
Foras Feasa ar Éirinn (The basis for
   a knowledge of Ireland) (Céitinn),
   1:34, 398
Force of Change, The (Mitchell),
   1:154
Ford, Alan, **1:**87
Ford, Patrick, **1:**253
Ford of the Biscuits, Battle at the
   (1594), **1:**466
foreign direct investment (FDI). *See*
   overseas investment
forestry policy. *See* woodlands
Forgaill, Dallán, **1:**164
forradh (royal seat), **2:**579
   Tara and, **2:**693–694
Four Courts garrison, **1:**93–94
"Four Horsemen," **1:**492
Fox, Charles James, **1:**391
   Catholic Association and, **1:**75
   Fitzgerald and, **1:**255
Foyle, Carlingford, and Irish Lights
   Commission, **1:**171
Foyle Fisheries Commission,
   1:129, 170, 171
*Fragments of Ancient Poetry Collected
   in the Highlands of Scotland and
   Translated from the Gaelic or Erse
   Language* (Macpherson), **2:**705
Frameworks Document (1995),
   1:129, 479, 487
France
   American Revolution and,
      1:204
   Franco-Irish forces in rebellion
      of 1798, **1:**207–208
   French and rebellion of 1798,
      2:544
   Irish colleges in, **1:**323–325
   Irish in army of, **2:**749
   See also French Revolution
franchise
   Catholics and, **1:**77, 205, 280
   in the constitution, **1:**106
   for farmers, **1:**311
   nineteenth-century extension
      of, **1:**213
   property ownership and, **1:**209
Francini brothers, **1:**35–36
Franciscans
   and *Annals of the Four Masters,*
      1:20
   Irish Franciscan College of Saint
      Anthony in Louvain, **1:**21
   Plunkett's conflict with, **2:**527

and schools, **2:**620
Fred Olsen Energy, **2:**658
Freeman's Journal (newspaper),
   1:451, 465
Freemasonry, **2:**542
Free Presbyterian Church of Ulster,
   2:517
Free State parliament. *See* Dáil
   Éireann
Free State Provisional Government
   Collins in, **1:**97
   proclamation at the beginning
      of the Civil War (1922), **2:**950
      (d)
free trade
   Grattan and, **1:**204–205
   between Ireland and Britain,
      1:167–168
   See also Anglo-Irish Free Trade
      Agreement of 1965
Fréine, Seán de, **1:**374
French language, use by Norman
   elite, **1:**470
French Revolution
   Defenderism and, **1:**131
   Fitzgerald and, **1:**255
   Irish colleges abroad and, **1:**325
   radicalizing effects of, **1:**205
   Second Reformation and, **2:**653
   Tandy and, **2:**693
   United Irishmen and, **2:**731,
      732
   welcomed by the northern
      Presbyterians, **2:**543
Freney, James, **1:**84, 85
Friel, Brian, **1:**40, 41, 153, 154
   Hiberno-English in, **1:**295
fruit trees, planting of, **2:**768
Frye, Thomas, **1:**37
fulachta fiadh, **1:**63
funeral rituals. *See* burial customs;
   keening; tombs; wake
furniture-making, **1:**37

≈ **G**

Gaelic. *See* Irish language
Gaelic Athletic Association (GAA),
   1:266–268
   ban, **1:**259, **259–260; 2:**547
   codification of sports in, **2:**675
   Collins in, **1:**96
   on cricket, **2:**674
   Cusack and, **1:**122
   education and, **1:**196
   Irish Parliamentary Party and,
      1:303
   social life and, **2:**664
   town life and, **2:**708

Gaelic Catholic state, making of, **1:260–262**
Gaelic football, **1:**266; **2:**674, 675
  women's, **2:**676
Gaelic games, **1:**267
Gaelic inheritance customs. *See* tanistry
Gaelic Irish dynasties, recovery of, **1:**262–263
Gaelic Journal/Irisleabhar na Gaedhilge, **1:**264, 265, 269, 401
Gaelic League, **1:**264–265, **268–270**, 401; **2:**547
  Collins in, **1:**96
  de Valera in, **1:**135
  and education, **1:**190, 196, 198
  foundation of, **1:**38
  Irish Parliamentary Party and, **1:**303
  official paper of, **1:**465
  and study of Irish on Great Blasket Island, **1:**49, 50
  women in, **2:**759
Gaelic Recovery, **1:262–264**
  accelerated by Bruce invasion, **1:**65
Gaelic revival, **1:264–266**, 374; **2:**547–548
Gaelic revivalism. *See* Gaelic Athletic Association; Gaelic League
Gaelic society in the late Middle Ages, **1:270–273**
Gaelic Union, **1:**264, 401
Gaeltacht, **1:**373, 375, 377
  autobiographies from, **1:**265
  Cosgrave's letter on the Commission on the Gaeltacht, **2:**956–957 *(d)*
Gaffikin, Thomas, **2:**910–911 *(d)*
Gageby, Douglas, **1:**424
Gaill, **1:**178
Galilei, Alessandro, **2:**585
  country houses by, **1:**113
Gallagher, Brian, **1:**129
Gallagher, Michael, **1:**169
Gallagher, Rory, **1:**457
Gallic Wars (Caesar), **1:**79
Gall (pilgrim exile), **1:**163
Galway under Tudors, **2:**736
Gamble, John, **2:**881–884 *(d)*
Gandon, James, **1:**35, 273
  Custom House (Dublin), **1:**274
Gaodhal, An (periodical), **1:**264
gardens and gardening
  country house and, **1:**114–115
  Huguenots and, **2:**591
Gardiner, Luke, **1:**273
Gaughan, Michael, **1:**307
gavelkind, custom of, **1:**272, 380

Geertz, Clifford, **2:**541
General Agreement on Tariffs and Trade (GATT)
  Anglo-Irish Free Trade Agreement of 1965 and, **1:**17
  Celtic Tiger economy and, **1:**81
General Collection of the Ancient Music of Ireland (Bunting), **1:**37, 455
Geographic Information Systems (GIS), Ordnance Survey and, **1:**511
geology
  Eiscir Riata, **1:**208–209
  map of, **1:***360*
George I
  Hanoverian succession and, **1:**203
  King and, **1:**344
George III
  incapacitation of, **1:**205
  opposition to Catholic emancipation, **1:**75; **2:**544
George IV, Catholic emancipation campaign and, **1:**75–76
Georgian style
  art and architecture of Georgian Dublin, **1:273–275**
  country houses in, **1:**114
Geraldines
  Desmond rebellions and, **1:**133–134
  Fitzgerald and, **1:**255
Gerard, William, **2:**807–808 *(d)*
"German Attack on Neutral States" (de Valera), **2:**970 *(d)*
Gernon, Luke, **1:**224; **2:**831–833 *(d)*
Giants Ring, **2:**683
  Gifford, Lord, **1:**51
Gilbert, Sir Humphrey
  colonial theory of, **1:**98
  Desmond rebellions and, **1:**133
Gildas, **1:**296
Gillespie, Raymond, **2:**611
Gillray, James, **2:**732
Ginkel, Godard van Reede, **1:**337–338
Giraldus Cambrensis, **1:**431, 472
  on barbarism of Irish indigenous culture, **1:**22
  Expugnatio Hibernica, **1:**223; **2:**788 *(d)*
  The Topography of Ireland, **1:**223; **2:**786–788 *(d)*
Giraldus (Gerald) of Wales. *See* Giraldus Cambrensis
Give Them Stones (Beckett), **1:**404
Gladstone, William Ewart, **1:**371
  Church of Ireland under, **1:**88

  and Home Rule, **1:**213, 302; **2:**5471:301–302
    on Home Rule bill of 1886, **2:**922–924 *(d)*
    Home Rule bills, **2:**725–726
  and land acts, **1:**352, 357
  "Manchester Martyrs" and, **1:**252
  Parnell's fall and, **1:**302
  Punch cartoon of, **1:***353*
  tenant right and, **2:**700
  on universities, **1:**197
Glass Act (1746), effects of, **2:**710
Glenn Máma, Battle of (999), **1:**123
Glenstal Abbey conference, **1:**184
glibs, **1:***217*
"God Save Ireland" (song, Sullivan), **2:**687, 906–907 *(d)*
Gold in the Streets (Charabanc), **1:**153
gold objects of Bronze Age, **1:**62, 63; **2:**577, 578
  gold collar from Gleninsheen, Co. Clare, **1:***63*
Goldsmith, Oliver, **1:**33, 34, 390
goldsmiths, Huguenots as, **2:**590
golf, **2:**674
"Gol na mBan san Ár," **1:**453
Gonne, Maud, **1:275**, 388, 402, 422; **2:**762
  Clarke and, **1:**95
  and "Easter 1916" (Yeats), **2:**936
  Yeats and, **2:**769
Goodacre, Hugh, **1:**201
Good Behavior (Keane), **1:**254, 403
Good Friday Agreement of 1998. *See* Belfast Agreement of 1998
Good Shepherd Sisters, **2:**621
Gookin, Vincent, **2:**841–842 *(d)*
Gore-Booth, Constance. *See* Markievicz, Countess Constance
Gothic architecture, **1:**26
Gothic novels, **1:**38
  Anglo-Irish Gothic, **1:**392–393
Gothic Revival–style country houses, **1:**113
Goulding, Cathal, **1:**330
government from 1690 to 1800, **1:275–277**
Government of Ireland Act (Britain, 1920), **1:**480, 482, 484; **2:**549, 728, 939–942 *(d)*
  Carson and, **1:**73
  Commonwealth and, **1:**99
  economic relations and, **1:**170, 172
  repeal of, **1:**488
Government of Ireland Bill of 1886, **1:**301

Government of the Tongue, The
(Heaney), **1:**294
Gow, Nathaniel, **1:**454
Gow, Neil, **1:**454
Gowran master, **2:**653
Graces, The, **1:277–279; 2:**599,
607
New English opposition to,
2:607
Old English and, **1:**502
Graham, James, **2:**670
Grammar of the Irish Language
(O'Donovan), **1:**500
Grand Canal, **2:**714
grand juries
as local government, **1:**405–406
Protestant landlords and, **2:**586
Grand Tour, **1:**232
Grania (Gregory), **1:**402
Grant of Prince John to Theobald
Walter of Lands in Ireland
(1185), **2:**785–786 *(d)*
Granuaile (Grace O'Malley),
1:279–280
Grattan, Henry, **1:280–281;**
2:*540*
Flood's disagreement with,
1:205, 257, 280
free trade and, **1:**204–205
and veto controversy, **2:**739,
740
Graunt, John, **2:**523
Gray, David, **1:**463
Gray, Jane, **2:**753
Gray, John, **1:**465
Great Awakening (1859), **1:**430
Great Britain, Irish emigration to,
1:433, 435, 439
*Great Case of Transplantation
Discussed, The* (Gookin), **2:**841–
842 *(d)*
Great Clare Gold Find of 1854,
2:578
Great Depression, **1:**174
American migration and, **1:**146
migration to Britain and,
1:141–142
Northern Ireland and, **1:**321
protectionism and, **1:**320
shipbuilding industry and,
2:658
women's economic rights and,
1:227
Great Famine (1845–1850),
1:281–284; 2:575
Church of Ireland in, **1:**88
clearances, **1:**245, 245–247;
2:564
country houses after, **1:**115
devotional revolution and,
1:137–138

as ecological disaster, **2:**568
effect on politics, **2:**545–546
and emigration, **1:**435
to Australia, **1:**139, 140
to Britain, **1:**141
to North America, **1:**144–
145
impact on Young Irelanders,
2:771
Independent Irish Party and,
1:311
Indian corn and, **1:**313–314,
314
industrialization and, **1:**318
and Irish language, **1:**373
impact on Gaelic literature,
1:400
undermining of scribal
culture, **1:**400
Irish stereotypes and, **1:**223
marriage and family in, **1:**241–
242
nationalist genocide
interpretation of
Mitchel and, **1:**445
Quakers during, **2:**622
Second Reformation and, **2:**654
severity of, **1:***281*
social change and, **2:**663
sodalities and confraternities,
2:668
and split in Anglo-Irish
literature, **1:**392
subdivision and subletting of
holdings, **2:**687
temperance movement and,
2:695
textile manufacture and, **1:**238
tourism and, **2:**705
trade unions and, **2:**712
Great Hunger, The (Kavanagh),
1:40; **2:**529
Great Northern Railway, **1:**170
Great O'Neill, The (O'Faolain),
1:466
Greatorex, Valentine, **1:284–285**
Great Reform Bill (1832), franchise
in, **1:**209
Great War. *See* World War I
Greek Revival–style country
houses, **1:**113
Green Helmet, The (Yeats), **2:**769
Greenhills conference, **1:**184
"Green Tea" (Le Fanu), **1:**392
Greenwich Mean Time, **2:**716
Greg, Thomas, **1:**495
Gregg, Archbishop John Allen
Fitzgerald, **2:**588
Gregg, John, **1:**410
Gregory, Lady Isabella Augusta,
1:39, 388, 389, *402*

and Abbey Theatre, **1:**388
drama of, **1:**151
Hyde and, **1:**308, 309
interest in national identity,
1:402
Gregory the Great, **1:**289
Grenville, Sir Richard, **1:**98
Grenville, Lord (William
Wyndham), **1:**75
Grey de Wilton, Lord (Arthur
Grey)
Desmond rebellions and, **1:**134
letter to Elizabeth, **2:**808–809
(d)
religious reform under, **1:**220
Spenser and, **2:**673
Spenser secretary to, **2:**813
Grey, Leonard (lord deputy), **2:**534
Fitzgerald and, **1:**256
religious reform under, **1:**220;
2:592
surrender and regrant policy,
2:689
greyhound racing, **2:**676
Griffin, Gerald, **1:**38
Griffith, Arthur, **1:287–288**
and Anglo-Irish Treaty of 1921,
1:18, 19, 55
speech in favor of, **2:**948–
949 *(d)*
arrest of, **2:**661
in the Civil War, **1:**92
Collins and, **1:**96, 97
Cosgrave and, **1:**110
and Gaelic League, **1:**268
Gonne and, **1:**275
on industrialization, **1:**321
influence of Young Ireland on,
2:772
on Irish neutrality, **1:**462
and National Council of Sinn
Féin, **2:**929
address to the first annual
convention of, **2:**927–929
(d)
nationalism of, **2:**548
negotiations with Lloyd George,
2:549
Sinn Féin and, **2:**531, 660
Grimm, Jakob, **1:**500
Grogan, Nathaniel, **1:**36
gross domestic product (GDP)
in Celtic Tiger economy, **1:**81
definition of, **1:**81
interwar era, **1:**174
overseas investment and, **1:**511
gross national product (GNP)
in Celtic Tiger economy, **1:**81,
177; **2:**557
Civil War and, **1:**92

North *vs.* South, **1**:175
Guests of the Nation (O'Connor), **1**:40, 253–254
guilds
    apprenticeships and, **1**:185
    Catholic Association and, **1**:74
    Catholics in, **1**:78
    dowries and, **1**:239–240
    metalworkers in, **1**:428
    Old English *vs.* New English in, **1**:221
    trade unions and, **2**:712
    urban craftworkers in, **1**:35–36
Guinnane, Timothy W., **1**:242
Guinness, Arthur, **1**:288
Guinness Book of World Records, **1**:288
Guinness Brewing Company, **1**:61, **288**, 315
    workforce at, **1**:319
Gulliver's Travels (Swift), **1**:33, 84; **2**:689, 690, *690*
Gúm, An (publication office), **1**:265

~ **H**

hagiography, **1:289–291**
    Céli-Dé and, **1**:90
    in early Christianity, **1**:161, 163
    Saint Patrick in, **2**:649–650
    study of, **1**:324–325
Haicéad, Pádraigín, **1**:34, 398
Hail and Farewell (Moore), **1**:39
Halifax, earl of (George Montague-Dunck), **2**:748
Hall, Mr. and Mrs. Samuel Carter, on Irish society before the Great Famine, **2**:893–896 *(d)*
Hamilton, Gustavus, **1**:335
Hamilton, James, **2**:700
Hamilton, Letitia Mary, **2**:741
Hand, John, **1**:514
handball, **2**:675–676
"Handbook for Princes" (*De rectoribus Christianis*) (Sedulius), **1**:297
Handel, George Frideric
    in Ireland, **1**:37
    première of the *Messiah*, **1**:455
Hanoverian succession, **1**:203
Harbour Commissioners (Cork), **1**:110
Hardiman, James, **1**:500
Harland, Edward, **2**:657–658
Harland and Wolff shipyard, **1**:319; **2**:657, *657*–658
Harley MS 913, **1**:431

Harper's Weekly, **2**:616
Harrigan, Ned, **1**:146
Harrington, Sir John, **1**:224
Harrington, Timothy Charles, **2**:386, 728
Harris, Frank, **2**:749
Harris, Matt, **1**:371
Harry Lorrequer (Lever), **1**:392
Hart, Tony, **1**:146
Hartlib, Samuel, **1**:57
Haughey, Charles, **1**:226; **2**:532, 562
    accusations of political corruption, **2**:557
    contraception and, **1**:149
    and Northern Ireland, **2**:556
Haughey's Fort, **1**:214
Haverty, Joseph Patrick, **1**:454
Haw Lantern, The (Heaney), **1**:294
health
    home births, **1**:243
    Indian corn and, **1**:313–314
    potato as as healthy diet, **2**:644
    secularization and, **2**:656
    social change and, **2**:666–667
    textile manufacture and, **1**:238
health and safety legislation
    and local government, **1**:406
    See also Mother and Child Scheme
health and welfare since 1950, state provisions for, **1:291–294**
Health (Family Planning) Bill (1980), **1**:149
Healy, Cahir, **2**:559
Healy, Robert, **1**:36
Healy, Timothy Michael, **1**:451
    Catholic hierarchy and, **2**:636
    Irish Parliamentary Party and, **1**:303–304
Heaney, Seamus, **1**:41, **294–295**; **2**:529
    Hewitt's influence on, **2**:983
    Hiberno-English in, **1**:295
    Kavanagh's influence on, **1**:40; **2**:529
    "Punishment," **2**:1005 *(d)*
    on Yeats, **2**:770
Hearts of Flint, **1**:496
Hearts of Gold, **1**:496
Hearts of Oak. *See* Oakboys and Steelboys
Hearts of Steel. *See* Oakboys and Steelboys
Heath, Sir Edward, **1**:486; **2**:722, 725
Heather Blazing, The (Tóibín), **1**:41, 254
Heather Field, The (Martyn), **1**:388
hedgerows, planting of, **1**:364; **2**:768

hedge schools, **1:186–188**
    Irish language in, **1**:190
Hell Box, The (Delanty), **2**:530
Hempson, Denis, **1**:37, 455
henges, **2**:683
Hennessy, D. C., **2**:598
Henry, Françoise, **2**:579
Henry, Paul, **2**:741, 742
    Launching the Currach, **2**:*742*
Henry II
    Alexander II and, **2**:782–784 *(d)*
    colonization of Ireland under, **1**:215
    and *Laudabiliter* (Adrian IV), **2**:782 *(d)*
    and Norman conquest of Ireland, **1**:411–412, 469, 471
    O'Connors and, **1**:499
Henry III
    courts under, **1**:215
    and Great Charter of Ireland, **2**:790–791 *(d)*
Henry of London, **1**:473
Henry VI, **2**:801
Henry VII, **2**:534
    surrender and regrant policy of, **2**:688
Henry VIII
    church and state under, **1**:218, 219
    Council of Trent and, **1**:111
    declared king of Ireland, **2**:534, 605
    decrees prohibiting music, **1**:453
    education under, **1**:185
    Fitzgerald and, **1**:255, 256
    Old English and, **1**:501
    Reformation, **2**:592, 605
    reform under, **1**:200
    surrender and regrant policy, **2**:689
Henry V (Shakespeare), Irish depicted in, **1**:223, 295
Herbert, William, **1**:98
hereditary legal families, **1**:59–60
hereditary scholars, **1**:396
Hermitage excavations, **2**:679
hermits, **1**:90, 290
Hervey, Frederick, **1**:87–88
Hewitt, John, **2**:983 *(d)*
Hiberniae Delineatio (Petty), **1**:225; **2**:523
Hibernian Antiquarian Society, **1**:22
Hiberniensis (Ruben and Cú Chuimne), **1**:59
Hiberno-English, **1:295**
    Middle English literature, **1:430–431**

Hiberno-Latin culture, **1:296–297**
Hiberno-Norse artistic tradition, **1**:476
Hickson, Robert, **2**:657
Hidden Symptoms (Madden), **1**:404
"Hierophilus" letters (MacHale), **1**:343, 411
Higgins, Aidan, **1**:40, 254
  on country houses, **1**:115
Higgins, Rita Ann, **1**:41, 403, 404; **2**:530
High Church tradition, **1**:88
High Crosses, **1**:29–30, **297–298**, *298*; **2**:651
  revival of interest in, **1**:31
higher education. *See* education
High Ground (McGahern), **1**:40
High Island (Murphy), **2**:529
high kings, **1**:165, 346
  disputed successions decided by Normans, **1**:474
  O'Connors of Connacht, **1**:498–499
  of Tara, **1**:165; **2**:693–695
high-technology industry, **1**:176
  Celtic Tiger and, **1**:83
  indigenous, **1**:321
  overseas investment in, **1**:512–513
Hill, Derek, **1**:41
Hillery, Patrick, **1**:233
hillforts from Bronze Age, **1**:63
Hillsborough Agreement. *See* Anglo-Irish Agreement of 1985
Hincks, William, **1**:420; **2**:641
His Follie (Beacon), **1**:369
Hisperica famina (Western sayings), **1**:296–297, 449
Histoire du Roy d'Angleterre Richard II (Creton), **2**:629
Historiæ Catholicæ Iberniæ Compendium (O'Sullivan Beare), **2**:809–810 *(d)*
Historical Cycle. *See* Cycle of Kings
Historical Memoirs of the Irish Bards (Walker), **1**:35
History of Ireland, The: The Heroic Period (O'Grady), **1**:264
History of Ireland (Mitchel), **1**:445
History of Jack Connor (Chagineau), **1**:33
History of the Irish Rebellion (Temple), **1**:224
Hobson, Bulmer, **2**:520
Hoche, Lazare, **1**:206
Holbrooke, William Henry, **1**:498
Holinshed, Raphael, **1**:223
Holl, F., **2**:746
Holland, Denis, **1**:465
Holt, Joseph, **1**:207

Holy Cross Abbey, sculpture at, **2**:653
Holy Ghost Fathers, **2**:620, 634
Holy Pictures (Boylan), **1**:403
holy wells, **1**:362
  pilgrimages to, **2**:617
  pilgrims at, in *Harper's Weekly*, **2**:*616*
Home Government Association (HGA), **1**:299; **2**:546, 907, 908
homelessness, **1**:229
Home Rule
  Carson on, **1**:73
  Commonwealth and, **1**:99
  Craig and, **1**:116
  development of, **2**:686
  Irish in Britain and, **1**:142
  opposition to
    Basil Brooke and, **1**:64
    by Southern unionists, **2**:930–932 *(d)*
  Orange Order and, **1**:509–510
  Parnell and, **2**:518
  separate administrations in Belfast and Dublin, **1**:484
  shipbuilding industry and, **2**:658
  social status and, **1**:209
  women and debate, **2**:762
Home Rule and the land question at Cork, Parnell on, **2**:919–920 *(d)*
Home Rule at Wicklow, Parnell on, **2**:920–921 *(d)*
Home Rule bill of 1886, Gladstone on, **2**:922–924 *(d)*
Home Rule Confederation of Great Britain, **1**:300
Home Rule Conference (1873), resolutions adopted at, **2**:907–908 *(d)*
Home Rule League, **2**:907
  Butt and, **1**:70
Home Rule movement and the Irish Parliamentary Party
  1870 to 1891, **1:299–302**
  1891 to 1918, **1:302–306**
Home Rule Party, **1**:349; **2**:548
  and Catholic clergy, **2**:614
  electoral success of, **1**:213
  formation of, **1**:299–300
  IRB and, **1**:252–253
  Parnell and, **2**:547
  Sinn Féin and, **2**:660, 661
  and temperance movement, **2**:695
homosexuality
  decriminalization of, **1**:229; **2**:557
  in literature, **1**:254

Hone, Evie, **2**:*742*
Hone, Horace, **1**:36
Hone, Nathaniel, **1**:36, 41
Honorius III (pope), **1**:473
honor-price, **1**:60, 346
Hood (Donoghue), **1**:404
Hooghe, Romeyn de, **1**:202
Hooke, Luke Joseph, **1**:325
Hooker, John, **2**:811 *(d)*
Hope, James, **1**:215
Hopkins, Gerard Manley, **1**:294
Horgan, John, **2**:1003
horses
  horse fairs, **1**:422
  introduction of, **2**:577
  racing, **2**:664, 674
Horslips, The, **1**:457
hospitals
  building program, **1**:292
  built under Tudors, **2**:736
  private care in, **1**:292–293
  secularization and, **2**:656
  towns and, **2**:708
Hostage, The (Behan), **1**:153
Hoult, Nora, **1**:403
household
  formation, **2**:565, 566
  size, **1**:244
House of Splendid Isolation, The (O'Brien), **1**:404
housework, **2**:757
housing
  of Catholics in Northern Ireland, **1**:485
  improvements in, **2**:664
  local-authority houses, **2**:757
  Neolithic, **2**:680
  of the poor in eighteenth century, **2**:643, *643*
  segregation in, **2**:666
  subsidized cottages
    county-council cottage schemes, **2**:647
    for laborers in nineteenth century, **2**:646
  thatched, **2**:664
  Young on, **2**:858–860 *(d)*
Howard, Gorges Edmond, **1**:391
Howlett, David, **1**:296
How Many Miles to Babylon? (Johnston), **1**:404
Hoyle, Joshua, **2**:717
Hughes, John, **1**:144–145
Hughes, Ted, **1**:294
Huguenots, **1**:88, 236
  immigration to Ireland, **2**:589–590
  industrialization and, **1**:315
Humanae Vitae, **1**:148; **2**:638
humanism, education and, **1**:185

Human Rights Act of 1998, **1:**229
Human Rights Commission, **1:**229
Humbert, Jean-Joseph
   in rebellion of 1798, **1:**207
   Tandy and, **2:**693
Hume, John, **1:306–307**, 479,
   482, 492; **2:**556, 560
   Belfast Agreement and, **1:**331
   and Bloody Sunday, **1:**51, 52
   conversations with Adams, **1:**3,
      487
   and peace process, **1:**487
Hume-Adams dialogue (1988–
   1994), **1:**3, 487
Hunger Strikes (1981), **1:307–
   308; 2:**686
   Adams's political role in, **1:**2–3
   and beginning of peace process,
      2:556
   Provisional IRA and, **1:**486
   Sinn Féin and, **1:**331
Hunt Commission (1969), **2:**639
Hunterston Brooch, **1:**417
Hurley, Michael, **1:**183
hurling, **2:**674, 675
   1995 All-Ireland Hurling Final,
      1:267
   Gaelic Athletic Association and,
      1:266
   Mr. and Mrs. Samuel Carter
      Hall on, **2:**893–896 *(d)*
Hussey, Thomas, **2:**628
Hutchinson, Billy, **1:**409
Hutchinson, Pearse, **1:**40; **2:**529
Hyde, Douglas, **1:**38, **308–309,**
   388; **2:***587*
   and Gaelic League, **1:**268
   modern editor of Raiftearaí,
      2:597
   "Necessity for De-Anglicising
      Ireland, The," **1:**264–265;
      2:925–927 *(d)*
Hynes, Eugene, **1:**138
Hynes, Garry, **1:**154

∼ **I**

Iarla, Gearóid, **1:**470
Illusionist, The (Johnston), **1:**403
Image of Irelande, The (Derricke),
   1:35, 224, *224*, 225, 369; **2:**810–
   811 *(d)*
Imaginaire Irlandais, L' (exhibition),
   2:744
Imperial Orange Council, **1:**510
In a Glass Darkly (Le Fanu), **1:**392
In a Little World of Our Own
   (Mitchell), **1:**154
Inchiquin truce, **2:**630

income
   EU, **1:**235
   farmers', **1:**248
   inequality of, **2:**667
Independent (newspaper), **1:**424
Independent Group, **1:**424
Independent International
   Commission on
   Decommissioning (IICD), **1:**129
Independent Ireland since 1922,
   2:550–558. *See also* Irish Free
   State; Republic of Ireland
Independent Irish Party, **1:311–
   313,** 357
Independent Labour Party, **1:**349–
   350
Independent News and Media,
   1:424, 425
Independent Newspapers, **1:**424
Independent Opposition. *See*
   Independent Irish Party
Independents (religion), **2:**594, 608
Indian corn (maize), **1:313–314**
Industrial Development Acts
   (1986–1998), **1:**322
Industrial Development Authority
   (IDA), **1:**175. *See also* Investment
   and Development Agency
   Celtic Tiger economy and, **1:**81,
      177
   outward-looking strategy and,
      1:320–321
   overseas investment and, **1:**512
   in state enterprise, **2:**676
Industrial Development Board,
   overseas investment and, **1:**513
industrialization, **1:314–319**
   Celtic Tiger and, **1:**83
   in Cork, **1:**109
   farming families and, **1:**248–
      249
   Fianna Fáil in, **2:**712–713
   railways and, **2:**715
   shipbuilding, **2:**656–658
   textile manufacture, **1:**237–239
   town development and, **2:**709
industry
   deindustrialization, **1:**172, 175–
      176
   in Dublin, **1:**155
   migration and, **1:**144
   protectionism and, **1:**173–174
   since 1920, **1:319–321**
inflation, **1:**169
Informer, The (O'Flaherty), **1:**254
Ingersoll, Ralph, **1:**425
Inghínidhe na hÉireann (Daughters
   of Ireland), **2:**762
   foundation by Gonne, **1:**275
   Markievicz and, **1:**422

In High Germany (Bolger), **1:**153
Inishfallen Crosier, **1:**428
Inis Pádraig, synod of (1148), **1:**91
In Night's City (Nelson), **1:**404
Innocent XI (pope), on Battle of the
   Boyne, **1:**58
"Inquisitio 1584" (Mhac an tSaoi),
   2:1009 *(d)*
Institute of the Blessed Virgin
   Mary, **2:**621
Institutes (Calvin), **1:**71
Insurrection Act (1796), **2:**543,
   869–871 *(d)*
Intentions (Wilde), **2:**749
*Interest of England in the Irish
   Transplantation Stated, The*
   (Lawrence), **2:**842–844 *(d)*
*Interest of Ireland in Its Trade and
   Wealth* (Lawrence), **1:**225
Intergovernmental Conference,
   Anglo-Irish Agreement of 1985
   and, **1:**17
Intermediate Board of Education,
   1:195, 196
   female education and, **1:**199
Intermediate Education Act (1878),
   1:193, 195
International Commission on
   Decommissioning, **1:**129
International Financial Services
   Centre (IFSC), Dublin, **1:**82, 83
   overseas investment and, **1:**512
International Fund for Ireland,
   1:492
   Anglo-Irish Agreement of 1985
      and, **1:**17
International Workers of the
   World, **1:**104, *105*
internment
   Faulkner and, **1:**249–250
   introduced in the South, **1:**489
   in Northern Ireland, **2:**725
      Provisional IRA and, **1:**485–
         486
   used by Craig, **2:**559
In the Name of the Father (film,
   Sheridan), **1:**42
Investment and Development
   Agency (IDA Ireland), **1:322**
   employment and, **1:**511
   overseas investment and,
      1:511–513
Investment in Education (Lynch),
   1:175
Invest Northern Ireland (INI),
   1:513
Invisible Worm, The (Johnston),
   1:404
Iona
   abbots of, **1:**165

Iona CONTINUED
  Columba and, **1**:163
  hagiography and, **1**:289–290
  literary production of, **1**:164
  Viking attacks on, **1**:165–166
Iosogán (Pearse), **1**:265
IRA. *See* Irish Republican Army
IRB. *See* Irish Republican
  Brotherhood; Irish Revolutionary
  Brotherhood
*Ireland, 1912–1985: Politics and
  Society* (Lee), **2**:971
Ireland, John, **1**:146
*Ireland: Social, Political, and
  Religious* (de Beaumont), **2**:892–
  893 *(d)*
Ireland Act (Britain, 1949), **1**:128–
  129, 484, 490; **2**:559, 975
  Declaration of a Republic and,
    1:127–129
Ireland Is Building (brochure),
  1:440
Ireland's Natural History (Boate),
  1:224–225
Ireton, Henry, **1**:117
Irish, The (O'Faolain), **1**:473
Irish Act of Union (1800), **2**:877–
  880 *(d)*
Irish Agricultural Labourers'
  Union, **1**:350
Irish Agricultural Organisation
  Society, **2**:528
Irish Amateur Athletics
  Association, **1**:266
Irish America, **1**:252–253
Irish-American society, **1**:438
Irish Archaeological Society, **1**:500
Irish Association of Women
  Graduates and Candidate
  Graduates, **1**:199
Irish brigade, **1**:311
Irish Catholic (newspaper), **2**:668
  Sullivan brothers and, **2**:688
Irish Church Disestablishment Act
  (1869), **1**:88
Irish Church Temporalities Act
  (1833), **1**:88
Irish Citizen Army, **1**:350, 407
  Connolly and, **1**:105
  Easter Rising, **2**:683–685
  Markievicz member of, **1**:422
  women in, **2**:759
"Irish Collection of Canons"
  (*Collectio canonum hibernensis*),
  1:164
Irish colleges abroad, **1**:323–326
  in Paris, **1**:324
  at Rome, **1**:408
Irish Confederation, **2**:772
  Mitchel and, **1**:445

Irish Congress of Trade Unions,
  2:713
Irish Constitutional Convention
  (1917–1918), **2**:727
  Plunkett's chairing of, **2**:528
Irish Council of Churches (ICC),
  1:183
Irish Countrywomen's Association,
  1:248; **2**:757, 760
Irish Creamery Milk Suppliers'
  Association, **1**:248
Irish Daily Independent (newspaper),
  1:465
Irish Dominion League, **2**:528
Irish Exhibition of Living Art
  (IELA) (1943), **2**:742–743
Irish Family Planning Association,
  1:149; **2**:1000
Irish Farmers' Association, **1**:248
Irish Feminist Information, **2**:761
Irish Folklore Commission (1935–
  1970), **1**:457
  source for traditional popular
    religion, **2**:6135
Irish Folklore Society, **1**:309
Irish Folk Song Society, **1**:457
Irish Football Association (IFU),
  2:675
Irish Free State
  becoming Republic of Ireland,
    1:490
  Catholic Church
    and social services, **1**:260
  and Catholic Church, **2**:636
  Civil War, **1**:92–93, 94
  in the Commonwealth, **1**:99–
    101
  Conditions of Employment Act
    and, **1**:101
  constitution of, **1**:105–107
  constitution of 1922, **2**:951–
    954 *(d)*
    equal citizenship of women,
      2:759
  contraception in, **1**:148
  Cosgrave in, **1**:110
  economic relations and, **1**:170
  Eucharistic Congress and, **1**:233
  Gaelic Athletic Association in,
    1:267
  as a Gaelic Catholic state,
    1:260–262
  great seal of, **1**:100
  immigration to, in twentieth
    century, **1**:441
  IRA and, **1**:329
  Irish-language education in,
    1:190, 265
  Irish pound and, **1**:326–327
  and local government, **1**:406

name fire, **1**:490
  Protestants in, **2**:587, 588–589
  social change in, **2**:663–667
  twentieth-century emigration
    from, **1**:440
  women's working rights in,
    2:759
Irish Georgian Society, **1**:114, 115
Irish House of Commons (Wheatley),
  2:540, 542
Irish Housewives' Association,
  2:760
Irish Hudibras, **1**:33
Irish independence, declaration of
  (1919), **2**:937–938 *(d)*
Irish Independent (newspaper),
  1:424, 425
  Murphy and, **1**:451
Irish Inter-Church Meeting, **1**:183
Irish-Ireland movement, **1**:269
Irish Ladies' Hockey Union, **2**:676
Irish Land and Labour Association,
  1:350
Irish language
  Book of Common Prayer in, **1**:86
  catechisms published in, **1**:112
  Celtic influence in, **1**:79, 80
  decline of, **1**:372–375, 386;
    2:644
  Gaelic League on, **1**:190
  hagiography, **1**:290
  Hiberno-English, **1**:295
  Hyde and, **1**:308–309
  MacHale's interest in, **1**:411
  newspaper columns in, **1**:465
  O'Conor and, **1**:499–500
  O'Donovan and, **1**:500
  percentage of speakers, **1**:376
  popular literature in, **1**:84–85
  in schools, **1**:189, 190, 196,
    198, 260
  since 1922, **1**:375–377
    cultural and political
      importance in the Irish Free
      State, **1**:260; **2**:956
    government strategy to
      enhance social and legal
      status of, **1**:375
    new literate culture among
      urban English speakers,
      1:387
  study of, **1**:324–325
  Tridentine catechism in, **1**:222
  See also literature: Gaelic
Irish law. *See* Brehon laws
Irish Literary Revival, **1**:22, 253–
  254
  Joyce on, **1**:340
Irish Literary Society, **1**:388
Irish Literary Theatre, **1**:388

foundation of, **1**:151
Irish Literature (McCarthy et al., ed.), **1**:389
Irish Loyal and Patriotic Union, **2**:726
"Irishman, The" (Orr), **1**:33–34
"Irishman in Coventry, An" (Hewitt), **2**:983 *(d)*
Irishman (newspaper), **1**:465
Irish Melodies (Moore), **1**:37–38
Irish Messenger of the Sacred Heart, **2**:668
Irish National Alliance, **1**:388
Irish National Caucus (INC), **1**:491
Irish National Land League, **2**:546
  constituency structures and, **1**:213
  Davitt and, **1**:126–127
  founding of, **1**:371
  Home Rule and, **1**:300
  and Land Acts, **1**:353, 357
  "lawless law" as code of behavior, **1**:372
  of Mayo, **1**:371
  Parnell and, **2**:518
  preceded by Land League of Mayo, **1**:371
  proposals for land-reform legislation, **1**:371
  Sullivan brothers and, **2**:687–688
Irish National Liberation Army (INLA), **1**:330–331, 410
Irish Nationalist Party
  Ascendancy and, **2**:586
  educational arrangement with Catholic hierarchy, **2**:635–636
Irish National Teachers' Organisation, **1**:191
Irish National Theatre Society, **1**:38, 151
Irish Northern Aid Committee (NORAID), **1**:308, 491
Irish parliament
  constituencies of, **1**:*210–212*
  creation of new boroughs to engineer compliant and Protestant Commons majority, **2**:537–538
  extinguished by Irish Act of Union, **2**:877–880 *(d)*
  Flood and, **1**:257
  granted legislative independence in 1782, **1**:277; **2**:584
  Grattan's parliament, **1**:205
  under Henry III, **1**:215, 217
  modeled on the British parliament, **2**:540
  obstructionism in, **1**:299–300
  Protestant Ascendancy and, **2**:584

reforms of, **1**:205, 257
  1690 to 1800, **1**:276
Irish Parliamentary Party (IPP)
  Easter Rising and, **2**:684–685
  formation of, **1**:209, 213
  and Gaelic Athletic Association, **1**:266
  Home Rule and, **1**:299–306
    banner, **1**:*303*
  and labor movement, **1**:350
  Liberal Party alliance with, **1**:301
  Parnell and, **1**:301–303; **2**:518, 919
  and Plan of Campaign, **2**:524
  pledge, **2**:925 *(d)*
  Redmond and, **2**:601
  Sinn Féin and, **2**:661
  Sullivan brothers and, **2**:688
  1870 to 1891, **1**:299–302
  1891 to 1918, **1**:302–306
  Ulster Catholics in, **2**:558
Irish People (newspaper), **1**:69, 250–251, 465
  Stephens and, **2**:678
Irish planning system, **2**:647
Irish polity
  ceremonial affirmations of, **2**:542
  composition of, **2**:539–541
Irish Popular Superstitions (Wilde), **2**:616
Irish pound, **1**:326–329
Irish Press, **1**:424, 425
Irish Press Group, **1**:424–425
Irish Reformation Parliament (1536–1537), **2**:534, 592
Irish Republic, **2**:555–556
  coalition governments in, **2**:556–557
  Proclamation of (1916), **2**:935–936 *(d)*
Irish Republican Army (IRA), **1**:329–331, 479; **2**:548–549
  aggressive dismantling by British, **2**:725
  in Anglo-Irish War (1919–1921), **1**:92; **2**:685–686
  British and, **2**:549
  campaign for Irish unity, **2**:561
  cease-fires, **1**:479–480
    1994, **1**:3; **2**:1012–1013 *(d)*
    1997, **2**:1013 *(d)*
  Civil War and, **1**:91, 93–94
  Craig and, **1**:116
  decommissioning and, **1**:129–130; **2**:717
  de Valera and, **1**:136
  estates burned by, **1**:232
  Faulkner and, **1**:249–250

  GAA members and, **1**:267
  hunger strikes, **1**:307–308
  impact of Bloody Sunday on recruiting of, **1**:52
  loyalist paramilitary groups compared to, **1**:410
  opposition to partition of Ireland, **1**:483
  proclamation at the beginning of the Civil War (1922), **2**:949–950 *(d)*
  Sinn Féin and, **2**:661
  Special Powers Act, **2**:672
  Trimble and, **2**:717
  See also Provisional IRA
Irish Republican Brotherhood (IRB), **1**:250–253; **2**:905
  Clarke in, **1**:95
  Collins in, **1**:96
  Davitt and, **1**:126–127
  Easter Rising, **2**:683–685
  and funeral of O'Donovan Rossa, **2**:932
  and Gaelic Athletic Association, **1**:266
  and Gaelic League, **1**:269–270
  Lemass in covert unit of, **1**:382
  Pearse and, **2**:520
  and proclamation of the Irish Republic, **2**:935–936 *(d)*
  Stephens in, **2**:678
  unionists and, **1**:304
Irish Republican Socialist Party, **1**:349
Irish Revolutionary Brotherhood (IRB), **2**:905–906
Irish Rosary (periodical), **2**:668
Irish Rugby Football Union (IRFU), **2**:675
Irish School of Ecumenics, **1**:183
Irish Shipping (est. 1941), **2**:676
Irish society
  consumer society, **2**:667
  liberalization of, **2**:557–558
  Mr. and Mrs. Samuel Carter Hall on Irish society before the famine, **2**:893–896 *(d)*
  rural society, **2**:642–644, 858–860 *(d)*
    before Great Famine, **2**:900–902 *(d)*
  social change since 1922, **2**:663–668
    EU and, **1**:234
    Irish Americans and, **1**:147
  from 1500 to 1690, **1**:178–182
  from 1750 to 1950, **2**:563–572
Irish Steel, **2**:677

Irish Stock Exchange (ISEQ), **1**:83
Irish Sugar Company, **2**:677
Irish Theatre Company, **1**:151
Irish Times (newspaper), **1**:253, 424; **2**:589
Irish Tourist Association, **2**:705–706
Irish Trade Board, **1**:81
Irish Trade Union Congress (ITUC), **1**:349
   IWWU and, **1**:332
   O'Brien and, **1**:497
   trade unions and, **2**:712
Irish Traditional Music Archive, **1**:457
Irish Transport and General Workers' Union (ITGWU), **1**:350, 378, 407
   anglicization and, **2**:712
   Connolly in, **1**:104, *105*
   IWWU and, **1**:332
   O'Brien and, **1**:497
Irish Unionist Alliance. *See* Irish Loyal and Patriotic Union
Irish Universities Act (1908), **1**:198
   and Catholic Church, **2**:634
Irish vernacular law. *See* Brehon laws
Irish Volunteer movement, **1**:204, 443–444
   Orange Order and, **1**:507
   Tandy in, **2**:693
Irish Volunteers
   changing their name to Irish Republican Army, **1**:329, 685–686; **2**:548
   Collins in, **1**:96
   Cumann na mBan and, **1**:121–**122**
   de Valera in, **1**:135
   Easter Rising and, **2**:684–685
   and Home Rule, **1**:305; **2**:548
   Irish Parliamentary Party and, **1**:304
   Sinn Féin and, **2**:660–661
   women's auxiliary, **2**:759, 762
Irish Warriors and Peasants Armed for War (Dürer), **1**:*217*
Irishwomen United, **2**:761
Irish Women Workers' Union (IWWU), **1**:**332–333**
   Conditions of Employment Act and, **1**:101
Irish Worker (newspaper), **1**:350
Irish World (newspaper), **1**:253
Irisleabhar na Gaedhilge. See Gaelic Journal
Irlande, Libre, L' (Gonne), **1**:275
Iron Age, **1**:27

Celtic culture, **1**:361
   Hallstatt tradition, **2**:579
      La Tène style and, **1**:80, *80*
   La Tène culture, **2**:579
   royal sites, **2**:579
ironwork, **1**:426
   prehistorical, **2**:579
Irrus Domnainn, **1**:*345*, 347
Isamnium, **1**:214
Isidore of Seville, **1**:296
Itinerary, An (Moryson), **2**:829–831 *(d)*
Ivory, Thomas, **1**:35
IWWU. *See* Irish Women Workers' Union

~ J

J. K. L. (bishop of Kildare and Leighlin). *See* Doyle, James Warren
Jackson, Kenneth, **1**:49, 50
   on *Táin Bó Cúailnge*, **2**:691–692
Jacobites and the Williamite wars. *See* Williamite wars
Jail Journal, or Five Years in British Prisons (Mitchel), **1**:392, 445
James I, **2**:537
   Church of Ireland under, **1**:87
   colonization under, **1**:98
   political and religious policies of, **1**:221–222
   and Ulster plantations, **1**:369
James II, **2**:538
   and Battle of the Boyne, **1**:57, *202*, 202–203
   Catholics under, **1**:222
   Council of Trent and, **1**:112
   Dublin Philosophical Society and, **1**:158
   exile, **1**:58
   King on Protestants under, **1**:344
   Old English and, **1**:502
   and religion in Ireland, **2**:609
   Sarsfield and, **2**:650–651
   siege of Derry and, **1**:131
   Trinity College and, **2**:718
James V, **1**:255
James VI
   colonization under, **1**:98
   and Presbyterianism, **2**:580
Jebb, John, **1**:88
Jeffersonian Democratic-Republicans, **1**:144
Jellett, Mainie, **1**:41; **2**:742
   Decoration, **2**:743
Jellicoe, Anne, **1**:193
Jenkinson, Biddy, **1**:403

Jerpoint Abbey, **2**:652
Jervas, Charles, **1**:36
Jesuits. *See* Society of Jesus
Jewish community, **1**:**338–339**
Jocelyn of Furness on St. Patrick, **2**:650
John, king, **1**:469
   Cork charter by, **1**:108
   law under, **1**:215
John, prince
   grant of civil liberties to Dublin (1192), **2**:788–790 *(d)*
   grant of lands to Theobald Walter (1185), **2**:785–786 *(d)*
John Bull's Other Island (Shaw), **1**:153
John of Salisbury, **2**:782
John Paul II (pope)
   ecumenism and, **1**:184
   visit to Ireland, **2**:655
Johnson, Esther, **2**:690
Johnson, Lionel, **1**:388
Johnson, Thomas, **2**:938–939 *(d)*
Johnston, Denis, **1**:153
Johnston, Francis, **1**:35
   country houses by, **1**:113
Johnston, Jennifer, **1**:403, 404
   on country houses, **1**:115
Johnston, William, **1**:465
   Orange Order and, **1**:509
Joint Committee of Women's Societies and Social Workers, **2**:760
Joint Group on Social Problems, **1**:183
joint-stock companies
   banks, **1**:46
   linen trade, **1**:317, 318
jointures replacing dowries, **1**:240
Jones, Henry, **2**:594
Jones, Marie, **1**:*152*, 154, 405
Jones, Michael, **1**:69
   Cromwellian conquest and, **1**:117
Jonson, Ben, **2**:673
Jordan, Eithne, **2**:743
Jordan, Neil, **1**:42
Joseph II (Habsburg emperor), **1**:325
Journal to Stella (Swift), **2**:690
Joyce, Giorgio, **1**:339
Joyce, James, **1**:39, 253, **339–340**, 388, 391
   Cusack and, **1**:122
   Dubliners, **1**:253
   Finnegans Wake, **1**:253
   Hiberno-English in, **1**:295
   A Portrait of the Artist as a Young Man, **1**:253
   on Swift, **2**:690

Ulysses, **1**:122, 253
on Vallancey, **1**:22–23
Joyce, Lucia, **1**:339
Joyriders (Reid), **1**:405
Judicial Separation and Family
Law Reform Act (1989), **1**:150
Juno and the Paycock (O'Casey),
1:152–153, 389
Jus Primatiale (Plunkett), **2**:527
justiciars, **1**:215, 217

≈ K

Katie Roche (Deevy), **1**:402
Kavanagh, Patrick, **1**:40; **2**:529
on Ireland between the world
wars, **2**:570
Kay, James, **1**:237
Keane, John B., **1**:153
Keane, Molly, **1**:254, 402, 403
on country houses, **1**:115
Kearney, H. F., **2**:695
Keating, Geoffrey, **1**:34, 396, 398,
400
Keating, Seán, **2**:741–742
keening, **1**:66; **2**:617
songs, **1**:453
Kellogg-Briand Pact (1928), **1**:100
Kells, monastery at, **1**:166
Kells, Synod of, **1**:91
Kelly, Alison, **1**:240
Kelly, Hugh, **1**:390
Kelly, "King," **1**:146
Kelly, Maeve, **1**:403, 404
Kelly, Mathew, **1**:240
Kelly, Oisín, **2**:742
Kelly, Thomas, **1**:251
Kenmare, fourth viscount (Thomas
Browne), **1**:74
Kenmare as estate town, **2**:709
Kennedy, Arthur, **1**:282
Kennedy, Dennis, **1**:128
Kennedy, Eamon, **2**:735
Kennedy, Edward, **1**:491, 492
Kennedy, John F.
Irish Americans and, **1**:147
visit of, **1**:341
Keogh, Dermot, **1**:341
Keogh, John, **1**:341–343
denounced, **1**:312
Keogh, William, **1**:311
Kerrigan, Colm, **2**:695
Kettle, Tom, **1**:286
Kickham, Charles J., **1**:250
Kildare
Desmond rebellions and, **1**:133
monasteries, **1**:448
hagiography of, **1**:289–290
pilgrimage site, **1**:449

Kildare, earl of, as king's deputy,
2:534
Kildare Place Society, **1**:343, 385
education and, **1**:187
opposition to, **1**:188
publications of, **1**:85
Kildare rebellion (1534–1535),
2:534
Fitzgerald and, **1**:255–256
Kilkenny, Confederation of. *See*
Confederation of Kilkenny
Killeen, The (Leland), **1**:404
Killian (pilgrim exile), **1**:163
Kilmainham Treaty (1882), **1**:300
Kilmallock as Norman settlement,
2:709
Kilnasaggart pillar, **2**:651
Kilroy, Thomas, **1**:153
Kiltegan Fathers (St. Patrick's
Missionary Society), **2**:620
Kincora (Gregory), **1**:151
King, William, **1**:344
Church of Ireland under, **1**:87
Kingdom of Ireland (1691–1800),
2:539
King Goshawk and the Birds
(O'Duffy), **1**:254
King of Spain's Daughter, The
(Deevy), **1**:153, 402
kings and kingdoms from 400 to
800 C.E., **1**:344–348
King's and Queen's Corporation for
the Linen Manufacture in
England, **2**:640
"king's English rebels," **2**:533, 689
"king's Irish enemies," **2**:533, 689
King's Stables, **1**:214
Kinsale, Battle of (1601), **2**:537
accounts of, **2**:819–820 *(d)*
and Irish emigration to Spain,
2:751
Kinsella, Thomas, **1**:40; **2**:529
on Yeats, **2**:770
Kirke, Percy, **1**:131
Knife in the Wave, The (O'Malley),
1:41; **2**:530
Knights of Columbus, **1**:146
Knights of Labor, **1**:146
Knights of the Plough, **1**:350
knitting industry, **2**:754
Knockaulin (royal site), **1**:214
Knowth mounds, **2**:681
Knox, Alexander, **1**:88
Krapp's Last Tape (Beckett), **1**:47

≈ L

laborers, **2**:642
subsidized cottages for, **2**:646

labor movement, **1**:349–351
American, **1**:146
childcare and, **1**:293
IWWU and, **1**:332–333
O'Brien in, **1**:496–497
social change and, **2**:665
welfare system and, **1**:291–292
"What Is Our Programme?"
(Connolly), **2**:933–935 *(d)*
See also trade unions
Labour Court, trade unions and,
2:713
Labour Party, **1**:350; **2**:532
Bennett in, **1**:332
in independent Ireland, **2**:532
move to the center, **2**:556
and Irish unity, **2**:562
O'Brien and, **1**:497
Sinn Féin and, **2**:661
trade unions and, **2**:712
Lacy, Hugh de, **1**:472, 473
Ladies' Collegiate School, **1**:198
Ladies' Land League, **1**:351, 351–
352, 372; **2**:759, 761
Lagan College, **1**:192
Lagan navigation, **2**:714
Lake, Gerard, **1**:508
Lake, The (Moore), **1**:253
lake dwellings (crannogs), **1**:362;
2:578
Lally, Isaac, **1**:186
Lalor, James Fintan, **1**:356
"Lament for Eoghan Rua O'Neill,"
1:453
laments written for funeral rituals,
1:399
Land Act of 1887, **1**:301
Land Acts, Ordnance Survey and,
1:511
Land Acts of 1870 and 1881,
1:352–354, 356–357, 372
country houses and, **1**:115
Davitt and, **1**:127
estates and demesnes under,
1:232
Land Act of 1870, **2**:645
Land Act of 1881, **1**:301;
2:915–918 *(d)*
Home Rule and, **1**:300
Parnell and, **2**:518
tenant right and, **2**:700
land agents, **1**:246
land agitation. *See* Irish National
Land League; Plan of Campaign
Land Commission, **1**:352
Ordnance Survey and, **1**:511
Landgartha (Burnell), **1**:390
landholdings
by Catholics, **1**:77–78; **2**:521,
540

landholdings CONTINUED
    right to purchase restored, **2**:860–861 *(d)*
    change in pattern after Great Famine, **2**:546
Land Law (Ireland) Act of 1881. *See* Land Acts of 1870 and 1881
Land League. *See* Irish National Land League
Landlord and Tenant (Ireland) Act (1870). *See* Land Acts of 1870 and 1881
land movement, women in, **2**:759
Land of Cokaygne, The, **1**:431
Land of Spices, The (O'Brien), **1**:402
Land Purchase Acts
    Land Purchase Act (Ashbourne Act) of 1885, **1**:357
    Land Purchase Act of 1888, **1**:301
    Land Purchase Acts of 1903 and 1909, **1**:354–355, 357
        Congested Districts Board and, **1**:104
        Punch cartoon of 1903, **1**:*354*
land questions, **1**:355–359; **2**:546–547
    Congested Districts Board and, **1**:104
    Home Rule and, **1**:299–306
    Irish Tithe Act and, **1**:332
    seventeenth-century, **1**:180–181
    Stuart monarchy and, **1**:180
    tenant right and, **2**:697–700
    tithe war and, **2**:701–703
land reform
    Protestant Ascendancy and, **2**:586
    Quakers and, **2**:623
landscape and settlement, **1**:359–367
    clachans, **1**:94–95
    estates and demesnes, **1**:230–232
    family life and, **1**:241–242
    famine clearances, **1**:245, 245–247
    farming families, **1**:247–249
    industrialization and, **1**:316
    Stone Age, **2**:678–683
    subdivision and subletting of holdings, **2**:686–687
land settlements from 1500 to 1690, **1**:367–371
    Cromwellian conquest and, **1**:117–118
    Desmond rebellions and, **1**:133–135

economy and, **1**:178
Land War of 1879 to 1882, **1**:371–372
    Davitt and, **1**:127
Lanfranc, archbishop of Canterbury, **1**:471
Langrishe, Go Down (Higgins), **1**:40, 254
Lantern Slides (O'Brien), **1**:254
Laoi Oisín ar Thír na nÓg (Oisin's song about the land of youth) (Ó Coimín), **1**:34–35
Laois-Offaly plantation, **1**:366
"Laoithe Fiannaíochta," **1**:453
Larcom, Thomas, **1**:500
Larkin, Emmet, on devotional revolution, **1**:136–137, 138
Larkin, James, **1**:350, **377–378**, *378*, 407
    anglicization and, **2**:712
    Connolly and, **1**:104, *105*
    IWWU and, **1**:332
    O'Brien and, **1**:497
Larkin, James, Jr., **1**:497
Larkin, Michael, **1**:252, *252*
Larne gunrunning, **1**:73
Last Conquest of Ireland (Perhaps), The (Mitchel), **1**:445
Last Poems and Two Plays (Yeats), **2**:769
Last Resorts (Boylan), **1**:403
Last September, The (Bowen), **1**:40, 254, 403, 404
La Tène style, **1**:80, *80*, 415, 416, 417, 426
    aniconic fertility stones, **2**:578
    gods and religion, **2**:579–580
Latham, James, **1**:36
Latin
    arrival of in Ireland, **1**:379
    and early Irish church, **1**:415, 450
    Hiberno-Latin culture and, **1**:296–297
    O'Donovan and, **1**:500
    and Old Irish literacy, **1**:378–380
La Touche, David Digues, **2**:590
Laud, William
    Calvinism and, **1**:71–72
    Trinity College and, **2**:717–718
Laudabiliter (Adrian IV), **1**:412, 419, 446; **2**:782 *(d)*
Launching the Currach (Henry), **2**:742
Lauri, Lorenzo, **1**:232
Laverty, Maura, **1**:402
Lavery, Sir John, **1**:41
Lavin, Mary, **1**:254, 403, 404
law

banking and, **1**:45
common law established by Normans, **1**:473
Danelaw, **1**:166
early tracts on, **1**:164–165
excise legislation and distilling, **1**:61
under King John, **1**:215
kingship and, **1**:346
legal change in the sixteenth and seventeenth centuries, **1**:380–382
marriage, **1**:239, 240
monastic, **1**:164
of succession, **1**:202
towns and English, **2**:707
on women's economic rights, **1**:226–228
See also Brehon laws; canon law; penal laws; poor law
Lawrence, Richard
    The Interest of England in the Irish Transplantation Stated, **2**:842–844 *(d)*
    Interest of Ireland in Its Trade and Wealth, **1**:225
Law Reports (Davies), **1**:380, 381
Lay Up Your Ends (Jones), **1**:154, 404
Leabhar na Uidhre. See Book of the Dun Cow
Leabhar Sgéulaigheachta (Hyde), **1**:309
League of Nations
    Commonwealth and, **1**:99, 100–101
    Cosgrave's speech on Ireland's admission to, **2**:955–956 *(d)*
    de Valera and, **1**:136
        "Failure of the League of Nations" (de Valera), **2**:963–965 *(d)*
    Free State and, **2**:554
Lebor Gabála Érenn (Book of invasions), **1**:79, 396, 459
Lebor na hUidhre. See Book of the Dun Cow
le Brocquy, Louis, **2**:742
    Study towards an Image of W. B. Yeats, **2**:743
Lectures on the Manuscript Materials of Ancient Irish History (O'Curry), **1**:401
Ledwich, Edward, **1**:23
Lee, John, **1**:323
Lee, Joseph, on de Valera's "National Thanksgiving" speech, **2**:971
Leech, William, **2**:741
Leenane Trilogy (McDonagh), **1**:154

Leerssen, Joep, **1**:22
Le Fanu, Joseph Sheridan, **1**:38, 392
   on country houses, **1**:115
Lefroy, Thomas, **1**:343
Legge, Hector, **1**:128–129
Legion of Mary, **1**:418; **2**:669
Leibniz, Gottfried Wilhelm, **1**:344
"Léig dod chomhmhórtas dúinn" (Give up your vying with us) (Ó Dubhthaigh), **1**:397
Leinster
   revolt in, **1**:220
   Richard II in, **2**:628
Leix-Offaly plantation, **2**:536. *See also* Laois-Offaly plantation
Leix (Laois) plantation
   formation of, **1**:219
   revolt in, **1**:220
Leland, Mary, **1**:404
Leland, Thomas, **1**:499
Lemass, Seán, **1**:17, **382–383**, 490–491
   economy and, **1**:81, 170–171; **2**:555
   meeting with O'Neill, **2**:555, 560, 724
   and neutrality, **1**:463
   and Northern Ireland, **2**:560
   O'Neill and, **1**:505, *506*
   speech at the European Economic Community (1962), **2**:984–987 *(d)*
   and United Nations, **2**:734
Lentin, Ronit, **1**:404
Leo III (pope), **1**:30
L'Escalopier, Jean, **1**:324
Letters on the State of Ireland (Doyle), **1**:150
Letter to (the soldiers of) Coroticus (St. Patrick), **1**:161
Lever, Charles, **1**:392
   on country houses, **1**:115
Lhuyd, Edward, **1**:79
Lia Fáil (Stone of Destiny), **1**:309; **2**:694
   Tara and, **2**:694
Liberal Party
   in electoral politics, **1**:213
   Home Rule and, **1**:213
   Irish Parliamentary Party and, **1**:301, 303–304
   and temperance movement, **2**:695
Liber Angeli (Book of the angel), **1**:449
Liber de mensura orbis terrae (Book on the measurement of the earth) (Dicuil), **1**:297
libraries

cathedral, **1**:88
Library of Ireland, **1**:159
Lichfield Gospels, **1**:417
Liddy, James, **1**:40; **2**:529
Life and Adventures of James Freney, The, **1**:84, 85
life expectancy, **2**:666
Life of Anthony, The (Athanasius), **1**:90
Life of Freney the Robber, The, **1**:159
Life of Jeremiah Grant, The, **1**:84
Life of John Buncle, The (Armory), **1**:33
Life of Michael Collier, The, **1**:84
Life of St. Patrick (Muirchú), **2**:778–780 *(d)*
Liffey Swim, The (Jack B. Yeats), **2**:741
Lighthouse, The (Donovan), **2**:530
Limerick
   housing in, **2**:757
   under Stuarts, **2**:737
   Viking settlement in, **1**:476
Limerick, Treaty of (1691), **1**:338; **2**:540, 844–846 *(d)*
   ratification of, **1**:202
   revolution settlement and, **1**:201
   Sarsfield and, **2**:651
Limerick Reporter (newspaper), **1**:464
Lindisfarne Gospels, **1**:416
Lindisfarne monastery, **1**:163–164
Linen and Hempen Manufacturers of Ireland, **1**:237, 315–316
Linen Board, **1**:315–316; **2**:640
   industrialization and, **1**:237, 317
linen trade and industry, **2**:640–641
   agriculture and, **1**:4
   American migration and, **1**:143
   bleachers, **1**:316, 317; **2**:640
   Chartres's linen mill in Belfast, **2**:752
   contraction of cottage-based industry
      and Great Famine, **1**:281
   cottage industry, **2**:*641*
   decline of, **1**:174, 175, 238
   effect of technical advances in spinning, **1**:7
   in eighteenth century, **2**:566
   export, **1**:7, 317
   home weaver, **2**:*640*
   Huguenots in, **2**:590
   industrialization of, **1**:237–239, 315–316, 318–319
   narrow or bandle linen, **2**:752
   in Northern Ireland after World War II, **1**:485

overseas investment and, **1**:513
   proto-industrial production, **2**:752
   tenant right, or Ulster custom, **2**:698, *698*
   trade policy and, **2**:710
   weaver colonies, **1**:232
   Woollen Act (1699) and, **1**:6
Lionel of Antwerp, earl of Ulster and duke of Clarence, **1**:474; **2**:791
Lisburn, Co. Antrim, **2**:642
literacy
   chapbooks and popular literature in shaping, **1**:84–85
   Christianity and, **1**:161
   immigration to Australia and, **1**:140
   importance to repeal movement, **2**:623
   Kildare Place Society and, **1**:343
   national levels of, **1**:386
   national schools and, **1**:190
   and popular culture, **1**:383–387
   Duffy in, **1**:159
Literary and Historical Essays (Davis), **1**:159
Literary History of Ireland, A (Hyde), **1**:309
Literary Renaissance (Celtic Revival), **1**:387–389
literature
   Anglo-Irish
      beginnings of tradition, **1**:389–391
      literature since 1800, **1**:37–42
      in the nineteenth century, **1**:391–393
   chapbooks and popular, **1**:84–85
   country houses in, **1**:115
   early modern from 1500 to 1800, **1**:32–37
   English, on Ireland, **1**:223–226
   fiction, modern, **1**:253–255
      twentieth-century novels, **1**:41
   Gaelic
      Anglo-Normans as patrons of, **1**:263
      early and medieval literature, **1**:393–396
      early modern before the Stuarts (1500-1603), **1**:396–397
      literary revival, **1**:263–264
      in the nineteenth century, **1**:399–401

literature CONTINUED
from 1607 to 1800, **1:397–399**
Hiberno-Latin culture and, 1:296–297
Hyde and, 1:308–309
Irish stereotypes in, 1:223–226
Kildare Place Society and, 1:343
Middle English, **1:430–431**
modern Irish since 1800, **1:37–42**
monasteries and, 1:164
O'Donovan and, 1:500
short stories
in Gaelic, 1:265
twentieth-century, 1:40
Táin Bó Cúailnge, 2:691–692
twentieth-century, 1:39–41
women writers, **1:401–405**
See also drama; poetry
literature, Norman French. *See* Norman French literature
Literature in Ireland (MacDonagh), 1:388
Lithgow, William, 2:833 (d)
Lives and Actions of the Most Notorious Irish Tories, Highwaymen, and Rapparees, 1:84
live wakes. *See* American wakes
living standards
American immigrants, 1:146
Celtic Tiger and, 1:176
current, 2:667
Irish in Britain, 1:141–142
North *vs.* South, 1:173, 175, 177
World War II and, 1:168
Lloyd George, David, 2:727
and Anglo-Irish Treaty of 1921, 1:18, 19, 20, 55
de Valera and, 1:135
and Griffith, 2:948
negotiations with Sinn Féin in 1921, 2:549
Lloyd, Joseph, 1:264
local government
established by Normans, 1:473
and ratepayers' franchise, 1:480, 483
since 1800, **1:405–407**
of towns under Tudors, 2:735–736
Local Government Act (Northern Ireland, 1922), 2:723
Local Government Act of 1898, 1:109, 406; 2:586
Irish Parliamentary Party and, 1:303–304
Locke, John
influence on Toland, 2:704

Molyneux and, 1:446
Lockout of 1913, 1:350, 378, **407**
Markievicz and, 1:422
Murphy and, 1:452
Loftus, Adam, 2:717
Logan, Michael (Ó Lócháin), 1:264
Logue, Cardinal Michael, 2:636
Lóeguire, King, conversion by Saint Patrick and, 1:163
Lombard, Peter, 1:291, **408**
London
Irish Literary Renaissance in, 1:388
Irish migration to, 1:169
role of in trade, 2:711
London, Treaty of (1641), Solemn League and, 2:670
Londonderry. *See* Derry
Londonderry Corporation, 1:506
London Hibernian Society
education and, 1:187
publications of, 1:85
Lonely Passion of Judith Hearne, The (Moore), 1:40, 254
Lonesome West, The (McDonagh), 1:154
Longley, Michael, 1:41; 2:529
Hewitt's influence on, 2:983
lord lieutenant, importance of, 1:277
Lord of the Dance, 1:457
Loreto College, 1:199
Loreto Sisters, 2:621
Loughcrew cemetery, 2:576, 682
Lough Derg (Kavanagh), 1:40; 2:529
Lough Gur hinge, 2:683
Louis XIII (France), colleges under, 1:324
Louis XIV (France), Williamite wars and, 1:335, 337
Louth as anglicized territory, 1:218
Louvain
Irish scholars in, 1:21, 398
Peter Lombard in, 1:408
Love à la Mode (Macklin), 1:34
Love Songs of Connacht (Hyde), 1:38, 309
Loyalist Prisoners' Aid, 1:409
Loyalist Prisoners of War, 1:409
loyalists
Dublin bombing, 2:556
paramilitaries after 1965, **1:408–410**
and street ballads, 1:43
See also Progressive Unionist Party; Ulster Defence Association
Loyalist Volunteer Force (LVF), 1:409

Loyal National Repeal Association, 2:623
Loyal Orange Order. *See* Orange Order
Luby, Thomas Clarke, 1:250
Lucas, Charles, 1:391
Catholic Committee and, 1:74
undertaker system and, 1:204
Lucas, Frederick, 1:313
Ludlow, Edmund, 2:846–847 (d)
Lundy, Robert, 1:131
Lynch, Jack, 1:491; 2:556, 562
European Union and, 1:233
statement by the taoiseach (1969), 2:991–992 (d)
Lynch, John, 2:829 (d)
Lynch, Liam, 1:94
death during Civil War, 2:954
Lynch, Patrick, 1:175
Lynnott, Phil, 1:457
Lyons, F. S. L., 1:463
Lyric Players, 1:153
Lyric Theatre, 1:153
Lysaght, Sean, 1:41; 2:530

∽ M

Maastricht Treaty on European Union (1992), 1:234
McAdoo, Henry, 1:89
mac Áeda, Domnall, 2:721
Mac Aingil, Aodh, 1:398
McAleese, Dermot, 1:169
McAleese, Mary, 1:184; 2:766
Mac an Bhaird, Eóghan Ruadh, 1:396
Mac an Bhaird, Fearghal Óg, 1:396
Macartney, George, 1:276
McAteer, Eddie, 1:306; 2:560
McAuley, Catherine, 1:452; 2:621, 668
MacBride, John, 1:275; 2:936
MacBride, Seán, 1:489; 2:735
Declaration of a Republic and the 1949 Ireland Act and, 1:128
and Mother and Child Scheme, 1:451
and NATO, 1:463
MacBride principles, 1:228
Mac Bruaideadha, Tadhg mac Dáire, 1:398
McCabe, Edward, 1:352; 2:745
McCabe, Patrick, 1:41, 254
McCabe, William Putnam, 1:215
Emmet and, 1:215
McCall, P. J., 1:44
McCann, Colum, 1:41, 254
MacCarthaig, king of Desmond, 1:469

MacCarthaigh, Finghín, **1**:290
McCarthy, Eugene, **1**:323
MacCarthy, Justin, **1**:335, 389
MacCarthy dynasty, **1**:262
mac Cerbaill, Diarmait, **2**:721
MacColla, Alasdair, **2**:670
mac Colmáin, Faelán, **1**:347
McCone, Kim, **1**:458
Mac Conraoi, Seán, **2**:597, 598
McCooey, Art, **1**:496
McCormack, William J., **2**:585
McCormick, Finbar, **2**:599
McCormick, Mrs. Harold, **1**:339
McCracken, Henry Joy, **1**:207
Mac Craith Aindrias, **1**:399
Mac Cumhaigh, Art, **1**:453
MacCurtain, Tomás, **1**:109
MacDermott Roe family, **1**:72–73
MacDomhnaill, Seán Clárach, **1**:454
McDonagh, Martin, **1**:154
MacDonagh, Thomas, **1**:388
MacDonnell, Randall, **2**:670
mac Finguine, Cathal, **1**:347
McGahern, John, **1**:40, 254
MacGearailt, Piaras, **1**:454
McGee, Mary, **2**:1000
McGee v. the Attorney General and the Revenue Commissioners (1973), **1**:148–149; **2**:1000–1003 (d)
MacGibbon, Maurice, **1**:111
MacGill, Patrick, **1**:254
MacGilpatrick, Barnaby, **1**:447
MacGiolla, Phádraig (Lord Fitzpatrick of Upper Ossory), **2**:535
Mac Giolla Ghunna, Cathal Buí, **1**:34
MacGonigal, Maurice, **2**:741, 742
MacGowan, Shane, **1**:457–458
McGrath, Thomas, **1**:138
McGrath, William, **1**:408
McGraw, John, **1**:146
MacGreevy, Thomas, **1**:40; **2**:529
MacGregor, James, **1**:397
Mac Gréil, Mícheál, **1**:184
Mac Grianna, Séamas, **1**:265
McGuckian, Medbh, **1**:41, 404, 405; **2**:529
McGuinness, Frank, **1**:154
McGuinness, Martin, **1**: *3*, 130
McGuinness, Norah, **1**:41
MacHale, John, **1**:411, 452
    Cullen and, **1**:120; **2**:634
    Duffy and, **1**:312–313
    education and, **1**:189
    Kildare Place Society and, **1**:343
    Second Reformation and, **2**:654
Macha Sanreth, **1**:214
MacIntyre, Tom, **1**:153

Mack, Connie, **1**:146
McKeague, John, **1**:409
McKeown, Ciaran, **2**:520
McKeown, Sean, **2**:735
Macklin, Charles, **1**:34, 390
MacKnight, James, **1**:465
Mac Liammóir, Micheál, **1**:153, 265
Maclise, Daniel, **1**:38
    The Marriage of Aoife and Strongbow, **1**:39
Mac Lochlainn, Muirchertach, **1**:499
    and high kingship, **1**:412
mac Longsig, Flaithbertach, **2**:721
mac Lorcáin, Cenétig, **1**:123
MacLysaght, Edward, **1**:265
mac Mael Ruanaid, Mael Sechnaill, **2**:721
MacMahon, Hugh
    execution of, **1**:466, 503–504
McMahon, Timothy G., **1**:269
MacMahons and rebellion of 1641, **2**:599–600
McManus, Henry, **1**:*384*
MacManus, Terence Bellew, **1**:250
McMichael, Gary, **1**:409
McMichael, John, **1**:409
Mac Murchada, Diarmait. *See* MacMurrough, Dermot
Mac Murchadha, Diarmaid. *See* MacMurrough, Dermot
MacMurrough, Art, **1**:263
    and Richard II, **2**:628
MacMurrough, Dermot
    and the Anglo-Norman invasion, **1**:411–413, 468–469, 471
    banishment of, **1**:499
MacMurrough Kavanagh, Art Oge, treaty with Richard II, **2**:800–801 (d)
MacMurrough (Mac Murchadha) family, **1**:263, 475
MacNamara, Kevin, **1**:183
MacNeice, Louis, **1**:40; **2**:528
    on Yeats, **2**:770
MacNeill, Agnes, **1**:121
MacNeill, Eoin, **1**:296
    as Boundary Commissioner, **1**:46, 55
    foundation of Gaelic League, **1**:264–265, 268
    as leader of the Irish Volunteers, **1**:304
    and World War I, **1**:285
McNeill, James, **1**:56
    Eucharistic Congress and, **1**:232
McNeill, Janet, **1**:403
McNeill, Tom, **2**:599

MacNeven, William James, **2**:873–877 (d)
mac Óengusso, Longsech, **2**:721
McPherson, Conor, **1**:41, 154
Macpherson, James, **1**:35, 460
    tourism and, **2**:705
McQuaid, John Charles, **1**:413
    on contraception, **1**:148
    de Valera and, **2**:554, 636–637
    and Mother and Child Scheme, **1**:451
        letter to Costello, **2**:976–978 (d)
Macra na Feirme (Sons of the Farms), **1**:248
Macrory, Patrick, **1**:406
MacStiofáin, Seán, **1**:330
MacSweenys, feast at the, **1**:*272*
McSwiney, Mary, **1**:121
MacSwiney, Terence
    death of, **1**:109
    hunger strike, **1**:307; **2**:686
MacUllick, Sean MacEdmund, elegy on the hanging of, **2**:1009
Madden, Deirdre, **1**:41, 254, 403, 404
Madoc (Muldoon), **2**:530
Máel-Máedóc Úa Morgair. *See* Malachy, Saint
Maelsechnaill I, **1**:30
Magauran, Edmund, **1**:111
Magee, William, **2**:654
Mageoghegan (Meic Eochagáin) dynasty, **1**:263
Magherafelt board of guardians, **2**:518
Magh Léna, Battle of, **1**:208
Magna Carta Hiberniae (The Great Charter of Ireland) (1216), **2**:790–791 (d)
Magna Carta sent to Ireland, **1**:215
magnates, Gaelic and Anglo-Irish, **1**:414–415
Maguire, Anne, **2**:520
Maguire, Hugh, **1**:221
Maguire, John Francis, **1**:465
Maguires and rebellion of 1641, **2**:599
Maher, Alice, **2**:743
Mahon, Derek, **1**:41; **2**:529
    Hewitt's influence on, **2**:983
    on Yeats, **2**:770
Mai, The (Carr), **1**:154, 403
mail service and transport, **2**:714–715
maize. *See* Indian corn
Major, John, **1**:488
    and Bloody Sunday, **1**:51
Major Barbara (Shaw), **1**:153

Makem, Tommy, **1**:456
Malachy, Saint, **1**:290, 471
Malby, Sir Nicholas, **1**:134
Malcolm, Elizabeth, **2**:695
Malcolme, John, **1**:1
Malin as plantation village, **2**:709
Mallin, Michael, **1**:422
Mallon, Seamus, **2**:723
Mallory, Jim, **2**:599
Malone Dies (Beckett), **1**:40, 47,
  253
Malone Ridge excavations, **2**:679
Malton, Thomas, **1**:36
"Manchester Martyrs," **1**:252, *252*
Mangan, James Clarence, **1**:38
  and the *Nation*, **2**:770
  Ordnance Survey and, **1**:500
manorial villages, **2**:709
manuscript writing and
  illumination, **1**:29, **415–417**,
  450
  Brehon laws and, **1**:59
  in Irish, **1**:379–380
  Irish glosses of Latin texts,
    1:379
  medieval
    illustrations in, **1**:32
    influence of metalwork, **1**:27
  in romanesque style, **1**:31
  tradition of Irish production,
    1:386
    in nineteenth century,
      1:399–400
*Man Who Was Marked by Winter,
  The* (Meehan), **2**:530
Many Young Men of Twenty (Keane),
  1:153
Maps of the Roads of Ireland (Taylor
  and Skinner), **2**:705
Már, Colmán, **2**:721
"Marbhna Luimní," **1**:453
Marianism, **1**:417–419**
  after Vatican II, **2**:637
  devotional revolution and,
    1:138
  in sodalities and confraternities,
    2:668, 669
Marian restoration (1553), **1**:419
Marino Casino, Clontarf, **1**:113
markets and fairs
  in the eighteenth and nineteenth
    centuries, **1**:420–422
    fair at Donnybrook, **1**:*421*
    markets of Banbridge, Co.
      Down, **1**:*420*
    town life and, **2**:707
  and linen, **2**:640
  livestock, **1**:*9*
  under Tudors, **2**:736
Markievicz, Countess Constance,
  1:407, **422–423**; **2**:661, 760

Clarke and, **1**:95
and politics, **2**:764
in prison with Gonne, **1**:275
Maro, Virgilius, **1**:297
Marob, Nicolas, **1**:324
marriage
  age at, **1**:*243*, 243–244; **2**:570
  among second-generation Irish
    in America, **1**:146
  in Australia, **1**:140
  divorce and, **1**:148–150
  fertility, marriage, and the
    family since 1950, **1**:242–
    244
  intermarriage and re-
    gaelicization, **1**:475
  in Middle Ages, **1**:272
  mixed, **1**:182
  patterns
    from 1500 to 1690, **1**:239–
      241
    from 1690 to 1921, **1**:241–
      242
  rates of, **2**:663–664, 665–666
    from 1500 to 1690, **1**:239–241
    from 1690 to 1921, **1**:241–242
    since 1950, **1**:242–244, *243*
  welfare system and, **1**:293
  women's economic rights and,
    1:226–228
  Young on, **2**:858–860 *(d)*
*Marriage of Aoife and Strongbow,
  The* (Maclise), **1**:39
Married Women's Status Act of
  1957, **1**:226
Marsh, Narcissus, **1**:87
  Trinity College and, **2**:718
Marshal, William, **1**:454, 473
Marshall, George C., **1**:423
Marshall Aid, **1**:423
Marstrander, Carl, **1**:49
Martin, Mary, **2**:621
Martin, Violet ("Martin Ross"),
  1:254, 392
  on country houses, **1**:115
Martin, William, **1**:279
Martyn, Edward, **1**:388
  drama of, **1**:151
martyrologies, **1**:290
Martyrology of Donegal (Ó Cléirigh),
  1:21
Martyrology of Oengus, **1**:290
Martyrology of Tallaght, **1**:90, 290
Mary Lavelle (O'Brien), **1**:402, 404
Mary I
  church and state under, **1**:219
  colonization under, **1**:98
Mason, Roy, **1**:487
Massue, Henry, **2**:590
Match at Football, A (Concanen),
  1:391

Maternity (Protection of
  Employees) Act of 1981, **1**:227
Mathew, Theobald, **2**:623, 635
  Rice and, **2**:628
  temperance medal, **2**:*696*
  temperance movement, **2**:668–
    669, 695
Matrimonial Causes Act (1939),
  1:148
Matrimonial Causes Order (1978),
  1:148
Maturin, Charles Robert, **1**:38,
  392
  on country houses, **1**:115
Maude, Caitlin, **1**:403
Mayhew, Patrick, **1**:487
Maynooth Castle and the Kildare
  rebellion, **1**:256
Maynooth College (Royal College
  of St. Patrick), **1**:198, 325, **423–
  424**
  Cullen and, **1**:121
  in overseas missions, **1**:514
  Troy and, **2**:719
Meagher, Thomas Francis, **2**:771,
  772
  speech on the use of physical
    force, **2**:902–903 *(d)*
Medb
  Cruachain and, **1**:118
  Cú Chulainn and, **1**:119, 120
media
  and popularization of Irish
    music, **1**:456
  since 1960, **1**:424–426**
    secularization and, **2**:656
  See also newspapers; radio;
    television
Medical Missionaries of Mary,
  2:621
medicine
  Catholic Church on, **1**:292–293
  Dublin Philosophical Society
    and, **1**:158
  education in, **1**:197–198
  social change and, **2**:666–667
  welfare programs and, **1**:292–
    293
Meehan, Paula, **1**:41, 403, 404;
  2:530
Meeting the British (Muldoon),
  2:529
Melmoth the Wanderer (Maturin),
  1:38, 392
Memoirs of Edmund Ludlow, The,
  2:846–847 *(d)*
Memoirs of Miss Sidney Biddulph
  (Sheridan), **1**:391
merchants
  Catholic, **1**:77–79**

revolution settlement and, **1**:202–203
guilds, **2**:736
Huguenots as, **2**:590
Merriman, Brian, **1**:34, 38, 399
"merry wake," **2**:617
Mesolithic communities, **1**:361; **2**:575
Messingham, Thomas, **1**:325
metalwork
Beaker metalworkers, **2**:577
bronze work, **1**:426
early and medieval, **1**:426–429
early medieval, **1**:27–28, 426–427
Viking period, **1**:427–428
See also ironwork
Methodism, **1**:429–430
Church of Ireland and, **1**:88; **2**:612
evangelicalism and revivals, **1**:236
missions, **1**:513
Second Reformation and, **2**:653
Methven, Eleanor, **1**:152
Mhac an tSaoi, Máire, **1**:403; **2**:733
"Inquisitio 1584," **2**:1009 (d)
Michael Collins (film, Jordan), **1**:42
Michael Robartes and the Dancer (Yeats), **2**:769
Middle English literature, **1**:430–431
middlemen, **2**:686–687
Midleton, first earl of (St. John Brodrick), **2**:727
Midsummer Night Madness and Other Stories (O'Faolain), **1**:40, 253
midwives, **2**:757
migration
Celtic Tiger and, **1**:176
Dublin, **1**:156
immigration since 1950, **1**:439–442
industrialization and, **1**:317–318
Jewish, **1**:339
music and, **1**:454
population change, 1841–1926, **1**:437
seasonal, **1**:442; **2**:569
See also emigration
military forces
standing army under Charles II, **2**:627
from 1690 to 1800, **1**:443–444
Tudor economy and, **1**:179–180

militias, **1**:443–444; **2**:541
Catholics granted right to join, **2**:543
Mill, John Stuart, on land question, **1**:356, 358
millenarianism in speech delivered at a United Irish meeting in Ballyclare, Co. Antrim, **2**:868 (d)
Miller, David W., **1**:137–138
Miller, Henry, **2**:700
Miller, Kerby A., **1**:145
Millevoye, Lucien, **1**:275
Milligan, Alice, **1**:402
and Gaelic League, **1**:268
Milton, John, **1**:223
Toland biography of, **2**:704
"Mise Raifteraí" (I am Raifteraí) (Raifteraí), **1**:38
Mission to Lepers, **1**:513
Mitchel, John, **1**:392, **445**
helps to form Irish Confederation, **2**:625
Pearse's affinity for, **2**:520
portrait, **1**:445
and Young Ireland, **2**:771, 772
Mitchell, Gary, **1**:154
Mitchell, George, **1**:480, 488, 492; **2**:723
decommissioning and, **1**:129
Mixed Marriage (Ervine), **1**:153
Mnemosyne Lay in Dust (Clarke), **1**:40; **2**:529
"Modest Proposal, A" **2**:689, 690
Mógh Nuadhat, **1**:208
Molesworth, Robert, **2**:704
Molloy, Frances, **1**:404
Irish colleges abroad and, **1**:325
Molloy, M. J., **1**:153
Molloy (Beckett), **1**:40, 47, 253
Molly, Frances, **1**:404
Molly Maguires, **1**:16
Molony, Helena, **1**:121
Molyneux, James, **2**:716–717
Molyneux, Samuel, **1**:158
Molyneux, Thomas, **1**:157, 158
Molyneux, William, **1**:33, **446**
Case of Ireland's Being Bound by Acts of Parliament in England Stated, **1**:203
Darcy and, **1**:125
Dublin Philosophical Society and, **1**:157, 158
on Toland, **2**:704
Monaghan settlement, **1**:221
monarchy, **1**:446–448
Old English on, **1**:501–502
O'Mahony on, **1**:503
Solemn League and, **2**:670
surrender and regrant policy, **2**:688–689

monasteries, **1**:362
beehive stone huts on Skellig Michael, **1**:24
foundations after 1400, **2**:592
in Gothic style, **1**:26
See also monasticism; religious orders
Monasternenagh, Battle of (1579), **1**:134
monasticism
Céli-Dé (Culdees), **1**:90
church reform and, **1**:89
Columba and, **1**:163
Council of Trent and, **1**:112
dissolution of, **1**:219
in the early Middle Ages, **1**:448–450
education and, **1**:163–164, 185
female, **1**:192–194
education of nuns, **1**:200
Eiscir Riata and, **1**:208
hagiography and, **1**:289–290
Irish colleges abroad and, **1**:323–326
literature in, **1**:223
See also monasteries; religious orders
Mondello Park, **2**:676
money and coinage
in early trade, **1**:179
EU policy on, **1**:234
Irish pound, **1**:326–329
king and, **1**:344
Wood's halfpence, **1**:203, 204
Money Bill Dispute (1753–1756), **1**:204
Mongán mac Fiachnai, **1**:164
Montague, John, **1**:40; **2**:529
Moore, Brian, **1**:40, 254
Moore, Christy, **1**:457
Moore, George Augustus, **1**:39, 388, 393
on country houses, **1**:115
A Drama in Muslin, **1**:253
Esther Waters, **1**:253
The Lake, **1**:253
The Untilled Field, **1**:253
Moore, George Henry
Duffy and, **1**:312–313
Ecclesiastical Titles Bill and, **1**:311
Moore, Michael, **1**:325
Moore, Thomas, **1**:37–38, 455
Carolan and, **1**:73
Moore Hall, Co. Mayo, **1**:113
Mór, Art, **1**:475
Mór, MacCarthy, **1**:133
morality, public
Catholic influence on, **1**:260–261; **2**:636–637

morality, public CONTINUED
  Marianism and, **1:**418
Moran, D. P., **1:**268
Moravians, **1:**236
  missions, **1:**513
Morda, Máel (king of Leinster),
  1:96
More, Hannah, **1:**85
More Pricks than Kicks (Beckett),
  1:47
Morgan, Sidney Owenson, Lady,
  1:38, 392
Morley, Thomas, on rebellion of
  October 1641, **2:**838–839 *(d)*
Morning after Optimism, The
  (Murphy), **1:**40
Morning News, **2:**687
Morning Post (newspaper), **1:**56
Morphey, Garrett, **1:**36
Morrison, James, **1:**456
Morrison, Richard, **1:**35
Morrison, Van, **1:**42, 457; **2:**667
Morrissy, Mary, **1:**403
mortality
  maternal, **2:**757
  and population explosion,
    2:565
  potato and, **2:**573
  rural, **2:**646
Mortimer, Roger, **2:**628, 629
Moryson, Fynes, **1:**224
  An Itinerary, **2:**829–831 *(d)*
  on Irish music, **1:**453
mother and child crisis, **1:**450–
  451; **2:**637, 656
  Browne and, **2:**555
  McQuaid and, **1:**413
    letter to Costello, **2:**976–978
      (d)
Mother of Pearl (Morrissy), **1:**403
motor racing, **2:**676
Mountjoy, eight baron (Charles
  Blount), **2:**537, 737
  and Battle of Kinsale, **2:**819
  and Nine Years War, **1:**468
Mountjoy (ship), **1:**131
Mount Sandel excavations, **2:**679
Moynihan, Daniel Patrick, **1:**492
MS Harley 913, **1:**431
Muirchú
  Life of St. Patrick, **2:**778–780 *(d)*
  on Saint Patrick, **1:**163, 289
Muldoon, Paul, **1:**41; **2:**529, 1010
Mullins, George, **1:**36
Mulready, William, **1:**38–39
multinational enterprises, **1:**177;
  2:557
Municipal Corporations Act of
  1840, **1:**109, 156; **2:**586
Munro, Henry, **1:**207

Munster
  high kingship of, **1:**165
  recusants' revolt of 1603,
    2:607
  revolt in 1560s, **1:**220
  Spenser and, **2:**673
Munster plantation, **1:**5, 366, 368
  Desmond rebellions and, **1:**134
  massacre of settlers (1598),
    2:810 *(d)*
"Munster Republic," **1:**94
Murdoch, Rupert, **1:**425
Murlands of Castlewellan, **1:**317
Murphaeid, The (Dunkin), **1:**33
Murphy, Arthur, **1:**390
Murphy, Father John, **1:**153
  in rebellion of 1798, **1:**207
Murphy, Lenny, **1:**409
Murphy, Martin, **1:**465
Murphy, Richard, **1:**40; **2:**529
Murphy, Tom, **1:**40, 41, 153
Murphy, William Martin, **1:**350,
  378, 407, **451–452**
Murphy (Beckett), **1:**47
Murphy (brewery), **1:**61
Murray, Charlie, **1:**167
Murray, Christopher, **1:**153
Murray, Daniel, **1:**452; **2:**634
  education and, **1:**189
  MacHale and, **1:**411
music
  from 1500 to 1800, **1:**37
  Carolan in, **1:**72–73
  early modern music, **1:**452–
    455
  Fleadh Cheoil, **1:**256–257
  GAA ban on "foreign music,"
    1:259
  harp music, **1:**72–73
  hymn on St. Patrick, **1:**296
  Irish Americans and, **1:**147
  modern, **1:**455–457**
  patronage in the Middle Ages,
    1:272–273
  popular, **1:**457–458**
  tourism and, **2:**706
  twentieth-century, **1:**41–42
musical instruments, **1:**455
  "Brian Boru's Harp," **1:**453
My Cousin Justin (Barrington),
  1:403
Myles Wright Report, **1:**157
myth and saga, **1:**458–460**
  Cú Chulainn, **1:**119–120**
  sagas, **1:**393–395
    cycles, **1:**459–460
    and manuscript tradition,
      1:400
  Táin Bó Cúailnge, **2:**691–692
mythological cycles, **1:**459

N

na gCopaleen, Myles. *See* O'Brien,
  Flann
Nagle, Honora (Nano), **1:**461;
  2:621, 634
Napier, Oliver, **1:**477
Napoleon Bonaparte and Act of
  Union, **1:**208
Napoleonic wars
  estates and farming in, **1:**232
  migration during, **1:**141, 144
Narrative of a Recent Journey
  (Bennett), **2:**903–904 *(d)*
Narrative of a Residence in Ireland
  (Plumptre), **2:**884–885 *(d)*
Nary, Cornelius, **1:**325
Nath Í (high king), **1:**347
nation, as modern construct,
  2:609
National Archives Act (1986),
  2:556
National Bank, **1:**46
National Board of Education,
  2:758
  Daniel Murray on, **1:**452
  organization of, **1:**187–188
  religion and, **2:**614
  Second Reformation and, **2:**654
National Brotherhood of Saint
  Patrick, **1:**250
National Covenant of 1638, **2:**669
National Democratic Party
  (Northern Ireland), **2:**560
National Development Plan, **1:**322
National Health Service in
  Northern Ireland, **2:**757
National Insurance Act (1911),
  1:16
nationalism
  apologistic, **1:**22
  Catholic Church and, **2:**635
  curriculum and, **1:**196
  economic, **1:**174
  Emmet and, **1:**214–215
  famine clearances and, **1:**247
  Irish-American culture and,
    1:145
  Irish Parliamentary Party and,
    1:302–306
  Keogh in, **1:**312
  land question and, **1:**358
  in modern drama, **1:**151–153
  recovery of, after Great Famine,
    2:546
  in the 1890s, **2:**547–548
  Sadleir in, **1:**312
  Sinn Féin and, **2:**660–662
  Sullivan brothers and, **2:**687–
    688

trade unions and, **2**:712–713
in voting, **2**:665
Nationalist Party, **1**:306; **2**:560
closing down the *Irishman*,
1:465
United Irish League machine
for, **2**:730
See also Irish Nationalist Party;
Irish Parliamentary Party
National Land League. *See* Irish
National Land League
National Land League of Mayo,
2:911–914 *(d)*
National League Party, **2**:559
national literary festival. *See*
Oireachtas
National Literary Society, **1**:38
Hyde's presidential address to,
2:925–927 *(d)*
National Press (newspaper), **1**:465
National Roads Authority, **2**:716
"National Thanksgiving" (de
Valera), **2**:971–974 *(d)*
National Trust, **1**:115
National Union of Dock Labourers,
1:350, 377, 407
National University of Ireland,
1:198, 423
women in, **1**:199
National Volunteers, **1**:444
and World War I, **1**:285
National Wage Agreement (1970)
and trade unions, **2**:713
Nation (newspaper), **1**:38, 313,
384, 464–465
Davis and, **1**:125–126
foundation of, **2**:770
Mitchel on staff of, **1**:445;
2:771
patriotic songs published in,
1:44
Sullivan brothers and, **2**:687–
688
women's contributions to,
2:761
writers in, **1**:392
"Nation Once Again, A" (Davis),
1:392
Native Americans, **1**:143
nativism, American, **1**:144, 145
NATO, **1**:463, 464
Navan Fort. *See* Emain Macha
(Navan Fort)
Navigation Acts (1660), **2**:710
and Irish economy, **1**:6
Navigatio Sancti Brendani (Voyage
of Saint Brendan), **1**:290
Neal(e), John, **1**:73
Neal(e), William, **1**:73
"Necessity for De-Anglicising
Ireland, The" (Hyde), **1**:264–265,
308–309; **2**:925–927 *(d)*

Neilson, Samuel, **1**:461–462
United Irishmen under, **1**:206
Nelson, Brian, **1**:4410
Nelson, Dorothy, **1**:404
Nemed school, **1**:165
neoclassical style in country
houses, **1**:113
Neolithic communities, **1**:361;
2:575, 680
Ne Temere decree, **1**:182
neutrality, **1**:462–464
New and Selected Poems (Cronin),
2:529
Newcastle Lyons as manorial
village, **2**:709
New Catholic Association, **1**:76
"New Departure," **1**:300, 371
New Description of Ireland, A (Rich),
2:824–825 *(d)*
New English
and agricultural innovations,
1:5
and Church of Ireland, **2**:607,
610
guilds and, **1**:221
opposition to the Graces, **2**:607
in towns under Tudors, **2**:736
"New Ferry, The" (Whyte), **1**:33
Newfoundland, Irish settlers in,
1:431, 432; **2**:750
Newgrange, **2**:576, *681*, 681, 682,
683
New Ireland Forum (1984), **1**:492;
2:556
New Irish Library, **1**:388
New Light movement
Abernathy and, **1**:1
evangelicalism and revivals,
1:236
in Presbyterianism, **2**:581
Westminster Confession and,
1:71
Newman, John Henry, **2**:634
Catholic University and, **1**:197
Cullen and, **1**:120
New Poems (Yeats), **2**:769
Newry navigation, **2**:714
newspapers, **1**:386, **464–466**
British, **1**:425
Catholic Association and, **1**:76
Connolly and, **1**:104–105
duties on, **1**:85
Fenian, **1**:250–251
on hunger strikes, **1**:308
in Irish, **1**:377
IWWU and, **1**:332
railways and, **2**:715–716
Stephens and, **2**:678
Sullivan brothers and, **2**:687–
688

New York City, Irish in, **1**:144,
146
New York Street Flax Spinning
Company, **1**:318
New Zealand, Irish emigration to,
1:435, 440
Niall of the Nine Hostages, **1**:165
Nice Treaty, **1**:233, 464
Nicholls, Kenneth, **1**:475
Nicholson, Asenath, on rural
society before Great Famine,
2:900–902 *(d)*
Ní Chonaill, Eibhlín Dubh, **1**:34,
399
Ní Chuilleanáin, Eiléan, **1**:403
NICRA. *See* Northern Ireland Civil
Rights Association
Ní Dhomhnaill, Nuala, **1**:41, 403;
2:530
"Feis," **2**:1010–1012 *(d)*
Ní Dhuibhne, Éilís, **1**:404
Night in November, A (Jones),
1:405
Ní Mhionacháin, Máiréad, **1**:374
1916 Rising. *See* Easter Rising
(1916)
Nine Years War (1593–1603),
1:368, 380, **466–468**
Desmond rebellions and, **1**:134
fusion of religion and politics,
2:606
Old English in, **1**:221; **2**:536
O'Neill and, **1**:504
origins of, **1**:221
Trinity College and, **2**:717
Nobel Peace Prize
of Corrigan and Williams,
2:520
of Hume and Trimble, **1**:306
No Country for Young Men
(O'Faolain), **1**:404
Noígiallach, Niall, **2**:721
Noise from the Woodshed, A
(Dorcey), **1**:404
No Mate for the Magpie (Molloy),
1:404
Non-Subscribing Irish Presbyterian
Church, **2**:581
Norman conquest and
colonization, **1**:**468–470**, 499
and architecture, **1**:31
colonization and landscape,
1:362, 364
Cork and, **1**:108
in Dublin, **1**:155–156
gaelicization as part of, **1**:263
and Gaelic resurgence, **1**:471–
475
Irish church under, **1**:91
and metalwork, **1**:428

Norman conquest and colonization
CONTINUED
    O'Connors and, **1**:499
    roads under, **2**:714
    sculpture and, **2**:652
    town development and, **1**:366;
        2:709
Norman French literature, **1**:470–
471
Norris, Sir John (lord president of
    Munster), **2**:673
Norse settlement, **1**:475–477
    Battle of Clontarf and, **1**:96
    Brian Boru and, **1**:123
North America, Irish emigration
    to, **2**:750
    in 1600s, **1**:431
    in 1700s, **1**:431–432
    in 1800s, **1**:433–434, 435
    in twentieth century, **1**:440
    See also Canada; United States
North-Eastern Boundary Bureau,
    1:55
Northern Bank, **1**:45, 46
Northern Ireland
    administration under direct
        rule, **2**:722
    Anglo-Irish Treaty of 1921 and,
        1:18
    border with Republic of Ireland,
        1:*483*
    and Boundary Commission,
        1:55
    constitutional settlements from
        Sunningdale to Good Friday,
        1:477–480
    creation of, **1**:73–74, 482–483
    deindustrialization of, **1**:172,
        175–176
    discrimination and the
        campaign for civil rights,
        1:480–482
    economic autonomy of, **1**:172
    Gaelic Athletic Association in,
        1:267
    history since 1920, **1**:482–488
    immigration to, in twentieth
        century, **1**:441
    and local government, **1**:406
    O'Neill on community relations
        in, **2**:987–989 *(d)*
    Parliament
        Sir Basil Brooke (Viscount
            Brookeborough) prime
            minister and member of,
            1:64
        boycotted by minority
            nationalists from 1922 to
            1925, **2**:559
    police force in, **2**:639

policy of the Dublin
    government from 1922 to
    1969, **1**:489–491
sectarian housing policy, **2**:757
social change in, **2**:663–667
twentieth-century emigration
    from, **1**:440
United States and Northern
    Ireland since 1970, **1**:491–
    493
women in politics in, **2**:766
Northern Ireland Act of 1974,
    2:722
Northern Ireland Act of 1998,
    1:229
Northern Ireland Affairs Select
    Committee, **2**:722
Northern Ireland Civil Rights
    Association (NICRA), **1**:2, 481,
    485; **2**:560
    Hume and, **1**:306
Northern Ireland Committee,
    2:722
    trade unions and, **2**:713
Northern Ireland Council for
    Integrated Education (NICIE),
    1:192
Northern Ireland Emergency
    Powers Act, **2**:672
Northern Ireland Forum (1996),
    2:723
    women in, **2**:764
Northern Ireland Human Rights
    Commission, **1**:229
Northern Ireland Labour Party,
    1:64
Northern Ireland Office (NIO),
    2:722
Northern Ireland Women's
    Coalition, **2**:764, 765
Northern Ireland Women's Rights
    Movement (NIWRM), **2**:763
Northern Spring, A: Fivemiletown
    (Ormsby), **2**:530
Northern Star (newspaper)
    Neilson and, **1**:462
    United Irishmen and, **2**:731
North (Heaney), **2**:1005
North-South Ministerial Council,
    1:488
"Notes of His Report" (Gerard),
    2:807–808 *(d)*
Nowlan, Alderman James, **1**:266,
    267
nuclear-nonproliferation initiative
    by Ireland, **2**:734
Nuclear Nonproliferation Treaty
    (1968)
    Ireland and, **2**:555, 734
Nugent rebellion of 1581, **2**:606

nursing, **2**:759
    women's religious orders and,
        2:621

∼ O

Oakboys and Steelboys, **1**:495–
496
    tenant right and, **2**:700
oath-taking
    Confederation of Kilkenny and,
        1:103
    as form of political ritual,
        2:543
    Solemn League and, **2**:670
*Object Lessons: The Life of the
    Woman and the Poet in Her Time*
    (Boland), **1**:41; **2**:530
Oblates of Mary Immaculate,
    2:620
Ó Bradaigh, Ruairí, **1**:330, 331
Ó Braonáin, Seán, **1**:400
O'Brennan, Martin, **1**:465
Ó Briain, Donal Mór (king of
    Thomond), **1**:469, 472
Ó Briain, Tadhg, **1**:474
Ó Briain, Terdelvacus (Turlough),
    1:471
O'Brien, Conor Cruise, **2**:733, 735,
    1009
O'Brien, Edna, **1**:40, 254, 403, 404
O'Brien, Flann (pseud. of Brian
    O'Nolan), **1**:40, 253, 391
    Joyce and, **1**:340
O'Brien, Kate, **1**:402
O'Brien, Lucius, **1**:22
O'Brien, Mary, **1**:391
O'Brien, Muirchertach, **1**:123, 499
O'Brien, Murrough, as first earl of
    Thomond, **1**:447; **2**:535
O'Brien, Murrough, first earl of
    Inchiquin, **1**:103
O'Brien, Turlough, **1**:338
O'Brien, William (politician),
    1:465, **496–497**; **2**:524
    Congested Districts Board and,
        1:104
    Cork under, **1**:109
    Irish Parliamentary Party and,
        1:303–304
    and United Irish League, **2**:728
O'Brien, William (trade unionist),
    1:496–497
O'Brien, William, Brett trial and,
    1:252, *252*
O'Briens and the O'Flahertys, The
    (Morgan), **1**:38
Ó Broin, Fiach MacAodha, **1**:453
Ó Bruadair, Dáibhí, **1**:34, 398, 453

Ó Bruaideadha, Maoilín Óg, **1:**397

Observe the Sons of Ulster Marching toward the Somme (McGuinness), **1:**154

O'Byrne, Feagh MacHugh, **1:**220

Ó Cadhain, Máirtín, **1:**40, 253, 254, 265

Ó Caoimh, Pádraig, **1:**267

O'Casey, Sean, **1:**39, 152–153, 389

   Hiberno-English in, **1:**295

Ó Catháin, Rory Dall, **1:**454

Ó Cearbhalláin, Toirdhealbhach. *See* Carolan, Turlough

Ó Cearnaigh, Nioclás, **1:**400

Ó Cearnaigh, Seán, **1:**397

Ó Cianáin, Tadhg, on Flight of the Earls (1607), **2:**821–822 (d)

Ó Cléirigh, Conaire, **1:**21

Ó Cléirigh, Cúchoigríche, **1:**21

Ó Cléirigh, Lughaidh, **1:**20, 398

Ó Cléirigh, Micheál, **1:**21, 34, 398

O'Clery, Michael, **1:**291

Ó Coilgligh, Ciarán, **2:**597

Ó Coimín, Mícheál, **1:**34

Ó Conaire, Pádraic, **1:**265, 269

Ó Conchobair, Ruaidrí (high king). *See* O'Connor, Roderic (Rory)

O'Connell, Daniel, **1:**22, 434, **497–498; 2:**725

   Butt and, **1:**299

   campaign publications of, **1:**85

   Catholic Association with dues of one penny a month, **2:**610

   Catholic emancipation campaign and, **1:**75, 76; **2:**545

   and Catholic Relief Act of 1829, **2:**888–890 (d)

   Cooke and, **1:**108

   Davis and, **1:**126

   Doyle and, **1:**150, 151

   Independent Irish Party and, **1:**311

   Irish-American culture and, **1:**145

   Irish party under, **1:**209, 213

   Irish stereotypes and, **1:**223

   Kildare Place Society and, **1:**343

   and land question, **1:**356

   in parliament, **1:**209

   portrait by Holbrooke, **1:**498

   Rice and, **2:**628

   Second Reformation and, **2:**654

   speech on repeal of the Act of Union at "monster meeting" at Mullingar, **2:**896–899 (d)

   support by MacHale, **1:**411

   Tara meeting, **2:**694

   tithe war and, **2:**703

use of Catholic clergy as political agitators, **2:**634

use of press, **1:**464

and veto controversy, **2:**739, 740

Young Ireland's differences with, **2:**770–771, 902

O'Connell, John, **2:**625

O'Connell, William, **1:**146

O'Connor, Aedh, **1:**474

O'Connor, Arthur, statement made with Emmet and MacNeven on United Irishmen, **2:**873–877 (d)

O'Connor, Cathal Crobderg, **1:**499

O'Connor, Frank, **1:**40, 253–254

O'Connor, John, **1:**428

O'Connor, Roderic (Rory), **1:**472, 474, 499

   and Norman conquest of Ireland, **1:**263, 412, 469

   and Treaty of Windsor (1175), **2:**784–785 (d)

O'Connor, Turloch Mór, **1:**499

O'Connors of Connacht, **1:498–499**

   High Crosses and, **1:**298

   surrender and regrant among, **1:**219

O'Conor, Cathal (Red-Hand), **1:**474

O'Conor, Charles, of Balenagare, **1:**22, 74, **499–500; 2:**631

O'Conor, Roderic (Rory), **1:**41; **2:**741

O'Conor, Rory. *See* O'Connor, Roderic

O'Conor, Thomas, **1:**500

Ó Corráin, Donnchadh, **1:**458

Ó Criomhthain, Séan, **1:**50

Ó Criomhthain, Tomás (O'Crohan), **1:**50, *50*, 265, 374

   autobiography

     final chapter, **2:**957–959 (d)

Ó Crualaoich, Gearóid, **2:**617

Ó Cuív, Brian, **1:**373

O'Curry, Anthony, **1:**500

O'Curry, Eugene, **1:**401, 500

   on *Táin Bó Cúailnge*, **2:**691

Ó Dálaigh, Aonghus Fionn, **1:**397

Ó Dálaigh, Cearbhall, **2:**582

Ó Dálaigh, Gofraidh Fionn, **1:**395

Ó Dálaigh, Seosamh, **1:**49, 50

O'Daly, Daniel, **1:**324

O'Dea mitre and gold crozier (1418), **1:**31

Ó Dineen, Domnall, **1:**291

Ó Direáin, Máirtín, **1:**40; **2:**529

Ó Domhnaill, Aodh Ruadh, **1:**325

Ó Donnchadha, Tadhg, **1:**264

O'Donnell, Frank Hugh, **1:**388

Home Rule and, **1:**299–300

O'Donnell, Godfrey, **1:**474

O'Donnell, Hugh Roe, **1:**397

O'Donnell, Mael Seachlainn, **1:**474

O'Donnell, Manus (Maghnus Ó Domhnaill), **1:**34, 290, 397

O'Donnell, Mary, **1:**41; **2:**530

O'Donnell, Patrick, **2:**636

O'Donnell, Peadar, **1:**254

   IRA and, **1:**330

O'Donnell, Red Hugh, **1:**466, 467, 468

   attack of the English of Connacht, **2:**809–810 (d)

   Hugh O'Neill and, **1:**503, 504

O'Donovan, John, **1:**400, **500**

   Ordnance Survey Letters, **1:**511

O'Donovan Rossa, Jeremiah

   graveside panegyric by Pearse, **2:**932–933 (d)

   IRB and, **1:**250, 253

O'Driscoll, Dennis, **1:**41; **2:**530

Ó Dubhagáin, Seán Mór, **1:**263

Ó Dubhthaigh, Eoghan, **1:**397

O'Duffy, Eimar, **1:**40, 254

O'Duffy, Eoin, **1:**111

Ó Duibhgeannáin, Cúchoigríche, **1:**21

O'Dwyer, Edward Thomas, **2:**524

O'Faolain, Julia, **1:**404

O'Faolain, Sean, **1:**40, 253

   on Fenian Cycle, **1:**459–460

   on Hugh O'Neill, **1:**466, 503

   on Norman law, **1:**473

O'Farrell, Elizabeth, **1:**121

O'Farrell dynasty, **1:**262–263

O'Farrelly, Agnes, **1:**121

Offaly plantation

   formation of, **1:**219

   Laois-Offaly (Leix-Offaly) plantation, **1:**366; **2:**536

   revolt in, **1:**220

Offences against the Persons Act (1861), **1:**148

Office of Public Works, **1:**115

O'Flaherty, Donal-an-Choghaidh (of the Battles), **1:**279

O'Flaherty, Liam, **1:**254, 265

O'Flynn dynasty, **1:**263

Ó Gadhra, Feargal, **1:**21

Ogham system of writing, **1:**27, 161, 378; **2:**580

Ó Gnímh, Fear Flatha, **1:**34

O'Grady, Standish James, **1:**264, 388

   on Cú Chulainn, **1:**119

O'Growney, Eugene, **1:**264

   and Gaelic League, **1:**268

Ó Guithín, Micheál, **1:**50; **2:**965

Ogulla, well of, **1:**119

O'Hagan, Thomas, **2:**634
O'Hanlon, Redmond, **1:**84
Ó hAodha, Seán, **1:**374
O'Healy, Cashel, **1:**111
O'Healy, Patrick, **1:**111
Ó Heodhasa, Bonaventura, **1:**398
Ó hEódhasa, Eochaidh, **1:**34, 272–273, 396
O'Higgins, Kevin, **1:**56
    assassination of, **1:**329
    Cosgrave and, **1:**110
    League of Nations and, **1:**100
Ó hUiginn, Domhnall Óg, **1:**397
Ó hUiginn, Pilib Bocht, **1:**270
Ó hUiginn, Tadhg Dall, **1:**34, 395
    political use of traditional material, **1:**396
O'Hurley, Dermot, **1:**111
Oidheadh Chloinne Tuireann (Tragic fate of the children of Tuireann), **1:**459
Oidheadh Chloinne Lir (Tragic fate of the children of Lir), **1:**397, 459
oil crises, **1:**175
Oireachtas (national literary festival), **1:**269, 270
    competitions, **1:**265
Oireachtas Committee, **1:**150
O'Keefe law case (1875), **2:**745
O'Keeffe, John, **1:**390
O'Keeffe, Patrick, **1:**500
O'Kelly, Seán T.
    and "Democratic Programme" of Dáil Éireann, **2:**938–939 (d)
    Republic of Ireland bill and, **1:**128
Ó Laoghaire, Peadar, **1:**265, 269
Old English, **1:**500–502
    Campion on, **1:**223
    the cess and, **1:**219, 220
    and Church of Ireland, **1:**219; **2:**607
    "church papistry" among, **1:**86
    in Confederation of Kilkenny, **2:**835
    education of priests and, **1:**323
    and the Graces, **1:**277
    in guilds, **1:**221
    in Irish Confederate War, **2:**608
    and Nine Years War, **1:**221, 468; **2:**536
    Old Irish and, **1:**222
    and plantations, **1:**278, 368
    and rebellion of 1641, **2:**600
    and recusancy, **2:**536
    under Restoration (1666–1688), **2:**627
    Stuarts and, **1:**221–222
Old Irish uprising, **1:**222
"Old Lights," **1:**71

evangelicalism and revivals, **1:**236
    in Presbyterianism, **2:**581
Old Testament. *See* Bible
O'Leary, John, **1:**388; **2:**769
    IRB and, **1:**250
Oliver, J. A., **2:**518
Ó Longáin, Micheál Óg, **1:**400
Ó Longáin scribal family, **1:**401
Olsen, Fred, **2:**658
Ó Luínse, Amhlaoibh, **1:**374
Olympic, **2:**657, 657
O'Mahony, Conor, S.J., **1:**502–503
O'Mahony, Francis, **1:**20
O'Mahony, John
    IRB and, **1:**250, 251, 253
    Stephens and, **2:**678
O'Malley, Grace. *See* Granuaile
O'Malley, Mary, **1:**41; **2:**530
    Lyric Players, **1:**153
O'Malley, Owen Dubhdara, **1:**279
Ó Maolchonaire, Fearfeasa, **1:**21
Ó Maolchonaire, Flaithrí, **1:**398
O'More, Onie, **1:**466
O'More clan, surrender and regrant in, **1:**219
Óm sceol ar ardmhagh Fáil ní chodlaim oídhche (With this news of Ireland's pain I cannot sleep) (Céitinn), **1:**398
On Baile's Strand (Yeats), **1:**151, 388
Ó Neachtain, Seán, **1:**35, 399
Ó Neachtain, Tadhg, **1:**399
Ó Neachtain circle (Dublin), **1:**499
One Bread, One Body, **1:**184
O' Neill, Aedh, **1:**474
O'Neill, Art McBaron, **1:**466
Ó Néill, Brian, **1:**474
O'Neill, Conn, lord of Tyrone, **1:**240
    becoming first earl of Tyrone, **1:**447; **2:**535
Ó Neill, Domhnall, **1:**65
O'Neill, Francis, **1:**457
O'Neill, Henry, **1:**504
O'Neill, Hugh, second earl of Tyrone, **1:**380, 467, 468, **503–504**; **2:**536, 606
    Catholic restoration and, **1:**221
    death of, **1:**20
    demands of, **2:**818–819 (d)
    and Nine Years War, **1:**466
    Old English and, **1:**502
    Peter Lombard agent of, **1:**408
    surrender to Mountjoy, **2:**537
Ó Néill, Niall Mór, **1:**475
O'Neill, Niall Oge, treaty with Richard II, **2:**799–800 (d)

O'Neill, Owen Roe, **1:**504–505; **2:**600, 601
    Confederation of Kilkenny and, **1:**103
O'Neill, Sir Phelim, **2:**599
O'Neill, Shane, **1:**179
    marriages of, **1:**239
    Sidney and, **2:**659
    surrender and regrant, **1:**220
O'Neill, Terence, **1:**408, 482, 485, **505–507**, *506*; **2:**518
    on community relations in Northern Ireland, **2:**987–989 (d)
    Faulkner and, **1:**249
    Lemass and, **1:**171, 382, 491; **2:**555, 560
    and nationalist politics, **2:**560
    as prime minister, **2:**724
    Trimble and, **2:**716
    "Ulster at the Crossroads," **2:**989–991 (d)
O'Neill, Tip, **1:**491, 492
O'Neill, Turlough Luineach
    Hugh O'Neill and, **1:**503, 504
    Sidney and, **2:**659
On Raferty's Hill (Carr), **1:**154
"On the Holy Places" (*De Locis Sanctis*) (Adomnán), **1:**164
"On the Study of Celtic Literature" (Arnold), **1:**22
Opened Ground: Selected Poems, 1966–1996 (Heaney), **2:**529
O'Rahilly, Nancy, **1:**121
O'Rahilly, T. F., **2:**691
oral tradition and literacy, **1:**384
Orange commemorations
    honoring deaths in Somme Battle, **1:**286
    remembering the Battle of the Boyne, **1:**59
"Orange Horses" (Kelly), **1:**403, 404
Orangeism and yeomanry, **1:**444
Orange Order, **2:**610–611, 732
    in Canada, **1:**147
    in electoral politics, **1:**213
    Independent Orange Order, **1:**510
    marching in Belfast in 1888, **2:**726
    opposition to the Act of Union, **2:**544
    origins, 1784 to 1800, **1:**507–509
    and patron-client culture, **2:**543
    processions in 1935, **2:**724
    and religion, **2:**612
        High Church tradition, **1:**88
    since 1800, **1:**509–510**

state assistance to, **1**:206
and unionism, **2**:726
Orange Volunteers, **1**:409
Ó Rathaille, Aogán, **1**:34, 399, 453
Ordnance Survey, **1**:**511**
O'Donovan and, **1**:500
Ordnance Survey Letters (O'Donovan), **1**:500, 511
Ordnance Survey Memoirs, **1**:511
O'Reilly, Tony, **1**:424
O'Reilly, William, **1**:270
O'Reilly dynasty, **1**:262
and rebellion of 1641, **2**:599–600
Organisation for Economic Co-operation and Development (OECD)
Celtic Tiger and, **1**:81
tourism and, **2**:706
orchards, **2**:768
Ó Riada, Seán, **1**:456
Ó Ríordáin, Seán, **1**:40; **2**:529
Ormond (Edgeworth), **1**:392
Ormond, twelfth earl and first duke (James Butler), **1**:35, 68–69; **2**:630
Ormond family
Desmond rebellions and, **1**:133–134
gaelicization of, **1**:263
Sidney and, **2**:659
Ormond Peace, first (March 1646), **1**:68–69
Rinuccini attempts to prevent, **2**:630
Ormond Peace, second (January 1649), **1**:69
Rinuccini and, **2**:630
Ormsby, Frank, **1**:41; **2**:529
O'Rourke, Brian, **1**:221
O'Rourke, Brian Oge, **1**:221
O'Rourke, Kevin, **1**:242
Orpen, Goddard H., **1**:472
Orpen, William, **1**:41; **2**:741
Orr, James, **1**:33
Orr, William, execution of, **1**:206
Ó Ruairc, Tigernán, **1**:412
Osborne, Walter, **1**:41
Ó Searcaigh, Cathal, **1**:41; **2**:530
O'Shea, Katharine, **1**:301; **2**:519, 525, 547
O'Shea, W. H., **1**:301
O'Sheerin, Thomas, **1**:324
Ossianic Cycle. *See* Fenian Cycle
Ó Súilleabháin, Amhlaoibh, **1**:400
Ó Súilleabháin, Eoghan Rua, **1**:34, 454
aislings of, **1**:399
Ó Súilleabháin, Mícheál, **1**:456
Ó Súilleabháin, Muiris, **1**:50, 265

autobiography, **2**:960–962 *(d)*
Ó Súilleabháin, Tomás Rua, **1**:455
O'Sullivan, Maurice. *See* Ó Súilleabháin, Muiris
O'Sullivan, Sonia, **2**:676
O'Sullivan, Tadhg, **2**:733
O'Sullivan, Timothy, **1**:84–85
O'Sullivan Beare, Philip, **2**:809–810 *(d)*
O'Toole, Fintan, **1**:153
O'Toole, Luke, **1**:266, 267
Ottawa Economic Conference (1932), **1**:100
Ó Tuama, Seán, **1**:399, 454
Our Lady's Sodality, **1**:418
Ourselves Alone (Devlin), **1**:404
outdoor relief to sick and poor, **2**:564, 621
overseas investment, **1**:**511–513**
Celtic Tiger and, **1**:81–82
European Union and, **1**:234–235
industry since 1920 and, **1**:320–321
share of, **1**:*512*
overseas missions, **1**:**513–515**
Irish Catholic Church, **2**:622
Methodist, **1**:430
of monasteries, **1**:448

∼ P

Pacata Hibernia (Stafford), on siege of Kinsale, **2**:819–820 *(d)*
Paddy Clarke Ha Ha Ha (Doyle), **1**:41, 254
Paddy's Resource, **1**:44
painting
landscape painting, **1**:36; **2**:741–742
portraiture, **1**:36
twentieth-century, **1**:41
Paisley, Ian, **1**:64, 408, 485; **2**:**517–518**, 724
Palatines, **1**:88, 236
immigration, **2**:591
Pale. *See* English Pale
Palladius (bishop), **2**:604
Hiberno-Latin culture and, **1**:296
sent by Celestine I (pope) to Ireland, **2**:603
St. Patrick and, **2**:649
pantheism, Toland and, **2**:704
paramilitary organizations
loyalists after 1965, **1**:**408–410**
United Irishmen reorganized as, **2**:732

See also Irish Republican Army (IRA)
Paris Peace Conference, **2**:685
Parker, Dame Dehra, **2**:**518**, 764
Parker, Henry, **2**:518
Parker, Stewart, **1**:153
Parliament Act (1911), **2**:548
Parliament Chloinne Tomáis (The parliament of Thomas's clan), **1**:398; **2**:537
Parnell, Anna, **1**:351, *351*; **2**:761
Parnell, Charles Stewart, **1**:70, 358; **2**:**518–519**, *519*
call at Ennis for agrarian militancy, **2**:914–915 *(d)*
Cork under, **1**:109
Davitt and, **1**:127
Cork under, **1**:109
and Irish National Land League, **1**:371
fall of, **1**:301–302
GAA support of, **1**:266
and Home Rule, **1**:299–300
on Home Rule and the land question at Cork, **2**:919–920 *(d)*
on Home Rule at Wicklow, **2**:920–921 *(d)*
Home Rule Party under, **1**:213
and Irish National Land League, **1**:371; **2**:546–547
land war and, **1**:300
Murphy's opposition to, **1**:451
obstructionism of, **1**:299–300
and Plan of Campaign, **2**:525
and press, **1**:465
Redmond and, **2**:601
Sullivan brothers and, **2**:688
Times allegations against, **1**:301
Parnell, Fanny, **2**:761
Parnell, Thomas, **1**:390
"Parson's Revels" (Dunkin), **1**:33
partition of Ireland, **2**:559, 727–728
constitution of 1937 on, **1**:106
de Valera's antipartition strategy, **1**:489
opposition of IRA, **1**:483
Partnership for Peace (NATO), Ireland and, **1**:464
Passionists, **2**:620
passive resistance, tithe war and, **2**:701, 703
pastoral economy, **1**:4–5, 6–7
Patrick, Saint, **1**:379, 448; **2**:580, 603, **649–650**
Armagh monastery and, **1**:449; **2**:649–650
Confessio (Declaration), **1**:161, 289; **2**:603, 777–778 *(d)*

Patrick, Saint CONTINUED
de Courcy on, **2**:650
documents on, **1**:291
in hagiography, **1**:289, 290
Hiberno-Latin culture and, **1**:296
life by Muirchú, **1**:289; **2**:778–780 (d)
mastery of biblical style, **1**:296
preface to Senchas Már, **1**:393
well of Ogulla and, **1**:119
writings of, **1**:161
writings on, **1**:161, 163
Patriot King, The; or Irish Chirgh (Dobbs), **1**:391
Patriot politics, **1**:280; **2**:541
economics in, **1**:203–204
Flood in, **1**:257
free trade and, **1**:204–205
legislative independence and, **1**:205
patronage
Anglo-Normans as patrons of Gaelic literature, **1**:263
aristocratic during Counter-Reformation, **1**:112
in the Middle Ages, **1**:272–273
of Protestant Ascendancy, **2**:584
of Raiftearaí, **2**:597
patron-client relationship in Irish politics, **2**:541, 543
Patten Commission, **2**:639
pattern. See pilgrimages
Patterns in Comparative Religion (Eliade), **2**:616–617
Paul III (pope), Fitzgerald and, **1**:255
Paulin, Tom, **1**:41; **2**:529
Paul IV (pope), **1**:111
payment-by-results policy, **1**:190, 195–196
Payne, Robert, **1**:224
Peace movement in Northern Ireland, **2**:519–520
Peace People, **2**:520
peace process, 1990–1998, **1**:487–488
Pearce, Sir Edward Lovett, **1**:35
Castletown House, **2**:585
country houses by, **1**:113–114
Parliament House (Dublin), **1**:273, 276
Pearse, Padraic. See Pearse, Patrick H.
Pearse, Patrick H., **1**:119–120, 407; **2**:520–521, 548
Connolly and, **1**:105
and Gaelic League, **1**:269
influence of Young Ireland on, **2**:772

O'Donovan Rossa's graveside panegyric, **2**:932–933 (d)
peat harvesting, **1**:7, 361
hand cutting, **1**:53
Peel, Sir Robert, **1**:424; **2**:614
Catholic emancipation campaign and, **1**:76
colleges created by, **1**:196–197
and Great Famine, **1**:282–283
Indian corn and, **1**:313
O'Connell and, **1**:498
"Peel's brimstone," **1**:314
Peep o' Day Boys, **1**:130; **2**:542
Orange Order and, **1**:507
Peig (Sayers), **1**:50, 265
Pelagius, **1**:297
pellagra, **1**:313, 314
Pembroke township, **1**:156
penal laws, **2**:521–522
Act to prevent the further growth of popery (1704), **2**:521, 847–853 (d)
Catholic emancipation campaign and, **1**:75–77
dismantling of, **2**:522
Catholic Relief Act (1778), **2**:857–858 (d)
education and, **1**:186–188
family under, **1**:240
Protestant Ascendancy and introduction of, **2**:584
revolution settlement and, **1**:201–202
role of Irish parliament in enacting, **2**:540
and Roman Catholic Church, **2**:613, 631
songs on, **1**:453
See also Catholic Relief Acts
Pennsylvania, Irish in, **1**:143
Pentecost (Parker), **1**:153
"People's Budget," **1**:304
People's Democracy, **1**:482, 485
Periphyseon: On the Division of Nature (Eriugena), **1**:297
Perrot, Sir John
Desmond rebellions and, **1**:133
religious reform under, **1**:220
Persian Gulf War (1990–1991), Ireland and, **1**:464
Pestalozzi, Heinrich, **1**:187
Petrie, George, **1**:500
Petty, William, **1**:6; **2**:522–524, 523
Down Survey, **1**:500
Dublin Philosophical Society and, **1**:157
Hiberniae Delineatio, **1**:225
on plantation, **1**:370
The Political Anatomy of Ireland, **1**:225

survey by, **1**:117
Peyton, Patrick, **2**:637
Pezron, Paul-Yves, **1**:79
Phaire, Robert, **1**:284
Pharaoh's Daughter (Ní Dhomhnaill), **1**:41; **2**:530
Philadelphia, Irish in, **1**:145
Philadelphia Here I Come (Friel), **1**:40, 153
Philosophical Enquiry into the Origin of Our Ideas of the Sublime and the Beautiful, A (Burke), **1**:36
Philosophical Survey of the South of Ireland, A (Campbell), **1**:225; **2**:854–857 (d)
Physico-Historical Society, **1**:158
Picture of Dorian Gray, The (Wilde), **1**:38; **2**:748
"Pierce's Cave" (O'Sullivan), **2**:960–962 (d)
Pigott, Richard, **1**:465
Pike Theatre, **1**:153
pilgrimages, **2**:664
held on saint's day, **2**:617
at holy wells, **2**:616, 617
as part of popular religion, **2**:611
tourism and, **2**:705
pilgrim exiles, **1**:163, 290
Pilkington, Laetitia, **1**:390
Pilkington, Matthew, **1**:390
Pim, Jonathan, **2**:623
Píobairí Uilleann, Na, **1**:456
Pioneers of the Sacred Heart, **2**:635
Pioneer Total Abstinence Association, **2**:553, 669, 695–696
Pious Miscellany (O'Sullivan), **1**:84–85
Pirrie, William, **2**:657
Pitt, William (the Younger), **1**:2, 277
Catholic emancipation campaign and, **1**:75
on commercial union, **1**:205
Maynooth College and, **1**:325
resignation, **2**:544
Pius V (pope), **1**:111
Pius IX (pope)
condemnation of Fenianism, **2**:635
Cullen and, **1**:121
and Marianism, **1**:418
Pius XI (pope), **1**:107
place-names
commemorating druidic sanctuaries, **2**:579
field-naming, **1**:364
and Norse settlement, **1**:476–477

Plan of Campaign (1886–1891),
  1:301; **2:524–527**
  condemnation by Pope Leo XIII,
    2:635
  Walsh and, **2**:745
plantations, **1**:367–368
  before 1622, map of, **1**:*368*
  Cromwellian, **1**:370
  estates and demesnes, **1**:230–
    231
  King's County (Offaly), **1**:219
  Old English and, **1**:278, 368
  policy of, **2**:605
  Queen's County (Laois), **1**:219
  revolt in, **1**:220
  towns around, **2**:709
  See also Munster plantation;
    Offaly plantation; Ulster
    plantations
Playboy of the Western World, The
  (Synge), **1**:39, 152, 388
Playboy riots, **1**:152
playhouses, **1**:34
Plays Pleasant and Unpleasant
  (Shaw), **1**:38
Plough and the Stars, The (O'Casey),
  1:39, 152–153, 389
plows
  difference between Gaelic Ireland
    and former colonial areas, **1**:4
  horse-drawn, **1**:12
Plumptre, Anne, **2**:884–885 *(d)*
Plunket, William Conyngham,
  2:740
Plunkett, Oliver, **2**:527, **527–528**
  Council of Trent and, **1**:112
  execution of, **1**:222
Plunkett, Sir Horace Curzon,
  2:528
Plunkett family and carving, **1**:31–
  32
pocket gospel books, **1**:29, 417
Poems, 1963–1983 (Longley), **2**:529
Poems, 1956–1986 (Simmons),
  2:529–530
Poems and Ballads of Young Ireland
  (Yeats, ed.), **2**:769
Poems of Ossian (Macpherson),
  1:460
Poems (Yeats), **2**:769
poetry
  on Columba, **1**:164
  courtly love poetry, **1**:34, 395
  courts of poetry, **1**:399
  early and medieval, **1**:395
  eighteenth-century, **1**:398–399
  folk, **1**:34
  Heaney, **1**:294–295
  in Irish, **2**:530
  in Middle English, **1**:430–431

modern, **2:528–530**
  patronage in Middle Ages,
    1:272–273
  Spenser, **2**:673
  twentieth-century, **1**:40–41
  women's, **1**:41, 403; **2**:530
  See also bardic poetry; *individual*
    poems
Poetry and Ireland (Yeats and
  Johnson), **1**:388
Pogues, The, **1**:457
poitín (poteen), **1**:61
Pole, Cardinal Reginald, **1**:419
Police Act for Northern Ireland
  (2000), **1**:229
police force
  Catholics in, **1**:228, 229
  Dublin, **2**:685, 686
  Northern Ireland, **2**:639
  See also Royal Irish
    Constabulary; Royal Ulster
    Constabulary
Police Service of Northern Ireland,
  2:639
Political Anatomy of Ireland, The
  (Petty), **1**:225; **2**:523
Political Arithmetic (Petty), **2**:523
Political Monitor, The; or Regent's
  Friend (O'Brien), **1**:391
political parties in independent
  Ireland, **2:531–533**
political theory, kingship in early,
  1:165
politics
  beginning of fusion of religion
    and, **2**:606
  impact of the Northern Ireland
    crisis on Southern politics,
    2:560–562
  independent Ireland since 1922,
    2:550–558
  kingship in early, **1**:165
  marriage in, **1**:239
  nationalist politics in Northern
    Ireland, **2:558–560**
  pre-Viking kingdoms, **1**:345,
    346
  role of newspapers in political
    agitations, **1**:386
  1500 to 1690, **2:533–539**
  1690 to 1800—a Protestant
    kingdom, **2:539–545**
  1800 to 1921—challenges to
    the union, **2:545–550**
  town life and, **2**:707
  women in, **2**:759 (*See also*
    Markievicz, Countess
    Constance)
    politics as family tradition,
      2:765

Politics, Law, and Order in
  Nineteenth-Century Ireland
  (Crossman), **1**:301
polity, concept of, **2**:539
Pollock, Frederick, **1**:381
Pomes Penyeach (Joyce), **1**:340
Poor Clares, **2**:621
poor law
  boards and local government,
    1:406
    Protestant landlords and,
      2:586
  inadequacy during Great
    Famine, **1**:282, 283
  and local government, **1**:406
  workhouse system, **2**:564
Poor Law Amendment Act of
  1847, **2:564**
  famine clearances, **1**:246, 247
  Gregory clause, **1**:246, 247;
    2:564
Poor Soldier, The (O'Keeffe), **1**:390
Popery Act of 1704. *See* Act to
  prevent the further growth of
  popery (1704)
popery laws. *See* penal laws
Popish Plot crisis (England, 1678–
  1681), **2**:609, 626
  Plunkett and, **2**:527, 538
popular culture
  American, **1**:146
  Cusack in, **1**:122
  Irish American, **1**:147
  social change and, **2**:665
popular religion, **2**:611
popular songs. *See* balladry; ballads
population
  American, **1**:143
  Belfast, **1**:48, 49, 319
  Celtic Tiger and, **1**:83
  changes
    1841–1926, **1**:*437*
    decline between 1851 to
      1911, **1**:8
    decline from 1851 to 1926,
      1:435
    explosion from 1750 to
      1845, **2**:565, **572–574**
  Cork, **1**:108–109, 315; **2**:707,
    708
  decline after Great Famine,
    2:569
  depopulation through
    emigration in Free State,
    2:554
  Dublin, **1**:155, 156, 180, 273;
    2:707, 708
  economic development and,
    1:180
  economy and society from
    1750 to 1950, **2:564–572**

population CONTINUED
estimates, 1812–1951, **2:**565
farm subdivision and, **1:**232
fertility rates and, **1:**244
industrialization and, **1:**314,
315
Irish-born in Australia, **1:**140
Irish-born in Britain, **1:**141–
142
Irish in Scotland, **1:**142
Jewish, **1:**338, 339
Northern Ireland, **1:**173, 175,
177
Roman Catholics as percentage
of, **2:**618
social change and, **2:**663, 665–
666
Southern Ireland, **1:**173, 175
in towns and villages, **2:**710
transport and, **2:**714
of women, **1:**142
*Population of Ireland, 1750 to 1845,
The* (Connell), **1:**241
portable gallows, **1:**496
Portable Virgin, The (Enright),
1:254
*Portrait of the Artist as a Young
Man, A* (Joyce), **1:**39–40, 253,
339, 340
Post Office, transport and, **2:**714–
715
potato, **1:**281; **2:574–575**
blight (*Phytophthora infestans*),
2:567–568
cultivation of, **2:**566–568
as healthy diet, **2:**644
as less important in diet after
Great Famine, **2:**645–646
in nineteenth century, **1:**4, 8
growing reliance on, before
1845, **2:**644
and population growth, **2:**566,
572–573
potato land often exempt from
tithe, **2:**701
in seventeenth century, **1:**4, 5
shortages before Great Famine,
2:568
poteen, **2:**695
pottery. *See* ceramics
Powderly, Terence, **1:**146
Power, Albert, **2:**742
Power, Ambrose, **2:**748
Power, John O'Connor, **1:**371
Home Rule and, **1:**299–300
Powis Commission, **1:**190
Poynings' Law (1494), **2:**541,
803–804 (*d*)
amendment to, **1:**205; **2:**541
Irish parliament constrained by,
1:276

Precursor Society of Ireland, **2:**623
prehistoric and Celtic Ireland,
1:361; **2:575–580**
Celtic migrations and, **1:**79–81
Cruachain, **1:118–119**
Cú Chulainn, **1:119–120**
Dún Ailinne, **1:159–160**
Eman Macha, **1:**214
Stone Age, **2:**673–683
Táin Bó Cúailnge, **2:**691–692
Tara, **2:**579, **693–695**
Prejudice and Tolerance in Ireland
(Mac Gréil), **1:**184
Prendergast, Kathy, **1:**41; **2:**743
Prendergast, Maurice de, **1:**412
Preoccupations (Heaney), **1:**294
Presbyterianism, **2:580–582**, 604
Calvinism in, **1:**71–72
colonization and, **1:**98
Cooke in, **1:107–108**
dissenters in, **1:**202; **2:**581
education and, **1:**189
evangelicalism and revivals,
1:235–236; **2:**581
Oakboys and Steelboys, **1:**495–
496
Second Reformation and, **2:**654
Solemn League and Covenant,
2:669–670
Westminster catechism, **1:**84
Presbyterians
in Belfast, **2:**542
legal restrictions on, **2:**521
ministers granted the *regium
donum* by government, **2:**581,
594, 608, 613
in Northern Ireland, **2:**581
political rituals of, **2:**542
and repeal movement, **2:**611
revival in 1859, **2:**613
Secession Synods, **2:**612
Presentation Brothers, **2:**628
Presentation Order. *See* Sisters of
the Presentation of the Blessed
Virgin Mary
presidency of Irish Republic,
2:582–583
press
journalists and Gaelic League,
1:268
magazines, **1:**159
regulation in eighteenth
century, **1:**464
See also newspapers
Preston, Thomas, **1:**103
Pride of Life, The, **1:**431
primogeniture
legitimate *vs.* illegitimate
children in, **1:**240
tanistry replaced by, **2:**535

printing
cheap-book trade, **1:**387
increased ownership of printed
matter, **1:**386
in Irish, **1:**386, 387
first book, **1:**397
single-sheet ballads, **1:**385
small books, **1:**385
Prior, James, **1:**478
prisoners, women's support of,
2:763
privatization, **2:**677
*Proceedings of the Royal Irish
Academy*, **1:**23
process-servers, violence against,
2:701, 702
Programme for Economic
Expansion, **1:**167; **2:**555
and agriculture, **1:**13
farming in, **1:**248
Programme for National Recovery,
2:713
Progressive Democrats, **2:**532, 556
creation of, **2:**562
Progressive Unionist Party (PUP),
1:408, 409, 479
property rights
in Brehon laws, **1:**380
tenant right, or Ulster custom,
2:697–700
Ulster plantations and, **1:**180
of women, **1:**226–228
See also landholdings
proportional representation, **2:**583
constitution and, **1:**106, 107
in Northern Ireland, **2:**559
in Republic of Ireland, **2:**765
Prosper of Aquitaine, **1:**161; **2:**603
on St. Patrick, **2:**649
protectionism, **1:**320
"Protestant Action Force," **1:**409
Protestant Ascendancy, **1:**275;
2:610–611
in Cork, **1:**109
country houses and, **1:113–
116**, *114*
Cromwellian conquest and,
1:118
decline, 1800 to 1930, **2:586–
588**
definition of, **2:**584
estates and demesnes, **1:**230–
232
Irish Tithe Act and, **1:**332
marriage among, **1:**240
as part of Irish polity, **2:**539
penal legislation and, **1:**87
preservation of, **1:**209
tithe war and, **2:**701–703
1690 to 1800, **2:583–585**

Trinity College and, **1**:196;
  2:718
Williamite wars and, **1**:338
women's view of Ireland from,
  1:225
Protestant Established Church. *See*
Church of Ireland
"Protestant Parliament and a
Protestant State, A," Craig on,
2:962–963 *(d)*
Protestant Reformation, **2**:591–
593
  Calvinism in, **1**:71–72
  education and, **1**:185
  education of priests and, **1**:323
  Elizabeth I and, **1**:85–87; **2**:806
    (d)
  English policy and, **1**:219
  failure in Ireland, **2**:604
  family under, **1**:240
  Trinity College and, **2**:717
Protestants
  and art, **1**:35
  in Belfast, **1**:48
  community in Southern Ireland
    since 1922, **2**:588–589
  and Gaelic League, **1**:269
  immigrants, **2**:589–591
  and rebellion of 1641, **2**:600–
    601
  and rebellion of 1798, **2**:544
  See also Baptists; Church of
    Ireland; Methodists;
    Presbyterians; Religious
    Society of Friends
proto-industrialism, female and
child labor in, **2**:751–753
Provincial Bank, **1**:46
Provisional IRA, **1**:485–486; **2**:725
  cease-fire of 1994, **1**:487
  cease-fire of 1997, **1**:488;
    2:723
  See also decommissioning;
    Adams, Gerry; Irish
    Republican Army
Ptolemy
  on Celts, **1**:79
  on Emain Macha, **1**:214
Public Dance Halls Act (Ireland,
1935), **1**:261
public examinations, education and
  payment-by-results and, **1**:190,
  195–196
  women and, **1**:193–194
public-works programs during
Great Famine, **2**:569
publishing
  and censorship, **1**:261
  Duffy in, **1**:159
pubs, **2**:664

"Punishment" (Heaney), **2**:1005
  (d)
PUP. *See* Progressive Unionist Party
Purchase of Land Act of 1891,
  1:104
Puritan sectaries, **2**:593–595
Purse of Coppers, A (O'Faolain),
  1:253
putting-out system
  innovation and, **1**:238
  textile industrialization and,
    1:237

∼ Q

Quadragesimo Anno (Pius XI),
  1:106–107
Quakers. *See* Religious Society of
Friends
quangos, **2**:722
quarterage dispute, **2**:707
  Catholic Committee and, **1**:74
  Catholic merchants in, **1**:78
Queen's Colleges, **1**:196–197
  bill, **2**:771
  Cork, **1**:109
  repeal movement and, **2**:625
  women at, **1**:199
  See also National University of
    Ireland
Queen's Institute, **1**:198
Queen's University Belfast, **1**:196–
197, 198
  women at, **1**:199
Quinn, J. F., **2**:695

∼ R

racial discrimination, **1**:229–230
Radcliffe, Thomas, **2**:658–659
radio, **1**:424, 425
  broadcasts by de Valera, **2**:959–
    960 *(d)*, 971–974 *(d)*
  Irish-language, **1**:377
  and popularization of Irish
    music, **1**:456
Radio Éireann, **1**:424
Raiftearaí, Antaine (Anthony
  Raftery), **1**:38, 400, 455; **2**:597–
  598
railways
  development of, **2**:715–716
  textile industrialization and,
    1:318
Railway Station Man, The
  (Johnston), **1**:403
raised bogs. *See* bogs and drainage
Raleigh, Sir Walter
  colonial theory of, **1**:98

Desmond rebellions and, **1**:134
ranch war, **2**:730
Rath Breasail, synod of, **1**:90–91
Rathcormac, tithe war and, **2**:703
Rathcroghan
  cemetery at, **1**:119
  as royal site, **1**:214
Rathlin Island massacre, **1**:221
Rathmines township, **1**:156
raths, **1**:362; **2**:598–599
  clachans and, **1**:95
  as sacred sites, **2**:616
Rat Pit, The (MacGill), **1**:254
Raven, Thomas, Derry sketch by,
  1:*132*
Raymond le Gros, **1**:412
rayon manufacture, **1**:238; **2**:754
Rea, Stephen, **1**:154
Reading Made Easy, **1**:84
reading rooms, **1**:464
Reagan, Ronald, **1**:491, 492
Reasons Most Humbly Offered
  (Toland), **2**:704
Rebellion of 1641, **1**:370; **2**:599–
601
  massacre of Protestants, **2**:*600*
    ceremonies recalling, **2**:584
  O'Neill and, **1**:504–505
  and Presbyterianism, **2**:593
  A Remonstrance . . . , Being the
    Examinations of Many Who
    Were Eye-Witnesses of the Same,
    and Justified upon Oath by
    Many Thousands (Morley),
    2:838–839 *(d)*
  Solemn League and, **2**:670
  Trinity College and, **2**:718
  A True and Credible Relation
    (anon.) **2**:837–838 *(d)*
Rebellion of 1798, **2**:610
  and Act of Union of 1800, **1**:2,
    277
  American migration and, **1**:144
  Orange Order and, **1**:508
  Quakers during, **2**:622
  Tone in, **2**:705
  United Irishmen in, **1**:206–207;
    2:544
Recollections of Fenians and
  Fenianism (O'Leary), **1**:388
Recollections of the Life of John
  O'Keeffe (O'Keeffe), **1**:390
recusancy
  among Gaelic and Old English,
    2:536
  in Munster revolt of 1603,
    2:607
Red Branch Cycle. *See* Ulster Cycle
Red Branch heroes, **1**:119
Redemptorist Archconfraternity of
  the Holy Family, **2**:620

Redemptorists, 2:620
Red Hand Commandos, 1:409
Red Hand Defenders, 1:409
Redmond, John, 2:601–602, 602, 636, 730
    Carson and, 1:73
    Home Rule and, 1:304–305
    Irish Parliamentary Party under, 1:303–304
    and Irish Volunteers during World War I, 1:285
Redmond, Willie, 1:286
Redress of Poetry, The (Heaney), 1:294
Re-Equipment of Industry Act (1951), 1:238
Rees, Merlyn, 1:307, 486
Reflections on the Revolution in France (Burke), 1:391
Reformation. See Protestant Reformation
Regan, Morice, 1:472
Regio, 1:214
Reid, Christina, 1:154, 405
Reid, Nano, 2:743
Relatives' Action Committee (RAC), 1:307–308; 2:763
religion
    devotional revolution, 1:136–139
    ecumenism and, 1:182–184
    evangelicalism and revivals, 1:235–236
    financal links with, 1:45
    from 1500 to 1690, 2:604–609
    hunger strikes and, 1:307–308
    importance in towns under Tudors, 2:736
    kingship in, 1:344
    overseas missions, 1:513–515
    policies on (1534–1690), 1:218–223
    religious geography, 2:618–619
    in sculpture, 2:651–653
    secularization and, 2:654–656
    since 1690, 2:609–615
    social change and, 2:664–665
    sodalities and confraternities, 2:668–669
    1500 to 1690, 2:604–609
    traditional popular religion, 2:615–618
    tripartite division of Irish society, 2:610
    in voting, 2:665
    See also Baptists; Church of Ireland; Methodists; Presbyterianism; Presbyterians; Religious Society of Friends; Roman Catholic Church

religious conflicts
    Confederation of Kilkenny and, 1:102–104
    funerals and, 1:66
religious freedom
    constitution on, 1:106
    Treaty of Limerick (1691) and, 1:338
religious geography, 2:618–619
Religious Obedience Founded on Personal Persuasion (Abernathy), 1:1
religious orders
    decline in, 2:666
    dissolution of religious communities under Henry VIII, 2:592
    establishment of seminaries, 2:633
    men's, 2:619–620
    new orders under Daniel Murray, 1:452
    in overseas missions, 1:514
    Roman decrees of 1743 and 1751 restricting activities of, 2:633
    sculpture and, 2:652–653
    secularization and, 2:656
    towns and, 2:709
    women's, 2:621–622, 633
        and education, 2:758
        and Marian cult, 1:418
    See also monasticism
Religious Society of Friends (Quakers), 2:594, 604, 608, 622–623
    in education, 1:187
    Kildare Place Society and, 1:343
reliquaries, 1:427
Reliques of Irish Poetry (Charlotte Brooke), 1:35, 391
Remembering Light and Stone (Madden), 1:41, 254
Remonstrance . . . , Being the Examinations of Many Who Were Eye-Witnesses of the Same, and Justified upon Oath by Many Thousands, A (Morley), 2:838–839 (d)
Renunciation Act (Britain, 1783), 2:863–864 (d)
Repeal Association
    Davis in, 1:125
    Mitchel and, 1:445, 445
    O'Connell and, 1:498
    reading rooms, 1:464
repeal movement, 2:623–625
    Butt as opponent of, 1:69
    Davis in, 1:125–126
    federalism as alternative to repeal, 2:899–900 (d)

"monster meetings," 2:624–625; 896
    banning of Clontarf meeting, 2:625
    at Tara, 2:624
    and press, 1:464
Report of the Commission on the Status of Women, 1:226–227
Representative Church Body, 1:88–89
Republican cease-fire order (1923), 2:954–955 (d)
republicanism
    after Anglo-Irish Agreement of 1985, 2:723
    Cú Chulainn and, 1:120
    education and, 1:187
    IRA and, 1:329
    Tone and, 2:704–705
Republican Labour Party (Northern Ireland), 2:560
Republic of Ireland, 1:490
    amendments of constitution as part of Belfast Agreement, 1:488; 2:560–561
    border with Northern Ireland, 1:483
    free-for-all maternity and infant-care system, 2:757
    proportional representation in, 2:765
    urbanization in, 1:367
    women parliamentary representation, 2:765–766
Republic of Ireland (1653–1660), 2:538
Republic of Ireland Act, 2:975
Republic of Ireland bill, Costello on, 2:975–976 (d)
Responsibilities (Yeats), 2:769
Restoration Ireland, 2:538, 626–627
    Protestant Ascendancy in, 2:584
    Solemn League and, 2:671
Restoration of Order in Ireland Act (ROIA) (1920), 2:671
Resurrection of Hungary, The (Griffith), 1:287
revivals. See evangelicalism and revivals
Reynolds, Albert, 1:487; 2:556
Reynolds, Thomas, 1:255
Rhymers' Club, 1:388
Ribbonmen, 1:355
RIC. See Royal Irish Constabulary
Ricciardelli, Gabrielle, 1:36
Rice, Edmund Ignatius, 2:620, 628, 634
Rice, Lena, 2:676

Rich, Barnaby, **2**:824–825 *(d)*
Richard II, **2:628–629**
　fleet of, **2**:*629*
　treatises with Irish chieftains in
　　1395, **2**:799–801 *(d)*
Riders to the Sea (Synge), **1**:152
Rightboys, political reform and,
　1:205
right to vote of Catholics, **2**:543,
　864–866 *(d)*
ringforts. *See* raths
Rinuccini, Giovanni Battista,
　2:629–630
　aims of missions, **2**:608
　Confederation of Kilkenny and,
　　1:102–103
　O'Neill and, **1**:505
　1640s revolt and, **1**:222
Ripley Bogle (Wilson), **1**:41, 254
Ritchie, William, **2**:657
Rithmus Facture Ville de Rosse,
　1:470
Rivals, The (Sheridan), **1**:34
Riverdance, **1**:457
River That Carries Me, The (Dorcey),
　1:404
Road to Brightcity, The, **1**:254
Roberts, Thomas, **1**:36
Robinson, Lennox, **1**:153
Robinson, Mary, **2:630–631**, 735,
　766
　contraception and, **1**:148
　election as president, **2**:557,
　　582
　on the family planning bill,
　　2:1003–1004 *(d)*
Robinson, Peter, **2**:517
Robinson, Richard, **1**:88
Robinson, Thomas, **1**:*207*
Robinson, William, **1**:35
　gardens of, **1**:115
Robinson Crusoe (Defoe), **1**:84
Roche, David (Viscount Fermoy),
　2:673
Rolleston, T. W., **1**:388
Roman Catholic Church, **2**:604,
　607–608
　anglicization of, **1**:472–473
　de Beaumont on Irish
　　Catholicism, **2**:892–893 *(d)*
　building program following
　　Catholic emancipation in
　　1829, **1**:366
　clergy
　　educational deal with Parnell,
　　　2:614
　　education and training,
　　　2:634
　　and Mother and Child
　　　Scheme, **2**:976

　and National Education
　　Board, **2**:614
　nomination of bishops,
　　2:613, 633
　scandals, **2**:638
　training, **1**:323–326
　and United Irish League,
　　2:730
　and clerical celibacy, **1**:270
　constitution on, **1**:106–107
　Counter-Reformation
　　Lombard and, **1**:408
　diocesan system, **1**:217–218
　Edwardian reform and, **1**:201
　establishment of parish system,
　　2:611
　Eucharistic Congress, **1**:232–
　　233
　Gaelic dynasties in, **1**:270
　and Home Rule Party, **2**:614
　household-based piety at
　　"stations," **2**:611, *632*
　Irish-American, **1**:144, 145,
　　146–147
　law in Latin, **1**:59
　opposition to ritual public
　　mourning and wakes, **2**:617
　organization in Ireland, **2**:631–
　　632
　overseas missions, **1**:513–514
　parish
　　churches before Reformation,
　　　2:591
　　missions, **1**:418
　in rural society, **2**:644
　scandals of, **2**:557
　secularization and, **2**:654–656
　seventeenth-century growth of,
　　1:222
　social change and, **2**:666–667
　on social welfare, **1**:292–293
　temperance movement, **2**:695–
　　696
　1690 to 1829, **2:631–632**
　1829 to 1891, **2:632–635**
　1891 to present, **2:635–639**
　town life and, **2**:708
　university education and, **2**:634
　See also Catholics; devotional
　　revolution; Trent, Council of;
　　Tridentine Catholicism
Romanesque style
　architecture, **1**:25, 30–31
　sculpture, **2**:652, *652*
Roman times in Ireland, **2**:580
Rome, Treaty of, **1**:235
Ronan, Sean, **2**:733
Rooney, William, **1**:287
Roosevelt, Franklin D., and Irish
　neutrality, **1**:463

Roosevelt, Theodore, Plunkett and,
　2:528
Rosa Mundi (Dorgan), **2**:530
ROSC (international exhibition),
　2:743
Ross, Martin. *See* Martin, Violet
Rothe, David
　Council of Trent and, **1**:112
　Irish colleges abroad and, **1**:325
Rothe House (Kilkenny city), **1**:35
Rough Field, The (Montague), **1**:40;
　2:529
Rough Magic Theatre Company,
　1:154
round towers, **1**:25, *25*
Row, Thomas, **2**:750
Royal Canal, **2**:714
Royal College of Saint Patrick at
　Maynooth. *See* Maynooth College
Royal Commission of Inquiry into
　Primary Education, **1**:190
Royal Commissions on University
　Education in Ireland, **1**:198, 199
Royal Dublin Society
　and tree planting, **2**:768
　and woodlands, **1**:364
Royal Engineers Artillery, **1**:511
Royal Hibernian Academy, **2**:742
Royal Hospital, Kilmainham
　(Dublin), **1**:35
Royal Irish Academy, **1**:22
　hagiography at, **1**:291
　O'Conor and, **1**:499
　O'Donovan and, **1**:500
Royal Irish Constabulary (RIC),
　1:301; **2**:639
　attacks on, **2**:685, 686
Royal Society of London, **2**:523
Royal Ulster Constabulary (RUC),
　1:483; **2:639**
　attacking a civil-rights
　　demonstration, **1**:*481*
　controlled by first Northern
　　Ireland government, **2**:723
Royal University of Ireland, **1**:197,
　198
　women in, **1**:193, 199
RTÉ (Radio Telefís Éireann), **1**:424,
　425
　Guinness's use of, **1**:288
Rúain, Maél, **1**:90
Ruben, **1**:59
RUC. *See* Royal Ulster
　Constabulary
rugby, **2**:675
rug mantles, **1**:4
rundale, **1**:95; **2**:648
　land held in, **2**:573
　tenant right, or Ulster custom,
　　2:697–698

rural industry, **2**:640–642
rural life
  Catholic dominance in, **1**:84
  government in, **1**:405
  Nicholson on, before Great
    Famine, **2**:900–902 *(d)*
  1690 to 1845, **2**:642–644
  1850 to 1921, **2**:644–647
  women in, **2**:758
rural settlement and field systems,
  2:647–648
  clachans, **1**:94–95
  rundale, **1**:95
Russell, George. *See* AE
Russell, John, **1**:283
Russell, T. W., **2**:729
Russell, Thomas, **1**:215

~ S

Sabbatarianism, **2**:665
  temperance and, **2**:696
Sadleir, John
  denounced, **1**:312
  Ecclesiastical Titles Bill and,
    1:311
sagas. *See* myth and saga
"Sailing to Byzantium" (Yeats),
  1:39; **2**:528
Saint Angela's College, **1**:199
Saint Anne's, Shandon, **1**:109
Saint Anthony's College, **1**:323,
  324
Saint Columb's House at Kells,
  1:25
Saint Enda's school established by
  Pearse, **2**:520
Saint Fin Barre's Cathedral (Cork),
  1:108; **2**:652
Saint Isidore's College, **1**:323
Saint Leger, Anthony, **1**:447;
  2:534–535
  church and state under, **1**:218,
    219
  Old English and, **1**:501
  and religious reformation,
    2:592
  surrender and regrant policy,
    2:689
Saint Louis convent, **1**:194
Saint Louis Sisters, **2**:621
Saint Mary's Pro-Cathedral
  (Dublin), **2**:156, 719
Saint Mary's University College,
  1:194
  women in, **1**:199
Saint Patrick, problem of, **2**:649–
  650
Saint Patrick's Bell, **1**:426

Saint Patrick's Cathedral (Dublin),
  1:26, *156*
  Second Reformation and, **2**:654
  Swift at, **2**:689, 690
Saint Patrick's College, Maynooth,
  1:325, 423–424
Saint Ruth, Charles Chalmont,
  marquis de, **1**:337–338
saints, research on lives of Irish,
  1:21
Salamanca college, **1**:186, 323,
  325
Salkeld, William, **1**:381
Sanders, Nicholas, **1**:134
Sands, Bobby, **1**:308
Saor Éire, **1**:329
Sarsfield, Genet, **1**:239
Sarsfield, Patrick, **2**:650–651
  Williamite wars and, **1**:*337*,
    338
Saunderson, Edward, **1**:116
Saville, Lord, and Bloody Sunday,
  1:51, 52
Saxey, William, on massacre of
  Munster settlers, **2**:810 *(d)*
Sayers, Peig, **1**:50, 265
  "Scattering and Sorrow,"
    2:965–968 *(d)*
scalpeens, **1**:247
"Scattering and Sorrow" (Sayers),
  2:965–968 *(d)*
Scenery of Ireland (Fisher), **1**:36
School Attendance Act (1926),
  2:755
School for Scandal, The (Sheridan),
  1:34
schools
  boarding schools, **1**:199
    convent, **1**:192–193
    of Huguenots, **2**:590
  built under Tudors, **2**:736
  cathedral schools, **1**:185
  Charter Schools, **1**:186–187
  diocesan schools, **1**:185, 186
  hedge schools, **1**:186–188, 383
  and Irish language, **1**:*189*, 190,
    196, 198, 260
    Irish-immersion primary
      schools, **1**:377
  model schools, **1**:190
  national schools, **1**:188–191,
    189
    Catholic Church and, **2**:634
    Dalkey School Project, **1**:191
  parish schools, **1**:185
  pension day schools, **1**:192–193
  See also education
Science Foundation Ireland, **1**:83
Scotland, seasonal employment in,
  1:442

Scots Covenanters
  Confederation of Kilkenny and,
    1:102, 103
  Solemn League and Covenant,
    2:669–671
Scots-Irish emigration, **1**:433;
  2:581
Scottish Presbyterians, **2**:607
  and agriculture, **1**:5
  as Dissenters, **2**:608, 610
  prosecuted for nonconformity,
    2:593
  separating from Church of
    Ireland, **2**:608
  settling in Ireland, **1**:431
    in Ulster, **2**:580, 594
Scottish Radio Holdings, **1**:424,
  425
Scottus, Clemens, **1**:297
Scottus, Joseph, **1**:297
Scottus, Muredach, **1**:297
Scottus, Sedulius, **1**:297
scriptoria (copying rooms), **1**:448
Scully, Sean, **2**:743
sculpture
  early and medieval, **2**:651–
    653, *652*
  modern, **2**:742
  See also High Crosses
scutch mills, **1**:237
SDLP. *See* Social Democratic and
  Labour Party
Séadna (Words) (Ó Laoghaire),
  1:265
"Seán Ó Duibhir A'Ghleanna,"
  1:453
Sea Ordnance, **2**:662
*Seasonable Thoughts Relating to Our
  Civil and Ecclesiastical Constitution*
  (O'Conor), **1**:499
Season for Mothers, A (Burke),
  1:403
Secession Synod, **2**:581
  Cooke and, **1**:107
Sechnaill, Maél II, **1**:123
Second Great Awakening,
  American migration and, **1**:144
Second Reformation, **2**:613, 653–
  654
  Doyle and, **1**:150–151
  evangelicalism and revivals,
    1:236
  Kildare Place Society and, **1**:343
  tithe war and, **2**:701
Second Vatican Council (1962–
  1965)
  ecumenism and, **1**:182, 183,
    184
  on education, **1**:191
  Irish Americans and, **1**:147

Irish Catholicism and, **2:**637
  on sodalities and confraternities, **2:**669
  welfare system and, **1:**293
Secreta Secretorum, **1:**431
Sectarianism: A Discussion Document, **1:**183
sectarian tensions, Methodism and, **1:**429
secularization, **2:654–656**
Secundinus, **1:**296
Sedgefield, Battle of, **2:**650–651
Seeing Things (Heaney), **1:**294
Select Committee for Antiquities of the Dublin Society, **1:**499
Selected Poems (Clarke), **1:**40; **2:**529
"Senility" (Lavin), **1:**404
Senchas Már ("Great Tradition"), **1:**60, 165, 393
Servant of the Queen, A (Gonne), **1:**275
servants. *See* domestic service
servitors, **1:**369
Sétanta, **1:**119. *See also* Cú Chulainn
settlements
  British settlement plans and towns, **1:**366–367
  in Bronze Age, **1:**361
  in Early Bronze Age, **1:**63
  eighteenth-century regions, **1:***365*
  of Huguenots, **2:**590
  medieval, **1:***363*
  Neolithic, **1:**361
  stone fortresses, in Bronze Age, **2:**578
  twenty-first century regions, **1:***366*
Seven Champions of Christendom, The, **1:**84, 85
Seven Wise Masters of Rome, The, **1:**84
Seven Years' War, Catholic Committee and, **1:**74
sewing industry, **1:**318
  women in, **2:**753
sex discrimination, **1:**228
Sex Discrimination Act (Northern Ireland, 1976), **2:**763
Sex Discrimination (Election of Candidates) Act (2001), **2:**766
Sexton, Thomas, **2:**730
Sexual Discrimination Act (Britain), extension to Northern Ireland, **2:**763
Seymour, Dermot, **2:**743
Sgáthán Shacramuinte na hAithridhe (Mirror of the sacrament of repentance) (Mac Aingil), **1:**398

Shadow of a Gunman, The (O'Casey), **1:**39, 152–153, 389
Shadwell, Charles, **1:**390
Shadwell, Thomas, **1:**33
Shakespeare, William
  Henry V, **1:**223
  Irish depicted in, **1:**223, 295
"Shankill Butchers," **1:**409
Shannon Airport, **2:**676
Shannon Electricity Scheme, **1:**320
Shape of Water, The (Boran), **2:**530
Sharp, Anthony, **2:**622
Shaw, George Bernard, **1:**38, 153
shebeens, **2:**695
Sheehy, Nicholas, **2:**747
Sheppard, Oliver, **2:**742
  Cú Chulainn sculpture, **1:**120
Sheridan, Frances, **1:**391
Sheridan, Jim, **1:**42
Sheridan, Richard Brinsley, **1:**33, 34, 390, 391
Sheridan, Thomas, **1:**34
Sheridan, Thomas, the Elder, **1:**390
She Stoops to Conquer (Goldsmith), **1:**34
shipbuilding, **2:656–658**
  Belfast, **1:**318–319
  decline of, **1:**174, 175
  in Northern Ireland after World War II, **1:**485
  overseas investment and, **1:**513
  World War II and, **1:**321
shire system, **1:**217
Siabhradh Mhic na Míchomhairle (The hallucination of the Son of Ill-Counsel), **1:**398
Sidney, Henry, **1:**367–368; **2:658–660**, 736
  Desmond rebellions and, **1:**133
  economic diversification under, **1:**179–180
  Shane O'Neill and, **1:**220
  surrender and regrant and, **1:**219
Siege of Tamor, The (Howard), **1:**391
Síl Muiredaig, the O'Connors and, **1:**498–499
Síl nAeda Sláine, **1:**348; **2:**721
silver
  early medieval use of, **1:**27–28
  Huguenots as silversmiths, **2:**590
  silverware, **1:**37
  silver work, **1:**426
Silver Tassie, The (O'Casey), **1:**153
Simmons, James, **2:**529–530
Simms, George, **1:**89
Simple Lessons in Irish (O'Growney), **1:**268

Single European Market, **1:**177
Sinn Féin, National Council of, first annual convention
  Griffith's address, **2:**927–929 *(d)*
  resolutions adopted at the public meeting following, **2:**929 *(d)*
Sinn Féin movements and parties, **1:**478, 479, 486, 492; **2:**548
  to 1922, **2:660–662**
  Adams and, **1:**2, 3
  after World War I, **1:**287
  Civil War and, **1:**91
  Collins in, **1:**96
  in Cork, **1:**109
  Cosgrave in, **1:**110
  Cumann na mBan and, **1:121–122**
  Dáil Éireann, **2:**685, *685*
  on decommissioning, **1:**130
  delegates at Anglo-Irish Treaty of 1921 negotiations, **1:**55
  de Valera and, **1:**135–136
  Easter Rising and, **2:**684–685
  education and, **1:**196
  electoral success of, **1:**213
  Griffith and foundation of party, **1:**287
  Home Rule and, **1:**305
  Hume and, **1:**306
  hunger strikes, **1:**307–308, 331
  IRA and, **1:**329
  Irish-American culture and, **1:**145
  in Northern Ireland, **2:**560
    nationalist vote, **2:**562
  and peace process, **1:**487, 488; **2:**723
  rejection of legitimacy of Free State, **2:**532
  state enterprise and, **2:**676
  strength of, **1:**331
  trade unions and, **2:**712
Sinn Féin (newspaper), **2:**929
Sinn Féin Party renamed Workers' Party, **2:**562
Sinn Féin *simpliciter*, **2:**562
Síogaí Rómhánach, An (The Roman fairy) (anon.), **1:**398
Sion Mills, **1:**317
Sisters of Charity, **1:**452; **2:**621
Sisters of Mercy, **1:**452; **2:**621, 634, 668
Sisters of the Charitable Instruction. *See* Sisters of the Presentation of the Blessed Virgin Mary
Sisters of the Holy Faith, **2:**621
Sisters of the Presentation of the Blessed Virgin Mary, **1:**461; **2:**621, 634

Sisters of the Sacred Heart, **2**:621, 634

Six Nations Championship, **2**:675

Skeffington, Hannah Sheehy, **1**:407

Skeffington, William, **2**:534, 592

Skinner, Andrew, **2**:705

Slammerkin (Donoghue), **1**:254, 404

Small Garland of Pious and Godly Songs (Wadding), **1**:33

Smiddy, Timothy, **1**:100

Smith, Erasmus, **2**:**662–663**

Smith, Jean Kennedy, **1**:492

Smith, Sir Roger, **2**:662

Smith, Thomas, **1**:368
 colonization under, **1**:98, 220–221

Smith O'Brien, William, **2**:771, 772
 arrest of, **2**:772
 and Irish Confederation, **1**:445; **2**:625
 Stephens and, **2**:678

Smock Alley (Dublin), **1**:33

Smollett, Tobias, **1**:223

Smyth, Hugh, **1**:409

soccer, **2**:675

social classes
 and Brehon laws, **1**:60
 in Cork, **1**:109
 in Dublin, **1**:157
 effect of changes in class structure on religion, **2**:612
 employment and, **2**:665
 Home Rule movement and, **1**:209
 marriage and, **1**:239
 middle-class
  merchants, **1**:78
  towns and, **2**:707, 708
 Mr. and Mrs. Samuel Carter Hall on, **2**:893–896 (d)
 and religion, **2**:611–613
 in rural society, **2**:642
 social change and, **2**:665
 social mobility in Irish-American culture, **1**:145
 socioeconomic status of Catholics *vs.* Protestants, **1**:229–230
 sport and leisure and, **2**:674, 675
 Young on, **2**:858–860 (d)

Social Democratic and Labour Party (SDLP), **1**:477, 478, 485
 Faulkner and, **1**:250
 Hume and, **1**:306
 in Northern Ireland, **2**:556
  formation under Fitt, **2**:560

and peace process, **1**:487

social-insurance system, **1**:292–293

socialism
 Connolly and, **1**:104
 papal encyclical on, **1**:106–107

Socialist Women's Group, **2**:763

Social Welfare Act of 1974, **1**:227

social-welfare reform in Northern Ireland, **1**:484

Société des Bollandistes, **1**:289

Society for Promoting the Education of the Poor of Ireland. *See* Kildare Place Society

Society for the Preservation of the Irish Language, **1**:264, 401

Society for the Propagation of the Gospel, **1**:513

Society for the Relief of Distressed Roomkeepers, **2**:628

Society of African Missions, **1**:514; **2**:620

Society of Dublin Painters, **2**:742

Society of Jesus, **2**:607
 education and, **1**:185; **2**:634
 Irish colleges abroad and, **1**:323, 325
 O'Mahony, **1**:502–503
 sodalities and confraternities, **2**:669
 suppression of, **1**:325
 university of, **1**:186, 197

Society of United Irishmen. *See* United Irishmen

Socinianism Truly Stated (Toland), **2**:704

sodalities and confraternities, **2**:620, **668–669**
 and Marian cult, **1**:418

Sodality of Our Lady, **2**:669

Solemn League and Covenant (1643), **2**:**669–671**

Solemn League and Covenant (1912), **2**:930–931 (d)
 women signatories of, **2**:759

Solon His Follie (Beacon), **2**:812–813 (d)

Someone to Watch over Me (McGuinness), **1**:154

Somerville, Edith, **1**:254, 392
 on country houses, **1**:115

Somewhere over the Balcony (Charabanc), **1**:154

Songdogs (McCann), **1**:41, 254

Song of Dermot and the Earl, **1**:470, 472

songs
 at American wakes, **1**:15
 fairs and, **1**:422
 love, **1**:453

patriotic song, **1**:44
 political, **1**:453, 455
 See also ballads

Songs Ascribed to Raftery (Hyde and Gregory), **1**:309

Songs on the Death of Children (Lentin), **1**:404

"Sons of Clanricard, The" (Hooker), **2**:811 (d)

"souperism," **2**:654

soup kitchens, during Great Famine, **1**:283; **2**:569

Souter, Camille, **1**:41

South Africa, Irish emigration to, **1**:435

South American Missionary Society, **1**:513

Spain
 Catholics supported by, **1**:221
 Irish colleges in, **1**:323–326
 Irish in army of, **2**:749
 memorial presented to, on behalf of the Irish Catholics, **2**:828–829 (d)
 and Nine Years War, **1**:467, 468

Spanish Armada, **1**:221

Speaker's Conference, **2**:722

Special Air Service, **1**:331

Special Powers Act (1922), **2**:**671–672**

speech advocating consideration of Home Rule by the House of Commons (Butt), **2**:908–910 (d)

Speeches from the Dock, **2**:687

speech in favor of the Anglo-Irish Treaty of December 1921 (Griffith), **2**:948–949 (d)

speech on the use of Physical Force (Meagher), **2**:902–903 (d)

Spence, Gusty, **1**:408, 409

Spenser, Edmund, **1**:369; **2**:673
 on barbarism of Irish indigenous culture, **1**:22
 colonial theory of, **1**:98
 on Cork, **1**:108
 Desmond rebellions and, **1**:134
 Faerie Queene, **1**:224
 on Irish music, **1**:453
 on plantations, **1**:368
 A View of the Present State of Ireland, **1**:98, 224, 369; **2**:813–818 (d)

Speranza. *See* Elgee, Jane Francesca

spinning, **2**:641, 752–753
 wet-spinning process, **1**:237–238, 317

Spirit Level, The (Heaney), **1**:294

Spirit of the Nation (songbook), **1**:44; **2**:770

Spokesong (Parker), **1:**153
sport and leisure, **2:674–676**
    Cusack and, **1:**122
    social change and, **2:**664
Spreading the News (Gregory),
    1:151, 388
Spring, Dick, **2:**556
Stafford, Thomas, on siege of
    Kinsale, **2:**819–820 *(d)*
stagecoaches, **2:**714–715, *715*
Stagg, Frank, **1:**307
stained glass, **2:**742
*Stair Éamainn Uí Chléire (The
    History of Éamonn Ó Clery)* (Ó
    Neachtain), **1:**399
standard of living. *See* living
    standards
Standing Advisory Commission on
    Human Rights (SACHR), **1:**228–
    229
Stanihurst, Richard, **1:**223
    influenced by Campion's
    "Histories of Ireland," **2:**806
Stanley, Edward, **1:**187, 188
Stapelton, Michael, **1:**35
    plaster work of, **1:**114
Staples, Edward, **1:**201; **2:**593
Starkie, William, **1:**190
state enterprise, **2:676–677**
stately homes. *See* Big Houses
statement by the taoiseach (1969)
    (Lynch), **2:**991–992 *(d)*
*State of the Protestants of Ireland
    under the Late King James's
    Government* (King), **1:**344
Station Island (Heaney), **1:**294
stations, practice of, in Catholic
    Church, **2:**611, *632*
Statute of Westminster (1931),
    1:100
Statutes of Kilkenny (1366),
    1:470, 474; **2:**791–799 *(d)*
    on hurling, **2:**674
Steelboys, **1:495–496; 2:**747
Steele, Richard, **1:**33, 390
Steenkirk, Battle of (1692), **2:**651
Stepdaughter, The (Blackwood),
    1:403
Stephen Hero (Joyce), **1:**340
Stephens, James, **1:**40, 254, 465;
    2:678, 906
    IRB under, **1:**250–252
Sterne, Laurence, **1:**33, 391
Stir-Fry (Donoghue), **1:**404
Stoker, Bram, **1:**38, 392
Stone Age settlement, **2:678–683**
stone carvings, early medieval,
    1:29–30
stone circles, **1:**63
stonemasons, **1:**31

Stones in His Pocket (Jones), **1:**154
Storm (O'Donnell), **1:**254
Stormont regime, **1:**182, 480
    deindustrialization after World
    War I, **1:**172
    economic relations and, **1:**170
    effect of Bloody Sunday on,
    1:52
    Faulkner and, **1:**249–250
    suspended by Heath, **1:**486
story cycles, **1:**397
Story of the Night, The (Tóibín),
    1:254
Stout, Matthew, **2:**599
Stowe Missal, **1:**417
Strong, Eithne, **1:**403
Structural Funds (EU), **1:**83
struggle for independence from
    1916 to 1921, **2:683–686**
Stuart, Henry Villiers, **1:**76
stuccodores, **1:**36, 114
*Study towards an Image of W. B.
    Yeats* (Le Brocquy), **2:**743
subdivision and subletting of
    holdings, **2:686–687**
succession
    Gaelic, replaced by English
    tenure, **2:**535
    kingship and, **1:**346
    laws on, **1:**202
    surrender and regrant policy,
    2:689
Succession Act of 1965, **1:**226
Sudan Interior Mission, **1:**513
Sudan United Mission, **1:**513
suffrage movement, **2:**759–760
Sullivan, Alexander Martin, **1:**465;
    2:687–688
Sullivan, John L., **1:**146
Sullivan, Timothy Daniel, **1:**465;
    2:687–688
    and words to "God Save
    Ireland," **2:**906–907 *(d)*
Sulpicius Severus, **1:**289
Sunday Independent (newspaper),
    1:424, 425
    on repeal of External Relations
    Act, **1:**128–129
Sunday Observance Act of 1765,
    2:674
Sunday Press (newspaper), **1:**424
Sunningdale Agreement of 1973,
    1:409, 487
    connection to the Belfast
    Agreement of 1998, **1:**477
    Faulkner and, **1:**250
    Republic of Ireland and, **2:**561
    Social Democratic and Labour
    Party and, **2:**560
    Trimble and, **2:**716

"supergrass" trials, **1:**331
surrender and regrant, **1:**219–220,
    447; **2:**534–535, **688–689**
    Old English and, **1:**501
Swanzy, Mary, **2:**742
Sweeney Astray (Heaney), **1:**294
Swift, Jonathan, **1:**33, 390;
    2:548, **689–690**
    categorization of, **1:**223
    Drapier's Letters, **1:**204
    on Erastianism, **1:**88
    Irish accent and, **1:**295
Sydney, Henry (Viscount Sydney
    and earl of Romney), **1:**201
Symons, Arthur, **1:**388
Synge, John Millington, **1:**39, 151
    and Abbey Theatre, **1:**388;
    2:769
    Hiberno-English in, **1:**295
    *The Playboy of the Western
    World*, **1:**152, 388
    Riders to the Sea, **1:**152

∼ T

Tablet (newspaper), **1:**313
Taibhdhearc na Gaillimhe, **1:**153
Tailteann Games, **2:**675
*Táin Bó Cúailnge (Cattle Raid of
    Cooley)*, **1:**459; **2:691–692**
    on Cú Chulainn, **1:**119
Talbot, Peter, **2:**527
Talbot, Richard, earl of Tyrconnell,
    2:538
    as viceroy, **1:**335
    Old English and, **1:**502
Tale of a Tub (Swift), **2:**690
Tales from Bective Bridge (Lavin),
    1:254
Tales of the O'Hara Family (Banim
    and Banim), **1:**38
Tallaght monastic community,
    1:90, 290
Tandy, James Napper, **2:693**
    and embargo on British goods,
    1:204
tanistry, **1:**272, 367, 380
    replaced by primogeniture,
    2:535
    surrender and regrant policy,
    2:689
Tara, **2:693–695**
    high king of, **1:**165
    prehistoric, **2:**579
    Rath na Ríogh (Fort of the
    Kings), **2:**694
    roads to, **2:**714
Tara, kingship of. *See* Uí Néill high
    kings

Tara Brooch, **1:**27, 427, *427*
  illumination style similar to,
    1:416
Tara (paramilitary organization),
  1:408
taxation
  in Restoration Ireland, **2:**627
  See also cess
Taylor, George, **2:**705
Taylor, Jeremy, **1:**223
Tea at Four O'Clock (McNeill),
  1:403
Teach Cormaic (Cormac's House),
  2:693–694
teachers
  Kildare Place Society and, **1:**343
  salary of, **1:**195
  training of, **1:**190
Teagasg Criosdaidhe, An (Ó
  Heodhasa), **1:**398
tea trade, **2:**711
Telesis report (1982), **1:**320–321
television, **1:**425
  Irish-language, **1:**377
  launch of Irish, **1:**424
  Lynch's 1969 statement,
    2:991–992 *(d)*
  1968 speech by O'Neill, **2:**989–
    991 *(d)*
temperance movements, **2:**623,
  635, **695–697**
  sodalities and confraternities in,
    2:668–669
Temple, Sir John
  History of the Irish Rebellion,
    1:224
  on rebellion of 1641, **2:**601
Temple, William, **2:**717
tenant-defense associations, **1:**371
tenant farmers, **2:**642
  championed by Butt, **1:**69
  housing of, **1:**365
  Independent Irish Party and,
    1:311
  mass evictions during Great
    Famine, **1:***283*
  and purchase of their farms,
    2:645
  rise of, after Great Famine,
    2:546
  United Irish League and, **2:**729
Tenant League
  attempt to unite Catholic and
    Protestant farmers, **2:**546
  Butt and, **1:**69, 299
  Duffy and, **1:**312–313
  Independent Irish Party and,
    1:311–312
  and press, **1:**465
  resolution adopted at 1852
    conference, **2:**905 *(d)*

and the "three Fs," **2:**904
tenant movement, **1:***312*
  Independent Irish Party and,
    1:311–313
tenant right, or Ulster custom,
  2:697–700
  Butt and, **2:**908
  defense of, **1:**356
  Oakboys and Steelboys, **1:**495–
    496
  sales of (1873–1880), **2:**699
Tenant-Right Conference (1850),
  resolutions adopted at, **2:**904–
    905 *(d)*
tennis, **2:**676
Test Act (1704), **2:**594
textile industry
  decline in handicraft, **2:**567
  factory-based textile
    manufacture, **1:237–239**
    children in, **2:**753
  homespun-tweed industry,
    2:754
  power looms, **2:**753
  women and children in, **2:**751
Thatcher, Margaret, **1:**491, 492
  and Anglo-Irish Agreement of
    1985, **1:**16; **2:**1005
  economic policies of, **1:**169
  Irish pound and, **1:**328
  state enterprise and, **2:**677
"theater state," **2:**541–542
*Theatre de tous les peuples et nations
  de la terre avec leurs habits et
  ornemens divers . . .* , **1:**471
Theatre Royal at Crow Street
  (Dublin), **1:**33
Thérèse of Lisieux, Saint, **2:**666
*Thesaurus Antiquitatem
  hibernicarum* (Thesaurus of Irish
  antiquities), **1:**291
Third Policeman, The (O'Brien),
  1:40, 253
Thirty-Nine Articles (1563), **1:**71,
  72
This Side of Brightness (McCann),
  1:41
Thompson, E. P., on Defenderism,
  1:130
Thompson, Sam, **1:**153
Thomson, George, **1:**50
"three Fs"
  Irish Tenant League and, **2:**904
  and land laws, **1:**352, 357;
    2:518, 915
Three Songs of Home (Curtis), **2:**530
"Three Sorrows of Storytelling,"
  1:459
Thurles, Synod of (1850), **1:**452
  Cullen and, **1:**120

sodalities and confraternities,
  2:668
Thurneyson, Rudolf, **2:**691
Thurston, Katherine Cecil, **1:**402
Tievebulliagh excavations, **2:**679
timber industry, **2:**768
  seventeenth-century, **1:**180
time, standardization of, **2:**715–
  716
Time (magazine), Lemass on cover
  of, **1:***382*
"Time Will Tell" (de Valera),
  2:945–948 *(d)*
Tinkers. *See* Travellers
Tinker's Wedding, The (Synge),
  1:389
Tiomna Nuadh, An (New
  Testament), **1:**397
Tipperary Joint Stock Bank, **1:**46
Tiréchan, **1:**289
  on Saint Patrick, **1:**163
Tiresias (Clarke), **1:**40; **2:**529
Titanic, **2:**657, *657*
Titanic Quarter, **2:**658
Tithe Act of 1838, **1:332**
  tithe war and, **2:**703
tithe on corn and second Whiteboy
  rebellion, **2:**748
tithe war (1830–1838), **2:701–
  703**
  Doyle in, **1:**151
  Tithe Act of 1838 and, **1:**332
tobacco trade, **2:**711
Tochmarc Étaíne (The wooing of
  Étaín), **1:**459
Tod, Isabella, **1:**193
Today FM (radio station), **1:**425
Todhunter, John, **2:**769
Tóibín, Colm, **1:**41, 254
tOileánach, An (The Islandman) (Ó
  Criomhthain), **1:**265, 374;
  2:957–959 *(d)*
Toland, John, **2:703–704**
Toleration Act (1719), **2:**595
"To Mary and Her Son" (Blathmac,
  Son of Cú Brettan), **2:**780–781
  (d)
tombs
  of Bronze Age, **2:**577
  court tombs, **2:**576, 680, 682–
    683
  Deerpark tombs, **2:**682
  gravestones, **1:**67
  individual burials, **2:**577
  megalithic, **1:**361; **2:**576, 577,
    680–683
  passage tombs, **2:**576, 680–682
  portal tombs, **2:**577, 680, 682–
    683
Tone, Theobald Wolfe, **2:**548, *704*,
  704–705

Keogh and, **1:**342
negotiating for French fleet, **1:**206
Pearse's affinity for, **2:**520
Tandy and, **2:**693
Topography of Ireland, The (Giraldus Cambrensis), **1:**223, 472; **2:**786–788 *(d)*
Tóruigheacht Chalmair (The pursuit of Calmar) (Ó Súilleabháin), **1:**400
Toryism
    demise of, **1:**203
    Home Rule and, **1:**299–300
    Swift and, **2:**689–690
Tóstal, An (The gathering), **2:**706
Total Discourse of His Rare Adventures, The (Lithgow), **2:**833 *(d)*
Tour in Ireland (Young), **1:**225
tourism, **2:**705–707
    Celtic Tiger and, **1:**83
    in Dublin, **1:**155
    economic development and, **1:**177
    railways and, **2:**715–716
    shipbuilding and, **2:**658
    state enterprise and, **2:**676
    the "Troubles" and, **1:**171
Tourist Traffic Acts, **2:**705, 706
"Towards Changes in the Republic" (FitzGerald), **2:**993–1000 *(d)*
Tower, The (Yeats), **2:**769
tower houses, **1:**26, 32, 35
town charters, **2:**709
Townend, Paul, **2:**695
towns and villages, **2:**709–710
    Black Death (1348–1350) effect on, **1:**263
    government of, **1:**405
    markets in, **1:**420
    Normans and, **1:**366, 470
    town life from 1690 to the early twentieth century, **2:**707–708
    town planning, **1:**35
    under Tudors, **2:**735–736
    Vikings and, **1:**476
    See also urban life, crafts, and industry from 1500 to 1690
Townshend, George, fourth viscount Townshend, **1:**204
    appointment as viceroy, **1:**276
Tractatus de Purgatorio Sancti Patricii (Tract on Saint Patrick's purgatory), **2:**650
trade
    Bronze Age, **1:**80–81
    Catholics and, **2:**522
    Cork in, **1:**108

Irish pound and, **1:**327–328
trade and trade policy from 1691 to 1800, **2:**710–711
    Catholic merchants in, **1:**77–78
transport and, **2:**714–716
with West Indies, **1:**181
trade pact with U.K. (1948), and agriculture, **1:**12
Trade Union Congress, **1:**233
trade unions, **2:**712–713
    American, **1:**146
    Conditions of Employment Act and, **1:**101
    women and, **2:**759
    See also labor movement
Traits and Stories of the Irish Peasantry (Carleton), **1:**38, 392; **2:**632
Translations (Friel), **1:**40, 154
transport
    canal construction, **1:**361
    Mr. and Mrs. Samuel Carter Hall on, **2:**893–896 *(d)*
    road, canal, rail, **2:**714–716
    shipbuilding, **2:**656–658
    towns and, **2:**707, 710
Transport Workers' Union, **1:**303
Travellers
    at horse fairs, **1:**422
    Maeve Kelly on world of, **1:**404
Travels (Brereton), **2:**834–835 *(d)*
travel writing, **1:**225
Travers, Walter, **1:**71
    Trinity College and, **2:**717
Treason Felony Act, **2:**672
Treatise of Ireland (Dymmok), **1:**224
Tremayne, Edmund, **2:**659
Trench, Power, **1:**88
Trent, Council of, **1:**111–113
    devotional revolution and, **1:**138
    education of priests and, **1:**323–326
    Elizabethan church and, **1:**86–87
    family under, **1:**240
    Gaelic catechism and, **1:**222
Trevelyan, Charles, **1:**283
Trevor, William, **1:**40, 254
    on country houses, **1:**115
Trí Biorghaoithe an Bháis (The three shafts of death) (Céitinn), **1:**398
"Tricolour Riots" (Belfast, 1964), **1:**2
Tridentine Catholicism, **2:**606, 611, 633
    Baltinglass and, **1:**220
    Desmond rebellions and, **1:**133

education and, **1:**186
Jesuit education and, **1:**325
literature, **1:**223–224
O'Neill in, **1:**503–504
triumph over popular religion, **2:**634
Trimble, David, **1:**306, 479; **2:716–717,** 723
Trinitarian Orphan Society, **2:**628
Trinity College, **2:**589, **717–718**
    Bedell provost at, **1:**47
    Calvinism and, **1:**71
    Catholic rejection of, **1:**111–112, *197, 198*
    clergical education at, **1:**86, 88, 186
    Dublin Philosophical Society and, **1:**158
    ecumenism and, **1:**182
    evangelicalism and revivals, **1:**236
    hagiography at, **1:**291
    Historical Society, **1:**68
    O'Donovan and, **1:**500
    Protestant Ascendancy and, **1:**196
    Robinson and, **2:**630
    Smith and, **2:**662
    subdivision and subletting of holdings, **2:**686–687
    Ussher and, **2:**738
    women at, **1:**200
Tripartite Life of Saint Patrick, **1:**290; **2:**649
Tristam Shandy (Sterne), **1:**33
"Troubles," **2:**549
    and art, **2:**743
    ecumenism and, **1:**183
    education and, **1:**191
    foreign investment during, **1:**321
    impact of Northern crisis on Irish Republic, **2:**556, **560–562**
    IRA and, **1:**330, *330–331*
    Lynch's statement at the beginning of, **2:**991–992 *(d)*
    Orange Order and, **1:**507, 510
    overseas investment and, **1:**321, 513
    Special Powers Act, **2:**671–672
    tourism and, **1:**171
    trade unions and, **2:**713
    and women's parliamentary representation, **2:**765
Troy, John, **2:718–719**
Trustees of the Linen and Hempen Manufacturers of Ireland. *See* Linen Board
Tuam Cathedral, sculpture in, **2:**652

Tuatha tribal units, **1**:361
tuberculosis, **1**:*292*
Tudor era
  economy in, **1**:179–180
  Fitzgerald and, **1**:255–256
  and Irish towns, **2**:735–736
  political and religious reforms, **1**:219
  surrender and regrant policy, **2**:688–689
  and system of devolved administration, **2**:534
Tudor Revival–style country houses, **1**:115
Turf Club, **2**:674
turf harvesting, **1**:7; **362**
Turner, Victor, **2**:617
TV3, **1**:425
Twelfth of July commemorations, Orange Order and, **1**:507, 509, 510
Two Bokes of the Histories of Ireland (Campion), **1**:223; **2**:806–807 *(d)*
Tynan Hinkson, Katharine, **1**:388
Tyrconnell, earl of. *See* Talbot, Richard
Tyrell, Richard, **1**:466
Tyrellspass, **1**:359
Tyrie, Andy, **1**:409
Tyrone House, Co. Galway, **1**:113
Tyrone navigation, **2**:714
Tyrone's demands (O'Neill), **2**:818–819 *(d)*
Tyrone's rebellion (1598). *See* Nine Years War

~ U

U2, **1**:42, *458*; **2**:667
Ua Dunáin, Maél Muire, **1**:90
Ua Morgair (Malachy), Maél Maédóc, **1**:91
UDA. *See* Ulster Defence Association
UDP. *See* Ulster Democratic Party
Uí Briúin, **1**:347
Uí Chennselaig, **1**:347
Uí Fáilgi, **1**:347
Uí Gabla, **1**:347
Uí Garrchon, **1**:347
Uí Máil, **1**:347
Uí Néill high kings, **1**:165, 346, 347–348, 412; **2**:**721**
  Brian Boru and, **1**:123
  High Crosses and, **1**:298
  St. Patrick and, **1**:163
  Tara and, **2**:693–694
Ulster
  Calvinism in, **1**:71

"dragooning" of, **1**:206
industrialization in, **1**:314, 315–319; **2**:571
as symbol of liberty, **1**:217
Oakboys and Steelboys in, **1**:495–496
physical topography of, **2**:*619*
politics under direct rule in, **2**:721–723
population growth in, **2**:566
religious geography of, **2**:618–619, *619*
religious revivals in, **1**:236
unionists weakended by 1884 franchise extension, **2**:586–587
urbanization, **2**:571
Ulster, General Synod of, **2**:614
Ulster, Synod of, **2**:581
  Cooke and, **1**:107
"Ulster at the Crossroads" (O'Neill), **2**:989–991 *(d)*
Ulster Bank, **1**:46
Ulster Canal, **2**:714
Ulster Covenant, Carson and, **1**:73
Ulster custom. *See* tenant right
Ulster Cycle, **1**:161, 459
  Emain Macha in, **1**:214
  Táin Bó Cúailnge in, **2**:691–692
"Ulster Day" ceremony (1912), **2**:930
Ulster Defence Association (UDA), **1**:409, 479
  Cú Chulainn and, **1**:120
  increase in membership after direct rule, **2**:722
Ulster Defence Regiment (UDR), **2**:639, 724
Ulster Democratic Unionist Party (UDP), **1**:479
"Ulster Freedom Fighteers," **1**:409
Ulster Group Theatre, **1**:153
Ulster Literary Theatre, **1**:153
Ulster Loyalist Democratic Party (Ulster Democratic Party), **1**:409
Ulster plantations, **1**:367
  colonial theory and, **1**:98
  conditions of (1610), **2**:822–823 *(d)*
  Derry in, **1**:*132*
  A Direction for the Plantation of Ulster (Blennerhasset), **2**:823–824 *(d)*
  economy of, **1**:180
  immigrants and exploitation of flax, **2**:640
Ulster Political Research Group, **1**:409
Ulster Presbyterians, **2**:610
  farmer alliance with United Irish League, **2**:729

Gamble on, **2**:881–884 *(d)*
migration, **1**:432–433
Ulster Protestant Volunteers (UPV), **1**:408
Ulster Rising (1641), **2**:538
Ulster Special Constabulary (USC), **1**:483; **2**:559, 639
Ulster Unionist Council, **2**:727
  Craig and, **1**:116
  Orange Order and, **1**:510
Ulster Unionist Party (UUP), **1**:477, 478.1:480; **2**:**723–725**
  Carson and, **1**:73
  decommissioning and, **1**:129–130
  Faulkner and, **1**:249–250
  Irish Parliamentary Party and, **1**:304
  O'Neill and, **1**:505–507
  and temperance movement, **2**:695
  Trimble and, **2**:716–717
Ulster United movement, **1**:462
Ulster Vanguard, **2**:722
Ulster Volunteer Force (UVF) (est. 1913), **1**:479; **2**:931
  Brooke and, **1**:64
  Carson and, **1**:73
  creation in 1913, **2**:727
  incorporation in British Army during World War I, **1**:284; **2**:727
  legislative independence and, **1**:205
  nursing units organized by Parker, **2**:518
  opposition to Home Rule, **2**:548
  women and, **2**:762
Ulster Volunteer Force (UVF) (est. 1965), **1**:408, 479
Ulster Volunteer resolutions (1782), **2**:861–862 *(d)*
Ulster Women's Unionist Council (UWUC), **2**:759, 762
  Parker and, **2**:518
Ulster Workers' Council (UWC)
  Hume and, **1**:306
  strike (1974), **1**:477, 478
Ulster Young Militants, **1**:409
Ultramontanism, **2**:668
Ulysses (Joyce), **1**:40, 122, 253, 339
Uncle Silas (Le Fanu), **1**:38, 392
undertaker system, **1**:204, 230, 276, 369; **2**:584
unemployment
  Catholic, **1**:228
  Celtic Tiger economy and, **1**:81
  in interwar years, **1**:484
  in Irish Republic, **2**:555

Unfair Dismissals Act of 1977, **1:**227

Unfortunate Fursey, The (Wall), **1:**254

Union, Act of. *See* Act of Union

unionism
after Anglo-Irish Agreement of 1985, **2:**723
Carson and, **1:**73–74
Irish Unionist Party, **1:**73
opposition to Home Rule, **2:**930–932 *(d)*
Paisley and, **2:**517
Parker and, **2:**518
from 1885 to 1922, **2:**725–**728**
women active in, **2:**762

United Ireland (newspaper), **1:**465; **2:**688
manifesto of the Plan of Campaign published in, **2:**524

United Irish League, **1:**16
campaigns, **2:**728–**731**
Irish Parliamentary Party and, **1:**303, 304
land war, **2:**729
Tandy in, **2:**693

United Irishman (newspaper), **1:**287, 445

United Irishmen, **1:**48
of Ballynahinch, Co. Down grievances of, **2:**867–868 *(d)*
in Belfast, **2:**731
created by Presbyterians, **2:**610
Defenderism and, **1:**131
Fitzgerald and, **1:**255
foundation, **2:**731
Insurrection Act and, **2:**869–871 *(d)*
Keogh in, **1:**342
and oath-taking, **2:**543
Orange Order and, **1:**508
propaganda materials of, **1:**85
and reform of system of representation, **2:**543
statement by Emmet, O'Connor, and MacNeven on (1798), **2:**873–877 *(d)*
United Irishmen organization (1797), **2:**871–873 *(d)*

United Irish parliamentary reform plan (1794), **2:**866–867 *(d)*

United Irish societies from 1791 to 1803, **2:**731–**733**
caricature by Gillray, **2:**732
Emmet in, **1:**214–215
leaders of, arrested, **1:**205
in rebellion of 1798, **1:**206–208
Tone in, **2:**704–705

United Irishwomen, **2:**757

United Kingdom of Great Britain and Ireland, **2:**539
creation of, **1:**1–2, 277; **2:**544

United Nations, **2:**733–**735**
Irish Republic member of, **2:**555
peacekeeping missions, Ireland and, **1:**463; **2:**555–556, 734–735
Robinson as Commissioner for Human Rights, **2:**630

United Nations Conference on Trade and Development (UNCTAD), **1:**512

United States
Civil War
"cotton famine," **1:**318
Fenian movement and, **1:**251–252
Congressional Ad Hoc Committee on Irish Affairs, **1:**491
decommissioning process and, **1:**129
Fenian Brotherhood in, **1:**250–**253**
Irish Americans, **1:**142–148
in American Revolution, **1:**143–144
in Civil War, **1:**145
and Democratic Party, **1:**147
Irish question, **1:**491
Kennedy visit, **1:**341, 342
manufacturing investment by, **1:**169, 177, 511–512, 513
and Northern Ireland since 1970, **1:**491–493
Second Reformation and, **2:**653
Stephens and, **2:**678
textile exports to, **1:**317–318
trade with, **1:**181; **2:**711

University College (Cork), **1:**109

University College (Dublin), **1:**197

University Education Act (1879), **1:**197

University of Evora, **1:**502

Unnamable, The (Beckett), **1:**40, 47, 253

Untilled Field, The (Moore), **1:**39, 253

urbanization, **1:**366–367
Catholic landowning and, **1:**77–78
estates and demesnes and, **1:**231–232

urban life, crafts, and industry from 1500 to 1690, **2:**735–**738**

USC. *See* Ulster Special Constabulary

Ussher, James, **2:**738
Calvinism and, **1:**71

Trinity College and, **2:**717

UUP. *See* Ulster Unionist Party

UVF. *See* Ulster Volunteer Force (est. 1913); Ulster Volunteer Force (est. 1965)

UWC. *See* Ulster Workers' Council

UWUC. *See* Ulster Women's Unionist Council

～ V

Valentine and Orson, **1:**84

Valentine M'Clutchy (Carleton), **1:**392

Vallancey, Charles, **1:**22

Vandeleur, Hector, **2:**525

Van der Hagen, William, **1:**36

Van Diemen's Land (Tasmania), **1:**139

Van Dyck, Anthony, **2:**746

Vanguard organization, **1:**409
Trimble and, **2:**716
Ulster Vanguard, **2:**722

Vanishing Country Houses of Ireland, **1:**115

Verse in English from Eighteenth-Century Ireland, **1:**390

veto controversy, **2:**739–**740**

Viatores Christi, **1:**514

Vicar of Wakefield (Goldsmith), **1:**33

Vico, Giambattisto, **1:**339

Victoria College, **1:**200

Victorian Baronial style country houses, **1:**115

Victorious of Aquitaine, **1:**89

View of the Present State of Ireland, A (Spenser), **1:**98, 224, 369; **2:**673, 813–818 *(d)*

Views of Dublin (Malton), **1:**36

Vikings
and architecture, **1:**30
art motif, **1:**476
in Dublin, **1:**155–156
early Christianity and, **1:**165–166
hagiography and, **1:**290
and metalwork, **1:**427
and monastic centers, **1:**362, 475
ninth-century poem about, **2:**781 *(d)*
roads under, **2:**714
town development and, **2:**709
first urban overseas trading settlements, **1:**362, 475
See also Norse settlement

"Vikings, The" (anon.), **2:**781 *(d)*

villages. *See* towns and villages

Vincentians, **2**:620

Violence in Ireland, **1**:183

Virgilius Maro Grammaticus, **1**:379

Virgin Mary
  apparitions of, **1**:418; **2**:634
    in Lourdes, **1**:418
  cult of, **2**:637
  See also Marianism

Visions and Beliefs in the West of Ireland (Gregory and Yeats), **1**:388

visual arts, modern, **2:741–744**

Vita Prima Sanctae Brigidae (First life of Saint Brigit), **1**:289

Vita Sanctae Brigidae (Life of Saint Brigit of Kildare) (Cogitosus), **1**:289

Vita Tripartita, **1**:290

Vocation of John Bale to the Bishopery of Ossorie (Bale), **2**:804–806 *(d)*

Voluntary Health Insurance Board, **1**:293

Volunteer corps, **1**:204

Volunteer Missionary Movement, Irish branch, **1**:514

Volunteers
  alliance with the Patriot Party, **2**:541
  in Belfast, **2**:542
  in Dublin
    demonstration by, **1**:444
    1779 parade, **2**:541
  nonelite Protestants in, **2**:542

"Voyage of Bran, The" *(Immram Brain)*, **1**:164

∼ W

W. and R. Jacob (biscuit makers), **1**:315

Wadding, Luke, **1**:33, 291
  Irish colleges abroad and, **1**:325
  Saint Isidore's and, **1**:323

Waiting for Godot (Beckett), **1**:40, 47, 153, 253

wakes, **2**:617
  from 1500 to 1690, **1**:66
  See also American wakes

Walker, George, **1**:131

Walker, Joseph, **1**:22, 35

Walker, William, **1**:349–350

Wall, Maureen, **1**:77–78

Wall, Mervyn, **1**:40, 254

Walled Garden, The (Dunne), **1**:403

Walsh, Peter, **1**:324–325

Walsh, William Joseph, **2**:636, **745**

and educational policy, **2**:635
  on female education, **1**:194
  and Plan of Campaign, **2**:524

Walter, Theobald, grant of Prince John to, **2**:785–786 *(d)*

Wanderings of Oisin and Other Poems, The (Yeats), **2**:769

Ward, Hugh, **1**:21
  in education, **1**:324
  hagiography and, **1**:291

Ward, Mary, **2**:621

Ware, Sir James, **1**:291

Warner, Ferdinando, **1**:499

War of Independence (1919–1921). *See* Anglo-Irish War (1919–1921)

War of the Three Kingdoms (1638–1652), **2**:537, 669

War of the Two Kings. *See* Williamite wars

Waterford
  Mountjoy and, **2**:737
  Viking settlement in, **1**:476

Waterford, synod at (1646), **2**:630

Waterfront Hall (Belfast), **1**:49

water power and linen industry, **2**:640

Watson-Wentworth, Charles, second marquis of Rockingham, **1**:68

Watt, J. A., **1**:473

Waugh, Samuel, **1**:*438*

Way of the World, The (Congreve), **1**:34

Way-Paver, The (Devlin), **1**:404

Weather Permitting (O'Driscoll), **2**:530

Weaver, Harriet Shaw, **1**:339

weavers, **2**:753

Weekly News, **2**:687, 688

Week of Prayer for Christian Unity, **1**:184

Weir, The (McPherson), **1**:154

welfare system (and poor relief)
  economic relations and, **1**:172
  famine clearances, **1**:246–247
  institutional care and religious orders, **2**:621
  in Northern Ireland, introduction of British welfare state, **2**:560
  secularization and, **2**:656
  social change and, **2**:666–667
  state provisions since 1950, **1**:291–294
  women's economic rights in, **1**:226–228

Well of the Saints, The (Synge), **1**:39

Welsh immigration to Ireland, **1**:431

Wentworth, Thomas, first viscount and first earl of Strafford, **1**:278; **2**:538, **745–746**
  absolutism of, **1**:222
  Calvinism and, **1**:72
  and Church of Ireland, **2**:608
  Darcy and, **1**:125
  Old English and, **1**:502
  portrait by Van Dyck, **2**:746
  and religous conformity, **2**:593
  Solemn League and, **2**:670
  Ussher and, **2**:738

Werburgh Street Theatre (Dublin), **1**:33

Wesley, John, **1**:429
  Church of Ireland and, **1**:88
  evangelicalism and revivals, **1**:236
  portrait, **1**:429

West, Robert, **1**:35
  stucco work by, **1**:114

West, Trevor, **2**:1003

Westminster Confession, **1**:71
  Irish articles of 1615 in, **1**:72
  Smith and, **2**:662

Wexford rebellion of 1798, **2**:544
  account by Cloney, **2**:890–892 *(d)*

What Are You Like? (Enright), **1**:404

Whately, Richard, **1**:452

Wheatley, Francis, **2**:*540, 542*

Whigs, **1**:280
  formation of Whig Club, **1**:205
  O'Connell and, **1**:209, 213, 498
  Swift and, **2**:690
  Toland and, **2**:704

whiskey, **1**:61

Whistle in the Dark, A (Friel), **1**:153

Whitaker, T. K., **1**:382, 491
  Celtic Tiger economy and, **1**:81
  and *Economic Development* report, **1**:167, 168, 175; **2**:979–983 *(d)*

Whitby, Synod of (664), **1**:90

White, Peter, **1**:408

White, Stephen, **1**:291

White, Thomas, **1**:323

Whiteboys and Whiteboyism, **1**:355; **2**:566, **746–748**
  Bush, John, on, **2**:853–854 *(d)*
  communitarian rituals of, **2**:542
  Defenderism compared with, **1**:130–131
  tithe war and, **2**:701, 703
  trade unions and, **2**:712

Whitefield, George, **1**:236

Whitelaw, William, **1**:2, 486; **2**:722, 725

White Linen Hall, Belfast, **1:**316
White Woman Street (Barry), **1:**153
Whyte, Lawrence, **1:**391
Whyte, Samuel, **1:**33
Wiclow Mountains, The (O'Keeffe), **1:**390
Wide Streets Commission, **1:**156, 274
Widgery report on Bloody Sunday, **1:**52
widows, power of, **2:**758
Wilde, Jane Francesca. *See* Elgee, Jane Francesca
Wilde, Oscar, **1:**38, 388, 393; **2:**748–749
Carson and, **1:**73
Wilde, William, **2:**616
Wild Geese, **2:**749–751. *See also* emigration
Wild Irish Girl, The (Morgan), **1:**392
"Wild Swans at Coole, The" (Yeats), **1:**39; **2:**528, 769
Wilfrid of York, **1:**90
William III (William of Orange)
and Battle of the Boyne, **1:**57, 202, 202–203; **2:**539
Huguenots in armies of, **2:**590
revolution settlement and, **1:**201–203
siege of Derry and, **1:**131
trade under, **1:**202–203
and Treaty of Limerick, **2:**844–846 *(d)*
Williamite land settlement, **2:**584
Williamite wars, **1:**335–338, **335–338**, *336*
Catholic Committee and, **1:**74
economy and, **1:**181
king in, **1:**344
Old English and, **1:**502
Quakers during, **2:**622
Sarsfield in, **2:**650–651
siege of Derry and, **1:**131
trade and, **2:**711
Williams, Betty, **2:**520
Williams, Peer, **1:**381
William the Marshall, **2:**790
Wilson, Harold, **1:**17, 485
Wilson, Robert MacLiam, **1:**41, 254
Wilson, Woodrow, Easter Rising and, **2:**685
Wind among the Reeds, The (Yeats), **2:**769
Winding Stair, The (Yeats), **2:**769
Windsor, Treaty of (1175), **2:**784–785 *(d)*
O'Connors and, **1:**499
Winter, Brenda, **1:***152*

Winter, Dan, **1:***508, 509*
Winter, Samuel, **2:**594
Trinity College and, **2:**718
Wintering Out (Heaney), **1:**294
Without My Cloak (O'Brien), **1:**402
Woffington, Peg, **1:**34
Wolfe, David, **1:**111
Wolff, Gustav, **2:**657
women
and constitution of 1937, **2:**554
economic rights of, **1:**226–228
education, **1:**198–200
secondary education, **1:**192–194
at Trinity College, **2:**718
effect of Irish membership in EEC on status of, **2:**557
emigration, **1:**438, 441; **2:**570, 756
to Australia, **1:**140
to Britain, **1:**142; **2:**757
family planning and, **1:**148–149
family size and, **1:**242
in farming, **1:**248, 249
fertility rates and, **1:**242–244, *243*
inheritance by, **1:**240
in Irish society since 1800, **2:**756–761
keeners, **1:**66
life expectancy of, **2:**666
in manufacturing, **1:**315, 316, 318–319
marriage
abandonment by husbands, **1:**239
age at, **1:***243*, 243–244
and work, **2:**755
medical care for, **1:**292–293
and Methodism, **1:**429
in nationalist and unionist movements in the early twentieth century, **2:**761–763
and peace movement in Northern Ireland, **2:**519
and poetry, **2:**530
and politics
in local government, **1:**406
parliamentary representation since 1922, **2:**764–766
population of, **1:**142
and religious vocation, **2:**758
in early Middle Ages, **1:**448
ordination of, **1:**89
Report of the Commission on the Status of Women (1972), **2:**992–993 *(d)*
secularization and, **2:**656

social change and, **2:**663–665, 665
in sports, **2:**676
St. Patrick on, **2:**649
suffrage
Connolly and, **1:**105
enactment of, **1:**209
in textile manufacture, **1:**238
at Trinity College, **2:**718
welfare system and, **1:**292–293
women's movement
impact on women's parliamentary representation, **2:**765–766
in Northern Ireland, **2:**763–**764**
and work
Conditions of Employment Act and, **1:**101
employment, **1:**244, 293
in the industrial workforce, **2:**751–754**
as migrant workers, **1:**442
since the mid-nineteenth century, **2:**754–756
Workers' Union, Irish Women (IWWU), **1:**332–333
writers
dramatists, **1:**154
twentieth-century, **1:**401–**405**
views of Ireland literature by, **1:**225
Women against Imperialism, **2:**763
Women Caring Trust, **2:**519
Women's Coalition, **1:**229
Women's declaration (1912), **2:**762
Women's Liberation Movement, **2:**760, 760–761
contraception and, **1:**148
Women's National Health Association, **2:**757
Women's Political Association (Republic of Ireland), **2:**761, 765
Women's World Day of Prayer, **1:**184
Women Together, **2:**519
woodcarvers, **1:**31
woodlands, **1:**364; **2:**766–769
clearing of, **1:**5, 6
in the seventeenth century, **2:**767
forestry policy in the Republic, **2:**768
King's and Queen's counties (Offaly and Laois), **2:**767
Wood of the Whispering, The (Molloy), **1:**153

Woods, Thomas, **1**:344
Woods, Vincent, **1**:154
"Wood's halfpence," **1**:203, 204
Woodward, Richard, **2**:739
Woolen Act (1699), **2**:710
    and Irish economy, **1**:6
woolen exports, **2**:641
    in Restoration Ireland, **2**:627
    under William III, **1**:202–203
woolen industry
    in eighteenth century, **2**:566
    women and children in, **2**:640,
        751–752
Wootton, Henry, **1**:47
Workers' Republic (newspaper),
    1:104; **2**:933
Workman, Clark, and Company,
    2:657–658
Workman Clark shipyard, **1**:319
Works of William Balke, The (Yeats
    and Ellis, ed.), **2**:769
World Council of Churches, **1**:183
World of Love, A (Bowen), **1**:403
World Trade Organization,
    agricultural trade and, **1**:99
World War I, **1**:285–287; **2**:548
    Clarke in German plot, **1**:95
    Easter Rising and, **2**:684
    economy and, **1**:172, 173
    Home Rule and, **1**:304–305
    neutrality mooted by Roger
        Casement, **1**:462
    opposition to conscription in
        Ireland, **1**:*285*, 286
    plough-up campaign, **1**:8
    and prosperity in rural Ireland,
        2:646
    Redmond and, **2**:601–602
    social change and, **2**:663
    Somme, Battle of the (1916),
        Orange Order and, **1**:510
World War II
    Anglo-Irish Economic War and,
        1:168
    Beckett during, **1**:47
    de Valera and, **1**:136
    economy and, **1**:170, 173, 174–
        175
    "German Attack on Neutral
        States" (de Valera), **2**:970 *(d)*
    IRA and, **1**:330

Irish neutrality, **1**:462–463,
    489; **2**:554
Jewish community after, **1**:339
Northern Ireland and, **1**:321,
    484
protectionism and, **1**:320
shipbuilding industry and,
    2:658
social change and, **2**:665
welfare after, **1**:291–292
Worsley, Benjamin, **1**:117
Worth, Edward, **2**:594
Wright, Billy, **1**:409
writing
    ogham script, **1**:27, 161, 378;
        2:580
    seventh-century British
        influence, **2**:604
"Writing out of Doors" (anon.),
    2:781–782 *(d)*
Würzburg codex, **1**:297, 379
Wyatt, James, **1**:113
Wyche, Cyril, **1**:158
Wyndham, George, **1**:*354*
Wyndham, William, **1**:75
Wyndham Land Act of 1903
    Irish Parliamentary Party and,
        1:303–304
    United Irish League and, **2**:730
    See also Land Purchase Acts of
        1903 and 1909
Wyse, John, **1**:499
Wyse, Thomas, **1**:74

~ X

X case (1992), **1**:150

~ Y

Year of the Knife, The (Casey),
    2:530
Yeats, Jack B., **1**:41; **2**:741, 742
    illustrator of *The Aran Islands*,
        1:388
    Liffey Swim, The, **2**:741
Yeats, John B., **1**:41
Yeats, William Butler, **1**:38, 39,
    387, 388, 393; **2**:528–529, **769**–
    770

and Abbey Theatre, **1**:388
on country houses, **1**:115
denunciations of Murphy,
    1:452
on divorce ban, **1**:260–261
drama of, **1**:151
"Easter 1916," **1**:39; **2**:769,
    936–937 *(d)*
and Gonne, **1**:275
Hiberno-English in, **1**:295
Hyde and, **1**:308
and Irish Literary Renaissance,
    1:388
Joyce and, **1**:339
opposition to censorship, **1**:261
Yellow Book of Lecan, **1**:396
Yellow Ford, Battle of (1598),
    1:466, 467
    Hugh O'Neill and, **1**:504
Yelverton's Act (1782), **2**:862–863
    (d)
yeomanry, **1**:444; **2**:543
Yonge, James, **1**:431
York, Richard, duke of, **2**:801
Youghal, sacking of (1579), **1**:134
Young, Arthur, **1**:454
    on Irish rural society and
        poverty, **2**:858–860 *(d)*
    Tour in Ireland, **1**:225
Young Citizen Volunteers, **1**:409
Young Ireland
    as cultural movement, **1**:44
    Davis in, **1**:125–126
    dissatisfaction with O'Connell,
        2:545, 625, 902
    education and, **1**:196
    IRB and, **1**:250
    and the Irish Confederation,
        2:770–772
    and *Nation*, **1**:464
    "rebellion" of 1848, **2**:545, *771*
    Romanticism and its influence
        on, **2**:545
    women in, **2**:761
Young Ireland (magazine), **2**:687

~ Z

Zola, Émile, **1**:253